W9-CFA-348

Subject Matter Number (ISA#)
and Document Title   *General Assurance and Auditing*

AUDITING
An International Approach
SECOND CANADIAN EDITION

Jack C. Robertson, Ph.D., C.P.A., C.F.E.
C.T. Zlatkovich, Centennial Professor
The University of Texas at Austin

Wally J. Smieliauskas, Ph.D., C.P.A., C.F.E.
University of Toronto

McGraw-Hill
Ryerson

Toronto Montréal Boston Burr Ridge, IL Dubuque, IA Madison, WI
New York San Francisco St. Louis Bangkok Bogotá Caracas
Kuala Lumpur Lisbon London Madrid Mexico City Milan
New Delhi Seoul Singapore Sydney Taipei

McGraw-Hill
Ryerson Limited

A Subsidiary of The McGraw·Hill Companies

Auditing: An International Approach
Second Canadian Edition

Copyright © 2001, 1998 by McGraw-Hill Ryerson Limited, a Subsidiary of The McGraw-Hill Companies. All rights reserved. No part of this publication may be reproduced or transmitted in any form or by any means, or stored in a data base or retrieval system, without the prior written permission of McGraw-Hill Ryerson Limited, or in the case of photocopying or other reprographic copying, a licence from CANCOPY (the Canadian Copyright Licensing Agency), 6 Adelaide Street East, Suite 900, Toronto, Ontario, M5C 1H6.

ISBN: 0-07-087137-X

1 2 3 4 5 6 7 8 9 10   TCP   0 9 8 7 6 5 4 3 2 1

Printed and bound in Canada.

Care has been taken to trace ownership of copyright material contained in this text; however, the publisher will welcome any information that enables them to rectify any reference or credit for subsequent editions.

This book includes quotations and adaptations from publications copyrighted by the American Institute of Certified Public Accountants. Such passages have been reprinted or adapted with permission of the AICPA. Material from the Uniform CPA Examinations and Unofficial Answers, copyright 1962–1986 and 1989–1994 by the American Institute of Certified Public Accountants, is reprinted or adapted with permission.

Material from the Certificate of Management Accounting Examinations, copyright 1974 through 1984 by the Institute of Management Accounting, is reprinted or adapted with permission.

Material from CGAAC Examinations, copyright 1994–1996, is reprinted or adapted with the permission of the Certified General Accountants Association of Canada.

Excerpts from the *CICA Handbook* and their publications are reprinted with permission from The Canadian Institute of Chartered Accountants, Toronto, Canada. Any changes to original CICA material cited in this textbook are the sole responsibility of J.C. Robertson, W.J. Smieliauskas, and McGraw-Hill Ryerson Limited and have not been reviewed by or endorsed by the CICA.

Material from the Institute of Chartered Accountants of Ontario's School of Accountancy Admission Examination Questions, copyright 1986–1995, is reprinted or adapted with the permission of the Institute of Chartered Accounts of Ontario, copyright ICAO.

Vice President and Editorial Director: Pat Ferrier
Senior Sponsoring Editor: Nicole Lukach
Developmental Editor: Katherine Goodes
Supervising Editor: Alissa Messner
Copyeditor: Catharine Haggert
Senior Marketing Manager: Jeff MacLean
Production Coordinator: Madeleine Harrington
Compositor: Bookman Typesetting Co. Inc.
Cover Design: Dianna Little
Cover Image: © Lois and Bob Schlowsky/Stone
Printer: Transcontinental Printing Group

Canadian Cataloguing in Publication Data

Robertson, Jack C.
    Auditing : an international approach

2nd Canadian ed.
First ed. published under title: Auditing & other assurance engagements.
Includes index.
ISBN 0-07-087137-X

1. Auditing.   I. Smieliauskas, Wally.   II. Title.   III. Title: Auditing & other assurance engagements.

HF5667.R616 2001   657'.45   C00-932431-3

J. C. Robertson dedicates this book to
Charles T. Zlatkovich
Professor Emeritus
C. Aubrey Smith Professorship
Educator
Mentor
The University of Texas at Austin

W. J. Smieliauskas dedicates this book to
Fabrice and Adrian

ABOUT THE AUTHORS

Jack C. Robertson is the C.T. Zlatkovich Centennial Professor at the University of Texas at Austin, where he has been a member of the faculty since 1970. In 1988 he was the Visiting Erskine Fellow in the Department of Accountancy at the University of Canterbury in Christchurch, New Zealand. He has given invited presentations in Jerusalem, Tel Aviv, Christchurch, Dunedin, Wellington, Kyoto, and Kobe.

Professor Robertson is a Certified Public Accountant (Texas) and has worked in industry, public accounting, and government (Academic Fellow in the SEC Office of the Chief Accountant).

Professor Robertson is a member of the American Institute of CPAs, the Texas Society of CPAs, and the American Accounting Association. He has served on committees and task forces of the AICPA and TSCPA, and he has been active in the AAA — serving as secretary, vice-chairman, and chairman of the Auditing Section and as chairman of the Auditing Standards Committee and the Committee on Liaison with the SEC. In the TSCPA he has been active on the Professional Ethics Committee.

Professor Robertson's research and writing interests include auditing and financial reporting subjects. His books are *Auditing, Cost Accounting for Small Manufacturers,* and *Business Income Determination Through Use of Current Cost Accounting.* He has published numerous articles on educational and technical topics in such journals as the *Accounting Review;* the *Journal of Accountancy; Journal of Accounting, Auditing, and Finance;* the *CPA Journal; Accounting Horizons; Auditing: A Journal of Practice and Theory;* and *Research in Accounting Regulations.*

At the University of Texas, Professor Robertson has developed three new auditing courses that have served as national models for courses elsewhere. Prior to his appointment as the C.T. Zlatkovich Centennial Professor, he held the Price Waterhouse Auditing Professorship (1979–85). Professor Robertson is listed in *Who's Who in America.*

Wally J. Smieliauskas is a professor of accounting at the University of Toronto, where he has been a member of the faculty since 1979. In 1987 he served as chair of the CAAA's Expectation Gap Task Force, which made a submission to the MacDonald Commission. Also in 1987, he co-chaired the CAAA conference that had as invited speaker Nobel laureate Herbert Simon.

Professor Smieliauskas is a certified public accountant and has worked in industry and public accounting. He spent his 1986–87 sabbatical year with the firm of Deloitte & Touche.

Professor Smieliauskas is a member of the American Institute of Certified Public Accountants, the Canadian Academic Accounting Association, and the Association of Fraud Examiners.

Professor Smieliauskas's research and writing interests include auditing and the role of accounting in society. He has published numerous articles on educational and technical topics in such journals as *Accounting Review, Contemporary Accounting Research, Journal of Accounting Research, Journal of Accounting Literature,* and *Auditing: A Journal of Practice and Theory.* In 1999, the Canadian Academic Accounting Association published his research monograph entitled "A Framework for Assurance Evidence and Its Role in Accounting."

At the University of Toronto, Professor Smieliauskas developed the first degree-credit introductory auditing course (in 1981) and the first advanced auditing course (in 1990). In 1988 he was the first director of the MBA Co-op Program in Professional Accounting, a position he held until 1993. The program is designed to facilitate the entry of undergraduates from various fields into the profession, and to provide a broader management education as well as specialized training in accounting, auditing, and tax topics. It has evolved to become the Master of Management & Professional Accounting (MMPA) Program now offered through the University of Toronto's Mississauga campus.

CONTENTS

PART II

BASIC CONCEPTS AND TECHNIQUES OF AUDITING

95

Chapter 8   **Auditing in a Computer Environment**   **248**

PART III
AUDIT APPLICATIONS
291

Chapter 9   **Revenue and Collection Cycle**   **292**

Chapter 10   *Acquisition and Expenditure Cycle Including Audit of Accounts Payable and Inventory Existence*   **338**

Chapter 11   *Production and Payroll Cycle Including Audit of Inventory Valuation and Capital Assets*   **384**

Chapter 12   ***Finance and Investment Cycle***   **430**

Chapter 13   ***A Strategic Systems Approach to the Financial Audit***   **470**

Chapter 14   ***Completing the Audit***   **488**

PART IV

PROFESSIONAL SERVICES AND RESPONSIBILITIES

527

PART V

SPECIALIZED TOPICS
819

PREFACE TO THE SECOND CANADIAN EDITION

This exciting second Canadian edition of *Auditing: An International Approach* (formerly titled *Auditing and Other Assurance Engagements)* provides the student with the necessary skills to move from knowledge of accounting principles to the professional practice of accounting and auditing in the working world. The study of *auditing* is a cutting-edge learning experience that includes accounting calculations and journal entries of previous accounting courses coupled with the process of gathering evidence and making judgements about the fair presentation of financial statement balances (that have already been produced by accountants). Special care has been taken to ensure that Canadian and International auditing issues have been solidly addressed throughout the text.

To support this focus of knowledge and procedure the authors have addressed the subject of auditing on both conceptual and procedural levels. At the conceptual level, students learn about the social role of auditing. This includes services offered in internal, governmental and public accounting practice and the professional standards for behaviour and technical competence. On the procedural level, the programs and procedures for defining auditing objectives, gathering evidence, making decisions and exercising professional scepticism are presented.

With this brand new second edition the author has endeavoured to clearly reflect the exciting and current challenges inherent in accounting and auditing practice, particularly in public accounting firms. Clients who pay the fees expect *value* — consulting advice, recommendations for improvements in the business and an audit report. On the other hand, public users of these clients' financial statements expect *effective service* — they expect auditors to be objective sceptics working to monitor the business management and blow the whistle on fraudulent financial statements. These dual challenges of service to clients and service to the public merge the business and professional aspects of public accounting practice.

Throughout the 1990s, the practice of accounting and auditing has expanded its horizons in keeping with the changes in the real world of business management. This book incorporates the important aspects of this expansion — mainly other assurance engagements. It provides thorough coverage of the general concept of assurance engagements (Chapters 2 and 15) as well as specific applications (Chapters 15, 18, 19 as well as Chapter 21 on the book's Web site). Overall, the student will come away with a well-rounded learning experience in the field of auditing.

WHAT'S NEW IN THE SECOND CANADIAN EDITION

This Second Canadian edition has a number of compelling features designed with the student in mind. Each concept has been carefully developed/revised to facilitate the ease and enjoyment of the auditing learning experience. The following is a complete list of these integral features:

- A fresh new international orientation with an emphasis on financial auditors' decision-making processes. These include:
  - recognizing problems and developing auditing objectives,
  - gathering evidence with auditing procedures, and
  - making judgements about the fair presentation of financial statement assertions.
- A comprehensive referencing to international standards in auditing.
- A unique chapter on fraud awareness.
- A chapter on the new strategic systems approaches to auditing (SSA audits).
- Comprehensive coverage of the new assurance engagement concept provides up-to-date information for the accounting student.

- A Web site chapter on electronic commerce, the Internet and related assurance services.
- A theoretical framework for professional accountants' Codes of Conduct lends support to the current theme of this textbook.
- A discussion of audit of derivatives, integration of the learning objectives and the review checkpoints.
- Various anecdotes, asides and "casettes" all enrich the text material.

KEY FEATURES

International Auditing

The most compelling change to this new edition is the incorporation of international auditing standards, which are found throughout the text. This brings the student to the leading edge of auditing and responds to the increasing focus on international standards in the real world of business management. The author has also included Canadian standards and some American standards, providing essential and comparative information to the student.

Fraud Auditing

This book was the first to contain full-chapter coverage of fraud auditing, an increasingly important topic in the new century. With the rapid global growth in white-collar crime, especially that related to fraudulent financial reporting, auditors will likely have to take more responsibility for fraud detection. The basic purpose of the fraud chapter is to create awareness of, and sensitivity to, the signs and signals of potential errors, irregularities, frauds and corruption. The chapter contains some unique insights on extended auditing and investigation procedures.

Strategic Systems Approach to Auditing (SSA Audits)

Steven Salterio, Associate Professor at the University of Waterloo's School of Accountancy, has contributed some very thought-provoking sections to this new edition as well. Through his expert authoring of Chapter 13, he introduces Strategic Systems Approach to Auditing (SSA Audits) — an exciting and potentially radically different approach to auditing. This unique treatment further supports the authors' commitment to ensure that this is the most current and pivotal text on the market.

The basic purpose of this material is to create awareness of, and sensitivity to, the signs and signals of potential errors, irregularities and frauds based on a thorough understanding of the strategic aspects of the clients business. Chapter 13 contains some unique insights on using competitive strategy techniques to plan effective and efficient audits.

Learning Aids

Each chapter and section in *Auditing: An International Approach* contains a number of pedagogical features that both enhance and support the learning experience. They include the following:

- Professional Standards References
  Each chapter references the relevant professional standards for the chapter topics. The inside front and back covers list these standards and other library resources used by professional auditors.
- Learning Objectives
  Each chapter opens with a presentation of pertinent learning objectives for the following text. These are repeated as marginal notes within the chapters.

- Anecdotes and Asides
  Illustrative anecdotes and asides can be found throughout the text. Some are located within the chapter text, while others stand alone to add realism and interest to the student. The result is a real-world flavour to the treatment of auditing.
- Review Checkpoints
  Instead of placing review questions at the end of each chapter, we have placed *review checkpoints* (questions) within each chapter so those students can test themselves as they proceed. These checkpoint islands make the text user-friendly by effectively breaking each chapter into smaller sections.

Casettes

The "casettes" are a unique feature to this book that are presented as *short stories* structured to reveal error, irregularity or fraud in an account. An *audit approach* follows. The audit approach describes an audit objective, desirable controls, and test of controls procedures and audit of balance procedures that can result in discovering the situation. The casettes occur in the "applications" chapters (Chapters 9–12 and Chapter 17).

The purpose of the casettes is to enliven the study of auditing. They replace the typical lengthy exposition of auditing fundamentals with illustrative situations based on real events. There are 25 casettes with auditing approaches in the applications chapters. Another 20 casettes are in the end-of-chapter discussion case sections. In these, the case stories are told and the students' assignment is to write the audit approach sections.

Key Terms

Throughout the book, key terms are highlighted in boldface print. An alphabetical key terms reference list with definitions is in the back of the text.

Kingston Case

The Kingston Company case is a practice case that has been moved from the text (1st edition) to a CD for easier use and more portability for the student. The company description starts in Chapter 4 and continues through Chapters 12, 14, and 20. Assignments related to the Kingston case connect many of the technical topics in a logical sequence of auditing engagement activities. However, there are numerous exercises, problems and discussion cases at the end of each chapter that are unrelated to the Kingston Company. To enhance clarity, the case material is integrated throughout the text, including references to the problem material on the CD.

ORGANIZATION
. . . .

Part I — Introduction to Auditing and Public Practice

Part I has three chapters. They cover the basic orientation to the accounting profession: assurance standards, generally accepted auditing standards and quality control standards; the standard unqualified audit report and major types of qualifications (technical modifications are a chapter appendix).

Part II — Basic Concepts and Techniques of Auditing

Part II follows the normal progression of financial auditing topics. Chapter 4 lays the groundwork with explanations of financial assertions, general types of procedures and working paper documentation. Chapter 5 continues the early audit planning considerations with technical material on preliminary analytical procedures, audit risk and materiality. Chapter 6 takes up the stream of planning and performing audit work with coverage of control risk assessment. Chapter 7 maintains the flow of planning topics with generalized and non-statistical explanations of audit sampling. Chapter 8 introduces basic concepts of computer auditing and control.

Part III — Audit Applications

Part III contains five chapters that address the details of audit work on specific accounts and assertions (including a chapter on unique features of SSA audits) and one chapter that wraps it all up with audit completion considerations. Chapters 9–14 are the accounting-cycle chapters and organize the control structure and account balances for comprehensive understanding. Chapter 14, aptly titled "Completing the Audit," concentrates on client representation letters, lawyers' letters, subsequent events, subsequent discovery of facts, financial statement adjustments and related party transactions.

Part IV — Professional Services and Responsibilities

The five chapters in Part IV can stand alone or be integrated with the preceding and following chapters. They deal separately with non-audit services rendered by public accounting firms; the context, methodology and reports of governmental and internal auditors and fraud awareness auditing. The last chapter has benefitted from the author's association with the Association of Certified Fraud Examiners. The two chapters on auditor responsibilities cover legal liability and professional codes of conduct. It was felt that these two topics are better understood after students have gained some knowledge of audit theory and practice.

Part V — Specialized Topics

Part V covers the technical topics. Chapter 21 covers computer audit planning and procedural applications. It fills out the introductory computer audit material in Chapter 8. Chapter 20 covers test on controls using attribute sampling and presents a thorough treatment of variables sampling for the audit of balances with dollar-unit sampling carrying the chapter content. Chapter 21 is not included in the hard copy of this text but is available to all adopters on the text Web site.

PROFESSIONAL STANDARDS
· · · · · · · · · · · ·

This textbook contains numerous references to authoritative statements on auditing standards and to standards governing other areas of practice. Even so, the text tries to avoid the mere repetition of passages from the standards, concentrating instead on explaining their substances and operational meaning in the context of making auditing decisions. Instructors and students may wish to supplement the text with current editions of pronouncements published by the International Federation of Accountants (IFAC), the Canadian Institute of Chartered Accountants (CICA), the Certified General Accountants Association of Canada (CGAAC) and the Institute of Internal Auditors (IIA).

SUPPLEMENTS
· · · · · · · · · · ·

Several additional resources for introductory auditing courses are available for instructors and students.

- **Instructor's Resource Guide.** The *Instructor's Resource Guide* includes a description of the Kingston Company case and a set of syllabi for organizing topical coverage. Each chapter contains suggested answers for all the review checkpoints, multiple-choice questions, Kingston Case assignments, exercises and problems and discussion cases. Blank forms for some homework assignments can be removed and copied for the students.
- **Computerized Test Bank.** The *Computerized Test Bank* contains numerous objectives, short-answer and essay questions.
- **PowerPoint® Presentation Slides.** The *PowerPoint® Presentation Slides* illustrate chapter concepts with the aid of presentation graphics software.

ACKNOWLEDGEMENTS

· · · · · · · · · · · ·

The International Federation of Accountants (IFAC), the Certified General Accountants Association of Canada (CGAAC) and the Canadian Institute of Chartered Accountants (CICA) have generously given permission for liberal quotations from official pronouncements and other publications, all of which lend authoritative sources to the text. In addition, several publishing houses, professional associations and accounting firms have granted permissions to quote and extract from their copyrighted material. Their co-operation is much appreciated because a great amount of significant auditing thought exists in this wide variety of sources.

A special acknowledgement is due Mr. Joseph T. Wells, former chairman of the National Association of Certified Fraud Examiners. He created the Certified Fraud Examiner (CFE) designation. Mr. Wells is a well-known authority in the field of fraud examination education and his entrepreneurial spirit has captured the interest of fraud examination professionals throughout North America.

Special acknowledgement is also due to Steven E. Salterio at the University of Waterloo for his contribution to the strategic systems approaches to auditing (SSA audits) material used in this edition, especially Chapter 13.

This book could not have been completed without the co-operation and input of many students in my auditing courses at the University of Toronto over the years 1992 through 1999. I am particularly indebted to Enola Stoyle for material that was adapted in various forms in this text.

I am grateful for the invaluable advice provided by Sylvia Smith, Diane Hillier, Jan Munro, Greg Shields and Karen Duggan. My experience with these talented individuals convinced me that Canada likely has the most productive standard setters in the world on a per person basis. They are keeping Canada at the forefront of practice globally and are an important influence on international standard setting. I sincerely hope the CICA will continue to actively represent the Canadian perspective in the global arena of standard setting.

I would also like to thank my colleagues at the University of Toronto for providing a stimulating, supportive environment for this work, especially Donna Losell, Manfred Schneider, Len Brooks, Ann Kittler and Irene Wiecek. In addition, the excellent typing provided by Maria and Michelle Raz over numerous revisions of this manuscript is greatly appreciated.

The reviews and suggestions provided by several professors have been of significant help in completing this textbook. Sincere appreciation is also due to Marcia McCann (Ryerson Polytechnic University), Margaret Kelly (University of Manitoba), Charlotte Heywood (Wilfrid Laurier University), Barbara Treholm (University of New Brunswick), Kate Bewley (York University), Donna Losell (University of Toronto), John Edds (Brock University), Dani Moss (Durham College), Dan. A. Simniuc (University of British Columbia), Richard Rennie (University of Regina), Susan McIsaac (Doan Raymond and Mount Allison University), Michael Maingot (University of Ottawa), Mohamed Ibrahim

(Concordia University) and Karim Jamal (University of Alberta). Their attention to reviews greatly enhanced several portions of the text.

Also, both authors would like to thank the excellent editorial and support staff at McGraw-Hill Ryerson who helped make this edition possible. They include Jennifer Lamantia, Nicole Lukach, Bonnie Moran, Katherine Goodes, Christine Lomas and Alissa Messner. A special acknowledgement is extended to Catharine Haggert for her skilful editorial work throughout the production process.

Wally J. Smieliauskas
University of Toronto

For the Student

ONLINE QUIZZING

Do you understand the material? You'll know after taking an Online Quiz! Try the Multiple Choice and True/False questions for each chapter. They're auto-graded with feedback and the option to send results directly to faculty.

WEB LINKS

This section references various Web sites including all company Web sites linked from the text.

MICROSOFT® POWERPOINT® PRESENTATIONS

View and download presentations created for each text. Great for pre-class preparation and post-class review.

INTERNET APPLICATION QUESTIONS

Go online to learn how companies use the Internet in their day-to-day activities. Answer questions based on current organization Web sites and strategies.

Your Internet companion to the most exciting educational tools on the Web!

The Online Learning Centre can be found at:
www.mcgrawhill.ca/college/robertson

PART I

INTRODUCTION TO AUDITING AND PUBLIC PRACTICE

CHAPTER 1

Learning Objectives

Learning objectives are statements of what you should be able to do after you have studied each chapter of this textbook, examined related professional standards, answered the review checkpoints in each chapter and completed assigned homework problems. For example, in an auto mechanics school one learning objective would be: "Be able to take a carburetor apart and put it back together in 15 minutes."

Learning objectives for auditing, however, are not this task specific. The learning objectives are given at the beginning of each chapter and are restated within the chapter at appropriate places. As you study each part of the chapter, you can use them as general reference points.

Chapter 1 gives you an introduction to professional accounting practice. Other accounting courses helped you learn the principles and methods of accounting; now you are starting a study of the ways and means of practising accounting and auditing outside the classroom. Your objectives are to be able to:

1. Distinguish auditing from accounting.

2. Chronicle the historical development of auditing standards, including the criticisms of the profession and its responses.

3. Define and explain auditing, especially its role in information risk reduction.

4. Describe the audits and auditors in governmental, internal and operational auditing.

5. Describe the organization of public accounting firms and identify the various services they offer.

6. Provide an overview of international and U.S. auditing (Appendix 1A).

7. Describe alternative theories of the role of auditing in society (Appendix 1B).

8. List and explain the requirements for becoming a public accountant (Appendix 1C).

9. Describe the accounting and auditing activities of the professional accounting organizations (Appendix 1C).

PROFESSIONAL PRACTICE

USER DEMAND FOR RELIABLE INFORMATION
· · · · · · · · · · · ·

Accounting

LEARNING OBJECTIVE
1. Distinguish *auditing* from *accounting*.
The following three underlying conditions affect demand by users for accounting information:

1. **Complexity.** A company's transactions can be numerous and complicated. Users of financial information are not trained to collect and compile it themselves. They need the services of professional accountants.
2. **Remoteness.** Users of financial information are usually separated from a company's accounting records by distance and time, as well as by lack of expertise. They need to employ full-time professional accountants to do the work they cannot do for themselves.
3. **Consequences.** Financial decisions are important to the state of investors' and other users' wealth. Decisions can involve large dollar amounts and massive efforts. The consequences are so important that good information, obtained through the financial reports prepared by accountants, is an absolute necessity.

Accounting is the process of recording, classifying and summarizing into financial statements a company's transactions that create assets, liabilities, equities, revenues and expenses. It is the means of satisfying users' demands for financial information that arise from the forces of complexity, remoteness and consequences. The function of **financial reporting** is to provide statements of financial position (balance sheets), statements of results of operations (income statements), cash flow statements and accompanying disclosure notes (footnotes) to outside decision makers who have no internal source of information like the management of the company has. A company's accountants are the producers of such financial reports. In short, accounting tries to record and summarize economic reality for the benefit of economic decision makers (the users).

Auditing

Financial decision makers usually obtain their accounting information from companies that want to obtain loans or sell stock. This source of information creates a potential **conflict of interest**, which is a condition that creates society's demand for audit services. Users need more than just information; they need reliable information. Preparers and issuers (directors, managers, accountants and others employed in a business) might benefit by giving false, misleading or overly optimistic information. The potential conflict has become real often enough to create a natural scepticism on the part of users. Thus, they depend on professional auditors to serve as objective intermediaries who will lend some credibility to financial information. This "lending of credibility" is also known as **providing assurance**, and external auditing of financial statements is described as an **assurance engagement**.

Auditing does not include the function of financial report production. That function is performed by a company's accountants under the direction of its management. Auditors obtain evidence that enables them to determine whether the information in the financial statements is reliable. Auditors then report to the users that the information is reliable by expressing an opinion that the company's presentation of financial position, results of operations and changes in financial position is in accordance with generally accepted accounting principles (GAAP), or some other disclosed basis of accounting. This opinion is the assurance provided by the assurance function, as it relates to the traditional financial statements.

Independent auditors work for clients. A **client** is the person (company, board of directors, agency or some other person or group) who retains the auditor and pays the fee. In financial audits the client and the auditee usually are the same economic entity. **Auditee** is the actual designation of the company or other entity whose financial statements are being audited. Occasionally the client and the auditee are different. For example, if Conglomerate Corporation hires and pays the auditors to audit Newtek Company in connection with a proposed acquisition, Conglomerate is the client and Newtek is the auditee.

Reliable financial information helps make capital markets efficient and helps people understand the consequences of a wide variety of economic decisions. Independent auditors practising the assurance function are not, however, the only auditors at work in the economy. Bank examiners, Canada Customs and Revenue Agency auditors, provincial regulatory agency auditors (e.g., auditors with a province's Commissioner of Insurance), internal auditors employed by a company and the Auditor General of Canada all practise auditing in one form or another.

R E V I E W
CHECKPOINTS

1.1 What conditions create demand for financial reports, and who produces financial reports for external users?

1.2 What is assurance? What condition creates demand for assurance to financial reports?

1.3 What is the difference between a client and an auditee?

1.4 What is the difference between auditing and accounting?

BRIEF HISTORY OF AUDITING

LEARNING OBJECTIVE
2. Chronicle the historical development of auditing standards, including the criticisms of the profession and its responses.

Auditors have been around for a long time. As long as there has been civilization, there has been a need for some types of record-keeping to implement accountability. In fact, it was the need to keep records of ownership of quantities of goods that led to the development of writing and arithmetic. The first number systems and the first written words were developed as symbols to keep track of merchandise either collected as taxes or used in trade. It was centuries later that literature and mathematics evolved separately, far removed from this initial accountability application. For example, the first proto-Greek written script, Linear B, was essentially developed for keeping records of business transactions and palace inventories in Mycenaean Greece of 1400–1300 B.C. It was only in 800–700 B.C. that a further evolved writing system was used to record some of the earliest works of Western literature, the *Iliad* and the *Odyssey*. By then in Greece writing had evolved to the point of recording outstanding deeds and social events and not just commercial transactions. Similarly, accounting and measuring evolved into more abstract mathematics. This pattern of the gradual evolution of writing had been seen in many even earlier civilizations, starting with the Sumerians (3000 B.C.), the Egyptians (2500 B.C.), the first Indus River civilization (2500 B.C.) and the start of the Xia dynasty in China (2300 B.C.).

Auditing accompanied the development of accounting, and the first recorded auditors were the spies of King Darius of ancient Persia (522 to 486 B.C.). These auditors acted as "the King's ears" checking on the behaviour of provincial satraps. The word *auditor* comes from the Latin word "to hear" because in ancient times auditors listened to the oral reports of responsible officials (stewards) to owners or those having authority, and confirmed the accuracy of the reports. Over the centuries this role of auditors as verifiers of official reports evolved to include that of verifying written records. By A.D. 1500 double-entry bookkeeping had evolved to the point of being documented by Luca Pacioli of Italy in the first known book on accounting. Pacioli also recommended that the accounting records be verified by auditors. By the early nineteenth century auditors acting as independent outside experts were frequently called upon to investigate and report on business failures or to settle business disputes. Independence is a key characteristic of the auditor that we will discuss in some detail throughout this book. For now think of it as conditions necessary to obtain an objective appraisal of the subject matter at issue. If the auditor showed any bias in his or her investigation, or even if there was merely the suspicion of bias, the effectiveness of the auditor's report would be greatly reduced.

Modern auditing began in 1844 when the British Parliament passed the Joint Stock Companies Act, which for the first time required that corporate directors report to shareholders via an audited financial statement, the balance sheet. In 1844 the auditor was required neither to be an accountant nor to be independent, but in 1900 a new Companies Act was passed that required an independent auditor.

The first public accountants' organization was the Society of Accountants in Edinburgh, organized in 1854, and Scotland and England became the leaders in establishing an accounting profession. As a result of the British lead, the first North American association of accountants, later to become the Institute of Chartered Accountants of Ontario, was organized in 1879 in Toronto. The Quebec Order became the first legally incorporated accounting association in North America in 1880. The Canadian Institute of Chartered Accountants (CICA) began under federal incorporation laws in 1902. And the Certified General Accountants Association of Canada was incorporated by an Act of Parliament in 1913.

Following British precedents, the first legislation requiring audits in Canada was the Ontario Corporations Act of 1907. This was followed by the Federal Corporation Act of 1917. Until 1930 Canadian practice followed the British model, focusing on the procedures that were followed to process a transaction (transaction oriented); these procedures largely relied on internal evidence.

After the 1929 stock market crash and the Great Depression of the 1930s, Canadian practice was increasingly influenced by developments in the United States. U.S. practice had evolved since the late nineteenth century toward a process of collecting evidence as to assets and liabilities or what is frequently referred to as a balance sheet audit. As a result of extensive misleading financial reporting that contributed to the stock market crash of 1929 and the world depression of the 1930s, the U.S. passed legislation in 1933 and 1934 that greatly influenced auditing around the world. The U.S. Securities Acts of 1933 and 1934 created the Securities and Exchange Commission (SEC), which regulated the major stock exchanges in the United States. Companies wishing to trade shares on the New York Stock Exchange or the American Stock Exchange were required to issue audited income statements as well as balance sheets. In addition, because of the earlier problems with misleading financial reports of the 1920s, the emphasis switched to fairness of presentation of these financial statements, and the auditor's role was to verify the fairness of presentation.

In 1941, as a result of experience in the McKesson and Robbin's fraud case (discussed in Chapter 17), the SEC recommended references to "generally accepted audit standards (GAAS)" in the auditor's report and mandated more extensive reliance on external evidence. This created a need to better define audit standards and objectives. This process was begun in 1948 by the American Institute of Certified Public Accountants (AICPA).

These developments in the United States greatly influenced Canadian auditing as well as auditing in the rest of the world. For example, in 1946 the CICA began its own standards for financial statement disclosure in Bulletin #1. A series of bulletins were issued over the next 20 years covering accounting and auditing matters. In 1968 these bulletins were reorganized into a single volume called the *CICA Handbook*. Revisions and additions to the *Handbook* have been made with such regularity since then that in the 1990s the *Handbook* was split into two volumes, one containing the accounting recommendations (*Sections* 1000 to 5000), and another covering the assurance and related services recommendations (*Sections* 5000 and higher) for both the private and public sectors.

An important development of standard setting in Canada was the adoption of Bulletins of the CICA in the Ontario (1953) and Federal Corporation Acts. In 1965 the Ontario Securities Act gave the Ontario Securities Commission (OSC) responsibility to regulate the Toronto Stock Exchange, Canada's largest. In 1972 an OSC Policy Statement mandated the use of the *CICA Handbook* to determine generally accepted accounting principles (GAAP). These requirements were soon incorporated in the *Ontario Securities Act* of 1978 and the *Canadian Business Corporation Act* of 1975. As a result of these developments, the status of *Handbook Recommendations* carries the force of law in Canadian reporting.

In contrast, the accounting and auditing standards developed by the American Institute of Certified Public Accountants (AICPA) and the Financial Accounting Standards Board (FASB) do not have comparable legal status in the United States. There, the SEC has the legal authority to set accounting standards for all the U.S. stock exchanges; however, the SEC has for the most part delegated this authority to the FASB and the AICPA. See Appendix 1A for more details on U.S. developments.

The failure of two Alberta banks in the first half of the 1980s and the resultant enquiry by the Estey Commission in 1985 raised questions about the effectiveness of audit and accounting standards in Canada. In response, the CICA helped organize the Macdonald Commission, which enquired into the public accounting profession. The commission's report came out in 1988 with 50 recommendations for improving accounting and auditing practice to help reduce a perceived "expectations gap" between what the public expects of auditors and what auditors can deliver. As a result of these recommendations the CICA attempted to reduce the gap through promulgation of new standards related to the auditor's report, auditor responsibility for detecting fraud and documentation of internal control evaluations. These recommendations are covered in the relevant chapters throughout this text.

Similar expectations gap standards were developed in the United States as a result of business and audit failures there, especially with respect to the savings and loan industry. A fundamental difference between the U.S. and Canadian environments, however, is the extent of government involvement in monitoring the profession. In the U.S. there have been several congressional investigations in the last two decades, with pressure being exerted through the Securities and Exchange Commission, which acts as a regulator of the profession (see Appendix 1A). In Canada, on the other hand, the government and regulators by and large have relied on the CICA standard-setting process to address public concerns.

Both countries' systems, however, are still far from perfect as indicated by recent criticisms of the profession by regulators. (See box below.) For this and other reasons the profession must continue evolving in response to changes in the business environment, and changes in public expectations. The profession is thus a dynamic and constantly changing one, and practicing auditors must expect to be engaged in a lifelong learning process.

For example, an August 31, 2000 report by a U.S. *Panel on Audit Effectiveness* may prove to be influential globally. This report is directed to the United States' Securities and Exchange Commission and encourages the development of international standards that can be used around the world. The purpose of the report is to address the types of problems noted in the box below. The report has as one of its major recommendations that all audits of financial statements include some "forensic-type" procedures in order to "enhance the prospects of detecting material financial statement fraud." Traditionally, forensic-type procedures have been restricted to specialized investigative engagements. (See Chapter 19 for more discussion of forensic-type procedures.)

R E V I E W
CHECKPOINTS

1.5 What single event can be said to have prompted the development of generally accepted auditing standards?

1.6 Identify the major changes to the auditing profession since 1945.

DEFINITIONS OF AUDITING

Academic Accountants' Definition of Auditing

LEARNING OBJECTIVE
3. Define and explain auditing, especially its role in information risk reduction.

The American Accounting Association (AAA) Committee on Basic Auditing Concepts (1971) prepared a comprehensive definition of auditing:

> Auditing is a systematic process of objectively obtaining and evaluating evidence regarding assertions about economic actions and events to ascertain the degree of correspondence between the assertions and established criteria and communicating the results to interested users.

"Stocks Watchdog Issues Warning to Auditors"

Questionable accounting practices cited

FROM CANADIAN PRESS

Canada's most powerful securities regulator has issued a harsh warning to auditors who connive in what legendary investor Warren Buffett has derided as "bold, imaginative accounting."

David Brown, chairman of the Ontario Securities Commission, told a luncheon of the Institute of Chartered Accountants of Ontario yesterday that the commission is "troubled" by an erosion of investor confidence in corporate financial reports.

"Commission members and staff, investors and analysts alike are expressing a growing frustration that a variety of problems appear to be not only persisting but flourishing," Brown told the accountants.

He specifically cited inconsistencies in the accounting treatment of costs, senior management compensation, short amortization periods and writeoffs of such intangibles as goodwill. And he stressed that the problems are not isolated.

OSC staff "regularly encounter situations in which reporting issuers and their auditors stretch the interpretation of accounting standards beyond all reasonable limits," Brown said.

And he warned the accountants that they could face a regulatory crackdown and the OSC might impose rules overriding the profession's own handbook of standards.

"An extraordinary level of trust is reposed in the auditor — a trust that is unparalleled amongst professionals with the possible exception of judges. There are few external checks and balances," he said.

"If the commission is to continue with its current approach, it must be satisfied that the standards-setting process, and the public accounting firms who are also important players in that process, are acting independently and in the public interest. We have a growing concern that this may not be the case."

On the corporate side, "I am very much aware of the pressures public companies face today."

In an environment in which share prices can decline dramatically on the basis of reported earnings in a single quarter, the temptation to distort earnings to meet expectations is enormous," Brown said.

"Operating in our public capital markets is not, however, an unqualified right. It carried responsibilities, and one of the most fundamental is to provide full, true and plain disclosure on a timely basis. I appeal to corporate managers and corporate directors to become part of the solution rather than part of the problem."

Brown's concern echoes statements by U.S. Securities and Exchange Commission head Arthur Levitt and a recent diatribe by Buffett in the annual report of his Berkshire Hathaway holding company.

"Clearly the attitude of disrespect that many executives have today for accurate reporting is a business disgrace," Buffett wrote.

"And auditors have done little on the positive side. Though auditors should regard the investing public as their client, they tend to kowtow instead to the managers who choose them and dole out their pay."

Source: Toronto Star, June 10, 1999, B12.

This definition contains several ideas important in a wide variety of audit practices. The first and most important concept is the perception of auditing as a systematic process that is purposeful and logical and is based on the discipline of a structured approach to decision making. Auditing is not haphazard, unplanned or unstructured.

The audit process, according to this definition, involves obtaining and evaluating evidence that consists of all the influences that ultimately guide auditors' decisions, and relates to assertions about economic actions and events. When beginning an audit engagement, an external auditor is given financial statements and other disclosures by management and thus obtains management's assertions about economic actions and events (assets, liabilities, revenue, expense). Evidence is then acquired which either substantiates or contradicts these management assertions.

External auditors generally begin work with explicit representations from management—assertions of financial statement numbers and information disclosed in footnotes. Other auditors, however, are typically not so well provided with explicit representations. An internal auditor, for example, may be assigned to "evaluate the cost effectiveness of the company's policy to lease, rather than to purchase, heavy equipment." A governmental auditor may be assigned to determine, for example, whether goals of creating an environmental protection agency have been met by the agency's activities. Often times, these latter two types of auditors must develop the explicit standards of performance for themselves.

The purpose of obtaining and evaluating evidence is to ascertain the degree of correspondence between the assertions and established criteria. Auditors will ultimately communicate their findings to interested users. To communicate in an efficient and understandable manner, there must be a common basis for measuring and describing financial information. Such a basis constitutes the established criteria essential for effective communication.

Established criteria may be found in a variety of sources. For external auditors, governmental auditors and Canada Customs and Revenue Agency inspectors, the criteria largely consist of the generally accepted accounting principles (GAAP). Canada Customs and Revenue Agency inspectors also rely heavily on criteria specified in federal tax acts. Governmental auditors may rely on criteria established in legislation or regulatory agency rules. Bank examiners and provincial insurance board auditors look to definitions and rules of law. Internal and governmental auditors rely a great deal on financial and managerial models of efficiency and economy as well as on generally accepted accounting principles (GAAP). All auditors rely to some extent on elusive criteria of general truth and fairness.

Exhibit 1–1 depicts an overview of financial statement auditing.

Audit Objective and the Auditor's Report

The American Accounting Association definition is broad and general enough to encompass external, internal and governmental auditing. Although the Canadian Institute of Chartered Accountants (CICA) has not defined auditing, its Audit Handbook Recommendation, "Audit of Financial Statements—an introduction" (*Section* 5090), sets forth the main objective of a financial audit:

> The objective of the audit of financial statements is to express an opinion whether the financial statements present fairly, in all material respects, the financial position, results of operation and changes in financial position in accordance with generally accepted accounting principles, or in special circumstances another appropriate disclosed basis of accounting. Such an opinion is not an assurance as to the future viability of an entity nor an opinion as to the efficiency or effectiveness with which its operations, including internal control, have been conducted. . . . In the performance of an audit of financial statements, the auditor complies with generally accepted auditing standards (GAAS), which (as set out in Section 5100.02) relate to the auditor's qualifications, the performance of the audit and the preparation of his or her report.[1]

---

[1] The Auditing Recommendations of the *CICA Handbook* are authoritative CICA pronouncements on auditing theory and practice.

EXHIBIT 1–1   OVERVIEW OF FINANCIAL STATEMENT AUDITING

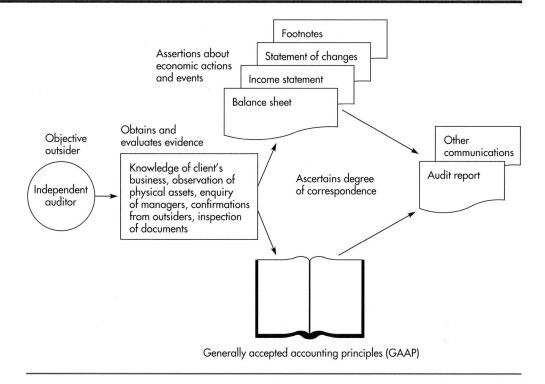

Generally accepted accounting principles (GAAP)

The CICA statement of objective restricts auditing interest to external auditors' audit of the traditional financial statements and their footnotes. However, as the needs of users change, new audit objectives and reports are created to meet new needs. Thus, the *CICA Handbook* also offers guidance on such divergent topics as reporting on control procedures at service organizations, on matters related to solvency and on examination of a financial forecast in a prospectus. A set of evolving "assurance standards" (presented in Chapter 2) may provide a framework to govern a wide range of assurance services.

The expression of the auditor's opinion on financial statements is found in the last paragraph of the audit report. A standard report is shown in Exhibit 1–2. (Chapter 3 explains this and other audit reports in more detail.)

EXHIBIT 1–2   AUDITOR'S REPORT

To the Shareholders of.........................

I have audited the balance sheet of .... as at ...., 20......, and the statements of income, retained earnings and changes in financial position for the year then ended. These financial statements are the responsibility of the company's management. My responsibility is to express an opinion on these financial statements based on my audit.

I conducted my audit in accordance with generally accepted auditing standards. Those standards require that I plan and perform an audit to obtain reasonable assurance whether the financial statements are free of material misstatement. An audit includes examining, on a test basis, evidence supporting the amounts and disclosures in the financial statements. An audit also includes assessing the accounting principles used and significant estimates made by management, as well as evaluating the overall financial statement presentation.

In my opinion, these financial statements present fairly, in all material respects, the financial position of the company as at ...., 20......, and the results of its operations and the changes in its financial position for the year then ended in accordance with generally accepted accounting principles.

City   (signed).....................................

Date   Chartered Accountants

A Definition of Auditing Relating to "Risk Reduction"

Although it is sometimes difficult to distinguish between a definition and a theory, most statements of theory begin with a definition. A theoretical viewpoint currently gaining popularity is that auditing is a "risk-reduction activity." The definition that supports this view is: Auditing is a process of reducing (to a socially acceptable level) the information risk to users of financial statements.

Economic activity takes place in an atmosphere of **business risk**. This risk is the chance a company takes that inflation will rise, taxes will increase, customers will buy from competitors, government grants will be lost, employees will go on strike and the like. Countering these negative examples are similar uncertainties that favourable events will occur. Auditors do not directly influence a company's business risk but they are responsible for proper disclosure of these risks in the financial statements. As the complexity of the business world grows, auditors are finding that they must increasingly focus their efforts in understanding the client's business risks. This understanding is necessary if the increased business complexity is to be properly reflected in the financial statements.

Information risk refers to the failure of the financial statements to appropriately reflect the economic substance of business activities, including business risks and uncertainties. In particular, information risk from the auditor's perspective is the risk (probability) that the financial statements distributed by a company will be materially false and misleading. Financial analysts and investors depend on financial reports for making stock purchase and sale decisions. Creditors (suppliers, banks and so on) use them to decide whether to give trade credit and bank loans. Labour organizations use financial reports to help determine a company's ability to pay wages. Government agencies and Parliament use them in preparing analyses of the economy and in making laws concerning taxes, subsidies and the like. These various users cannot take it on themselves to determine whether financial reports are reliable and, therefore, low on the information-risk scale. The users do not have the expertise, resources or time to enter thousands of companies to satisfy themselves about the veracity of financial reports; thus, they hire independent auditors to perform the assurance function and reduce the information risk. Auditors assume the social role of attesting to published financial information, thereby offering users the valuable service of assurance that the information risk is low. This role of auditors has been institutionalized through laws and regulations as discussed earlier on the history of the profession.

This risk-reduction definition may appear very general. As your study of auditing continues, you will find that auditors perform many tasks whose primary objective is to reduce the risk of giving an inappropriate opinion on financial statements. Auditors are careful to work for trustworthy clients, to gather and analyse evidence about the data in financial statements and to take steps to ensure that audit personnel report properly on the financial statements when adverse information is known. Subsequent chapters of this book will have more to say about various information-risk-reduction activities.

R E V I E W
CHECKPOINTS

1.7 Define and explain auditing. What would you answer if asked by an anthropology major: "What do auditors do?"

1.8 What is the essence of the risk-reduction theory (definition) of auditing?

1.9 Who cares about information risk reduction?

OTHER KINDS OF AUDITS AND AUDITORS

LEARNING OBJECTIVE
4. Describe the audits and auditors in governmental, internal and operational auditing.

The AAA, CAAA, CICA and the risk-reduction definitions clearly apply to the financial audit practice of independent external auditors who practise auditing in public accounting firms. The word *audit*, however, is used in other contexts to describe broader kinds of work.

The variety of audit work performed by different kinds of auditors causes some problems with terminology. Hereafter in this textbook, "independent auditor," "external auditor," "chartered accountant (CA)," "certified general accountant (CGA)" and "public accountant (PA)" will refer to people doing audit work with public accounting firms. In the governmental and internal contexts discussed below, auditors are identified as governmental auditors, operational auditors and internal auditors. While many of these auditors are chartered accountants or certified general accountants, the initials *PA, CA* and *CGA* in this book will refer to auditors in public practice. (Governmental and internal audit work is covered in more detail in Chapter 18.)

Operational and Internal Auditing

The Institute of Internal Auditors defined internal auditing and stated its objective as follows:

> Internal auditing is an independent appraisal function established within an organization to examine and evaluate its activities as a service to the organization. The objective of internal auditing is to assist members of the organization in the effective discharge of their obligations. To this end, internal auditing furnishes them with analyses, appraisals, recommendations, counsel, and information concerning the activities reviewed.

Internal auditing is practised by auditors employed by an organization, such as a bank, hospital, city government or industrial company. Some internal auditing activity is known as **operational auditing**. Operational auditing (also known as **performance auditing** and **management auditing**) refers to the study of business operations for the purpose of making recommendations about the economic and efficient use of resources, effective achievement of business objectives and compliance with company policies. The goal of operational auditing is to help managers discharge their management responsibilities and improve profitability.

Operational and internal auditors also perform audits of financial reports for internal use, much as external auditors audit financial statements distributed to outside users. Thus, some internal auditing work is similar to the auditing described elsewhere in this textbook. In addition, the expanded-scope services provided by internal auditors include: (1) reviews of control systems that ensure compliance with company policies, plans and procedures and with laws and regulations; (2) appraisals of the economy and efficiency of operations; and (3) reviews of effectiveness in achieving program results in comparison to pre-established objectives and goals.

Operational auditing is included in the definition of internal auditing cited above. In a similar context a PA may consider operational auditing performed by independent PA firms as a distinct type of management consulting service whose goal is to help a client improve the use of its capabilities and resources to achieve its objectives. So, internal auditors consider operational auditing integral to internal auditing, and external auditors define it as a type of management consulting service offered by public accounting firms.

Internal auditors need to be independent of the line managers in an organization, much like the external auditors need to be independent of the company management. Independence helps internal auditors be objective. They can make recommendations for correction of poor business decisions and practices, and they can praise good decisions and practices. If they were responsible for making the decisions or carrying out the practices, they could hardly be credible in the eyes of upper-management officers to whom they report. Consequently, the ideal organizational arrangement is to have internal auditors with no other responsibilities than to audit and to report to a very high level in the organization, such as a financial vice president and the audit committee of the board of directors. This arrangement is a type of internal independence that enhances the appraisal function (internal audit) within a company.

Governmental Auditing

The Office of the Auditor General of Canada (OAG) is an accounting, auditing and investigating agency of Parliament, headed by the Auditor General. In one sense, OAG auditors are the highest level of internal auditors for the federal government as a whole. Many provinces have audit agencies similar to the OAG. These provincial auditors answer to provincial legislatures and perform the same types of work described under governmental auditing below. In another sense, the OAG and similar provincial auditors are really external auditors with respect to government agencies they audit because they are organizationally independent.

Many government agencies have their own internal auditors and inspectors: for example, most federal ministries (Defense Ministry, Canada Customs and Revenue Agency) and provincial agencies (education, welfare, controller). Well-managed local governments (cities, regions, townships) also have internal audit staffs.

Governmental and internal auditors have much in common. The OAG shares with internal auditors the same elements of expanded-scope services. The OAG, however, emphasizes the accountability of public officials for the efficient, economical and effective use of public funds and other resources. The CICA sets accounting and auditing standards for all public sector audit engagements including the federal, provincial and local levels of government. Public sector audits can be described as comprehensive auditing as follows:

> Public Sector auditing includes financial, compliance and value-for-money (VFM) audits. . . . Financial statement audits determine (1) whether financial statements present fairly the financial position, results of operations . . . in accordance with generally accepted accounting principles, and (2) compliance audits determine whether the [audited] entity has complied with laws and regulations. . . . VFM audits include economy and efficiency and effectiveness audits.

In this definition you can see the audit function applied to financial reports and a compliance audit function applied with respect to laws and regulations. All government organizations, programs, activities and functions were created by law and are surrounded by regulations that govern the things they can and cannot do. For example, in some provinces there are serious problems of health card abuse and fraud by ineligible persons. A hospital cannot simply provide free services to anyone since there are regulations about eligibility of tourists and visitors from other countries. A compliance audit of such a service involves a study of the hospital's procedures and performance in determining eligibility and treatment of patients. Nationwide, such programs involve millions of people and billions of taxpayers' dollars.

Also in this definition you see value-for-money or VFM audits, a category that includes economy, efficiency and effectiveness audits. Government is always concerned about accountability for taxpayers' resources, and value-for-money audits are a means of seek-

---

SOME EXAMPLES OF RECOMMENDATIONS BASED ON VALUE-FOR-MONEY AUDITS CONDUCTED BY THE ONTARIO PROVINCIAL AUDITOR

HEALTH CARE: Stronger efforts needed to control undesirable patterns of practice by health care providers.

INSURANCE: Cost effectiveness of Ontario Insurance Commission monitoring activities was considered adequate.

EDUCATION: Need to improve procedures for availability of programs to exceptional children.

YOUNG OFFENDERS: Suggested improvements to documentation before releasing young offenders.

CRIMINAL LAW: Several recommendations made for better utilization of courtroom and judicial resources.

Source: The Office of the Provincial Auditor of Ontario.

ing to improve accountability for the efficient and economical use of resources and the achievement of program goals. Value-for-money audits, like internal auditors' operational audits, involve studies of the management of government organizations, programs, activities and functions.

Comprehensive governmental auditing is auditing that goes beyond an audit of financial reports and compliance with laws and regulations to include economy and efficiency and effectiveness audits. The public sector standard on the elements of comprehensive auditing is similar to the internal auditors' view. (These elaborations are presented in Chapter 18.)

The audit of a governmental organization, program, activity or function may involve financial auditing, compliance auditing, or VFM auditing, or all of them (a comprehensive audit). Public Sector standards do not require all engagements to include all types of audits. The scope of the work is supposed to be determined according to the needs of those who use the audit results.

Regulatory Auditors

For the sake of clarity, other kinds of auditors deserve separate mention. You probably are aware of tax auditors employed by the Canada Customs and Revenue Agency. These auditors take the "economic assertions" of taxable income made by taxpayers in their tax returns and audit these returns to determine their correspondence with the standards found in the Income Tax Act. They also audit for fraud and tax evasion. Their reports can either clear a taxpayer's return or claim that additional taxes are due.

Federal and provincial bank examiners audit banks, trust companies and other financial institutions for evidence of solvency and compliance with banking and other related laws and regulations. In 1985 these examiners as well as external auditors made news as a result of the failures of two Alberta banks—the first Canadian bank failures in over 60 years.

. . . .

R E V I E W
CHECKPOINTS

1.10 What is operational auditing? How does the CICA view operational auditing?

1.11 What are the elements of comprehensive auditing?

1.12 What is compliance auditing?

1.13 Name some other types of auditors in addition to external, internal and governmental auditors.

. . . .

PUBLIC ACCOUNTING
. . . .

The Accounting Profession

LEARNING OBJECTIVE

5. Describe the organization of public accounting firms and identify the various services they offer.

There are a number of professional associations representing accountants. In addition to the provincial Institutes of Chartered Accountants (the chartered accountants organization in Quebec is called Order of Chartered Accountants of Quebec), there are the Certified General Accountants Associations, the Societies of Management Accountants, and the Institute of Internal Auditors. Each of these provincial organizations also has a national coordinating and standard setting body: the Canadian Institute of Chartered Accountants (CICA), the Certified General Accountants' Association of Canada (CGAAC), the Society of Management Accountants of Canada (SMAC) and the Institute of Internal Auditors (IIA) which is an international organization with Canadian Chapters. Each of these organizations has developed their own professional designations as follows: the Chartered Accountants (CAs), Certified Management Accountants (CMAs), Certified General Accountants (CGAs) and Certified Internal Auditors (CIAs). The requirements for obtaining these various designations vary greatly and it is best to consult your provincial organization or local chapter for the details.

Generally the distinguishing features of these various designations are as follows: CAs have traditionally been oriented to providing auditing and related public accounting services for even the largest companies, CMAs have traditionally been oriented primarily to providing private management and internal accounting services, CIAs are oriented primarily to provide private internal audit services to larger organizations, and CGAs aim to provide all types of services, although they have been prohibited from doing external audits in some provinces. There is considerable overlap among all these accounting professionals in that they provide accounting, tax and management advisory work, with CAs and CGAs primarily oriented to providing these services to the public while CMAs and CIAs are oriented to provide these services to their full-time employer companies.

Recently, CGAs and CMAs have been obtaining public practice rights throughout Canada. The only exceptions now are the provinces of Ontario and Prince Edward Island, but even here there have been some moves toward accommodation. It is therefore more appropriate to talk about public accountants as PAs instead of CA's in a book about external auditing. Although we will use the more generic term *PA* throughout the book, many of our illustrations will be based on standards set by the CICA. The reason for this is that the CICA's standards are given legal standing in the courts through the various Federal and Provincial Corporation Acts, and through various regulatory policy statements. In addition, when CGAs and CMAs practice public accounting, their guides refer to the use of the *CICA Handbook* standards in the performance of public accounting services. Appendix 1C provides illustrations of public accounting standard setting activities and requirements.

Public Accounting Firms

Many people think of public accounting in terms of the "big" accounting firms. (As of July 2000, there were the "Big Five": Ernst & Young, Deloitte & Touche, KPMG, Price Waterhouse Coopers and Arthur Andersen & Co. Notwithstanding this perception, public accounting is practised in thousands of practice units ranging in size from sole proprietorships (individuals who "hang out the shingle") to international firms employing thousands of professionals. Many students look on public accounting as the place to begin a career: for three to ten years they gain intimate knowledge of many different business enterprises; they then select the industry segment in which to pursue their interests. Public accounting experience provides an excellent background to almost any business career.

Public accounting firms do business in a competitive environment. They are in business to make profits, yet they are also in the profession to perform public accounting services in the public/social interest. This duality—profit motive and professional responsibility—creates tensions between the need to perform quality services and the desire to make a profit.[2] As the 1980s closed and the 1990s began, public accounting felt the lingering effects of a national recession. Business sagged in some services, and some large public accounting firms trimmed partners and staff from their payrolls. One large accounting firm in the United States actually declared bankruptcy, reportedly pushed over the brink by lawsuits looming over malpractice claims. At the same time, some public accounting firms experienced growth, particularly in their taxation and consulting services.

Public accounting as a whole is a major employer of PAs performing assurance services, tax services and consulting services. Exhibit 1–3 shows a typical organization of a PA firm. PA firms differ in their organization. Some have other departments than those shown, such as small-business advisory and compensation consulting. Some PA firms have other names for their staff and management positions. The exhibit shows the most typical organizational structure for a larger PA firm.

---

[2] Note that this dichotomy exists in most professions: doctors often diagnose an illness and treat it; architects act on behalf of the owners of buildings and often also as general contractors.

EXHIBIT 1–3   PA FIRM ORGANIZATION

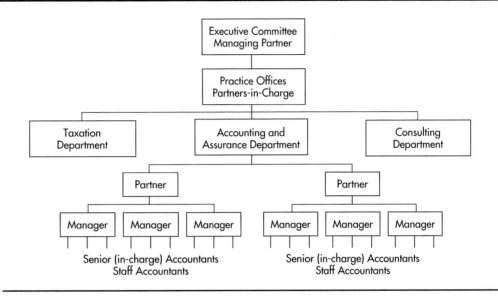

Assurance Services

Audits of traditional financial statements are the most frequent type of assurance services for public companies and for most large and medium nonpublic companies. Auditing amounts to around 30 to 40 percent of the business of most PA firms—a percentage that has shrunk dramatically in just two decades. Most of this textbook is about the audit of traditional financial statements.

Accounting and review services are the "nonaudit" or other services, performed frequently for medium and small businesses and not-for-profit organizations. A great deal of nonaudit work is done by small public accounting practice units. PAs can be associated with clients' financial statements without giving the standard audit report. They can perform compilation, which consists of writing up the financial statements from a client's books and records, without performing any evidence-gathering work. They can perform review, a semiaudit service in which some evidence-gathering work is performed, but which is lesser in scope than an audit. (Compilation and review standards are explained in more detail in Chapter 15.)

Assurance services are also performed on information in presentations other than traditional financial statements. Since assurance is the lending of credibility by an independent party (assurer, auditor) to the representations made by one person or organization to another, demand for numerous kinds of PA organizations has arisen. Public accountants have provided assurance to vote counts (Academy Awards), to the dollar amount of prizes claimed to have been given in sweepstakes advertisements, to investment performance statistics and to characteristics claims for computer software programs. These nontraditional services are governed by special sections of the *CICA Handbook,* or covered by the broader set of standards for assurance engagements (explained in more detail in Chapter 2) that are not covered by more specific standards. Henceforth, any reference to *Handbook Section* or *Section* is intended to mean sections of the *CICA Handbook.*

Taxation Services

Local, provincial, national and international tax laws are often called accountant and lawyer full-employment acts. The laws are complex, and PAs perform services of tax planning and tax return preparation in the areas of income, sales, property and other taxation. A large proportion of the practice in small accounting firms is tax practice. Tax laws change frequently, and tax practitioners must spend considerable time in continuing education and self-study to keep current with them.

Consulting Services

All accounting firms handle a great deal of consulting. The firm of Arthur Andersen & Company even separated its consulting practice under the name of Andersen Consulting. Consulting and management advisory services are the great "open end" of public accounting practice, placing accountants in direct competition with the non-PA consulting firms. The field is virtually unlimited, and a list of consulting activities could not possibly do justice to all of them. Indeed, accounting firms have created consulting units with professionals from other fields—lawyers, actuaries, engineers and advertising executives, to name a few. Many of the large accounting firms have tried to become "one-stop shopping centres" for clients' auditing, taxation and business advice needs.

In large PA firms the consulting department is quite often independent from the auditing and accounting department, performing engagements that do not directly interact with the audits performed by other professionals. In contrast, the OAG has on staff an equally wide range of expertise; but all its combined expertise goes into the audits and studies performed for Parliament. The OAG does not distinguish audits from consulting work, instead marshalling all its abilities to study the wide range of social, agricultural, defence, engineering and personnel activities it gets charged to investigate.

Regulation of Public Accounting

Regulation of public accounting, as with most professional groups, is a provincial matter. Most provinces have laws, public accountancy acts, that specify who can be allowed to practise public accounting in the province. For example, Ontario's Public Accounting Act licenses only CAs to perform audits and reviews. The Ontario act allows CAs to self-regulate, within constraints brought on by the Ontario Securities Commission and other regulators, as well by as the courts. Alberta's Public Accounting Act of 1988 licenses CMAs and CGAs, as well as CAs; British Columbia and Quebec license CAs and CGAs; while Saskatchewan and Manitoba have no public accountancy laws, effectively allowing anyone to practice. In a province like Saskatchewan, the various designations act as certificates signalling to the public that certain educational and experience requirements have been met, but legally anyone is allowed to practise public accounting. In such provinces market demand determines the relative success of the various designations. There may also be other legislation such as corporation acts that specify, for example, that CAs must perform the annual audits of a public corporation. Such legislation effectively creates demand for public accounting services, to be provided by the affected accounting association.

The general trend in provincial public accountancy legislation in recent years has been to open up public accounting to CGAs and CMAs as well as CAs. For example, currently there is a proposal before the Attorney General of Ontario to reform the Public Accounting Act to allow CGAs and CMAs to practise audits under controlled conditions in order to better serve the public interest. There is a desire to increase accessibility of public accounting services at reasonable cost while maintaining standards. The concern is to protect the public interest, particularly that of vulnerable third parties.

In addition to the self-regulatory system described above, there are other factors that have great influence on the profession. These include the legal system in which the profession operates (discussed in Chapter 17) and regulators that have an impact on practising auditors. These regulators include at the federal level the Superintendent of Financial Institutions, who has the prime responsibility for monitoring and protecting the public interest vis-à-vis the financial services industry falling under the jurisdiction of the Federal Bank Act. At the provincial level there are the securities commissions, which are charged with the responsibility of investor protection and with ensuring the fairness and efficiency of the capital markets in a province. There are securities commissions in every province and territory. Due to the division of powers between the provinces and the federal government, there is no national-level securities commission in Canada comparable to the SEC in the United States.

The Ontario Securities Commission (OSC) has responsibility for the biggest and most developed capital markets in Canada. It will be used as an illustration of the impact a regulator can have on public accounting. The OSC has three principal activities in ensuring the orderly functioning of capital markets within its jurisdiction, such as the Toronto Stock Exchange:

1. Registration of persons trading in securities and commodity futures contracts.
2. Reviewing and clearing of prospectuses.
3. Enforcement of the Securities Act and Commodity Futures Act.

Activities 2 and 3 have the most impact on public accountants. The staff of the OSC include the chief accountant and a chief forensic accountant who works under the director of enforcement. The Office of the Chief Accountant is responsible for the formulation of financial reporting policy and for monitoring the application of accounting principles and auditing standards by report issuers and their auditors. Financial statements are reviewed on a selective basis, and up to one-quarter of companies reviewed receive comment letters relating to inadequacies in their financial reports. The companies' auditors are also informed of problems noted. If the financial reporting problems are severe enough, the Enforcement Branch is notified.

An example of an Enforcement Branch report affecting an auditor follows:

> An investigation of National Business Systems Inc. resulted in the withdrawal of the company's financial statements for the year ended September 30, 1987. Revised financial statements were required because of "misrepresentations, new information which either was not available or was withheld at the time of the audit of the Original 1987 Statements and matters for which the original accounting was inappropriate". The shareholders equity in the revised financial was $22 million, a reduction of $56 million from the original figure of $78 million reported to shareholders. (*OSC 1988 Annual Report*; p. 18)

The office also monitors auditing and accounting standards-setting of the CICA, and provides input on emerging issues and commentary on proposed standards. In addition, since 1989 the OSC has issued Staff Accounting Communiques (SACs), which are intended to explain the OSC staff's views on specific reporting issues. Although the SACs have no official OSC approval, OSC staff are likely to challenge any treatment that is inconsistent with an SAC. In recent years the OSC, by publishing the results of its monitoring program, filing complaints to provincial disciplinary committees and through its representation on CICA standard-setting boards, has made a significant, ongoing impact on the profession.

There are other regulators that touch the profession. For example, the Canadian Investor Protection Fund, which is sponsored by the Toronto, Montreal, Vancouver and Alberta stock exchanges, and by the Toronto Future Exchange, as well as by the Investment Dealers Association of Canada, is a trust established to protect customers in the event of the financial failure of a member firm (any member of a sponsoring organization, and some American bond dealers that trade in Canada). In recent years Fund staff have taken a more active supervisory role. The Fund oversees regular, monthly, quarterly and annual reporting, periodic surprise visits to the offices of a member firm and at least one surprise financial questionnaire a year. The Fund can fine and set sanctions if a member firm violates capital, reporting or other requirements. The Fund develops policy statements that address standards for internal control within member firms. Auditors have to be aware of these standards when auditing member firms. Internal control reports are discussed in more detail in Chapter 15.

Another regulator that affects Canadian auditors whose client firms have dealings with U.S. securities markets is the SEC. In recent years many Canadian companies have gone to American and other international markets to raise cash through initial public offerings (IPOs). Many Canadian companies are finding it cheaper to raise money on public markets in other countries, because if they did so in Canada they would need to file regulatory documents in each province. This increases the cost of financing in Canada. At this writing, Finance Minister Paul Martin is exploring the idea of creating a national securities regulation in order to make Canadian securities markets more competitive.[3] The impact of the SEC on auditors is discussed in Appendix 1A.

---

[3] A. Freeman and K. Hawlett, "Keep IPO's at home: Martin." *The Globe and Mail*, Toronto (March 8, 1996), B1.

Finally, there are regulators such as provincial ministries of the environment and natural resources, which have an indirect impact on the profession through restrictions they place on client activities that the clients themselves may need to disclose as part of the client's business risk.

It is clear from this brief review that the profession is facing an increasingly complex regulatory environment and that auditors will have to be increasingly sensitized to regulator concerns in order to do a proper audit.

REVIEW
CHECKPOINTS

1.14 Identify several types of professional accountants and their organizations.

1.15 What are some examples of assurance services rendered on representations other than traditional financial statements?

1.16 What are the three major areas of public accounting services?

SUMMARY

This chapter began by defining auditing and distinguishing it from accounting. The practice of public accounting is rooted in the history of auditing, which started in Canada shortly before 1900. Events since the mid-1970s, in the form of various company failures and related litigation and enquiries, have propelled auditors in public practice into a phase of far-reaching change.

Auditing is practised in numerous forms by various practice units including PA firms, the Canada Customs and Revenue Agency, the OAG, internal audit departments in companies and several other types of regulatory auditors. Fraud examiners, many of whom are internal auditors and inspectors, have found a niche in auditing-related activities.

Many auditors aspire to become CAs, CGAs, CMAs or CIAs; this involves passing rigorous examinations, obtaining practical experience and maintaining competence through continuing professional education. Each of these groups has a large professional organization that governs the professional standards and quality of practice of its members.

When you begin a study of auditing, you may be eager to attack the nitty-gritty of doing financial statement audit work. These technical topics begin in Chapter 4. Instructors can choose to cover chapters in a different sequence than the one offered, but the next chapters introduce you to generally accepted audit standards and audit reports. Technical material starts in Chapter 4 and continues through Chapter 14. You are then introduced to other services and reports, professional ethics, legal liability, governmental and internal auditing and fraud awareness auditing. The book concludes with more advanced coverage of computer auditing and statistics.

Although the textbook will enable you to learn about auditing, instructors are seldom able to duplicate a practice environment in a classroom setting. You may feel frustrated about knowing "how to do it." This frustration is natural because auditing is done in the field under pressure of time limits and in the surroundings of client personnel, paperwork and accounting information systems. The textbook can provide a foundation and framework for understanding auditing, but nothing can substitute for the first few months of work when the classroom study comes alive in the field.

MULTIPLE-CHOICE QUESTIONS FOR PRACTICE AND REVIEW

1.17 When people speak of the assurance function, they are referring to the work of auditors in:
  a. Lending credibility to a client's financial statements.
  b. Detecting fraud and embezzlement in a company.
  c. Lending credibility to an auditee's financial statements.

d. Performing a program results audit in a government agency.

1.18 Company A hired Sampson & Delila, CAs, to audit the financial statements of Company B and deliver the audit report to Megabank. Which is the client?
a. Megabank.
b. Sampson & Delila.
c. Company A.
d. Company B.

1.19 According to the CICA, the objective of an audit of financial statements is:
a. An expression of opinion on the fairness with which they present financial position, results of operations and cash flows in conformity with generally accepted accounting principles.
b. An expression of opinion on the fairness with which they present financial position, results of operations and cash flows in conformity with accounting standards promulgated by the Financial Accounting Standards Board.
c. An expression of opinion on the fairness with which they present financial position, result of operations and cash flows in conformity with accounting standards promulgated by the CICA Accounting Standards Committee.
d. To obtain systematic and objective evidence about financial assertions and report the results to interested users.

1.20 Bankers who are processing loan applications from companies seeking large loans will probably ask for financial statements audited by an independent PA because:
a. Financial statements are too complex for them to analyse themselves.
b. They are too far away from company headquarters to perform accounting and auditing themselves.
c. The consequences of making a bad loan are very undesirable.
d. They generally see a potential conflict of interest between company managers

who want to get loans and their needs for reliable financial statements.

1.21 Operational audits of a company's efficiency and economy of managing projects and of the results of programs are conducted by whom?
a. Management advisory services departments of PA firms in public practice.
b. The company's internal auditors.
c. Governmental auditors employed by the federal government.
d. All of the above.

1.22 Independent auditors of financial statements perform audits that reduce and control:
a. The business risks faced by investors.
b. The information risk faced by investors.
c. The complexity of financial statements.
d. Quality reviews performed by other PA firms.

1.23 The primary objective of compliance auditing is to:
a. Give an opinion on financial statements.
b. Develop a basis for a report on internal control.
c. Perform a study of effective and efficient use of resources.
d. Determine whether auditee personnel are following laws, rules, regulations and policies.

1.24 Which of the following forms of auditing is considered to have the most limited objectives?
a. Operational auditing.
b. Performance auditing.
c. Management auditing.
d. Financial statement auditing.

1.25 Auditing standards are officially issued by the:
a. Financial Accounting Standards Board.
b. CICA Accounting and Review Services Committee.
c. CICA Auditing Standards Executive Committee.
d. CICA Assurance Standards Board.

EXERCISES AND PROBLEMS

1.26 **Controller as Auditor.** The chairman of the board of Hughes Corporation proposed that the board hire as controller a PA who had been the manager on the corporation's audit performed by a firm of independent accountants. The chairman thought that hiring this person would make the annual audit unnecessary and would consequently result in

saving the professional fee paid to the auditors. The chairman proposed to give this new controller a full staff to conduct such investigations of accounting and operating data as necessary. Evaluate this proposal.

1.27 **Controller as Auditor.** Put yourself in the position of the person hired as controller in the above situation. Suppose the chairman of the board moves to discontinue the annual audit because Hughes Corporation now has your services on a full-time basis. You are invited to express your views to the board. Explain how you would discuss the nature of your job as controller and your views on the discontinuance of the annual audit.

1.28 Logic and Method. Identify four major factors affecting information risk that make the need for independent audits important in today's business world. Give two examples for each of the factors.

1.29 Logic and Method. Auditors must have a thorough knowledge of generally accepted accounting principles (GAAP) if they are to properly perform an audit of the financial statements of a company. Explain why this is so. Use capital leases as an example of the need for this knowledge.

1.30 Operational Auditing. Bigdeal Corporation manufactures paper and paper products and is trying to decide whether to purchase and merge Smalltek Company. Smalltek has developed a process for manufacturing boxes that can replace other containers that use fluorocarbons for expelling a liquid product. The price may be as high as $45 million. Bigdeal prefers to buy Smalltek and integrate its products, while leaving the Smalltek management in charge of day-to-day operations. A major consideration is the efficiency and effectiveness of the Smalltek management. Bigdeal wants to obtain a report on the operational efficiency and effectiveness of the Smalltek sales, production and research and development departments.

Required:
Who can Bigdeal engage to produce this operational audit report? Several possibilities exist. Are there any particular advantages or disadvantages in choosing among them?

1.31 Definition of Financial Position. Every independent auditor's opinion refers to the presentation of financial position in conformity with generally accepted accounting principles. Search the authoritative accounting and economics literature (or conduct interviews with practising auditors) and find the official definition of "financial position." Determine whether the definition(s) is adequate for you and defend your support or criticism of the definition.

1.32 Auditor as Guarantor. Your neighbour invited you to lunch yesterday. Sure enough, it was no "free lunch" because he wanted to discuss the annual report of the Dodge Corporation. He owns Dodge shares and just received the annual report. He says: "Price Waterhouse prepared the audited financial statements and gave an unqualified opinion, so my investment must be safe."

Required:
What misconceptions does your neighbour seem to have about the auditor's role with respect to Dodge Corporation?

1.33 Identification of Audits and Auditors. Audits may be characterized as (*a*) financial statement audits, (*b*) compliance audits—audits of compliance with control policies and procedures and with laws and regulations, (*c*) economy and efficiency audits and (*d*) program results audits. The work can be done by independent (external) auditors, internal auditors or governmental auditors. Below is a list of the purposes or products of various audit engagements:
1. Render a public report on the assumptions and compilation of a revenue forecast by a sports stadium/racetrack complex.
2. Determine the fair presentation in conformity with GAAP of an advertising agency's financial statements.
3. Report on how better care and disposal of vehicles confiscated by drug enforcement agents could save money and benefit law enforcement.
4. Determine costs of municipal garbage pickup services compared to comparable service subcontracted to a private business.
5. Audit tax shelter partnership financing terms.
6. Study a private aircraft manufacturer's test pilot performance in reporting on the results of test flights.
7. Conduct periodic examination of a bank for solvency.
8. Evaluate the promptness of materials inspection in a manufacturer's receiving department.

Required:
Prepare a three-column schedule showing: (1) Each of the engagements listed above; (2) the type of audit (financial statement, compliance, economy and efficiency, or program results); and (3) the kind of auditors you would expect to be involved.

1.34 Analysis and Judgment. As part of your regular year-end audit of a publicly held client, you must estimate the probability of success of its proposed new product line. The client has experienced financial difficulty during the last few years and—in your judgment—a successful introduction of the new product line is necessary for the client to remain a going concern.

There are five steps, all of which are necessary for successful introduction of the product: (1) successful labour negotiations between the construction firms contracted to build the necessary addition to the present plant and the building trades unions; (2) successful defence of patent rights; (3) product approval by the Health Branch; (4) successful negotiation of a long-term raw material contract with a foreign supplier; and (5) successful conclusion of distribution contract talks with a large national retail distributor.

In view of the circumstances, you contact experts, who have provided your audit firm with reliable estimates in the past. The labour relations expert estimates that there is an 80 percent chance of successfully concluding labour negotiations before the strike deadline. Legal counsel advises that there is a 90 percent chance of successfully defending patent rights. The expert on Health Branch product approvals estimates a 95 percent chance of approval. The experts in the remaining two areas estimate the probability of successfully resolving (*a*) the raw materials contract and (*b*) the distribution contract talks to be 90 percent in each case. Assume these estimates are reliable.

Required:

What is your assessment of the probability of successful product introduction? (Hint: You can assume the five steps are independent of each other.)

APPENDIX 1A

OVERVIEW OF INTERNATIONAL AND U.S. AUDITING

. . . .

International Auditing

LEARNING OBJECTIVE
6. Provide an overview of international and U.S. auditing.

Many of the large public accounting firms are worldwide organizations that have grown rapidly in the last few decades paralleling the increased economic integration of their global clientele. Developments such as the North American Free Trade Agreement (NAFTA), the evolution of the European Economic Union and other free trade zones, and the pervasive effects of technological change are all contributing to increased global harmonization of auditing and accounting standards. For these reasons the International Federation of Accountants (IFAC) was created in 1977. The IFAC is increasingly mirroring the activities at an international level what national institutes have been doing domestically. In particular, the IFAC publishes its own handbook on auditing standards that recommends international standards on auditing (ISAs). ISAs cover such issues as basic principles of auditing, auditor's reports, professional independence, reliance on other auditors abroad and professional qualifications.

The issue is whether ISAs will achieve worldwide acceptance. This increasingly looks likely. For example, the *CICA Handbook* has a section (*Section* 5101) providing a comparison between the *Handbook* and ISAs. The CICA's policy is to adopt ISAs as is unless Canadian conditions require a different standard, and to keep existing practice until the CICA adopts a new ISA. *Section* 5101 either notes a significance difference between an ISA and a *Handbook Section(s)*, or makes the statement that there is no significant difference. Generally, the remaining significant differences between the *Handbook* and the ISAs are that the ISAs tend to focus more on (1) financial information instead of financial statements, (2) procedures rather than broader standards, (3) rules of professional conduct (something not covered in the *CICA Handbook*), (4) working paper documentation, (5) engagement letters, (6) reliance on other auditors, (7) management representatives, and (8) special purpose auditor reports. The CGAs have published their own GAAP guide, which, in addition to the *CICA Handbook,* references U.S. and IASC standards and notes key differences between the Canadian requirements and those of the IASC and the United States.

As the world becomes more interdependent, many concepts and terms used in other countries will become increasingly accepted in Canadian practice. Indeed, many large firms already use manuals and training materials reflecting international practice. This textbook makes use of those terms and concepts and does not restrict itself to those currently used in the *CICA Handbook.*

U.S. Auditing

In the United States the early formal development of accounting and auditing were mixed together. Working with the Federal Trade Commission, the Federal Reserve Board and the New York Stock Exchange, the American Institute of Accountants (later renamed the American Institute of Certified Public Accountants) produced these bulletins designed to systematize accounting and auditing:

1917— Federal Reserve Board, "Uniform Accounting: A Tentative Proposal Submitted by the Federal Reserve Board."

1918— Federal Reserve Board, "Approved Methods for the Preparation of Balance Sheet Statements."

1929— Federal Reserve Board, "Verification of Financial Statements."

1934— New York Stock Exchange, "Audits of Corporate Accounts."

1936— American Institute of Accountants, "Examination of Financial Statements by Independent Public Accountants."

These first 20 years were marked by interest in both accounting and auditing and by co-operation between the American Institute and government agencies. In 1939 the American Institute went its own way by creating the Committee on Auditing Procedure to deal exclusively with auditing matters. This committee launched the Statements on Auditing Procedure series, the first of which (1939) was titled "Extensions of Auditing Procedure."

Generally accepted auditing standards, however, were not known by that name until 1947. Following an investigation of the McKesson and Robbins fraud in the late 1930s and the auditors' failure to detect it, the Securities and Exchange Commission in the United States passed a rule requiring auditors to report that their audits were "in accordance with generally accepted auditing standards." The Committee on Auditing Procedure got busy (after being delayed by World War II) and published in 1947 the "Tentative Statements of Auditing Standards—Their Generally Accepted Significance and Scope."

Standard-setting for auditors has been the responsibility of the American Institute ever since, although the names have changed. In 1972 the AICPA Auditing Standards Executive Committee replaced the Committee on Auditing Procedure, and the series of auditing pronouncements was renamed *Statements on Auditing Standards*. Following an extensive study by the Commission on Auditors' Responsibilities (Cohen Commission), the committee's name was changed to the AICPA Auditing Standards Board (1978), which remains the AICPA's senior technical committee on auditing matters. (The name of the series, *Statements on Auditing Standards (SAS)*, was not changed.) The Cohen Commission was formed at a time when auditors were coming under criticism from the U.S. Congress. In the early 1970s several spectacular business failures and alleged audit failures drew the attention of senators and representatives, and they proposed a federal takeover of the regulation of accounting and auditing. Accountants abhor federal regulation, and the Cohen Commission report paved the way for several reforms that defused the congressional concerns, including the creation of the AICPA private companies practice section and the SEC practice section (discussed later in this appendix).

However, trouble would not go away. In the 1980s more business and audit failures led to creation of the National Commission on Fraudulent Financial Reporting (Treadway Commission). In 1987 this commission made numerous recommendations concerning auditors' responsibilities. Many of these recommendations were enacted by the Auditing Standards Board in several Statements on Auditing Standards, known generally as the expectation gap auditing standards. The main thrust of these new statements (issued in 1988 and numbered 53–61) was to increase auditors' responsibilities for detecting and reporting errors, irregularities, illegal acts, and frauds, and to enhance accounting firms' monitoring of the quality of their audit practices.

Congressional interest in the auditing profession continues to this day. Bank and savings and loan failures have heightened this interest. The Oversight and Investigations

THOUGHTS FROM "THE ACCOUNTING ESTABLISHMENT"

Selected Recommendations

Congress should exercise stronger oversight of accounting practices and more leadership in establishing proper goals and practices.

Congress should amend the Federal securities laws to restore the right of individuals to sue independent auditors for negligence.

Congress should consider methods of increasing competition among accounting firms for selection as independent auditors.

The Federal Government should directly establish financial accounting standards for publicly-owned corporations.

The Federal Government should establish auditing standards used by independent auditors.

Federal standards of conduct for auditors should prohibit representation of client interests and management advisory services for audit clients.

The Federal Government should define the responsibilities of independent auditors so that they clearly meet the expectations of Congress, the public, and courts of law.

Source: Staff Study by the Subcommittee on Reports, Accounting, and Management of the Senate Committee on Government Operations, 95th Congress, Document No. 95-34, March 31, 1977.

Subcommittee of the House Energy and Commerce Committee (chaired by Representative John Dingell, Democrat, Michigan) has held many hearings focusing on the effectiveness of independent accountants who perform audits. Legislation has been introduced that would, among other things, (1) require auditors to make special reports when clients commit illegal acts, (2) require the SEC to prescribe methods to be used by auditors to detect and report illegal activities, and (3) require the SEC to prescribe methods to detect illegal acts and related party transactions, and to evaluate companies' going-concern status. Only time will tell the nature and extent of new regulation of the auditing profession.

The AICPA currently regulates itself through the Division for CPA Firms. This division consists of two sections: the Private Companies Practice Section (PCPS) and the SEC Practice Section (SECPS). Accounting firms can volunteer to join one or both of the sections. Rules for membership include requirements for an average of 40 hours of continuing professional education (CPE) each year for professional employees and a peer review every three years. A peer review or quality review is a study of a firm's quality policies and procedures followed by a report on the firm's quality of audit practice. Both sections have peer review committees that review the work and reports of the peer reviewers. In addition, the SECPS has a Public Oversight Board (POB) that is like a board of outside directors. The POB consists of prominent people who serve as representatives of the public at large, overseeing the self-regulation of firms that audit companies registered with the U.S. Securities and Exchange Commission. Auditors of SEC-registered companies are required to be members of the SEC Practice Section. (Professionals working in accounting firms that audit SEC companies and are not members of SECPS cannot remain members of the AICPA.) The goal of this requirement is to ensure the high quality of audits of public companies. The SECPS membership consists of about 1,000 accounting firms that employ about 127,000 professionals and audit the 14,000 public companies.

The report discussed at the beginning of this chapter, recommending forensic-type procedures on all audits, was prepared by a panel appointed by the POB at the request of the SEC. This Panel on Audit Effectiveness was charged with thoroughly examining the current audit model, and the final version of its report will eventually influence audit practice around the world.

Quality Control Standards

From 1977 to 1982, the AICPA also had a Quality Control Standards Committee. This senior committee was dissolved after it issued its *Statement on Quality Control Standards No. 1 (QCS 1)*. The AICPA believed that, because the work of quality control and self-regulation was being handled well by the Division for Firms, a separate committee was no longer needed. Nevertheless, *QCS 1* remains as an authoritative practice standard. In 1987 the AICPA designated the Quality Review Executive Committee as a senior technical committee. This body develops policies and procedures for the peer review programs, and it currently provides the technical support for the reviews of accounting firms' quality controls.

Accredited Personal Financial Specialists

For many years the AICPA resisted proposals to accredit persons as specialists (e.g., tax specialists, consulting specialists). The ice was broken, however, in 1987. After the Colorado Society of CPAs instituted a successful specialization course and examination, the AICPA authorized the specialty designation of "Accredited Personal Financial Specialist" (APFS). Among the requirements are a one-day examination, 250 hours of personal financial planning experience in each of the past three years, and six reference letters from other professionals and clients. APFSs must also meet continuing education requirements, have valid CPA certificates in their states and maintain membership in the AICPA. Examinations are given annually and may be given more often in the future if demand is great enough. The AICPA has a Personal Financial Planning Executive Committee that has been designated by council as a senior technical committee to make official pronouncements relating to personal financial planning practice.

APPENDIX 1B

ALTERNATIVE THEORIES OF THE ROLE OF AUDITING IN SOCIETY

LEARNING OBJECTIVE

7. Describe alternative theories of the role of auditing in society.

In the chapter we defined *auditing* as an information-risk reducing activity. This definition follows from the information hypothesis that is used to explain the demand for external audits. Under the information hypothesis, audit services are demanded to reduce the information risk to users of financial statements. Information risk is the risk that user decisions may be based on incorrect information. Thus, auditors are demanded to reduce losses due to faulty decisions resulting from errors or irregularities in the financial statements. Losses to investors may also arise because of failure to disclose all the facts about a firm by company management. Auditors help assess whether this information asymmetry is alleviated through proper disclosure. Less-accurate information may also deter investment, so auditing may also alleviate underinvestment in the capital markets and result in better resource allocation in the economy.

Another hypothesis that has been proposed to explain the sources of demand for audits is the monitoring hypothesis. The monitoring hypothesis is based on the principal-agent framework of economic theory. Agency theory predicts that utility-maximizing agents (the managers), if unchecked, will consume more resources than optimal. However, investors with rational expectations will take such behaviour into account in pricing a firm's securities. As a result, the agents have the incentive to contract for mechanisms to monitor their opportunistic behaviour. The hiring of an external auditor is one such mechanism. This theory predicts that management will demand audits whenever the cost of monitoring their activities is less than the wage loss management suffers without the monitoring. The presumption here is that the owners of the firm will pay managers more with monitoring of their activities than without monitoring.

The insurance hypothesis predicts that auditors are demanded so that they may be sued in case there is a business failure. Auditing thus provides investors a form of insurance. If an investor purchases securities on the basis of audited financial statements and subsequently sustains losses, the law provides some degree of recourse against the auditor. In this way the auditor can, depending on how the court's reasoning works, function as an indemnifier against investment losses.

The degree of recourse depends on the legal system in force. Under a negligence-based concept, some form of audit failure needs to be proved. Moreover, for registration statements under SEC laws (covered in Chapter 17), the burden of proof is on the auditor to demonstrate that due care was observed in the audit task. Recent court cases in the United States seem to abandon the negligence concept in favour of an implied warranty concept. Under the implied warranty concept, the issue of whether the auditor is negligent is irrelevant. The auditor is responsible once it can be proved that the audited financial statement is wrong. This concept is concerned with accident (audit failure) prevention, compensating the injured and a better distribution of losses. Under implied warranty the audit fee may be little more than a fee for insurance against otherwise uninsurable business risk (e.g., due to management incompetence). We say "may" because it all depends on how courts interpret "wrong" financial statements: if "wrong" financial statements mean failure to anticipate *any* adverse business event, then auditors are responsible for insuring business losses. If, on the other hand, "wrong" financial statements mean failure to disclose only those adverse events for which there is information at the time of audit, then auditors are effectively liable only for information risk. So, much depends on court interpretation and the amount of damages awarded to the plaintiffs. The punitive damage award system in the United States—with its high multiples of actual damages—is close to the kind of system that would make auditors insurers of business risk. It is assumed that any auditor-insured business risk is then passed on in the form of fee increases to all clients. Clients in turn pass these costs on to society via increased prices for their products. In this way risks faced by investors are passed on to society—that is, business risk is socialized.

Each of these theories helps explain some aspect of the audit environment and some of the reasons audits are demanded. These theories are best viewed as complementary rather than mutually exclusive. These theories also appear to apply in different degrees in different countries and different legal systems. For example, in the United States the risk of an auditor being sued has traditionally been about 10 times that of the risk in Canada. This suggests that the insurance hypothesis may be a more important explanation of the demand for audits in the American business environment than in the Canadian business environment.

Each of these theories can provide a justification for reduced information risk. Clearly under the monitoring and information hypotheses, information risk is to be reduced for the principals and other users respectively. Under the insurance hypothesis it may be less obvious why information risk should be reduced. Under a negligence-based liability system, if the auditor can prove due care in reducing information risk, then the auditor will reduce the possibility of legal liability. Even under the implied warranty concept of insurance, reduced information risk will reduce the risk of legal liability because there is a lower chance of an audit failure or "accident" to cause the liability. Thus, despite the different explanations these hypotheses provide, they all have in common the auditor's need to reduce information risk. Some estimate that information risk is a significant component of cost of capital for many firms. A reduction in information risk thus has the tangible effect of reducing a firm's cost of capital.

APPENDIX 1C

HOW TO BECOME A PA

- -

Education

First, we discuss the education requirements for the CA designation. The provincial institutes, which are self-regulating in each province, set the education requirements for taking the CA examination and receiving a CA designation. The majority of provinces currently require a bachelor's degree, with some minimal credits in accounting.

In addition to entry-level education requirements, the provincial institutes, in conjunction with the CICA, have available optional continuing-education courses. However, with the North American Free Trade Agreement (NAFTA) and globalization of public accounting services there will be increasing harmonization of educational requirements in public accounting. For these reasons it is instructive to look at other countries' systems, especially that of the United States, which tends to lead global practice. At present with respect to continuing professional education, the AICPA and most states require 120 contact hours (not semester or quarter-college hours) of continuing professional education (CPE) over three-year reporting periods, with no less than 20 hours in any one year. CPAs who are not in public practice generally face fewer continuing-education requirements (the AICPA requires 90 hours over three-year reporting periods with no less than 15 hours in any one year.) These continuing-education hours are obtained in a variety of ways—AICPA continuing-education courses, state CPA society-sponsored courses, in-house training in CPA firms and industry, college courses and private-provider courses. These types of courses range in length from one hour to two days, depending on the subject. Although similar courses are also being offered by provincial institutes, at the current time CPE is done on a voluntary basis by most CAs. Check with your provincial institute.

CGAs and CMAs also have a university degree requirement that varies by province. Check with your provincial association or society for more details.

PA Examination

The Uniform Final Examination is prepared by the Examinations Division of the CICA. It is administered in September each year throughout Canada and Bermuda. The examination covers business law, auditing, accounting practice and theory. These topics are covered in depth separately as well as being integrated in a comprehensive case format reflecting a realistic professional setting. Because qualifications for taking the CA examination vary from province to province, you should contact your provincial institute for information. CGA examinations are designed to provide an in-depth assessment of knowledge and skills in accounting, auditing, finance and taxation. Students take the various level exams after completing a specific program of courses. Check your provincial association for more details. CMA students must also pass a comprehensive entrance exam on accounting and management knowledge gained through university studies, as well as a case presentation and board report upon completion of the program.

Experience

Most provinces and territories require persons who have attained the education level and passed the CA Examination to have a period of experience before they are awarded CA designations. Experience requirements vary among provinces, but the most common system requires two years for holders of bachelor's degrees and one year for holders of master's degrees. While a few provinces require that the experience be obtained in a public accounting firm, most of them accept experience in other organizations (provincial auditor, Canada Customs and Revenue Agency) as long as the applicant performs work requiring accounting judgment and is supervised by a competent accountant, preferably a CA.

CGAs and CMAs also have experience requirements that vary among provinces.

Provincial Certificate and Licence

The CICA does not issue CA certificates or licences to practice. There is no national CA certificate. Most provinces and territories have public accountancy laws and provincial institutes to administer them. These are the agencies that make physical arrangements to give the CA examination (called the Uniform Final Examination or UFE), collect the examinations, receive the grades from the CICA grading service and notify candidates whether they passed or failed. After satisfying provincial requirements for education and experience, successful candidates are awarded the CA designation by a province. Thereafter, provincial institutes regulate the behaviour of CAs under their jurisdiction (enforcing provincial rules of professional conduct) and supervise practice inspection.

Provincial associations and societies regulate the practice of CGAs and CMAs respectively. This regulation includes enforcing the provincial rules of professional conduct and administering subject area and national exams as well as the programs of professional education courses.

R E V I E W
C H E C K P O I N T S

1.35 Can you see any justification for requiring 150 semester-hours of university courses for PAs?

1.36 How much continuing education is required of PAs?

1.37 Why do you think experience is required by all provinces to be a PA?

1.38 What are some of the functions of a provincial institute, association or society?

THE NATIONAL AND PROVINCIAL ORGANIZATION OF PAs

LEARNING OBJECTIVE

9. Describe the accounting and auditing activities of the professional accounting organizations.

Public recognition of PAs as professionals is enhanced by the existence of professional organizations both nationally (CICA, CGAAC, SMAC) and provincially. The provincial institutes' societies and associations have responsibility for setting and enforcing standards of qualification, standards of adherence and standards of enforcement. The standards of qualification relate to enrolment, education and examination of students, and each provincial institute society and association has responsibility for administering each aspect of qualification through various committees, such as in Ontario the Education Coordination Committee and Applications Committee of the ICAO. Each ICAO committee is assisted by at least one full-time staff member of ICAO.

Standards of adherence relate to the system of practice inspection that a province may have to monitor the quality of audit practice. The objective is to provide feedback to members on the quality of their work, and, if needed, recommendations for additional training. There are also practice advisory services and consultation services provided to members on request, usually for sole practitioners or smaller firms. The standards of enforcement relate to the activities of professional conduct, discipline and appeals as discussed in Chapter 16. Activities of provincial institutes also include lobbying activities with provincial governments for changes to legislation in such areas as securities regulation, corporation acts and taxation. Since 1991 there have also been various Co-ordination Committees set up to co-ordinate issues such as rules of professional conduct and education across the various provinces. A partial organization chart of the Institute of Chartered Accountants of Ontario (ICAO) is shown in Exhibit 1C–1 as an illustration. This chart reflects the management and senior staff of the Institute, many of whom act in an advisory capacity to related committees.

Regulation 44 of the Canada Business Corporation Act requires that financial statements of companies subject to the Act be prepared in accordance with the recommendations of the *CICA Handbook.* Thus the CICA has primary responsibility for standards of practice, including the setting of accounting, auditing and other assurance standards through the

EXHIBIT 1C–1   PARTIAL ORGANIZATION CHART OF THE INSTITUTE OF CHARTERED ACCOUNTANTS
OF ONTARIO

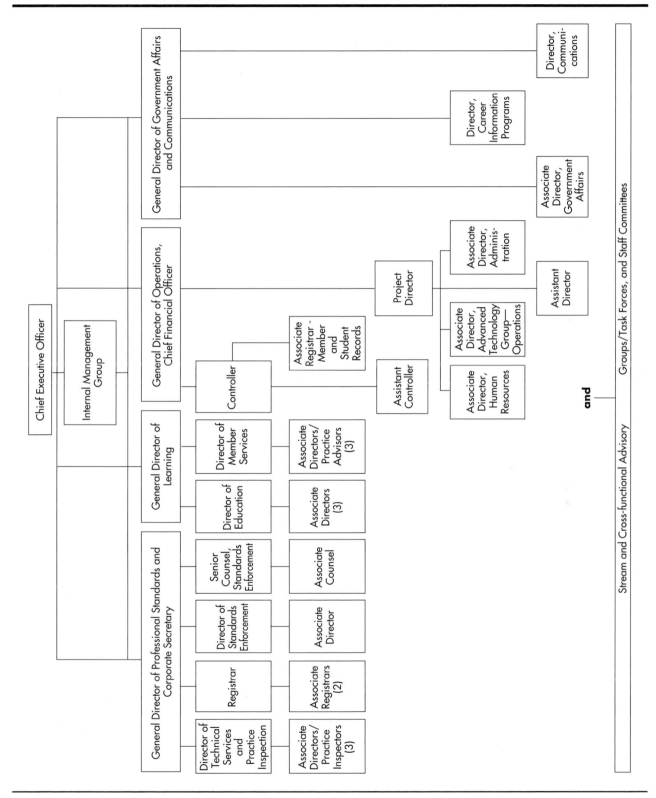

E X H I B I T 1C–2   **PARTIAL CICA ORGANIZATION CHART**

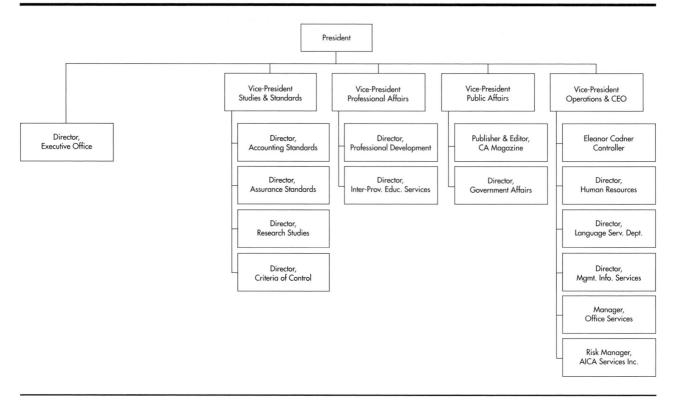

Handbook. However, the CICA also has other objectives, such as to maintain the highest national and international stature as a professional organization; in co-operation with the provincial Institutes, to develop and maintain a body of knowledge and to prepare the uniform final exam; and to promote international harmonization of principles, standards and practices of the profession.

To achieve these various objectives the CICA operates through numerous committees and groups. A list of some of the more important committees follows:

1. Accounting Research and Auditing Standards Committees
2. Federal Legislation Committee
3. Management Consultants and Taxation Committees

CICA Organization

A partial organization chart is shown in Exhibit 1C–2. It highlights the CICA divisions most closely related to accounting and auditing practice.

The national organizations of CGAs and CMAs also engage in similar activities, setting national standards or guides, including programs of basic research. However, currently only the CAs have gotten to the point of developing their own audit standards.

R E V I E W
C H E C K P O I N T S

1.39 Identify the type of standards set by the CICA.

1.40 Identify the type of standards set by provincial institutes of CAs.

1.41 Identify at least two other activities of the CICA besides standard setting.

1.42 Identify two interprovincial issues that require co-ordination by provincial institutes.

CHAPTER 2

Learning Objectives

Chapter 1 gave you a general introduction to professional accounting practice. Chapter 2 explains three sets of interrelated practice standards for audit services offered by PAs in public practice. Your objectives are to be able to:

1. Name the various practice standards for internal, governmental and independent auditors, and identify their sources.

2. Discuss the reasons for having general assurance standards and give some examples of assurance subject matters.

3. Write and explain the eight CICA generally accepted auditing standards (GAAS), and explain how GAAS was or was not followed in specific fact situations.

4. Describe the standard unqualified audit report in terms of its communication of audit standards and other messages.

5. Interpret GAAS in the context of a computer environment.

6. Explain some characteristics of "professional scepticism."

7. List and explain the important requirements of quality control standards for a PA firm.

ASSURANCE, AUDIT AND QUALITY CONTROL STANDARDS

PRACTICE STANDARDS

LEARNING OBJECTIVE
1. Name the various practice standards for internal, governmental and independent auditors, and identify their sources.

Practice standards are general guides for the quality of professional work. The North American accounting and auditing profession has many sets of standards, depending upon which sets are included or excluded in a particular count. This chapter deals directly with three sets: assurance standards, as suggested by various sections of the *CICA Handbook*; generally accepted auditing standards, issued by the CICA Assurance Standards Board; and quality control standards as reflected in firm peer review, and in provincial Institutes' practice inspection manuals and the CICA's *Guide for Developing Quality Control Systems in Public Accounting*.

Other chapters in this textbook explain other sets of standards. Chapter 16 covers the Rules of Professional Conduct. The CICA Recommendations for Compilation and Review Services are explained in Chapter 15. The CICA's public sector audit standards and the internal audit standards (Institute of Internal Auditors) are in Chapter 18. *Professional Standards and Practices for Certified Fraud Examiners* (Association of Certified Fraud Examiners) are in an appendix to Chapter 19.

Another set of auditing standards is known as the International Standards of Auditing (ISA), issued by the International Auditing Practices Committee of the International Federation of Accountants. In the international community, accountants and regulators have a great interest in **harmonization**—that is, making the standards co-ordinated, if not uniform, throughout the world. The ISAs are a first step in this direction. They are cited in this textbook along with the Canadian generally accepted auditing standards. Some differences exist, however. The *CICA Handbook* has summaries of the points on which the ISA's are more demanding or conflict with Canadian generally accepted auditing standards (*Section* 5101). Also CGA-Canada has prepared a guide relating CICA Standards to ISA and U.S. Standards.

You will find very few references to the accounting recommendations in this textbook. The CICA issues accounting standards but this book concentrates on auditing and the practice of accounting, not on the accounting rules themselves. An overview of the audit standard-setting process is provided in the next section.

OVERVIEW OF AUDITING STANDARD-SETTING PROCESS OF CICA[1]

The Vice-President Studies and Standards has overall responsibility for standard setting as indicated in Exhibit 1C–2 in Chapter 1. There are four directors, each reporting to the Vice-President Studies and Standards with various technical and support staff, in each of the following areas: (1) Accounting Standards, (2) Assurance Standards, (3) Criteria for Control, and (4) Research Studies.

In order to ensure due process, a number of key steps are taken in developing standards:

1. Identification of need and setting of priorities.
2. Preliminary investigation—if necessary, by means of a Study or Report.
3. Development and approval of a Project Proposal.

---

[1] This section is based on information supplied by CICA on their standard-setting process.

   4. Setting up and briefing of volunteer group (task force).

   5. The development of the draft Statement of Principles.

   6. The distribution of the draft Statement of Principles to "Associates."

   7. Approval by the respective standard-setting board/committee of the Statement of Principles.

   8. The development of the Exposure Draft.

   9. Approval by the respective standard-setting board/committee of the Exposure Draft.

   10. Processing of the comments on the Exposure Draft and meetings with respondents.

   11. Approval by the respective standard-setting board/committee of the final Standard in English and French.

   12. Production and distribution of the final Standard.[2]

The boards referred to in steps 7, 9 and 11 are made up of volunteer members, who are appointed for three-year terms as voting members, as well as staff of the CICA, who are nonvoting members. Volunteer efforts are critical to the CICA's standard-setting efforts: an estimated 5,400 volunteer days are contributed annually by some 850 volunteers. The formal objectives of the boards most relevant to this text are stated as follows:

   1. The Assurance Standards Board's objective is to develop and promulgate recommended performance and reporting standards and practice guidance on auditing and related services in the best interests of the profession and the public as a whole, for both the public and private sectors.

   2. The Criteria of Control Committee's objective is to develop criteria that will permit management to assess and report on control systems and publish such guidance as it considers to be in the best interests of the public, including users, preparers and auditors of control reports.

   3. The Studies Advisory Committee provides leadership and direction to the studies activity by supporting and monitoring the progress of projects initiated by the standard-setting boards and by identifying and stimulating research on other topics and themes that are likely to be of concern to the accounting profession.[3]

The entire process normally takes at least two years, and projects that are preceded by studies take the longest. An overview of the process is given in Exhibit 2–1.

More timely guidance is provided by Auditing Guidelines. Auditing Guidelines do not go through the full due process of a Standard and they do not have the same authority as *Handbook Recommendations.* The Boards issue Guidelines to clarify existing standards or provide guidance in their application on a timely basis.

· ·

R E V I E W
CHECKPOINTS

2.1 What are the practice standards, and who issues them for external auditors of financial statements? internal auditors? government auditors?

2.2 What are the practice standards, and who issues them for external nonaudit assurance engagements? quality of CA firms' audit practice? fraud examination work? consulting services? tax services? (Refer also to Chapter 1.)

· ·

[2] Ibid, p. 5.
[3] Ibid, p. 2.

EXHIBIT 2–1   PROJECT DEVELOPMENT PROCESS

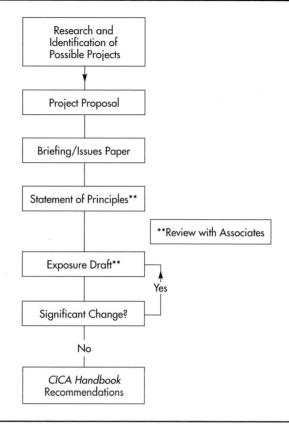

*Boards/Committees may vote not to re-expose.
**Review with associates takes place at either the draft Statement of Principles or draft Exposure Draft stage or both.

ASSURANCE STANDARDS

* * * * * * * * * * *

LEARNING OBJECTIVE

2. Discuss the reasons for having general assurance standards and give some examples of assurance subject matters.

In March 1997 the CICA issued *Section* 5025, "Standards for Assurance Engagements." The significance of this standard, the first of its kind in the world, arises from the fact that it is intended to provide an umbrella framework for all existing and future audit-type engagements. This means the standard is intended to provide a framework for auditing and related engagements for a large variety of subject matters besides financial statement audits. Over time this framework should influence the future evolution of the rest of the *Handbook*. Its importance therefore cannot be overemphasized.

An assurance engagement is defined in *Section* 5025.03–.04 as follows:

> An engagement where, pursuant to an accountability relationship between two or more parties, a practitioner is engaged to issue a written communication expressing a conclusion concerning a subject matter for which the accountable party is responsible. An accountability relationship is a prerequisite for an assurance engagement. An accountability relationship exists when one party (the "accountable party") is answerable to and/or is responsible to another party (the "user") for a subject matter or voluntarily chooses to report to another party on a subject matter. The accountability relationship may arise either as a result of an agreement or legislation, or because a user can be expected to have an interest in how the accountable party has discharged its responsibility for a subject matter.

The assurance standard does not supersede exisiting audit and review standards, but it will probably influence future changes to more specific standards. In the meantime the assurance framework is expected to provide guidance for expanding assurance service to new "subject matters" not currently covered in the *Handbook*.

The general relationships are given in the box above.

An assertion is a statement about some relevant aspect of a subject matter—for example, that a building exists as of a certain point in time. The assurance standards in *Section 5025* are quite broad in that they can be applied to assertions that are unwritten and only implied (called direct reporting engagements) as well as to written assertions (called attestation engagements):

> In an attest engagement the practitioner's conclusion will be on a written assertion prepared by the accountable party. The assertion evaluates using suitable criteria, the subject matter for which the accountable party is responsible. In a direct reporting engagement, the practitioner's conclusion will evaluate directly using suitable criteria, the subject matter for which the accountable party is responsible. . . . In these standards, the accountable party is referred to as management. Depending on a circumstance, the user could include a variety of stakeholders such as shareholders, creditors, customers, the board of directors, the audit committee, legislators or regulators. The practitioner is the person who has overall responsibility for the assurance engagement. (*Handbook Sections* 5025.05–.06)

These relationships are illustrated in the box below.

For example, the practitioner of *Section* 5025.06 in a financial statement assurance engagement has traditionally been referred to as an external auditor. Since most of this textbook deals with financial statement audits, we will continue using the traditional terminology for much of the text. After we have become familiarized with other assurance services in Chapter 15, we will discuss the assurance standards in more detail. In this chapter we focus on existing auditing standards and provide an overall comparison between the auditing standards (GAAS) and the new assurance standard.

The assurance standard was written long after the generally accepted auditing standards for financial statement audits (GAAS). In Exhibit 2–2 you can see the ideas borrowed from the existing GAAS.

The major differences lie in the areas of practitioner competence, internal control and reporting. With respect to practitioner competence, the GAAS presume knowledge of accounting and require training and proficiency as an auditor (meaning an auditor of financial statements, since that was the only kind of assurance engagement being performed when

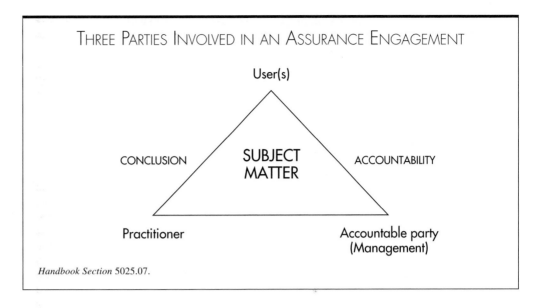

THREE PARTIES INVOLVED IN AN ASSURANCE ENGAGEMENT

User(s)

CONCLUSION   SUBJECT   ACCOUNTABILITY
                    MATTER

Practitioner   Accountable party
                                                (Management)

Handbook Section 5025.07.

E X H I B I T 2–2   COMPARISON OF ASSURANCE AND AUDIT STANDARDS
                         (The numbers are in the sequence of the more familiar and specific GAAS)

Assurance Standards	Auditing Standards
1. The practitioner should seek management's acknowledgment of responsibility for the subject matter as it relates to the objective of the engagement. If the practitioner does not obtain management's acknowledgment, the practitioner should: (a) obtain other evidence that an accountability relationship exists, such as a reference to legislation or a regulation; (b) consider how the lack of management's acknowledgment might affect his or her work and conclusion; and (c) disclose in his or her report that acknowledgment of responsibility has not been obtained. The assurance engagement should be performed with due care and with an objective state of mind. The practitioner and any other persons performing the assurance engagement should have adequate proficiency in such engagements. The practitioner and any other persons performing the assurance engagement should collectively possess adequate knowledge of the subject matter. In addition, when a specialist is involved, the practitioner should consider whether the practitioner's involvement in the engagement and knowledge of the subject matter elements involving the specialist is sufficient to enable the practitioner to discharge his or her responsibilities.	1. The examination should be performed and the report prepared by a person or persons having adequate technical training and proficiency in auditing, with due care and with an objective state of mind.
2. The work should be adequately planned and the practitioner should ensure that any other persons performing the assurance engagement are properly supervised.	2. The work should be adequately planned and properly executed using sufficient knowledge of the entity's business as a basis. If assistants are employed they should be properly supervised. 3. A sufficient understanding of internal control should be obtained to plan the audit. When control risk is assessed below maximum, sufficient appropriate audit evidence should be obtained through tests of controls to support the assessment.
4. The practitioner should consider the concept of significance and the relevant components of engagement risk when planning and performing the assurance engagement. Sufficient appropriate evidence should be obtained to provide the practitioner with a reasonable basis to support the conclusion expressed in his or her report.	4. Sufficient appropriate audit evidence should be obtained, by such means as inspection, observations, enquiry, confirmation, computation and analysis, to afford a reasonable basis to support the content of the report.
5,6,7,8. As a minimum the practitioner's report should: (a) identify to whom the report is directed; (b) describe the objective of the engagement and the entity or portion thereof, the subject matter and the time period covered by the engagement; (c) in an attest report, identify management's assertion; (d) describe the responsibilities of management and the practitioner;	5. The report should identify the financial statements and distinguish between the responsibilities of management and the responsibilities of the auditor.

(continued)

E X H I B I T 2–2   **COMPARISON OF ASSURANCE AND AUDIT STANDARDS (continued)**

Assurance Standards	Auditing Standards
(e) identify the applicable standards in accordance with which the engagement was conducted; (f) identify the criteria against which the subject matter was evaluated; (g) state a conclusion that conveys the level of assurance being provided and/or any reservation the practitioner may have; (h) state the date of the report; (i) identify the name of the practitioner (or firm); and (j) identify the place of issue.	6. The report should describe the scope of the auditor's examination.
7. The reservation should be expressed in the form of a qualification of conclusion or a denial of conclusion when the practitioner is unable to obtain sufficient appropriate evidence to evaluate one or more aspects of the subject matter's conformity with the criteria. When the practitioner: (a) in a direct reporting engagement, concludes that the subject matter does not conform with criteria; or (b) in an attest engagement, concludes that the assertion prepared by management does not present fairly the criteria used or the conformity of the subject matter with the criteria or essential information has not been presented or has been presented in an inappropriate manner, he or she should express a reservation in the form of a qualification of conclusion or an adverse conclusion.	7. The report should contain either an expression of opinion on the financial statements or an assertion that an opinion cannot be expressed. In the latter case, the reasons therefor should be stated.
8. A reservation should be expressed when the practitioner: (a) is unable to obtain sufficient appropriate evidence to evaluate one or more aspects of the subject matter's conformity with the criteria; (b) in a direct reporting engagement, concludes that the subject matter does not conform with the criteria; or (c) in an attest engagement concludes that (i) the assertion prepared by management does not present fairly the criteria used, (ii) the assertion prepared by management does not present fairly the subject matter's conformity with the criteria, or (iii) essential information has not been presented or has been presented in an inappropriate manner. A reservation should provide an explanation of the matter giving rise to the reservation and, if reasonably determinable, its effect on the subject matter.	8. Where an opinion is expressed, it should indicate whether the financial statements present fairly, in all material respects, the financial position, results of operations and changes in financial position in accordance with an appropriate disclosed basis of accounting, which except in special circumstances should be generally accepted accounting principles. The report should provide adequate explanation with respect to any reservation contained in such opinion.
A. Before undertaking an assurance engagement, the practitioner should have a reasonable basis for believing the engagement can be completed in accordance with the standards in this *Section*. B. The practitioner should identify or develop criteria that are suitable for evaluating the subject matter. When generally accepted criteria consistent with the objective of the engagement exist, the practitioner should use them in forming his or her conclusion except when and only when, the intended users of practitioner's report are an identifiable limited group of users and he or she is satisfied such users agree their needs are met by using criteria other than generally accepted criteria. In such cases, the practitioner's report should not include a reservation with respect to generally accepted criteria but should include a caution that the report is intended only for the use of the intended users. When there are no generally accepted criteria consistent with the objective of the engagement, criteria from sources in paragraph 5025.41 (d) and (e) should be used. The practitioner should assess the suitability of these criteria because they lack authoritative support. In these circumstances, the practitioner should attempt to obtain, from intended users and management, acknowledgment that the criteria are suitable for the engagement. When such acknowledgment cannot be obtained, the practitioner should consider the effect if any on his or her work and report. In no circumstances should the practitioner perform the engagement using criteria which, in his or her judgment, would result in a report that would be misleading to intended users. C. The practitioner should document matters that in his or her professional judgment are important in providing evidence to support the conclusion expressed in his or her report.	

A, B, C, designates *Section* 5025 Standards that are not directly comparable to a GAAS standard.

the GAAS were written). On the other hand, the assurance standards are more general, requiring training and proficiency in assurance engagements and knowledge of the "subject matter of the engagement." The assurance service refers to the ability to recognize the information being asserted, to determine the evidence relevant to the assertions, and to make decisions about the correspondence of the information asserted with suitable criteria. The "knowledge of the subject matter" is not confined to accounting and financial assertions because assurance engagements may cover a wide variety of information. Note, however, that the first assurance standard does not allow auditors to provide assurance on assertions beyond their level of competence, for example, adherence to complex legal contracts.

The assurance standards, unlike GAAS, have no requirement regarding an understanding of the internal control structure for an information system. Considerations of internal control are implicit in the task of obtaining sufficient evidence for financial statement audits. However, some kinds of assured information may not have an underlying information control system in the same sense as a financial accounting and reporting system.

Reporting is different because assurance engagements on nonfinancial information do not depend upon generally accepted accounting principles. These are the only criteria for financial statement audits. The assurance standards speak of "evaluation against suitable criteria" and "accordance with generally accepted criteria" and they leave the door open for assurance engagements on a wide variety of informational assertions. An illustration of how far assurance engagements can go is provided in the *Wall Street Journal* article excerpt given in the box below.

The assurance standards shown in Exhibit 2–2 provide guidance and a broad framework for a wide variety of assurance engagements PAs can perform in public practice.

Many people appreciate the value of auditors' assurance to historical financial statements, and they have found other representations for PAs to assure, as illustrated in the box on page 40.

A main objective in developing the assurance standards is to provide a general framework for, and set reasonable boundaries around, the assurance services offered by public accountants. Whether these standards actually "set boundaries" remains to be seen. After all, before the assurance standards were published, public accountants were using the

---

FORE!

Wilson Sporting Goods Company is using PAs to prove that amateur golfers can hit Wilson's Ultra golf ball farther than they can hit competitors' golf balls. Wilson says the PAs certify that Wilson's Ultra outdistances its competitors by an average of 5.7 yards per drive.

Competitors aren't impressed by Wilson's accountants. "I can walk off a golf ball's distance as well as any accountant," says Harry Groome, an accountant executive with Ayer, Inc., the ad agency for the Maxfli gold balls made by Dunlop Slazenger Corporation. "Using a PA is an odd way to measure a golf drive."

Marlene Baddeloo, a manager for the Chicago office of Coopers & Lybrand, which oversees the golf-ball competitions sponsored by Wilson, agrees "that anyone could pace off a golf driving range to see how far a ball goes." But she says Coopers staffers since last May have checked that Wilson employees haven't doctored the results at more than 30 driving ranges. "We also make sure the amateurs participating aren't affiliated with Wilson or its competitors and haven't been paid to participate," she adds.

The use of accountants may upset Wilson's competitors, but it sure makes the accountants happy. "Our personnel love . . . {to} wear shorts and spend the day out in the air," says Ms. Baddeloo. "I get a lot of volunteers."

Source: Lee Burton, "After This, CPAs May Take Over Instant-Replay Duties for Football." *The Wall Street Journal,* July 19, 1991, p. B1.

EXAMPLES OF ASSURANCE ENGAGEMENTS

- Insurance claims data.
- Labour data for union contract negotiation.
- Newspaper and magazine audience and circulation data.
- Integrity and security of a computer network.
- Investment performance statistics.
- GST and real estate tax bases.
- Political contributions and expenditures.
- Financial feasibility of a rapid transit system.
- Cost justification for a utility rate increase.
- Regulator's questionnaire on business ethics and conduct.

Source: Courtesy of Alan Winters.

GAAS audit standards as a point of departure for other assurance engagements. New assurance opportunities must now use the assurance standards as the point of departure.

R E V I E W
C H E C K P O I N T S

2.3 What is the purpose served by assurance standards?

2.4 What are the major differences between assurance standards and the generally accepted auditing standards?

2.5 Define an "assurance engagement."

2.6 What is the theoretical essence of an "assurance service?"

GENERALLY ACCEPTED AUDITING STANDARDS (GAAS)

LEARNING OBJECTIVE

3. Write and explain the eight CICA generally accepted auditing standards (GAAS), and explain how GAAS was or was not followed in specific fact situations.

The CICA's generally accepted auditing standards (GAAS) were first written as a short statement of eight standards. Since 1975, these eight have been augmented by additional explanations and requirements in the Auditing Recommendations of the *Handbook*. The eight basic standards are shown below, classified as the general standard, examination standards and reporting standards. (*Handbook Section* 5100).

The Auditing Recommendations of the *Handbook* are issued from time to time in a numbered series. Officially they are considered "interpretations" of the eight basic standards; but, for all practical purposes, they are also GAAS. Any auditor who does not follow *Handbook* directives can be judged to have performed a deficient audit.

The auditing standards literature also includes a series of Guidelines. Although officially considered less authoritative and less binding than the Recommendations, auditors still must justify any departures from them. For the most part, the Guidelines give technical help.

The *IFAC Handbook*, which was first discussed at the end of Chapter 1, does not have anything comparable to *CICA Handbook Section* 5100. Instead of general standards the IFAC's International Standards on Auditing (ISAs) tend to be more detailed, but these detailed standards address the issues summarized by the general standards. The IFAC also issues International Audit Practice Statements (IAPSs) which like the CICA's Audit Guidelines (AUGs) are intended to provide more practical assistance in implementing the standards. Throughout this book we will list any ISASs or IAPSs relevant to a particular topic along with Handbook Sections and AUGs. Currently, the *CICA Handbook* is generally more comprehensive than the *IFAC Handbook*.

Handbook Section 5101.07–.08 notes that for international engagements an auditor may be required to audit in conformity with both the *CICA* and *IFAC Handbooks*. In planning the audit in such situations the auditor should be aware of any differences between the two Handbooks.

Auditing standards are quite different from auditing procedures. Auditing procedures are the particular and specialized actions auditors take to obtain evidence in a specific audit engagement. **Auditing standards** are audit quality recommendations that remain the same through time and for all audits, including audits of computerized accounting systems. Procedures may vary, depending on the complexity of an accounting system (whether manual or computerized), on the type of company and on other situation-specific factors. This difference is the reason audit reports refer to an audit "conducted in accordance with generally accepted auditing standards," rather than in accordance with auditing procedures. Considerable judgment is required to apply audit procedures in specific situations.

GAAS General Standard

The general standard of GAAS relates to the personal integrity and professional qualifications of auditors (Section 5100.02 of the *Handbook*).

Competence

The first general standard requires competence—adequate technical training and proficiency—as an auditor. This competence starts with education in accounting, because auditors hold themselves out as experts in accounting standards and financial reporting. It continues with on-the-job training in developing and applying professional judgment in real-world audit situations. This stage is practice in performing the assurance function, in which auditors learn to (1) recognize the underlying assertions being made by the management of a company in each element (account) in the financial statements, (2) decide which evidence is relevant for supporting or refuting the truth of the assertions, (3) select and perform procedures for obtaining the evidence, and (4) evaluate the evidence and decide whether the management assertions correspond to reality and GAAP. Auditors must be thoughtfully prepared to encounter a wide range of judgment on the part of management accountants, varying from true objective judgment to the occasional extreme of deliberate misstatement.

GENERALLY ACCEPTED AUDITING STANDARDS (*Handbook Section* 5100)

Generally Accepted Auditing Standards are as follows:

General standard

The examination should be performed and the report prepared by a person or persons having adequate technical training and proficiency in auditing, with due care and with an objective state of mind.

Examination standards

1. The work should be adequately planned and properly executed. If assistants are employed they should be properly supervised.
2. A sufficient understanding of internal control should be obtained to plan the audit. When control risk is assessed below maximum, sufficient appropriate audit evidence should be obtained through tests of controls to support the assessment.
3. Sufficient appropriate audit evidence should be obtained, by such means as inspection, observation, enquiry, confirmation, computation, and analysis, to afford a reasonable basis to support the content of the report.

Reporting standards

1. The report should identify the financial statements and distinguish between the responsibilities of management and the responsibilities of the auditor.
2. The report should describe the scope of the auditor's examination.
3. The report should contain either an expression of opinion on the financial statements or an assertion that an opinion cannot be expressed. In the latter case, the reason therefor should be stated.
4. Where an opinion is expressed, it should indicate whether the financial statements present fairly, in all material respects, the financial position, results of operations and changes in financial position in accordance with an appropriate disclosed basis of accounting, which except in special circumstances should be generally accepted accounting principles. The report should provide adequate explanation with respect to any reservation contained in such opinion.

Objectivity

The general standard also requires an objective state of mind. In this sense objectivity is a matter of intellectual honesty and impartiality. Auditors are expected to be unbiased and impartial with respect to the financial statements and other information they audit. They are expected to be fair both to the companies and executives who issue financial information and to the outside persons who use it. This type of objectivity in assurance services is achieved through the maintenance of professional independence. There are two aspects of independence: independence in fact and independence in appearance. Independence in fact is a mental attitude that is essential for an objective state of mind. Independence in appearance is another matter and is addressed in more detail in the Rules of Professional Conduct (Chapter 16). The appearance of independence—avoiding financial and managerial relationships with clients—is important because the appearances are all the public users of audit reports can see. They cannot see inside auditors' heads to detect the "mental attitude." Independence must be zealously guarded because the general public will grant social recognition of professional status to auditors only as long as they are perceived to be independent.

Some critics of the public accounting profession say the fact that auditors are paid by their clients is an undesirable arrangement. They argue that it is impossible to be independent from the party paying the fee. Accountants have generally not taken such criticism seriously because the alternative would be some form of public government control of accounting fees, and very few people want government involvement. In addition, as noted in Chapter 1 public accounting is not alone among professions that face such a dilemma. Medical doctors, lawyers and architects face similar dilemmas. What is unique about auditors is that, although a company pays the auditor, the auditors' real clients are the third-party users of financial statements. The auditor therefore needs to sort out responsibilities to the company from responsibilities to third parties. Addressing such ethical conflicts in a competent manner is part of what makes public accounting a profession. See Chapter 16 for more details.

The notion of individual independence is more specific in the conduct of each audit engagement. In essence, an individual auditor must not subordinate his or her judgment to others and must stay away from influences that might bias judgment. In more specific terms, auditors must preserve their independence in the "Three Aspects" presented in the following box.

Due Professional Care

The exercise of due professional care requires observance of the general standard and the field work standards. Auditors must be competent and independent; they must plan and supervise the audit, understand the auditee's control structure and obtain sufficient competent evidence if they are to be properly careful. Their training should include computer auditing techniques because of the importance and pervasiveness of computers in the business world.

Due care in an audit is best understood in the context of the prudent auditor. The idea of a prudent professional practitioner is present in other social science theories—for example, the "economic person" of economic theory and the "reasonable person" in law. Mautz and Sharaf summarized the qualities of the prudent auditor:

> A prudent practitioner [auditor] is assumed to have a knowledge of the philosophy and practice of auditing, to have the degree of training, experience, and skill common to the average independent auditor, to have the ability to recognize indications of irregularities, and to keep abreast of developments in the perpetration and detection of irregularities. Due audit care requires the auditor to acquaint himself with the company under examination, the accounting and financial problems of the company . . . to be responsive to unusual events and unfamiliar circumstances, to persist until he has eliminated from his own mind any reasonable doubts he may have about the existence of material irregularities, and to exercise caution in instructing his assistants and reviewing their work. (Mautz and Sharaf, *The Philosophy of Auditing*, American Accounting Association, 1961, p. 140.)

Due professional care is a matter of what auditors do and how well they do it. A determination of proper care must be reached on the basis of all facts and circumstances in a

THREE ASPECTS OF PRACTICAL INDEPENDENCE

Programming Independence

Auditors must remain free from interference by client managers who try to restrict, specify or modify the procedures auditors want to perform, including any attempt to assign personnel or otherwise control the audit work. Occasionally, client managers try to limit the number of auditors permitted in a location.

Investingative Independence

Auditors must have free access to books, records, correspondence and other evidence. They must have the co-operation of management without any attempt to interpret or screen evidence. Sometimes, client managers refuse auditors' requests for access to necessary information.

Reporting Independence

Auditors must not let any feelings of loyalty to the client or auditee interfere with their obligation to report fully and fairly. Neither should the client management be allowed to overrule auditors' judgments on the appropriate content of an audit report. Disciplinary actions have been taken against auditors who go to a client management conference with a preliminary estimate for a financial adjustment and emerge after agreeing with management to a smaller adjustment.

LESSONS AUDITORS IGNORE AT THEIR OWN RISK

Litigation is an exacting and uncompromising teacher, but it provides auditors with some hard and useful lessons. The tuition is the high cost of malpractice insurance, legal fees, adverse court decisions, embarrassing publicity and stress.
- There is no substitute for knowledge of the client's business.
- There is no substitute for effective, ongoing, substantial supervision of the work of people assigned to the engagement.
- The partner in charge of the engagement must constantly emphasize the importance of integrity, objectivity and professional scepticism in carrying out the audit.

Source: Hall and Renner, "Lessons That Auditors Ignore at Their Own Risk," *Journal of Accountancy*, July 1988, pp. 50–58.

*All material from the *Journal of Accountancy* appearing in this textbook is reprinted with permission by the American Institute of Certified Public Accountants, Inc. Opinions of the authors are their own and do not necessarily reflect policies of the AICPA.

particular case. When an audit firm's work becomes the subject of a lawsuit, the question of due audit care is frequently at issue (as you will see in the law cases in Chapter 17).

R E V I E W
C H E C K P O I N T S

2.7 What is the difference between auditing standards and auditing procedures?

2.8 By what standard would a judge determine the quality of due professional care? Explain.

2.9 What are the three specific aspects of independence that an auditor should carefully guard in the course of a financial statement audit?

GAAS Examination Standards

The three examination standards set forth general quality criteria for conducting an audit. Auditors cannot effectively satisfy the general standard requiring due professional care if they have not also satisfied the standards of field work.

Planning and Supervision

Section 5150 contains several lists of considerations for planning and supervising an audit. They are all concerned with (1) preparing an audit program and supervising the audit work, (2) obtaining knowledge of the client's business, and (3) dealing with differences of opinion among the audit firm's own personnel.

A written audit program is desirable. An **audit program** is a list of the audit procedures the auditors need to perform to produce the evidence needed for good audit decisions. The procedures in an audit program should be stated in enough detail to instruct the assistants about the work to be done. (You will see detailed audit programs later in this textbook.)

An understanding of the client's business is an absolute necessity. An auditor must be able to understand the events, transactions and practices characteristic of the business and of the management that may have a significant effect on the financial statements. This knowledge helps auditors identify areas for special attention (the places where errors, irregularities or frauds might exist), evaluate the reasonableness of accounting estimates made by management, evaluate management's representations and answers to enquiries and make judgments about the appropriateness of accounting principles choices (*Section* 5140).

Where does an auditor get this understanding of a business? By being there; by work in other companies in the same industry; by conducting interviews with management and other client personnel; by reading extensively—CICA accounting and audit guides, the *CGAAC Public Practice Manual*, industry publications, other companies' financial statements, business periodicals and textbooks; by getting a thorough familiarization presentation by the partner in charge of the audit before beginning the engagement; and by being observant and letting on-the-job experience sink into long-term memory. Auditors are increasingly structuring their understanding of the client's business through use of knowledge acquisition frameworks from strategic management. These strategic management frameworks (covered in more detail in Chapter 4) provide a structured approach to gaining deep knowledge of the client's business and industry.

There is no guarantee that all the auditors on an audit team will always agree among themselves on audit decisions, which range from inclusion or omission of procedures to conclusions about the fair presentation of an account or the financial statements as a whole. When differences of opinion arise, audit personnel should consult with one another and with experts in the firm to try to resolve the disagreement. If resolution is not achieved, the audit firm should have procedures to allow an audit team member to document the disagreement and to dissociate himself or herself from the matter. Particularly in a situation where there are disagreements, the basis for the final audit decision on the matter should be documented in the working papers for later reference.

Timing is important for audit planning. To have time to plan an audit, auditors should be engaged before the client's fiscal year-end. The more advance notice auditors can have, the better they are able to provide enough time for planning. An early appointment benefits both auditor and client. The audit team may be able to perform part of the audit at an **interim date**—a date some weeks or months before the fiscal year-end—and thereby make the rest of the audit work more efficient. At an interim date, auditors can perform preliminary analytical procedures, do a preliminary assessment of internal control risk, test the controls and audit some account balances. Advance knowledge of problems can enable auditors to alter the audit program as necessary so that year-end work (performed on and after the fiscal year-end date) can be more efficient. Advance planning for the observation of physical inventory and for the confirmation of accounts receivable is particularly important.

Too Late

FastTrak Corporation got mad at its auditor because the partner in charge of the engagement would not agree to let management use operating lease accounting treatment for some heavy equipment whose leases met the criteria for capitalization. FastTrak fired the auditors 10 weeks after the company's balance sheet date, then started contacting other audit firms to restart the audit. However, the audit report was due at the OSC in six weeks. Every other audit firm contacted by FastTrak refused the audit because it could not be planned and performed properly on such short notice with such a tight deadline.

Internal Control Assessment

The second examination standard requires an understanding of the client's internal control. Internal control consists of a company's control environment, accounting system and control procedures. The existence of a satisfactory internal control system reduces the probability of errors and irregularities in the accounts. This in turn provides the foundation for the work auditors do in an assessment of control risk. Control risk is the probability that a material misstatement (error or irregularity) could occur and not be prevented or detected on a timely basis by the company's internal control structure policies and procedures (*Section* 5210).

Internal control may be defined simply as a system's capability to prevent or detect material data processing errors or fraud and provide for their correction on a timely basis. Auditors need to know enough about the client's control system to assess the control risk.

The primary purpose of control risk assessment is to help the auditors develop the audit program, which specifies the nature, timing and extent of the audit procedures for gathering evidence about the account balances that will go into the financial statements. The second field work standard presumes two necessary relationships: (*a*) good internal control reduces the control risk, and an auditor thus has a reasonable basis for minimizing the extent of subsequent audit procedures; (*b*) conversely, poor internal control produces greater control risk, and an auditor must increase the extent of subsequent audit procedures. If auditors were to assume no relationship between the quality of controls and the accuracy of output, then an assessment of control risk would be pointless. Audit efficiency would be lost in many cases. (Chapter 6 explains the work involved in control risk assessment.)

Control Lapse Contributes to Duplicate Payments

All Points Trucking processed insurance claims on damages to shipments in transit on its trucks, paying them in a self-insurance plan. After payment, the claims documents were not marked "paid." Later, the same documents were processed again for duplicate payments to customers, who kicked back 50 percent to a dishonest All Points employee. The auditors learned that the documents were not marked "paid," concluded that the specific control risk of duplicate payments was high, extended their procedures to include a search for duplicate payments in the damage expense account, found them, and traced the problem to the dishonest employee. Embezzlements of $35,000 per year were stopped.

Sufficient, Appropriate Evidential Matter

Evidence is the heart of assurance function work for audits of financial statements and for assurance to nonfinancial information. The third examination standard requires auditors to obtain enough evidence to justify the decision about an opinion on financial statements. **Evidence** is all the influences upon the minds of auditors that ultimately guide their decisions. Evidence includes the underlying accounting data and all available corroborating information (*Section* 5300). Appropriate evidence—evidence that is reliable and relevant— may be quantitative or qualitative; it may be objective or subjective; it may be absolutely compelling to a decision or it may only be mildly persuasive. The audit team's task is to collect and evaluate sufficient appropriate evidence to afford a reasonable and logical basis for audit decisions.

The standard refers to "sufficient," rather than "absolute," evidence. Auditors do not audit all of a company's transactions and events. They audit data samples and make audit decisions by inference, in most cases.

The standard takes a broad brush to procedures for gathering evidence—inspection, observation, enquiry and confirmation. This is not a complete enumeration of evidence-gathering procedures. (Chapter 4 contains a more thorough explanation of audit objectives and procedures.)

R E V I E W
C H E C K P O I N T S

2.10 What three elements of planning and supervision are considered essential in audit practice?

2.11 Why does the timing of an auditor's appointment matter in the conduct of a financial statement audit?

2.12 For what reasons does an auditor obtain an understanding of the internal control system?

2.13 Define audit *evidence*.

GAAS Reporting Standards

LEARNING OBJECTIVE

4. Describe the standard unqualified audit report in terms of its communication of audit standards and other messages.

The ultimate objective of independent auditors—the report on the audit—is guided by the four GAAS reporting standards. These four deal with generally accepted accounting principles (GAAP), auditor and management responsibilities, adequate disclosure and report content. Auditing standards dictate use of a "standard report." (The standard unqualified audit report is shown in Exhibit 2–3 [same as Exhibit 1–2], and you should review it in relation to the discussion that follows.)

"Unqualified," in the name of the report, means "good" in the sense that the auditors are not calling attention to anything wrong with the audit work or the financial statements. "Qualified" means "bad" in the sense that the financial statements contain a departure from GAAP or the scope of the audit work was limited. (You will study "qualified" audit reports in Chapter 3.) All standard **unqualified reports** contain these features:

1. **Title.** The title should refer to the auditor, thus indicating that the report is based on an audit examination and not some other types of engagement.

2. **Address.** The report shall be addressed to the client, which occasionally may be different from the auditee.

3. **Notice of audit.** A sentence should identify the financial statements and declare that they were audited. This appears in the introductory paragraph.

4. **Responsibilities.** The report should state management's responsibility for the financial statements and the auditor's responsibility for the audit report. These statements are also in the introductory paragraph.

EXHIBIT 2–3   **AUDITOR'S REPORT**

To the Shareholders of...............

I have audited the balance sheet of .... as at ...., 20....., and the statement of income, retained earnings and changes in financial position for the year then ended. These financial statements are the responsibility of the company's management. My responsibility is to express an opinion on these financial statements based on my audit.

I conducted my audit in accordance with generally accepted auditing standards. Those standards require that I plan and perform an audit to obtain reasonable assurance whether the financial statements are free of material misstatement. An audit includes examining, on a test basis, evidence supporting the amounts and disclosure in the financial statements. An audit also includes assessing the accounting principles used and significant estimates made by management, as well as evaluating the overall financial statement presentation.

In my opinion, these financial statements present fairly, in all material respects, the financial position of the company as at ...., 20....., and the results of its operations and the changes in its financial position for the year then ended in accordance with generally accepted accounting principles.

City   (signed) ....

Date   Chartered Accountant

5. **Description of the audit.** The second paragraph (scope paragraph) should declare that the audit was conducted in accordance with generally accepted auditing standards and describe the principal characteristics of an audit.

6. **Opinion.** The report shall contain an opinion (opinion paragraph) regarding conformity with generally accepted accounting principles.

7. **Signature.** The auditor shall sign the report, manually or otherwise.

8. **Date.** The report shall be dated with the date when all significant field work was completed.

Generally Accepted Accounting Principles (GAAP)

The fourth reporting standard refers to generally accepted accounting principles, or GAAP, which is used in most circumstances. In the audit report, this standard is shown to be met with the opinion sentence in the opinion paragraph: "In our opinion, the financial statements . . . present fairly in all material respects the financial position . . . and the results of operations and changes in financial position . . . in accordance with generally accepted accounting principles." In this opinion sentence, auditors make a statement of fact about their belief (opinion). Auditors are the professional experts, so users of financial statements rely upon the audit opinion.

However, determining the appropriate GAAP in a company's circumstances is not always an easy matter. Students often think of *Handbook Recommendations* on accounting standards as the complete body of GAAP. Not so. GAAP consists of all the accounting methods and procedures that have substantial authoritative support. The *Handbook* is only one source of such support, albeit the highest and most powerful. It is widely recognized that "the meaning of 'present fairly in accordance with GAAP' in the audit report" sets forth a hierarchy of authoritative support for various sources of GAAP.

Handbook Recommendations cover many accounting issues and problems. When the *Handbook* covers an issue, its standards are considered generally compelling. However, the *Handbook* has not covered all conceivable accounting matters. When a conclusion about GAAP cannot be found in *Handbook Recommendations,* auditors usually go down a hierarchy to find the next highest source of support for a client's accounting solution to a financial reporting problem. Reference can be made to positions on accounting matters by the affected provincial Securities Commission. Reference can also be made to other countries' authoritative pronouncements such as the U.S.'s Financial Accounting Standards Board (FASB) announcements, industry audit and accounting guides, consensus positions of the CICA's Emerging Issues Committee, and other accounting literature.

The unqualified opinion sentence contains these implicit messages: (*a*) the accounting principles in the financial statements have general acceptance (authoritative support); (*b*) the accounting principles used by the company are appropriate in the circumstances; (*c*) the financial statements and notes are informative of matters that may affect their use, understanding and interpretation (full disclosure accounting principle); (*d*) the classification and summarization in the financial statements is neither too detailed nor too condensed for users; and (*e*) the financial statements are accurate within practical materiality limits (*Section* 5130 or *ISA* 320 and 400). This last feature refers to materiality and accuracy. Auditors and users do not expect financial account balances to be absolutely accurate to the penny. Accounting is too complicated, and too many estimates are used in financial statements to expect absolute accuracy. After all, many financial reports use numbers rounded to the thousands, even millions, of dollars! Everyone agrees that financial figures are "fair" as long as they are not "materially" misstated—that is, misstated by enough to make a difference in users' decisions. (Chapter 5 discusses "materiality" in more detail.)

Consistency

The fourth reporting standard calls for explicit reporting in accordance with GAAP except in special circumstances. Prior to 1991, all audit reports contained a sentence confirming that GAAP had been "consistently applied" when no changes in the application of accounting principles had been made. This sentence referred to a company's use of the same accounting procedures and methods from year to year. However, an official pronouncement (*Section* 1506) governs the accounting and disclosure of a company's change of accounting principles.

In 1991 the fourth reporting standard was changed to allow the audit report to be silent (i.e., implicit) about consistency when no accounting changes had been made or any changes that were made were properly disclosed in the financial statements. This change has created a conflict with U.S. reporting standards for clients falling within the jurisdiction of SEC filing requirements. A CICA Guideline suggests that this conflict is best resolved by providing information on the conflict to U.S. readers in documents submitted to the SEC. See the CICA Guideline (AUG-21) on Canada–U.S. reporting differences.

Adequate Disclosure

The fourth reporting standard also has a second implicit report element. The standard requires auditors to use professional judgment to decide whether the financial statements and related disclosures contain all the important accounting information users need for their decisions. Disclosure of information not specified completely in sources of authoritative support may be necessary. Auditors may need to deal with a rare and unusual fact situation that nobody has encountered before. Using this standard, auditors have latitude for determining what is important and what is not. Likewise, users of financial statements also have the right to claim that certain information is necessary for adequate disclosure. In fact, many lawsuits are brought forward on the issue that certain necessary information was not disclosed, and auditors must show reasons for lack of disclosure.

When auditors believe that some information is necessary for adequate disclosure, yet the company refuses to disclose it, a departure from GAAP exists. A "qualified opinion" is usually written, and the reason for the departure (missing disclosure) is described in the audit report. Sometimes the missing disclosure is added to the audit report itself.

Report Content

The third reporting standard states the requirements concerning an opinion. There are two elements in the first sentence:

1. The report shall contain either an expression of opinion on the financial statements or an assertion that an opinion cannot be expressed.

The first sentence divides opinion statements into two classes: (*a*) opinions on statements taken as a whole (i.e., unqualified, adverse and qualified opinions) and (*b*) the denial of opinion. An **adverse opinion** is the opposite of an unqualified opinion. It states that the financial statements are not in accordance with GAAP. A **denial of opinion** is an auditor's declaration that no opinion is given. The standard applies to financial statements as a whole, that is, the standard applies equally to a set of financial statements and footnotes and to each individual financial statement and footnote. The second sentence adds the requirement to explain why an opinion cannot be expressed:

2. In the latter case, the reasons therefor should be stated.

Combining reporting standards three and four, an explanation is required whenever there is a report reservation. Thus, when the adverse opinion, qualified opinion or denial of opinion is rendered, all the substantive reasons for doing so must be explained. An additional paragraph is generally used for such an explanation.

The first two reporting standards relate to auditor responsibilities and the need to identify the financial statements covered by the opinion. Every time PAs (even when acting as accountants associated with unaudited financial statements) are associated by name or by action with financial statements, they must report on their work and responsibility. The character of the work is usually described by the standard reference to an audit in accordance with generally accepted auditing standards. But if an audit has been restricted in some way or if the statements are simply unaudited, the auditor must say so.

The "degree of responsibility" is indicated by the form of the opinion. Auditors take full responsibility for their opinion about conformity with GAAP when they give either an unqualified or an adverse opinion. They take no responsibility whatsoever when they give a denial of opinion. They take responsibility when they give the qualified opinions for all matters except those stated as the reasons for the qualification. (Qualified and adverse opinions and denials of opinion are discussed more fully in Chapter 3.)

REVIEW CHECKPOINTS

2.14 What are the eight important features of a standard unqualified audit report?

2.15 Identify various authoritative support for GAAP with an indication of their ranking.

2.16 Do auditors take any responsibility for clients' choices of accounting principles?

2.17 What four kinds of audit opinion statements are identified in this chapter? What is the message of each one?

2.18 What messages are usually implicit in a standard audit report?

AUDITING STANDARDS IN A COMPUTER ENVIRONMENT

LEARNING OBJECTIVE
5. Interpret GAAS in the context of a computer environment.

The auditing standards (GAAS) were written without any special reference to the use of computers in accounting. Nevertheless, the general and field work standards guide audit quality in a computer environment as well as in a manual accounting system environment. Some interpretation, however, will help you put the standards in context.

General Standard

To be considered adequately trained and proficient, auditors must have a working knowledge of the functions of computerized accounting and control systems. Levels of required knowledge include a minimum competency expected of new staff accountants; a supervisory capability expected of senior accountants, managers and partners; and a technical expertise expected of computer audit specialists.

New staff accountants should be familiar with computer terminology, be able to comprehend the flow of transactions in clients' computerized systems, be able to read and understand system and logic flowcharts and know the nature of common organizational arrangements in computer departments. Supervising accountants must have knowledge beyond these fundamentals so they can decide what level of technical support is needed and can review the audit plans of computer audit specialists and the results of their work in relation to the audit engagement as a whole. Computer audit specialists, usually trained in special technical courses and given extensive job experience, are the people who need to know how to work directly with the computers.

Sufficient training and proficiency in computer auditing are necessary to enable auditors to make their own evaluations and decisions about the computer operations in a client's accounting system. Without knowledge of computers, independence is threatened. An auditor must be technically proficient and exercise suitable professional scepticism to avoid being inappropriately influenced by experts' technical explanations and terminology. At the very least, supervisory auditors should know enough about computers to be able to recognize situations calling for the technical assistance of computer audit specialists. With specialists at work, the engagement can be completed as a team effort.

Examination Standards

The exercise of due audit care in an engagement depends on observance of the three examination standards. Special care is required when assigning personnel to the job and planning the audit. Among other things, the audit planner needs to know (*a*) the computer systems in use so compatible audit tools can be provided; (*b*) the extent of internal auditor involvement in reviewing and controlling computer operations so the extent of audit effort can be estimated; and (*c*) the computer department schedule so that access to the client's files and systems can be arranged. Above all, the partner in charge of the audit needs to plan ahead to arrange for the appropriate level of expertise needed for supervision of computer audit specialists and for the level of expertise needed for review of their work.

Probably the most complex task is performing an assessment of control risk. Computer audit expertise is required for all but the simplest computer systems. The ability to evaluate manual control over input data and over output distribution usually is not sufficient. Computerized accounting applications typically have control features built into both the systems and program software. Some members of the audit team must be able to evaluate the operations of such controls using the computer. Clients spend a great amount of money developing systems and controls, and they expect auditors to be able to understand them.

Computerized accounting systems lend themselves to computer-assisted methods of gathering sufficient appropriate evidence. Auditors can program a computer to scan a client's files and identify unusual items (e.g., loans receivable with credit balances, debits in revenue accounts and credits in expense accounts), to recalculate accounting calculations (e.g., depreciation) made by the client, and to select accounts receivable for confirmation and print the confirmation information. These are examples of computer-assisted audit methods for obtaining sufficient appropriate evidential matter.

Reporting Standard

The technical problems and opportunities presented by the computer environment add complications to the general standards and field work standards. However, the reporting standards are not affected by the technology of the accounting system. It matters not whether the financial statements were produced by chiselling them on stone or by engraving them on paper with a laser beam: reporting requirements regarding conformity with generally accepted accounting principles, consistency, adequate disclosure and report content remain the same. When a standard audit report is written, the output of the system, not its process, is the subject of the report.

R E V I E W
CHECKPOINTS

2.19 Do the general standards of generally accepted auditing standards apply when the client uses a computerized accounting system? examination standards? reporting standards? Explain.

2.20 What is considered the most complex task for auditing in a computer environment?

PROFESSIONAL SCEPTICISM

LEARNING OBJECTIVE

6. Explain some characteristics of "professional scepticism."

"Professional scepticism" is a buzz phrase that appears frequently in auditing literature and speech. **Professional scepticism** is an auditor's tendency not to believe management assertions, a tendency to ask management to "prove it" (with evidence). Professional scepticism is inherent in applying due care in accordance with the general standards. The business environment that has seen errors, irregularities and fraud in financial reports dictates this basic aspect of professional scepticism: "A potential conflict of interest always exists between the auditor and the management of the enterprise under audit."

Holding a belief that a potential conflict of interest always exists causes auditors to perform procedures to search for errors, irregularities and frauds that would have a material effect on financial statements. This requirement tends to make audits more extensive and more expensive. The extra work is not needed in the vast majority of audits where no errors, irregularities or frauds exist. Nevertheless, auditors have had to react in all audits to the misdeeds perpetrated by a few people.

Even so, auditors must be careful when exercising professional scepticism and when holding a belief regarding a potential conflict of interest. Once an audit is under way and procedures that are designed to search for errors, irregularities and frauds have been performed and none have been found, the audit team must be willing to accept the apparent fact there is no evidence that the potential conflict is a real one. Overtones of suspicion can be dispelled by evidence.

Still, due audit care requires professional scepticism on the part of auditors—a disposition to question all material assertions made by management whether oral, written or incorporated in the accounting records. However, this attitude of scepticism must be balanced with an open mind about the integrity of management. Auditors should neither blindly assume that every management is dishonest nor thoughtlessly assume management to be perfectly honest. The key lies in auditors' objectivity and in the audit attitude toward gathering the evidence necessary to reach reasonable and supportable audit decisions.

R E V I E W
CHECKPOINTS

2.21 Why should auditors act as though there is always a potential conflict of interest between the auditor and the management of the enterprise under audit?

QUALITY CONTROL STANDARDS

LEARNING OBJECTIVE

7. List and explain the important requirements of quality control standards for a PA firm.

Generally accepted auditing standards must be observed in each audit engagement conducted by a PA firm. Thus, each PA firm needs to observe GAAS in conducting its entire audit practice. While GAAS relate to the conduct of each audit engagement, quality control standards govern the quality of a PA firm's audit practice as a whole. Quality control can be defined as actions taken by a public accounting firm to evaluate compliance with professional standards. And a "system of quality control" is designed to provide reasonable assurance of conforming with professional standards. Professional standards include GAAS as covered in the *CICA Handbook* as well as Provincial Rules of Conduct.

Elements of Quality Control

The International Federation of Accountants (IFAC) has identified four basic elements of quality control. These are listed and explained briefly in Exhibit 2–4. In contrast, the AICPA has identified nine basic elements of quality control. These are as follows: (1) Independence, (2) Assigning personnel to engagements, (3) Consultation, (5) Supervision, (5) Hiring, (6) Professional development, (7) Advancement, (8) Acceptance and continuation of engagements, and (9) Inspection.

Canada currently does not have codified quality control standards. Both the 1978 Adams Report (the *Report of the Special Committee to Examine the Role of the Auditor*) and the 1988 Macdonald Commission Report (*Report of the Commission to Study the Public's Expectations of Audits*) recommended the development of quality control standards and that PA firms establish systems of quality control conforming with these standards. More recently several regulatory agencies have taken initiatives to discipline substandard performance of professional staff in PA firms and criticized the individual-level focus of the provincial disciplinary process. In response provincial Institutes are amending their bylaws to bring firms as well as individuals within the disciplinary process. This expanded disciplinary process will require new guidelines for evaluating systems of quality control. Increasing litigation is also putting pressure on firms to develop good systems of quality control so that they can demonstrate compliance with professional standards and thus minimize the loss from litigation. Recently, the International Federation of Accountants has issued a policy statement proposing that members' bodies provide more guidance on quality control systems. There is thus increasing need for developing codified quality control standards in Canada. A recent CICA study entitled "Guide for Developing Quality Control Systems in Public Accounting" proposes a quality control framework based on five key components or areas: clients, personnel, engagement procedures, practice administration and a quality control review program.

Exhibit 2–5 illustrates the implementation of a quality control systems as proposed by the CICA study using the five key components as a framework. The study proposes that the areas of clients and engagement procedures be given top priority when implementing a system in stages. The right-hand columns in Exhibit 2–5 reflect the suggested priority in setting up a firmwide quality control system. Note in Exhibit 2–5 that the five key components or quality control areas have been subdivided into a series of refined elements that allow firms to better articulate all the different aspects of quality control. This refined list of elements may be viewed as an improvement on Exhibit 2–4 and thus as a better framework for quality control. However, the Exhibit 2–5 framework is not a standard at the current time, but indicates where a Canadian codified framework may be headed. Note that this framework can be extended to include tax and management advisory services, and one controversy is the extent to which these other services should also be considered in the quality control system.

Whatever framework is used, firms can use these or similar criteria in developing their policies and procedures for quality control, and the related documentation. When a peer review or quality review is conducted, the reviewers "audit" the PA firm's statement of poli-

EXHIBIT 2–4   **ELEMENTS OF QUALITY CONTROL (ISA 220)**

1. Quality control policies and procedures should be implemented at both the level of the audit firm and on individual audits.
2. The audit firm should implement quality control policies and procedures designed to insure that all audits are conducted in accordance with ISAs or relevant national standards of practices.
3. The firm's general quality control policies and procedures should be communicated to its personnel in a manner that provides reasonable assurance that the policies and procedures are understood and implemented.
4. The auditor should implement those quality control procedures which are, in the context of the policies and procedures of the firm, appropriate to the individual audit. In particular, delegated work should be properly directed, supervised and reviewed.

EXHIBIT 2–5   IMPLEMENTING A QUALITY CONTROL SYSTEM

Quality Control Area/Elements	First Priority	Second Priority
A. Clients (refer to Chapter 5)		
1. Independence and Objectivity	✔	
2. Prohibited Investments	✔	
3. Conflicts of Interest	✔	
4. Confidentiality	✔	
5. Acceptance and Continuance	✔	
6. New Client Proposals	✔	✔
B. Personnel (refer to Chapter 6)		
1. Hiring		✔
2. Assignment		✔
3. Performance Evaluation		✔
4. Advancement		✔
5. Continuing Professional Education	✔	
6. Restriction of Professional Staff Activities	✔	
C. Engagement Procedures (refer to Chapter 7)		
1. Engagement Letters	✔	
2. Planning and Execution	✔	
3. Documentation	✔	
4. Supervision and Review	✔	
5. Resolution of Differences of Opinion		✔
6. Consultation with Peers		✔
7. Independent Review	✔	
8. Management Letters	✔	
D. Practice Administration (refer to Chapter 8)		
1. Use of Firm Name		✔
2. Access to Client Files	✔	
3. Security of Confidential Information	✔	
4. Retention of Files		✔
5. Software Usage and Security		✔
6. Technical Reference Materials	✔	
7. Litigation and Professional Conduct		✔
8. Advertising and Promotion		✔
9. Solicitation of Clients	✔	
E. Quality Control Review Program (refer to Chapter 9)		
1. Internal Review		✔
2. Monitoring Client Services		✔
3. Monitoring Quality Control		✔
4. Premerger Review		✔
Total Elements	17	16

*Same as Exhibit 4–2 in CICA's *Guide for Developing Quality Control Systems in Public Accounting*, p. 35.

cies and procedures designed to ensure compliance with the elements of Exhibits 2–4 and 2–5 or similar criteria. These statements of policy and procedures may vary in length and complexity, depending on the size of the PA firm. (Students who wish to know these policies and procedures in detail when interviewing for a job should ask for a copy of the firm's "quality control document.")

Practice Inspection, Peer Review and Quality Reviews

Practice inspection, peer review and quality reviews are "audits of the auditors." Practice inspection is the name given to the system of reviewing and evaluating practice units' audit files and other documentation by an independent external party. The main objective of practice inspection is to evaluate conformity of members' work with the *CICA Handbook* and professional, ethical principles and rules of conduct (covered in Chapter 16). The practice unit can be an individual or an entire office, in which case the individual members of the office are evaluated relative to their level of responsibility. Provincial Institutes' practice inspection programs apply to all members and consist of several steps:

1. Selection of practice unit for inspection (a practice unit can be a PA firm, an office of a firm or a sole practitioner).

2. Completion of practice inspection questionnaires gathering general information about the practice and quality control systems of the practice unit.

3. Assignment of inspector.

4. Inspection of a sample of engagement files.

5. Report of inspection—each report focuses on an individual in a practice unit.

6. Follow-up reviews.

7. A report to the professional conduct committee if necessary.[4]

There are some minor variations among provincial practice inspection programs relating to types of engagements reviewed and the way the inspection reports are prepared. The overall focus is on an individual member's performance, and the orientation is more educational than disciplinary in character, although serious deficiencies of professional practice could lead to a complaint with a professional conduct committee. This is further discussed in Chapter 16. Practice inspections are a useful complement to a firm's system of quality control. Their success is reflected in the fact that many countries have followed this Canadian model, including Ireland, Norway, Hong Kong and Australia.

Peer reviews or quality reviews are a review and evaluation of the quality of the overall practice. They are thus aimed more at the firm level rather than at individuals. A peer review involves an extensive study of a firm's quality control document, including interviews with audit personnel and selection of audit engagements for detailed study of the quality of work and of adherence to GAAS and quality control standards. Peer reviews can cost from $500 to $50,000. A firm's peer review usually is done by another PA firm engaged by the firm reviewed. The reviewers issue a report giving conclusions about the firm's compliance with quality control standards and making recommendations about ways to improve the audit practice.

A quality review has the same objective as a peer review, but it is less extensive. Quality reviews usually are requested by the smaller PA firms. They cost from $1,000 to $5,000.

Peer reviews and quality reviews are more common in the United States, where they are mandated not only by the SEC but also by the AICPA Practice Sections (see Appendix 1A). In particular, the SEC Practice Section oversees the peer review process of firms wishing to practise for the SEC. This includes all firms issuing shares in U.S. stock exchanges and therefore affects some Canadian companies and their auditors.

SEC Practice Section members are required to report to the SEC any litigation against the firm or its personnel alleging audit deficiencies involving public companies or regulated financial institutions. The SEC obtains lawsuit documents related to the litigation, but it does not attempt to try the case. The SEC's goal is to determine whether the litigation has any bearing on quality control deficiencies in the public accounting firm. In Canada sometimes a regulator such as the OSC will ask that a PA firm or individual be reviewed by a provincial Institute reviewer. This is usually in response to a complaint made to the regulator, but it sometimes arises from regular monitoring of annual reports and filings submitted to the regulator.

The extent of work involved in practice inspection, peer review or quality review is greatly influenced by the quality of documentation concerning the quality control system. Generally, if the quality control documentation is good and the reviewer can rely on exten-

---

[4] CICA, *Guide for Developing Quality Control Systems in Public Accounting*, CICA, 1993, p. 17.

sive internal monitoring of quality control, less work is required than if documentation is poor and the reviewer must rely more on his or her own detailed inspection of files.

A recent survey of one aspect of quality control, the use of accounting consultation units, among the largest five public accounting firms in Canada shows considerable variation in the characteristics of these units.[5] Accounting consultation units (ACUs) act as internal consultants at the firm's national offices. They assist practice office partners throughout the country in making difficult financial accounting judgments, including choosing among different alternatives in GAAP and disclosure issues. Some ACUs are proactive, encouraging consultation before the client enters into a transaction. These proactive ACUs tend to have more extensive staffs and databases, and emphasize creation of knowledge by compiling information on consultations already completed.

Other ACUs, however, are more passive, reacting to each consultation as a unique case and making relatively little use of databases available to them. There is no special emphasis on consultation before the client enters a transaction, and the focus is on the best technical accounting solution rather than the reasons for the transaction. There is relatively little, if any, documentation at the ACU of the consultation for future reference. These more passive ACUs tend to be driven by practice office partner needs rather than audit client needs, as is the case with the proactive ACUs. Interestingly, the proportion of proactive versus passive ACUs is evenly split among the large firms, and these differences in role are not reflected in the formal descriptions as written in the firm manuals. ACUs are an interesting example of qualitative differences among PA firms. Future research is needed to determine whether these qualitative difference in ACUs have an impact on overall audit firm performance.

. . . .

R E V I E W
C H E C K P O I N T S

2.22   What is the meaning of quality control as it relates to a PA firm?

2.23   Consider the following quality control policy and identify the quality control element to which it relates: "Designate individuals as specialists to serve as authoritative sources; provide procedures for resolving differences of opinion between audit personnel and specialists."

2.24   What is the practice inspection, and what roles does it play in the quality control self-regulation of the profession?

. . . .

SUMMARY
. . . .

The assurance standards are the general framework for applying the "assurance engagements" to a wide range of subjects. They are the quality guides for general assurance work. Theoretically, they could serve as quality guides for independent audits of financial statements. However, they were created long after GAAS for audits of financial statements, and therefore GAAS remains the predominant framework for most engagements.

Financial statement auditors are most concerned with the eight GAAS standards because they are the direct guides for the quality of everyday audit practice. The general standard sets requirements for auditors' competence, objectivity and due professional care. The three examination standards set requirements for planning and supervising each audit, obtaining an understanding of the client's internal controls and obtaining sufficient appropriate evidence to serve as a basis for an audit report. The four reporting standards cover requirements for GAAP, auditor and management responsibilities, adequate disclosure and report content.

---

[5] S. Salterio and R. Denham, "Organizational Memory in Public Accounting Firms: The Role of Accounting Consultation Units," University of Alberta Working Paper (presented at the 1995 CAAA Conference in Montreal).

These GAAS have been widely copied. When you study Chapter 18, on public sector and internal auditing, you will see that the CICA and internal audit standards incorporate all the GAAS and many elements of assurance concepts. All auditors have some common ground in generally accepted auditing standards.

GAAS are applicable in computer accounting systems as well as in manual systems. Compliance with the GAAS general and field work standards is more complex because of the technological complexity of computer systems. However, the GAAS reporting standards are not affected.

In all matters relating to financial statement audits, auditors are advised to have a sense of professional scepticism. This attitude is reflected in a "prove it with evidence" response to management representations, to answers to enquiries and to financial statement assertions themselves.

While assurance standards and GAAS govern the quality of work on each individual engagement, the quality control elements guide a PA firm's audit practice taken as a whole. Quality control is the foundation of the self-regulatory system of peer review, practice inspection and quality review. The nine elements of independence, assigning personnel, consultation, supervision, hiring, professional development, advancement, acceptance and continuance of clients, and inspection are usually the objects of a firm's policies and procedures for assuring that GAAS are followed faithfully in all aspects of the firm's practice.

As an auditor, you must have a thorough understanding of these practice standards, especially GAAS. All practical problems can be approached by beginning with a consideration of the practice standards in question. Auditing standards do not exist in a vacuum. They are put to work in numerous practical applications. Practical applications of the standards will be shown in subsequent chapters on audit program planning, execution of auditing procedures, gathering evidence and making auditing decisions.

MULTIPLE-CHOICE QUESTIONS FOR PRACTICE AND REVIEW

2.25 It is always a good idea for auditors to begin an audit with the professional scepticism characterized by the assumption that:
a. A potential conflict of interest always exists between the auditor and the management of the enterprise under audit.
b. In audits of financial statements, the auditor acts exclusively in the capacity of an auditor.
c. The professional status of the independent auditor imposes commensurate professional obligations.
d. Financial statements and financial data are verifiable.

2.26 When Client Company prohibits auditors from visiting selected branch offices of the business, this is an example of interference with:
a. Reporting independence.
b. Investigative independence.
c. Auditors' training and proficiency.
d. Audit planning and supervision.

2.27 After the auditors learned of Client Company's failure to record an expense for obsolete inventory, they agreed to a small adjustment to the financial statements because the Client president told them the company would violate its debt agreements if the full amount were recorded. This is an example of a lack of:
a. Auditors' training and proficiency.
b. Planning and supervision.
c. Audit investigative independence.
d. Audit reporting independence.

2.28 The primary purpose for obtaining an understanding of the company's internal controls in a financial statement audit is:
a. To determine the nature, timing and extent of auditing procedures to be performed.
b. To make consulting suggestions to the management.
c. To obtain direct sufficient appropriate evidential matter to afford a reasonable basis for an opinion on the financial statements.
d. To determine whether the company has changed any accounting principles.

2.29 Auditors' activities about which of these generally accepted auditing standards are not affected by the auditee's utilization of a computerized accounting system?

a. The audit report shall state whether the financial statements are presented in accordance with GAAP.

b. The work is to be adequately planned and assistants, if any, are to be properly supervised.

c. Sufficient appropriate evidential matter is to be obtained . . . to afford a reasonable basis for an opinion regarding the financial statements under audit.

d. The audit is to be performed by a person or persons having adequate technical training and proficiency as an auditor.

2.30 Which of the following is not found in the standard unqualified audit report on financial statements?

a. An identification of the financial statements that were audited.

b. A general description of an audit.

c. An opinion that the financial statements present financial position in conformity with GAAP.

d. An emphasis paragraph commenting on the effect of economic conditions on the company.

2.31 The assurance standards do not contain a requirement that auditors obtain:

a. Adequate knowledge in the subject matter of the assertions being examined.

b. An understanding of the auditee's internal control structure.

c. Sufficient evidence for the conclusions expressed in an attestation report.

d. Independence in mental attitude.

2.32 Auditor Jones is studying a company's accounting treatment of a series of complicated transactions in exotic financial instruments. She should look for the highest level of authoritative support for proper accounting in:

a. Provincial Securities Commission Staff Position Statements.

b. CICA industry audit and accounting guides.

c. CICA recommendations in the *Handbook.*

d. Emerging Issues Committee Consensus Statements.

2.33 Which of the following is not an example of a quality control procedure likely to be used by a public accounting firm to meet its professional responsibilities to clients?

a. Completion of independence questionnaires by all partners and employees.

b. Review and approval of audit plan by the partner in charge of the engagement just prior to signing the auditor's report.

c. Evaluating professional staff after the conclusion of each engagement.

d. Evaluating the integrity of management for each new audit client.

2.34 Which of the following concepts is not included in the wording of the auditor's standard report?

a. Management's responsibility for the financial statements.

b. Auditor's responsibility to assess significant estimates made by management.

c. Extent of auditor's reliance on the client's internal controls.

d. Examination of evidence on a test basis.

2.35 Which of the following is not mandatory when performing an audit in accordance with Generally Accepted Auditing Standards?

a. Proper supervision of assistants.

b. Efficient performance of audit procedures.

c. Understanding the client's system of internal controls.

d. Adequate planning of work to be performed.

EXERCISES AND PROBLEMS

2.36 **Audit Independence and Planning.** You are meeting with executives of Cooper Cosmetics Corporation to arrange your firm's engagement to audit the corporation's financial statements for the year ending December 31. One executive suggests the audit work be divided among three staff members. One person would examine asset accounts, a second would examine liability accounts and the third would examine income and expense accounts to minimize audit time, avoid duplication of staff effort and curtail interference with company operations.

Advertising is the corporation's largest expense, and the advertising manager suggests that a staff member of your firm, whose uncle owns the advertising agency that handles the corporation's advertising, be assigned to examine the Advertising Expense account. The staff member has a thorough knowledge of the rather complex contact between Cooper Cosmetics and the advertising agency.

Required:

a. To what extent should a PA follow the client's suggestions for the conduct of an audit? Discuss.

b. List and discuss the reasons why audit work should not be assigned solely according to asset, liability and income and expense categories.

c. Should the staff member of your PA firm whose uncle owns the advertising agency be assigned to examine advertising costs? Discuss.

2.37 Examination Standards. You have accepted the engagement of auditing the financial statements of the C. Reis Company, a small manufacturing firm that has been your client for several years. Because you were busy writing the report for another engagement, you sent a staff accountant to begin the audit, with the suggestion that she start with the accounts receivable. Using the prior year's working papers as a guide, the auditor prepared a trial balance of the accounts, aged them, prepared and mailed positive confirmation requests, examined underlying support for charges and credits, and performed other work she considered necessary to obtain evidence about the validity and collectibility of the receivables. At the conclusion of her work, you reviewed the working papers she prepared and found she had carefully followed the prior year's working papers.

Required:

The opinion rendered by a PA states that the audit was made in accordance with generally accepted auditing standards.

List the three generally accepted standards of field work. Relate them to the above illustration by indicating how they were fulfilled or, if appropriate, how they were not fulfilled.

(ICAO adapted)

2.38 Time of Appointment and Planning. Your public accounting practice is located in a town of 15,000 population. Your work, conducted by you and two assistants, consists of compiling clients' monthly statements and preparing income tax returns for individuals from cash data and partnership returns from books and records. You have a few corporate clients; however, service to them is limited to preparation of income tax returns and assistance in year-end closings where bookkeeping is deficient.

One of your corporate clients is a retail hardware store. Your work for this client has been limited to preparing the corporation income tax return from a trial balance submitted by the bookkeeper.

On December 26 you receive from the president of the corporation a letter containing the following request:

> We have made arrangements with the First National Bank to borrow $500,000 to finance the purchase of a complete line of appliances. The bank has asked us to furnish our auditor's certified statement as of December 31, which is the closing date of our accounting year. The trial balance of the general ledger should be ready by January 10, which should allow ample time to prepare your report for submission to the bank by January 20. In view of the importance of this certified report to our financing program, we trust you will arrange to comply with the foregoing schedule.

Required:

From a theoretical viewpoint, discuss the difficulties that are caused by such a short-notice audit request.

(AICPA adapted)

2.39 Reporting Standards. PA Musgrave and his associates audited the financial statements of North Company, a computer equipment retailer. Musgrave conducted the audit in accordance with the general and field work standards of generally accepted auditing standards and therefore wrote a standard audit description in his audit report. Then he received an emergency call to fill in as a substitute tenor in his barbershop quartet.

No one else was in the office that Saturday afternoon, so he handed you the complete financial statements and footnotes and said: "Make sure it's OK to write an unqualified opinion on these statements. The working papers are on the table. I'll check with you on Monday morning."

Required:

In general terms, what must you determine in order to write an unqualified opinion paragraph for Musgrave's signature?

2.40 GAAS in a Computer Environment. The Lovett Corporation uses an IBM mainframe computer system with peripheral optical reader and high-speed laser printer equipment. Transaction information is initially recorded on paper documents (e.g., sales invoices) and then read by optical equipment that produces a magnetic disk containing the data. These data file disks are processed by a computer program, and printed listings, journals and general ledger balances are produced on the high-speed printer equipment.

Required:

Explain how the audit standard requiring "adequate technical training and proficiency" is important for satisfying the general and field work standards in the audit of Lovett Corporation's financial statements.

2.41 Audit Report Language. The standard unqualified report contains several important sentences and phrases. Give an explanation of why each of the following phrases is used instead of the alternative language indicated.

1. Address: "To the Board of Directors and Stockholders" instead of "To Whom It May Concern."

2. "We have audited the balance sheet of Anycompany as of December 31, 1997, and the related statements of income, retained earnings and cash flows for the year then ended" instead of "We have audited the attached financial statements."

3. "We conducted our audit in accordance with generally accepted auditing standards" instead of "Our audit was conducted with due audit care appropriate in the circumstances."

4. "In our opinion, the financial statements referred to above present fairly . . . in conformity with generally accepted accounting principles" instead of "The financial statements are true and correct."

2.42 Authoritative Support. Auditors' reports on financial statements contain an opinion on the conformity of the statements with generally accepted accounting principles (GAAP). An audit decision on GAAP includes the determination of whether an accounting treatment is "generally accepted," and this determination is made by finding the authoritative support for the accounting treatment.

Required:

List in order of priority the sources of authoritative support an auditor can consult when faced with a decision about GAAP.

2.43 Deficiencies and Omissions in an Audit Report. On completion of all field work on September 23, 1998, the following report was written by Betsy Ross to the directors of Continental Corporation.

To the Board of Directors.
Continental Corporation:

The accompanying balance sheet of Continental Corporation and the related statements of income and retained earnings as of July 31, 1998, are the responsibility of management. In accordance with your instructions, we have conducted a complete audit. We planned and performed the audit to obtain reasonable assurance about whether the financial statements are free of material misstatement. An audit includes examining, on a test basis, evidence supporting the amounts and disclosures in the financial statements. An audit also includes assessing the accounting principles used and significant estimates made by management, as well as evaluating the overall financial statement presentation. We believe that our audit provides a reasonable basis for our opinion.

In many respects this was an unusual year for the Continental Corporation. The weakening of the economy in the early part of the year and the strike of plant employees in the summer led to a decline in sales and net income. After making several tests of the sales records, nothing came to our attention that would indicate sales have not been properly recorded.

In our opinion, with the explanation given above, and with the exception of some minor errors we consider immaterial, the aforementioned financial statements present the financial position of Continental Corporation at July 31, 1998, and the results of its operations, and its cash flows for the year then ended, in conformity with generally accepted accounting principles.

Betsy Ross & Co., PA
July 31, 1998

Required:

List and explain the deficiencies and omissions in Ross's audit report.

2.44 Management Fraud Conflict of Interest. Many cases of management fraud probably go undetected even when competent annual audits are performed. The reason, of course, is that generally accepted auditing procedures are not always designed and executed specifically to detect executive-level management fraud. Please give your own estimate of the prevalence of executive-level management fraud as requested below.

1. Based on your perceptions of business, is the incidence of significant executive-level management fraud more than

10 in each 1,000 clients (i.e., 1 percent) audited by Big Six accounting firms? Answer *a* or *b*.

   a. Yes, more than 10 in each 1,000 Big Six clients have significant executive-level management fraud.

   b. No, fewer than 10 in each 1,000 Big Six clients have significant executive-level management fraud.

2. What is your estimate of the number of Big Six clients per 1,000 that have significant executive-level management fraud?

DISCUSSION CASES

. . . .

2.45 Investment Performance Assurance. Nancy Drew is the president of Mystery Capital Management, Inc. Mystery manages $1.2 billion in two mutual funds, one a stock fund and the other a bond fund. Competition for investors' money is fierce, and hundreds of money management companies compete by advertising their funds' performance statistics. Recently, the Ontario Securities Commission (OSC) has criticized the advertisements for misrepresenting the returns investors can actually earn. In addition to the investment performance statistics, money management firms also advertise the amounts of their fees, usually representing no-load or low-fee arrangements, but they often do not advertise the other expenses allowed under OSC rules.

   Ms. Drew has retained your PA firm to give an opinion on the fair presentation of Mystery Capital Management's investment performance statistics and expense ratios used in its advertisements. The plan is to present your report in the company's advertisements.

Required:
For each of the assurance standards, state its applicability in relation to the engagement.

2.46 Auditing Standards Case Study. Ray, the owner of a small company, asked Holmes, PA, to conduct an audit of the company's records. Ray told Holmes that the audit was to be completed in time to submit audited financial statements to a bank as part of a loan application. Holmes immediately accepted the engagement and agreed to provide an auditor's report within three weeks. Ray agreed to pay Holmes a fixed fee plus a bonus if the loan was granted.

   Holmes hired two accounting students to conduct the audit and spent several hours telling them exactly what to do. Holmes told the students not to spend time reviewing the controls but, instead, to concentrate on proving the mathematical accuracy of the ledger accounts and on summarizing the data in the accounting records that support Ray's financial statements. The students followed Holmes's instructions and after two weeks gave Holmes the financial statements, which did not include footnotes. Holmes reviewed the statements and prepared an unqualified auditor's report. The report, however, did not refer to generally accepted accounting principles or to the fact that Ray had changed to the accounting standard for capitalizing interest.

Required:
Briefly describe each of the generally accepted auditing standards and indicate how the action(s) of Holmes resulted in a failure to comply with each standard.

(AICPA adapted)

2.47 Quality Control Standards. Each of the following quality control policies and procedures is typical of ones that can be found in PA firms' quality control documents. Identify each of them with one of the elements of quality control required by the Quality Control Standards.

   a. Review semiannual performance reports with individuals and assess their progress in relation to job performance, future objectives, assignment preferences and career opportunities.

   b. Publish guidelines for review of each audit report, including determination of the adequacy of evidence shown in the working papers, conformity of the report with professional standards and review of the report by a partner not otherwise connected with the audit engagement.

   c. Maintain or provide access to adequate reference libraries and designated experts by (1) maintaining technical manuals and internal technical newsletters and (2) advising staff personnel of the degree of authority accorded internal experts' opinions and the procedures to be followed for resolving disagreements with experts.

d. Consider the experience and training of the engagement personnel in relation to the complexity or other requirements of the engagement and the extent of supervision to be provided.

e. Review recruiting results annually to determine whether goals and personnel needs are being achieved.

f. Distribute new professional pronouncements (IAGs, EIC, others), and encourage personnel at all levels to take continuing professional education courses.

g. A special team will review a selection of completed audits for compliance with professional standards, including generally accepted auditing standards, generally accepted accounting principles and the firm's quality control policies and procedures.

h. Obtain from personnel periodic, written representations listing their investments, outside business relationships and employment of their close relatives.

i. A firm management committee shall annually review client relationships in light of changes in management, directors, ownership, legal counsel, financial condition, litigation status, nature of client's business and scope of the engagement.

CHAPTER 3

Learning Objectives

This chapter covers the most frequent variations in audit reports.

Management has the primary responsibility for the fair presentation of financial statements in conformity with generally accepted accounting principles. Auditors have primary responsibility for their own audit reports on the financial statements. You must know the standard unqualified report as a starting place, since this chapter explains reasons for changing the standard language when auditors cannot give this "clean opinion."

Your objectives, with respect to variations in audit reports, are to be able to:

1. Determine whether an accountant is associated with financial statements.

2. Explain the general meaning of the three "levels of assurance."

3. Write a detailed description of the meaning of the scope paragraph and the opinion paragraph in a standard unqualified audit report.

4. Write a qualified, an adverse and a denial report for a given description of accounting facts and audit circumstances.

5. Write an audit report with an unqualified opinion but containing additional explanation or modified wording for specific issues allowed by auditing standards.

6. Explain why auditors have standards for reporting on the "application of accounting principles."

7. List and explain the effects of materiality on audit report choices.

8. Write an audit report in which a principal auditor refers to the work of another independent auditor (Appendix 3A).

9. Write the required modifications when a report on prior-year comparative financial statements is changed (Appendix 3A).

10. Describe the type of report issued when an audit engagement is limited (Appendix 3A).

11. Explain auditors' reporting responsibilities in connection with "other information" and supplementary information (Appendix 3A).

12. Describe the reporting requirements involved in auditors' association with condensed financial information (Appendix 3A).

REPORTS ON AUDITED FINANCIAL STATEMENTS

ASSOCIATION WITH FINANCIAL STATEMENTS

LEARNING OBJECTIVE
1. Determine whether an accountant is associated with financial statements.

Auditing standards require a report to be rendered in all cases where a PA's name is **associated with financial statements**. As a PA, you are associated with financial statements when (1) you have consented to the use of your name in connection with the statements; or (2) you have prepared or performed some other services with respect to the statements, even if your name is not used in any written report (*Handbook Section* 5020.04).

The concept of association is far-reaching. PAs are associated with financial statements and must render reports even in such cases as these: (1) financial statements are merely reproduced on an accountant's letterhead, (2) financial statements are produced by the accountant's computer as part of a bookkeeping service, and (3) a document containing financial statements merely identifies an accountant as the public accountant or auditor for the company. The reason a report is required is that most users of financial statements assume that an audit has been conducted and that "everything is OK" whenever an independent accountant is known to be involved with financial statements. Consequently, an obligation exists to inform the users about the nature of the work performed, if any, and the conclusions the accountant has made about the financial statements. This outline is summarized in more detail in Appendix 3A.

R E V I E W
CHECKPOINTS

3.1 Why should public accountants issue a report whenever they are associated with financial statements?

LEVELS OF ASSURANCE

LEARNING OBJECTIVE
2. Explain the general meaning of the three "levels of assurance".

In practice, accountants and auditors can render three basic types of conclusions about financial statements. These three are known as the **levels of assurance**. The highest level is considered to be the audit assurance exemplified by the standard unqualified report (sometimes known as the clean opinion). Its opinion sentence reads: "In our opinion, the accompanying financial statements present fairly, in all material respects." This opinion sentence is sometimes called **positive assurance** because it is a forthright and factual statement of the PA's opinion based on an audit. Although the *CICA Handbook* does not explicitly state how much assurance an auditor provides in an audit opinion, it does discuss assurance in terms of auditor objectives. (See *Handbook Section* 5130.02.)

The middle level is known as **negative assurance**. A negative assurance conclusion is typical in the review report on unaudited nonfinancial statements, thus: "Based on my review, nothing has come to my attention that causes me to believe that these financial statements are not, in all material respects, in accordance with generally accepted accounting principles" (*Section* 8200.04 of the *Handbook*). This conclusion is called negative because it uses the backdoor phrase "nothing has come to my attention" to give assurance about conformity with GAAP. Auditing standards prohibit the use of negative assurance in reports on audited financial statements because it is considered too weak a conclusion for the audit effort involved (*Section* 5400.15). However, negative assurance is permitted in reviews of unaudited financial statements, in letters to underwriters and in reviews of interim financial information. (More details about review reports on unaudited financial statements are in Chapter 15.)

E X H I B I T 3–1   LEVELS OF ASSURANCE

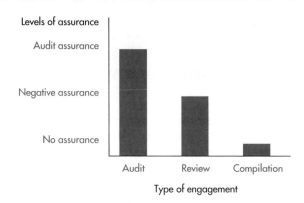

The lowest level of assurance is a no assurance engagement. The most common examples are compilation engagements, which can be considered a form of specified procedures engagements. Compilation engagements are not considered to be assurance engagements because the practitioner is not required to audit, review or otherwise attempt to verify the accuracy or completeness of the information provided by management. The practitioner is, therefore, not expressing a conclusion on the reliability of the statements compiled. The auditors' involvement in compiling the financial statements is presumed, however, to add accounting credibility to the financial statements even though there is no audit credibility or assurance provided. (More details about compilation reports on unaudited financial statements are in Chapter 15).

The levels of assurance are depicted in Exhibit 3–1. It should be noted that audit, review and compilation engagements are intended to provide the specified assurance levels given in Exhibit 3–1. As we will see in discussing the denial of opinion, under some conditions not even an audit engagement can provide much assurance.

R E V I E W
C H E C K P O I N T S

3.2 What is the most important distinction between an auditor's opinion on financial statements and other PA communications?

3.3 What is negative assurance? When is negative assurance permitted?

STANDARD UNQUALIFIED REPORT AND VARIATIONS

LEARNING OBJECTIVE

3. Write a detailed description of the meaning of the scope paragraph and opinion paragraph in a standard unqualified audit report.

The standard unqualified report contains three basic segments: (1) the introductory paragraph, (2) the scope paragraph and (3) the opinion paragraph. An example is given in Exhibit 3–2. The technical details of this report were introduced in Chapter 2. The ISA equivalent report is given in Appendix 3B.

Meaning of the Introductory, Scope and Opinion Paragraphs

Many users understand the audit report by counting the paragraphs! Crude as this may seem, it makes some sense because the three standard paragraphs are supposed to convey the same messages for all audits.

EXHIBIT 3-2   **AUDITOR'S REPORT (from *Handbook Section* 5400.26)**

To the Shareholders of ....

I have audited the balance sheet of .... as at ...., 20.........., and the statements of income, retained earnings and cash flow for the year then ended. These financial statements are the responsibility of the company's management. My responsibility is to express an opinion on these financial statements based on my audit.

I conducted my audit in accordance with generally accepted auditing standards. Those standards require that I plan and perform an audit to obtain reasonable assurance whether the financial statements are free of material misstatement. An audit includes examining, on a test basis, evidence supporting the amounts and disclosure in the financial statements. An audit also includes assessing the accounting principles used and significant estimates made by management, as well as evaluating the overall financial statement presentation.

In my opinion, these financial statements present fairly, in all material respects, the financial position of the company as at ...., 20.........., and the results of its operations and the changes in its financial position for the year then ended in accordance with generally accepted accounting principles.

City   (signed) ....
Date   Chartered Accountant

Introductory Paragraph

The introductory paragraph declares that an audit has been conducted and identifies the financial statements. These identifications are important because the opinion paragraph at the end is an opinion on these financial statements. If one or more of the basic financial statements is not identified in the introductory paragraph, the opinion paragraph likewise should not offer any opinion on it (them). The introductory paragraph also gives notice of management's responsibility for the financial statements and the auditors' responsibility for the audit report (*Handbook Section* 5400.08).

Scope Paragraph

Auditors must render a fair presentation of their own work, as well as an opinion on the financial statements. The scope paragraph is the auditor's report of the character of the work in the audit. This portion of the report is vitally important for disclosure of the quality and extent of the audit itself.

The sentence "I conducted my audit in accordance with generally accepted auditing standards" refers primarily to the general and field work standards. Its message is that (1) the auditors were trained and proficient, (2) the auditors were independent, (3) due professional care was exercised, (4) the work was planned and supervised, (5) a sufficient understanding of the internal control structure was obtained, and (6) sufficient appropriate evidential matter was obtained. To the extent that one or more of these general and field work standards is not actually satisfied during an audit, the scope paragraph must be qualified. A qualification in this paragraph means the addition of words explaining exactly which standard was not satisfied. Such qualifications may be caused by lack of sufficient appropriate evidence, such as restrictions on procedures imposed by the client (*Section* 5510). In practice, auditors always change the standard opinion paragraph language when the scope paragraph is qualified.

The scope paragraph contains general descriptions of the audit work in addition to the reference to generally accepted auditing standards. It makes special mention of the auditors' assessment of the choice of accounting principles and the evaluation of the overall financial statement presentation. The scope paragraph also lists any conditions that prevented the auditor from getting sufficient appropriate evidence. Such conditions can indicate areas of improvement in the client's system of record keeping.

Opinion Paragraph

Users of audited financial statements are generally most interested in the opinion paragraph. It is actually one long sentence. This sentence contains the auditors' conclusions about the financial statements. It is the public manifestation of the private audit decision process.

The third and fourth reporting standards are incorporated in the opinion sentence:

1. The standard report states that the financial statements are presented in accordance with generally accepted accounting principles.

2. The standard report, by its silence, regards the financial statement disclosures as reasonably adequate.

3. The standard report contains an expression of opinion regarding the financial statements.

4. An "overall opinion" is expressed in the standard report, so no reasons for not doing so need to be stated.

5. The scope paragraph gives the "clear-cut indication of the character of the audit examination," and the degree of responsibility is unqualified positive assurance.

With regard to the fourth reporting standard, other examples later in this chapter will show how auditors assert that an opinion cannot be expressed (denial of opinion) and how audit responsibility can be limited (qualified opinion).

When reading the reporting standards, you should understand the term "financial statements" to include not only the traditional balance sheet, income statement and cash flow statement, but also all the footnote disclosures and additional information (e.g., earnings per share calculations) that are integral elements of the basic financial presentation required by GAAP. The first and fourth standards are explicit in the standard report. The second and third standards are effectively on an implicit reporting basis—that is, the report comments on consistency only when accounting principles have been changed *and* disclosures are considered inadequate. The adequacy of disclosures may be judged by GAAP requirements; but auditors also must be sensitive to the information needs of investors, creditors and other users when considering the need to disclose information that is not explicitly required by GAAP. Disgruntled investors often use the "lack of informative disclosure" criterion as a basis for lawsuits.

Reservation in the Audit Report

Subsequent sections of this chapter explain the major variations on the standard report. These are referred to as reservations in the auditor's report. There are two basic reasons for giving a report other than the standard unqualified audit report.

When the financial statements contain a departure from GAAP, including inadequate disclosure, the auditors must choose between a qualified opinion and an adverse opinion. The choice depends on the materiality (significance) and pervasiveness of the effect of the GAAP departure.

When there is a scope limitation (extent of audit work has been limited), and the auditors have not been able to obtain sufficient appropriate evidence on a particular account balance or disclosure, the auditors must choose between a qualified opinion and a denial of opinion. The choice depends on the materiality of the matter for which evidence is not sufficient.

R E V I E W
C H E C K P O I N T S

3.4 Think about the standard unqualified introductory and scope paragraphs: (*a*) What do they identify as the objects of the audit? (*b*) What is meant by this sentence: "We conducted our audit in accordance with generally accepted auditing standards"?

3.5 What are the major reasons for changing the standard unqualified report?

AUDIT REPORT RESERVATIONS
. . . .

LEARNING OBJECTIVE
4. Write a qualified, an ad-
    verse and a denial report
    for a given description
    of accounting facts and
    audit circumstances.

Audit reports other than the standard unqualified audit report are called audit report reservations. The most common report reservations are called **qualified reports** because they
contain an opinion paragraph that does not give the positive assurance that everything in
the financial statements is in conformity with GAAP. The three basic types of qualified
reports are different.

GAAP Departure Reports

A company's management can decide to present financial statements containing an
accounting treatment or disclosure that is not in conformity with GAAP. The reasons are
varied. Management may not wish to capitalize leases and show the related debt, may calculate earnings per share incorrectly, may not accrue unbilled revenue at the end of a
period, may make unreasonable accounting estimates or may be reluctant to disclose all the
known details of a contingency. Whatever the reason, the fact is a departure from GAAP.
Now the auditor must decide the type of opinion to render.

   If the departure is immaterial or insignificant, it can be treated as if it did not exist. The
audit opinion can be unqualified. What is considered immaterial under the circumstances
is a matter of auditor's professional judgment.

   If in the auditor's judgment the departure is material enough to potentially affect users'
decisions based on the financial statements, the opinion must be qualified. In this case, the
qualification takes the "except-for" language form. The opinion sentence begins: "In my
opinion, except for the [nature of the GAAP departure explained in the report], the financial statements present fairly, in all material respects . . . in accordance with generally

---

E X H I B I T 3–3   **(from *Handbook Section* 5510.A, Example A)**

Departure from generally accepted accounting principles—no depreciation recorded. When the auditor has determined that a qualification is the type of reservation required, the following wording may be appropriate.

AUDITOR'S REPORT

To the Shareholders of ....

I have audited the balance sheet of .... as at ...., 20.........., and the statements of income,
retained earnings and cash flows for the year then ended. These financial statements are the responsibility of the company's management. My responsibility is to express an opinion of these financial statements based on my audit.

I conducted my audit in accordance with generally accepted auditing standards. Those standards require that I plan and
perform an audit to obtain reasonable assurance whether the financial statements are free of material misstatement. An
audit includes examining, on a test basis, evidence supporting the amounts and disclosures in the financial statements.
An audit also includes assessing the accounting principles used and significant estimates made by management, as well
as evaluating the overall financial statement presentation.

Note .... describes the depreciation policy with respect to the company's manufacturing plants and equipment. The
note also indicates that the company is not depreciating its head office building, which it acquired 5 years ago, on the
grounds that it is not a producing asset and is maintaining its value as a potential rental or resale property. In this respect
the financial statements are not in accordance with generally accepted accounting principles. The estimated useful life
of similar buildings is usually considered to be between 30 and 40 years. If depreciation had been provided on the
basis of an estimated useful life of, say, 35 years, depreciation for the current year would have been increased by
$..........(20..........$..........), net income after taxes would have been decreased by $..........(20..........$..........),
accumulated depreciation would have been increased by $..........(20..........$..........) and the balance of deferred
income taxes and the closing balance of retained earnings would have been reduced by $..........(20..........$..........)
and $..........(20..........$..........) respectively.

In my opinion, except for the effects of the failure to record depreciation as described in the preceding paragraph, these
financial statements present fairly, in all material respects, the financial position of the company as at ....,
20.........., and the results of its operations and the changes in its financial position for the year then ended in accordance with generally accepted accounting principles.

(signed).....................................
(CHARTERED ACCOUNTANT)

---

accepted accounting principles." This except-for form of GAAP departure qualification isolates a particular departure, but says that the financial statements are otherwise in conformity with GAAP. The nature of the GAAP departure can be explained in a separate paragraph (called the reservation paragraph) in the audit report between the scope paragraph and the opinion paragraph (*Handbook Section* 5510.28).

In the except-for qualified report, the introductory and scope paragraphs are the same as the standard unqualified report. They are not changed. After all, the audit has been performed without limitation, and the auditors have sufficient appropriate evidence about the financial statements, including the GAAP departure.

GAAP-departure report examples are hard to find in published financial statements. Most published statements come under the jurisdiction of the provincial securities commissions, which require public companies to file financial statements in conformity with GAAP without any departures. Exhibit 3–3 shows a GAAP departure due to a failure to record depreciation.

However, if the GAAP departure is (1) more than material or "so significant that they overshadow the financial statements" (what we'll call here "super-material"), or (2) pervasive, affecting numerous accounts and financial statement relationships, an adverse opinion should be given. An adverse opinion is exactly the opposite of the unqualified opinion. In this type of opinion, auditors say the financial statements do not present financial position, results of operations and changes in financial position in conformity with generally accepted accounting principles. The introductory and scope paragraphs should not be qualified because, in order to decide to use the adverse opinion, the audit team must possess all evidence necessary to reach the decision. When this opinion is given, all the substantive reasons must be disclosed in the report in the reservation paragraph(s) (*Section* 5510.28).

Because of the securities commission requirements, adverse opinions are hard to find. The example in Exhibit 3–4 is an adverse opinion due to a disagreement between the audi-

EXHIBIT 3–4   **ADVERSE REPORT (from *Handbook Section* 5510.11)**

Departure from generally accepted accounting principles—disagreement on carrying value of a long-term investment. When the auditor has determined that an adverse opinion is the type of reservation required, the following wording may be appropriate. (For an adverse opinion, "present fairly" in the opinion paragraph, need not be modified with the phrase "in all material respects")

AUDITOR'S REPORT

To the Shareholders of ....

I have audited the balance sheet of .... as at ...., 20.........., and the statements of income, retained earnings and cash flows for the year then ended. These financial statements are the responsibility of the company's management. My responsibility is to express an opinion of these financial statements based on my audit.

I conducted my audit in accordance with generally accepted auditing standards. Those standards require that I plan and perform an audit to obtain reasonable assurance whether the financial statements are free of material misstatement. An audit includes examining, on a test basis, evidence supporting the amounts and disclosures in the financial statements. An audit also includes assessing the accounting principles used and significant estimates made by management, as well as evaluating the overall financial statement presentation.

The company's investment in X Company Ltd., its only asset, which is carried at a cost of $10,000,000, has declined in value to an amount of $5,850,000. The loss in the value of this investment, in my opinion, is other than a temporary decline and in such circumstances, generally accepted accounting principles require that the investment be written down to recognize the loss. If this decline in value had been recognized, the investment, net income for the year and retained earnings would have been reduced by $4,150,000.

In my opinion, because the write-down has not been made for the significant decline in value of the investment described in the preceding paragraph, these financial statements do not present fairly the financial position of the company as at ...., 20.......... and the results of its operations and the changes in its financial position for the year then ended in accordance with generally accepted accounting principles.

(signed)......................................
CHARTERED ACCOUNTANT

Date
City

tor and management on the carrying value of a long-term investment. The departure from GAAP is considered to be super-material, or well in excess of what would be considered material for an "except for" qualification.

As a practical matter, auditors generally require more evidence to support an adverse opinion than to support an unqualified opinion. Perhaps this phenomenon can be attributed to auditors' reluctance to be bearers of bad news. However, audit standards are quite clear on the point that, if an auditor has a basis for an adverse opinion, the uncomfortable position cannot be relieved by giving a denial of opinion.

R E V I E W
C H E C K P O I N T S

3.6 With reference to evidence, what extent of evidence is required as a basis for the unqualified opinion? for an adverse opinion? for an opinion qualified for GAAP departure?

3.7 What effect does the materiality of a GAAP departure have on the auditors' reporting decision?

Scope Limitation Reports

Auditors are in the most comfortable position when they have all the evidence needed to make a report decision, whether the opinion is to be unqualified, adverse or qualified for a GAAP departure. However, two kinds of situations can create **scope limitations**, which are conditions where the auditors are unable to obtain sufficient appropriate evidence. The two arise from (1) management's deliberate refusal to let auditors perform some procedures and (2) circumstances, such as late appointment of auditor, in which some procedures cannot be performed.

If management's refusal or the circumstances affect the audit in a minor, immaterial way, or if sufficient appropriate evidence can be obtained by other means, the audit can be considered to be unaffected, and the report can be unqualified as if the limitation had never occurred.

Management's deliberate refusal to give access to documents or decision to otherwise limit the application of audit procedures is the most serious condition. It casts doubt on management's integrity. (Why does management refuse access or limit the work?) In most such cases, excluding ones in which the limitation clearly relates to financial matters already known to be immaterial, the audit report is qualified or an opinion is denied, depending upon the materiality of the financial items affected.

Exhibit 3–5 shows two reports that illustrate the auditors' alternatives. The illustrated failure to take physical counts of inventory might have been a deliberate management action, or it might have resulted from other circumstances (such as the company not anticipating the need for an audit and appointing the auditor after the latest year-end).

In Panel A the opinion is qualified, using the except-for language form. Here the lack of evidence is considered material but not "super-material" to overwhelm the meaning of a qualified audit opinion and the usefulness of the unaffected parts of the financial statements. The proper qualification phrase is: "In our opinion, except for the effects of adjustments, if any, as might have been determined to be necessary had we been able to examine evidence regarding the inventories, the financial statements present fairly, in all material respects, . . . in conformity with generally accepted accounting principles." This report "carves out" the inventory from the audit reporting responsibility, taking no audit responsibility for this part of the financial statements.

Notice that the introductory paragraph in Panel A is the same as for an unqualified report. However, the scope paragraph is qualified because the audit was not entirely completed in accordance with generally accepted auditing standards. Specifically, sufficient appropriate evidence about the inventories was not obtained. Whenever the scope paragraph is qualified for an important omission of audit work, the opinion paragraph should also be qualified.

E X H I B I T 3–5   SCOPE LIMITATION REPORTS

Panel A: Qualified Opinion

Auditor's Report

To the Shareholders of
X Company:

(Standard introductory paragraph here)

Except as discussed in the following paragraph, we conducted our audits in accordance with generally accepted auditing standards. . . . (Remainder of paragraph the same as the standard unqualified scope paragraph) . . .

The Company did not make a count of its physical inventory in 2002 or 2001, stated in the accompanying financial statements at $10 million as of December 31, 2002, and at $15 million as of December 31, 2001, and we were unable to observe the physical quantities on hand. The Company's records do not permit the application of other auditing procedures to the audit of the inventories.

In our opinion, except for the effects of such adjustments, if any, as might have been determined to be necessary had we been able to examine evidence regarding the inventories described above, the financial statements referred to above present fairly, in all material respects, the financial position of X Company at December 31, 2002 and 2001, and the results of operations and cash flows for the years then ended in conformity with generally accepted accounting principles.

/s/ Auditor signature
January 29, 2003

Panel B: Denial of Opinion

Auditor's Report

To the Shareholders of
X Company:

We were engaged to audit the accompanying balance sheets of X Company as of December 31, 2002 and 2001, and the related statements of income, retained earnings and cash flows for the years then ended. These financial statements are the responsibility of the Company's management.

(Scope paragraph omitted)

The Company did not make a count of its physical inventory in 2002 or 2001, stated in the accompanying financial statements at $10 million as of December 31, 2002, and at $15 million as of December 31, 2001, and we were unable to observe the physical quantities on hand. The Company's records do not permit the application of other auditing procedures to the audit of the inventories.

Since the Company did not take physical inventories and we were not able to apply other auditing procedures to satisfy ourselves as to inventory quantities and cost, the scope of our work was not sufficient to enable us to express, and we do not express, an opinion on these financial statements.

/s/ Auditor signature
January 29, 2003

In Panel B the situation is considered fatal to the audit opinion. The inventories are too large and too important in this case to say "except for adjustments, if any." The audit report then must be a denial of opinion. In the U.S. and in international standards (ISA 700) a denial of opinion is referred to as a disclaimer of opinion.

It is very important to remember that scope limitation reservations arise only when it is not possible to obtain compensating assurance from alternative audit procedures. If, for example, in Panel A and Panel B the auditor had been able to satisfy himself or herself through alternative procedures that the inventory was materially accurate, then an unqualified opinion could have been issued for both panels. Thus, scope limitation reports are issued only if in the auditor's judgment there are insufficient alternative procedures to compensate for the restriction.

To summarize, we can view audit reservations as arising from two types of circumstances: audit deficiencies or scope limitations, and accounting deficiencies resulting from a GAAP departure. Audit deficiencies can result in either a qualification or denial of opinion, depending on the significance of the scope limitation. In an audit deficient reservation both the scope and opinion paragraphs are affected. An accounting deficiency, on the other hand, can result in either a qualification or adverse opinion, depending on the significance of the GAAP departure. In an accounting deficiency reservation only the opinion paragraph is affected.

OTHER RESPONSIBILITIES WITH A DENIAL

A denial of opinion because of severe scope limitation or because of association with unaudited financial statements carries some additional reporting responsibilities. In addition to the denial, these guides should be followed:

1. If the PA should learn that the statements are not in conformity with generally accepted accounting principles (including adequate disclosures), the departures should be explained in the denial.

2. If prior years' unaudited statements are presented, the denial should cover them as well as the current-year statement.

It should be stressed that both auditor and client work to avoid a report reservation. There may be much discussion and negotiation between the auditor and client management to avoid a report reservation. This negotiation is discussed in more detail in Chapter 15 after we have considered the available evidence at the end of the engagement.

. . . .

REVIEW CHECKPOINTS

3.8 What are the differences between a report qualified for a scope limitation and a standard unqualified report?

3.9 What are the differences between a report in which the opinion is denied because of scope limitation and a standard unqualified report?

3.10 What are unaudited statements? In connection with unaudited statements, which general reporting guides should the auditor follow for public companies?

. . . .

Effects of Lack of Independence

Independence is the foundation of the audit function. When independence is lacking, an audit in accordance with generally accepted auditing standards is impossible. When the auditors lack independence they should resign or not accept an audit engagement by the Rules of Professional Conduct (discussed in Chapter 17). An audit is not simply the application of tools, techniques and procedures of auditing; it is also the independence in mental attitude of the auditors. This idea is reflected in the general standard and in provincial Codes of Professional Conduct, an example of one of which is the Ontario Institutes Rule 204, titled "Objectivity."

> Rule 204.1: A member engaged as an auditor to express an opinion on financial statements or on financial or other information shall hold himself or herself free of any influence, interest or relationship, which, in respect of the engagement, impairs the member's professional judgment or objectivity or which in view of a reasonable observer would impair the member's professional judgment or objectivity.

This rule applies to the auditors of financial statements. The criteria for determining independence are discussed in Chapter 16.

. . . .

REVIEW CHECKPOINTS

3.11 If an auditor is not independent with respect to a public company client, what should he or she do?

. . . .

UNQUALIFIED OPINION WITH EXPLANATION OR MODIFICATION

LEARNING OBJECTIVE

5. Write an audit report with an unqualified opinion but containing additional explanation or modified wording for specific issues allowed by auditing standards.

Several circumstances may permit an unqualified opinion paragraph, but they raise the need to consider additional information and additional paragraphs to the standard report. Five such situations are covered in this section.

- Consistency. Effects of various changes in accounting and the appropriate disclosure.
- *Section* 5400.22 Report. An unqualified opinion under *Section* 5400.22, justifying a departure from an official pronouncement.
- Emphasis Paragraph(s). Additional explanatory paragraphs that "emphasize a matter" of importance.
- Uncertainty. Paragraph that draws attention to accounting and disclosure for contingencies.
- Going Concern. Paragraph that draws attention to problems of being able to continue as a going concern.

Consistency

There is no longer a need to make reference to consistency even when there are changes in accounting principles as long as the changes are properly disclosed in the financial statements (*Section* 5400.17).

Other changes that do not require consistency references in the audit report are the following: (1) changes in accounting estimates, (2) error corrections that do not involve a change in accounting principles, (3) changes in the classification or aggregation of financial statement amounts, (4) changes in the format or basis of the statement of changes in financial position (e.g., from a balancing format to a net change format), and (5) changes in the subsidiaries included in consolidated financial statements as a result of forming a new subsidiary, buying another company, spinning off or liquidating a subsidiary or selling a subsidiary. However, failure to disclose any of these changes could amount to a GAAP departure and could present a different reason for qualifying the opinion.

When evaluating a change in accounting principle, auditors must be satisfied that management's justification for the change is reasonable. In the United States there is an additional requirement that the change be to a "preferable" principle. The U.S. standard "Accounting Changes" states:

> The presumption that an entity should not change an accounting principle may be overcome only if the enterprise justifies the use of an alternative acceptable accounting principle on the basis that it is preferable.

A change from accelerated depreciation to straight-line "to increase profits" may be preferable from management's viewpoint, but such a reason is not reasonable justification for most auditors. If the U.S. auditors cannot agree that a change in accounting principle is preferable, then an opinion qualification based on a departure from GAAP is appropriate. (The SEC in the United States requires auditors to submit a letter stating whether the change is to a preferable principle—one that provides a better measure of business operations.)

Section 5400.22 Report

The unqualified opinion depends upon GAAP for standards of financial accounting. However, *Handbook Section* 5400.22 provides for the possibility that adherence to *Handbook Recommendations* might create misleading financial statements:

> When there is a departure from a Handbook Recommendation and the auditor concludes that following the Recommendation would result in misleading financial statements, the auditor should express his or her opinion without reservation, provided the related disclosure is adequate.

Emphasis Paragraph

Sometimes auditors opt to add additional information in the auditor's report. This type of addition to the audit report is known as the **emphasis of a matter** paragraph. Beyond the standard unqualified report wording, auditors have one avenue for enriching the information content in an audit report. They can add one or more paragraphs to emphasize a matter they believe readers should consider important or useful. An emphasis paragraph can be added when the auditor intends to write an unqualified opinion paragraph. Indeed, the matter emphasized is not supposed to be mentioned in the standard unqualified opinion sentence.

Currently (May 2000) there are some limits on the content of an emphasis paragraph. For example *Handbook Sections* 5701 and 5510.19 specifically prohibit reference to contingencies on going concern issues if they are already properly disclosed in the financial statements. In addition the *Handbook* specifically mentions that the following information may be provided in a final paragraph: information required by statute (*Section* 5701.03); unaudited comparative figures (*Section* 5701.10); and comparative figures reported on by other auditors (*Section* 5701.11). However, since the time *Section* 5701 was issued, several new issues have evolved that may expand the content of an emphasis paragraph. These issues include foreign reporting requirements, use of another appropriate disclosed basis of accounting besides GAAP, and, possibly, going concern issues if the current standards are revised in conformity with international standards. An example of additional comments attached to but distinct from the auditor's report, relating to Canadian GAAP and foreign reporting requirements, is shown in Exhibit 3–6.

Reporting on Uncertainties

In an earlier part of this chapter, you studied scope limitations in which management or circumstances prevented the auditors from obtaining sufficient appropriate evidence about a part of the financial statements. A different type of evidence deficiency arises when uncertainties exist. An auditing "uncertainty" is similar to an accounting "contingency," which is defined in *Handbook Section* 3290.02:

> A contingency is . . . an existing condition, or situation, involving uncertainty as to possible gain ("gain contingency") or loss ("loss contingency") to an enterprise that will ultimately be resolved when one or more future events occur or fail to occur. Resolution of the uncertainty may confirm the acquisition of an asset or the reduction of a liability or the loss or impairment of an asset or the incurrence of a liability.

Section 3290 sets forth accounting and disclosure standards for contingencies. One of the most common contingencies involves the uncertain outcome of litigation pending against the company. Audit uncertainties include not only lawsuits but also such things as the value of fixed assets held for sale (e.g., a whole plant or warehouse facility) and the status of assets involved in foreign expropriations.

E X H I B I T 3–6   **EXAMPLE OF ADDITIONAL COMMENTS PARAGRAPH (from *CICA Handbook* Aug-21 Appendix)**

Comments by Auditor for U.S. Readers on Canada–U.S. Reporting Difference

In the United States, reporting standards for auditors require the addition of an explanatory paragraph (following the opinion paragraph) when the financial statements are affected by conditions and events that cast substantial doubt on the company's ability to continue as a going concern, such as those described in Note .... to the financial statements. My report to the shareholders dated ...., 20.......... is expressed in accordance with Canadian reporting standards which do not permit a reference to such events and conditions in the auditor's report when these are adequately disclosed in the financial statements.

City
Date

(signed) ....
CHARTERED ACCOUNTANT

Auditors may perform procedures in accordance with generally accepted auditing standards, yet the uncertainty and lack of evidence may persist. The problem is that it is impossible to obtain audit "evidence" about the future. The concept of audit evidence includes information knowable at the time a reporting decision is made and does not include predictions about future resolution of uncertainties. Consequently, auditors should not change (modify or qualify) the introductory, scope or opinion paragraphs of the standard unqualified report when contingencies and uncertainties exist. When the audit has been performed in accordance with generally accepted auditing standards, and the auditor has done all the things possible in the circumstances, no alteration of these standard paragraphs is necessary as long as the uncertainty has been properly disclosed.

When significant uncertainties about future events exist about such matters as tax deficiency assessments, contract disputes, recoverability of asset costs, lawsuits and other important contingencies, they should be explained clearly and completely in footnotes to the financial statements. These disclosures are as much a part of management's responsibility as the balance sheet, income statement and statement of changes in financial position. *Handbook Section* 5510.46 advises that:

> when a contingency is accounted for and disclosed in accordance with GAAP it is not appropriate to draw attention to the contingency by expressing a reservation of opinion or by mentioning it in a separate paragraph following the auditor's standard report.

In the United States, however, the auditor may decide to add a paragraph to the report as a "red flag" drawing attention to the uncertainty.

Uncertainty situations may cause audit reports to be qualified for departures from GAAP, if (1) management's disclosure of the uncertainty is inadequate, (2) management uses inappropriate accounting principles to account for the uncertainty, and (3) management makes unreasonable accounting estimates in connection with the effects of the uncertainty. The audit report also may be qualified because of a scope limitation regarding available evidence about an uncertainty.

Reporting on "Going-Concern" Problems

Generally accepted accounting principles are based on the going-concern concept, which means the entity is expected to continue in operation and meet its obligations as they become due, without substantial disposition of assets outside the ordinary course of business, restructuring of debt, externally forced revisions of its operations (e.g., a bank reorganization forced by the Superintendent of Financial Institutions) or similar actions. Hence, an opinion that financial statements are in conformity with GAAP means that continued existence may be presumed for a "reasonable time" not to exceed one year beyond

---

"SUBJECT-TO" OPINIONS PRIOR TO 1980

From the early 1960s until 1980, auditors gave "subject-to" opinions for uncertainty situations. The opinion sentence was qualified with these words: "In our opinion, subject to the effects of such adjustments, if any, as might have been determined had the outcome of the uncertainty discussed in the preceding paragraph been known . . ." The explanatory paragraph was placed before the opinion paragraph, and the opinion was considered qualified. You may see this form of "subject to" opinion when you use reports issued in 1980 and earlier. However, the audit standards were changed in 1980, and now (1) the "subject to" wording is prohibited, (2) the explanatory paragraph is no longer used, and (3) the opinion sentence itself is unqualified.

the date of the financial statements ("The Going Concern Assumption," 1991 CICA Research Report). This one-year time horizon is reiterated in the CICA's Exposure Draft on going concern issues, released in March 1996.

Dealing with questions of going concern, or lack thereof, is difficult because auditors are forced to evaluate matters of financial analysis, business strategy and financial forecasting. Most managements are unwilling to give up and close their businesses without strong attempts to survive. Sometimes, survival optimism prevails until the creditors force bankruptcy proceedings and liquidation. Auditors are generally reluctant to puncture any balloons of optimism. Managers and auditors both view news of financial troubles in an audit report (an attention-directing paragraph or a disclaimer based on going-concern doubt) as a "self-fulfilling prophecy" that causes bankruptcy. However fallacious this view might be, it still prevails and inhibits auditors' consideration of going-concern questions.

Auditors are responsible for determining whether there is a significant doubt about a company's ability to continue as a going concern. No careful auditor should ignore signs of financial difficulty and operate entirely on the assumption that the company is a going concern. Financial difficulties, labour problems, loss of key personnel, litigation and other such things may be important signals. Likewise, elements of financial flexibility (salability of assets, lines of credit, debt extension, dividend elimination) may be available as survival strategies. (In U.S. auditing standards these elements of financial flexibility and management strategy are known as **mitigating factors** that may reduce the financial difficulties.)

Accounting and finance research efforts have produced several bankruptcy prediction models. These models use publicly available financial information to classify companies into "fail" and "nonfail" categories. At least one auditing firm uses such a model as an analytical review tool. Auditing standards, however, make no mention of research models, specifying instead many company-specific considerations and elements of internal information for analysis. (One bankruptcy prediction model is described briefly in the appendix to Chapter 5 of this textbook.)

Auditor's responsibilities for the going-concern assumption are currently the same as for contingencies (*Section* 5510.53). However, the recent CICA Research Study, "The Going Concern Assumption," gives recommendations leaning toward U.S. practice except that it quantifies key threshold probabilities whereas U.S. standards do not. The key audit recommendations of the CICA's going concern study are as follows:

1. Require auditors on every audit to perform procedures to provide reasonable assurance about the validity of the "going-concern" assumption.

2. Evaluate results of procedures performed.

3. If significant (20–50% probability) or substantial doubts (50% or greater probability) are raised, assess management's plans to address these matters, considering if they can be effectively implemented. (Note: The very existence of such plans should call "going concern" into question.)

4. Expand the auditor's reporting responsibilities when doubt about the validity of the "going-concern" assumption becomes substantial. Include an explanatory paragraph even if doubt is adequately disclosed in the notes.

5. Issue an adverse opinion where substantial doubt exists and disclosure is inadequate.

6. Issue an adverse opinion if virtually certain, and GAAP no longer applies.

According to this study five types of audit reports may be used when going-concern problems exist. The first is a standard report with no additional explanatory paragraphs as long as doubts are significant or less and properly disclosed in the notes to the financial statements. The second is a standard report with an unqualified opinion paragraph and an additional explanatory paragraph(s) to direct attention to management's disclosures about the problems. This second type of standard report would be used when there are substantial doubts and the company has properly disclosed these problems in the notes.

The third type of report is an adverse opinion that arises from failure to disclose substantial doubts, or when it is virtually certain that the company will fail to continue as a going concern, and GAAP no longer applies.

A fourth type of report is a qualification for a GAAP departure if the auditor believes the company's disclosures about financial difficulties and going-concern problems are inadequate. Such a report is shown in Exhibit 3–7. The fifth type of report is a report qualified for a scope limitation if evidence that does exist or did exist is not made available to the auditors, leading to the "except for adjustments, if any" type of qualified opinion explained earlier in this chapter. These different reports arise from the refined classification scheme reflected by the Going-Concern Study recommendations.

So what is current GAAS regarding going concern? The current *Handbook* recommendation that applies is *Section* 5510.53, which effectively states that if there is a "going concern" problem, an unqualified opinion is given as long as the problem is adequately disclosed. If the facts are not adequately disclosed, then the auditor should issue a reservation of the audit opinion. An illustration of an "except for" qualification reservation is shown in Exhibit 3–7.

As of this writing (Sept. 1999) there are Auditing (issued September 1995) and Accounting (issued March 1996) Exposure Drafts related to going concern. The Accounting Exposure Draft uses a significant doubt concept similar to that described above from the CICA Research Study. However, the Auditing Exposure Draft uses the term factors that "cast doubt" on the entity's ability to continue as a going concern. It is not clear whether "cast doubt" is comparable to "significant doubt," and perhaps this will be clarified in the final standards. One thing that is clear in the current standards is that contingencies related to going concern that are appropriately disclosed in the financial statements are specifically prohibited as a subject matter for an emphasis paragraph (*Handbook*

E X H I B I T 3–7   **AQUALIFIED REPORT EXPLAINING GOING CONCERN PROBLEMS (from *Handbook* Section 5510.F)**

Departure from generally accepted accounting principles—inadequate disclosure of matters affecting the company's ability to continue as a going concern. When the auditor has determined that a qualification is the type of reservation required, the following wording may be appropriate.

AUDITOR'S REPORT

To the Shareholders of ....

I have audited the balance sheet of .... as at ...., 20-1 and the statements of income, retained earnings and cash flows for the year then ended. These financial statements are the responsibility of the company's management. My responsibility is to express an opinion on these financial statements based on my audit.

I conducted my audit in accordance with generally accepted auditing standards. Those standards require that I plan and perform an audit to obtain reasonable assurance whether the financial statements are free of material misstatement. An audit includes examining, on a test basis, evidence supporting the amounts and disclosures in the financial statements. An audit also includes assessing the accounting principles used and significant estimates made by management, as well as evaluating the overall financial statement presentation.

The accompanying financial statements, in my opinion, do not draw attention explicitly to doubts concerning the company's ability to realize its assets and discharge its liabilities in the normal course of business. These doubts arise because it is uncertain whether the company will be able to refinance long-term debt in the amount of $.................... due on ...., 20-2 in view of the existence of recurring operating losses in the past five years and the deficiency in working capital of $.................... as at ...., 20-1. If refinancing cannot be arranged, it is not known whether the company can sell its hotel property for an amount sufficient to realize its carrying value of $.................... and to generate adequate funds to repay this debt.

In my opinion, except for the omission of the disclosure described in the preceding paragraph, these financial statements present fairly, in all material respects, the financial position of the company as at ...., 20-1 and the results of its operations and the change in its financial position for the year then ended in accordance with generally accepted accounting principles.

(signed) ....
CHARTERED ACCOUNTANT

Date
City

Sections 5510.49 and 5510.52). Whether this will continue to be the case depends on the final form of the Going Concern Standards.

REPORTING ON THE APPLICATION OF ACCOUNTING PRINCIPLES

LEARNING OBJECTIVE

6. Explain why auditors have standards for reporting on the "application of accounting principles."

The subject of "reporting on the application of accounting principles" touches a sensitive nerve in the public accounting profession. It arose from clients' shopping for an auditor who would agree to give an unqualified audit report on a questionable accounting treatment. "Shopping" often involved auditor-client disagreements, after which the client said: "If you won't agree with my accounting treatment, then I'll find an auditor who will." These disagreements often involved early revenue recognition and unwarranted expense or loss deferral. A few cases of misleading financial statements occurred after shopping resulted in clients' switching to more agreeable auditors. However, the practice is not entirely undesirable, because "second opinions" on complex accounting matters often benefit from consultation with other PAs.

Handbook Section 7600 established procedures for dealing with requests for consultation from parties other than an auditor's own clients. These parties can include other companies (nonclients who are shopping), lawyers, investment bankers and perhaps other people. *Section* 7600 is applicable in these situations:

- When preparing a written report or giving oral advice on specific transactions, either completed or proposed.
- When preparing a written report or giving oral advice on the type of audit opinion that might be rendered on specific financial statements.
- When preparing a written report on hypothetical transactions.

The standard does not apply to conclusions about accounting principles offered in connection with litigation support engagements or expert witness work, nor does it apply to advice given to another PA in public practice. It also does not apply to an accounting firm's expressions of positions in newsletters, articles, speeches, lectures, and the like, provided that the positions do not give advice on a specific transaction or apply to a specific company.

The basic requirements are to consider the circumstances of the request for advice, its purpose and the intended use of the report of the advice; to obtain an understanding of the form and substance of the transaction in question; to review applicable GAAP; to consult with other professionals if necessary; and to perform research to determine the existence of creditable analogies and precedents (e.g., find the authoritative support). When the request for advice comes from a business that already has another auditor, the consulting PA should consult with the other auditor to learn all the facts and circumstances.

Written reports are required and should include these elements:

- Description of the nature of the engagement and a statement that it was performed in accordance with standards for such engagements.
- Statement of relevant facts and assumptions, and the sources of information.
- Statement of the advice—the conclusion about appropriate accounting principles or the type of audit report, including reasons for the conclusions, if appropriate.
- Statement that a company's management is responsible for proper accounting treatments, in consultation with its own auditors.
- Statement that any differences in facts, circumstances or assumptions might change the conclusions.

The purpose of the *Section* 7600 standards is to impose some discipline on the process of shopping/consultation and to make it more difficult for companies to seek out a "willing" auditor.

3.12 Why might "opinion shopping" be suspect? beneficial?

3.13 What must a PA do when reporting on the application of accounting principles?

Summary

LEARNING OBJECTIVE
7. List and explain the effects of materiality on
audit report choices.

This chapter began at the beginning: setting forth the requirement that auditors must report whenever they are "associated with" financial statements. This report can take different forms in different circumstances—audit assurance, negative assurance and no assurance. These levels of assurance are further explained in terms of (1) reports qualified for (*a*) scope limitations, and (*b*) departures from GAAP; (2) adverse reports resulting from GAAP departures; and (3) denials of opinion resulting from lack of independence and lack of sufficient appropriate evidence.

Throughout this chapter's explanation of the auditors' choices of reports, the materiality dimension played an important role. When an auditor makes decisions about the audit report, immaterial or unimportant information can be ignored and treated as if it did not exist. However, when inaccuracies, departures from GAAP, accounting changes and uncertainties have a large enough financial impact, the standard audit report must be changed. In practice, when an auditor decides a matter is material enough to make a difference, a further distinction must be made between "lesser materiality" and "greater materiality." Lesser materiality means that the item in question is important and needs to be disclosed or that the opinion needs to be qualified for it. The information cannot simply be ignored. Greater materiality means that the item in question is very important and has an extreme impact on the reporting decision.

Auditing standards refer to several basic circumstances that cause departures from the standard unqualified audit report. These circumstances are shown in Exhibit 3–8 in relation to the influence of materiality. You can see that each report qualified when the item is of lesser materiality becomes a disclaimer or an adverse report when the item involves greater materiality. The exception is the lack of independence issue, where materiality does not make a difference.

Audit reports can also be modified and expanded with additional paragraphs. Such additions to the audit report arise from the need for an "emphasis of a matter" paragraph. The final topic in the chapter is "shopping" for accounting principles and auditors. Standards exist to raise the public perception that auditors are careful about competing among one another on the basis of professional opinions.

E X H I B I T   3–8   **INFLUENCE OF MATERIALITY ON AUDIT REPORTS**

	Required Type of Report	
Circumstances for Departure from Standard Report	Lesser Materiality	Greater Materiality
Departure from GAAP	Qualified "except for": Separate paragraph discloses reasons and effects.*	Adverse Opinion: Separate paragraph discloses reasons and effects.
Limitation on scope (lack of evidence)	Qualified Opinion: Refers to possible effects on financials.	Denial of Opinion: Separate paragraph explains limitations.
Uncertainty	Unqualified Opinion**	Unqualified Opinion**

*Where the departure is necessary to make the financials not misleading, an unqualified opinion is issued with an explanation of the circumstances.
**Unless there is a failure to properly disclose the uncertainty.

3.14 Explain the effect of greater or lesser materiality on an auditor's report when the client uses an accounting method that departs from generally accepted accounting principles.

3.15 Explain the effect of greater or lesser materiality on an auditor's report when there is a scope limitation.

3.16 Explain the effect of greater or lesser materiality on an auditor's report when there is a material uncertainty associated with the financial statements.

3.17 Identify the levels of assurance associated with auditor's reports.

3.18 Under what conditions would an auditor use an "emphasis of a matter" paragraph?

MULTIPLE-CHOICE QUESTIONS FOR PRACTICE AND REVIEW

3.19 A PA developed a system for clients to enter transaction data by remote terminal into the PA's computer. The PA's system processes the data and prints monthly financial statements. When delivered to the clients, these financial statements should include:
a. A standard unqualified audit report.
b. An adverse audit report.
c. A report containing a description of the character of the examination and the degree of responsibility the PA is taking.
d. A description of the remote terminal system and of the controls for ensuring accurate data processing.

3.20 According to the CICA, what is the objective of an audit of financial statements?
a. An expression of opinion on the fairness with which they present financial position, results of operations and cash flows in conformity with GAAP.
b. An expression of opinion on the fairness with which they present financial position, results of operations and cash flows in conformity with FASB.
c. An expression of opinion on the fairness with which they present financial position, results of operations and cash flows in conformity with GAAS.
d. To obtain systematic and objective evidence about financial assertions and report the results to interested users.

3.21 Some of the GAAS reporting standards require certain statements in all audit reports ("explicit") and others require statements only under certain conditions ("implicit" basis). Which combination shown below correctly describes these features of the reporting standards?

Standards	(a)	(b)	(c)	(d)
1. GAAP	Explicit	Explicit	Implicit	Implicit
2. Consistency	Implicit	Explicit	Explicit	Implicit
3. Disclosure	Implicit	Implicit	Explicit	Explicit
4. Report	Explicit	Explicit	Implicit	Implicit

3.22 A PA finds that the client has not capitalized a material amount of leases in the financial statements. When considering the materiality of this departure from GAAP, the PA's reporting options are:
a. Unqualified opinion or denial of opinion.
b. Unqualified opinion or qualified opinion.
c. Emphasis paragraph with unqualified opinion or an adverse opinion.
d. Qualified opinion or adverse opinion.

3.23 An auditor has found that the client is suffering financial difficulty and that the going-concern status is seriously in doubt. Even though the client has placed good disclosures in the financial statements, the PA must choose between the following audit report alternatives:
a. Unqualified report with a going-concern explanatory paragraph or denial of opinion.
b. Denial of opinion.
c. Qualified opinion or adverse opinion.
d. Standard unqualified report.

3.24 A company accomplished an early extinguishment of debt, and the auditors believe that recognition of a huge loss distorts the financial statements and causes them to be misleading. The auditors' reporting choices are:
a. Explain the situation and give an adverse opinion.
b. Explain the situation and give a denial of opinion.
c. Explain the situation and give an unqualified opinion, relying on Rules of

APPENDIX 3B

ISA 700

· ·

Auditor's Report

(Appropriate addressee)

We have audited the accompanying balance sheet of the ABC Company as of December 31, 20X1, and the related statements of income and cash flows for the year then ended. These financial statements are the responsibility of the Company's management. Our responsibility is to express an opinion on these financial statements based on our audit.

We conducted our audit in accordance with International Standards on Auditing (or refer to relevant national standards or practices). Those Standards require that we plan and perform the audit to obtain reasonable assurance about whether the financial statements are free of material misstatement. An audit includes examining, on a test basis, evidence supporting the amounts and disclosures in the financial statements. An audit also includes asserting the accounting principles used and significant estimates made by management, as well as evaluating the overall financial statement presentation. We believe that our audit provides a reasonable basis for our opinion.

In our opinion, the financial statements give a true and fair view of (or 'present fairly, in all material respects,') the financial position of the Company as of December 31, 20X1, and of the results of its operations and its cash flows for the year then ended in accordance with . . . (and comply with . . .).

AUDITOR

Date
Address

PART II

BASIC CONCEPTS AND TECHNIQUES OF AUDITING

CHAPTER 4

Learning Objectives

Chapter 4 and Chapter 5 cover the underlying concepts of audit field work and their role in planning an independent audit of financial statements. Chapter 4 deals with the pre-engagement arrangements for an audit, the important task of understanding the client's business and industry, the organization of financial statements and the management assertions in them, the theory of evidence, the general forms of evidence-gathering procedures and the working papers that document the audit. After studying Chapter 4, you should be able to:

1. List and describe the activities auditors undertake before beginning an audit.

2. Identify the procedures and sources of information the auditors can use to obtain knowledge of a client's business and industry.

3. Name the principal accounts in each cycle in accounting and business processes.

4. Describe and define the five principal management assertions in financial statements, and explain their role for establishing audit objectives.

5. Explain audit evidence in terms of its appropriateness and relative strength of persuasiveness.

6. List and describe six general types of audit techniques for gathering evidence.

7. Discuss the effectiveness of various audit procedures.

8. Review an audit working paper for proper form and content.

AUDIT OBJECTIVES, PROCEDURES AND WORKING PAPERS

AUDIT PLANNING

Many activities are involved in planning an audit of financial statements. This chapter covers some of them, and succeeding chapters cover others. For organizational purposes, the first aspects of planning are divided into activities, concepts and tools. They are explained in Chapters 4 and 5 as follows:

OVERVIEW OF CHAPTERS 4 AND 5

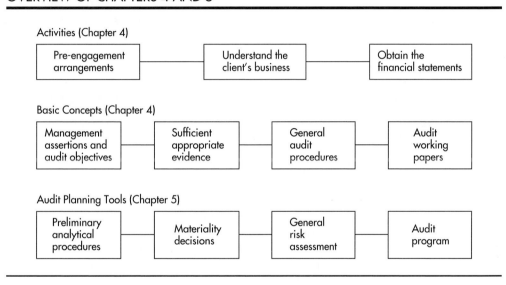

Discussion of the activities, concepts and tools continues in Chapter 6 (Assessing Control Risk) and Chapter 7 (Audit Sampling). Technical topics of statistical sampling are in Chapter 20, and computer auditing topics are in Chapters 8 and 21. Audit applications in specific accounts and cycles are in Chapters 9 to 14.

PRE-ENGAGEMENT ARRANGEMENTS

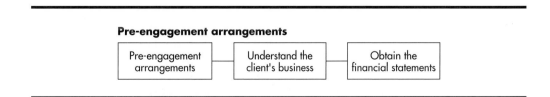

LEARNING OBJECTIVE

1. List and describe the activities auditors undertake before beginning an audit.

Auditors undertake several activities before beginning any audit work on a client's financial statements. In general, these can be called the first risk management activities. Risk in an audit engagement generally refers to the probability of something going wrong. Auditors try to reduce risk by carefully managing the engagement. The flip side of risk management is quality management, which was discussed in Chapter 2 under the heading of "Quality Control Standards." The topics discussed next can best be understood in the context of risk management and quality management.

Client Selection and Retention

An important element of an accounting firm's quality control policies and procedures is a system for deciding to accept a new client and, on a continuing basis, deciding whether to resign from audit engagements. Accounting firms are not obligated to accept undesirable clients, nor are they obligated to continue to audit clients when relationships deteriorate or when the management comes under a cloud of suspicion. For example, an auditor may think twice about accepting an engagement with management that has a poor business reputation or where an assumption of management good faith cannot be made.

Client acceptance and retention policies and procedures include (1) obtaining and reviewing financial information about the prospective client—annual reports, interim statements, registration statements, annual information forms and reports to regulatory agencies; (2) enquiring of the prospective client's banker, legal counsel, underwriter or other

---

SEMI-TECH AUDITOR QUIT OVER 'LACK OF TRUST'

The Toronto Stock Exchange suspended all trading in Semi-Tech Corp. yesterday, even as it emerged the firm's former auditors had served notice in late 1997 that they were quitting over a "breakdown of trust" with the Toronto holding company and Singer, its principal subsidiary.

Neither the investing public nor regulators have been told why Ernst & Young was replaced.

The fact surfaced only after the two companies fled into U.S. bankruptcy protection this month—revealing a patchwork of questionable acquisitions, unusual deals and a history of related-company transactions that appear to lack many of the usual controls.

Court documents filed in the United States and Canada show the unravelling of the international empire stitched together by Hong Kong businessman James Ting has been years in the making—and the change of auditors was a key trouble sign.

Minutes of a meeting of Semi-Tech's audit committee in November, 1997, show the company was warned by Robert Long of Ernst & Young that the auditors were "unhappy" with financial reporting and wanted out.

"Mr. Long confirmed Ernst & Young would not conduct the Singer audit and they wished to be replaced as auditors of Semi-Tech Corp. and Singer," the minutes say.

"The reason given was a breakdown of trust between these entities and Ernst & Young," the minutes say.

"He said their replacement should be speedy or they would have to act on their own. He said that the stated reason for the change in auditors should be a breakdown in the relationship with Ernst & Young."

Singer had a stock market value of about $663-million (US) at the time, while Semi-Tech was valued at about $88-million.

Shares in the two firms—once the darlings of investors from New York to Hong Kong—have been trading for pennies in recent days in both New York and Toronto. In addition, Deloitte & Touche, the replacement auditor, has now suspended all work on Singer's 1998 financials pending an investigation of a troubling Russian transaction.

Source: The Financial Post, September 24, 1999.

persons who do business with the company for information about the company and its management; (3) communicating with the predecessor auditor, if any, for information on the integrity of management, on disagreements with management about accounting principles, auditing procedures or similar matters, and on the reasons for a change of auditors; (4) considering whether the engagement would require special attention or involve unusual risks; (5) evaluating the accounting firm's independence with regard to the prospective client; and (6) considering the need for special skills (e.g., computer auditing or specialized industry knowledge).

Decisions to continue auditing a client are similar to acceptance decisions, except that the accounting firm will have more first-hand experience with the company. Retention reviews may be done periodically (say, annually) or upon occurrence of major events, such as changes in management, directors, ownership, legal counsel, financial condition, litigation status, nature of the client's business or scope of the audit engagement. In general, conditions that would have caused an accounting firm to reject a prospective client may develop and lead to a decision to discontinue the engagement. For example, a client company may expand and diversify on an international scale to the extent that a small accounting firm may not have the competence to continue the audit. It is not unusual to see newspaper stories about accounting firms dropping clients after directors or officers admit to falsification of financial statements or to theft and misuse of corporate assets.

Communication Between Predecessor and Successor Auditors

When companies change auditors, the former auditor is the predecessor, and the new auditor is the successor. Experience has shown that clients have fired their auditors because of arguments about the scope of the audit or the acceptability of accounting principles. Sometimes these arguments involve auditors' access to necessary evidence, questions of early revenue recognition or disputes over deferral of expenses and losses. More frequently, however, a change in business ownership or a concern over fees is the reason for a change.

The Rules of Professional Conduct of the provincial Institutes require a successor auditor to initiate contact with, and attempt to obtain basic information directly from, the predecessor. The reason for this is that the former auditor knows a great deal about the client and can give the new auditor information that will be useful in (1) deciding whether to accept the new client and become the successor auditor, and (2) planning the audit.

The Rules of Professional Conduct require the predecessor auditor to respond to communications from the successor. However, client consent will determine the amount of client information that is conveyed. Note that the file belongs to the auditor, not the client. However, confidentiality remains even when the auditor–client relationship ends. It is common practice for the successor auditor to explain the situation and the standards to the client and to ask that consent be given to permit the former auditor to speak. If this consent is refused, the successor auditor should be wary.

With consent, the predecessor auditor can speak freely. It is not unusual to have a cordial change of auditors and see the successor conduct interviews with the predecessor auditor's staff and obtain copies of the predecessor auditor's working papers. This exchange greatly facilitates the successor's first-time audit.

A change of auditors could cause the successor auditor's report to be modified from the standard form. It is important to note that the predecessor–successor situation is not the "using the work and reports of other independent auditors" topic explained in Appendix 3A. That situation involved the engagement of two or more audit firms auditing the financial statements for the same year. The predecessor–successor situation arises in the topic of "reporting on comparative statements" (Appendix 3A). In this case the successor auditor may be reporting on the current year, but the client may present the prior-year financial statements audited by the predecessor. The successor's report should disclose this fact in a separate paragraph of the auditor's report following the opinion paragraph or in the notes to the financial statements (*Handbook Section* 5701.11).

Engagement Letters

When a new audit client is accepted, an **engagement letter** (Exhibit 4–1) should be prepared. (The letter should be obtained each year from continuing clients.) This letter sets forth the terms of the engagement, including an agreement about the fee to be charged. Normally fees are based on the time required to perform the services. Such time estimates require some familiarity with the accounting system. The engagement letter is in effect the audit contract. It may contain special requests and assignments to be undertaken by the auditors, or it may be a rather standard letter stating that an audit of financial statements will be performed in accordance with generally accepted auditing standards. An engagement letter is highly recommended as a means of reducing the risk of misunderstandings with the client and as a means of avoiding legal liability for claims that the auditors did not perform the work promised. For example, agreeing on a completion date in advance can reduce disappointments later in the engagement. Also, there may be changes in fees and services provided so that it is usually advisable to prepare engagement letters even for continuing clients. A typical engagement letter is illustrated in Exhibit 4–1.[1]

Staff Assignment

When a new client is obtained, most accounting firms assign a full-service team to the new client. For larger clients, this team usually consists of the audit engagement partner (the person with final responsibility for the audit); the audit manager; one or more senior audit staff members; staff assistants or PA students; any statistics, computer and industry specialists (if needed); a tax partner; a consulting services partner; and a second audit partner. The tax and consulting partners are consultants to the audit team if the engagement does not include other specific tax and consulting work contracted by the client. For smaller clients the team may consist of only one or two people, the partner and a staff assistant, especially if the public accounting firm itself is small.

Getting Tough in the Engagement Letter

Ivan F. Boesky's limited partnership is seeking a new auditing firm after Mr. Boesky's longtime auditors imposed stringent new conditions for remaining on the job. The CPA firm of Oppenheim, Appel, Dixon & Company reportedly sent an "engagement letter" to the limited partnership requesting assurances that Mr. Boesky, the general partner, and the SEC would answer all questions asked by the auditor. Such questions could involve sensitive areas the SEC is still investigating. This was one of the conditions the accounting firm presented as necessary for its continuance as auditor. [Mr. Boesky was later convicted and sentenced to prison for securities violations.]

Representatives of other accounting firms said: "If we couldn't get assurances that we would be told all the facts relevant to the audit, I doubt we would want to take the risk of taking such an engagement," and "We prefer that the Boesky limited partnership doesn't come to us; there are people we just can't afford to be associated with because we have to maintain our own reputation."

Source: The Wall Street Journal, January 23, 1987.

---

[1] *International Standard on Auditing* 210 (ISA 210) "Terms of Audit Engagements," gives detailed guidance. The international standards are issued by the International Auditing Practice Committee of the International Federation of Accountants. They are not enforceable under the provincial Rules of Conduct. Canadian generally accepted auditing standards do not require engagement letters for audits, although they are recommended for some other types of engagements.

EXHIBIT 4–1   **ENGAGEMENT LETTER**

Anderson, Olds & Watershed
Public Accountants
Toronto, Ontario
July 15, 2003

Mr. Larry Lancaster,
Chairman
Kingston Company
Kingston, Ontario

Dear Mr. Lancaster:

This will confirm our understanding of the arrangements for auditing the Kingston Company financial statements for 2003.

Our work will consist of an audit of the balance sheet at December 31, 2003, and the related statements of income, retained earnings and changes in financial position for the year ending that date. Our audit will be made in accordance with generally accepted auditing standards and will include such tests of the accounting records and such other auditing procedures as we consider necessary.

Our audit will be conducted in accordance with generally accepted auditing standards. The audit will include examining, on a test basis, evidence supporting the amounts and disclosure in the financial statements. The audit also includes assessing the accounting principles used and significant estimates made by management, as well as evaluating the overall financial statement presentation.

We will plan the audit to detect material errors and irregularities that may affect your financial statements. However, our work is subject to the unavoidable risk that errors, irregularities and illegal acts, including fraud and theft, if they exist, will not be detected. We expect to obtain reasonable but not absolute assurance that material misstatements do not exist in the financial statements. Our findings regarding misstatements that indicate significant weaknesses in internal control, including the design or operation of the entity's financial reporting process, will be reported to the audit committee of your board of directors in a separate letter at the close of the audit.

At your request, we will perform the following other services: (1) timely preparation of all required corporate tax returns and (2) a review and report on the company's methods for assessing your environmental performance information system in accordance with the CICA Study "Reporting on Environmental Performance."

We will provide your staff with a package of blank schedules needed by our staff during the audit. The delivery dates have been discussed and mutually agreed upon. We understand that your staff will prepare all the schedules in the package, all the financial statements and notes thereto and the Ontario Securities Commission Annual Information Form for our review. The scope of our services does not include preparation of any of these financial statements.

Mr. Dalton Wardlaw will be the partner in charge of all work performed for you. He will inform you immediately if we encounter any circumstances that could significantly affect our fee estimate of $60,000 discussed with you on July 1, 2003. He is aware of the due date for the audit report, February 15, 2004. You should feel free to call on him at any time.

If the specifications above are in accordance with your understanding of the terms of our engagement, please sign below and return the duplicate copy to us. We look forward again to serving you as public accountants.

Sincerely yours,

Ann Anderson, PA

Accepted by _____   Date _____

Firm policy may require that a second audit partner review the work of the audit team. This partner is supposed to have a detached professional point of view because he or she is not directly responsible for keeping the client happy.[2]

Time Budget

The partner and manager in charge of the audit prepare a plan for the timing of the work and set the number of hours that each segment of the audit is expected to take. This time

---

[2] A second audit partner is required for audits of financial statements filed with the U.S. Securities and Exchange Commission. On SEC engagements, the audit engagement partner is required to rotate to other clients so that he or she does not remain in charge of a particular client for more than seven years.

budget is based on last year's performance for continuing clients, taking changes in the client's business into account. In a first-time audit, the budget may be based on a predecessor auditor's experience or on general experience with similar companies. A simple time budget is shown below.

	Audit Time Budget (hours)	
	Interim	Year-End
Knowledge of the business	15	
Internal audit familiarization	10	
Assessment of control risk	30	10
Audit program planning	25	
Related parties investigation	5	15
Client conferences	10	18
Cash	10	15
Accounts receivable	15	5
Inventory	35	20
Accounts payable	5	35
Representation letters		20
Financial statement review		25
Report preparation		12
Total	160	175

The time budget is illustrative, not complete. Real-time budgets are much more detailed. Some specify the expected time by level of staff people on the team (partner, manager, in-charge accountant, staff assistant, specialist). The illustration shows time at interim and at year-end.

Interim audit work refers to procedures performed several weeks or months before the balance sheet date.

Year-end audit work refers to procedures performed shortly before and after the balance sheet date. Audit firms typically spread the workload out during the year by scheduling interim audit work so that they will have enough time and people available when several audits have year-ends on the same date (December 31 is common). For many audit firms, the audit "busy season" runs from October through June of the following year. The interim work can consist of both internal control risk assessment work (*Handbook Section* 5210.20) and audit of balances as they exist at the early date (*Section* 5300.36).

Everyone who works on the audit reports the time taken to perform procedures for each segment of the audit. These time reports are recorded by budget categories for the purposes of (1) evaluating the efficiency of the audit team members, (2) compiling a record for billing the client, and (3) compiling a record for planning the next audit. Time budgets create job pressures. Staff members are under pressure to "meet the budget," and beginning auditors often experience frustration as they learn how to do audit work efficiently.

R E V I E W
CHECKPOINTS

4.1 What sources of information can a PA use in connection with deciding whether to accept a new audit client?

4.2 Why does a successor auditor need to obtain the client's consent for a predecessor auditor to give information about the former audit client?

4.3 What benefits are obtained by having an engagement letter?

4.4 What persons and skills are normally assigned to a "full-service" audit team?

4.5 What is interim audit work? year-end audit work?

UNDERSTANDING THE CLIENT'S BUSINESS

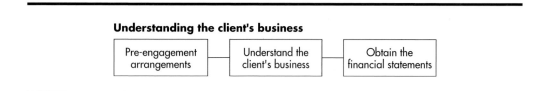

Understanding the client's business

| Pre-engagement arrangements | Understand the client's business | Obtain the financial statements |

LEARNING OBJECTIVE

2. Identify the procedures and sources of information that auditors can use to obtain knowledge of a client's business and industry.

Knowledge and understanding of the client's business in the context of the client's industry is very important in an audit. Therefore, auditing standards require the audit team to obtain a sufficient understanding of the business to plan and perform the audit work (*Handbook Section* 5140.07 or ISA 310.4–8). The understanding and planning culminate in an audit program, which is a list of the audit procedures believed necessary to obtain sufficient, appropriate evidence that will serve as the basis for the audit report. Auditing standards state: "The auditor should document matters which in his or her opinion are important in providing evidence to support the content of his or her report" (*Handbook Section* 5140.01). A mental program "in my head" is not sufficient.

The auditor's objectives in obtaining knowledge of the business are the following:

1. Design and execute an effective audit that identifies and addresses all the significant risks of a material misstatement in the financial statements.

2. Design and execute an efficient audit that provides sufficient appropriate audit evidence in the most economical manner.

3. Enhance the accuracy of the auditor's evaluation of audit findings and the evidence supporting them.

4. Provide better ancillary services to the client.[3]

In order to achieve these objectives, auditors must understand the broad economic environment in which the client operates, including such things as the effects of national economic policies (e.g., price regulations and import/export restrictions), the geographic location and its economy (Alberta's predominantly resource-based economy, Ontario's manufacturing-based economy), and developments in taxation and regulatory areas (e.g., deregulation in agriculture and air transport, approval processes in the drug and chemical industries). Industry characteristics are important. There is a great deal of difference in the production and marketing activities of banks, insurance companies, mutual funds, supermarkets, hotels, oil and gas, agriculture, manufacturing and so forth. No auditors are experts in all these businesses. Audit firms typically have people who are expert in one or two industries and rely on them to manage audits in those industries. Indeed, some PA firms have a reputation for having many audit clients in a particular industry, while other PA firms have a larger presence in other industries.

Greater knowledge of business is required because auditors are increasingly expected to use integrative reasoning in reaching their conclusions. Accounting is supposed to reflect the economic substance of transactions and this usually requires asking the right business questions of management. Effective questioning requires strong knowledge of the business.

Strategic Business Approaches to Auditing

A recent trend in audit practice is to base more of the audit on knowledge of the business. These newer approaches are referred to by various names and involve high level knowledge of management strategy and other management topics. We will refer to these newer approaches as strategic systems approaches to auditing or SSA audits. While no generally

---

[3] Shields, G., "Knowledge of the Clients' Business" *CA Magazine*, August 1994, pp. 56–57.

accepted definition of SSA audits has yet evolved, they can be characterized as top-down approaches that start with an understanding of corporate strategy and the business as a whole to determine the effects on the financial statements. In contrast, the traditional financial statement audit has focused on a bottom-up approach that gathers evidence on individual transactions and aggregates them to the financial statement level.

Most of this textbook follows the traditional approach, however, SSA audit differences are noted in several areas and Chapter 13 is devoted exclusively to providing a more complete overview of SSAs. At the time of this writing SSAs are used to some extent in three of the Big Five PA firms. SSAs have not yet filtered down to the smaller PA firms, nor are SSAs reflected in official pronouncements. The differences between SSA audits and traditional audits will be clarified as we continue through our study of financial auditing.

Methods and Sources of Information

Numerous sources of information are available for obtaining the understanding of the client's business and industry. The field of strategic management has produced a number of frameworks that audit firms are adopting to structure their acquisition of knowledge of client's business and industry. These approaches, while integral to the SSA audit, are also being used by many accounting firms following the traditional audit approach to ensure their auditors have a comprehensive understanding of their client and its industry. Appendix 4A provides an introduction to two such frameworks. The sources of client information can be categorized by the methods auditors use.

Enquiry, Including Prior Working Papers

For continuing audits, information about the client is available in the permanent file section of the current working papers (discussed later in this chapter) and in prior audit working papers. Personnel who worked on the audit in prior years are available to convey their understanding of the business. Enquiry and interviews with the company's management, directors and audit committee can bring auditors up to date on changes in the business and the industry. Such interviews with client personnel have the multiple purposes of building personal working relationships (which includes observations about the co-operation and integrity of client managers), obtaining general understanding and probing gently for problem areas in the financial statements.

One very important aspect of the enquiry-based familiarization is obtaining information for planning the computer-based audit work. Almost all organizations use computers in data processing to some extent. The audit team needs to determine the extent of computer use on significant accounting transactions, the complexity of the computer system, the organization of the computer processing activities and the availability of data and system documentation.

POTENTIAL TROUBLE SPOTS

- Aggressive management attitude in financial reporting.
- Inadequate or inconsistent profitability relative to industry.
- Unusual related party transactions.
- Constant crisis conditions in operating areas, such as frequent/excessive back orders shortages, delays and understaffed departments.
- Bonuses or management profit based on short-term financial results.
- Overemphasis on quantified targets that are linked to management compensations.

Source: CICA Handbook Section 5135A.

Another important aspect of enquiry is to obtain an understanding of the needs of the users of the client's financial statements. Part of this is obtained when assessing whether to accept the engagement, but an important part is also obtained at this enquiry stage. The information obtained from enquiries of management, when combined with analysis of management's financial statements (covered later), helps the auditor to assess user needs in terms of what is significant for the users. The materiality concept is a way of quantifying significance for users. Materiality is discussed in more detail in Chapter 5.

Observation

At the same time that enquiries and interviews take place, the audit team can take a tour of the company's physical facilities. This is the time to keep eyes open for activities and things that should be reflected in the accounting records. For example, an auditor might notice a jumbled pile of materials and parts in the warehouse and make a mental note to check for its inventory condition and valuation. The tour is the time to see company personnel in their normal workplaces. Later, the auditors will meet these same people in more directed evidence-gathering circumstances.

Study

Numerous sources for reading material are available. A good start can be found in CICA and AICPA industry accounting and auditing guides. These guides explain the typical transactions and accounts used by various kinds of businesses and not-for-profit organizations. They were written by accountants for accountants. In addition, most industries have specialized trade magazines and journals. You may not choose to read *Canadian Grocer* for pleasure, but magazines of this special type are very valuable for learning and main-

---

SOURCES OF BUSINESS AND INDUSTRY INFORMATION

General Information

Statistics Canada (including economic forecasts)
Dun & Bradstreet Principal International Businesses.
Standard & Poor's Register of Corporations, Directors, and Executives.
CICA Industry Guides, Audit Risk Alerts

Value Line Investment Survey.
Moody's manuals (various industries).
CFO Magazine
Standard & Poor's Corporation Records.
Analysts' reports.
Dunn & Bradstreet, *Key Business Ratios.*
Firm libraries, universities, dissertations on specialized industry topics.

Communications Media

Canadian Journal of Communication
Broadcasting-Cablecasting Yearbook (annual).
Advertising Age (twice weekly).
Broadcasting (weekly).
Publishers Weekly (weekly).
Variety (weekly).
Web sites, trade associations, conferences. (See inside back cover for industry and business statistics websites).

taining an industry expertise. Specific information about public companies can be found in registration statements and annual report filings with the provincial securities commissions.

General business magazines and newspapers often contribute insights about an industry, a company and individual corporate officers. Many are available, including such leaders as *Canadian Business*, *Report on Business Magazine*, *Business Week*, *Forbes*, *Harvard Business Review*, *Barron's*, *The Wall Street Journal*, and of course the business sections of newspapers such as the *Globe and Mail* and the *National Post*. Practising auditors typically read several of these regularly. A selection of other public information sources is shown in the above box.

Special note should be made of the newest and increasingly important information source for auditors—the Internet. For example, client information can be obtained from the client's Web site. Client's increasingly post financial statement and other information on their Web sites. In addition, industry information as well as information on comparable companies can be obtained on the Internet. This allows the auditor to better improve his or her knowledge of the business and the usefulness of analytical procedures.

Other Aspects of Understanding the Business

The general understanding discussed above can lead to some specific areas for further investigation and planning.

First-Time Audits

A first audit requires more work than a repeat engagement. If an existing company has been operating for a while, but has never been audited, the additional work includes an audit of the beginning balances in the balance sheet accounts. In other words, the starting place for the audited accounting must be established with reliable account balances. Such accounts as inventory, fixed assets and intangible assets affect the current-year income and cash flow statements. This work may involve going back to audit several years' transactions that make up the permanent account balances.

Internal Auditors

Audit efficiency can be realized by working in tandem with internal auditors. Independent auditors should understand a company's internal audit activities as they relate to the system of internal control. Internal auditors can also assist with performance of parts of the audit under the supervision of the independent audit team. External auditors' co-operation with internal auditors is explained in more detail in Chapter 18.

Analysis

The auditors' own analysis of the client's financial statements can contribute a significant understanding of the business and how it has operated for the period covered by the financial statements. Analytical procedures (e.g., ratio and comparison analyses) applied at the beginning of the audit can point out specific areas of audit risk. These applications are explained in more detail in Chapter 5.

Specialists

The understanding of the business can lead to information that indicates the need to employ specialists on the audit. **Specialists** are persons skilled in fields other than accounting and auditing—actuaries, appraisers, legal counsel, engineers and geologists—who are not members of the audit team. Auditors are not expected to be expert in all fields of knowledge that may contribute information to the financial statements. When specialists are engaged, auditors must know about their professional qualifications and reputations. A specialist should be unrelated to the company under audit, if possible. Auditors must obtain an understanding of the specialist's methods and assumptions. Provided some additional auditing work is done on the accounting information used by the specialist, auditors may use the specialist's work in connection with audit decisions (*Handbook Section* 5360).

R E V I E W
CHECKPOINTS

4.6 What are some of the types of knowledge and understanding about a client's business and industry an auditor is expected to obtain?

4.7 What are some of the methods and sources of information for understanding a client's business and industry?

MANAGEMENT'S FINANCIAL STATEMENTS

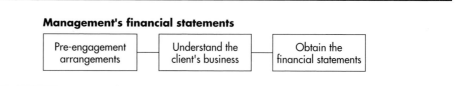

Management's financial statements

Pre-engagement arrangements	Understand the client's business	Obtain the financial statements

LEARNING OBJECTIVE

3. Name the principal accounts in each cycle in accounting and business processes.

Two points need to be made about the financial statements: (1) the management of the company is responsible for preparing them, thus they contain management's assertions about economic actions and events; and (2) the numbers in them are produced by the company's control system, which includes the accounting system, and the numbers can be found in the company's trial balance. The relation of the trial balance to the financial statements is shown in Exhibit 4–2, and the relation of the financial statements to assertions is illustrated in Exhibit 4–3.[4] (These exhibits use the trial balance of the Kingston Company, which is the subject of the case study located on the CD-ROM that accompanies this textbook.)

The illustrative Kingston trial balance is short and simple. Real companies have trial balances with hundreds of accounts, and the number of them creates an organization problem for the auditors. To simplify the audit plan, auditors typically group the accounts into several cycles. A **cycle** is a set of accounts that go together in an accounting system. This book uses these four cycles: (1) revenue and collection cycle; (2) acquisition and expenditure cycle; (3) production and conversion cycle; and (4) finance and investment cycle. Briefly, Cycle 1 deals with the record-keeping for the sales activities of the firm, Cycle 2 deals with the record-keeping for purchasing, Cycle 3 deals with the recordkeeping for manufacturing and cost accounting and Cycle 4 deals with the recordkeeping involving all the financing activities of the firm.

Using the revenue and collection cycle as an example, the idea of the cycle organization is to group together accounts related to one another by the transactions that normally affect them all. This cycle starts with a sale to a customer along with the recording of an account receivable, which is later collected in cash or provided in an allowance for doubtful accounts. Auditors find it easier to audit such related accounts with a co-ordinated set of procedures instead of attacking each account as if it existed alone. All the cycles are discussed in more detail in Chapters 9 through 12.

---

[4] In Exhibit 4–2 and thereafter, the term *amortization* is the general term for allocating capital asset costs over the years' benefited in accordance with *Handbook Section* 3060. Historically and internationally, specialized names for amortization have evolved in practice. *Depreciation* is amortization when applied to tangible capital assets, such as machinery and buildings, while the term *depletion* tends to be used for natural resources. In practice, amortization tends to be used in the more restricted sense of applying to intangible assets and premium or discount on long-term debt. Consistent with the *Handbook*, however, we treat all these allocations as specialized names for amortization.

EXHIBIT 4–2A   KINGSTON COMPANY TRIAL BALANCE, DECEMBER 31, 2002

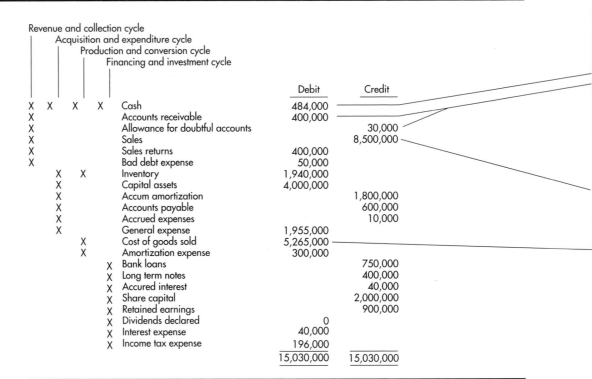

Revenue and collection cycle
  Acquisition and expenditure cycle
    Production and conversion cycle
      Financing and investment cycle

					Debit	Credit
X	X	X	X	Cash	484,000	
X				Accounts receivable	400,000	
X				Allowance for doubtful accounts		30,000
X				Sales		8,500,000
X				Sales returns	400,000	
X				Bad debt expense	50,000	
	X	X		Inventory	1,940,000	
	X			Capital assets	4,000,000	
	X			Accum amortization		1,800,000
	X			Accounts payable		600,000
	X			Accrued expenses		10,000
	X			General expense	1,955,000	
		X		Cost of goods sold	5,265,000	
		X		Amortization expense	300,000	
			X	Bank loans		750,000
			X	Long term notes		400,000
			X	Accrued interest		40,000
			X	Share capital		2,000,000
			X	Retained earnings		900,000
			X	Dividends declared	0	
			X	Interest expense	40,000	
			X	Income tax expense	196,000	
					15,030,000	15,030,000

In Exhibit 4–2, the Kingston accounts are rearranged into an order not normally seen in a trial balance. This is done to illustrate the idea of the cycles. You can see that some accounts are in more than one cycle. For example, the cash account is represented in all the cycles, because: (*a*) cash receipts are involved in cash sales and collections of accounts receivable (revenue and collection cycle), (*b*) cash receipts are involved in deposit of stock issuance and loan proceeds (finance and investment cycle), (*c*) cash disbursements are involved in buying inventory and capital assets and paying for expenses (acquisition and expenditure cycle), and (*d*) cash disbursements are involved in paying wages and overhead expenses (production and conversion cycle).

When placed in the financial statements, the accounts and their descriptive titles make the assertions that are the focal points of audit procedures. Exhibit 4–2 carries the accounts forward to the financial statements.

· ·

REVIEW
CHECKPOINTS
4.8 What are four of the major "cycles" in an accounting system? What accounts can be identified with them?

· ·

MANAGEMENT ASSERTIONS AND AUDIT OBJECTIVES

· · · · · · · · · · · · ·

Management assertions and audit objectives

EXHIBIT 4–2B   **KINGSTON COMPANY UNAUDITED FINANCIAL STATEMENTS**

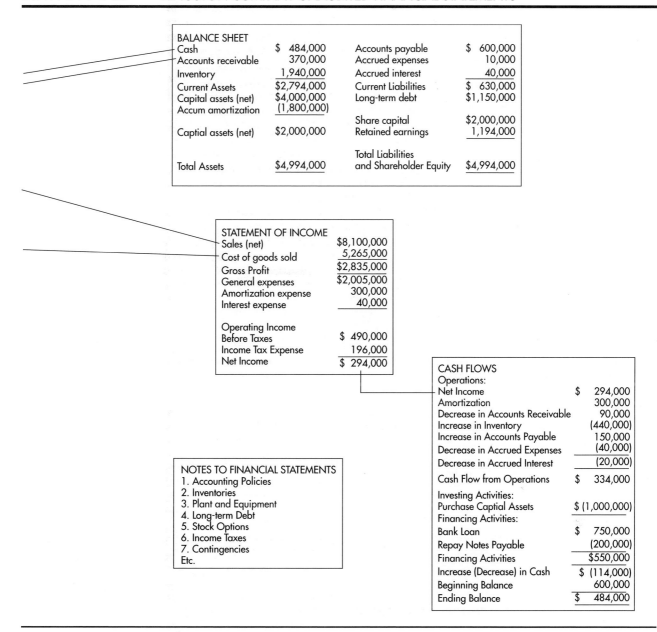

BALANCE SHEET

Cash	$ 484,000	Accounts payable	$ 600,000
Accounts receivable	370,000	Accrued expenses	10,000
Inventory	1,940,000	Accrued interest	40,000
Current Assets	$2,794,000	Current Liabilities	$ 630,000
Capital assets (net)	$4,000,000	Long-term debt	$1,150,000
Accum amortization	(1,800,000)		
		Share capital	$2,000,000
Captial assets (net)	$2,000,000	Retained earnings	1,194,000
		Total Liabilities	
Total Assets	$4,994,000	and Shareholder Equity	$4,994,000

STATEMENT OF INCOME

Sales (net)	$8,100,000
Cost of goods sold	5,265,000
Gross Profit	$2,835,000
General expenses	$2,005,000
Amortization expense	300,000
Interest expense	40,000
Operating Income	
Before Taxes	$ 490,000
Income Tax Expense	196,000
Net Income	$ 294,000

NOTES TO FINANCIAL STATEMENTS
1. Accounting Policies
2. Inventories
3. Plant and Equipment
4. Long-term Debt
5. Stock Options
6. Income Taxes
7. Contingencies
Etc.

CASH FLOWS

Operations:	
Net Income	$ 294,000
Amortization	300,000
Decrease in Accounts Receivable	90,000
Increase in Inventory	(440,000)
Increase in Accounts Payable	150,000
Decrease in Accrued Expenses	(40,000)
Decrease in Accrued Interest	(20,000)
Cash Flow from Operations	$ 334,000
Investing Activities:	
Purchase Captial Assets	$ (1,000,000)
Financing Activities:	
Bank Loan	$ 750,000
Repay Notes Payable	(200,000)
Financing Activities	$550,000
Increase (Decrease) in Cash	$ (114,000)
Beginning Balance	600,000
Ending Balance	$ 484,000

LEARNING OBJECTIVE

4. Describe and define the five principal management assertions in financial statements, and explain their role for establishing audit objectives.

As you study this section, keep in mind this scheme of things:

- Management's accounting system produces a trial balance.

- Management arranges the trial balance in financial statements and thereby makes certain assertions about the financial statements.

- Auditors take the assertions as focal points for the audit work.

- The practical audit objectives are to obtain and evaluate evidence about these five assertions made by management in financial statements. We will start with five very general assertions here:
  1. Existence or occurrence.
  2. Completeness.
  3. Rights and obligations.
  4. Valuation or allocations.
  5. Presentation and disclosure.

EXHIBIT 4–3   MANAGEMENT ASSERTIONS ABOUT INVENTORY

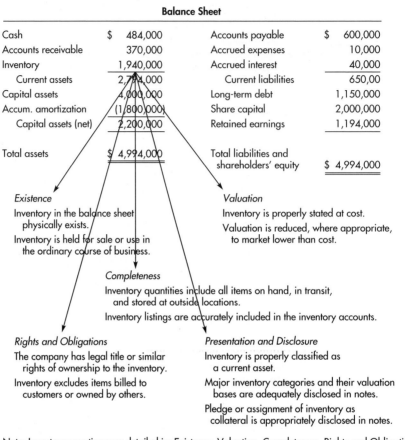

Balance Sheet

Cash	$ 484,000	Accounts payable	$ 600,000
Accounts receivable	370,000	Accrued expenses	10,000
Inventory	1,940,000	Accrued interest	40,000
Current assets	2,794,000	Current liabilities	650,00
Capital assets	4,000,000	Long-term debt	1,150,000
Accum. amortization	(1,800,000)	Share capital	2,000,000
Capital assets (net)	2,200,000	Retained earnings	1,194,000
Total assets	$ 4,994,000	Total liabilities and shareholders' equity	$ 4,994,000

Existence
Inventory in the balance sheet physically exists.
Inventory is held for sale or use in the ordinary course of business.

Valuation
Inventory is properly stated at cost.
Valuation is reduced, where appropriate, to market lower than cost.

Completeness
Inventory quantities include all items on hand, in transit, and stored at outside locations.
Inventory listings are accurately included in the inventory accounts.

Rights and Obligations
The company has legal title or similar rights of ownership to the inventory.
Inventory excludes items billed to customers or owned by others.

Presentation and Disclosure
Inventory is properly classified as a current asset.
Major inventory categories and their valuation bases are adequately disclosed in notes.
Pledge or assignment of inventory as collateral is appropriately disclosed in notes.

Note: Inventory assertions are detailed in: Existence, Valuation, Completeness, Rights and Obligations, and Presentation and Disclosure. See *Audit of Inventories*, CICA, 1986.

Exhibit 4–3 illustrates the five general assertions in some detail with relation to the inventory in the balance sheet. The sections that follow describe and define the assertions more fully.

Existence or Occurrence

The audit objective related to existence is to establish with evidence that assets, liabilities and equities actually exist and that revenue and expense transactions actually occurred. Occurrence is the existence assertion for transactions. Thus, auditors will count cash and inventory, confirm receivables and payables and perform other procedures to obtain evidence related to their specific objectives of determining whether cash, inventory, receivables, insurance in force and other assets actually exist. Beginning students must be careful at this point, however, because the finding of existence alone generally proves little about the other four assertions. (Chapter 9 contains a special note on existence assertion audit procedures.)

Cutoff

A special aspect of existence or occurrence is cutoff. Cutoff refers to recognizing assets and liabilities as of a proper date and accounting for revenue, expense and other transactions in the proper period. Simple cutoff errors can occur (1) when late December sales invoices are recorded for goods not actually shipped until January or (2) when cash receipts are recorded through the end of the week (e.g., Friday, January 4) and the last batch for the year should have been processed on December 31. In auditor's jargon, the cutoff date refers to the client's year-end balance sheet date.

Proper cutoff means accounting for all transactions that occurred during a period and neither postponing some recordings to the next period nor accelerating next period transactions into the current-year accounts.

Completeness

The objective related to completeness is to establish with evidence that all transactions and accounts that should be presented in the financial reports are included. Thus, auditors' specific objectives include obtaining evidence to determine whether, for example, all the inventory on hand is included, all the inventory consigned out is included, all the inventory consigned in is excluded, all the notes payable are reported and so forth. Auditing this assertion means auditing what is not there, so verifying this assertion creates special difficulties for the auditor. A verbal or written management representation saying that all transactions are included in the accounts is not considered a sufficient basis for deciding whether the completeness assertion is true. Auditors need to obtain persuasive evidence about completeness. (Chapter 10 contains a special note on completeness assertion audit procedures.)

Cutoff

The completeness assertion also has a special cutoff aspect. Both completeness and cutoff mean that all the transactions of a period should be recorded in the proper period and not shifted to another. Incomplete accounting and coincident cutoff errors include such things as (1) failure to record accruals for expenses incurred but not yet paid, thus understating both expenses and liabilities; (2) failure to record purchases of materials not yet received and, therefore, not included in the ending inventory, thus understating both inventory and accounts payable; and (3) failure to accrue unbilled revenue through the fiscal year-end for customers on a cycle billing system, thus understating both revenue and accounts receivable.

Rights and Obligations

The objective related to rights and obligations is to establish with evidence that amounts reported as assets of the company represent its property rights and that the amounts reported as liabilities represent its obligations. In plainer terms the objective is to obtain evidence about ownership and owership. You should be careful about ownership, however, because the idea includes assets (rights) for which a company does not actually hold title. For example, an auditor will have a specific objective of obtaining evidence about the amounts capitalized for leased property. Likewise, the owership idea includes "accounting liabilities" a company may not yet be legally obligated to pay. For example, specific objectives would include obtaining evidence about the obligations under a capitalized lease or the estimated liability for product guarantees.

Valuation or Allocation

The objective related to valuation or allocation is to determine whether proper values have been assigned to assets, liabilities, equities, revenue and expense. Auditors, thus, obtain evidence about specific valuations by reconciling bank accounts, comparing vendors' invoices to inventory prices, obtaining lower-of-cost-or-market data, evaluating collectibility of receivables and so forth. Many valuation and allocation decisions amount to decisions about the proper application of GAAP.

Presentation and Disclosure

Auditors also must determine whether accounting principles are properly selected and applied and whether disclosures are adequate. This objective relates to the presentation and disclosure assertion. Specific objectives include proper current and long-term balance sheet classification, and footnote disclosure of accounting policies. The presentation and disclosure objective is the meeting place for accounting principles and audit reporting standards. Footnote disclosure is the one area where management and auditors have the most disagreements and where professional judgment is essential.

A Compliance Assertion

Although not normally listed as a separate assertion, compliance with laws and regulations is very important for a business, and disclosure of known noncompliance is sometimes necessary for presentation of financial statements in conformity with generally accepted accounting principles. Auditors gather evidence about specific objectives related to financial laws and regulations, such as provincial securities acts, tax withholding regulations, minimum wage laws, wage and price guidelines, credit allocation regulations, income tax laws and specialized industry regulations. Compliance with legal terms of the company's private contracts (e.g., merger agreements and bond indentures) is also important for financial statement presentations. The importance of this assertion has recently been elevated through the issuance of *Section* 5136 of the *Handbook,* "Misstatements—Illegal Acts," which provides additional guidance on dealing with this assertion. When the sole purpose of an engagement is to audit compliance with various laws regulations, or rules, the engagement is called a compliance audit. This type of engagement is discussed in Chapter 15.

Compliance with laws and regulations is also a required characteristic of governmental audits, such as those by the Auditor General and provincial auditors. It is generally an objective for internal auditors with respect to managerial policies. Compliance auditing is a major topic in Chapter 18 (Governmental and Internal Auditing).

Importance of Assertions

Financial statement assertions are important and fairly complicated. They are the management assertions subject to audit and the focal points for audit procedures. When audit procedures are specified, you should be able to relate the evidence produced by each procedure to one or more specific objectives tailored to specific assertions. The way to begin planning a list of audit procedures is to ask: "Which assertion(s) does this procedure produce evidence about?" Then, "Does the list of procedures (the audit program) cover all the assertions?" The extent to which a particular procedure is used, however, will be determined by qualitative factors (discussed later in this chapter), the cost of the procedure, the risks associated with each assertion and materiality. Risk and materiality are covered in Chapter 5.

You can simplify the five major assertions by calling them existence, completeness, ownership, valuation and presentation. Just do not forget that each of them has additional aspects. Auditing standards explicitly identify the following assertions: existence, occurrence, completeness, ownership, valuation, measurement and statement presentation, where measurement relates to valuation of transactions and allocation of transactions to the proper period and occurrence relates to the existence of transactions. In essence there are five assertions for assets and liabilities: existence, completeness, ownership, valuation and statement presentation; and four assertions for revenue and expenses: occurrence, completeness, measurement and statement presentation (*Handbook Section* 5300.17).

· ·

R E V I E W
CHECKPOINTS

4.9   List and briefly explain the five major assertions that can be made about assets and liabilities and auditors' objectives related to each.

4.10 Why should auditors think about a "compliance assertion" that is not listed in the auditing standards about assertions (*Handbook Section* 5300.17)?

. . . .

SUFFICIENT APPROPRIATE EVIDENCE IN AUDITING

. . . .

Sufficient appropriate evidence in auditing

LEARNING OBJECTIVE

5. Explain audit evidence in terms of its appropriateness and relative strength of persuasiveness.

After obtaining the financial statements, auditors proceed to the task of specifying procedures for gathering evidence about the assertions in them. However, before studying these procedures, you need to understand some features of evidence in auditing.

The third examination standard requires auditors to obtain sufficient appropriate evidential matter as a reasonable basis for an opinion on financial statements (*Handbook Section* 5100.02 or ISA 500.7). The accounting records (journals, ledgers, accounting policy manuals, computer files and the like) are evidence of the bookkeeping/accounting process but are not sufficient appropriate supporting evidence for the financial statements. Evidence corroborating these records must be obtained through auditors' direct personal knowledge, examination of documents and the enquiry of company personnel. The purpose of gathering and analysing evidence is to support the decision on whether the financial statements conform to GAAP.

Appropriateness of Evidence

Appropriateness of evidence relates to the qualitative aspects of evidence. To be considered **appropriate,** evidence must be relevant and reliable. To be *relevant,* audit evidence must assist the auditor in achieving the audit objectives. This means relevant evidence must relate to at least one of the assertions. If evidence does not relate to one of the management assertions, the evidence is not relevant to the auditor.

The *reliability* of audit evidence depends on its nature and source. The following hierarchy of evidential matter will help you understand the relative reliability and, when combined with relevance, the overall persuasive power or appropriateness of different kinds of evidence. The hierarchy starts with the strongest form of evidence and proceeds to the weakest.

1. An auditor's direct, personal knowledge, obtained through physical observation and his or her own mathematical computations, is generally considered the most reliable evidence.

2. Documentary evidence obtained directly from independent external sources (external evidence) is considered very reliable.

3. Documentary evidence that has originated outside the client's data processing system but that has been received and processed by the client (external-internal evidence) is generally considered reliable. However, the circumstances of internal control quality are important.

4. Internal evidence consisting of documents that are produced, circulated and finally stored within the client's information system is generally considered low in reliability. However, internal evidence is used extensively when it is produced under satis-

factory conditions of internal control. Sometimes, internal evidence is the only kind available. Internal evidence is also generally easy to obtain and, therefore, tends to be less costly than other evidence.

5. Spoken and written representations given by the client's officers, directors, owners and employees are generally considered the least reliable evidence. Such representations should be corroborated with other types of evidence.

Auditors must be careful about the appropriateness of evidence. When specifying audit procedures for gathering evidence, the best initial approach is to seek the evidence of the highest reliability. If physical observation and mathematical calculation are not relevant to the account or are impossible or too costly, then move down the hierarchy to obtain the best evidence available. The evidence is best in the sense that it is the most appropriate or persuasive evidence under the circumstances. That is, it is the most reliable evidence that can be obtained in a cost-effective manner relative to a particular audit objective.

Sufficiency of Evidence

Sufficiency is a question of how much appropriate evidence is enough. The auditing profession has no official standard, leaving the matter of sufficiency to auditors' professional judgment. Realistically, however, audit decisions must be based on enough evidence to stand the scrutiny of other auditors (supervisors and reviewers) and outsiders (such as critics and judges). The real test of sufficiency is whether you can persuade someone else that your evidential base is strong enough to reach the same conclusions you have reached. The fact that important evidence is difficult or costly to obtain is not an acceptable reason for failing to obtain it.

With these aspects of evidence in mind, you are now ready to study the general procedures for obtaining evidence.

. . . .

R E V I E W
C H E C K P O I N T S

4.11 How are external, external-internal and internal documentary evidence generally defined?

4.12 What's the problem with evidence obtained from related parties?

. . . .

RELATED PARTIES AND THE APPROPRIATENESS OF EVIDENCE

Handbook Section 3840 contains extensive definitions and accounting standards concerning disclosure of balances and transactions that a company has with related parties. This note, however, deals only with the audit evidence aspect of related parties.

The Audit Guideline "Related Party Transactions and Economic Dependence" put the matter in perspective by stating: "The auditor should be aware that the substance of a particular transaction could be significantly different from its form and that financial statements should recognize the substance of particular transactions, rather than merely their legal form." Auditors are supposed to identify related party relationships and transactions and obtain evidence that the financial accounting and disclosure for them are proper.

The audit problem with related parties is that evidence obtained from them should not be considered highly reliable in terms of persuasiveness. The source of the evidence may be biased. Hence, auditors should obtain evidence of the purpose, nature and extent of related party transactions and their effect on financial statements; and the evidence should extend beyond enquiry of management.

GENERAL AUDIT PROCEDURES
• • • • • • • • • • • •

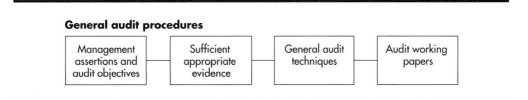

General audit procedures

| Management assertions and audit objectives | Sufficient appropriate evidence | General audit techniques | Audit working papers |

LEARNING OBJECTIVE

6. List and describe six general types of audit techniques for gathering evidence.

Auditors use six basic types of evidence and auditing standards, and identify six general techniques to gather it. The six techniques identified in *Handbook Section* 5300.22 (and also in the third examination standard) are (1) computation, (2) observation, (3) confirmation, (4) enquiry, (5) inspection, and (6) analysis. In practice many auditing firms subdivide these techniques into more specific procedures. One or more of these techniques may be used no matter what account balance, control procedure, class of transactions or other information is under audit. Auditors arrange the techniques or more specific procedures in an audit program, which is basically a list of procedures. Exhibit 4–4 shows the six types of evidence and the techniques most closely related to each.

Computation

Computation consists of performing independent calculations, or recalculating the calculations previously performed by a client. This produces compelling mathematical evidence. A client calculation is either right or wrong. Client calculations performed by computer programs can be recalculated using computer auditing software, with differences printed out for further audit investigation. Mathematical evidence can serve the objectives of both existence and valuation for financial statement amounts that exist principally as calculations—for example, depreciation, pension liabilities, actuarial reserves, statutory bad debt reserves and product guarantee liabilities. Recalculation, in combination with other procedures, also is used to provide evidence of valuation for all other financial data. Computation provides the auditor with evidence that is highly reliable with respect to mathematical accuracy.

Observation

Observation consists of looking at the application of policy or procedures by others. It provides highly reliable evidence as to performance or conditions at a given point in time but does not necessarily reflect performance at other times or over long time periods. The technique of observation is utilized whenever auditors view the client's physical facilities and

EXHIBIT 4–4   AUDIT TECHNIQUES AND RELATED TYPES OF EVIDENCE

Audit Techniques	Types of Evidence
1. Computation.	1. Auditor's calculations.
2. Observation.	2. Physical observation.
3. Confirmation.	3. Statements by independent parties.
4. Enquiry.	4. Statements by client personnel.
5. Inspection.	5a. Documents prepared by independent parties.
	5b. Documents prepared by the client.
	5c. Physical inspection of tangible assets.
6. Analysis.	6. Data interrelationships

personnel on an inspection tour, or watch personnel carry out accounting and control activities, or participate in a surprise petty cash count or payroll distribution. Physical observation can also produce a general awareness of events in the client's offices.

Confirmation

Confirmation consists of an enquiry, usually written, to verify accounting records. Confirmation by direct correspondence with independent parties is a procedure widely used in auditing. For example, confirmation is recommended for accounts receivable by *Section 5303* of the *CICA Handbook*. Confirmation can produce evidence of existence and ownership and sometimes of valuation and cutoff. Most transactions involve outside parties and, theoretically, written correspondence could be conducted even on such items as individual paycheques. However, auditors limit their use of confirmation to major transactions and balances about which outside parties could be expected to provide information. A selection of confirmation applications includes:

- Banks—account balances.
- Customers—receivables balances.
- Borrowers—note terms and balances.
- Agents—inventory or consignment or in warehouses.
- Lenders—note terms and balances.
- Policyholders—life insurance contracts.
- Vendors—accounts payable balances.
- Registrar—number of shares of stock outstanding.
- Legal counsel—litigation in progress.
- Trustees—securities held, terms of agreements.
- Lessors—lease terms.

The important general points about confirmations are these:

- Confirmation letters should be printed on the client's letterhead, or a facsimile, and signed by a client officer.
- Auditors should be very careful that the recipient's address is reliable and not subject to alteration by the client in such a way as to misdirect the confirmation.
- The request should seek information the recipient can supply, like the amount of a balance or the amounts of specified invoices or notes.
- Confirmations should be controlled by the audit firm, not given to client personnel for mailing. Direct communication is required by auditing standards.
- Responses should be returned directly to the audit firm, not to the client.

Confirmations of receivables and payables may take several forms. Two widely used forms are positive confirmation and negative confirmation. The positive confirmation requests a reply in all cases, whether the account balance is considered correct or incorrect. The negative confirmation requests a reply only if the account balance is considered incorrect. Auditors should try to obtain replies from all positive confirmations by sending second and third requests to nonrespondents. If there is no response to positive confirmations, or if the response to either positive or negative confirmations specifies an exception to the client's records, the auditors should investigate with other audit procedures, such as examining whether there is subsequent collection on the account or examination of internal evidence supporting the recording of the receivable. Cash and accounts receivable confirmations, as well as limitations, and issues arising from the use of faxes in confirmation procedures, are explained more fully in Chapter 9. Accounts payable confirmations are mentioned briefly in Chapter 10, with reference to the audit of the completeness of liability recording.

WHO'S LYING NOW?

This news item was released at the time of the U.S. Senate hearings on the Clarence Thomas nomination to the U.S. Supreme Court, after Anita Hill's information about sexual harassment became public (1991).

****

Psychologist Paul Ekman has spent 30 years studying the art of lying. He knows the averted eyes, fleeting facial expressions and hesitations that characterize a person at war with the truth.

After viewing the Thomas–Hill contradictory testimony, Ekman concluded: "Whichever one started out lying is now totally convinced of what they are saying. People who have an enormous stake in distorting the truth can . . . convince themselves that what they prefer to believe truly happened. Most people think they can tell when someone is lying, but they can't." A study showed that police, judges, and even FBI agents cannot reliably separate truth tellers from liars.

Source: News item from *Los Angeles Times* Service, October 13, 1991.

****

So, what can most auditors do? The best strategy is first to distinguish new assertions from "evidence." Most responses to enquiries produce more management assertions about facts, estimates, or judgments. This best strategy then verifies the new assertions with other, independent evidence.

Enquiry

Enquiry generally involves the collection of oral evidence from independent parties and client officials. Statements must be obtained in the written representation letter for all important enquiries. (Representation letters are covered in detail in Chapter 14.) Auditors use enquiry procedures during the early office and plant tour and when conferences are conducted. Evidence gathered by formal and informal enquiry of persons working for the client generally cannot stand alone as convincing, and auditors must corroborate responses with other findings based on other procedures. Such corroboration may include making further enquiries from other appropriate sources within the entity. Consistent responses from different sources provide an increased degree of assurance. Sometimes, however, the auditor will encounter conflicting evidence in the form of a negative statement where someone volunteers adverse information, such as an admission of theft, irregularity or use of an accounting policy that is misleading. In these situations the auditor will have to use considerable judgment in reconciling the conflicting evidence or in deciding what additional evidence to gather. Scepticism and a critical attitude are important aspects of professional judgment, and the auditor may sometimes get into situations similar to that described in the box above. The last paragraph in the box above suggests one way of dealing with conflicting evidence from enquiries.

Enquiries, interviews and oral evidence generally are being viewed as increasingly important within the profession. (S. Smith, "A Matter of Evidence," *CA Magazine*, October 1994, pp. 57–58.) This arises from the recognition that client's explanations are an important way of obtaining an understanding of the business and the nature of specific transactions. Oral evidence has always been viewed as critical evidence in public sector auditing. The new SSA audits are also putting increasing stress on enquiry as a means to a better understanding the client's strategy, and the risks and controls associated with it. Client managements' explanations can be compared with that of other client employees, as well as that of industry experts and other sources of corroborating evidence. There also are a variety of techniques to increase the reliability of enquiries as a source of audit evidence. For example, see T.R. Craig, "Effective Interviewing Skills for Auditors," *Journal of Accountancy*, July 1991, pp. 121–126.

Inspection

Inspection consists of looking at records and documents or at assets having physical substances. It encompasses procedures of varying degrees of thoroughness such as examining, perusing, reading, reviewing, scanning, scrutinizing and vouching.

Physical inspection of tangible assets provides reliable evidence of existence and may provide tentative evidence of condition and valuation. The same is true of physical inspection of formal documents having intrinsic value, such as securities certificates. Records and documents not having an intrinsic market value, such as invoices or purchase orders, have varying degrees of reliability for different assertions depending on their source.

Much auditing work involves gathering evidence by examining authoritative documents prepared by independent parties and by the client. Such documents can provide at least some evidence regarding all the assertions.

Documents Prepared by Independent Outside Parties

A great deal of documentary evidence is external–internal. Convincing documentation is that prepared or validated by other parties and sent to the client. The signatures, seals, engravings and other distinctive stylistic attributes of formal authoritative documents make such sources more reliable (less susceptible to alteration) than ordinary documents prepared by outsiders. Some examples of both types of documents are listed below:

Formal Authoritative Documents	**Ordinary Documents**
1. Bank statements.	1. Vendor's invoices.
2. Cancelled cheques.	2. Customers' purchase orders.
3. Insurance policies.	3. Loan applications.
4. Notes receivable.	4. Notes receivable (on unique forms and on standard bank forms).
5. Securities certificates.	5. Insurance policy applications.
6. Indenture agreements.	6. Simple contracts.
7. Elaborate contracts.	7. Correspondence.
8. Title papers (e.g., autos).	

Documents Prepared and Processed Within the Entity Under Audit

Documentation of this type is internal evidence. Some of these documents may be quite informal and not very authoritative or reliable. As a general proposition, the reliability of these documents depends on the quality of internal control under which they were produced and processed. Some of the most common of these documents are:

Internal Documents

1. Sales invoice copies.	7. Shipping documents.
2. Sales summary reports.	8. Receiving reports.
3. Cost distribution reports.	9. Requisition slips.
4. Loan approval memos.	10. Purchase orders.
5. Budgets and performance reports.	11. Credit memoranda.
6. Documentation of transactions with subsidiary or affiliated companies.	12. Transaction logs.
	13. Batch control logs (computer).

A Particular Inspection Procedure: Vouching—Examination of Documents

The important point about vouching in the examination of documents is the direction of the search for audit evidence. In vouching, an item of financial information is selected from an account (e.g., the posting of a sales invoice in a customer's master file record); then the auditor goes backward through the accounting and control system to find the source documentation that supports the item selected. The auditor finds the journal entry or data input list, the sales summary, the sales invoice copy and the shipping documents, and, finally, the customer's purchase order. Vouching of documents can help auditors decide whether all recorded data are adequately supported (the existence/occurrence assertion), but vouching does not provide evidence to show whether all events were recorded. (This latter problem is covered by tracing.)

A Particular Inspection Procedure: Tracing—Examination of Documents

In the examination of documents, tracing takes the opposite direction from vouching. When an auditor performs tracing, he or she selects sample items of basic source documents and proceeds forward through the accounting and control system (whether computer or manual) to find the final recording of the accounting transactions. For example, samples of payroll payments are traced to cost and expense accounts, sales invoices to the sales accounts, cash receipts to the accounts receivable subsidiary accounts and cash disbursements to the accounts payable subsidiary accounts.

Using tracing, an auditor can decide whether all events were recorded (the completeness assertion), and complement the evidence obtained by vouching. However, you must be alert to events that may not have been captured in the source documents and not entered into the accounting system. For example, the search for unrecorded liabilities for raw materials purchases must include examination of invoices received in the period following the fiscal year-end and examination of receiving reports dated near the year-end. (The "search for unrecorded liabilities" is explained in detail in Chapter 10.)

A Particular Inspection Procedure: Scanning

Scanning is the way auditors exercise their general alertness to unusual items and events in clients' documentation. A typical scanning directive in an audit program is "Scan the expense accounts for credit entries; vouch any to source documents."

In general, scanning is an "eyes-open" approach of looking for anything unusual. The scanning procedure usually does not produce direct evidence itself, but it can raise questions for which other evidence must be obtained. Scanning can be accomplished on computer records using computer audit software to select records to be printed out for further audit investigation. Typical items discovered by the scanning effort include debits in revenue accounts, credits in expense accounts, unusually large accounts receivable write-offs, unusually large paycheques, unusually small sales volume in the month following the year-end and large cash deposits just prior to year-end. Scanning can contribute some evidence related to the existence of assets and the completeness of accounting records, including the proper cutoff of material transactions.

Scanning is valuable when sampling methods are applied in audit decisions. When a sample is the basis for selecting items for audit, the risk of choosing a sample that does not reflect the entire population of items always exists. Such an event may cause a decision error. Auditors subjectively reduce this detection risk by scanning items not selected in the sample.

Analysis

Analysis consists of

(a) identifying the components of a financial statement item or account so that particular characteristics of these components can be considered in designing the nature, timing and extent of other audit procedures; and

(b) performing analytical procedures, which are techniques by which the auditor:
- (i) studies and uses meaningful relationships among elements of financial and non-financial information to form expectations about what amounts recorded in the accounts should be;
- (ii) compares such expectations with the recorded amounts; and
- (iii) uses the results of this comparison to help determine what, if any, other audit procedures are needed to obtain sufficient appropriate audit evidence that the recorded amounts are not materially misstated. [*Handbook Section* 5300.01]

The difference between part (a) of the definition of analysis and scanning is that analysis relates to a higher level of aggregation—comparison of components of a financial statement—whereas scanning relates to the detail records about a particular component.

Auditors can evaluate financial statement accounts by analysis. The methods of study and comparison are known as analytical procedures. Auditors can use analysis when (a) planning the audit (i.e., at the beginning), (b) during the executing phase of the audit as a substantive procedure to verify assertions about specific account balances or classes of transactions, and (c) when performing the final review and evaluation of the financial statements before the audit report is issued (i.e., at the end of the audit). *Handbook Sections* 5301.11 and 5301.27 require that analysis be used at the planning (beginning) stage and at the end of the audit.

Analysis is the "other" category in the list of six auditing techniques. Analytical procedures are "everything else an auditor can think to do" that does not meet the definitions of computation, observation, confirmation, structured enquiry or inspection. The procedures themselves range from simple comparisons to application of complex mathematical estimation models. They can be used to obtain evidence on any of the management assertions, but the assertions most affected are completeness, valuation, measurement or allocation, and statement presentation (D.G. Smith, *Analytical Review*, Chapter 2, CICA, 1983).

Analytical procedures can be classified into these five general forms:

1. Comparison of current-year account balances to balances of one or more comparable periods.
2. Comparison of the current-year account balances to anticipated results found in the company's budgets and forecasts.
3. Evaluation of the relationships of current-year account balances to other current-year balances for conformity with predictable patterns based on the company's experience.
4. Comparison of current-year account balances and financial relationships (e.g., ratios) with similar information for the industry in which the company operates.
5. Study of the relationships of current-year account balances with relevant nonfinancial information (e.g., physical production statistics).

Auditors need to be careful to use independent, reliable information for comparison to current-year financial accounts. Thus, the sources of information for analytical procedures are very important:

- Financial account information for comparable prior period(s). Company budgets and forecasts.
- Financial relationships among accounts in the current period.
- Industry statistics.
- Nonfinancial information, such as physical production statistics.

Because analytical procedures are loosely defined, many auditors consider the evidence they produce to be "soft." Therefore, auditors, professors and students tend to concentrate on computation, observation, confirmation, inspection of assets and vouching of documents that are perceived to produce "hard" evidence. However, you should resist this distinction. Analytical procedures are, in fact, quite effective.

SOME EXAMPLES OF ANALYTICAL PROCEDURES

Auditors noticed large quantities of rolled steel in the company's inventory. Several 30,000-kilogram rolls were entered in the inventory list. The false entries were detected because the auditor knew the company's fork-lift trucks had a 10,000-kilogram lifting capacity.

****

Auditors compared the total quantity of vegetable oils the company claimed to have inventoried in its tanks to the storage capacity reported in national export statistics. The company's "quantity on hand" amounted to 90 percent of the national supply and greatly exceeded its own tank capacity.

****

Last year's working papers showed that the company employees had failed to accrue wages payable at the year-end date. A search for the current accrual entry showed it had again been forgotten.

****

Auditors programmed a complex regression model to estimate the electric utility company's total revenue. They used empirical relations of fuel consumption, meteorological reports of weather conditions and population census data in the area. The regression model estimated revenue within close range of the reported revenue.

Hylas and Ashton collected evidence on misstatements requiring financial statement adjustment in a large number of audits.[5] They were interested primarily in describing the audit procedures used to detect the misstatements. Their definition of analytical procedures was broad. It included data comparisons, predictions based on outside data, analyses of interrelationships among account balances, "reasonableness tests," "estimates," and cursory review of financial statements in the audit planning stage. They also had two procedure categories called expectations from prior years (which involves the carry over of analytical and detail knowledge about continuing audit clients) and discussions with client personnel.

They found that auditors gave credit for misstatement discovery to analytical procedures for 27.1 percent of all misstatements. They gave credit to "expectations" and "discussions" for another 18.5 percent. Altogether, the so-called soft procedures accounted for detection of 45.6 percent of the misstatements. All of these procedures typically are applied early in the audit, so you should not infer that other kinds of audit procedures would or would not have detected the same misstatements. The detection success of other procedures depends on the results of the early applied procedures because, as this study was designed, even a good physical observation procedure did not get credit for "discovery" of a misstatement that already had been discovered using analytical procedures.

Auditors must consider the value of analytical procedures, especially since they are usually less costly than more detailed, document-oriented procedures. Also, the "hard evidence" procedures have their own pitfalls. Auditors may not be competent to "see" things they are supposed to observe. Clients can manipulate confirmations by giving auditors the addresses of conspirators or by asking customers just to "sign it and send it back." An audit program consists of several different types of procedures, and analytical procedures deserve a prominent place.

---

[5] R.E. Hylas and R.H. Ashton, "Audit Detection of Financial Statement Errors," *Accounting Review*, October 1982, pp. 751–65.

POTHOLES IN THE AUDIT PROCEDURE ROAD

Computation:

An auditor calculated inventory valuations (quantities times price), thinking the measuring unit was gross (144 units each), when the client had actually recorded counts in dozens (12 units each), thus causing the inventory valuation to be 12 times the proper measure.

Inspection of Assets:

While inspecting the fertilizer tank assets in ranch country, the auditor was fooled when the manager was able to move them to other locations and place new numbers on them. The auditor "inspected" the same tanks many times.

Confirmation:

The insurance company executive gave the auditor a false address for a marketable securities confirmation, intercepted the confirmation, then returned it with no exceptions noted. The company falsified $20 million in assets.

Enquiry:

Seeking evidence of the collectibility of accounts receivable, the auditors "audited by conversation" and took the credit manager's word about the collection probabilities on the over-90-day past-due accounts. They sought no other evidence.

Inspection by Examination of Documents:

The auditors did not notice that the bank statement had been crudely altered. (Can you find the alteration in the bank statement in Exhibit 19–3 in Chapter 19?)

Inspection by the Scanning Procedure:

The auditors extracted a computer list of all the bank's loans over $1,000. They neglected to perform a similar scan for loans with negative balances, a condition that should not occur. The bank had data processing problems that caused many loan balances to be negative, although the trial balance balanced!

The box above illustrates problems that can arise in evaluating evidence obtained with "hard evidence" procedures.

REVIEW CHECKPOINTS

4.13 What is meant by "vouching"? by "tracing"? and by "scanning"?

4.14 What can auditors do to improve the effectiveness of confirmation requests?

4.15 What are the five types of general analytical procedures?

4.16 Are analytical procedures very effective for discovering errors and irregularities?

EFFECTIVENESS OF AUDIT PROCEDURES

LEARNING OBJECTIVE
7. Discuss the effectiveness of various audit procedures.

Audits are supposed to be designed to provide reasonable assurance of detecting misstatements that are material to the financial statements (see *Handbook Section* 5090.04). When misstatements exist, and auditors do a good job of detecting them, adjustments will be made to management's unaudited financial statements before an audit report is issued. How often does this happen? Wright and Ashton obtained information on 186 audits performed by KPMG Peat Marwick during 1984–85.[6] The reported frequency of audit adjustments is shown in Exhibit 4–5.

[6] Data for Exhibit 4–5 and the other, related exhibits come from Arnold Wright and Robert H. Ashton, "Identifying Audit Adjustments with Attention-Directing Procedures," *The Accounting Review*, October 1989, pp. 710–28.

EXHIBIT 4–5   FREQUENCY OF AUDIT ADJUSTMENTS (sample of audits from one audit firm)

Number of Audit Adjustments*	Number of Audits	Percent of Audits
Zero or 1	22	12%
2–5	30	16
6–10	45	24
More than 10	89	48
Total	186	100%

*Total number of adjustments detected regardless of size or nature.

What kinds of misstatements did the auditors find? Wright and Ashton reported the data for 23 accounts. A selection of them is shown in Exhibit 4–6. The misstatements consisted of both understatements and overstatements. (However, you should remember that these are not "good" or "bad" descriptions. Overstatement of assets and understatement of liabilities both cause shareholders' equity to be overstated.) Since they come from respondents in one public accounting firm, these data may not be generalizable to all audits. In this case, however, the overstatements/understatements look mixed in the current assets, understatements are in the majority in the noncurrent assets, understatements appear to be in the majority in the liabilities and understatements appear to be in the majority in the expense accounts.

As you can see, discovery of misstatements in management's unaudited financial statements is not unusual. How do the auditors do it? What procedures do they find effective? Wright and Ashton compiled data on seven "initial events" that identified misstatements in financial statements. They were called "initial events" instead of "audit procedures" because they were the first work that identified misstatements, and all of them did not correspond exactly with specific procedures auditors would list in an audit program. Exhibit 4–7 shows the initial events that indicated misstatements that required adjustment. The so-called "soft" information from expectations based on prior-year experience, analytical procedures and client enquiry accounted for an overall 50 percent of the discovered misstatements. (These data are consistent with the earlier Hylas-Ashton study. See footnote 5.)

EXHIBIT 4–6   SUMMARY OF MISSTATEMENTS (selected accounts)

Account	Number of Misstatements	
	Overstatement	Understatement
Cash	6	10
Securities	21	17
Accounts receivable	48	22
Inventory	24	32
Property, plant	14	23
Other noncurrent	11	24
Accounts payable	21	25
Accrued liabilities	17	40
Other current liabilities	10	13
Long-term liabilities	12	24
Revenue	32	30
Cost of goods sold	38	45
Selling expense	11	16
Gen and admin. expense	39	52

Note: The effect of adjustments on income was that 43 percent of the adjustments reduced the reported income, while 28 percent increased the reported income. The other 29 percent of the adjustments were reclassifications that neither reduced nor increased income.

EXHIBIT 4–7   INITIAL EVENTS THAT IDENTIFIED ADJUSTMENTS

Initial Event	Number of Adjustments	Percent
Tests of details: examination of transaction amounts and descriptions, account balance details, workups to support account balances, data on various reconciliations	104	28.7%
*Expectations from the prior year	78	21.5
*Analytical procedures: comparison of current unaudited balances with balances of prior years, predictions of current balances based on exogenous data, analyses of interrelationships	56	15.5
*Client enquiry	48	13.3
Test of detail: checks for mathematical accuracy	35	9.7
General audit procedures	8	2.2

*These were the three "attention-directing procedures" that accounted for 50.3 percent of the identified adjustments.

Nevertheless, detail audit procedures also were effective. Wright and Ashton note that the "ordering effect" (the fact that the attention-directing procedures come first) biases the results against showing that detail procedures might have detected the misstatements if they had not already been detected. They note further that (1) few adjustments were initially signalled by confirmations or inventory observation and (2) simple methods of comparison and client enquiry detected many misstatements.

Analysis takes on a much more prominent role in SSA audits. In SSA audits analysis is used independently by the auditor to develop a knowledge of the business sufficient to second-guess management abilities to carry out their plans and to second-guess management estimates. If the auditor's independently derived conclusions correspond with that of management's assertions, then the auditor is assumed to have obtained sufficient assurance for these assertions. Thus the auditor relies much more on analysis in SSA audits than in traditional audits.

R E V I E W
C H E C K P O I N T S

4.17 Is there any pattern in auditors' experience in finding overstatements and understatements in accounts?

4.18 List several types of audit work (initial events, audit procedures) in their order of apparent effectiveness for identifying financial statement misstatements. Where would you put accounts receivable confirmation and inventory observation on the list?

AUDIT WORKING PAPERS

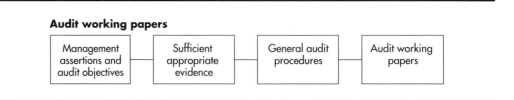

Audit working papers

Management assertions and audit objectives — Sufficient appropriate evidence — General audit procedures — Audit working papers

LEARNING OBJECTIVE

8. Review an audit working paper for proper form and content.

An audit is not complete without preparation of proper working paper documentation. Working papers are the auditors' record of compliance with generally accepted auditing standards. They should contain support for the decisions regarding procedures necessary in the circumstances and all other important decisions made during the audit. Even though the auditor is the legal owner of the working papers, professional ethics require that those papers not be transferred without consent of the client because of the confidential information recorded in them. Detailed auditing standards concerning working papers are in *Handbook Section* 5145 or ISA 90.

Working papers can be classified into three categories: (1) permanent file papers, (2) audit administrative papers, and (3) audit evidence papers. The last two categories are often called the "current file" because they relate to the audit of one year.

Permanent File Papers

The "permanent file" contains information of continuing interest over many years' audits of the same client. This file can be used year after year, whereas each year's current audit evidence papers are filed away after they have served their purpose. Documents of permanent interest and applicability include (1) copies or excerpts of the corporate charter and bylaws or partnership agreements; (2) copies or excerpts of continuing contracts, such as leases, bond indentures and royalty agreements; (3) a history of the company, its products and its markets; (4) excerpts of minutes of shareholders' and directors' meetings on matters of lasting interest; and (5) continuing schedules of accounts whose balances are carried forward for several years, such as share capital, retained earnings, partnership capital and the like. Copies of prior years' financial statements and audit reports also may be included. The permanent file is a ready source of information for new personnel on the engagement who must familiarize themselves with the client.

Audit Administrative Papers

Administrative papers contain the documentation of the early planning phases of the audit. They usually include the engagement letter, staff assignment notes, conclusions related to understanding the client's business, results of preliminary analytical procedures, initial assessments of audit risks and initial assessments of audit materiality. Many accounting firms follow the practice of summarizing these data in an engagement planning memorandum.

Audit planning and administration also includes work on the preliminary assessment of control risk and preparation of a written audit program. In general, the following items are usually among the administrative working papers in each year's current file:

1. Engagement letter.
2. Staff assignments.
3. Client organization chart.
4. Memoranda of conferences with management.
5. Memoranda of conferences with the directors' audit committee.
6. Preliminary analytical review notes.
7. Initial risk assessment notes.
8. Initial materiality assessment notes.
9. Engagement planning memorandum.
10. Audit engagement time budget.
11. Internal control questionnaire and control analyses.
12. Management controls questionnaire.
13. Computer controls questionnaire.
14. Internal control system flowcharts.
15. Audit program.
16. A working trial balance of general ledger accounts.

17. Working paper record of preliminary adjusting and reclassifying entries.

18. Memoranda of review notes and unfinished procedures (all cleared by the end of the field work).

The SSA audit results in a very different set of working papers being generated. Chapter 13 provides more details.

Audit Evidence Papers

The current-year audit evidence working papers contain the specific assertions under audit, the record of the procedures performed, the evidence obtained and the decisions made in the course of the audit. (See Exhibit 4–8.) These papers communicate the quality of the audit, so they must be clear, concise, complete, neat, well indexed and informative. Each separate working paper (or multiple pages that go together) must be complete in the sense that it can be removed from the working paper file and considered on its own, with proper cross-reference available to show how the paper co-ordinates with other working papers. Working papers may be in the form of magnetic tape or disks, or film, or photographs; they may be handwritten or stored on computer.

E X H I B I T 4–8   **CURRENT WORKING PAPER FILE**

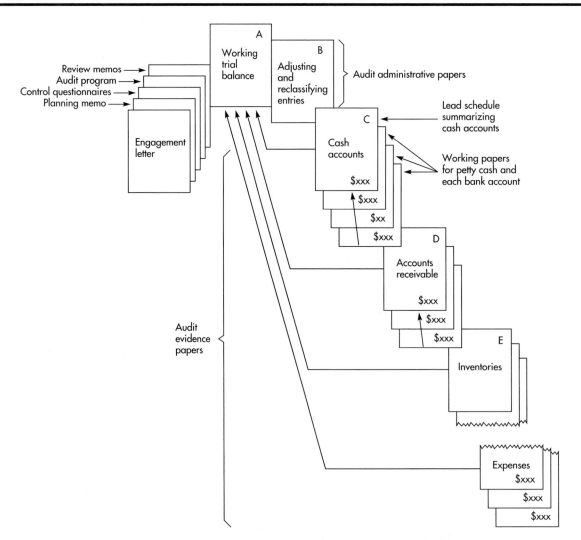

The most important facet of the current audit evidence papers is the requirement that they show the auditors' decision problems and conclusions. The papers must record the management assertions that were audited (book values or qualitative disclosures), the evidence gathered about them and the final decisions. Auditing standards (*Section* 5145) recommend that the working papers show (1) evidence that the work was adequately planned and supervised; (2) a description of audit evidence obtained include memoranda, check lists, questionnaires, flowcharts, audit programs, schedules, correspondence and extracts of legal documents; (3) evidence of the evaluation and disposition of misstatements; and (4) copies of letters or notes concerning audit matters reported to the client (*Handbook Section* 5145.05 or ISA 230.11). Common sense also dictates that the working papers be sufficient to show that the financial statements conform to GAAP and that the disclosures are adequate. The working papers also should explain how exceptions and unusual accounting questions were resolved or treated. (Notice in Exhibit 4–9 the auditor's confirmation

EXHIBIT 4–9   ILLUSTRATIVE WORKING PAPER

of the disputed account payable liability.) Taken altogether, these features should demonstrate that all the auditing standards were observed.

Working Paper Arrangement and Indexing

Every auditing organization has a different method of arranging and indexing working papers. In general, however, the papers are grouped in order behind the trial balance according to balance sheet and income statement captions. Usually, the current assets appear first, followed by fixed assets, other assets, liabilities, equities, income and expense accounts. The typical arrangement is shown in Exhibit 4–8.

Several working paper preparation techniques are quite important for the quality of the finished product. The points explained below are illustrated in Exhibit 4–9.

- *Indexing.* Each paper is given an index number, like a book page number, so it can be found, removed, and replaced without loss. For example, an index number can consist of a section letter (e.g., "C") and a page number within that section (e.g., C-"2"). This allows for each section to be given to different audit teams and for easy expansion within a given section without affecting other sections.
- *Cross-indexing.* Numbers or memoranda related to other papers carry the index of other paper(s) so that the connections can be followed.
- *Heading.* Each paper is titled with the name of the company, the period under audit date, and a descriptive title of the contents of the working paper.
- *Signatures and initials.* The auditor who performs the work and the supervisor who reviews it must sign the papers so that personnel can be identified.
- *Dates of audit work.* The dates of performance and review are recorded on the working papers so that reviewers of the papers can tell when the work was performed.
- *Tick marks and explanations.* "Tick marks" are the auditor's shorthand for abbreviating comments about work performed. Tick marks always must be accompanied by a full explanation of the auditing work.

Audit Working Paper Software

Specialized working paper software is becoming very common in public practice. Electronic working papers can boost productivity by automating many documentation tasks (for example, automatically carrying over adjustments to related working paper documents and the financial statements). Good electronic working paper software integrates the audit information and allows easy access, review and changes to the format, content or order of the files. Because more and more client data is already in electronic form, it is logical to integrate this data with electronic working paper files. For example, a working paper program can directly import a trial balance from ACCPAC and generate lead sheets automatically. In addition, the use of electronic working papers with laptop computers eliminates the need for voluminous file boxes and suitcases, and allows for electronic communication and sharing of information among staff and continuous monitoring and review of everyone's work even from a distance by a supervisor. The entire audit process can be re-engineered to be more efficient (for example, through use of standard templates and electronic questionnaires).

Audit working paper software can also facilitate analysis. Links can be established to other databases, or even websites so that data or information from these sources can be cross referenced or transferred to the working papers. Thus, not only various staff work but also various other sources of information can be integrated to support the auditor's opinion.

Some problems are associated with computer generated working papers, however, including costs of hardware, software, training and the continuous upgrading with advances in technology. Also, some copies of original source documents such as important contracts still need to be kept in hard copy form. Common working paper software used in public practice includes CaseWare and Lotus Notes.

4.19   What information would you expect to find in a permanent audit file? in the front of a current working paper file?

4.20   What is considered the most important content of the auditor's current audit working papers?

Summary

This chapter discussed two types of topics. The first was a set of activities auditors undertake when beginning an audit engagement. These pre-engagement activities start with the work of deciding whether to accept a new client and become its auditor and, on an annual basis, deciding whether to continue as auditor for existing clients. Public accounting firms are not obligated to provide audits to every organization that asks for one, and they regularly exercise discretion about the organizations with which they wish to associate. The investigation may involve the co-operative task of communicating with the former (predecessor) auditor of the organization. Once a client is accepted, the pre-engagement work continues with the preparation of an engagement letter, and the assignment of partners, managers, and staff to the job, and the preparation of a time budget for the audit.

The activities part of the chapter also covered the important process of obtaining an understanding of the client's business and industry. Methods and sources of information were explained. The last part of the activities was a brief explanation of the financial statements and of the grouping of accounts into cycles for purposes of organizing the audit.

The second set of topics in the chapter related to the basic practical concepts involved in performing audits. The financial statements were explained in terms of the primary assertions management makes in them, and these assertions were identified as the focal points of the auditors' procedural evidence-gathering work. The theory of sufficient, appropriate evidence was introduced with an explanation of the relative strengths and persuasiveness of various types of evidence. Next, the general procedures for obtaining evidence were outlined. This explanation of procedures was enriched with additional notes about the ways in which procedures can be misapplied. Analytical procedures were introduced, and their power was illustrated with some empirical research findings based on actual audit results. The chapter closed with some basic pointers about the form, content and purpose of audit working papers.

Multiple-Choice Questions For Practice And Review

Questions 4.21 to 4.23 are located on the CD-ROM that accompanies this textbook.

4.24   An audit engagement letter should normally include the following matter of agreement between the auditor and the client:
 a. Schedules and analyses to be prepared by the client's employees.
 b. Methods of statistical sampling the auditor will use.
 c. Specification of litigation in progress against the client.
 d. Client representations about availability of all minutes of meetings of the board of directors.

4.25   When a successor auditor initiates communications with a predecessor auditor, the successor should expect:

 a. To take responsibility for obtaining the client's consent for the predecessor to give information about prior audits.
 b. To conduct interviews with the partner and manager in charge of the predecessor audit firm's engagement.
 c. To obtain copies of some or all of the predecessor auditor's working papers.
 d. All of the above.

4.26   Generally accepted auditing standards require that auditors prepare and use:
 a. A written engagement letter on all audits.
 b. Written client consents to discuss audit matters with successor auditors.
 c. A written audit program.

    d. Written time budgets and schedules for performing each audit.

4.27 The revenue cycle of a company generally includes these accounts:
    a. Inventory, accounts payable and general expenses.
    b. Inventory, general expenses and payroll.
    c. Cash, accounts receivable and sales.
    d. Cash, notes payable and capital stock.

4.28 When auditing the existence assertion for an asset, auditors proceed from the:
    a. Financial statement numbers back to the potentially unrecorded items.
    b. Potentially unrecorded items forward to the financial statement numbers.
    c. General ledger back to the supporting original transaction documents.
    d. Supporting original transaction documents to the general ledger.

4.29 The objective in an auditor's review of credit ratings of a client's customers is to obtain evidence related to management's assertion about:
    a. Compliance.
    b. Existence or occurrence.
    c. Rights and obligations
    d. Valuation or allocation

4.30 Jones, PA, is planning the audit of Rhonda's Company. Rhonda verbally asserts to Jones that all the expenses for the year have been recorded in the accounts. Rhonda's representation in this regard:
    a. Is sufficient evidence for Jones to conclude that the completeness assertion is supported for the expenses.
    b. Can enable Jones to minimize his work on the assessment of control risk for the completeness of expenses.
    c. Should be disregarded because it is not in writing.
    d. Is not considered a sufficient basis for Jones to conclude that all expenses have been recorded.

4.31 The evidence considered most competent by auditors is best described as:
    a. Internal documents, such as sales invoice copies produced under conditions of strong internal control.
    b. Written representations made by the president of the company.
    c. Documentary evidence obtained directly from independent external sources.
    d. Direct personal knowledge obtained through physical observation and mathematical recalculation.

4.32 Confirmations of accounts receivable provide evidence primarily about these two assertions:
    a. Completeness and valuation.
    b. Valuation and rights and obligations.
    c. Rights and obligations and existence.
    d. Existence and completeness.

4.33 When planning an audit, which of the following is not a factor that affects auditors' decisions about the quantity, type and content of audit working papers?
    a. The auditors' need to document compliance with generally accepted auditing standards.
    b. The existence of new sales contracts important for the client's business.
    c. The auditors' judgment about their independence with regard to the client.
    d. The auditors' judgments about materiality.

4.34 An audit working paper that shows the detailed evidence and procedures regarding the balance in the accumulated depreciation account for the year under audit will be found in the:
    a. Current file evidence working papers.
    b. Permanent file working papers.
    c. Administrative working papers in the current file.
    d. Planning memorandum in the current file.

4.35 An auditor's permanent file working papers would most likely contain:
    a. Internal control analysis for the current year.
    b. The latest engagement letter.
    c. Memoranda of conference with management.
    d. Excerpts of the corporate charter and by-laws.

EXERCISES AND PROBLEMS

4.36 Communications Between Predecessor and Successor Auditors. Assume that your client was audited last year by PA Diggs. Your client was generally pleased with the services provided by Diggs, but he thinks the audit work was too detailed and interfered excessively with normal office routines. You have asked your client to inform Diggs of the decision to change auditors, but he does not wish to do so.

Required:

List and discuss the steps you should follow with regard to dealing with a predecessor auditor and a new client before accepting the engagement. (Hint: Use the independence rules of conduct for a complete response to this requirement.)

4.37 Audit Planning. Walter Wolf was pleased. He had been with the firm of Riding, Hood & Co. less that a year-and-a-half since graduation from university and had received excellent performance reviews on every engagement. Now he was being given "in charge" responsibility on an audit. It was a small client, but it felt good to have the firm show such confidence in him. He planned to show that the firm had made the right decision.

Walter thought back to some of the advice his seniors had given him. Two comments in particular stood out as key steps to a successful audit:

- Careful attention to planning the audit pays dividends. Time spent on audit planning is never wasted.
- Avoid being a mechanical auditor by focusing on management's assertions embodied in the financial statements and the related audit objectives when planning audit tests.

Required:

a. Develop a list of tasks that Walter should perform in planning this audit engagement, before any audit testing begins.

b. *Handbook Section* 5300 lists seven management assertions embodied in financial statements. List and briefly describe the associated audit objectives that relate to these assertions.

(ICAO adapted)

Classes of Transactions	General Ledger Accounts
Cash receipts	Cash
Cash disbursements	Accounts receivable
Credit sales	Allowance for doubtful
Sales returns and allowances	accounts
Purchases on credit	Inventory
Purchase returns	Capital assets
Uncollectible account write-offs	Accounts payable
	Long-term debt
	Sales revenue
	Investment income
	Expenses

4.38 Understand the Business—Transactions and Accounts. In the table above, the left column names several "classes of transactions." The right column names several general ledger accounts.

Required:

Identify the general ledger accounts that are affected by each class of transactions.

Approach:

Match the classes of transactions with the general ledger accounts where their debits and credits are usually entered.

4.39 General Audit Procedures and Financial Statement Assertions. The six general audit procedures produce evidence about the principal management assertions in financial statements. However, some procedures are useful for producing evidence about certain assertions, while other procedures are useful for producing evidence about other assertions. The assertion being audited may influence the auditors' choice of procedures.

Required:

Prepare a two-column table with the six general procedures listed on the right. Opposite each one, write the management assertions most usefully audited by using each procedure.

4.40 Financial Assertions and Audit Objectives. You were engaged to examine the financial statements of Kingston Company for the year ended December 31.

Assume that on November 1, Kingston borrowed $500,000 from North Country Bank to finance plant expansion. The long-term note agreement provided for the annual payment of principal and interest over five years. The existing plant was pledged as security for the loan.

Due to the unexpected difficulties in acquiring the building site, the plant expansion did not begin on time. To make use of the borrowed funds, management decided to invest in stocks and bonds, and on November 16 the $500,000 was invested in securities.

Required:

What are the audit objectives for the audit of the investments in securities at December 31?

Approach:

Develop specific assertions related to securities (assets) based on the five general assertions.

4.41 Appropriateness of Evidence and Related Parties. Johnson & Company, PAs, audited the Guaranteed Trust Company. M. Johnson had the assignment of evaluating the collectibility of real estate loans. Johnson was working on two particular loans: (1) a $4 million loan secured by the Smith Street Apartments and (2) a $5.5 million construction loan on the Baker Street Apartments now being built. The appraisals performed by the Guaranteed Appraisal Partners, Inc., showed values in excess of the loan amounts. Upon enquiry, Mr. Bumpus, the trust company vice president for loan acquisition, stated: "I know the Smith Street loan is good because I myself own 40 percent of the partnership that owns the property and is obligated on the loan."

Johnson then wrote in the working papers: (1) the Smith Street loan appears collectible; Mr. Bumpus personally attested to knowledge of the collectibility as a major owner in the partnership obligated on the loan, (2) the Baker Street loan is assumed to be collectible because it is new and construction is still in progress, (3) the appraised values all exceed the loan amounts.

Required:
a. Do you perceive any problems with related party involvement in the evidence used by M. Johnson? Explain.
b. Do you perceive any problems with M. Johnson's reasoning or the appropriateness of evidence used in that reasoning?

4.42 Relative Appropriateness of Evidence. The third generally accepted standard of audit fieldwork requires that auditors obtain sufficient appropriate evidential matter to afford a reasonable basis for an opinion regarding the financial statements under examination. In considering what constitutes sufficient appropriate evidential matter, a distinction should be made between underlying accounting data and all corroborating information available to the auditor.

Required:
What presumptions can be made about:
a. The relative appropriateness of evidence obtained from external and internal sources.
b. The role of internal control with respect to internal evidence produced by a client's data processing system.
c. The relative persuasiveness of auditor observation and recalculation evidence compared to the external, external-internal and internal documentary evidence.

(AICPA adapted)

4.43 Relative Appropriateness of Evidence.
1. Classify the following evidential items by type (direct knowledge, external and so on), and rank them in order of appropriateness:
   a. Amounts shown on monthly statements from creditors.
   b. Amounts shown on "paid on account" in the voucher register.
   c. Amount of "discounts lost expense" computed by the auditor from unaudited supporting documents.
   d. Amounts shown in letters received directly from creditors.
2. Classify the following evidential items by type (direct knowledge, external and so on), and rank them in order of appropriateness.
   a. Amounts shown on a letter received directly from an independent bond trustee.
   b. Amounts obtained from minutes of board of directors' meetings.
   c. Auditors' computation of bond interest and amortization expense when remaining term and status of bond are audited.
   d. Amounts shown on cancelled cheques.

4.44 Audit Procedures. Auditors frequently refer to the terms *standards* and *procedures*. Standards deal with measures of the quality of performance. Standards specifically refer to the generally accepted auditing standards expressed in the Statements on Auditing Standards. Procedures specifically refer to the methods or techniques used by auditors in the conduct of the examination. Procedures are also expressed in the Statements on Auditing Standards.

Required:
List seven different types of procedures auditors can use during an audit of financial statements and give an example of each.

4.45 Confirmation Procedure. A PA accumulates various kinds of evidence on which to base the opinion on financial statements. Among this evidence are confirmations from third parties.

Required:
a. What is an audit confirmation?
b. What characteristics of the confirmation process and the recipient are important if a PA is to consider the confirmation evidence competent?

4.46 Audit Procedure Terminology. Identify the types of procedures(s) employed in each situation described below (vouching, tracing, recalculation, observation and so on):

1. An auditor uses computer software to select vendors' accounts payable with debit balances and compares amounts and computation to cash disbursements and vendor credit memos.

2. An auditor examines property insurance policies and checks insurance expense for the year. The auditor then reviews the expense in light of changes and ending balances in captial asset accounts.

3. An auditor uses computer software to test perpetual inventory records for items that have not been used in production for three months or more. The client states that the items are obsolete and have already been written down. The auditor checks journal entries to support the client's statements.

4. An auditor tests cash remittance advices to see that allowance and discounts are appropriate and that receipts are posted to the correct customer accounts in the right amounts and reviews the documents supporting unusual discounts and allowances.

5. An auditor watches the client take a physical inventory. A letter is also received from a public warehouser stating the amounts of the client's inventory stored in the warehouse. The company's cost flow assumption, FIFO,

is then tested by the auditor's computer software program.

4.47 Audit Working Papers. The preparation of working papers is an integral part of a PA's audit of financial statements. On a recurring engagement, PAs review their audit programs and working papers from their prior audit while planning the current audit to determine usefulness for the current-year work.

Required:

a. (1) What are the purposes or functions of audit working papers? (2) What records may be included in audit working papers?

b. What factors affect the PA's judgment of the type and content of the working papers for a particular engagement?

c. To comply with generally accepted auditing standards, a PA includes certain evidence in his or her working papers; for example, "evidence that the audit was planned and work of assistants was supervised and reviewed." What other evidence should a PA include in audit working papers to comply with generally accepted auditing standards?

d. How can a PA make the most effective use of the preceding year's audit programs in a recurring audit?

(AICPA adapted)

DISCUSSION CASES

4.48 Client Selection. You are a PA in a regional accounting firm that has 10 offices in three provinces. Mr. Shine has approached you with a request for an audit. He is president of Hitech Software and Games, Inc., a five-year-old company that has recently grown to $40 million in sales and $20 million in total assets. Mr. Shine is thinking about going public with a $17 million issue of common shares, of which $10 million would be a secondary issue of shares he holds. You are very happy about this opportunity because you know Mr. Shine is the new president of the Symphony Society board and has made quite a civic impression since he came to your medium-size city seven years ago. Hitech is one of the growing employers in the city.

Required:

a. Discuss the sources of information and the types of enquiries you and the firm's partners can make in connection with accepting Hitech as a new client.

b. Does the profession require any investigation of prospective clients?

c. Suppose Mr. Shine has also told you that 10 years ago his closely held hamburger franchise business went bankrupt, and upon investigation you learn from its former auditors (your own firm) that Shine played "fast and loose" with franchise-fee income recognition rules and presented such difficulties that your office in another city resigned from the audit (before the bankruptcy). Do you think the partner in charge of the audit practice should accept Hitech as a new client?

4.49 Predecessor and Successor Auditors. The president of Allpurpose Loan Company had a genuine dislike for external auditors. Almost any conflict generated a towering rage. Consequently, the company changed auditors often.

Wells & Ratley, PAs, was recently hired to audit the 2003 financial statements. The W&R firm succeeded the firm of Canby & Company, which had obtained the audit after Albrecht & Hubbard had been fired. A&H audited the 2002 financial statements and rendered a report that contained an additional paragraph explaining an uncertainty about Allpurpose Loan Company's loan loss reserve. Goodby A&H! The president then hired Canby & Company to audit the 2003 financial statements, and Art Canby started the work. But before the audit could be completed, Canby was fired, and W&R was hired to complete the audit. Canby & Company did not issue an audit report because the audit was not finished.

Required:

Does the Wells & Ratley firm need to initiate communications with Canby & Company? with Albrecht & Hubbard? with both? Explain your response in terms of the purposes of communications between predecessor and successor auditors.

4.50 Potential Audit Procedure Failures. For each of the general audit procedures of (*a*) recalculation, (*b*) physical observations, (*c*) confirmation (accounts receivable, securities or other assets), (*d*) verbal enquiry, (*e*) examination of internal documents, and (*f*) scanning, discuss one way the procedure could be misapplied or the auditors could be misled in such a way as to render the work (audit evidence) mis-

leading or irrelevant. Give examples different from the examples in Chapter 4.

4.51 Risk of Misstatement in Various Accounts. Based on information you have available in Chapter 4:

a. Which accounts may be most susceptible to overstatement? to understatement?

b. Why do you think a company might permit asset accounts to be understated?

c. Why do you think a company might permit liability accounts to be overstated?

d. Which direction of misstatement is most likely: income overstatement or income understatement?

4.52 Working Paper Review. The schedule in Exhibit 4.52–1 was prepared by the controller of World Manufacturing, Inc., for use by the independent auditors during their examination of World's financial statements. All procedures performed by the audit assistant were noted in the bottom "Legend" section, and it was initialled properly, dated and indexed, and then submitted to a senior member of the audit staff for review. Internal control was reviewed and is considered to be satisfactory.

Required:

a. What information essential to the audit of marketable securities is missing from the schedule?

b. What essential audit procedures were not noted as having been performed by the audit assistant?

Approach:

Write specific assertions based on the five general assertions, then look to the working paper for documentation of evidence related to each one.

(AICPA adapted)

E X H I B I T 4.52–1   MARKETABLE SECURITIES (World Manufacturing, Inc., year ended December 31, 2002)

Description of Security			Serial No.	Face Value of Bonds	General Ledger 1/1	Purchased in 2002	Sold in 2002	Cost	General Ledger 12/31	12/31 Market	Pay Date(s)	Amt. Received	Accruals 12/31
Corp. Bonds	%	Yr. Due										*Dividend and Interest*	
											1/15	300**b,d**	
A	6	09	21-7	10,000	9,400**a**				9,400	9,100	7/15	300**b,d**	275
D	4	03	73-0	30,000	27,500**a**				27,500	26,220	12/1	1,200**b,d**	100
G	9	06	16-4	5,000	4,000**a**				4,000	5,080	8/1	450**b,d**	188
R**c**	5	03	08/2	70,000	66,000**a**		57,000**b**	66,000					
S**c**	10	07	07-4	100,000		100,000**e**			100,000	101,250	7/1	5,000**b,d**	5,000
					106,900	100,000	57,000	66,000	140,900	141,650		7,250	5,563
					a,f	**f**	**f**	**f**	**f,g**	**f**		**f**	**f**

Stocks

											3/1	750**b,d**	
P 1,000 shs			1,044		75,00**a**				7,500	7,600	6/1	750**b,d**	
Common											9/1	750**b,d**	
											12/1	750**b,d**	250
											3/1	750**b,d**	
U 50 shs			8,530		9,700**a**				9,700	9,800	2/1	800**b,d**	
Common											8/1	800**b,d**	667
					17,200				17,200	17,400		4,600	917
					a,f				**f,g**	**f**		**f**	**f**

Legends and comments relative to above:
a = Beginning balances agreed to 2001 working papers.
b = Traced to cash receipts.
c = Minutes examined (purchase and sales approved by the board of directors).
d = Agreed to 1099.
e = Confirmed by tracing to broker's advice.
f = Totals footed.
g = Agreed to general ledger.

APPENDIX 4A

FRAMEWORKS FOR STRATEGIC ANALYSIS

There are many frameworks for performing strategic analysis. Among them are product life cycle analysis, SWOT (Strength, Weaknesses, Opportunities and Threats) analysis, PEST (Political-Legal, Economic, Social and Technological) analysis and Porter's Five Forces model. This appendix covers two common approaches, an environment-centred approach (PEST analysis) and the firm's position in the industry (Porter's Five Forces model). Many auditing students complete a course in strategic management that will cover all of these and more in detail.

PEST analysis

PEST refers to four contextual categories that form the environment in which a firm operates:

- Political-Legal factors
- Economic factors
- Social factors
- Technological factors.

Overall, the PEST analysis should be a "broad brush." The factors that are considered in a PEST analysis may include:

1) **Political factors:** (a) government stability, (b) taxation policy, (c) government spending, (d) government relations with other countries, (e) industrial policy (e.g., towards privatization, regulation and nationalization).
   Legal factors: (a) employment law, (b) monopolies and mergers legislation, (c) environmental protection laws, (d) foreign trade regulations.

2) **Economic factors:** (a) inflation, (b) employment, (c) disposable income, (d) business cycles, (e) interest rates, (f) GNP growth rates, (g) exchange rates, (h) energy and basic raw materials prices.

3) **Social and cultural factors:** (a) population demographics, (b) income distribution, (c) levels of education, (d) lifestyle changes, (e) attitudes to work and leisure, (f) consumerism, (g) social mobility.

4) **Technological factors:** (a) new discoveries/developments in our own or related (e.g., supplier) industry, (b) speed of technology transfer (diffusion), (c) government spending on research, (d) rates of obsolescence.

The PEST analysis addresses the "big picture" in which a firm operates. It provides the context in which to perform a more detailed industry level analysis.

Porter's Five Forces Model

In order to understand the client's position in the industry, Porter's Five Forces Model aids in understanding the competitive pressures at work on the firm.[7] The intensity of these pressures as a whole will determine relative industry profitability and greatly influence relative firm profit potential. Exhibit 4–11 shows the relationship among the five forces.

- **Threat of new entrants** is largely determined by such factors as: economies of scale, proprietary product differences, brand identity, buyer switching costs, capital requirements, access to distribution, absolute cost advantages, government policy and new entrants' fear of retaliation.

---

[7] For more details see Chapter 1 of M. Porter. *Competitive Advantage.* Free Press, 1985.

E X H I B I T 4–11   PORTER'S FIVE FORCES

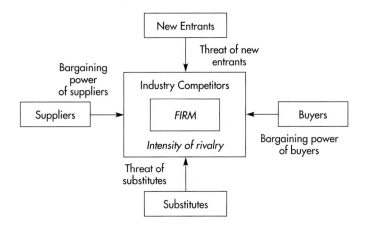

- **Bargaining power of buyers** is largely determined by two factors: bargaining leverage and price sensitivity. Bargaining leverage is mainly determined by buyer concentration versus firm concentration, buyer volume, buyer switching costs relative to firm switching costs, buyer information and the ability of firm to backward integrate. Price sensitivity is largely governed by price of component versus total purchases needed to make product, product differences, brand identity, impact of component on quality/performance and buyer profits.
- **Threat of substitutes** is mostly determined by relative price performance of substitute products, buyer switching costs and buyer propensity to substitute.
- **Bargaining power of suppliers** is mainly determined by differentiation of inputs, switching costs of suppliers and firms in the industry, presence of substitute inputs, supplier concentration, importance of volume to supplier, cost relative to total purchases in the industry and threat of forward integration of supplier versus backward integration of firms in the industry.
- **Intensity of competitor rivalry** is largely determined by industry growth, intermittent overcapacity, fixed costs/value added, product differences, branch identity, switching costs, concentration and balance, informational complexity, diversity of competitors and exit barriers from industry.

Upon completing this analysis, the auditor has the information necessary to understand the firm's strategy and position in the industry.

CHAPTER 5

Learning Objectives

Chapter 5 continues the coverage of audit fieldwork planning started in Chapter 4. This chapter deals with some of the tools of planning—the application of analytical procedures at the beginning of an audit, the materiality determination and tolerable misstatement assignment decisions and the assessment of risks with reference to the audit risk model, all leading up to the preparation of audit programs. After studying Chapter 5, you should be able to:

1. Perform analytical procedures using unaudited financial statements to identify potential problems in the accounts.

2. Analyse a materiality determination case and decide upon a maximum amount of misstatement (planning materiality) acceptable in a company's financial statements.

3. Assign an overall planning materiality amount to the tolerable misstatement amounts for particular accounts.

4. Describe the conceptual audit risk model and explain the meaning and importance of its components in terms of professional judgment and audit planning.

5. Describe the content and purpose of audit programs.

AUDIT PLANNING WITH ANALYTICAL PROCEDURES,

RISKS AND MATERIALITY

AUDIT PLANNING

After the auditors finish the pre-engagement arrangements, understand the audit client's business and industry and obtain the unaudited financial statements, certain planning tools can be used to guide and direct the audit work. In this chapter these audit tools are classified as preliminary analytical procedures, materiality decisions, general risk assessment and audit programs. The usefulness of the first three is to help the auditors design the audit programs. For our study purposes, the topics are arranged in the following sequence.

Audit planning tools

The activities, concepts and tools introduced in Chapters 4 and 5 continue in Chapter 6 (Control Risk Assessment) and Chapter 7 (Audit Sampling). Basic sampling concepts are covered in Chapter 7 and basic computer audit concepts are covered in Chapter 8. More advanced topics in computer audit and sampling are covered in Chapters 20 and 21, respectively. Audit applications in specific accounts and cycles are in Chapters 9 to 14.

PRELIMINARY ANALYTICAL PROCEDURES

According to auditing standards, analytical procedures should be applied in the beginning planning stages of each audit (*Section* 5301.11) and as part of the overall evaluation at the end of the audit (*Section* 5301.27). ISA 520.2 gives the same requirements. These procedures were introduced in Chapter 4 and described in terms of five general types of procedures. For review, they are:

1. Comparison of current-year account balances to balances for one or more comparable periods.
2. Comparison of the current-year account balances to anticipated results found in the company's budgets and forecasts.
3. Evaluation of the relationships of current-year account balances to other current-year balances for conformity with predictable patterns based on the company's experience.
4. Comparison of current-year account balances and financial relationships (e.g., ratios) with similar information for the industry in which the company operates.
5. Study of the relationships of current-year account balances with relevant nonfinancial information (e.g., physical production statistics).

139

WHAT'S IN THE MINUTES OF MEETINGS?

Boards of directors are supposed to monitor the client's business. The minutes of their meetings and the meetings of their committees (e.g., executive committee, finance committee, compensation committee, audit committee) frequently contain information of vital interest to the independent auditors. Some examples:

- Amount of dividends declared.
- Authorization of officers' salaries.
- Authorization of stock options and other "perk" compensation.
- Acceptance of contracts, agreements, lawsuit settlements.
- Approval of major purchases of property and investments.
- Discussions of merger and divestiture progress. Authorization of financing by share issues, long-term debt and leases.
- Approval to pledge assets as security for debts.
- Discussion of negotiations on bank loans and payment waivers.
- Approval of accounting policies and accounting for estimates and unusual transactions.
- Authorizations for individuals to sign bank cheques.

Auditors take notes or make copies of important parts of these minutes and compare them with information in the accounts and disclosures (e.g., compare the amount of dividends declared to the amount paid, compare officers' authorized salaries to amounts paid, compare agreements to pledge assets to proper disclosure in the notes to financial statements).

Because of the importance that the minutes have in determining what needs to be disclosed in order to obtain fair presentation, denial of access to the minutes of the board of directors meeting constitutes a major scope restriction by the client. Such denial is a common source of opinion reservation.

Analytical procedures can take many forms, ranging from simple to complex. For the more simple and easily applied procedures, auditors have begun to define a wide range of early information-gathering activity as "analytical procedures," including: (*a*) review of adjustments proposed in prior years' audits; (*b*) conversations with client personnel; (*c*) reading and study of the minutes of the meetings of directors and committees of the board of directors (e.g., executive committee, finance committee, compensation committee, audit committee); (*d*) review of the corporate charter and bylaws or partnership agreement; (*e*) review of contracts, agreements and legal proceedings; (*f*) and many other activities that do not fit the strict definition of the five general types of analytical procedures. The purpose of this work is "attention directing"—to alert the audit team to problems (errors, irregularities) in the account balances and disclosures. The effectiveness of some of these activities was reviewed in Chapter 4 (see Exhibit 4–7).

Other analytical procedures can be complex, including mathematical time series and regression calculations, complicated comparisons of multiyear data, and trend and ratio analyses. In the sections that follow, two of the more complicated general analytical procedures are emphasized: (number 1) comparison of current year account balances to balances for one or more comparable periods, and (number 3) evaluation of the relationships of current-year account balances to other current-year balances for conformity with predictable patterns based on the company's experience.

More mathematical approaches to analytical review are covered in Chapter 20.

5.1 What are the five types of general analytical procedures?

5.2 What is the purpose of performing preliminary analytical procedures in the audit planning stage?

5.3 What official documents and authorizations should an auditor read when performing preliminary analytical procedures?

5.4 What important information can be found in directors' minutes about officers' compensation? Business operations? Corporate finance? Accounting policies and control?

ANALYSIS OF UNAUDITED FINANCIAL STATEMENTS

LEARNING OBJECTIVE

1. Perform analytical procedures using unaudited financial statements to identify potential problems in the accounts.

Horizontal analysis refers to changes of financial statement numbers and ratios across two or more years. Vertical analysis refers to financial statement amounts expressed each year as proportions of a base, such as sales for the income statement accounts and total assets for the balance sheet accounts. Auditors look for relationships that do not make sense as indicators of problems in the accounts, and they use such indicators to plan further audit work.

Attention Directing

In the planning stage, analytical procedures are used to identify potential problem areas so that subsequent audit work can be designed to reduce the risk of missing something important. The application demonstrated below thus can be described as attention directing—pointing out accounts that may contain errors and irregularities. The insights derived from preliminary analytical procedures do not provide direct evidence about the numbers in the financial statements. They only help the audit team plan the audit program.

An Organized Approach

With an organized approach—a standard starting place—preliminary analytical procedures can provide considerable familiarity with the client's business. Many auditors start with comparative financial statements and calculate common-size statements (vertical analysis) and year-to-year change in balance sheet and income statement accounts (horizontal analysis). This is the start of describing the financial activities for the current year under audit. Exhibit 5–1 contains financial balances for the prior year (consider them audited) and the current year (consider them unaudited at this stage). Common-size statements (vertical) are shown in parallel columns, and the dollar amount and percentage change (horizontal) are shown in the last two columns. These are some basic beginning analytical data.

Describe the Financial Activities

After generating these basic financial data, the next step is to describe the financial changes and relationships you can see in the data. According to the unaudited financial statements in Exhibit 5–1, the company increased the net income by increasing sales 10 percent, reducing cost of goods sold as a proportion of sales and controlling other expenses. At least some of the sales growth appears to have been prompted by easier credit (larger accounts receivable) and more service (more equipment in use). The company also used much of its cash and borrowed more to purchase the equipment, to make its payment on the long-term debt, and to pay dividends.

EXHIBIT 5-1   ANYCOMPANY, INC.—PRELIMINARY ANALYTICAL PROCEDURES DATA

	Prior Year		Current Year		Change	
	Balance	Common Size	Balance	Common Size	Amount	Percent Change
Assets						
Cash	$ 600,000	14.78%	$ 200,000	4.12%	($ 400,000)	−66.67%
Accounts receivable	500,000	12.32	900,000	18.56	400,000	80.00
Allowance doubtful accounts	(40,000)	−0.99	(50,000)	−1.03	(10,000)	25.00
Inventory	1,500,000	36.95	1,600,000	32.99	100,000	6.67
Total current assets	2,560,000	63.05	2,650,000	54.63	90,000	3.52
Equipment	3,000,000	73.89	4,000,000	82.47	1,000,000	33.33
Accumulated amortization	(1,500,000)	−36.95	(1,800,000)	−37.11	(300,000)	20.00
Total assets	$4,060,000	100.00%	$4,850,000	100.00%	$ 790,000	19.46%
Liabilities and Equity						
Accounts payable	$ 500,000	12.32%	$ 400,000	8.25%	($ 100,000)	−20.00%
Bank loans, 11%	0	0.00	750,000	15.46	750,000	
Accrued interest	60,000	1.48	40,000	0.82	(20,000)	−33.33
Total current liabilities	560,000	13.79	1,190,000	24.53	630,000	112.50
Long-term debt, 10%	600,000	14.78	400,000	8.25	(200,000)	−33.33
Total liabilities	1,160,000	28.57	1,590,000	32.78	430,000	37.07
Share capital	2,000,000	49.26	2,000,000	41.24	0	0.00
Retained earnings	900,000	22.17	1,260,000	25.98	360,000	40.00
Total liabilities and equity	$4,060,000	100.00%	$4,850,000	100.00%	$ 790,000	19.46%
Income						
Sales (net)	$9,000,000	100.00%	$9,900,000	100.00%	$ 900,000	10.00%
Cost of goods sold	6,750,000	75.00	7,200,000	72.73	450,000	6.67
Gross margin	2,250,000	25.00	2,700,000	27.27	450,000	20.00
General expense	1,590,000	17.67	1,734,000	17.52	144,000	9.06
Amortization	300,000	3.33	300,000	3.03	0	0.00
Operating income	360,000	4.00	666,000	6.46	306,000	85.00
Interest expense	60,000	0.67	40,000	0.40	(20,000)	−33.33
Income taxes (40%)	120,000	1.33	256,000	2.59	136,000	113.33
Net income	$ 180,000	2.00%	$ 370,000	3.74%	$ 190,000	105.56%

Ask Relevant Questions

The next step is to ask: "What could be wrong?" and "What errors and irregularities, as well as legitimate explanations, could account for these financial results?" For this explanation we will limit attention to the accounts receivable and inventory accounts. At this point some other ratios can help support the analysis. Exhibit 5–2 contains several familiar ratios. (Appendix 5A at the end of this chapter contains these ratios and their formulas.)

Question: Are the accounts receivable collectible? (Alternative: Is the allowance for doubtful accounts large enough?) Easier credit can lead to more bad debts. The company has a much larger amount of receivables (Exhibit 5–1), the days' sales in receivables has increased significantly (Exhibit 5–2), the receivables turnover has decreased (Exhibit 5–2), and the allowance for doubtful accounts is smaller in proportion to the receivables (Exhibit 5–2). If the prior-year allowance for bad debts at 8 percent of receivables was appropriate, and conditions have not become worse, perhaps the allowance should be closer to $72,000 than $50,000. The auditors should work carefully on the evidence related to accounts receivable valuation.

Question: Could the inventory be overstated? (Alternative: Could the cost of the goods sold be understated?) Overstatement of the ending inventory would cause the cost of goods sold to be understated. The percentage of cost of goods sold to sales shows a decrease (Exhibits 5–1 and 5–2). If the 75 percent of the prior year represents a more accurate cost

EXHIBIT 5–2   ANYCOMPANY, INC.—SELECTED FINANCIAL RATIOS

	Prior Year	Current Year	Percent Change
Balance Sheet Ratios			
Current ratio	4.57	2.23	−51.29%
Days' sales in receivables	18.40	30.91	67.98
Doubtful accounts ratio	0.0800	0.0556	−30.56
Days' sales in inventory	80.00	80.00	0.00
Debt/equity ratio	0.40	0.49	21.93
Operations Ratios			
Receivables turnover	19.57	11.65	−40.47
Inventory turnover	4.50	4.50	0.00
Cost of goods sold/sales	75.00%	72.73%	−3.03
Gross margin percentage	25.00%	27.27%	9.09
Return on beginning equity	6.62%	12.76%	92.80
Financial Distress Ratios (Altman, 1968, Appendix 5A)			
Working capital/total assets	0.49	0.30	−38.89
Retained earnings/total assets	0.22	0.26	17.20
EBIT/total assets	0.09	0.14	54.87
Market value of equity/total debt	2.59	1.89	−27.04
Net sales/total assets	2.22	2.04	−7.92
Discriminant Z score	4.96	4.35	−12.32

of goods sold, then the income before taxes may be overstated by $225,000 (75 percent of $9.9 million minus $7.2 million unaudited cost of goods sold). The days' sales in inventory and the inventory turnover remained the same (Exhibit 5–2), but you might expect them to change in light of the larger volume of sales. Careful work on the physical count and valuation of inventory appears to be needed.

Other questions can be asked and other relationships derived when industry statistics are available. Industry statistics can be obtained from such services as Statistics Canada, Dun & Bradstreet and Robert Morris Associates. These statistics include industry averages for important financial yardsticks, such as gross profit margin, return on sales, current ratio and debt/net worth. A comparison with client data may reveal out-of-line statistics, indicating a relatively strong feature of the company, a weak financial position or possibly an error or misstatement in the client's financial statements. However, care must be taken with industry statistics. A particular company may or may not be well represented by industry averages.

Comparing reported financial results with internal budgets and forecasts also can be useful. If the budget or forecast represents management's estimate of probable future outcomes, planning questions can arise for items that fall short of or exceed the budget. If a company expected to sell 10,000 units of a product but sold only 5,000 units, the auditors would want to plan a careful lower-of-cost-or-market study of the inventory of unsold units. If 15,000 were sold, an auditor would want to audit for sales validity. Budget comparisons can be tricky, however. Some companies use budgets and forecasts as goals, rather than as expressions of probable outcomes. Also, meeting the budget with little or no shortfall or excess can result from managers manipulating the numbers to "meet the budget." Auditors must be careful to know something about a company's business conditions from sources other than the internal records when analysing comparisons with budgets and forecasts. This is especially important under the new SSA audits (see Appendix 5B).

Funds Flow Analysis

If the client has not already prepared the statement of changes in financial position, the auditors can use the comparative financial statements to prepare one. The analysis of changes in financial position enables the auditors to see the crucial information of funds flow from operating, investment and financing activities. A funds flow deficit from operations may signal financial difficulty. Companies fail when they run out of cash (no surprise) and are unable to pay their debts when they become due.

You can use the information in Exhibit 5–1 to prepare a statement of changes in financial position (or "cash flow statement" as per *Section* 1540.01). This is an exercise in a technique you learned in earlier accounting courses.

Analytical Procedures Requirements

Even though particular analytical procedures are not required by audit standards, the timing of required application is specified in two instances. Analytical procedures applicable in the circumstances are required (1) at the beginning of an audit—the planning stage application of analytical procedures discussed in this chapter—and (2) at the end of an audit when the partners in charge review the overall quality of the work and look for apparent problems.

A recent study found that analytical procedures are most effective when used in an integrative fashion with other sources of information, especially when accompanied by a strong knowledge of the client's business. "Auditors must combine different types of knowledge (accounting, general business, industry and client-specific) and issues (operating, financing and investing) into a whole. This skill is needed whether analytical procedures are used for planning, substantive testing or overall review purposes, but it appears to be most critical at overall review, where the auditor's goal is to examine the financial statements to determine whether they make sense taken as a whole." (E. Hirst, L. Koonce, F. Philipps, *CA Magazine*, August 1998, p. 41.)

. . . .

R E V I E W
CHECKPOINTS

5.5 What are the steps auditors can use to apply comparison and ratio analysis to unaudited financial statements?

5.6 What are some of the ratios that can be used in preliminary analytical procedures?

5.7 Is anything questionable about the relationship between retained earnings and income as shown in Exhibit 5–1?

. . . .

PRELIMINARY ASSESSMENT OF PLANNING MATERIALITY
. . . .

Audit planning tools

| Preliminary analytical procedures | Preliminary materiality decisions | Preliminary risk assessment | Audit programs |

LEARNING OBJECTIVE

2. Analyse a materiality determination case and decide upon a maximum amount of misstatement (planning materiality) acceptable in a company's financial statements.

When planning an audit, auditors should think about "planning materiality" as the largest amount of uncorrected dollar misstatement that could exist in published financial statements, yet they would still fairly present the company's financial position and results of operations in conformity with GAAP. Accounting firms, however, differ greatly on how to carry out this idea. Some believe in the "blunt instrument" approach to auditing—just beat the accounts to death for the evidence. Some of these auditors go to an engagement and start performing procedures without bothering with theoretical niceties of making preliminary materiality estimates. Some firms tell their staffs to "think about it, but don't try to put a number on it." Some firms guide their staffs with directions about how to use numbers to quantify a preliminary materiality amount.

Financial Statement Materiality

So what is materiality, and how can you deal with it? The concept of materiality pervades financial accounting and reporting in this context: Information is material and should be disclosed if it is likely to influence the economic decisions of financial statement users. The emphasis is on the users' point of view, not on accountants' and managers' points of view. Thus, material information is a synonym for important or significant information (ISA 320).

Financial statement measurements and information in some footnote disclosures are not perfectly accurate. However, you should not leap to the unwarranted conclusion that financial reports are inherently imprecise and inaccurate. Some numbers are not perfectly accurate because mistakes exist in them, and some are not perfectly accurate because they are based on estimates. Everyone acknowledges that people make mistakes—billing a customer the wrong amount, using the wrong prices to compile an inventory, making a mathematical mistake in an amortization calculation. Furthermore, many financial measurements are based on estimates; for example, the estimated depreciable lives of fixed assets or the estimated amount of uncollectible accounts receivable. However, this imprecise nature of accounting should not be taken as licence to be sloppy about clerical accuracy or negligent in accounting judgments (e.g., see box on next page).

Auditors are limited by the nature of accounting. Some amount of inaccuracy is permitted in financial statements because (1) unimportant inaccuracies do not affect users' decisions and hence are not material, (2) the cost of finding and correcting small errors is too great, and (3) the time taken to find them would delay issuance of financial statements. As a leading accountant once said, summing up materiality thought: "If it doesn't really matter, don't bother with it."[1] Accounting numbers are not perfectly accurate, but accountants and auditors want to maintain that financial reports are materially accurate and do not contain material misstatements.

Materiality Judgment Criteria

Many accountants wish that definitive, quantitative materiality guides could be issued, but many also fear the rigidity of such guides. The CICA offers some rules of thumb in its "Applying Materiality and Audit Risk Concepts in Conducting an Audit" Guideline (AUG–7):

1. 5–10% of income before taxes   [paragraph 6]
2. 1/2% to 1% of assets
3. 1/2% to 5% of equity   [paragraph 8]
4. 1/2% to 1% of revenue
5. 1/2% to 5% of gross profit

The CICA suggests that if income is used it should be adjusted for abnormal or extraordinary items. Also, if income is negative or close to zero a "normalized income based on some averaging could be used." But caution should be used in "normalizing" so that it is reasonable. If it is difficult to justify normalized income such as when income is negative or too small relative to other items, then a different basis such as rules 2 to 5 should be used instead of rule 1. The rules of thumb can't just be applied mechanically as auditors must consider a number of factors in setting materiality. Some of the more common factors auditors use in making materiality judgments are these:

---

[1] Ernest L. Hicks, "Materiality," *Journal of Accounting Research*, Autumn 1964, p. 158.

AUDIT CONSIDERATIONS FOR ACCOUNTING ESTIMATES

An accounting estimate is an approximation of a financial statement number, and estimates are often included in financial statements. (See *Handbook Section* 5305 or ISA 540.3.)

Examples include net realizable value of accounts receivable, market (lower than cost) of inventory, amortization expense, property and casualty insurance loss reserves, percentage-of-completion contract revenues, pension expense and warranty liabilities.

Management is responsible for making accounting estimates. Auditors are responsible for determining that all appropriate estimates have been made, that they are reasonable and that they are presented in conformity with GAAP and adequately disclosed.

Part of the audit process entails the auditors producing their own estimate and comparing it to management's estimate. Often, consideration of a range for an amount is involved. For example, management may estimate an allowance for doubtful accounts to be $50,000, and the auditors may estimate that the allowance could be $40,000 to $55,000. In this case management's estimate is within the auditors' range of reasonableness. However, the auditors should take note that the management estimate leans toward the conservative side (more than the auditors' $40,000 lower estimate, but not much less than the auditors' higher $55,000 estimate). If other estimates exhibit the same conservatism, and the effect is material, the auditors will need to evaluate the overall reasonableness of the effect of all estimates taken together.

If the auditors develop an estimate that differs (e.g., a range of $55,000 to $70,000 for the allowance that management estimated at $50,000), the preferred treatment is to consider the difference between management's estimate and the closest end of the auditors' range as an error (in this case, error = $5,000 = auditors' $55,000 minus management's $50,000). The remaining difference to the farthest end of the range ($15,000 = $70,000 − $55,000) is noted and reconsidered in combination with the findings on all management's estimates.

The best evidence of the reasonableness of estimates is the actual subsequent experience of the company with the financial amounts estimated at an earlier date. Keeping track of the accuracy of management's earlier estimates could provide the auditor with important information on the expected accuracy of future estimates.

Absolute Size

An amount of potential misstatement may be important regardless of any other considerations. Not many auditors use absolute size alone as a criterion because a given amount, say $50,000, may be appropriate in one case and too large or too small in another. Yet, some auditors have been known to say: "$1 million or some other large number is material, no matter what."

Relative Size

The relationship of potential misstatement to a relevant base number is often used. Potential misstatements in income statement accounts usually are related to net income either before or after taxes. If income fluctuates widely, a "normalized" or average income over recent years may be substituted for the current-year net income, or the relationship may be to the trend change of income. The base for nonprofit entities may be gross revenue or contributions or a figure important in the statement of changes in financial position. Potential misstatements in balance sheet accounts may be related to a subtotal number, such as current assets or net working capital. Some auditors prefer the total gross margin as a uniform base because it is less subject to year-to-year fluctuations than the net income number.

Nature of the Item or Issue

An important qualitative factor is the descriptive nature of the item or issue. An illegal payment is important primarily because of its nature as well as because of its absolute or relative amount. A misstatement in segment information may be small in relation to the total business but important for analysis of the segment. Generally, potential errors in the more liquid assets (cash, receivables and inventory) are considered more important than potential errors in other accounts (such as capital assets and deferred charges). Other qualitative factors include whether a misstatement affects the trend of earnings, whether analysts' forecasts are met and whether a loan covenant is violated. Such qualitative factors can be very important as noted by SEC Chairman Arthur Levitt: "Missing an earnings projection by a penny, for example, can result in a loss of millions in market capitalization."

Circumstances

Auditors generally place extra emphasis on lesser permitted misstatement in financial statements that will be widely used (publicly held companies) or used by important outsiders (bank loan officers). Auditors' liability is a relevant consideration. When management can exercise discretion over an accounting treatment, auditors tend to exercise more care and use a more stringent materiality criterion. Troublesome political events in foreign countries also can cause auditors to try to be more accurate with measurements and disclosures. However, these matters relate as much to risks as they do to financial statement materiality.

Cumulative Effects

Auditors must evaluate the sum of known or potential misstatements. Considering five different $15,000 mistakes that all increase net income as immaterial is inappropriate when the net income-based materiality limit is $50,000.

MATERIALITY ALLOCATION VERSUS NONALLOCATION

. . . .

LEARNING OBJECTIVE

3. Assign an overall planning materiality amount to the tolerable misstatement amounts for particular accounts.

To plan the audit of various accounts, some auditors assign part of the planning materiality to each account. The amount assigned to an account is called the **tolerable misstatement** for that account. The tolerable misstatement is the amount by which a particular account may be misstated (error not discovered by auditors!), yet still not cause the financial statements taken as a whole to be materially misleading. Thus, tolerable misstatement for each account is based on the overall financial statement materiality.

The extent to which tolerable misstatement is "based on" the overall materiality amount may vary from auditor to auditor. One method assigns tolerable misstatement amounts that add up to twice the overall materiality. The theory is that actual financial misstatements in accounts can be both overstatements and understatements, and the two directions will tend to balance out. Another is to assign tolerable misstatement in amounts such that the square root of the sum of the squared tolerable misstatements is equal to the overall materiality. The theory here is that the different misstatements behave like random errors in a calculation of statistical variance. Another method is to assign tolerable misstatement amounts that exactly add up to materiality. This method assumes that the worst case is that all the errors in the account balances have the same directional effect on income (i.e., overstatement of understatement, but not some of both). All these approaches are examples of materiality allocation. The simplest approach, however, is to not allocate but to use the same overall materiality level for the entire audit. This approach also results in the least testing and is implied by the *CICA Handbook.* This simplest approach is the one used in this textbook. Thus, tolerable misstatements will be set equal to overall materiality, and there is no difference between accounting and auditing materiality.[2] These issues are covered in more detail in Chapter 20.

Consider a materiality judgement for the current-year financial information of Anycompany, Inc., shown in Exhibit 5–1. The judgement involves centring attention on the most impor-

---

[2] Depending on factors used in setting overall materiality, there may be secondary materiality levels (less than overall materiality) necessary to satisfy the requirements of certain specific users (for example, a bank that has negotiated loan covenants as part of the loan agreement). In these situations a secondary materiality level(s) may apply to some restricted accounts (e.g., current assets) but overall materiality to all the rest. See D. Leslie's *Materiality, The Concept and Its Application to Auditing,* CICA, 1985, Chapter 2.

A Possible Relative Size Materiality Determination Illustrated

Suppose the auditors take the influence of earnings per share (EPS) on share price as an important consideration in determining materiality. For illustrative purposes, suppose the model for share price determination is a simple EPS multiple. (This is not to suggest that share prices actually are determined by such a simple method as multiplying the EPS in all cases. Analysts and investors use many other valuation models beyond the scope of this illustration.)

Assume that Anycompany, Inc., whose financial statements are in Exhibit 5–1, has 100,000 shares outstanding and its shares trade at a 14 price-earning multiple, thus indicating a share price of $51.80. (Share price = EPS ($3.70 = $370,000/100,000) *14 = $51.80.) The auditors must make a judgment about how much investors could overpay for the shares, yet it would not make any difference to them, say 5 percent to 10 percent.

	Low (5%)	High (10%)
Indicated share price (14 × $3.70)	$ 51.80	$ 51.80
Price materiality judgment	2.59	5.18
Adjusted share price	49.21	46.62
Adjusted earnings per share (divide by 14 multiple)	3.52	3.33
Indicated net income (multiply by 100,000 shares)	352,000	333,000
Add pretax accounts that can be audited completely:		
Interest expense	40,000	40,000
Income tax expense (40%)	234,667	222,000
Indicated pretax income*	626,667	595,000
Unaudited pretax income	666,000	666,000
Indicated planning materiality based on pretax income	39,333	71,000

*Calculate the pretax income, which, when reduced by interest expense and 40 percent income taxes, produces the indicated net income (after-tax).

tant financial decisions that may be related to the use of the financial statements. This centre of attention can be different for different audits. In some cases the centre of attention may be the current asset-liability position of a company in financial difficulty seeking to renew its bank loans. Such a company may be experiencing operating losses, and the balance sheet, rather than the income statement, is of utmost importance. In other cases the income statement and the net income number may be the most important because the company is growing and issuing shares to the public, so that decisions based on income performance are of greatest importance. The illustration boxed above shows a calculation of overall materiality based on an assumed effect of income misstatement on the share price. If the auditors decide the shares could be mispriced by 10 percent, and nobody would care, then the income before taxes and interest could be overstated (or understated) by as much as $71,000.

While the overall materiality assessment may frequently start with an expression of materiality for an income statement number, the materiality is audited in relation to one or more balance sheet accounts. The reason for this phenomenon is that income misstatements in the double-entry bookkeeping system leave a "dangling debit" or a "dangling credit" loose somewhere in the balance sheet accounts, and the audit challenge is to find it. If there is no dangling debit or credit, then the other side of the misstatement transaction has gone through the income statement, probably causing misstatement in two accounts (opposite directions), with no net effect on the net income bottom line. (For example, if fictitious credit sales were recorded, and the fictitious accounts receivable were written off as bad debt expense, both the revenue and expense would be overstated but the income would not be misstated.)

Even though we will not use materiality allocation in this text, readers should remember the term "tolerable misstatement." Tolerable misstatement is the part of the overall materiality number assigned to an account. Since here we do not assign overall materiality, tolerable misstatement is synonymous with overall materiality. The word "tolerable" is also frequently associated with the level of control deviations that is presumed to lead to material misstatements. Tolerable in this context is discussed in more detail in Chapter 7.

Materiality and Planning

The major reason for thinking about materiality at the planning stage is to try to fine-tune the audit for effectiveness and efficiency. Thinking about it in advance helps to avoid surprises. Suppose that near the end of an audit the partner decided that individual and aggregate misstatements over $40,000 should be considered material, but then realized that the nature, timing and extent of audit procedures resulted in an acceptable assurance for errors only below $70,000. More work should be done, and now it is very late to do it. Conversely, an audit team might **overaudit**—perform more audit work than is necessary, thinking in terms of detecting $70,000 in total misstatement, when accuracy to the nearest $100,000 is satisfactory.

The concept of materiality is used by auditors in three ways: (1) as a guide to planning the audit program—directing attention and audit work to the important, uncertain or material error-prone items and accounts; (2) as a guide to evaluation of the evidence; and (3) as a guide for making decisions about the audit report. An important point is that materiality in auditing is perceived in terms of both potential misstatement (in a planning sense) and known or estimated misstatement (in an evaluation and reporting decision sense). An account, such as inventory, is not necessarily material in an audit context because of its size or its place in the financial statements. The importance derives from the potential for, and effect of, misstatements that might exist in the account. The preliminary analytical procedures should give the auditors some insights about where potential misstatements lie. Chapter 20 discusses the role of materiality in evaluating the results of audit tests on different accounts.

R E V I E W
C H E C K P O I N T S

5.8   What is "material information" in accounting and auditing? What is "planning materiality" in an audit context?

5.9   Do auditing standards require auditors to express planning materiality as a specific dollar amount?

5.10 What do you think is the best objective evidence of the reasonableness of an accounting estimate? Use the allowance for doubtful accounts receivable as an example.

5.11 What benefits are claimed for auditors' preliminary assessment of materiality as a matter of audit planning? Is $500,000 a material amount of misstatements to leave uncorrected in financial statements?

PRELIMINARY ASSESSMENT OF AUDIT RISKS

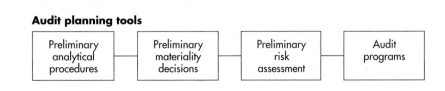

Audit planning tools

Preliminary analytical procedures — Preliminary materiality decisions — Preliminary risk assessment — Audit programs

LEARNING OBJECTIVE
4. Describe the conceptual audit risk model and explain the meaning and importance of its components in terms of professional judgment and audit planning.

Knowledge of the client's business from preliminary analytical procedures can help auditors identify problem areas and make overall risk assessments. However, some more specific risks also need to be assessed. These are known as inherent risk, control risk, detection risk and audit risk. Since several adjectives are used to describe these risks, you should not speak of "risk" without a modifier (*inherent, control,* and so on) to specify the one you mean. Audit risk is a function of inherent risk, control risk and detection risk. Audit risk is related to information risk (discussed in Chapter 1) associated with the financial statements. We discuss audit risk in more detail after first considering each of its components.

Inherent Risk

Inherent risk is the probability that material misstatements have occurred, regardless of the existence of internal control, in transactions entering the accounting system used to develop financial statements, or that material misstatements have occurred in an account balance (*Section* 5130.11, ISA 400.4, and Audit Guideline "Applying Materiality and Audit Risk Concepts in Conducting an Audit"). Put another way, inherent risk is the risk of material misstatements occurring in the first place. Inherent risk is a characteristic of the client's business, the major types of transactions and the effectiveness of its accountants. Auditors do not create or control inherent risk. They can only try to assess its magnitude.

An assessment of inherent risk can be based on a variety of information. Auditors may know that material misstatements were discovered during the last year's audit, so inherent risk will be considered higher than it would be if last year's audit had shown no material misstatements. Auditors may believe the client's accounting clerks tend to misunderstand GAAP and the company's own accounting policies, thus suggesting a significant probability of mistakes in transaction processing. The nature of the client's business may produce complicated transactions and calculations generally known to be subject to data processing and accounting treatment error. (For example, real estate, franchising and oil and gas transactions are frequently complicated and subject to accounting error. Some kinds of inventories are harder than others to count, value and keep accurately in perpetual records.) Some accounts (e.g., cash and inventory) are more susceptible to embezzlement, theft or other loss than are other accounts (e.g., land or prepaid expenses). The important relationship you should understand is that audit care and attention should be greater where inherent risk is judged to be higher.

Auditor experience has shown that due to management optimism and bias, asset and income accounts tend to have a higher inherent risk of overstatement than understatement; and that liability accounts have a higher inherent risk of understatement than overstatement. Due to these predilections and biases, audit procedures that are more effective in detecting overstatements, such as vouching, are more widely used with asset and income accounts. At the same time, audit procedures that are more effective in detecting understatements, such as tracing subsequent payments, are more likely to be used with liability accounts. Thus, the inherent and relative risks determine the importance of various procedures for different accounts.

Control Risk

Control risk is the risk that the client's internal control will not prevent or detect a material misstatement. More specifically, control risk is the probability that the client's internal control policies and procedures will fail to detect or prevent material misstatements, provided any enter the accounting system in the first place (*Section* 5130.11, ISA 400.5, and Audit Guideline "Applying Materiality and Audit Risk Concepts in Conducting an Audit"). Auditors do not create or control the control risk. They can only evaluate a company's control system and assess the probability of failure to detect material misstatements. An auditor's assessment of control risk is based on the study and evaluation of the company's control system. You will study this process in detail in Chapter 6.

INHERENT RISK ARISING FROM ECONOMIC CONDITIONS

Economic conditions have improved in 1994 and should continue to do so in 1995. Businesses are experiencing increased levels of exports, improved profitability from cost reduction activities, consumer spending increases and a recovery in the manufacturing sector.

While this environment eliminates some of the concerns entities faced during the depths of the recession, auditors should be aware of the following factors when assessing the risk of material misstatement in an entity's financial statements.

- Increased exporting may lead to increased foreign exchange exposure with related unrecorded foreign exchange liabilities. Management may have more difficulty collecting accounts receivable arising from foreign as compared to domestic sales and fail to make adequate provision for doubtful accounts.
- Productivity improvement and cost reduction activities may have eroded the segregation of duties and increased staff workloads, bringing a drop in the attention paid to internal controls. Management's operating style, its control methods and an entity's organization structure are three important control environment factors. Re-engineering an entity's operations may adversely affect each of these control factors.
- Lenders have become much more selective in the entities they finance, and debt covenants are more restrictive than before. This may make it more difficult for entities to finance their debt loads and expansion plans.
- Entities are introducing new technology to improve the quality of their products and reduce the costs of production. Technological obsolescence is accelerating and can affect the carrying values of productive assets, inventories and other assets.
- Some sectors of the economy are recovering more slowly than others. Entities may continue to experience adverse operating results and find themselves in financial difficulty. In addition, many commercial and industrial buildings still have high vacancy rates and depressed selling prices. Such capital assets should be written down when the long-term expectation is that the net carrying amount will not be recovered.

Source: CICA, *Audit Risk Alert*—December 1994.

Inherent risk is difficult to evaluate, and sometimes its assessment can be combined with the evaluation of control risk. The problems arise from the fact that internal controls "work" only when errors, irregularities and other misstatements occur. Also, some controls are preventive in nature and so tend to reduce inherent risk. Exhibit 5–3 shows the combinations of original errors and control effectiveness, or lack thereof.

Control effectiveness conclusions and risk assessments may be made on a preliminary basis for planning purposes. Auditors often carry over preconceived notions about control risk when they perform the audit on a client year after year. This carryover is known as **anchoring** the control risk assessment (starting with knowledge of last year's conclusions), and it represents (1) a useful continuity of experience with a particular client and (2) a potential pitfall if conditions change for the worse and the auditor fails to acknowledge the deterioration of control.

Control risk should not be assessed so low that auditors place complete reliance on controls and do not perform any other audit work.

Many auditors conclude their control risk assessment decisions with descriptive assessments (e.g., high, moderate, low), and some auditors put probability numbers on them (e.g., 1.0, 0.50, 0.30).

EXHIBIT 5–3   INTERNAL CONTROL CONDITIONS AND CONCLUSIONS

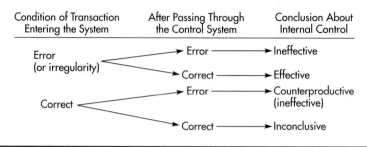

Source: Adapted from L. E. Graham, "Audit Risk-Part III," *CPA Journal*, October 1985, p. 39.

Detection Risk

Detection risk is the risk that any material misstatement that has not been corrected by the client's internal control will not be detected by the auditor (*Handbook Section* 5130.10, ISA 400.6 and Audit Guideline "Applying Materiality and Audit Risk Concepts in Conducting an Audit"). In contrast to inherent risk and control risk, auditors are responsible for performing the evidence-gathering procedures that manage and control detection risk. These audit procedures represent the auditors' opportunity to detect material misstatements that can cause financial statements to be misleading.

In subsequent chapters you will study substantive procedures. These are the procedures used to detect material misstatements in dollar amounts and disclosures presented in the financial statements and footnotes. The two categories of substantive procedures are (1) audit of the details of transactions and balances and (2) analytical procedures applied to produce circumstantial evidence about dollar amounts in the accounts. Detection risk is realized when procedures in these two categories fail to detect material misstatements.

Audit Risk

In an overall sense, **audit risk** is the probability that an auditor will fail to express a reservation that financial statements are materially misstated. The profession assumes audit risk can at best be controlled at a low level, not eliminated, even when audits are well planned and carefully performed. The risk is much greater in poorly planned and carelessly performed audits. The relationship between audit risk and business risk was discussed in Appendix 1B. Planned audit risk may vary depending on client circumstances. Generally, the more risky the client or the more that users rely on the audited financial statements, the lower the planned audit risk. As the risk of being sued for material misstatement goes up, the planned audit risk goes down to compensate for the increased risk associated with the engagement. Many accounting firms have developed internal guidelines for setting planned levels of audit risk.

The auditing profession has no hard standard for an acceptable level of overall audit risk, except that it should be "appropriately low" and involve the exercise of professional judgment. In quantitative terms "most auditors would strive to limit such risks to no more than 5 percent" (CICA Guideline AUG-7, "Applying Materiality and Audit Risk Concepts in Conducting an Audit," paragraph 16). However, auditors would be appalled to think that even 1 percent of their audits would be bad. For a large firm with 2,000 audit clients, 1 percent would mean 20 bad audits per year! But on the other hand, not all audits have material misstatements, so using 5 percent planned audit risk on *every* engagement may lead to a much lower level of bad audits. For example, if the risk of material misstatement is 5 percent, then with 5 percent audit risk the number of bad audits would be $.05 \times .05 = .0025 = 1/4\%$.

The concept of audit risk also applies to individual account balances and disclosures. Here the risk is that material misstatement is not discovered in an account (e.g., the inventory total) or in a disclosure (e.g., a pension plan footnote explanation). Audit risk is most often utilized in practice with regard to individual balances and disclosures. You should keep this context in mind when you study the risk model summary presented next. Audit risk of 0.05 at the account level, used by many CA firms, is presented as an illustrative audit risk.

In summary, audit risk is the same whether applied to financial statements as a whole or to individual account balances. Thus, for example, if audit risk is set at .05 it is used for all accounts as well as for financial statements as a whole.

Risk Model—A Summary

The foregoing concepts of audit risks can be expressed in a model that assumes the elements of audit risk are independent. Thus, the risks are multiplied as follows:

Audit risk (AR) = Inherent risk (IR) $\times$ Control risk (CR) $\times$ Detection risk (DR)

An intuitive explanation for this formula can be given as follows. Audit risk is the probability that the audit fails to detect a material misstatement. This will occur only under the following circumstances: (1) there is a material misstatement to start with (probability of which is inherent risk), (2) the internal controls fail to detect and correct the material misstatement (probability of which is control risk), and (3) the audit procedures also fail to detect the material misstatement (probability of which is detection risk). The audit fails only if all three events occur and the probability of this happening is the product of the three risks as given above. Audit risk is thus the probability that the audit fails.

Auditors want to perform an audit of a particular balance or disclosure well enough to hold the audit risk (AR) to a relatively low level (e.g., 0.05, which means that on average 5 percent of audit decisions when there is a material misstatement will be wrong). As such, AR is a quality criterion based on professional judgment. All the other risk assessments are estimates based on professional judgment and evidence.

For example, suppose an auditor thought a particular inventory balance was subject to great inherent risk of material misstatement (say, IR = 0.90) and that the client's internal control was not very effective (say, CR = 0.70). If he or she wanted to control audit risk at a low level (say, AR = 0.05), the other procedures would need to be designed so that detection risk (DR) did not exceed 0.08 (approximately). According to the model, this example would produce the following results:

$$AR = IR \times CR \times DR$$

$$0.05 = 0.90 \times 0.70 \times DR$$

Solving for DR: DR = 0.08

The practical problem here is knowing whether the audit has been planned and performed well enough to hold the detection risk as low as 0.08. Despite the simplicity of the risk model, it is only a conceptual tool. Auditors have few ways to calculate detection risk, so the model represents more of a way to think about audit risks than a way to calculate them. However, several accounting firms use this model to calculate risks and the related sample sizes.

The model produces some insights, including these:

1. Auditors cannot rely entirely on an estimate of zero inherent risk to the exclusion of other evidence-gathering procedures. Thus, you cannot have the condition:

$$AR = IR \ (=0) \times CR \times DR = 0$$

2. Auditors cannot place complete reliance on internal control to the exclusion of other audit procedures. Thus, you cannot have the condition:

$$AR = IR \times CR \ (= 0) \times DR = 0$$

3. Audits would not seem to exhibit due audit care if the risk of failure to detect material misstatements were too high, for example:

$$AR = IR \ (= 0.80) \times CR \ (= 0.80) \times DR \ (= 0.50) = 0.32$$

4. Auditors can choose to rely almost exclusively on evidence produced by substantive procedures, even if they think inherent risk and control risk are high. For example, this combination is acceptable (provided AR = 0.05 is acceptable):

$$AR = IR \ (= 1.00) \times CR \ (= 1.00) \times DR \ (= 0.05) = 0.05$$

Despite the precision implied by the mathematical depiction of the audit risk model, in reality applying it is difficult and highly judgmental. The objective in an audit is to limit audit risk (AR) to a low level, as judged by the auditor. This is done by assessing inherent risk (IR) and control risk (CR) along a spectrum. Often in practice this assessment is reduced to three levels: high risk, moderate risk or low risk. The greater the inherent and control risks, the lower the detection risk needs to be, resulting in "more" procedures ("more" includes their nature and timing as well as their extent) that the auditor would need to carry out. At the end of the day, the objective is to limit audit risk (AR) to an appropriately low level, thus enabling the auditor to achieve *high assurance* that the financial statements are free of material misstatement. It is also important to remember that the model incorporates the concept of materiality in its definition and that materiality enters throughout the risk assessment process. Chapters 7 and 20 give more details on the audit risk model.

R E V I E W
CHECKPOINTS

5.12 What are the four audit risks an auditor must consider? What does each involve?

5.13 What is anchoring with regard to auditors' judgments about the quality or effectiveness of internal control?

5.14 What are some of the effects of bad economic times that produce risks that auditors should be alert to detect in clients' financial statements?

5.15 What is the difference between "audit risk in an overall sense" and "audit risk applied to individual account balances?"

PLANNING MEMORANDUM

Auditors usually prepare a **planning memorandum** summarizing the preliminary analytical review and the materiality assessment with specific directions about the effect on the audit. This planning memo also usually includes information about (1) investigation or review of the prospective or continuing client relationship, (2) needs for special technical or industry expertise, (3) staff assignment and timing schedules, (4) the assessed level of control risk, (5) significant industry or company risks, (6) computer system control environment, (7) utilization of the company's internal auditors, (8) identification of unusual accounting principles problems, and (9) schedules of work periods, meeting dates with client personnel and completion dates. The memo summarizes all the important overall planning information.

All the planning becomes a basis for preparing the audit program. An **audit program** is a specification of procedures that auditors use to guide the work of inherent and control risk assessment and to obtain sufficient competent evidence that serves as a basis for the audit report.

AUDIT PROGRAMS

. . . .

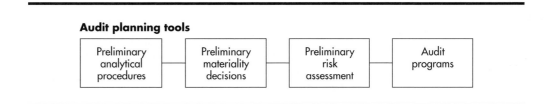

Audit planning tools

Preliminary analytical procedures — Preliminary materiality decisions — Preliminary risk assessment — Audit programs

LEARNING OBJECTIVE

5. Describe the content and purpose of audit programs.

Auditors use two kinds of audit programs, each with a different objective. One contains the specification of procedures for obtaining an understanding of the client's business and management's control system, and for assessing the inherent risk and the control risk related to the financial account balances. For identification purposes we will call this program the "internal control program." The other contains the specification of substantive procedures for gathering direct evidence on the assertions (i.e., existence, completeness, valuation, rights and obligations, presentation and disclosure) about dollar amounts in the account balances. For identification, we will call this one the "balance-audit program."

These audit programs combine all the considerations of audit planning heretofore discussed in Chapter 4 and Chapter 5, including:

- Understanding the client's business and industry.
- Assertions and objectives embodied in the client's financial statements.
- Persuasive strengths of evidence.
- General procedures for obtaining evidence, expressed as specific procedures and directives.
- Preliminary analytical procedures for identifying specific risk areas in the unaudited financial statements.
- Preliminary materiality decisions and tolerable misstatement assignments.
- Preliminary risk assessments.

In actual field situations these audit programs are very lengthy. Special program documents may contain separate listings of procedures and questionnaires on the company's internal control environment, internal control procedures, management control and computer control. The audit programs contain numerous detailed specifications of procedures the auditors intend to perform as the work progresses. The two boxes below abstract elements of audit programs for illustrative purposes. They put in perspective the sequence of topics you have read about in Chapter 4 and Chapter 5.

The technical parts of internal control risk assessment programs are too detailed to cover at this stage. They are explained more fully in subsequent chapters.

The balance-audit program consists of several programs, each applicable to a particular account. Auditors first subdivide the financial statements into cycles (as explained in Chapter 4), then turn attention to the accounts in each cycle. The procedures in these audit programs are designed to obtain evidence about the existence or occurrence, completeness, valuation, rights and obligations, and presentation and disclosure assertions implicit in each account title and balance. The box below contains brief specifications of procedures for auditing accounts receivable. You can see in them the elements of the general techniques (e.g., confirmation, computation, enquiry, inspection and the assertions toward which they are directed). This type of audit program is presented later in more detail in Chapter 7.

An illustration of a partial program in the revenue and collection cycle is given in the box below.

UNDERSTAND THE BUSINESS, INHERENT RISK, CONTROL RISK

- Communicate with predecessor auditors.
- Study prior-year audit working papers, CICA and AICPA audit and accounting guides and industry publications concerning the company and its industry.
- Interview management with regard to business and accounting policies.
- Evaluate the competence and independence of the company's internal auditors.
- Determine the need for specialists on the engagement.
- Determine the extent of significant computer applications in the company's accounting system.
- Obtain the financial statements and make decisions about the planning materiality appropriate in the circumstances.
- Perform preliminary analytical procedures to identify risk areas in the financial statement accounts.
- Assess the inherent risk in general and with respect to particular accounts.

****

- Obtain an understanding of the company's internal control through interviews, observations and tests of controls (more on this topic in Chapter 6).
- Perform detail test of control procedures, if necessary (more on this topic in Chapters 6 and 7, and Chapter 20 for more advanced issues).
- Assess the control risk (more on this topic in Chapters 6 and 7, and Chapter 20 for more advanced issues).
- Use the control risk assessment to design the nature, timing and extent of substantive audit procedures (more on this topic in Chapters 6 and 7, and Chapter 20 for advanced issues).

BALANCE SHEET AUDIT PROGRAM IN REVENUE AND COLLECTION CYCLE

Accounts Receivable

- Prepare and send confirmations on a sample of customers' accounts receivable. Analyse the returns.
- Obtain an aged trial balance of the receivables. Calculate and analyse the age status of the accounts and the allowance for uncollectible accounts.
- Interview the credit manager concerning the past-due accounts. Obtain credit reports and financial statements for independent analysis of overdue accounts.
- Vouch receivables balances to cash payments received after the confirmation date.
- Read loan agreements and make note of any pledge of receivables, sales with recourse or other restrictions or contingencies related to the receivables.
- Read sales contracts for evidence of customers' rights of return or price allowance terms.
- Obtain written representations from the client concerning pledges for collateral, related party receivables, collectibility and other matters related to accounts receivable.

These audit procedures are intended to enable auditors to conduct the work in accordance with the three CICA examination standards concerning planning and supervision of the audit, obtaining an understanding of the control structure and obtaining sufficient competent evidence to serve as a basis for the audit report. The exact specification of the procedures, the arrangement for their timing (i.e., when they are performed) and the determination of their extent (i.e., the sample sizes of data examined, such as the number of customer accounts receivable to confirm) all depend upon the activities, concepts and tools of audit planning.

. . . .

R E V I E W   5.16   Two kinds of audit programs have been identified. What are they? What is the objec-
C H E C K P O I N T S   tive of each?

5.17   What is meant by the terms nature, timing and extent of audit procedures?

. . . .

SUMMARY

. . . .

The several topics under the heading of "audit planning" started in Chapter 4 with pre-engagement activities, understanding the client's business and industry, and obtaining the financial statements and organizing the accounts into cycles for efficient audit work. Chapter 4 also introduced the basic concepts of management assertions and audit objectives, qualities of evidence, general types of audit procedures and audit working papers. The concepts are part of the theoretical foundation for performing audits.

Chapter 5 continued the series of audit planning topics by explaining several technical tools of planning. These tools are part of the nitty-gritty of audit work. They start with preliminary analytical procedures applied to the client's unaudited financial statements. The analytical process includes getting the financial data, calculating common-size and comparative financial statements, calculating ratios, describing the company's financial activities and asking relevant questions. This analysis enables auditors to look for problem areas and signs of potential misstatement in the financial statements. Detecting signs of problems enables the auditors to plan procedures for the audit program to follow up and to determine whether misstatements, errors, irregularities or frauds have affected the fair presentation of the financial balances.

The technical planning tools include auditors' determination of materiality with relation to the financial statements taken as a whole. Materiality in this sense is defined as the largest amount of uncorrected dollar misstatement that could exist in published financial statements, yet the statements would still fairly present the company's financial position and results of operations in conformity with GAAP. A method of calculating materiality based on judgments about acceptable misstatement was presented to connect income misstatement to earnings-per-share misstatements and an effect on share prices.

Risk assessment is the common language of auditing. The audit risk model was explained, and its elements of inherent risk, control risk, detection risk and audit risk were defined. Implications of the risk model were explored in relation to limits on the risks permitted in practical applications.

The closing topic was a brief preview of audit programs. Programs were categorized as "internal control programs" and "balance-audit programs." The illustrations were not complete programs for conducting any particular audit, but they showed the general nature and content of audit programs.

Now the stage is set to take up a more detailed explanation of the theory and process of auditing internal control. The next chapter deals with the task of control risk assessment.

MULTIPLE-CHOICE QUESTIONS FOR PRACTICE AND REVIEW

Questions 5.18 to 5.20 are located on the CD-ROM that accompanies this textbook.

5.21 Analytical procedures are generally used to produce evidence from:
a. Confirmations mailed directly to the auditors by client customers.
b. Physical observation of inventories.
c. Relationships among current financial balances and prior balances, forecasts and nonfinancial data.
d. Detailed examination of external, external-internal and internal documents.

5.22 Auditors perform analytical procedures in the planning stage of an audit for the purpose of:
a. Deciding the matters to cover in an engagement letter.
b. Identifying unusual conditions that deserve more auditing effort.
c. Determining which of the financial statement assertions are the most important for the client's financial statements.
d. Determining the nature, timing and extent of audit procedures for auditing the inventory.

5.23 Which of the following match-ups of types of analytical procedures and sources of information makes the most sense?

	Type of Analytical Procedure	Source of Information
a.	Comparison of current account balances with prior-periods statistics	Physical production
b.	Comparison of current account balances with expected balances	Company's budgets and forecasts
c.	Evaluation of current account balances with relation to predictable historical patterns	Published industry ratios
d.	Evaluation of current account balances in relation to nonfinancial information	Company's own comparative financial statements

5.24 Analytical procedures can be used in which of the following ways?
a. As a means of overall review at the end of an audit.
b. As "attention directing" methods when planning an audit at the beginning.
c. As substantive audit procedures to obtain evidence during an audit.
d. All of the above.

5.25 Analytical procedures used when planning an audit should concentrate on:
a. Weaknesses in the company's internal control procedures.
b. Predictability of account balances based on individual transactions.
c. Five major management assertions in financial statements.
d. Accounts and relationships that may represent specific potential problems and risks in the financial statements.

5.26 When a company that has $5 million current assets and $3 million current liabilities pays $1 million of its accounts payable, its current ratio will:
a. Increase.
b. Decrease.
c. Remain unchanged.

5.27 When a company that has $3 million current assets and $5 million current liabilities pays $1 million of its accounts payable, its current ratio will:
a. Increase.
b. Decrease.
c. Remain unchanged.

5.28 When a company that has $5 million current assets and $5 million current liabilities pays $1 million of its accounts payable, its current ratio will:
a. Increase.
b. Decrease.
c. Remain unchanged.

5.29 When a company that sells its products for a (gross) profit increases its sales by 15 percent and its cost of goods sold by 7 percent, the cost of goods sold ratio will:
a. Increase.
b. Decrease.
c. Remain unchanged.

5.30 Which of the following is not a benefit claimed for the practice of determining materiality in the initial planning stage of starting an audit?
a. Being able to fine-tune the audit work for effectiveness and efficiency.
b. Avoiding the problem of doing more work than necessary (overauditing).
c. Being able to decide early what kind of audit opinion to give.
d. Avoiding the problem of doing too little work (underauditing).

5.31 It is appropriate and acceptable under generally accepted auditing standards for an auditor to:
   a. Assess both inherent and control risk at 100 percent and achieve an acceptably low audit risk by performing extensive detection work.
   b. Assess control risk at zero and perform a minimum of detection work.
   c. Assess inherent risk at zero and perform a minimum of detection work.
   d. Decide that audit risk can be 40 percent.

5.32 Auditors are not responsible for accounting estimates with respect to:
   a. Making the estimates.
   b. Determining the reasonableness of estimates.
   c. Determining that estimates are presented in conformity with GAAP.
   d. Determining that estimates are adequately disclosed in the financial statements.

5.33 Tolerable misstatement in the context of audit planning means:
   a. Amounts that should be disclosed if they are likely to influence the economic decisions of financial statement users.
   b. The largest amount of uncorrected dollar misstatement that could exist in published financial statements, yet they would still fairly present the company's financial position and results of operations in conformity with GAAP.
   c. Part of the overall materiality amount for the financial statements assigned to a particular account.
   d. A dollar amount assigned to an account as required by auditing standards.

5.34 The risk that the auditors' own work will lead to the decision that material misstatements do not exist in the financial statements, when in fact such misstatements do exist, is:
   a. Audit risk.
   b. Inherent risk.
   c. Control risk.
   d. Detection risk.

5.35 Auditors are responsible for the quality of the work related to management and control of:
   a. Inherent risk.
   b. Relative risk.
   c. Control risk.
   d. Detection risk.

5.36 The auditors assessed a combined inherent risk and control risk at 0.75 and said they wanted to achieve a 0.15 risk of failing to detect misstatements in an account equal to the $17,000 tolerable misstatement assigned to the account. What detection risk do the auditors plan to use for planning the remainder of the audit work?
   a. 0.20.
   b. 0.10.
   c. 0.75.
   d. 0.00.

5.37 An audit program contains:
   a. Specifications of audit standards relevant to the financial statements being audited.
   b. Specifications of procedures the auditors believe appropriate for the financial statements under audit.
   c. Documentation of the assertions under audit, the evidence obtained and the conclusions reached.
   d. Reconciliation of the account balances in the financial statements with the account balances in the client's general ledger.

EXERCISES AND PROBLEMS

5.38 Analytical Review Ratio Relationships. The following situations represent errors and irregularities that could occur in financial statements. Your requirement is to state how the ratio in question would compare (greater, equal or less) to what the ratio "should have been" had the error or irregularity not occurred.
   a. The company recorded fictitious sales with credits to sales revenue accounts and debits to accounts receivable. Inventory was reduced and cost of goods sold was increased for the profitable "sales." Is the current ratio greater than, equal to or less than what it should have been?
   b. The company recorded cash disbursements paying trade accounts payable but held the cheques past the year-end date—meaning that the "disbursements" should not have been shown as credits to cash and debits to accounts payable. Is the current ratio greater than, equal to or less than what it should have been? Consider cases in which the current ratio before the improper "disbursement" recording would have been

(1) greater than 1:1, (2) equal to 1:1, and (3) less than 1:1.

c. The company uses a periodic inventory system for determining the balance sheet amount of inventory at year-end. Very near the year-end, merchandise was received, placed in the stockroom, and counted, but the purchase transaction was neither recorded nor paid until the next month. What was the effect on inventory, cost of goods sold, gross profit and net income? How were these ratios affected, compared to what they would have been without the error: current ratio (remember three possible cases), gross margin ratio, cost of goods sold ratio, inventory turnover and receivables turnover?

d. The company is loathe to write off customer accounts receivable, even though the financial vice president makes entirely adequate provision for uncollectible amounts in the allowance for bad debts. The gross receivables and the allowance both contain amounts that should have been written off long ago. How are these ratios affected compared to what they would be if the old receivables were properly written off: current ratio, days' sales in receivables, doubtful account ratio, receivables turnover, return on beginning equity, working capital/total assets?

e. Since last year, the company has reorganized its lines of business and placed more emphasis on its traditional products while selling off some marginal businesses merged by the previous go-go management. Total assets are 10 percent less than they were last year, but working capital has increased. Retained earnings remained the same because the disposals created no gains, and the net income after taxes is still near zero, the same as last year. Earnings before interest and taxes remained the same, a small positive EBIT. The total market value of the company's equity has not increased, but that is better than the declines of the past several years. Proceeds from the disposals have been used to retire long-term debt. Net sales have decreased 5 percent because the sales decrease resulting from the disposals has not been overcome by increased sales of the traditional products. Is the discriminant Z score of the current year higher or lower than that of the prior year?

5.39 **Auditing an Accounting Estimate.** Suppose management estimated the lower-of-cost-or-market valuation of some obsolete inventory at $99,000, and wrote it down from $120,000, recognizing a loss of $21,000. The auditors obtained the following information: The inventory in question could be sold for an amount between $78,000 and $92,000. The costs of advertising and shipping could range from $5,000 to $7,000.

Required:

a. Would you propose an audit adjustment to the management estimate? Write the appropriate accounting entry.

b. If management's estimate of inventory market (lower than cost) had been $80,000, would you propose an audit adjustment? Write the appropriate accounting entry.

5.40 **Calculate a Planning Materiality Amount.** The auditors were planning the work on the financial statements of the Mary Short Cosmetics Company. The unaudited financial statements showed $515,000 net income after providing an allowance of 35 percent for income taxes. The company had no debt and no interest expense. Mary Short's shares are traded over the counter, and investors have generally assigned a price-earnings multiple of 16 to the shares. Press releases by the company have enabled analysts to estimate the income for the year at about 515,000, which was forecast by the company at the beginning of the year. There are 750,000 shares outstanding, and the last quoted price for them was $11.

The auditors have decided that a 6 percent mispricing error in the shares would not cause investors to change their buying and selling decisions.

Required:

Calculate the "planning materiality" the auditors could allow, based on the income before income taxes.

5.41 **Audit Risk Model.** Audit risks for particular accounts and disclosures can be conceptualized in this model: Audit risk (AR) = Inherent risk (IR) × Internal control risk (CR) × Detection risk (DR). Use this model as a framework for considering the following situations and deciding whether the auditor's conclusion is appropriate.

1. Ohlsen, PA, has participated in the audit of Limberg Cheese Company for five years, first as an assistant accountant and

the last two years as the senior accountant. He has never seen an accounting adjustment recommended. He believes the inherent risk must be zero.

2. Jones, PA, has just (November 30) completed an exhaustive study and evaluation of the internal control system of Lang's Derfer Foods, Inc. (fiscal year ending December 31). She believes the control risk must be zero because no material errors could possibly slip through the many error-checking procedures and review layers used by Lang's.

3. Fields, PA, is lazy and does not like audit jobs in Toronto, anyway. On the audit of Hogtown Manufacturing Company, he decided to use detail procedures to audit the year-end balances

very thoroughly to the extent that his risk of failing to detect material errors and irregularities should be 0.02 or less. He gave no thought to inherent risk and conducted only a very limited review of Philly's internal control system.

4. Shad, PA, is nearing the end of a "dirty" audit of Allnight Protection Company. Allnight's accounting personnel all resigned during the year and were replaced by inexperienced people. The controller resigned last month in disgust. The journals and ledgers were a mess because the one computer specialist was hospitalized for three months during the year. Thankfully, Shad thought, "I've been able to do this audit in less time than last year when everything was operating smoothly."

Discussion Cases

5.42 Analytical Review. Kermit Griffin, an audit manager, had begun a preliminary analytical review of selected statistics related to the Majestic Hotel. His objective was to obtain an understanding of this hotel's business in order to draft a preliminary audit program. He wanted to see whether he could detect any troublesome areas or questionable accounts that might require special audit attention. Unfortunately, Mr. Griffin caught the flu and was hospitalized. From his sickbed he sent you the schedule he had prepared (Exhibit 5.42–1). He has asked you to write a memorandum identifying areas of potential misstatements or other matters that the preliminary audit program should cover.

Required:
Write a memorandum describing Majestic's operating characteristics compared to the "industry average" insofar as you can tell from the statistics. Does this analytical

review identify any areas that might present problems in the audit?

This assignment gives you some practice using the number 4 general type of analytical procedures discussed in the chapter: "Comparison of current year account balances and financial relationships (e.g., ratios) with similar information for the industry in which the company operates."

5.43 Analytical Review. The use of analytical procedure is becoming more frequent as auditors strive to improve the efficiency with which they conduct their audit examinations.

Required:
a. What are the two required uses of analytical procedures in an audit?
b. List the basic steps in the process of performing analytical procedures.
c. What is the auditor's objective in using analytical procedures in each stage of the audit?

(CGAAC Adapted)

EXHIBIT 5.42–1   **MAJESTIC HOTEL PRELIMINARY ANALYTICAL PROCEDURES FYE 3/31/0Y**

The Majestic Hotel, East Apple, British Columbia, compiles operating statistics on a calendar-year basis. Hotel statistics, below, were provided by the controller, A. J. Marcello, for 200X. The parallel column contains industry average statistics obtained from the National Hotel Industry Guide.

Average annual percent of rooms occupied, Majestic (percent)

	Majestic (percent)	Industry (percent)
Sales:		
Rooms	60.4%	63.9%
Food and beverage	35.7	32.2
Other	3.9	3.9
Costs:		
Rooms department	15.2%	17.3%
Food and beverage	34.0	27.2
Administrative & general	8.0	8.9
Management fee	3.3	1.1
Advertising	2.7	3.2
Real estate taxes	3.5	3.2
Utilities, repairs, maintenance	15.9	13.7
Profit per sales dollar	17.4%	25.4%
Rooms dept. ratios to room sales dollars:		
Salaries and wages	18.9%	15.7%
Laundry	1.0	3.7
Other	5.3	7.6
Profit per rooms sales dollar	74.8%	73.0%
Food/beverage (F/B) ratios to F/B sales dollars:		
Cost of food sold	42.1%	37.0%
Food gross profit	57.9	63.0
Cost of beverages sold	43.6	29.5
Beverages gross profit	56.4	70.5
Combined gross profit	57.7	64.6
Salaries and wages	39.6	32.8
Music and entertainment	—	2.7
Other	13.4	13.8
Profit per F/B sales dollar	4.7	15.3
Average annual percent of rooms occupied	62.6	68.1
Average room rate per day	$160	$120
Number of rooms available per day	200	148

APPENDIX 5A

SELECTED FINANCIAL RATIOS

. . . .

Balance Sheet Ratios	Formula*
Current ratio	$\dfrac{\text{Current assets}}{\text{Current liabilities}}$
Days' sales in receivables	$\dfrac{\text{Ending net receivables}}{\text{Credit sales}} \times 360$
Doubtful account ratio	$\dfrac{\text{Allowance for doubtful accounts}}{\text{Ending gross receivables}}$
Days' sales in inventory	$\dfrac{\text{Ending inventory}}{\text{Cost of goods sold}} \times 360$
Debt ratio	$\dfrac{\text{Current and long-term debt}}{\text{Shareholder equity}}$

Operations Ratios	
Receivables turnover	$\dfrac{\text{Credit sales}}{\text{Ending net receivables}}$
Inventory turnover	$\dfrac{\text{Cost of goods sold}}{\text{Ending inventory}}$
Cost of goods sold ratio	$\dfrac{\text{Cost of goods sold}}{\text{Net sales}}$
Gross margin ratio	$\dfrac{\text{Net sales} - \text{Cost of goods sold}}{\text{Net sales}}$
Return on beginning equity	$\dfrac{\text{Net income}}{\text{Shareholder equity (beginning)}}$

Financial Distress Ratios (Altman, 1968)	Formula*
(X_1) Working capital ÷ Total assets	$\dfrac{\text{Current assets} - \text{Current liabilities}}{\text{Total assets}}$
(X_2) Retained earnings ÷ Total assets	$\dfrac{\text{Retained earnings (ending)}}{\text{Total assets}}$
(X_3) Earnings before interest and taxes ÷ Total assets	$\dfrac{\text{Net Income} + \text{Interest expense} + \text{Income tax expense}}{\text{Total assets}}$
(X_4) Market value of equity ÷ Total debt	$\dfrac{\text{Market value of common and preferred shares}}{\text{Current liabilities and long-term debt}}$
(X_5) Net sales ÷ Total assets	$\dfrac{\text{Net sales}}{\text{Total assets}}$
Discriminant Z score (Altman, 1968)	$1.2 \times X_1 + 1.4 \times X_2 + 3.3 \times X_3 + 0.6 \times X_4 + 1.0 \times X_5$

*These ratios are shown to be calculated using year-end, rather than year-average, numbers for such balances as accounts receivable and inventory. Other accounting and finance reference books may contain formulas using year-average numbers. As long as no dramatic changes have occurred during the year, the year-end numbers can have much audit relevance because they reflect the most current balance data. For comparative purposes, the ratios should be calculated on the same basis for all the years being compared.
In the Anycompany example in Exhibits 10–1 and 10–2, the market value of the equity in the calculations is $3 million.

The discriminant Z score is an index of a company's "financial health." The higher the score, the more healthy the company. The lower the score, the closer financial failure approaches. The score that predicts financial failure is a matter of dispute. Research suggests that companies with scores above 3.0 never go bankrupt. Generally, companies with scores below 1.0 experience financial difficulty of some kind. The score can be a negative number. It should be stressed that these ratios are indicators only, and therefore need to be combined with in-depth analysis before any final conclusions can be reached.

APPENDIX 5B

STRATEGIC SYSTEMS APPROACHES TO AUDITING

· ·

Chapter 13 provides a primer and more complete overview on SSA audits. Here the differences between SSA audits and more traditional approaches with respect to auditing planning, analytical procedures, materiality and risk assessment are noted.

The strategic systems approaches to auditing (SSA audits) generally do not view audit planning as a separate phase of the audit. Because of the importance of the knowledge of business, enquiries and analysis in obtaining assurance in SSA audits, the planning phase becomes less distinguishable from the rest of the audit in terms of obtaining assurance. In SSA audits, the auditor develops his or her own assurance propositions about the client financial statements based on a deep knowledge base that includes strategic analysis, analysis of business processes, a continuous business risk assessment analysis and a detailed business measurement analysis. Throughout the audit, these auditor generated propositions about the client's financial statements are compared to management's assertions. If the management's assertions are consistent with the auditor generated propositions, then the auditor may have obtained significant, perhaps sufficient, assurance for those assertions.

The SSA auditor starts his or her audit by performing a strategic analysis of the client using strategic management tools such as those described in Appendix 4B. Understanding the strategy of the client helps the auditor understand client business risks in detail. At the end of the strategic analysis the SSA auditor should be able to answer the following questions:

1. What is the client's strategy?
2. Is it sustainable?
3. What are the business risks/threats to the client?
4. How does the client manage those risks?
5. What are the gaps in the client's risk management approach?
6. Do those gaps affect the financial statements?

The answers to these questions suggest two courses of action for the SSA auditor. First, the SSA auditor sees how these business risks are reflected in the financial statements and second, the SSA auditor sees what business processes are in place that both generate and attempt to control the business risk. This analysis leads the auditor to the most novel aspect of the SSA approach to auditing, an in-depth analysis of key business processes (e.g., supply chain product management) that generate transactions, accounting estimates and contingencies that contain potentially a high risk of misstatement.

In considering the answers to questions five and six the auditor considers audit risk and materiality assessments in light of the insights provided by the SSA audit.

More details about how the SSA audit approach differs are found in Chapter 13.

CHAPTER 6

Learning Objectives

Two major themes from Chapters 4 and 5 are carried forward into this chapter. They are understanding the client's business and control risk. Chapter 6 also makes use of the concepts of management assertions and their related audit objectives, general audit procedures and audit working papers (Chapter 4); and of risk assessment and audit programs (Chapter 5). This chapter takes these topics and molds them into the process of internal control evaluation and control risk assessment. After studying Chapter 6, you should be able to:

1. Explain primary and secondary reasons for conducting an evaluation of a client's internal controls.

2. Distinguish between management's and auditors' responsibility regarding a company's internal control structure.

3. Define and describe the three basic elements of internal control, and specify some of their component characteristics.

4. Identify and give examples of seven internal control objectives, and associate them with the five management assertions in financial account balances.

5. List and explain the control procedures companies use to achieve control objectives.

6. Explain the phases of an evaluation of control and risk assessment and the documentation and extent of audit work required.

7. Write procedures for an audit program, following the general form of a detail test of control procedure.

8. Define and explain reasonable assurance and cost-benefit in the context of control risk assessment.

9. Adapt the concepts and processes of control risk assessment to small businesses.

INTERNAL CONTROL EVALUATION:

ASSESSING CONTROL RISK

INTRODUCTION

Internal control evaluation and control risk assessment is a very important part of the work in every audit of financial statements. Generally accepted auditing standards emphasize internal control in the second examination standard: "A sufficient understanding of internal control should be obtained to plan the audit." (*Handbook Section* 5100.02, or see ISA 400.2 for equivalent wording). Auditing standards describe the elements of internal controls and specify the extent of the auditors' work necessary to satisfy the second examination standard. When control risk is assessed below maximum, sufficient appropriate evidence should be obtained from tests of controls to support the assessment (*Handbook Section* 5100.02, or see ISA 400.31 for the equivalent wording).

The elements are control environment and control systems. Control systems include accounting systems. For our purposes we will treat the accounting system as a separate element. The extent of work involves obtaining an understanding of all three elements, documenting the understanding and performing tests of controls, if needed. Exhibit 6–1 puts these elements and this work in perspective for Chapter 6.

Chapter 6 presents a general introduction to the theory and definitions for internal control evaluation and control risk assessment. Chapter 7 (Audit Sampling) covers audit sampling for detail test of control procedures, and Chapter 20 covers the more technical topic of statistical attribute sampling for tests of controls. Computer-technical topics of the role of control in planning are covered in Chapter 8 (Auditing in a Computer Environment). Specific applications of control risk assessment are covered in the specific accounts and cycles in Chapters 9 to 13.

REASONS FOR INTERNAL CONTROL EVALUATION

LEARNING OBJECTIVE
1. Explaining primary and secondary reasons for conducting an evaluation of a client's internal controls.

Handbook Section 5200.03 defines internal control as "consisting of the policies and procedures established and maintained by management to assist in achieving its objective of ensuring, as far as practical, the orderly and efficient conduct of the entity's business." (See ISA 400.8 for a more detailed but consistent definition.) However, *Section* 5200.07 makes clear that "internal control relevant to the audit is comprised of those policies and procedures established and maintained by management that affect control risk relating to specific financial statement assertions at the account balance or class of transactions level." (An equivalent statement is made in ISA 400.9.) We will refer to these audit relevant controls as *accounting controls* and the rest of the internal control as *management controls*. The auditor is thus primarily interested in accounting controls. You can properly infer that accounting controls enable a company to safeguard its assets and prepare financial statements in conformity with generally accepted accounting principles. However, management is also interested in internal controls to assess adherence to management policy and promotion of operational efficiencies, and develops management controls to meet these objectives as well. **Control risk** arises from failures in internal control. Specifically, "control risk is the risk that the client's internal control will not prevent or detect material mis-

E X H I B I T 6–1   INTERNAL CONTROL EVALUATION AND CONTROL RISK ASSESSMENT

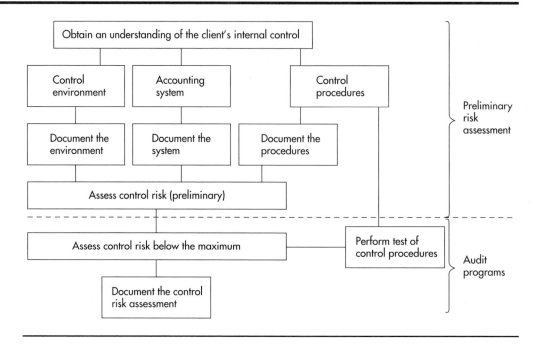

statement" (*Section* 5130.10 or ISA 400.5). Control risk is a characteristic of the client's internal control. The auditors' task is to assess it; that is, to assign an evaluation to it. Many auditors conclude their internal control risk assessment decisions with descriptive assessments (e.g., high, moderate, low), and some auditors put probability numbers on them (e.g., 1.0, 0.50, 0.30).

The primary reason for conducting an evaluation of a company's internal control and assessing control risk is to give the auditors a basis for planning the audit and determining the nature, timing and extent of audit procedures in the account balance audit program. Note that this means the auditor's primary concern with regard to internal controls is the impact controls have on safeguarding the company's assets and the accuracy of the accounting records (accounting controls). This is the basis on which the auditors have prepared a preliminary audit program and have ideas about the work they want to do, including the extreme possibility of concluding that the client may not be auditable. This preliminary program might be last year's audit program or an off-the-shelf "standard program" that will need to be modified for client-specific preliminary analytical review, materiality and risk assessments. Exhibit 6–1 outlines the process. The impact of this process on the rest of the audit is discussed later with Exhibit 6–10.

In the preliminary risk assessment phase, the auditor begins by making an assessment of the general controls associated with the overall control environment and the accounting system. If the general controls appear to be reliable, the auditor will then make a preliminary evaluation of the more specific procedures. Tests of controls are not performed unless the auditor feels he or she can rely on controls and most such tests relate to specific accounting cycles. The rest of this chapter discusses this process in more detail.

An **account balance audit program** is a specification (list) of procedures designed to produce evidence about the assertions in financial statements. Each procedure should have identifiable characteristics of nature, timing and extent, as well as a direct association with one or more financial statement assertions. The **nature** of procedures refers to the six general techniques: computation, confirmation, enquiry, inspection, observation and analysis. The **timing** of procedures is a matter of when they are performed: at "interim" before the balance sheet date or at "year-end" shortly before and after the balance sheet date. The **extent** of procedures refers to the amount of work done when the procedures are performed.

EXHIBIT 6–2   ACCOUNTS RECEIVABLE BALANCE-AUDIT PROGRAM (PARTIAL ILLUSTRATION)

Assertions/Procedures	Nature	Timing	Extent
Existence/Cutoff: Accounts receivable are authentic obligations owed to the company and represent sales made before December 31.			
1. Obtain a trial balance of customers' accounts. Select 75 for positive confirmation.	Confirmation	November 1 (interim date)	Limited sample
2. Obtain a year-end trial balance of customer accounts. Compare to the November 1 trial balance and investigate significant changes by vouching large increases to sales invoices and bills of lading.	Analytical procedures Document vouching	December 31 (year-end)	All customer accounts
3. Select all the sales invoices recorded in the last five days of the year, and vouch to bills of lading for December shipping date.	Document vouching	December 31 (year-end)	Last five days' sales
Completeness/Cutoff: Accounts receivable include all amounts owed to the company at December 31.			
4. Send positive confirmations to customers with zero balances.	Confirmation	December 31 (year-end)	All zero balance accounts
5. Select all the bills of lading dated in the last five days of the year, and trace to sales invoices recorded in December.	Document tracing	December 31 (year-end)	Last five days' shipments

Exhibit 6–2 contains five procedures for auditing two accounts receivable assertions. These procedures are part of an account balance audit program. The existence and completeness subheadings and the columns in the exhibit were added to help you see the connections to financial statement assertions and to the nature, timing and extent of the procedures.

Restricting Account Balance Audit Procedures

The procedures presented in Exhibit 6–2 show some restrictions of the timing and extent of work, which suggest a low control risk, specifically:

* Confirmation of a sample of customer accounts receivable before year-end, instead of confirmation of all accounts as of December 31.

* Vouching the last 5 days' recorded sales to bills of lading for cutoff evidence, instead of vouching the last 15 days' sales.

* Tracing the last 5 days' shipments to recorded sales invoices for cutoff evidence, instead of tracing the last 15 days' shipments.

You should assume the auditors think this is an efficient program. An alternative program, which would require more time and greater audit cost, would (1) confirm all the customer accounts as of December 31; (2) omit the analytical comparison of the December accounts receivable trial balance because the confirmation was done as of December 31; (3) select all the sales invoices recorded in the last 15 days for vouching to December bills of lading; (4) send positive confirmations to customers with small balances and zero balances; and (5) select all bills of lading dated in the last 15 days for tracing to December sales invoices.

The preliminary audit program presented in Exhibit 6–2, therefore, depends on a low control risk related to the company's internal control structure. The audit task is to assess the inherent and internal control risks of material misstatement (error or irregularity) that slip into the accounts receivable total through the improper or omitted recording of sales and charges to customers. If the risks are too high, some procedures may need to be changed to provide for greater extent (larger samples) and better timing (confirmation moved to December 31). Likewise, if the risk of omitted sales is not high, the confirmation of zero-balance receivables might be omitted, or negative confirmations might be used instead of positive confirmations. In general, a good system of internal control should result in less audit work than a bad system of internal control. Thus, it is possible to obtain audit efficiencies from good internal controls: less testing and audit work spread over a longer time period.

Communicating Internal Control Weaknesses

A secondary reason to evaluate internal control is to formulate constructive suggestions for improvements. Auditors become involved in system design consulting by including their suggestions in a management letter to the client. Officially, the profession considers these suggestions a part of the audit and does not define the work as a management consulting service. Clients are free to decide whether to act on the suggestions. A management letter is written at the end of the field work. (See Exhibit 13–10 in Chapter 13.) *Handbook Section* 5220 requires communication to management of all significant weaknesses in internal control. In addition, *Section* 5750, "Communication of Matters Identified During the Financial Statement Audit," requires the communication of (1) nontrivial misstatements, (2) fraud, and (3) consequential illegal or possibly illegal acts. However, neither of these sections requires communication in writing—oral communication is sufficient. Thus, when management letters are prepared, *Sections* 5750 and 5220 do not require that their subject matters be included in the management letter.

The management letter *can* include these identified matters; it's just that *Sections* 5750 and 5220 *do not require* management letters to do so. These sections make no explicit mention of management letters. We will call the contents of management letters reportable matters and define these as items the auditor believes should be communicated to the client in writing. (For example, see S. Smith's article, "More Than a Drop in the Bucket," in *CA Magazine,* February 1993, pp. 50–52). For some financial institution regulators, auditors have a "well-being" reporting requirement that includes reporting on significant internal control weaknesses (CICA Guideline AUG–17, "Transactions or Conditions Reportable Under the 'Well-Being Reporting Requirement' in Federal Institutions Legislation"). This Guideline uses the specific term "reportable condition." Thus, a type of reportable matter by our definition is a reportable condition. Examples of reportable conditions include:

- Absence of appropriate segregation of duties.
- Absence of appropriate reviews and approvals of transactions.
- Evidence of failure of control procedures.
- Evidence of intentional management override of control procedures by persons in authority to the detriment of control objectives.
- Evidence of wilful wrongdoing by employees or management, including manipulation, falsification or alteration of accounting records.

Communications of reportable conditions and matters are discussed more fully in Chapter 14. ISA 1007.19 requires auditors to make management aware of material weaknesses in internal controls.

Report of Significant Weakness

Reportable matters include the serious condition called a significant weakness in internal control, which is defined as a deficiency such that a material misstatement is not likely to be prevented or detected in the current or future financial statements of the entity.

Although auditors are not obligated to provide assurance for reportable matters and significant weaknesses, they often communicate ones that come to their attention in the normal performance of the audit. Written communications are preferred, but sometimes

> "The objective of my audit was to obtain reasonable assurance that the financial statements were free of material misstatement and was not designed for the purpose of identifying matters to communicate. Accordingly my audit would not usually identify all such matters that may exist and it is inappropriate to conclude that no matters exist.
>
> During the course of my audit of _____ for the year ended _____ I did not identify any of the following matters: misstatements, other than trivial errors; fraud; misstatements that may cause future financial statements to be materially misstated; illegal or possibly illegal acts, other than ones considered inconsequential; or significant weaknesses in internal control.
>
> This communication is prepared solely for the information of management and is not intended for any other purpose. I accept no responsibility to a third party who relies on this communication."
>
> *Source: CICA Handbook Section* 5750.22, "Communication of Matters Identified During the Financial Statement Audit" (June 1997).

auditors communicate reportable conditions orally, in which case a memorandum of the oral report should be placed in the working papers. However, because the potential for misinterpretation is great, *Section* 5750 recommends that even if no reportable conditions are found in the audit, a carefully worded report should be prepared stating that no specific matters were noted during the audit. See the box above.

R E V I E W
C H E C K P O I N T S

6.1 What are the primary and secondary reasons for conducting an evaluation of an audit client's internal control?

6.2 What is an account balance, substantive audit procedure? Define and explain the nature, timing and extent features of account balance audit procedures in general.

6.3 What is a reportable condition regarding internal control?

Management Versus Auditor Responsibility

LEARNING OBJECTIVE

2. Distinguish between management's and auditors' responsibility regarding a company's internal controls.

A company's management is responsible for its control environment, for its accounting system, and for establishing and maintaining a system of internal control procedures. Continuous managerial supervision and modification are elements of management's responsibility. Management is not only responsible for the internal control that supports the production of financial statements but also is responsible for the internal control that achieves all the other objectives of the business. This broader concept of internal control is exemplified by a definition proposed by the Institute of Internal Auditors, as shown in the box below.

External auditors' communications of *reportable* conditions and material weaknesses are intended to help management carry out its responsibilities for internal control monitoring and change. However, external auditors' observations and recommendations are usually limited to external financial reporting matters.

External auditors are not responsible for designing effective internal control for audit clients. They are responsible for evaluating existing internal controls and assessing the control risk in them. "Designing systems" refers to formulating the plan of organization, the policies and procedures, and other matters important in creating and managing internal control. Accounting firms undertake control design as consulting engagements but consider such work to be separate and apart from the audit engagement responsibility.

INTERNAL CONTROL DEFINITION (IIA)

Internal control is the process by which an entity's board of directors, management and/or other personnel obtain reasonable assurance that the following control objectives will be achieved:

1. Significant financial, managerial and operating information reported internally and externally is accurate, reliable and timely.
2. The activities of the organization are in compliance with policies, plans, standards and procedures, and with applicable laws and regulations.
3. Resources are adequately protected.
4. Resources are acquired economically and used efficiently (or cost-effectively).
5. The organization's plans, goals and objectives are achieved.

Commentary: Emphasis is added in number 1 (italicized words) to isolate the external auditors' primary interest in internal control. You can see by the other parts of number 1 and numbers 2 through 5 that managers' and internal auditors' interests in control are much broader.

Source: The Institute of Internal Auditors, letter to Committee of Sponsoring Organizations of the Treadway Commission (June 14, 1991).

External auditors' basis for knowing about reportable conditions and material weaknesses is found in their familiarity with the types of errors, irregularities, frauds and misstatements that can occur in any account balance or class of transactions. Clearly, hundreds of innocent errors and not-so-innocent fraud schemes are possible. (Many of these are discussed in Chapter 18, on Fraud Awareness Auditing.) Instead of trying to learn hundreds of possible errors and irregularities, it is better to start with seven general categories of them. Exhibit 6–3 shows a typology of seven categories, with some examples. The external auditors' task of control risk assessment involves finding out what the company does to prevent, detect and correct these potential errors and irregularities. You will encounter the flip side of these when you study control objectives later in the chapter.

. . . .

REVIEW
CHECKPOINTS

6.4 What are some of the elements of breadth that characterize managerial and internal audit interest in internal control over and above the external auditors' interest in internal control?

EXHIBIT 6–3

GENERAL CATEGORIES AND EXAMPLES OF ERRORS AND IRREGULARITIES (misstatements)

1. Invalid transactions are recorded: Fictitious sales are recorded and charged to nonexistent customers.
2. Valid transactions are omitted from the accounts: Shipments to customers never get recorded.
3. Unauthorized transactions are executed and recorded: A customer's order is not approved for credit, yet the goods are shipped, billed and charged to the customer without requiring payment in advance.
4. Transaction amounts are inaccurate: A customer is billed and the sale is recorded in the wrong amount because the quantity shipped and the quantity billed are not the same and the unit price is for a different product.
5. Transactions are classified in the wrong accounts: Sales to a subsidiary company are recorded as sales to outsiders instead of intercompany sales, or the amount is charged to the wrong customer account receivable record.
6. Transaction accounting is incomplete: Sales are posted in total to the accounts receivable control account, but some are not posted to individual customer account records.
7. Transactions are recorded in the wrong period: Shipments made in January (next year) are backdated and recorded as sales and charges to customers in December; shipments in December are recorded as sales and charges to customers in January.

6.5 How do external auditors help managers meet their responsibilities for internal control?

6.6 Define control risk. What seven types of errors or irregularities is internal control intended to prevent, detect or correct?

INTERNAL CONTROL ELEMENTS

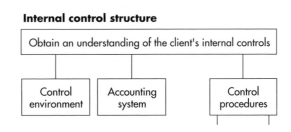

LEARNING OBJECTIVE

3. Define and describe the three basic elements of internal control, and specify some of their component characteristics.

For purposes of explanation, internal control is divided into three elements: The **control environment** is a set of characteristics that defines good control working relationships in a company. The **accounting system** contains policies and procedures for recording transactions properly. The **control procedures** are specific error-checking routines performed by company personnel. In combination, these three parts provide the policies and procedures designed to prevent, detect and correct material errors, irregularities, frauds and misstatements.

Control Environment

The control environment is characterized by management attitudes, structure (organization chart), effective communication of control objectives and supervision of personnel and activities. The following are elements of internal control environments:

- Management's philosophy and operating style.
- Company organization structure.
- Functioning of the board of directors, particularly its audit committee.
- Methods of assigning authority and responsibility.
- Management's monitoring methods, including internal auditing. Personnel policies and practices.
- External influences (e.g., examinations by bank regulatory agencies).
- Control environment for computerized systems also includes the organizational and logical controls that control access to computers and computer files, and authorization of changes to program and data files. Generally, such environmental controls can be characterized as preventive controls in the sense that they are there to prevent misstatements from arising in the first place. Preventive controls are more cost effective than controls designed to detect or correct misstatements that have entered the system. This is one reason why auditors tend to focus the preliminary evaluation on environmental controls. Another reason is the pervasive impact environmental controls have on the accounting cycles affected.

Since management fraud in financial statements became a topic for acceptable discussion in the mid-1980s, "tone at the top" has become a buzzword for the necessary condition for good internal control. The "tone" is virtually identical to the control environment. A wide

---

CRITERIA OF CONTROL (COCO) BOARD OF THE CICA

All control rests ultimately on people assuming responsibility for their decisions and actions. Organizational values that people find acceptable encourage them to assume responsibility for the continuous improvement of their organization.

Shared ethical values influence all behaviour in an organization. Together with an understanding of mission and vision, they constitute the basic identity that will shape the way an individual, group, organization or board will operate, and they provide stability over time. Shared values contribute to control because they provide a guide for individual, group or team decision-making, action and policy.

The values and preferences of senior management and the board of directors greatly influence an organization's objectives and systems. These values and preferences address issues such as:

- good corporate citizenship;
- commitment to truth and fair dealing;
- commitment to quality and competence;
- leadership by example;
- compliance with laws, regulations, rules and organizational policy;
- respect for the privacy of client, organization and employee information;
- fair treatment of and respect for individuals;
- fair relationships with competitors;
- integrity of transactions and records; and
- a professional approach to financial reporting.

Ethical values are part of an organization's culture and provide an unwritten code of conduct against which behaviour is measured. A formal, written code of conduct offers a means of consistent communication of the standards of ethical behaviour. People can be asked periodically to confirm their understanding and observance of the code.

Source: COCO, *Guidance on Control* (November 1995), pp. 14, 15.

---

variety of activities characterize the control environment. For example, the organization structure indicates to the auditor who has the immediate responsibility to authorize payments in payroll processing. Some aspects of the control environment, however, are hard for auditors to understand and document, such as management's philosophy. The box above illustrates some criteria to consider in evaluating the human factor in the control environment.

Accounting System

An accounting system processes transactions, records them in journals and ledgers (either computerized or manual), and produces financial statements without necessarily guaranteeing their accuracy. Nevertheless, the accounting policies and procedures often contain important elements of control. The accounting instruction of "Prepare sales invoices only when shipment has been made," is a control so long as the people performing the work follow the instruction. The control part of this policy could be expressed: "Prepare sales invoices and record them only when a shipping document is matched."

All accounting systems, whether computerized or manual, consist of four essential functions—data preparation, data entry, transaction processing and report production and distribution.

Data preparation is the analysis of transactions and their "capture" for accounting purposes. The "capture" amounts to creation of source documents, such as sales invoices, credit memos, cash receipts listings, purchase orders, receiving reports, negotiable cheques and the like. These source documents provide the information for data entry. However, in some computerized accounting systems the paper source documents are not produced first. Transactions may be entered directly on a keyboard, or electronic equipment may capture the transaction information. Your long-distance telephone charges are initially captured by the telephone company's computers using your telephone number, the location called and the duration of the call.

Data entry often consists of accounting personnel using a batch of source documents to enter transaction information on a keyboard into an accounting software program. This process may produce a "book of original entry," another name for a journal, such as the sales journal, purchases journal, cash receipts journal, cash disbursements journal, general journal and others. In advanced paperless systems, electronic equipment may enter the accounting information automatically without producing an intermediate journal. Your long-distance telephone call is entered automatically into the telephone company's revenue and receivable accounts. Your monthly telephone bill is later produced from the accounting information.

Transaction processing usually refers to posting the journals to the general ledger accounts, using the debits and credits you learned in other accounting courses. The posting operation updates the account balances. When all data are entered and processed, the account balances are ready for placement in reports.

Report production and distribution is the object of the accounting system. The account balances are put into internal management reports and external financial statements. The internal reports are management's feedback for monitoring and control of operations. The external reports are the financial information for outside investors, creditors and others.

The accounting system produces a trail of accounting operations, from transaction analyses to reports. Often, this is called the audit trail. You can visualize that it starts with the source documents and proceeds through to the financial reports. Auditors often follow this trail frontwards and backwards! They will follow it backwards from the financial reports to the source documents to determine whether everything in the financial reports is supported by appropriate source documents. They will follow it forward from source documents to reports to determine that everything that happened (transactions) got recorded in the accounts and reported in the financial statements.

Control procedures are client procedures (both computerized and manual) imposed on the accounting system for the purpose of preventing, detecting and correcting errors and irregularities that might enter and flow through to the financial statements. For example, a control procedure related to the accounting policy cited above would be: "At the end of each day, the billing supervisor reviews all the sales invoices to see that the file copy has a bill of lading copy attached."

Minimum requirements for a good control-oriented accounting system include a chart of accounts and some written definitions and instructions about measuring and classifying transactions. In most organizations such material is incorporated in computer systems documentation, computer program documentation, systems and procedures manuals, flowcharts of transaction processing and various paper forms. A company's internal auditors and systems staff often review and evaluate this documentation. Independent auditors may review and study their work instead of doing the same tasks over again.

Accounting manuals should contain statements of objectives, policies and procedures. Management should approve statements of specific accounting and control objectives and ensure that appropriate procedures are used to accomplish them. In general, the overriding objective of an accounting system is to produce financial statement assertions that are correct. Therefore, the objective of accounting is to produce correct statements of existence or occurrence, completeness, valuation, rights and obligations and presentation and disclosure. An accounting system cannot accomplish this objective without an integrated set of control procedures.

· ·

R E V I E W
C H E C K P O I N T S
6.7 What are some of the important characteristics of "tone at the top" and control environment?

6.8 Where can an auditor find a client's documentation of the accounting system?

6.9 What is the audit trail? Of what use is it in the audit process?

· ·

CONTROL OBJECTIVES AND PROCEDURES
· · · · · · · · · · ·

LEARNING OBJECTIVE

4. Identify and give examples of seven internal control objectives, and associate them with the five management assertions in financial account balances.

While the objective of the accounting system is to produce financial statement assertions that are true, principally in account balances, the overriding objective of control procedures is to process transactions correctly. Correctly processed transactions produce correct account balances, which in turn help produce accurate and reliable assertions in the financial statements.

These connections are shown in Exhibit 6–4. The new information in this exhibit is a list of control objectives. There are many control objective listing schemes. This is one of the shortest.

Control Objectives

Each of the control objectives is a reverse expression of the seven types of errors and irregularities shown in Exhibit 6–3. The presentation in Exhibit 6–5 summarizes each of the seven objectives, with a general statement of the objective and a specific example (accounts receivable/sales transaction processing context). The explanations that follow tell you some more about these objectives and give some examples of client procedures designed to accomplish them.

Validity refers to ensuring that recorded transactions are ones that should have been recorded. The client's procedure can be to require matching of shipping documents with sales invoices before a sale is recorded. This procedure is supposed to prevent the recording of undocumented (possibly fictitious) sales.

Completeness refers to ensuring that valid transactions are not omitted entirely from the accounting records. If sales are represented by shipments, then no shipping documents should be left unmatched with sales invoices. Transaction documents (e.g., shipping documents) are often prenumbered. Accounting for the numerical sequence of prenumbered shipping documents is a control procedure designed to achieve the completeness objective.

Authorization refers to ensuring that transactions are approved before they are recorded. Credit approval for a sale transaction is an example. Sometimes, you may need to ponder the nature of authorization for some transactions. For example, what "authori-

E X H I B I T 6–4   CONTROL OBJECTIVES AND FINANCIAL STATEMENT ASSERTIONS

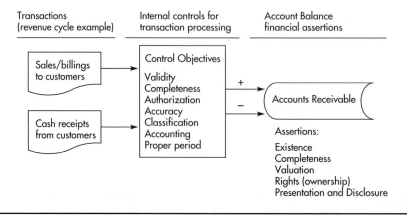

EXHIBIT 6–5   INTERNAL CONTROL OBJECTIVES

Objectives	General	Specific Example (accounts receivable/sales)
Validity	Recorded transactions are valid and documented.	Recorded sales are supported by invoices, shipping documents and customer orders.
Completeness	All valid transactions are recorded, and none are omitted.	All shipping documents are prenumbered and matched with sales invoices daily.
Authorization	Transactions are authorized according to company policy.	Credit sales over $1,000 are given prior approval by the credit manager.
Accuracy	Transaction dollar amounts are properly calculated.	Sales invoices contain correct quantities and are mathematically correct.
Classification	Transactions are properly classified in the accounts.	Sales to subsidiaries and affiliates are classified as intercompany transactions.
Accounting	Transaction accounting is complete.	All sales on credit are charged to customers' individual accounts.
Proper period	Transactions are recorded in the proper period.	Sales of the current period are charged to customers in the current period, and sales of the next period are charged in the next period.

zation" is needed to record a cash receipt? Usually none—companies are happy to accept payments—but a sales manager may need to approve a good customer taking a discount after the discount period has elapsed.

Management must establish criteria for recognizing transactions in the accounting system and for supervisory approval of transactions. A control system should permit accounting to proceed only for authorized transactions and should bar unauthorized transactions.

Authorization may be general and may be delegated to a fairly low level of management. For example, (1) all shipments amounting to more than $1,000 in value require credit approval and (2) all sales can be recorded in the accounting department upon receipt of a copy of a shipping ticket. Some authorizations may be quite tacit. For example, listing the payments received on account when the mail is opened may be sufficient authorization to accept and record cash receipts. Some authorizations may be very important and defined specifically by the board of directors. For example, sales of major assets or responsibility for signing the company name to a loan agreement may be authorized specifically in the minutes of the board of directors.

Accuracy refers to ensuring that dollar amounts are calculated correctly. A manual or computer check for billing the same quantity shipped, at the correct list price, with correct multiplication and addition of the total, is intended to control for accuracy. (This objective, rather than the completeness one, covers errors of billing at too low a price or for a smaller quantity than shipped.) **Classification** refers to ensuring that transactions are recorded in the right accounts, charged or credited to the right customers (including classification of sales to subsidiaries and affiliates, as mentioned in Exhibit 6–5), entered in the correct segment product line or inventory description and so forth. Classification may be confused with accuracy, but remember that accuracy refers to the accounting numbers.

Accounting is a general category concerned with ensuring that the accounting process for a transaction is performed completely and in conformity with GAAP. For example, a clerk can balance the total of individual customers' receivables with the control account to determine whether all charges and credits to the control account also have been entered in individual customers' accounts. (Classification is the control over whether the entries got into the right customers' accounts in the right time period and accuracy is the control category related to use of correct numbers.) Control over accounting, in general, is a useful category if you cannot identify a control problem in one of the other categories.

Proper period refers to ensuring that the accounting for transactions is in the period in which they occur. This control objective is very closely related to the cutoff aspect of the existence and completeness assertions. Procedurally, the client's accountants must be alert to the dates of transactions in relation to month-, quarter-, and year-end. Proper period accounting (cutoff) is a pervasive problem. You will see it mentioned in relation to all kinds of transactions—sales, purchases, inventories, expense accruals, income accruals and others.

Control Objectives and Assertions

The control objectives are closely connected to management's assertions in financial statements. An association of the control objectives with the five assertions is shown in Exhibit 6–6. The Xs in the exhibit show the primary relevance of control objectives to assertions.

To interpret Exhibit 6–6, associate the achievement of control objectives with the probability that an assertion may be materially misstated. For example, if a company has strong control over the validity of recorded sales and cash receipts transactions, if it has an effective system of credit authorization and if it ensures that sales transactions are correctly recorded in the proper period, then the control risk related to the existence/occurrence assertions for sales and accounts receivable balances may be assessed low.

However, an auditor may find that some, but not all, of the control objectives for a particular account balance (i.e., set of assertions) are achieved. For example, the situation cited above may coexist with failure to achieve control over the completeness of recording sales transactions and accounts receivable amounts. In such a case, the preliminary audit program may be changed to require more work related to the completeness of accounts receivable (the assertion for which control risk is high) and be unchanged for the work on the existence of accounts receivable (the assertion for which control risk is low).

The final evaluation of a company's internal control is the assessment of the control risk (CR) related to each assertion. Control risk is the CR element in the audit risk model: $AR = IR \times CR \times DR$. This assessment is an auditor's expression of the effectiveness of the control system for preventing, detecting and correcting specific errors and irregularities in management's financial statement assertions.

Control Procedures

LEARNING OBJECTIVE
5. List and explain the control procedures companies use to achieve control objectives.

Companies use numerous detailed accounting and control procedures designed to achieve the control objectives. All detail procedures are directed, one way or another, toward preventing, detecting and correcting the seven general kinds of errors, irregularities, frauds and misstatements that can occur.

Control procedures can be complicated. Exhibit 6–7 presents an overview of the discussion that follows. The discussion is organized under the headings of general control procedures, segregation of technical responsibilities and error-checking procedures.

EXHIBIT 6–6   ASSOCIATION OF CONTROL OBJECTIVES AND FINANCIAL STATEMENT ASSERTIONS

| Control Objectives | *Financial Statement Assertions* | | | | |
	Existence, Occurrence	Completeness	Valuation	Rights, Obligations	Presentation and Disclosure
Validity	X			X	
Completeness		X		X	
Authorization	X		X	X	
Accuracy			X		
Classification					X
Accounting					X
Proper Period	X	X			

E X H I B I T 6–7   OVERVIEW OF CONTROL PROCEDURES

General Control Procedures

While the "tone at the top" (control environment) is pervasive, the control procedures of capable personnel, segregation of responsibilities, controlled access and periodic comparison are always important in a company's internal controls. General controls like environmental controls are primarily preventive in nature and have a pervasive impact on the various accounting cycles. For these reasons, auditors tend to focus on environmental and general controls in the preliminary evaluation of internal controls.

Capable Personnel.   The most important feature of control is the people who make the system work. A company's personnel problems sometimes create internal control problems. High turnover in accounting jobs means that inexperienced people are doing the accounting and control tasks, and they generally make more mistakes than experienced people. New accounting officers and managers (financial vice president, controller, chief accountant, plant accountant, data processing manager) may not be familiar enough with company accounting and may make technical and judgmental errors. Sometimes accounting officers and employees are fired because they refuse to go along with improper accounting procedures desired by a higher level of management. In general, accounting personnel changes may be a warning signal.

Segregation of Responsibilities.   A very important characteristic of reliable internal control is an appropriate segregation of functional responsibilities. Sometimes this characteristic is called division of duties. Proper segregation of responsibilities is a necessary condition for making detailed clerical control procedures effective.

Four kinds of functional responsibilities should be performed by different departments, or at least by different persons on the company's accounting staff:

1. *Authorization to execute transactions.* This duty belongs to people who have authority and responsibility for initiating the recordkeeping for transactions. Authorization may be general, referring to a class of transactions (e.g., all purchases), or it may be specific (e.g., sale of a major asset).

2. *Recording of transactions.* This duty refers to the accounting and recordkeeping function (bookkeeping) which in most organizations is delegated to a computer system. (People who control the computer processing are the recordkeepers.)

3. *Custody of assets involved in the transactions.* This duty refers to the actual physical possession or effective physical control of property.

4. *Periodic reconciliation of existing assets to recorded amounts.* This duty refers to making comparisons at regular intervals and taking appropriate action with respect to any differences.

Incompatible responsibilities are combinations of responsibilities that place a person alone in a position to create and conceal errors, irregularities and misstatements in his or her normal job. Duties should be so divided that no one person can control two or more functional responsibilities. The first and fourth responsibilities are management functions, the second is an accounting function, and the third is a custodial function. If different departments or persons are forced to deal with these different facets of transactions, then two benefits are obtained: (1) Irregularities are made more difficult because they would require collusion of two or more persons, and most people hesitate to seek the help of others to conduct wrongful acts, and (2) innocent errors are more likely to be found and flagged for correction. The old saying is that "two heads are better than one." The flip side of this is that the more people are assigned to control duties, the better are the controls and the higher the cost of the controls. Any control system will reflect compromises of benefits versus the costs.

Supervision is an important element of control procedures. You can readily imagine a company having clerks and computers to carry out the accounting and control procedures. Equally important is management's provision for supervising the work. A supervisor could, for example, oversee the credit manager's performance or could periodically compare the sum of customers' balances to the accounts receivable control account total. Supervisors or department heads can correct errors found by the clerical staff and make or approve accounting decisions. Supervision is important as management's means of monitoring and maintaining a system of internal control.

Controlled Access.   Physical access to assets and important records, documents and blank forms should be limited to authorized personnel. Such assets as inventory and securities should not be available to persons who have no need to handle them. Likewise, access to cost records and accounts receivable records should be denied to people who do not have a recordkeeping responsibility for them.

Some blank forms are very important for accounting and control, and their availability should be restricted. Someone not involved in accounting for sales should not be able to pick up blank sales invoices and blank shipping orders. A person should not be able to obtain blank cheques (including computer-paper blank cheques) unless he or she is involved in cash disbursement activities. Sometimes, access to blank forms is the equivalent of access to, or custody of, an important asset. For example, someone who has access to blank cheques has a measure of actual custody and access to cash. In computerized systems, controlled access is achieved through the use of physically secure hardware and software and the use of passwords to control electronic access.

Periodic Comparison.   Management has responsibility for the recorded accountability of assets and liabilities. Managers should provide for periodic comparison of the recorded amounts with independent evidence of existence and valuation. Internal auditors and other people on an accounting staff can perform periodic comparison on a regular basis. However, the people who perform these periodic comparisons should not also have responsibility for authorization of related transactions, accounting or recordkeeping or custodial responsibility for the assets.

Periodic comparisons may include counts of cash on hand, reconciliation of bank statements, counts of securities, confirmation of accounts receivable and accounts payable and other such comparison operations undertaken to determine whether accounting records—the recorded accountability—represent real assets and liabilities. A management that performs frequent periodic comparisons has more opportunities to detect errors in the records than a management that does not. The frequency, of course, is governed by the costs and benefits. One should not try to count, compare or confirm assets with great frequency (say, weekly) unless those assets are especially susceptible to loss or error or unless they are unusually valuable. In other words, if the inherent risk is high the control risk should be made commensuratively lower so that the product of the two is constant, e.g., if IR = 1 then CR should be closer to .05 than if IR = .1: $IR \times CR = 1 \times .05 = .1 \times .5 = .05$, assuming planned material misstatement after controls is to be maintained at a constant .05 despite variation in IR.

Subsequent action to correct differences is also important. Periodic comparison and action to correct errors lowers the risk that material misstatements will remain in the accounts. Such comparisons are frequently assigned to internal auditors and other employees.[1]

Segregation of Technical Responsibilities

Most companies use computer-based accounting and control systems. In large companies the essential separation of responsibilities involves the duties of analysts, programmers and operators. The duties associated with these and other important roles are defined as follows:

Systems Analyst.   Analyses requirements for information. Evaluates the existing system and designs new or improved data processing. Outlines the system and prepares specifications that guide the programmers. Prepares documentation of the application system.

Programmer.   Flowcharts the logic of the computer programs required by the overall system designed by the systems analyst. Codes the logic in the computer program. Prepares documentation of the program. A programmer should not be allowed to make any unauthorized coding changes. This invites abuse such as fraud through a computerized payroll function. To reduce this risk it is therefore necessary to have all program changes authorized and documented by the systems analyst.

Computer Operator.   Operates the computer for each accounting application system according to written operating procedures found in the computer operation instructions.

Data Conversion Operators.   Prepares data for machine processing. Previously these individuals operated keypunch machines and produced punched cards; now these operators usually convert visible source data to magnetic tape or disk, operate optical-character reading equipment, or use data transmission terminals. In advanced computer systems, the data conversion operators will likely be accounting clerks entering transactions from the accounting department into remote terminals.

Librarian.   Two types of librarian functions may be found in a computer facility—one for system and program documentation and the other for the actual programs and data files. The purpose of the system/program documentation library is to maintain control over documentation of the design and operation stages of computer information systems. The purpose of the program/data library is to maintain control over the data files and programs

---

[1] Wayne Alderman and James Deitrick have described how companies with active internal auditors have fewer financial statement adjustments recommended by independent auditors than companies without active internal auditors. See "Internal Audit Impact of Financial Information Reliability," *The Internal Auditor*, April 1981, pp. 43–56.

PROGRAMMER AND OPERATOR COMBINED

A programmer employed by a large savings and loan association in the United States wrote a special subroutine that could be activated by a command from the computer console. The computation of interest on deposits and certificates was programmed to truncate calculations at the third decimal place. The special subroutine instructed the program to accumulate the truncated mills, and, when processing was complete, to credit the amount to the programmer-operator's savings account. Whenever this person was on duty for the interest calculation run, she could "make" several hundred dollars! She had to be on duty to manipulate the control figures "properly" so the error of overpaying interest on her account would not be detected by the control group. She was a programmer with computer operation duties.

---

actually used from day to day. In many systems this second library function is done automatically with software.

Control Group.   The control group receives input from user departments, logs the input and transfers it to data conversion, reviews documentation sequence numbers, reviews and processes error messages, monitors actual processing, compares control totals to computer output and distributes output.

Separation of the duties performed by analysts, programmers and operators is important. The general idea is that anyone who designs a processing system should not do the technical programming work, and anyone who performs either of these tasks should not be the computer operator when "live" data is being processed. Persons performing each function should not have access to each other's work, and only the computer operators should have access to the equipment. Computer systems are susceptible to manipulative handling, and the lack of separation of duties along the lines described should be considered a serious weakness in general control. The control group or similar monitoring by the user departments can be an important compensating factor for weaknesses arising from lack of segregation of duties in computerized systems.

Error-Checking Routines

The numerous techniques used to check for errors in accounting data can be categorized as (1) input controls, (2) processing controls, and (3) output controls. The weakest point in computer systems is input—the point at which transaction data are transformed from hardcopy source documents into machine-readable cards, tape or disk, or when direct entry is made with a communication device such as a remote terminal. When undetected errors are entered originally, they may not be detected during processing, and, if detected, they are troublesome to correct. For this reason preventive controls at *input* tend to be the most cost effective. *Processing control* refers to error-condition check routines written into the computer program. *Output control* refers primarily to control over the distribution of reports, but feedback on errors and comparison of input totals to output totals also are part of this "last chance" control point.

Input Control Procedures.   Input controls are designed to provide reasonable assurance that data received for processing by the computer department have been authorized properly and converted into machine-sensible form, and that data have not been lost, suppressed, added, duplicated or otherwise improperly changed. These controls also apply to correction and resubmission of data initially rejected as erroneous. The following control areas are particularly important:

- **Input authorized and approved.**   Only properly authorized and approved input should be accepted for processing by the computer center. Authorization usually is a clerical (noncomputer) procedure involving a person's signature or stamp on a transaction document. However, some authorizations can be general (e.g., a management policy of automatic approval for sales under $500), and some authorizations can be computer-controlled (e.g., automatic production of a purchase order when an inventory item reaches a predetermined reorder point).

- **Check digits.**   Numbers often are used in computer systems in lieu of customer names, vendor names and so forth. One common type of number validation procedure is the calculation of a check digit. A check digit is an extra number, precisely calculated, that is tagged onto the end of a basic identification number, such as an employee number. The basic code with its check digit sometimes is called a self-checking number. An electronic device can be installed on a data input device or the calculation can be programmed. The device or the program calculates the correct check digit and compares it to the one on the input data. When the digits do not match, an error message is indicated on the device or printed out on an input error report. Check digits are used only on identification numbers (not quantity or value fields) to detect coding errors or keying errors such as the transposition of digits (e.g., coding 387 as 837).[2]

Data Conversion.   Conversion of data into machine-sensible form is a source of many errors. Control procedures include the following:

- **Record counts.** Counts of records are tallies of the number of transaction documents submitted for data conversion. The known number submitted can be compared to the count of records produced by the data-conversion device (e.g., the number of sales transactions or count of magnetic records coded). A count mismatch indicates a lost item or one converted twice. Record counts are used as batch control totals and also are used during processing and at the output stage—whenever the comparison of a known count can be made with a computer-generated count.

- **Batch financial totals.** These totals are used in the same way as record counts, except the batch total is the sum of some important quantity or amount (e.g., the total sales dollar in a batch of invoices). Batch totals are also useful during processing and at the output stage.

- **Batch hash totals.** These totals are similar to batch number totals, except the hash total is not meaningful for accounting records (e.g., the sum of all the invoice numbers on invoices submitted to the data input operator).

Edit or Validation Routines.   Various computer-programmed editing or validation routines can be used to detect data conversion errors. Some of these are listed below:

- **Valid character tests.** These tests are used to check input data fields to see if they contain numbers when they are supposed to have numbers and alphabetic letters where they are supposed to have letters.

- **Valid sign tests.** Sign tests check data fields for appropriate plus or minus signs.

---

[2] One check digit algorithm is the "Modulus 11 Prime Number" method:
   a. Begin with a basic number: 814973.
   b. Multiply consecutive prime number weights of 19, 17, 13, 7, 5, 3 to each digit in the basic code number:

8	1	4	9	7	3
×19	×17	×13	×7	×5	×3
= 152	+ 17	+ 52	+ 63	+ 35	+ 9 = 328

   Note: the sequence of weights is the same for all codes in given system.
   c. Add the result of the multiplication = 328.
   d. Determine the next higher multiple of 11, which is 330.
   e. Subtract the sum of the multiplication (330 – 328 = 2). This is the check digit.
   f. New account number: 8149732.

Now if this number is entered incorrectly, say it is keypunched as 8419732, the check digit will not equal 2 and an error will be indicated. [See J. G. Burch, Jr., F. R. Strater, Jr., and G. Grudniski, *Information Systems: Theory and Practice*, 5th ed. (New York: John Wiley & Sons, 1989), pp. 191–93.]

- **Missing data tests.** These edit tests check data fields to see if any are blank when they must contain data for the record entry to be correct.
- **Sequence tests.** These test the input data for numerical sequence of documents when sequence is important for processing, as in batch processing. This validation routine also can check for missing documents in a prenumbered series.
- **Limit or reasonableness tests.** These tests are computerized checks to see whether data values exceed or fall below some predetermined limit. For example, a payroll application may have a limit test to flag and reject any weekly payroll time record of 50 or more hours. The limit tests are a computerized version of scanning, the general audit procedure of reviewing data for indication of anything unusual that might turn out to be an error.

Error Correction and Resubmission.   Errors should be subject to special controls. Usually the computer department itself is responsible only for correcting its own errors (data conversion errors, for example). Other kinds of errors, such as those due to improper coding, should be referred to and handled by the user departments. It is a good idea to have a control group log the contents of error reports in order to monitor the nature, disposition and proper correction of rejected data. Unless properly supervised and monitored, the error-correction process itself can become a source of data input errors.

Processing Control Procedures.   Processing controls are designed to provide reasonable assurance that data processing has been performed as intended without any omission or double-counting of transactions. Many of the processing controls are the same as the input controls, but they are used in the actual processing phases, rather than at the time input is checked. Other important controls are the following:

- **Run-to-run totals.** Movement of data from one department to another or one processing program to another should be controlled. One useful control is run-to-run totals. Run-to-run refers to sequential processing operations—runs—on the same data. These totals may be batch record counts, financial totals and/or hash totals obtained at the end of one processing run. The totals are passed to the next run and compared to corresponding totals produced at the end of the second run.
- **Control total reports.** Control totals—record counts, financial totals, hash totals and run-to-run totals—should be produced during processing operations and printed out on a report. Someone (the control group, for example) should have the responsibility for comparing and/or reconciling them to input totals or totals from earlier processing runs. Loss or duplication of data thus may be detected. For example, the total of the balances in the accounts receivable master file from the last update run, plus the total of the credit sales from the current update transactions, should equal the total of the balances at the end of the current processing.
- **File and operator controls.** External and internal labels are means of assuring that the proper files are used in applications. The systems software should produce a log to identify instructions entered by the operator and to make a record of time and use statistics for application runs. These logs should be reviewed by supervisory personnel.
- **Limit and reasonableness tests.** These tests should be programmed to ensure that illogical conditions do not occur: for example, depreciating an asset below zero or calculating a negative inventory quantity. These conditions, and others considered important, should generate error reports for supervisory review. Other logic and validation checks, described earlier under the heading of input edit checks, also can be used during processing.

Output Control Procedures.   Output controls are the final check on the accuracy of the results of computer processing. These controls also should be designed to ensure that only authorized persons receive reports or have access to files produced by the system. Typical output control procedures are the following:

- **Control totals.** Control totals produced as output should be compared and/or reconciled to input and run-to-run control totals produced during processing. An independent control group should be responsible for the review of output control totals and investigation of differences.
- **Master file changes.** These changes should be reported in detail back to the user department from which the request for change originated because an error can be pervasive. For example, changing selling prices incorrectly can cause all sales to be priced wrong. Someone should compare computer-generated change reports to original source documents for assurance that the data are correct.
- **Output distribution.** Systems output should be distributed only to persons authorized to receive it. A distribution list should be maintained and used to deliver report copies. The number of copies produced should be restricted to the number needed.

R E V I E W
C H E C K P O I N T S

6.10 What are some of the characteristics that distinguish among control environment, accounting system and control procedures in an internal control system?

6.11 What four general kinds of functional responsibilities should be performed by different departments or persons in a control system with good division of duties?

6.12 Give some examples of periodic comparisons a company can perform to control the accuracy of its recorded accountability.

6.13 What is a client's control procedure?

6.14 Describe the typical duties of computer personnel.

6.15 Which duties should be segregated within the computer department?

6.16 What is a self-checking number? Can you give an example of one of your own?

6.17 Describe five types of edit or validation controls and give an example of each for fields on a sales invoice form (e.g., customer name and number, dollar amount of the sale, shipping document number field, invoice number).

PHASES OF A CONTROL EVALUATION

LEARNING OBJECTIVE

6. Explain the phases of an evaluation of control and risk assessment and the documentation and extent of audit work required.

The following sections describe the process of control evaluation in three phases. A major goal in audits is to be efficient. This means performing the work in minimum time and cost while still doing high-quality work to obtain sufficient, competent evidence. The allocation of work times between control evaluation and "year-end audit work" (e.g., the procedures in Exhibit 6–2) is a cost-benefit trade-off. Generally, the more auditors know about good controls, the less substantive year-end work they need to do. However, auditors do not necessarily need to determine the actual quality of a company's internal control structure. They only need to know enough to plan the other audit work. They can obtain only a minimum understanding of the control structure, assess a high control risk and perform extensive substantive balance-audit work. Alternatively, they can perform a complete evaluation of control, assess control risk to be low and minimize the balance-audit work. This trade-off is illustrated in Exhibit 6–8.

The three phases of work are described as if they are separate and distinct work packages performed before any account balance (substantive) audit work is started. In practice, work on the phases is often overlapping, and account balance-audit work is often done at a date before the company's fiscal year-end, at the same time some of the control evaluation work is being done. However, the analytical thinking process follows the sequence described hereafter.

EXHIBIT 6–8   AUDIT COST TRADE-OFF

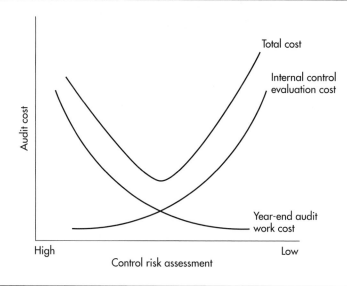

PHASE 1: UNDERSTANDING THE INTERNAL CONTROL

. . . .

Exhibit 6–9 puts the internal control evaluation phases in perspective. In Phase 1 documentation of the auditors' understanding of internal control is required, but the audit team can halt the control evaluation process for the efficiency or effectiveness reasons explained below. However, if the auditors want to justify a low risk assessment to restrict the substantive audit procedures, the evaluation must be continued in Phase 3, the testing phase.

Nature and Timing of Phase 1 Work

The Phase 1 obtaining-an-understanding work should be done early. It gives auditors an overall acquaintance with the control environment, the flow of transactions through the

EXHIBIT 6–9   PHASES OF RISK ASSESSMENT DIAGRAM

accounting system, and the effectiveness of some control procedures. It should produce general knowledge of the control environment along these lines:

- Managers' and directors' attitudes and actions regarding control.
- The client's organizational chart and personnel assignments.
- The segregation of functional responsibilities. Methods used to communicate responsibility and authority.
- Methods used to monitor and supervise the accounting system and the control procedures and to control access to assets and documents.
- The work assignments of internal auditors, if any.

It should also produce general knowledge of the flow of transactions through the accounting system along the following lines:

- The various classes of significant accounting transactions.
- The types of material errors and irregularities that could occur.
- Methods by which each significant class of transaction is:
  Authorized and initiated.
  Documented and recorded.
  Processed in the accounting system.
  Placed in financial reports and disclosures.

Auditors obtain an understanding of the internal controls through several sources of information. These sources include (1) previous experience with the company as found in last year's audit, (2) responses to enquiries directed to client personnel, (3) inspection of documents and records, and (4) observation of activities and operations made in a "walk-through" of one or a few transactions. Such "walk-through" tests of one transaction have traditionally been used to verify the accuracy of the auditor's flowchart or other description of the system.

The following box illustrates an actual system so bad it was considered unauditable.

UNDERSTANDING THE AUDITABILITY OF THE ACCOUNTS

Bad Books Block Audit for County

Travis County commissioners kept such poor financial records for four nonprofit corporations they controlled that an audit cannot be done, commissioners were told Tuesday. The four corporations are conduits for more than $630 million in low-interest financing for businesses. Public Accountant D. Holliday of Holliday & Associates struggled to find words to describe the corporations' records. "To say they are horrid is stretching it, because there weren't any records," Holliday told Commissioners Court members.

Among the findings were: (1) No records were kept of purchase and redemption of certificates of deposit for hundreds of thousands of dollars, (2) there may be certificates of deposit the county officials do not know exist, (3) bank statements were not kept, (4) checking accounts were not reconciled.

The former treasurer of the corporations said: "We had a very simple bookkeeping system. Money went in and went out. The system wasn't sophisticated because it wasn't needed."

Source: Austin American Statesman, August 19, 1987.

E X H I B I T 6–10   PHASES OF INTERNAL CONTROL EVALUATION

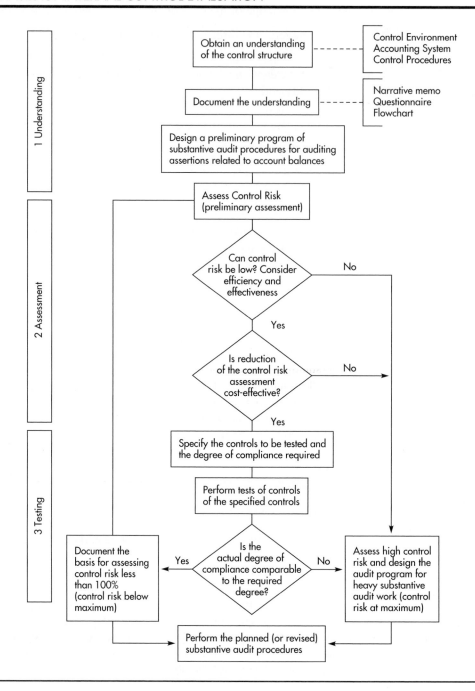

Stopping the Risk Assessment Work

Auditors can decide to stop the evaluation work in Phase 1 for either of two reasons, both of them co-ordinated with the final audit program. First, the audit team might conclude that no more evidence is needed to show that control is too poor to justify restrictions of subsequent audit procedures. This conclusion is equivalent to assessing control risk at 1.0 (100 percent or "at maximum") and specifying extensive account balance-audit procedures, such as confirmation of all customer accounts as of December 31. Essentially, this decision is a matter of audit **effectiveness**.

Second, the audit team might decide that more time and effort would be spent evaluating controls to lower the control risk assessment than could be saved through being able to justify less account balance work (providing the controls turn out to be working well). In other words, the cost of obtaining a low control risk assessment may be high. In this case the conclusion is also equivalent to assessing control risk at or near 1.0, but this time because the auditors lack knowledge about the controls and not because they have decided controls are poor. However, the result is the same: extensive year-end account balance-audit procedures are specified. For example, suppose the extensive evaluation of controls over the validity of charges to customers would take 40 hours. If controls were excellent, suppose then the sample confirmation as of November 1 (with subsequent review of the December 31 trial balance) would take 30 hours less to perform than confirmation of all accounts as of December 31. The additional work on controls is not economical. The decision to stop work on control risk assessment in this case is a matter of audit **efficiency**—deciding not to work 40 hours in order to save 30 hours.

Documentation of the Control Elements

Working paper documentation of a decision to assess control risk as 1.0 (no reliance on the control structure to restrict procedures) can consist only of a memorandum of that fact. However, for future reference in next year's audit, many firms prepare a memorandum explaining the effectiveness-related or efficiency-related reasons.

Working paper documentation also should include records showing the audit team's understanding of the internal controls. The understanding can be summarized in the form of questionnaires, narratives and flowcharts.

Internal Control Questionnaire and Narrative

The most efficient means of gathering evidence about the control structure is to conduct a formal interview with knowledgeable managers, using the checklist type of **internal control questionnaire** illustrated in Exhibit 6–11. This questionnaire is organized under headings that identify the control environment questions and the questions related to each of the seven control objectives. All questionnaires are not organized like this, so auditors need to know the general categories in order to know whether the questionnaire is complete. Likewise, if you are assigned to write a questionnaire, you will need to be careful to include questions about each control objective.

Internal control questionnaires are designed to help the audit team obtain evidence about the control environment and about the accounting and control procedures that are considered good error-checking routines. Answers to the questions, however, should not be taken as final and definitive evidence about how well control actually functions. Evidence obtained through the interview-questionnaire process is hearsay evidence because its source is generally a single person who, while knowledgeable, is still not the person who actually performs the control work. This person may give answers that reflect what he or she believes the system should be, rather than what it really is. The person may be unaware of informal ways in which duties have been changed or may be innocently ignorant of the system details. Nevertheless, interviews and questionnaires are useful when a manager tells of a weak feature. An admission of weak control is fairly convincing.

A strong point about questionnaires is that an auditor is less likely to forget to cover some important point. Questions generally are worded so that a "no" answer points out some weakness or control deficiency, thus making analysis easier.

One way to tailor these enquiry procedures to a particular company is to write a narrative description of each important control subsystem. Such a narrative would simply describe all the environmental elements, the accounting system and the control procedures. The narrative description may be efficient in audits of very small businesses.

EXHIBIT 6–11 INTERNAL CONTROL QUESTIONNAIRE—SALES TRANSACTION PROCESSING

Client _____ Audit Date _____

Client Personnel Interviewed _____

_____

Auditor _____ Date Completed _____

Reviewed by _____ Date Reviewed _____

Question	Answer			
	NA	Yes	No	Remarks
Environment:				
1. Is the credit department independent of the marketing department?				
2. Are sales of the following types controlled by the same procedures described below? Sales to employees, COD sales, disposals of property, cash sales and scrap sales.				
Validity Objective				
3. Is access to sales invoice blanks restricted?				
4. Are prenumbered bills of lading or other shipping documents prepared or completed in the shipping department?				
Completeness Objective				
5. Are sales invoice blanks prenumbered?				
6. Is the sequence checked for missing invoices?				
7. Is the shipping document numerical sequence checked for missing bills of lading numbers?				
Authorization Objective				
8. Are all credit sales approved by the credit department prior to shipment?				
9. Are sales prices and terms based on approved standards?				
10. Are returned sales credits and other credits supported by documentation as to receipt, condition, and quantity and approved a responsible officer?				
Accuracy Objective				
11. Are shipped quantities compared to invoice quantities?				
12. Are sales invoices checked for error in quantities, prices, extensions and footing, freight allowances and checked with customer's orders?				
13. Is there an overall check on arithmetic accuracy of period sales data by a statistical or product-line analysis?				
14. Are periodic sales data reported directly to general ledger accounting independent of accounts receivable accounting?				
Classification Objective				
15. Does the accounting manual contain instructions for classifying sales?				
Accounting Objective				
16. Are summary journal entries approved before posting?				
Proper Period Objective				
17. Does the accounting manual contain instructions to date sales invoices on the shipment date?				

Accounting and Control System Flowcharts

Another method for documenting auditors' understanding of accounting and control systems is to construct a flowchart. Many control-conscious companies will have their own flowcharts, usually prepared by internal auditors, and the external auditors can use them instead of constructing their own. Flowcharting is used widely by auditors. The advantages of flowcharts can be summarized by an old cliché: "A picture is worth a thousand words." Flowcharts can enhance auditors' evaluations, and annual updating of a chart is relatively easy—simply add or delete symbols and lines.

Construction of a flowchart takes time because an auditor must learn about the operating personnel involved in the system and gather samples of relevant documents. Thus, the information for the flowchart, like the narrative description, involves a lot of legwork and observation. When the flowchart is complete, however, the result is an easily evaluated, informative description of the system.

Exhibit 6–12 contains a few simple flowchart symbols. For any flowcharting application, the chart must be understandable to an audit supervisor. He or she should not need to consult a lengthy index of symbols to decipher a flowchart. A flowchart should be drawn with a template and ruler or with computer software. A messy chart is hard to read. The starting point in the system should, if possible, be placed at the upper left-hand corner. The flow of procedures and documents should be from left to right and from top to bottom, as much

E X H I B I T 6–12   STANDARD FLOWCHART SYMBOLS

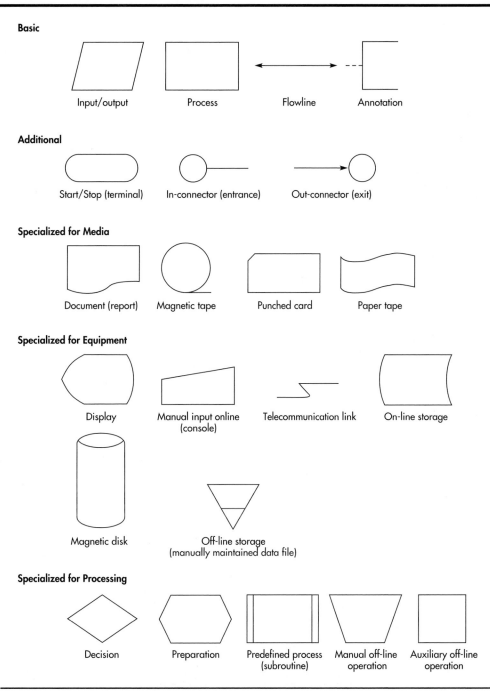

Basic

Input/output   Process   Flowline   Annotation

Additional

Start/Stop (terminal)   In-connector (entrance)   Out-connector (exit)

Specialized for Media

Document (report)   Magnetic tape   Punched card   Paper tape

Specialized for Equipment

Display   Manual input online (console)   Telecommunication link   On-line storage

Magnetic disk   Off-line storage (manually maintained data file)

Specialized for Processing

Decision   Preparation   Predefined process (subroutine)   Manual off-line operation   Auxiliary off-line operation as is possible. Narrative explanations should be written on the face of the chart as annotations or be written in a readily available reference key.

The flowchart should communicate all relevant information and evidence about segregation of responsibilities, authorization and accounting and control procedures in an understandable, visual form. Exhibit 6–13 contains a flowchart representation of the beginning stages of a sales and delivery processing system. This is a partial flowchart. The out-connectors shown by the circled A and B indicate continuation on other flowcharts. Ultimately, the flowchart ends showing entries in accounting journals and ledgers.

In Exhibit 6–13 you can see some characteristics of flowchart construction and some characteristics of this accounting system.[3] One general rule is to minimize the number of flowlines that cross each other.

By reading down the columns headed for each department, you can see that transaction initiation authority (both credit approval and sales invoice preparation) and custody of assets are separated. Notice that all documents have an intermediate or final resting place in a file. (Some of these files are in the flowcharts connected to A and B.) This flowchart feature gives auditors information about where to find audit evidence later.

A technological development that has helped make flowcharting more cost effective is specialized software that automates the flowcharting process. The box on page 193 illus-

E X H I B I T 6–13   CREDIT APPROVAL AND SALES PROCESSING, SHIPMENT AND DELIVERY

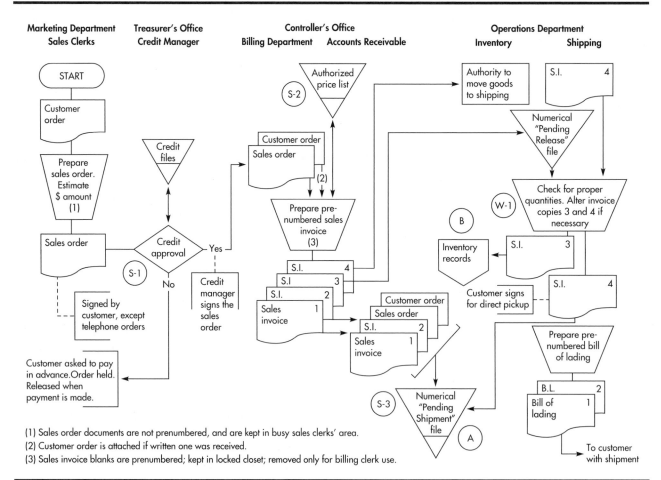

(1) Sales order documents are not prenumbered, and are kept in busy sales clerks' area.
(2) Customer order is attached if written one was received.
(3) Sales invoice blanks are prenumbered; kept in locked closet; removed only for billing clerk use.

[3] Accounting firms have various methods for constructing flowcharts. The illustrations in this book take the approach of describing an accounting subsystem completely. Some accounting firms use more efficient methods to flowchart only the documents, information flows and controls considered important for the audit.

ANALYSING AND DOCUMENTING INTERNAL CONTROL

We can bring to bear a variety of techniques and tools to assist clients in strengthening internal control. The most exciting of these methodologies is INFOCUS, our microcomputer package for analysing portions of an entity's internal controls and graphically portraying potential weaknesses. INFOCUS harnesses the microcomputer to combine flowcharting and narratives, blending attributes of both to achieve a unique approach to documenting and evaluating internal controls that is applicable regardless of size, complexity, type of business or nature of the entity.

Source: Grant Thornton open letter to clients, May 20, 1991.

---

trates some software used in practice. Regardless of the method used to develop the flowchart, an important way of verifying the accuracy of the flowchart is to perform a "walk through" test of the documents and procedures to verify that they are processed in the manner described in the flowchart.

This section concludes with a brief overview of how internal controls affect audit strategy:[4]

1. Most audit engagements involve some minimal reliance on internal controls, even if only on environmental controls affecting all cycles (for example, reconciliation of general ledger to subsidiary ledgers). Such general control reliance is particularly common in audits of small businesses. Note: Under *Section* 5205 and GAAS (*Section* 5100), auditors are *required* to understand internal controls in order to plan an audit.

2. Internal control is documented through narratives, questionnaires and flowcharts. These are corroborated through "walk-through" tests or tracing of a representative transaction.

3. In reaching a preliminary evaluation of internal control, the auditor must consider:
    (a) possible errors that may arise, and
    (b) the controls that exist to prevent or detect those errors.

    This requires application of professional judgment after obtaining the knowledge in point 2 above.

4. The review, preliminary evaluation and documentation must be applied to specific internal controls within an individual cycle. The specific controls, not the entire system as a whole, are tested for reliability. Only the specific controls on which auditors intend to rely need to be documented and tested.

5. If the auditor wishes to rely on internal controls above the minimal level (that is, control risk is *below* maximum as per *Section* 5210), tests of control need to be planned and executed. The decision to test the controls is a function of:
    (a) the evaluation of the design of the system, and
    (b) the cost-benefit tradeoffs of compliance testing, assuming the design is adequate.

In summary, if the auditor decides not to rely on internal controls beyond the minimal level (control risk at maximum), then there is no reduction in the extent of substantive audit procedures. This is referred to as the substantive audit approach in the *Handbook*. If, on a preliminary basis, the auditor does decide to rely on internal controls, testing of the controls is required. If the tests show the controls are operating effectively, then the auditor may reduce the extent of substantive audit procedures (control risk below maximum). This is referred to as the combined audit approach in the *Handbook*. Interim testing is primarily reserved for compliance testing (that is, tests of controls) when the auditor plans to rely on controls.

The combined and substantive audit approaches are covered in *Handbook Sections* 5205 and 5210, and further summarized in Exhibit 6–14.

---

[4] Summarized from J.M. Sylph, "How Internal Controls Affect Audit Strategy," *CAmagazine*, January 1983, pages 47–51.

E X H I B I T 6–14 AUDIT APPROACHES TO INTERNAL CONTROL

*Some auditing procedures performed to obtain the necessary understanding of internal control for audit planning puposes may also provide audit evidence that policies and procedures are operating effectively and therefore constitute tests of controls (5210.19).

Phase 2: Assessing the Control Risk

After completing Phase 1—obtaining an understanding of the internal control and designing a preliminary audit program—the audit team should be able to make a preliminary assessment of the control risk. One way to make the assessment is to analyse the control strengths and weaknesses. **Strengths** are specific features of good detail controls that would prevent, detect or correct material misstatements. **Weaknesses** are the lack of controls in particular areas that would allow material errors to get by undetected. The auditors' findings and preliminary conclusions should be written up for the working paper files.

Strengths and weaknesses should be documented in a working paper sometimes called a bridge working paper, so called because it connects (bridges) the control evaluation to subsequent audit procedures. The major strengths and weaknesses apparent in the flow chart (Exhibit 6–13) can be summarized as shown in Exhibit 6–15. On the flowchart the strengths are indicated by S-, and the weaknesses by W-. In the bridge working paper, the "audit program" column contains test of controls procedures for auditing the control strengths and suggestions about substantive account balance audit procedures related to the weaknesses (the last column in Exhibit 6–15). Auditors do not need to perform test of controls audit procedures on weaknesses just to prove they are weak places. Doing so would be inefficient.

In terms of control risk assessment, at this stage the control risk related to the inventory balance might be set very high (e.g., 0.8 or 0.9). The three control strengths, however, relate to good control over sales validity and accounts receivable accuracy. The auditors probably will want to rely on these controls to reduce the accounts receivable balance audit work. Test of controls procedures ought to be performed to obtain evidence about whether the

EXHIBIT 6–15   **BRIDGE WORKING PAPER**

Index   By _____ Date _____
                                  Reviewed _____ Date _____

KINGSTON COMPANY
Credit Approval, Sales Processing, Shipment and Delivery Control
December 31, 2002

	Strength/Weakness	Audit Implication	Audit Program
S-1	Credit approval on sales order.	Credit authorization reduces risk of bad debt loss and helps check on validity of customer identification.	Select a sample of recorded sales invoices, and look for credit manager signature on attached sales order.
S-2	Unit prices are taken from an authorized list.	Prices are in accordance with company policy, minimizing customer disputes.	Using the S-1 sample of sales invoices, vouch prices used thereon to the price lists.
S-3	Sales are not recorded until goods are shipped.	Cutoff will be proper and sales will not be recorded too early.	Using the S-1 sample of sales invoices, compare the recording date to the shipment date on attached bill of lading or copy 4. (Also, scan the "pending shipment" file for old invoices that might represent unrecorded shipments.)
W-1	Shipping personnel have transaction alteration (initiation) authority to change the quantities on invoices, as well as custody of the goods.	Dishonest shipping personnel can alone let accomplices receive large quantities and alter the invoice to charge them for small quantities. In this system, sales and accounts receivable would be understated, and inventory could be overstated.	The physical count of inventory will need to be observed carefully (extensive work) to detect material overstatement.

apparent strengths actually are performed well. The "audit program" segment of Exhibit 6–15 for each of the strengths is a statement of a test of controls audit procedure. Test of controls auditing (Phase 3) consists of procedures designed to produce evidence of how well the controls worked in practice. If they pass the auditor's criteria (the required degree of compliance), control risk can be assessed low. If they fail the test, the final conclusion is to assess a high control risk, revise the account balance audit plan to take the control weakness into account, and then proceed with the audit work. In summary, Phases 1 and 2 can be described as dealing with the evaluation of the *design* of the system assuming it operates properly, whereas Phase 3 is a test of the actual operation of the systems.

PHASE 3: PERFORMING TEST OF CONTROLS AUDIT PROCEDURES

LEARNING OBJECTIVE

7. Write procedures for an audit program, following the general form of a detail test of control procedure.

By the time auditors reach the third phase of an evaluation of internal control, they will have identified specific controls on which risk could be assessed very low (e.g., the strengths shown in Exhibit 6–15). To reduce the final risk assessment to a low level, auditors must determine (1) the required degree of company compliance with the control policies and procedures and (2) the actual degree of company compliance. The **required degree of compliance** is the auditors' decision criterion for good control performance. Knowing that compliance cannot realistically be expected to be perfect, auditors might decide, for example, that evidence of using bills of lading (shipping documents) to validate sales invoice recordings 96 percent of the time is sufficient to assess a low control risk for the audit of accounts receivable (looking for overstatement in receivables and sales).

Now the auditors can perform **test of controls procedures** to determine how well the company's controls actually functioned during the period under audit. A test of controls audit procedure is a two-part statement. Part 1 is an identification of the data population from which a sample of items will be selected for audit. Part 2 is an expression of an action taken to produce relevant evidence. In general, the action is (1) determine whether the selected items correspond to a standard (e.g., mathematical accuracy), and/or (2) determine whether the selected items agree with information in another data population. The test of controls procedures in Exhibit 6–15 show this two-part design.

One other important aspect of these audit procedures is known as the direction of the test. The procedures described in Exhibit 6–15 provide evidence about control over the validity of sales transactions. However, they do not provide evidence about control over completeness of recording all shipments. Another data population—the shipping documents—can be sampled to provide evidence about completeness. The direction of the test idea is illustrated in Exhibit 6–16. If completeness control is found to be strong, the audi-

EXHIBIT 6-16   **DIRECTION OF THE TEST OF CONTROLS AUDIT PROCEDURES**

TEST OF CONTROLS NECESSARY FOR
ASSESSING LOW CONTROL RISK

Enquiry alone generally will not provide sufficient evidential matter to support a conclusion about the effectiveness of design or operation of a specific [client] control procedure. When the auditor determines that a specific [client] control procedure may have a significant effect in reducing control risk to a low level for a specific assertion, he or she ordinarily needs to perform additional tests [of controls] to obtain sufficient evidential matter to support the conclusion about the effectiveness of the design or operation of that [client] control procedure.

Source: Handbook Section 5205.23.

---

tors can omit the year-end procedure of confirming customers' zero-balance accounts to search for unrecorded assets.

Some test of controls procedures involve **reperformance**—the auditors perform again the arithmetic calculations and the comparisons the company people were supposed to have performed. Some accountants, however, believe mere **inspection** is enough—the auditors just look to see whether the documents were marked with an initial, signature or stamp to indicate that they had been checked (some refer to this as "pure" tests of controls). They maintain that reperformance is not necessary.[5] A compromise is to perform both procedures (**dual-purpose tests**) on at least some of the tested transactions.

Some test of controls procedures depend on documentary evidence, like a sales entry supported by a bill of lading. Documentary evidence in the form of signatures, initials, checklists, reconciliation working papers and the like provides better evidence than procedures that leave no documentary tracks. Some control elements, such as segregation of employees' duties, may leave no documents behind. In this case, the best kind of procedures—reperformance of control operations—cannot be done, and the second procedure—observation—must be used. This procedure amounts to an auditor's unobtrusive eyewitness observation of employees at their jobs performing control operations.

Tests of controls procedures, when performed, should be applied to samples of transactions and control procedures executed throughout the period under audit. The reason for this requirement is that the conclusions about controls will be generalized to the whole period under audit.

. . . .

R E V I E W
CHECKPOINTS

6.18 Must the Phase 1 obtaining-an-understanding work of an evaluation of internal control always be followed by assessment and testing phases? Explain.

6.19 What are the advantages and disadvantages of documenting internal control by using (1) an internal control questionnaire, (2) a narrative memorandum, and (3) a flowchart?

6.20 What is a bridge working paper? Describe its content and its connection to the test of controls and account balance audit programs.

6.21 What is a test of controls audit procedure? What two parts are important in a written procedure?

6.22 What is the difference between inspection and reperformance in test of controls audit procedures?

. . . .

---

[5] When you go to work for an audit organization, one preference will prevail, but many auditors believe good evidence requires reperformance, where feasible, at least for part of the controls testing.

CONTROL EVALUATION AND COST/BENEFIT
. . . .

LEARNING OBJECTIVE

8. Define and explain reasonable assurance and cost-benefit in the context of control risk assessment.

An assessment of control risk should be co-ordinated with the final audit plan. The final account balance audit plan includes the specification (list) of **substantive audit procedures**, which were defined in Chapter 5 as the transaction detail audit and analytical procedures designed to detect material misstatements in account balances and footnote disclosures.

Internal controls are subject to cost-benefit considerations. Controls possibly could be made perfect, or nearly so, at great expense. A fence could be erected; locks could be installed; lighting could be used at night; television monitors could be put in place; guards could be hired. Each of these successive safeguards costs money, as does extensive supervision of clerical personnel in an office. At some point the cost of protecting the inventory from theft (or of supervisors' catching every clerical error) exceeds the benefit of control. Hence, control systems generally do not provide absolute assurance that the objectives of internal control are satisfied. **Reasonable assurance** is thought to be enough, and has been defined as follows: "The concept of reasonable assurance recognizes that the cost of an entity's internal [controls] should not exceed the benefits that are expected to be derived." The *CICA Handbook* notes this concept when it recognizes that internal control is designed to assist management to optimize the use of resources (*Sections* 5200–5220C).

Notwithstanding the common sense of the concept of reasonable assurance, auditors must be careful to determine whether a system contains any internal control weakness. Business managers can make estimates of benefits to be derived from controls and weigh them against the cost. Managers are perfectly free to make their own judgments about the necessary extent of controls. Managers can decide the degree of business risk they are willing to accept (refer to Appendix B of *Handbook Sections* 5200–5220). However, auditors should be aware that the "cost-benefit" and "reasonable assurance" concepts can sometimes be used loosely by a management to tolerate control deficiencies.

Since preparation of the final account balance audit plan is the primary aim and purpose, the evaluation of internal control must be documented in audit working papers. Documentation of the understanding of the internal control and the control risk assessment is required. These audit working papers can include internal control questionnaires, narrative descriptions, flowcharts, specifications of controls and compliance criteria, and the evidence produced by test of controls audit procedures.

You have studied tests of controls and substantive balance audit procedures as if they were easily distinguishable. Be advised, however, that the six general audit techniques described in Chapter 4 can be used both as test of controls procedures and as substantive procedures. Actually, you would be better advised to think in terms of test of controls and substantive **purposes** of a procedure instead of test of controls and substantive procedures. A single procedure may produce both control and substantive evidence and, thus, serve both purposes (hence the name **dual-purpose tests**, *Handbook Section* 5210.21). For example, a selection of recorded sales entries could be used (1) to vouch sales to supporting bills of lading and (2) to calculate the correct dollar amount of sales. The first datum is relevant information about control compliance. The second is dollar-value information that may help measure an amount of misstatement in the book balance of sales. Another example is the confirmation of accounts receivable procedure. This procedure has a primary substantive purpose, but, when confirmation replies tell about significant or systematic errors, the evidence is relevant to control evaluation as well as to dollar-value measurement. Most audit procedures serve dual purposes and yield evidence both about controls and about financial statement assertions.

. . . .

R E V I E W
CHECKPOINTS

6.23 What is the concept of reasonable assurance? Who is responsible for assessing it?

6.24 What audit problems can arise over management's beliefs about reasonable assurance?

6.25 What purposes are served by a "dual-purpose test?"

. . . .

Internal Control in Small Business

· · · · · · · · · · · ·

9. Adapt the concepts and processes of control risk assessment to small businesses.

The foregoing explanations of internal control characteristics contain an underlying thread of bureaucratic organization theory and a large-business orientation. A company must be large and employ several people (about 10 or more) to have a theoretically appropriate segregation of functional responsibilities and its accompanying high degree of specialization of work. Supervision requires people. The paperwork and computer control necessary in most large systems is extensive. Large organization control theory and practice also suggests that people performing in accounting and control roles do not engage in frequent personal interaction across functional responsibility boundaries. None of these theoretical dimensions fit small business very well.

Auditors should be careful to recognize the bureaucratic, large-business orientation of internal control theory. When the business under audit is small, some allowances must be made for size, the number of people employed and the control attitude expressed by important managers and owners. Although one should also keep in mind that the extensive downsizing taking place in the nineties has had a generally adverse impact on the general control environment with the consequence that critical elements of the control environment are taking on more relevance for larger businesses.

The key person in internal control in a small business is the owner-manager. Because the business is small, it does not exhibit the complexity that creates demand for elaborate internal control. A diligent owner-manager may be able to oversee and supervise all the important authorization, recordkeeping and custodial functions. He or she also may be able to ensure satisfactory data processing accuracy (ISA 400.48). Thus, an auditor evaluating control risk will study the extent of the owner-manager's involvement in the operation of the accounting and control system and evaluate the owner-manager's competence and integrity. This latter task emphasizes the importance of the "competent personnel" quality characteristic of internal control. Internal control questionnaires designed specifically for small businesses contain more items related to the owner-manager and other key personnel than do large-business questionnaires. The reason for this is that although small businesses may lack key elements of formal control such as segregation of duties, management involvement can compensate for lack of more formal controls.

As a small business begins to grow from, say, 4 people to 10 or 15, the transition to more formalized internal control tends to lag behind. The owner-manager may become overburdened with control duties and may tacitly delegate these to others. The intermediate-size stage represents a turning point where both owner-manager and auditor need to be very careful. At this point such measures as limited specialization and surety bonding of employees may help make the transition, and an auditor may offer many suggestions to the owner-manager as an added service.

In practice most auditors assess control risk at maximum in dealing with small business environments. This is probably due to cost/benefit considerations.

· ·

R E V I E W
C H E C K P O I N T S

6.26 Is the general theory of internal control embodied in the basic characteristics of reliable internal control equally applicable to large and small enterprises? Discuss.

6.27 What are the two main features of internal control in a small business?

· ·

Auditor's Responsibility to Detect and Communicate Misstatements

· · · · · · · · · · · ·

After the auditor's evaluation of internal controls, the auditor is in a strong position to assess the likelihood of material misstatements. Perhaps this then is a good point to review auditor responsibilities for detecting and communicating misstatements as per the guidance in *Handbook Section* 5135 or ISA 1007.16.

Financial misstatements can arise from error, fraud or other irregularities. A financial error is defined as an unintentional misstatement, whereas fraud and other irregularities are defined as intentional misstatements.

Intent is difficult to prove and for that reason "a misstatement arising from management's bias in selecting and applying accounting principles or in making accounting estimates would be considered an error." However, the audit also needs to be performed with professional scepticism, meaning the auditor:

1. Should be aware of factors that increase the risk of misstatement (see appendix); and
2. Should be sensitized to evidence that contradicts the assumption of management's good faith.

Note that many of the risk factors relate to poor internal controls.

If there are enough "red flags" present, the auditor will assess a higher inherent risk, and if control risk is also high, these higher assessments will cause the auditor to:

1. Obtain more reliable evidence.
2. Expand the extent of audit procedures performed.
3. Apply audit procedures closer to or as of the balance sheet date.
4. Require more extensive supervision of assistants and/or assistants with more experience and training.

In essence, if the auditor suspects that the financial statements are misstated, she or he should perform procedures to confirm or dispel that suspicion. These procedures are discussed in more detail in subsequent chapters.

Generally, the auditor is less likely to detect material misstatements arising from fraud because of the deliberate concealment involved. (Procedures for fraud detection are discussed in more detail in Chapter 19 and in various examples, which we call "casettes" in this book.) The auditor should inform the appropriate level of management whenever he or she obtains evidence of a nontrivial misstatement, and of weaknesses in internal control. The audit committee or board of directors should be informed of all significant misstatements.

The auditor should consider obtaining legal advice if he or she has doubts about communicating misstatements to third parties, particularly if the auditor resigned, or was removed, or was unable to report on the financial statements.

Internal Control in SSA Auditing

As indicated at the beginning of this chapter, most of the controls discussed in this chapter relate to controls that can be characterized as internal accounting controls. Accounting controls are those primarily oriented to maintaining accurate record keeping and safeguarding of assets. Internal accounting controls are those of primary interest to the traditional financial statement auditor.

There are other types of management controls, however, more geared to achieving broader operational objectives. You have studied examples of these in your management accounting courses: for example the controls consisting of the budgeting and any related variance analysis system. This concept of management internal controls can be extended to include the management controls of business risks that is the focus of SSA audits. In fact, the Criteria of Control (COCO) framework discussed in the box on page 174 represents the first steps to developing standards for evaluating the broader management control system.

COCO is discussed in more detail in Chapter 14. For now, we wish to emphasize that SSA auditors use COCO as one of a number of possible approaches to evaluating management control systems and their ability to control business risks. The SSA auditor puts more stress on strategic level controls and controls of business processes such as the supply chain to obtain assurance on the financial statement assertions. In short, SSA auditors rely much more on management controls than on accounting controls as compared to the traditional audit approaches. These and other differences in audit approaches are discussed in more detail in Chapter 13.

SUMMARY

This chapter explained the theory and practice of auditors' involvement with a client's "internal control." The purposes of auditor involvement are to assess the control risk in order to plan the substantive audit program and to report control deficiencies to management and the board of directors.

In theory a control system consists of three elements—the control environment, the accounting system, and the client's control procedures. Each of these is evaluated and documented in the audit working papers. The control environment was explained in terms of understanding the client's business. Elements of the accounting system were explained in conjunction with control procedures designed to prevent, detect and correct misstatements that occur in transactions. These misstatements were systematized in a set of seven categories of errors and irregularities that can occur. A reverse expression of them yielded the seven control objectives a company wishes to achieve. The control objectives were related to management's assertions found in financial statements.

Control procedures were covered extensively. They were organized under the headings of general control procedures (i.e., capable personnel, segregation of responsibilities, controlled access, periodic comparison and error-checking routines), segregation of technical responsibilities (computer-related jobs), and error-checking routine detail (11 input controls, 4 processing controls and 3 output controls). The explanations of these controls integrated computerized accounting systems with control practice.

Documentation of a control system was explained with reference to control questionnaires, flowcharts and narratives. Questionnaires and flowcharts were demonstrated. The understanding and the documentation were taken one step further to the test of controls phase and the cost reduction reasons for doing work to obtain a low control risk assessment. The assessed control risk was connected to the CR in the control risk model (Chapter 5).

Control evidence was linked to audit programs with a bridge working paper presentation. The nature of test of controls procedures was explained in terms of a two-part statement that dictated identification of the data population, from which control evidence is drawn, and the action taken to produce the relevant evidence.

The chapter closed with sections on cost-benefit and reasonable assurance considerations and on adaptation of control theory to small businesses. The Chapter 6 treatment of control risk assessment provided some basis for the theory and practice of audit sampling, which is covered next in Chapter 7.

MULTIPLE-CHOICE QUESTIONS FOR PRACTICE AND REVIEW

Questions 6.28 to 6.33 are located on the CD-ROM that accompanies this textbook.

6.34 The primary purpose for obtaining an understanding of an audit client's internal control structure is to:
   a. Provide a basis for making constructive suggestions in a management letter.
   b. Determine the nature, timing and extent of tests to be performed in the audit.
   c. Obtain sufficient appropriate evidential matter to afford a reasonable basis for an opinion on the financial statements under examination.

   d. Provide information for a communication of internal control structure-related matters to management.

6.35 What does management's internal control objectives include?
   a. Reducing the amount of testing done by the auditors.
   b. Allowing the auditor to assess control risk.
   c. Preventing and detecting fraud.

d. Implementing policies and procedures such that control risk is assessed below maximum.

6.36 Which of the following can an auditor observe as a general control procedure used by companies?
a. Segregation of functional responsibilities.
b. Management philosophy and operating style.
c. Open lines of communication to the audit committee of the board of directors.
d. External influences such as federal bank examiner audits.

6.37 A client's control procedure is:
a. An action taken by auditors to obtain evidence.
b. An action taken by client personnel for the purpose of preventing, detecting and correcting errors and irregularities in transactions.
c. A method for recording, summarizing and reporting financial information.
d. The functioning of the board of directors in support of its audit committee.

6.38 The control objective intended to reduce the probability that fictitious transactions get recorded in the accounts is:
a. Completeness.
b. Authorization.
c. Proper period.
d. Validity.

6.39 The control objective intended to reduce the probability that a credit sale transaction will get debited to cash instead of accounts receivable is:
a. Validity.
b. Classification.
c. Accuracy.
d. Completeness.

6.40 Which of the following employees normally would be assigned the operating responsibility for designing a computerized accounting system, including documentation of application systems?
a. Computer programmer.
b. Data processing manager.
c. Systems analyst.
d. Internal auditor.

6.41 When erroneous data are detected by computer program controls, such data may be excluded from processing and printed on an error report. The error report should most probably be reviewed and followed up by the:
a. Control group.
b. Systems analyst.

c. Supervisor of computer operations.
d. Computer programmer.

6.42 Totals of amounts in computer-record data fields that are not usually added but are used only for data processing control purposes are called:
a. Record totals.
b. Hash totals.
c. Processing data totals.
d. Field totals.

6.43 In updating a computerized accounts receivable file, which one of the following would be used as a batch control to verify the accuracy of the posting of cash receipts remittances?
a. The sum of the cash deposits plus the discounts less the sales returns.
b. The sum of the cash deposits.
c. The sum of the cash deposits less the discounts taken by customers.
d. The sum of the cash deposits plus the discounts taken by customers.

6.44 In most audits of large companies, internal control risk assessment contributes to audit efficiency, which means:
a. The cost of year-end audit work will exceed the cost of control evaluation work.
b. Auditors will be able to reduce the cost of year-end audit work by an amount more than the control evaluation costs.
c. The cost of control evaluation work will exceed the cost of year-end audit work.
d. Auditors will be able to reduce the cost of year-end audit work by an amount less than the control evaluation costs.

6.45 Which of the following is a device designed to help the audit team obtain evidence about the control environment and about the accounting and control procedures of an audit client:
a. A narrative memorandum describing the control system.
b. An internal control questionnaire.
c. A flowchart of the documents and procedures used by the company.
d. A well-indexed file of working papers.

6.46 A bridge working paper shows the connection between:
a. Control evaluation findings and subsequent audit procedures.
b. Control objectives and accounting system procedures.
c. Control objectives and company control procedures.
d. Financial statement assertions and test of control procedures.

6.47 Test of control audit procedures are required for:
   a. Obtaining evidence about the financial statement assertions.
   b. Accomplishing control over the validity of recorded transactions.
   c. Analytical review of financial statement balances.
   d. Obtaining evidence about the operating effectiveness of client control procedures.

EXERCISES AND PROBLEMS

6.48 Costs and benefits of control. The following questions and cases deal with the subject of cost-benefit analysis of internal control. Some important concepts in cost-benefit analysis are:

1. Measurable benefit. Benefits or cost savings may be measured directly or may be based on estimates of expected value. An expected loss is an estimate of the amount of a probable loss multiplied by the frequency or probability of the loss-causing event. A measurable benefit can arise from the reduction of an expected loss.
2. Qualitative benefit. Some gains or cost savings may not be measurable, such as company public image, reputation for regulatory compliance and customer satisfaction.
3. Measurable costs. Controls may have direct costs such as wages and equipment expenses.
4. Qualitative cost factors. Some costs may be indirect, such as lower employee morale created by overcontrolled work restrictions.
5. Marginal analysis. Each successive control feature may have marginal cost and benefit effects on the control problem.

Case A

Porterhouse Company has numerous bank accounts. Why might management hesitate to spend $10,000 (half of a clerical salary) to assign someone the responsibility of reconciling each account every month for the purpose of catching the banks' accounting errors? Do other good reasons exist to justify spending $10,000 each year to reconcile bank accounts monthly?

Case B

Harper Hoe Company keeps a large inventory of hardware products in a warehouse. Last year, $500,000 was lost to thieves who broke in through windows and doors. Josh Harper figures that installing steel doors with special locks and burglar bars on the windows at a cost of $25,000 would eliminate 90 percent of the loss. Hiring armed guards to patrol the building 16 hours a day at a current annual cost of $75,000 would eliminate all the loss, according to officials of the Holmes Security Agency. Should Josh arrange for one, both or neither of the control measures?

Case C

The Merry Mound Cafeteria formerly collected from each customer as he or she reached the end of the food line. A cashier, seated at a cash register, rang up the amount (displayed on a digital screen) and collected money. Management changed the system, and now a clerk at the end of the line operates an adding machine and gives each customer a paper tape. The adding machine accumulates a running total internally. The customer presents the tape at the cash register on the way out and pays.

The cafeteria manager justified the direct cost of $10,000 annually for the additional salary and $500 for the new adding machine by pointing out that he could serve 4 more people each weekday (Monday through Friday) and 10 more people on Saturday and Sunday. The food line now moves faster and customers are more satisfied. (The average meal tab is $6, and total costs of food and service are considered fixed.) "Besides," he said, "my internal control is better." Evaluate the manager's assertions.

Case D

Assume, in the Merry Mound situation cited above, that the better control of separating cash custody from the end-of-food-line recording function was not cost beneficial, even after taking all measurable benefits into consideration. As an auditor, you believe the cash collection system deficiency is a material weakness in internal control, and you have written it as such in your letter concerning reportable conditions, which Merry Mound's central administration engaged you to deliver. The local manager insists on inserting his own opinion on the cost-benefit analysis in the preface to the document that contains your report. Should you, in your report, express any opinion or evaluation on the manager's statement?

6.49 Cash Receipts Control. Sally's Craft Corner was opened in 1993 by Sally Moore, a fashion designer employed by Bundy's Department Store. Sally is employed full-time at Bundy's and travels frequently to shows and marts in Vancouver, Montreal and Toronto. She enjoys crafts, wanted a business of her own, and saw an opportunity in Vancouver. The Corner now sells regularly to about 300 customers, but business only began to pick up in 2000. The staff presently includes two salespeople and four office personnel, and Sally herself helps out on weekends.

Sales have grown, as has the Corner's reputation for quality crafts. The history is as follows:

	Sales	Discounts and Allowances	Net Sales
1996	$16,495	$500	$15,995
1997	18,575	550	18,025
1998	17,610	520	17,090
1999	18,380	570	17,810
2000	23,950	950	23,000
2001	29,470	1,480	27,990
2002	37,230	$2,230	35,000

With an expanding business and a need for inventory, the Corner is now cash poor. Prices are getting higher every month, and Sally is a little worried. The net cash flow is only about $400 per month after allowance of a 3 percent discount for timely payments on account. So she has engaged you as auditor and asks for any recommendations you might have about the cash flow situation. The Corner has never been audited.

During your review of internal control, you have learned the following about the four office personnel:

Janet Bundy is the receptionist and also helps customers. She is the daughter of the Bundy Department Store owner and a long-time friend of Sally. Janet helped Sally start the Corner. They run around together when Sally is in town. She opens all the mail, answers most of it herself, but turns over payments on account to Sue Kenmore.

Sue Kenmore graduated from high school and started working as a book-keeper-secretary at the Corner in 2000. She wants to go to university but cannot afford it right now. She is very quiet in the office, but you have noticed she has some fun with her friends in her new BMW. In the office

she gets the mailed-in payments on account from Janet, takes payments over the counter in the store, checks the calculations of discounts allowed, enters the cash collections in the cash receipts journal, prepares a weekly bank deposit (and mails it) and prepares a list (remittance list) of the payments on account. The list shows amounts received from each customer, discount allowed and amount to be credited to customers' account. She is also responsible for approving the discounts and credits for merchandise returned.

Ken Murphy has been the bookkeeper-clerk since 1996. He also handles other duties. Among them, he receives the remittance list from Sue, posts the customers' accounts in the subsidiary ledger, and gives the remittance list to David Roberts. Ken also prepares and mails customers' monthly statements. Ken is rather dull, interested mostly in hunting on weekends, but is a steady worker. He always comes to work in a beat-up pickup truck—an eyesore in the parking lot.

David Roberts is the bookkeeping supervisor. He started work in 1997 after giving up his small practice as a PA. He posts the general ledger (using the remittance list as a basis for cash received entries) and prepares monthly financial statements. He also approves and makes all other ledger entries and reconciles the monthly bank statement. He reconciles the customer subsidiary records to the accounts receivable control each month. David is very happy not to have to contend with the pressures he experienced in his practice as a PA.

Required:
a. Draw a simple flow chart of the cash collection and bookkeeping procedures.
b. Identify any reportable conditions or material weakness in internal control Explain any reasons why you might suspect that errors or irregularities may have occurred.
c. Recommend corrective measures you believe necessary and efficient in this business.

6.50 Tests of Control Procedure Specifications. To conduct tests of controls of a client's internal control procedures, auditors design a test of controls audit program. This audit program is a list of procedures to be performed, and each is directly related to an important client control procedure. Auditors perform the procedures to obtain evidence about the operating effectiveness of the client's control procedures.

The controls listed below relate to a system for processing sales transactions. Each numbered item indicates an error or irregularity that could occur and specifies a control procedure that could prevent or detect it.

Required:
a. Identify the control objective satisfied by the client's control procedure.
b. Write the audit program of test of controls procedures by specifying an effective procedure to produce evidence about the client's performance of the control procedure. [Hint: A test of controls procedure is a two-part statement consisting of (1) identification of a data population from which a sample can be drawn and (2) expression of an action to take.]

1. The company wants to avoid selling goods on credit to bad credit risks. Poor credit control could create problems with estimating the allowance for bad debts and a potential error by overstating the realizable value of accounts receivable. Therefore, the control procedure is: Each customer order is to be reviewed and approved for 30-day credit by the credit department supervisor. The supervisor then notes the decision on the customer order, which eventually is attached to copy 2 of the sales invoice and filed by date in the accounts receivable department. The company used sales invoices numbered 20,001 through 30,000 during the period under review.

2. The company considers sales transactions complete when shipment is made. The control procedures are: Shipping department personnel prepare prenumbered shipping documents in duplicate (sending one copy to the customer and filing the other copy in numerical order in the shipping department file). The shipping clerk marks up copy 3 of the invoice indicating the quantity shipped, the date and the shipping document number and sends it to the billing department where it is taken as authorization to complete the sales recording. Copy 3 is then filed in a daily batch in the billing department file. These procedures are designed to prevent the recording of sales (1) for which no shipment is made, or (2) before the date of shipment.

3. The company wants to control unit pricing and mathematical errors that could result in overcharging or undercharging customers, thus producing the errors of overstatement or understatement of sales revenue and accounts receivable. The accounting procedures are: Billing clerks use a catalogue list price to price the shipment on invoice copies 1, 2, and 3. They compute the dollar amount of the invoice. Copy 1 is sent to the customer. Copy 2 is used to record the sale and later is filed in the accounts receivable department by date. Copy 3 is filed in the billing department by date.

4. The company needs to classify sales to subsidiaries apart from other sales so the consolidated financial statement eliminations will be accurate. That is, the company wants to avoid the error of understating the elimination of intercompany profit and, therefore, overstating net income and inventory. The control procedure is: A billing supervisor reviews each invoice copy 2 to see whether the billing clerk imprinted sales to the company's four subsidiaries with a big red "9" (the code for intercompany sales). The supervisor does not initial or sign the invoices.

6.51 **Test of Controls Procedures and Errors/Irregularities.** The four questions below are taken from an internal control questionnaire. For each question, state (*a*) one test of controls procedure you could use to find out whether the control technique was really used, and (*b*) what error or irregularity could occur if the question were answered "no," or if you found the control was not effective.

1. Are blank (sales) invoices available only to authorized personnel?
2. Are (sales) invoices checked for the accuracy of quantities billed? Prices used? Mathematical calculations?
3. Are the duties of the accounts receivable bookkeeper separate from any cash functions?
4. Are customer accounts regularly balanced with the control account?

6.52 **Control Objectives and Procedures Associations.** Exhibit 6.52–1 contains an arrangement of examples of transaction errors (lettered *a–g*) and a set of client control procedures and devices (numbered 1–15). You should photocopy the Exhibit 6.52–1

E X H I B I T 6.52–1

a.	Sales recorded, goods not shipped
b.	Goods shipped, sales not recorded
c.	Goods shipped to a bad credit risk customer
d.	Sales billed at the wrong price or wrong quantity
e.	Product line A sales recorded as Product line B
f.	Failure to post charges to customers for sales
g.	January sales recorded in December

Control Procedures

1. Sales order approved for credit
2. Prenumbered shipping doc prepared, sequence checked
3. Shipping document quantity compared to sales invoice
4. Prenumbered sales invoices, sequence checked
5. Sales invoice checked to sales order
6. Invoiced prices compared to approved price list
7. General ledger code checked for sales product lines
8. Sales dollar batch totals compared to sales journal
9. Periodic sales total compared to same period accounts receivable postings
10. Accountants have instructions to date sales on the date of shipment
11. Sales entry date compared to shipping document date
12. Accounts receivable subsidiary totalled and reconciled to accounts receivable control account
13. Intercompany accounts reconciled with subsidiary company records
14. Credit files updated for customer payment history
15. Overdue customer accounts investigated for collection

page or obtain a full-size copy from your instructor for the following requirements.

Required:
a. Opposite the examples of transaction errors lettered a–g, write the name of the control objective clients wish to achieve to prevent, detect or correct the error.
b. Opposite each numbered control procedure, place an X in the column that identifies the error(s) the procedure is likely to control by prevention, detection or correction.

6.53 Control Objectives and Assertion Associations. Exhibit 6.52–1 contains an arrangement of examples of transaction errors (lettered *a–g*) and a set of client control procedures and devices (numbered 1–15).

Required:
For each error/control objective, identify the financial statement assertion most benefitted by the control.

6.54 Client Control Procedures and Audit Test of Control Procedures. Exhibit 6.52–1 contains an arrangement of examples of transaction errors (lettered *a–g*) and a set of client control procedures and devices (numbered 1–15).

Required:
For each client control procedure numbered 1–15, write an auditor's test of control procedure that could produce evidence on the question of whether the client's control procedure has been installed and is in operation.

DISCUSSION CASES

. . . .

6.55 Obtaining a "Sufficient" Understanding of Internal Control. The 12 partners of a regional-sized PA firm met in special session to discuss audit engagement efficiency. Jones spoke up, saying:

"We all certainly appreciate the firm-wide policies set up by Martin and Smith, especially in connection with the audits of the large clients that have come our way recently. Their experience with a large national firm has helped build up our practice. But I think the standard policy of conducting reviews and tests of internal control on all audits is raising our costs too much. We can't charge our smaller clients fees for all the time the staff spends on this work. I would like to propose that we give engagement partners discretion to decide whether to do a lot of work on assessing control risk. I may be an old mossback, but I think I can finish a competent audit without it."

Discussion on the subject continued but ended when Martin said, with some emotion: "But we can't disregard generally accepted auditing standards like Jones proposes!"

What do you think of Jones's proposal and Martin's view of the issue? Discuss.

6.56 Starting the "Logical Approach." One of the things you can do in a "logical approach" to the evaluation of internal control is to imagine what types of errors or irregularities could occur with regard to each significant class of transactions. Assume a company has the significant classes of transactions listed below. For each one, identify one or more errors or irregularities that could occur and specify the accounts that would be affected if proper controls were not specified or were not followed satisfactorily.

1. Credit sales transactions.
2. Raw materials purchase transactions.
3. Payroll transactions.
4. Equipment acquisition transactions.
5. Cash receipts transactions.
6. Leasing transactions.
7. Dividend transactions.
8. Investment transactions (short term).

6.57 Irregularity Opportunities. The Simon Blfpstk Construction Company has two divisions. The president, Simon, manages the roofing division. Simon has delegated authority and responsibility for management of the modular manufacturing division to John Gault. The company has a competent accounting staff and a full-time internal auditor. Unlike Simon, however, Gault and his secretary handle all the bids for manufacturing jobs, purchase all the materials without competitive bids, control the physical inventory of materials, contract for shipping by truck, supervise the construction activity, bill the customer when the job is finished, approve all bid changes and collect the payment from the customer. With Simon's tacit approval, Gault has asked the internal auditor not to interfere with his busy schedule.

Required:

Discuss this fact situation in terms of internal control and identify irregularities that could occur.

APPENDIX 6A

EXAMPLES OF FACTORS THAT MIGHT INCREASE THE RISK OF MATERIAL MISSTATEMENTS

The importance of the factors considered in assessing inherent and control risks, including the examples shown below, varies depending upon the size, complexity and ownership characteristics of the entity. The auditor assesses the risk of material misstatement in the financial statements by considering factors collectively. The presence of an individual factor would not necessarily indicate increased risk.

Corporate Environment
Ineffective board of directors or audit committee.
Management's poor business reputation.
Management operating and financial decisions dominated by a single person.
Aggressive management attitude in financial reporting.
Lack of formal code of conduct or its enforcement.

Financial Pressures
Business or industry decline (revenue or market share).
Inadequate or inconsistent profitability relative to industry.
Financial difficulties.
High debt-to-equity ratio, especially if the result of a recent acquisition.
Forthcoming debt or share offering.
Bonuses or management profit-sharing arrangements based on short-term financial results.
Existence of financial debt covenants.
Management places undue emphasis on meeting financial targets.
Overemphasis of quantified targets that are linked to management compensation.
Unrealistic budget pressures.
Rapidly changing conditions in entity's industry.
Sensitivity of operating results to economic factors, such as inflation, interest rates and unemployment.

Management Style
Constant crisis conditions in operating areas such as frequent/excessive back orders, shortages, delays, understaffed departments.
Turnover in key financial positions.
Organization decentralized without adequate monitoring.
Changed control, especially if a high price was paid.

Engagement Characteristics
Poor internal control.
Ineffective internal audit function.
Company does not correct material weaknesses that are possible to correct.
Inadequate control over accounting estimates (personnel lack of knowledge due to carelessness, inexperience or inadequate review).
Inadequate policies and procedures for security of assets, such as not limiting access to authorized employees, not investigating employees before hiring or not bonding employees.
Difficult-to-substantiate amounts or transactions.
New client, with no previous audit history or none available from predecessor.
Unusual related party transactions.
Nature of misstatements in prior period's financial statements.
Susceptibility of assets to misappropriation.

Source: From Appendix to *Handbook Section* 5135.

CHAPTER 7

Learning Objectives

Chapters 4 and 5 introduced several activities, concepts and tools for audit planning, and Chapter 6 introduced the theory and practice of control risk assessment. We now take up the general topic of audit sampling, which relies heavily on the concepts of materiality and risk—audit risk, inherent risk, control risk and detection risk. Audit sampling is not an audit procedure in the same class of the techniques explained in Chapter 4. It is a method of organizing the application of audit procedures and a method of organizing auditors' thoughts for decision making.

Chapter 7 introduces audit sampling as a general topic. Later, Chapter 20 will take you into the mathematical details of statistical sampling in auditing. After you study Chapter 7, you should be able to:

1. Define and explain the terms unique to audit sampling, including the fundamental technical differences between statistical sampling and non-statistical sampling.

2. Identify audit work considered to be audit sampling and distinguish it from work not considered to be audit sampling.

3. Develop a simple audit program for a test of controls audit of a client's internal control procedures.

   a. Specify objectives, deviation conditions, populations and sampling units.

   b. Determine sample size and select sampling units.

   c. Evaluate evidence from a test of controls audit.

4. Develop a simple audit program for an account balance audit considering the influence of risk and tolerable misstatement.

   a. Specify objectives and define a population for data.

   b. Determine sample size and select sampling units.

   c. Evaluate monetary error evidence from a balance audit sample.

AUDIT SAMPLING

INTRODUCTION TO AUDIT SAMPLING

LEARNING OBJECTIVE
1. Define and explain the terms unique to audit sampling, including the fundamental technical differences between statistical sampling and nonstatistical sampling.

Audit sampling is the application of an audit procedure to less than 100 percent of the items within an account balance population or class of transactions for the purpose of evaluating some characteristic of the balance or class (ISA 530.3). Testing is synonymous with sampling.[1] You have already seen the sampling idea incorporated in the explanation of a test of controls audit procedure, which was defined as a two-part statement consisting of (1) an identification of the data population from which a sample of items will be selected for audit and (2) an expression of an action taken to produce relevant evidence. To understand the definition of audit sampling, you must keep the following definitions in mind: Audit procedure refers to actions described as past audit techniques in Chapter 4 (computation, observation, confirmation, enquiry, inspection and analysis). An account balance refers to a control account made up of many constituent items; for example, an accounts receivable control account representing the sum of customers' accounts, an inventory control account representing the sum of various goods in inventory, a sales account representing the sum of many sales invoices or a long-term debt account representing the sum of several issues of outstanding bonds. A class of transactions refers to a group of transactions having common characteristics, such as cash receipts or cash disbursements, but which are not simply added together and presented as an account balance in financial statements.

Other definitions: A **population** is the set of all the elements that constitute an account balance or class of transactions. Each of the elements is a **population unit**; and when an auditor selects a sample, each element selected is called a sampling unit. A **sampling unit** can be a customer's account, an inventory item, a debt issue, a cash receipt, a cancelled cheque and so forth. A **sample** is a set of sampling units.

Sampling and the Extent of Auditing

Three aspects of auditing procedures are important—their nature, timing and extent. **Nature** refers to the six general techniques (computation, observation, confirmation, enquiry, inspection and analysis). **Timing** is a matter of when procedures are performed. More will be said about timing later in this chapter. Audit sampling is concerned primarily with matters of **extent**—the amount of work done when the procedures are performed. In the context of auditing standards, nature and timing relate most closely to the appropriateness of evidential matter, while extent relates most closely to the sufficiency (sample size) of evidential matter. The concept of testing is important to auditors because it is uneconomical to test client files exhaustively in many situations. It is common for client files on inventory and accounts receivable to contain thousands of accounting records. Testing is a means of gaining assurance that the amount of errors in large files is not material. The formal theory supporting the concept of testing is statistical sampling. However, courts approved the concept of testing long before statistical theories were introduced to auditing. The majority of testing in auditing was once done on a judgmental basis. But as accounting populations increased in size auditors became aware that statistical sample sizes could be much smaller than intuition would suggest. For this reason statistical sampling became increasingly popular in the 1970s and 1980s. Both judgmental and statistical testing methods are equally acceptable by auditing standards. The reason for the focus on statistics here is that there is a theory underlying statistics that formalizes the reasoning used

---

[1] *Terminology for Accountants*, 4th Ed., CICA, Toronto, 1992.

in pure judgmental testing. Note that both audit programs below can be performed on a statistical or nonstatistical basis.

TWO KINDS OF AUDIT PROGRAMS: TWO PURPOSES FOR AUDIT SAMPLING

Test of Controls Audit Program	Balance-Audit Program
Purpose Obtain evidence about client's control objective compliance	Purpose Obtain evidence about client's financial statement assertions
Validity Completeness Authorization Accuracy Classification Accounting Proper period	Existence/Occurrence Completeness Valuation Rights and obligations (ownership and owership) Presentation and disclosure
Sample Usually from a class of transactions (population), such as:	Sample Usually from items in an asset or liability balance (population), such as:
Cash receipts Cash disbursements Purchases (inventory additions) Inventory issues Sales on credit Expense details Welfare payments (eligibility)	Accounts receivable Loans receivable Inventory Small tool fixed assets Depositors' savings accounts Accounts payable Unexpired magazine subscriptions

Inclusions and Exclusions Related to Audit Sampling

LEARNING OBJECTIVE
2. Identify audit work considered to be audit sampling and distinguish it from work not considered to be audit sampling.

Look again at the audit sampling definition and to that part about audit sampling being "for the purpose of evaluating some characteristics of the balance or class." The meaning of these words is: An application of audit procedures is considered audit sampling if and only if the auditors' objective is to reach a conclusion about the entire account balance or transaction class (the population) on the basis of the evidence obtained from the audit of a sample drawn from the balance or class. If the entire population is audited, or if the purpose is only to gain general familiarity, the work is not considered to be audit sampling.

Perhaps the distinction between audit sampling and other methods can be perceived more clearly in terms of the following work that is not considered audit sampling.

- Complete (100 percent) audit of all the elements in a balance or class, by definition, does not involve sampling.

- Analytical procedures, in the nature of overall comparisons, ratio calculations and the like, are normally not applied on a sample basis.

- A **walk-through**—following one or a few transactions through the accounting and control systems in order to obtain a general understanding of the client's systems—is not audit sampling because the objective is not to reach a conclusion about a balance or class.

- Several procedures do not lend themselves to sampling methods; for example, enquiry of employees, obtaining written representations, obtaining enquiry responses in the form of answers on an internal control questionnaire, scanning accounting records for unusual items and observation of personnel and procedures.[2]

---

[2] "Audit Sampling," *Audit and Accounting Guide* (AICPA, 1983), pp. 1–3.

Several procedures are typically used in audit sampling applications. They are recalculation, physical observation of tangible assets, confirmation and document examination. These procedures most often are applied to the audit of details of transactions and balances.

Why Auditors Sample

Auditors utilize audit sampling when (1) the nature and materiality of the balance or class does not demand a 100 percent audit, (2) a decision must be made about the balance or class, and (3) the time and cost to audit 100 percent of the population would be too great. So, auditors use sampling because they need to perform efficient audits on a timely basis and cannot do so by auditing 100 percent. The two sampling designs used by auditors are statistical sampling and nonstatistical sampling.

Statistical Sampling

Auditors define **statistical sampling** as audit sampling that uses the laws of probability for selecting and evaluating a sample from a population for the purpose of reaching a conclusion about the population. The essential points of this definition are that (1) a statistical sample is selected at random, and (2) statistical calculations are used to measure and express the results. Both conditions are necessary for a method to be considered statistical sampling rather than nonstatistical sampling.

A **random sample** is a set of sampling units so chosen that each population item has an equal likelihood of being selected in the sample. You can use a random sample in a "nonstatistical sampling" design. However, you cannot use statistical calculations with a nonrandom sample. The mathematical laws of probability are not applicable for nonrandom samples, and basing such calculations on a nonrandom sample would be wrong.

A statistical calculation of sample size is not necessary for a method to be considered statistical sampling. You can use any sample size you feel appropriate in the circumstances. However, a preliminary estimate of sample size can be calculated using statistical models. (More on this subject is in Chapter 20.) A sampling method is statistical by virtue of random selection of the sample coupled with statistical calculation of the results.

WHEN TO USE STATISTICAL SAMPLING

Random numbers can be associated with population items.

Objective results that can be defended mathematically are desired.

Auditor has insufficient knowledge about the population to justify a basis for a nonstatistical sample.

A representative (random) sample is required.

Staff are adequately trained in statistical auditing.

Advantages of Statistical Sampling

Requires a precise and definite approach to the audit problem.

Incorporates evaluation that calculates a direct relation between the sample results and the entire population under audit.

Requires auditors to specify, and even quantify, particular judgments on risk and materiality.

Does not eliminate or reduce auditors' professional judgment.

Allows more objective control of audit risks. Results in better planning and documentation when properly implemented (but can be more time-consuming and costly because of the greater formalism required).

Nonstatistical Sampling

A good definition of **nonstatistical (judgmental) sampling** is audit sampling in which auditors do not utilize statistical calculations to express the results. The sample selection technique can be random sampling or some other selection technique not based on mathematical randomness. Auditors are fond of saying that nonstatistical sampling involves "consideration of sampling risk in evaluating an audit sample without using statistical theory to measure that risk." "Consideration" in this context means "giving sampling risk some thoughtful attention" without direct knowledge or measurement of its magnitude.

Sampling and Nonsampling Risk

Be careful not to confuse sampling and nonsampling risk with statistical and nonstatistical sampling. They are not related. When auditors perform procedures on a sample basis and obtain sufficient evidence, a conclusion about the population characteristic can still be wrong. For example, suppose an auditor selected 100 sales invoices for audit and found no errors or irregularities in any of them. The conclusion that a significant incidence of errors and irregularities does not exist in the entire population of sales invoices from which the sample was drawn might be wrong. How, you ask? Simple: The sample might not reflect the actual condition of the population. No matter how randomly or carefully the sample was selected, it might not be a good representation of the extent of errors and irregularities actually in the population.

Sampling risk is defined as the probability that an auditor's conclusion based on a sample might be different from the conclusion based on an audit of the entire population. You could audit a sample of sales invoices and decide, based on the sample, that the population of sales invoices contained few errors and irregularities. However, suppose some auditors with more time could audit all the sales invoices and find a large number of errors and irregularities. In such a case, your sample-based decision would have been proved wrong. Your sample apparently did not represent the population very well. Sampling risk expresses the probability of making a wrong decision based on sample evidence, and it exists in both sta-

---

WHEN TO USE NONSTATISTICAL SAMPLING

Association of population items with random numbers is difficult and expensive.

Strictly defensible results based on mathematics are not necessary.

Auditor has sufficient knowledge about the population to justify a basis for a nonstatistical sample with expectation of a reasonable conclusion about the population.

A representative (random) sample is not required; for example, because an efficient nonstatistical sample of large items leaves an immaterial amount unaudited.

The population is known to be diverse, with some segments especially error-prone.

Advantages of Nonstatistical Sampling

Permits a less rigidly defined approach to unique problems that might not fit into a statistical method.

Permits the auditors to reapply evaluation judgments based on factors in addition to the sample evidence.

Permits auditors to be vague and less than definite about, and omit quantification of, particular judgments on risk and materiality.

Permits auditors to assert standards of subjective judgment. (Thus, the alternative name is "judgment sampling.")

Manifestations of Nonsampling Risk

Performing inappropriate procedures: Auditors based the evaluation of inventory obsolescence on forecasted sales without adequately evaluating the forecast assumptions.

Failure to consider test results adequately: Auditor did not adequately investigate discrepancies in inventory counts and pricing, failing to draw the appropriate conclusions.

Neglecting the importance of analytical review: Auditor might have discovered client's failure to eliminate intercompany profits if year-to-year product mix, gross profit and recorded eliminations had been studied.

Failure to maintain control over audit procedures: Auditors' loose attitude permitted client employees to tamper with records selected for confirmation.

Lack of professional scepticism: Auditors accepted client's unsupported verbal representations instead of gathering independent evidence.

Source: Audit Risk, Coopers & Lybrand.

---

tistical and nonstatistical sampling methods. You cannot escape it in audit sampling. With statistical sampling, you can measure it, and you can control it by auditing sufficiently large samples. With nonstatistical sampling, you can "consider" it without measuring it. However, considering sampling risk without measuring it requires experience and expertise. Special aspects of sampling risk are discussed later in the sections on auditing control compliance and account balances.

Nonsampling risk is all risk other than sampling risk. You need to refer to the audit risk model (Chapter 5) to grasp the breadth of this definition:

Risk Model: $AR = IR \times CR \times DR$

Nonsampling risk can arise from:

- Misjudging the inherent risk (IR). An auditor who mistakenly believes that few material errors or irregularities occur in the first place will tend to do less work and, therefore, may fail to detect problems.

- Misjudging the control risk (CR). An auditor who is too optimistic about the ability of controls to prevent, detect and correct errors and irregularities will tend to do less work, with the same results as misjudging the inherent risk.

- Poor choice of procedures and mistakes in execution—related to detection risk (DR). Auditors can select procedures inappropriate for the objective (e.g., confirming recorded accounts receivable when the objective is to find unrecorded accounts receivable), can fail to recognize errors or irregularities when vouching supporting documents or can sign off as having performed procedures when the work actually was not done.

Nonsampling risk also represents the possibility of making a wrong decision. It exists both in statistical and in nonstatistical sampling. The problem is that nonsampling risk cannot be measured. Auditors control it—and believe it is reduced to a negligible level—through adequate planning and supervision of audit engagements and personnel, by having policies and procedures for quality control of their auditing practices and by having internal monitoring and external peer review of their own quality control systems.

One other distinction is important: External critics (judges, juries, peer reviewers) have few grounds for criticizing auditors who fall victim to sampling risk, provided that an audit sampling application is planned and executed reasonably well. Auditors are more open to criticism and fault-finding when erroneous audit decisions result from nonsampling risk.

Sampling Methods and Applications

Audit sampling is concerned with the amount of work performed and the sufficiency of audit evidence obtained. Audit sampling terminology contains many new concepts and definitions. The ones presented above, however, are general and apply to all phases of audit sampling. You need to know them so you can "speak the language."

Auditors design audit samples to deal with (1) auditing control for the purpose of assessing control risk and (2) auditing account balances for the purpose of getting direct evidence about financial statement assertions. The next major sections of this chapter explain these two designs. Each of the sections is organized in terms of (1) planning, (2) performing, and (3) evaluating audit sampling.

This chapter is presented in general terms, avoiding the mathematics of sampling, along the same lines as the *CICA Handbook Section* 5130 and Auditing Guideline "Applying Materiality and Audit Risk Concepts in Conducting an Audit," ISA 530 and the AICPA audit and accounting guide entitled "Auditing Sampling." If you want to crunch numbers, Chapter 20 (attribute sampling and variables sampling) should appeal to your technical needs. Chapter 20 can be viewed as a series of lengthy appendices to this chapter. Its coverage is limited mostly to technical details.

R E V I E W
C H E C K P O I N T S

7.1   Why do auditors sample?

7.2   What are the primary distinctions between statistical and nonstatistical sampling?

7.3   What is nonsampling risk? Give some examples.

7.4   What are test of controls audit procedures in general? What purpose do they serve?

7.5   Why must an audit sample be representative of the population from which it is drawn?

7.6   What control objectives should be achieved by a company's control structure?

7.7   What two types of audit programs are ordinarily used as written plans for audit procedures?

TEST OF CONTROLS FOR ASSESSING CONTROL RISK

LEARNING OBJECTIVE

3. Develop a simple audit program for a test of controls audit of a client's internal control procedures.

Auditors must assess the control risk to determine the nature, timing and extent of other audit procedures. Final evaluations of internal control are based on evidence obtained in the review and testing phases of an evaluation. Auditors' assessments of control risk are hard to describe because they always depend entirely on the circumstances in each specific situation. The judgments are usually very specific. For example, an auditor might learn that a company's validity control procedure to prevent recording of fictitious sales is to require the bookkeeper to match a shipping order with each sales invoice before recording a sale. Now suppose the test of control audit procedure of selecting recorded sales invoices and vouching them to shipping orders shows a number of mistakes (invoices without supporting shipping orders)—poor control, as performed. Sales might be overstated. One way to take this control deficiency into account is to perform more extensive work on accounts receivable using confirmation and enquiries and analytical review related to collectibility. (If sales are overstated, one result could be overstatement of receivables—the debit side of the accounting entry.)

The example above related a specific control (the validity-related control procedure of matching sales invoices with shipping orders) to a specific set of other audit procedures directed toward a possible problem (overstatement of sales and receivables). In a more general sense, auditors reach judgments about control risk along the lines shown in Exhibit 7–1. Some situations may call for a nonquantitative expression, and auditors sometimes

EXHIBIT 7–1 | AUDITOR'S ASSESSMENT OF CONTROL RISK

	Judgment Expression of Control Risk	
Evaluation of Internal Control	Nonquantitative	Quantitative
Excellent control, both as specified and in compliance.	Low (1)	10%–30%
Good control, but lacks something in specification or compliance.	Moderate (2)	20%–70%
Deficient control, either in specification or compliance or both.	High (3)	60%–95%
Little or no control.	Maximum	100%

If combining inherent and control risk evaluation is easier, then "low," "moderate," and "high" mean:
1. Low combined inherent and control risk.
2. Moderate combined inherent and control risk.
3. High combined inherent and control risk.

need a quantitative expression. The quantitative ranges overlap so you will not get the idea that auditors really can put exact numbers on these kinds of evaluations.

Audit sampling can be used as a method and plan for conducting the test of controls audit procedures. The application of sampling in test of controls auditing is a structured, formal approach embodied in seven steps. The seven-step framework helps auditors plan, perform and evaluate test of controls audit work. It also helps auditors accomplish an eighth step—careful documentation of the work—by showing each of the seven areas to be described in the working papers. The first seven steps are:

1. Specify the audit objectives.
2. Define the deviation conditions.
3. Define the population.
4. Determine the sample size.
5. Select the sample.
6. Perform the test of controls procedures.
7. Evaluate the evidence.

Plan the Procedures

LEARNING OBJECTIVE
3A. Specify objectives, deviation conditions, populations and sampling units.

The first three steps are planning steps that represent the **problem-recognition** phase of the sampling method. When a client describes the control system, the implicit assertion is: "These controls work; people comply with the control procedures and achieve the control objectives." The auditors' question (problem) is: "Is it so? Are the validity (and other) control objectives achieved satisfactorily?"

Test of controls audit work is always directed toward producing evidence of the client's performance of its own control procedures. Thus, auditors' procedures should produce evidence about the client's achievement of the seven control objectives.

1. Specify the Audit Objectives

Take a control procedure under the validity objective as an example—namely, the client's procedure of requiring a shipping order to be matched with a sales invoice before a valid sale is recorded. The specific objective of an auditor's test of controls audit procedure would be: Determine whether recorded sales invoices are supported by matched shipping orders. The audit procedure itself would be: Select a sample of recorded sales invoices and vouch them to supporting shipping orders.

The client's matching of sales invoices to shipping orders in the example is a **key control**—it is important. Auditors should identify and audit only the key controls. Incidental controls that are not important will not be relied on to reduce control risk and need not be audited for compliance. Auditing them for compliance just wastes time if they really do not have much impact on the control risk assessment.

2. Define the Deviation Conditions

The terms **deviation**, **error**, **occurrence** and **exception** are synonyms in test of controls sampling. They all refer to a departure from a prescribed internal control procedure in a particular case: for example, an invoice is recorded with no supporting shipping order (bill of lading). Defining the deviation conditions at the outset is important, so the auditors doing the work will know a deviation when they see one. As an assistant accountant, you would prefer to be instructed: "Select a sample of recorded sales invoices, vouch them to supporting shipping orders and document cases where the shipping order is missing" instead of "Check recorded sales invoices for any mistakes." The latter instruction does not define the deviation conditions well enough.

The example we are using is oversimplified. However, this vouching procedure for compliance evidence can be used to obtain evidence about several control objectives at the same time. The invoice can be compared to the shipping order for evidence of actual shipment (validity), reviewed for credit approval (authorization), prices compared to the price list (authorization and accuracy), quantity billed compared to quantity shipped (accuracy), recalculated (arithmetic accuracy), compared for correspondence of shipment date and record date (proper period), and traced to postings in the general ledger and subsidiary accounts (accounting). Exhibit 7–2 shows these deviation conditions laid out in a working paper designed to record the results of a test of controls audit of a sample of sales invoices.

EXHIBIT 7–2   TEST OF CONTROLS AUDIT DOCUMENTATION

Index __M 10.3__   By __J C__   Date __11-11-2002__
                                                         Review __J.D.__   Date __11-15-2002__

KINGSTON COMPANY
Test of Controls Over Recorded Sales
December 31, 2002

Invoice number	Date	Amount	Bill of lading	Credit approved	Approved prices	Quantities match	Arithmetic accurate	Dates match	Posted to customer
35000	Mar. 30	$ 3,000							
35050	Mar. 31	$ 800			X				
35100	Apr. 2	$ 1,200					Y		
35150	Apr. 3	$ 1,500			Y				
35200	Apr. 5	$ 400							
35250	Apr. 6	$ 300	X			X	Y	X	
32100	Jan. 3	$ 1,000							
32150	Jan. 4	$ 200							
34850	Mar. 25	Missing	X	X	X	X	X	X	
34900	Mar. 26	$ 100			Y				
34950	Mar. 27	$ 200							
Sample = 200		$98,000							
Uncorrected deviations			4	9	5	6	3	7	0

X = Uncorrected deviation.
Y = Deviation occurred but was detected and corrected later.

Time for some more terminology: Test of controls audit sampling also is called **attribute sampling**. Attribute sampling is audit sampling in which auditors look for the presence or absence of a control condition. In response to the audit question: "For each sales invoice in the sample, can a matched shipping order be found?" the answer can be only yes or no. With this definition, auditors can count the number of deviations and use the count when evaluating the evidence.

3. Define the Population

The specification of test of controls (compliance) audit objectives and the definition of deviation conditions usually define the **population**, which is the set of all elements in the balance or class of transactions. In the example the population consists of all the recorded sales invoices, and each invoice is a **population unit**. In **classical attribute sampling**, a sampling unit is the same thing as a population unit.[3]

Population definition is important because audit conclusions can be made only about the population from which the sample was selected. For example, evidence from a sample of recorded sales invoices (the population for our illustrative procedure) cannot be used for a conclusion about completeness. Controls related to the completeness objective (in this case, control over failure to record an invoice for goods shipped) can only be audited by sampling from a population representing goods shipped (the shipping order file) and not by sampling from the population of recorded invoices.

A complicating factor in population definition is the timing of the audit work. Test of controls audit procedures ideally should be applied to transactions executed throughout the period under audit because auditors want to reach a conclusion about control risk during the entire period. However, auditors often perform test of controls procedures at an **interim date**—a date some weeks or months before the client's year-end date—and at that time the entire population (say, recorded sales invoices for the year) will not be available for audit. Nothing is wrong with doing the work at an interim date, but auditors still cannot ignore the remaining period between the interim date and the year-end. Strategies for considering control in the period after the interim date are explained later.

Another complicating factor in population definition is the need to determine the correspondence of the **physical representation of the population** to the population itself. The physical representation of the population is the auditor's frame of reference for selecting a sample. It can be a journal listing of recorded sales invoices, a file drawer full of invoice copies, a magnetic disk file of invoices, or another physical representation. The sample actually will be selected from the physical representation, so it must be complete and cor-

---

A BALANCE-AUDIT APPLICATION OF ATTRIBUTE SAMPLING

Previous presentations have said that attribute test of controls samples usually are drawn from a class of transactions in order to obtain evidence about compliance with control objectives. Attribute sample also can be used sometimes for balance-audit purposes. This example suggests an attribute sample to obtain evidence about an ownership (rights) financial statement assertion.

Question: A lessor is in the business of leasing autos, large trucks, tractors and trailers. Is it necessary for the auditors to examine the titles to all the equipment?

Answer: It is not necessary, unless some extraordinary situation or circumstance is brought to light, for the auditors to examine titles to all the equipment. Random test verification of title certificates or proper registration of vehicles should be made.

Source: AICPA Technical Practice Aids, 8330.02.

---

[3] Dollar-unit sampling, however, defines a different sampling unit. Dollar-unit sampling (DUS) is discussed in Chapter 20.

respond with the actual population. The physical representation of the recorded sales invoice as a list in a journal is fairly easy to visualize. However, an auditor should make sure that periodic listings (e.g., monthly sales journals) are added correctly and posted to the general ledger sales accounts. Now, a selection of individual sales invoices from the sales journal is known to be from the complete population of recorded sales invoices. You should be careful, however. Some physical frames may not be so easy to assess for complete correspondence to a population of interest.

Perform the Procedures

LEARNING OBJECTIVE
3B. Determine sample size and select sampling units.

The next three performance steps represent the **evidence-collection** phase of the sampling method. These steps are performed to get the evidence.

The sample size determination and sample selection steps explained in this section might be considered planning steps; but since they require a little more action, they also can be considered performance. The distinction is not crucial. They are merely the next things to do.

4. Determine the Sample Size

Sample size—the number of population units to audit—should be determined thoughtfully. Some auditors operate on the "magic number theory" (e.g., select 30, because that's what we have always used on this audit). Be careful, however, because a magic number may or may not satisfy the need for enough evidence. A magic number may also be too large. Auditors must consider four influences on sample size: sampling risk, tolerable deviation rate, expected population deviation rate and population size.

Sampling Risk.   Earlier, sampling risk was defined as the probability that an auditor's conclusion based on a sample might be different from the conclusion based on an audit of the entire population. In other words, when using evidence from a sample, an auditor might reach a wrong conclusion. He or she might decide that (1) control risk is very low when, in fact, it is not, or (2) control risk is very high when, in fact, it is not so bad. The more you know about a population (from a larger sample), the less likely you are to reach a wrong conclusion. Thus, the larger the sample, the lower the sampling risk of making either of the two decision errors. More will be said about these risks in the section on evaluation.

In terms of our example, the important sampling risk is the probability that the sample will reveal few or no recorded sales invoices without supporting shipping orders when, in fact, the population contains many such deviations. This result leads to the erroneous conclusion that the control worked well. The probability of finding few or no deviations when many exist is reduced by auditing a larger sample. Thus, sample size varies inversely with the amount of sampling risk an auditor is willing to take.

Tolerable Deviation Rate.   Auditors should have an idea about the correspondence of rates of deviation in the population with control risk assessments. Perfect control compliance is not necessary, so the question is: What rate of deviation in the population signals control risk of 10 percent? 20 percent? 30 percent? and so forth, up to 100 percent? Suppose an auditor believes that $90,000 of sales invoices could be exposed to control deviations without causing a minimum material misstatement in the sales and accounts receivable balances. If the total gross sales is $8.5 million, this judgment implies a **tolerable deviation rate** of about 1 percent ($90,000/$8.5 million). Since this 1 percent rate marks the minimum material misstatement, it indicates a low control risk (say, 0.05), and it justifies a great deal of reliance on internal control in the audit of the sales and accounts receivable balances.

However, there can be more than one tolerable deviation rate. Each successively higher rate is associated with a higher control risk. Continuing with our example, higher tolerable deviation rates could be associated with higher control risks as follows:[4]

---

[4] Accounting firms have different policies for associating tolerable deviation rates with control risk categories. Some start with a minimum rate of 1 percent, and others start with higher rates.

Deviation Rate	Control Risk
1%	0.05
2	0.10
4	0.20
6	0.30
8	0.40
10	0.50
12	0.60
14	0.70
16	0.80
18	0.90
20	1.00

Since sample size varies inversely with the tolerable deviation rate, the auditor who wants to assess control risk at 0.05 (tolerable rate = 1 percent) will need to audit a larger sample of sales transactions than another auditor who is willing to assess control risk at 0.40 (tolerable rate = 8 percent). The desired control risk level and its tolerable rate is a matter of auditor choice.

The tolerable rate is not a fixed rate until the auditor decides what control risk assessment suits the audit plan. Then it becomes a decision criterion involved in the sampling application. Some auditors express the tolerable rate as a number (necessary for statistical calculation of sample size), while others do not put a number on it. Chapter 20 contains more explanation about the determination of various tolerable rates.

Expected Population Deviation Rate.   Auditors usually know or suspect some control performance conditions. Sometimes they have last year's audit experience with the client; sometimes they have information from a predecessor auditor. They have information about the client's personnel, the working conditions and the general control-environment. This knowledge contributes to an **expectation about the population deviation rate**, which is an estimate of the ratio of the number of expected deviations to population size. Suppose the auditors discovered 1 percent deviation in last year's audit. The expected population deviation rate could then be 1 percent. Auditors can also stipulate a zero expected deviation rate, which will produce a minimum sample size for audit.

The expected rate is important in a commonsense perspective. If auditors had reason to expect more deviations than they could tolerate, there would be no reason to perform any test of controls audit procedures. Thus, the expected rate must be less than the tolerable rate. Also, the closer the expected rate is to the tolerable rate, the larger the sample will need to be to reach a conclusion that deviations do not exceed the tolerable rate. Consequently, the sample size varies directly with the expected deviation rate (especially in terms of larger samples when the expected rate nears the tolerable rate). Some auditors will express the expected rate as a number (necessary for statistical calculations of sample size), while others will not put a number on it.

Population Size.   Common sense probably tells you that samples should be larger for bigger populations (a direct relationship). Strictly speaking, your common sense is accurate. As a practical matter, however, an appropriate sample size for a population of 100,000 units may be only 2 or 3 sampling units larger than an appropriate sample size for a 10,000-unit population. Not much difference! The power of the mathematics of probability is at work. The explanations in Chapter 20 are based on populations of 1,000 or more. However, you will need to be careful and make extra calculations when dealing with populations of fewer than 1,000 units.

The preceding discussion of sample size determinants is intended to give you a general understanding of the four influences on sample size. These influences are applicable to both statistical and nonstatistical sampling. A summary is presented in Exhibit 7–3. For further information about how to calculate a sample size, refer to Chapter 20.

E X H I B I T 7–3   SAMPLE SIZE RELATIONSHIPS: TEST OF CONTROLS AUDITING

	Predetermined Sample Size Will Be		
Sample Size Influence	High Rate or Large Population	Low Rate or Small Population	Sample Size Relationship
1. Acceptable sampling risk	Smaller	Larger	Inverse
2. Tolerable deviation rate	Smaller	Larger	Inverse
3. Expected population deviation rate	Larger	Smaller	Direct
4. Population	Larger*	Smaller*	Direct

*Effect on sample size is quite small for population of 1,000 or more.

5. Select the Sample

Auditing standards express two requirements for samples: (1) Sampling units must be selected from the population to which an audit conclusion will apply, ideally from transactions executed throughout the period under audit, and (2) a sample must be representative of the population from which it is drawn. In this context a **representative sample** is one that mirrors the characteristics of the population. Auditors, however, cannot guarantee representativeness. After all, that is what sampling risk is all about—the probability that the sample might not mirror the population well enough.

Auditors can try to attain representativeness by selecting random samples. A sample is considered **random** if each unit in the population has an equal probability of being included in the sample.

Intentional or accidental exclusion of a segment of a population can render a sample nonrepresentative. A popular way to select random samples is to associate each population unit with a unique number (easily done if the population units are prenumbered documents), then obtain a selection of random numbers to identify the sample units. You can use a printed random number table (see Appendix 20A) or a computerized random number generator to obtain a list of random numbers. This method is known as **unrestricted random selection**.

Another popular method is called **systematic random selection**. You need to know the population size and have a predetermined sample size to use it. The process is (1) obtain a random starting place in the physical representation (list of sales invoices recorded in a sales journal, for example) and select that unit, then (2) count through the file and select every *k*th unit, where *k* = Population size divided by Sample size. For example, if 10,000 invoices, numbered from 32071 to 42070, were issued, and you want a sample of 200, first use a random number table to get a starting place, say at invoice #35000, then select every *k*th = 10,000 divided by 200 = 50th invoice. So the next would be #35050, then #35100 . . ., then #42050, then #32100, #32150, and so on. (At the end of the list, you cycle back through the invoices #32071 through #34950.) Most systematic samples are selected using five or more random starts, as described in Chapter 20. (See the example in Exhibit 7–2).

Sample selection is the first step where a distinction between statistical and nonstatistical audit sampling is crucial. For statistical sampling evaluation, the sample must be random.

In nonstatistical plans, auditors sometimes use sample selection methods whose randomness and representativeness cannot be evaluated easily. **Haphazard selection** refers to any unsystematic way of selecting sample units; for example, closing your eyes and dipping into a file drawer of sales invoices to pick items. The problem is that you may pick only the dog-eared ones that stick out, and they may be different from most of the other invoices in the drawer. Also, you cannot describe your method so someone else can **replicate** it—reperform your selection procedure and get the same sample units. Some auditors describe haphazard sampling as a method of choosing items without any special reason for including or excluding items, thus obtaining a representative sample. However, haphazard selection should be considered only as a last resort because it is hard to document and impossible to replicate.

Another method is **block sampling**, which is the practice of choosing segments of contiguous transactions; for example, choosing the sales invoices processed on randomly chosen days, say February 3, July 17 and September 29. Implicitly, the block sampling auditor has defined the population unit as a business day (260 to 365 of them in a year) and has selected three—not much of a sample. Block sampling is undesirable because it is hard to get a representative sample of blocks efficiently. When you have enough blocks, you have a huge number of invoices to audit for compliance.

6. Perform the Test of Controls Procedures

Now you are ready to obtain the evidence. A **test of controls audit program** consists of procedures designed to produce evidence about the effectiveness of a client's internal control performance. The test of controls procedures listed in the box on the next page can be performed to determine how well the control procedures were followed on the transactions affecting accounts receivable. After each action part of a procedure, the parenthetical note tells you the control objective the auditor is testing.

R E V I E W
C H E C K P O I N T S

7.8   In test of controls auditing, why is it necessary to define a compliance deviation in advance? Give seven examples of compliance deviations.

7.9   Which judgments must an auditor make when deciding on a sample size for test of controls audit sampling? Describe the influence of each judgment on sample size.

7.10   What criterion must be met if a sample is to be considered random?

7.11   Name and describe four sample selection methods.

7. Evaluate the Evidence

LEARNING OBJECTIVE
3C. Evaluate evidence from a test of controls audit.

The final step represents the **evidence evaluation** phase of the sampling method. First, you recognized the problem as the task of determining whether each specified key control procedure worked satisfactorily. Then you gathered relevant compliance evidence. Now you need to evaluate the evidence and make justifiable decisions about the control risk.

Test of controls audit sampling is undertaken to provide evidence of whether a client's internal control procedures are being followed satisfactorily. Compliance evidence, therefore, is very important for the conclusion about control risk. When auditors evaluate sample-based compliance evidence, they run the sampling risks of making one of two decision errors: assessing the control risk too low or assessing the control risk too high. These two decision errors are related to the idea of sampling risk presented earlier.

The **risk of assessing the control risk too low** is the probability that the compliance evidence in the sample indicates low control risk when the actual (but unknown) degree of compliance does not justify such a low control-risk assessment. Assessing the control risk too low can lead to auditors' failure to do additional work that should be done. Assessing the control risk too low creates a threat to the effectiveness of the audit.

The **risk of assessing the control risk too high** is the probability that the compliance evidence in the sample indicates high control risk when the actual (but unknown) degree of compliance would justify a lower control-risk assessment. Assessing the control risk too high tends to trigger more audit work than was planned originally. Assessing the control risk too high threatens the efficiency of the audit.

Audit efficiency is certainly important, but audit effectiveness is considered more important. For this reason, auditing standards require auditors to allow for a low level of risk of assessing the control risk too low, especially when this decision error could cause an auditor to do significantly less work on the related account balances. These risks and decisions are illustrated in Exhibit 7–4. Keeping these risks in mind, the evaluation of evidence consists of calculating the sample deviation rate, comparing it to the tolerable rate and following up all the deviations discovered.

TEST OF CONTROLS AUDITING

1. Select a sample of recorded sales invoices and:
   a. Determine whether a bill of lading is attached (evidence of validity).
   b. Determine whether credit was approved (evidence of authorization).
   c. Determine whether product prices on the invoice agree with the approved price list (evidence of authorization and accuracy).
   d. Compare the quantity billed to the quantity shipped (evidence of accuracy).
   e. Recalculate the invoice arithmetic (evidence of accuracy).
   f. Compare the shipment date with the invoice record date (evidence of proper period).
   g. Trace the invoice to posting in the general ledger control account and in the correct customer's account (evidence of accounting).
   h. Note the type of product shipped and determine proper classification in the right product-line revenue account (evidence of classification).

2. Select a sample of shipping orders and:
   a. Trace them to recorded sales invoices (evidence of completeness).
   b. The procedures in 1b, 1c, 1d, 1e, 1f, and 1h also could be performed on the sales invoices produced by this sample. However, the work need not be duplicated.

3. Select a sample of recorded cash receipts and:
   a. Trace them to deposits in the bank statement (evidence of validity).
   b. Vouch discounts taken by customers to proper approval or policy (evidence of authorization).
   c. Recalculate the cash summarized for a daily report or posting (evidence of accuracy).
   d. Trace the deposit to the right cash account (evidence of classification).
   e. Compare the date of receipt to the recording date (evidence of proper period).
   f. Trace the receipts to postings in the correct customers' accounts (evidence of accounting).

4. Select a sample of daily cash reports or another source of original cash records and:
   a. Trace to the cash receipts journal (evidence of completeness).
   b. The procedures in 3b, 3c, 3d, 3e, and 3f also could be performed on this cash receipts sample. However, the work need not be duplicated.

5. Scan the accounts receivable for postings from sources other than the sales and cash receipts journals (e.g., general journal adjusting entries, credit memos). Vouch a sample of such entries to supporting documents (evidence of validity, authorization, accuracy and classification).

This program describes the **nature** of the procedures. Each is a specific application of one of the general techniques.

Calculate the Sample Deviation Rate

The first piece of hard evidence is the sample deviation rate. Suppose an auditor selected 200 recorded sales invoices and vouched them to shipping orders (bills of lading), finding four without shipping orders. The sample deviation rate is 4/200 = 2 percent. This is the best single-point estimate of the actual, but unknown, deviation rate in the population. However, you cannot say that the deviation rate in the population is exactly 2 percent. Chances are the sample is not exactly representative; the actual but unknown population deviation rate could be lower or higher.

> ## SUPERSEDED TERMINOLOGY:
> ## OVERRELIANCE AND UNDERRELIANCE
>
> Several years ago, professional terminology was changed from reference to "reliance on control" to "assessment of control risk." However, old habits die hard, and you will probably encounter these uses of control terminology:
>
> **Overreliance** is the result of realizing the risk of assessing control risk too low. When auditors think control risk is low, when in fact it is higher, they will *overrely* on internal control and restrict other audit procedures when they actually should perform more work.
>
> **Underreliance** is the result of realizing the risk of assessing control risk too high. When auditors think control risk is high, when in fact it is lower, they will *underrely* on internal control and perform more audit work when less work would suffice.

Judge the Deviation Rate in Relation to the Tolerable Rate and the Risk of Assessing the Control Risk Too Low

Suppose the auditor in the example believed the tolerable rate was 8 percent to justify a control risk assessment of CR = 0.40. In a nonstatistical sampling application, this auditor is supposed to think about the sample deviation rate (2 percent) in relation to the tolerable rate (8 percent), and he or she is supposed to think about the risk (of assessing control risk too low) that the actual, but unknown, deviation rate in the population exceeds 8 percent. The decision in a nonstatistical evaluation depends on the auditor's experience and expertise. In our example a nonstatistical auditor might conclude that the population deviation rate probably does not exceed 8 percent because the sample deviation rate of 2 percent is so much lower.

In a statistical sample evaluation, an auditor does things that are more explainable in a textbook. He or she establishes decision criteria by (1) assigning a number to the risk of assessing the control risk too low, say 10 percent, and (2) assigning a number to the tolerable rate, say 8 percent. Then a statistical table is used to calculate a sampling error–adjusted upper limit, which is the sample deviation rate adjusted upward to allow for the idea that the actual population rate could be higher. In this example the adjusted limit (call it UEL for "upper error limit") can be calculated to be 4 percent. This finding can be interpreted to mean: "The probability is 10 percent that the actual but unknown population deviation rate is greater than 4 percent." The decision criterion was: "The actual but unknown population deviation rate needs to be 8 percent or lower, with 10 percent risk of assessing

EXHIBIT 7–4   THE TEST OF CONTROLS AUDIT SAMPLING DECISION MATRIX

Decision Alternatives (based on sample deviation rate)	Actual Population Deviation Rate	
	Less than Tolerable Rate	Greater than Tolerable Rate
The deviation rate is less than the tolerable rate, so the control is performed satisfactorily.	Correct decision.	Control risk too low decision error.
The deviation rate is greater than the tolerable rate, so the control is not performed satisfactorily.	Control risk too high decision error.	Correct decision.

the control risk too low." So the decision criterion is satisfied, and the control risk assessment (0.40) associated with the 8 percent tolerable rate can be justified.[5]

Follow Up All the Deviations

All the evaluation described so far has been mostly quantitative in nature, involving counts of deviations, deviation rates and tolerable rate and risk judgment criteria. Qualitative evaluation is also necessary in the form of following up all the deviations to determine their nature and cause. A single deviation can be the tip of the iceberg—the telltale sign of a more pervasive deficiency. Auditors are obligated by the standard of due audit care to investigate known deviations so that nothing important will be overlooked.

The qualitative evaluation is sometimes called **error analysis** because each deviation from a prescribed control procedure is investigated to determine its nature, cause and probable effect on financial statements. The analysis is essentially judgmental and involves auditors' determination of whether the deviation is (1) a pervasive error in principle made systematically on all like transactions or just a mistake on the particular transaction; (2) a deliberate or intentional control breakdown, rather than unintentional; (3) a result of misunderstanding of instructions or careless inattention to control duties; or (4) directly or remotely related to a money amount measurement in the financial statements. You can see that different qualitative perceptions of the seriousness of a deviation would result from error analysis findings.

When the decision criteria are not satisfied and the preliminary conclusion is that the control risk is high, the auditors need to decide what to do next. The deviation follow-up can give auditors the obligation to do more account balance audit work by changing the nature, timing and extent of other audit procedures—that is, by not limiting the work in reliance on the client's particular internal control procedures. If the audit manager hesitates to make this commitment to do more audit work, he or she can enlarge the sample and perform the test of controls audit procedures on more sample units in hopes of deciding that the control risk is actually lower. However, when faced with the preliminary "nonreliance" decision, you should never manipulate the quantitative evaluation by raising the tolerable rate or the risk of assessing the control risk too low. Supposedly, these two decision criteria were carefully determined in the planning stage, so now only new information would be a good basis for easing them.

Timing of Test of Controls Audit Procedures

Earlier in the chapter, you learned that auditors can perform the test of controls audit procedures at an interim date—a date some weeks or months before the client's year-end date. When test of controls auditing is timed early, an audit manager must decide what to do about the remaining period (e.g., the period October through December after doing test of controls auditing in September for a December 31 year-end audit).

The decision turns on several factors: (1) The results of the work at interim might, for example, indicate poor control performance and high control risk; (2) enquiries made after interim may show that a particular control procedure has been abandoned or improved; (3) the length of the remaining period may be short enough to forego additional work or long enough to suggest a need for continuing the test of controls audit; (4) the dollar amounts affected by the control procedure may have been much larger or much smaller than before; (5) evidence obtained about control as a byproduct of performing substantive procedures covering the remaining period may show enough about control performance that separate work on the control procedure performance may not be necessary; or (6) work performed by the company's internal auditors may be relied on with respect to the remaining period.

---

[5] Changing the example to suppose 11 deviations were found creates a problem for the nonstatistical sampler. He or she must think harder about the evidence (a 5.5 percent sample rate) in relation to the tolerable rate (8 percent) and acceptable risk. The statistical sampler can measure the UEL at 8.3 percent, which is greater than the 8 percent tolerable rate at 10 percent risk of overreliance. The control fails the decision criterion test. Chapter 20 contains more information about making these calculations using statistical tables and formulas.

Depending on the circumstances indicated by these, an audit manager can decide to (1) continue the test of controls audit work because knowledge of the state of control performance is necessary to justify restriction of other audit work or (2) stop further test of controls audit work because (*a*) compliance evidence derived from other procedures provides sufficient evidence or (*b*) information shows the control has failed, control risk is high, and other work will not be restricted. Whatever the final judgment, considerations of audit effectiveness and efficiency should always be uppermost in the audit manager's mind.

. . . .

R E V I E W
C H E C K P O I N T S

7.12 Why should auditors be more concerned in test of controls auditing with the risk of assessing the control risk too low (overreliance) than with the risk of assessing the control risk too high (underreliance)?

7.13 What important decision must be made when test of controls auditing is performed and control risk is evaluated at an interim date several weeks or months before the client's fiscal year-to-date?

. . . .

SUBSTANTIVE PROCEDURES FOR AUDITING ACCOUNT BALANCES

. . . .

LEARNING OBJECTIVE

4. Develop a simple audit program for an account balance audit considering the influence of risk of material misstatement.

When audit sampling is used for auditing the assertions in account balances, the main feature of interest is the monetary amount of the population units, not the presence or absence of control deviations, as is the case with attribute sampling. Test of controls auditing is a part of the evaluation of internal control. **Substantive tests of details auditing** is the performance of procedures to obtain direct evidence about the dollar amounts and disclosures in the financial statements.

Substantive-purpose procedures include (1) analytical procedures and (2) test (audit) of details of transactions and balances. Analytical procedures involve overall comparisons of account balances with prior balances, financial relationships, nonfinancial information, budgeted or forecasted balances and balances derived from estimates calculated by auditors (refer to the discussion of analytical procedures in Chapters 4 and 5). Analytical procedures are usually not applied on a sample basis. So, substantive procedures for auditing details are the normal procedures used in account balance audit sampling.

Risk Model Expansion

Up to now you have worked with a conceptual risk model that had a single term for "detection risk"—DR. The detection risk is actually a combination of two risks: Analytical procedures risk (APR) is the probability that analytical procedures will fail to detect material errors, and the risk of incorrect acceptance (RIA) is the probability that test-of-detail procedures will fail to detect material errors. The two types of procedures are considered independent, so detection risk is $DR = APR \times RIA$, and the expanded risk model is:

$$AR = IR \times CR \times APR \times RIA$$

This model is still a conceptual tool. The expansion of it did not make auditing any less professional. It can now be used to help you understand some elements of sampling for auditing the details of account balances. First, recognize that auditors exercise professional judgment in assessing the inherent risk (IR), control risk (CR), analytical procedures risk (APR), and audit risk (AR). If these four risks are given, you can then manipulate the model to express the risk of incorrect acceptance (RIA):

$$RIA = \frac{AR}{IR \times CR \times APR}$$

With AR, IR, and APR held constant, RIA varies inversely with CR; that is, the higher the planned control risk (CR), the lower the planned risk of incorrect acceptance (RIA), and vice versa.

More About Sampling Risk

Substantive-purpose procedures are performed to produce the evidence necessary to enable an auditor to decide whether an account balance is or is not fairly presented in conformity with GAAP. Thus, auditors run the sampling risks of making one of two decision errors. The **risk of incorrect acceptance (RIA)** represents the decision to accept a balance as being materially accurate when, in fact (unknown to the auditor), the balance is materially misstated. The other decision error risk is the **risk of incorrect rejection**, and represents the decision that a balance is materially misstated when, in fact, it is not. These sampling risk relationships are shown in Exhibit 7–5.

Incorrect Acceptance

The risk of incorrect acceptance is considered the more important of the two decision error risks. When an auditor decides an account book balance is materially accurate (hence, needs no adjustment or change), the audit work on that account is considered finished, the decision is documented in the working papers, and the audit team proceeds to work on other accounts. When the account is, in fact, materially misstated, an unqualified opinion on the financial statements may well be unwarranted. Incorrect acceptance damages the effectiveness of the audit.

Incorrect Rejection

When an auditor decides an account book balance is materially misstated, some more audit work on that account is performed to determine the amount of an adjustment to recommend. The risk is that the book balance really is a materially accurate representation of the (unknown) actual value. At this point the event of incorrect rejection is about to be realized, and the audit manager may be inclined to recommend an adjustment that is not needed.

Incorrect rejection is not considered to be as serious an error as incorrect acceptance. When auditors first begin to think a balance may contain a material misstatement, efforts will be made to determine why the misstatement occurred and to estimate the amount. Thus, more evidence will be sought by the audit team or provided by the client. The data will be reviewed for a source of systematic error. The amounts of discovered errors will be analysed carefully. Client personnel may be assigned to do a complete analysis to determine a more accurate account balance.

If the initial decision was, in fact, a decision error of incorrect rejection, this other work should allow the auditors to determine whether the recorded amount is really misstated or the sample was not representative. Hence, incorrect rejection is not considered as serious as incorrect acceptance because steps will be taken to determine the amount of error and the erroneous decision has a chance to be reversed. Incorrect rejection thus affects the efficiency of an audit by causing unnecessary work.

EXHIBIT 7–5   THE ACCOUNT BALANCE AUDIT SAMPLING DECISION MATRIX

	Unknown Actual Account Balance is	
Decision Alternatives (based on sample evidence)	Materially* accurate.	Materially* misstated.
The book value of the account is materially accurate.	Correct decision.	Incorrect acceptance.
The book value of the account is materially misstated.	Incorrect rejection.	Correct decision.

*Materially in this context refers to the "material misstatement" assigned to the account balance.

Materiality and Tolerable Misstatement

Determining a threshold for the materiality of misstatements in financial statements is a tough problem under any circumstances. Audit sampling for substantive audit of particular account balances adds another wrinkle. Auditors also must decide on an amount of material misstatement, which is a judgment of the amount of monetary misstatement that may exist in an account balance or class of transactions and cause the financial statements to be materially misstated. Audit risk (AR in the risk model), therefore, is the risk that all the audit work on an account balance will not result in discovery of material misstatement. This concept is further discussed in Chapter 20.

SAMPLING STEPS FOR ACCOUNT BALANCE AUDIT

Audit sampling for the audit of account balances is structured much like the steps you studied in connection with test of controls audit sampling. As the steps are explained, an example related to auditing receivables is used. Remember, the example used with regard to test of controls sampling was the audit of a control procedure designed to prevent the recording of sales invoices without shipping orders. Now we move on to the next stage of work that can produce independent evidence of sales overstatement resulting from a breakdown of the control or from other causes. The seven-step framework explained in the next sections helps auditors plan, perform and evaluate account balance detail audit work. It also helps auditors accomplish an eighth step—careful documentation of the work—by showing each of the seven areas to be described in the working papers. The first seven steps are the following:

1. Specify the audit objectives.
2. Define the population.
3. Choose an audit sampling method.
4. Determine the sample size.
5. Select the sample.
6. Perform the substantive-purpose procedures.
7. Evaluate the evidence.

Plan the Procedures

LEARNING OBJECTIVE
4A. Specify objectives and define a population for data.

The three planning steps represent the **problem-recognition** phase of the sampling method. When a client presents the financial statements, the assertions include (for example): "The trade accounts receivable exist and are bona fide obligations owed to the company" (ownership); "All the accounts receivable are recorded" (completeness); "They are stated at net realizable value" (valuation); and "They are properly classified as current assets, presented and disclosed in conformity with GAAP." Each assertion represents a hypothesis (problem) to be tested; for example, "The trade accounts receivable exist as bona fide obligations owed to the company." A test of this hypothesis is the objective. The set of recorded accounts receivable is the population of data.

1. Specify the Audit Objectives
When performing accounts receivable confirmations on a sample basis, the specific objective is to decide whether the client's assertions about existence, rights (ownership) and valuation are materially accurate. In this context the auditing is viewed as **hypothesis testing**—the auditors hypothesize that the book value is materially accurate about existence, ownership and valuation. The evidence will enable them to accept or reject the hypothesis. The audit objective is to determine the monetary misstatement found by comparing the recorded balances to the balances determined from the evidence.

Accountants can use similar sampling methods for **dollar-value estimation objective**, which is the job of helping a client obtain an estimate of an amount. Examples include estimation of inventory FIFO values and data for current cost accounting information.[6] In dollar-value estimation, the objective is to develop a basic measurement, not to audit the balance or amount. Audit sampling, in the following discussion, adopts the objective of hypothesis testing.

2. Define the Population

Auditors need to be sure the definition of the population matches the objectives. Defining the population as the recorded accounts receivable balances suits the objective of obtaining evidence about existence, ownership and valuation. This definition also suits the related objective of obtaining evidence about sales overstatement. In the case of accounts receivable, each customer's account balance is a population unit. However, if the objectives were to obtain evidence about completeness and sales understatement, the recorded accounts receivable would be the wrong population.

Ordinarily, the sampling unit is the same as the population unit. Sometimes, however, it is easier to define the sampling unit as a smaller part of a population unit. For example, if the client's accounting system keeps track of individual invoices charged to customers, an auditor may want to audit a sample of invoices by confirming them with customers instead of working with each customer's balance.

Since a sample will be drawn from a physical representation of the population (e.g., a printed trial balance or magnetic disk file of customers' accounts), the auditors must determine whether it is complete. Footing the trial balance and reconciling it to the control account total will accomplish the job.

Auditing standards require auditors to use their judgment to determine whether any population units should be removed from the population and audited separately (not sampled) because taking sampling risk (risk of incorrect acceptance or incorrect rejection) with respect to them is not justified. Suppose the accounts receivable in our example amounted to $400,000, but six of the customers had balances of $10,000 or more, for a sum of $100,000. The next-largest account balance is less than $10,000. The six accounts are considered **individually significant items** because each of them exceeds the material misstatement amount, and they should be removed from the population and audited completely.

In the jargon of audit sampling related to account balances, subdividing the population is known as **stratification**. The total population is subdivided into subpopulations by account balance size. For example, a small number of accounts totalling $75,000 may be identified as the first (large balance) stratum when four strata are defined. Three more strata may be defined, each containing a total of approximately $75,000 of the recorded balances, but each made up of a successively larger number of customer accounts whose average balance is successively smaller. Stratification can be used to increase audit efficiency (smaller total sample size). A stratification example appears in the following box.

3. Choose an Audit Sampling Method

You already have been introduced to statistical and nonstatistical sampling methods. At this point, an auditor must decide which to use. If he or she chooses statistical sampling, another choice needs to be made. In statistical sampling, classical variables sampling methods that utilize normal distribution theory are available. Dollar-unit sampling, which utilizes attribute sampling theory, also can be used. Some of the technical characteristics of the statistical methods are explained more fully in Chapter 20.

The calculation examples shown later in this chapter use the dollar-unit sampling method. This calculation is relatively simple and illustrates the points adequately. Moreover, dollar-unit sampling is used more often in practice.

---

[6] Don Leslie, Albert Teitlebaum, and Rodney Anderson, *Dollar Unit Sampling* (Toronto: Copp, Clark, Pitman, 1979), pp. 244–49.

STRATIFICATION EXAMPLE

The stratification below subdivides the population into a first stratum of six individually significant accounts and four other strata, which each have approximately one-fourth ($75,000) of the remaining dollar balance. You can see the typical situation in which the accounts of smaller value are more numerous.

The example also shows one kind of allocation of a sample size of 90 to the last four strata. Such a stratification is referred to as *stratified sampling*. When each stratum gets one-fourth of the sample size, the sample is skewed toward the higher-value accounts: The second stratum has 23 in the sample out of 80 in the stratum, and the fifth stratum has 23 out of 910 in the stratum.

Stratum	Book Value	Number	Amount	Sample
1	Over $10,000	6	$100,000	6
2	$625–$9,999	80	75,068	23
3	$344–$624	168	75,008	22
4	$165–$343	342	75,412	22
5	$1–$164	910	74,512	23
		1,506	$100,000	96

This kind of stratification takes care of the normal situation in which the variability of the account balances and errors in them tend to be larger in the high-value accounts than in the low-value accounts. As a consequence, the sample includes a larger proportion of the high-value accounts (23/80) and a smaller proportion of the low-value accounts (23/910). In addition to size or variability, stratification can be based on other qualitative characteristics the auditor considers important, such as transactions stratified by individual, location, date, product and so forth.

Perform the Procedures

LEARNING OBJECTIVE
4B. Determine sample size and select sampling units.

The next three steps represent the **evidence-collection** phase of the sampling method. These steps are performed to get the evidence.

Figuring sample size for account balance auditing requires consideration of several influences. The main reason for figuring a sample size in advance is to help guard against underauditing (not obtaining enough evidence) and overauditing (obtaining more evidence than needed). Another important reason is to control the cost of the audit. An arbitrary sample size could be used to perform the accounts receivable confirmation procedures; but if it turned out to be too small, sending and processing more confirmations might be impossible before the audit report deadline. Alternative procedures then could become costly and time-consuming. A predetermined sample size is not as important in other situations where the auditors can increase the sample simply by choosing more items available for audit in the client's office.

4. Determine the Sample Size

Whether using statistical or nonstatistical sampling methods, auditors first need to establish decision criteria for the risk of incorrect acceptance, the risk of incorrect rejection and the material misstatement. Also, auditors may want to estimate the expected dollar amount of misstatement. These decision criteria should be determined before any evidence is obtained from a sample.

a. Risk of Incorrect Acceptance (RIA).   This risk is assessed in terms of the audit risk model, which can be your guide. An acceptable risk of incorrect acceptance depends on the assessments of inherent risk, control risk and analytical procedures risk. The risk of incorrect acceptance varies inversely with the combined product of the other risks. The larger the combined product of the other risks, the smaller is the allowable risk of incorrect acceptance.

Suppose, for example, two different auditors independently assess the client's control risk and their own analytical procedures and arrive at the following conclusions. Assume both auditors believe an appropriate audit risk—AR—is 0.05:

Auditor A believes the inherent risk is high (IR = 1.0), the control risk is moderate (CR = 0.50), and analytical procedures will not be performed (APR = 1.0). Audit procedures need to be so planned that the risk of incorrect acceptance will be about 10 percent.

$$RIA = AR/(IR*CR*APR) = 0.05/(1.0*0.50*1.0) = 0.10$$

Auditor B believes the inherent risk is high (IR = 1.0), the control risk is very low (CR = 0.20), and analytical procedures will not be performed (APR = 1.0). Audit procedures need to be so planned that the risk of incorrect acceptance will be about 25 percent.

$$RIA = AR/(IR*CR*APR) = 0.05/(1.0*0.20*1.0) = 0.25$$

Use the model with caution. The lesson you should learn from these examples is that auditor A's account balance sampling work must provide less risk than that of auditor B. Since sample size varies inversely with the risk of incorrect acceptance, auditor A's sample will be larger. In fact, when the control risk is lower, as in auditor B's evaluation, the acceptable risk of incorrect acceptance (RIA) is higher. Thus, auditor B's sample of customers' accounts receivable can be smaller than auditor A's sample.

b. Risk of Incorrect Rejection.   Like the risk of incorrect acceptance, the risk of incorrect rejection exists both in statistical and nonstatistical sampling applications. It can be controlled, usually by auditing a larger sample. So, sample size varies inversely with the risk of incorrect rejection. The determination of the risk of incorrect rejection is discussed in Chapter 20.

c. Material Misstatement.   The material misstatement—usually the same as the overall materiality of misstatements—also must be considered in nonstatistical as well as statistical sampling applications. In statistical sampling, material misstatement must be expressed as a dollar amount or as a proportion of the total recorded amount. The sample size varies inversely with the amount of misstatement considered material. The greater the material misstatement, the smaller the sample size needed.

d. Expected Dollar Misstatement.   Auditors may want to estimate an "expected dollar misstatement" amount. The estimate may be based on last year's audit findings or on other knowledge of the accounting system. Expectations of dollar misstatement have the effect of increasing the sample size. The more dollar misstatement expected, the larger the sample size should be. Sample sizes should be larger when more dollar misstatement is expected. So, sample size varies directly with the amount of expected dollar misstatement.

e. Variability Within the Population.   Auditors using nonstatistical sampling must take into account the degree of dispersion among unit values in a population. The typical skewness of some accounting populations needs to be taken into account. **Skewness** is the concentration of a large proportion of the dollar amount in an account in a small number of the population items. In our illustration, $100,000 (25 percent) of the total accounts receivable is in six customers' accounts while the remaining $300,000 is in 1,500 customers' accounts.

As a general rule, auditors should be careful about populations whose unit values range widely, say from $1 to $10,000. Obtaining a representative sample in such a case, as you might imagine, would take a larger sample than if the range of the unit values were only from $1 to $500. Sample size should vary directly with the magnitude of the variability of population unit values. Populations with high variability should be stratified, as previously shown in the stratification example.

Auditors using classical statistical sampling methods must obtain an estimate of the population **standard deviation**, which is a measure of the population variability. When using dollar-unit sampling, the variability is taken into account with the expected dollar misstatement, and no separate estimate of a standard deviation needs to be made. This is because in dollar-unit sampling the unit of selection is each recorded dollar, rather than the account balance. Thus there is no variability in the population of recorded items as viewed by dollar-unit sampling. It is the potential errors that are considered variable. See Chapter 20 for more details.

These five influences, plus the influence of population size on sample size, are summarized in Exhibit 7–6.

5. Select the Sample

As was the case with test of controls audit samples, account balance samples must be representative. Nothing is new about the selection methods. You can use unrestricted random selection and systematic selection to obtain the random samples necessary for statistical applications. Haphazard and block selection methods have the same drawbacks as they have in test of controls audit samples.

6. Perform the Substantive-Purpose Procedures

The basic assertions in a presentation of accounts receivable are that they exist, they are complete (no receivables are unrecorded), the company has the right to collect the money, they are valued properly at net realizable value and they are presented and disclosed properly in conformity with GAAP. A **substantive-purpose audit program** consists of account balance–related procedures designed to produce evidence about these assertions. The substantive-purpose procedures listed in the following box can be performed to obtain the evidence. The parenthetical notes identify the assertion addressed by the procedure.

The confirmation procedures should be performed for all the sampling units. The other procedures should be performed as necessary to complete the evidence relating to existence, ownership and valuation. The important thing is to audit all the sample units. You cannot simply discard one that is hard to audit in favour of adding to the sample a customer whose balance is easy to audit. This action might bias the sample. Sometimes, however, you will be unable to audit a sample unit. Suppose a customer did not respond to the confirmation requests, sales invoices supporting the balance could not be found and no payment was received after the confirmation date. Auditing standards contain the following guidance:

- If considering the entire balance to be misstated will not alter your evaluation conclusion, then you do not need to work on it anymore. Your evaluation conclusion may be to accept the book value, as long as the account is not big enough to change the conclusion. Your evaluation conclusion already may be to reject the book value, so that considering another account misstated just reinforces the decision.

E X H I B I T 7–6   SAMPLE SIZE RELATIONSHIPS: AUDIT OF ACCOUNT BALANCES

| | Predetermined Sample Size Will Be | | |
Sample Size Influence	High Rate or Large Amount	Low Rate or Small Amount	Sample Size Relation
1. Risk of incorrect acceptance	Smaller	Larger	Inverse
2. Risk of incorrect rejection	Smaller	Larger	Inverse
3. Tolerable misstatement	Smaller	Larger	Inverse
4. Expected misstatement	Larger	Smaller	Direct
5. Population variability	Larger	Smaller	Direct
6. Population size	Larger	Smaller	Direct

ACCOUNT BALANCE AUDITING

1. Confirm a sample of the receivables, investigate exceptions and follow up nonrespondents by vouching sales charges and cash receipts to supporting documents (evidence of existence, rights and valuation).

2. Obtain an aged trial balance of the receivables. Audit the aging accuracy on a sample basis. Calculate and analyse the age status of the accounts and the allowance for uncollectible accounts in light of current economic conditions and the company's collection experience (evidence of valuation).

3. Discuss past-due accounts with the credit manager. Obtain credit reports and financial statements for independent analysis of large overdue accounts (evidence of valuation).

4. Vouch receivables balances to cash received after the cutoff date (evidence of existence, rights and valuation).

5. Distinguish names of trade customers from others (officers, directors, employees, affiliates) and determine that the two classifications are reported separately (evidence of presentation and disclosure).

6. Read loan agreements and note any pledge of receivables, sales with recourse or other restrictions or contingencies related to the receivables (evidence of presentation and disclosure).

7. Read sales contracts for evidence of customers' rights of return or price allowance terms (evidence of presentation and disclosure).

8. Obtain written representations from the client concerning pledges for collateral, related party receivables, collectibility and other matters relating to accounts receivable (detail assertions in writing).

This program describes the **nature** of the procedures. Each is a specific application of one of the seven general procedures. However, this list does not include a procedure dealing explicitly with the completeness assertion. You can obtain completeness evidence with the dual-purpose nature of the completeness procedures done in the test of controls audit work (see test of controls procedures 2 and 4). The list also excludes analytical procedures based on interrelationships with budget, forecast, industry or historical data. More specific situational facts would need to be known to be specific about analytical procedures work.

- If considering the entire balance to be misstated would change an acceptance decision to a rejection decision, you need to do something about it. Since the example seems to describe a dead end, you may need to select more accounts (expand the sample), perform the procedures on them (other than confirmation) and re-evaluate the results.

REVIEW CHECKPOINTS

7.14 Write the expanded risk model. What risk is implied for "test of detail risk" when inherent risk = 1.0, control risk = 0.40, analytical procedures risk = 0.60, audit risk = 0.048, tolerable misstatement = $10,000, and the estimated standard deviation in the population = $25?

7.15 When auditing account balances, why is an incorrect acceptance decision considered more serious than an incorrect rejection decision?

7.16 What should be the relationship between tolerable misstatement in the audit of an account balance and the amount of monetary misstatement considered material to the overall financial statements?

7.17   What general set of audit objectives can you use as a frame of reference to be specific about the particular objectives for the audit of an account balance?

7.18   What audit purpose is served by stratifying an account balance population and by removing some units from the population for 100 percent audit attention?

7.19   What is the influence on dollar-value variables sample sizes of the risk of incorrect acceptance? of the risk of incorrect rejection? of the tolerable misstatement? of the population variability and the population size?

· ·

7. Evaluate the Evidence

LEARNING OBJECTIVE
4C. Evaluate monetary error evidence from a balance audit sample.

The final step represents the **evidence evaluation** and decision-making phase of the sampling method. Your decisions about existence, ownership and valuation need to be justifiable by sufficient, competent quantitative and qualitative evidence. You should be concerned first with quantitative evaluation of the evidence. Qualitative follow-up is also important and is discussed later. The basic steps in quantitative evaluation are these:

- Figure the total amount of actual monetary error found in the sample. This amount is the **known misstatement**.
- Project the known misstatement to the population. The projected amount is the **likely misstatement**.
- Compare the likely misstatement (also called the "projected misstatement") to the material misstatement for the account and consider: the risk of incorrect acceptance that likely misstatement is calculated to be less than material misstatement even though the actual misstatement in the population is greater; or the risk of incorrect rejection that likely misstatement is calculated to be greater than material misstatement, even though the actual misstatement in the population is smaller.

Amount of Known Misstatement

Now you need some illustrative numbers. Hypothetical audit evidence from a sample is shown in Exhibit 7–7. The example cited earlier said that total accounts receivable is $400,000, and $100,000 of the total is in six large balances, which are to be audited separately. The remainder is in 1,500 customer accounts whose balances range from $1 to $9,999. Suppose the audit team selected 90 of these accounts and applied the confirmation or vouching procedures to each of them. The evidence showed $136 of actual misstatement representing net overstatement of the recorded amounts (Exhibit 7–7). This amount is the known misstatement for this sample of 90 customer accounts.

Project the Known Misstatement to the Population

To make a decision about the population, the known misstatement in the sample must be projected to the population. The key requirement for projecting the known misstatement to the population is that the sample must be representative. If the sample is not representative, a projection produces a nonsense number. Take an extreme example: Remember that all of the six largest accounts ($100,000 in total) were audited. Suppose one of them contained a $600 disputed amount. Investigation showed the customer was right, management agreed, so the $600 is the amount of known misstatement. If an auditor takes this group of six accounts as being representative of the population, projecting the $100 average misstatement to 1,506 accounts ($100 × 1,506) would project a total misstatement of $150,600, compared to the recorded accounts receivable total of $400,000. This projection is neither reasonable nor appropriate. The six large accounts are not representative of the entire population of 1,506 accounts. Nothing is wrong with the calculation method. The nonrepresentative "sample" is the culprit in this absurd result.

A projection based on a sample applies only to the population from which the sample was drawn. Consider the sample of 90 accounts from the population of 1,500. The average difference is $1.51 (overstatement of the recorded amount), so the projected likely mis-

EXHIBIT 7–7   HYPOTHETICAL SAMPLE DATA

Sample Item	Audited Amount	Recorded Amount	Difference* (Recorded – Audited)
1	$691	$691	$0
*	*	*	*
*	*	*	*
*	*	*	*
6	372	508	136
*	*	*	*
*	*	*	*
*	*	*	*
23	136	141	5
*	*	*	*
*	*	*	*
*	*	*	*
50	62	62	0
*	*	*	*
*	*	*	*
*	*	*	*
90	135	130	(5)
Totals	$18,884	$19,020	$136
Averages:			
Audited amount	$209.82		
Recorded amount		$211.33	
Difference			$1.51

*A positive difference is an account overstatement, and a negative difference is an account understatement.

statement is $2,267 (overstatement), provided the sample is representative. This projection method is called the average difference method, expressed in equation form as:

Projected likely misstatement (under the average difference method) =
((Dollar amount of misstatement in the sample)/(Number of sampling units)) *
(Number of population units)

In the example:

Projected likely misstatement (under the average difference method) =
($136/90)*1,500 = $2,267 (overstatement)

How can you tell whether a sample is representative? You cannot guarantee representativeness, but you can try to attain it by selecting a random sample and by carefully subdividing (stratifying) the population according to an important characteristic, such as the size of individual customers' balances. When the population is stratified, each stratum is more homogeneous according to account size than the population as a whole, and the known misstatement in each can be projected. Combining them into a single projection is shown in the stratification calculation example shown below.

You can also inspect the sample to see whether it shows the characteristics of the population. In the example, for instance, the average recorded amount of the population is $200 ($300,000 divided by 1,500); the average in the illustrative unstratified sample is $211.33 (a little high). You also can look to see whether the sample contains a range of recorded amounts similar to the population that ranged from $1 to $9,999. With statistics you can calculate the standard deviation of the sample recorded amounts and compare it to the standard deviation of the population.

The dollar-unit sampling projection method automatically takes into account the stratification of the population. You can project using the dollar-unit sampling method, expressed in equation form as follows:

STRATIFICATION CALCULATION EXAMPLE

Projected Likely Misstatement: Average Difference Method

Stratification of a population is said to be more efficient because you can usually calculate a smaller projected likely misstatement with the same sample size than would have been used in an unstratified sample (as illustrated in this chapter), or you can usually calculate the same projected likely misstatement with a smaller stratified sample. The example below illustrates a typical situation of finding larger misstatements in the larger accounts, resulting in a projected likely misstatement smaller than the $7,350 illustrated in the chapter for an unstratified sample ($600 in the six largest customers plus $6,750 projected from the sample of 90 from the other 1,500 customers).

The calculation of projected likely misstatements (PLM), using the difference method, is applied separately to each stratum. Then, the amounts are added to get the whole sample result.

Stratum	Number	Amount	Sample	Misstatement*	PLM
1	6	$100,000	6	$ −600	$ −600
2	80	75,068	23	−274	−953
3	168	75,008	22	−66	−504
4	342	75,412	22	−88	−1,368
5	910	75,512	23	23	910
	1,506	$400,000	96	$−1,005	$−2,515

*A positive misstatement indicates overstatement of the book value, and a negative misstatement indicates understatement.

Projected likely misstatement (dollar-unit method) = (Sum of the proportionate amount of misstatements or taintings of all dollar units in error in the sample) * (Recorded amount in the population)

Taintings are discussed in more detail in Chapter 20. In the example here:

Projected likely misstatement (dollar-unit method) =
$300,000 * (1/90) * ((136/508) + (5/141) − (5/130)) = $883 (overstatement)

The difference in the two projected likely misstatements illustrates the importance of having representative sampling. Auditors also need to be very careful about the adequacy of the sample size. You can see that small samples which produce large or small dollar differences can distort both the average difference and the average dollar-unit ratio, thus distorting the projected likely misstatement. One way to exercise care is to take the sampling risks into account.

Consider Sampling Risks

The risks of making wrong decisions (incorrect acceptance or incorrect rejection) exist in both nonstatistical and statistical sampling. The smaller the sample, the greater both risks. Common sense tells you that the less you know about a population because of a small sample, the more risk you run of making a wrong decision.

The problem is to consider the risk that the projected likely misstatement ($883 overstatement for the sample of 90 accounts in the example using the dollar-unit sampling method) could have been obtained even though the actual total misstatement in the population is greater than the material misstatement ($10,000 in the example). Auditing guidance suggests you can use your experience and professional judgment to consider the risk. If the projected likely misstatement is considerably less than tolerable misstatement, chances are good that the total actual misstatement in the population is not greater than tolerable misstatement. However, when projected likely misstatement is close to tolerable misstatement (say, $9,000, compared to $10,000), the chance is not so good, and the risk of incorrect acceptance may exceed the acceptable risk (RIA) that an auditor initially established as a decision criterion.

A similar situation exists with respect to the risk of incorrect rejection. Suppose the sample results had produced a projected likely misstatement of $15,000 overstatement. Now the question is: "What is the risk that this result was obtained even though the actual misstatement in the population is $10,000 or less?" Again, the judgment depends on the size of the sample and the kinds and distribution of misstatements discovered.

Auditors take the rejection decision as a serious matter and conduct enough additional investigation to determine the amount and adjustment required. Hence, the risk of incorrect rejection is mitigated by additional work necessary to determine the amount and nature of an adjustment. In the example, if the sample of 90 customers' accounts had shown total misstatement of $900 (yielding the $15,000 projected misstatement using the average difference method), most auditors would consider the evidence insufficient to propose a significant adjustment. (Incidentally, however, correction of the $900 should not by itself be a sufficient action to satisfy the auditors.)

When using nonstatistical sampling, auditors utilize their experience and expertise to take risks into account. Statistical samplers can add statistical calculations to these considerations of sampling risk. Further explanation of statistical calculations is in Chapter 20.

Qualitative Evaluation

The numbers are not enough. Auditors are required to follow up each monetary difference to determine whether it arose from (*a*) misunderstanding of accounting principles, (*b*) simple mistakes or carelessness, (*c*) an intentional irregularity, or (*d*) management override of an internal control procedure. Auditors also need to relate the differences to their effect on other amounts in the financial statements. For example, overstatements in accounts receivable may indicate overstatement of sales revenue.

Likewise, you should not overlook the information that can be obtained in account balance auditing about the performance of internal control procedures—the dual-purpose characteristic of auditing procedures. Deviations (or absence of deviations) discovered when performing substantive procedures can help confirm or contradict an auditor's previous conclusion about control risk. If many more monetary differences arise than expected, the control risk conclusion may need to be revised, and more account balance auditing work may need to be done.

Knowledge of the source, nature and amount of monetary differences is very important. Such knowledge is required to explain the situation to management and to direct additional work to areas where adjustments are needed. The audit work is not complete until the qualitative evaluation and follow-up is done.

Evaluate the Amount of Misstatement

Handbook Section 5130 and the CICA Auditing Guideline on Materiality and Audit Risk requires the aggregation of known misstatement ("identified misstatement" in the Guideline) and projected likely misstatement ("likely aggregate misstatement" in the Guideline). The aggregation is the sum of (*a*) known misstatement in the population units identified for 100 percent audit (in the example, the six accounts totalling $100,000, with $600 overstatement discovered), and (*b*) the projected likely misstatement for the population sampled (in the example, the $883 overstatement projected using the dollar-unit sampling method). The theory underlying (*b*) is that the projected likely misstatement is the best single estimate of the amount that would be determined if all the accounts in the sampled population had been audited. You can see the importance of sample representativeness in this regard. This aggregation ($883 overstatement in the example) should be judged in combination with other misstatements found in the audit of other account balances to determine whether the financial statements taken as a whole need to be adjusted and, if so, in what amount.

The evaluation of amounts is not over yet, however. One thing that cannot be said about the projected likely misstatement is that it is the exact amount that would be found if all the units in the population were audited. The actual amount might be more or less, and the problem arises from **sampling error**—the amount by which a projected likely misstatement amount could differ from an actual (unknown) total as a result of the sample not being exactly representative. Of course, auditors are most concerned with the possibility that the actual total misstatement might be considerably more than the projected likely misstatement.

This sampling phenomenon gives rise to the concept of **possible misstatement** (the third kind, in addition to known and likely misstatement), which is interpreted in auditing standards as the further misstatement remaining undetected in the units not selected in the sample. Nonstatistical auditors resort to experience and professional judgment in considering additional possible misstatement. Statistical auditors, however, can utilize some statistical calculations to measure possible misstatement, as explained in Chapter 20.

In Chapter 20 the basic example shows how to calculate a possible misstatement. For the illustration here the possible misstatement is in the amount of $6,331. For now treat this as a given. Thus, the aggregation of known, projected and possible misstatement is $600 + $884 + $6,331 = $7,814. This total suggests that the misstatement in the account does not exceed the amount considered material ($10,000). If the possible misstatement were higher, say $9,000, the total would be $10,483, and the evidence would suggest that the misstatement in the account exceeds $10,000.

Timing of Substantive Audit Procedures

Account balances can be audited, at least in part, at an interim date. When this work is done before the company's year-end date, auditors must extend the interim-date audit conclusion to the balance sheet date. The process of **extending the audit conclusion** amounts to nothing more (and nothing less) than performing substantive-purpose audit procedures on the transactions in the remaining period and on the year-end balance to produce sufficient competent evidence for a decision about the year-end balance.

Substantive procedures must be performed to obtain evidence about the balance after the interim date. You cannot audit a balance (say, accounts receivable) as of September 30, then without further work accept the December 31 balance. Internal control must be well designed and performed adequately. If the company's internal control over transactions that produce the balance under audit is not particularly strong, you should time the substantive detail work at year-end instead of at interim.

BALANCE-AUDIT SAMPLING FAILURE

The company owned surgical instruments that were loaned and leased to customers. The auditors decided to audit the existence of the assets by confirming them with the customers who were supposed to be holding and using them. From the population of 880 instruments, the auditors selected 8 for confirmation, using a sampling method that purported to produce a representative selection.

Two confirmations were never returned, and the auditors did not follow up on them. One returned confirmation said the customer did not have the instrument in question, and the auditors were never able to find it. Nevertheless, the auditors concluded that the $3.5 million recorded amount of the surgical instrument assets was materially accurate.

Judges who heard complaints on the quality of the audit work concluded that it was not performed in accordance with generally accepted auditing standards (GAAS) because the auditors did not gather sufficient evidence concerning the existence and valuation of the surgical instruments. GAAS requires auditors to project the sample findings to the population. The auditors did not do so. They never calculated (nonstatistical) the fact that $1,368,750 of the asset amount could not be confirmed or found to exist. The sample of eight was woefully inadequate both in sample size and in the proportionately large number of exceptions reported. There was a wholly insufficient statistical basis for concluding that the account was fairly stated under generally accepted accounting principles.

Source: U.S. Securities and Exchange Commission, *Administrative Proceeding File No. 3-6579* (Initial Decision, June 1990).

If rapidly changing business conditions might predispose managers to misstate the accounts (try to slip one by the auditors), the work should be timed at year-end. In most cases careful scanning of transactions and analytical review comparisons should be performed on transactions that occur after the interim date.

As an example, accounts receivable confirmation can be done at an interim date. Subsequently, efforts must be made to ascertain whether controls continued to be reliable. You must scan the transactions of the remaining period, audit any new large balances and update work on collectibility, especially with analysis of cash received after the year-end.

Audit work is performed at interim for two reasons: (1) to spread the accounting firms' workload so that not all the work on clients is crammed into December and January and (2) to make the work efficient and enable companies to report audited financial results soon after the year-end. Some well-organized companies with well-planned audits report their audited figures as early as five or six days after their fiscal year-ends.

R E V I E W
C H E C K P O I N T S

7.20 What kind of evidence evaluation consideration should an auditor give to the dollar amount of a population unit that cannot be audited?

7.21 What are the three basic steps in quantitative evaluation of monetary amount evidence when auditing an account balance?

7.22 What are two methods of projecting the known misstatement to the population?

7.23 What are some of the signs that an unstratified random sample is actually representative of the population from which it was drawn?

7.24 The projected likely misstatement may be calculated, yet further misstatement may remain undetected in the population. How can auditors take the further misstatement under consideration when completing the quantitative evaluation of monetary evidence?

7.25 What additional considerations are in order when auditors plan to audit account balances at an interim date several weeks or months before the client's fiscal year-end date?

Summary

Audit sampling was explained in this chapter as an organized method to make decisions. Two kinds of decisions were shown—assessment of control risk and the decision about whether financial statement assertions in an account balance are fairly presented. The method is organized by two kinds of audit programs to guide the work on these two decisions—the test of controls audit program and the balance-audit program. The audit sampling itself can be attribute sampling for test of controls and balance-audit (variables) sampling for auditing the assertions in an account balance.

Audit sampling is a method of organizing the application of audit procedures and a disciplined approach to decision problems. Both types of sampling were explained in basic terms of planning the audit procedures, performing the audit procedures and evaluating the evidence produced by the audit procedures. The latter process was reinforced with some difference and dollar-unit sampling projections of misstatement amounts. Mathematical consideration of sampling error ("possible misstatement," "further misstatement remaining undetected") was postponed to Chapter 20.

Risk in audit decisions was explained in the context of nonsampling and sampling risk, with sampling risk further subdivided into two types of decision errors: (1) assessing control risk too low and incorrect acceptance of a balance and (2) assessing control risk too high and incorrect rejection of an account balance. The first pair damages the effectiveness of audits, and the second pair damages the efficiency of audits.

Dollar-valued materiality was incorporated in the balance-audit sampling in terms of the material misstatement assigned to the audit of a particular account. The connection of material misstatement to the tolerable deviation rate in test of controls sampling was postponed to Chapter 20.

Audit programs for test of controls procedures and balance-audit procedures were illustrated. Separate sections explained the application of procedures at an interim date. Thus, the chapter covered the nature, timing and extent of audit procedures. One of the goals of this chapter was to enable students to be able to understand these procedural programs in the context of audit sampling.

MULTIPLE-CHOICE QUESTIONS FOR PRACTICE AND REVIEW

Questions 7.26 to 7.30 are located on the CD-ROM that accompanies this textbook.

7.31 In an audit sampling application, an auditor:
 a. Performs procedures on all the items in a balance and makes a conclusion about the whole balance.
 b. Performs procedures on less than 100 percent of the items in a balance and formulates a conclusion about the whole balance.
 c. Performs procedures on less than 100 percent of the items in a class of transactions for the purpose of becoming familiar with the client's accounting system.
 d. Performs analytical procedures on the client's unaudited financial statements when planning the audit.

7.32 Auditors consider statistical sampling to be characterized by the following:
 a. Representative sample selection and non-mathematical consideration of the results.
 b. Carefully biased sample selection and statistical calculation of the results.
 c. Representative sample selection and statistical calculation of the results.
 d. Carefully biased sample selection and nonmathematical consideration of the results.

7.33 In audit sampling applications, sampling risk is:
 a. Characteristic of statistical sampling applications but not of nonstatistical applications.
 b. The probability that the auditor will fail to recognize erroneous accounting in the client's documentation.
 c. The probability that accounting errors will arise in transactions and enter the accounting system.
 d. The probability that an auditor's conclusion based on a sample might be different from the conclusion based on an audit of the entire population.

7.34 When auditing the client's performance of control to accomplish the completeness objective related to ensuring that all sales are recorded, auditors should draw sample items from:

 a. The sales journal list of recorded sales invoices.
 b. The file of shipping documents.
 c. The file of customer order copies.
 d. The file of receiving reports for inventory additions.

7.35 Nelson Williams was considering the sample size needed for a selection of sales invoices for the test of controls audit of the LoHo Company's internal controls. He presented the following information for two alternative cases:

	Case A	Case B
Acceptable risk of underreliance	High	Low
Acceptable risk of overreliance	High	Low
Tolerable deviation rate	High	Low
Expected population deviation rate	Low	High

Nelson should expect the sample size for Case A to be:
 a. Smaller than the sample size for Case B.
 b. Larger than the sample size for Case B.
 c. The same as the sample size for Case B.
 d. Not determinable relative to the Case B sample size.

7.36 Nelson next considered the sample size needed for a selection of customers' accounts receivable for the substantive audit of the total accounts receivable. He presented the following information for two alternative cases:

	Case X	Case Y
Acceptable risk of incorrect acceptance	Low	High
Acceptable risk of incorrect rejection	Low	High
Tolerable dollar misstatement in the account	Small	Large
Expected dollar misstatement in the account	Large	Small
Estimate of population variability	Large	Small

Nelson should expect the sample size for Case X to be:
a. Smaller than the sample size for Case Y.
b. Larger than the sample size for Case Y.
c. The same as the sample size for Case Y.
d. Not determinable relative to the Case Y sample size.

7.37 Which of the following should be considered an audit procedure for obtaining evidence?
a. An audit sampling application in accounts receivable selection.
b. The accounts receivable exist and are valued properly.
c. Sending a written confirmation on a customer's account balance.
d. Nonstatistical consideration of the amount of difference reported by a customer on a confirmation response.

7.38 When calculating the total amount of misstatement relevant to the analysis of an account balance, an auditor should add to the misstatement discovered in individually significant items the following:
a. The projected likely misstatement and the additional possible misstatement estimate.
b. The known misstatement in the sampled items.
c. The known misstatement in the sampled items, the projected likely misstatement and the additional possible misstatement estimate.
d. The additional possible misstatement estimate.

7.39 Eddie audited the LoHo Company's inventory on a sample basis. She audited 120 items from an inventory compilation list and discovered net overstatement of $480. The audited items had a book (recorded) value of $48,000. There were 1,200 inventory items listed, and the total inventory book amount was $490,000. Which of these calculations is (are) correct:
a. Known misstatement of $4,800 using the difference method.
b. Projected likely misstatement of $480 using the ratio method.
c. Projected likely misstatement of $4,900 using the ratio method.
d. Projected likely misstatement of $4,800 using the difference method.

7.40 Steve Katchy audited the client's accounts receivable, but he could not get any good information about customer 102's balance. The customer responded to the confirmation saying, "Our system does not provide detail for such a response." The sales invoice and shipping document papers have been lost, and the customer has not yet paid. Steve should:
a. Get another customer's account to consider in the sample.
b. Treat customer 102's account as being entirely wrong (overstated), if doing so will not affect his audit conclusion about the receivables taken altogether.
c. Require adjustment of the receivables to write off customer 102's balance.
d. Treat customer 102's account as accurate because there is no evidence saying it is fictitious.

7.41 The risk of incorrect acceptance in balance-audit sampling and the risk of assessing control risk too low in test of controls sampling both relate to:
a. Effectiveness of an audit.
b. Efficiency of an audit.
c. Control risk assessment decisions.
d. Evidence about assertions in financial statements.

7.42 An advantage of statistical sampling is that it helps an auditor:
a. Eliminate nonsampling risk.
b. Reapply evaluation judgments based on factors in addition to the sample evidence.
c. Be precise and definite in the approach to an audit problem.
d. Omit quantification of risk and materiality judgments.

7.43 To determine the sample size for a balance-audit sampling application, an auditor should consider the tolerable misstatement, the risk of incorrect acceptance, the risk of incorrect rejection, the population size and the:
a. Expected monetary misstatement in the account.
b. Overall materiality for the financial statements taken as a whole.
c. Risk of assessing control risk too low.
d. Risk of assessing control risk too high.

EXERCISES AND PROBLEMS

· ·

7.44 Sampling and Nonsampling Audit Work. The accounting firm of Mason & Jarr performed the work described in each separate case below. The two partners are worried about properly applying standards regarding audit sampling. They have asked your advice.

Required:

Write a report addressed to them, stating whether they did or did not observe the essential elements of audit sampling standards in each case:

a. Mason selected three purchase orders for raw materials from the LIZ Corporation files. He started at this beginning point in the accounting process and traced each one through the accounting system. He saw the receiving reports, purchasing agent's approvals, receiving clerks' approvals, the vendors' invoices (now stamped paid), the entry in the cash disbursement records and the cancelled cheques. This work gave him a firsthand familiarity with the cash disbursement system, and he felt confident about understanding related questions in the internal control questionnaire completed later.

b. Jarr observed the inventory taking at SER Corporation. She had an inventory list of the different inventory descriptions with the quantities taken from the perpetual inventory records. She selected the 200 items with the largest quantities and counted them after the client's shop foreman had completed his count. She decided not to check out the count accuracy on the other 800 items. The shop foreman miscounted in 16 cases. Jarr concluded the rate of miscount was 8 percent, so as many as 80 of the 1,000 items might be counted wrong. She asked the foreman to recount everything.

c. CSR Corporation issued seven series of short-term commercial paper notes near the fiscal year-end to finance seasonal operations. Jarr confirmed the obligations under each series with the independent trustee for the holders, studied all seven indenture agreements and traced the proceeds of each issue to the cash receipts records.

d. At the completion of the EH&R Corporation audit, Mason obtained written representations, as required by auditing

standards, from the president, the chief financial officer and the controller. He did not ask the chief accountant at headquarters or the plant controllers in the three divisions for written representations.

7.45 Test of Controls Audit Procedure Objectives and Control Deviations. This exercise asks you to specify test of controls audit procedure objectives and define deviations in connection with planning the test of controls audit of Kingston Company's internal controls. (In assignment 7.50, the requirement is to specify the client's control objectives and write test of controls audit procedures.)

Required:

a. For each control cited below, state the objective of an auditor's test of controls audit procedure.

b. For each control cited below, state the definition of a deviation from the control.

1. The credit department supervisor reviews each customer's order and approves credit by making a notation on the order.

2. The billing department must receive written notice from the shipping department of actual shipment to a customer before a sale is recorded. The sales record date is supposed to be the shipment date.

3. Billing clerks carefully look up the correct catalogue list prices for goods shipped and calculate and recheck the amounts billed on invoices for the quantities of goods shipped.

4. Billing clerks review invoices for intercompany sales and mark each one with the code "9," so that they will be posted to intercompany sales accounts.

7.46 Timing of Test of Controls Audit Procedures. Auditor Magann was auditing the authorization control over cash disbursements. She selected cash disbursement entries made throughout the year and vouched them to paid invoices and cancelled cheques bearing the initials and signatures of people authorized to approve the disbursements. She performed the work on September 30, when the company had issued cheques numbered from 43921 to 52920. Since 9,000 cheques had been issued in nine months, she reasoned that 3,000 more could be issued in the three months before the December 31 year-end. About 12,000 checks had been issued last year. She wanted to take one sample of 100 disbursements for the entire year, so she selected 100 random numbers in the sequence 43921 to 55920. She audited the 80 cheques in the sample that were issued before September 30, and she held the other 20 randomly selected cheque numbers for later use. She found no deviations in the sample of 80—a finding that would, in the circumstances, cause her to assign a low (20 percent) control risk to the probability that the system would permit improper charges to be hidden away in expense and purchase/inventory accounts.

Required:

Take the role of Magann and write a memo to the audit manager (dated October 1) describing the audit team's options with respect to evaluating control performance for the remaining period, October through December.

7.47 Evaluation of Quantitative Test of Controls Evidence. Assume you audited control compliance in the Kingston Company for the deviations related to a random selection of sales transactions, as shown below. For different sample sizes, the number of deviations was as follows:

Required:

For each deviation and each sample, calculate the rate of deviation in the sample (sample deviation rate).

7.48 Stratification Calculation of Projected Likely Misstatement Using the Ratio Method. The stratification calculation example in the chapter shows the results of calculating the projected likely misstatement using the difference method. Assume the results shown in Exhibit 7.48–1 were obtained from a stratified sample.

Required:

Apply the ratio calculation method to each stratum to calculate the projected likely misstatement (PLM). What is PLM for the entire sample?

7.49 Determining Risk of Incorrect Acceptance. In the dialogue between the Kingston auditors, Fred said: "Our analytical procedures related to receivables didn't show much. The total is down, consistent with the sales decline, so the turnover is up a little. If any misstatement is in the receivables total, it may be too small to be obvious in the ratios." Then Jack said: "That's good news if the problems are immaterial. Too bad we can't say analytical procedures reduce our audit

	Sample Sizes									
	30	60	80	90	120	160	220	240	260	300
Missing sales invoice	0	0	0	0	0	0	0	0	0	0
Missing bill of lading	0	0	0	0	0	1	2	2	3	3
No credit approval	0	3	6	8	10	14	17	23	26	31
Wrong prices used	0	0	0	0	2	4	8	9	9	12
Wrong quantity billed	1	2	4	4	4	5	5	5	5	5
Wrong invoice arithmetic	0	0	0	0	1	2	2	2	2	3
Wrong invoice date	0	0	0	0	0	2	2	2	2	2
Posted to wrong account	0	0	0	0	0	0	0	0	0	0

EXHIBIT 7.48–1

				Sample Results	
Stratum	Population Size	Recorded Amount	Sample	Recorded Amount	Misstatement Amount*
1	6	$100,000	6	$100,000	$ −600
2	80	75,068	23	21,700	−274
3	168	75,008	22	9,476	−66
4	342	75,412	22	4,692	−88
5	910	74,512	23	1,973	23
	1,506	$400,000	96	$137,841	$−1,005

*A negative misstatement indicates overstatement of the book value, and a positive misstatement indicates understatement.

risk. What about internal control?" Fred responded: "I say it's about a 50–50 proposition. Sometimes control seemed to work well, sometimes it didn't. I noticed a few new people doing the invoice processing last week when we were here for a conference. Incidentally, I lump the inherent risk problems and internal control risk problems together when I think about internal

control risk. Anyway, firm policy is to plan a sample for a low overall audit risk for the receivables."

Required:

Based on this dialogue information, use the expanded risk model to determine a test of detail risk. Relate this risk to sample size determination.

Discussion Cases

· ·

7.50 Application to Accounts Receivable. Toni Tickmark has been assigned to plan the audit of the Cajuzzi Corporation, and is currently planning the circularization (confirmation) of accounts receivable. Cajuzzi sells a number of products in the personal health care field but its mainstay is a portable whirlpool unit for use in bathtubs called the "Ecstasizer." Offering the same therapeutic muscle-relaxing benefits as built-in units costing up to four times more, the Ecstasizer has been an outstanding success and is largely responsible for the 14% jump in sales this year.

Cajuzzi has five major categories of customers: wholesalers, department store chains, drug stores, hardware stores and sporting goods stores. Because the health care industry is highly competitive and a number of "clones" are appearing on the market, Cajuzzi has an aggressive sales strategy coupled with fairly liberal credit policies. Viewing on-site store displays as its primary advertising media, Cajuzzi actually gives each customer a display unit for demonstration purposes. These costs are charged to promotion expense. It is the stated objective of the company to have every store in the country displaying its products.

New customers are extended credit using a very liberal credit policy and terms are net 30. Cajuzzi will not stop shipments unless balances are more than 120 days old. Customers' credit status is returned to normal as soon as the overdue balances are paid. Cajuzzi is loathe to write off any account unless the customer is actually insolvent or has given intent not to pay.

Schedule A contains a five-year summary of key financial data, and Schedule B has a summary of accounts receivable

at the year-end circularization date (06/30/02).

This is the second year that Toni's firm has been the auditor of Cajuzzi, and her first year on the engagement. Last year's working papers showed that the 50 largest accounts were circularized, which was coverage of 20% ($2,600,000). Overstatement of accounts receivable of $190,000 was discovered, but no adjustment was proposed as the error was deemed immaterial.

Required:

a. Critique last year's approach to the circularization of receivables and the subsequent disposition of errors discovered.

b. What is meant by random (representative) selection, and why is it the most fundamental principle of sampling theory? Under what conditions is nonrandom selection appropriate?

c. What is meant by the terms *sampling error* and *non-sampling error?* What steps can the auditor take to control these?

d. Design a sampling plan for the circularization of receivables for Cajuzzi at 06/30/02.

Cajuzzi's product line includes the following:

- Bathtub whirlpool units.
- Exercise equipment (rowers, bikes and mini-gyms).
- Heating pads, massage units and footbaths.
- Air purifiers and ionizers.
- "Healthware" cooking utensils.
- Skin care products and vitamin supplements.
- Track suits, footwear and sportswear.

SCHEDULE A
Cajuzzi—Five-Year Financial Summary
(in $000s)

	1998	1999	2000	2001	2002
Sales	84,000	85,000	83,000	86,000	98,000
A/R (6/30)	11,000	12,500	12,000	13,000	18,000
Allowance for doubtful accounts	1,260	1,275	1,245	1,290	1,470
Pre-tax income	3,300	2,400	3,200	3,900	5,000
Total assets	25,000	25,000	26,000	26,000	29,000

SCHEDULE B
Cajuzzi—Accounts Receivable Summary
June 30, 2002

Range	Number of Customers	Total $
$100,000–$500,000	6	$ 1,800,000
75,000–99,999	20	1,700,000
50,000–74,999	35	2,000,000
25,000–49,999	30	1,100,000
15,000–24,999	100	1,900,000
10,000–14,999	120	1,400,000
Less than 10,000	16,220	8,100,000
	16,531	$18,000,000

Cajuzzi—Aged Trial Balance at 06/30/02

0–30 days	31–60 days	61–90 days	91–120 days	More than 120 days
$8,350,000	$5,740,000	$2,105,000	$1,350,000	$455,000

(ICAO adapted)

7.51 Statistical Confirmation of Receivables.
You are about to commence the audit of Delta Ltd. This is the first time you have worked in the field without direct supervision by a senior, and you are of course anxious to do a good job. The senior has preceded you in visiting the client and has left you an audit file containing the following:

- An internal control questionnaire indicating no serious deficiencies in internal control over accounts receivable.
- An aged accounts receivable listing prepared by the client.
- A confirmation control schedule.
- Returned confirmations.

The confirmation control shows the following information:

- Number of accounts in the receivables subledger at December 31 = 65.
- Number of positive confirms mailed = 15.
- Number of negative confirms mailed = 30.

The client year-end, December 31, was selected as the circulation date. Trade terms are 2/10, net/30. Confirmation results are as follows:

1. Eight positive confirms returned indicating full agreement.
2. One positive confirm returned indicating the balance was correct but this is the outstanding balance as at November 30, 2002, not December 31, 2002.
3. One positive confirm returned stating the balance was correct but should also reflect a credit memo issued January 5, 2003.
4. One positive confirm returned stating the company uses an open invoice system and is unable to respond.
5. One positive confirm responding that the amount shown is incorrect because it does not reflect the 2% cash discount taken January 3, 2003.
6. One positive and three negative confirms returned by the post office marked "No Such Address."
7. One positive confirm stating that the balance was correct but that the com-

pany refuses to pay because of defective product quality.

8. One positive confirm not returned, even after two follow-up requests.
9. Two negative confirms returned with no notations made by customers.
10. One negative confirm returned stating the customer owed more than the balance shown.
11. One negative confirm returned stating that the balance was correct but asking for an extension of credit terms.
12. One negative confirm returned stating "sue us."

The *first* page of the aged trial balance supplied by the client for Delta as at December 31 is shown in the table on the next page.

Notes made by the senior indicate the following additional information:
• Abbey is an employee of Delta.
• The $700 Babbitt account represents a consignment shipment.

• The $500 October balance of Cabal has been formalized by a note receivable.
• The Cadenza balance represents a deposit. No shipments have been made to them yet.

Another note in the working paper file indicates that the client asked you not to send confirmation requests to Dacron Ltd. because they are worried about jeopardizing the ongoing collection efforts for the $3,000 past-due balance. Also, you were requested not to circularize Cadaver because Delta is extremely happy to have such a large account and wants to avoid bothering them in any way.

Required:

Analyse the evidence already obtained and describe any further procedures required to complete the audit of accounts receivable.

(ICAO adapted)

Account	Balance	Dec	Nov	Oct	Prior
	(CR)				
Aardwark Enterprises	$4,200	$2,100	$2,100		
Abacus Inc.	900				$900
Abalone Co.	5,500	1,000	3,200	$1,200	
Abbey, Fred	<600>	<600>			
Abstract Enterprises	1,100	500	400		200
Babbitt Inc.	700	700			
Bacchus Co.	6,000	2,000	4,000		
Cabal Ltd.	1,000			500	500
Cacao Enterprises	<900>				<900>
Cadaver Inc.	30,000	30,000			
Cadenza Co.	<1,200>	<1,200>			
Dacron Ltd.	3,100	100		3,000	
Subtotal (first page)	$49,800	$34,600	$9,700	$4,700	$800

7.52 Projected Likely Misstatement. When Marge Simpson, PA, audited the Candle Company inventory, a random sample of inventory types was chosen for physical observation and price testing. The sample size was 80 different types of candle and candle-making inventory. The entire inventory contained 1,740 types, and the amount in the inventory control account was $166,000. Simpson already had decided that a misstatement of as much as $6,000 in the account would not be material. The audit work revealed the following eight errors in the sample of 80.

Book Value	Audit Value	Error Amount
$600.00	$622.00	$(22.00)
15.50	14.50	(1.00)
65.25	31.50	(33.75)
83.44	53.45	(29.99)
16.78	15.63	(1.15)
78.33	12.50	(65.83)
13.33	14.22	$(.89)
93.87	39.87	(54.00)
$966.50	$803.67	$(162.83)

The negative difference indicates overstatement of the recorded amount.

Required:
Calculate the projected likely misstatement using the difference method. Discuss the decision choice of accepting or rejecting the $166,000 book value (recorded amount) without adjustment.

CHAPTER 8

Learning Objectives

Computers are used by almost all audit clients. Thus, computer auditing is practised, to a greater or lesser extent, in almost all audits. Computers introduce electronic technology in four phases of the audit process: (1) planning the audit, (2) obtaining an understanding of the control structure and control risk, (3) testing controls, and (4) using the computer to obtain substantive evidence about account balances.

Chapter 8 covers the basic concepts in all four phases with focus on simple systems. Chapter 21 covers topics related to more complex computer systems. After you study Chapter 8, you should be able to:

1. Explain how a computer accounting system differs from a manual accounting system.

2. List and discuss additional matters of planning auditors should consider for clients who use computers.

3. Describe how the phases of control risk assessment are affected by computer processing.

4. Describe and explain general control procedures and place the application control procedures covered in Chapter 6 in the context of computerized "error checking routines."

5. Describe the characteristics and control problems of micro-minicomputer installations.

6. Explain the differences between auditing around the computer, auditing through the computer and auditing with the computer.

7. Explain how the auditor can perform the test of control's audit of computerized controls in a simple computer system.

8. Describe the use of generalized audit software.

9. Describe how microcomputers can be used as an audit tool.

AUDITING IN A COMPUTER ENVIRONMENT

COMPUTER ENVIRONMENT
. . . .

LEARNING OBJECTIVE
1. Explain how a computer accounting system differs from a manual accounting system.

This chapter does not mark the first place you have seen the computer environment mentioned. A computer orientation and computer terminology has been integrated in several prior chapters. The first was in the Chapter 2 section "Auditing Standards in a Computer Environment." It would be a good idea to review those few pages now to set the stage for Chapter 8. Later, you will see references to Chapter 6 and several computer control procedures.

The *CICA Handbook* prefers the use of the term "electronic data processing," or EDP for short, when referring to computer systems. Here we use the term "computer auditing/processing" interchangeably with "EDP auditing/processing."

An auditing text cannot describe fully all the complexities of EDP or computer processing of business transactions. This chapter assumes you have had a course in computer concepts and general computer data processing. The purpose of this section is to review the basic elements of a computer system, to define some terms that will be used subsequently and to describe some of the control considerations unique to automated systems.

Although the term "computer auditing" has a certain mystique, there is no fundamental difference between computer auditing and the auditing described elsewhere in this book. To be more specific, when a computer is used to process the transactions:

- The definition of auditing is not changed.
- The purposes of auditing are not changed.
- The generally accepted auditing standards are not changed.
- The assertions of management embodied in financial statements are not changed.
- The control objectives are not changed.
- The requirement to gather sufficient appropriate evidence is not changed.
- The independent auditor's report on financial statements is not changed.

Therefore, everything you have learned from previous chapters is valid; only the method of processing and storing accounting data has changed. When the automation of transactions becomes more complex, auditing firms need to employ audit specialists who understand computer technology and who are aware of basic audit purposes. These "computer auditors" are members of the audit team and are called upon when the need for their skills arises, just as statistical sampling specialists or industry specialists are available when their expertise is needed. All auditors should have enough familiarity with computer processing and controls to enable them to complete the audit of simple systems and to work with computer audit specialists. (From EDP Audit Guideline "Auditing in an EDP Audit Environment." Henceforth such Guidelines will be referred to as they are in the *CICA Handbook* as "EDP–" with an appropriate number, in this case EDP–1.)

Elements of a Computer-Based System

In a manual accounting system, transaction processing can be readily followed and typically is supported by paper documents—approvals, vouchers, invoices and records of accountability, such as perpetual inventory records. Similar documents often exist in a computer system, but in many cases they are available only in machine-sensible form. Further, the basic records (ledgers and journals) of a computer-based accounting system frequently are machine-sensible data files that cannot be read or changed without a computer.

A computer-based hardware system includes the following elements:

1. *Hardware.* The physical equipment or devices that constitute a computer. These may include the central processing unit, optical reader, tape drives, disk devices, printers, terminals and other devices.

2. *Software.*
   a. System programs. Programs that perform generalized functions for more than one application. These programs, sometimes referred to as supervisory programs, typically include "operating systems," which control, schedule and maximize efficient use of the hardware; "data management systems," which perform standardized data-handling functions for one or more application programs; and "utility" programs that can perform basic computer operations, such as sorting records. System programs generally are developed by the hardware supplier or by software development companies. Examples of system programs include the many versions of DOS, Windows and Linux.
   b. Application (user) programs. Sets of computer instructions that perform data processing tasks. These programs usually are written within the organization or purchased from an outside supplier.

3. *Documentation.* A description of the system and its control structure in relation to input, data processing, output, report processing, logic and operator instructions.

4. *Personnel.* Persons who manage, design, program, operate or control data processing systems.

5. *Data.* Transactions and related information entered, stored and processed by the system.

6. *Control Procedures.* Procedures designed to ensure the proper recording of transactions and to prevent or detect errors and irregularities.

According to auditing standards, the establishment and maintenance of internal controls is an important responsibility of management (see *Handbook Section* 5200.03). The policies and procedures included as elements of a computer-based system are part of that responsibility. The audit team's responsibility is to make an assessment of the control risk in the system. Management can meet its responsibility and assist auditors in the following ways: (1) by ensuring that documentation of the system is complete and up to date, (2) by maintaining a system of transaction processing that includes an audit trail, and (3) by making computer resources and knowledgeable personnel available to the auditors to help them understand and audit the system.

Effect of Computer Processing

The method used to process accounting transactions will affect a company's organizational structure and will influence the procedures and techniques used to accomplish the objectives of internal control. When computers are used, special control considerations are relevant for evaluating the control environment and control procedures. The following are characteristics that distinguish computer processing from manual processing:

- *Transaction trails.* Some computer systems are so designed that a complete transaction trail useful for audit purposes may exist only for a short time or only in computer-readable form. (A transaction trail is a chain of evidence provided through coding, cross-references and documentation connecting account balances and other summary results with the original transaction documents and calculations.)

- *Uniform processing of transactions.* Computer processing uniformly subjects like transactions to the same processing instructions. Consequently, computer processing virtually eliminates the occurrence of random errors normally associated with manual processing. Conversely, programming errors (or other similar systematic errors in either the computer hardware or software) will result in all like transactions being processed incorrectly when those transactions are processed under the same conditions. This uniformity of processing characteristics causes a subtle change in the nature of audit testing of controls. The stress in auditing computerized files will be to test a small number of unusual or exceptional transactions rather than a large number of similar transactions, as is the case in manual systems. Of course, the test transactions should also include examples of the most typical, common transactions. Use of such strategies implies auditors will also need to get assurance that the software tested has not been tampered with between tests. This assurance is obtained through justified reliance on control systems that are in place to prevent unauthorized changes and to document all changes to the software.

- *Segregation of functions.* Many internal control procedures once performed by different individuals in manual systems may be concentrated in computer systems. Therefore, individuals who have access to the computer may be in a position to perform incompatible functions. As a result, other control procedures may be required in computer systems to achieve the degree of control ordinarily accomplished by segregating functions in manual systems. These may include such techniques as use of password control procedures to prevent incompatible functions from being performed by individuals who have access to assets and access to records through an on-line terminal. The concentration of record-keeping activities normally associated with computer centres requires a change in the approach to auditing that puts more emphasis on the evaluation of internal controls of the computer centre.

- *Potential for errors and irregularities.* The potential for individuals, including those performing control procedures, to gain unauthorized access or alter data without visible evidence, as well as to gain access (direct or indirect) to assets, may be greater in computerized accounting systems than in manual systems (partly due to the lack of segregation of duties noted above). Less human involvement in handling transactions processed by computers can reduce the potential for observing errors and irregularities. Errors or irregularities made in designing or changing application programs can remain undetected for long periods.

- *Potential for increased management supervision.* Computer systems offer management a wide variety of analytical tools that may be used to review and supervise the operations of the company. The availability of these additional controls may enhance the entire system of internal control and, therefore, reduce the control risk. For example, traditional comparisons of actual operating ratios with those budgeted, as well as reconciliation of accounts, frequently are available for management review on a more timely basis when such information is computerized. Additionally, some programmed applications provide computer operating statistics that may be used to monitor the actual processing of transactions.

- *Initiation or subsequent execution of transactions by computer.* Certain transactions may be initiated or executed automatically by a computer system. The authorization of these transactions or procedures may not be documented in the same way as those in a manual accounting system, and management's authorization of those transactions may be implicit in its acceptance of the design of the system.

Also review Chapter 6 for more details on aspects of computer operations relevant for auditors.

. . . .

R E V I E W
C H E C K P O I N T S

8.1 How can management meet its responsibility for establishing and maintaining an internal control system and assist the auditors at the same time?

8.2 What are the important differences between manual and computer accounting systems?

. . . .

Planning

· · · · · · · · · · · ·

In addition to the audit planning considerations presented in Chapters 4 and 5, auditors should consider the methods employed by a client to process significant accounting information, including the use of such outside organizations as data processing service centres. The client's methods influence the design of the accounting system and the nature of the internal control procedures.

The extent to which computer processing is used in significant accounting applications as well as the complexity of the processing also may influence the nature, timing and extent of audit procedures (EDP–1). Accordingly, when evaluating the effect of a client's computer processing on an audit of financial statements, auditors should consider such matters as:

- The extent to which the computer is used in each significant accounting application (e.g., sales and billing, payroll).
- The complexity of the computer operations used by the entity (e.g., batch processing, on-line processing, outside service centres).
- The organizational structure of the computer processing activities.
- The availability of data required by the auditor.
- The computer-assisted audit techniques available to increase the efficiency of audit procedures.
- The need for specialized skills.

Extent to Which Computers Are Used

The extent to which computers are used in each significant accounting application should be considered in audit planning. Significant accounting applications are those relating to accounting information that can materially affect the financial statements. When computers are used to process significant accounting applications, the audit team may need computer-related skills to understand the flow of these transactions. The nature, timing and extent of audit procedures also may be affected by the level of computer use. Computer applications are so common and pervasive that virtually every transaction is typically computerized. Historically, payroll, accounts receivable, accounts payable and inventory were the first applications to be computerized.

Complexity of Computer Operations

The complexity of the computer operations used by a client, including the use of an outside service centre, should be considered in audit planning. When assessing the complexity of computer processing, the audit manager should consider his or her training and experience relative to the methods of data processing used by the client. If significant accounting applications are processed at outside service centres, it may be necessary to coordinate audit procedures with service auditors. (Refer to Chapter 14 for a discussion of service auditors.)

Other matters may be considered when assessing the complexity of computer processing. The computer hardware utilized by the entity may show the degree of complexity involved. The degree to which various computerized systems appear to share common files or are otherwise integrated affects the complexity of computer operations because these characteristics may cause all such integrated systems to be considered significant accounting applications. In some computerized systems a transaction trail may be available only in computer-readable form for short periods and possibly in a complex form. These considerations affect the type and timing of audit evidence gathered, and thus affect audit planning.

Organizational Structure of Computer Processing

The organizational structure of a client's computer processing activities can have significant effects on how the auditor plans to conduct the work. Clients differ greatly in their approaches to organizing these activities. The degree of centralization inherent in the organizational structure especially may vary.

A highly centralized organizational structure generally will have all significant computer processing activities controlled and supervised at a central location. The control environment, the computer hardware and the computer systems may be uniform throughout the company. Auditors may be able to obtain most of the necessary computer processing information by visiting the central location. At the other extreme, a highly decentralized organizational structure generally allows various departments, divisions, subsidiaries or geographical locations to develop, control and supervise computer processing activities in an autonomous fashion. In this situation the computer hardware and the computer systems usually will not be uniform throughout the company. Thus, auditors may need to visit many locations to obtain the necessary audit information. To assess the potential for appropriate segregation of functions, auditors may wish to consider the number of people involved with computer processing activities within the company, as well as the apparent level of computer-related knowledge possessed by these personnel.

Availability of Data

Computer systems provide an ability to store, retrieve and analyse much more data than is practical in manual systems. Input data, certain computer files and other data required by the audit team may exist only for short periods or only in computer readable form. In some computer systems hard-copy input documents may not exist at all because information is entered directly. The data retention policies adopted by a client may require auditors to arrange for some information to be retained for review. Alternatively, auditors may need to plan to perform audit procedures at a time when the information is still available.

In addition, certain information generated by the computer system for management's internal purposes may be useful in performing analytical procedures. For example, due to the ease of storage, the client may save sales information by month, by product and by salesman. Such information can be used with analytical procedures to determine whether the revenue amounts are reasonable.

Use of Computer-Assisted Audit Techniques

Computer-assisted audit techniques (CAATs per EDP–1, EDP–2 and ISA 1009) may be used to increase the efficiency of certain audit procedures and also may provide auditors with opportunities to apply certain procedures to an entire population of accounts or transactions. There are two main categories of CAATs: (1) audit software and (2) test data (EDP–2 or ISA 1009.4). The use of these techniques requires advance planning and may require individuals with specialized skills as members of the audit team. These techniques are further discussed later in this chapter.

Need for Specialized Skills

To determine the need for specialized computer skills, all aspects of a client's computer processing should be considered. In planning the engagement, the audit manager may conclude that certain specialized skills are needed to consider the effect of computer processing on the audit, to understand the flow of transactions or to design and perform audit procedures. For example, specialized skills relating to various methods of data processing, programming languages, software packages or computer-assisted audit techniques may be needed. Audit managers and partners should possess sufficient computer knowledge to know when to call on specialists and to understand and supervise their work.

. . . .

8.3 In addition to the planning matters considered in a manual accounting system, what additional ones should be considered when computer processing is involved?

8.4 What are the general characteristics of transactions that are typically computerized? typically not computerized?

. . . .

PHASE 1: COMPUTER SYSTEM UNDERSTANDING
. . . .

LEARNING OBJECTIVE

3. Describe how the phases of control risk assessment are affected by computer processing.

The purpose of the Phase 1 understanding is to obtain sufficient knowledge of the control environment, the accounting system and the control procedures to determine whether internal control provides a basis for planning the nature, timing and extent of substantive audit procedures. The Phase 1 obtaining-an-understanding work should be designed to provide an understanding of the control environment and the flow of transactions through the accounting system, including a general knowledge of (*a*) the organizational structure, (*b*) the methods used by the client to communicate responsibility and authority, and (*c*) the methods used by management to supervise the system, including the existence of an internal audit function, if any. Each of these elements of the control environment may be affected by computer processing.

The Organizational Structure

The auditors' understanding of the organizational structure of a company should include an understanding of the organization of its computer function. This understanding should contribute to the overall assessment of control risk. In reviewing the organization structure of a company's computer function, auditors should obtain and evaluate:

- A description of the company's computer resources, including details of computer equipment used, the use of an outside services centre, if any, and locations from which the computer resources can be accessed.

- A description of the organizational structure of computer operations as it relates to personnel within the computer department, and the interaction with personnel in other departments.

The description of computer resources should give auditors (1) an overview of computer operating activities, (2) knowledge of access to computer resources used to process accounting information, and (3) knowledge of company policies regarding access only by authorized personnel. Auditors should enquire about the division of responsibilities between systems and programming staff and operations personnel to assess the segregation of duties. They should understand the existence and organization of the control function and its assigned responsibilities. Auditors should identify the position the computer function has in the overall organization structure, as well as understand the interaction between user departments and the computer department. Such an understanding helps the auditor to decide on the reliance to put on system controls and the effect of such reliance on substantive procedures.

Methods Used to Communicate Responsibility and Authority

In connection with understanding the methods used by the client to communicate responsibility and authority, the auditor should obtain information about the existence of (*a*) accounting and other policy manuals, including computer operations and user manuals, and (*b*) formal job descriptions for computer department personnel. Related user personnel job descriptions may be helpful. Auditors should gain an understanding of how the client's computer resources are managed and how priorities for their use are determined. Auditors also should gain an understanding of the extent to which other departments within the company have a clear understanding of how they must comply with computer processing-related standards and procedures.

Methods Used by Management to Supervise the System

As part of the Phase 1 review, auditors should learn the procedures management uses to supervise the computer operation, including:

- The existence of systems design and documentation standards and the extent to which they are used.
- The existence and quality of procedures for system and program modification, systems acceptance approval and output modification (such as changes in reports or files).
- The procedures limiting access to authorized information, particularly with respect to sensitive information.
- The availability of financial and other reports, such as budget/performance reviews for use by management.
- The existence of an internal audit function and the degree of its involvement in reviewing computer-produced accounting records and related controls and its involvement in systems development control evaluation and testing.

After the audit team gains an understanding of the control environment, the obtaining-an-understanding phase should be continued by obtaining an understanding of the accounting system—the flow of transactions.

Understanding the Accounting System

An understanding of the flow of transactions through the accounting system is required to support the design of substantive audit procedures. Gaining the understanding of the flow of transactions for each significant accounting application begins with referring to the client's description of the accounting applications. Descriptions should include the user's manuals and instructions, file descriptions, system flowcharts and narrative descriptions.

The audit team may find that internal audit personnel or other client personnel already have prepared documentation relating to the flow of transactions. This documentation may be adequate for purposes of understanding the accounting system. Early in the audit planning, the internal auditors and other client personnel should be consulted to determine whether they have documentation that can be useful.

PHASE 2: ASSESSING THE CONTROL RISK
. . . .

The distinction between the understanding phase and the control risk assessment phase is useful for your understanding of the audit work. However, most auditors in practice do the two together, not as separate and distinct work packages.

Control risk assessment, when a computer is used, involves:

- Identifying specific control objectives based on the types of misstatements that may be present in significant accounting applications.
- Identifying the points in the flow of transactions where specific types of misstatements could occur.
- Identifying specific control procedures designed to prevent or detect these misstatements.

COMPUTER IMPACT ON INTERNAL CONTROL

Traditional segregation of duties may be impaired because an individual employee may be able to perform incompatible functions, such as making and concealing an error.

The number of people who handle a transaction is typically reduced, often to just the individual employee who enters the data into the computer. Control can be maintained only if additional controls are in the computer system.

In a simple environment, an individual manager can be responsible for managing and ensuring the quality of the gathering, processing and use of data. In computer systems, an individual manager may be responsible for only a portion of the processing and control. Unless carefully defined and monitored, this sharing of control responsibilities can result in loss of overall control.

Source: Adapted from Deloitte & Touche handbook.

- Identifying the control procedures that must function to prevent or detect the misstatements.
- Evaluating the design of control procedures to determine whether it suggests a low control risk and whether test of controls audit procedures on them may be cost effective.

Identifying specific control objectives is no different than in a manual data processing system. However, the process of identifying the points in the flow of transactions where misstatements could occur is different in a computer system in comparison to a manual system. For example, when a computer is used, these points (see Exhibit 8–1) are places where misstatements could occur:

1. Activities related to source data preparation are performed, causing the flow of transactions to include authorization and initial execution.
2. Noncomputerized procedures are applied to source data, such as a manual summarization of accounting data (preparation of batch totals).
3. Source data are converted into computer-readable form.
4. Input files are identified for use in processing.
5. Information is transferred from one computer program to another.
6. Computer-readable files are used to supply additional information relating to individual transactions (e.g., customer credit reports).
7. Transactions are initiated by the computer.
8. Output files are created or master files are updated.
9. Master files are changed (records added, deleted or modified) outside the normal flow of transactions within each cycle through file maintenance procedures.
10. Output reports or files are produced.
11. Errors identified by control procedures are corrected.

Once the audit team has identified the points where a misstatement might occur, specific control objectives can be related to such points. For example, one possible misstatement might involve billing customers with incorrect prices because a wrong file has been used. One way to state a control objective relating to this type of misstatement is: "Appropriate price information should be used during the billing process." As will be discussed later in this chapter, the controls associated with prevention, detection or correction of these misstatements can be grouped into three broad categories: input, processing and output controls. Input controls are the ones associated with preventing misstatements of the type

EXHIBIT 8–1   COMPUTER ACCOUNTING: POINTS OF VULNERABILITY TO MISSTATEMENT ERRORS

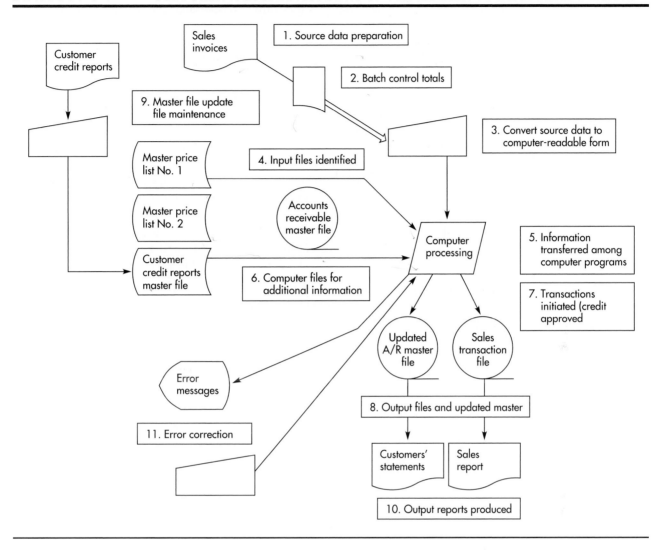

numbered 1 through 4 above. Processing controls are primarily designed to detect misstatements of the type numbered 5 through 8 above. Output controls are primarily designed to correct misstatements of the type numbered 9 through 11 above.

Once points where misstatements could occur in the flow of transactions are identified, auditors should focus on specific control procedures that may prevent or detect such misstatements. Control procedures should be considered in terms of specific control objectives. For example, for the objective of using appropriate price information, one control procedure might be "The billing application program should identify the correct price file through matching the file name in the program to the name on the header label." (Header labels are described later.)

In a computerized accounting system, control procedures may have characteristics that differ from manual control procedures designed to accomplish the same control objectives. For example, in a manual system, credit approval usually is indicated by affixing an authorized signature to a source document, such as a customer's order or invoice. In a computerized system, however, approval can be accomplished by utilizing an approved password that releases a credit sale transaction by assigning a special code to it. The password provides access to programs that permit initiating a specific type of transaction or changing master files. In such a case, although the control objective is identical in the manual and computerized systems, the methods used to achieve the objective and the visible evidence of conformity with authorized procedures differ considerably and the audit approach may be significantly different.

The information gathered about the client's control environment, the accounting system and the control procedures should enable the auditor to reach one of the following conclusions about control risk:

- Control risk may be assessed low, and it seems efficient to perform tests of controls audit procedures. Control procedures designed to prevent or detect misstatements apparently can be audited for compliance in a cost-effective manner. In this situation the auditors continue with test of controls auditing discussed later in this chapter.

- Control risk may be assessed low, but audit inefficiencies would occur if controls were tested. Control policies and procedures appear to be good, but test of controls auditing is not cost effective. In this case the auditors would concentrate attention on the substantive audit procedures.

- Control risk may be assessed high. Control structure policies and procedures do not appear to be sufficient to prevent or detect material misstatements. In this case the auditors will concentrate on substantive audit procedures.

If controls do not appear to be good, the auditors should proceed with the design of substantive audit procedures. In making this evaluation, it may be possible to identify specific control procedures that provide a low risk assessment with regard to some but not all assertions. In such situations the auditors may achieve some audit objectives through a combination of tests of controls and substantive auditing, while other audit objectives may be achieved through substantive procedures alone.

REVIEW CHECKPOINTS

8.5 How is the understanding of the control environment affected when a computer is used in data processing?

8.6 What sources of information can auditors use to obtain an understanding of the flow of transactions through a client's computerized accounting system?

8.7 What five general tasks are involved in computer system control risk assessment?

8.8 Categorize the 11 points of vulnerability to misstatement errors in terms of manual input, computer processing and error correction activities in a computer system.

SIMPLE COMPUTER SYSTEMS: CHARACTERISTICS AND CONTROL CONSIDERATIONS

LEARNING OBJECTIVE
4. Describe and explain general control procedures and place the application control procedures covered in Chapter 6 in the context of computerized "error checking routines."

The controls described in this section relate to a simple computer system, although many of the controls are applicable to more advanced systems described in Chapter 21. A simple system is one where all processing occurs at a central processing facility, usually a personal computer (PC), or as part of a local area network (ISA 1001.5). At most there are three or four people involved in the operations of a simple system.

Characteristics of a Simple Computer System

Batch processing (also called **serial** or **sequential processing**) means that all records to be processed are collected in groups (batches) of like transactions. The computer operator (or the operating system) obtains the programs and master files from the computer library. Following the instructions in the run manual, all like transactions then are processed utilizing the same programs and the same master files. For example, all payroll records are run at one time, and the input is in the form of a magnetic disk containing employees' identification numbers and hours worked. The programs edit and validate the input and match good transactions against the employee master file for pay rate and deduction information. Programs will execute the processing to compute the payroll, print cheques, update year-to-date records, and summarize payroll information for management. After completion of the run, the programs and data files will be returned to storage (magnetic disk) and the output of cheques and reports will be distributed.

Batches may be collected at a central computer site or other locations. Input transactions may be entered via terminals and stored on magnetic tape or disks. Regardless of the method, batch processing is characterized by grouping like transactions to be processed in batches, all using the same programs. The master files take the place of subsidiary and general ledgers in manual systems. The batches of transactions are similar to journals in a manual system. All transactions in a batch may be listed in printed output. However, the detail of transactions usually is not printed and the familiar journal is nonexistent. Instead, summary entries are prepared for updating general ledger master files. Many smaller systems now provide the on-line processing capability that traditionally has been associated with advanced systems (see Chapter 21). *On-line* has a variety of meanings as discussed in Chapter 21, but a meaning that is relevant for all systems is the following: Data processing is termed on-line (or direct access or random) where transactions can be input into computer processing from the point of origin without first being sorted.

Master files contain records with two general types of fields—**static** fields, such as employee number and pay rate, and **dynamic** fields, such as year-to-date gross pay and account balances. Most of the computer processing of accounting data involves changing these fields in the master file records. The dynamic fields are changed in **update** processing, as was described for batch processing of payroll. Update processing does not change the static fields. The static fields are changed by **file maintenance** processing, which will add or delete entire records (e.g., add new employee) or change fields (e.g., new pay rate). Auditors are concerned with authorization and controls over both types of changes.

General Control Procedures

Control procedures in a computerized accounting system may be classified into two types—general controls and application controls (EDP–3 or ISA 1001.35–.36, and ISA 1008). **General control procedures** relate to all or many computerized accounting activities—for example, controls over access to computer programs and data files. **Application control procedures** relate to individual computerized accounting applications—for example, programmed validation controls for verifying customers' account numbers and credit limits. The general controls are presented first because they usually are considered early in the audit.

Organization and Physical Access

The proper segregation of functional responsibilities—authority to authorize transactions, custody of assets, recordkeeping and periodic reconciliation—is as important in computer systems as in manual systems. However, computer systems involve such functions as systems analysis, programming, data conversion, library functions and machine operations that are unique. Therefore, further separation of duties is recommended. These separate functions were explained in Chapter 6, but they are also an integral part of computer system control. It is a good idea to review the Chapter 6 section "Segregation of Technical Responsibilities" at this time.

The physical security of computer equipment, and limited access to computer program files and data files, are as important as segregation of technical responsibilities. Access controls help prevent improper use or manipulation of data files, unauthorized or incorrect use of computer programs and improper use of the computer equipment.

The librarian function or librarian software should control access to systems documentation and access to program and data files by using a checkout log (a record of entry and use) or password to record the use by authorized persons. Someone who possesses both documentation and data files will have enough information to alter data and programs for his or her own purposes.

Organization and Physical Access: Selected Questionnaire Items

Preliminary

Prepare or have the client prepare a "Computer Profile," which should include an organization chart, hardware and peripheral equipment, communication network, major application processes (batch or on-line), significant input and output files, software used and a layout of the data centre.

Organization

Are the following functions performed by different individuals so that proper segregation of duties exists?

a. Application programming, computer operation and control of data files?

b. Application programming and control and reconciliation of input and output?

Are computer operators rotated periodically from shift to shift?

Are programmers and systems analysts rotated periodically from application to application?

Data and Procedural Control

Is there a separate group within the computer department to perform control and balancing of input and output?

Are there written procedures for setting up input for processing?

Is there a formal procedure for distribution of output to user departments?

Access Control

Is access to the computer room restricted to authorized personnel?

Are operators restricted from access to program and application documentation?

Does access to on-line files require that specific passwords be entered to identify and validate the terminal user?

Locked doors, security passes, passwords and check-in logs (including logs produced by the computer) can be used to limit access to the computer system hardware. Having definite schedules for running computer applications is another way to detect unauthorized access, because the computer system software can produce reports that can be compared to the planned schedule. Variations then can be investigated for unauthorized use of computer resources.

Weakness or absence of organizational and access controls decreases the overall integrity of the computer system. The audit team should be uncomfortable when such deficiencies exist and should weigh their impact when evaluating control risk. Some typical questions asked by auditors are shown in the box above. A full set of questions, of which these are a part, is one method that auditors use to review and document the organization and access control of a computer facility.

Documentation and Systems Development

Documentation is the means of communicating the essential elements of the data processing system. The following purposes may be served by computer system documentation:

- Provide for management review of proposed application systems.
- Provide explanatory material for users.
- Instruct new personnel by providing background on previous application systems and serve as a guideline for developing new applications.
- Provide the data necessary for answering enquiries about the operation of a computer application.
- Serve as one source of information for an evaluation of controls.
- Provide operating instructions.
- Simplify program revision by providing details of processing logic.
- Supply basic information for planning and implementing audit software or other auditing techniques.[1]

Auditors review the documentation to gain an understanding of the system and to determine whether the documentation is adequate. Of utmost importance in this area of the review is whether systems development and documentation standards have been established by the client. Unless written standards exist, it is very difficult to determine whether the systems development controls and the documentation are adequate. The **systems development and documentation standards manual** prepared by management should contain standards that ensure (1) proper user involvement in the systems design and modification process, (2) review of the specifications of the system, (3) approval by user management and data processing management, and (4) controls and auditability.

Armed with the manual describing systems development standards, auditors first evaluate the standards to determine whether they are adequate and then review the documentation to determine whether the standards are followed. This review actually accomplishes a test of controls audit of systems development standards (and controls), as well as providing an understanding of how a particular system works. This kind of work may require the knowledge and skills of a computer audit specialist.

Auditors are interested in the following elements of the documentation of accounting applications: application description, problem definition, programs description, acceptance testing records, computer operator instructions, user department manual, change and modification log, and listing of controls. For example, the **application description** usually contains system flowcharts, description of all inputs and outputs, record formats, lists of computer codes and control features. The application system flowcharts frequently can be adapted to audit working paper flowcharts where the flow of transactions can be followed and control points noted. Copies of record formats of significant master files frequently are obtained for use in computer-assisted audit techniques described later.

The **program description** should contain a program flowchart, a listing of the program source code (such as C++ or BASIC), and a record of all program changes. Auditors should review this documentation to determine whether programmed controls such as input validations exist.

The **acceptance testing records** may contain test data that can be used by auditors when performing their own tests of controls audit procedures. The users' manual should indicate manual procedures and controls in the user departments that submit transactions and receive the output. The log of changes and modifications is important to auditors because it should provide assurance that the application systems have been operating as described for the period under review and that all changes and modifications have been authorized.

The **controls section** of the documentation also is very important. Here all the computer controls described in other sections are repeated along with manual controls that affect the application program. Careful review by auditors of this section should provide a complete overview of the entire control over the processing of transactions in a particular application and of how the general controls are carried out in the application.

---

[1] Gordon B. Davis, Donald L. Adams, and Carol A. Schaller, *Auditing and EDP*, 2nd ed. (New York: AICPA, 1983), p. 59.

DOCUMENTATION AND SYSTEMS DEVELOPMENT: SELECTED QUESTIONNAIRE ITEMS

Development

Does a written priority plan exist for development of new systems and changes to old systems?

Do the design and development of a new system involve the users as well as computer personnel?

Is there a formal review and approval process at the end of each significant phase in developing a new system?

Documentation

Do written standards exist for documentation of new systems and for changing documentation when existing systems are revised?

Does the following documentation exist for each application?

- System flowchart.
- Record layouts.
- Program edit routines.
- Program source listing.
- Operator instructions.
- Approval and change record.

Hardware

Modern computer equipment is very reliable. Machine malfunctions that can go undetected are relatively rare. You are not expected to be a computer systems engineer, but you should be familiar with some of the hardware controls so that you can converse knowledgeably with computer personnel.

The most important hardware control now incorporated in all computers is a **parity check**. The parity check ensures that the coding of data internal to the computer does not change when it is moved from one internal storage location to another. An additional hardware control commonly found is an **echo check**. It involves a magnetic read after each magnetic write "echoing" back to the sending location and comparing results. Many computers also contain dual circuitry to perform arithmetic operations twice. Auditors (and management) cannot do much about the absence of such controls but should be concerned primarily with operator procedures when such errors occur (for example, the Pentium processor chip flaw that was widely publicized in late 1994 and early 1995). Modern computers are largely self-diagnostic. Therefore, written procedures should exist for all computer malfunctions, and all malfunctions should be recorded along with their causes and resolutions.

Another significant area of auditor interest is **preventive maintenance**. Auditors should determine whether maintenance is scheduled and whether the schedule is followed and documented. Maintenance frequently is under contract with the computer vendor. In such cases, auditors should review the contract as well as the record of regular maintenance work. Other general evidence on hardware reliability may be obtained from a review of operating reports and downtime logs.

Data File and Program Control and Security

Controls over physical access to the computer hardware were described earlier in this chapter in conjunction with organization controls. Equally important and sensitive is control over access, use and security of the data files and programs. Since magnetic storage media can be erased or written over, controls are necessary to ensure that the proper file is being used and that the files and programs are appropriately backed up. **Backup** involves a retention system for files, programs and documentation so that master files can be reconstructed in case of accidental loss and so that processing can continue at another site if the computer centre is lost to fire or flood. Thus, backup files must be stored offsite, away from the main computer.

Some of the more important security and retention control techniques and procedures are listed and explained next.

External Labels. These labels are paper labels on the outside of a file (diskettes, cartridges, portable disk packs or magnetic tapes). The label identifies the contents, such as "Accounts Receivable Master File," so the probability of using the file inappropriately (e.g., in the payroll run) is minimized.

Header and Trailer Labels. These labels are special internal records on magnetic tapes and disks. They are magnetic records on the tape or disk; but, instead of containing data, they hold label information similar to the external file label. Therefore, the header and trailer labels are sometimes called **internal labels**. Their function is to prevent use of the wrong file during processing. The header label will contain the name of the file and relevant identification codes. The trailer label gives a signal that the end of the file has been reached. Sometimes these trailer labels are designed to contain accumulated control totals to serve as a check on loss of data during operation; for example, the number of accounts and the total balance of an accounts receivable file.

File Security. Security is enhanced by many physical devices, such as storage in fireproof vaults, backup in remote locations and files sorted in computer-readable, printed or microfilm form. In the majority of cases, the exposure to risk of loss warrants insurance on program and data files.

File Retention. Retention practices are related closely to file security; but, in general, retention may provide the first line of defence against relatively minor loss, while security generally consists of all measures taken to safeguard files against total loss. In essence, the problem is how to reconstruct records and files once they have been damaged. One of the most popular methods is the **grandfather-father-son** concept. This involves the retention of backup files, such as the current transaction file and the prior master file, from which the current master file can be reconstructed. Exhibit 8–2 illustrates the file retention plan. Particularly important files may be retained to the great-grandfather generation if this is considered necessary.

Disk files are more difficult to reconstruct than tape files because the process of updating old records with new information is "destructive." The old or superseded data on a record are removed (destroyed) when new data are entered in the same place on a disk. One means of reconstruction is to have a disk file "dumped" onto tape or cartridge periodically (each day or each week). This file copy, along with the related transaction file also retained, can serve as the father to the current disk file (son).

Application Control Procedures

In this book the computerized application control procedures have been integrated with the introduction to control risk assessment topics in Chapter 6. Exhibit 6–6 in Chapter 6 gives a summary list of the "error checking routines," and the chapter text explains them. These are the application control procedures. It would be a good idea to review them at this time and put them in the context of technical computer auditing.

The designation "application controls" comes from the fact that they are used in each "application"—sales and billing, purchasing, payroll and other specific accounting applications. The application controls are organized under three categories—input controls, processing controls and output controls. The brief sections below put some computer system questionnaire items in the context of these control procedures.

E X H I B I T 8-2   GRANDFATHER, FATHER AND SON IN MAGNETIC TAPE FILES

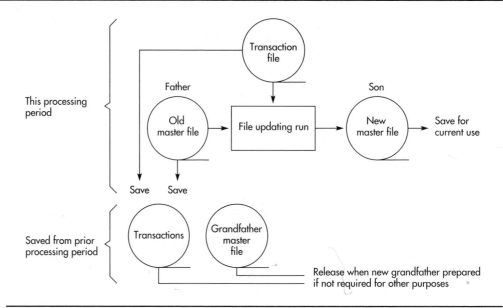

Input Controls

In Chapter 6 the input controls procedures are:

- Input authorization.
- Check digits.
- Record counts.
- Batch financial totals.
- Batch hash totals.
- Valid character tests.
- Valid sign tests.
- Missing data tests.
- Sequence tests.
- Limit/reasonableness tests.
- Error resubmission.

Some typical questionnaire items that may be asked during a review of input controls are shown in the next box. These questions should be asked about each significant accounting application. Input controls are primarily preventive in nature, and with the increasing complexity of computer systems, auditors are placing increasing importance on the input controls. This follows from the "garbage in, garbage out" or GIGO philosophy. It is generally more cost effective for a system to prevent misstatements rather than detect and correct misstatements once they have entered the system.

Processing Controls

In Chapter 6, the processing control procedures are:

- Run-to-run totals.
- Control total reports.
- File logs.
- Limit/reasonableness tests.

INPUT CONTROL PROCEDURES: SELECTED QUESTIONNAIRE ITEMS

Authorization of Transactions

Have procedures been established to ensure that only authorized transactions are accepted, such as (*a*) written approval on source documents? (*b*) general authorizations to process all of the user's transactions? and (*c*) use of identification numbers, security codes and passwords for remote terminal users?

Completeness of Input

Are control totals established by the user prior to submitting data for processing?
   Does someone verify that input data are received on a timely basis from the user and physically controlled in the computer centre?

Data Conversion

Have procedures been established to exercise proper control over processing rejected transactions, including (*a*) positive identification of rejected records? (*b*) review of the cause of rejection? (*c*) the correction of rejected records? (*d*) review and approval of the correction? and (*e*) prompt reentry of the correction at a point where it will be subjected to the same input controls as the original data?

Processing controls are primarily oriented to detecting misstatements. Some typical questionnaire items are in the first two boxes on the next page.

Output Controls

In Chapter 6 the output control procedures are:

- Control totals.
- Master file changes.
- Output distribution.

Output controls are primarily oriented to correcting misstatements already in the system. Some typical questionnaire items are in the third box on the next page.

Control Risk Assessment in Simple Computer Systems

Apparent weakness in any of the input, processing and output control procedures is a matter of concern. However, absence of a control at the input stage may be offset by other controls at later stages (EDP–3). For example, if check digits are not calculated when the input is prepared, but transaction numbers are compared to master file numbers and nonmatches are rejected and printed in an error report, the control is likely to be satisfactory and effective. Of course, it usually is more efficient to catch errors early, rather than late; but control still can be considered effective for the accounting records and financial statements. Internal auditors, however, may be very interested in when controls are applied, since they are concerned about the efficiency of computer operations.

Material weaknesses in manual and computer controls become a part of the independent auditor's assessment of control risk. Lack of input controls may permit data to be lost or double-counted, and poor processing control can permit accounting calculation, allocation and classification errors to occur. Poor output controls over distribution of reports and

---

PROCESSING CONTROL PROCEDURES:
SELECTED QUESTIONNAIRE ITEMS

Completeness

Are programmed control procedures (run-to-run totals) included in each job step during the processing cycle?

Do application programs test the terminal identification or password, or both, for access authorization to that specific program?

Are control totals maintained on all files, and are these verified by the update or file maintenance application program each time a file is used in processing?

File Control

Do application programs check for internal header and trailer labels?

Are disk or cartridge files subjected to adequate on-site and off-site backup support?

Are test data files documented, up to date and kept separate from live data files?

OUTPUT CONTROL PROCEDURES:
SELECTED QUESTIONNAIRE ITEMS

Are input control totals reconciled to output totals?

Are input changes to master files compared item by item to output reports of these changes?

Do written distribution lists exist for all output reports from each application?

Are all output files appropriately identified with internal and external labels?

---

other output (negotiable cheques, for example) can be the source of misstatements that could make financial statements materially misleading.

The purpose of the review of internal control is to gain an understanding of the flow of transaction processing and to determine strengths (controls) and weaknesses (lack of controls) that need to be considered in planning substantive audit procedures. In a computer environment the general control procedures must be reviewed if any application system contains important computer controls. Based on the audit documentation (working papers) of the computer controls and manual controls, the audit manager must determine whether processing is accurate and complete. The audit documentation may consist of questionnaires, such as those illustrated in this chapter, and flowcharts. The general control procedures and the controls in each application system may be subject to tests of controls auditing to determine whether the controls operate effectively. Generally, most auditors find it cost effective to follow a strategy of evaluating general and environmental controls before evaluating the more specific application controls. The reasoning for this is that the controls having a more pervasive impact and preventive in nature are the more important controls.

R E V I E W
CHECKPOINTS

8.9   What are the four categories of general control procedures?

8.10   What general familiarity do auditors obtain with the preliminary information sought in the "organization and physical access" questionnaire?

8.11   What is the typical content of application description documentation for a computerized accounting system? of the program description documentation? of the acceptance testing records documentation? of the controls section documentation?

8.12   What is the difference between an external label and an internal label in magnetic file media? What is the purpose of each?

8.13   What aspects of documentation, file security and retention control procedures are unique to computer systems?

8.14   Describe the purposes of computer system documentation. Why should the auditor review the computer system documentation?

8.15   What does an auditor need to know about computer hardware controls?

8.16   What is a self-checking number? Can you give an example of one of your own? (Refer to Chapter 6.)

Micro-Minicomputer Environment (Small Business)

LEARNING OBJECTIVE
5. Describe the characteristics and control problems of microminicomputer installations.

The term "micro-minicomputer" is used herein to describe a family of computers that includes small business computers, personal computers or PCs, and intelligent terminals (EDP–4 or ISA 1001). These small computers can have any or all of the characteristics of advanced systems.

Computer activity involving micro-minicomputers should be included in the assessment of control risk. Since the control objectives do not change, the internal control questionnaires illustrated in this chapter and the audit techniques discussed in Chapter 21 are relevant but may have to be tailored to the micro-minicomputer installation. The following explanations are designed to assist you in appreciating how the questionnaires, flowcharts and audit techniques may have to be modified by directing attention to potential problems and controls normally affecting micro-minicomputers.

Major Characteristics

Micro-minicomputers may be elements of a distributed system or a stand-alone system doing all the data processing for a business. The latter is considered here. The control environment, and not the computer technology, is the important aspect for auditors (EDP–4). Many small businesses use these resources:

- *Utility programs.* Purchased utility programs are used extensively to enter and change data.
- *Disks.* Magnetic disks are used extensively for accounting file storage.
- *Terminals.* Terminals and micro-minicomputers are used for transaction data entry, enquiry and other interactive functions.
- *Software packages.* Purchased software packages are used extensively, rather than internally developed application software.
- *Documentation.* Available system, program, operation and user documentation may be limited or nonexistent.
- *Cartridge or magnetic tape backup.* Is used extensively as long-term backup file storage.

In a micro-minicomputer installation, the most significant control weakness is a lack of segregation of duties. This potential weakness may be compounded by the lack of control procedures in the operating system and application programs. Simply turning on the system may provide access to all the files and programs, with no record of use. The next box highlights these control problems.

Micro-Minicomputer Control Considerations

Most of the control problems can be traced to the lack of segregation of duties and the lack of computerized control procedures. It follows that most of the auditors' control considerations and procedures are designed to overcome these deficiencies. Auditors should consider the entire control structure, including manual controls, and look for compensating control strengths that might offset apparent weaknesses. The various control considerations and techniques are discussed below under headings similar to the general control procedures discussed previously—organizational, operations and processing, and systems development and modification.

Organizational Control Procedures

The environment in a micro-minicomputer installation is similar to the one-person book-keeping department because the system analysis, design and programming functions are available using off-the-shelf software, with rudimentary client set-up and modification using one or two people. The main controls involve limiting the concentration of functions, to the extent possible, and establishing proper supervision. The situation is a computerized version of internal control in a small business as described in Chapter 6. You should review

---

CONTROL PROBLEMS IN
MICRO-MINICOMPUTER ENVIRONMENTS

Lack of Segregation of Accounting Functions

People in user departments may initiate and authorize source documents, enter data, operate the computer and distribute output reports.

Lack of Segregation of Computer Functions

Small organizations may not separate the functions of programming and operating the computer. Programs and data are often resident on disk at all times and accessible by any operator.

Lack of Physical Computer Security

The computer often is located in the user department instead of in a separate secure area. Ease of access and use is desired, and access to hardware, programs and data files may not be restricted.

Lack of Computer Knowledge

Individuals responsible for data processing sometimes have limited knowledge of computers, relying instead on packaged software and utility programs with convenient user manuals. Computer professionals may be assigned to monitor mainframe systems but not the micro-minicomputers.

that section at this time if you do not recall it. The implementation of the other control procedures discussed below will help offset control weaknesses caused by lack of segregation of duties.

Operation Control Procedures

In micro-minicomputer installations, the most important controls are those over on-line data (accounting transactions) entry.

Restricting Access to Input Devices.   Terminals may be physically locked and keys controlled. The utilization of various levels of passwords to access files, initiate changes and invoke programs should be strictly followed.

Standard Screens and Computer Prompting.   The computer can be programmed to produce a standard screen format when a particular function is called. The operator must complete all blanks as prompted by the computer, thus ensuring that complete transactions are entered before they are processed.

On-line Editing and Sight Verification.   The input edit and validation controls discussed previously can be programmed to occur at time of input. In some installations the data on the screen are not released until the data have been sight-verified and the operator signals the computer to accept the entire screen.

Processing Control Procedures

The processing can be controlled by artificially creating the files equivalent to the grandfather-father-son retention concept found in batch systems. The procedures that could ensure that the data processed are in balance, that an adequate audit trail is maintained and that recovery is possible include the following.

Transaction Logs.   Transaction entry through the terminal should be captured automatically in a computerized log. The transaction logs (for each terminal or each class of terminals) should be summarized into the equivalent of batch totals (counts of transactions, financial totals or hash totals).

Control Totals.   Master files should contain records that accumulate the number of records and financial totals. The update processing automatically should change these control records.

Balancing Input to Output.   The summary of daily transactions and the master file control totals from the micro-minicomputer should be balanced to manual control totals maintained by the accounting department. If this external balancing is not feasible, techniques similar to the auditor's analytical procedures can be employed to test for reasonableness.

Audit Trail.   The transaction logs and periodic dumps of master files should provide an audit trail and means for recovery. In addition, some micro-minicomputer installations have systems software that can provide a log of all files accessed and all jobs processed.

Systems Development and Modification

The control objectives and techniques in a micro-minicomputer installation are no different than on a larger system, even though the environment is different. Many application programs will be purchased from computer manufacturers or software vendors not completely familiar with control techniques. Purchased programs should be reviewed carefully and tested before acquisition and implementation. However, once the auditor becomes familiar with widely used off-the-shelf accounting software packages such as ACCPAC or MYOB, this knowledge can be used in the review of systems of other clients using the same software.

There are a variety of programming languages and application generators used in micro/minicomputer systems (C++, DBase) and programming ability may develop within the user group. Most microcomputers have "menu-type" micro-instructions, which are simple to use without technical training. Further, the programming is in an interpretative

Three types of systems are encountered in small businesses: microcomputers, local area networks (LANs), and certain multi-user systems. Where microcomputers are used to process accounting records, the computers often "stand alone" and run a single software package purchased from a software vendor. Where computers are linked together, they form a LAN, again usually running packaged software. In fewer cases, the computers are linked together using a multi-user operating system, such as UNIX, and run custom software especially developed for the business, usually by an outside developer or consultant.

Access controls are important for all of these scenarios, as are backup procedures. The greater the number of users, the greater the opportunity for using access controls for enforcing division of duties. Program development controls are significant only for custom software.

As a minimum, a small business audit file should include a brief memo addressing each of these areas, identifying, for example, whether passwords are being used and how they are administered; whether and by whom programs are changed; and whether backups are made and stored off site. The more complex the system, the more fully the areas need to be addressed.

Source: Trites, G. *Audit of a Small Business*, CICA, 1994, pp. 46–47.

language, which means it remains in the computer program library in source code form that is easy to change. Development standards and modification authorization become even more important than in larger systems. Since most programming will be done through terminals, special passwords should be required to access programs and only authorized personnel should be issued these passwords. The box above identifies key issues of general controls in small business systems.

There is some controversy about the effect of computerization in small businesses and whether such computerization increases or decreases control risk. The International Federation of Accountants suggests that computerization in small businesses leads to increased control risk because of the increased risk of incompatible duties being performed. However, S. J. Gaston argues that adequate general controls can be achieved with "appropriate segregation of duties of only three or four employees" when combined with proper use of user identification and password capabilities.[2] Such general controls, when combined with "reasonably effective application controls," can result in a reduced level of control risk.[3]

R E V I E W CHECKPOINTS

8.17 Which important duties are generally not segregated in small business computer systems?

8.18 What control techniques can a company use to achieve control over the operation of a micro-minicomputer accounting system?

8.19 What control techniques can a company use to achieve control over the computer processing of accounting data in a micro-minicomputer system?

8.20 What are the major characteristics and control problems in micro-minicomputer installations?

[2] S. J. Gaston, *Managing and Controlling Small Computer Systems Including LANS* (Toronto, CICA, 1992) p. XIX
[3] G. Trites, *Audit of a Small Business* (Toronto, CICA, 1994), pp. 47–48.

EVALUATION APPROACHES FOR COMPUTER SYSTEMS

LEARNING OBJECTIVE

6. Explain the differences between auditing around the computer, auditing through the computer and auditing with the computer.

When businesses started using computers, two terms were coined to describe the nature of auditing work on computer systems. The first term, "auditing around the computer," came to mean that auditors were attempting to isolate the computer—to treat it like a "black box"—and to find audit assurance by vouching data from output to source documents and by tracing from source documents to output. As long as the computer was used as a speedy calculator, this method generally was considered adequate. In fact, it may be satisfactory today in a case where the computer system is used simply as a calculator and printer. Nothing is inherently wrong with auditing around the computer if auditors are satisfied with the control structures and are able to gather sufficient evidence. However, auditing around the computer becomes unacceptable if this approach is used because of lack of auditor expertise regarding computer processing.

The second term that has evolved is "auditing through the computer." It refers to the auditor's actual evaluation of the hardware and software to determine the reliability of operations that cannot be viewed by the human eye. Auditing through has become more common in practice because more and more computer systems do not operate as speedy calculators but have significant control procedures built into their systems. Thus, ignoring a computer system and the controls built into it would amount to ignoring important features of internal control.

More recently, two new terms have been used to describe the auditor's approach to computer systems: (1) "auditing without the computer" and (2) "auditing with the computer." The first approach consists of using visible evidence, such as the input source data, the machine-produced error listings, the visible control points (e.g., use of batch totals) and the detailed printed output. The second approach is also referred to as computer-assisted audit techniques (CAATs) as per EDP–1, EDP–2 and ISA 1009. When auditing a simple computer system, CAATs refers to such audit techniques as the use of the following (EDP–2):

- Tests of details of transactions and balances—for example, the use of audit software to test all (or a sample) of the transactions in a computer file.
- Analytical review procedures—for example, the use of audit software to identify unusual fluctuations or items.
- Tests of general EDP controls—for example, the use of test data to test access procedures to the program libraries.
- Compliance tests of EDP application controls—for example, the use of test data to test the functioning of a programmed procedure.

Exhibit 8–3 shows the scheme of auditing around the computer. The auditors select a sample of source documents for a tracing procedure to test the controls over recording sales transactions. The client's computer system processes the transactions, but the auditor treats it like a "black box," interested only in the correspondence of the input (customer's order, quantity shipped and amount billed) to the output (debit to accounts receivable, credit to sales revenue).

TESTS OF COMPUTER CONTROLS IN SIMPLE BATCH SYSTEMS

LEARNING OBJECTIVE

7. Explain how the auditor can perform the test of controls audit of computerized controls in a simple computer system.

In the simple batch systems described earlier, adequate evidence of control performance frequently exists in the printed output and logs (thus, auditing around the computer is possible). For example, input error reports usually will contain examples of each type of error the edit routines are designed to detect. A sample of each type of error can be traced to the error log maintained by the computer control group and to evidence of correction and resubmission. Likewise, printed documentation may exist of compliance with authorized procedures required for execution of transactions or for changes to master files.

EXHIBIT 8–3   EXAMPLE OF AUDITING AROUND THE COMPUTER

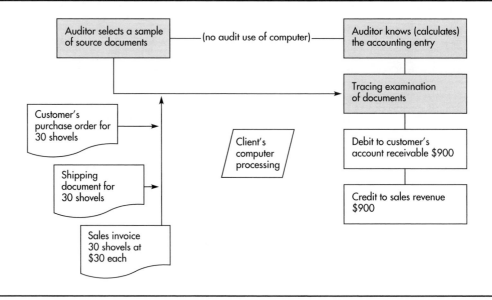

However, external auditors occasionally must use the computer as an audit tool to test the controls within the application programs of even simple systems. (Internal auditors more frequently utilize these techniques.) Thus, a consideration of the use of the computer as an "auditor's assistant" in test of controls audit procedures is the next topic for you to study.

Two Approaches for Using the Computer in Test of Controls Audit Procedures

Auditors can use two approaches to audit through the computer and with the computer to test controls: (1) audit the programmed processing controls with simulated data and (2) audit the programmed controls with live data reprocessed with an audit program. The auditing of programmed control procedures with simulated data generally is referred to as test data, while the reprocessing of live data to test program controls is called parallel simulation.

Test Data

The basic concept of test data is that once a computer is programmed to handle transactions in a certain logical way, it will faithfully handle every transaction exactly the same way. This is the uniformity principle we introduced at the beginning of the chapter. Therefore, the audit team need only prepare a limited number of simulated transactions (some with "errors" and some without) to determine whether each control operates as described in the program documentation.

A **test deck** is a sample of one of each possible combination of data fields that may be processed through the real system. Test deck is a term that refers to the earliest days of computer system operation when all input was prepared on punched card media. Today, simulated test data will more likely be on a disk. Test data also may be entered into an on-line system through computer terminals. The purpose of using test data is to determine whether controls operate as described in questionnaire responses and program flowcharts. Test transactions may consist of abstractions from real transactions and of simulated transactions generated by the auditors' imagination.[4] The auditors must prepare a worksheet list-

---

[4] This may be an oversimplification because computer systems may have multiple controls that create thousands of error combinations and possible test transactions. Computerized test data generators are available to help auditors overcome the magnitude of the test data creation task.

ing each transaction and the predicted output based on the program documentation. Then these test transactions must be converted to the normal machine-sensed input form, and arrangements must be made to process the transactions with the actual program used for real transactions.

Auditors must be very familiar with the nature of the business and the logic of the programs to anticipate all data combinations that might exist as transaction input or that might be generated by processing. They must be able to assign degrees of audit importance to each kind of error-checking control method. Further, they must ensure that the test data do not get commingled with real transactions and change the actual master files.

Consider an example of processing sales transactions. Assume that the objective of the test is to check the controls over accuracy of input data. The problem is to assemble a set of transactions that includes important error conditions in order to determine whether the input and processing controls can detect them.

For example, the audit team can create hypothetical transactions with the following conditions:

1. No customer code number.
2. Invalid customer code number (wrong check digit).
3. Bill of lading document number not entered.
4. Sales amount greater than $25,000.
5. Sales amount equal to zero.
6. Sales amount less than zero.

These six conditions generate many possible combinations of transactions. An example of 15 of them is shown in a decision table presented with problem 21.24 (Exhibit 21.24–1) at the end of Chapter 21. The auditors know that transactions having no customer number or no bill of lading document number (missing data test), an invalid customer code number (self-checking number test), a sales amount greater than $25,000 (limit test), a sales amount equal to zero (missing data test) or a sales amount less than zero (sign test) should produce error messages. Transactions with valid conditions should not. The auditors arrange to run these simulated transactions on the client's system and to find out whether the controls operate.

Test data are processed at a single point in time with the client program that is supposed to have been used during the period under audit. After the analysis of test output, the audit manager still must make an inference about processing throughout the entire period. In order to do so, he or she must be satisfied by a review of documentation that any program changes have been authorized and correctly made. Some auditors occasionally perform test data procedures on an irregular, surprise basis during the year.

Exhibit 8–4 shows the scheme of testing controls with test data. (You should compare it to Exhibit 8–3, the example of auditing around the computer.) The auditors create source document input that can contain accurate as well as erroneous conditions, in this case a shipment of fewer units than the customer ordered. The auditors know the desired outcome—an error message that the quantity shipped and the quantity billed do not match, perhaps with an accounting entry to charge the customer for the shipped quantity. If this result does not appear from the processing of the test data, the auditors can conclude that the processing control over accurate sales recording contains a deficiency (weakness). The auditors are testing the control procedures embedded in the computer program, and they are using the actual processing program for the test. When using test data, the auditor can focus on unusual transactions or error conditions rather than a large number of similar transactions. The reasoning is that if the program handles one transaction correctly, then it will handle other similar transactions the same way. However, the test deck provides a control test only at a specific point in time. In order to rely on the program controls for a period of time, the auditor will also need to obtain assurance that general controls such as controls over program changes are in place and operating over the same time period.

E X H I B I T 8–4   **EXAMPLE OF AUDITING CONTROLS WITH TEST DATA (through the computer)**

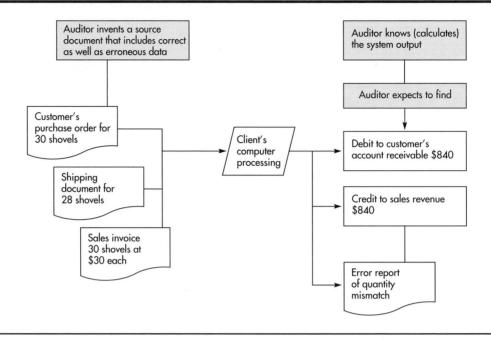

Parallel Simulation

In parallel simulation the audit team prepares a computer program (utilizing generalized audit software described later in this chapter) designed to process client data properly. The result of the auditors' processing of real client data is compared with the result of the real data processed by the actual client program. The concept of this method is illustrated in Exhibit 8–5.

To test the controls contained in computer programs, auditors have the options of (1) using the client's real programs, (2) having client personnel write special programs, or (3) writing their own special programs to collect evidence that the controls work. The first option would be used in the test data technique described in the previous section. The second option requires close supervision and testing to ensure that the client's personnel have prepared the audit program correctly. The third option is parallel simulation, and it requires significant programming expertise of the audit staff or close liaison with expert independent programmers.

However, with **generalized audit software** the parallel simulation option has become much more attractive. The generalized audit software programs consist of numerous prepackaged subroutines that can perform most tasks needed in auditing and business applications. The auditor's programming task consists of writing simple instructions that call up one or more of the subroutines. Thus, there is no need to write complete, complex programs, and the expertise to use the generalized software can be acquired in one week of training. (You will get a closer look at these generalized audit software programs and their capabilities later in this chapter.)

Using the generalized audit program capabilities, an auditor can construct a system of data processing that will accept the same input as the real program, use the same files, and attempt to produce the same results. This simulated system will contain all the controls the auditor believes appropriate, and, in this respect, the thought process is quite similar to the logic that goes into preparing test data. The simulated-system output then is compared to the real-system output for correspondence or difference, and at this point the audit evidence is similar to the evidence obtained by using test data with the real program: conclusions can be reached about the error-detection capabilities of the real system.

EXHIBIT 8–5   SYSTEM CONCEPT OF PARALLEL SIMULATION

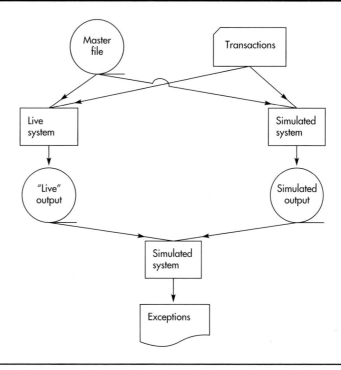

Another way to create a parallel system is to conduct a thorough technical audit of the controls in the client's actual program, then keep a copy of it secure in the auditors' files. Actual client data later can be processed using this audited copy of the client's program (e.g., at times later in the year under audit or in the following year audit). The goal is to determine whether output from the program the client actually used in processing data produces satisfactory accounting output when compared to the output from the auditors' controlled copy of the program. This approach is often called **controlled reprocessing**, and it is a version of parallel simulation.

The first audit application of parallel simulation may be very costly, although it probably will be more efficient than auditing without the computer or utilizing test data. Real economies are realized, however, in subsequent audits of the same client.

The audit team must take care to determine that the real transactions selected for processing are "representative." Thus, some exercise in random selection and identification of

---

PARALLEL SIMULATION

A parallel simulation of Kingston Company's sales invoice and accounts receivable processing system revealed that invoices that showed no bill of lading or shipment reference were processed and charged to customers with a corresponding credit to sales. Further audit of the exceptions showed that the real-data processing program did not contain a missing-data test and did not provide error messages for lack of shipping references. This finding led to (1) a more extensive test of the sales invoice population with comparison to shipping documents and (2) a more extensive audit of accounts receivable for customers who were charged with such sales.

important transactions may be required in conjunction with parallel processing. The illustration in the box above is based on the illustrative sales–accounts receivable system described in the Kingston Company case study that accompanies this chapter.

The ultimate goal of the computer methods of test of controls auditing is to reach a conclusion about the actual operation of controls in a computer system. This conclusion allows the audit manager to assess the control risk and determine the nature, timing and extent of substantive audit procedures for auditing the related account balances. This control risk assessment decision is crucial, particularly in computer systems, because subsequent audit work may be performed using machine readable files that are produced by the computerized information system. The data processing control over such files is important since their content is utilized later in computer-assisted work using generalized audit software.

R E V I E W
CHECKPOINTS

8.21 What is the difference between auditing "through the computer" and auditing "with the computer"?

8.22 What is the difference between the computerized test of controls audit procedures of "test data" and "parallel simulation"?

8.23 "The use of the test data technique to test the client's application control procedures is unprofessional. We don't enter fake transactions into a client's manual system. Why should we do it in their computer system?" Evaluate this position and question posed by an audit partner.

8.24 What is "controlled reprocessing?"

8.25 Why is the auditors' test of computer controls and assessment of related control risk considered "crucial?"

GENERALIZED AUDIT SOFTWARE

LEARNING OBJECTIVE
8. Describe the use of generalized audit software.

Generalized audit software (GAS) programs are a set of functions that may be utilized to read, compute and operate on machine-readable records. Audit software provides access to audit evidence that otherwise would be unavailable. This part of the chapter builds on the computer-related concepts and terminology, and the tests of controls auditing covered in the previous sections of this chapter. However, the emphasis is shifted from the assessment of control risk to the techniques of using the computer to assist with gathering substantive evidential matter about transaction details and account balances.

You need to know about generalized audit software (GAS) because it is used on most audits where the client's accounting records are stored in computer files or a database. The following material does not attempt to prepare you to use any particular generalized audit software because each audit organization has its own GAS and will provide the training to use its particular package. Instead, this section provides you with an understanding of what GAS packages can accomplish and, most important, where the general auditor needs to be involved in a GAS application.

Auditing with the Computer

The audit problems following assessment of control risk in a computer environment are to gain access to machine-readable detail records, to select samples of items for manual or computer audit procedures, to perform calculations and analyses of entire data files and to produce audit working papers of the work performed. GAS packages were first developed by CA firms in the mid-1960s for specific application to audit engagements and have been improved and adapted with the changes in technology. The essential advantages of a generalized audit software package are:

Original programming is not required. The generalized package consists of a set of pre-programmed editing, operating and output subroutines.

The required programming is easy. A simple, limited set of programming instructions using preprinted specification forms is used to call up the subroutines in the package. Training time is short. About one week of intensive training is sufficient to learn how to program a GAS package.

For special-purpose analysis of data files, GAS is more efficient than special programs written from scratch because of the little time required for writing the instructions to call up the appropriate functions of the generalized audit software package. Also, the same software can be used on various clients' computer systems. Control and specific tailoring are achieved through the auditors' own ability to program and operate the system. A large number of GAS packages are currently available through CA firms and consulting firms.

Audit Procedures Performed by Generalized Audit Software

Computer accounting applications capture and generate voluminous amounts of data that usually are available only on machine-readable records. GAS can be used to access the data and organize it into a format useful to the audit team. Audit software can be used with four of the six basic audit techniques of *Section* 5100.02 of the *Handbook.*[5]

1. Computation.   Verification of calculations can be done by the computer with more speed and accuracy than by hand. The audit software can be used to test the accuracy of client computations and to perform analytical procedures to evaluate the reasonableness of account balances. Examples of this use are to (*a*) recalculate depreciation expense, (*b*) re-calculate extensions on inventory items, (*c*) compute file totals, and (*d*) compare budgeted, standard and prior-year data with current-year data.

2. Confirmation.   Auditors can program statistical or judgmental criteria for selecting customers' accounts receivable, loans and other receivables for confirmation. The GAS can be used to print the confirmations and get them ready for mailing. It can do everything except carry them to the post office!

3a. Inspection.   GAS can compare audit evidence from other sources to company records efficiently. The audit evidence must be converted to machine-readable form and then can be compared to the company records on computer files. Examples are (*a*) comparing inventory test counts with perpetual records, (*b*) comparing adjusted audit balances on confirmed accounts receivable to the audit file of book balances, and (*c*) comparing vendor statement amounts to the company's record of accounts payable.

3b. Inspection.   Auditors can use GAS to examine records to determine quality, completeness, consistency and correctness. This is the computer version of scanning the records for exceptions to the auditors' criteria. For example, GAS can scan (*a*) accounts receivable balances for amounts over the credit limit, (*b*) inventory quantities for negative or unreasonably large balances, (*c*) payroll files for terminated employees, and (*d*) loan files for loans with negative balances.

4a. Analysis.   Comparing data on separate files can be accomplished by GAS to determine whether compatible information is in agreement. Differences can be printed out for investigation and reconciliation. Examples are comparing (*a*) payroll details with personnel records, (*b*) current and prior inventory to details of purchases and sales, (*c*) paid vouchers to check disbursements, and (*d*) current and prior-year fixed asset records to identify dispositions.

4b. Analysis.   GAS can summarize and sort data in a variety of ways. Examples are (*a*) preparing general ledger trial balances, (*b*) sorting inventory items by location to facilitate observations, and (*c*) summarizing inventory turnover statistics for obsolescence analysis.

---

[5] CICA, *Application of Computer-Assisted Audit Techniques Using Microcomputers,* CICA (Toronto, 1994), p. 16.

Using Generalized Audit Software

For the most part, the widely used GAS packages are very similar. Regardless of the particular GAS used, five distinct phases are involved in developing a GAS application: (1) define audit objectives, (2) plan the application, (3) design the application, (4) code and test the application, and (5) process the application and evaluate the results.

1. Define the Audit Objective

The first step in applying GAS is to determine specific audit objectives. GAS should be viewed as a special tool providing auditors with a means to accomplish their objectives, not as an objective in itself.

For example, the general audit objectives might be to audit management's assertions that the accounts receivable balance represents detail accounts which exist, are complete and are valued correctly. Based on these general objectives, specific procedures may include footing the accounts subsidiary ledger master file, selecting a sample of accounts for confirmation, preparing an aged trial balance and investigating accounts with overdue balances.

2. Feasibility and Planning

Feasibility should be considered in three ways: (1) Is the use of audit software technically feasible? (2) Are alternative ways to accomplish the audit task available? (3) Which of the alternatives is the most practical and economical? If the use of GAS is technically feasible, other considerations as listed in the next box must be weighed.

Audit software may be the most practical way to achieve the audit objective, but it is seldom the only way. Audit resources (qualified people and their time) must be allocated carefully to achieve efficient and effective results. Using GAS requires considerable investment in time and effort and may be efficient only when repeated use is anticipated on return engagements. Obviously the data must be available. The desired files, especially detailed transaction files, often are retained only for a short time. The availability of data files and the degree of client co-operation normally would be determined during the general and application controls review. Client co-operation in turn could be affected by such issues as client concerns over the security of confidential or sensitive data, including the risk of auditors introducing computer viruses into client computers.

After determining the feasibility of using GAS, the audit manager should determine specifically how it will be used, establish control procedures for all subsequent steps and arrange the logistics with the data center. Specific planning steps are listed in the box on the next page.

The planning phase is also the time to define the workpapers that will document the GAS application. The audit manager, not the computer auditor specialist, should determine what computer output representing coding and testing should be retained in the workpapers. The computer output may be in the form of computer-readable workpapers, such as audit files on disk.

3. Application Design

Developing a GAS application is much like the client's procedures for developing a new application system. However, a complete description of the application phase is beyond the

---

FEASIBILITY CONSIDERATIONS

Cost-effectiveness of hardware and software.
Technical complexity including access to client data.
Availability of qualified audit software staff.
Other issues including client concern about data security.

Source: Application of Computer-Assisted Audit Techniques Using Microcomputers, CICA (Toronto, 1994), p. 20.

Planning Steps

Set application objectives.
Determine content and accessibility of the client's files.
Define transactions to test procedures and output requirements.
Identify client personnel to provide technical assistance.
Determine computer and software needs.
Prepare GAS application budgets and timetables.
Execute GAS application.
Evaluate the results.

Source: EDP Audit Guideline on Computer-Assisted Audit Techniques (EDP–2, p. 7).

---

scope of this book. It should be undertaken only by specially trained audit staff. The application design expands the ideas developed during the feasibility and planning stage into detailed descriptions necessary for preparing coded computer instructions. The documentation of the application design phase includes the GAS application system flowchart, logic descriptions, detailed report layouts, list of control points and procedures, record formats and a test plan. Frequently, the auditor must obtain a computer dump of a few records of each client file to ensure that subsequent coding is based on accurate information. The application must be thoroughly tested with sample client data or simulated data until the audit manager is confident that the GAS application works as desired. The client's file should not be used for testing; the auditor should obtain a copy for testing purposes.

4. Coding and Testing

Most GAS packages have an extensive repertoire of powerful instructions to facilitate processing data files and preparing audit output. The coding is done on specially designed forms (or computer screens for on-line coding).

Coding converts the application design into specific operational requirements (computer language) of the package in use. As coding progresses, the sequence and the logic should be challenged and reviewed. The coding must be converted to a machine-readable form, and all syntax errors must be removed (errors due to failure to follow the rules of the package). Then the coded instructions must be compiled (converted into the hardware machine language like any computer program).

Once the coding errors are removed, the logic must be tested. Testing is very similar to the test data approach used in test of controls auditing of client programs described earlier in this chapter. The test plan defined in the design phase should be extensive enough to test each logic path and anticipate all variations of client data.

5. Processing and Evaluation

The foregoing phases are usually accomplished during interim work—before the year-end. Thus, everything is tested and ready for processing of the year-end balances. The processing phase involves (1) verifying that the status of the client file has not changed, (2) obtaining a copy of the client file, (3) processing the GAS application against the copy of the client's file(s), and (4) reviewing results, updating working papers, and retaining audit files. The audit team should carefully monitor and control the actual processing and the output. Control procedures established during the design phase should be followed. Planned totals should be compared to results and the totals logged on control working papers. The audit manager should review the output for reasonableness and clarity. Finally, the documentation workpapers of the application must be completed and filed.

Special care must be taken to leave adequate documentation for subsequent use on a repeat engagement. (In a sense this documentation is the "audit trail of the audit.") The working papers frequently will contain a list of suggested modifications for next year's audit.

In summary, following the feasibility and planning phase, a GAS application should be designed to achieve specific audit objectives. The reliability of general application computer controls, the availability of client files, access to the computer and technical assistance and estimated costs and the availability of GAS-trained audit staff must be evaluated. The noncomputer-trained auditor should be actively involved in the definition of audit objectives and the application plan. The computer auditor will utilize the application design to link the coding and testing to the planning phase. Results of testing should be reviewed by the audit manager. In the processing phase audit software is run under control of the computer auditor to process copies of client files and produce audit results.

Planning and testing are the most critical tasks in the development of a GAS application. If planning is not adequate, the audit objectives may not be achieved. Problems are likely to occur in subsequent phases and require excessive time and effort to correct. Testing must be adequate or the probability of success is low. Once processing is commenced after year-end, it is extremely difficult to correct errors and deficiencies.

Many larger companies have internal auditors skilled in using GAS. Independent (external) auditors may utilize the internal auditors to develop and run the GAS application under supervision and review of the external audit manager.

Generalized Audit Software Limitations

Notwithstanding the powers of the computer, several good auditing procedures are outside its reach. The computer cannot observe and count physical things (inventory, for example), but it can compare auditor-made counts to the computer records.

The computer cannot examine external and internal documentation; thus, it cannot vouch accounting output to sources of basic evidence. An exception would exist in an advanced computer system that stored the basic source documents on magnetic or optical media. The auditor would have to test the controls over creation of the files but then would have no choice but to treat the file as a basic "document" source. This is discussed further in Chapter 21. When manual vouching is involved, computer-assisted selection of sample items is a great efficiency. Probably the biggest problem auditors encounter in using CAATs is obtaining the data in a format that can be used on their computers. Issues that must be addressed in advance include compatibility of the client's with the auditor's system, data structures in the client's system and availability of client staff to download the data for use by the auditor.[6] Finally, the computer cannot conduct an enquiry in the limited sense that the enquiry procedure refers to questionnaires and conversations.

. . . .

R E V I E W
CHECKPOINTS

8.26   What is generalized audit software?

8.27   What advantages are derived from using generalized audit software to perform recalculations? to select samples and print confirmations?

8.28   What are five audit procedures that can be performed using generalized audit software?

8.29   What are the phases of developing an application using generalized audit software? What are the noncomputer auditor's responsibilities in each phase?

8.30   Why are the testing and planning tasks the most critical when using generalized audit software?

8.31   When a generalized audit software application is planned, which member of the audit team should have the responsibility of deciding about the computer output that should be retained in the working papers?

8.32   Evaluate the following statement by a senior computer auditor: "The time to be thinking about generalized audit software procedures is at the beginning when we obtain an understanding of the control structure."

. . . .

[6] Trites, G. *Audit of a Small Business*, CICA (Toronto, 1994), pp. 50–51.

USING THE MICROCOMPUTER AS AN AUDIT TOOL

LEARNING OBJECTIVE

9. Describe how the microcomputer can be used as
an audit tool.

The microcomputer has revolutionized auditing. You have probably already learned to use the microcomputer to prepare accounting schedules with spreadsheet software and to use word processing software to prepare your class papers. The audit microcomputer software makes use of these same microcomputer software tools to prepare auditing working papers, audit programs and audit memos.

Several GAS have been designed for use on microcomputers, two of the most common in Canada being Interactive Data Extraction and Analysis (IDEA), which is sold and supported by the CICA, and ACL, which is sold by a West Coast vendor. These programs are relatively easy to use since little or no programming is required to use these packages.[7]

The microcomputer is being used regularly in small and large public accounting firms to perform such clerical steps as preparing the working trial balance, posting adjusting entries, grouping accounts that represent one line item on the financial statement into lead schedules, computing comparative financial statements and common ratios for analytical review, preparing supporting workpaper schedules and producing draft financial statements. Many of the large firms also are using the microcomputer to assess control risk, perform sophisticated analytical functions on individual accounts, access public and firm databases for analysis of unusual accounting and auditing problems and utilize decision support software in making complex evaluations. Exhibit 8–6 illustrates the different phases a typical public accounting firm or internal audit department may go through in the use of the microcomputer as an audit tool.

In addition to the various uses of the microcomputer listed in Exhibit 8–6, you can expect a highly integrated microcomputer-based audit process, one that will allow future auditors to control and document the audit from the engagement letter to the audit report and accompanying financial statements. The preliminary audit program will be generated automatically following answers to internal control questionnaires and other programmed audit risk evaluators. The accounting data for the trial balance will be entered into the microcomputer workpapers automatically, and all lead schedules and supporting workpapers will be generated. Related analytical procedure workpapers will be produced using not only client data but also related industry data (most likely downloaded from the Internet), with suggestions made to update the preliminary audit program. Virtually every element of this integrated microcomputer audit is currently in use or being developed. The integration and the degree of sophistication will develop further uses of the microcomputer as an audit tool. In particular, the availability of audit software enables the auditor to:

- simulate all or part of the process by which the data supporting management's assertions were compiled.
- extract information for substantive tests and tests of controls, based on the client's data supporting the subject matter of the engagement.
- prepare information directly relevant to high inherent and control risk items (e.g., approvals of limits for high risk customers).[8]

As a result of acquisition of microcomputers or computer services by even the smallest business, information in electronic format has become the norm. It is now standard for auditors to make effective use of microcomputers in small business audits. Some of the opportunities for using a microcomputer in a small business audit relate to trial balance and financial statement software, preparation of audit programs, planning and administration, and computer-assisted audit techniques (CAATs). Common applications of CAATs in small businesses include accounts receivable, confirmation and aging, footing and extending inventory files, and selecting inventory items for price testing. The ability of CAATs to

---

[7] Ibid, p. 50.

[8] CICA, *Application of Computer-Assisted Audit Techniques Using Microcomputers*, CICA, 1994, p. 17.

EXHIBIT 8–6   PHASES FOR THE USE OF THE MICROCOMPUTER AS AN AUDIT TOOL

Applications	Goals and Objectives	Software Available
Phase 1: Automating the Audit Process		
Trial balance and working papers	Overall audit efficiency.	Automated workpapers vendor supplied, developed by PA firms and others.
Adjusting and updating financial data	Automation of time-consuming activities.	
Time and budget data	Improved control.	Vendor supplied.
Audit program, memo and report generation	Efficient and more readable.	Word processing.
Phase 2: Basic Auditing Functions		
Spreadsheet analysis working papers	Efficiency in common working papers.	Vendor supplied, firm-developed uses.
Analytical review	Improved overall analysis	Part of automated workpaper packages.
Sampling planning, selection and evaluation	Evidence collection and evaluation efficiency.	Statistical, firm developed.
Phase 3: Advanced Auditing Functions		
Analytical procedures for specific accounts	Improved auditor analysis.	Firm developed.
Access to client files on larger computers	Ability to download directly into automated workpaper software.	Vendor supplied or firm developed.
Access to firm and public databases	Provide auditor with reference information.	Micro as a terminal, tele communication.
GAS functions	Mainframe GAS workpapers downloaded to micro.	Firm developed.
Modelling and decision support systems	Improved auditor decisions.	Firm-developed decision support systems.
Audit-file collection. Continuous monitoring	Use the techniques in Chapter 21.	Embedded Audit Modules

Source: Adapted from Clinton E. White, "The Microcomputer as an Audit Tool," *Journal of Accountancy.* (As modified.)

check an entire file with little additional effort is a major advantage because it allows the auditor to obtain a higher degree of audit assurance, at little additional cost.

REVIEW CHECKPOINTS

8.33 What audit tasks can be accomplished with microcomputer word processing?

8.34 Describe automated workpaper software that can be used with microcomputers.

8.35 How could microcomputer spreadsheet packages be used to generate supporting workpapers, such as bank reconciliations, that could be used on more than one audit?

SUMMARY

Computer auditing is not something for future consideration. It is encountered in almost all audits today. Even though computer technology changes the accounting system and the control environment, it does not change the basic auditing standards. Qualities of competence, independence, due care, planning, control risk assessment and sufficient competent evidence are not changed. However, the nuances and aspects of achieving them must be tailored to a world of computers.

It is very tempting to compare computer accounting systems and computer-oriented auditing to manual accounting and manual auditing. Chapter 8 tried to avoid overworking these comparisons because computers are a way of life, not a departure from a basic manual world. Nevertheless, audit planning begins with learning about a client's extent of computer use—the type of personnel organization, computer equipment and the significant accounting applications.

Numerous general and specific control procedures were explained, starting with the "general control procedures" and proceeding to the "application control procedures." However, the application control procedures were not in Chapter 8. They were introduced in Chapter 6, where internal control was also introduced; thus, computer control concepts were integrated with control considerations in all audits. These application procedures were then cross-referenced in Chapter 8 for review/study from Chapter 6. Some control questionnaire items were added to them in Chapter 8.

A useful distinction was made in this chapter between simple computer systems and advanced computer systems. The simple systems are characterized as batch systems, and the advanced systems are ones that have sophisticated data communication, database integration, automatic transaction initiation or an unconventional audit trail. The brief introduction to advanced systems serves as a warning about the complexities of large-scale computer systems.

This chapter also had a section with a small business orientation to micro-minicomputer systems. Their characteristics and typical control problems were described. This section was similar to the small business section in Chapter 6, where students were warned not to expect to find all the bureaucratic features of big business control in small clients.

Multiple-Choice Questions for Practice and Review

· ·

Questions 8.36 to 8.38 are located on the CD-ROM that accompanies this textbook.

8.39 In an electronic data processing system, automated equipment controls or hardware controls are designed to:
  a. Arrange data in a logical sequential manner for processing purposes.
  b. Correct errors in the computer programs.
  c. Monitor and detect errors in source documents.
  d. Detect and control errors arising from use of equipment.

8.40 A good example of application (user) computer software is:
  a. Payroll processing program.
  b. Operating system program.
  c. Data management system software.
  d. Utility programs.

8.41 Which of the following statements most likely represents a disadvantage for a company that performs its accounting using microcomputers?
  a. It is usually difficult to detect arithmetic errors.
  b. Unauthorized persons find it easy to access the computer and alter the data files.
  c. Transactions are coded for account classifications before they are processed on the computer.
  d. Random errors in report printing are rare in packaged software systems.

8.42 A procedural control used in the management of a computer centre to minimize the possibility of data or program file destruction through operator error includes:
  a. Control figures.
  b. Crossfooting tests.
  c. Limit checks.
  d. External labels.

8.43 Which of the following is not a characteristic of a batch-processed computer system?
  a. The collection of like transactions that are sorted and processed sequentially against a master file.
  b. Keyboard input of transactions, followed by machine processing.
  c. The production of numerous printouts.
  d. The posting of a transaction, as it occurs, to several files, without intermediate printouts.

8.44 What is the computer process called when data processing is performed concurrently with a particular activity and the results are available soon enough to influence the particular course of action being taken or the decision being made?
  a. Batch processing.
  b. Real-time processing.
  c. Integrated data processing.
  d. Random access processing.

8.45 The client's computerized exception-reporting system helps an auditor to conduct a more efficient audit because it:
a. Condenses data significantly.
b. Highlights abnormal conditions.
c. Decreases the tests of computer controls requirements.
d. Is efficient computer input control.

8.46 Auditors often make use of computer programs that perform routine processing functions, such as sorting and merging. These programs are made available by software companies and are specifically referred to as:
a. Compiler programs.
b. Supervisory programs.
c. Utility programs.
d. User programs.

8.47 In the weekly computer run to prepare payroll cheques, a cheque was printed for an employee who had been terminated the previous week. Which of the following controls, if properly utilized, would have been most effective in preventing the error or ensuring its prompt detection?
a. A control total for hours worked, prepared from time cards collected by the timekeeping department.
b. Requiring the treasurer's office to account for the numbers of the prenumbered cheques issued to the computer department for the processing of the payroll.
c. Use of the check digit for employee numbers.
d. Use of a header label for the payroll input sheet.

EXERCISES AND PROBLEMS

8.48 Computer Internal Control Questionnaire Evaluation. Assume that, when conducting procedures to obtain an understanding of the control structure in the Denton Seed Company, you checked "No" to the following internal control questionnaire items (selected from those illustrated in the chapter):
- Does access to on-line files require specific passwords to be entered to identify and validate the terminal user?
- Are control totals established by the user prior to submitting data for processing? (Order entry application subsystem.)
- Are input control totals reconciled to output control totals? (Order entry application subsystem.)

Required:
Describe the errors, irregularities or misstatements that could occur due to the weaknesses indicated by the lack of controls.

8.49 Check Digit. Suppose that a credit sale was made to John Q. Smyth, customer account number 8149732. The last digit is a check calculated by the "Modulus 11 Prime Number" method. The data entry operator made an error and keyed in the customer as 8419732.

Required (refer to Chapter 11):
a. Calculate the check digit for the number that was keyed in.
b. How would the self-checking number control detect this data input error?

8.50 Explain Computer Control Procedures. At a meeting of the corporate audit committee attended by the general manager of the products division and you, representing the internal audit department, the following dialogue took place:

Jones (committee chair): Mr. Marks had suggested that the internal audit department conduct an audit of the computer activities of the products division.

Smith (general manager): I don't know much about the technicalities of computers, but the division has some of the best computer people in the company.

Jones: Do you know whether the internal controls protecting the system are satisfactory?

Smith: I suppose they are. No one has complained. What's so important about controls anyway, as long as the system works?

Jones turns to you and asks you to explain computer control policies and procedures.

Required:
Address your response to the following points:
a. State the principal objective of achieving control over (1) input, (2) processing, and (3) output.
b. Give at least three methods of achieving control over (1) source data, (2) processing, and (3) output.

8.51 File Retention and Backup. You have audited the financial statements of the Solt Manufacturing Company for several years and are making preliminary plans for the audit for the year ended June 30. This year, however, the company has installed and used a computer system for processing a portion of its accounting data.

The following output computer files are produced in the daily processing runs:

1. Cash disbursements sequenced by cheque number.
2. Outstanding payables balances (alphabetized).
3. Purchase journals arranged by (*a*) account charged and (*b*) vendor.

Company records, as described above, are maintained on magnetic tapes. All tapes are stored in a restricted area within the computer room. A grandfather-father-son policy is followed in retaining and safeguarding tape files.

Vouchers (with supporting invoices, receiving reports, and purchase order copies) are filed by vendor code. Another purchase order copy and the cheques are filed numerically.

Required:

a. Explain the grandfather-father-son policy. Describe how files could be reconstructed when this policy is used.
b. Discuss whether company policies for retaining and safeguarding the tape files provide adequate protection against losses of data.

8.52 Separation of Duties and General Control Procedures. You are engaged to examine the financial statements of Horizon Incorporated, which has its own computer installation. During the preliminary understanding work, you found that Horizon lacked proper segregation of the programming and operating functions. As a result, you intensified the evaluation of the internal control structures surrounding the computer and concluded that the existing compensating general control procedures provided reasonable assurance that the objectives of internal control were being met.

Required:

a. In a properly functioning computer environment, how is the separation of the programming and operating functions achieved?
b. What are the compensating general control procedures that you most likely found?

(AICPA adapted)

8.53 Advanced Computer Systems Control Procedures. The revenue ministry of one province is developing a new computer system for processing provincial income tax returns of individuals and corporations. The new system features direct data input and enquiry capabilities. Identification of taxpayers is provided by using the social insurance number for individuals and the federal identification number for corporations. The new system should be fully implemented in time for the next tax season. The new system will serve three primary purposes as described below:

1. Data will be input into the system directly from tax returns through terminals located at the central headquarters of the Department of Taxation.
2. The returns will be processed using the main computer facilities at central headquarters. The processing includes:
   a. Verification of mathematical accuracy.
   b. Auditing the reasonableness of deductions, tax due, and so forth through the use of edit routines; these routines also include a comparison of the current year's data with the prior year's data.
   c. Identification of returns that should be considered for audit by revenue agents of the department.
   d. Issuing refund cheques to taxpayers.
3. Enquiry service will be provided to taxpayers on request through the assistance of Tax Department personnel at five regional offices. A total of 50 terminals will be placed at the regional offices. A taxpayer will be allowed to determine the status of his or her return or get information from the last three years' returns by calling or visiting one of the department's regional offices.

The provincial revenue minister is concerned about data security over and above protection against natural hazards such as fire and flood. He is concerned with protection against the loss or damage of data during data input or processing. Also, both he and the provincial attorney general have discussed the general problem of data confidentiality. Both officials want to have all potential problems identified before the system is fully developed and implemented so that the proper controls can be incorporated into the new system.

Required:

a. Describe the potential confidentiality problems that could arise in each of the following three areas of processing and recommend the corrective action(s) to solve the problem: (1) Data input. (2) Processing of returns. (3) Data enquiry.

b. The provincial revenue minister wants to incorporate control procedures to provide data security against the loss, damage or improper input or use of data during data input and processing. Identify the potential problems (other than of natural hazards such as fire and flood) for which the Department of Taxation should develop controls, and recommend the possible controls for each problem identified.

(CMA adapted)

8.54 Computer Frauds and Missing Control Procedures. The following are brief stories of actual employee thefts and embezzlements perpetrated using computers.

Required:

What kind of control procedures were missing or inoperative that might have prevented or detected the fraud?

a. An accounts payable terminal operator at a subsidiary company fabricated false invoices from a fictitious vendor, and entered them in the parent company's central accounts payable/cash disbursement system. Five cheques totalling $155,000 were issued to the "vendor."

b. A bank provided custodial and record-keeping services for several mutual funds. A proof-and-control department employee substituted his own name and account number for those of the actual purchasers of some shares. He used the computerized recordkeeping and correction system to conceal and shift balances from his name and account to names and accounts of the real investors when he needed to avoid detection because of missing amounts in the investors' accounts.

c. The university computer system was entered. Vandals changed many students' first name to "Susan," student telephone numbers were changed to the number of the university president, grade point averages were modified and some academic files were deleted completely.

d. A computer operator at a state-run horse race betting agency set the computer clock back three minutes. After the race was won, he quickly telephoned bets to his girlfriend, an input clerk at the agency, gave her the winning horse and the bet amount, and won every time!

DISCUSSION CASES

8.55 Control Weaknesses and Recommendations—Frontenac Sales Corporation. George Beemster, CPA, is examining the financial statements of the Frontenac Sales Corporation, which recently installed a computer. The following comments have been extracted from Mr. Beemster's notes on computer operations and the processing and control of shipping notices and customer invoices:

To minimize inconvenience, Frontenac converted without changing its existing data processing system, which utilized tabulating equipment. The computer company supervised the conversion and provided training to all computer department employees in systems design, operations and programming.

Each computer run is assigned to a specific employee who is responsible for making program changes, running the program and answering questions. This procedure has the advantage of eliminating the need for records of computer operations because each employee is responsible for her or his own computer runs.

At least one computer department employee remains in the computer room during office hours, and only computer department employees have keys to the computer room.

Systems documentation consists of those materials furnished by the computer company—a set of record formats and program listings. These and the tape library are kept in a corner of the computer department.

The company considered the desirability of programmed controls but decided to retain the manual controls from its existing system.

Company products are shipped directly from public warehouses, which forward shipping notices to general accounting. There, a billing clerk enters the prices of the items and accounts for the numerical sequence of shipping notices from each warehouse. The billing clerk also prepares daily adding machine tapes ("control tapes") of the units shipped and the unit prices.

Shipping notices and control tapes are forwarded to the computer department for input and processing. Extensions are made on the computer. Output consists of invoices (in six copies) and a daily sales register. The daily sales register shows the aggregate totals of units shipped and unit prices, which the computer operator compares to the control tapes.

All copies of the invoice are returned to the billing clerk. The clerk mails three copies to the customer, forwards one copy to the warehouse, maintains one copy in a numerical file, and retains one copy in an open invoice file that serves as a detail accounts receivable record.

Required:

Describe the weaknesses in the internal control structure over information and data flows and the procedures for processing shipping notices and customer invoices. Recommend some improvements in these control policies and procedures. Organize your answer sheet with two columns, one headed "Weaknesses" and the other headed "Recommended Improvements."

(AICPA adapted)

8.56 Flowchart Control Points. Each number of the flowchart in Exhibit 8.56–1 locates a control point in the labour processing system. Make a list of the control points, and for each point, describe the type or kind of internal control procedure that ought to be specified.

8.57 Internal Control Considerations in a Microcomputer Environment.

INTRODUCTION

The second standard of field work requires that an audit include "a sufficient understanding of the internal control to plan the audit and to determine the nature, timing and extent of tests to be performed."

Given the increasing use of microcomputers by many businesses today, auditors must know about the potential internal control weaknesses inherent in a microcomputer environment. Such knowledge is crucial if the auditor is to make a proper assessment of the related control risk and to plan an effective and efficient audit approach.

Required:

In the following case study, assume that you are participating in the audit of Calgary Appliance Company and that the background information below has been obtained during the planning phase. You have been asked to (1) consider the potential effects on internal control that have

been introduced by the microcomputer application and (2) assess how those internal control effects may alter the audit plan for the current year.

BACKGROUND INFORMATION

Calgary Appliance is a wholesale distributor of electric appliances. The company's sales in each of the last two years have been approximately $40 million. All accounting applications are handled at the company's corporate office.

The data processing operations have historically centred around an on-site minicomputer. The computer applications include accounts payable and cash disbursements, payroll, inventory and general ledger. Accounts receivable and fixed asset records have been prepared manually in the past. Internal controls in all areas have been considered strong in the last few years.

During the past year, financial management decided to automate the processing of sales, accounts receivable and fixed asset transactions and accounting. Management also concluded that purchasing a microcomputer and related available software was more cost effective than increasing the minicomputer capacity and hiring a second computer operator. The controller and accounting clerks have been encouraged to find additional uses for the microcomputer and to "experiment" with it when they are not too busy.

The accounts receivable clerk is enthusiastic about the microcomputer, but the fixed asset clerk seems somewhat apprehensive about it because he has no prior experience with computers. The accounts receivable clerk explained that the controller had purchased a "very easy to use" accounts receivable software application program for the microcomputer, which enables her to input the daily information regarding billings and payments received quickly and easily. The controller has added some programming of his own to the software to give it better report-writing features.

During a recent demonstration, the accounts receivable clerk explained that the program required her only to input the customer's name and invoice amount in the case of billings, or the customer's name and cheque amount in the case of payments. The microcomputer then automatically updates the respective customer's account balance. At the end of every month, the accounts receivable trial balance is printed and reconciled by the clerk to the general ledger balance. The reconciliation is reviewed by the controller.

EXHIBIT 8.56–1

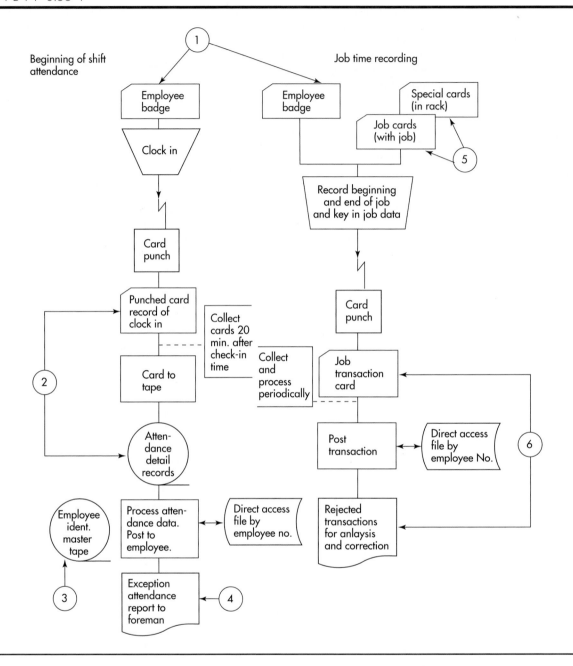

The fixed asset program also was purchased from an outside vendor. The controller indicated that the software package had just recently been put on the market and that it was programmed to compute tax depreciation based on recent changes in the federal tax laws. He also stated that, because of the fixed asset clerk's reluctance to use the microcomputer, he had input all the information from the fixed asset manual records. He indicated, however, that the fixed asset clerk would be responsible for the future processing related to the fixed assets files and for generating the month-end and year-end reports used to prepare the related accounting entries.

The various accounts receivable and fixed asset diskettes are all adequately labelled as to the type of program or data file. They are arranged in an organized manner in a diskette holder located near the microcomputer.

(Adapted from a case contributed by Price Waterhouse to The Auditor's Report.*)*

8.58 Use of CAATs. Jane Ford has just joined the public practice firm in which you are employed as a junior staff member. The two of you are meeting with Jay Birch, who will be the senior on your next (starting tomorrow) audit. Jane is very enthusiastic about her first audit assignment, which will provide an opportunity to use CAATs. She says to Jay, "We should use CAATs for every audit of a client who has an EDP system. That's the only way to go."

Jay relies, "It's not quite that simple—there are a number of considerations we have to bear in mind when we're deciding whether to use CAATs."

Required

Elaborate on Jay's comment to Jane.

(CGAAC adapted)

8.59 General Controls. Les Tough has been assigned to assist you with the audit of Nercando Inc. Les will be making an initial visit to the client's office in a few days to familiarize himself with the company's operations. Nercando is an owner-managed business that has its accounting applications performed in a microcomputer environment. One of Les's tasks will be to make a preliminary assessment of Nercando's EDP internal control system and inform you so that you may incorporate that information into your audit planning. Les is somewhat unsure of what he should be looking for with respect to the EDP internal control system, and asks you for some direction.

Required:

Draft a memo to Les giving him guidance as to how to evaluate the general EDP internal control environment and the concerns that may exist in the case of a small, owner-managed company such as Nercando.

(CGAAC adapted)

PART III

AUDIT APPLICATIONS

CHAPTER 9

Learning Objectives

This chapter contains a concise overview of a cycle for processing customer orders and making sales, delivering goods and services to customers, accounting for customer accounts receivable, collecting and depositing cash received from customers, and reconciling bank statements. A series of short cases is used to show the application of audit procedures in situations where errors, irregularities and frauds might be discovered. The chapter ends with special technical notes on the existence assertion, using confirmations and auditing bank reconciliations. After completing this chapter, you should be able to:

1. Describe the revenue and collection cycle, including typical source documents and controls.

2. Give examples of detail test of controls procedures for auditing control over customer credit approval, delivery, accounts receivable accounting, cash receipts accounting and bank statement reconciliation.

3. Describe some common errors, irregularities and frauds in the revenue and collection cycle, and design some audit and investigation procedures for detecting them.

4. Explain the importance of the existence assertion for the audit of cash and accounts receivable, and describe some procedures for obtaining evidence about the existence of assets.

5. Identify and describe considerations for using confirmations in the audit of cash and accounts receivable.

6. Design and perform substantive audit procedures for the audit of a bank statement reconcilation, and tell how auditors can search for lapping and kiting.

REVENUE AND COLLECTION CYCLE

REVENUE AND COLLECTION CYCLE: TYPICAL ACTIVITIES

LEARNING OBJECTIVE
1. Describe the revenue and collection cycle, including typical source documents and controls.

Exhibit 9–1 shows the activities and transactions involved in a revenue and collection cycle. The basic activities are (1) receiving and processing customer orders, including credit granting; (2) delivering goods and services to customers; (3) billing customers and accounting for accounts receivable; (4) collecting and depositing cash received from customers; and (5) reconciling bank statements. As you follow the exhibit, you can track some of the highlighted elements of a control structure.

Sales and Accounts Receivable Authorization

Exhibit 9–2 represents a computerized system for processing customer orders. Company personnel receive the customer's purchase order and create a sales order, entering it in a computer terminal. The computer system then performs automatic authorization procedures—determining whether the customer is a "regular" or a new customer, approving credit, and checking the availability of inventory to fill the order. (If inventory is short, a back order is entered.) When these authorizations are embedded in a computer system, access to the master files for additions, deletions and other changes must be limited to responsible persons. If these controls fail, orders might be processed for fictitious customers, credit might be approved for bad credit risks and packing slips might be created for goods that do not exist in the inventory.

When a customer order passes these authorizations, the system (1) creates a record in the pending order master file, (2) produces a packing slip that is transmitted to the stockroom and shipping department, and (3) updates the inventory master file to show the commitment (removal) of the inventory. At this stage the pending order and the packing slip should be numbered in a numerical sequence so that the system can determine later whether any transactions have not been completed (completeness objective of control). The packing slip is the storeskeeper's authorization to release goods to the shipping department and the shipping department's authorization to release goods to a trucker or to the customer.

Another authorization in the system is the price list master file. It contains the product unit prices for billing customers. Persons who have power to alter this file have the power to authorize price changes and customer billings.

Custody

Physical custody of goods starts with the storeroom or warehouse where inventory is kept. Custody is transferred to the shipping department upon the authorization of the packing slip that orders storeskeepers to release goods to the shipping area. As long as the system works, custody is under proper control. However, if the storeskeepers or the shipping department personnel have the power to change the quantity shown on the packing slip, they can cause errors in the system by billing the customer for too small or too large a quantity. (This power combines custody with a recording function. A computer record or "log" of such changes will create an electronic paper trail.)

"Custody" of accounts receivable records themselves implies the power to alter those records directly or to enter transactions to alter them (e.g., transfers, returns and allowance credits, write-offs). Personnel with this power have a combination of authorization and recording responsibility. (A computer "log" of such entries will create an electronic paper trail).

EXHIBIT 9–1   REVENUE AND COLLECTION CYCLE

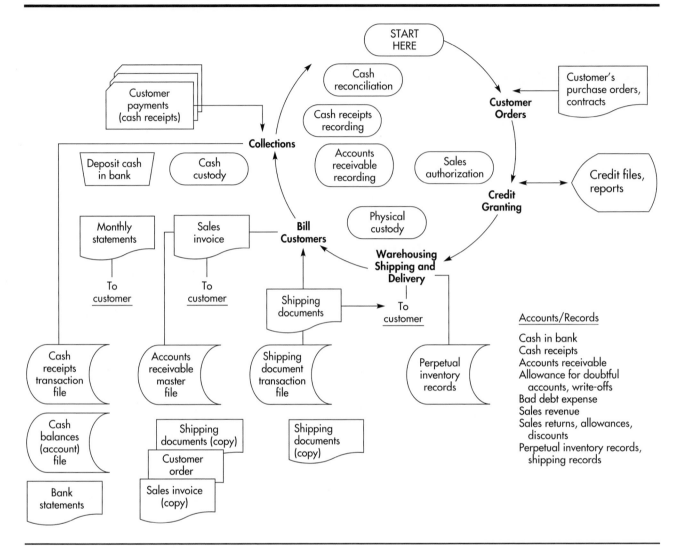

Recording

When delivery or shipment is complete, the shipping personnel enter the completion of the transaction in a terminal, and the system (1) produces a bill of lading shipping document, which is evidence of an actual delivery/shipment; (2) removes the order from the pending order master file; and (3) produces a sales invoice (prenumbered the same as the order and packing slip) that bills the customer for the quantity shipped, according to the bill of lading. Any personnel who have the power to enter or alter these transactions or to intercept the invoice that is supposed to be mailed to the customer have undesirable combinations of authorization, custody and recording responsibilities; they can "authorize" transaction changes and record them by making entries in systems under their control.

Periodic Reconciliation

The most frequent reconciliation is the comparison of the sum of customers' unpaid balances with the accounts receivable control account total. Usually, this reconciliation is done with an aged trial balance. An aged trial balance is a list of the customers and their balances, with the balances classified in columns headed for different age categories (e.g., current, 10–30 days past due, 31–60 days past due, 61–90 days past due, over 90 days past

EXHIBIT 9–2   SALES AND ACCOUNTS RECEIVABLE: COMPUTER PROCESSING

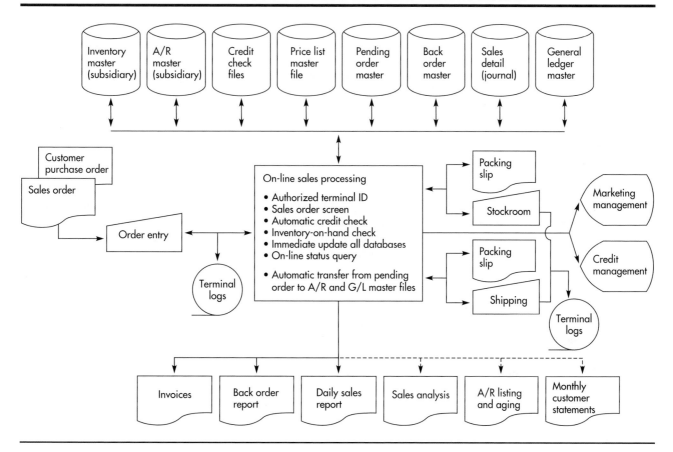

due). Internal auditors can perform periodic comparison of the customers' obligations (according to the customers) with the recorded amount by sending confirmations to the customers. (Refer to the special note on confirmations at the end of this chapter.)

Cash Receipts and Cash Balances Authorization

There are numerous ways to receive cash—over the counter, through the mail, by electronic funds transfer and by receipt in a "lockbox." In a lockbox arrangement, a fiduciary (e.g., a bank) opens the box, lists the receipts, deposits the money and sends the remittance advices (stubs showing the amount received from each customer) to the company. Most companies need little "authorization" to accept a payment from a customer! However,

---

Price Fixing

The company's computer programmer was paid off by a customer to cause the company to bill the customer at prices lower than list prices. The programmer wrote a subroutine that was invoked when the billing system detected the customer's regular code number. This subroutine instructed the customer billing system to reduce all unit prices 9.5 percent. The company relied on the computer billing system, and nobody ever rechecked the actual prices billed.

SHIPPING EMPLOYEE CAUGHT BY COMPUTER!

A customer paid off a shipping department employee to enter smaller quantities than actually shipped on the packing slip and bill of lading. This caused the customer's invoices to be understated. Unknown to the employee, a computer log recorded all the entries that altered the original packing slip record. An alert internal auditor noticed the pattern of "corrections" made by the shipping employee. A trap was laid by initiating fictitious orders for this customer, and the employee was observed making the alterations.

---

authorization is important for approving customers' discounts and allowances taken. Exhibit 9–3 shows some cash receipts processing procedures in a manual accounting setting. (It is easier to describe these procedures as manual ones instead of as a variety of computerized procedures.) You can see the "approval of discounts" noted in Exhibit 9–3.

Custody

Someone always gets the cash and cheques in hand and thus has custody of the physical cash for a time. Control over this custody can vary. Companies can rotate people through the custody responsibility so that one person does not have this custody all the time; they can have rotating teams of two or more people so that they would need to collude with one another to steal money; they can make arrangements outside the company for actual cash custody (e.g., the lockbox arrangement). Since this initial custody cannot be avoided, it is always good control to prepare a list of the cash receipts as early in the process as possible, then separate the actual cash from the bookkeeping documents. The cash goes to the cashier or treasurer's office, where a bank deposit is prepared and the money is sent to the bank. The list goes to the accountants, who record the cash receipts. (This list simply may be a stack of the remittance advices received with the customers' payments. You yourself prepare a "remittance advice" each time you write the "amount enclosed" on the top part of your credit card billing, tear it off, and enclose it with your cheque.)

Recording

The accountants who record cash receipts and credits to customer accounts should not handle the cash. They should use the remittance list to make entries to the cash and accounts receivable control accounts and to the customers' accounts receivable subsidiary account records. In fact, it is a good error-checking procedure to have control account and subsidiary account entries made by different people; then later the accounts receivable entries and balances can be compared (reconciled) to determine whether the proper source documents (remittance lists) were used to make error-free accounting entries. A further segregation would be to prevent the person who receives and lists cheques from having access to cash, bank accounts or receivables accounts. Some computerized accounting programs post the customers' accounts automatically by keying in the customer identification number.

Periodic Reconciliation

It is important that bank account reconciliations be prepared carefully. Deposit slips should be compared to the details on cash remittance lists, and the totals should be traced to the general ledger entries. Likewise, paid cheques should be traced to the cash disbursements listing (journal). This care is required to establish that all receipts recorded in the books were deposited and that credit was given to the right customer. The reconciliation should be done by someone other than the accountant, such as the office manager or administrative assistant. (Refer to the special note on auditing bank reconciliations at the end of this chapter.)

EXHIBIT 9–3   CASH RECEIPTS PROCESSING

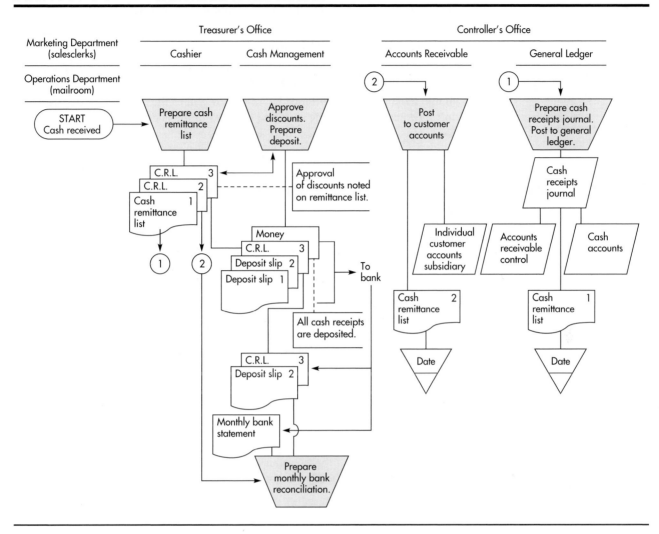

CAREFUL RECONCILIATION
(Refer to Exhibit 9–3)

Suppose the cashier who prepares the remittance list had stolen and converted Customer A's cheques to personal use. It might work for a short time until Customer A complained that the company had not given credit for payments. The cashier knows this. So, the cashier later puts Customer B's cheques in the bank deposit, but shows Customer A on the remittance list; thus, the accountants give Customer A credit. So far, so good for preventing Customer A's Complaint. But now Customer B needs to be covered. This "lapping" of customer payments to hide an embezzlement can be detected by a bank reconciliation comparison of the cheques deposited (Customer B) with the remittance credit recorded (Customer A). Sometimes the lapping is covered by issuing a credit slip for customer B. This illustrates the importance of proper authorization and control of credit slips.

9.1 What is the basic sequence of activities and accounting in a revenue and collection cycle?

9.2 What purpose is served by prenumbering sales orders, shipping documents (packing slips and bills of lading) and sales invoices?

9.3 Why is controlled access to computer terminals and master files (such as credit files and price lists) important in a control structure?

9.4 Why should a list of cash remittance be made and sent to the accounting department? Wouldn't it be easier to send the cash and cheques to the accountants so that they can enter the credits to customers' accounts accurately?

AUDIT EVIDENCE IN MANAGEMENT REPORTS AND DATA FILES

Computer processing of revenue and cash receipts transactions makes it possible for management to generate several reports that can provide important audit evidence.

Pending Order Master File

This file contains sales transactions that were started in the system but are not yet completed, thus not recorded as sales and accounts receivable. Old orders may represent shipments that actually were made, but for some reason the shipping department did not enter the shipping information (or entered an incorrect code that did not match the pending order file). The pending orders can be reviewed for evidence of the completeness of recorded sales and accounts receivable.

Credit Check Files

The computer system may make automatic credit checks, but up-to-date maintenance of the credit information is very important. Credit checks on old or incomplete information are not good credit checks. A sample of the files can be tested for current status. Alternatively, the company's records on updating the files can be reviewed for evidence of updating operations.

Price List Master File

The computer system may produce customer invoices automatically; but if the master price list is wrong, the billings will be wrong. The computer file can be compared to an official price source for accuracy. (The company should perform this comparison every time the prices are changed.)

Sales Detail (Sales Journal) File

This file should contain the detail sales entries, including the shipping references and dates. The file can be scanned for entries without shipping references (fictitious sales?) and for

---

PEAKS AND VALLEYS

During the year-end audit, the independent auditors reviewed the weekly sales volume reports classified by region. They noticed that sales volume was very high in Region 2 the last two weeks of March, June, September, and December. The volume was unusually low in the first two weeks of April, July, October, and January. In fact, the peaks far exceeded the volume in all the other six regions. Further investigation revealed that the manager in Region 2 was holding open the sales recording at the end of each quarterly reporting period in an attempt to make the quarterly reports look good.

match of recording dates with shipment dates (sales recorded before shipment?). This file contains the population of debit entries to the accounts receivable.

Sales Analysis Reports

A variety of sales analyses can be produced. Sales classified by product lines is information for the business segment disclosures. Sales classified by sales employee or region can show unusually high or low volume that may bear further investigation if error is suspected.

Accounts Receivable Aged Trail Balance

The list of accounts receivable balances is the accounts receivable. If the control account total is larger than the sum in the trial balance, too bad. A receivable amount that cannot be identified with a customer cannot be collected! The trial balance is used as the population for selection of accounts for confirmation. (See the special note on the existence assertion and the special note on using confirmations at the end of this chapter.) The aging information is used in connection with assessing the allowance for doubtful accounts. (An aged trial balance is in Exhibit 9–8, presented later.) The aged trial balance can also provide useful feedback to the credit department for follow up.

Cash Receipts Journal

The cash receipts journal contains all the detail entries for cash deposits and credits to various accounts. It contains the population of credit entries that should be reflected in the credits to accounts receivable for customer payments. It also contains the adjusting and correcting entries that can result from the bank account reconciliation. These entries are important because they may signal the types of accounting errors or manipulations that happen in the cash receipts accounting.

. . . .

R E V I E W
C H E C K P O I N T S

9.5 What computer-based files could an auditor examine to find evidence of unrecorded sales? of inadequate credit checks? of incorrect product unit prices?

9.6 Suppose you selected a sample of customers' accounts receivable and wanted to find supporting evidence for the entries in the accounts. Where would you go to vouch the debit entries? What would you expect to find? Where would you go to vouch the credit entries? What would you expect to find?

. . . .

CONTROL RISK ASSESSMENT
. . . .

LEARNING OBJECTIVE

2. Give examples of detail test of controls procedures for auditing control over customer credit approval, delivery, accounts receivable accounting, cash receipts accounting and bank statement reconciliation.

Control risk assessment is important because it governs the nature, timing and extent of substantive audit procedures that will be applied in the audit of account balances in the revenue and collection cycle. These account balances (listed in the corner of Exhibit 9–1) include:

Cash in bank.

Accounts receivable.

Allowance for doubtful accounts.

Bad debt expense.

Sales revenue.

Sales returns, allowances, discounts.

General Control Considerations

Control procedures for proper segregation of responsibilities should be in place and operating. By referring to Exhibit 9–1, you can see that proper segregation involves authorization of sales and credit by persons who do not have custody, recording or reconciliation duties. Custody of inventory and cash is in persons who do not directly authorize credit, record the accounting entries or reconcile the bank account. Recording (accounting) is performed by persons who do not authorize sales or credit, handle the inventory or cash, or perform reconciliations. Periodic reconciliations should be performed by people who do not have authorization, custody or recording duties related to the same assets. Combinations of two or more of these responsibilities in one person, one office or one computerized system may open the door for errors, irregularities and frauds.

A common feature of cash management is to require that persons who handle cash be insured under a fidelity bond. A fidelity bond is an insurance policy that covers most kinds of cash embezzlement losses. Fidelity bonds do not prevent or detect embezzlement, but the failure to carry the insurance exposes the company to complete loss when embezzlement occurs. Auditors may recommend fidelity bonding to companies that do not know about its coverage. However, a company can collect from the bonding agency only if it can prove its losses—another good reason for internal controls.

In addition, the control structure should provide for detail control checking procedures. For example: (1) policy should provide that no sales order should be entered without a customer order; (2) a credit-check code or manual signature should be recorded by an authorized means; (3) access to inventory and the shipping area should be restricted to authorized persons; (4) access to billing terminals and blank invoice forms should be restricted to authorized personnel; (5) accountants should be under orders to record sales and accounts receivable when all the supporting documentation of shipment is in order, and care should be taken to record sales and receivables as of the date the goods and services were shipped and the cash receipts on the date the payments are received; (6) customer invoices should be compared with bills of lading and customer orders to determine that the customer is sent the goods ordered at the proper location for the proper prices, and that the quantity being billed is the same as the quantity shipped; (7) pending order files should be reviewed in a timely fashion to avoid failure to bill and record shipments; and (8) bank statements should be reconciled in detail monthly.

Information about the control structure often is gathered by completing an internal control questionnaire. Control risk assessment was introduced in Chapter 6. You should now refer to Exhibit 6–9 to review an internal control questionnaire for sales transaction control. A selection of other questionnaires for both general (manual) controls and computer controls over cash receipts and accounts receivable is in Appendix 9A. You can study these questionnaires for details of desirable control policies and procedures. They are organized under headings that identify the important control objectives—environment, validity, completeness, authorization, accuracy, classification, accounting and proper period recording.

Another way to obtain general information about internal controls is called a "walk-through," or a "sample of one." In this work the auditors take a single example of a transaction and "walk it through" from its initiation to its recording in the accounting records. The revenue and collection cycle walk-through involves following a sale from the initial

---

FICTITIOUS REVENUE

A Mississauga computer peripheral equipment company was experiencing slow sales, so the sales manager entered some sales orders for customers who had not ordered anything. The invoices were marked "hold," while the delivery was to a warehouse owned by the company. The rationale was that these customers would buy the equipment eventually, so why not anticipate the orders! (However, it's a good idea not to send them the invoices until they actually make the orders, hence the "hold.") The "sales" and "receivables" were recorded in the accounts, and the financial statements contained overstated revenue and assets.

customer order through credit approval, billing, and delivery of goods, to the entry in the sales journal and subsidiary accounts receivable records, and finally to its subsequent collection and cash deposit. Sample documents are collected, and employees in each department are questioned about their specific duties. The purposes of a walk-through are to (1) verify or update the auditors' understanding of the client's sales/accounts receivable accounting system and control procedures and (2) learn whether the controls the client reported in the internal control questionnaire are actually in place. The walk-through, combined with enquiries, can contribute evidence about appropriate separation of duties, which might be a sufficient basis for assessing control risk slightly below the maximum. However, a walk-through is too limited in scope to provide evidence of whether the client's control procedures were operating effectively during the period under audit. A larger sample of transactions for detail testing of control performance is necessary to justify a low control risk assessment based on actual control performance evidence.

Detail Test of Controls Audit Procedures

An organization should have input, processing and output control procedures in place and operating to prevent, detect, and correct accounting errors. You studied the general control objectives in Chapter 6 (validity, completeness, authorization, accuracy, classification, accounting and proper period recording). Exhibit 9–4 puts these in the perspective of revenue cycle activity with examples of specific objectives. You should study this exhibit carefully. It takes control objectives out of the abstract and expresses them in specific examples related to controlling sales accounting.

Auditors can perform detail test of controls audit procedures to determine whether controls that are said to be in place and operating actually are being performed properly by company personnel. A detail test of control procedure consists of (1) identification of the data population from which a sample of items will be selected for audit and (2) an expression of the action that will be taken to produce relevant evidence. In general, the actions in detail test of control audit procedures involve vouching, tracing, observing, scanning and recalculating. A specification of such procedures is part of an audit program for obtaining evidence useful in a final control risk assessment. If personnel in the organization are not performing their control procedures very well, auditors will need to design substantive

EXHIBIT 9–4   INTERNAL CONTROL OBJECTIVES: REVENUE CYCLE (SALES)

General Objectives	Examples of Specific Objectives
1. Recorded sales are *valid* and documented.	Customer purchase orders support invoices. Bills of lading or other shipping documentation exist for all invoices. Recorded sales in sales journal supported by invoices.
2. Valid sales transactions are *recorded* and none omitted.	Invoices, shipping documents and sales orders are prenumbered and the numerical sequence is checked. Overall comparisons of sales are made periodically by a statistical or product-line analysis.
3. Sales are *authorized* according to company policy.	Credit sales approved by credit department. Prices used in preparing invoices are from authorized price schedule.
4. Sales invoices are *accurately* prepared.	Invoice quantities compared to shipment and customer order quantities. Prices checked and mathematical accuracy independently checked after invoice prepared.
5. Sales transactions are properly *classified*.	Sales to subsidiaries and affiliates classified as intercompany sales and receivables. Sales returns and allowances properly classified.
6. Sales transaction *accounting* is proper.	Credit sales posted to customer's individual accounts. Sales journal posted to general ledger account. Sales recognized in accordance with generally accepted accounting principles.
7. Sales transactions are recorded in the *proper period*.	Sales invoices recorded on shipment date.

audit procedures to try to detect whether control failures have produced materially misleading account balances.

Test of controls audit procedures can be used to audit the accounting for transactions in two directions. This dual-direction testing involves samples selected to obtain evidence about control over completeness in one direction and control over validity in the other direction. The completeness direction determines whether all transactions that occurred were recorded (none omitted), and the validity direction determines whether recorded transactions actually occurred (were valid). An example of the first direction is the examination of a sample of shipping documents (from the file of all shipping documents) to determine whether invoices were prepared and recorded. An example of the second direction is the examination of a sample of sales invoices (from the file representing all recorded sales) to determine whether supporting shipping documents exist to verify the fact of an actual shipment. The content of each file is compared with the another. The example is illustrated in Exhibit 9–5. (The A-1-b and A-3-b codes correspond to the test of controls procedures in Exhibit 9–6).

Exhibit 9–6 contains a selection of test controls audit procedures. Many of these procedures can be characterized as steps taken to verify the content and character of sample documents from one file with the content and character of documents in another file. These steps are designed to enable the audit team to obtain objective evidence about the effectiveness of controls and about the reliability of accounting records. These samples are usually attribute samples designed along the lines you studied in Chapter 7.

On the right, Exhibit 9–6 shows the control objectives tested by the audit procedures. Thus, the test of controls procedures produce evidence that helps auditors determine whether the specific control objectives listed in Exhibit 9–4 were achieved.

Summary: Control Risk Assessment

The audit manager must evaluate the evidence obtained from an understanding of the internal control structure and from test of controls audit procedures. The initial process of obtaining an understanding of the control structure and the later process of obtaining evidence from actual test of controls are two of the phases of control risk assessment work (see Exhibit 6–8 in Chapter 6).

If the control risk is assessed very low, the substantive audit procedures on the account balances can be limited in cost-saving ways. For example, the accounts receivable confirmations can be sent on a date prior to the year-end, and the sample size can be fairly small.

On the other hand, if tests of controls reveal weaknesses (such as posting sales without shipping documents, charging customers the wrong prices and recording credits to customers without supporting credit memos), the substantive procedures will need to be designed to lower the risk of failing to detect material error in the account balances. For

EXHIBIT 9–5   DUAL DIRECTION OF TEST AUDIT SAMPLES

EXHIBIT 9–6   TEST OF CONTROLS AUDIT PROCEDURES FOR SALES, CASH RECEIPTS AND
RECEIVABLES

	Control Objective
A. Sales	
1. Select a sample of shipping documents:	
a. Scan for missing numbers.	Completeness
b. Trace to related sales invoices.	Completeness
2. Scan sales invoices for missing numbers in the sequence.	Completeness
3. Select a sample of recorded sales invoices (sales journal):	
a. Perform recalculations to verify arithmetic accuracy.	Accuracy
b. Vouch to supporting shipping documents. Note dates and quantities.	Validity Accuracy Proper period
c. Vouch prices to approved price lists.	Authorization
d. Vouch credit approval.	Authorization
e. Trace posting to general ledger and proper customer account.	Accounting
4. Observe customer order handling and invoice preparation work.	Environment
B. Cash Receipts	
1. Select a sample of recorded cash receipts (cash receipts journal):	
a. Vouch to deposit slip and remittance list.	Validity
b. Trace to bank statement.	Validity
c. Trace posting to general ledger accounts.	Accounting
d. Trace posting to subsidiary accounts.	Accounting
2. Select a sample of remittance lists (or daily cash reports):	
a. Trace to cash receipts journal.	Completeness
b. Trace journal posting to general ledger.	Accounting
c. Trace to bank statement.	Accuracy
3. Observe the work habits of cashiers and their interactions with persons who keep cash records.	Environment
C. Accounts Receivable	
1. Trace sales invoices to accounts receivable posting (procedure A-3-*e* above).	Accounting
2. Trace cash receipts to accounts receivable posting (procedure B-1-*d* above).	Accounting
3. Select a sample of credit memos.	
a. Review for proper approval.	Authorization
b. Trace to posting in customers' accounts.	Accounting
4. Select a sample of customers' accounts:	
a. Vouch debits to supporting sales invoices.	Validity
b. Vouch credits to supporting cash receipts documents and approved credit memos.	Validity
5. Observe mailing of monthly customer statements.	Validity

example, the confirmation procedure may need to be scheduled on the year-end date with
a large sample of customer accounts. Descriptions of major deficiencies, control weaknesses and inefficiencies may be incorporated in a management letter to the client.

R E V I E W
C H E C K P O I N T S

9.7   What account balances are included in a review and collection cycle?

9.8   What specific control policies and procedures (in addition to separation of duties and
responsibilities) should be in place and operating in a control structure governing revenue recognition and cash accounting?

9.9   What is a "walk-through" of a sales transaction? And how can the walk-through work
complement the use of an internal control questionnaire?

9.10 What are the two important characteristics of a detail test of control procedure? What
"actions" are typically contemplated by such a procedure?

9.11 What is "dual direction test of controls sampling?"

AUDIT CASES: SUBSTANTIVE AUDIT PROCEDURES

. . . .

LEARNING OBJECTIVE

3. Describe some common errors, irregularities and frauds in the revenue and collection cycle, and design some audit and investigation procedures for detecting them.

The audit procedures to gather evidence on account balances are called "substantive procedures." Some amount of substantive audit procedures ought to follow the assessment of control risk. Auditors should not place total reliance on controls to the exclusion of other procedures. Substantive audit procedures differ from test of controls audit procedures in their basic purpose. Substantive procedures are designed to obtain direct evidence about the dollar amounts in account balances, while test of controls procedures are designed to obtain evidence about the company's performance of its own control procedures. Sometimes an audit procedure can be used for both purposes simultaneously, and then it is called a **dual-purpose procedure.**

The goal in performing substantive procedures is to detect evidence of errors, irregularities and frauds if any exist in the accounts as material overstatements or understatements of account balances. In the remainder of this part of the chapter, the approach is to use a set of casettes (little cases) that contain specific examples of test of controls and substantive audit procedures (recalculation, observation, confirmation, enquiry, vouching, tracing, scanning and analytical review). The case stories are used instead of listing schemes and detection procedures in the abstract. If you like lists of details, a selection of detail substantive procedures for cash and accounts receivable is in Appendix 9B.

The "casettes" follow a standard format, which first tells about an error, irregularity or fraud situation. This part is followed by an audit approach section that tells about the audit objective (assertion), controls, test of controls and audit of balances (substantive procedures) that could be considered in an approach to the situation. The audit approach section presumes that the auditors do not know everything about the situation. (As a student of the case, you have "inside information.") These are the parts of the case situation description for each casette:

Method: A cause of the misstatement (accidental error, intentional irregularity or fraud attempt), which usually is easier to make because of some kind of failure of controls.

Paper trail: A set of telltale signs of erroneous accounting, missing or altered documents, or a "dangling debit" (the false or erroneous debit that results from an overstatement of assets).

Amount: The dollar amount of overstated assets and revenue, or understated liabilities and expenses.

The audit approach section contains these parts:

Audit objective: A recognition of a financial statement assertion for which evidence needs to be obtained. The assertions are about existence of assets, liabilities, revenues and expenses; their valuation; their complete inclusion in the account balances; the rights and obligations inherent in them; and their proper presentation and disclosure in the financial statements. (These assertions were introduced in Chapter 4.)

Control: A recognition of the control procedures that should be used by an organization to prevent and detect errors and irregularities.

DUAL-PURPOSE NATURE OF ACCOUNTS RECEIVABLE CONFIRMATIONS

Accounts receivable confirmation is a substantive procedure designed to obtain evidence of the existence and gross amount (valuation) of customers' balances directly from the customer. If such confirmations show numerous exceptions, auditors will be concerned with the controls over the details of sales and cash receipts transactions even if previous control evaluations have seemed to show little control risk.

Test of controls: Ordinary and extended procedures designed to produce evidence about the effectiveness of the controls that should be in operation.

Audit of balances: Ordinary and extended substantive procedures designed to find signs of errors, irregularities and frauds in account balances and classes of transactions.

At the end of the chapter, some similar discussion cases are presented, and you can write the audit approach to test your ability to design audit procedures for the detection of errors, irregularities and frauds.

CASETTE 9.1
THE CANNY CASHIER

Problem

Cash embezzlement caused overstated accounts receivable, overstated customer discounts expense and understated cash sales. Company failed to earn interest income on funds "borrowed."

Method

D. Bakel was the assistant controller of Sports Equipment, Inc. (SEI), an equipment retailer. SEI maintained accounts receivable for school districts in the region; otherwise, customers received credit by using their own credit cards.

Bakel's duties included being the company cashier, who received all the incoming mail payments on school accounts and the credit card account and all the cash and cheques taken over the counter. Bakel prepared the bank deposit (and delivered the deposit to the bank), listing all the cheques and currency, and also prepared a remittance worksheet (daily cash report) that showed amounts received, discounts allowed on school accounts and amounts to credit to the accounts receivable. Bakel also reconciled the bank statement. No one else reviewed the deposits or the bank statements except the independent auditors.

Bakel opened a bank account in the name of Sport Equipment Company (SEC), after properly incorporating the company in the Department of Corporate Affairs' office. Over-the-counter cash and cheques and school district payments were taken from the SEI receipts and deposited in the SEC account. (None of the customers noticed the difference between the rubber stamp endorsements for the two similarly named corporations, and neither did the bank.) SEC kept the money awhile, earning interest; then Bakel wrote SEC cheques to SEI to replace the "borrowed" funds, in the meantime taking new SEI receipts for deposit to SEC.

Bakel also stole payments made by the school districts, depositing them to SEC. Later, Bakel deposited SEC cheques in SEI, giving the schools credit, but approved an additional 2 percent discount in the process. Thus, the schools received proper credit later, and SEC paid in less by the amount of the extra discounts.

Paper Trail

SEI's bank deposits systematically showed fairly small currency deposits. Bakel was nervous about taking too many cheques, so cash was preferred. The deposit slips also listed the SEC cheques because bank tellers always compare the deposit slip listing to the cheques submitted. The remittance worksheet showed different details: Instead of showing SEC cheques, it showed receipts from school district and currency, but not many over-the-counter cheques from customers. The transactions became complicated enough that Bakel had to use the microcomputer in the office to keep track of the school districts that needed to get credit. There were no vacations for this hard-working cashier because the discrepancies might be noticed by a substitute, and Bakel needed to give the districts credit later.

Amount

Over a six-year period, Bakel built up a $150,000 average balance in the Sport Equipment Company (SEC) account, which earned a total of $67,500 interest that should have been earned by Sports Equipment, Inc. (SEI). By approving the "extra" discounts, Bakel skimmed 2 percent of $1 million in annual sales, for a total of $120,000. Since SEI would have had net income before taxes of about $1.6 million over this six years (about 9 percent on the sales dollar), Bakel's embezzlement took about 12.5 percent of the income.

AUDIT APPROACH

Objective

Obtain evidence to determine whether the accounts receivable recorded on the books represent claims against real customers in the gross amounts recorded.

Control

Authorization related to cash receipts, custody of cash, recording cash transactions and bank statement reconciliation should be separate duties designed to prevent errors, irregularities and frauds. Some supervision and detail review of one or more of these duties should be performed as a next-level control designed to detect errors, irregularities and frauds if they have occurred. For example, the remittance worksheet should be prepared by someone else, or at least the discounts should be approved by the controller; the bank reconciliation should be prepared by someone else.

Bakel had all the duties. (While recording was not actually performed, Bakel provided the source document—the remittance worksheet—the other accountant used to make the cash and accounts receivable entries.) According to the company president, the "control" was the diligence of "our" long-time, trusted, hard-working assistant controller. Note: An auditor who "thinks like a crook" to imagine ways Bakel could commit errors, irregularities or fraud could think of this scheme for cash theft and accounts receivable lapping.

Test of Controls

Since the "control" purports to be Bakel's honest and diligent performance of the accounting and control procedures that might have been performed by two or more people, the test of controls is an audit of cash receipts transactions as they relate to accounts receivable credit. The dual-direction samples and procedures are these:

Validity direction: Select a sample of customer accounts receivable, and vouch payment credits to remittance worksheets and bank deposits, including recalculation of discounts allowed in comparison to sales terms (2 percent), classification (customer name) identification and correspondence of receipt date to recording date.

Completeness direction: Select a sample of remittance worksheets (or bank deposits), vouch details to bank deposit slips (trace details to remittance worksheets if the sample is bank deposits) and trace forward to complete accounting posting in customer accounts receivable.

Audit of Balance

Since there is a control risk of incorrect accounting, perform the accounts receivable confirmation as of the year-end date. Confirm a sample of school district accounts, using positive confirmations.

Blank confirmations may be used. Since there is a control risk, the "sample" may be all the accounts, if the number is not too large.

As prompted by notice of an oddity (noted in the discovery summary below), use the telephone book, chamber of commerce directory and a visit to a local Ministry of Industry and Trade office to determine the location and identity of Sport Equipment Company.

Discovery Summary

The test of controls samples showed four cases of discrepancy, one of which looked like this:

Bank Deposit Slip

Jones	25
Smith	35
Hill Dist.	980
Sport Equip	1,563
Currency	540
Deposit	3,143

Cash Remittance Report

Name	Amount	Discount	AR	Sales
Jones	25	0	0	25
Smith	35	0	0	35
Hill Dist.	980	20	1,000	0
Marlin Dist.	480	20	500	0
Waco Dist.	768	32	800	0
Currency	855	0	0	855
Totals	3,143	72	2,300	915

The auditors sent positive confirmations on all 72 school district accounts. Three of the responses stated that the districts had paid the balances before the confirmation date. Follow-up procedures on their accounts receivable credit in the next period showed they had received credit in remittance reports, and the bank deposits had shown no cheques from the districts but had contained a cheque from Sports Equipment Company.

Investigation of SEC revealed the connection of Bakel, who was confronted and then confessed.

CASETTE 9.2
THE TAXMAN ALWAYS RINGS TWICE

Problem

Overstated receivables for property taxes in a school district because the tax assessor stole some taxpayers' payments.

Method

J. Shelstad was the tax assessor–collector in the Ridge School District, serving a large metropolitan area. The staff processed tax notices on a computer system and generated 450,000 tax notices each October. An office copy was printed and used to check off "paid" when payments were received. Payments were processed by computer and a master file of "accounts receivable" records (tax assessments, payments) was kept on the computer hard disk.

Shelstad was a good personnel manager, who often took over the front desk at lunchtime so the teller staff could enjoy lunch together. During these times, Shelstad took payments over the counter, gave the taxpayers a counter receipt, and pocketed some of the money, which was never entered in the computer system.

Shelstad resigned when he was elected to the Ridge school board. The district's assessor–collector office was eliminated upon the creation of a new regionwide tax agency.

Paper Trail

The computer records showed balances due from many taxpayers who had actually paid their taxes. The book of printed notices was not marked "paid" for many taxpayers who had received counter receipts. These records and the daily cash receipts reports (cash receipts journal) were available at the time the independent auditors performed the most recent annual audit in April. When Shelstad resigned in August, a power surge permanently destroyed the hard disk receivables file, and the cash receipts journals could not be found.

The new regional agency managers noticed that the total of delinquent taxes disclosed in the audited financial statements was much larger than the total turned over to the region's legal counsel for collection and foreclosure.

Amount

Shelstad had been the assessor–collector for 15 years. The "good personnel manager" pocketed 100–150 counter payments each year, in amounts of $500–$2,500, stealing about $200,000 a year for a total of approximately $2.5 million. The district had assessed about $800–$900 million per year, so the annual theft was less than 1 percent. Nevertheless, the taxpayers got mad.

AUDIT APPROACH

Objective

Obtain evidence to determine whether the receivables for taxes (delinquent taxes) represent genuine claims collectible from the taxpayers.

Control

The school district had a respectable system for establishing the initial amounts of taxes receivable. The professional staff of appraisers and the independent appraisal review board established the tax base for each property. The school board set the price (tax rate). The computer system authorization for billing was validated on these two inputs.

The cash receipts system was well designed, calling for preparation of a daily cash receipts report (cash receipts journal that served as a source input for computer entry). This report was always reviewed by the "boss," Shelstad.

Unfortunately, Shelstad had the opportunity and power to override the controls and become both cash handler and supervisor. Shelstad made the decisions about sending delinquent taxes to the county attorney for collection, and the ones known to have been paid but stolen were withheld.

Test of Controls

The auditors performed dual-direction sampling to test the processing of cash receipts.

Validity direction: Select a sample of receivables from the computer hard disk, and vouch (1) charges to the appraisal record, recalculating the amount using the authorized tax rate and (2) payments, if any, to the cash receipts journal and bank deposits. (The auditors found no exceptions.)

Completeness direction: Select a sample of properties from the appraisal rolls, and determine that tax notices had been sent and tax receivables (charges) recorded in the computer file. Select a sample of cash receipts reports, vouch them to bank deposits of the same amount and date, and trace the payments forward to credits to taxpayers' accounts. Select a sample of bank deposits, and trace them to cash receipts reports of the same amount and date. In one of these latter two samples, compare the details on bank deposits to the details on the cash receipts reports to determine whether the same taxpayers appear on both documents. (The auditors found no exceptions.)

Audit of Balance

Confirm a sample of unpaid tax balances with taxpayers. Response rates may not be high, and follow-up procedures determining the ownership (county title files) may need to be performed, and new confirmations may need to be sent.

Determine that proper disclosure is made of the total of delinquent taxes and the total of delinquencies turned over to the region's legal counsel for collection proceedings.

Discovery Summary

Shelstad persuaded the auditors that the true "receivables" were the delinquencies turned over to the region's legal counsel. The confirmation sample and other work was based on this population. Thus, confirmations were not sent to fictitious balances that Shelstad knew had been paid, and the auditors never had the opportunity to receive "I paid" complaints from taxpayers.

The new managers of the regional tax district were not influenced by Shelstad. They questioned the discrepancy between the delinquent taxes in the audit report and the lower amount turned over for collection. Since the computer file was not usable, the managers had to use the printed book of tax notices, where paid accounts had been marked "paid." (Shelstad had not marked the stolen ones "paid" so the printed book would agree with the computer file.) Tax due notices were sent to the taxpayers with unpaid balances, and they began to show up bringing their counter receipts and loud complaints.

In a fit of audit overkill, the independent auditors had earlier photocopied the entire set of cash receipt reports (cash journal). They were thus able to determine that the counter receipts (all signed by Shelstad) had not been deposited or entered. Shelstad was prosecuted and sentenced to a jail term.

CASETTE 9.3
BILL OFTEN, BILL EARLY

Problem

Overstated sales and receivables, understated discounts expense and overstated net income resulted from recording sales too early and failure to account for customer discounts taken.

Method

McGossage Company experienced profit pressures for two years in a row. Actual profits were squeezed in a recessionary economy, but the company reported net income decreases that were not as severe as other companies in the industry.

Sales were recorded in the grocery products division for orders that had been prepared for shipment but not actually shipped until later. Employees backdated the shipping documents. Gross profit on these "sales" was about 30 percent. Customers took discounts on payments, but the company did not record them, leaving the debit balances in the customers' accounts receivable instead of charging them to discounts and allowances expense. Company accountants were instructed to wait 60 days before recording discounts taken.

The division vice president and general manager knew about these accounting practices, as did a significant number of the 2,500 employees in the division. The division managers were under orders from headquarters to achieve profit objectives they considered unrealistic.

Paper Trail

The customers' accounts receivable balances contained amounts due for discounts the customers already had taken. The cash receipts records showed payments received without credit for discounts. Discounts were entered monthly by a special journal entry.

The unshipped goods were on the shipping dock at year-end with papers showing earlier shipping dates.

Amount

As misstatements go, some of these were on the materiality borderline. Sales were overstated 0.3 percent and 0.5 percent in the prior and current year, respectively. Accounts receivable were overstated 4 percent and 8 percent. But the combined effect was to overstate the division's net income by 6 percent and 17 percent. Selected data were:

	One Year Ago		Current Year	
	Reported	Actual	Reported	Actual
Sales	$330.0	$329.0	$350.0	$348.0
Discounts expense	1.7	1.8	1.8	2.0
Net income	6.7	6.3	5.4	4.6

AUDIT APPROACH

Objective

Obtain evidence to determine whether sales were recorded in the proper period and whether gross accounts receivable represented the amounts due from customers at year-end. Obtain evidence to determine whether discounts expense was recognized in the proper amount in the proper period.

Control

The accounting manual should provide instructions to record sales on the date of shipment (or when title passes, if later). Management subverted this control procedure by having shipping employees date the shipping papers incorrectly.

Cash receipts procedures should provide for authorizing and recording discounts when they are taken by customers. Management overrode this control instruction by giving instructions to delay the recording.

Test of Controls

Questionnaires and enquiries should be used to determine the company's accounting policies. It is possible that employees and managers would lie to the auditors to conceal the policies. It is also possible that pointed questions about revenue recognition and discount recording policies would elicit answers to reveal the practices.

For detail procedures: Select a sample of cash receipts, examine them for authorization, recalculate the customer discounts, trace them to accounts receivable input for recording of the proper amount on the proper date. Select a sample of shipping documents and vouch them to customer orders, then trace them to invoices and to recording in the amounts receivable input with proper amounts on the proper date. These tests follow the tracing direction—starting with data that represent the beginning of transactions (cash receipts, shipping) and tracing them through the company's accounting process.

Audit of Balance

Confirm a sample of customer accounts. Use analytical relationships of past years' discount expense to a relevant base (sales, sales volume) to calculate an overall test of the discounts expense.

Discovery Summary

The managers lied to the auditors about their revenue and expense timing policies. The sample of shipping documents showed no dating discrepancies because the employees had inserted incorrect dates. The analytical procedures on discounts did not show the misstatement because the historical relationships were too erratic to show a deficient number (outlier). However, the sample of cash receipts transactions showed that discounts were not calculated and recorded at time of receipt. Additional enquiry led to discovery of the special journal entries and knowledge of the recording delay. Two customers in the sample of 65 confirmations responded with exceptions that turned out to be unrecorded discounts.

Two other customers in the confirmation sample complained that they did not owe for late invoices on December 31. Follow-up showed the shipments were goods noticed on the shipping dock. Auditors taking the physical inventory noticed the goods on the shipping dock during the December 31 inventory-taking. Inspection revealed the shipping documents dated December 26. When the auditors traced these shipments to the sales recording, they found them recorded "bill and hold" on December 29. (These procedures were performed and the results obtained by a successor audit firm in the third year!)

CASETTE 9.4
THANK GOODNESS IT'S FRIDAY

Problem

Overstated sales caused overstated net income, retained earnings, current assets, working capital and total assets. Overstated cash collections did not change the total current assets or total assets but they increased the amount of cash and decreased the amount of accounts receivable.

Method

Alpha Brewery Corporation generally has good control policies and procedures related to authorization of transactions for accounting entry, and the accounting manual has instructions for recording sales transactions in the proper accounting period. The company regularly closes the accounting process each Friday at 5 p.m. to prepare weekly management reports. The year-end date (cutoff date) is December 31, and, in 2000, December 31 was a Monday. However, the accounting was performed through Friday as usual, and the accounts were closed for the year on January 4.

Paper Trail

All the entries were properly dated after December 31, including the sales invoices, cash receipts and shipping documents. However, the trial balance from which the financial statements were prepared was dated December 31, 2000, even though the accounts were actually closed on January 4. Nobody noticed the slip of a few days because the Friday closing was normal.

Amount

Alpha recorded sales of $672,000 and gross profit of $268,800 over the January 1–4 period. Cash collections on customers' accounts came in the amount of $800,000.

AUDIT APPROACH

Objective

Obtain evidence to determine the existence, completeness and valuation of sales for the year ended December 31, 2000, and the cash and accounts receivable as of December 31, 2000.

Control

The company had in place the proper instructions to people to date transactions on the actual date on which they occurred and to enter sales and cost of goods sold on the day of shipment and to enter cash receipts on the day received in the company offices. An accounting supervisor should have checked the entries through Friday to make sure the dates corresponded with the actual events, and that the accounts for the year were closed with Monday's transactions.

Test of Controls

In this case the auditors need to be aware of the company's weekly routine closing and the possibility that the intervention of the December 31 date might cause a problem. Asking the question "Did you cut off the accounting on Monday night this week?" might elicit the "Oh, we forgot!" response. Otherwise, it is normal to sample transactions around the year-end date to determine whether they were recorded in the proper accounting period.

The procedure: Select transactions 7–10 days before and after the year-end date, and inspect the dates on supporting documentation for evidence of accounting in the proper period.

Audit of Balance

The audit for sales overstatement is partly accomplished by auditing the cash and accounts receivable at December 31 for overstatement (the dangling debit location). Confirm a sample of accounts receivable. If the accounts are too large, the auditors expect the debtors to say so, thus leading to detection of sales overstatements.

Cash overstatement is audited by auditing the bank reconciliation to see whether deposits in transit (the deposits sent late in December) actually cleared the bank early in January. Obviously, the January 4 cash collections could not reach the bank until at least Monday, January 7. That's too long for a December 31 deposit to be in transit to a local bank.

The completeness of sales recordings is audited by selecting a sample of sales transactions (and supporting shipping documents) in the early part of the next accounting period (January 2001). One way that sales of 2000 could be incomplete would be to postpone recording December shipments until January, and this procedure will detect them if the shipping documents are dated properly.

The completeness of cash collections (and accounts receivable credits) are audited by auditing the cash deposits early in January to see whether there is any sign of holding cash without entry until January.

In this case the existence objective is more significant for discovery of the problem than the completeness objective. After all, the January 1–4 sales, shipments, and cash collections did not "exist" in December 2000.

Discovery Summary

The test of controls sample from the days before and after December 31 quickly revealed the problem. Company accounting personnel were embarrassed, but there was no effort to misstate the financial statements. This was a simple error. The company readily made the following adjustment:

	Debit	Credit
Sales	$672,000	
Inventory	403,200	
Accounts receivable	800,000	
Accounts receivable		$672,000
Cost of goods sold		403,200
Cash		800,000

R E V I E W
C H E C K P O I N T S

9.12 What are the goals of dual-direction sampling in regard to an audit of the accounts receivable and cash collection system?

9.13 In the case of "The Canny Cashier," name one bank reconciliation control procedure that could have revealed signs of embezzlement.

9.14 What feature(s) of a cash receipts internal control system would be expected to prevent the cash receipts journal and recorded cash sales from reflecting more than the amount shown on the daily deposit slip?

9.15 In the case of "The Taxman Always Rings Twice," what information could have been obtained from confirmations directed to the real population of delinquent accounts?

9.16 In the case of "Bill Often, Bill Early," what information might have been obtained from enquiries? from detail test of controls procedures? from observations? and from confirmations?

9.17 With reference to the case of "Thank Goodness It's Friday," what contribution could an understanding of the business and the management reporting system have made to discovery of the open cash receipts journal cutoff error?

SPECIAL NOTE: THE EXISTENCE ASSERTION

LEARNING OBJECTIVE

4. Explain the importance of the existence assertion for the audit of cash and accounts receivable, and describe some procedures for obtaining evidence about the existence of assets.

When considering assertions and obtaining evidence about accounts receivable and other assets, auditors must put emphasis on the existence and rights (ownership) assertions. (For liability accounts, the emphasis is on the completeness and obligations assertions, as will be explained in Chapter 10.) This emphasis on existence is rightly placed because companies and auditors sometimes have gotten into malpractice trouble by giving unqualified reports on financial statements that overstated assets and revenues and understated expenses. For example, credit sales recorded too early (fictitious sales?) result in overstated accounts receivable and overstated sales revenue; failure to amortize prepaid expense results in understated expenses and overstated prepaid expenses (current assets).

Discerning the population of assets to audit for existence and ownership is easy because the company has asserted their existence by putting them on the balance sheet. The audit procedures described in the following sections can be used to obtain evidence about the existence and ownership of accounts receivable and other assets.

Recalculation

Think about the assets that depend largely on calculations. They are amenable to auditors' recalculation procedures. Expired prepaid expenses are recalculated, using auditors' vouching of basic documents, such as loan agreements (prepaid interest), rent contracts (prepaid rent) and insurance policies (prepaid insurance). Goodwill and deferred expenses are recalculated by using original acquisition and payment document information and term (useful life) estimates. A bank reconciliation is a special kind of calculation, and the company's reconciliation can be audited. (See the special note on auditing a bank reconciliation later in this chapter.)

Physical Observation

Inventories and fixed assets can be inspected and counted (more on inventory observation is in Chapter 10). Titles to autos, land and buildings can be vouched, sometimes using public records in a regional government office. Petty cash and undeposited receipts can be observed and counted, but the cash in the bank cannot. Securities held as investments can be inspected if held by the company.

Confirmation

Letters of confirmation can be sent to banks and customers, asking for a report of the balances owed the company. Likewise, if securities held as investments are in the custody of banks or brokerage houses, the custodians can be asked to report the names, numbers and quantity of the securities held for the company. In some cases inventories held in public warehouses or out on consignment can be confirmed with the other party. (Refer to the special note on confirmations later in this chapter.)

Verbal Enquiry

Enquiries to management usually do not provide very convincing evidence about existence and ownership. However, enquiries always should be made about the company's agreements to maintain compensating cash balances (may not be classifiable as "cash" among the current assets), about pledge or sale of accounts receivable with recourse in connection with financings and about pledge of other assets as collateral for loans.

Examination of Documents (Vouching)

Evidence of ownership can be obtained by studying the title documents for assets. Examination of loan documents may yield evidence of the need to disclose assets pledged as loan collateral.

Scanning

Assets are supposed to have debit balances. A computer can be used to scan large files of accounts receivable, inventory and fixed assets for uncharacteristic credit balances. Usually, such credit balances reflect errors in the recordkeeping—customer overpayments, failure to post purchases of inventory, depreciation of assets more than cost. The names of

---

SIMPLE ANALYTICAL COMPARISON

The auditors prepared a schedule of the monthly credit sales totals for the current and prior years. They noticed several variations, but one, in November of the current year, stood out in particular. The current-year credit sales were almost twice as large as in any prior November. Further investigation showed that a computer error had caused the November credit sales to be recorded twice in the control accounts. The accounts receivable and sales revenue were materially overstated as a result.

debtors can be scanned for officers, directors and related parties, amounts for which need to be reported separately or disclosed in the financial statements.

Analytical Procedures

A variety of analytical comparisons may be employed, depending on the circumstances and the nature of the business. Comparisons of asset and revenue balances with recent history may help detect overstatements. Such relationships as receivables turnover, gross margin ratio and sales/asset ratios can be compared to historical data and industry statistics for evidence of overall reasonableness. Account interrelationships also can be used in analytical review. For example, sales returns and allowances and sales commissions generally vary directly with dollar sales volume, bad debt expense usually varies directly with credit sales volume and freight expense varies with the physical sales volume. Accounts receivable write-offs should be compared with earlier estimates of doubtful accounts.

REVIEW CHECKPOINTS

9.18 Why is it important to place emphasis on the existence and rights (ownership) assertions when auditing cash and accounts receivable?

9.19 Which audit procedures are usually the most useful for auditing and existence and rights assertions? Give some examples.

SPECIAL NOTE: USING CONFIRMATIONS

LEARNING OBJECTIVE
5. Identify and describe considerations for using confirmations in the audit of cash and accounts receivable.

The confirmation audit procedure was introduced in Chapter 4. This special note gives some details about using confirmations in the audit of cash and accounts receivable. The use of confirmations for cash balances and trade accounts receivable is considered a generally accepted audit procedure (*Section* 5303.28 or ISA 501.19). However, auditors may decide not to use them if suitable alternative procedures are available and applicable in particular circumstances. Auditors should document justifications for the decision not to use confirmations for trade accounts receivable in a particular audit. Justifications include (1) receivables are not material; (2) confirmations would be ineffective, based on prior years' experience or knowledge that responses could be unreliable; and (3) other substantive test of details procedures provide sufficient appropriate evidence and the auditor has assessed the combined level of inherent risk and control risk associated with the financial statement assertions being audited as low.

Confirmations of Cash and Loan Balances

The standard bank confirmation form is shown in Exhibit 9–7. This form is used to obtain bank confirmation of deposit and loan balances. (Other confirmation letters are used to

---

A DECISION NOT TO USE ACCOUNTS RECEIVABLE CONFIRMATIONS

Sureparts Manufacturing Company sold all its production to three auto manufacturers and six aftermarket distributors. All nine of these customers typically paid their accounts in full by the 10th day of each following month. The auditors were able to vouch the cash receipts for the full amount of the accounts receivable in the bank statements and cash receipts records in the month following the Surepart year-end. Confirmation evidence was not considered necessary in these circumstances.

E X H I B I T 9–7   BANK CONFIRMATION

Bank Confirmation

Areas to be completed by client are marked §, while those to be completed by the financial institution are marked †

FINANCIAL INSTITUTION §	CLIENT (LEGAL NAME) §
(Name, branch and full mailing address)	
	The financial institution is authorized to provide the details requested herein to the below-noted firm of accountants
	§ _____
	Client's authorized signature
CONFIRMATION DATE §	Please supply copy of the most recent credit facility agreement (initial if required) § _____
(All information to be provided as of this date)	
(See Bank Confirmation Completion Instructions)	

1. LOANS AND OTHER DIRECT AND CONTINGENT LIABILITIES (If balances are nil, please state)

NATURE OF LIABILITY/ CONTINGENT LIABILITY †	INTEREST (Note rate per contract)		DUE DATE †	DATE OF CREDIT FACILITY AGREEMENT †	AMOUNT AND CURRENCY OUTSTANDING †
	RATE †	DATE PAID TO †			

ADDITIONAL CREDIT FACILITY AGREEMENT(S) _____
Note the date(s) of any credit facility agreement(s) not drawn upon and not referenced above † _____

2. DEPOSITS/OVERDRAFTS

TYPE OF ACCOUNT §	ACCOUNT NUMBER §	INTEREST RATE §	ISSUE DATE (If applicable) §	MATURITY DATE (If applicable) §	AMOUNT AND CURRENCY (Brackets if Overdraft) †

EXCEPTIONS AND COMMENTS (See Bank Confirmation Completion Instructions)†

STATEMENT OF PROCEDURES PERFORMED BY FINANCIAL INSTITUTION †
The above information was completed in accordance with the Bank Confirmation Completion Instructions.

_____   BRANCH CONTACT _____
Authorized signature of financial institution   Name and telephone number

Please mail this form directly to our chartered accountant in the enclosed addressed envelope.

Name:
Address:
Telephone:
Fax:

Developed by the Canadian Bankers Association and The Canadian Institute of Chartered Accountants obtain confirmation of contingent liabilities, endorsements, compensating balance agreements, lines of credit and other financial instruments and transactions. The standard form and illustrative letters are reproduced in the PA's Professional Engagement Manuals.) A word of caution is in order: While financial institutions may note exceptions to the information typed in a confirmation and may confirm items omitted from it, the auditor should not put sole reliance on the form to satisfy the completeness assertion, insofar as cash and loan balances are concerned. Officers and employees of financial institutions cannot be expected to search their information systems for balances and loans that may not be immediately evident as assets and liabilities of the client company. However, it is a good idea to send confirmations on accounts the company represents as closed during the year to get the bank to confirm zero balances. (If a nonzero balance is confirmed by a bank, the auditors have evidence that some asset accounting has been omitted in the company records.)

Confirmation of Accounts and Notes Receivable

Confirmations provide evidence of existence and, to a limited extent, of valuation of accounts and notes receivable. The accounts and notes to be confirmed should be documented in the working papers with an aged trial balance. (An aged trial balance is shown in Exhibit 9–8, annotated to show the auditor's work.) Accounts for confirmation can be

EXHIBIT 9–8   ACCOUNTS RECEIVABLE AGED TRIAL BALANCE

```
D-2                       KINGSTON COMPANY            Prepared   JD
PG. 1 OF 15             ACCOUNTS RECEIVABLE           Date    1-12-03
                        December 31, 2002             Reviewed  Terri Tough
                                                      Date    1-17-03


                     --------- -------- Aged --------   Jan. 2003 Collection
                              30-60    61-90  Over 90               Past
                     Current  Days     Days   Days    Total  Current  Due
                     ----------------------------------------------------------
Able Hardware        12,337 X                         12,337 XPC "12,337
Baker Supply            712                              712      712
Charley Company       1,486 X    420 X                 1,906 XPC  1,486    420
Dogg General Store                             755       755

Welsch Windows                    531 X                  531 X NC         531
Zlat Stuff Place                                214       214            214

Balance per books   335,000  30,000  20,000  15,000 400,000  320,000  25,000
                                                          (J)
Billing errors      (11,000)         (1,000)        (12,000) (1)

Adjusted balance    324,000  30,000  19,000  15,000 388,000


   X  Traced to accounts receivable subsidiary ledger.

  PC  Positive confirmation mailed Jan. 4. Replies D-2.3

  NC  Negative confirmation mailed Jan. 4. Replies D-2.4

   u  No reply to positive confirmation, vouched charges to invoices.

   J  Traced to general ledger control account.

  (1) Billing error adjustment explained on working paper D-2.2

Note: See D-2.2 for analysis of doubtful accounts and our test
        of reasonableness
```

selected at random or in accordance with another plan consistent with the audit objectives. Statistical methods may be useful for determining the sample size. Generalized audit software to access computerized receivables files may be utilized to select and even to print the confirmations.

Two widely used confirmation forms are positive confirmations and negative confirmations. An example of a positive confirmation is shown in Exhibit 9–9. A variation of the positive confirmation is the blank form. A blank confirmation does not contain the balance; customers are asked to fill it in themselves. The blank positive confirmation may produce better evidence because the recipients need to get the information directly from their own records instead of just signing the form and returning it with no exceptions noted. (However, the effort involved may cause a lower response rate.)

The negative confirmation form for the same request shown in Exhibit 9–9 is in Exhibit 9–10. The positive form asks for a response. The negative form asks for a response only if something is wrong with the balance; thus, lack of response to negative confirmations is considered evidence of propriety.

The positive form is used when individual balances are relatively large or when accounts are in dispute. Positive confirmations may ask for information about either the account balance or specific invoices, depending on knowledge about how customers maintain their accounting records. The negative form is used mostly when inherent risk and control risk

E X H I B I T 9–9   **POSITIVE CONFIRMATION LETTER**

D-2.3

▲▲▲
KINGSTON COMPANY
Kingston, Ontario

January 5, 2003

Charley Company
Lake and Adams
Chicago, Illinois

Gentlemen:

Our auditors, Anderson, Olds & Watershed, are making their regular audit of our financial statements. Part of this audit includes direct verification of customer balances.

PLEASE EXAMINE THE DATA BELOW CAREFULLY AND EITHER CONFIRM ITS ACCURACY OR REPORT ANY DIFFERENCES DIRECTLY TO OUR AUDITORS USING THE ENCLOSED REPLY ENVELOPE.

This is not a request for payment. Please do not send your remittance to our auditors.

Your prompt attention to this confirmation request will be appreciated.

Sandra Carboy
Sandra Carboy, Controller

The balance due Kingston Company as of December 31, 2002, is $1,906. This balance is correct except as noted below:

It's correct. Will send payment as soon as possible

Date: *Jan. 7, 2003*   By: *P. "Charley" O'Quirk*

Title: *President*

EXHIBIT 9–10   NEGATIVE CONFIRMATION LETTER

KINGSTON COMPANY
Kingston, Ontario

January 5, 2003

Charley Company
Lake and Adams
Chicago, Illinois

Gentlemen:

Our auditors, Anderson, Olds & Watershed, are making their regular audit of our financial statements. Part of this audit includes direct verification of customer balances.

PLEASE EXAMINE THE DATA BELOW CAREFULLY AND COMPARE THEM TO YOUR RECORDS OF YOUR ACCOUNT WITH US. IF OUR INFORMATION IS NOT IN AGREEMENT WITH YOUR RECORDS, PLEASE STATE ANY DIFFERENCES ON THE REVERSE SIDE OF THIS PAGE, AND RETURN DIRECTLY TO OUR AUDITORS IN THE RETURN ENVELOPE PROVIDED. IF THE INFORMATION IS CORRECT, NO REPLY IS NECESSARY.

This is not a request for payment. Please do not send your remittance to our auditors.

Your prompt attention to this confirmation request will be appreciated.

Sandra Carboy

Sandra Carboy, Controller

As of December 31, 2002, balance due to Kingston Company: $1,906
Date of Origination: November and December, 2002
Type: Open trade account

---

are considered low, when a large number of small balances is involved, and when the client's customers can be expected to consider the confirmations properly. Frequently, both forms are used: positive confirmations are sent on some customers' accounts and negative confirmations on others. According to *Handbook Section* 6020.09: "For many audit engagements, a combination of positive requests for at least a sample of large accounts and negative requests for at least a sample of smaller accounts will provide a suitable coverage."

Getting confirmations delivered to the intended recipient is a problem that requires auditors' careful attention. Auditors need to control the confirmations, including the addresses to which they are sent. Experience is full of cases where confirmations were mailed to company accomplices, who provided false responses. The auditors should consider carefully features of the reply, such as postmarks, fax responses, letterhead, e-mail, telephone, or other characteristics, that may suggest false responses. Auditors should follow up electronic and telephone responses to determine their origin (e.g., returning the telephone call to a known number, looking up telephone numbers to determine addresses or using a criss-cross directory to determine the location of a respondent). Furthermore, the lack of response to a negative confirmation is no guarantee that the intended recipient received it unless the auditor carefully controlled the mailing.

The **response rate** for positive confirmations is the proportion of the number of confirmations returned to the number sent, generally after the audit team prompts recipients with second and third requests. Research studies have shown response rates ranging from 66 to 96 percent. Recipients seem to be able to detect account misstatements to varying degrees. Studies have shown **detection rates** (the ratio of the number of exceptions reported to auditors to the number of account errors intentionally reported to customers) ranging from 20 to 100 percent. Negative confirmations seem to have lower detection rates than positive confirmations. Also, studies show somewhat lower detection rates for misstatements favourable to recipients (i.e., an accounts receivable understatement). Overall, positive confirmations appear to be more effective than negative confirmations; but results depend on the type of recipients, the size of the account and the type of account being confirmed. Effective confirmation practices depend on attention to these factors and on prior years' experience with confirmation results on a particular client's accounts.

Effective confirmation also depends on using a "bag of tricks" to boost the response rate. Often, auditors merely send out a cold, official-looking request in a metered mail envelope and expect customers to be happy to respond. However, the response rate can be increased by using (1) a postcard sent in advance, notifying that a confirmation is coming; (2) special delivery mail; (3) first-class stamp postage (not metered); and (4) an envelope imprinted "Confirmation Enclosed: Please Examine Carefully." These devices increase the cost of the confirmation procedure, but the benefit is a better response rate.[1]

The audit team should try to obtain replies to all positive confirmations by sending second and third requests to nonrespondents. If there is no response or if the response specifies an exception to the client's records, the auditors should carry out document-vouching procedures to audit the account.

These alternative procedures include the vouching direction of finding sales invoice copies, shipping documents and customer orders that signal the existence of sales charges. They also include the tracing direction of finding evidence of customers' payments in subsequent cash receipts.

When sampling is used, all accounts in the sample should be audited. It is improper to substitute an easy-to-audit customer account not in the sample for one that does not respond to a confirmation request.

Confirmation of receivables may be performed at a date other than the year-end. When confirmation is done at an interim date, the audit firm is able to spread work throughout the year and avoid the pressures of overtime that typically occur around December 31. Also, the audit can be completed sooner after the year-end date if confirmation has been done earlier. The primary consideration when considering confirmation of accounts before the balance sheet date is the client's internal control over transactions affecting receivables. When confirmation is performed at an interim date, the following additional procedures should be considered:

1. Obtain a summary of receivables transactions from the interim date to the year-end date.

2. Obtain a year-end trial balance of receivables, compare it to the interim trial balance and obtain evidence and explanations for large variations.

3. Consider the necessity for additional confirmations as of the balance sheet date if balances have increased materially.

One final note about confirmations: Confirmations of accounts, loans and notes receivable may not produce sufficient evidence of ownership by the client (rights assertion). Debtors may not be aware that the auditor's client has sold their accounts, notes or loans receivable to financial institutions or to the public (collateralized securities). Auditors need to perform additional enquiry and detail procedures to get evidence of the ownership of the receivables and of the appropriateness of disclosures related to financing transactions secured by receivables.

---

[1] CICA, *Confirmation of Accounts Receivable, An Audit Technique Study* (Toronto, 1980), Chapter 5. See also Paul Caster, "The Role of Confirmations as Audit Evidence," *Journal of Accountancy*, February 1992, pp. 73–76.

Summary: Confirmations

Confirmations of cash balances, loans, accounts receivable and notes receivable are required, unless auditors can justify substituting other procedures in the circumstances of a particular audit. The bank confirmation is a standard positive form. Confirmations for accounts and notes receivable can be in positive or negative form, and the positive form may be a blank confirmation.

Auditors must take care to control confirmations to ensure that responses are received from the real debtors and not from persons who can intercept the confirmations to give false responses. Responses by fax, e-mail, telephone or other means not written and signed by a recipient should be followed up to determine their genuine origins. Second and third requests should be sent to prompt responses to positive confirmations, and auditors should audit nonresponding customers by alternative procedures. Accounts in a sample should not be left unaudited (e.g., "They didn't respond"), and easy-to-audit accounts should not be substituted for hard-to-audit ones in a sample. Various "tricks" can be used to raise the response rate.

Confirmations yield evidence about existence and gross valuation. However, the fact that a debtor admits to owing the debt does not mean the debtor can pay. Other procedures must be undertaken to audit the collectibility of the accounts. Nevertheless, confirmations can give some clues about collectibility when customers tell about balances in dispute. Confirmations of accounts, notes and loans receivable should not be used as the only evidence of the ownership (rights assertions) of these financial assets.

R E V I E W
CHECKPOINTS

9.20 List the information a PA should solicit in a standard bank confirmation enquiry sent to an audit client's bank.

9.21 Distinguish between "positive" and "negative" confirmations. Under what conditions would you expect each type of confirmation to be appropriate?

9.22 Distinguish between confirmation "response rate" and confirmation "detection rate."

9.23 What methods can be used to increase the response rate for receivables confirmations?

9.24 What are some of the justifications for not using confirmations of accounts receivable on a particular audit?

9.25 What special care should be taken with regard to examining the sources of accounts receivable confirmation responses?

SPECIAL NOTE: AUDIT OF BANK RECONCILIATIONS WITH ATTENTION TO LAPPING AND KITING

LEARNING OBJECTIVE

6. Design and perform substantive audit procedures for the audit of a bank statement reconciliation, and tell how auditors can search for lapping and kiting.

The company's bank reconciliation is the primary means of valuing cash in the financial statements. The amount of cash in the bank is almost always different from the amount in the books (financial statements), and the reconciliation purports to explain the difference. The normal procedure is to obtain the company-prepared bank reconciliation and audit it. Auditors should not perform the company's control function of preparing the reconciliation.

A client-prepared bank reconciliation is shown in Exhibit 9–11. The bank balance is confirmed and cross-referenced to the bank confirmation working paper (Exhibit 9–7). The reconciliation is recalculated, the outstanding cheques and deposits in transit are footed, and the book balance is traced to the trial balance (which has been traced to the general ledger). The reconciling items should be vouched to determine whether outstanding cheques really were not paid and that deposits in transit actually were mailed before the reconciliation date. The auditor's information source for vouching the bank reconciliation items is a **cutoff bank statement,** which is a complete bank statement including all paid cheques and deposit slips. The client requests the bank to send this bank statement directly to the auditor. It is usually for a 10– to 20–day period following the reconciliation date. (It also can be the next regular monthly statement, received directly by the auditors.)

The vouching of outstanding cheques and deposits in transit is a matter of comparing cheques that cleared in the cutoff bank statement with the list of outstanding cheques for evidence that all cheques that were written prior to the reconciliation date were on the list of outstanding cheques. The deposits shown in transit should be recorded by the bank in the first business days of the cutoff period. If recorded later, the inference is that the deposit may have been made up from receipts of the period after the reconciliation date. For large outstanding cheques not clearing in the cutoff period, vouching may be extended to other documentation supporting the disbursement. These procedures are keyed and described by tick marks in Exhibit 9–11.

Accounts Receivable Lapping

When the business receives many payments from customers, a detailed audit would include comparison of the cheques listed on a sample of deposit slips (from the reconciliation month and other months) to the detail of customer credits listed on the day's posting to customer accounts receivable (daily remittance list or other record of detail postings). This pro-

E X H I B I T 9–11   **BANK RECONCILIATION**

```
                         KINGSTON COMPANY
  C-2          BANK RECONCILIATION-NORTH COUNTRY BANK     Prepared  J.D. 1/10/03
                         General Account                  Reviewed  PRA 1/10/03
                            12/31/02
                        (Prepared by client)

Balance per bank statement                           506,100  c
Add:
   Deposit in transit as of 12/31/02                  51,240  n
Deduct outstanding checks:                           557,340

      Date      No.      Payee
     --------   ----    ------------------------
     12/10/01   842     Ace Supply Company          500  ✗
     11/31/02   1280    Ace Supply Company        1,800  ✓
     12/15/02   1372    Northwest Lumber Co.      30,760  ✓
     12/28/02   1412    Gibson & Johnson           7,270  ✗
     12/30/02   1417    North Country payroll     20,000  ✓
     12/30/02   1418    Ace Supply Company         2,820  ✓
     12/30/02   1419    Windy City Utilities       2,030  ✓
     12/30/02   1420    Howard Hardware Supply      8,160  ✓
                                                   -------
Balance per book                                    73,340
                                                   -------

                                                   484,000  f
                                                   -------
```

Note: *Obtained cutoff bank statement 1/9/03* (C-23) (T/B-1)
f   *Footed*
c   *Confirmed by bank, standard bank confirmation* (C-22)
n   *Vouched to cutoff bank statement, deposit recorded by bank on 1/3/02. Vouched to duplicate deposit slip validaged 1/3/03*
✓   *Vouched to paid check cleared with cutoff bank statement.*
✗   *Vouched to statement from attorneys.*
✗   *Amount in dispute per controller.*

cedure is a test for accounts receivable lapping. It is an attempt to find credits given to customers for whom no payments were received on the day in question. An example of this type of comparison is in the discovery summary section of Casette 9.1 ("The Canny Cashier").

Cheque Kiting

Auditors also should be alert to the possibility of "kiting." **Cheque kiting** is the practice of building up apparent balances in one or more bank accounts based on uncollected (float) cheques drawn against similar accounts in other banks. Kiting involves depositing money from one bank account to another, using a hot cheque. The depository bank does not know the cheque is on insufficient funds, but the deficiency is covered by another hot cheque from another bank account before the first cheque clears. Kiting is the deliberate floating of funds between two or more bank accounts. By this method a bank customer uses the time required for cheques to clear to obtain an unauthorized loan without any interest charge.

Professional money managers working for cash-conscious businesses try to have minimal unused balances in their accounts, and their efforts sometimes can look like cheque kites. Tight cash flows initiate kites, and intent to kite is the key for criminal charges. Kites evolve to involve numerous banks and numerous cheques. The more banks and broader geographical distance, the harder a perpetrator finds it to control a kite scheme.

Here is a simple illustration of how a kite scheme works:

Start with no money in Bank A and Bank B, and draw $5,000 cheques on each to "deposit" in the other:

	Bank A	Bank B	Total
Apparent balances	$5,000	$5,000	$10,000
Actual balances	0	0	0

Do it again with $8,000 cheques:

	Bank A	Bank B	Total
Apparent balances	$13,000	$13,000	$26,000
Actual balances	0	0	0

Make a $6,000 down payment on a Mercedes from Bank A:

	Bank A	Bank B	Total
Apparent balances	$7,000	$13,000	$20,000
Actual balances	(6,000)	0	(6,000)

At the same time that the first cheques for $5,000 clear, write some more, this time for $9,000 each:

	Bank A	Bank B	Total
Apparent balances	$11,000	$17,000	$28,000
Actual balances	(6,000)	0	(6,000)

Pay the balances ($28,000) to a travel agent and take a long trip (preferably to a country with no extradition treaty!):

	Bank A	Bank B	Total
Apparent balances	0	0	0
Actual balances	$(17,000)	$(17,000)	$(34,000)

These are some characteristic signs of cheque kiting schemes:

- Frequent deposits and cheques in same accounts.
- Frequent deposits and cheques in round amounts.
- Frequent deposits with cheques written on the same (other) banks.
- Short time lag between deposits and withdrawals.
- Frequent ATM account balance enquiries.
- Many large deposits made on Thursday or Friday to take advantage of the weekend.
- Large periodic balances in individual accounts with no apparent business explanation.
- Low average balance compared to high level of deposits.
- Many cheques made payable to other banks.
- Bank willingness to pay against uncollected funds.
- "Cash" withdrawals with deposit cheques drawn on another bank.
- Cheques drawn on foreign banks with lax banking laws and regulations.

Auditors can detect the above signs of cheque kiting by reviewing bank account activity. The only trouble is that criminal cheque kiters often destroy the banking documents. If a company cannot or will not produce its bank statements, with all deposit slips and cancelled cheques, the auditors should be wary.

If these cash transfers are recorded in the books, a company will show the negative balances that result from cheques drawn on insufficient funds. However, perpetrators may try to hide the kiting by not recording the deposits and cheques. Such manoeuvres may be detectable in a bank reconciliation audit. If auditors notice some sign of kiting, yet no uncleared items are on the reconciliation, a schedule of interbank transfers can be constructed from the cancelled cheques and the cleared deposits in the bank statements. This schedule shows each cheque amount, the name of the paying bank (with the book recording date and the cheque clearing date), and the name of the receiving bank (with the book deposit date and the bank clearing date). The purpose of this schedule is to see that both sides of the transfer transaction are recorded in the same period (and in the proper period). (An example is in Exhibit 9.62–1 with Discussion Case 9.62 at the end of the chapter.)

Summary: Bank Reconciliations, Lapping and Kiting

The combination of all the procedures performed on the bank reconciliation provides evidence of existence, valuation and proper cutoff of the bank cash balances. Auditors use a cutoff bank statement to obtain independent evidence of the proper listing of outstanding cheques and deposits in transit on a bank reconciliation.

Additional procedures can be performed to try to detect attempts at lapping accounts receivable collections and kiting cheques. For lapping these procedures include auditing the details of customer payments listed in bank deposits in comparison to details of customer payment postings (remittance lists). For kiting these procedures include being alert to the signs of kites and preparing a schedule of interbank transfers.

R E V I E W
C H E C K P O I N T S

9.26   What is a cutoff bank statement? How is it used by auditors?

9.27   What is "lapping?" What procedures can auditors employ for its detection?

9.28   What is "cheque kiting?" How might auditors detect kiting?

. . . .

SUMMARY

. . . .

The revenue and collection cycle consists of customer order processing, credit checking, shipping goods, billing customers and accounting for accounts receivable, and collecting and accounting for cash receipts. Companies reduce control risk by having a suitable separation of authorization, custody, recording and periodic reconciliation duties. Error-checking procedures of comparing customer orders and shipping documents are important for billing customers the right prices for the delivered quantities. Otherwise, many things could go wrong—ranging from making sales to fictitious customers or customers with bad credit to erroneous billings for the wrong quantities at the wrong prices at the wrong time.

Cash collection is a critical point for asset control. Many cases of embezzlement occur in this process. Illustrative cases in this chapter told the stories of some of these cash embezzlement schemes, including the practice of "lapping" accounts receivable.

Three topics were given special technical notes in the chapter. The existence assertion is very important in the audit of cash and receivables assets because misleading financial statements often have contained overstated assets and revenue. The use of confirmations got a special section in this chapter because confirmation is frequently used to obtain evidence of asset existence from outside parties, such as customers who owe on accounts receivable. The audit of bank reconciliations was covered in the context of an audit opportunity to recalculate the amount of cash for the financial statements and to look for signs of accounts receivable lapping and cheque kiting.

MULTIPLE-CHOICE QUESTIONS FOR PRACTICE AND REVIEW

. . . .

Questions 9.29 to 9.33 are located on the CD-ROM that accompanies this textbook.

9.34 Which of the following would be the best protection for a company that wishes to prevent the lapping of trade accounts receivable?

a. Segregate duties so that the bookkeeper in charge of the general ledger has no access to incoming mail.

b. Segregate duties so that no employee has access to both cheques from customers and currency from daily cash receipts.

c. Have customers send payments directly to the company's depository bank.

d. Request that customer's payment cheques be made payable to the company and addressed to the treasurer.

9.35 Which of the following internal control procedures will most likely prevent the concealment of a cash shortage from the improper write-off of a trade account receivable?

a. Write-off must be approved by a responsible officer after review of credit department recommendations and supporting evidence.

b. Write-offs must be supported by an aging schedule showing that only receivables overdue several months have been written off.

c. Write-offs must be approved by the cashier who is in a position to know if the receivables have, in fact, been collected.

d. Write-offs must be authorized by company field sales employees who are in a position to determine the financial standing of the customers.

9.36 Auditors sometimes use comparisons of ratios as audit evidence. For example, an unexplained decrease in the ratio of gross profit to sales may suggest which of the following possibilities?

a. Unrecorded purchases.

b. Unrecorded sales.

c. Merchandise purchases being charged to selling and general expense.

d. Fictitious sales.

9.37 An auditor is auditing sales transactions. One step is to vouch a sample of debit entries from the accounts receivable subsidiary ledger back to the supporting sales invoices. What would the auditor intend to establish by this step?

a. Sales invoices represent bona fide sales.

b. All sales have been recorded.

c. All sales invoices have been properly posted to customer accounts.

d. Debit entries in the accounts receivable subsidiary ledger are properly supported by sales invoices.

9.38 To conceal defalcations involving receivables, the auditor would expect an experienced bookkeeper to charge which of the following accounts?

a. Miscellaneous income.

b. Petty cash.

c. Miscellaneous expense.

d. Sales returns.

9.39 Which of the following would the auditor consider to be an incompatible operation if the cashier receives remittances?

a. The cashier prepares the daily deposit.

b. The cashier makes the daily deposit at a local bank.

c. The cashier posts the receipts to the accounts receivable subsidiary ledger cards.

d. The cashier endorses the cheques.

9.40 The audit working papers often include a client-prepared, aged trial balance of accounts receivable as of the balance sheet date. The aging is best used by the auditor to:

a. Evaluate internal control over credit sales.

b. Test the accuracy of recorded charge sales.

c. Estimate credit losses.

d. Verify the existence of the recorded receivables.

9.41 Which of the following might be detected by an auditor's cutoff review and examination of sales journal entries for several days prior to the balance sheet date?

a. Lapping year-end accounts receivable.

b. Inflating sales for the year.

c. Kiting bank balances.

d. Misappropriating merchandise.

9.42 Confirmation of individual accounts receivable balances directly with debtors will, of itself, normally provide evidence concerning the:

a. Collectibility of the balances confirmed.

b. Ownership of the balances confirmed.

c. Existence of the balances confirmed.

d. Internal control over balances confirmed.

9.43 Which of the following is one of the better auditing techniques an auditor might use to detect kiting between intercompany banks?

a. Review composition of authenticated deposit slips.

b. Review subsequent bank statements.

c. Prepare a schedule of the bank transfers.

d. Prepare a year-end bank reconciliation.

9.44 The best reason for prenumbering in numerical sequence such documents as sales orders, shipping documents and sales invoices is:

a. Enables company personnel to determine the accuracy of each document.

b. Enables personnel to determine the proper period recording of sales revenue and receivables.

c. Enables personnel to check the numerical sequence for missing documents and unrecorded transactions.

d. Enables personnel to determine the validity of recorded transactions.

9.45 When a sample of customer accounts receivable are selected for the purpose of vouching debits therein for validity evidence, the auditors will vouch them to:

a. Sales invoices with shipping documents and customer sales invoices.

b. Records of accounts receivable write-offs.

c. Cash remittance lists and bank deposit slips.

d. Credit files and reports.

9.46 In the audit of cash and accounts receivable, the most important emphasis should be on the:

a. Completeness assertions.

b. Existence assertion.

c. Obligations assertion.

d. Presentation and disclosure assertion.

9.47 When accounts receivable are confirmed at an interim date, the auditors need not be concerned with:

a. Obtaining a summary of receivables transactions from the interim date to the year-end date.

b. Obtaining a year-end trial balance of receivables, comparing it to the interim trial balance and obtaining evidence and explanations for large variations.

c. Sending negative confirmations to all the customers as of the year-end date.

d. Considering the necessity for some additional confirmations as of the balance sheet date if balances have increased materially.

9.48 The negative request form of accounts receivable confirmation is useful particularly when the:

	Assessed level of control risk relating to receivables is:	Number of small balances is:	Proper consideration by the recipient is:
a.	Low	Many	Likely
b.	Low	Few	Unlikely
c.	High	Few	Likely
d.	High	Many	Likely

(AICPA adapted)

9.49 When an auditor selects a sample of shipping documents and takes the tracing direction of a test to find the related sales invoice copies, the evidence is relevant for deciding:

a. Shipments to customers were invoiced.

b. Shipments to customers were recorded as sales.

c. Recorded sales were shipped.

d. Invoiced sales were shipped.

(AICPA adapted)

Exercises and Problems

9.50 Cash Receipts: Control Objectives and Control Examples. Prepare a table similar to Exhibit 9–4 (internal control objectives) for cash receipts.

9.51 Internal Control Questionnaire for Book Buy-Back Cash Fund. Taylor, a PA, has been engaged to audit the financial statements of University Books, Incorporated. University Books maintains a large, revolving cash fund exclusively for the purpose of buying used books from students for cash. The cash fund is active all year because the nearby university offers a large variety of courses with varying starting and completion dates throughout the year.

Receipts are prepared for each purchase. Reimbursement vouchers periodically are submitted to replenish the fund.

Required:

Construct an internal control questionnaire to be used in evaluating the system of internal control over University Books' buying back books using the revolving cash fund. The internal control questionnaire should elicit a yes or no response to each question. Do not discuss the internal controls over books that are purchased.

(AICPA adapted)

9.52 Test of Controls Audit Procedures for Cash Receipts. You are the in-charge auditor examining the financial statements of the Gutzler Company for the year ended December 31. During late October you, with the help of Gutzler's controller, completed an internal control questionnaire and prepared the appropriate memoranda describing Gutzler's accounting procedures. Your comments relative to cash receipts are as follows:

All cash receipts are sent directly to the accounts receivable clerk with no processing by the mail department. The accounts receivable clerk keeps the cash receipts journal, prepares the bank deposit slip in duplicate, posts from the deposit slip to the subsidiary accounts receivable ledger and mails the deposit to the bank.

The controller receives the validated deposit slips directly (unopened) from the bank. She also receives the monthly bank statement directly (unopened) from the bank and promptly reconciles it.

At the end of each month, the accounts receivable clerk notifies the general ledger clerk by journal voucher of the monthly totals of the cash receipts journal for posting to the general ledger.

Each month, with regard to the general ledger cash account, the general ledger clerk makes an entry to record the total debits to cash from the cash receipts journal. In addition, the general ledger clerk, on occasion, makes debit entries in the general ledger cash account from sources other than the cash receipts journal—for example, funds borrowed from the bank. Certain standard auditing procedures listed below already have been performed by you in the audit of cash receipts:

All columns in the cash receipts have been totalled and cross-totalled.

Postings from the cash receipts journal have been traced to the general ledger.

Remittance advices and related correspondence have been traced to entries in the cash receipts journal.

Required:

Considering Gutzler's internal control over cash receipts and the standard auditing procedures already performed, list all other auditing procedures that should be performed to obtain sufficient audit evidence regarding cash receipts control and give the reasons for each procedure. Do not discuss the procedures for cash disbursements and cash balances. Also, do not discuss the extent to which any of the procedures are to be performed. Assume adequate controls exist to ensure that all sales transactions are recorded. Organize your answer sheet as follows:

Other Audit Procedures	Reason for Other Audit Procedures

(AICPA adapted)

9.53 Cash Receipts: Weaknesses and Recommendations. The Pottstown Art League operates a museum for the benefit and enjoyment of the community. During hours when the museum is open to the public, two volunteer clerks positioned at the entrance collect a $5 admission fee from each nonmember patron. Members of the Art League are permitted to enter free of charge on presentation of their membership cards.

At the end of each day, one of the clerks delivers the proceeds to the treasurer. The treasurer counts the cash in the presence of the clerk and places it in a safe. Each Friday afternoon, the treasurer and one of the clerks deliver all cash held in the safe to the bank, and they receive an authenticated deposit slip that provides the basis for the weekly entry in the cash receipts journal.

The board of directors of the Pottstown Art League has identified a need to improve the system of internal control over cash admission fees. The board has determined that the cost of installing turnstiles or sales booths or otherwise altering the physical layout of the museum will greatly exceed any benefits that may be derived. However, the board has agreed that the sale of admission tickets must be an integral part of its improvement efforts.

Required:

The board of directors has requested your assistance. Prepare a report for presentation and discussion at their next board meeting that identifies the weaknesses in the existing system of cash admission fees and suggests recommendations.

(AICPA adapted)

9.54 Control Weaknesses: Computer. Ajax, Inc., an audit client, recently installed a new computer system to process the shipping, billing and accounts receivable records more efficiently. During interim work, an assistant completed the review of the accounting system and the internal controls. The assistant determined the following information concerning the new computer systems and the processing and control of shipping notices and customer invoices.

Each major computerized function (i.e., shipping, billing, accounts receivable) is permanently assigned to a specific computer operator who is responsible for making program changes, running the program and reconciling the computer log. Responsibility for the custody and control over the various databases and system documentation is randomly rotated among the computer operators on a monthly basis to prevent any one person from having access to the database and documentation at all times. Each computer programmer and computer operator has access to the computer room via a magnetic card and a digital code that is different for each card. The systems analyst and the supervisor of computer operators do not have access to the computer room.

The computer system documentation consists of the following items: program listings, error listings, logs and database dictionaries. To increase efficiency, batch totals and processing controls are not used in the system.

Ajax ships its products directly from two warehouses, which forward shipping notices to general accounting. There, the billing clerk enters the price of the item and accounts for the numerical sequence of the shipping notices. The billing clerk also prepares daily adding machine tapes of the units shipped and the sales amounts. Shipping notices and adding machine tapes forwarded to the computer department for processing the computer output consist of:

a. A three-copy invoice that is forwarded to the billing clerk.

b. A daily sales register showing the aggregate totals of units shipped and sales amounts that the computer operator compares to the adding machine tapes.

The billing clerk mails two copies of each invoice to the customer and retains the third copy in an open invoice file that serves as a detail accounts receivable record.

Required:
a. Prepare a list of weaknesses in internal control (manual and computer), and for each weakness make one or more recommendations.
b. Suggest how Ajax's computer processing over shipping and billing could be improved through the use of remote terminals to enter shipping notices. Describe appropriate controls for such an on-line data entry system.

CASH: SUBSTANTIVE AUDIT PROCEDURES

9.55 Bank Reconciliation. The following client-prepared bank reconciliation is being examined by you during an audit of the financial statements of Cynthia Company:

CYNTHIA COMPANY
Bank Reconciliation
Village Bank Account 2
December 31, 2002

Balance per bank (a):		$18,375.91
Deposits in transit (b):		
12/30	$1,471.10	
12/31	2,840.69	4,311.79
Subtotal		22,687.70
Outstanding cheques (c):		
837	6,000.00	
1941	671.80	
1966	320.00	
1984	1,855.42	
1985	3,621.22	
1987	2,576.89	
1991	4,420.88	(19,466.21)
Subtotal		3,221.49
NSF cheque Returned 12/29 (d):		200.00
Bank charges		5.50
Error cheque no. 1932		148.10
Customer note collected by the bank ($2,750 plus $275 interest (e):		(3,025.00)
Balance per books (f):		$550.09

Required:
Indicate one or more audit procedures that should be performed in gathering evidence in support of each of the items (a) through (f) above.

(AICPA adapted)

9.56 Sales Cutoff and Cutoff Bank Statement.
a. You wish to test Houston Corporaton's sales cutoff at June 30. Describe the steps you should include in this test.
b. You obtain a July 10 bank statement directly from the bank. Explain how

this cutoff bank statement should be used:
(1) In your review of the June 30 bank reconciliation.
(2) To obtain other audit information.

(AICPA adapted)

9.57 Bank Reconciliation—Cash Shortage. The Patrick Company had poor internal control over its cash transactions. Facts about its cash position at November 30 were the following:

The cash books showed a balance of $18,901.62, which included undeposited receipts. A credit of $100 on the bank statement did not appear on the books of the company. The balance according to the statement was $15,550.

When you received the cutoff bank statement on December 10, the following cancelled cheques were enclosed: No. 6500 for $116.25, No. 7126 for $150.00, No. 7815 for $253.25, No. 8621 for $190.71, No. 8623 for $206.80, and No. 8632 for $145.28. The only deposit was in the amount of $3,794.41 on December 7.

The cashier handles all incoming cash and makes the bank deposits personally. He also reconciles the monthly bank statement. His November 30 reconciliation is shown below.

Balance, per books, November 30		$18,901.62
Add: Outstanding cheques:		
8621	$190.71	
8623	206.80	
8632	145.28	442.79
		19,344.41
Less: Undeposited receipts		3,794.41
Balance per bank, November 30		15,550.00
Deduct: Unrecorded credit		100.00
True cash, November 30		$15,450.00

Required:
a. You suspect that the cashier has stolen some money. Prepare a schedule showing your estimate of the loss.
b. How did the cashier attempt to conceal the theft?
c. Based only on the information above, name two specific features of internal control that apparently were missing.
d. If the cashier's October 31 reconciliation is known to be in order and you start your audit on December 5, what

specific auditing procedures could you perform to discover the theft?

(AICPA adapted)

RECEIVABLES AND REVENUES: SUBSTANTIVE AUDIT PROCEDURES

9.58 Alternative Accounts Receivable Procedures. Several accounts receivable confirmations have been returned with the notation "verification of vendors statements is no longer possible because our data processing system does not accumulate each vendor's invoices." What alternative auditing procedures could be used to audit these accounts receivable?

(AICPA adapted)

9.59 Receivables Audit Procedures. The ABC Appliance Company, a manufacturer of small electrical appliances, deals exclusively with 20 distributors situated throughout the country. At December 31 (the balance sheet date) receivables from these distributors aggregated $875,000. Total current assets were $1.3 million.

With respect to receivables, the auditors followed the procedures outline below in the course of the annual audit of financial statements:

1. Reviewed the system of internal control and found it to be exceptionally good.
2. Reconciled the subsidiary and control accounts at year-end.
3. Aged accounts. None were overdue.
4. Examined details sales and collection transactions for the months of February, July and November.
5. Received positive confirmations of year-end balances.

Required:
Criticize the completeness or incompleteness of the above program, giving reasons for your recommendations concerning the addition or omission of any procedures.

(AICPA adapted)

9.60 Rent Revenue. You were engaged to conduct an audit of the financial statements of Clayton Realty Corporation for the year ending January 31. The examination of the annual rent reconciliation is a vital portion of the audit.

The following rent reconciliation was prepared by the controller of Clayton Realty Corporation and was presented to you. You subjected it to various audit procedures:

CLAYTON REALTY CORPORATION
Rent Reconciliation
For the Year Ended January 31

Gross apartment rents (Schedule A)	$1,600,800*
Less vacancies (Schedule B)	20,000*
Net apartment rentals	1,580,300
Less unpaid rents (Schedule C)	7,800*
Total	1,572,500
Add prepaid rent collected (Schedule D)	500*
Total cash collected	$1,573,000*

Schedules A, B, C and D are available to you but have not been illustrated. You have conducted an assessment of the control risk and found it to be low. Cash receipts from rental operations are deposited in a special bank account.

Required:
What substantive audit procedures should you employ during the audit in order to substantiate the validity of each of the dollar amounts marked by an asterisk(*)?

(AICPA adapted)

DISCUSSION CASES

9.61 Trinity Company—Defalcations. Assume that you are participating in the audit of the Trinity Company's financial statements. The situations described below came to your attention when you performed certain substantive audit procedures of account balance details.

1. The July sales journal indicated that customers were billed $140,000 during that month. This amount was posted as a debit to accounts receivable and a credit to sales. However, you tested the footing of the July sales journal and determined that the correct sum of the customer billings was $144,500.
2. You noted that an $8,500 debit posting had been entered in the miscellaneous expense account, but you could not vouch this posting to any "preceding" record (such as a purchases journal, payroll journal or general journal).
3. When you examined a voucher for the purchase of office supplies, you noted that the cheque signer had initialed the

vendor's invoice to indicate her approval, but the purchase order and receiving report had not been initialed or otherwise cancelled.

4. When you audited the reconciliation of the company's chequing account at year-end, you noted that a $6,000 cheque had been omitted from the list of outstanding cheques. The cheque had been issued and recorded as a disbursement during the previous month, but it had not yet cleared the bank.

Required:

1. Describe how each situation may indicate an attempted concealment of a defalcation.
2. Answer the following general questions:
   a. Are certain types of concealment "temporary" in the sense that further actions will be required to prevent detection?
   b. How might the direction of audit testing (testing for over- or understatement) be influenced by the auditor's responsibility to search for material defalcations?
   c. Can auditors rely exclusively on a good internal control structure to fulfill the responsibility to search for and detect material misstatements?
   d. Can auditors rely exclusively on analytical procedures to fulfill the responsibility to search for and detect material misstatements?

(Adapted from the case contributed by Deloitte Haskins & Sells to the Auditor's Report)

9.62 Interbank Transfers. EverReady Corporation is in the home building and repair business. Construction business has been in a slump, and the company has experienced financial difficulty over the past two years. Part of the problem lies in the company's desire to avoid laying off its skilled crews of bricklayers and cabinetmakers. Meeting the payroll has been a problem.

The auditors are engaged to audit the 2002 financial statements. Knowing of EverReady's financial difficulty and its business policy, the auditors decided to prepare a schedule of interbank transfers covering the 10 days before and after December 31, which is the company's balance sheet date.

First, the auditors used the cash receipts and disbursements journals to prepare part of the schedule shown in Exhibit 9.62–1. They obtained the information for everything except the dates of deposit and payment in the bank statements (disbursing date per bank and receiving date per bank). They learned that EverReady always transferred money to the payroll account at North Country Bank from the general account at North Country Bank. This transfer enabled the bank to clear the payroll cheques without delay. The only bank accounts in the EverReady financial statements are the two at North Country Bank.

Next, the auditors obtained the December 2002 and January 2003 bank statements for the general and payroll accounts at North Country Bank. They recorded the bank disbursement and receipt dates in the schedule of interbank transfers. For each

E X H I B I T 9.62–1   SCHEDULE OF INTERBANK TRANSFERS

C-5

EVERREADY CORPORATION
Schedule of Interbank Transfers
December 31, 2002

Prepared _____
Date _____
Reviewed _____
Date _____

	Disbursing Account				Receiving Account		
Check #	Bank	Amount	Date per Books	Date per Bank	Bank	Date per Books	Date per Bank
1417	North Country	10,463✓	24-Dec	24-Dec"	North Country payroll	24-Dec r	24-Decχ
1601	North Country	11,593✓	31-Dec✗	31-Dec"	North Country payroll	31-Dec r	31-Decχ
1982	North Country	9.971✓	08-Jan	08-Jan"	North Country payroll	08-Jan r	08-Janχ

✓ Traced from cash disbursements journal.
✗ Cheque properly listed as outstanding on bank reconciliation.
" Vouched to cheque cleared in bank statement.
r Traced from cash receipts journal.
χ Vouched deposit cleared in bank statement.
Note: We scanned the cash disbursements and cash receipts journals for cheques to and deposits from other bank accounts.

transfer these dates are identical because the accounts are in the same bank. An alert auditor noticed that the North Country Bank general account bank statement also contains deposits received from Commerce Bank and cancelled cheque number 1799 dated January 5 payable to Commerce Bank. This cheque cleared the Commerce Bank account on January 8 and was marked "transfer of funds." This led to new information.

NEW INFORMATION

Asked about the Commerce Bank transactions, EverReady's chief financial officer readily admitted the existence of an off-books bank account. He explained that it was used for financing transactions in keeping with normal practice in the construction industry. He gave the auditors the December and January bank statements for the account at Commerce Bank. In it, the auditors found the following:

Commerce Bank

Cheque #	Payable to	Amount	Dated	Cleared Bank
4050	North Country	10,000	23-Dec	29-Dec
4051	Chase Bank	12,000	28-Dec	31-Dec
4052	North Country	12,000	30-Dec	05-Jan
4053	Chase Bank	14,000	04-Jan	07-Jan
4054	North Country	20,000	08-Jan	13-Jan

Deposits		
Received from	Amount	Dated
Chase Bank	11,000	22-Dec
Chase Bank	15,000	30-Dec
North Country	10,000	05-Jan
Chase Bank	12,000	07-Jan

When asked about the Chase Bank transactions, EverReady's chief financial officer admitted the existence of another off-books bank account, which he said was the personal account of the principal shareholder.

He explained that the shareholder often used it to finance EverReady's operations. He gave the auditors the December and January bank statements for this account at Chase Bank; in it, the auditors found the following:

Chase Bank

Cheque #	Payable to	Amount	Dated	Cleared Bank
2220	Commerce Bank	11,000	22-Dec	28—Dec
2221	Commerce Bank	15,000	30-Dec	05—Jan
2222	Commerce Bank	12,000	07-Jan	12—Jan

Deposits		
Received from	Amount	Dated
Commerce Bank	12,000	28-Dec
Commerce Bank	14,000	04-Jan

An abbreviated calendar for the period is in Exhibit 9.62–2.

Required:

a. Complete the schedule of interbank transfers (working paper C-5, Exhibit 9.62–1) by entering the new information.

b. What is the actual cash balance for the four bank accounts combined, considering only the amounts given in this case information, as of December 31, 2002 (before any of the December 31 payroll cheques are cashed by employees)? As of January 8, 2003 (before any of the January 8 payroll cheques are cashed by employees)? (Hint: Prepare a schedule of "apparent balances" and "actual balances" illustrated in Chapter 17 to explain cheque kiting.)

9.63 Manipulated Bank Reconciliation. Caulco, Inc., is the audit client. You have obtained the client-prepared bank reconciliation as of February 28, 1998. (The bank statement and, thus, the dates are actual

E X H I B I T 9.62–2   CALENDAR

	S	M	T	W	T	F	S
December	20	21	22	23	24	25	26
2002	27	28	29	30	31	1	2
January	3	4	5	6	7	8	9
2003	10	11	12	13	14	15	16

documents, although the situation is contrived for the purposes of this problem.)

Required:

Cheque #2231 was the first cheque written in February. All earlier cheques cleared the bank, some in the January bank statement and some in the February bank statement.

Assume that the only February-dated cancelled cheques returned in the March bank statement are #2231; #2239 and #2231; #2240, showing the amounts listed in the February bank reconciliation. They cleared the bank on March 3 and March 2, respectively. The first deposit on the March bank statement was $1,097.69, credited on March 3. Assume further that all cheques entered in Caulco's cash disbursements journal through February 28 have either cleared the bank or are listed as outstanding cheques in the February bank reconciliation.

Examine the February bank statement in Exhibit 18–3 (Chapter 18). Determine whether anything is wrong with the bank statement and the bank reconciliation. If anything is wrong, prepare a corrected reconciliation and explain the problem.

9.64 Employee Embezzlement via Cash Receipts and Payment of Personal Expenses (duplicated in Chapter 18, Case 18.52). Instructions for Discussion Cases 9.64 and 9.65.

These cases are designed like the ones in the chapter. They give the problem, the method, the paper trail and the amount.

Your assignment is to write the audit approach portion of the case, organized around these sections:

Objective: Express the objective in terms of the facts supposedly asserted in financial records, accounts and statements. (Refer to discussion of assertions in Chapter 4).

Control: Write a brief explanation of desirable controls, missing controls and especially the kinds of "deviations" that might arise from the situation described in the case.

Test of controls: Write some procedures for getting evidence about existing controls, especially procedures that could discover deviations from controls. If there are no controls to test, then there are no procedures to perform; go then to the next section. A "procedure" should instruct someone about the source(s) of evidence to tap and the work to do.

Audit of balance: Write some procedures for getting evidence about the existence, completeness, valuation, ownership or disclosure assertions identified in your objective section above.

Discovery summary: Write a short statement about the discovery you expect to accomplish with your procedures.

THE EXTRA BANK ACCOUNT

Problem: Cash receipts pocketed and personal expenses paid from business account.

Method: The Ourtown Independent School District, like all others, had red tape

CAULCO, INC.
Bank Reconciliation
February 28, 1998

Balance per bank				$7,374.93
Deposit in transit				1,097.69
Outstanding cheques				

#	Date	Payee	Amount	
2239	Feb. 26	Alpha Supply	500.00	
2240	Feb. 28	L.C. Stateman	254.37	
Total outstanding				(754.37)
General ledger balance Feb. 28, 1998				$7,718.25

about school board approval of cash disbursements. To get around the rules and to make timely payment of some bills possible, the superintendent of schools had a school bank account that was used in the manner of a petty cash fund. The board knew about it and had given blanket approval in advance for its use to make timely payment of minor school expenses. The board, however, never reviewed the activity in this account. The business manager had sole responsibility for the account, subject to the annual audit. The account got money from transfers from other school accounts and from deposit of cafeteria cash receipts. The superintendent did not like to be bothered with details, and he often signed blank cheques so that the business manager would not need to run in for a signature all the time. The business manager sometimes paid her personal American Express credit card bills, charged personal items to the school's VISA account and pocketed some cafeteria cash receipts before deposit.

Paper trail: An informant called the state education audit agency and told the story that this business manager had used school funds to buy hosiery. When told of this story, the superintendent told the auditor to place no credibility in the informant, who is "out to get us." (The informant had been fired after an accusation of improper behaviour and later faced a similar charge at the next place of employment.) The business manager had in fact used the account to write cheques to "cash" (herself), put her own American Express bills in the school files (the school district had a VISA card, not American Express), and signed on the school card for gasoline and auto repairs during periods when school was not in session. (As for the hosiery, she purchased $700 worth with school funds one year.) The superintendent was genuinely unaware of the misuse of funds.

Amount: The business manager had been employed for six years, was trusted, and stole an estimated $15,000.

Required:

Write the audit approach section according to the instructions at the beginning of 9.64. You can assume that you received the informant's message.

9.65 Overstated Sales and Accounts Receivable. Follow the instructions given with Case 17.64. Write the audit approach section.

RING AROUND THE REVENUE

Problem: Sales were recorded early, sometimes at fictitiously high prices, overstating sales revenue, accounts receivable and income.

Method: Mattox Toy Manufacturing Company had experienced several years of good business. Income had increased steadily and the common shares were a favourite among investors. Management had confidently predicted continued growth and prosperity. But business turned worse instead of better. Competition became fierce.

In earlier years Mattox had accommodated a few large retail customers with the practice of field warehousing coupled with a "bill and hold" accounting procedure. These large retail customers executed noncancellable written agreements, asserting their purchase of toys and their obligation to pay. The toys were not actually shipped because the customers did not have available warehouse space. They were set aside in segregated areas on the Mattox premises and identified as the customers' property. Mattox would later drop-ship the toys to various retail locations upon instructions from the customers. The "field warehousing" was explained as Mattox serving as a temporary warehouse and storage location for the customers' toys. In the related bill-and-hold accounting procedure, Mattox prepared invoices billing the customers, delivered them to the customers, and recorded the sales and accounts receivable.

When business took the recent downturn, Mattox expanded its field warehousing and its bill-and-hold accounting practices. Invoices were recorded for customers who did not execute the written agreements used in previous arrangements. Some customers signed the noncancellable written agreements with clauses permitting subsequent inspection, acceptance and determination of discounted prices. The toys were not always set aside in separate areas, either, and this failure later gave shipping employees problems when it came to identifying shipments of toys that had been "sold" earlier and those that had not.

Mattox also engaged in overbilling. Customers who ordered close-out toys at discounted prices were billed at regular prices, even though the customers' orders showed the discounted prices agreed by Mattox sales representatives.

In a few cases, the bill-and-hold invoices and the close-out sales were billed and recorded in duplicate. In most cases the customers' invoices were addressed and mailed to specific individuals in the customers' management instead of the routine mailing to the customers' accounts payable departments.

Paper trail: The field warehousing arrangements were well known and acknowledged in the Mattox accounting manual. Related invoices were stamped "bill and hold." Customer orders and agreements were attached in a document file. Sales of close-out toys were stamped "close-out," indicating the regular prices (bases for salespersons' commissions) and the invoice prices. Otherwise, the accounting for sales and accounts receivable was unexceptionable. Efforts to record these sales in January (last month of the fiscal year) caused the month's sales revenue to be 35 percent higher than the January of the previous year.

In the early years of the practice, inventory sold under the field warehousing arrangements (both regular and closeout toys) was segregated and identified. The shipping orders for these toys left the "carrier name" and "shipping date" blank, even though they were signed and dated by a company employee in the spaces for the company representative and the carrier representative signature.

The lack of inventory segregation caused problems for the company. After the fiscal year-end, Mattox solved the problem by reversing $6.9 million of the $14 million bill and hold sales. This caused another problem because the reversal was larger than the month's sales, causing the sales revenue for that month to be a negative number!

Amount: Company officials' reasons for the validity of recognizing sales revenue and receivables on the bill-and-hold procedure and field warehousing were persuasive. After due consideration of the facts and circumstances, the company's own accountants agreed that the accounting practices appropriately accounted for revenue and receivables.

It was Mattox's abuse of the practices that caused financial statements to be materially misstated. In January of the year in question, the company overstated sales by about $14 million, or 5 percent of the sales that should have been recorded. The gross profit of $7 million on these sales caused the income to be overstated by about 40 percent.

9.66 Cut-Off Tests for Sales. In connection with an audit of the financial statements of a wholesale food distributor, a PA will perform cutoff tests in several areas, including merchandise receipts, sales transactions and cash.

Required:
a. Explain the general purpose of a cutoff test. To which management assertion(s) are such tests related?
b. Assume the financial statements of the wholesale distributor have never been audited. Must cutoff tests be performed for both the beginning and end, or only at the end of the fiscal year? Explain.
c. List four procedures the PA could perform in testing the cutoff of sales revenue at the end of the fiscal year. All of the company's sales are made on account.
d. Explain how the PA should test the cutoff of cash receipts at the end of the fiscal year.

(CGAAC adapted)

9.67 Audit of Receivables. You are the auditor of North Shore Linen Supply Company, which performs laundry services for restaurants and similar businesses. The company's drivers deliver clean linens (tablecloths, towels, uniforms, etc.) to each customer on a weekly basis, while picking up soiled goods for laundering and delivery the following week. All linens are the property of the customer, and the drivers carry a stock of standard items that are sold to customers who need to replace damaged goods, etc. You are planning your examination of the company's accounts receivable balances and determine the following:

1. There are 50 separate routes; each route consists of 25 to 40 customers, the number that can be serviced by a driver in one day.
2. Each driver maintains a route book. This consists of a loosely bound volume that, among other things, shows the detailed charges and credits to each customer's account.
3. Charges for laundry services are recorded on a preprinted, prenumbered invoice form at the plant and also recorded in the route book. The driver delivers the invoice to the customer with the clean goods. Charges for any linens sold are entered in the route books directly by the drivers.
4. Drivers are authorized to collect cash. Amounts collected are recorded in the route book, and the cash is remitted to a cashier at the plant at the end of each route. When collecting the cash, the

cashier verifies that the amount remitted agrees with the total credits recorded to the customers' accounts by the driver that day.

5. Some customers pay their accounts by cheque sent directly to the plant. The route books are updated when these cheques are received.

6. Last year's audit program for the selection of accounts receivable for confirmation states: "Select two accounts from each route by opening the route book twice, at random."

Required

a. List six weaknesses in internal controls in the system as described in the case. Do not include suggestions for improvements.

b. Would the procedure used last year to select a sample of accounts for confirmation produce a statistically valid random sample? Explain.

c. What form of customer confirmation request would be most appropriate in this situation? Discuss.

d. Would dollar-unit sampling be an appropriate method of determining sample size and selecting a sample of customer accounts for confirmation in this situation? Discuss.

(CGAAC adapted)

APPENDIX 9A
INTERNAL CONTROL QUESTIONNAIRES

· ·

E X H I B I T   9A–1   INTERNAL CONTROL QUESTIONNAIRE—CASH RECEIPTS PROCESSING

Environment:
1. Are receipts deposited daily, intact and without delay?
2. Does someone other than the cashier or accounts receivable bookkeeper take the deposits to the bank?
3. Are the duties of the cashier entirely separate from recordkeeping for notes and accounts receivable? From general ledger recordkeeping?
4. Is the cashier denied access to receivables records or monthly statements?

Validity objective:
5. Is a bank reconciliation performed monthly by someone who does not have cash custody or recordkeeping responsibility?
6. Are the cash receipts journal entries compared to the remittance lists and deposit slips regularly?

Completeness objective:
7. Does the person who opens the mail make a list of cash received (a remittance list)?
8. Are currency receipts controlled by mechanical devices? Are machine totals checked by the internal auditor?
9. Are prenumbers sales invoice or receipts books used? Is the numerical sequence checked for missing documents?

Authorization objective:
10. Does a responsible person approve discounts taken by customers with payments on account?

Accuracy objective:
11. Is a duplicate deposit slip retained by the internal auditor or someone other than the employee making up the deposit?
12. Is the remittance list compared to the deposit by someone other than the cashier?

Classification objective:
13. Does the accounting manual contain instructions for classifying cash receipts credits?

Accounting objective:
14. Does someone reconcile the accounts receivable subsidiary to the control account regularly (to determine whether all entries were made to customers' accounts)?

Proper period objective:
15. Does the accounting manual contain instructions for dating cash receipts entries the same day as the date of receipt?

E X H I B I T   9A–2   INTERNAL CONTROL QUESTIONNAIRE—SALES

Environment:
1. Is the credit department independent of the marketing department?
2. Are sales of the following types controlled by the same procedures described below? Sales to employees, COD sales, disposals of property, cash sales and scrap sales.

Validity objective:
3. Is access to sales invoice blanks restricted?
4. Are prenumbered bills of lading or other shipping documents prepared or completed in the shipping department?

Completeness objective:
5. Are sales invoice blanks prenumbered?
6. Is the sequence checked for missing invoices?
7. Is the shipping document numerical sequence checked for missing bills of lading numbers?

Authorization objective:
8. Are all credit sales approved by the credit department prior to shipment?
9. Are sales prices and terms based on approved standards?
10. Are returned sales credits and other credits supported by documentation as to receipt, condition, and quantity, and approved by a responsible officer?

Accuracy objective:
11. Are shipped quantities compared to invoice quantities?
12. Are sales invoices checked for error in quantities, prices, extensions and footing, freight allowances and checked with customers' orders?
13. Is there an overall check on arithmetic accuracy of period sales data by a statistical or product-line analysis?
14. Are periodic sales data reported directly to general ledger accounting independent of accounts receivable accounting?

Classification objective:
15. Does the accounting manual contain instructions for classifying sales?

Accounting objective:
16. Are summary journal entries approved before posting?

Proper period objective:
17. Does the accounting manual contain instructions to date sales invoices on the shipment date?

E X H I B I T 9A–3   INTERNAL CONTROL QUESTIONNAIRE—ACCOUNTS AND NOTES RECEIVABLE

Environment:
1. Are customers' subsidiary records maintained by someone who has no access to cash?
2. Is the cashier denied access to the customers' records and monthly statements?
3. Are delinquent accounts listed periodically for review by someone other than the credit manager?
4. Are written-off accounts kept in a memo ledger or credit report file for periodic access?
5. Is the credit department separated from the sales department?
6. Are notes receivable in the custody of someone other than the cashier or accounts receivable recordkeeper?
7. Is custody of negotiable collateral in the hands of someone not responsible for handling cash or keeping records?

Validity objective:
8. Are customers' statements mailed monthly by the accounts receivable department?
9. Are direct confirmations of accounts and notes obtained periodically by the internal auditor?
10. Are differences reported by customers routed to someone outside the accounts receivable department for investigation?
11. Are returned goods checked against receiving reports?

Completeness objective:
(Refer to completeness questions in the sales and cash receipts questionnaires.)
12. Are credit memo documents prenumbered and the sequence checked for missing documents?

Authorization objective:
13. Is customer credit approved before orders are shipped?
14. Are write-offs, returns and discounts allowed after discount date subject to approval by a responsible officer?
15. Are large loans or advances to related parties approved by the directors?

Accuracy objective:
16. Do the internal auditors confirm customer accounts periodically to determine accuracy?

Classification objective:
17. Are receivables from officers, directors and affiliates identified separately in the accounts receivable records?

Accounting objective:
18. Does someone reconcile the accounts receivable subsidiary to the control account regularly?

Proper period objective:
(Refer to proper period objective questions in the sales and cash receipts questionnaires.)

E X H I B I T 9A–4   SALES AND ACCOUNTS RECEIVABLE COMPUTER CONTROLS

- Each terminal performs only designated functions. For example, the terminal at the shipping dock cannot be used to enter initial sales information or to access the payroll database.
- An identification number and password (issued on an individual person basis) is required to enter the sales and each command that a subsequent action has been completed. Unauthorized entry attempts are logged and immediately investigated. Further, certain passwords have "ready only" (cannot change any data) authorization. For example, the credit manager can determine the outstanding balance of any account or view on-line "reports" summarizing overdue accounts receivable, but cannot enter credit memos to change the balances.
- All input information is immediately logged to provide restart processing should any terminal become inoperative during the processing.
- A transaction code calls up on the terminals a full screen "form" that appears to the operator in the same format as the original paper documents. Each clerk must enter the information correctly or the computer will not accept the transaction. This is called **on-line input validation** and utilizes validation checks, such as missing data, check digit and limit tests.
- All documents prepared by the computer are numbered, and the number is stored as part of the sales record in the accounts receivable database.
- A daily search of the pending order database is made by the computer, and sales orders outstanding more than seven days are listed on the terminal in marketing management.

APPENDIX 9B

SUBSTANTIVE AUDIT PROGRAMS

. . . .

E X H I B I T 9B–1 **AUDIT PROGRAM—SELECTED SUBSTANTIVE PROCEDURES—CASH**

1. Obtain confirmations from banks (standard bank confirmation).
2. Obtain reconciliations of all bank accounts.
   a. Trace the bank balance on the reconciliation to the bank confirmation.
   b. Trace the reconciled book balance to the general ledger.
   c. Recalculate the arithmetic on client-prepared bank reconciliations.
3. Review the bank confirmation for loans and collateral.
4. Ask the client to request cutoff bank statements to be mailed directly to the audit firm.
   a. Trace deposits in transit on the reconciliation to bank deposits early in the next period.
   b. Trace outstanding cheques on the reconciliation to cheques cleared in the next period.
5. Prepare a schedule of interbank transfers for a period of 10 business days before and after the year-end date. Document dates of book entry transfer and correspondence with bank entries and reconciliation items, if any.
6. Count cash funds in the presence of a client representative. Obtain a receipt for return of the funds.
7. Obtain written client representations concerning compensating balance agreements.

E X H I B I T 9B–2 **AUDIT PROGRAM FOR ACCOUNTS AND NOTES RECEIVABLE AND REVENUE: SELECTED SUBSTANTIVE PROCEDURES**

A. Accounts and Notes Receivable.
   1. Obtain an aged trial balance of individual customer accounts. Recalculate the total and trace to the general ledger control account.
   2. Send confirmations to all accounts over $X. Select a random sample of all remaining accounts for confirmation.
      a. Investigate differences reported by customers.
      b. Perform alternative procedures on accounts that do not respond to positive confirmation requests.
         (1) Vouch cash receipts after the confirmation date for subsequent payment.
         (2) Vouch sales invoices and shipping documents.
   3. Evaluate the adequacy of the allowance for doubtful accounts.
      a. Vouch a sample of *current* amounts in the aged trial balance to sales invoices to determine whether amounts aged current should be aged past due.
      b. Compare the current-year write-off experience to the prior-year allowance.
      c. Vouch cash receipts after the balance sheet date for collections on past-due accounts.
      d. Obtain financial statements or credit reports and discuss with the credit manager collections on large past-due accounts.
      e. Calculate an allowance estimate using prior relations of write-offs and sales, taking under consideration current economic events.
   4. Review the bank confirmations, loan agreements and minutes of the board for indications of pledged, discounted or assigned receivables.
   5. Inspect or obtain confirmation of notes receivable.
   6. Recalculate interest income and trace to the income account.
   7. Obtain written client representations regarding pledge, discount or assignment of receivables, and about receivables from officers, directors, affiliates or other related parties.
   8. Review the adequacy of control over recording of all charges to customers (completeness), audited in the sales transaction test of controls audit program.
B. Revenue
   1. Select a sample of recorded sales invoices and vouch to underlying shipping documents.
   2. Select a sample of shipping documents and trace to sales invoices.
   3. Obtain production records of physical quantities sold and calculate an estimate of sales dollars based on average sale prices.
   4. Compare revenue dollars and physical quantities with prior-year data and industry economic statistics.
   5. Select a sample of sales invoices prepared a few days before and after the balance sheet date and vouch to supporting documents for evidence of proper cutoff.

CHAPTER 10

Learning Objectives

This chapter contains a concise overview of a cycle for the acquisition of goods (inventory) and services (expenses), the acquisition of property, plant, and equipment (fixed assets) and the expenditure of cash (cash disbursements) in connection with paying for the purchases and acquisitions. A series of short cases is used to show the application of audit procedures in situations where errors, irregularities and frauds might be discovered. The chapter ends with special notes on inventory observation and accounts payable completeness. After completing this chapter, you should be able to:

1. Describe the acquisition and expenditure cycle, including typical source documents and controls.

2. Give examples of detail test of controls procedures for auditing the controls over purchase of inventory and services, acquisition of fixed assets and disbursement of cash.

3. Describe some common errors, irregularities and frauds in the acquisition and expenditure cycle, and design some audit and investigation procedures for detecting them.

4. Explain the importance of the completeness assertion for the audit of accounts payable liabilities, and list some procedures for a "search for unrecorded liabilities."

5. Identify and describe considerations involved in the audit observation of physical inventory-taking.

ACQUISITION AND EXPENDITURE CYCLE INCLUDING AUDIT

OF ACCOUNTS PAYABLE AND INVENTORY EXISTENCE

ACQUISITION AND EXPENDITURE CYCLE: TYPICAL ACTIVITIES

LEARNING OBJECTIVE

1. Describe the acquisition and expenditure cycle, including typical source documents and controls.

Exhibit 10–1 shows the activities and transactions involved in an acquisitions and expenditure cycle. The exhibit also lists the accounts and records typically found in this cycle.

The basic acquisition and expenditure activities are (1) purchasing goods and services and (2) paying the bills. As you follow the exhibit, you can track the elements of a control structure described in the sections below.

Authorization

Purchases are requested (requisitioned) by people who know the needs of the organization. A purchasing department seeks the best prices and quality and issues a purchase order to a selected vendor. Obtaining competitive bids is a good practice because it tends to produce the best prices and involves several legitimate suppliers in the process.

Cash disbursements are authorized by an accounts payable department's assembly (voucher) of purchase orders, vendor invoices and internal receiving reports to show a valid obligation to pay. Accounts payable obligations usually are recorded when the purchaser receives the goods or services ordered.

Cheques are signed by a person authorized by the management or the board of directors. A company may have a policy to require two signatures on cheques over a certain amount (e.g., $1,000). Vouchers should be marked "paid" or otherwise stamped to show that they have been processed completely so that they cannot be paid a second time.

Custody

A receiving department inspects the goods received for quantity and quality (producing a receiving report), then puts them in the hands of other responsible persons (e.g., inventory warehousing, fixed asset installation). Services are not "received" in this manner, but they are accepted by responsible persons. Cash "custody" rests largely in the hands of the person or persons authorized to sign cheques.

Another aspect of "custody" involves access to blank documents, such as purchase orders, receiving reports and blank cheques. If unauthorized persons can obtain blank copies of these internal business documents, they can forge a false purchase order to a fictitious vendor, forge a false receiving report, send a false invoice from a fictitious supplier and prepare a company cheque to the fictitious supplier, thereby accomplishing an embezzlement.

Recording

When the purchase order, vendor's invoice and receiving report are in hand, accountants enter the accounts payable, with debits to proper inventory, fixed asset and expense accounts, and with a credit to accounts payable. When cheques are prepared, entries are made to debit the accounts payable and credit cash.

EXHIBIT 10–1   **ACQUISITION AND EXPENDITURE CYCLE**

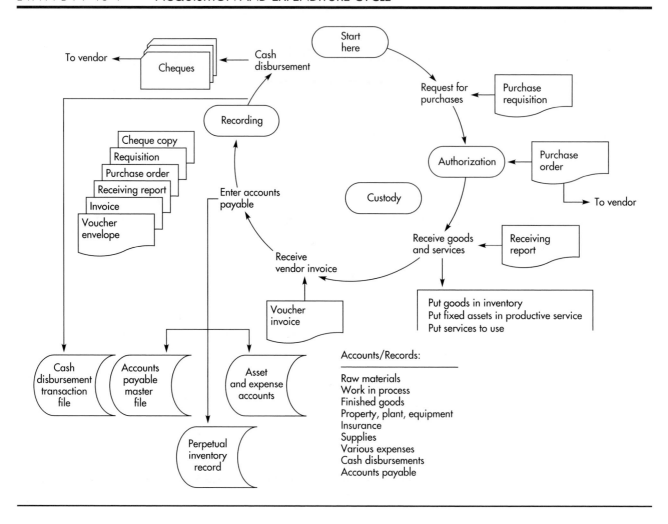

Periodic Reconciliation

A periodic comparison or reconciliation of existing assets to recorded amounts is not shown in Exhibit 10–1, but it occurs in several ways, including physical inventory-taking to compare inventory on hand to perpetual inventory records, bank account reconciliation to compare book cash balances to bank cash balances, inspection of fixed assets to compare to detail fixed asset records, preparation of an accounts payable trial balance to compare the detail of accounts payable to the control account and internal audit confirmation of accounts payable to compare vendors' reports and monthly statements to recorded liabilities.

TOO MUCH TROUBLE

A trucking company self-insured claims of damage to goods in transit, processed claims vouchers and paid customers from its own bank accounts. Several persons were authorized to sign cheques. One person thought it "too much trouble" to stamp the vouchers PAID and said: "That's textbook stuff anyway." Numerous claims were recycled to other cheque signers, and $80,000 in claims were paid in duplicate before the problem was discovered.

> ## Classify the Debits Correctly
>
> Invoices for expensive repairs were not clearly identified, so the accounts payable accountants entered the debits that should have been repairs and maintenance expense as capitalized fixed assets. This initially understated expenses and overstated income by $125,000 one year, although the incorrectly capitalized expenses were written off as depreciation in later years.

AUDIT EVIDENCE IN MANAGEMENT REPORTS

Computer processing of acquisition and payment transactions makes it possible for management to generate several reports that can provide important audit evidence.

Open Purchase Orders
Purchase orders are "open" from the time they are issued until the goods and services are received. They are held in an "open purchase order" file. Generally, no liability exists to be recorded until the transactions are complete. However, auditors may find evidence of losses on purchase commitments in this file if market prices have fallen below the purchase price shown in purchase orders.

Unmatched Receiving Reports
Normally, liabilities should be recorded on the date the goods and services are received and accepted by the receiving department or by another responsible person. Sometimes, however, vendor invoices arrive later. In the meantime, the accounts payable department holds the receiving reports "unmatched" with invoices, awaiting enough information to record an accounting entry. Auditors can inspect the "unmatched receiving report" file report to determine whether the company has material unrecorded liabilities on the financial statement date.

Unmatched Vendor Invoices
Sometimes, vendor invoices arrive in the accounts payable department before the receiving processing is complete. Such invoices are held "unmatched" with receiving reports, awaiting information that the goods and services were actually received and accepted. Auditors can inspect the "unmatched invoice file" and compare it to the "unmatched receiving report" file to determine whether liabilities are unrecorded. Systems failures and human coding errors can cause "unmatched" invoices and related "unmatched" receiving reports to sit around unnoticed when all the information for recording a liability is actually at hand.

Accounts Payable Trial Balance
This trial balance is a list of payable amounts by vendor, and the sum should agree with the accounts payable control account. (Some organizations keep records by individual invoices instead of vendor names, so the trial balance is a list of unpaid invoices. The sum still should agree with the control account balance.) The best kind of trial balance for audit purposes is one that contains the names of all the vendors with whom the organization has done business, even if their balances are zero. The audit "search for unrecorded liabilities" should emphasize the small and zero balances, especially for regular vendors, because these may be the places where liabilities are unrecorded.

All paid and unpaid accounts payable should be supported by a "voucher" or similar document. A "voucher" is a cover sheet, folder or envelope that contains all the supporting documents—purchase requisition (if any), purchase order (if any) vendor invoice, revenue estimates are revised. (The accounting amortization is very similar to depletion of a mineral resource, which depends upon estimates of recoverable minerals and current production.)

Candid Production was not too candid. For example, its recent film of *Bang the Drum Slowly* was forecast to produce $50 million total revenue over six years, although the early box office returns showed only $10 million in the first eight months in the theatres. (Revenue will decline rapidly after initial openings, and video and other revenues depend on the box office success of a film.)

Accounting "control" with respect to film cost amortization resides in the preparation and revision of revenue forecasts. In this case they were overly optimistic, showing the expense recognition and overstating assets and income.

Paper Trail

Revenue forecasts are based on many factors, including facts and assumptions about number of theatres, ticket prices, receipt-sharing agreements, domestic and foreign reviews and moviegoer tastes. Several publications track the box office records of movies. You can see them in newspaper entertainment sections and in industry trade publications. Of course, the production companies themselves are the major source of the information. However, company records also show the revenue realized from each movie.

Revenue forecasts can be checked against actual experience, and the company's history of forecasting accuracy can be determined by comparing actual to forecast over many films and many years.

Amount

Over a four-year period, Candid Productions postponed recognition of a $20 million amortization expense, thus inflating assets and income.

AUDIT APPROACH

Objective

Obtain evidence to determine whether revenue forecasts provide a sufficient basis for calculating film cost amortization and net asset value of films.

Control

Revenue forecasts need to be prepared in a controlled process that documents the facts and underlying assumptions built into the forecast. Forecasts should break down the revenue estimate by years, and the accounting system should produce comparable actual revenue data so that forecast accuracy can be assessed after the fact. Forecast revisions should be prepared in as much detail and documentation as original forecasts.

Test of Controls

The general procedures and methods used by personnel responsible for revenue forecasts should be studied (enquiries and review of documentation), including their sources of information both internal and external. Procedures for review of mechanical aspects (arithmetic) should be tested: Select a sample of finished forecasts and recalculate the final estimate.

Specific procedures for forecast revision also should be studied in the same manner. A review of the accuracy of forecasts of other movies with hindsight on actual revenues helps in a circumstantial way, but past accuracy on different film experiences may not directly influence the forecasts on a new, unique product.

Audit of Balance

The audit of amortization expense concentrates on the content of the forecast itself. The preparation of forecasts used in the amortization calculation should be studied to distinguish underlying reasonable expectations from "hypothetical assumptions." A hypothetical assumption is a statement of a condition that is not necessarily expected to occur, but nonetheless is used to prepare an estimate. For example, a hypothetical assumption is like an "if-then" statement: "If *Bang the Drum Slowly* sells 15 million tickets in the first 12 months of release, then domestic revenue and product sales will be $40 million, and foreign revenue can eventually reach $10 million." Auditors need to assess the reasonableness of the basic 15 million ticket assumption. It helps to have some early actual data from the film's release in hand before the financial statements need to be finished and distributed. For actual data, industry publications ought to be reviewed, with special attention paid to competing films and critics' reviews (yes, movie reviews!)

Discovery Summary

The auditors were not skeptical enough about optimistic revenue forecasts, and they did not weigh unfavourable actual/forecast history comparisons heavily enough. Apparently, they let themselves be convinced by exuberant company executives that the movies were comparable with *Gone with the Wind*! The audit of forecasts and estimates used in accounting determinations is very difficult, especially when company personnel have incentives to hype the numbers, seemingly with conviction about the artistic and commercial merit of their productions. The postponed amortization expense finally came home to roost in big write-offs when the company management changed.

. . . .

R E V I E W
C H E C K P O I N T S

10.12 Give some examples of "receiving departments."

10.13 When is a "blind purchase order" used as a receiving report document?

10.14 The cases on "Printing (Copying) Money," on "Real Cash Paid to Phony Doctors," and on "Retread Tires" all included fictitious people, businesses and locations. Where can an auditor obtain information about them?

10.15 How can analytical procedures be used for discovery of excess costs ("Receiving the Missing Oil") and understated expenses ("Amortize The Drum Slowly")?

10.16 What impact can related party transactions have in some cases of asset valuation?

10.17 How can it help an auditor to know the physical characteristics of inventoried assets?

10.18 Why is "professional scepticism" important for auditors? Give two case examples.

10.19 What evidence could the "verbal enquiry" audit procedure produce in "Printing (Copying) Money"? "Receiving the Missing Oil"? "Go for the Gold"? "Retread Tires"?

· ·

SPECIAL NOTE: THE COMPLETENESS ASSERTION
· · · · · · · · · · · ·

LEARNING OBJECTIVE

4. Explain the importance of the completeness assertion for the audit of accounts payable liabilities, and list some procedures for a "search for unrecorded liabilities."

When considering assertions and obtaining evidence about accounts payable and other liabilities, auditors must put emphasis on the completeness and obligations assertions. (For asset accounts the emphasis is on the existence and rights assertions.) This emphasis on completeness is rightly placed because companies typically are less concerned about timely recording of expenses and liabilities than they are about timely recording of revenues and assets. Of course, generally accepted accounting principles require timely accrual of liabilities and their associated expenses.

Evidence is much more difficult to obtain to verify the completeness assertion than the existence assertion. Auditors cannot rely entirely on a management assertion of completeness, even in combination with a favourable assessment of control risk. Substantive procedures, tests of details or analytical procedures ought to be performed. The **search for unrecorded liabilities** is a set of procedures designed to yield audit evidence of liabilities that were not recorded in the reporting period. Such a search ought normally to be performed up to the report date in the period following the audit client's balance sheet date.

The following is a list of procedures useful in the search for unrecorded liabilities. The audit objective is to search all the places where evidence of them might exist. If these procedures reveal none, the auditors can conclude that all material liabilities are recorded.

1. Scan the open purchase order file at year-end for indications of material purchase commitments at fixed prices. Obtain current prices and determine whether any adjustments for loss and liability for purchase commitments are needed.

2. List the unmatched vendor invoices and determine when the goods were received, looking to the unmatched receiving report file and receiving reports prepared after the year-end. Determine which invoices, if any, should be recorded.

3. Trace the unmatched receiving reports to accounts payable entries, and determine whether ones recorded in the next accounting period need to be adjusted to report them in the current accounting period under audit.

4. Select a sample of cash disbursements from the accounting period following the balance sheet date. Vouch them to supporting documents (invoice, receiving report) to determine whether the related liabilities were recorded in the proper accounting period.

5. Trace the liabilities reported by financial institutions to the accounts. (See the bank confirmation in Exhibit 9–7, Chapter 9. However, a bank really is not expected to search all its files to report all client liabilities to auditors, so the bank confirmation is not the best source of evidence of unrecorded debts.)

6. Study Canada Customs and Revenue Agency notices of assessment for evidence of income or other taxes in dispute, and decide whether actual or estimated liabilities need to be recorded.

7. Confirm accounts payable with vendors, especially regular suppliers showing small or zero balances in the year-end accounts payable. These are the ones most likely to be understated. (Vendors' monthly statements controlled by the auditors also may be used for this procedure.) Be sure to verify the vendors' addresses so that confirmations will not be misdirected—perhaps to conspirators in a scheme to understate liabilities.

8. Study the accounts payable trial balance for indications of dates showing fewer payables than usual recorded near the year-end. (A financial officer may be stashing vendor invoices in a desk drawer instead of recording them.)

9. Review the lawyers' responses to requests for information about pending or threatened litigation, and about unasserted claims and assessments (see Chapter 14). The lawyers' information may signal the need for contingent liability accruals or disclosures. *Handbook Section* 6560.07 recommends that such an enquiry letter be prepared by the client and sent by the auditor.

10. Use a checklist of accrued expenses to determine whether the company has been conscientious about expense and liability accruals, including accruals for wages, interest, utilities, sales and excise taxes, payroll taxes, income taxes, real property taxes, rent, sales commissions, royalties and warranty and guarantee expense.

11. When auditing the details of sales revenue, pay attention to the terms of sales to determine whether any amounts should be deferred as unearned revenue. (Enquiries directed to management about terms of sales, such as enquiries about customers' rights of cancellation or return, can be used to obtain initial information.)

12. Prepare or obtain a schedule of casualty insurance on fixed assets, and determine the adequacy of insurance in relation to asset market values. Inadequate insurance and self-insurance should be disclosed in the notes to the financial statements.

13. Confirm life insurance policies with insurance companies to ask whether the company has any loans against the cash value of the insurance. In this confirmation, request the names of the beneficiaries of the policies. If the insurance is for the benefit of a party other than the company, the beneficiaries may be creditors on unrecorded loans. Make enquiries about the business purpose of making insurance proceeds payable to other parties.

14. Review the terms of debt due within one year but classified long-term because the company plans to refinance it on a long-term basis. Holders of the debt or financial institutions must have shown (preferably in writing) a willingness to refinance the debt before it can be classified long-term. Classification cannot be based solely on management's expressed intent to seek long-term financing.

15. Apply analytical procedures appropriate in the circumstances. In general, accounts payable volume and period-end balances should increase when the company experiences increases in physical production volume or engages in inventory stockpiling. Some liabilities may be functionally related to other activities, for example, sales taxes are functionally related to sales dollar totals, payroll taxes to payroll totals, excise taxes to sales dollars or volume and income taxes to income.

· ·

R E V I E W   10.20   Describe the purpose and give examples of audit procedures in the "search for
CHECKPOINTS   unrecorded liabilities."

10.21   Explain the difference in approach in confirmation of accounts receivable and accounts payable.

10.22   In substantive auditing, why is the emphasis on the completeness assertion for liabilities instead of on the existence assertion as in the audit of assets?

· ·

SPECIAL NOTE: PHYSICAL INVENTORY OBSERVATION

LEARNING OBJECTIVE

5. Identify and describe considerations involved in the audit observation of physical inventory-taking.

In an audit engagement, the audit procedures for inventory and related cost of sales accounts frequently are extensive. A 96-page joint CICA–AICPA auditing technique study entitled *Audit of Inventories* (CICA, 1986) describes many facets of inherent risk and control risk, and of the process of obtaining evidence about inventory financial statement assertions. The significance of inventories is acknowledged in the following quotation:

> Generally, inventories reflect the characteristics of a business more than any other asset. Significant to manufacturing, wholesale, and retail organizations, inventories frequently are also material to the financial statements of service organizations. It has been estimated that, for some types of businesses, inventories constitute 20 to 25 percent of total assets and represent the largest current asset.[1]

A material error or irregularity in inventory has a pervasive effect on financial statements. Errors in inventory cause misstatements in current assets, working capital, total assets, cost of sales, gross margin and net income. While analytical procedures can help indicate inventory presentation problems, the auditors' best opportunity to detect inventory errors and irregularities is during the physical observation of the client's inventory count taken by company personnel. (Auditors observe the inventory-taking and make test counts, but they seldom actually take (count) the entire inventory.) Auditing standards express the requirement for inventory observation in *Section* 6030.04: "Usually, the checking of the quantities is accomplished most conveniently by observing and noting the counts made by the client's staff, but actual test counts are often undertaken by the auditors, before, during or after the client's physical stocktaking." ISA 501.5 expresses a similar requirement.

The remainder of this special note gives details about auditors' observation of physical inventory-taking. The first task is to review the client's inventory-taking instructions. The instructions should include the following:

1. Names of client personnel responsible for the count.
2. Dates and times of inventory-taking.
3. Names of client personnel who will participate in the inventory-taking.
4. Instructions for recording accurate descriptions of inventory items, for count and double-count, and for measuring or translating physical quantities (such as counting by measures of litres, barrels, meters, dozens).
5. Instructions for making notes of obsolete or worn items.
6. Instructions for the use of tags, punched cards, count sheets or other media devices and for their collection and control.
7. Plans for shutting down plant operations or for taking inventory after store closing hours, and plans for having goods in proper places (such as on store shelves instead of on the floor, or in a warehouse rather than in transit to a job).
8. Plans for counting or controlling movement of goods in receiving and shipping areas if those operations are not shut down during the count.
9. Instructions for computer compilation of the count media (such as tags, punch cards) into final inventory listings or summaries.
10. Instructions for pricing the inventory items.
11. Instructions for review and approval of the inventory count; notations of obsolescence or other matters by supervisory personnel.

These instructions characterize a well-planned counting operation. As the plan is carried out, the independent auditors should be present to hear the count instructions being given to the client's count teams and to observe the instructions being followed.

---

[1] James Carty, "Ask the Right Questions about Inventory," *World Accounting Report*, January 1984, p. 20.

Many physical inventories are counted at the year-end when the auditor is present to observe. The auditors can perform dual-direction testing by (1) selecting inventory items from a perpetual inventory master file, going to the location and obtaining a test count, which produces evidence for the existence assertion; and (2) selecting inventory from locations on the warehouse floor, obtaining a test count and tracing the count to the final inventory compilation, which produces evidence for the completeness assertion. If the company does not have perpetual records and a file to test for existence, the auditors must be careful to obtain a record of all the counts and use it for the existence-direction tests.

However, the following other situations frequently occur.

Physical Inventory Not on Year-End Date

Clients sometimes count the inventory on a date other than the balance sheet date, either before or after. When the auditors are present to make their physical observation, they follow the procedures outlined above for observation of the physical count. However, with a time period intervening between the count date and the year-end, additional roll-forward or rollback auditing procedures must be performed on purchase, inventory addition and issue transactions during that period. The inventory on the count date is reconciled to the year-end inventory by appropriate addition or subtraction of the intervening receiving and issue transactions.

Cycle Inventory Counting

Some companies count inventory on a cycle basis or use a statistical counting plan but never take a complete count on a single date. In these circumstances the auditors must understand the cycle or sampling plan and evaluate its appropriateness. In this type of situation the auditors are present for some counting operations. Only under unusual circumstances and as an "extended procedure" are auditors present every month (or more frequently) to observe all counts. Businesses that count inventory in this manner purport to have accurate perpetual records and carry out the counting as a means of testing the records and maintaining their accuracy.

The auditors must be present during some counting operations to evaluate the counting plans and their execution. The procedures for an annual count enumerated above are utilized, test counts are made and the audit team is responsible for a conclusion concerning the accuracy (control) of perpetual records.

Auditors Not Present at Client's Inventory Count

This situation can arise on a first audit when the audit firm is appointed after the beginning inventory already has been counted. The auditors must review the client's plan for the already completed count as before. Some test counts of current inventory should be made and traced to current records to make a conclusion about the reliability of perpetual records. If the actual count was recent, intervening transaction activity may be reconciled back to the beginning inventory.

However, the reconciliation of more than a few months' transactions to unobserved beginning inventories may be very difficult. The auditors may employ procedures utilizing such interrelationships as sales activity, physical volume, price variation, standard costs and gross profit margins for the decision about beginning inventory reasonableness. Nevertheless, much care must be exercised in "backing into" the audit of a previous inventory. If the auditors cannot satisfy themselves as to the beginning inventory balance, then a reservation in the auditor's report is normally called for (*Section* 6030.17).

Inventories Located Off the Client's Premises

The auditors must determine where and in what dollar amounts inventories are located off the client's premises, in the custody of consignees or in public warehouses. If amounts are material and if control is not exceptionally strong, the audit team may wish to visit these locations and conduct on-site test counts. However, if amounts are not material and/or if related evidence is adequate (such as periodic reports, cash receipts, receivables records, shipping records) and if control risk is low, then direct confirmation with the custodian may be considered sufficient appropriate evidence of the existence of quantities (*Section 6030.07*). Note that confirmation is normally expected by the CICA for two items—accounts receivable and off-premise inventories.

INVENTORY COUNT AND MEASUREMENT CHALLENGES

Examples	Challenges
Lumber.	Problem identifying quality or grade.
Piles of sugar, coal, scrap steel.	Geometric computations, aerial photos.
Items weighed on scales.	Check scales for accuracy.
Bulk materials (oil, grain, liquids in storage tanks).	Climb the tanks. Dip measuring rods. Sample for assay or chemical analysis.
Diamonds, jewellery.	Identification and quality determination problems. Ask a specialist.
Pulp wood.	Quantity measurement estimation. Aerial photos.
Livestock.	Movement not controllable. Count critter's legs and divide by four (two for chickens).

Source: (adapted): CICA, Audit of Inventories, *Auditing Procedure Study* (1986), p. 28.

Inventory Existence and Completeness

The physical observation procedures are designed to audit for existence and completeness (physical quantities) and valuation (recalculation of appropriate FIFO, specific item or other pricing at cost and lower-of-cost-or-market write-down of obsolete or worn inventory). After the observation is complete, auditors should have sufficient appropriate evidence of the following physical quantities and valuations:

- Goods in the perpetual records but not owned were excluded from the inventory compilation.
- Goods on hand were counted and included in the inventory compilation.
- Goods consigned-out or stored in outside warehouses (goods owned but not on hand) were included in the inventory compilation.
- Goods in transit (goods actually purchased and recorded but not yet received) were added to the inventory count and included in the inventory compilation.
- Goods on hand already sold (but not yet delivered) were not counted and were excluded from the inventory compilation.
- Goods consigned-in (goods on hand but not owned) were excluded from the inventory compilation.

R E V I E W
C H E C K P O I N T S

10.23 In the review of a client's inventory-taking instructions, for what characteristics are the auditors looking?

10.24 Explain dual-direction sampling in the context of inventory test counts.

10.25 What procedures are employed to audit inventory when the physical inventory is taken on a cycle basis or on a statistical plan, but never a complete count on a single date?

SUMMARY

The acquisition and expenditure cycle consists of purchase requisitioning, purchase ordering, receiving goods and services, recording vendors' invoices and accounting for accounts payable and making disbursements of cash. Companies reduce control risk by having a suitable separation of authorization, custody, recording and periodic reconciliation duties. Error-checking procedures of comparing purchase orders and receiving reports to vendor invoices are important for recording proper amounts of accounts payable liabilities. Supervisory control is provided by having a separation of duties between preparing cash disbursement cheques and actually signing them. Otherwise, many things could go wrong, ranging from processing false or fictitious purchase orders to failing to record liabilities for goods and services received.

Cash disbursement is a critical point for asset control. Many cases of embezzlement occur in this process. Illustrative cases in the chapter told of some embezzlement schemes, mostly involving payment of fictitious charges to dummy companies set up by employees.

Two topics had special technical notes in the chapter. The completeness assertion is very important in the audit of liabilities because misleading financial statements often have contained unrecorded liabilities and expenses. The "search for unrecorded liabilities" is an important set of audit procedures. The physical inventory observation audit work received a special section because actual contact with inventories (and fixed assets, for that matter) provides auditors with direct eyewitness evidence of important tangible assets.

MULTIPLE-CHOICE QUESTIONS FOR PRACTICE AND REVIEW

Questions 10.26 to 10.30 are located on the CD-ROM that accompanies this textbook.

10.31 When verifying debits to the perpetual inventory records of a nonmanufacturing company, an auditor would be most interested in examining a sample of purchase:
   a. Approvals.
   b. Requisitions.
   c. Invoices.
   d. Orders.

10.32 Which of the following is an internal control weakness for a company whose inventory of supplies consists of a large number of individual items?
   a. Supplies of relatively little value are expensed when purchased.
   b. The cycle basis is used for physical counts.
   c. The warehouse manager is responsible for maintenance of perpetual inventory records.
   d. Perpetual inventory records are maintained only for items of significant value.

10.33 An effective internal control procedure that protects against the preparation of improper or inaccurate cash disbursements would be to require that all cheques be:
   a. Signed by an officer after necessary supporting evidence has been examined.
   b. Reviewed by the treasurer before mailing.
   c. Sequentially numbered and accounted for by internal auditors.
   d. Perforated or otherwise effectively cancelled when they are returned with the bank statement.

10.34 A client's purchasing system ends with the recording of a liability and its eventual payment. Which of the following best describes the auditor's primary concern with respect to liabilities resulting from the purchasing system?
   a. Accounts payable are not materially understated.
   b. Authority to incur liabilities is restricted to one designated person.
   c. Acquisition of materials is not made from one vendor or one group of vendors.
   d. Commitments for all purchases are made only after established competitive bidding procedures are followed.

10.35 Which of the following is an internal control procedure that would prevent a paid disbursement voucher from being presented for payment a second time?
   a. Vouchers should be prepared by individuals who are responsible for signing disbursement cheques.
   b. Disbursement vouchers should be approved by a least two responsible management officials.
   c. The date on a disbursement voucher should be within a few days of the date the voucher is presented for payment.
   d. The official signing the cheque should compare the cheque with the voucher and should stamp "paid" on the voucher documents.

10.36 Which of the following procedures would best detect the theft of valuable items from an inventory that consists of hundreds of different items selling for $1 to $10 and a few items selling for hundreds of dollars?

a. Maintain a perpetual inventory of only the more valuable items with frequent periodic verification of the validity of the perpetual inventory record.

b. Have an independent CPA firm prepare an internal control report on the effectiveness of the administrative and accounting controls over inventory.

c. Have separate warehouse space for the more valuable items with frequent periodic physical counts and comparison to perpetual inventory records.

10.37 Budd, the purchasing agent of Lake Hardware Wholesalers, has a relative who owns a retail hardware store. Budd arranged for hardware to be delivered by manufacturers to the retail store on a COD basis, thereby enabling his relative to buy at Lake's wholesale prices. Budd was probably able to accomplish this because of Lake's poor internal control over:

a. Purchase requisitions.
b. Cash receipts.
c. Perpetual inventory records.
d. Purchase orders.

10.38 Which of the following is the best audit procedure for determining the existence of unrecorded liabilities?

a. Examine confirmation requests by creditors whose accounts appear on a subsidiary trial balance of accounts payable.

b. Examine a sample of cash disbursements in the period subsequent to the year-end.

c. Examine a sample of invoices a few days prior to and subsequent to the year-end to ascertain whether they have been properly recorded.

d. Examine unusual relationships between monthly accounts payable and recorded purchases.

10.39 When evaluating inventory controls with respect to segregation of duties, a PA would be least likely to:

a. Inspect documents.
b. Make enquiries.
c. Observe procedures.
d. Consider policy and procedure manuals.

10.40 An auditor will usually trace the details of the test counts made during the observation of the physical inventory taking to a final inventory compilation. This audit procedure is undertaken to provide evidence that items physically present and observed by the auditor at the time of the physical inventory count are:

a. Owned by the client.
b. Not obsolete.
c. Physically present at the time of the preparation of the final inventory schedule.
d. Included in the final inventory schedule.

10.41 Which of the following procedures is least likely to be performed before the balance sheet date?

a. Observation of inventory.
b. Review of internal control over cash disbursements.
c. Search for unrecorded liabilities.
d. Confirmation of receivables.

10.42 The physical count of inventory of a retailer was higher than shown by the perpetual records. Which of the following could explain the difference?

a. Inventory items had been counted but the tags placed on the items had not been taken off the items and added to the inventory accumulation sheets.

b. Credit memos for several items returned by customers had not been recorded.

c. No journal entry had been made on the retailer's books for several items returned to its suppliers.

d. An item purchased "FOB shipping point" had not arrived at the date of the inventory count and was not reflected in the perpetual records.

10.43 From the auditor's point of view, inventory counts are more acceptable prior to the year-end when:

a. Internal control is weak.
b. Accurate perpetual inventory records are maintained.
c. Inventory is slow moving.
d. Significant amounts of inventory are held on a consignment basis.

10.44 To determine whether accounts payable are complete, an auditor performs a test to verify that all merchandise received is recorded. The population for this test consists of all:

a. Vendors' invoices.
b. Purchase orders.
c. Receiving reports.
d. Cancelled cheques.

10.45 Which of the following internal control procedures most likely addresses the completeness assertion for inventory?

a. The work in process account is periodically reconciled with subsidiary inventory records.

b. Employees responsible for the custody of finished goods do not perform the receiving function.

c. Receiving reports are prenumbered and the numbering sequence is checked periodically.

d. There is a separation of duties between the payroll department and inventory accounting personnel.

(AICPA adapted)

Exercises and Problems

10.46 The essential characteristic of the liabilities control system is to separate the authorization and approval to initiate a transaction from the responsibility for recordkeeping. What would constitute the authorization for vouchers (accounts) payable recording? What documentary evidence could auditors examine as evidence of this authorization?

10.47 The use of prenumbered documents is an important feature for control to ensure that all valid transactions are recorded and none are omitted. How could auditors gather evidence that the control for completeness of cash disbursements was being used properly by a company?

10.48 Two "automatic transactions" can be produced in a computerized accounting system: (1) cheque printing and signature and (2) purchase order at a preprogrammed stock reorder point. Assume management is uncomfortable with the computer creating transactions. How could management delay these transactions until they were "viewed" and authorized?

10.49 Why should auditors be concerned with the adequacy of casualty insurance coverage of a client's physical property?

10.50 What evidence regarding inventories and cost of sales can the auditor typically obtain from verbal enquiry?

10.51 Auditors plan their audit procedures to gather evidence about management's assertions in the financial statements. In addition to the broad assertions, such as existence and completeness, specific assertions are made for each major account area. List 9 or 10 examples of such specific assertions for the fixed assets and related accounts.

10.52 Why should the Repairs and Maintenance expense account be audited at the same time as the fixed asset accounts?

10.53 Audit procedures may be classified as:
Physical observation.
Recalculation.
Confirmation.
Examination of documents (vouching and tracing).
Verbal enquiry.
Scanning.
Analytical procedures.

Required:

Describe how each procedure may be used to gather evidence on fixed assets and which broad financial statement assertion(s) (existence, completeness, rights, valuation or allocation, and presentation and disclosure) is being addressed by the use of the procedure.

TEST OF CONTROLS AUDIT PROCEDURES

10.54 Payable ICQ Items: Control Objectives, Test of Controls Procedures and Possible Errors or Irregularities. Listed below is a selection of items from the internal control questionnaire on payables shown in Appendix 10A.
1. Are invoices, receiving reports and purchase orders reviewed by the cheque signer?
2. Are cheques dated in the cheque register with the date of the cheque?
3. Are quantity and quality of goods received determined at time of receipt by receiving personnel independent of the purchasing department?
4. Are vendors' invoices matched against purchase orders and receiving reports before a liability is recorded?

Required:
For each one:
a. Identify the control objective to which it applies.
b. Specify one test of controls audit procedure an auditor could use to determine whether the control was operating effectively.

EXHIBIT 10.55–1   **MAYLOU CORPORATION—DOCUMENT FLOWCHART FOR PURCHASES**

c. Using your business experience, your logic or your imagination, or all three, give an example of an error or irregularity that could occur if the control was absent or ineffective.

10.55 Purchasing Control Procedures. Long, PA, has been engaged to examine and report on the financial statements of Maylou Corporation. During the review phase of the study of Maylou's system of internal control over purchases, Long was given the following document flowchart for purchases (see Exhibit 10.55–1).

Required:
Identify the procedures relating to purchase requisitions and purchase orders that Long would expect to find if Maylou's system of internal control over purchases is effective. For example, purchase orders are prepared only after giving proper consideration to the time to order and quantity to order. Do not comment on the effectiveness of the flow of documents as presented in the flowchart or on separation of duties.

(AICPA adapted)

10.56 Test of Controls Procedures for Cash Disbursements. The Runge Controls Corporation manufactures and markets electrical control systems: temperature controls, machine controls, burglar alarms and the like. Electrical and semiconductor parts are acquired from outside vendors, and systems are assembled in Runge's plant. The company incurs other administrative and operating expenditures. Liabilities for goods and services purchased are entered in a vouchers payable journal, at which time the debits are classified to the asset and expense accounts to which they apply. The company has specified control procedures for approving vendor invoices for payment, for signing cheques, for keeping records and for reconciling the chequing accounts. The procedures appear to be well specified and placed in operation. You are the senior auditor on the engagement, and you need to specify a program (list) of test of controls procedures to audit the effectiveness of the controls over cash disbursements.

Required:
Using the seven general internal control objectives, specify two or more test of controls procedures to audit the effectiveness of typical control procedures. (Hint: From one sample of recorded cash disbursements, you can specify procedures related to several objectives. See Exhibit 10–3 for examples of test of controls procedures over cash disbursements.) Organize your list according to the example shown below for the "completeness" objective.

(AICPA adapted)

Completeness Objective	Test of Controls Program
All valid cash disbursements are recorded and none are omitted.	Determine the numerical sequence of cheques issued during the period and scan the sequence for missing numbers. Scan the accounts payable records for amounts that appear to be too long outstanding indicating liabilities for which payment may have been made but not recorded properly).

LIABILITIES: SUBSTANTIVE PROCEDURES

10.57 Unrecorded Liabilities Procedures. You were in the final stages of your audit of the financial statements of Ozine Corporation for the year ended December 31, 2002, when you were consulted by the corporation's president. The president believes there is no point to your examining the 2003 voucher register and testing data in support of 2003 entries. He stated: (1) bills pertaining to 2002 that were received too late to be included in the December voucher register were recorded as of the year-end by the corporation by journal entry; (2) the internal auditor made tests after the year-end; and (3) he would furnish you with a letter certifying that there were no unrecorded liabilities.

Required:
a. Should your procedures for unrecorded liabilities be affected by the fact that the client made a journal entry to record 2002 bills that were received later? Explain.
b. Should your test for unrecorded liabilities be affected by the fact that a letter is obtained in which a responsible management official certifies that to the best of his knowledge all liabilities have been recorded? Explain.
c. Should your test for unrecorded liabilities be eliminated or reduced because of the internal audit work? Explain.
d. What sources, in addition to the 2003 voucher register, should you consider to locate possible unrecorded liabilities?

(AICPA adapted)

10.58 Accounts Payable Confirmations. Clark and his partner, Kent, both PAs, are planning their audit program for the audit of accounts payable on the LeClair Corporation's annual audit. Saturday afternoon they reviewed the thick file of last year's working papers, and both of them remembered all too well the six days they spent last year on accounts payable.

Last year, Clark had suggested that they mail confirmations to 100 of LeClair's suppliers. The company regularly purchases from about 1,000 suppliers and these account payable balances fluctuate widely, depending on the volume of purchase and the terms LeClair's purchasing agent is able to negotiate. Clark's sample of 100 was designed to include accounts with large balances. In fact, the 100 accounts confirmed last year covered 80 percent of the total accounts payable.

Both Clark and Kent spent many hours tracking down minor differences reported in confirmation responses. Nonresponding accounts were investigated by comparing LeClair's balance with monthly statements received from suppliers.

Required:
a. Identify the accounts payable audit objectives that the auditors must consider in determining the audit procedures to be performed.
b. Identify situations when the auditors should use accounts payable confirmations, and discuss whether they are required to use them.
c. Discuss why the use of large dollar balances as the basis for selecting accounts payable for confirmation may not be the most efficient approach, and indicate a more efficient sample selection procedure that could be followed when choosing accounts payable for confirmation.

INVENTORY AND FIXED ASSETS: SUBSTANTIVE PROCEDURES

10.59 Inventory Count Observation: Planning and Substantive Audit Procedures. Sammy Smith is the partner in charge of the audit of Blue Distributing Corporation, a wholesaler that owns one warehouse containing 80 percent of its inventory. Sammy is reviewing the working papers that were prepared to support the firm's opinion on Blue's financial statements. Sammy wants to be certain essential audit procedures are well documented in the working papers.

Required:
a. What evidence should Sammy expect to find that the audit observation of the client's physical count of inventory was well planned and that assistants were properly supervised?
b. What substantive audit procedures should Sammy find in the working papers that document management's assertions about existence and completeness of inventory quantities at the end of the year? (Refer to Appendix 18B for procedures.)

(AICPA adapted)

10.60 Sales/Inventory Cutoff. Your client took a complete physical inventory count under your observation as of December 15 and adjusted the inventory control account (perpetual inventory method) to agree with the physical inventory. Based on the count adjustments as of December 15 and after review of the transactions recorded from December 16 to December 31, you are almost ready to accept the inventory balance as fairly stated.

However, your review of the sales cut-off as of December 15 and December 31 disclosed the following items not previously considered:

Cost	Sales Price	Shipped	Date Billed	Credited to Inventory Control
$28,400	$36,900	12/14	12/16	12/16
39,100	50,200	12/10	12/19	12/10
18,900	21,300	1/2	12/31	12/31

Required:
What adjusting journal entries, if any, would you make for each of these items? Explain why each adjustment is necessary.

(AICPA adapted)

10.61 Statistical Sampling Used to Estimate Inventory. ACE Corporation does not conduct a complete annual physical count of purchased parts and supplies in its principal warehouse but, instead, uses statistical sampling to estimate the year-end inventory. Ace maintains a perpetual inventory record of parts and supplies. Management believes that statistical sampling is highly effective in determining inventory values and is sufficiently reliable that a physical count of each item of inventory is unnecessary.

Required:
a. List at least 10 normal audit procedures that should be performed to verify physical quantities whenever a client conducts a periodic physical count of all or part of its inventory (see Appendix 18B for procedures).
b. Identify the audit procedures you should use that change or are in addition to normal required audit procedures (in addition to those listed in your solution to part [a]) when a client utilizes statistical sampling to determine inventory value and does not conduct a 100 percent annual physical count of inventory items.

(AICPA adapted)

10.62 Inventory Procedures Using Generalized Audit Software. You are conducting an audit of the financial statements of a wholesale cosmetics distributor with an inventory consisting of thousands of individual items. The distributor keeps its inventory in its own distribution centre and in two public warehouses. A perpetual inventory computer database is maintained on a computer disk. The database is updated at the end of each business day. Each individual record of the perpetual inventory database contains the following data:

Item number.
Location of item.
Description of item.
Quantity on hand.
Cost per item.
Date of last purchase.
Date of last sale.
Quantity sold during year.

You are planning to observe the distributor's physical count of inventories as of a given date. You will have available a computer tape, provided by the client, of the above items taken from their database as of the date of the physical count. Your firm has a generalized audit software package that will run on the client's computer.

Required:
List the basic inventory auditing procedures and, for each, describe how the use of the general-purpose audit software package and the tape of the perpetual inventory database might be helpful to the auditor in performing such auditing procedures. (See Appendix 10B for substantive audit procedures for inventory.)

Organize your answer as follows:

Basic inventory auditing procedures	How general purpose audit software package and tape of the inventory tape file data might be helpful

(AICPA adapted)

10.63 Manufacturing Equipment and Accumulated Depreciation. In connection with a recurring examination of the financial statements of the Louis Manufacturing Company for the year ended December 31, you have been assigned the audit of the fixed assets accounts (Manufacturing Equipment, Manufacturing Equipment—Accumulated Depreciation, and Repairs to Manufacturing Equipment). Your review of Louis's policies and procedures has disclosed the following pertinent information:
1. The Manufacturing Equipment account includes the net invoice price plus related freight and installation costs for all of the equipment in Louis's manufacturing plant.

2. The Manufacturing Equipment—Accumulated Depreciation accounts are supported by a subsidiary ledger, which shows the cost and accumulated depreciation for each piece of equipment.

3. An annual budget for capital expenditures of $1,000 or more is prepared by the executive committee and approved by the board of directors. Capital expenditures over $1,000 that are not included in this budget must be approved by the board of directors, and variations of 20 percent or more must be explained to the board. Approval by the supervisor of production is required for capital expenditures under $1,000.

4. Company employees handle installation, removal, repair and rebuilding of the machinery. Work orders are prepared for these activities and are subject to the same budgetary control as other expenditures. Work orders are not required for external expenditures.

Required:

a. Prepare a list of the major specific objectives (assertions) for your audit of the Manufacturing Equipment, Manufacturing Equipment—Accumulated Depreciation, and Repairs of Manufacturing Equipment accounts. Do not include in this listing the auditing procedures designed to accomplish these objectives.

b. Prepare the portion of your audit program applicable to the review of current-year additions to the Manufacturing Equipment account. (You will find Appendix 18B helpful, although it does not specifically mention manufacturing equipment.)

(AICPA adapted)

DISCUSSION CASES

10.64 Peacock Company: Incomplete Flowchart of Inventory and Purchasing Control Procedures. Peacock Company is a wholesaler of soft goods. The inventory is composed of approximately 3,500 different items. The company employs a computerized batch processing system to maintain its perpetual inventory records. The system is run each weekend so that inventory reports are available on Monday morning for management use. The system has been functioning satisfactorily for the past 15 months, providing the company with accurate records and timely reports.

The preparation of purchase orders has been automatic as a part of the inventory system to ensure that the company will maintain enough inventory to meet customer demand. When an item of inventory falls below a predetermined level, a record of the inventory items is written. This record is used in conjunction with the vendor file to prepare the purchase orders.

Exception reports are prepared during the update of the inventory and the preparation of the purchase orders. These reports list any errors or exceptions identified during the processing. In addition, the system provides for management approval of all purchase orders exceeding a specified amount. Any exceptions or items requiring management approval are handled by supplemental runs on Monday morning and are combined with the weekend results.

A system flowchart of Peacock Company's inventory and purchase order procedure is in Exhibit 10.64–1.

Required:

a. The illustrated system flowchart (Exhibit 10.64–1) of Peacock Company's inventory and purchase order system was prepared before the system was fully operational. Several steps that are important to the successful operations of the system were inadvertently omitted from the chart. Now that the system is operating effectively, management wants the system documentation complete and would like the flowchart corrected. Describe the steps that have been omitted and indicate where the omissions have occurred. The flowchart does not need to be redrawn.

b. In order for Peacock's inventory/purchase order system to function properly, control procedures should be included in the system. Describe the type of control procedures Peacock Company should use in its system to ensure proper functioning, and indicate where these procedures would be placed in the system.

(CMA adapted)

EXHIBIT 10.64–1   **PEACOCK COMPANY—INVENTORY AND PURCHASE ORDER PROCEDURE**

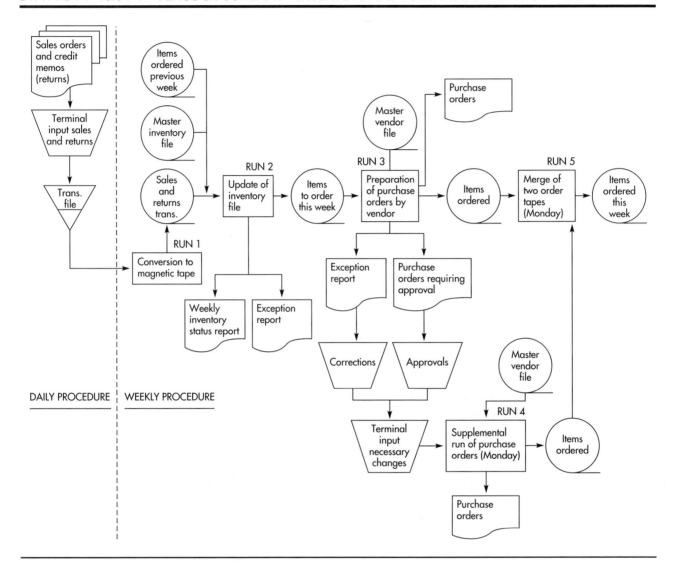

10.65 Inventory Evidence and Long-Term Purchase Contracts. During the audit of Mason Company, Inc., for the calendar year 2002, you noticed that the company produces aluminum cans at the rate of about 40 million units annually. On the plant tour, you noticed a large stockpile of raw aluminum in storage. Your inventory observation and pricing procedures showed this stockpile to be the raw materials inventory of 400 tons valued at $240,000 (LIFO cost). Enquiry with the production chief yielded the information that 400 tons was about a four-month supply of raw materials.

Suppose you learn that Mason had executed a firm long-term purchase contract with All Purpose Aluminum Company to purchase raw materials on the following schedule:

| | Quantity | |
Delivery Date	Quantity (tons)	Total Price
January 30, 2003	500	$300,000
June 30, 2003	700	420,000
December 30, 2003	1,000	500,000

Because of recent economic conditions, principally a decline in the demand for raw aluminum and a consequent oversupply, the price stood at 40 cents per pound as of January 15, 2003. Commodities experts predict that this low price will prevail for 12 to 15 months or until there is a general economic recovery.

Required:
a. Describe the procedures you would employ to gather evidence about this contract (including its initial discovery).
b. What facts recited in the problems are ones that you would have to discover for yourself in an audit?
c. Discuss the effect this contract has on the financial statements.

10.66 Deake Corporation: Property Accounting System. Deake Corporation is a medium-sized, diversified manufacturing company. Recently, Jack Richards was promoted to manager of the property accounting section. Richards is having difficulty responding to some of the requests from individuals in other departments for information about the company's fixed assets. Some of the requests are:

1. The controller has requested schedules of individual fixed assets to support the balances in the general ledger. Richards has furnished the necessary information, but it was late. The manner in which the records are organized makes it difficult to obtain information easily.
2. The maintenance manager wishes to verify the existence of a punch press he thinks was repaired twice. He has asked Richards to confirm the asset number and location of the press.
3. The insurance department wants data on the cost and book values of assets to include in its review of current insurance coverage.
4. The tax department has requested data that can be used to determine when Deake should switch depreciation methods for tax purposes.
5. The company's internal auditors have spent a significant amount of time in the property accounting section recently, attempting to audit the annual depreciation expense.

The property account records consist of a set of manual books. These records show the date the asset was acquired, the account number for the asset, the dollar amount capitalized and the estimated useful life of the asset for depreciation purposes.

After many frustrations, Richards has realized that his records are inadequate and that he cannot supply data when requested. He has decided to discuss his problem with the controller, Jim Castle.

Richards: Jim, something has got to give. My people are working overtime and can't keep up. You worked in property accounting before you became controller. You know I can't tell the tax, insurance and maintenance people everything they need to know from my records. Also, that internal auditing team is living in my area and that slows down the work pace. The requests of these people are reasonable, and we should be able to answer these questions and provide the needed data. I think we need a computerized property accounting system. I would like to talk to the information systems people to see if they can help me.

Castle: Jack, I think you have a good idea, but be sure you are personally involved in the design of any system so you get all the information you need.

Required:
a. Identify and justify four major objectives Deake Corporation's computerized property accounting system should possess to provide the data necessary to respond to requests for information by company personnel.
b. Identify the data that should be included in the computer record for each asset included in the property account.

(CMA adapted)

10.67 Grover Manufacturing—Purchasing Defalcation. On January 11 at the beginning of your annual audit of the Grover Manufacturing Company's financial statements for the year just ended December 31, the company president confides to you that an employee is living on a scale in excess of that which his salary would support.

The employee has been a buyer in the purchasing department for six years and has charge of purchasing all general materials and supplies. He is authorized to sign purchase orders for amounts up to $2,000. Purchase orders in excess of $2,000 require the countersignature of the general purchasing agent.

The president understands that the usual audit of financial statements is not designed to disclose immaterial fraud or conflicts of interest, although such events may be discovered. The president authorizes you, however, to expand your regular audit procedures and to apply additional audit procedures to determine whether there is any evidence that the buyer has been misappropriating company funds or has been engaged in activities that are a conflict of interest.

Required:

List the audit procedures that you would apply to the company records and documents in an attempt to:

1. Discover evidence within the purchasing department of defalcations being committed by the buyer. Give the purpose of each audit procedure.
2. Provide leads about possible collusion between the buyer and suppliers. Give the purpose of each audit procedure.

INSTRUCTIONS FOR DISCUSSION CASES 10.68–10.71.

These cases are designed like the ones in the chapter. They give the problem, the method, the paper trail and the amount. Your assignment is to write the audit approach portion of the case, organized around these sections:

Objective: Express the objective in terms of the facts supposedly asserted in financial records, accounts and statements. (Refer to discussion of assertions in Chapter 9.)

Control: Write a brief explanation of desirable controls, missing controls and especially the kinds of "deviations" that might arise from the situation described in the case.

Test of controls: Write some procedures for getting evidence about existing controls, especially procedures that could discover deviations from controls. If there are no controls to test, then there are no procedures to perform; go then to the next section. A "procedure" should instruct someone about the source(s) of evidence to tap and the work to do.

Audit of balance: Write some procedures for getting evidence about the existence, completeness, valuation, ownership or disclosure assertions identified in your objective section above. (Refer to Appendix 10B for suggestions.)

Discovery summary: Write a short statement about the discovery you expect to accomplish with your procedures.

10.68 Financial Reporting: Overstated Inventory and Profits (duplicated in Chapter 18: Case 18.56). Follow the instructions above. For this case, recalculate the income (loss) before taxes using the correct inventory figures. (Assume the correct beginning amount two years ago was $5.5 million.)

THE PHANTOM OF THE INVENTORY

Problem: Overstated physical inventory caused understated cost of goods sold and overstated net income, current assets, total assets and retained earnings.

Method: All Bright Company manufactured lamps. Paul M., manager of the Katherine Street plant, was under pressure to produce profits so that the company could maintain its loans at the bank. The loans were secured by the inventory of 1,500 types of finished goods, work in process and parts used for making lamps (bases, shades, wire, nuts, bolts and so on). Paul arranged the physical inventory counting procedures and accompanied the external audit team while the external auditors observed the count and made test counts after the company personnel had recorded their counts on tags attached to the inventory locations. At the auditors' request, Paul directed them to the "most valuable" inventory for their test count, although he did not show them all of the most valuable types. When the auditors were looking the other way, Paul raised the physical count on inventory tags the auditors would not include in their test counts. When everyone had finished each floor of the multistory warehouse, all the tags were gathered and sent to data processing for computer compilation and pricing at FIFO cost.

Paper trail: All Bright had no perpetual inventory records. All the record of the inventory quantity and pricing was in the count tags and the priced compilation, which was produced by the data processing department six weeks later. The auditors traced their test counts to the compilation and did not notice the raised physical quantities on the inventory types they did not test count. They also did not notice some extra (fictitious) tags Paul had handed over to data processing.

Amount: Paul falsified the inventory for three years before the company declared bankruptcy. Over that period, the inventory was overstated by $1 million (20 percent, two years ago), $2.5 million (45 percent, one year ago), and $3 million (42 percent, current year). The financial statements showed the following (dollars in 000s):

	Two Years Ago	One Year Ago	Current Year
Sales	$25,000	$29,000	$40,000
Cost of good sold	(20,000)	(22,000)	(29,000) Expenses
	(5,000)	(8,000)	(9,000)
Income (loss) before taxes	0	$ (1,000)	$ 2,500
Ending inventory	$ 6,00	$ 8,000	$10,200
Other current assets	9,000	8,500	17,500
Total assets	21,000	21,600	34,300
Current liabilities	5,000	5,500	13,000
Long-term debt*	5,500	6,600	9,300
Shareholder equity	10,500	9,500	12,000

*Secured by inventory pledged to the bank.

10.69 Purchase Kickbacks. Follow the instructions preceding Case 10.68. This time, let your initial objective be to select one vendor for investigation. Instead of a "test of controls" section, name the one vendor you would select from those in Exhibit 10.69–1 and tell your reasons. In the "test of balances" section, tell how you would investigate the situation. In the "discovery summary" section, speculate about how your investigation might reveal the culprit.

PURCHASING STARS

Problem: Kickbacks taken on books or supplies inventory purchases caused inflated inventory, cost of goods sold and expenses.

Method: Bailey Books, Inc., is a retail distributor of upscale books, periodicals and magazines. Bailey has 431 retail stores throughout the southeastern states. Three full-time purchasing agents work at corporate headquarters. They are respon-

E X H I B I T 10.69–1   SUMMARY OF PURCHASING ACTIVITY

Bailey Books, Incorporated
Selected Purchases 2000-2002

Vendor	Items Purchased	2000	2001	2002	Date of Last Bid	Percent of Purchases Bid (3-yr. Period)
Armour	Books	683,409	702,929	810,100	12/01/02	87%
Burdick	Sundries	62,443	70,949	76,722	—	—
Canon	Magazines	1,404,360	1,947,601	2,361,149	11/03/02	94
DeBois, Inc.	Paper	321,644	218,404	121,986	06/08/02	57
Elton books	Books	874,893	781,602	649,188	07/21/02	91
Fergeson	Books	921,666	1,021,440	1,567,811	09/08/02	81
Guyford	Magazines	2,377,821	2,868,988	3,262,49	10/08/02	81
Hyman, Inc.	Supplies	31,640	40,022	46,911	10/22/02	—
Intertec	Books	821,904	898,683	949,604	11/18/02	86
Jerrico	Paper	186,401	111,923	93,499	10/04/02	72
Julian-Borg	Magazine	431,470	589,182	371,920	02/07/02	44
King Features	Magazines	436,820	492,687	504,360	11/18/02	89
Lycorp	Sundries	16,280	17,404	21,410	—	—
Medallian	Books	—	61,227	410,163	12/15/02	99
Northwood	Books	861,382	992,121	—	12/07/01	—
Orion Corp.	Paper	86,904	416,777	803,493	11/02/01	15
Peterson	Supplies	114,623	—	—	N/A	N/A
Quick	Supplies	—	96,732	110,441	11/03/02	86
Robertson	Books	2,361,912	3,040,319	3,516,811	12/01/02	96
Steele	Magazines	621,490	823,707	482,082	11/03/02	90
Telecom	Sundries	81,406	101,193	146,316	—	—
Union Bay	Books	4,322,639	4,971,682	5,368,114	12/03/02	97
Victory	Magazines	123,844	141,909	143,286	06/09/02	89
Williams	Sundries	31,629	35,111	42,686	—	—

sible for purchasing all the inventory at the best prices available from wholesale jobbers. They can purchase with or without obtaining competitive bids. The three purchasing agents are R. McGuire in charge of purchasing books, M. Garza in charge of purchasing magazines and periodicals, and L. Collins (manager of purchasing) in charge of ordering miscellaneous items, such as paper products and store supplies.

One of the purchasing agents is suspected of taking kickbacks from vendors. In return, Bailey is thought to be paying inflated prices, which first go to inventory and then to cost of goods sold and other expense accounts as the assets are sold or used.

L. Collins is the manager in charge. Her duties do not include audit or inspection of the performance of the other two purchasing agents. No one audits or reviews Collins's performance.

Paper trail: The purchasing system is computerized, and detail records are retained. An extract from these records is in Exhibit 10.69–1.

Amount: This kickback scheme has been going on for two or three years. Several hundred thousand dollars may have been overpaid by Bailey Books.

(NACFE adapted)

10.70 **Fictitious Vendors, Theft and Embezzlement.** Follow the instructions preceding Case 10.68. Write the Audit Approach section.

LIKE A SON

Problem: Fictitious purchases, overstated inventory and inflated costs and expenses, causing misstated financial statements and operating losses.

Method: Simon Construction Company had two divisions. Simon, the president, managed the roofing division. Simon delegated authority and responsibility for management of the modular manufacturing division to John G. A widower, Simon had virtually adopted John when he ran away from an orphanage 20 years earlier, treating him like the son he never had, even building him a fine house on the outskirts of the city.

John and his secretary handled all the bids for manufacturing jobs, purchased all the material, controlled the physical inventory of materials, contracted for shipping by truck, supervised the construction activity, billed the customers when jobs were in progress and finished, approved all bid

changes and collected payments from the customers. With Simon's approval, John asked the company internal auditor not to interfere with his busy schedule. The secretary entered all the division's transactions into the computerized accounting system from a dedicated terminal in the manufacturing division office.

John did everything crooked, and the secretary was an accomplice. He rigged low bids and gave kickbacks to customers' purchasing agents, paid high prices to suppliers and took kickbacks, set up dummy companies to sell materials to Simon Construction at inflated prices, removed excess materials inventory and sold it and took the money, manipulated the inventory accounts to overstate the inventory and hide the thefts, and caused Simon Construction to pay trucking bills for a side business he owned. Simon exercised no control over John's operations.

Paper trail: Paper evidence was plentiful, if somebody looked for it. Bid records showed original low bids, later raised for basic construction (e.g., adding second floor, when the original request for bid included a second floor). Cheques payable to "cash" were endorsed by people known to be customers' purchasing agents. Prices paid for materials and supplies were higher than the list prices shown in the competing suppliers' price books kept in the manufacturing division library. John's kickbacks were deposited in his own bank account. Dummy companies were incorporated in the same province, with John and the secretary listed as original incorporators. The physical inventory shown in the accounts simply did not exist. Trucking bills showed deliveries to locations where the manufacturing division had no jobs in progress.

Amount: John drained $1.2 million from Simon Construction over a nine-year period before he was caught. Auditors were engaged to analyse the situation when Simon finally noticed the reported losses in the manufacturing division and had a violent argument with John.

10.71 **Liability Understatement.** Follow the instructions preceding Case 10.68. This time, along with your procedural solution, specify the discrepancies you notice by studying the excerpt from the accounts payable trial balance in Exhibit 10.71–1. Also, recalculate the income before taxes and write the adjusting journal entry you would propose.

EXHIBIT 10.71–1   **EXCERPT FROM ACCOUNTS PAYABLE TRIAL BALANCE: DECEMBER 31, 2002**

Voucher #	Vendor NaYme	Invoice #	Date Invoice	Date Due	Amount
26695	Industrial Uniforms	66681	01-Oct-02	01-Nov-02	112.11
26694	Industrial Uniforms	67127	08-Oct-02	08-Nov-02	112.11
27209	Industrial Uniforms	67582	15-Oct-02	15-Nov-02	112.11
27208	Industrial Uniforms	67981	22-Oct-02	22-Nov-02	112.11
27210	Industrial Uniforms	68462	29-Oct-02	29-Nov-02	112.11
27552	Industrial Uniforms	68972	05-Nov-02	05-Dec-02	112.11
27553	Industrial Uniforms	69463	12-Nov-02	12-Dec-02	112.11
27854	Industrial Uniforms	69851	19-Nov-02	19-Dec-02	112.11
29123	industrial Uniforms	70851	03-Dec-02	03-Jan-03	112.11
28095	Industrial Uniforms	71353	10-Dec-02	10-Jan-03	112.11
29437	Industrial Uniforms	71831	17-Dec-02	17-Jan-03	112.11
Vendor total					1,233.21
27484	B&B Experimental Co	17490	04-Nov-02	04-Dec-02	2,354.50
27550	B&B Experimental Co	17492	04-Nov-02	04-Dec-02	371.25
27559	B&B Experimental Co	17495	08-Nov-02	08-Dec-02	148.50
27560	B&B Experimental Co	17493	08-Nov-02	08-Dec-02	396.00
27741	B&B Experimental Co	17502	09-Nov-02	09-Dec-02	560.25
27475	B&B Experimental Co	17508	12-Nov-02	12-Dec-02	145.11
29494	B&B Experimental Co	17512	16-Nov-02	16-Dec-02	1,284.25
27556	B&B Experimental Co	17474	18-Nov-01	18-Nov-02	265.50
27662	B&B Experimental Co	17514	22-Nov-02	22-Dec-02	519.75
28084	B&B Experimental Co	17523	26-Nov-02	26-Dec-02	938.34
28085	B&B Experimental Co	17546	30-Nov-02	20-Dec-02	893.62
28086	B&B Experimental Co	17549	06-Dec-02	06-Jan-03	1,607.72
Vendor total					9,484.79
29377	Cameo Corp	44298	06-Dec-02	28-Feb-03	1,429.02
29379	Cameo Corp	44300	06-Dec-02	28-Feb-03	1,747.93
29378	Cameo Corp	44413	07-Dec-02	28-Feb-03	259.33
29374	Cameo Corp	44412	07-Dec-02	28-Feb-03	808.33
29380	Cameo Corp	44415	07-Dec-02	28-Feb-03	844.71
29382	Cameo Corp	44414	07-Dec-02	07-Feb-03	1,553.19
29372	Cameo Corp	44596	09-Dec-02	28-Feb-03	3,781.01
29371	Cameo Corp	44682	10-Dec-02	28-Feb-03	1,262.59
29383	Cameo Corp	44684	10-Dec-02	10-Feb-03	4,094.82
29381	Cameo Corp	44681	10-Dec-02	28-Feb-03	926.51
29385	Cameo Corp	44685	10-Dec-02	28-Feb-03	3,750.44
29373	Cameo Corp	44680	10-Dec-02	28-Feb-03	1,124.78
29370	Cameo Corp	44983	10-Dec-02	28-Feb-03	3,973.39
Vendor total					25,556.05
27120	Central Pension		15-Apr-02	15-Apr-02	10,558.23
27121	Central Pension		15-May-02	15-May-02	10,558.23
27122	Central Pension		15-Jun-02	15-Jun-02	10,558.23
27123	Central Pension		15-Jul-02	15-Jul-02	10,558.23
27124	Central Pension		15-Aug-02	15-Aug-02	10,558.23
27125	Central Pension		15-Sep-02	15-Sep-02	10,558.23
27126	Central Pension		15-Oct-02	15-Oct-02	10,588.23
Vendor total					73,907.61

THE BULGING DESK DRAWERS

Problem: Failure to record purchases of raw materials and expense items caused understated accounts payable, understated cost of goods sold, understated expenses and overstated income.

Method: All Bright Company manufactured lamps. L. Mendoza, the company financial vice president, knew the company was under pressure to produce profits in order to maintain its loans at the bank. One of the surest ways accountants know to produce profits with a pencil is to fail to record purchases. This keeps expenses off the books and understates cost of goods sold figured on a periodic inventory basis. (Cost of good sold = Beginning inventory + Purchases – Ending inventory.)

Mendoza opened the mail each day and removed the invoices from suppliers, putting them in the office desk drawer. Later, when the company could "afford it," some invoices were sent to the accounts payable department for recording. Mendoza did not always get them in sequence of arrival, but that didn't matter much to her. Anyway, the desk drawers were getting full.

The clerks in the accounts payable department knew about this manipulation. They would go through periods with very little to record, then a large stack of invoices would be delivered for recording. (Must have made a big sale, they gossiped.)

The clerks followed control procedures about matching invoices with receiving reports, and they always had a full file of "unmatched receiving reports" awaiting the arrival of invoices. Mendoza had the power to override controls that called for the timely recording of purchases, and the clerks could not record invoices they had not yet received.

Paper trail: The accounts payable clerks gave each invoice-receiving report-purchase order set a voucher number in numerical sequence. They dated the accounts payable and related debit recordings on the day they processed the vouchers. Their vouchers were always complete because they were under strict orders not to record any payables that were not supported by source documents.

The problem with the paper trail is that the recording did not get started until Mendoza delivered the invoices. However, there was a file of the unmatched receiving reports in the accounts payable department, forwarded from the receiving employees, and there was a trial balance of accounts payable produced for the auditors.

An excerpt from this trial balance is in Exhibit 10.71–1. The total accounts payable on the trial balance, not shown in Exhibit 10.71–1, was $1.8 million for the year ended December 31, 2002. (The signs of delayed recording of accounts payable are in the exhibit. Can you find them?)

Amount: Mendoza held back the recording of accounts payable for two years (the current year 2002, and one year ago 2001). One year ago, the accounts payable were understated by $500,000, of which $200,000 was unrecorded purchases for inventory and $300,000 was unrecorded operating expenses. In the current year (2002), the accounts payable were understated at December 31 by $750,000, of which $450,000 was for inventory purchases, and $300,000 was unrecorded operating expenses. The financial statements showed the following (dollars in 000s):

	Two Years Ago	One Year Ago	Current Year
Sales	$(25,000)	$(29,000)	$(40,500)
Cost of goods sold	(20,000)	(22,000)	(29,000)
Expenses	(5,000)	(8,000)	(9,000)
Income (loss)			
before taxes	0	$ (1,000)	$ (2,500)
Ending inventory	$ (6,000)	$ (8,000)	$(10,200)
Current assets	(9,000)	(8,500)	(17,500)
Total assets	(21,000)	21,600)	(34,300)
Current liabilities	(5,000)	(5,500)	(13,000)
Long-term debt*	(5,500)	(6,600)	(9,300)
Shareholder equity	(10,500)	(9,500)	(12,000)

*Secured by inventory pledged to the bank.

10.72 Audit of Capital Assets. At the beginning of her examination of the financial statements of Nuclear Data Ltd., a small manufacturer of nuclear particle analysers used in university research laboratories and the like, a PA and her audit team studied the company's business and industry. The company's shares were recently listed on the Vancouver Stock Exchange.

While performing analytical procedures, the PA noted that Nuclear Data's debt-to-equity ratio had increased substantially from 1:2 to 2:1 during the year. However, the rate of return on common equity also increased.

Profitability was improved relative to the previous year primarily because of excellent results in the fourth quarter. Not only were quarterly sales about 25 percent greater than in the previous fiscal year, but the gross margin also increased. The controller pointed out that one reason for the profitability improvement was the use of percentage-of-completion method to account for certain large pieces of equipment being built on special order for a major university. The equipment was about 75 percent complete at year-end, and 75 percent of the expected gross profit was therefore recorded in the current fical year.

A preliminary review of internal control showed that the documents and records were adequate, and that there was a system of authorization and approval for major purchases, sales, cash receipts and cash disbursements. However, because of the small size of the company, the number of personnel involved in processing transactions was very limited. Moreover, top management was by and large neither involved nor interested in the internal control system, concentrating instead on marketing, production and other operation matters.

Required:

a. Identify the various elements of the audit risk model and explain how (if at all) each element is affected in this case (that is, would increase or decrease relative to a normal or typical audit).

b. List six substantive audit procedures the PA should perform with respect to the items being accounted for on a percentage-of-completion basis in the financial statements.

c. The PA is thinking of using physical units attribute sampling in performing certain audit tests. Do you think the use of attribute sampling is appropriate in this case? Explain.

(CGAAC adapted)

APPENDIX 10A

INTERNAL CONTROL QUESTIONNAIRES

. . . .

E X H I B I T 10A–1   PURCHASING AND ACCOUNTS PAYABLE

Environment:
1. Is the purchasing department independent of the accounting department, receiving department and shipping department?
2. Are receiving report copies transmitted to inventory custodians? To purchasing? To the accounting department?

Validity objective:
3. Are vendors' invoices matched against purchase orders and receiving reports before a liability is recorded?

Completeness objective:
4. Are the purchase order forms prenumbered and is the numerical sequence checked for missing documents?
5. Are receiving report forms prenumbered and is the numerical sequence checked for missing documents?
6. Is the accounts payable department notified of goods returned to vendors?
7. Are vendors' invoices listed immediately upon receipt?
8. Are unmatched receiving reports reviewed frequently and investigated for proper recording?

Authorization objective:
9. Are competitive bids received and reviewed for certain items?
10. Are all purchases made only on the basis of approved purchase requisitions?
11. Are purchases made for employees authorized through the regular purchases procedures?
12. Are purchase prices approved by a responsible purchasing officer?
13. Are all purchases, whether for inventory or expense, routed through the purchasing department for approval?
14. Are shipping documents authorized and prepared for goods returned to vendors?
15. Are invoices approved for payment by a responsible officer?

Accuracy objective:
16. Are quantity and quality of goods received determined at the time of receipt by receiving personnel independent of the purchasing department?
17. Are vendors' monthly statements reconciled with individual accounts payable accounts?
18. In the accounts payable department, are invoices checked against purchase orders and receiving reports for quantities, prices and terms?

Classification objective:
19. Does the chart of accounts and accounting manual give instructions for classifying debit entries when purchases are recorded?

Accounting objective:
20. Is the accounts payable detail ledger balanced periodically with the general ledger control account?

Proper period objective:
21. Does the accounting manual give instructions to date purchase/payable entries on the date of receipt of goods?

E X H I B I T 10A–2   **CASH DISBURSEMENTS PROCESSING**

Environment:
1. Are persons with cash custody or cheque-signing authority denied access to accounting journals, ledgers and bank reconciliations?
2. Is access to blank cheques denied to unauthorized persons?
3. Are all disbursements except petty cash made by cheque?
4. Are cheque signers prohibited from drawing cheques to cash?
5. Is signing blank cheques prohibited?
6. Are voided cheques mutilated and retained for inspection?

Validity objectives:
7. Are invoices, receiving reports and purchase orders reviewed by the cheque signer?
8. Are the supporting documents stamped "paid" (to prevent duplicate payment) before being returned to accounts payable for filing?
9. Are cheques mailed directly by the signer and not returned to accounts payable department for mailing?

Completeness objective:
10. Are blank cheques prenumbered and is the numerical sequence checked for missing documents?

Authorization objective:
11. Do cheques require two signatures? Is there dual control over machine signature plates?

Accuracy objective:
12. Are bank accounts reconciled by personnel independent of cash custody or recordkeeping?

Classification objective:
13. Do the chart of accounts and accounting manual give instructions for determining debit classifications of disbursements not charged to accounts payable?
14. Is the distribution of charges double-checked periodically by an official? Is the budget used to check on gross misclassification errors?
15. Are special disbursements (e.g., payroll and dividends) made from separate bank accounts?

Accounting objective:
16. Is the bank reconciliation reviewed by an accounting official with no conflicting cash receipts, cash disbursements or recordkeeping responsibilities?
17. Do internal auditors periodically conduct a surprise audit of bank reconciliations?

Proper period objective:
18. Are cheques dated in the cash disbursements journal with the date of the cheque?

E X H I B I T 10A–3   **ACQUISITION AND EXPENDITURE COMPUTER CONTROLS**

- Each terminal performs only designated functions. For example, the receiving clerk's terminal cannot accept a purchase order entry.
- An identification number and password (used on an individual basis) is required to enter the nonautomatic purchase orders, vendors' invoices and the receiving report information. Further, certain passwords have "read only" authorization. These are issued to personnel authorized to determine the status of various records, such as an open voucher, but not authorized to enter data.
- All input immediately is logged to provide restart processing should any terminal become inoperative during the processing.
- The transaction codes call up a full-screen "form" on the terminals that appears to the operators in the same format as the original paper documents. Each clerk must enter the information correctly (on-line input validation) or the computer will not accept the data.
- All printed documents are computer numbered and the number is stored as part of the record. Further, all records in the open databases have the vendor's number as the primary search and matching field key. Of course, status searches could be made by another field. For example, the inventory number can be the search key to determine the status of a purchase of an item in short supply.
- A daily search of the open databases is made. Purchases outstanding for more than 10 days and the missing "document" records are printed out on a report for investigation of the delay.
- The cheque signature is printed, using a signature plate that is installed on the computer printer only when cheques are printed. A designated person in the treasurer's office maintains custody of this signature plate and must take it to the computer room to be installed when cheques are printed. This person also has the combination to the separate document storage room where the blank cheque stock is kept and is present at all cheque printing runs. The printed cheques are taken immediately from the computer room for mailing.

EXHIBIT 10A–4   INVENTORY TRANSACTION PROCESSING

Environment:
1. Are perpetual inventory records kept for raw materials? Supplies? Work in process? Finished goods?
2. Are perpetual records subsidiary to general ledger control accounts?
3. Do the perpetual records show quantities only? Quantities and prices?
4. Are inventory records maintained by someone other than the inventory stores custodian?
5. Is merchandise or materials on consignment-in (not the property of the company) physically segregated from goods owned by the company?

Validity objective:
6. Are additions to inventory quantity records made only on receipt of a receiving report copy?
7. Do inventory custodians notify the records department of additions to inventory?

Completeness objective:
8. Are reductions of inventory record quantities made only on receipt of inventory issuance documents?
9. Do inventory custodians notify inventory records of reductions of inventory?

Authorization objective:
Refer to question 6 above (additions).
Refer to question 8 above (reductions).

Accuracy objective:
10. If standard costs have been used for inventory pricing, have they been reviewed for current applicability?

Classification objective?
11. Are periodic counts of physical inventory made to correct errors in the individual perpetual records?

Accounting objective:
12. Is there a periodic review for overstocked, slow-moving or obsolete inventory? Have any adjustments been made during the year?
13. Are perpetual inventory records kept in dollars periodically reconciled to general ledger control accounts?

Proper period objective:
14. Does the accounting manual give instructions to record inventory additions on the date of the receiving report?
15. Does the accounting manual give instructions to record inventory issues on the issuance date?

EXHIBIT 10A–5   FIXED ASSET AND RELATED TRANSACTIONS PROCESSING

Environment:
1. Are detailed property records maintained for the various fixed assets?

Validity objective:
2. Is the accounting department notified of actions of disposal, dismantling or idling of a productive asset? For terminating a lease or rental?
3. Are fixed assets inspected periodically and physically counted?

Completeness objective:
4. Is casualty insurance carried? Is the coverage analysed periodically? When was the last analysis?
5. Are property tax assessments periodically analysed? When was the last analysis?

Authorization objective:
6. Are capital expenditure and leasing proposals prepared for review and approval by the board of directors or by responsible officers?
7. When actual expenditures exceed authorized amounts, is the excess approved?

Accuracy objective:
8. Is there a uniform policy for assigning depreciation rates, useful lives and salvage values?
9. Are depreciation calculations checked by internal auditors or other officials?

Classification objective:
10. Does the accounting manual contain policies for capitalization of assets and for expensing repair and maintenance?
11. Are subsidiary fixed assets records periodically reconciled to the general ledger accounts?
12. Are memorandum records of leased assets maintained?

Proper period objective:
13. Does the accounting manual give instructions for recording fixed asset additions on a proper date of acquisition?

E X H I B I T 10A–6   SELECTED COMPUTER QUESTIONNAIRE ITEMS: GENERAL AND APPLICATION
                          CONTROLS (capital assets)

General controls:

1. Are computer operators and programmers excluded from participating in the input and output control functions?
2. Are programmers excluded from operating the computer?
3. Is there a database administrator who is independent of computer operations, systems, programming and users?
4. Are computer personnel restricted from initiating, authorizing or entering transactions or adjustments to the general ledger master database or the subsidiary ledger master database?
5. Is access to the computer room restricted to authorized personnel?
6. Is on-line access to data and programs controlled through the use of department account codes, personal ID numbers and passwords?
7. Are systems, programs and documentation stored in a fireproof area?
8. Can current files, particularly master files, be reconstructed from files stored in an off-site location?

Fixed asset application controls:

1. Is terminal entry of fixed asset data done on the basis of up-to-date written instructions?
2. Are important fixed asset data fields subject to input validation tests—missing data tests, limit and range tests, check digits, valid codes and so forth?
3. Does the computer print an input error report? Is this returned to the accounting department for correction of errors?
4. Is an accounting department person assigned the responsibility for promptly correcting errors in fixed asset input data and re-entering the data for inclusion with the next batch?
5. Are batch control totals used to reconcile computer-processed fixed asset output to input control data?
6. Is fixed asset computer output reviewed for reasonableness, accuracy and legibility by the computer department personnel and the fixed asset accounting personnel?

APPENDIX 10B

SUBSTANTIVE AUDIT PROGRAMS

. . . .

E X H I B I T   10B–1   AUDIT PROGRAM FOR INVENTORY AND COST OF GOODS SOLD

A. Inventory
   1. Conduct an observation of the company's physical inventory count. Count a sample of inventory items and trace these counts to the final inventory compilation.
   2. Select a sample of inventory items. Vouch unit prices to vendors' invoices or other cost records. Recalculate the multiplication of unit times price.
   3. Scan the inventory compilation for items added from sources other than the physical count and items that appear to be large round numbers or systematic fictitious additions.
   4. Recalculate the extensions and footings of the final inventory compilation for clerical accuracy.
   5. For selected inventory items and categories, determine the replacement cost and the applicability of lower-of-cost-or-market valuation.
   6. Determine whether obsolete or damaged good should be written down:
      a. Enquire about obsolete, damaged, unsalable, slow-moving items.
      b. Scan the perpetual records for slow-moving items.
      c. During the physical observation, be alert to notice damaged or scrap inventory.
      d. Compare the listing of obsolete, slow-moving, damaged or unsalable inventory from last year's audit to the current inventory compilation.
   7. At year-end, obtain the numbers of the last shipping and receiving documents for the year. Use these to scan the sales, inventory/cost of sales and accounts payable entries for proper cutoff.
   8. Read bank confirmations, debt agreements and minutes of the board, and make enquiries about pledge or assignment of inventory to secure debt.
   9. Enquire about inventory out on consignment and about inventory on hand that is consigned in from vendors.
   10. Confirm or inspect inventories held in public warehouses.
   11. Recalculate the amount of intercompany profit to be eliminated in consolidation.
   12. Obtain written client representations concerning pledge of inventory as collateral, intercompany sales and other related-party transactions.
B. Cost of Sales
   1. Select a sample of recorded cost of sales entries and vouch to supporting documentation.
   2. Select a sample of basic transaction documents (such as sales invoices, production reports) and determine whether the related cost of goods sold was figured and recorded properly.
   3. Determine whether the accounting costing method used by the client (such as FIFO, LIFO, standard cost) was applied properly.
   4. Compute the gross margin rate and compare to prior years.
   5. Compute the ratio of cost elements (such as labour, material) to total cost of goods sold and compare to prior years.

E X H I B I T 10B–2   **AUDIT PROGRAM FOR CAPITAL ASSETS AND RELATED ACCOUNTS**

A. Capital Assets
    1. Summarize and foot detail capital asset subsidiary records and reconcile to general ledge control accounts(s).
    2. Select a sample of detail fixed asset subsidiary records:
       a. Perform a physical observation (inspection) of the assets recorded.
       b. Inspect title documents, if any.
    3. Prepare, or have client prepare, a schedule of capital asset additions and disposals for the period:
       a. Vouch to documents, indicating proper approval.
       b. Vouch costs to invoices, contracts or other supporting documents.
       c. Determine whether all costs of shipment, installation, testing and the like have been properly capitalized.
       d. Vouch proceeds (on dispositions) to cash receipts or other asset records.
       e. Recalculate gain or loss on dispositions.
       f. Trace amounts to detail fixed asset records and general ledger control account(s).
    4. Prepare an analysis of capital assets subject to investment tax credit for correlation with tax liability audit work.
    5. Observe a physical inventory-taking of the capital assets and compare with detail capital assets records.
    6. Obtain written representations from management regarding pledge of assets as security for loans and leased assets.
B. Depreciation
    1. Analyse amortization expense for overall reasonableness with reference to costs of assets and average depreciation rates.
    2. Prepare, or have client prepare, a schedule of accumulated amortization showing beginning balance, current amortization, disposals and ending balance. Trace to amortization expense and asset disposition analyses. Trace amounts to general ledger account(s).
    3. Recalculate amortization expense and trace to general ledger account(s).
C. Other Accounts
    1. Analyse insurance for adequacy of coverage.
    2. Analyse property taxes to determine whether taxes due on assets have been paid or accrued.
    3. Recalculate prepaid and/or accrued insurance and tax expenses.
    4. Select a sample of rental expense entries. Vouch to rent/lease contracts to determine whether any leases qualify for capitalization.
    5. Select a sample of repair and maintenance expense entries and vouch them to supporting invoices for evidence of property that should be capitalized.

E X H I B I T 10B–3   **AUDIT PROGRAM FOR ACCOUNTS PAYABLE**

1. Obtain a trial balance of recorded accounts payable as of year-end. Foot it and trace the total to the general ledger account. Vouch a sample of balances to vendors' statements. Review the trial balance for related-party payables.
2. When concerned about the possibility of unrecorded payables, send confirmations to creditors, especially those with small or zero balances and those with whom the company has done significant business.
3. Conduct a search for unrecorded liabilities by examining open vouchers, vendors' invoices an statements received and cash payments made for a period after year-end.
4. Enquire about terms that justify classifying payables as long term instead of current.
5. For estimated liabilities, such as warranties, determine and evaluate the basis of estimation, and recalculate the estimate.
6. Obtain written client representations about related party payables and pledges of assets as collateral for liabilities.

E X H I B I T 10B–4   **AUDIT PROGRAM FOR PREPAID, DEFERRED AND ACCRUED EXPENSES**

1. Obtain a schedule of all prepaid expenses, deferred costs and accrued expenses.
2. Determine whether each item is properly allocated to the current or future accounting periods.
3. Select significant additions to deferred and accrued amounts, and vouch them to supporting invoices, contracts or calculations.
4. Determine the basis for deferral and accrual, and recalculate the recorded amounts.
5. Study the nature of each item, enquire of management and determine whether the remaining balance will be recovered from future operations.
6. In other audit work on income and expenses, be alert to notice items that should be considered prepaid, deferred or accrued, and allocated to current or future accounting periods.
7. Scan the expense accounts in the trial balance and compare to prior year. Investigate unusual differences that may indicate failure to account for a prepaid or accrual item.
8. Study each item to determine the proper current or noncurrent balance sheet classification.

APPENDIX 10C

EDI SYSTEMS AND ACCOUNTS PAYABLE AUDITS

Rapid changes in information technology have had a great impact on how audits are conducted in various accounts. The CICA has documented some of these changes in an audit testing study, *Confirmation of Accounts Payable* (CICA, 1996). Advanced computerized systems are discussed in general terms in Chapter 21; this appendix provides merely a brief overview of the effects EDI systems have on accounts payable audits. EDI stands for electronic data interchange and is defined in the study as "an exchange of electronic business documents between economic trading partners, computer to computer, in a standard format."

The significance of EDI for the audit approach to accounts payable is summarized in pages 35–40 of the study as follows (the numbers in the margins indicate paragraph numbers from the study):

Partnership with Suppliers

10   EDI has introduced a new way of doing business, that is, business in partnership. EDI implementation requires the support of customers and/or suppliers, and they must agree with the entity on how transactions will be carried out. With respect to purchases, the entity must enter into agreements with each of its suppliers willing to trade by EDI. Depending on the integration level of applications, discussions deal with the various documents to be exchanged, as well as supply, delivery, billing or payment methods. It becomes preferable for entities to buy a given product from a limited number of suppliers, and they will thus forge closer business relationships. In some cases, the partnership goes even further: the customer communicates the sales or production forecasts for a product to the supplier to help the latter plan for the supply of the product and improve customer service . . .

Elimination of Statements of Account

11   Given these new ties between partners, certain documents, such as statements of account currently issued by suppliers, are no longer useful. As accounts payable balances become less significant and purchase terms are set in agreements, the partners will probably no longer feel the need for documents that summarize transactions and balances. The elimination of statements of account, however, also eliminates reliable external audit evidence regarding accounts payable at the end of the accounting period cycle. Several of the substantive procedures the auditor normally uses to audit accounts payable are based on this evidence. To obtain the required audit evidence, the auditor must now perform procedures based on other forms of evidence . . .

Billing of Accounts Payable

13   Systems integration and partnerships with suppliers can also change the way goods are billed. For example, price information can be extracted from a price catalogue managed jointly by the trading partners and incorporated into their respective applications. In such a case, the supplier does not send an electronic invoice. The pricing of purchases is based on information contained in the electronic notice of receipt issued by the customer (or in the electronic notice of shipment issued by the supplier) and the price catalogue. The auditor can no longer use supplier invoices, which previously constituted external evidence, and will probably have to rely on the proper functioning of the pricing process. The auditor will most likely verify application controls (as well as manual and physical controls), for example, controls to access and/or modify the price catalogue . . .

Audit Approach
Importance of controls in an integrated EDI environment

17   With EDI, entities depend more on computer systems, and while effective systems can lessen the risk of human error, the impact of any weakness in control may be magnified. Moreover, the accuracy, authorization and completeness of data produced by inte-

grated EDI systems are ensured mainly by programmed controls intended to prevent, rather than only detect, errors. It will be difficult to rely on evidence available essentially only in electronic form without auditing the functioning of controls—mainly programmed controls—which ensure the reliability and authenticity of such evidence.

18 The factors mentioned in the previous paragraph, the complexity of integrated EDI systems and the difficulty of implementing detection controls that involve external evidence can increase detection risk, and it is possible that an essentially substantive approach will no longer be efficient. By obtaining the assurance that control systems have operated effectively during the entire period, the auditor will be able to reduce control risk below maximum and accept a higher level of detection risk for a comparable audit risk. Under this approach, it will be necessary to design tests of controls to verify the effectiveness of controls. Since, in an integrated EDI environment, existing controls are, for the most part, electronic, the auditor will have to use computer-assisted audit techniques more frequently, for example, integrated test facilities, concurrent audit tools and embedded audit modules. In addition, tests of controls will probably have to be performed in real time and at different times during the period, so that the auditor can assess the effectiveness of internal control throughout the period and not only at one particular moment, such as the interim audit. In short, for entities whose EDI applications are integrated with other applications, it will likely be more effective to audit financial information using a control-based approach and computer-assisted audit techniques . . .

Confirmation

24 One might question the usefulness of accounts payable confirmation in an integrated EDI environment. If statements of account from suppliers are not available, if the value of accounts payable is no longer material and if other procedures can be used to verify balances more effectively, the auditor might decide that accounts payable confirmation is unnecessary.

25 Where the combined inherent and control risk associated with accounts payable is high, the auditor may need to perform substantive procedures that will provide more reliable audit evidence than that gathered from the review of subsequent payments. Accounts payable confirmation could be used to attain that objective. The fact that a supplier may be unable to determine the account balance at a specific date could be a major problem. To overcome this difficulty, the auditor could ask the client whether an agreement could be reached with the suppliers whereby they would retain (for a certain period of time) balance-related data at the client's year-end date . . .

27 Eventually, auditors, too, will probably use EDI in the performance of their duties. Confirmation requests could then take the form of electronic documents, and be transmitted by EDI to suppliers. In turn, the suppliers will forward their responses to the auditor's electronic mailbox, possibly through a value-added network. If auditors are to use EDI to confirm accounts payable, however, a set of standardized electronic documents will have to be developed.

CHAPTER 11

Learning Objectives

In the production and payroll cycle, materials, labour and overhead are converted into finished goods and services. This chapter separates the production and payroll cycle into two sections. Part I covers the production cycle, dealing with inventory valuation, amortization and cost of goods sold accounting. The audit of payrolls and labour cost accounting is in Part II. A few short cases are used to show the application of audit procedures in situations where errors, irregularities and frauds may be discovered. After completing this chapter, you should be able to:

1. Describe the production cycle, including typical source documents and controls.

2. Give examples of detail test of controls procedures for auditing the controls over conversion of materials and labour in a production process.

3. Describe some common errors, irregularities and frauds in the accounting for production costs and related cost of goods sold, and design some audit and investigation procedures for detecting them.

4. Describe the payroll cycle, including typical source documents and controls.

5. Give examples of detail test of controls procedures for auditing the controls over payroll.

6. Describe some common errors, irregularities and frauds in payroll, and design some audit and investigation procedures for detecting them.

Production and Payroll Cycle Including Audit of Inventory Valuation and Capital Assets

PART I: PRODUCTION CYCLE TYPICAL ACTIVITIES

LEARNING OBJECTIVE

1. Describe the production cycle, including typical source documents and controls.

Exhibit 11–1 shows the activities and accounting involved in a production cycle. The basic activities start with production planning, including inventory planning and management. Production planning can range from use of a sophisticated computerized long-range plan with just-in-time (JIT) inventory management to a simple ad hoc method ("Hey, Joe, we got an order today. Go make 10 units!"). Most businesses try to estimate or forecast sales levels and seasonal timing, and they try to plan facilities and production schedules to meet customer demand. As shown in Exhibit 11–1, the production cycle interacts with the acquisition cycle (Chapter 10) and the payroll cycle (later in this chapter) for the acquisition of fixed assets, materials, supplies, overhead and labour.

The physical output of a production cycle is inventory (starting with raw materials, proceeding to work-in-process, thence to finished goods). Most matters of auditing inventory and physical inventory-taking were explained in Chapter 9 and Chapter 10. Exhibit 11–1 shows the connection of inventory to the revenue and collection cycle (Chapter 9) in terms of orders and deliveries.

Most of the "transactions" in a production cycle are cost accounting allocations, unit cost determinations and standard cost calculations. These are internal transactions produced entirely within the company's accounting system. Exhibit 11–1 shows the elements of depreciation cost calculation, cost of goods sold determination and job cost analysis as examples of these transactions.

As you follow Exhibit 11–1, you can track the following elements of a control structure.

Authorization

The overall production authorization starts with production planning, which usually is based on a sales forecast. Production planning interacts with inventory planning to produce production orders. These production orders specify the materials and labour required and the timing for the start and end of production. Managers in the sales/marketing department and production department usually sign off their approval on plans and production orders. Since sales volume and inventory requirements change with economic conditions and company success or failure, these plans and approvals are dynamic. They are amended according to changing needs.

Authorization also can include plans and approvals for subcontracting work to other companies. The process of taking bids and executing contracts can be a part of the planning-authorization system.

The production order usually includes a bill of materials (a specification of the materials authorized for the production). This bill of materials is the source of authorization for the preparation of materials requisitions, and these requisitions are the authorization for the inventory custodian to release raw materials and supplies to the production personnel. These documents are the inventory recordkeepers' authorizations to update the raw materials inventory files to record the reductions of the raw materials inventory.

Later, when production is complete, the production reports, along with the physical units and the quality control test reports, are the authorizations for the finished goods inventory

EXHIBIT 11-1   **PRODUCTION CYCLE**

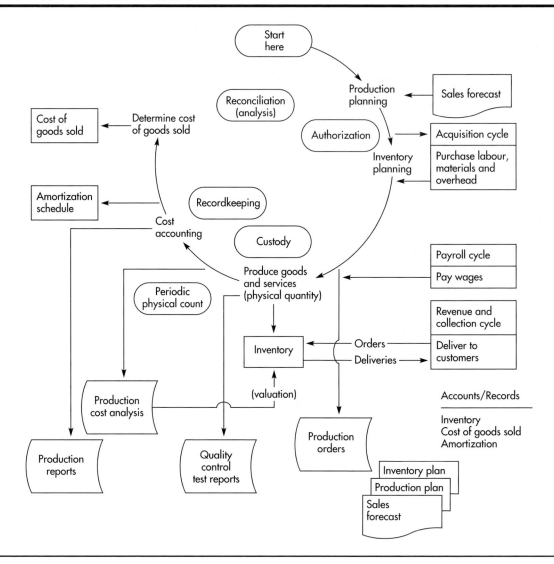

custodian to place the units in the finished goods inventory. These same documents are the inventory recordkeepers' authorization to update the inventory record files to record the additions to the finished goods inventory.

Custody

Supervisors and workers, skilled and unskilled, have physical custody of materials, equipment and labour while the production work is performed. They can requisition materials from the raw materials inventory, assign people to jobs and control the pace of work. In a sense they have custody of a "moving inventory." The work in process (an inventory category) is literally "moving" and changing form in the process of being transformed from raw materials into finished goods.

Control over this custody is more difficult than control over a closed warehouse full of raw materials or finished goods. Control can be exercised by holding supervisors and workers accountable for the use of materials specified in the production orders, for the timely completion of production, and for the quality of the finished goods. This accountability can be achieved with good cost accounting, cost analysis and quality control testing.

Overhead Allocation

The cost accounting department at Pointed Publications, Inc., routinely allocated overhead to book printing runs at the rate of 40 percent of materials and labour cost. The debit was initially to the finished books inventory, while the credit went to an "overhead allocated" account that was offset against other entries in the cost of goods sold calculation, which included all the actual overhead incurred. During the year 10 million books were produced and $40 million of overhead was allocated to them. The auditors noticed that actual overhead expenditures were $32 million, and 3 million books remained in the ending inventory.

The finding resulted in the conclusion that the inventory was overstated by $2.4 million, the cost of goods sold was understated by $2.4 million, and the income before taxes was overstated by 8.2 percent.

	Company Accounting	Proper Accounting
Books produced	10 million	10 million
Labour and material cost	$100 million	$100 million
Overhead allocated	$ 40 million	$32 million
Cost per book	$ 14.00	$13.20
Cost of goods sold		
Labour and materials cost	$100 million	$100 million
Overhead allocated to books	40 million	
Overhead incurred	32 million	32 million
Overhead credited to cost	(40 million)	
Ending inventory	(42 million)	(39.6 million)
Total cost of goods sold	$ 90 million	$ 92.4 million

Recordkeeping (Cost Accounting)

When production is completed, production orders and the related records of material and labour used are sent forward to the cost accounting department. Since these accounting documents may come from the production personnel, the effective separation of the record-keeping function depends upon its receiving independent notices from other places, especially notifications of materials issued from the inventory custodian and the labour costs assigned by the payroll department.

The cost accounting department produces analyses of cost-per-unit, standard cost and variances. Cost accounting also may determine the allocation of overhead to production in general, to production orders and to finished units. Depending on the design of the company's accounting system, these costs are used in inventory valuation and ultimately in determination of the cost of goods sold. Often the cost accounting department also is responsible for calculating the depreciation of fixed assets and the amortization of intangibles.

Periodic Reconciliation

The function of periodic reconciliation generally refers to comparison of actual assets and liabilities to the amounts recorded in the company accounts (e.g., comparing the physical count of inventory to the perpetual inventory records, comparing vendors' monthly statements to the recorded accounts payable). Exhibit 11–1 shows the periodic reconciliation of physical inventory to recorded amounts. The features and audit considerations of this reconciliation were covered in Chapter 10. The work in process inventory also can be observed, although the "count" of partially completed units is very judgmental. It can be costed at the labour, materials and overhead assigned to its stage of completion.

Most other periodic reconciliations in the production cycle take the form of analyses of internal information. After all, with the exception of the physical inventory, no external transactions or physical units are unique to production and cost accounting. These analyses include costing the production orders, comparing the cost to prior experience or to standard costs, and determining lower-of-cost-or-market (LCM) valuations. In a sense the LCM calculations are a "reconciliation" of product cost to the external market price of product units.

· ·

R E V I E W
CHECKPOINTS

11.1 What are the functions normally associated with the production and conversion cycle?

11.2 Why is an understanding of the production process, including the related data processing and cost accounting, important to auditors evaluating the control structure as part of their assessment of control risk?

11.3 Describe a "walk-through" of a production transaction from production orders to entry in the finished goods perpetual inventory records. What document copies would be collected? What controls noted? What duties separated?

11.4 Describe how the separation of (1) authorization of production transactions, (2) recording of these transactions, and (3) physical custody of inventories can be specified among the production, inventory and cost accounting departments.

11.5 What features of the cost accounting system would be expected to prevent the omission of recording materials used in production?

· ·

AUDIT EVIDENCE IN MANAGEMENT REPORTS AND FILES

· · · · · · · · · · · ·

Most production accounting systems produce timely reports that managers need to supervise and control production. These reports can be used by auditors as supporting evidence for assertions about work in process and finished goods inventories and about cost of goods sold.

Sales Forecast

Management's sales forecast provides the basis for several aspects of business planning, notably the planning of production and inventory levels. If the auditors want to use the forecast for substantive audit decisions, some work to obtain assurance about its reasonableness needs to be performed. This work is not an examination or compilation of a forecast as contemplated by the assurance services standards. All the auditors need to accomplish is to learn about the assumptions built into the forecast for the purpose of ascertaining their reasonableness. In addition, some work on the mechanical accuracy of the forecast should be performed to avoid an embarrassing reliance on faulty calculations.

THE SALY FORECAST

The auditors were reviewing the inventory items that had not been issued for 30 days or more, considering the need to write some items down to market lower than cost. The production manager showed them the SALY forecast that indicated continuing need for the materials in products that were expected to have reasonable demand. The auditors agreed that the forecasts supported the prediction of future sales of products at prices that would cover the cost of the slow-moving material items.

Unfortunately, they neglected to ask the meaning of SALY in the designation of the forecast. They did not learn that it means "Same As Last Year." It is not a forecast at all. The products did not sell at the prices expected, and the company experienced losses the following year that should have been charged to cost of goods sold earlier.

389

Forecasts can be used in connection with knowing the shape of management's plans for the year under audit, most of which will have already passed when the audit work begins. It will help the auditors understand the nature and volume of production orders and the level of materials inventory. Forecasts of the following year can be used in connection with valuing the inventory at lower-of-cost-or-market (e.g., slow-moving and potentially obsolete inventory), which influences the amount of cost of goods sold that is shown in the financial statements. Special care must be taken with using the forecast for the next year in connection with inventory valuation because an overly optimistic forecast can lead to a failure to write down inventory, accelerate the depreciation of capital assets and account for more cost of goods sold.

Production Plans and Reports

Based on the sales forecast, management should develop a plan for the amount and timing of production. The production plan provides general information to the auditors, but the production orders and inventory plan associated with the production plan are even more important. The production orders carry the information about requirements for raw materials, labour and overhead, including the requisitions for purchase and use of materials and labour. These documents are the initial authorizations for control of the inventory and production.

Production reports record the completion of production quantities. When coupled with the related cost-accounting reports, they are the company's record of the cost of goods placed in the finished goods inventory. In most cases auditors will audit the cost reports in connection with determining the cost valuation of inventory and cost of goods sold.

Amortization Schedule

The cost accounting department may be charged with preparing a schedule of the amortization (depreciation) of capital assets. In many companies such a schedule is long and complicated, involving large dollar amounts of asset cost and calculated amortization expense. It is not unusual to find the amount of amortization expense exceeding a company's net income. (In the statement of changes in financial position, the amortization added back to calculate the cash flow from operations can be larger than the net income carried forward from the income statement.) An abbreviated illustration of a fixed asset and amortization schedule is in the following table.

Fixed Assets and Amortization

| Description | Asset Cost (000s) | | | | Accumulated Amortization (000s) | | | |
	Beginning Balance	Added	Sold	Ending Balance	Beginning Balance	Added	Sold	Ending Balance
Land	10,000			10,000				
Bldg 1	30,000			30,000	6,857	857		7,714
Bldg 2		42,000		42,000		800		800
Computer A	5,000		5,000	0	3,750	208	3,958	0
Computer B		3,500		3,500		583		583
Press	1,500			1,500	300	150		450
Auto 1	15		15	0	15		15	0
Auto 2		22		22		2		2
Total	46,515	45,522	5,015	87,022	10,922	2,600	3,973	9,549

The amortization schedule is audited by recalculating the amortization expense, using the company's methods, estimates of useful life and estimates of residual value. (Problem 11.54 at the end of the chapter requires some work on the schedule presented above.) The asset acquisition and disposition information in the schedule gives the auditors points of departure for auditing the asset additions and disposals. When the schedule covers hundreds of assets and numerous additions and disposals, auditors can (*a*) use computer auditing methods to recalculate the amortization expense and (*b*) use sampling to choose additions and disposals for test of controls and substantive audit. The beginning balances of assets and accumulated amortization should be traced to the prior year's audit working papers. This schedule can be made into an audit working paper and placed in the auditor's files for future reference.

R E V I E W
CHECKPOINTS

11.6 When auditors want to use a client's sales forecast for general familiarity with the production cycle or for evaluation of slow-moving inventory, what kind of work should be done on the forecast?

11.7 If the actual sales for the year are substantially lower than the sales forecasted at the beginning of the year, what potential valuation problems may arise in the production cycle accounts?

11.8 What production cycle documentation supports the valuation of manufactured finished goods inventory?

11.9 What items in a client's fixed asset and amortization schedule give auditors points of departure (assertions) for audit procedures?

CONTROL RISK ASSESSMENT

LEARNING OBJECTIVE

2. Give examples of detail test of controls procedures for auditing the controls over conversion of materials and labour in a production process.

Control risk assessment is important because it governs the nature, timing and extent of substantive audit procedures that will be applied in the audit of account balances in the production cycle. These account balances include:

Inventory:
 Raw materials.
 Work in process.
 Finished goods.

Cost of goods sold.

Amortization:
 Amortization expense.
 Accumulated amortization.

Several aspects of the audit of purchased inventories and physical quantities are covered in Chapter 10 (acquisition and expenditure cycle). With respect to inventory valuation, this chapter points out the cost accounting function and its role in determining the cost valuation of manufactured finished goods.

General Control Considerations

Control procedures for proper segregation of responsibilities should be in place and operating. By referring to Exhibit 11–1, you can see that proper segregation involves authorization (production planning and inventory planning) by persons who do not have custody, recording or cost accounting and reconciliation duties. Custody of inventories (raw materials, work in process and finished goods) is in the hands of persons who do not authorize the amount or timing of production or the purchase of materials and labour, or perform the cost accounting recordkeeping or prepare cost analyses (reconciliations). Cost accounting (a recording function) is performed by persons who do not authorize production or have custody of assets in the process of production. However, you usually will find that the cost accountants prepare various analyses and reconciliations directly related to production activities. Combinations of two or more of the duties of authorization, custody, or cost accounting in one person, one office or one computerized system may open the door for errors, irregularities and frauds.

In addition, the control structure should provide for detail control checking procedures. For example: (1) production orders should contain a list of materials and their quantities, and they should be approved by a production planner/scheduler; (2) materials requisitions should be compared in the cost accounting department with the list of materials on the production order, and the materials requisitions should be signed by the production operator and the materials inventory storeskeeper; (3) labour time records on jobs should be signed by production supervisors, and the cost accounting department should reconcile these cost amounts with the labour report from the payroll department; (4) production reports of finished units should be signed by the production supervisor and finished goods inventory custodian and forwarded to cost accounting. These control operations track the raw materials and labour from start to finish in the production process. With each internal transaction, the responsibility and accountability for assets are passed from one person or location to another.

Complex computer systems to manage production and materials flow are found in many companies. Even though the technology is complex, the basic management and control functions of ensuring the flow of labour and materials to production and controlling waste should be in place. Manual signatures and paper production orders and requisitions may not exist. They may all be imbedded in computer-controlled manufacturing systems. Matters of auditing in a complex computer environment will need to be considered (refer to Chapter 21).

Internal Control Questionnaire

Information about the production cycle control structure often is gathered initially by completing an internal control questionnaire (ICQ). An ICQ for general (manual) controls is in Appendix 11A–1. This questionnaire can be studied for details of desirable control policies and procedures. It is organized with headings that identify the important control objectives—environment, validity, completeness, authorization, accuracy, classification, accounting and proper period recording. Problem 11.51 at the end of the chapter asks you to describe the errors and irregularities that can occur if certain ICQ items are not specified by a company. Problem 11.62 at the end of the chapter presents a computerized payroll system and asks for identification of control weaknesses (reference to control features in Chapters 6 and 8 will help).

Production Management—JIT

Considerable interest has arisen in just-in-time (JIT) manufacturing. JIT has been implemented in many companies, and auditors need to be familiar with its precepts and implications for auditing. Appendix 11B contains a brief explanation of JIT manufacturing.

OVERCHARGING THE GOVERNMENT

Government contracting periodically gets in the news through exposés of companies charging unrelated costs to government contracts of various kinds. Although the production plans and orders do not specify allowable costs for building the company baseball field or paying the company president's kennel fees while on business trips, costs like these have found their way into government contract reimbursement claims. Government contract auditors have found them, and companies have incurred penalties and requirements to reimburse the costs wrongly charged. Some companies summarily fire cost accountants who engage in cost manipulation on government contracts (McDonnell Douglas Company in the United States). Other organizations suffer in the glare of adverse publicity (Northrop Corporation, Massachusetts Institute of Technology, Stanford University).

Detail Test of Controls Audit Procedures

An organization should have detail control procedures in place and operating to prevent, detect and correct accounting errors. You studied the general control objectives in Chapter 6 (validity, completeness, authorization, accuracy, classification, accounting and proper period recording). Exhibit 11–2 puts these in the perspective of production activity with examples of specific objectives. You should study this exhibit carefully. It expresses the general control objectives in specific examples related to production.

Auditors can perform detail test of controls audit procedures to determine whether controls that are said to be in place and operating actually are being performed properly by company personnel. A detail test of control procedure consists of (1) identification of the data population from which a sample of items will be selected for audit and (2) an expression of the action that will be taken to produce relevant evidence. In general, the actions in detail test of control audit procedures involve vouching, tracing, observing, scanning and recalculating. A specification of such procedures is part of an audit program for obtaining evidence useful in a final control risk assessment. If personnel in the organization are not performing their control procedures very well, auditors will need to design substantive audit procedures to try to detect whether control failures have produced materially misleading account balances.

Exhibit 11–3 contains a selection of detail test of controls audit procedures for auditing controls over the accumulation of costs for work-in-process inventory. This is the stage of "inventory" while it is in the production process. Upon completion, the accumulated costs become the cost valuation of the finished goods inventory. The illustrative procedures presume the existence of production cost reports that are updated as production takes place, labour reports that assign labour cost to the job, materials-used and materials requisitions charging raw materials to the production order and overhead allocation calculations. Some or all of these documents may be in the form of computer records. The samples are usually attribute samples designed along the lines you studied in Chapter 7. On the right, Exhibit 11–3 shows the control objectives tested by the audit procedures.

Direction of the Test of Controls Procedures

The test of controls procedures in Exhibit 11–3 are designed to test the production accounting in two directions. One is the completeness direction, in which the control performance

EXHIBIT 11–2   **CONTROL OBJECTIVES (PRODUCTION CYCLE)**

General Objectives	Examples of Specific Objectives
1. Recorded production transactions are *valid* and documented.	Cost accounting separated from production, payroll and inventory control. Material use reports compared to raw material stores issue slips. Labour use reports compared to job time tickets.
2. Valid production transactions are *recorded* and none omitted.	All documents prenumbered and numerical sequence reviewed.
3. Production transactions are *authorized*.	Material use and labour use prepared by foreman and approved by production supervisor.
4. Production job cost transactions computations contain *accurate* figures.	Job cost sheet entries reviewed by person independent of preparation. Costs of inventory used and labour used reviewed periodically.
5. Labour and materials are *classified* correctly as direct or indirect.	Production foreman required to account for all material and labour used as direct or indirect.
6. Production *accounting* is complete.	Open job cost sheets periodically reconciled to the work-in-process inventory accounts.
7. Production transactions are recorded in the *proper period*.	Production reports of material and labour used prepared weekly and transmitted to cost accounting. Job cost sheets posted weekly and summary journal entries of work in process and work completed prepared monthly.

EXHIBIT 11–3   TEST OF CONTROLS AUDIT PROCEDURES FOR WORK-IN-PROCESS INVENTORY

	Control Objective
1. Reconcile the open production cost reports to the work-in-process inventory control account.	Completeness
2. Select a sample of open and closed production cost reports:	
a. Recalculate all costs entered.	Accuracy
b. Vouch labour costs to labour reports.	Validity
c. Compare labour reports to summary of payroll.	Accounting
d. Vouch material costs to issue slips and materials-used reports.	Validity
e. Vouch overhead charges to overhead analysis schedules.	Accuracy
f. Trace selected overhead amounts from analysis schedules to cost allocations and to invoices or accounts payable vouchers.	Validity
3. Select a sample of issue slips from the raw materials stores file:	
a. Determine if a matching requisition is available for every issue slip.	Completeness
b. Trace materials-used reports into production cost reports.	Completeness
4. Select a sample of clock timecards from the payroll file. Trace to job time tickets, labour reports and production cost reports.	Completeness
5. Select a sample of production orders:	
a. Determine whether production order was authorized.	Authorization
b. Match to bill of materials and manpower needs.	Completeness
c. Trace bill of materials to material requisitions, material issue slips, materials-used reports and production cost reports.	Completeness
d. Trace manpower needs to labour reports and production cost reports.	Completeness

of audit interest is the recording of all the production that was ordered to be started. Exhibit 11–4 shows that the sample for this direction is taken from the population of production orders found in the production planning department. The procedures trace the cost accumulation forward into the production cost reports in the cost accounting department. The procedures keyed in the boxes (5-*a*, *b*, *c*, *d*) are cross-references to the procedures in Exhibit 11–3. A potential finding with these procedures is the cancellation of some production because of technical or quality problems, which should result in write-off or scrap of some partially completed production units.

The other direction is the validity direction of the test. The control performance of interest is the proper recording of work in process and finished goods in the general ledger. Exhibit 11–5 shows that the sample for this test is from the production reports (quantity and cost) recorded in the inventory accounts. This sample yields references to production cost reports filed in the cost accounting department. From these basic records the recorded costs can be recalculated, vouched to labour reports, compared to the payroll and vouched to records of material used and overhead incurred. The procedures keyed in the boxes (2-*a*, *b*, *c*, *d*, *e*, *f*) are cross-references to the procedures in Exhibit 11–3. A potential finding with these procedures is improper valuation of the recorded inventory cost.

Summary: Control Risk Assessment

The audit manager or senior accountant in charge of the audit should evaluate the evidence obtained from an understanding of the internal control structure and from the test of controls audit procedures. If the control risk is assessed very low, the substantive audit procedures on the account balances can be limited in cost-saving ways. For example, the inventory valuation substantive tests can be limited in scope (i.e., smaller sample size), and overall analytical procedures can be used with more confidence in being able to detect material misstatements not otherwise evident in the accounting details.

On the other hand, if tests of controls reveal weaknesses, amortization calculation errors and cost accumulation errors, the substantive procedures will need to be designed to lower the risk of failing to detect material error in the inventory and cost of goods sold account

EXHIBIT 11-4   TEST OF PRODUCTION COST CONTROLS: COMPLETENESS DIRECTION

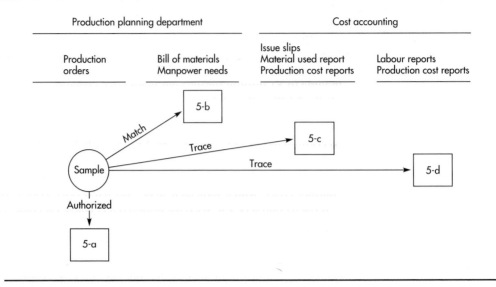

balances. For example, the amortization cost may need to be completely recalculated and reviewed again by the auditors. A large number of inventoried production reports may need to be selected for valuation calculations. Cost overruns will need to be investigated with reference to contract terms to determine whether they should be carried as assets (e.g., inventory or unbilled receivables) or written off. Descriptions of major deficiencies, control weaknesses and inefficiencies may be incorporated in a management letter to the client.

Computerized production cycle records are encountered frequently. Their complexity may range from simple batch systems, which automate the data processing, to transaction-driven integrated systems, which capture the production progress directly from automated devices on the production line. Computer audit techniques, such as test data, frequently are employed to audit controls in such systems, and generalized audit software may be employed to match data on different files. (Refer to Chapter 8 for these subjects.)

EXHIBIT 11-5   TEST OF PRODUCTION COST CONTROLS: VALIDITY DIRECTION

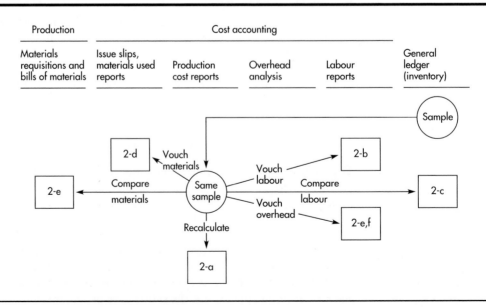

IMPROPER PRODUCTION LOSS DEFERRALS

According to the SEC, Litton Corporation incurred cost overruns on its shipbuilding contracts and postponed writing off a $128 million cost overrun by classifying it as an asset for financial reporting purposes. If it had been written off timelier, the net income of $1 million for the year would have become a substantial loss. Litton wrote off the $128 million later.

****

According to the SEC, International Systems & Controls Corporation (ISC) recorded and reported cost overruns on fixed price contracts, claims for price escalation, and kickback arrangements with suppliers as unbilled receivables. Additional uncollectible contract costs, which indicated losses on fixed price contracts, were buried in other unrelated contracts. ISC used the unbilled receivables account as a dumping ground for improper and questionable payments on the contracts. It tried to show them as legitimate reimbursable contract costs in order to avoid (*a*) writing them off as expense and (*b*) showing the true nature of the items. ISC used the unbilled receivables account to record cost overruns on fixed price contracts, misrepresenting them as an escalation payment due from the owner, but the contract did not provide for any such payment.

Source: I. Kellog, *How to Find Negligence and Misrepresentation in Financial Statements* (New York: Shepard's/McGraw-Hill, 1983), pp. 208–9, 302–3.

R E V I E W
C H E C K P O I N T S

11.10 What are the primary functions that should be segregated in the production cycle?

11.11 Describe the two general characteristics of a test of controls audit procedure.

11.12 How does the production order document (or computer record) provide a control over the quantity of materials used in production?

11.13 Where might an auditor find accounting records of cost overruns on contracts? of improper charges? of improperly capitalized inventory?

11.14 Evaluate the following statement made by an auditing student: "I do not understand cost accounting; therefore, I want to get a job with an auditing firm where I will only have to know financial accounting."

11.15 From what population of documents would an auditor sample to determine whether all authorized production was completed and placed in inventory or written off as scrap? to determine whether finished goods inventory was actually produced and properly costed?

AUDIT CASES: SUBSTANTIVE AUDIT PROCEDURES

LEARNING OBJECTIVE

3. Describe some common errors, irregularities and frauds in the accounting for production costs and related cost of goods sold, and design some audit and investigation procedures for detecting them.

The audit of account balances consists of procedural efforts to detect errors, irregularities and frauds that may exist in the balances, thus making them misleading in financial statements. If such misstatements exist, they are characterized by the following features:

Method: A cause of the misstatement (accidental error, intentional irregularity or fraud attempt), which is usually made easier by some kind of failure of controls.

Paper trail: A set of telltale signs of erroneous accounting, missing or altered documents or a "dangling debit" (the false or erroneous debit that results from an overstatement of assets).

Amount: The dollar amount of overstated assets and revenue, or understated liabilities and expenses.

Each audit program for the audit of an account balance contains an audit approach that may enable auditors to detect misstatements in account balances. Each application of procedures contains these elements:

Audit objective: A recognition of a financial statement assertion for which evidence needs to be obtained. The assertions are about existence of assets, liabilities, revenue and expenses; their valuation; their complete inclusion in the account balances; the rights and obligations inherent in them; and their proper presentation and disclosure in the financial statements. (These assertions were introduced in Chapter 4.)

Control: A recognition of the control procedures that should be used by an organization to prevent and detect errors and irregularities.

Test of controls: Ordinary and extended procedures designed to produce evidence about the effectiveness of the controls that should be in operation.

Audit of balance: Ordinary and extended substantive procedures designed to find signs of errors, irregularities and frauds in account balances and classes of transactions.

The next portion of this chapter consists of two "casettes" (little cases) that first set the stage with a story about an error, irregularity or fraud—its method, paper trail (if any) and amount. This part of the casette gives you the "inside story," which auditors seldom know before they perform the audit work. The second part of the casette, under the heading of the audit approach, tells a structured story about the audit objective, desirable controls, test of control procedures, audit of balance procedures and discovery summary. The audit approach segment illustrates how audit procedures can be applied and the discoveries they may enable auditors to make. At the end of the chapter, some similar discussion cases are presented, and you can write the audit approach to test your ability to design audit procedures for the detection of errors, irregularities and frauds.

CASETTE 11.1
UNBUNDLED BEFORE ITS TIME

Problem

Production "sold" as finished goods before actual unit completion caused understated inventory, overstated cost of goods sold, overstated revenue and overstated income.

Method

Western Corporation assembled and sold computer systems. A systems production order consisted of hardware and peripheral equipment specifications and software specifications with associated performance criteria. Customer contracts always required assembly to specifications, installation, hardware testing, software installation and software testing, after which the customer could accept the finished installation and pay the agreed price for the entire package. Completion of an order usually took three to eight months.

For internal accounting purposes, Western "unbundled" the hardware and software components of the customer orders. Production orders were split between the two components. Standard production processing and cost accounting were performed as if the two components were independent orders. When the hardware was installed and tested (with or without customer acceptance), Western recorded part of the contract price as sales revenue and the related cost of goods sold. The amount "due from customers" was carried in an asset account entitled "unbilled contract revenue." No billing statement was sent to the customer at this time.

When the software component was completed, installed, tested and accepted, the remainder of the contract price was recorded as revenue, and the cost of the software was recorded as cost of goods sold. A billing statement was sent to the customer. The "unbilled contract revenue," which now matched the customer's obligation, was moved to "accounts receivable."

During the time either or both of the order components were in process (prior to installation at the customer's location), accumulated costs were carried in a work-in-process inventory account.

Paper Trail

Customer orders and contracts contained all the terms relating to technical specifications, acceptance testing and the timing of the customer's obligation to pay. Copies of the technical specification sections of the contracts were attached to the separate hardware and software production orders prepared and authorized in the production planning department. During production, installation and testing, each of these production orders served as the basis for the production cost accumulation and the subsidiary record of the work-in-process inventory. At the end the production report along with the accumulated costs became the production cost report and the supporting documentation for the cost of goods sold entry.

Amount

Western Corporation routinely recorded the hardware component of contracts too early, recognizing revenue and cost of goods sold that should have been postponed until later when the customer accepted the entire system. In the last three years, the resulting income overstatement amounted to 12 percent, 15 percent and 19 percent of the reported operating income before taxes.

AUDIT APPROACH

Objective

Obtain evidence of the actual occurrence of cost of goods sold transactions, thereby yielding evidence of the completeness of recorded inventory.

Control

The major control lies in the production planning department approval of orders that identify a total unit of production (in this case, the hardware and software components combined). Nothing is wrong with approving separate orders for efficiency of production, but they should be cross-referenced so that both production personnel and the cost accounting department can see them as separate components of the same order unit.

Test of Controls

While the company conducted a large business, it had relatively few production orders (200–250 charged to cost of goods sold during each year). A sample of completed production orders should be taken and vouched to the underlying customer orders and contracts. The purpose of this procedure includes determining the validity of the production orders in relation to customer orders and determining whether the cost of goods sold was recorded in the proper period. (Procedures to audit the accuracy and completeness of the cost accumulation also are carried out on this sample.)

Even though the auditors can read the customer contracts, enquiries should be made about the company's standard procedures for the timing of revenue and cost of goods sold recognition.

Audit of Balances

The sample of completed production orders taken for the test of controls also can be used in a "dual purpose test" to audit the details of the cost of goods sold balance. In connection with the balance audit, the primary points of interest are the validity and completeness of the dollar amounts accumulated as cost of the contracts and the proper cutoff for recording the cost.

The existence of the "unbilled contract revenue" asset account in the general ledger should raise a red flag. Such an account always means that management has made an estimate of a revenue amount that has not been determined according to contract and has not yet been billed to the customer in accordance with contract terms. Even though the revenue is "unbilled," the related cost of goods sold still should be in the cost of goods sold account. While accounting theory and practice permit recognizing unbilled revenue in certain cases (e.g., percentage of completion for construction contracts), the accounting has been known to harbour abuses in some cases.

Discovery Summary

When the company decided to issue shares to the public, a new audit firm was engaged. These auditors performed the dual-purpose procedures outlined above, made the suggested enquiries and investigated the "unbilled contract revenue" account. They learned about management's unbundling policy and insisted that the policy be changed to recognize revenue only when all the terms of the contract were met. (The investigation yielded the information about prior years' overstatements of revenue, cost of goods sold and income.) Part of the reason for insisting on the change of policy was the finding that Western did not have a very good record of quality control and customer acceptance of software installation. Customer acceptance was frequently delayed several months while systems engineers debugged software. On several occasions Western solved the problems by purchasing complete software packages from other developers.

CASETTE 11.2
WHEN IN DOUBT, DEFER!

Problem

SaCom Corporation deferred costs under the heading of work in process, military contract claims and R&D test equipment, thus overstating assets, understating cost of goods sold and overstating income. Disclosure of the auditor's fees was manipulated and understated.

Method

SaCom manufactured electronic and other equipment for private customers and government military defence contracts. Near the end of the year, the company used a journal entry to remove $170,000 from cost of goods sold and to defer it as tooling, leasehold improvements and contract award and acquisition costs.

The company capitalized certain expenditures as R&D test equipment ($140,000) and as claims for reimbursement on defence contracts ($378,000).

In connection with a public offering of securities, the auditors billed SaCom $125,000 for professional fees. The underwriters objected. The auditors agreed to forgive $70,000 of the fees, and SaCom agreed to pay higher fees for work the following year (150 percent of standard billing rates). SaCom disclosed audit fees in the registration statement in the amount of $55,000. This amount was paid from the proceeds of the offering.

Paper Trail

The $170,000 deferred costs consisted primarily of labour costs. The company altered the labour time records in an effort to provide substantiating documentation. The auditors knew about the alterations. The cost was removed from jobs that were left with too little labour cost in light of the work performed on them.

The R&D test equipment cost already had been charged to cost of goods sold with no notice of deferral when originally recorded. Deferral was accomplished with an adjusting journal entry. The company did not have documentation for the adjusting entry, except for an estimate of labour cost (44 percent of all labour cost in a subsidiary was capitalized during the period).

The claim for reimbursement on defence contracts did not have documentation specifically identifying the costs as being related to the contract. (Auditors know that defence department auditors insist on documentation and justification before approving such a claim.)

The audit fee arrangement was known to the audit firm, and it was recorded in an internal memorandum.

Amount

SaCom reported net income of about $542,000 for the year, an overstatement of approximately 50 percent.

AUDIT APPROACH

Objective

Obtain evidence of the validity of production costs deferred as tooling, leasehold improvements, contract award and acquisition costs, R&D test equipment and claims for reimbursement on defence contracts.

Control

The major control lies in the procedures for documenting the validity of cost deferral journal entries.

Test of Controls

The test of controls procedure is to select a sample of journal entries, suspect ones in this case, and vouch them to supporting documentation. Experience has shown that nonstandard adjusting journal entries are the source of accounting errors and irregularities more often than standard repetitive accounting for systematic transactions. This phenomenon makes the population of adjusting journal entries a ripe field for control and substantive testing.

Audit of Balances

The account balances created by the deferral journal entries can be audited in a "dual-purpose procedure" by auditing the supporting documentation. These balances were created entirely by the journal entries, and their "existence" as legitimate assets, deferrals and reimbursement claims depends on the believability of the supporting explanations. In connection with the defence contract claim, auditors can review it with knowledge of the contract and the extent of documentation required by government contract auditors. (As a separate matter, the auditors could "search for unrecorded liabilities," but they already know about the deferred accounting fees, anyway.)

Discovery Summary

By performing the procedures outlined above, the manager and senior and staff accountants on the engagement discovered all the questionable and improper accounting. However, the partners in the firm insisted on rendering unqualified opinions on the SaCom financial statements without adjustment. One partner owned 300 shares of the company's stock in the name of a relative (without the consent or knowledge of the relative). Another audit partner later arranged a bank loan to the company to get $125,000 to pay past-due audit fees. This partner and another, and both their wives, guaranteed the loan. (When the bank later disclosed the guarantee in a bank confirmation obtained in the course of a subsequent SaCom audit, the confirmation was removed from the audit working paper file and destroyed.)

The SEC investigated, and, among other things, barred the audit firm for a period (about six months) from accepting new audit clients who would file financial statements with the SEC. The SEC also barred the partners involved in supervising various portions of the audit work from involvement with new audit clients for various periods of time. (Adapted: ASR 196.) In addition the partners had violated several rules of professional conduct and were therefore subject to disciplinary action by their provincial institute (see Chapter 16 for discussion of Rules of Professional Conduct).

REVIEW
CHECKPOINTS

11.16 In a production situation similar to the Western Corporation in the "Unbundled Before Its Time" case, what substantive audit work should be done on a sample of completed production orders (cost reports) recorded as cost of goods sold?

11.17 What red flag is raised when a company has an "unbilled contract revenue" account in its general ledger?

11.18 Why should auditors always select the client's adjusting journal entries for detail audit?

11.19 Is there anything wrong about auditors helping clients obtain bank loans to pay their accounting firm's fees?

. . . .

Part II: Payroll Cycle Typical Activities

. . . .

LEARNING OBJECTIVE

4. Describe the payroll cycle, including typical source documents and controls.

Every company has a payroll. It may include manufacturing labour, research scientists, administrative personnel or all of these. Subsidiary operations, partnerships and joint ventures may call it "management fees" charged by a parent company or general partner. Payroll can take different forms. Personnel management and the payroll accounting cycle not only include transactions that affect the wage and salary accounts but also the transactions that affect pension benefits, deferred compensation contracts, compensatory stock option plans, employee benefits (such as health insurance), payroll taxes and related liabilities for these costs. It is very important that auditors verify the payroll systems compliance with local, provincial and federal laws regarding deductions, overtime rules (after 8 hours in a day or 40 in a week), minimum hours, etc. Very large liabilities can arise from failures to comply.

Exhibit 11–6 shows a payroll cycle. It starts with hiring (and firing) people and determining their wage rates and deductions, then proceeds to attendance and work (timekeeping) and ends with payment followed by preparation of governmental (tax) and internal reports. One of these internal reports is a report of labour cost to the cost accounting department, which is how the payroll cycle is linked with cost accounting in the production cycle. Five functional responsibilities should be performed by separate people or departments. They are:

- Personnel and Labour Relations—hiring and firing.
- Supervision—approval of work time.
- Timekeeping and Cost Accounting—payroll preparation and cost accounting.
- Payroll Accounting—cheque preparation and related payroll reports.
- Payroll Distribution—actual custody of cheques and distribution to employees.

The elements that follow are part of the payroll control structure.

Authorization

A personnel or labour relations department that is independent of the other functions should have transaction initiation authority to add new employees to the payroll, to delete terminated employees, to obtain authorizations for deductions (such as insurance, saving bonds, withholding tax exemptions on federal form TD1), and to transmit authority for pay rate changes to the payroll department.

Authorization also takes place in the supervision function. All pay base data (hours, job number, absences, time off allowed for emergencies and the like) should be approved by an employee's immediate supervisor.

Authorization is also a feature of the timekeeping and cost accounting function. Data on which pay is based (such as hours, piece-rate volume, incentives) should be accumulated independent of other functions.

Custody

The main feature of custody in the payroll cycle is the possession of the paycheques, cash or electronic transfer codes used to pay people. (Electronic transfer codes refer to the practice by some organizations of transferring pay directly into employees' bank accounts.) A payroll distribution function should control the delivery of pay to employees so that

EXHIBIT 11–6   PAYROLL CYCLE

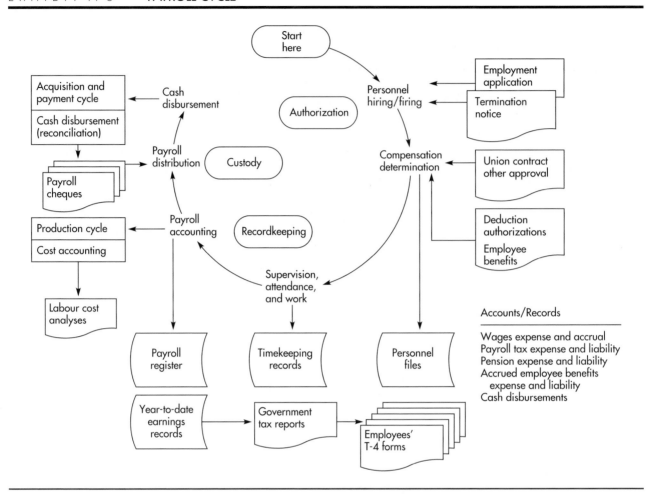

unclaimed cheques, cash or incomplete electronic transfers are not returned to persons involved in any of the other functions.

There are elements of custody of important documents in the supervision function and in the timekeeping function. Supervisors usually have access to time cards or time sheets that provide the basis for payment to hourly workers. Likewise, the timekeeping devices (e.g., time clocks, supervisory approval of time cards or time sheets, electronic punch-in systems) have a type of custody of employees' time-base for payroll calculations.

APPROVAL OF FICTITIOUS OVERTIME

A supervisor at Austin Stoneworks discovered that she could approve overtime hours even though an employee had not worked 40 regular-time hours. She made a deal with several employees to alter their work timecards and split the extra payments. Over a 12-year period, the supervisor and her accomplices embezzled $107,000 in excess payments.

The employees' time cards were not reviewed after being approved by the supervisor. The company's payroll computer program did not have a valid data combination test that paid overtime only after 40 regular-time hours were paid.

Recordkeeping

The **payroll accounting** function should prepare individual paycheques, pay envelopes or electronic transfers using rate and deduction information supplied by the personnel function and base data supplied by the timekeeping-supervision functions. Persons in charge of the authorization and custody functions should not also prepare the payroll. They might be tempted to pay fictitious employees.

Payroll accounting maintains individual year-to-date earnings records and prepares the provincial and federal tax reports (income tax and Canada or Quebec Pension Plan withholding, unemployment insurance reports and annual T-4 forms). The payroll tax returns (e.g., the federal T-4 summary that reports taxes withheld, unemployment insurance returns) and the annual T-4 summary to employees are useful records for audit recalculation and overall testing (analytical) procedures. They should correspond to company records. Most company employees responsible for these reports are reluctant to manipulate them.

Periodic Reconciliation

The payroll bank account can be reconciled like any other bank account. Otherwise, there is not much to count or observe in payroll to accomplish a traditional reconciliation—comparing "real payroll" to recorded wage cost and expense. However, one kind of reconciliation in the form of feedback to the supervision function can be placed in operation. Some companies send to each supervisor a copy of the payroll register, showing the employees paid under the supervisor's authority and responsibility. The supervisor gets a chance to reapprove the payroll after it is completed. This provides an opportunity to notice whether any persons not approved have been paid and charged to the supervisor's accountability.

The payroll report sent to cost accounting can be reconciled to the labour records used to charge labour cost to production. The cost accounting function should determine whether the labour paid is the same as the labour cost used in the cost accounting calculations.

Employees on Fixed Salary

The functional duties and responsibilities described above relate primarily to nonsalaried (hourly) employees. For salaried employees, the system is simplified by not having to col-

---

NOT ENOUGH CONTROL, NO FEEDBACK, BYE-BYE MONEY

Homer had been in payroll accounting for a long time. He knew it was not uncommon to pay a terminated employee severance benefits and partial pay after termination. Homer received the termination notices and the data for the final paycheques. But Homer also knew how to keep the terminated employee on the payroll for another week, pay a full week's compensation, change the electronic transfer code, and take the money for himself. The only things he could not change were the personnel department's copy of the termination notices, the payroll register, and the individual employee pay records used for withholding tax and TD1 forms.

Fortunately, nobody reconciled the cost accounting labour charges to the payroll. The supervisors did not get a copy of the payroll register for postpayment approval, so they did not have any opportunity to notice the extra week. Nobody ever reviewed the payroll with reference to the termination notices. Former employees never complained about more pay and withholding reported on their T-4s than they actually received.

Homer and his wife Marge retired comfortably to a villa in Spain on a nest egg that had grown to $450,000. After his retirement, the company experienced an unexpected decrease in labour costs and higher profits.

lect timekeeping data. In nonmanufacturing businesses, the cost accounting operations may be very simple or even nonexistent.

The relative importance of each of the above five areas should be determined for each engagement in light of the nature and organization of the company's operations.

R E V I E W
CHECKPOINTS

11.20 What functional responsibilities are associated with the payroll cycle?

11.21 Describe a "walk-through" of the payroll transaction flow from hiring authorization to payroll cheque disbursement. What document copies would be collected? What controls noted?

11.22 In a payroll system, which duties should be separated?

11.23 What features of a payroll system can be expected to prevent or detect payment of a fictitious employee? omission of payment to an employee?

AUDIT EVIDENCE IN MANAGEMENT REPORTS AND FILES

Payroll systems produce numerous reports. Some are internal reports and bookkeeping records. Others are government tax reports.

Personnel Files

The personnel and labour relations department keeps individual employee files. The contents usually include an employment application, a background investigation report, a notice of hiring, a job classification with pay rate authorization and authorizations for deductions (e.g., health insurance, life insurance, retirement contribution, union dues, T-4 form for income tax exemptions). When employees retire, quit or are otherwise terminated, appropriate notices of termination are filed. These files contain the raw data for important pension and post-retirement benefit accounting involving an employee's age, tenure with the company, wage record and other information used in actuarial calculations.

A personnel file should establish the reality of a person's existence and employment. The background investigation report (prior employment, references, social insurance number validity check, credentials investigation, perhaps a private investigator's report) is important for employees in such sensitive positions as accounting, finance and asset custody. One of the primary system controls is capable personnel. Experience is rich with errors, irregularities and frauds perpetrated by people who falsify their credentials (identification, education, prior experience, criminal record and the like). An additional protection from this risk is to obtain a suretyship bond for employees through an insurance company.

WHERE DID HE COME FROM?

The controller defrauded the company for several million dollars. As it turned out, he was no controller at all. He didn't know a debit from a credit. The fraudster had been fired from five previous jobs where money had turned up missing. He was discovered one evening when the president showed up unexpectedly at the company and found a stranger in the office with the controller. The stranger was doing all of the accounting for the bogus controller.

Source: National Association of Certified Fraud Examiners, "Auditing for Fraud."

Timekeeping Records

Employees paid by the hour or on various incentive systems require records of time, production, piecework or other measures of the basis for their pay. (Salaried employees do not require such detail records.) Timekeeping or similar records are collected in a variety of ways. The old-fashioned time clock is still used. It accepts an employee's time card and imprints the time when work started and ended. More sophisticated systems perform the same function without the paper time card. Production employees may clock in for various jobs or production processes in the system for assigning labour cost to various stages of production. These records are part of the cost accounting for production labour.

Timekeeping records should be approved by supervisors. This approval is a sign that employees actually worked the hours (or produced the output) reported to the payroll department. The payroll department should find a supervisor's signature or initials on the documents used as the basis for periodic pay. In computer systems this approval may be automatic by virtue of the supervisory passwords used to input data into a computerized payroll system.

Payroll Register

The payroll "register" is a special journal. It typically contains a row for each employee with columns for the gross regular pay, gross overtime pay, income tax withheld, Employment Insurance (EI) and Canada Pension Plan (CPP) or Quebec Pension Plan (QPP) withheld, other deductions and net pay. The net pay amount usually is transferred from the general bank account to a special imprest payroll bank account. The journal entry for the transfer of net payroll, for example, is:

        Payroll Bank Account 25,774
            General Bank Account 25,774

The payroll cheque amounts are accumulated to create the payroll posting to the general ledger, like this example:

        Wages clearing account 40,265
            Employee income taxes payable 7,982
            Employee Canada Pension plan 3,080
            Employment Insurance premium payable 2,100
            Life insurance premium payable .1,329
            Payroll bank account 25,774

The payroll register is the primary original record for payroll accounting. It contains the implicit assertions that the employees are real company personnel (existence assertion), that they worked the time or production for which they were paid (rights/ownership assertion), that the amount of the pay is calculated properly (valuation assertion), and that all

---

LOOK AT THE ENDORSEMENTS

An assistant accountant was instructed to "look at" the endorsements on the backs of a sample of cancelled payroll cheques.

She noticed three occurrences of the payee's signature followed by a second signature. Although scrawled almost illegibly, the second signatures were identical and were later identified as the payroll accountant's handwriting. The payroll accountant had taken unclaimed cheques and converted (stolen) them. When cashing these "third-party cheques," banks and stores had required the payroll accountant to produce identification and endorse the cheques that already had been "endorsed" by the employee payee.

The lesson: Second endorsements are a red flag.

the employees were paid (completeness assertion). The presentation and disclosure assertion depends on the labour cost analysis explained below.

Payroll department records also contain the cancelled cheques (or a similar electronic-deposit record). The cheques will contain the employees' endorsements on the back.

Labour Cost Analysis

The cost accounting department can receive its information in more than one way. Some companies have systems that independently report time and production work data from the production floor directly to the cost accounting department. Other companies let their cost accounting department receive labour cost data from the payroll department. When the data is received independently, it can be reconciled in quantity (time) or amount (dollars) with a report from the payroll department. This is a type of reconciliation to make sure the cost accounting department is using actual payroll data and that the payroll department is paying only for work performed.

The cost accounting department (or a similar accounting function) is responsible for the "cost distribution." This is the most important part of the presentation and disclosure assertion with respect to payroll. The cost distribution is an assignment of payroll to the accounts where it belongs for internal and external reporting. Using its input data, the cost accounting department may make a distribution entry like this:

Production job A	14,364
Production job B	3,999
Production process A	10,338
Selling expense	8,961
General and administrative expense	2,603
Wages clearing account	40,265

Payroll data flows from the hiring process, through the timekeeping function, into the payroll department, thence to the cost accounting department and finally to the accounting entries that record the payroll for inventory cost determination and financial statement presentation. The same data is used for various governmental and tax reports.

Governmental and Tax Reports

Payroll systems have complications introduced by the provincial and federal income and pension plan laws. Several reports are produced. These can be used by auditors in tests of controls and substantive tests of the balances produced by accumulating numerous payroll transactions.

Year-to-Date Earnings Records

The year-to-date (YTD) earnings records are the cumulative subsidiary records of each employee's gross pay, deductions and net pay. Each time a periodic payroll is produced, the YTD earnings records are updated for the new information. The YTD earnings records

---

BEWARE THE "CLEARING ACCOUNT"

"Clearing accounts" are temporary storage places for transactions awaiting final accounting. Like the wages clearing account illustrated in the entries above, all clearing accounts should have zero balances after the accounting is completed.

A balance in a clearing account means that some amounts have not been classified properly in the accounting records. If the wages clearing account has a debit balance, some labour cost has not been properly classified in the expense accounts or cost accounting classifications. If the wages clearing account has a credit balance, the cost accountant has assigned more labour cost to expense accounts and cost accounting classifications than the amount actually paid.

are a subsidiary ledger of the wages and salaries cost and expense in the financial statements. Theoretically, like any subsidiary and control account relationship, their sum (e.g., the gross pay amounts) should be equal to the costs and expenses in the financial statements. The trouble with this reconciliation idea is that there are usually many payroll cost/expense accounts in a company's chart of accounts. The production wages may be scattered about in several different accounts, such as inventory (work in process and finished goods), selling, general and administrative expenses.

However, these YTD records provide the data for periodic governmental and tax forms. They usually can be reconciled to the tax reports.

Companies in financial difficulty have been known to try to postpone payment of employee taxes, UIC, and CPP or QPP withheld. However, the consequences can be serious. The Canada Customs and Revenue Agency can and will padlock the business and seize the assets for nonpayment. After all, the withheld taxes belong to the employee's accounts with the government, and the employers are obligated to pay over the amounts withheld from employees along with a matching share for the Canada Pension Plan.

Employee T-4 Reports

The T-4 slip is the annual report of gross salaries and wages and the income, pension plan and Employment Insurance withheld. Copies are filed with the Canada (or Quebec) Pension Plan and the Canada Customs and Revenue Agency, and copies are sent to employees for use in preparing their income tax returns. The T-4s contain the annual YTD accumulations for each employee. They also contain each employee's address and social insurance number. In certain procedures (described later), auditors can use the name, address, social insurance number, and dollar amounts to obtain evidence about the existence of employees. The T-4s can be reconciled to the payroll tax reports.

REVIEW CHECKPOINTS

11.24 What important information can be found in employees' personnel files?

11.25 What is important about background checks using the employment applications submitted by prospective employees?

11.26 What payroll cycle documentation supports the validity and accuracy of payroll transactions?

11.27 Which government tax returns can be reconciled in total with employees' year-to-date earnings records? reconciled in total, but not in detail?

11.28 What is the purpose of examining endorsements on the back of payroll cheques?

CONTROL RISK ASSESSMENT

LEARNING OBJECTIVE

5. Give examples of detail test of controls procedures for auditing the controls over payroll.

The major risks in the payroll cycle are:

- Paying fictitious "employees" (invalid transactions, employees do not exist).
- Overpaying for time or production (inaccurate transactions, improper valuation).
- Incorrect accounting for costs and expenses (incorrect classification, improper or inconsistent presentation and disclosure).

The assessment of payroll system control risk normally takes on added importance because most companies have fairly elaborate and well-controlled personnel and payroll functions. The transactions in this cycle are numerous during the year yet result in small amounts in balance sheet accounts at year-end. Therefore, in most audit engagements the review of controls and test of controls audit of transaction details constitute the major portion of the evidence gathered for these accounts. On most audits the substantive audit procedures devoted to auditing the payroll-related account balances are very limited.

General Control Considerations

Control procedures for proper segregation of responsibilities should be in place and operating. By referring to Exhibit 11–6, you can see that proper segregation involves authorization (personnel department hiring and firing, pay rate and deduction authorizations) by persons who do not have payroll preparation, paycheque distribution or reconciliation duties. Payroll distribution (custody) is in the hands of persons who neither authorize employees' pay rates or time, nor prepare the payroll cheques. Recordkeeping is performed by payroll and cost accounting personnel who do not make authorizations or distribute pay. Combinations of two or more of the duties of authorization, payroll preparation and recordkeeping, and payroll distribution in one person, one office or one computerized system may open the door for errors, irregularities and frauds.

In addition, the control structure should provide for detail control checking procedures. For example: (1) periodic comparison of the payroll register to the personnel department files to check hiring authorizations and terminated employees not deleted, (2) periodic rechecking of wage rate and deduction authorizations, (3) reconciliation of time and production paid to cost accounting calculations, (4) reconciliation of YTD earnings records with tax returns, and (5) payroll bank account reconciliation.

Computer-Based Payroll

Complex computer systems to gather payroll data, calculate payroll amounts, print cheques and transfer electronic deposits may be found in many companies. Even though the technology is complex, the basic management and control functions of ensuring a flow of data to the payroll department should be in place. Various paper records and approval signatures may not exist. They may all be imbedded in computerized payroll systems. Matters of auditing in a complex computer environment will need to be considered (refer to Chapter 20).

Internal Control Questionnaire

Information about the payroll cycle control structure often is gathered initially by completing an internal control questionnaire (ICQ). An ICQ for general (manual) controls is in Appendix 11A–2. This questionnaire can be studied for details of desirable control policies and procedures. It is organized with headings that identify the important control objectives—environment, validity, completeness, authorization, accuracy, classification, accounting and proper period recording. Problem 11.62 at the end of the chapter presents a computerized payroll system and asks for identification of control weaknesses (reference to control features in Chapters 6 and 8 will help).

Detail Test of Controls Audit Procedures

An organization should have detail control procedures in place and operating to prevent, detect and correct accounting errors. You studied the general control objectives in Chapter 6 (validity, completeness, authorization, accuracy, classification, accounting and proper period recording). Exhibit 11–7 puts these in the perspective of the payroll functions with examples of specific objectives. You should study this exhibit carefully. It expresses the general control objectives with specific examples related to payroll.

Auditors can perform detail test of controls audit procedures to determine whether controls that are said to be in place and operating actually are being performed properly by company personnel. A detail test of control procedure consists of (1) identification of the data population from which a sample of items will be selected for audit and (2) an expression of the action that will be taken to produce relevant evidence. In general, the actions in detail test of control audit procedures involve vouching, tracing, observing, scanning and recalculating. A specification of such procedures is part of an audit program for obtaining evidence useful in a final control risk assessment. If personnel in the organization are not performing

EXHIBIT 11-7   CONTROL OBJECTIVES (PERSONNEL AND PAYROLL CYCLE)

General Objectives	Examples of Specific Objectives
1. Recorded payroll transactions are *valid* and documented.	Payroll accounting separated from personnel and timekeeping. Time cards indicate approval by supervisor's signature. Payroll files compared to personnel files periodically.
2. Valid payroll transactions are *recorded* and none are omitted.	Employees' complaints about paycheques investigated and resolved (written records maintained and reviewed by internal auditors).
3. Payroll names, rates, hours and deductions are *authorized*.	Names of new hires or terminations reported immediately in writing to payroll by the personnel department. Authorization for deductions kept on file. Rate authorized by union contract, agreement or written policy and approved by personnel officer.
4. Payroll computations contain *accurate* gross pay, deductions and net pay.	Payroll computations checked by person independent of preparation. Totals of payroll register reconciled to totals of payroll distribution by cost accounting.
5. Payroll transactions are *classified* correctly as direct or indirect labour or other expenses.	Employee classification reviewed periodically. Overall charges to indirect labour compared to direct labour and total product costs periodically.
6. Payroll transaction *accounting* is complete.	Details of employee withholding reconciled periodically to liability control accounts and tax returns. Employee tax expense and liabilities prepared in conjunction with payroll.
7. Payroll costs and expenses are recorded in the *proper period*.	Month-end accruals reviewed by internal auditors. Payroll computed, paid and booked in timely manner.

their control procedures very well, auditors will need to design additional procedures to try to detect whether control failures have produced payments to fictitious employees, over-payments for time or production or incorrect accounting for costs and expenses.

Exhibit 11–8 contains a selection of detail test of controls audit procedures for auditing controls over payroll. Most of the illustrative procedures involve manual records, and B-5 refers to computerized systems. The samples are usually attribute samples designed along the lines you studied in Chapter 7, although payroll testing also can be designed in terms of variables sampling for substantive evidence of dollar errors and irregularities (also in Chapter 7). On the right, Exhibit 11–8 shows the control objectives tested by the audit procedures.

Direction of the Test of Controls Procedures

The test of controls procedures in Exhibit 11–8 are designed to test the payroll accounting in two directions. One is the completeness direction, in which the control performance of audit interest is the matching of personnel file content to payroll department files and the

---

COVERT SURVEILLANCE

This sounds like spy work, and it indeed has certain elements of it.

Auditors can test controls over employees' clocking into work shifts by making personal observations of the process—observing whether anybody clocks in with two time cards or with two or more electronic entries, or leaves the premises after clocking in.

The auditors need to be careful not to make themselves obvious. Standing around in a manufacturing plant at 6 a.m. in the standard blue pinstripe suit uniform is as good as printing "Beware of Auditor" on your forehead. People then will be on their best behaviour, and you will observe nothing unusual.

Find an unobtrusive observation post. Stay out of sight. Use a video camera. Get a knowledgeable office employee to accompany you to interpret various activities. Perform an observation that has a chance of producing evidence of improper behaviour.

EXHIBIT 11–8   TEST OF CONTROLS AUDIT PROCEDURES FOR PAYROLL

	Control Objective
A. Personnel Files and Compensation Documents	
1. Select a sample of personnel files:	
a. Review personnel files for complete information on employment date, authority to add to payroll, job classification, wage rate and authorized deductions.	Authorization Classification Authorization
b. Trace pay rate to union contracts or other rate authorization. Trace salaries to directors' minutes for authorization.	Authorization
c. Trace pay rate and deduction information to payroll department files used in payroll preparation.	Completeness
2. Obtain copies of pension plans, stock options, profit sharing and bonus plans. Review and extract relevant portions that relate to payroll deductions, fringe benefit expenses, accrued liabilities and financial statement disclosure.	Validity Completeness Authorization Accuracy Accounting
B. Payroll	
1. Select a sample of payroll register entries:	
a. Vouch employee identification, pay rate and deductions to personnel files or other authorizations.	Authorization
b. Vouch hours worked to clock time cards and supervisor's approval.	Validity Authorization
c. Recalculate gross pay, deductions, net pay.	Accuracy
d. Recalculate a selection of periodic payrolls.	Accuracy
e. Vouch to cancelled payroll cheque. Examine employees' endorsement.	Accuracy Validity
2. Select a sample of clock time cards. Note supervisor's approval and trace to periodic payroll registers.	Authorization Completeness
3. Vouch a sample of periodic payroll totals to payroll bank account transfer vouchers and vouch payroll bank account deposit slip for cash transfer.	Accounting
4. Trace a sample of employees' payroll entries to individual payroll records maintained for tax reporting purposes. Reconcile total of employees' payroll records with payrolls paid for the year.	Completeness Accuracy
5. Review computer-printed error messages for evidence of the use of check digits, valid codes, limit tests and other input, processing and output application controls. Investigate correction and resolution of errors.	
6. Trace payroll information to management reports and to general ledger account postings.	Accounting
7. Obtain control of a periodic payroll and conduct a surprise distribution of paycheques.	Validity
C. Cost Distribution Reports	
1. Select a sample of cost accounting analyses of payroll:	
a. Reconcile periodic totals with payroll payments for the same periods.	Completeness
b. Vouch to time records.	Validity
2. Trace cost accounting labour cost distributions to management reports and postings in general ledger and subsidiary account(s).	Accounting Classification
3. Select a sample of labour cost items in (a) ledger accounts and/or (b) management reports. Vouch to supporting cost accounting analyses.	Validity

payroll register. Exhibit 11–9 shows that the sample for this direction is taken from the population of personnel files. The procedures trace the personnel department authorizations to the payroll department files (procedure A-1–c).

The other direction is the validity direction of the test. The control performance of interest is the preparation of the payroll register. Exhibit 11–9 shows that the sample for this test is from the completed payroll registers. The individual payroll calculations are vouched to the personnel files (procedure B-1–a).

Computerized Payroll Processing

Payroll processing and payroll register preparation are usually the first computer applications a business implements. Payroll preparation is basically the same for all businesses, and many off-the-shelf computer programs are available. The files in a personnel and payroll database and the related record files (data elements) auditors should expect to find include:

EXHIBIT 11–9   DUAL DIRECTION TEST OF PAYROLL CONTROLS

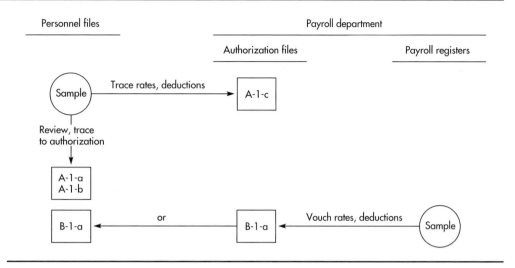

- Reference files:

    Personnel master—employee name and number, date hired, education, skills, employment history, tax withholding factors.

    Payroll master—employee number, name, department, address, compensation class, deduction codes.

    Compensation table—compensation classes matched to hourly rates.

    Deduction tables—deduction codes matched to amounts or formulas.

- Dynamic files:

    Employee earnings records—employee number, compensation class, gross pay (YTD), deductions (YTD), net pay (YTD).

    Deduction, withholding and tax—employee number, Social Insurance number, tax (QTD and YTD).

    Time card transactions—employee number, compensation class, hours (regular and overtime), time period, shop or department.

    Cost distribution—job or department, employee number, job or process number, labour costs, benefit costs.

Generalized audit software can be used extensively in the test of controls procedures in the payroll cycle. Files can be matched (e.g., personnel master file and payroll master file),

---

OVERT SURVEILLANCE

Surprise Payroll Distribution

Auditors may perform a surprise observation of a payroll distribution in connection with tests for overstatement. Such an observation involves taking control of paycheques and accompanying a company representative as the distribution takes place. The auditor is careful to see that each employee is identified and that only one cheque is given to each individual. Unclaimed cheques are controlled, and in this manner the auditor hopes to detect any fictitious persons on the payroll. Auditors need to be extremely careful to notice any duplication of employee identification or instance of one person attempting to pick up two or more cheques.

and unmatched records and differences in common fields can be printed out. Statistical samples of files can be selected and printed for vouching to union contracts or to other authorizations. Statistical samples can be selected for recalculation, using the generalized software or printed out as working papers for tracing and vouching, using the procedures in Exhibit 11–8.

In both manual and computer systems, the test of controls audit of transaction details is highly important because the evidence bears heavily on the reliability of internal management reports and analyses. In turn, reliance on these reports and analyses, along with other analytical relationships, constitutes a major portion of the substantive audit of payroll, compensation costs and labour costs assigned to inventory and costs of goods sold.

The test of controls procedures are designed to produce evidence of the following:

- Adequacy of personnel files, especially the authorizations of pay rate and deductions used in calculating pay.
- Accuracy of the periodic payrolls recorded in accounts and in employees' cumulative wage records. The procedures tend to centre on the periodic payroll registers.
- Accuracy of cost accounting distributions and management reports. The cost accounting for labour costs must be reasonably accurate because good management reports contribute to cost control. The auditor who wishes to rely on the cost accounting system must determine whether it contains and transmits accurate information.

Computerized payroll and cost accounting systems are encountered frequently. Their complexity, however, ranges from an application of simply writing payroll cheques to an integrated system that prepares management reports and cost analyses based on payroll and cost distribution inputs. Computerized audit techniques, such as the use of test data, frequently are employed to test controls in such systems. Parallel simulation may be applied efficiently to test an integrated system. Refer to Chapter 8 for an explanation of these computerized procedures.

Summary: Control Risk Assessment

The audit manager or senior accountant in charge of the audit should evaluate the evidence obtained from an understanding of the internal control structure and from the test of controls audit procedures. If the control risk is assessed very low, the substantive audit procedures on the account balances can be limited in cost-saving ways. As examples: a surprise payroll distribution may be considered unnecessary; the auditors may decide it is appropriate to place considerable reliance on management reports generated by the payroll system.

On the other hand, if tests of controls reveal weaknesses, improper segregation of duties, inaccurate cost reports, inaccurate tax returns or lax personnel policies, then substantive procedures will need to be designed to lower the risk of failing to detect material error in the financial statements. The problem in payroll is that the irregularities of paying fictitious employees and overpaying for fraudulent time records do not normally misstate the financial statements as long as the improper payments are expensed. (The losses are expensed, as they should be!) The only misstatement is failing to distinguish and disclose "payroll fraud losses" from legitimate wages expense and cost of goods sold, but such losses are usually immaterial in a single year's financial statements, anyway. Nevertheless, auditors habitually perform procedures designed to find payroll fraud. It is more of a service to clients than a crucial part of the effort to detect material misstatements in financial statements.

· ·

R E V I E W
CHECKPOINTS

11.29   What are the most common errors and irregularities in the personnel and payroll cycle? Which control characteristics are auditors looking for to prevent or detect these errors?

11.30   What's wrong with an auditor standing by the plant gate and time clock at starting time to observe employees checking in for work shifts?

11.31   How can an auditor determine whether the amount of labour cost charged to production was actually paid to employees?

11.32   Why might an auditor conduct a surprise observation of a payroll distribution? What should be observed?

11.33   Assume the processing of payroll is accomplished with a computer utilizing the files described in this chapter. Which files could be matched for audit purposes utilizing generalized audit software?

- -

AUDIT CASES: SUBSTANTIVE AUDIT PROCEDURES

LEARNING OBJECTIVE

6. Describe some common errors, irregularities and frauds in payroll, and design some audit and investigation procedures for detecting them.

The audit of account balances consists of procedural efforts to detect errors, irregularities and frauds that may exist in the balances, thus making them misleading in financial statements. If such misstatements exist, they are characterized by the following features:

Method: A cause of the misstatement (accidental error, intentional irregularities, or fraud attempt), which usually is made easier by some kind of failure of controls.

Paper trail: A set of telltale signs of erroneous accounting, missing or altered documents or a "dangling debit" (the false or erroneous debit that results from an overstatement of assets).

Amount: The dollar amount of overstated assets and revenue, or understated liabilities and expenses.

Each audit program for the audit of an account balance or class of transactions like payroll contains an audit approach that may enable auditors to detect errors, irregularities and frauds. Each application of procedures contains these elements:

Audit objective: A recognition of a financial statement assertion for which evidence needs to be obtained. The assertions are about existence of assets, liabilities, revenue and expenses; their valuation, their complete inclusion in the account balances; the rights and obligations inherent in them; and their proper presentation and disclosure in the financial statements. (These assertions were introduced in Chapter 9.)

Control: A recognition of the control procedures that should be used by an organization to prevent and detect errors and irregularities.

Test of controls: Ordinary and extended procedures designed to produce evidence about the effectiveness of the controls that should be in operation.

Audit of balance: Ordinary and extended substantive procedures designed to find signs of errors, irregularities and frauds in account balances and classes of transactions.

The next portion of this chapter consists of two "casettes" (little cases) that first set the stage with a story about an error, irregularity or fraud—its method, paper trail (if any) and amount. This part of the casette gives you the "inside story," which auditors seldom know before they perform the audit work. The second part of the casette, under the heading of the audit approach, tells a structured story about the audit objective, desirable controls, test of control procedures, audit of balance procedures and discovery summary. The audit approach segment illustrates the manner in which audit procedures can be applied and the discoveries they may enable auditors to make. At the end of the chapter, some similar discussion cases are presented, and you can write the audit approach to test your ability to design audit procedures for the detection of errors, irregularities and frauds.

CASETTE 11.3
TIME CARD FORGERIES

Problem

False claims for work time caused the overpayment of wages.

Method

A personnel leasing agency assigned Nurse Jane to work at Municipal Hospital. She claimed payroll hours on agency time cards, which showed approval signatures of a county nursing shift supervisor. The shift supervisor had been terminated by the county several months prior to the periods covered by the time cards in question. Nurse Jane worked one or two days per week but submitted time cards for a full 40-hour work week.

The leasing agency paid Nurse Jane, then billed Municipal Hospital for the wages and benefits. Supporting documents were submitted with the leasing agency's bills.

Paper Trail

Each hospital work station keeps ward shift logs, which are sign-in sheets showing nurses on duty at all times. Nurses sign in and sign out when going on and going off duty.

Municipal Hospital maintains personnel records showing, among other things, the period of employment of its own nurses, supervisors and other employees.

Amount

Nurse Jane's wages and benefits were billed to the hospital at $22 per hour. False time cards overcharging about 24 extra hours per week cost the hospital $528 per week. Nurse Jane was assigned to Municipal Hospital for 15 weeks during the year, so she caused overcharges of about $7,900. However, she told three of her crooked friends about the procedure, and they overcharged the hospital another $24,000.

AUDIT APPROACH

Audit Objective

Obtain evidence to determine whether wages were paid to valid employees for actual time worked at the authorized pay rate.

Control

Control procedures should include a hiring authorization putting employees on the payroll. When leased employees are used, this authorization includes contracts for nursing time, conditions of employment and terms including the contract reimbursement rate. Control records of attendance and work should be kept (ward shift log). Supervisors should approve time cards or other records used by the payroll department to prepare paycheques.

In this case the contract with the leasing agency provided that approved time cards had to be submitted as supporting documentation for the agency billings.

Test of Controls

Although the procedures and documents for control were in place, the controls did not operate because nobody at the hospital ever compared the ward shift logs to time cards, and nobody examined the supervisory approval signatures for their validity. The scam was easy in the leasing agency situation because the nurses submitted their own time cards to the agency for payment. The same scam might be operated by the hospital's own employees if they, too, could write their time cards and submit them to the payroll department.

Auditors should make enquiries (e.g., internal control questionnaire) about the error-checking procedures performed by hospital accounting personnel. Test of control audit procedures are designed to determine whether control procedures are followed properly by the organization. Since the comparison and checking procedures were not performed, there is nothing to test.

However, the substantive tests described below are identical to the procedures that could be called "tests of controls," but in this case they are performed to determine whether nurses were paid improperly (a substantive purpose).

Audit of Balances

Select a sample of leasing agency billings and their supporting documentation (time cards). Vouch rates billed by the agency to the contract for agreement to proper rate. Vouch time claimed to hospital work attendance records (ward shift logs). Obtain handwriting examples of supervisors' signatures and compare them to the approval signatures on time cards. Use personnel records to determine whether supervisors were actually employed by the hospital at the time they approved the time cards. Use available work attendance records to determine whether supervisors were actually on duty at the time they approved the time cards.

Discovery Summary

The auditors quickly found that Nurse Jane (and others) had not signed in on ward shift logs for days they claimed to have worked. Further investigation showed that the supervisors who supposedly signed the time cards were not even employed by the hospital at the time their signatures were used for approvals. Handwriting comparison showed that the signatures were not written by the supervisors.

The leasing agency was informed and refunded the $31,900 overpayment proved by the auditors. The auditors continued to comb the records for more! (Adapted from vignette published in *Internal Auditor*, April 1990.)

CASETTE 11.4
THE WELL-PADDED PAYROLL

Problem

Embezzlement with fictitious people on the payroll.

Method

Maybelle had responsibility for preparing personnel files for new hires, approval of wages, verification of time cards and distribution of payroll cheques. She "hired" fictitious employees, faked their records and ordered cheques through the payroll system. She deposited some cheques in several personal bank accounts and cashed others, endorsing all of them with the names of the fictitious employees and her own.

Paper Trail

Payroll creates a large paper trail with individual earnings records, T-4 tax forms, payroll deductions for taxes, insurance and pension plans, and payroll tax reports. She mailed all the T-4 forms to the same post office box.

Amount

Maybelle stole $160,000 by creating some "ghosts," usually 3 to 5 out of 112 people on the payroll, and paying them an average of $256 per week for three years. Sometimes the ghosts quit and were later replaced by others. But she stole "only" about 2 percent of the payroll funds during the period.

AUDIT APPROACH

Objective

Obtain evidence of the existence and validity of payroll transactions.

Control

Different people should be responsible for hiring (preparing personnel files), approving wages, and distributing payroll cheques. "Thinking like a crook" leads an auditor to see that Maybelle could put people on the payroll and obtain their cheques.

Test of Controls

Audit for transaction authorization and validity. Random sampling may not work because of the small number of ghosts. Look for the obvious. Select several weeks' cheque blocks, account for numerical sequence (to see whether any cheques have been removed), and examine cancelled cheques for two endorsements.

Audit of Balances

There may be no "balance" to audit other than the accumulated total of payroll transactions, and the total may not appear out of line with history because the fraud is small in relation to total payroll and has been going on for years.

Conduct a surprise payroll distribution; follow up by examining prior cancelled cheques for the missing employees. Scan personnel files for common addresses.

Discovery Summary

Both the surprise distribution and the scan for common addresses provided the names of 2–3 exceptions. Both led to prior cancelled cheques (which Maybelle had not removed and the bank reconciler had not noticed) that carried Maybelle's own name as endorser. Confronted, she confessed.

REVIEW CHECKPOINTS

11.34 What good are control documents and control procedures if company personnel do not use them to prevent, detect and correct payroll errors, irregularities and frauds?

11.35 How can an auditor find out whether payroll control documents and control procedures were followed by client personnel?

11.36 Give some examples of payroll control omissions that would make it easy to "think like a crook" and see opportunities for errors, irregularities and frauds.

11.37 What difference is there, if any, between tests of controls and tests (audit) of balances in the payroll area?

SUMMARY

The production and payroll cycle consists of two parts that are closely related. Production involves production planning; inventory planning; acquisition of labour, materials and overhead (acquisition and payment cycle); custody of assets while work is in process and when finished products are stored in inventory; and cost accounting. Payroll is a part of every business and an important part of every production cycle. Management and control of labour costs are important. The payroll cycle consists of hiring, rate authorization, attendance and work supervision, payroll processing and paycheque distribution.

Production and payroll information systems produce many internal documents, reports and files. A dozen or more of these sources of audit information were described in the chapter. This cycle is characterized by having mostly internal documentation as evidence and by having relatively little external documentary evidence. Aside from the physical inventory in the production process, the accounts in the production and payroll cycle are intangible. They cannot be observed, inspected, touched or counted in any meaningful way. Most audit procedures for this cycle are analytical procedures and dual-purpose procedures that test both the company's control procedures and the existence, valuation and completeness assertions made by accumulating the results of numerous labour and overhead transactions.

Companies reduce control risk by having a suitable separation of authorization, custody, recording and periodic reconciliation duties. Error-checking procedures of analysing production orders and finished production cost reports are important for proper determination of inventory values and proper valuation of cost of goods sold. Without these procedures, many things could go wrong, ranging from overvaluing the inventory to understating costs of production by deferring costs that should be expensed.

Cost accounting is a central feature of the production cycle. Illustrative cassettes in this chapter told the stories of financial reporting manipulations and of the audit procedures that detected them.

Payroll accounting is a critical operation for expenditure control. Many cases of embezzlement occur during this process. Illustrative cassettes in the chapter told the stories of some fictitious employees and false-time embezzlements and thefts.

MULTIPLE-CHOICE QUESTIONS FOR PRACTICE AND REVIEW

Questions 11.38 and 11.39 are located on the CD-ROM that accompanies this textbook.

11.40 When an auditor tests a company's cost accounting system, the auditor's procedures are designed primarily to determine that:
a. Quantities on hand have been computed based on acceptable cost accounting techniques that reasonably approximate actual quantities on hand.
b. Physical inventories are in substantial agreement with book inventories.
c. The system is in accordance with generally accepted accounting principles and is functioning as planned.
d. Costs have been properly assigned to finished goods, work in process and cost of goods sold.

11.41 The auditor tests the quantity of materials charged to work-in-process by vouching these quantities to:
a. Cost ledgers.
b. Perpetual inventory records.
c. Receiving reports.
d. Material requisition.

11.42 Effective internal control over the payroll function should include procedures that segregate the duties of making salary payments to employees and:
a. Controlling unemployment insurance claims.
b. Maintaining employee personnel records.
c. Approving employee fringe benefits.
d. Hiring new employees.

11.43 Which of the following is the best way for an auditor to determine that every name on a company's payroll is that of a bona fide employee presently on the job?
a. Examine personnel records for accuracy and completeness.
b. Examine employees' names listed on payroll tax returns for agreement with payroll accounting records.

c. Make a surprise observation of the company's regular distribution of pay-cheques.

d. Control the mailing of annual T-4 tax forms to employee addresses in their personnel files.

11.44 It would be appropriate for the payroll accounting department to be responsible for which of the following functions?

a. Approval of employee time records.

b. Maintenance of records of employment, discharges and pay increases.

c. Preparation of periodic governmental reports as to employees' earnings and withholding taxes.

d. Temporary retention of unclaimed employee paycheques.

11.45 One of the auditor's objectives in observing the actual distribution of payroll cheques is to determine that every name on the payroll is that of a bona fide employee. The payroll observation is an auditing procedure that is generally performed for which of the following reasons?

a. The professional standards that are generally accepted require the auditor to perform the payroll observation.

b. The various phases of payroll work are not sufficiently segregated to afford effective internal control.

c. The independent auditor uses personal judgment and decides to observe the payroll distribution on a particular audit.

d. The standards that are generally accepted by the profession are interpreted to mean that payroll observation is expected on an audit unless circumstances dictate otherwise.

11.46 During the year, a bookkeeper perpetrated a theft by preparing erroneous T-4 forms. The bookkeeper's UIC withheld was overstated by $500 and the UIC withheld from all other employees was understated. Which of the following is an audit procedure that would detect such a fraud?

a. Multiplication of the applicable rate by the individual gross taxable earnings.

b. Utilizing Form T-4 and withholding charts to determine whether deductions authorized per pay period agree with amounts deducted per pay period.

c. Footing and crossfooting of the payroll register followed by tracing postings to the general ledger.

d. Vouching cancelled cheques to federal tax report.

11.47 A common audit procedure in the audit of payroll transactions involves vouching selected items from the payroll journal to employee time cards that have been approved by supervisory personnel. This procedure is designed to provide evidence in support of the audit proposition that:

a. Only bona fide employees worked and their pay was properly computed.

b. Jobs on which employees worked and their pay was properly computed.

c. Internal controls relating to payroll disbursements are operating effectively.

d. All employees worked the number of hours for which their pay was computed.

11.48 To minimize the opportunities for fraud, unclaimed cash payroll should be:

a. Deposited in a safe deposit box.

b. Held by the payroll custodian.

c. Deposited in a special bank account.

d. Held by the controller.

11.49 An effective client internal control procedure to prevent lack of agreement between the cost accounting for labour cost is and the payroll paid is:

a. Reconciliation of totals on production job time tickets with job reports by the employees responsible for the specific jobs.

b. Verification of agreement of production job time tickets with employee clock cards by a payroll department employee.

c. Preparation of payroll transaction journal entries by an employee who reports to the personnel department director.

d. Custody of pay rate authorization forms by the supervisor of the payroll department.

(AICPA adapted)

11.50 In a computerized payroll system, an auditor would be least likely to use test data to test controls related to:

a. Missing employee numbers.

b. Proper signature approval of overtime by supervisors.

c. Time tickets with invalid job numbers.

d. Agreement of hours per clock card with hours on time tickets.

(AICPA adapted)

EXERCISES AND PROBLEMS

PRODUCTION AND CONVERSION CYCLE

11.51 ICQ Items: Possible Error or Irregularity Due to Weakness. Refer to the internal control questionnaire (Appendix 11A–1) and assume the answer to each question is no. Prepare a table matching questions to errors or irregularities that could occur because of the absence of the control. Your column headings should be:

Question	Possible Error or Irregularity Due to Weakness

11.52 Test of Controls Audit Procedures Related to Controls and Objectives. Each of the following test of control audit procedures may be performed during the audit of the controls in the production and conversion cycle. For each procedure: (*a*) identify the internal control procedure (strength) being tested, and (*b*) identify the internal control objective(s) being addressed.

1. Balance and reconcile detail production cost sheets to the work-in-process inventory control account.
2. Scan closed production cost sheets for missing numbers in the sequence.
3. Vouch a sample of open and closed production cost sheet entries to (*a*) labour reports and (*b*) issue slips and materials-used reports.
4. Locate the material issue forms. Are they prenumbered? kept in a secure location? available to unauthorized persons?
5. Select several summary journal entries in the work-in-process inventory: (*a*) vouch to weekly labour and material reports and to production cost sheets, and (*b*) trace to control account.
6. Select a sample of the material issue slips in the production department file. Examine for:
   a. Issue date/materials-used report date.
   b. Production order number.
   c. Foreman's signature or initials.
   d. Name and number of material.
   e. Raw material stores clerk's signature or initials.
   f. Matching material requisition in raw material stores file. Note date of requisition.
7. Determine by enquiry and inspection if cost clerks review dates on report of units completed for accounting in the proper period.

11.53 Control over Departmental Labour Cost in a Job-Cost System. The Brown Printing Company accounts for the services it performs on a job-cost basis. Most jobs take a week or less to complete and involve two or more of Brown's five operating departments. Actual costs are accumulated by job. To ensure timely billing, however, the company prepares sales invoices based on cost estimates.

Recently, several printing jobs have incurred losses. To avoid future losses, management has decided to focus on cost control at the department level. Since labour is a major element of cost, management has proposed the development of a department labour cost report. This report will originate in the payroll department as part of the biweekly payroll and then go to an accounting clerk for comparison to total labour cost estimates by department. If the actual total department labour costs in a payroll are not much more than the estimated total departmental labour cost during that period, the accounting clerk will send the report to the department foreman. If the accounting clerk concludes that a significant variance exists, the report will be sent to the assistant controller. The assistant controller will investigate the cause when time is available, and recommend corrective action to the production manager.

Required:
Evaluate the proposal:
a. Give at least three common aspects of control with which the department labour cost report proposal complies. Give an example from the case to support each aspect cited.
b. Give at least three common aspects of control with which the departmental labour cost report proposal does not comply. Give an example from the case to support each aspect cited.

(CIA adapted)

11.54 Audit the Fixed Asset and Depreciation Schedule. Bart's Company has prepared the fixed asset and depreciation schedule shown in Exhibit 11.54–1. The following information is available:

EXHIBIT 11.54–1

Fixed Assets and Amortization

| Description | Asset Cost (000s) | | | | Accumulated Amortization (000s) | | | |
	Beginning Balance	Added	Sold	Ending Balance	Beginning Balance	Added	Sold	Ending Balance
Land	10,000			10,000				
Bldg. 1	30,000			30,000	6,857	857		7,714
Bldg. 2		42,000		42,000		800		800
Computer A	5,000		5,000	0	3,750	208	3,958	0
Computer B		3,500		3,500		583		583
Press	1,500			1,500	300	150		450
Auto 1	15		15	0	15		15	0
Auto 2		22		22		2		2
Total	46,515	45,522	5,015	87,022	10,922	2,600	3,973	9,549

- The land was purchased eight years ago when Building 1 was erected. The location was then remote but now is bordered by a major freeway. The appraised value is $35 million.
- Building 1 has an estimated useful life of 35 years and no residual value.
- Building 2 was built by a local contractor this year. It also has an estimated useful life of 35 years and no residual value. The company occupied it on May 1 this year.
- The Computer A system was purchased January 1 six years ago, when the estimated useful life was eight years with no residual value. It was sold on May 1 for $500,000.
- The Computer B system was placed in operation as soon as the Computer A system was sold. It is estimated to be in use for six years with no residual value at the end.
- The company estimated the useful life of the press at 20 years with no residual value.
- Auto 1 was sold during the year for $1,000.
- Auto 2 was purchased on July 1. The company expects to use it five years and then sell it for $2,000.
- All amortization is calculated on the straight-line method using months of service.

Required:

a. Audit the amortization calculations. Are there any errors? Put the errors in the form of an adjusting journal entry, assuming 90 percent of the amortization on the buildings and the press has been charged to cost of goods sold and

10 percent is still capitalized in the inventory, and the other amortization expense is classified as general and administrative expense.

b. List two audit procedures for auditing the fixed asset additions.

c. What will an auditor expect to find in the "gain and loss on sale of assets" account? What amount of cash flow from investing activities will be in the statement of cash flows?

PAYROLL CIRCLE

11.55 ICQ Items: Errors That Could Occur from Control Weaknesses. Refer to the internal control questionnaire on a payroll system (Exhibit 11A–2) and assume the answer to each question is no. Prepare a table matching the questions to errors or irregularities that could occur because of the absence of the control. Your column headings should be:

Question Number	Possible Error or Irregularity Due to Weakness

11.56 ICQ Items: Control Objectives, Test of Controls Procedures and Possible Errors or Irregularities. Listed below is a selection of items from the payroll processing internal control questionnaire in Exhibit 11A–2.

1. Are names of terminated employees reporting in writing to the payroll department?
2. Are authorizations for deductions, signed by the employees, on file?
3. Is there a timekeeping department (function) independent of the payroll department?

4. Are timekeeping and cost accounting records (such as hours, dollars) reconciled with payroll department calculations of wage and salaries?

Required:

For each question above:

a. Identify the control objective to which the question applies.

b. Specify one test of controls audit procedure an auditor could use to determine whether the control was operating effectively (see Exhibit 11–8 for procedures).

c. Using your business experience, your logic and/or your imagination, give an example of an error or irregularity that could occur if the control were absent or ineffective.

11.57 Test of Controls Audit Procedures, Evaluation of Possible Diversion of Payroll Funds. The Generous Loan Company has 100 branch loan offices. Each office has a manager and four or five subordinates who are employed by the manager. Branch managers prepare the weekly payroll, including their own salaries, and pay employees from cash on hand. Employees sign the payroll sheet signifying receipt of their salary. Hours worked by hourly personnel are inserted in the payroll register sheet from time cards prepared by the employees and approved by the manager.

The weekly payroll register sheets are sent to the home office along with other accounting statements and reports. The home office compiles employee earnings records and prepares all federal and provincial salary reports from the weekly payroll sheets.

Salaries are established by home office job-evaluation schedules. Salary adjustments, promotions and transfers of full-time employees are approved by a home office salary committee based on the recommendations of branch managers and area supervisors. Branch managers advise the salary committee of new full-time employees and terminated employees. Part-time and temporary employees are hired without advising the salary committee.

Required:

a. Prepare a payroll audit program to be used in the home office to audit the branch office payrolls of the Generous Loan Company. See Exhibit 11–8 for sample audit procedures.

b. Based on your review of the payroll system, how might funds for payroll be diverted?

(AICPA adapted)

11.58 Major Risks in Payroll Cycle. Prepare a schedule of the major risks in the payroll cycle. Identify the control objectives and the financial statement assertions related to each. Lay out a three-column schedule like this:

Payroll Cycle Risk	Control Objective	Assertion

11.59 Payroll Authorization in a Computer System. Two accountants were discussing control procedures and test of control auditing for payroll systems. The senior accountant in charge of the engagement said: "It is impossible to determine who authorizes transactions when the payroll account is computerized."

Required:

Evaluate the senior accountant's statement about control in a computerized payroll system. List the points in the flow of payroll information where authorization takes place.

11.60 Payroll Processed by a Service Bureau. Assume that you are the audit senior conducting a review of the payroll system of a new client. In the process of interviewing the payroll department manager, she makes the following statement: "We don't need many controls since our payroll is done outside the company by Automated Data Processing, a service bureau."

Required:

Evaluate the payroll department manager's statement and describe how a service bureau affects an auditors' review of controls. You may want to refer to Chapter 6.

DISCUSSION CASES
. . . .

11.61 Croyden Factory, Inc.: Evaluation of Flowchart for Payroll Control Weaknesses. A PA's audit working papers contain a narrative description of a segment of the Croyden Factory, Inc., payroll system and an accompanying flowchart (Exhibit 11.61–1) as follows:

EXHIBIT 11.61–1   CROYDEN, INC., FACTORY PAYROLL SYSTEM

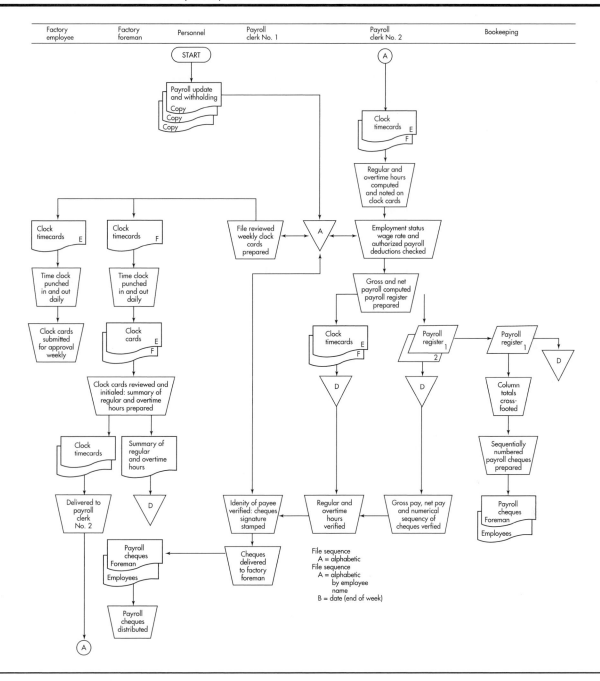

NARRATIVE:

The internal control system, with respect to the personnel department, is well functioning and is not included in the accompanying flowchart.

At the beginning of each workweek, payroll clerk No. 1 reviews the payroll department files to determine the employment status of factory employees. Clerk No. 1 then prepares clock time cards and distributes them as each individual ar-

rives at work. This payroll clerk, who also is responsible for custody of the cheque signature stamp machine, verifies the identity of each payee before delivering signed cheques to the foreman.

At the end of each workweek, the foreman distributes payroll cheques for the preceding workweek. Concurrent with this activity, the foreman reviews the current week's employee timecards, notes the regular and overtime hours worked on a summary form, and initials the clock time cards. The foreman then delivers all time cards and unclaimed payroll cheques to payroll clerk No. 2.

Required:

a. Based on the narrative and accompanying flowchart (Exhibit 11.61–1), what are the weaknesses in the system of internal control?

b. Based on the narrative and accompanying flowchart, what enquiries should be made with respect to clarifying the existence of possible additional weaknesses in the system of internal control?

Note: Do not discuss the internal control system of the personnel department.

(AICPA adapted)

11.62 Vane Corporation: Control Weaknesses in Computerized Payroll System. The Vane Corporation is a manufacturing concern that has been in business for the past 18 years. During this period, the company has grown from a very small family-owned operation to a medium-sized manufacturing concern with several departments. Despite this growth, a substantial number of the procedures employed by Vane have been in effect since the business was started. Just recently, Vane has computerized its payroll function.

The payroll function operates in the following manner. Each worker picks up a weekly time card on Monday morning and writes in his or her name and identification number. These blank cards are kept near the factory entrance. The workers write on the time card the times of their daily arrival and departure. On the following Monday, the factory foremen collect the completed time cards for the previous week and send them to data processing.

In data processing the time cards are used to prepare the weekly payroll transaction file. This file is used to update the master payroll file, which is maintained on magnetic tape sequenced by worker identification number. After the payroll file is updated and the cheques are prepared, the cheques are written by the computer on the regular chequing account and imprinted by a signature plate with the treasurer's signature. The cheques are sent to the factory foremen who distribute them to the workers or hold them for absent workers to pick up later.

The foremen notify data processing of new employees and terminations. Any changes in hourly pay rate or any other changes affecting payroll usually are communicated to data processing by the foremen.

The workers also complete a job time ticket for each individual job they work on each day. The job time tickets are collected daily and sent to cost accounting, where they are used to prepare a cost distribution analysis.

Further analysis of the payroll function reveals the following:

1. A worker's gross wages never exceed $300 per week.
2. Raises never exceed 55 cents per hour for the factory workers.
3. No more than 20 hours of overtime are allowed each week.
4. The factory employs 150 workers in 10 departments.

The payroll function had not been operating smoothly for some time but even more problems have surfaced since the payroll was computerized. The foremen have indicated that they would like a weekly report indicating worker tardiness, absenteeism and idle time, so that they can determine the amount of productive time lost and the reason for the lost time. The following errors and inconsistencies have been encountered the past few pay periods:

1. A worker's paycheque was not processed properly because he had transposed two numbers in his identification number when he filled out his time card.
2. A worker was issued a cheque for $1,531.80 when it should have been $153.18.
3. One worker's paycheque was not written, and this error was not detected until the paycheques for that department were distributed by the foreman.
4. Part of the master payroll file was destroyed when the tape reel was inadvertently mounted on the wrong tape drive and used as a scratch tape. Data processing attempted to re-establish the destroyed portion from original source documents and other records.
5. One worker received a paycheque for an amount considerably larger than he should have. Further investigation revealed that 84 had been keyed instead of 48 for hours worked.
6. Several records on the master payroll file were skipped and not included in the updated master payroll file. This was not detected for several pay periods.

E X H I B I T 11.63–1   **DIAGRAM OF PAYROLL TEST OF CONTROLS**

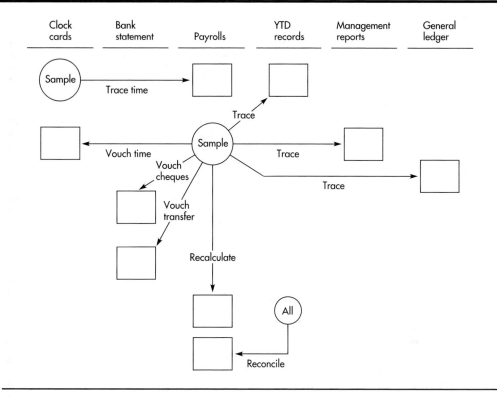

7. In processing nonroutine changes, a computer operator included a pay rate increase for one of his friends in the factory. By chance, this was discovered by another employee.

Required:

Identify the control weaknesses in Vane's payroll procedures and in the computer processing as it is now conducted. Recommend the necessary changes to correct the system. Arrange your answer in the following columnar format:

Control Weaknesses	Recommendations
1.	1.

11.63 Payroll Test of Controls. The diagram in Exhibit 11.63–1 describes several payroll test of control procedures. It shows the direction of the tests, leading from samples of clock cards, payrolls and cumulative year-to-date earnings records to blank squares.

Required:

For each blank square in Exhibit 11.63–1, write a payroll test of controls procedure and describe the evidence it can produce. (Hint: Refer to Exhibit 11–8 in Chapter 11.)

11.64 Cost Accounting Test of Controls. The diagram in Exhibit 11.64–1 describes several cost accounting test of control procedures. It shows the direction of the tests, leading from samples of cost accounting analyses, management reports and the general ledger to blank squares.

Required:

For each blank square in Exhibit 11.64–1, write a cost accounting test of controls procedure and describe the evidence it can produce. (Hint: Refer to Exhibit 11–8 in Chapter 11.)

11.65 Inventory and Deferred Cost Overstatement.

INSTRUCTIONS FOR DISCUSSION CASES 11.65–11.67:

These cases are designed like the ones in the chapter. They give the problem, the method, the paper trail and the amount. Your assignment is to write the audit approach portion of the case organized around these sections:

Objective: Express the objective in terms of the facts supposedly asserted in financial records, accounts and statements. (Refer to discussion of assertions in Chapter 4.)

EXHIBIT 11.64–1 DIAGRAM OF COST ACCOUNTING TEST OF CONTROLS

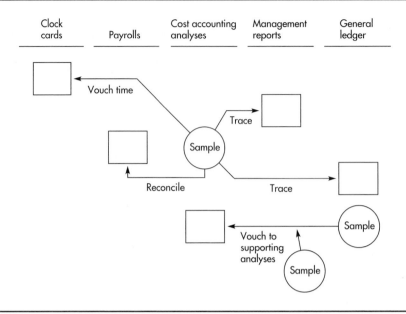

Control: Write a brief explanation of desirable controls, missing controls and especially the kinds of "deviations" that may arise from the situation described in the case.

Test of controls: Write some procedures for getting evidence about existing controls, especially procedures that could discover deviations from controls. If there are no controls to test, then there are no procedures to perform; go then to the next section. A "procedure" should instruct someone about the source(s) of evidence to tap and the work to do.

Audit of balance: Write some procedures for getting evidence about the existence, completeness, valuation, ownership or disclosure assertions identified in your objective section above.

Discovery summary: Write a short statement about the discovery you expect to accomplish with your procedures.

TOYING AROUND WITH THE NUMBERS

Problem: Mattel, Inc., a manufacturer of toys, failed to write off obsolete inventory, thereby overstating inventory, and improperly deferred tooling costs, both of which understated cost of goods sold and overstated income.

Method: "Excess" inventory was identified by comparing types of toys (wheels, general toys, dolls, games), parts and raw materials with the forecasted sales or use. Lower-of-cost-or-market (LCM) determi-

nations then were made to calculate the obsolescence write-off. Obsolescence was expected, and the target for the year was $700,000. The first comparison computer run showed $21 million "excess" inventory! The company "adjusted" the forecast by increasing the quantities of expected sales for many toy lines. (Forty percent of items had forecasted sales greater than the recent actual sales experience.) Another "adjustment" was to forecast toy closeout sales not at reduced prices but at regular prices. Also, certain parts were labelled "interchangeable" without the normal reference to a new toy product. These "adjustments" to the forecast reduced the "excess" inventory exposed to LCM valuation and write-off.

The cost of setting up machines, preparing dies and other preparations for manufacture are "tooling costs." They benefit the lifetime run of the toy manufactured. The company capitalized them as prepaid expenses and amortized them in the ratio of current-year sales to expected product lifetime sales (much like a natural resource depletion calculation). To get the amortization cost lower, the company transferred unamortized tooling costs from toys with low forecasted sales to ones with high forecasted sales. This caused the year's amortization ratio to be smaller, the calculated cost write-off lower and the cost of goods sold lower than it should have been.

Paper trail: The computer-forecast runs of expected use of interchangeable parts provided a space for a reference to the code number of the new toy where the part would be used. Some of these references contained the code number of the part itself, not a new toy. In other cases the forecast of toy sales and parts use contained the quantity on hand, not a forecast number.

In the tooling cost detail records, unamortized cost was classified by lines of toys (similar to classifying asset cost by asset name or description). Unamortized balances were carried forward to the next year. The company changed the classifications shown at the prior year-end to other toy lines that had no balances or different balances. In other words, the balances of unamortized cost at the end of the prior year did not match the beginning balances of the current year, except that the total prepaid expense amount was the same.

Amount: For lack of obsolescence write-offs, inventory was overstated $4 million. The company recorded a $700,000 obsolescence write-off. It should have been about $4.7 million, as later determined.

The tooling cost manipulations overstated the prepaid expense by $3.6 million.

The company reported net income (after taxes) of $12.1 million in the year before the manipulations took place. If pretax income was in the $20–$28 million range in the year of the misstatements, the obsolescence and tooling misstatements alone amounted to about 32 percent income overstatement.

11.66 Inadequate Payroll Time Records. Follow the instructions accompanying Discussion Case 11.65.

PAYROLL IN THE BLUE SKY

Problem: SueCan Corporation deferred costs under the heading of defence contract claims for reimbursement and deferred tooling labour costs, thus overstating assets, understating cost of goods sold and overstating income.

Method: SueCan manufactured electronic and other equipment for private customers and government defence contracts. Near the end of the year, the company used a journal entry to remove $110,000 from cost of goods sold and defer it as deferred tooling cost. This $110,000 purported to be the labour cost associated with preparing tools and dies for long production runs.

The company opened a receivables account for "cost overrun reimbursement receivable" as a claim for reimbursement on defence contracts ($378,000).

Paper trail: The company altered the labour time records for the tooling costs in an effort to provide substantiating documentation. Company employees prepared new work orders numbered in the series used late in the fiscal year and attached labour time records dated much earlier in the year. The production orders originally charged with the labour cost were left completed but with no labour charges!

The claim for reimbursement on defence contracts did not have documentation specifically identifying the labour costs as being related to the contract. There were no work orders. (Auditors know that Defence Ministry auditors insist on documentation and justification before approving such a claim.)

Amount: SueCan reported net income of about $442,000 for the year, an overstatement of approximately 60 percent.

11.67 Employee Embezzlement via Padded Payroll. Follow the instructions accompanying Discussion Case 11.65. In this case (11.67, aka 19.53) your assignment is to analyse the payroll register and see if you can identify any of the ghosts. (This register is short, and you can try to do the analysis visually.

This case is a duplication of Discussion Case 19.53 in Chapter 19 (Ghost Riders on the Payroll). It involves an examination of some payroll information for fictitious employees using fraud auditing knowledge from Chapter 19. Case 19.53 is at the end of Chapter 19.

Required:

Analyse the payroll register in Exhibit 19.53–1 and identify the questionable employees who might be ghosts on the payroll.

11.68 Payroll Flowchart Control Points. This is a cross-reference to Discussion Case 8.47 in Chapter 8 (Audit Planning in a Computer Environment). Case 8.47 presents a flowchart of a computerized payroll process and asks for a list of the control points and control procedures.

11.69 Audit of Inventory. During his examination of the inventories and related accounts of Consumer Electronics, manufacturer and distributor of small appliances, a PA encountered the following:

a. During the inventory observation, the PA noticed several trucks loaded with finished goods parked at the shipping dock. He noted that the contents of the trucks were excluded from the physical inventory.

b. The finished goods inventory at the company's plant included several products for which there was a high volume of goods on hand, with many of the cartons being old and covered with dust. In response to the PA's questions, the plant manager stated that there was no problem as "all of these goods will eventually be sold although some price incentives may be necessary."

c. While reviewing the complex calculations used to develop the unit production costs of items in finished goods, the PA noted that the costs of the company's electrical engineering depart-ment, which had been treated as period expenses in previous years, were included as part of manufacturing overhead in the current year.

d. The company installed a computerized perpetual inventory system during the year. The PA noted that numerous year-end quantities as per the perpetual records differed from the actual physical inventory counts. In part because of these problems, the company took a complete physical inventory at year-end.

Required:

Describe the additional audit procedures (if any) that the PA should perform to obtain sufficient appropriate evidence in each of the above situations.

(CGAAC adapted)

APPENDIX 11A

INTERNAL CONTROL QUESTIONNAIRES

· ·

EXHIBIT 11A–1   PRODUCTION AND COST ACCOUNTING TRANSACTION PROCESSING

Environment:
1. Is access to blank production order forms denied to unauthorized persons?
2. Is access to blank bills of materials and manpower needs forms denied to unauthorized persons?
3. Is access to blank material requisitions forms denied to unauthorized persons?

Validity objective:
4. Are material requisitions and job time tickets reviewed by the production supervisor after the foreman prepares them?
5. Are the weekly direct labour and materials-used reports reviewed by the production supervisor after preparation by the foreman?

Completeness objective:
6. Are production orders prenumbered and the numerical sequence checked for missing documents?
7. Are bills of materials and manpower needs forms prenumbered and the numerical sequence checked for missing documents?
8. Are material requisitions and job time tickets prenumbered and the numerical sequence checked for missing documents?
9. Are inventory issue slips prenumbered and the numerical sequence checked for missing documents?

Authorization objective:
10. Are production orders prepared by authorized persons?
11. Are bills of materials and manpower needs prepared by authorized persons?

Accuracy objective:
12. Are differences between inventory issue slips and materials-used reports recorded and reported to the cost accounting supervisor?
13. Are differences between job time tickets and the labour report recorded and reported to the cost accounting supervisor?
14. Are standard costs used? If so, are they reviewed and revised periodically?
15. Are differences between reports of units completed and products-received reports recorded and reported to the cost accounting supervisor?

Classification objective:
16. Does the accounting manual give instructions for proper classification of cost accounting transactions?

Accounting objective:
17. Are summary entries reviewed and approved by the cost accounting supervisor?

Proper period objective:
18. Does the accounting manual give instructions to date cost entries on the date of use? Does an accounting supervisor review monthly, quarterly and year-end cost accruals?

EXHIBIT 11A–2   **PAYROLL PROCESSING**

Environment:
1. Are all employees paid by cheque?
2. Is a special payroll bank account used?
3. Are payroll cheques signed by persons who neither prepare cheques nor keep cash funds or accounting records?
4. Is the payroll bank account reconciled by someone who does not prepare, sign or deliver paycheques?
5. Are payroll department personnel rotated in their duties? required to take vacations? bonded?
6. Is there a timekeeping department (function) independent of the payroll department?

Validity objective:
7. Are names of terminated employees reported in writing to the payroll department?
8. Is the payroll compared to personnel files periodically?
9. Are cheques distributed by someone other than the employee's immediate supervisor?
10. Are unclaimed wages deposited in a special bank account or otherwise controlled by a responsible officer?
11. Do internal auditors conduct occasional surprise distributions of paycheques?

Completeness objective:
12. Are names of newly hired employees reported in writing to the payroll department?
13. Are blank payroll cheques prenumbered and the numerical sequence checked for missing documents?

Authorization objective:
14. Are all wage rates determined by contract or approved by a personnel officer?
15. Are authorizations for deductions, signed by the employees, on file?
16. Are time cards or piecework reports prepared by the employee approved by his or her supervisor?
17. Is a time clock or other electromechanical or computer system used?
18. Is the payroll register sheet signed by the employee preparing it and approved prior to payment?

Accuracy objective:
19. Are timekeeping and cost accounting records (such as hours, dollars) reconciled with payroll department calculations of hours and wages?
20. Are payrolls audited periodically by internal auditors?

Classification objective:
21. Do payroll accounting personnel have instructions for classifying payroll debit entries?

Accounting objective:
22. Are individual payroll records reconciled with quarterly tax reports?

Proper period objective:
23. Are monthly, quarterly and annual wage accruals reviewed by an accounting officer?

APPENDIX 11B

JUST-IN-TIME MANUFACTURING

· ·

Just-in-time (JIT) manufacturing has been implemented by many companies and is being promoted by management consultants. The presentation in this appendix is a management consulting explanation intended to promote an accounting firm's expertise. As you study this explanation, notice that the 10 principles deal with matters of efficiency and effectiveness of production operations. They are not phrased in terms of audit interest; even so, the design of manufacturing operations is always of interest for auditors.

Following the 10 principles, you can notice mention of some standard production accounting documents (e.g., bills of materials, routing orders, inventory records, production forecasts). JIT alters the management of production, but it retains many familiar features of production accounting.

Just-in-Time: Eliminating Waste and Reducing Cost*

In manufacturing, waste is defined as anything other than the minimum amount of equipment, materials, space and workers' time needed to make a product. It is anything that does not add value to the final product.

The more waste a manufacturer cuts from his operations, the more time he can devote to assuring product quality, reducing lead time, cutting costs and increasing profitability.

That's why increasing numbers of companies are adopting just-in-time (JIT) manufacturing as a strategy to achieve a competitive advantage and increased profit.

JIT can be applied to manufacturing operations of any size or configuration. Any process or activity that adds value is a candidate for JIT, whether it is performed by a small job shop or a large mass-production facility.

JIT enables managers to solve deep-rooted operating problems. It enables management to stop "putting out fires," running from one crisis to another and papering over problems by accumulating inventory.

Instead, it can uncover root cause problems, solve them and allow the company to move on to new challenges.

The 10 Principles

JIT is based on 10 principles.

1. Reduce manufacturing lead time. Ideally, a manufacturer's cycle time or lead time should equal its process time. Any additional time is "waste." If it takes eight days to produce a product, but only one hour to actually make it on a machine, the remaining seven days and 23 hours are waste.

2. Cut inventories to a minimum. Companies use inventory to hide problems. They increase inventory to hide problems. They increase inventory to make certain product is available when problems occur. Eliminate the inventory and management will be forced to solve problems.

3. Synchronize all production processes to the rate of customer demand. If a customer orders 10 pieces, but a manufacturer can make 100 more economically, it makes 100; 90 of them go to inventory.

   This is wasteful. Make the manufacturing of 10 pieces the most economical lot size.

---

* *Source: Manufacturing Issues,* vol. 3, no. 1 (Winter 1992), (Chicago: Grant Thornton). Reprinted with permission of Grant Thornton.

4. Use demand flows to control the shop. Today, most factories operate on a "push" system: If operator 2 produces his product faster than operator 3 needs it, the product is "pushed" to operator 3 and waits in a queue.

   JIT is a "pull" system: When operator 3 is done with his work, he sends signals to operator 2 and requests more work.

5. Reduce lot sizes and setup times. Most manufacturers produce a variety of products. If they slash inventories and work-in-process, they must be prepared to produce these various products more often and in small lot sizes. That means they must reduce setup time.

6. Strive for linear production. Instead of labouring all week to ship everything in a mad rush on Friday, maintain the same pace of production, day in and day out. Match the production pace with consumer demand.

   JIT optimizes the total operation. Each department performs at the same level to meet customer requirements. No longer do departments have individual performance requirements. The entire organization is measured against common performance criteria.

7. Make it right the first time. Rejects and scrap are pure waste.

8. Eliminate waste, in the form of rework.

9. Dedicate work cells to product families. Have the same workers work on a family of related products. It's a more efficient use of their time and your facilities.

10. Form partnerships with vendors. Have vendors guarantee more-frequent deliveries, in smaller quantities, with higher quality. In exchange, you will be in the position to give the vendor more business.

Some ways to go about this include reducing the number of vendors for a given part, issuing a blanket order to a vendor for a year's worth of product or involving key vendors in production planning.

The end result will be a successful partnership with both companies in a win-win situation.

Implementing JIT

The biggest obstacle to implementing JIT is people's natural resistance to change.

The best way to overcome this resistance is to conduct a JIT pilot program on a specific family of products. Pick a pilot of modest difficulty. Its success has the best chance of convincing nonbelievers, which could be most of the factory.

To oversee the pilot program, create a steering committee, task groups and continuous improvement teams. They do not replace line management; their job is to implement JIT.

The steering committee consists of people who can allocate resources, make decisions and review or approve recommendations made to them. The committee may or may not include the CEO, but will likely include the plant manager and should definitely include a union representative (if applicable). The steering committee appoints a co-ordinator, who will direct the JIT implementation.

The task groups are made up of line management and workers. Their job is to solve specific problems and achieve improvements within a given time frame. Once they've identified their problems and defined and implemented the solutions, they disband.

The continuous improvement teams are an ongoing group. They focus on trying continually to improve the process and to eliminate waste in a given area of activity.

The steering committee should meet once or twice a month, but the task groups and continuous improvement teams should meet more frequently. Once a week or more frequently is typical for both.

Education and human relations programs about JIT are essential for effective implementation. Explain to your employees what you are trying to do and how it will affect them.

Understand their concerns about the change and do everything possible to eliminate their anxieties. Be sure that the union representatives, where applicable, are involved in important decisions.

Be open and upfront with all employees about the progress of the implementation and any problems encountered. Invite their help and ideas. You are trying to instill in them a sense of teamwork. Their ideas and insights are crucial to the success of the implementation. Recognize and reward ideas and initiatives generated by team members.

Taking the Steps

Once the task groups are in place, their job is to look at the operations included in the pilot program and to tear them down into components. Everything should be open to review and possible change. There should be no "sacred cows."

The task group should identify all the steps in the manufacturing process and the equipment involved. It ought to examine bills of materials, routing, inventories, setup time and staffing levels. It should compare production forecasts for the pilot project with capabilities.

Performance measures then are benchmarked prior to implementation, and all improvement is measured against that performance.

Goals are established to enable the employees to view their improvement on a day-to-day basis. Team leaders and management should be positive and respond promptly to issues raised in the task groups and teams.

Once a pilot has been implemented, the continuous improvement team takes over. It monitors the area's performance and works to improve it even more. The team should have the authority to make changes. The quickest way for them to fail at their job is to deny them that authority.

Continuous improvement teams are crucial to the success of JIT. They insure that the hard-won gains made by the other committees are held to and continually improved on. They insure that the company continues to expand the waste-cutting benefits of the JIT philosophy.

Generally, it takes about 14 weeks to 21 weeks to implement a JIT pilot program. The biggest and most time-consuming step is diagnosing the things that need to be changed.

But the process gets easier. Once the first pilot project is completed, the next one will take less time and effort. All involved will have learned a great deal from the pilot.

CHAPTER 12

Learning Objectives

The finance and investment cycle comprehends a company's ways and means of planning for capital requirements and raising the money by borrowing, selling shares and entering into acquisitions and joint ventures. Dividend, interest and income tax payments are in this cycle. It also includes the accounts for investments in marketable securities, joint ventures and partnerships, and subsidiaries. The finance part of the cycle deals with getting money into the company. The investment part of the cycle deals with the disposition of money in investment accounts. After completing this chapter, you should be able to:

1. Describe the finance and investment cycle, including typical source documents and controls.

2. Give examples of test of controls procedures for obtaining information about the controls over debt and owner equity transactions and investment transactions.

3. Describe some common errors, irregularities and frauds in the accounting for capital transactions and investments, and design some audit and investigation procedures for detecting them.

FINANCE AND INVESTMENT CYCLE

FINANCE AND INVESTMENT CYCLE: TYPICAL ACTIVITIES

LEARNING OBJECTIVE

1. Describe the finance and investment cycle, including typical source documents and controls.

The finance and investment cycle contains a large number of accounts and records, ranging across tangible and intangible assets, liabilities, deferred credits, shareholders' equity, gains and losses, expenses and related taxes such as income tax, goods and service tax (GST) and provincial sales tax (PST). The major accounts and records are listed in Exhibit 12–1. These include some of the more complicated topics in accounting—equity method accounting for investments, consolidation accounting, goodwill, income taxes and financial instruments, to name a few. It is not the purpose of this chapter to explain the accounting for these balances and transactions. The chapter concentrates on a few important aspects of auditing them. Exhibit 12–1 shows a skeleton outline of the finance and investment cycle. Its major functions are financial planning and raising capital; interacting with the acquisition and expenditure, production and payroll, and revenue and collection cycles; and entering into mergers, acquisitions and other investments.

Debt and Shareholder Equity Capital

Transactions in debt and shareholder equity capital are normally few in number but large in monetary amount. They are handled by the highest levels of management. The control-related duties and responsibilities reflect this high-level attention.

Authorization

Financial planning starts with the chief financial officer's (CFO's) cash flow forecast. This forecast informs the board of directors and management of the business plans, the prospects for cash inflows and the needs for cash outflows. The cash flow forecast usually is integrated with the capital budget, which contains the plans for asset purchases and business acquisitions. A capital budget approved by the board of directors constitutes the authorization for major capital asset acquisitions (acquisition cycle) and investments.

Sales of share capital and debt financing transactions usually are authorized by the board of directors. All the directors must sign registration documents for public securities offerings. However, authority normally is delegated to the CFO to complete such transactions as periodic renewals of notes payable and other ordinary types of financing transactions without specific board approval of each transaction. Auditors should expect to find the authorizing signatures of the chief executive officer (CEO), CFO, chair of the board of directors and perhaps other high-ranking officers on financing documents.

Many financing transactions are "off the balance sheet." Companies can enter into obligations and commitments that are not required to be recorded in the accounts. Examples of such authorizations include leases, endorsements on discounted notes or on other companies' obligations, letters of credit, guarantees, repurchase or remarketing agreements, commitments to purchase at fixed prices, commitments to sell at fixed prices and certain kinds of stock options. These are among the business and financing options available to companies. They cause problems in financial reporting and disclosure.

Custody

In large companies custody of share certificate books is not a significant management problem. Large companies employ banks and trust companies to serve as registrars and transfer agents. A registrar keeps the shareholder list and, from time to time, determines the shareholders eligible to receive dividends (shareholders of record on a dividend record

EXHIBIT 12-1   FINANCE AND INVESTMENT CYCLE

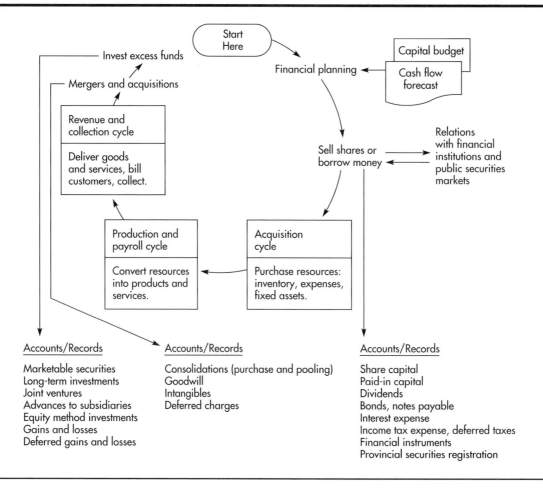

Accounts/Records

Marketable securities
Long-term investments
Joint ventures
Advances to subsidiaries
Equity method investments
Gains and losses
Deferred gains and losses

Accounts/Records

Consolidations (purchase and pooling)
Goodwill
Intangibles
Deferred charges

Accounts/Records

Share capital
Paid-in capital
Dividends
Bonds, notes payable
Interest expense
Income tax expense, deferred taxes
Financial instruments
Provincial securities registration

---

date) and those entitled to vote at the annual meeting. A transfer agent handles the exchange of shares, cancelling the shares surrendered by sellers and issuing new certificates to buyers. It is not unusual to find the same bank or trust company providing both services.

Small companies often keep their own shareholder records. A share certificate book looks like a chequebook. It has perforated stubs for recording the number of shares, the owner's name and other identification, and the date of issue. Actual unissued share certificates are attached to the stubs, like unused cheques in a chequebook. The missing certificates are the ones outstanding in the possession of owners. Custody of the share certificate book is important because the unissued certificates are like money or collateral. If improperly removed, they can be sold to buyers who think they are genuinely issued or can be used as collateral with unsuspecting lenders.

Lenders have custody of debt instruments (e.g., leases, bonds and notes payable). A CFO may have copies, but they are merely convenience records. However, when a company repurchases its debt instruments, these come into the custody of trustees or company officials, usually the CFO. Until they are cancelled and destroyed, it is possible to misuse them by improperly reselling them to unsuspecting investors.

Recordkeeping

Records of notes and bonds payable are maintained by the accounting department and the CFO or controller. The recordkeeping procedures should be similar to those used to account for vendor accounts payable: payment notices from lenders are compared to the accounting records, due dates are monitored, interest payments are set up in vouchers for

---

THE BRE-X SCANDAL
Shares close at 8.5¢—'it's just a shell now'

Bre-X Minerals Ltd. stock plunged 98% in minutes yesterday as angry investors wiped almost $700 million off the company's market capitalization and sent the the one-time market darling back to the ranks of the penny stocks.

It was the first time Bre-X shares have traded since the report by **Strathcona Mineral Services Ltd.** blew the whistle on a massive "falsification of assay values" at the supposedly huge Busang gold find in Indonesia.

The volume was so heavy it choked the Toronto Stock Exchange's communications system, leading officials to halt Bre-X trades and leave shareholders cooling their heels for more than an hour before trading in the stock resumed.

When the dust settled, the Calgary exploration company—valued at $6.8 billion a year ago—saw its market capitalization reduced to $18.6 million from $707.4 million on Friday.

Bre-X president David Walsh has insisted he was not part of any scam, and has hired former assistant RCMP commissioner Rod Stamler and forensic accountant Robert Lindquist to search out an explanation.

Bre-X's New York public relations firm, Hill & Knowlton Inc., left the account after viewing the Strathcona report that said the fraud was on a scale "without precedent in the history of mining."

A New York law firm, Wechsler Harwood Halebian & Feffer LLP, yesterday become at least the 10th to file a class-action suit against Bre-X.

Shaken investors on both sides of the border were lining up to get into lawsuits as they struggled to come to terms with their losses. [The sheer size of the damage claims against Bre-X ranks Busang among the biggest financial frauds in history, larger than the collapse of Barings Securities, the Bank of Credit and Commerce International and the Sumitomo copper trading scam.]

"What do I hope to recover? I guess all of it," said Dan Depaola, a Toronto sales representative who bought 3,000 shares about a month ago, after the stock collapsed. "But that's impossible, I know that. So anything, really. It's such a blow."

He didn't take the chance to dump his shares yesterday. "What's the point? The commissions are going to cost more."

Source: Sandra Rubin, *The Financial Post,* May 7, 1997, p. 6.

---

payment and accruals for unpaid interest are made on financial reporting dates. If the company has only a few bonds and notes outstanding, no subsidiary records of notes are kept. All the information is in the general ledger accounts. (Companies with a large number of bonds and notes may keep control and subsidiary accounts, as is done for accounts receivable.) When all or part of the notes become due within the next year, the CFO and controller have the necessary information for properly classifying current and long-term amounts.

Another class of credit balances is treated here under the heading of "recordkeeping," for which the functions of authorization, custody and reconciliation are not easy to describe. They are the "calculated liabilities and credits"—lease obligations, deferred income taxes, pension and post-retirement benefit liabilities and foreign currency translation gains and losses, to name a few. These are accounting creations, calculated according to accounting rules and using basic data from company plans and operations. Management usually enjoys considerable discretion in structuring leases, tax strategies, pension plan and employee benefit terms, foreign holdings and the like. These accounting calculations often involve significant accounting estimates made by management. Company accountants try to capture the economic reality of these calculated liabilities by following generally accepted accounting principles.

Periodic Reconciliation

A responsible person should periodically inspect the share certificate book to determine whether the only missing certificates are the ones known to be outstanding in the possession of bona fide owners. If necessary, company officials can confirm the ownership of shares with the holders of record. Reports with similar information content can be obtained from registrars and transfer agents to verify that the company's record of the number of shares outstanding agrees with the registrars' number. (Without this reconciliation, counterfeit shares handled by the transfer agent and recorded by the registrar might go unnoticed.)

Ownership of bonds can be handled by a trustee having duties and responsibilities similar to those of registrars and transfer agents. Confirmations and reports from bond trustees can be used to reconcile the trustee's records to the company's records.

Investments and Intangibles

A company can have many investments or only a few, and can have a large variety or a limited set of types of investments. Intangible assets may be in the form of purchased assets (e.g., patents, trademarks) or in the form of accounting allocations (e.g., goodwill, deferred charges). The sections below are phrased in the context of a manufacturing or service company for which investments and intangibles are fairly incidental in the business. Financial institutions (banks, trust companies), investment companies, mutual funds, insurance companies and the like have more elaborate systems for managing their investments and intangibles.

Authorization

All investment policies should be approved by the board of directors or its investment committee. It is not unusual to find board or executive committee approval required for major individual investment transactions. However, auditors should expect to find a great deal of variation across companies as to the nature and amount of transactions that must have specific high-level approval. The board of directors always is closely involved in major acquisitions, mergers and share buy-back plans.

Custody

Custody of investments and intangibles depends on the nature of the assets. Some investments, such as shares and bonds, are represented by negotiable certificates. The actual certificates may be kept in a brokerage account in a "house name" (the brokerage company), and, in this case, "custody" rests with the company official who is authorized to order the buy, sell and delivery transactions. They also may be in the actual possession of the owner (client company). If they are kept by the company, they should be in a safe or a bank safe-deposit box. Only high-ranking officers (e.g., CFO, CEO, president, chair of board) should have combinations and keys.

Other kinds of investments do not have formal negotiable certificates, and "custody" may take the form of "management responsibility" instead of actual physical handling. Examples are joint ventures and partnerships in which the client company is a partner. Venture and partnership agreements are evidence of these investments, but they usually are merely filed with other important documents. Misuse of them is seldom a problem because they are not readily negotiable. Real custody rests with management's supervision and monitoring of the venture or partnership operations.

Having "custody" of most intangibles is like trying to keep Jell-O in your pocket—good in theory but messy in practice. However, patents, trademarks, copyrights and similar legal intangible rights may be evidenced in legal documents and contracts. These seldom are negotiable, and they usually are kept in ordinary company files. Accounting intangibles like goodwill and deferred charges (deferred tax credits and pension obligations on the liability side) are in the custody of the accountants who calculate them. Company mangers may be assigned responsibility to protect exclusive rights granted by various intangibles.

AUTHORIZATION: HERE TODAY, GONE TOMORROW

The treasurer of Travum County had many responsibilities as a chief financial officer. She invested several million dollars of county funds with a California-based investment money manager. Soon thereafter, news stories of the money manager's expensive personal lifestyle and questionable handling of client's funds began to circulate, indicating that clients could lose much of their investments. At the same time, news stories about the treasurer's own credit-card spending habits were published locally, indicating that she had obtained a personal credit card by using the county's name.

Although no county funds were lost and no improper credit-card bills were paid, the county commissioners temporarily suspended the treasurer's authority to choose investment vehicles for county funds.

Recordkeeping

The procedures for purchase of share and bond investments involve the voucher system described in the acquisition and expenditure cycle (Chapter 10). Authorization by the board of directors or other responsible officials is the approval for the accounting department to prepare the voucher and the cheque. The treasurer or CFO signs the cheque for the investment. If the company has few investments, no subsidiary records are maintained and all information is kept in the general ledger accounts. If the company has many investments, a control account and subsidiary ledger may be maintained.

The recordkeeping for many kinds of investments and intangibles can be complicated. The complications arise not so much from the original recording of transactions as from the maintenance of the accounts over time. This is the place where complex accounting standards for equity method accounting, consolidations, goodwill, intangibles amortization and valuation, deferred charges, deferred taxes, pension and postretirement benefit liabilities and various financial instruments enter the picture. High-level accountants who prepare financial statements get involved with the accounting rules and the management estimates required to account for such investments and intangibles. Management plans and estimates of future events and minute interpretations of the accounting standards often become elements of the accounting maintenance of these balances. These decisions are ripe areas for overstatement of assets, understatement of liabilities and understatement of expenses.

Periodic Reconciliation

The most significant reconciliation opportunity in the investments and intangibles accounts is the inspection and count of negotiable securities certificates. This reconciliation is similar to a physical inventory in that it consists of an inspection of certificates on hand, along with comparison to the information recorded in the accounts. (When securities are held by a brokerage firm, the "inspection" is accomplished with a written confirmation.)

A securities count is not a mere handling of bits of paper. A securities count "inventory" should include a record of the name of the company represented by the certificate, the interest rate for bonds, the dividend rate for preferred shares, the due date for bonds, the serial numbers on the certificates, the face value of bonds, the number or face amount of bonds and shares and notes on the name of the owner shown on the face of the certificate or on the endorsements on the back (should be the client company). Companies should perform this reconciliation reasonably often and not wait for an annual visit by the independent auditors. A securities count in a financial institution that holds thousands of shares in multimillion-dollar asset accounts is a major undertaking.

When auditors perform the securities inspection and count, the same kind of information should be recorded in the audit working papers. An example of these elements in an audit working paper is in Problem 4.52 at the end of Chapter 4. You can see several elements of evidence in the information: existence is established by handling the securities, ownership is established by viewing the client name as owner, valuation evidence is added by finding the cost and market value (see the example in Problem 4.52). If a security certificate is not available for inspection, it may be pledged as collateral for a loan and in the hands of a creditor. It can be confirmed or inspected, if the extended procedure of visiting the creditor is necessary. The pledge as collateral may be important for a disclosure note. A securities count and reconciliation is important for management and auditors because companies have been known to try to substitute others' securities for missing ones. If securities have been sold, then replaced without any accounting entries, the serial numbers will show that the certificate recorded in the accounts is not the same as the ones on hand.

R E V I E W
C H E C K P O I N T S

12.1 Do you believe that losses hidden by fraudulent overstatement of assets should be corrected with prior period adjustment accounting after discovery?

12.2 When a management carefully crafts a lease agreement to barely fail the tests for lease capitalization and liability recognition, do you believe that auditors should insist on capitalization anyway?

12.3 What would constitute the authorization for notes payable? What documentary evidence could auditors examine as evidence of this authorization?

12.4 Define and give five examples of "off-balance-sheet information." Why should auditors be concerned with such items?

12.5 What features of a client's share capital are of importance in the audit?

12.6 What information about share capital could be confirmed with outside parties? How could this information be corroborated by the auditors?

12.7 What procedures can auditors employ in the audit of investment securities to obtain the names of the issuers, the number of shares held, certificate numbers, maturity value and interest and dividend rates?

12.8 Describe the procedures and documentation of a controlled count of client's investment securities. What information should be included in an audit working paper?

12.9 What is a "destruction certificate?"

· ·

CONTROL RISK ASSESSMENT
· · · · · · · · · · · ·

LEARNING OBJECTIVE

2. Give examples of test of controls procedures for obtaining information about the controls over debt and owner equity transactions and investment transactions.

In the finance and investment cycle, auditors look for control procedures, such as authorization, custody, recordkeeping and periodic reconciliation. They especially look for information about the level of management involved in these functions. Tests of controls generally amount to enquiries and observations related to these features. Samples of transactions for detail tests of control performance are not normally a part of the control risk assessment work as they can be in the revenue and collection cycle, in the acquisition and expenditure cycle, and in the production and payroll cycle. Because finance and investment transactions are usually individually material, each transaction usually is audited in detail. Reliance on control does not normally reduce the extent of substantive audit work on finance and investment cycle accounts. However, lack of control can lead to performance of significant extended procedures.

General Control Considerations

Control procedures for suitable handling of responsibilities (note the avoidance of the idea of "proper segregation") should be in place and operating. By referring to the discussion accompanying Exhibit 12–1, you can tell that these responsibilities are basically in the hands of senior management officials. You also can tell that different companies may have widely different policies and procedures.

It is hard to have a strict segregation of functional responsibilities when the principal officers of a company authorize, execute and control finance and investment activities. It is not very realistic to maintain that a CEO can authorize investments but cannot have access to shareholder records, securities certificates and the like. Real segregation of duties can be found in middle management and lower ranks, but it is hard to create and enforce in upper-level management.

In light of this problem of control, a company should have compensating control procedures. A compensating control is a control feature used when a standard control procedure (such as strict segregation of function responsibilities) is not specified by the company. In the area of finance and investment, the compensating control feature is the involvement of two or more persons in each kind of important functional responsibility.

If involvement by multiple persons is not specified, then oversight or review can be substituted. For example, the board of directors can authorize purchase of securities or creation of a partnership. The CFO or CEO can carry out the transactions, have custody of certificates and agreements, manage the partnership or the portfolio of securities, oversee the recordkeeping and make the decisions about valuations and accounting (authorizing the journal entries). These are rather normal management activities, and they combine several responsibilities. The compensating control can exist in the form of periodic reports to the board of directors, oversight by the investment committee of the board and internal audit involvement in making a periodic reconciliation of securities certificates in a portfolio with the amounts and descriptions recorded in the accounts.

Control over Accounting Estimates

An accounting estimate is the amount included in financial statements to approximate the effect of past business transactions or events on the present status of an asset or liability. The use of accounting estimates in financial reporting is common. Examples include such items as allowance for doubtful receivables, loss provisions and amortization of capital assets. Accounting estimates can have a significant or pervasive effect on reported results, either individually or when considered in the aggregate (*Handbook Section* 5305.02 and ISA 540.4).

Accounting estimates often are included in basic financial statements because (1) the measurement of some amount of valuation is uncertain, perhaps depending upon the outcome of future events, or (2) relevant data cannot be accumulated on a timely, cost-effective basis. Some examples of accounting estimates in the finance and investment cycle are shown in the box on the next page.

A client's management is responsible for making estimates and should have a process and control structure designed to reduce the likelihood of material misstatements in them. Specific relevant aspects of such a control structure include:

- Management communication of the need for proper accounting estimates.
- Accumulation of relevant, sufficient and reliable data for estimates.
- Preparation of estimates by qualified personnel.
- Adequate review and approval by appropriate levels of authority.
- Comparison of prior estimates with subsequent results to assess the reliability of the estimation outcomes.
- Consideration by management of whether particular accounting estimates are consistent with the company's operational plans.

Auditors' test of controls over the production of estimates amounts to enquiries and observations related to the features listed immediately above. Such enquiries are: Who prepares estimates? When are they prepared? What data are used? Who reviews and approves the estimates? Have you compared prior estimates with subsequent actual events? Observations include study of data documentation, study of comparisons of prior estimates

---

FINANCE AND INVESTMENT CYCLE ESTIMATES

Financial instruments: Valuation of securities, classification into trading versus investment portfolios, probability of a correlated hedge, sales of securities with puts and calls.

Accruals: Compensation in stock option plans, actuarial assumptions in pension costs.

Leases: Initial direct costs, executory costs, residual values, capitalization interest rate.

Rates: Imputed interest rates on receivables and payables.

Other: Losses and net realizable value on segment disposal and business restructuring, fair values in nonmonetary exchanges.

with subsequent actual experience and study of intercompany correspondence concerning estimates and operational plans.

The audit of an estimate starts with the test of controls, much of which has a bearing on the substantive quality of the estimation process and of the estimate itself. Further substantive audit procedures include recalculating the mathematical estimate, developing an auditor's own independent estimate based on alternative assumptions and comparing the estimate to subsequent events to the extent they are known before the end of the field work.

Control Risk Assessment for Notes Payable

From the preceding discussion, you can tell that test of controls audit procedures take a variety of forms—enquiries, observations, study of documentation, comparison with related data, such as tax returns, and detail audit of some transactions. The detail audit of transactions, however, is a small part of the test of controls because of the nature of the finance and investment transactions, their number (few), and their amount (large). However, some companies have numerous debt financing transactions, and in such cases a more detailed approach to control risk assessment can be used, including the selection of a sample of transactions for control risk assessment evidence.

An internal control questionnaire for notes payable is in Exhibit 12–2. It illustrates typical questions about the control objectives. These enquiries give auditors insights into the client's specifications for review and approval of major financing transactions, the system of accounting for them and the provision for error-checking review procedures.

Auditors can select a sample of notes payable transactions for detail test of controls, provided that the population of notes is large enough to justify sample-based auditing. Exhibit 12–3 lists a selection of such procedures, with notation of the relevant control objectives shown on the right.

Summary: Control Risk Assessment

The audit manager or senior accountant in charge of the audit should evaluate the evidence obtained from an understanding of the internal control structure and from test of controls audit procedures. These procedures can take many forms because management systems for finance and investment accounts can be quite varied among clients. The involvement of

---

E X H I B I T 12–2   INTERNAL CONTROL QUESTIONNAIRE: NOTES PAYABLE

Environment:
1. Are notes payable records kept by someone who cannot sign notes or cheques?
Validity objective:
2. Are paid notes cancelled, stamped "paid" and filed?
Completeness objective:
3. Is all borrowing authorization by the directors checked to determine whether all notes payable are recorded?
Authorization objective:
4. Are direct borrowings on notes payable authorized by the directors? by the treasurer or by the chief financial officer?
5. Are two or more authorized signatures required on notes?
Accuracy objective:
6. Are bank due notices compared with records of unpaid liabilities?
Classification objective:
7. Is sufficient information available in the accounts to enable financial statement preparers to classify current and long-term debt properly?
Accounting objective:
8. Is the subsidiary ledger of notes payable periodically reconciled with the general ledger control account(s)?
Proper period objective:
9. Are interest payments and accruals monitored for due dates and financial statement dates?

EXHIBIT 12–3   TEST OF CONTROLS AUDIT PROCEDURES FOR NOTES PAYABLE

	Control Objective
1. Read directors' and finance committee's minutes for authorization of financing transactions (such as short-term notes payable, bond offerings).	Authorization
2. Select a sample of paid notes:	
a. Recalculate interest expense for the period under audit.	Accuracy
b. Trace interest expense to the general ledger account.	Completeness
c. Vouch payment to cancelled cheques.	Validity
3. Select a sample of notes payable:	
a. Vouch to authorization by directors or finance committee.	Authorization
b. Vouch cash receipt to bank statement.	Validity

senior officials in a relatively small number of high-dollar transactions makes control risk assessment a process tailored specifically to the company's situation. Some companies enter into complicated financing and investment transactions, while others keep to the simple transactions.

However, some control considerations can be generalized. Control over management's production of accounting estimates is characterized by some common features. In some cases, such as a company with numerous notes payable transactions, samples of transactions for detail testing can be used to produce evidence about compliance with control policies and procedures.

In general, substantive audit procedures on finance and investment accounts are not limited in extent. It is very common for auditors to perform substantive audit procedures on 100 percent of these transactions and balances. The number of transactions is usually not

---

AN ESTIMATED VALUATION BASED ON FUTURE DEVELOPMENT

Gulf & Western Industries (G&W) sold 450,000 shares of Pan American stock from its investment portfolio to Resorts International (Resorts). Resorts paid $8 million plus 250,000 shares of its unregistered common stock. G&W recorded the sale proceeds as $14,167,500, valuing the unregistered Resorts shares at $6,167,500, which was approximately 67 percent of the market price of Resorts shares at the time ($36.82 per share). G&W reported a gain of $3,365,000 on the sale.

Four years later, Resorts shares fell to $2.63. G&W sold its 250,000 shares back to Resorts in exchange for 1,100 acres of undeveloped land on Grand Bahamas Island. For its records, Resorts got a broker-dealer's opinion that its 250,000 shares were worth $460,000. For property tax assessment purposes, the Bahamian government valued the undeveloped land at $525,000.

G&W valued the land on its books at $6,167,500, which was the previous valuation of the Resorts shares. The justification was an appraisal of $6,300,000 based on the estimated value of the 1,100 acres when ultimately developed (i.e., built into an operating resort and residential community). However, G&W also reported a loss of $5,527,000 in its tax return (effectively valuing the land at $640,500). The SEC accused G&W of failing to report a loss of $5.7 million in its financial statements. Do you think the loss should have appeared in the G&W income statement?

Source: I. Kellog, *How to Find Negligence and Misrepresentation in Financial Statements* (New York: Shepard's/McGraw Hill, 1983), p. 279.

large, and the audit cost is not high for complete coverage. Nevertheless, control deficiencies and unusual or complicated transactions can cause auditors to adjust the nature and timing of audit procedures. Complicated financial instruments, pension plans, exotic equity securities, related party transactions and nonmonetary exchanges of investment assets call for procedures designed to find evidence of errors, irregularities and frauds in the finance and investment accounts. The next section deals with some of the finance and investment cycle assertions, and it has some cases for your review.

R E V I E W
C H E C K P O I N T S

12.10 What is a compensating control? Give some examples for finance and investment cycle accounts.

12.11 What are some of the specific relevant aspects of management's control over the production of accounting estimates? What are some enquiries auditors can make?

12.12 When a company has produced an estimate of an investment valuation based on a nonmonetary exchange, what source of comparative information can an auditor use?

12.13 If a company does not monitor notes payable for due dates and interest payment dates in relation to financial statement dates, what misstatements can appear in the financial statements?

12.14 Generally, how much emphasis is placed on adequate internal control in the audit of long-term debt? of share capital? of contributed surplus? and of retained earnings?

ASSERTIONS, SUBSTANTIVE PROCEDURES AND AUDIT CASES

LEARNING OBJECTIVE

3. Describe some common errors, irregularities and frauds in the accounting for capital transactions and investments, and design some audit and investigation procedures for detecting them.

This part of the chapter covers the audit of various account balances and gains and losses. It is presented in three sections—owners' equity, long-term liabilities and related accounts, and investments and intangibles. As in previous chapters, some casettes illustrating errors, irregularities and frauds are used to describe useful audit approaches. In addition, this chapter gives some assertions and procedures related to accounts in the cycle.

The cases begin with a description containing these elements:

Method: A cause of the misstatement (mistaken estimate or judgment, accidental error, intentional irregularity or fraud attempt), which usually is made easier by some kind of failure of controls.

Paper trail: A set of telltale signs of erroneous accounting, missing or altered documents or a "dangling debit" (the false or erroneous debit that results from an overstatement of assets).

Amount: The dollar amount of overstated assets and revenue, or understated liabilities and expenses.

Each audit program for the audit of an account balance contains an Audit Approach that may enable auditors to detect misstatements in account balances. Each application of procedures contains these elements:

Audit objective: A recognition of a financial statement assertion for which evidence needs to be obtained. The assertions are about the existence of assets, liabilities, revenue and expenses; their valuation; their complete inclusion in the account balances; the rights and obligations inherent in them; and their proper presentation and disclosure in the financial statements. (These assertions were introduced in Chapter 4.)

Control: A recognition of the control procedures that should be used by an organization to prevent and detect errors and irregularities.

Test of controls: Ordinary and extended procedures designed to produce evidence about the effectiveness of the controls that should be in operation.

Audit of balance: Ordinary and extended substantive procedures designed to find signs of mistaken accounting estimates, errors, irregularities and frauds in account balances and classes of transactions.

The cases first set the stage with a story about an accounting estimate, error, irregularity or fraud—its method, paper trail (if any) and amount. This part of the casette gives you the "inside story," which auditors seldom know before they perform the audit work. The second part of the casette, under the heading of Audit Approach, tells a structured story about the audit objective, desirable controls, test of control procedures, audit of balance procedures and discovery summary. The Audit Approach segment illustrates how audit procedures can be applied and the discoveries they may enable auditors to make. At the end of the chapter, some similar discussion cases are presented, and you can write the Audit Approach to test your ability to design audit procedures for the detection of mistaken accounting estimates, errors, irregularities and frauds.

Owners' Equity

Management makes assertions about the existence, completeness, rights and obligations, valuation and presentation and disclosure of owners' equity. Typical specific assertions include:

1. The number of shares shown as issued is in fact issued.

2. No other shares (including options, warrants and the like) have been issued and not recorded or reflected in the accounts and disclosures.

3. The accounting is proper for options, warrants and other share issue plans, and related disclosures are adequate.

4. The valuation of shares issued for noncash consideration is proper, in conformity with accounting principles.

5. All owners' equity transactions have been authorized by the board of directors.

An illustrative program of substantive audit procedures for owners' equity is in Exhibit 12A–1.

Documentation

Owners' equity transactions usually are well documented in minutes of the meetings of the board of directors, in proxy statements and in securities offering registration statements. Transactions can be vouched to these documents, and the cash proceeds can be traced to the bank accounts.

Confirmation

Share capital may be subject to confirmation when independent registrars and transfer agents are employed. Such agents are responsible for knowing the number of shares authorized and issued and for keeping lists of shareholders' names. The basic information about share capital—such as number of shares, classes of shares, preferred dividend rates, conversion terms, dividend payments, shares held in the company name, expiration dates and terms of warrants and share dividends and splits—can be confirmed with the independent agents. Many of these items can be corroborated by the auditors' own inspection and reading of share certificates, charter authorizations, directors' minutes and registration statements. However, when there are no independent agents, most audit evidence is gathered by vouching share record documents (such as certificate book stubs). When circumstances call for extended procedures, information on outstanding shares may be confirmed directly with the holders.

CASETTE 12.1
UNREGISTERED SALE OF SECURITIES

Problem

A. T. Bliss & Company (Bliss) sold investment contracts in the form of limited partnership interests to the public. These "securities" sales should have been under a public registration filing with the OSC, but they were not.

Method

Bliss salespeople contacted potential investors and sold many of them limited partnership interests. The setup deal called for these limited partnerships to purchase solar hot water heating systems for residential and commercial use from Bliss. All the partnerships entered into arrangements to lease the equipment to Nationwide Corporation, which then rented the equipment to end users. The limited partnerships were, in effect, financing conduits for obtaining investors' money to pay for Bliss's equipment. The investors depended on Nationwide's business success and ability to pay under the lease terms for their return of capital and profit.

Paper Trail

Bliss published false and misleading financial statements, which used a non-GAAP revenue recognition method and failed to disclose cost of goods sold. Bliss overstated Nationwide's record of equipment installation and failed to disclose that Nationwide had little cash flow from end users (resulting from rent-free periods and other inducements). Bliss knew—and failed to disclose to prospective investors—the fact that numerous previous investors had filed petitions with the federal tax court to contest the disallowance by Revenue Canada (now the Canada Customs and Revenue Agency) of all their tax credits and benefits claimed in connection with their investments in Bliss's tax-sheltered equipment lease partnerships.

Amount

Not known, but all the money put up by the limited partnership investors was at risk largely not disclosed to the investors.

AUDIT APPROACH

Audit Objective

Obtain evidence to determine whether capital fundraising methods comply with provincial securities laws and whether financial statements and other disclosures are not misleading.

Control

Management should employ experts—lawyers, underwriters and accountants—who can determine whether securities and investment contract sales do or do not require registration.

Test of Controls

Auditors should learn the business backgrounds and securities-industry expertise of the senior managers. Study the minutes of the board of directors for authorization of the fund-raising method. Obtain and study opinions rendered by lawyers and underwriters about the legality of the fund-raising methods. Enquire about management's interaction with the OSC in any presale clearance. (The OSC will give advice about the necessity for registration.)

Audit of Balances

Auditors should study the offering documents and literature used in the sale of securities to determine whether financial information is being used properly. In this case the close relationship with Nationwide and the experience of earlier partnerships give reasons for extended procedures to obtain evidence about the representations concerning Nationwide's business success (in this case, lack of success).

Discovery Summary

The auditors gave unqualified reports on Bliss's materially misstated financial statements. They apparently did not question the legality of the sales of the limited partnership interests as a means of raising capital. They apparently did not perform procedures to verify representations made in offering literature respecting Bliss or Nationwide finances. Two partners in the audit firm were enjoined from violations of the securities laws. They resigned from practice before the OSC and were ordered not to perform any assurance services for companies making filings with the OSC. They later were expelled from the ICAO for failure to co-operate with the Disciplinary Committee in its investigation of alleged professional ethics violations.

CASETTE 12.2
TAX LOSS CARRYFORWARDS

Problem

Aetna Life & Casualty Insurance Company had losses in its taxable income operations in 1981 and 1982. Confident that future taxable income would absorb the loss, the company booked and reported a tax benefit for the tax loss carryforward. The OSC maintained that the company understated its tax expense and understated its liabilities (Aetna reported the tax benefit as a negative liability). Utilization of the loss carryforward was not "virtually certain," as required by *Handbook Section 3470.46*.

Method

Aetna forecasted several more years of taxable losses (aside from its nontaxable income from tax-exempt investments), then forecasted years of taxable income, eventually offsetting the losses and obtaining the benefit of the tax law allowing losses to be carried forward to offset against future taxable income. The company maintained there was no reasonable doubt that the forecasts would be achieved.

Paper Trail

The amounts of tax loss were clearly evident in the accounts. Aetna made no attempt to hide the facts. The size of the portfolio of taxable investments and all sources of taxable income and deductions were well known to the company accountants, management and independent auditors.

Amount

At first, the carryforward tax benefit was $25 million, soon growing to over $200 million, then forecast to become an estimated $1 billion before it was forecast to reverse by being absorbed by future taxable income. In 1983, the first full year affected, Aetna's net income was 35 percent lower than 1981, instead of 6 percent lower with the carryforward benefit recognized.

AUDIT APPROACH

Audit Objective

Obtain evidence to determine whether realization of the benefits of the tax loss carryforward are "virtually certain."

Control

The relevant control in this case concerns the assumptions and mathematics involved in preparing the forecasts used to justify the argument for recording the tax loss carryforward benefit. These forecasts are the basis for an accounting estimate of "virtually certain realization."

Test of Controls

Auditors should make enquiries and determine: Who prepared the forecasts? When were they prepared? What data were used? Who reviewed and approved the forecast? Is there any way to test the accuracy of the forecast with actual experience?

Audit of Balances

Aside from audit of the assumptions underlying the forecast and recalculations of the compilation, the test of balances amounted to careful consideration of whether the forecast, or any forecast, could meet the test required by accounting standards. The decision was a judgment of whether the test of "virtually certain realization" was met.

The auditors should obtain information about other situations in which recognition of tax loss carryforward benefits were allowed in financial statements. Other companies have booked and reported such benefits when gains from sales of property were realized before the financial statement was issued and when the loss was from discontinuing a business line, leaving other businesses with long profit histories and prospects in operation.

Discovery Summary

The OSC was tipped off to Aetna's accounting recognition of the tax loss carryforward benefit by a story in *Financial Post* magazine, which described the accounting treatment. Aetna and its auditors argued on the basis of the forecasts. The OSC countered that the forecasts did not provide assurance beyond any reasonable doubt that future taxable income would be sufficient to offset the loss carry-forward and would be earned during the carry-forward period prescribed by the tax laws, as prescribed by Section 3490.43 of the *CICA Handbook*. For this reason, the OSC concluded that the "virtually certain realization" was not established. The OSC won the argument. Aetna revised its previously issued quarterly financial statements, and the company abandoned the attempt to report the tax benefit.

Long-term Liabilities and Related Accounts

The primary audit concern with the verification of long-term liabilities is that all liabilities are recorded and that the interest expense is properly paid or accrued. Therefore, the assertion of completeness is paramount. Alertness to the possibility of unrecorded liabilities during the performance of procedures in other areas frequently will uncover liabilities that have not been recorded. For example, when fixed assets are acquired during the year under audit, auditors should enquire about the source of funds for financing the new asset.

E X H I B I T 12–4   **OFF-BALANCE SHEET COMMITMENTS**

Type of Commitment	Typical Procedures and Sources of Evidence
1. Repurchase or remarketing agreements.	1. Vouching of contracts, confirmation by customer, enquiry of client management.
2. Commitments to purchase at fixed prices.	2. Vouching of open purchase orders, enquiry of purchasing personnel, confirmation by supplier.
3. Commitments to sell at fixed prices.	3. Vouching of sales contracts, enquiry of sales personnel, confirmation by customer.
4. Loan commitments.	4. Vouching of open commitment file, enquiry of loan officers.
5. Lease commitments.	5. Vouching of lease agreement, confirmation with lessor or lessee.

Management makes assertions about existence, completeness, rights and obligations, valuation and presentation and disclosure. Typical specific assertions relating to long-term liabilities include:

1. All material long-term liabilities are recorded.
2. Liabilities are properly classified according to their current or long-term status. The current portion of long-term debt is properly valued and classified.
3. New long-term liabilities and debt extinguishments are properly authorized.
4. Terms, conditions and restrictions relating to non-current debt are adequately disclosed.
5. Disclosures of maturities for the next five years and the capital and operating lease disclosures are accurate and adequate.
6. All important contingencies are either accrued in the accounts or disclosed in footnotes.

An illustrative program of substantive audit procedures for notes payable and long-term debt is in Appendix Exhibit 12A–2.

Confirmation

When auditing long-term liabilities, auditors usually obtain independent written confirmations for notes and bonds payable. In the case of notes payable to banks, the standard bank confirmation may be used. The amount and terms of bonds payable, mortgages payable and other formal debt instruments can be confirmed by requests to holders or a trustee. The confirmation request should include questions not only of amount, interest rate and due date but also about collateral, restrictive covenants and other items of agreement between lender and borrower. Confirmation requests should be sent to lenders with whom the company has done business in the recent past, even if no liability balance is shown at the confirmation date. Such extra coverage is a part of the search for unrecorded liabilities. (Refer to Chapter 10 for more on the "search for unrecorded liabilities.")

Off-Balance Sheet Financing

Confirmation and enquiry procedures may be used to obtain responses on a class of items loosely termed "off-balance sheet information." Within this category are terms of loan agreements, leases, endorsements, guarantees and insurance policies (whether issued by a client insurance company or owned by the client). Among these items is the difficult-to-define set of "commitments and contingencies" that often pose evidence-gathering problems. Some common types of commitments are shown in Exhibit 12–4.

Footnote disclosure should be considered for the types of commitments shown in Exhibit 12–4. Some of them can be estimated and valued and, thus, can be recorded in the accounts and shown in the financial statements themselves (such as losses on fixed-price purchase commitments and losses on fixed-price sales commitments).

Analytical relationships interest expense generally is related item by item to interest-bearing liabilities. Based on the evidence of long-term liability transactions (including those that have been retired during the year), the related interest expense amounts can be recalculated. The amount of debt, the interest rate and the time period are used to determine whether the interest expense and accrued interest are properly recorded. By comparing the audit results to the recorded interest expense and accrued interest accounts, auditors may be able to detect (1) greater expense than their calculations show, indicating some interest paid on debt unknown to them, possibly an unrecorded liability; (2) lesser expense than their calculations show, indicating misclassification, failure to accrue interest or an interest payment default; or (3) interest expense equal to their calculations. The first two possibilities raise questions for further study, and the third shows a correct correlation between debt and debt-related expense. Examples of working papers showing this interrelationship and recalculation of interest expense and other notes payable procedures are presented in Problems 12.27 and 12.56 at the end of the chapter.

Deferred Credits—Calculated Balances

Several types of deferred credits depend on calculations for their existence and valuation. Examples include (1) deferred profit on installment sales involving the gross margin and the sale amount; (2) deferred income taxes and investment credits involving tax-book timing differences, tax rates and amortization methods; and (3) deferred contract revenue involving contract provisions for prepayment, percentage-of-completion revenue recognition methods or other terms unique to a contract. All of these features are incorporated in calculations that auditors can check for accuracy.

Casette 12.3
Off-Balance Sheet Inventory Financing

Problem

Verity Distillery Company used the "product repurchase" ploy to convert its inventory to cash, failing to disclose the obligation to repurchase it later. Related party transactions were not disclosed.

Method

Verity's president incorporated the Veritas Corporation, making himself and two other Verity officers the sole shareholders. The president arranged to sell $40 million of Verity's inventory of whiskey in the aging process to Veritas, showing no gain or loss on the transaction. The officers negotiated a 36-month loan with a major bank to get the money Veritas used for the purchase, pledging the inventory as collateral. Verity pledged to repurchase the inventory for $54.4 million, which amounted to the original $40 million plus 12 percent interest for three years.

Paper Trail

The contract of sale was in the files, specifying the name of the purchasing company, the $40 million amount and the cash consideration. Nothing mentioned the relation of Veritas to the officers. Nothing mentioned the repurchase obligation. However, the sale amount was unusually large.

Amount

The $40 million amount was 40 percent of the normal inventory. Verity's cash balance was increased 50 percent. While the current asset total was not changed, the inventory ratios (e.g., inventory turnover, day's sales in inventory) were materially altered. Long-term liabilities were understated by not recording the liability. The ploy was actually a secured loan with inventory pledged as collateral, but this reality was neither recorded nor disclosed. The total effect would be to keep debt off the books, to avoid recording interest expense and later to record inventory at a higher cost. Subsequent sale of the whiskey at market prices would not affect the ultimate income results, but the unrecorded interest expense would be buried in the cost of goods sold. The net income in the first year when the "sale" was made was not changed, but the normal relationship of gross margin to sales was distorted by the zero-profit transaction.

	Before Transaction	Recorded Transaction	Should Have Recorded
Assets	$530	$530	$570
Liabilities	390	390	430
Shareholder Equity	140	140	140
Debt/Equity ratio	2.79	2.79	3.07

AUDIT APPROACH

Audit Objective

Obtain evidence to determine whether all liabilities are recorded. Be alert to undisclosed related party transactions.

Control

The relevant control in this case would rest with the integrity and accounting knowledge of the senior officials who arranged the transaction. Authorization in the board minutes might detail the arrangements; but, if they wanted to hide it from the auditors, they also would suppress the telltale information in the board minutes.

Test of Controls

Enquiries should be made about large and unusual financing transactions. This may not elicit a response because the event is a sales transaction, according to Verity. Other audit work on controls in the revenue and collection cycle may turn up the large sale. Fortunately, this one sticks out as a large one.

Audit of Balances

Analytical procedures to compare monthly or seasonal sales probably will identify the sale as large and unusual. This identification should lead to an examination of the sales contract. Auditors should discuss the business purpose of the transaction with knowledgeable officials. If being this close to discovery does not bring out an admission of the loan and repurchase arrangement, the auditors nevertheless should investigate further. Even if the "customer" name is not a giveaway, a quick enquiry at the corporate search branch of the provincial ministry of consumer and commercial relations for corporation records (on-line in some databases) will show the names of the officers, and the auditors will know the related party nature of the deal. A request for the financial statements of Veritas should be made.

Discovery Summary

The auditors found the related party relationship between the officers and Veritas. Confronted, the president admitted the attempt to make the cash position and the debt/equity ratio look better than they were. The financial statements were adjusted to reflect the "should have recorded" set of figures shown above.

Investments and Intangibles

Companies can have a wide variety of investments and relationships with affiliates. Investments accounting may be on the cost method, equity method without consolidation or full consolidation, depending on the size and influence represented by the investment. Purchase-method consolidations usually create problems of accounting for the fair value of acquired assets and the related goodwill. Specific assertions typical of a variety of investment account balances are these:

1. Investment securities are on hand or are held in safekeeping by a trustee (existence).
2. Investment cost does not exceed market value (valuation).
3. Significant influence investments are accounted for by the equity method (valuation).
4. Purchased goodwill is properly valued (valuation).
5. Capitalized intangible costs relate to intangibles acquired in exchange transactions (valuation).
6. Research and development costs are properly classified (presentation).
7. Amortization is properly calculated (valuation).
8. Investment income has been received and recorded (completeness).
9. Investments are adequately classified and described in the balance sheet (presentation).

An illustrative program of substantive audit procedures for investments, intangibles and related accounts is in Appendix Exhibit 12A–3.

Unlike the current assets accounts, which are characterized by numerous small transactions, the noncurrent investment accounts usually consist of a few large entries. This difference has internal control and substantive audit procedure implications. The impact on the auditors' consideration of the control environment is concentration on the authorization of transactions, since each individual transaction is likely to be material in itself and the authorization will give significant information about the proper classification and accounting method. The controls usually are not reviewed, tested and evaluated at an interim date but are considered along with the year-end procedures when the transactions and their authorizations are audited.

A few of the trouble spots in audits of investments and intangibles are in the box below.

Confirmation

The practice of obtaining independent written confirmation from outside parties is fairly limited in the area of investments, intangibles and related income and expense accounts. Securities held by trustees or brokers should be confirmed, and the confirmation request should seek the same descriptive information as that obtained in a physical count by the auditor (described earlier in this chapter).

Enquiries About Intangibles

Company counsel can be queried about knowledge of any lawsuits or defects relating to patents, copyrights, trademarks or trade names. This confirmation can be sought by a specific request in the enquiry letter to the law firm. (Chapter 13 contains more information regarding the enquiry letter to the law firm.)

Income from Intangibles

Royalty income from patent licences received from a single licencee may be confirmed. However, such income amounts usually are audited by vouching the licencee's reports and related cash payment.

Inspection

Investment property may be inspected in a manner similar to the physical inspection of fixed assets. The principal goal is to determine actual existence and condition of the property. Official documents of patents, copyrights and trademark rights can be inspected to see that they are, in fact, in the name of the client.

Documentation Vouching

Investment costs should be vouched to brokers' reports, monthly statements or other documentary evidence of cost. At the same time, the amounts of sales are traced to gain or loss accounts, and the amounts of sales prices and proceeds are vouched to the brokers' statements. Auditors should determine what method of cost-out assignment was used (i.e., FIFO, specific certificate or average cost) and whether it is consistent with prior-years' transactions. The cost of real and personal property likewise can be vouched to invoices or other documents of purchase, and title documents (such as on land, buildings) may be inspected.

Market valuation of securities may be required in some cases. While a management may assert that an investment valuation is not impaired, subsequent sale at a loss before the end of audit field work will indicate otherwise. Auditors should review investment transactions subsequent to the balance sheet date for this kind of evidence about lower-of-cost-or-market valuation.

Vouching may be extensive in the areas of research and development (R&D) and deferred software development costs. The principal evidence problem is to determine whether costs are properly classified as assets or as R&D expense. Recorded amounts generally are selected on a sample basis, and the purchase orders, receiving reports, payroll records, authorization notices and management reports are compared to them. Some R&D costs may resemble non-R&D cost (such as supplies, payroll costs), so auditors must be very careful in the vouching to be alert for costs that appear to relate to other operations.

External Documentation

By consulting quoted market values of securities, auditors can calculate market values and determine whether investments should be written down. If quoted market values are not available, financial statements related to investments must be obtained and analysed for evidence of basic value. If such financial statements are unaudited, evidence indicated by them is considered to be extremely weak.

Income amounts can be verified by consulting published dividend records for quotations of dividends actually declared and paid during a period (e.g., Moody's and Standard & Poor's dividend records). Since auditors know the holding period of

---

Trouble Spots in Audits of Investments and Intangibles

- Valuation of investments at lower of cost, market or value impairment that is other than temporary.
- Determination of significant influence relationship for equity method investments.
- Proper determination of goodwill in purchase-method consolidations. Reasonable amortization life for goodwill.
- Realistic distinction between purchase and pooling consolidations.
- Capitalization and continuing valuation of intangibles and deferred charges.
- Realistic distinctions of research, feasibility and production milestones for capitalization of software development costs.
- Adequate disclosure of restrictions, pledges or liens related to investment assets.

securities, dividend income can be calculated and compared to the amount in the account. Any difference could indicate a cutoff error, misclassification, defalcation or failure to record a dividend receivable. In a similar manner, application of interest rates to bond or note investments produces a calculated interest income figure (making allowance for amortization of premium or discount if applicable).

Equity Method Investments

When equity method accounting is used for investments, auditors will need to obtain financial statements of the investee company. These should be audited statements. Inability to obtain financial statements from a closely held investee may indicate that the client investor does not have the significant controlling influence required by *Handbook Section* 3050.06–.08. When available, these statements are used as the basis for recalculating the amount of the client's share of income to recognize in the accounts. In addition, these statements may be used to audit the disclosure of investees' assets, liabilities and income presented in footnotes (a disclosure recommended when investments accounted for by the equity method are material).

Amortization Recalculation

Amortization of goodwill and other intangibles should be recalculated. Like depreciation, amortization ex-pense owes its existence to a calculation, and recalculation based on audited costs and rates is sufficient audit evidence.[1]

Merger and acquisition transactions should be reviewed in terms of the appraisals, judgments and allocations used to assign portions of the purchase price to tangible assets, intangible assets, liabilities and goodwill. In the final analysis, nothing really substitutes for the inspection of transaction documentation, but verbal enquiries may help auditors to understand the circumstances of a merger.

Questions about lawsuits challenging patents, copyrights or trade names may produce early knowledge of problem areas for further investigation. Likewise, discussions and questions about research and development successes and failures may alert the audit team to problems of valuation of intangible assets and related amortization expense. Responses to questions about licensing of patents can be used in the audit of related royalty revenue accounts.

Equiries About Management Intentions

Enquiries should deal with the nature of investments and the reasons for holding them. Management's expressed intention that a marketable security investment be considered a long-term investment may be the only available evidence for classifying it as long term and not as a current asset. The classification will affect the accounting treatment of market values and the unrealized gains and losses on investments.

---

[1] Under section 3060.31 of the *Handbook* the official terminology is now "capital assets" and "amortization" although "depreciation" still receives common use when reference is to amortization of tangible capital assets.

CASETTE 12.4
A CONSOLIDATION BY ANY OTHER NAME

Problem

Digilog, Inc., formed another company named DBS International (DBSI), controlled it and did not consolidate its financial position and results of operations in the Digilog financial statements. Digilog income was overstated, and assets and liabilities were understated.

Method

Digilog, Inc. formed DBSI as a separate corporation to market Digilog's microcomputer equipment. DBSI was formed separately to avoid the adverse impact of reporting expected startup losses in Digilog's financial statements. Instead of owning shares in DBSI, Digilog financed the company with loans convertible at will into 90 percent of DBSI's stock. (Otherwise, the share ownership was not in Digilog's name.) Since Digilog did not control DBSI (control defined as 50 percent or more ownership), DBSI was not consolidated, and the initial losses were not reported in Digilog's financial statements. See *Handbook Section* 1590.08 for the usual presumptions concerning the level of ownership leading to control.

Paper Trail

Formation of DBSI was not a secret. It was authorized. Incorporation papers were available. Loan documents showing the terms of Digilog's loans to DBSI were in the files.

Amount

Several hundred thousand dollars of losses in the first two years of DBSI operations were not consolidated. Ultimately, the venture became profitable and was absorbed into Digilog.

AUDIT APPROACH

Audit Objective

Obtain evidence to determine whether proper accounting methods (cost, equity, consolidation) are used for investments.

Control

The relevant control in this case would rest with the integrity and accounting knowledge of the senior officials who arranged the transaction. Proper documentation of authorization and financing and operating transactions between the two corporations should be in the companies' files.

Test of Controls

Enquiries should be made about large and unusual financing transactions. Minutes of the board of directors' meetings should be studied to find related authorizations. These authorizations and supporting papers signal the accounting issues and the interpretations of generally accepted accounting principles required in the circumstances.

Audit of Balances

The central issue in this case was the interpretation of accounting standards regarding required consolidation. Existence, completeness, valuation and ownership were not problematic audit issues. Unless these are extenuating factors (*Handbook Section* 1590.08), accounting standards require consolidation of over-50 percent owned subsidiaries, and prohibits consolidation of subsidiaries owned less than 50 percent. Digilog's purpose in financing DBSI with loans instead of direct share ownership was to skirt the 50 percent "ownership" criterion, thus keeping the DBSI losses out of the Digilog consolidated financial statements. The "test of the balance" (decision of whether to require consolidation) amounted to an interpretation of the substance versus form of "ownership" through convertible notes instead of direct shareholding.

Discovery Summary

Digilog, with concurrence of its independent audit firm, adopted the narrow interpretation of "ownership." Since Digilog did not "own" DBSI stock, DBSI was not "controlled," and its assets, liabilities and results of operations were not consolidated. The regulator disagreed and took action on the position that the convertible feature of the loans and the business purpose of the DBSI formation were enough to attribute control to Digilog. The company was enjoined from violating certain reporting and antifraud provisions of the provincial securities act and was required to amend its financial statements for the years in question (consolidating DBSI). The regulator also took action against the audit firm partner in charge of the Digilog audit.

R E V I E W
C H E C K P O I N T S

12.15   What are some of the typical assertions found in owners' equity descriptions and account balances?

12.16   How can confirmations be used in auditing shareholder capital accounts? in auditing notes and bonds payable?

12.17   What are some of the typical assertions found in the long-term liability accounts?

12.18   What procedures do auditors employ to obtain evidence of the cost of investments? of investment gains and losses? of investment income?

12.19   Why are auditors interested in substantial investment losses occurring early in the period following year-end?

12.20   What is the concept of "substance versus form" in relation to financing and investment transactions and balances? (Refer to the off-balance sheet and consolidation cases in the chapter.)

12.21   What are some of the "trouble spots" for auditors in the audits of investments and intangibles?

OTHER ASPECTS OF CLEVER ACCOUNTING AND FRAUD

The types of clever accounting and fraud that must be considered are those affecting the fair presentation of material equity accounts, investments and intangibles. Improper accounting presentations are engineered more frequently by senior officials than by middle management or lower ranks. Top management personnel who deal with the transactions involved in investments, long-term debt and shareholders' equity are not subject to the same kind of control as lower-level employees, and they generally are able to override detail procedural controls.

Long-Term Liabilities and Owners' Equity

The kinds of clever accounting and fraud connected with liability and owners' equity accounts differ significantly from those associated with asset and revenue accounts. Few employees are tempted to steal a liability, although fictitious liabilities may be created as a means of misdirecting cash payments into the hands of an officer. Auditors should be alert for such fictions in the same sense that they are alert to the possibility of having fictitious accounts receivable.

Although there are opportunities for employee fraud against the company, the area of liabilities and owners' equity also opens up possibilities for company fraud against outsiders. This class of fraud is most often accomplished through material misrepresentations or omissions in financial statements and related disclosures.

Officers and employees can use share or bond instruments improperly. Unissued shares or bonds and treasury stock may be used as collateral for personal loans. Even though the company may not be damaged or suffer loss by this action (unless the employee defaults and the securities are seized), the practice is unauthorized and is contrary to company interests. Similarly, employees may gain access to shareholder lists and unissued coupons and cause improper payments of dividends and interest on securities that are not outstanding.

Proper custodial control of securities (either by physical means, such as limited-access vaults, or by control of an independent disbursing agent) prevents most such occurrences. An auditing procedure of reconciling authorized dividend and interest payments (calculated using declared dividend rates, coupon interest rates and known quantities of outstanding securities) to actual payments detects unauthorized payments. If the company did not perform this checking procedure, auditors should include it among their own analytical recalculation procedures. Many liability, equity and off-balance-sheet transactions are outside the reach of normal internal control procedures, which can operate effectively over ordinary transactions (such as purchases and sales) processed by clerks and machines. Auditors generally are justified in performing extensive substantive auditing of long-term liability, equity and other high-level managed transactions and agreements since control depends in large part on the integrity and accounting knowledge of management.

Income tax evasion and fraud result from actions taken by managers. Evasion and fraud may be accomplished (1) by simple omission of income, (2) by unlawful deductions (such as contributions to political campaigns, capital cost allowance on nonexistent assets or capital cost allowance in excess of cost), or (3) by contriving sham transactions for the sole purpose of avoiding taxation. Auditors should be able to detect errors of the first two categories if the actual income and expense data have been sufficiently audited in the financial statements. The last category—contrived sham transactions—is harder to detect because a dishonest management can skilfully disguise them. Some of the procedures outlined in Chapter 19 may be useful and effective.

Financial statements may be materially misstated by reason of omission or understatement of liabilities and by failure to disclose technical defaults on loan agreement restrictions. These restrictions or test covenants can be very important to the viability of the client because if they are violated, creditors can force the client into bankruptcy. Hence auditor knowledge of these restrictions and comparison with the client's current financial condition is very important for pinpointing audit risk areas and for properly assessing the going concern assumption. The procedures you have learned to discover unrecorded liabilities through a "search for unrecorded liabilities" may be used to discover such omissions and understatements (Chapter 10). If auditors discover that loan agreement terms have been violated, they should bring the information to the client's attention and insist on proper disclosure in notes to the financial statements. In both situations (liability understatement and loan default disclosure), management's actions, reactions and willingness to adjust the financial figures and to make adverse disclosures are important insights for auditors' subjective evaluation of managerial integrity. An accumulation of inputs relevant to managerial integrity can have an important bearing on the auditors' perceptions of relative risk for the audit engagement taken as a whole.

Intent is difficult to prove and for that reason "a misstatement arising from management's bias in selecting and applying accounting principles or in making accounting estimates would be considered an error" (*Section* 5135). However, the audit also needs to be performed with professional skepticism, meaning the auditor:

(*a*) should be aware of factors that increase the risk of misstatement; and

(*b*) should be sensitized to evidence that contradicts the assumption of management's good faith.

If there are enough "red flags" present, the auditor will assess a higher inherent risk and for a given control risk these higher assessments will cause the auditor to:

(*a*) obtain more reliable evidence.

(*b*) expand the extent of audit procedures performed.

(*c*) apply audit procedures closer to or as of the balance sheet date.

(*d*) require more extensive supervision of assistants and/or assistants with more experience and training.

In essence, if the auditor suspects that the financial statements are misstated, he or she should perform procedures to confirm or dispel that suspicion.

Generally, the auditor is less likely to detect material misstatements arising from fraud because of the deliberate concealment involved.

The auditor should inform the appropriate level of management whenever he or she obtains evidence of a nontrivial misstatement; and the audit committee or board of directors should be informed of all significant misstatements (*Section* 5135).

A company, its individual managers and the auditors can violate securities regulations if they are not careful. Chapter 17 covers the general framework of regulation by provincial securities commissions. Auditors must know the provisions of the securities laws to the extent that they can identify situations that constitute obvious fraud, and so that they can identify transactions that may be subject to the law. Having once recognized or raised questions about a securities transaction, auditors should not act as their own lawyer. The facts should be submitted to competent legal counsel for an opinion. Even though auditors are not expected to be legal experts, they have the duty to recognize obvious instances of impropriety and to pursue investigations with the aid of legal experts.

Similarly, auditors should assist clients in observing securities commission rules and regulations on matters of timely disclosure. In general, the timely disclosure rules are phrased in terms of management's duties, and they do not require auditors to carry out any specific procedures or to make any specific disclosures. The regulations' purpose is to require management to disseminate to the public any material information, whether favourable or unfavourable, so that investors can incorporate it in their decision making. Various rule provisions require announcements and disclosures very soon after information becomes known. Often, relevant situations arise during the year when the independent auditors are not present, so, of course, they cannot be held responsible or liable. However, in other situations, auditors may learn of the information inadvertently or the auditors' advice may be sought by the client. In such cases auditors should advise their clients, consistent with the requirements of law and regulations.

Presently, pressures are on the auditors to discover more information about off-balance sheet contingencies and commitments and to discover the facts of management involvement with other parties to transactions. Auditors' knowledge of contingencies and commitments that are not evidenced in accounting records depends in large part on information the management and its legal counsel will reveal. Nevertheless, certain investigative procedures are available (Chapter 19). The current pressures on auditors to discover more information is a part of the public pressure on auditors to take more responsibility for fraud detection.

Investments and Intangibles

Theft, diversion and unauthorized use of investment securities can occur in several ways. If safekeeping controls are weak, securities simply may be stolen, in which case the theft becomes a police problem rather than an auditing problem. Somewhat more frequent are diversions, such as using securities as collateral during the year, returning them for a count, then giving them back to the creditor without disclosure to the auditor. If safekeeping methods require entry signatures (as at a safe-deposit vault), auditors may be able to detect the in-and-out movement. The best chance of discovery is that the creditor will confirm the collateral arrangement. In a similar manner, securities may be removed by an officer and sold, then repurchased before the auditors' count. The auditors' record of the certificate numbers should reveal this change, since the returned certificates (and their serial numbers) will not be the same as the ones removed. The rapid growth in use of derivative securities as investments and hedges has created new and rather unique problems for auditors, not the least of which is lack of familiarity with these financial instruments. Appendix Exhibit 12A–4 provides an overview of the recent global problems in this area.

Cash receipts from interest, royalties on patent licences, dividends and sales proceeds may be stolen. The accounting records may or may not be manipulated to cover the theft. In general, this kind of defalcation should be prevented by cash receipts control; but, since these receipts usually are irregular and infrequent, the cash control system may not be as effective as it is for regular receipts on trade accounts. If the income accounts are not manipulated to hide stolen receipts, auditors will find less income in the account than the amount indicated by their audit calculations based on other records, such as licence agreements or published dividend records. If sales of securities are not recorded, auditors will notice that securities are missing when they try to inspect or confirm them. If the income accounts have been manipulated to hide stolen receipts, vouching of cash receipts will detect the theft, or vouching may reveal some offsetting debit buried in some other account.

Accounting values may be manipulated in a number of ways, involving purchase of assets at inflated prices, leases with affiliates, acquisitions of patents for shares given to an inventor or promoter, sales to affiliates and fallacious decisions about amortization. Business history has recorded several cases of non-arm's-length transactions with promoters, officers, directors and controlled companies (even "dummy" companies) designed to drain the company's resources and fool the auditors.

In one case a company sold assets to a dummy purchaser set up by a director to bolster sagging income with a gain. The auditors did not know that the purchaser was a shell. All the documents of sale looked in order, and cash sales proceeds had been deposited. The auditors were not informed of a secret agreement by the seller to repurchase the assets at a later time. This situation illustrates a very devious manipulation. All transactions with persons closely associated with the company (related parties) should be audited carefully with reference to market values, particularly when a nonmonetary transaction is involved (such as shares exchanged for patent rights). Sales and lease-back and straight lease transactions with insiders likewise should be audited carefully.

R E V I E W
CHECKPOINTS

12.22   What is the single most significant control consideration in connection with clever accounting and fraud in finance and investment cycle accounts?

12.23   Which is more likely to exist in the finance and investment cycle accounts: (1) fraud against the company? or (2) fraud by the company in financial or tax reporting? Explain.

12.24   What should an auditor do when violation of securities laws is suspected?

12.25   What is the danger for auditors when company officials engage in undisclosed related party transactions?

SUMMARY

The finance and investment cycle contains a wide variety of accounts—share capital, dividends, long-term debt, interest expense, tax expenses and deferred taxes, financial instruments, marketable securities, equity method investments, related gains and losses, consolidated subsidiaries, goodwill and other intangibles. These accounts involve some of the most technically complex accounting standards. They create most of the difficult judgments for financial reporting.

Transactions in these accounts generally are controlled by senior officials. Therefore, internal control is centred on the integrity and accounting knowledge of these officials. The procedural controls over details of transactions are not very effective because the senior managers can override them and order their own desired accounting presentations. As a consequence, auditors' work on the assessment of control risk is directed toward the senior managers, the board of directors and their authorizations and design of finance and investment deals.

Fraud and clever accounting in the finance and investment cycle get directed most often to producing misleading financial statements. While theft and embezzlement can occur, the accounts in this cycle frequently have been the ones subject to manipulation and spurious valuation for the purpose of reporting financial position and results of operations better than the reality of companies' situations. Off-balance-sheet financing and investment transactions with related parties are explained as ripe areas for fraudulent financial reporting.

This chapter ends the book's coverage of audit applications for various cycles and their accounts. Chapter 14 contains several topics involved in putting the finishing touches on an audit.

MULTIPLE-CHOICE QUESTIONS FOR PRACTICE AND REVIEW

Questions 12.26 and 12.27 are located on the CD-ROM that accompanies this textbook.

12.28 Jones was engaged to examine the financial statements of Gamma Corporation for the year ended June 30, 2003. Having completed an examination of the investment securities, which of the following is the best method of verifying the accuracy of recorded dividend income?
  a. Tracing recorded dividend income to cash receipts records and validated deposit slips.
  b. Utilizing analytical review techniques and statistical sampling.
  c. Comparing recorded dividends with amounts appearing on federal tax returns.
  d. Comparing recorded dividends with a standard financial reporting service's record of dividends.

12.29 When a large amount of negotiable securities is held by the client, planning by the auditor is necessary to guard against:
  a. Unauthorized negotiation of the securities before they are counted.
  b. Unrecorded sales of securities after they are counted.
  c. Substitution of securities already counted for other securities which should be on hand but are not.
  d. Substitution of authentic securities with counterfeit securities.

12.30 In connection with the audit of an issue of long-term bonds payable, the auditor should:

  a. Determine whether bondholders are persons other than owners, directors or officers of the company issuing the bond.
  b. Calculate the effective interest rate to see if it is substantially the same as the rates for similar issues.
  c. Decide whether the bond issue was made without violating state or local law.
  d. Ascertain that the client has obtained the opinion of counsel on the legality of the issue.

12.31 Which of the following is the most important consideration of an auditor when examining the shareholders' equity section of a client's balance sheet?
  a. Changes in the share capital account are verified by an independent share transfer agent.
  b. Stock dividends and stock splits during the year under audit were approved by the shareholders.
  c. Stock dividends are capitalized at par or stated value on the dividend declaration date.
  d. Entries in the share capital account can be traced to resolutions in the minutes of the board of directors' meetings.

12.32 If the auditor discovers that the carrying amount of a client's investments is overstated because of a loss in value that is other than a temporary decline in market value, the auditor should insist that:

   a. The approximate market value of the investments be shown in parentheses on the face of the balance sheet.

   b. The investments be classified as long term for balance sheet purposes with full disclosure in the footnotes.

   c. The loss in value be recognized in the financial statements.

   d. The equity section of the balance sheet separately shows a charge equal to the amount of the loss.

12.33 The primary reason for preparing a reconciliation between interest-bearing obligations outstanding during the year and interest expense in the financial statements, is to:

   a. Evaluate internal control over securities.

   b. Determine the validity of prepaid interest expense.

   c. Ascertain the reasonableness of imputed interest.

   d. Detect unrecorded liabilities.

12.34 The auditor should insist that a representative of the client be present during the inspection and count of securities in order to:

   a. Lend authority to the auditor's directives.

   b. Detect forged securities.

   c. Co-ordinate the return of all securities to proper locations.

   d. Acknowledge the receipt of securities returned.

12.35 When independent share transfer agents are not employed and the corporation issues its own shares and maintains share records, cancelled share certificates should:

   a. Be defaced to prevent reissuance and attached to their corresponding stubs.

   b. Not be defaced, but segregated from other share certificates and retained in a cancelled certificates file.

   c. Be destroyed to prevent fraudulent reissuance.

   d. Be defaced and sent to the federal finance minister.

12.36 When a client company does not maintain its own share capital records, the auditor should obtain written confirmation from the transfer agent and registrar concerning:

   a. Restrictions on the payment of dividends.

   b. The number of shares issued and outstanding.

   c. Guarantees of preferred share liquidation value.

   d. The number of shares subject to agreements to repurchase.

(AICPA adapted)

12.37 All corporate share capital transactions should ultimately be traced to the:

   a. Minutes of the board of directors.

   b. Cash receipts journal.

   c. Cash disbursements journal.

   d. Numbered share certificates.

12.38 A corporate balance sheet indicates that one of the corporate assets is a patent. An auditor will most likely obtain evidence of this patent by obtaining a written representation from:

   a. A patent lawyer.

   b. A regional patent office.

   c. The patent inventor.

   d. The patent owner.

12.39 An audit program for the examination of the retained earnings account should include a step that requires verification of the:

   a. Market value used to charge retained earnings to account for a two-for-one share split.

   b. Approval of the adjustment to the beginning balance as a result of a write-down of an account receivables.

   c. Authorization for both cash and share dividends.

   d. Gain or loss resulting from disposition of treasury shares.

EXERCISES AND PROBLEMS

INVESTMENTS AND INTANGIBLES

12.40 **ICQ for Equity Investments.** Cassandra Corporation, a manufacturing company, periodically invests large sums in marketable equity securities. The investment policy is established by the investment committee of the board of directors. The treasurer is responsible for carrying out the investment committee's directives. All securities are stored in a bank safe-deposit vault.

   Your internal control questionnaire with respect to Cassandra's investments in equity securities contains the following three questions:

1. Is investment policy established by the investment committee of the board of directors?
2. Is the treasurer solely responsible for carrying out the investment committee's directive?
3. Are all securities stored in a bank safe-deposit vault?

Required:

In addition to the above three questions, what questions should your internal control questionnaires include with respect to the company's investment in marketable equity securities? (Hint: Prepare questions to cover the control objectives—validity, completeness, authorization, accuracy, classification, accounting and proper period.)

(AICPA adapted)

12.41 Noncurrent Investment Securities. You are engaged in the audit of the financial statements of Bass Corporation for the year ended December 31, and you are about to begin an audit of the noncurrent investment securities. Bass's records indicate that the company owns various bearer bonds, as well as 25 percent of the outstanding common shares of Commercial Industrial, Inc. You are satisfied with evidence that supports the presumption of significant influence over Commercial Industrial, Inc. The various securities are at two locations as follows:

1. Recently acquired securities are in the company's safe in the custody of the treasurer.
2. All other securities are in the company's bank safe deposit box. All securities in Bass's portfolio are actively traded in a broad market.

Required:

a. Assuming that the system of internal control over securities is satisfactory, what are the objectives (specific assertions) for the audit of the noncurrent securities?
b. What audit procedures should you undertake with respect to the audit of Bass's investment securities?

(AICPA adapted)

12.42 Securities Examination and Count. You are in charge of the audit of the financial statements of the Demot Corporation for the year ended December 31. The corporation has had the policy of investing its surplus funds in marketable securities. Its share and bond certificates are kept in a safe-deposit box in a local bank. Only the president and the treasurer of the corporation have access to the box.

You were unable to obtain access to the safe-deposit box on December 31 because neither the president nor the treasurer was available. Arrangements were made for your assistant to accompany the treasurer to the bank on January 11 to examine the securities. Your assistant has never examined securities that were being kept in a safe-deposit box and requires instructions. Your assistant should be able to inspect all securities on hand in an hour.

Required:

a. List the instructions that you would give to your assistant regarding the examination of the share and bond certificates kept in the safe-deposit box. Include in your instructions the details of the securities to be examined and the reasons for examining these details.
b. After returning from the bank, your assistant reports that the treasurer had entered the box on January 4 to remove an old photograph of the corporation's original building. The photograph was loaned to the local chamber of commerce for display purposes. List the additional audit procedures that are required because of the treasurer's action.

(AICPA adapted)

12.43 Securities Procedures. You were engaged to examine the financial statements of Ronlyn Corporation for the year ended June 30. On May 1 the corporation borrowed $500,000 from the Second National Bank to finance plant expansion. However, due to unexpected difficulties in acquiring the building site, the plant expansion had not begun as planned. To make use of the borrowed funds, management decided to invest in shares and bonds; on May 16 the $500,000 was invested in securities.

Required:

In your audit of investments, how would you:

a. Audit the recorded dividend or interest income?
b. Determine market value?
c. Establish the authority for security purchases?

(AICPA adapted)

12.44 Research and Development. The Hertle Engineering Company depends on innovation of new product development to maintain its position in the market for drilling tool equipment. The company conducts an extensive research and development program for this purpose, and it consistently charges research and development costs to current operations in accordance with Statement on Financial Accounting Standards No. 2.

The company began a project called Project Able in January 2001 with the goal of patenting a revolutionary drilling bit design. Work continued until October 2002 when the company applied for a patent. Costs were charged to the research and development expense account in both years, except for the cost of a computer program that engineers plan to use in Project Baker, scheduled to start in December 2002. The computer program was purchased from Computeering, Inc., in January 2001 for $45,000.

Required:

a. Give an audit program for the audit of research and development costs on Project Able. Assume that you are auditing the company for the first time at December 31, 2002.

b. What evidence would you require for the audit of the computer program that has been capitalized as an intangible asset? As of December 31, 2002, this account has a balance of $40,000 (cost less $5,000 amortized as a part of Project Able).

(AICPA adapted)

12.45 Intangibles. Sorenson Manufacturing Corporation was incorporated on January 3, 2001. The corporation's financial statements for its first year's operations were not examined by a PA. You have been engaged to audit the financial statements for the year ended December 31, 2002, and your examination is substantially completed.

A partial trial balance of the company's accounts is given below:

The following information relates to accounts which may yet require adjustment:

1. Patents for Sorenson's manufacturing process were purchased January 2, 2002, at a cost of $68,000. An additional $17,000 was spent in December 2002 to improve machinery covered by the patents and charged to the patents

SORENSON MANUFACTURING CORPORATION
Trial Balance at
December 31, 2002

	Trial Balance	
	Debit	Credit
Cash	$11,000	
Accounts receivable	42,500	
Allowance for doubtful accounts		$ 500
Inventories	38,500	
Machinery	75,000	
Equipment	29,000	
Accumulated depreciation		10,000
Patents	85,000	
Leasehold improvements	26,000	
Prepaid expenses	10,500	
Organization expenses	29,000	
Goodwill	24,000	
Licensing Agreement No. 1	50,000	
Licensing Agreement No. 2	49,000	

account. The patents had a remaining legal term of 17 years.

2. On January 3, 2001, Sorenson purchased two licensing agreements, which at that time were believed to have unlimited useful lives. The balance in the licensing agreement No. 1 account included its purchase price of $48,000 and $2,000 in acquisition expenses. Licensing agreement No. 2 also was purchased on January 3, 2001, for $50,000, but it has been reduced by a credit of $1,000 for the advance collection of 1998 revenue from the agreement.

In December 2001 an explosion caused a permanent 60 percent reduction in the expected revenue-producing value of licensing agreement No. 1, and in January 2002 a flood caused additional damage, which rendered the agreement worthless.

A study of licensing agreement No. 2 made by Sorenson in January 2002 revealed that its estimated remaining life expectancy was only 10 years as of January 1, 2002.

3. The balance in the goodwill account includes $24,000 paid December 30, 2001, for an advertising program, which it is estimated will assist in increasing Sorenson's sales over a period of four years following the disbursement.

4. The leasehold improvement account includes (*a*) the $15,000 cost of improvements, with a total estimated useful life of 12 years, which Sorenson, as tenant, made to leased premises in January 2001; (*b*) movable assembly line equipment costing $8,500, which was installed in the leased premises in December 2002; and (*c*) real estate taxes of $2,500 paid by Sorenson which, under the terms of the lease, should have been paid by the landlord. Sorenson paid its rent in full during 2002. A 10-year nonrenewable lease was signed January 3, 2001, for the leased building that Sorenson used in manufacturing operations.
5. The balance in the organization expenses account includes preoperating costs incurred during the organizational period.

Required:
Prepare adjusting entries as necessary.

(AICPA adapted)

LONG-TERM LIABILITIES AND COMMITMENTS

12.46 Long-Term Note. You were engaged to examine the financial statements of Ronlyn Corporation for the year ended June 30. On May 1 the corporation borrowed $500,000 from the Second National Bank to finance plant expansion. The long-term note agreement provided for the annual payment of principal and interest over five years. The existing plant was pledged as security for the loan.

Due to unexpected difficulties in acquiring the building site, the plant expansion had not begun as planned. To make use of the borrowed funds, management decided to invest in shares and bonds, and on May 16 the $500,000 was invested in securities.

Required:
a. What are the audit objectives in the examining of long-term debt?
b. Prepare an audit program for the examination of the long-term note agreement between Ronlyn and Second National Bank.

(AICPA adapted)

12.47 Long-Term Financing Agreement. You have been engaged to audit the financial statements of Broadwall Corporation for the year ended December 31, 2002. During the year, Broadwall obtained a long-term loan from a local bank pursuant to a financing agreement, which provided that:
1. Loan was to be secured by the company's inventory and accounts receivable.
2. Company was to maintain a debt-to-equity ratio not to exceed 2:1.
3. Company was not to pay dividends without permission from the bank.
4. Monthly installment payments were to commence July 1, 2002.

In addition, during the year the company also borrowed, on a short-term basis, from the president of the company, substantial amounts just prior to the year-end.

Required:
a. For the purposes of your audit of the financial statements of Broadwall Corporation, what procedures should you employ in examining the described loans? Do not discuss internal control.
b. What financial statement disclosures should you expect to find with respect to the loan from the president?

12.48 Bond Indenture Covenants. The following covenants are extracted from the indenture of a bond issue. The indenture provides that failure to comply with its terms in any respect automatically advances the due date of the loan to the date of noncompliance (the regular date is 20 years hence). Give any audit steps or reporting requirements you believe should be taken or recognized in connection with each of the following:
1. "The debtor company shall endeavour to maintain a working capital ratio of 2:1 at all times, and, in any fiscal year following a failure to maintain said ratio, the company shall restrict compensation of officers to a total of $500,000. Officers for this purpose shall include chairman of the board of directors, president, all vice presidents, secretary and treasurer."
2. "The debtor company shall keep all property which is security for this debt insured against loss by fire to the extent of 100 percent of its actual value. Policies of insurance comprising this protection shall be filed with the trustee."
3. "The debtor company shall pay all taxes legally assessed against property which is security for this debt within the time provided by law for payment without penalty and shall deposit

receipted tax bills or equally acceptable evidence of payment of same with the trustee."

4. "A sinking fund shall be deposited with the trustee by semiannual payments of $300,000, from which the trustee shall, in his discretion, purchase bonds of this issue."

(AICPA adapted)

OWNERS' EQUITY

12.49 Common Share and Treasury Share Audit Procedures. You are the continuing auditor of Sussex, Inc., and are beginning the audit of the common share and treasury share accounts. You have decided to design substantive audit procedures with reliance on internal controls.

Sussex has no-par, no-stated-value common shares, and acts as its own registrar and transfer agent. During the past year, Sussex both issued and reacquired shares of its own common stock, some of which the company still owned at year-end. Additional common share transactions occurred among the shareholders during the year.

Common share transactions can be traced to individual shareholders' accounts in a subsidiary ledger and to a share certificate book. The company has not paid any cash or share dividends. There are no other classes of shares, share rights, warrants or option plans.

Required:
What substantive audit procedures should you apply in examining the common share and treasury share accounts? Organize your answer as a list of audit procedures organized by the financial statement assertions. (See Appendix Exhibit 20A–1 for examples of substantive procedures for owners' equity.)

(AICPA adapted)

12.50 Shareholders' Equity. You are a PA engaged in an examination of the financial statements of Pate Corporation for the year ended December 31. The financial statements and records of Pate Corporation have not been audited by a PA in prior years.

The shareholders' equity section of Pate Corporation's balance sheet at December 31 follows:

Shareholders' equity:	
Share capital—10,000 shares of $10 par value authorized; 5,000 shares issued and outstanding	$ 50,000
Capital contributed in excess of par value of share capital	32,580
Retained earnings	47,320
Total shareholders' equity	$129,900

Pate Corporation was founded in 1992. The corporation has 10 shareholders and serves as its own registrar and transfer agent. There are no capital share subscription contracts in effect.

Required:
a. Prepare the detailed audit program for the examination of the three accounts composing the shareholders' equity section of Pate Corporation's balance sheet. Organize the audit program under broad financial statement assertions. (Do not include in the audit program the audit of the results of the current year's operations.)

b. After every other figure on the balance sheet has been audited, it may appear that the retained earnings figure is a balancing figure and requires no further audit work. Why don't auditors audit retained earnings as they do the other figures on the balance sheet? Discuss.

(AICPA adapted)

DISCUSSION CASES

12.51 Oil Leases Exchanged for Capital Shares. Al and Billy Bob formed the Wildcat Corporation and transferred to it oil leases owned equally by them for which they had paid $30 in capitalized fees. They also had paid $1,280 for delay lease rentals, which they had charged to expense in the year paid by them as individuals. Al and Billy Bob had no other

costs or expenses applicable to these leases.

At the time of the transfer, there were favourable geological and geophysical reports on the property, but there had been no production in the area. The board of directors of the Wildcat Corporation issued $300,000 par value common shares for the leases, one half the shares going to

Al and one half to Billy Bob. Al and Billy Bob then donated one half of their respective shares to the corporate treasury to be sold at par for working capital.

Required:

a. Discuss the proper balance sheet presentation of the leases and of the capital and donated shares.

b. What audit procedures would you apply to the leases? (Consider the audit objectives in planning the proper audit procedures.)

c. Must this share issue be reported or registered with the SEC? Explain.

(AICPA adapted)

12.52 Intercompany and Interpersonal Investment Relations. You have been engaged to audit the financial statements of Hardy Hardware Distributors, Inc., as of December 31. In your review of the corporate nonfinancial records, you have found that Hardy Hardware owns 15 percent of the outstanding voting common shares of Hardy Products Corporation. Upon further investigation, you learn that Hardy Products Corporation manufactures a line of hardware goods, 90 percent of which is sold to Hardy Hardware.

Mr. James L. Hardy, president of Hardy Hardware, has supplied you with objective evidence that he personally owns 30 percent of the Hardy Products voting shares and that the remaining 70 percent is owned by Mr. John L. Hardy, his brother and president of Hardy Products. James L. Hardy also owns 20 percent of the voting common shares of Hardy Hardware Distributors. Another 20 percent is held by an estate of which James and John are beneficiaries, and the remaining 60 percent is publicly held. The shares are listed on the American Stock Exchange.

Hardy Hardware consistently has reported operating profits greater than the industry average. Hardy Products Corporation, however, has a net return on sales of only 1 percent. The Hardy Products investment always has been reported at cost, and no dividends have been paid by the company. During the course of your conversations with the Hardy brothers, you learn that you were appointed as auditor because the brothers had a heated disagreement with the former auditor over the issues of accounting for the Hardy Products investment and the prices at which goods have been sold to Hardy Hardware.

For Discussion

a. Identify the issues in this situation as they relate to (1) conflicts of interest and (2) controlling influences among individuals and corporations.

b. Should the investment in Hardy Products Corporation be accounted for on the equity method?

c. What evidence should the auditor seek with regard to the prices paid by Hardy Hardware for products purchased from Hardy Products Corporation?

d. What information would you consider necessary for adequate disclosure in the financial statements of Hardy Hardware Distributors?

INSTRUCTIONS FOR DISCUSSION CASES 12.53–12.54—.

These cases are designed like the ones in the chapter. They give the problem, the method, the paper trail and the amount. Your assignment is to write the Audit Approach portion of the case, organized around these sections:

Objectives: Express the objective in terms of the facts supposedly asserted in financial records, accounts and statements. (Refer to discussion of assertions in Chapter 4.)

Control: Write a brief explanation of control considerations, especially the kinds of manipulations that may arise from the situation described in the case.

Test of controls: Write some procedures for getting evidence about existing controls, especially procedures that could discover management manipulations. If there are no controls to test, then there are no procedures to perform; go then to the next section. A "procedure" should instruct someone about the source(s) of evidence to tap and the work to do.

Audit of balance: Write some procedures for getting evidence about the existence, completeness, valuation, ownership or disclosure assertions identified in your objective section above.

Discovery summary: Write a short statement about the discovery you expect to accomplish with your procedures.

12.53 Related Party Transaction "Goodwill."

HIDE THE LOSS UNDER THE GOODWILL

Problem: A contrived amount of goodwill was used to overstate assets and disguise a loss on discontinued operations.

Method: Gulwest Industries, a public company, decided to discontinue its unprofitable line of business of manufacturing sporting ammunition. Gulwest had capitalized the start-up cost of the business, and, with its discontinuance, the

$7 million deferred cost should have been written off.

Instead, Gulwest formed a new corporation named Amron and transferred the sporting ammunition assets (including the $7 million deferred cost) to it in exchange for all the Amron shares. In the Gulwest accounts the Amron investment was carried at $12.4 million, which was the book value of the assets transferred (including the $7 million deferred cost).

In an agreement with a different public company (Big Industrial), Gulwest and Big created another company (BigShot Ammunition). Gulwest transferred all the Amron assets to BigShot in exchange for (1) common and preferred shares of Big, valued at $2 million, and (2) a note from BigShot in the amount of $3.4 million. Big Industrial thus acquired 100 percent of the shares of BigShot. Gulwest management reasoned that it had "given" Amron shares valued at $12.4 million to receive shares and notes valued at $5.4 million, so the difference must be goodwill. Thus, the Gulwest accounts carried amounts for Big Industrial shares ($2 million), BigShot note receivable ($3.4 million), and goodwill ($7 million).

Paper trail: Gulwest directors included in the minutes an analysis of the sporting ammunition business's lack of profitability. The minutes showed approval of a plan to dispose of the business, but they did not use the words "discontinue the business." The minutes also showed approval of the creation of Amron, the deal with Big Industrial along with the formation of BigShot, and the acceptance of Big's shares and Bigshot's note in connection with the final exchange and merger.

Amount: As explained above, Gulwest avoided reporting a write-off of $7 million by overstating the value of the assets given in exchange for the Big Industrial shares and the BigShot Ammunition note.

12.54 Related Party Transaction Valuation. Follow the instructions accompanying Case 12.53. Write the audit approach section of the case.

IN PLANE VIEW

Problem: Whiz corporation overstated the value of shares given in exchange for an airplane and, thereby, understated its loss on disposition of the shares. Income was overstated.

Method: Whiz owned 160,000 Wing Company shares, carried on the books as an investment in the amount of $6,250,000. Whiz bought a used airplane from Wing, giving in exchange (1) $480,000 cash and (2) the 160,000 Wing shares. Even though the quoted market value of the Wing shares was $2,520,000, Whiz valued the airplane received at $3,750,000, indicating a share valuation of $3,270,000. Thus, Whiz recognized a loss on disposition of the Wing shares in the amount of $2,980,000.

Whiz justified the airplane valuation with another transaction. On the same day it was purchased, Whiz sold the airplane to the Mexican subsidiary of one of its subsidiary companies (two layers down; but Whiz owned 100 percent of the first subsidiary, which in turn owned 100 percent of the Mexican subsidiary). The Mexican subsidiary paid Whiz with US$25,000 cash and a promissory note for US$3,725,000 (market rate of interest).

Paper trail: The transaction was within the authority of the chief executive officer, and company policy did not require a separate approval by the board of directors. A contract of sale and correspondence with Wing detailing the terms of the transaction were in the files. Likewise, a contract of sale to the Mexican subsidiary, along with a copy of the deposit slip, and a memorandum of the promissory note was on file. The note itself was kept in the company vault. None of the Wing papers cited a specific price for the airplane.

Amount: Whiz overvalued the Wing shares and justified it with a related party transaction with its own subsidiary company. The loss on the disposition of the Wing shares was understated by $750,000.

12.55 Loss Deferral on Hedged Investments. This case contains complexities that preclude writing the entire Audit Approach according to the instructions accompanying Case 12.53. Instead, respond to these requirements:
a. What is the objective of the audit work on the investment account described in the Sharp Hedge Clippers case?
b. What is your conclusion about the propriety of deferring the losses on the hedged investments sales and the futures contracts? about the proper carrying amount of the investment in the balance sheet?
c. Do you believe the successor auditors were independent? competent? Discuss the practice of "shopping around" for an unqualified audit report.

SHARP HEDGE CLIPPERS

Problem: Southeastern Savings & Loan Company (Southeastern) overstated its assets and income by improperly deferring losses on hedged investment transactions.

Method: In the course of its normal operations, Southeastern held investments in 15 percent and 16 percent GNMA certificates. Fearing an increase in interest rates and a consequent loss in the market value of these investments, Southeastern sought to hedge by selling futures contracts for U.S. Treasury bonds. If market interest rates increased, the losses in the GNMA investments would be offset by gains in the futures contracts.

However, interest rates declined, and Southeastern was caught in an odd market quirk. The value of the GNMAs increased with the lower interest rates, but not very much. (GNMAs are certificates in pools of government-backed mortgages, which pass through the interest and principle collections to the certificate holders.) As interest rates declined, the market perceived that the underlying mortgages would be paid off more quickly, that investors would receive all their proceeds earlier than previously expected, and that they would need to reinvest their money at the now-lower interest rates. Consequently, the 15 percent and 16 percent GNMAs held by Southeastern began trading as if the expected maturity were 4–5 years instead of the previously expected 8–12 years, which means that their prices did not rise as much as other interest-sensitive securities. On the other hand, the U.S. Treasury bonds with fixed maturity dates fell in price, and the futures hedge generated large losses.

Southeastern sold its 15 percent and 16 percent GNMAs and realized a $750,000 gain. Before and after these sales, the company purchased 8.0–12.5 percent GNMAs. The goal was to be invested in substantially different securities, ones that had a market return and the normal 8–12-year expected life payout. Later, Southeastern closed out its Treasury bond futures and realized a loss of $3.7 million. Still later, Southeastern sold GNMA futures contracts to hedge the investment in the 8.0–12.5 percent GNMA investments. The net loss of about $3 million was deferred in the balance sheet, instead of being recognized as a loss in the income statement.

Paper trail/accounting principles: The accounting for these transactions is complex and requires some significant judgments. In general, no gain or loss is recognized when the security sold is simultaneously replaced by the same or substantially the same security (a "wash" transaction), provided that any loss deferral does not result in carrying the investment at an amount greater than its market value. When a futures hedge is related to the securities sold, gains and losses on the futures contracts must be recognized when the hedged securities are sold, unless the sale of the hedged securities is part of a wash sale.

The significant accounting judgment is the identification of the disposition and new investment as a wash transaction. In turn, this requires a determination of whether the sale and reinvestment is "simultaneous" and involves "substantially the same security."

The "paper trail" is littered with information relevant to these judgments:

Criterion	Southeastern Transaction
Timing: Simultaneous sale/ purchase or purchase/sale.	Some of the 15 percent and 16 percent GNMAs were sold six weeks after the 8.0–12.5 percent GNMAs were purchased.
Substantial similarity: Same issuer.	Both the securities sold and the securities purchased were GNMAs.
Similar market yield.	The yields on the two different GNMA series differed by about 3 percentage points.
Similar contractual maturity date.	The contractual maturity dates were the same.
Similar prospects for redemption.	The market priced and sold the 15 percent and 16 percent GNMAs as though payback would occur in 4–5 years and the 8.0–12.5 percent GNMAs as though payback would occur in 8–12 years.
Carrying value: Asset carrying amount, including any deferred loss, shall not exceed securities' market value.	Asset value in financial statements exceeded the market value.

Paper trail/auditor involvement: Southeastern's independent auditors concluded that the losses should not be deferred. Southeastern fired the auditors and reported the disagreement in the 8-K report filed with the SEC. After consulting other auditors, who agreed with the former auditors, Southeastern found a PA firm whose local partners would give an unqualified audit report on financial statements containing the deferral.

In February the auditors who disagreed with the deferral were fired. The new auditors were hired on February 18 to audit the financial statements for the year ended the previous December 31. The unqualified audit report was dated March 28, 39 days after the new auditors were engaged by Southeastern's audit committee.

The new auditors were well aware of the accounting judgments required. They knew the former auditors and another PA firm had concluded that the losses should not be deferred. They saw memoranda of the disagreement and the conclusion in the predecessor's working papers. They

spoke with the predecessor partner on the engagement.

12.56 Long-Term Debt Working Paper Review. The long-term debt working paper in Exhibit 12.56–1 was prepared by client personnel and audited by AA, an audit staff assistant, during the calendar year 2002 audit of Canadian Widgets, Inc., a continuing audit client. You are the engagement supervisor, and your assignment is to review this working paper thoroughly.

Required:

Identify and prepare a list explaining the deficiencies that should be discovered in the supervisory review of the long-term debt working paper.

(AICPA adapted)

E X H I B I T   12.56–1

CANADIAN WIDGETS, INC.
Working Papers December 31, 2002

Index	K1	
	Initials	Date
Prepared by	AA	3/22/02
Approved by		

Lender	Interest Rate	Payment Terms	Collateral	Balance 12/31/01	2002 Borrowings	2002 Reductions	Balance 12/31/02	Interest paid to	Accrued Interest Payable 12/31/02	Comments
⓪ First Commercial Bank	12%	Interest only on 25th of month, principal due in full 1/1/06, no prepayment penalty	Inventories	$ 50,000 ✓	$300,000 1/31/02 A	$100,000 6/30/02 ⊕	$ 250,000 CX	12/25/02	$2,500 NR	Dividend of $80,000 paid 9/2/02 (W/P N-3) violates a provision of the debt agreement, which thereby permits lender to demand immediate payment; lender has refused to waive this violation.
⓪ Lender's Capital Corp.	Prime plus 1%	Interest only on last day of month, principal due in full 3/5/04	2nd Mortgage on Park St. Building	100,000 ✓	50,000 A	—	200,000 C	12/31/02	—	
⓪ Gigantic Building & Loan Assoc.	12%	$5,000 principal plus interest due on 5th of month, due in full 12/31/13	1st Mortgage on Park St. Building	720,00 ✓	—	60,000 ⊖	660,000 C	12/5/02	5,642 R	Prime rate was 8% to 9% during the year.
⓪ J. Lott, majority shareholder	0%	Due in full 12/13/05	Unsecured	300,000 ✓	—	100,000 N	200,000 C	—	—	
				$1,170,000 F	$350,000 F	$260,000 F	$1,310,000 T/B F		$8,142 T/B F	

Tick-mark legend

F   Readded, foots correctly.
C   Confirmed without exception, W/P K-2.
CX Confirmed with exception, W/P K-3.
NR Does not recompute correctly.
A   Agreed to loan agreement, validated bank deposit ticket, and board of directors authorization, W/P W-7.
⊖   Agreed to cancelled cheques and lender's monthly statements.
N   Agreed to cash disbursements journal and cancelled cheques dated 12/31/02, clearing 1/8/03.
T/B Traced to working trial balance.
✓   Agreed to 12/31/01 working papers.
⓪   Agreed interest rate, term, and collateral to copy of note and loan agreement.
⊕   Agreed to cancelled cheques and board of director's authorization, W/P W-7.

Overall Conclusions

Long-term debt, accrued interest payable, and interest expense ae correct and complete at 12/31/02.

Interest costs for long-term debt

Interest expense for year	$ 281,333 T/B
Average loan balance outstanding	$1,406,667 R

Five year maturities (for disclosure purposes)

Year end		
	12/31/03	$ 60,000
	12/31/04	260,000
	12/31/05	260,000
	12/31/06	310,000
	12/31/07	60,000
	Thereafter	360,000
		$1,310,000
		F

Reclassification entry for current portion proposed (See RJE-3)

Borrowed additional $100,000 from J. Lott on 1/7/03.

12.57 Audit of Pension Expense. Clark, PA, has been engaged to perform the audit of Kent Ltd.'s financial statements for the current year. Clark is about to commence auditing Kent's employee pension expense. Her preliminary enquiries concerning Kent's pension plan lead her to believe that some of the actuarial computations and assumptions are so complex that they are beyond the competence ordinarily required of an auditor. Clark is considering engaging Lane, an actuary, to assist with this portion of the audit.

Required:

a. According to CGA–Canada Guideline No. 1. Audit Evidence or Other Standards, what is the confidence required for reliance to be placed on other professionals? What is the additional condition for reliance on other auditors?

b. What are Clark's responsibilities with respect to the findings of Lane, if she wishes to rely on those findings?

c. Distinguish between the circumstances where it is and is not appropriate for Clark to refer to Lane in the auditor's report.

(CGAAC adapted)

APPENDIX 12A
SUBSTANTIVE AUDIT PROGRAMS

· ·

EXHIBIT 12A–1   **AUDIT PROGRAM FOR OWNERS' EQUITY**

1. Obtain an analysis of owners' equity transactions. Trace additions and reductions to the general ledger.
   a. Vouch additions to directors' minutes and cash receipts.
   b. Vouch reductions to directors' minutes and other supporting documents.
2. Read the directors' minutes for owners' equity authorization. Trace to entries in the accounts. Determine whether related disclosures are adequate.
3. Confirm outstanding common and preferred shares with share registrar agent.
4. Vouch stock option and profit-sharing plan disclosures to contracts and plan documents.
5. Vouch treasury stock transactions to cash receipts and cash disbursement records and to directors' authorization. Inspect treasury stock certificates.
6. When the company keeps its own share records:
   a. Inspect the share record stubs for certificate numbers and number of shares.
   b. Inspect the unissued certificates.
   c. Obtain written client representations about the number of shares issued and outstanding.

EXHIBIT 12A–2   **AUDIT PROGRAM FOR NOTES PAYABLE AND LONG-TERM DEBT**

1. Obtain a schedule of notes payable and other long-term debt (including capitalized lease obligations) showing beginning balances, new notes, repayment and ending balances. Trace to general ledger accounts.
2. Confirm liabilities with creditor: amount, interest rate, due date, collateral and other terms. Some of these confirmations may be standard bank confirmations.
3. Review the standard bank confirmation for evidence of assets pledged as collateral and for unrecorded obligations.
4. Read loan agreements for terms and conditions that need to be disclosed and for pledge of assets as collateral.
5. Recalculate the current portion of long-term debt and trace to the trial balance, classified as a current liability.
6. Study lease agreements for indications of need to capitalize leases. Recalculate the capital and operating lease amounts for required disclosures.
7. Recalculate interest expense on debts and trace to the interest expense and accrued interest accounts.
8. Obtain written representations from management concerning notes payable, collateral agreements and restrictive covenants.

EXHIBIT 12A–3   **AUDIT PROGRAM FOR INVESTMENTS AND RELATED ACCOUNTS**

A. Investments and related accounts.
   1. Obtain a schedule of all investments, including purchase and disposition information for the period. Reconcile with investment accounts in the general ledger.
   2. Inspect or confirm with a trustee or broker the name, number, identification, interest rate and face amount (if applicable) of securities held as investments.
   3. Vouch the cost of recorded investments to brokers' reports, contracts, cancelled cheques and other supporting documentation.
   4. Vouch recorded sales to brokers' reports and bank deposit slips, and recalculate gain or loss on disposition.
   5. Recalculate interest income and look up dividend income in a dividend reporting service (such as Moody's or Standard & Poor's annual dividend record).
   6. Obtain market values of investments and determine whether any write-down or write-off is necessary. Scan transactions soon after the client's year-end to see if any investments were sold at a loss. Recalculate the unrealized gains and losses required for marketable equity securities disclosures.
   7. Read loan agreements and minutes of the board, and enquire of management about pledge of investments as security for loans.
   8. Obtain audited financial statements of joint ventures, investee companies (equity method of accounting), subsidiary companies and other entities in which an investment interest is held. Evaluate indications of significant controlling influence. Determine proper balance sheet classification. Determine appropriate consolidation policy in conformity with accounting principles.
   9. Obtain written representations from the client concerning pledge of investment assets as collateral.
B. Intangibles and related expenses.
   1. Review merger documents for proper calculation of purchased goodwill.
   2. Enquire of management about legal status of patents, leases, copyrights and other intangibles.
   3. Review documentation of new patents, copyrights, leaseholds and franchise agreements.
   4. Vouch recorded costs of intangibles to supporting documentation and cancelled cheque(s).
   5. Select a sample of recorded R&D expenses. Vouch to supporting documents for evidence of proper classification.
   6. Recalculate amortization of goodwill, patents and other intangibles.

E X H I B I T   12A–4   DERIVATIVE SECURITIES—AN EXAMPLE OF NEW RISKS THAT MANAGEMENT AND AUDITORS FACE

Unless otherwise indicated this Appendix exhibit is a composite of the following articles:

John Saunders, "Derivatives: The biggest betting game," *The Globe and Mail*. March 4, 1994, A1, A10.

Douglas Gould, "Questions Mount in Barings Saga," *The Globe and Mail*. February 28, 1995, B10.

Bonnie McKennon, "Derivatives Rules Adequate: Palmer," *The Globe and Mail*. March 3, 1995, B4.

John Putridge, "Trader Incentives Under Attack," *The Globe and Mail*. March 3, 1995, B4.

Madelaine Drohan, "Barings Trader Lands in German Court," *The Globe and Mail*. March 3, 1995, B1, B4.

An increasingly important aspect of many larger company operations is derivative trading. The reason for this growth is that derivatives allow companies to manage risks better; however, as recent events at Orange County, California, and Barings Bank in the United Kingdom have shown, derivatives can also create risks where none existed previously. Derivatives are "securities" whose values depend on the values of other more basic variables. An IBM stock option is a derivative security because its value depends on the price of IBM shares; a wheat futures contract is a derivative security because its value depends on the price of wheat and so on.[2]

When derivatives are used to offset natural business risks, such as fluctuations in the price of commodities, interest rates or currency exchange rates, they are called hedges. Hedges play an important role in optimizing business risks, and derivatives trading room operations of many corporations are becoming an increasingly critical function for the success (or failure) of the corporations. Thus, the control of derivatives trading within a company is becoming increasingly critical to the success and well-being of the entire company. For example, when things go wrong it's usually because employees "go rogue" (engage in a covert gamble) or simply do not know what they are doing—the Barings Bank case appears to be a classic example. There you had England's oldest (233 years old) bank, Barings plc, which played a key role in financing the completion of the CP transcontinental railway in 1885—suddenly collapsed because it lost $1.26 billion in three weeks before anyone noticed. How could this happen? A Barings employee, Mr. Leeson, with or without the approval of others—facts that are to be determined in court—was able to commit the bank to ruinous speculations on the direction of Tokyo's Nikko 225 stock index, among other things.

"It appears that over a period of a few weeks Barings' Singapore office acquired thousands of futures contracts representing billions of dollars on the Singapore International Monetary Exchange and on the Osaka futures market.

"Most of Barings' exposure apparently was in 'long' contracts, which means Barings was obliged to buy Nikkon index stocks at current prices, before the contracts expired at March 10, 1995. Obviously, Barings hoped the market would rise so it could sell the contracts at a profit. The Japanese stock market had been weak for quite a while and Barings gambled that the market would rebound when it kept weakening, Barings gambled further by selling more long contracts. Unfortunately for Barings throughout the period the Nikkei index kept dropping."[3]

The Barings episode is only one in a series of huge losses in derivatives experienced by various organizations around the world: Orange County California, Proctor & Gamble Co., the German Conglomerate Metallgesellschaft AG, Kashima Oil in Japan, Wall Street Investment firm Kidder Peabody & Co. Inc. Derivative trading has mushroomed in popularity around the world despite these risks. For example, the daily volume of derivatives trading on the London International Financial Futures Exchange has grown from 100,000 derivatives in 1987 to 600,000 in 1994.

A unique aspect of the Barings case is that the transactions went through exchanges that involved intermediaries who acted as guarantors. These should have required Barings to provide deposits on both the Osaka and Singapore exchanges. The Barings fiasco will provide an interesting "stress test" on the clearing corporations in Singapore and Osaka to see whether they and their members will be able to meet the obligations they have guaranteed.

Part of the problem in assessing derivatives risk is that so many new transactions have evolved that the actual risks and obligations and rights have not had time to be tested in the courts.

There are two major types of derivatives transactions, over the counter and open markets. Over the counter or off-exchange derivatives are individually tailored and privately negotiated contracts. They are frequently crafted by investment banks or brokerage firms for their client's special needs.

Canadian banks have been identified as having particularly strong internal controls to prevent the types of collapses as Barings. John Palmer, the federal Superintendent of Financial Institutions, commented that Canadian banks have been more conservative in engaging in derivatives transactions, as well as financially stronger than their foreign rivals. However, because of the increased derivatives activities, the office is working with the industry in drafting guidelines for internal controls to control risks by ensuring that bets are adequately hedged and not concentrated in any one country or stock exchange. It is important that these controls be closely monitored too so that they maintain their strength.

Since derivatives transactions take place with lightning speed involving thousands of daily transactions with huge amounts of money, it creates new challenges for management and regulators. A major part of the problem is that "derivatives basically enable you to execute transactions more efficiently and save the economy money. For example, through swap transactions banks can protect themselves against interest rate changes that could turn financing mismatches into disasters. The benefit to Canadians is five-year, fixed rate mortgage loans based on short-term, low-cost savings deposits.

"Derivatives get their beauty and deadliness from the same sources: speed and power. They came into their own with the advent of desktop computers, which make split-second calculations feasible. For better or worse, they generally let players commit themselves to large positions faster and with greater leverage (and thus risks)—a bigger bang for the buck—than is possible in other markets.

"But that is also why both dealers and customers need to maintain tight controls."

Selling uncovered options is a particularly risky game because the buyer pays only a specific sum, while the seller's losses are almost unlimited if the bet goes the wrong way.

Normally treasurers get involved in these transactions—or ought to get involved in them—as a function of a hedging strategy, and one of the things that amazes me is the lack of understanding at a basic level of management in otherwise sophisticated corporations.

One risk is what I would call the hero syndrome, where you've got the guy who's making so much money (for the firm) that everyone's afraid to question him.

Another temptation is to bend the rules in quest of a big win and then double up on losing bets. It's like gambling with other people's money. You think I'll win it back tomorrow and put it back in the kitty, but you never do. Desperate people do desperate things. . . . You just don't know what will make somebody snap."

To minimize risk, traders must be kept on a short lease, according to the director of trading room operations at the Mutual Group. No trader should be allowed to handle payment or recordkeeping functions as Mr. Leeson is suspected to have done in Singapore, possibly with the help of his wife, Lisa, who worked in the back office.

All traders should take at least four weeks' vacation a year, partly to get them away from the office long enough that secret schemes are likely to come to light and partly to relieve the stress of the job.

One result of the recent derivatives fiasco is the rethinking of the practice of paying instant rewards to market high flyers. You're beginning to get incentive structures to senior people in investment houses that go toward medium-term performance, in other words, deferred compensation and bonuses. Conceivably one effect of the Barings collapse would be to cut down on frequent moves and on immediate incentives and immediate gratification. The collapse of Barings was not only a function of "control problems" but also "the trading and investment bank culture." It's a world where players can earn hundreds of thousands, even millions of dollars a year in bonuses, and where, increasingly, they are moving from firm to firm lured by even bigger rewards.

There is a breed of young, aggressive traders and the real problem is not that they are trying to make money but that the system puts a tremendous amount of pressure on the short-run realization of profits. And the bonus structure itself forces a lot of this on individual performance inside firms.

Regulators in the United Kingdom concerned about explosive growth and a handful of big losses in the derivatives business may limit the amount of speculative trading commercial banks can do for their own account.

A *Financial Times* editorial said regulators should try to prevent bank deposits covered by taxpayer financial deposit insurance from being used for speculation. "There is no reason why taxpayers' money should be used to support banks' taste for gambling," it said.

The attitude of Canadian regulators, on the other hand, is that little can be done on a day-to-day basis other than monitoring bank controls. Regulators can oversee how the banks' own controls are working, but they can't monitor the hundreds of traders and thousands of daily transactions that financial institutions make. The regulators' focus is to ensure that controls are in place and that procedures are in place to monitor adherence to these controls.

The Canadian regulators' view is that the Barings collapse was caused by a series of blunders, not inadequate controls.

According to Susan LaBorge, "Derivatives are an essential part of risk management and so if you didn't do certain kinds of things with derivatives, you'd actually increase the risk to a bank. You'd have far more volatility in results because of interest rate mismatches and various risks on foreign exchange that we really don't want our institutions to take, so derivatives are a very useful risk-management tool."

She does worry that small institutions, such as trust companies, may lack the skills and internal safeguards required for some types of derivatives trading. In fact, the fact that Barings traditionally was not a big player in the market and hadn't developed the internal controls for dealing with it explains part of the apparent weaknesses in internal controls at the Barings bank. Risk management controls that are too weak can open the way to fraud. Also, if treasury departments are treated as profit centres, managers have more incentive to take more speculative risks.

Part of the problem is that organizations often ask traders to monitor their own derivatives exposure. This lax monitoring system gives traders leeway to play with valuations.

Banks have more stringent systems in place to prevent tellers from executing fraudulent transactions than they have for traders. This reflects the rapidity with which trader activities have grown in terms of importance and risks. Such rapidity that management and regulators only now are aware of the potentially new risks being created by trader activities.

Optimal control of these new risks is not achieved by banning derivatives—derivatives bring too many benefits. Instead the optimal approach is to more carefully monitor and control exposure to the new risks. The right expertise is needed to put the right restraint in place, and this requires new types of professionals that are only now becoming identified.

Problems with derivatives trading are also evident in Canada. According to a March 4, 1995, article in the *Toronto Star*, the following are some signs of trading fiascos in Canada.

– In April 1994 CIBC Wood Gundy fired its interim head of capital markets trading. His strategy on a portfolio of financial derivatives based on Canadian interest rates cost the brokerage an estimated $12 million.

– Also in April 1994 a derivatives trader at Credit Swiss Canada "hit the bricks" after reportedly losing between $15 million and $21 million.

– In July 1994 the Bank of Montreal U.S. subsidiary, Harris Bancorp Inc., wrote off $46 million in trading-related losses.

And according to an article in *Report on Business*, A10, March 4, 1995, an investigative accountant in Canada helped to reconstruct dealings in which a Canadian company treasurer blew "several million dollars" about three years ago selling uncovered foreign exchange options.

The loss did not destroy the company, but it could have done. Apparently it was only luck of the market forces that losses were only several million rather than several hundred millions, yet the risks were there nonetheless.[4]

In fact, these derivatives' losses are part of a longer tradition of trading losses that have plagued Canadian financial institutions over the decades. A March 4, 1995, article in the Business Section of the *Toronto Star* entitled, "So It Can't Happen Here, Eh?" details an Ontario financial institutional failure similar to Barings. For example, the Ontario Bank failure of 1906 ($1 million in damages—$7 million at current dollars) and the Osler brokerage failure of 1987 ($57 million in damages), as well as the more recent derivatives' trading losses all have in common good regulation but poor enforcement. A trusted employee is loosely supervised and breaches the trust. Something goes wrong and there's an overwhelming urge to win it back. That means placing bigger bets, which lead to bigger losses.[5]

Greed will always be around. But one way of reducing speculative trading risk is to change the way top traders are rewarded. Instead of instant payoffs, some of the bonus money could be deferred over several years. That reduces short-run pressures and the temptation to make the big play. However, with respect to derivatives trades, special technical controls also need to be developed: a framework for evaluating the effects of derivatives dealings on firm capital, regular audited reports on credit risks assumed by the firm in their derivative tradings, and last but not least, making sure hedge positions do not get over-exposed. Overexposure results in creation of new risk rather than risk minimization through proper hedging. Hence, there should be "very" close monitoring of hedging activities. For example, the very fact that a hedged position produces a gain means there is an exposed position. Just as easily as you produce gains, therefore, you can also produce losses. Hence, constant monitoring of trading activities to test if

EXHIBIT 12A–4   (*continued*)

they meet firm objectives and operate within firm guidelines is a key to controlling trading losses. Since many of these trades take place very quickly and electronically, this suggests that many of the controls should be built into the electronic network so that, for example, if a capital requirement is violated, a trade should be automatically terminated. Such sophisticated computer controls can only be implemented at the design stage of system development and only through extensive consultation with management and finance specialists so that both operating control and auditability objectives of electronic trading can be met with reasonable effectiveness. This is just another example of the increased complexity of the environment the auditor must learn to operate in.

In a recent audit alert (see box below) the CICA provided suggestions to PAs on auditing derivatives, given the high-profile risks in this area.

[2]John Hull, *Introductions to Future and Option Markets*, Prentice Hall, Englewood Cliffs, New Jersey, 1991, p. 12.
[3]Douglas Gould, "Questions Mount in Barings Saga," *Globe and Mail*, February 28, 1995, p. B10.
[4]Ibid, p. A10.
[5]Adam Mayers, "So It Can't Happen Here, Eh?" *Toronto Star*, March 4, 1995, pp. C1 and C3.

The following are examples of unique, inherent risk factors associated with derivatives:
- Many derivatives are not recognized in the financial statements. As a result, there is an increased risk that derivatives, and related fees, premiums, commissions, receivables and payables will not be collected and recorded by control systems.
- Because derivatives are financial instruments whose values are derived from underlying market rates or indexes, their values change as those rates or indexes change. Increase in the volatility of interest rates, commodity prices and foreign currency rates may cause wide fluctuations in the values of derivatives.
- Entities use derivatives to (*a*) manage risk—that is to hedge, and (*b*) to speculate. Derivatives used for hedging purposes may be accounted for differently from those used to speculate.

The following are steps that the auditor might consider taking when auditing an entity involved with derivative financial instruments.
- Obtain an understanding of the nature and extent of the use of derivatives to determine whether they may have a significant effect on the audit or on the financial statements.
- Make preliminary decisions on the materiality of derivatives and the level of inherent risk during the planning stage of the audit.
- Ensure that audit staff who will be performing audit procedures on derivatives have an appropriate level of knowledge and experience.
- Consider whether it is necessary to use the work of a specialist (see "Using the work of a specialist," *Section* 5360 of the *CICA Handbook* for guidance).
- Consider the extent to which it is appropriate to use the work of internal audit (see *Section* 5230, "Using the work of internal audit").
- Obtain an understanding of the control-environment factors affecting derivative activities (see *Section* 5200.11 of the *Handbook* for examples).

The extent of an entity's use of derivatives and the relative complexity of the instruments used are important in determining the level of sophistication that is necessary for an entity's control and monitoring systems for derivative activities. To assist the auditor in understanding the control environment, the following questions, adapted from material developed by the American Institute of Certified Public Accountants, could be used in discussion with top management, the board of directors and the audit committee:
- — Has the board established a clear and internally consistent risk management policy, including appropriate risk limits? In particular, if the entity is a financial institution, has the entity incorporated into its risk management programs the guidance issued by Office of the Superintendent of Financial Institutions' Derivatives Best Practices and the Canada Deposit Insurance Corporation's Standards of Sound Business Practice?

— Are management's strategies and implementation policies consistent with the board's authorization?

— Do controls exist to ensure that only authorized transactions take place and that unauthorized transactions are quickly detected and appropriate action is taken?

— Are the magnitude, complexity and risks of the entity's derivatives commensurate with the entity's objectives?

— Are personnel with authority to engage in and monitor derivative transactions well qualified and appropriately trained?

— Do the right people have the right information to make decisions?

Source: "Auditing derivatives financial instruments," Studies and Standards Alert, *CA Magazine,* January/February 1995, p. 66.

The CICA recommends that the sample letter in the following box be used for confirming information related to derivative instruments.

Sample Letter 2

REQUEST FOR STATEMENT DETAILING
OUTSTANDING DERIVATIVE INSTRUMENTS

[Client letterhead]

[Date]
[Financial institution official responsible for account]
[Financial institution name]
[Financial institution address]

Dear [financial institution official responsible for account]:

In connection with their audit of our financial statements for the year ended March 31, 1997, our auditors, CA & Co. have requested a statement summarizing all derivative financial instruments entered into by the company and outstanding at March 11, 1997. Derivative financial instruments include futures, foreign exchange contracts, forward rate agreements, interest rate swaps and options contracts, or other financial instruments with similar characteristics.

In your response, please include the following information for each instrument:

1. The principal, stated, face or other similar amount (sometimes also referred to as the notional amount) on which future payments are based.

2. The date of maturity, expiration or execution.

3. Any early settlement options, including the period in which, or date at which the options may be exercised and the exercise price or range of prices.

4. Any options to convert the instrument into, or exchange it for, another financial instrument or some other asset or liability, including the period in which, or date at which the options may be exercised and the conversion or exchange ratio(s).

5. The amount and timing of scheduled future cash receipts or payments of the principal amount of the instrument, including installment repayments and any sinking fund or similar requirements.

6. The stated rate or amount of interest, dividend or other periodic return on principal and the timing of payments.

7. Any collateral held or pledged.

8. The currency of the cash flows if these are other than Canadian funds.

9. Where the instrument provides for an exchange, information noted in 1 to 8 above for the instrument to be acquired in the exchange.

10. Any condition of the instrument or an associated convenant that, if contravened, would significantly alter any of the other terms.

Please mail the above noted information directly to our auditors in the enclosed addressed envelope. Should you wish to discuss any details of this confirmation request with our auditors, please contact (name of audit staff member) at (111) 222-3333, or by fax at (111) 222-3334.

Yours truly,

[Authorized signatory of the client]

Source: CICA and Canadian Bankers Association

CHAPTER 13

Learning Objectives

Chapters 9–12 of this book have concentrated on presenting the transaction cycle approach to auditing. In Chapters 1–6 the concept of the strategic systems approach (SSA) to auditing was briefly introduced (see in particular Chapters 4 and 5 and their appendices). It was indicated that at least three of the largest PA firms are adopting this approach in whole or in part to their financial statement audit. Obviously one chapter cannot cover SSA auditing in the same depth as the transactions cycle approach was covered in the preceding chapters. After studying Chapter 13 you should be able to:

1. Describe the concept of business risk.

2. Discuss how the PA gains understanding of business risk through strategic analysis and business process analysis.

3. Describe the types of risk assessment and reduction procedures carried out by an SSA auditor.

4. Explain how the PA links business risk to audit risk and the nature of the audit evidence acquired.

5. Relate analysis of business performance to the financial statements.

6. Describe how an SSA audit complies with GAAS (generally accepted auditing standards).

A STRATEGIC SYSTEMS APPROACH

TO THE FINANCIAL AUDIT[1]

BUSINESS RISK

LEARNING OBJECTIVE

1. Describe the concept of business risk.

The SSA audit requires the auditor to focus on "auditing the business as management runs it" as opposed the more traditional approach that focuses the auditor's attention on accounting transactions and cycles. Therefore, the SSA auditor focuses on understanding business risk. Business risk can be defined as an event or action that will adversely affect an organization's ability to achieve its business objectives and execute its strategies. For example, the development of the microcomputer and its word processing capabilities reduced dramatically the market for electric typewriters therefore threatening the business objectives of many firms in the typewriter business. The SSA auditor seeks to understand management's perception of the firm's business risk as well as independently reach a conclusion on the completeness of management's assessment. The next section explains how this conclusion is reached.

ANALYSIS OF THE BUSINESS

LEARNING OBJECTIVE

2. Discuss how the PA gains understanding of business risk through strategic analysis and business process analysis.

There are two parts of business analysis, the first is strategic analysis and the second is business process analysis. The goal of both is the same: to learn about management's analysis of the risks the business faces and to enable the auditor to determine if management's analysis identifies all material business risks.

Strategic Analysis

The SSA auditor begins the strategic analysis by gaining an understanding from senior client management (for example, chief executive officer, chief operating officer) about what are their business objectives, key strategies employed to achieve those objectives and risks that threaten achievement of those objectives. In for-profit entities objectives are normally some combination of profitability and growth. Other entities might have much more complex objectives: for example, an inner city health clinic's goals may revolve around providing medical services to immigrant populations that are under-served by the traditional means of medical service delivery. Strategies involve the way the organization establishes systems and processes to achieve the business objectives at a more detailed implementation level. Common strategies include being an industry cost leader (i.e., having the lowest costs), differentiating your products from those of your competitors (i.e., finding some element of the product that a large subset of purchasers value and delivering it to them). The appendix to this chapter discusses further common business strategies and the risks associated with them.

After documenting senior management's strategies the auditor seeks to determine if these strategies guide the lower levels of management of the organization. The SSA auditor does this by interviewing managers of the various business units in the organization to determine

---

[1] Prepared by: S. Salterio, December 7, 1999

471

whether their individual unit's activities are consistent with the strategy described by top management. This deepens the auditor's knowledge of how the strategies are implemented and whether there are gaps between what top management says is the strategy and what business unit managers are attempting to carry out. For example, is top management's strategy for increasing customer satisfaction with their retail shopping experience reflected in the actions of store level management when they are deciding staffing plans? The auditor also enquires as to what the lower levels of management perceive as the risks that might threaten the successful implementation of the business strategies.

Once the SSA auditor has a sound understanding of what client management's objectives, strategies and risks are, the auditor needs to assess the completeness of management's analysis. In particular the auditor considers whether management has identified all of the risks that might have a material effect on the business. The SSA auditor approaches this task by carrying out an independent analysis of the environment of the business and an industry analysis. Two common tools for carrying out such analysis, PEST analysis and Porter's five forces model, were introduced in the appendix to Chapter 4. If management's analysis is found to be incomplete, additional discussions with senior management are undertaken and depending on the outcome of such discussions, additional audit procedures may have to be carried out as will be explained later in this chapter.

The strategic analysis also serves another purpose. It is the beginning of the auditor's development of a set of in-depth, knowledge-driven propositions about what amounts and relationships between amounts the auditor will find in the financial statements. The strategic analysis also may suggest certain disclosures need to be considered in the financial statement notes.

Business Process Analysis

An important way that management tries to minimize business risks is by designing well-thought-out business processes. Business processes can be defined as a structured set of activities within the entity that are designed to produce a specific output in accordance with the business strategy. Exhibit 13–1 shows an example of some of the typical business processes for an airline company. The theory underlying business process analysis has its origins in value chain analysis. Exhibit 13–2 describes value chains. If the business process produces the output in the way that the strategy intended it to do, it is more likely that the business will achieve its objectives and not fall prey to the various risks.

Every business that is audited will have a number of processes and sub-processes as part of the set of activities that it carries out in creating value for its customers. The auditor, via interviews with various operating managers, defines what processes exist in a particular client. SSA auditors are aided in this task with generic process models that outline typical business processes found in clients in a particular industry. The SSA auditor must choose only those processes that are key to the business and then within each process choose key sub-processes to examine in detail since it is not cost-effective to audit all processes. The choice of key processes can be made by considering the following factors.

EXHIBIT 13–1   EXAMPLES OF BUSINESS PROCESSES AND SUB-PROCESSES FOR A PASSENGER AIRLINE COMPANY

- Market and sell services.
  1. Develop a marketing plan
  2. Form and continue alliances with other airlines.
  3. Establish positive customer contact.
- Provide transportation services.
- Acquire, maintain and manage assets.
- Manage safety and risk.

EXHIBIT 13–2   **VALUE CHAIN ANALYSIS**

Value chain analysis is described as "a framework for analyzing the contribution of individual activities in a business to the overall level of customer value the firm produces, and ultimately to the firm's financial performance."[1] The diagram shows the traditional, functional way of viewing business in vertical columns (e.g., research and development, or "R & D"). Value chain analysts claim that these functional areas are not the source of the firm's competitive advantage. It is how the firm organizes these functions to accomplish the activities of the business that determines whether a strategy is successfully implemented. The diagram shows processes (e.g., "add and keep customers") as cutting horizontally across the various functional areas. The processes are action oriented in keeping with the idea of finding what activities cause the customer to value the products or services delivered by a business.

Value Chains and Traditional Business Functions

R & D Sales Purchasing HR Production Distribution Finance

Add and keep customers

Obtain and fill orders

Launch new products

Provide operating resources

Generate cash flow

Satisfy stakeholders

[1] Michael Porter, *Competitive Advantage: Creating and Sustaining Superior Performance* (New York: Free Press, 1985).

- **Strategic relevance.** How vital is the process is to the strategy and objectives of the client? The more vital the process is, the more likely it will be considered "key."
- **Inherent business risk.** This risk is the likelihood of a business risk occurring, ignoring the effects of the client's control environment (as explained below). The more likely the process is to contain business risks as identified in the strategic analysis, the more likely the process will be considered "key." Some factors that might be taken into account in determining the level of inherent business risk are:
  - Complexity of the process.
  - Management judgement needed in the process.
  - Likelihood the process will generate nonroutine transactions.
  - Extent of management judgement over these nonroutine transactions.
- **Control environment.** This aspect reflects the SSA auditor's assessment of the overall attitude, awareness and commitment of management concerning the importance of control and its emphasis within the entity. The types of factors considered include:
  - Management philosophy and operating style.
  - Organizational structure.
  - Management control systems.
  - Systems development controls.
  - Personnel policies.

The auditor would subjectively weigh each of the three factors (strategic relevance, inherent business risk and control environment) in selecting which processes are key business processes for a particular client.

For each of the key business processes the SSA auditor would learn, via interviews of management, the following:

- Process objectives (the roles the process plays in achieving the entity's business objectives).
- Process activities.
- Classes of accounting transactions and systems employed.
- Process risks.
- Process controls (those management controls that the deal with the identified process risks).

The SSA auditor would develop and compare an independent analysis of process risks with management's analysis. If management's analysis is found to be incomplete, additional discussions with appropriate operating management, and potentially senior management, are undertaken. Depending on the outcome of such discussions, additional audit procedures may have to be carried out as explained later in this chapter. Process risks are also examined to see if they increase the previously identified business risks.

The process analyses continue to deepen the auditor's understanding of the business that began in the strategic analysis. This additional depth of understanding should allow the auditor to develop even more precise estimates of the amounts and relationships among the amounts that should be found in the financial statements. The process analyses may also suggest disclosures that should be present in the notes to the financial statements.

R E V I E W
CHECKPOINTS

13.1 What is business risk? Give an example of a business risk that affects the airline industry.

13.2 What are the two parts that make up business analysis? What is the goal of business analysis?

13.3 Why does the auditor learn about management's strategies? Who does the auditor learn about strategy from? How does the auditor develop independent analysis of the risks associated with the strategy?

13.4 What is the purpose of business process analysis? What factors influence the auditor's choice of business processes to analyze? What information does the auditor seek to learn about business processes?

RISK ANALYSIS AND REDUCTION

LEARNING OBJECTIVE

3. Describe the types of risk assessment and reduction procedures carried out by an SSA auditor.

An SSA auditor is constantly evaluating risk during the SSA audit. The auditor learns about management's understanding of business and process risks, independently assesses the completeness of this understanding and designs audit procedures to ensure the risk is reduced to an appropriately low level. The auditor knows that management has to take certain risks to achieve rewards in the marketplace. Those are the risks management accepts from being in business. Other risks, however, can be managed in any of four ways:

1. Avoided by not performing those business activities that would cause the risk to occur.
2. Reduced to an acceptable level via management controls embedded in business processes.
3. Ignored on a cost/benefit basis.
4. Transferred to another party via a contract (e.g., insurance).

After understanding the business risks, the auditor needs to consider which risks are high. The SSA auditor considers two factors in this analysis, the likelihood of the risk occurrence and the magnitude of the risk. Each risk is qualitatively judged according to a three-point scale on likelihood of occurrence ("unlikely," "possible" or "probable") and magnitude of risk ("insignificant," "moderate" and "significant.") When considered together these two assessments result in classifying a risk as "low," "medium" or "high." Exhibit 13–3 shows

EXHIBIT 13-3   INITIAL RISK ASSESSMENT

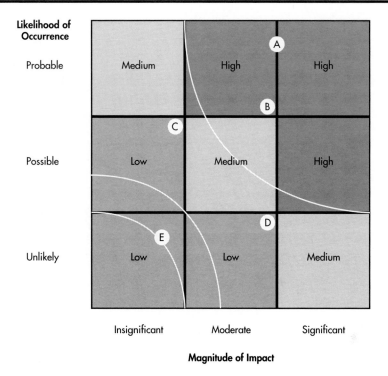

a graphical representation of the assessment process. For example, the business risk represented by point A indicates a risk that is probable to occur and if it did occur it would have a significant effect. Therefore, the auditor would classify the risk at point A as a high risk. The business risk represented by point E indicates a business risk that is unlikely to occur and if it did occur be insignificant in size. Hence the auditor would classify this risk as low.

Most business risks are managed through well-designed business processes although some fall into the ignored or transferred category. The auditor examines the risks that threaten to prevent the entity from carrying out of the process effectively (i.e., process risk). The auditor then tests the controls that management has in place to ensure efficient and effective functioning of the key business processes. Controls in this sense are wider than the traditional internal controls discussed in Chapter 6. Here the reference to "controls" is similar to that employed by the CICA Criteria of Control Committee, which defines control as "those elements of an organization (including its resources, systems, processes, culture, structure and tasks) that, taken together, support people in the achievement of the organization's objectives." See Exhibit 13–4 for examples of management controls. The SSA auditor has to test these controls, often by determining if the key performance indicators employed by management are effective at controlling the process and whether management is actually using the controls.

EXHIBIT 13-4   EXAMPLES OF MANAGEMENT CONTROLS

- Budget systems.
- Forecasting systems.
- Physical measures of process performance (e.g., defect rates).
- Quality enhancement programs.
- Performance indicators (both financial and nonfinancial).
- Process monitoring activities.
- Traditional accounting internal controls.

EXHIBIT 13–5   RISK ASSESSMENT AFTER CONSIDERING MANAGEMENT CONTROLS

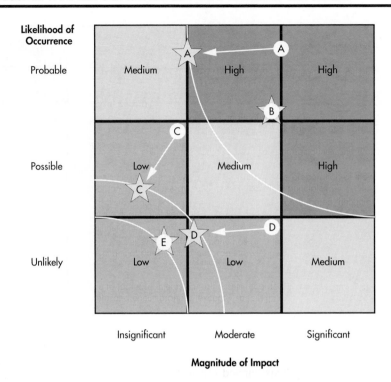

After testing the management controls, the auditor considers the results that effective functioning of controls have on the original risk analysis. Exhibit 13–5 shows the auditor reassessing business risk after examining and testing the management controls. The business risk referred to as point C has been moved by the auditor from an overall risk judgment of near medium to well into the low category. The auditor has reclassified the business risk referred to as point A from being a clearly high risk to a medium to high risk. Note, however, that controls did not reduce the risks associated with point B. All the risks that are not moved into the low category by management controls are referred to as "residual risks" and need to be subject to further audit scrutiny. These residual risk categories effectively represent categories for which the control risks are high. That is, the controls fail to offset the inherent risks associated with the category.

R E V I E W
C H E C K P O I N T S

13.5 What five ways can business risks be managed? How are business risks analyzed?

13.6 What is the relationship between business risks and business processes? Why does the auditor test the controls management has in place over business processes?

13.7 Do auditors in an SSA audit normally test traditional accounting internal controls?

BUSINESS RISK AND AUDIT RISK

LEARNING OBJECTIVE
4. Explain how the PA links business risk to audit risk and the nature of the audit evidence acquired.

The objective of a financial statement audit is to render an opinion on whether the financial statements, taken as a whole, are materially in accordance with generally accepted accounting standards. Audit risk, as discussed in Chapter 5, is the risk that the auditor fails to express a reservation of opinion when the financial statements are misstated. The residual business risks must be analyzed further to determine whether they result in an unacceptably high audit risk. First, the residual business risks are related to significant classes of accounting transactions. Second, the specific audit objectives (e.g., existence—see Chapter 4) regarding those classes of transactions must be considered. Third, the risk that these transactions will be misstated as a result of the residual business risk must be assessed. If the risk that the class of transaction is materially misstated is greater than low then the auditor must design additional substantive audit procedures to gain evidence that the misstatement risk is reduced to an appropriately low level. On a very focused basis the auditor would apply substantive tests as discussed in Chapters 9–12 and gather additional audit evidence with which to develop an opinion.

BUSINESS PERFORMANCE ANALYSIS AND THE FINANCIAL STATEMENTS

LEARNING OBJECTIVE

5. Relate analysis of business performance to the financial statements.

The preceding risk analysis and reduction procedures provide higher quality evidence than the routine accounting transactions that processes generate as part of the normal business activities. This analysis also provides some evidence with respect to nonroutine accounting transactions (ones that occur infrequently) as well as to accounting estimates. However, a key part of the risk of material misstatement of the financial statements is that the financial statements will not capture the underlying business reality in conformance with generally accepted accounting principles. Therefore, the SSA auditor considers carefully whether the analysis of business performance is consistent with the performance portrayed in the financial statements. The auditor develops expectations about the contents of the financial statements through the analysis carried out in business analysis and risk assessment and reduction. Business performance analysis integrates these analyses by considering financial performance measures and nonfinancial performance measures and the interrelationships among the two.

Financial Performance

Financial performance begins with a traditional financial analysis similar to that presented in Chapters 4 and 5 under the heading of analytical procedures. The SSA auditor has expectations about what such a financial analysis should discover based on the previous audit analyses. A financial analysis would include examining key sets of financial statement ratios (e.g., short-term liquidity ratios—see Appendix 5A for details), examining trends over time in those ratios and considering the interrelationships among the ratios for consistency.

Financial performance analysis continues with a review of the significant accounting policy choices made by management and benchmarking those choices with significant competitors in the industry. Here the auditor is attempting to gain an understanding of the degree of conservatism of management's accounting policy selection. In particular the auditor considers the revenue recognition policy in for-profit entities as this has been found to be a key area of abuse when apparently successful companies suddenly fail. See Exhibit 13–6 for examples. Should the accounting policies diverge significantly from industry norms, the auditor will re-perform the quantitative financial performance analysis after

E X H I B I T 13–6   ACCOUNTING REVENUE RECOGNITION "GIMMICKS"

- Recording revenue before it is earned.
- Creating fictitious revenue.
- Boosting profits with nonrecurring transactions.
- Shifting current expenses to a later period.
- Failing to record or disclose liabilities.
- Shifting current income to a later period.
- Shifting future expenses to an earlier period.

adjusting the financial statements to accounting policies common in the industry. The results are then compared with industry benchmarks. This analysis may suggest areas where the auditor has to do additional audit work to reduce audit risk to an appropriately low level or suggest that management modify its accounting policies and practices.

Also part of the financial analysis is consideration of the quality of the earnings in for-profit companies. Quality of earnings refers to the client's ability to replicate its earnings, both in terms of the amounts and the trends over relatively long periods of time. Exhibit 13–7 lists factors thought to be indicative of high earnings quality. Indications of low-quality earnings may result in the auditor performing additional audit procedures to reduce risk to an appropriately low level or suggest changes to the financial statements prepared by management.

Nonfinancial Performance

Through the key process analysis the SSA auditor has developed a deep understanding of the nonfinancial performance measures employed in various business processes. Nonfinancial performance analysis builds on that understanding by analyzing in greater depth the relationships among the resources the business has available, the process by which the business uses those resources and the ability of the firm to compete in the markets in which it sells products or services. Based on the business analysis, the SSA auditor already has information about resources available to the entity and the business processes. The auditor locates information about how the firm is performing in the markets the firm competes in. Tools that the auditor can use in this analysis include: developing a "balanced scorecard" for the client and benchmarking the client firm with others in the industry. Exhibit 13–8 explains the concept of a balanced scorecard and your management accounting classes will provide more in-depth understanding. The scorecard reflects measures of resources (learning and growth), processes (internal business) and markets (customer related) in addition to relating all three to financial performance.

A key part of the nonfinancial performance analysis is determining whether the resources available to the firm combined with the relative efficiency and effectiveness of the business processes are consistent with the marketplace results. For example, a firm is competing in a technological industry with a high rate of change. The firm does not have up-to-date equipment or top engineers (both examples of resources). Its business processes are benchmarked as below industry average in performance. Therefore, the firm should have below-average market performance in terms of market share or customer satisfaction. This pattern would reflect a set of consistent results and increase the auditor's confidence in the assessment of audit risk.

Interrelationships Between Financial and Nonfinancial Performance

The SSA auditor considers whether the financial results and the nonfinancial performance measures portray the same picture of the client's business. If the client's financial state-

---

E X H I B I T 13–7   HIGH QUALITY EARNINGS

1. Earnings management practices that are not used by firms with high quality earnings:
   a. Using accounting accruals to smooth income increases over time.
   b. Structuring business transactions to ensure an outcome desired by management on accounting income for the period.
   c. Making management choices based primarily on short-term profitability.
2. High quality earnings have operating cash flows and income recognized closely together over time.
3. Indicators of high quality earnings include:
   a. Consistency of accounting accruals from year to year.
   b. Accounting policy changes reduce income.
   c. Short time lag between income recognition and the cash resulting transaction being received by the business.

EXHIBIT 13–8   THE BALANCED SCORECARD

The balanced scorecard contains measures related to financial performance, customer relations, internal business processes, and measures related to learning and growth in the organization. Financial measures are those measures particularly relevant to the business unit (e.g., revenues per employee for a sales unit, or research and development expense for a pharmaceutical division). Measures related to customers include results of customer surveys, sales from repeat customers and customer profitability. Internal business process measures relate specifically to the operational processes of the business unit. For example, a petroleum distributor may measure investment in new product development and dealer quality. The final set of performance measures, those related to learning and growth, relate to employee capabilities, information systems capabilities and employee motivation and empowerment. The scorecard is a strategic management tool that should explicate the drivers of performance, as well as provide measures of performance.

ments show increasing sales and increasing gross margins there should be market share increases, resource advantages or process efficiencies found in the nonfinancial measures that support these financial results. Again, should discrepancies be found, additional substantive audit work may need to be carried out to reduce audit risk to an appropriately low level. This analysis also provides the auditor with the knowledge to consider going-concerns issues and other areas of completing the audit as discussed in Chapter 14.

REVIEW
CHECKPOINTS

13.8   What is the relationship between business risk and audit risk? What is a residual business risk? How does the auditor deal with residual business risks?

13.9   What are the three components of business performance analysis? Why does the auditor perform business performance analysis?

13.10   What are the activities carried out by the auditor in a financial performance analysis? When would the auditor design and carry out additional substantive audit procedures as a result of performance analysis?

13.11   What are the activities carried out by the auditor as part of nonfinancial performance analysis? Why does the auditor emphasize the consistency of the nonfinancial performance measures?

13.12   What is the auditor's objective when examining the interrelationship between the financial performance measures and the nonfinancial performance measures?

THE SSA AUDIT AND GENERALLY ACCEPTED AUDITING STANDARDS

LEARNING OBJECTIVE

6. Describe how an SSA audit complies with GAAS (generally accepted auditing standards).

An SSA audit complies fully with the general and three examination standards of GAAS introduced in Chapter 2. Obviously the auditor would have to be trained in the strategic management knowledge employed as the theory underlying a SSA audit. While the concept of internal control employed in an SSA audit is the broader concept of management control, the SSA auditor certainly has an in-depth knowledge of controls and relies on them when testing the management controls. The SSA auditor also gathers whatever additional substantive evidence is needed based on the residual risk analysis and business performance analysis to support the content of the auditor's report. Currently, the SSA auditor prepares no additional reports beyond what is envisioned in current standards and thus is fully compliant with the reporting standards of GAAS.

The SSA audit tends to put more reliance on enquiry-type evidence and knowledge of the business than traditional audits. In recognition of this the CICA completed a research report in March 2000 entitled *Audit Enquiry* in which it identified ways of making audit enquiry a more reliable type of evidence. For example, to make the type of assessments required by the balanced scorecard as discussed in Exhibit 13–8, an auditor's primary source of information would be enquiries of the client's management, other employees and perhaps even others from outside the client organization such as regulators or former employees.

It's usually necessary to assess the reliability of the process used to make the client's accounting estimates. This frequently involves discussions with various of the client's senior executives. The CICA research report gives an illustration involving enquiry of VP's in customer service, manufacturing, quality controls, marketing and finance to assess the adequacy of an allowance for warranty claims

To make the integration and synthesis of the whole range of estimates used in financial reporting feasible it may be necessary to create special environments for the audit team that facilitate sharing of enquiry evidence. "Debriefings following interviews and site visits should encourage perceptions and intuitive feelings to be brought out, and information challenged to help identify inconsistencies and gaps . . . and answer colleagues' questions about their findings and impressions . . . The objective, of course, is an integration of findings, capitalizing on the synergy that can come from focused group effort."[2]

Several PA firms have developed audit management centres (AMC's) to create environments to gather the many aspects of SSA audits that rely heavily on enquiry. In AMC's a variety of media are used to bring together multi-sensory sources of relevant information such as models, graphs, pictures, narrative information in the form of real time progress reports and videoconferencing capabilities for widely scattered team members in other locations. An audit team working through an AMC is more likely to identify relevant patterns and key issues. They do this by building on one another's insights, sharing knowledge and using the available information fully. AMC's are thus one way of making SSA approaches requiring audit team members with a range of specialized skills, such as financial engineering and e-commerce, more feasible.

SUMMARY

Chapter 13 provides a broad-brush introduction to a new approach to auditing known as the strategic systems audit. This approach to auditing has been adopted in whole or in part by at least three of the Big Five PA firms. The SSA audit revolves around the concept of business risk and its relationship to audit risk. The auditor documents business risks affecting the client through strategic analysis and business process analysis. The SSA auditor then analyzes these risks, considers and tests the controls over the risks and determines what are the remaining or residual business risks. These residual risks are then analyzed for their effect on audit risk and additional substantive procedures are designed, if needed, to reduce the audit risk to an appropriately low level. The audit concludes with a detailed assessment of business performance to ensure that actual business performance is reflected in the financial statements in accordance with generally accepted auditing standards.

---

[2] CICA. *Audit Enquiry.* CICA. March 2000. page 24.

APPENDIX 13A

THREE GENERIC STRATEGIES

A Canadian teaching at Harvard University, Michael Porter, developed a framework for analyzing strategies in his book *Competitive Strategy*. There, he outlined what he called three generic strategies: cost leadership, differentiation and the application of both of those strategies to a narrow part of the industry, which he denoted as a "focus" strategy.

Cost Leadership

This is perhaps the easiest strategy to understand. The firm tries to become the lowest-cost producer in the industry while producing products/services with all the necessary features the buyer wants. This allows the firm to charge at or near industry average prices and, combined with its low costs, results in above-normal profits. If the cost leader does not have all the features normally required by buyers, then the cost leader's profits may be eroded significantly as it must make price concessions to make up for the lack of features. So while costs are the focus of this strategy, the firm must still pay attention to all the features that a buyer wishes the product to have.

Differentiation

In this strategy the firm attempts to be unique in its industry along some dimension(s) that are widely valued by buyers. That is, the product or service has some unique feature for which the buyer is willing to pay a price premium. Of course this does not mean that cost is not important, as the cost of the unique feature must be less than the price premium to result in above-average profits. Further, all other costs combined need to be at or below industry average to have above-average profits. While a differentiation strategy focuses on unique features that appeal to a broad variety of buyers, costs must still be carefully managed.

Focus

Both cost leadership and differentiation are applied to the products or services for the industry. A focuser is different, in that it attempts to optimize its product or service for a narrow segment of the industry. The focus can either be on cost leadership or on differentiation. The segments focused on must have unique needs that cannot readily be satisfied by broad-based competitors.

Porter argues that if you are not following one of these three generic strategies, in the long run you will be "caught in the middle" as competitors who are following one of the three strategies take away your profitable customers. In other words, careful implementation of one of these three strategies, taking into account the industry environment and the firm's resources, results in obtaining a sustainable competitive advantage.

Each of these generic strategies has risks associated with it, as outlined in the table below:

Risks of Cost Leadership	Risks of Differentiation	Risks of Focus
Cost leadership is not sustained because: • Competitors imitate. • Technology changes. • Other bases for cost leadership erode.	Differentiation is not sustained because: • Competitors imitate. • Bases for differentiation become less important to buyers.	Competitors imitate: The target segment becomes unattractive as demand disappears or the basis of segmentation disappears.
Features that must be present in the product or service change and the cost leader does not make the changes.	The cost of the differentiated feature rises above the price premium or other costs rise relative to industry average.	Broadly targeted competitors overwhelm the segment: • The segment differences with other segments narrow. • The advantages of a broad line increase.
Cost focusers achieve even lower costs in each segment they service, eaving no room for a broad-based cost leader.	Differentiation focusers achieve even greater differentiation in segments, leaving no room for a broad-based differentiator.	New focusers sub-segment the industry even further.

SLEEMAN BREWERIES LTD.

Introduction

In 1984 John Sleeman began to build a brewing company whose goal was to dominate the craft brewing market in Canada by producing excellent ales and lagers. John began by acquiring the trademark symbol of the beaver on the maple leaf, and then he obtained the exclusive rights to distribute a unique bottle. John wanted his first product, based on an old family recipe, to be a traditional ale called "Sleeman Cream Ale." He incorporated the company under the name of The Sleeman Brewing and Malting Company Limited.

In 1988, a credit crunch came for the fledgling company when a significant creditor suddenly began to feel uneasy about the prospects for repayment based primarily on sales of Sleeman Cream Ale. John looked to the United States for a partner and found that partner in the Stroh Brewing Company who purchases shares in Sleeman. Along with the financial support and expertise of the company came the enthusiasm, energy and determination of Doug Berchtold, currently COO of Sleeman, a seasoned veteran from the senior financial ranks of Stroh.

John, Doug and all of the management and employees worked very hard in 1989 and subsequent years, adding new products and increasing brewing capacity. Additional ales and lagers were added incrementally and the company grew in market share and volume. In 1995 it repurchased all the shares that Stroh had acquired. In 1996 after a reverse takeover of Okanagan Spring Brewery, Sleeman became a publicly traded company on the Toronto Stock Exchange, listed under the trading symbol, ALE.

The introduction of Honey Brown Lager in 1997 proved far more successful than anyone had hoped. It nearly doubled their market share and caused Sleeman to break ground on a new brewhouse expansion of 300,000 hectolitres (hl) (90 million bottles), bringing their total capacity in Guelph to 500,000 hl. Honey Brown Lager appealed to an increasing number of female consumers looking for an alternative to the traditional beer products. It has significantly stimulated the growth of Sleeman and has actually led to the expansion of the overall craft market size through a modest contraction of the traditional beer and ale market. Throughout the period 1988 to 1999 Sleeman had expanded by the introduction of its own products and the acquisition of smaller craft brewers either by purchase of shares or assets. Sleeman is now the largest craft brewer in Canada and is larger than the next four smaller craft brewers combined.

Today's Beer Industry

Ontario is the largest consumer of beer and ale in Canada (in 1996, Statistics Canada reports that Ontarians consumed 7.6 million hl, compared to the total Canadian consumption of 20.3 million hl). In the province of Ontario, the provincial government creates a barrier for entry into the market through the operation of the Brewers Retail and the LCBO retail stores as the only two distribution outlets for beer and ale products. Brewers Retail (BRI) is owned by Labatt (43 percent), Molson (54 percent) and Sleeman (3 percent), these three companies form the "Shareholders." The LCBO is owned entirely by the province.

BRI requires every producer to distribute their products to each individual retail outlet from which they want to sell, or pay BRI a transfer fee for doing so. The shareholders of BRI (including Sleeman) have the critical mass necessary to avoid most transfer fees while most other breweries must pay the $15/hl charge. In addition, Brewers Retail collects and sorts bottle returns. The average bottle is used twenty times before it is crushed and recycled. Molson and Labatt receive the traditional brown bottle back. As Sleeman uses its own distinctive bottles, they are returned to them via Brewers Retail. If a new entrant uses their own distinctive bottle, these bottle returns are either sorted for a fee by BRI or crushed and recycled without being returned. It is usually too costly for a new entrant to use anything but the traditional brown bottle, almost guaranteeing that their product is indistinguishable from Molson's and Labatt's products.

The current economic factors of low inflation, low interest rates, good GNP growth rates and stable raw material costs have created a stable business environment for the beer and ale industry in general. The reason the overall market is changing has much more to do with social and cultural factors than economic ones. The population demographics in the three key areas of Ontario, Quebec and the Western provinces of Alberta and British Columbia are changing. The baby boomers are getting older, and older people do not drink as much beer as their younger counterparts. The boomers have more money than any previous generation and they use it in different ways. Today, consumers will spend more money on a product if it is perceived to either be fashionable or increase the quality of life.

One of the biggest differences in the market is the adoption of a healthier lifestyle in which drinking to excess is discouraged. This approach is reinforced by the adoption by the government of stringent anti-drink and driving legislation and enforcement. Also, the ability to motivate people to drink alcohol in general is closely monitored by the government and the main advertising message that is allowed is one of socially responsible drinking. All these factors together have created an environment where the traditional beer market is shrinking and the craft market is expanding. The craft beer and ale market has managed to take advantage of the change in demographics to reinforce the image that it is distinctly different than the traditional beer and ale market in Canada.

In addition to increased laws over drinking and driving government also uses the brewing industry to collect additional tax revenues. Through a policy of aggressive taxation at the retail level, the government benefits from substantial revenues and provides no special subsidies or other tax relief for the industry.

There is little new in the way of technology to the beer and ale industry. The process has changed very little in several hundred years. The ingredients are one of the primary factors that make one product distinct from another. The physical process of combining, heating and fermenting the mixture changes from one company to another and this also changes the texture and the flavor of one product over another. The shelf life of a bottle is established by brewers to be ninety days; so in all provinces in Canada, most beer and ale that is over ninety days is pulled from the shelves and discarded. This rule has more to do with chemistry than any other factor: beer and ale begin to degenerate in chemical composition after that time.

The next largest factor after chemistry that differentiates one beer or ale from another is advertising and image. This is where the craft industry has been able to make the largest inroads on the traditional beer industry. Craft brewers require higher gross margins due to lower volumes and higher unit overhead costs, and fortunately the baby boomers are willing to pay the higher per bottle price that keeps the craft brewers in business.

The price for craft market products has an upper limit and a lower limit set in the market place. The upper limit is the price of imported beer and ale. These imported products are perceived to be premium products, some of the more common ones are Heineken and Guinness. They are priced higher due to a combination of freight, higher tariff duties and a higher price that reflects their global image. The craft industry has quality products, but these products are not perceived by the purchasing public at this time as providing the necessary "badging" to command a price greater than the premium imports.

The domestic beer industry giants, Labatt and Molson, set the lower limit on prices. They set a price for beer that is the same within a defined geopolitical region, such as the Maritimes, Ontario, Quebec and Western Canada. Frequently, but not always, that price is the same throughout Canada. The price of domestic beer is increasing at a faster rate than the premium imports are increasing, thus decreasing the price spread between the two. This "price squeeze" has caused the craft industry to put more emphasis on image and less emphasis on price as the price spread declines.

The consumer has little, if any, ability to affect price. The most that a consumer can do if one product becomes too expensive for them is to switch to a lower priced product. The bargaining power of suppliers is also almost non-existent. The ingredients for beer and ale can be found in plentiful supply in almost every region in Canada. As a result of these market forces, the Canadian craft beer producers' ability to satisfy gross margin requirements through price increases is declining. This trend has accelerated the consolidation of small brewers to increase volumes. Sleeman now has a presence either through direct production or distribution in every province of Canada. As a craft beer producer, its products occupies a market and price niche above the traditional beer market and below the premium imports.

Sleeman's Strategy

It is Sleeman's intention to remain the premier craft brewer in Canada and to be identified by consumers as the first alternative to traditional beer and ale consumption. Some of the key differences between the craft industry and the beer industry are described briefly in the table below, along with the relative position of Sleeman.

SUMMARY OF BEER AND ALE INDUSTRY IN CANADA

Industry	Annual Volumes (hectolitres; hl)	Number of Products	Distribution of Product	Annual Sales Dollars (000s)	Ownership
Craft	Under 100,000	Less than six	Local or regional	$50–$10,000	Private; closely held
Sleeman	600,000	More than ten	Local, regional or national	$75,000	Public; closely held
Traditional	Over 5,000,000	More than ten	National	Over $300,000	Public; widely held

Although their marketing image is that of a family owned craft brewer they share characteristics of both industries. This places them in the delicate position of balancing the image of the craft brewer while approaching the size of the traditional brewers. They accomplish this by acquiring small regional brewers and optimizing their production, marketing and distribution, while leaving the unique market attributes of the brewery intact. This approach created a collective of small regional craft brewers. The method most often used to improve profits after an acquisition is to perform clerical, data entry, production, distribution and sales at the local level, and consolidate the senior management from sales, marketing, finance and procurement processes at the Guelph location. This requires strong internal controls at the local levels since all data is input at the local level. Sleeman relies on good controls to reduce its administrative presence at the acquired company and to ensure that the acquired companies conform to Sleeman's policies and procedures. Sleeman has used this approach very successfully in the past and expects to use it in all future acquisitions.

As the number of acquisitions has increased, so has Sleeman's confidence in their ability to predict earnings based on past and projected sales and earnings. The asset base of the companies they acquire is typical of the craft industry. The land and buildings are generally from five to fifty years of age, and in some cases the family may have owned the land for more than fifty years. Each of the acquisitions is specifically chosen to complement the existing product line on either a regional or national basis. Sleeman seeks to acquire only those companies that can add value to its existing product portfolio. It has historically sought companies that have premium products that are well defined to a particular region or province. Many of the acquisitions are not in a growth stage when Sleeman makes the acquisition since inappropriately qualified senior management often stifles the potential growth. Sleeman uses its expertise to further develop and market the regional brands thus adding value to its own brands.

Sleeman also makes certain that the acquired products do not simply reduce the sales of the existing Sleeman product line. The new products must be capable of sustaining their own sales growth once Sleeman takes over, but not by stealing market from other Sleeman products. Many small companies attempt product diversification, but the company resources and their markets are too small to support the diversification endeavor. Frequently, a rationalization of the existing product lines within the acquired company takes place once Sleeman gains control. Sleeman will reduce the number of products the acquired company sells and concentrate only on those products that have the most potential. This sometimes results in Sleeman shedding one or more of its own products if it feels that the newly acquired product will increase overall sales. Thus Sleeman constantly renews itself with each new product or acquisition.

Another strategic issue that Sleeman looks at closely is the ability to expand to new markets. The Canadian market is saturated and although the craft brewers can take from the existing beer market, even that market is only so large. The two most obvious markets that Sleeman would like to expand to are Europe and the United States. To the extent that the target has a market image in the either the US or Europe, it enhances its likelihood of selection within the Sleeman family.

Additional Current Issues

John reviewed the 1998 financial statements; they were the best of any year that the company had been in business. The three-year audited comparative financial statements (Exhibit 13A-1) showed the success that had been achieved by concentrating on the core lines of ale and lager. Their next product launch was not to take place until the late spring of 2000, but preliminary market research showed that it had the potential to double the size of the overall craft industry market. This increase was at the expense of the large breweries like Molson and Labatt since the overall consumption of the beer industry had actually declined over the last few years. It meant that even with the introduction of competitors' products in the next two or three years, Sleeman could potentially capture a full twelve to fifteen percent of the total market of the entire beer, ale and lager industry. The cost to Labatt and Molson would be significant and would lead to the very real threat of intense price and marketing retaliation from each of them. John doubted that Sleeman could survive if both of the two industry giants decided to wage a full-scale price and advertising war against Sleeman.

John questioned the market research for the new product and he had gone so far as to engage another marketing firm to verify the original test results. Although the second firm never saw the results of the original firm's research and the test subjects and the testing methods were not the same, the results were quite similar.

Sleeman had expanded in the 1990s as fast as its infrastructure would allow. John pondered the ramifications of expanding to one million hectolitres at the Guelph plant. This was the minimum size they needed to go to if the market predictions were as accurate as they appeared to be. The initial product launch of new product would take almost 250,000 hectolitres, and their existing 1999 production of 450,000 hectolitres at the Guelph plant would take a significant portion of the existing capacity. They had just finished putting the final touches on the new brewhouse and that was to have kept them free from production bottlenecks for the next three to five years. There was even a suggestion from Allan Brash, Vice president of Operations, that Sleeman consider taking advantage of the economies of scale and expand by two million hectolitres. That would put it at almost half the capacity of either of Labatt or Molson.

During the current year, Sleeman's former partner, Stroh Brewing Company, sold its brewing interests to Pabst Brewing. Pabst was now looking for a Canadian partner to continue the business of importing the Stroh family of brands into Canada. Based on Stroh's former relationship with Sleeman, Pabst approached Sleeman. John was now considering whether to enter this relationship that would involve mainly importing beer from the U.S. but also some additional production of certain Stroh brands in Canada. The Stroh products primarily appeal to a very price conscious customer who would not normally purchase Sleeman's high quality craft brews.

EXHIBIT 13A–1   **SLEEMAN BREWERIES LTD.**

Audited Balance Sheets
December 26, 1998, December 27, 1997, and December 28, 1996
All dollar amounts are in thousands

	1998	1997	1996
Assets			
Current:			
Accounts Receivable	$ 10,299	$10,342	$ 6,643
Inventories, WIP & Finished Goods	4,789	3,435	3,466
Bottle Deposits	7,183	5,032	4,149
Prepaid Expenses	1,303	473	717
Total Current Assets	$ 23,574	$19,282	$14,975
Property, Plant & Equipment	41,865	33,365	28,356
Long Term Investments	3,308	4,631	4,006
Deferred Income Taxes	566	–	–
Intangible Assets	36,342	13,980	14,631
Total Assets	$105,655	$71,258	$61,968
LIABILITIES AND SHAREHOLDERS' EQUITY			
Current:			
Bank Indebtedness	$ 2,547	$281	$ 3,733
Accounts Payable & Accrued	17,483	14,029	9,032
Current Portion of LTD	4,745	3,821	2,655
Total Current Liabilities	$ 24,775	$18,131	$15,420
Long Term Debt Obligations	29,465	19,156	17,389
Deferred Income Taxes	–	1,510	969
	$ 54,240	$38,797	$33,778
Shareholders' Equity:			
Share Capital	38,310	26,110	25,670
Retained Earnings	13,105	6,351	2,520
Total Equity	$ 51,415	$32,461	$28,190
Total Liabilities and Equity	$105,655	$71,258	$61,968

SLEEMAN BREWERIES LTD.

Audited Income Statements and Statements of Retained Earnings
Years ended December 26, 1998, December 27, 1997 and December 28, 1996
Dollar amounts are in thousands, except per share data

	1998	1997	1996
Net Revenue	$ 76,023	$54,061	$39,217
Cost of Goods Sold	34,575	26,080	19,737
Gross Margin	$ 41,448	$27,981	$19,480
Selling, General & Administrative Expense	26,302	18,663	13,897
Earnings before: Interest, Income Taxes, Depreciation and Amortization	$ 15,146	$ 9,318	$ 5,583
Depreciation & Amortization Expense	3,697	3,135	2,335
Interest Expense	2,112	1,442	1,441
Earnings before Income Taxes	$ 9,337	$ 4,741	$ 1,807
Income Taxes	2,582	911	325
Net Earnings	$ 6,755	$ 3,830	$ 1,482
Retained Earnings, Beginning of Year	6,350	2,520	1,038
Retained Earnings, End of Year	$ 13,105	$ 6,350	$ 2,520
Earnings per share—Basic	$0.44	$0.29	$0.14
Earnings per share—Fully Diluted	$0.43	$0.28	$0.14

What would be public think about a premium craft brewer as an importer/brewer of a price-oriented brand? Would the public perceive Sleeman to be a craft brewer if they expanded their capacity to over two million hectolitres for their own high quality craft products? Even at one million they were in a transitional world between all their traditional competitors and the two industry giants in Canada. On a worldwide basis Labatt was owned by Interbrew, the head office is in central Europe, which has a worldwide capacity of 50 million hectolitres and is one of the largest brewers in the world. Sleeman did not intend to compete with Interbrew, and John was concerned what the effect might be if they were to be perceived as a serious threat to Labatt.

DISCUSSION QUESTIONS

Based on your understanding of the strategic systems approach to auditing, answer the following questions.

1. What are Sleeman's key business objectives? Why are these objectives being pursued?

2. What is Sleeman's strategy for achieving its objectives? What are the key factors that have shaped the current degree of success or failure of this strategy? Does Sleeman's strategy appear to be working?

3. What are the key threats (business risks) to the sustainability of Sleeman's strategy?

4. What are Sleeman's core products and services?

5. Who are Sleeman's customers?

6. Within which markets does Sleeman's operate?

7. What are the key business processes at Sleeman?

8. Analysis of a key business process begins with defining its objectives or, in other words, explaining management's vision for how the process contributes to the overall business objectives. What are the process objectives for Sleeman's mergers and acquisitions management process? What risks threaten Sleeman's achievement of mergers and acquisition process objectives? How might those risks effect Sleeman's financial statements?

9. Identify some critical success factors (CSFs) for the mergers and acquisitions process. Speculate about what key performance indicators (KPIs) Sleeman's might use to control its mergers and acquisitions process.

CHAPTER 14

Learning Objectives

This chapter covers the process of completing the field work and gathering up the loose ends of the audit. The following principal items are covered:

- Completing the audit of revenue and expense.
- Consideration of contingencies and obtaining letters from the client's lawyers.
- Obtaining written client representations.
- Events subsequent to the balance sheet date and events subsequent to the audit report date.
- Final wrap-up of the audit (audit review).

Your learning objectives relative to these topics are to be able to:

1. Describe the related balance sheet account group where the audit of the major revenue and expense accounts normally is associated.

2. Describe the use of analytical procedures to audit revenue and expense accounts.

3. Explain the use of the client representation letter and the lawyer's letter as an audit is completed.

4. Describe the reasons why written client representations are obtained, and list the four items that are included without regard to a materiality criterion.

5. Given a set of facts and circumstances, classify a subsequent event by type and describe the proper treatment in the financial statements.

6. Specify the sequence of decisions and actions auditors must consider upon discovery (after the issuance of the report) of information about facts that may have existed at the date of the auditors' report.

7. Specify the considerations and procedures applied by auditors upon concluding (after the audit report date) that one or more auditing procedures were omitted.

8. Explain the final audit steps involving adjusting entries, second-partner review and the management letter.

COMPLETING THE AUDIT

INTRODUCTION
. . . .

This chapter covers the completion of the audit cycle. The chapter reviews the issues, techniques, procedures and documents that are normally considered in effectively and efficiently completing an audit. At the completion of the audit, the audit opinion should be properly supported by the audit evidence as reflected in the audit files. The audit of the nominal or flow accounts reflected in the income statement, statement of changes in financial position and statement of changes in retained earning cannot be completed until year-end when all the transactions for the period have also been completed. As a result some year-end audit procedures relate to revenue and expense accounts for the period. This part of the year-end audit is covered in the first half of the chapter.

As well, some audit procedures relate to the year-end amounts on the balance sheet. The audit of these amounts has already been covered in the earlier part of this text relating to the different accounting cycles. However, there are procedures unique to the year-end such as audit for subsequent events, contingencies, commitments or contractual obligations, overall evaluation of audit results, proper presentation and disclosure issues that need to be considered before signing off on the audit file. These and related issues are covered in the second half of the chapter.

AUDIT OF REVENUE AND EXPENSE
. . . .

LEARNING OBJECTIVE
1. Describe the related balance sheet account group where the audit of the major revenue and expense accounts normally is associated.

As the field work nears its end, the major revenue and expense accounts will have been audited in connection with related balance sheet accounts. Now auditors need to consider other revenue and expense accounts. The broad financial statement assertions are the bases for specific assertions and audit objectives for these accounts. Typical specific assertions for the revenue and expense accounts are:

1. Revenue accounts represent all the valid transactions recorded correctly in the proper account, amount and period.
2. The accounting for consignments and goods sold with rights of return is in conformity with accounting principles.
3. Expense accounts represent all the valid expense transactions recorded correctly in the proper account, amount and period.
4. Revenues, expenses, cost of goods sold, and extraordinary, unusual or infrequent transactions are adequately classified and disclosed.

Revenue
The following types of revenue and related topics already will have been audited, either in whole or in part, at the completion stage of the engagement.

Revenue and Related Topics	Related Account Groups
Sales and sales returns.	Receivables.
Lease revenue.	Capital assets and receivables.
Franchise revenue.	Receivables, intangibles.
Dividends and interest.	Receivables, investments.
Gain, loss on asset disposals.	Fixed assets, receivables and investments.

Rental revenue.	Receivables and investments.
Royalty and licence revenue.	Receivables and investments.
Long-term sales commitments.	Revenue and receivables.
Product line reporting.	Revenue and receivables.
Accounting policy disclosure.	Revenue and receivables.

To the extent these revenue items already have been audited, the working papers should show cross-reference indexing to the revenue account in the trial balance. The accounts that have not been audited completely will be evident. Auditors should ascertain by reference to the trial balance that they have a list of all the revenue and gain or loss accounts and their amounts.

Audit Procedures

LEARNING OBJECTIVE

2. Describe the use of analytical procedures to audit revenue and expense accounts.

According to the CICA study "Analytical Review" (authored by D.G. Smith, 1983), analytical procedures can be used at these points during the audit: (1) at the planning stage, (2) during the overall evaluation of the financial statements at the end of the audit, and (3) as a substantive test procedure. The use of analytical procedures as part of the overall evaluation at the end of the audit is the most common use of analytical review in practice. This overall verification "can be an effective means of obtaining assurance as to the reasonableness of reported results. There is a broad spectrum of overall verification procedures, many particular to a specific industry, which provides a range of assurance from virtually 100% assurance to reasonable approximation" (D.J. Smith [1983; p. 3]). *Section 5301.27* requires use of analytical procedures to assist in evaluating the overall financial statement presentation upon substantial completion of the audit.

Analytical procedures can be used to compare the revenue accounts and amounts to prior-year data and to multiple-year trends to ascertain whether any unusual fluctuations are present. Comparisons also should be made to budgets, monthly internal reports and forecasts to ascertain whether events have occurred that require explanation or analysis by management. These explanations would then be subjected to audit. For example, a sales dollar increase may be explained as a consequence of a price increase that can be corroborated by reference to price lists used in the test of controls audit of sales transactions.

Auditors also should ascertain whether account classifications, aggregations and summarizations are consistent with those of the prior year. This information will have a bearing on the consistency issue in financial reporting.

All "miscellaneous" or "other" revenue accounts and all "clearing" accounts with credit balances should be analysed. Account analysis in this context refers to the identification of each important item and amount in the account, followed by document vouching and enquiry to determine whether amounts should be classified elsewhere. All clearing accounts should be eliminated and the amounts classified as revenue, deferred revenue, liabilities, deposits or contra-assets.

Miscellaneous revenue and other suspense accounts can harbour many accounting errors. Proceeds from sale of assets, insurance premium refunds, insurance proceeds and other receipts simply may be credited to such an account. Often, such items reveal unrecorded asset disposals, expiration of insurance recorded as prepaid or other asset losses covered by insurance. Exhibit 14–1 lists common audit procedures for revenue accounts.

Unusual Transactions

Significant audit evidence and reporting problems can arise with transactions designed by management to manufacture earnings. Frequently, such transactions are run through a complicated structure of subsidiaries, affiliates and related parties. Generally, the amounts of revenue are large. The transactions themselves may not be concealed, but certain guarantees may have been made by management and not revealed to the auditors. The timing of the transactions may be arranged carefully to provide the most favourable income result.

EXHIBIT 14-1   AUDIT PROGRAM FOR REVENUES AND EXPENSES

REVENUES

1. Obtain analyses of sales, cost of goods sold and gross profit by product line, department, division or location.
   a. Trace amounts to the general ledger.
   b. Compare the analyses to prior years and seek explanations for significant variations.
   c. Determine one or more standard markup percentages and calculate expected gross profits. Enquire for explanations of significant variations compared to actual results.
2. Co-ordinate procedures for audit of revenue with evidence obtained in other audit programs:

Sales and sales returns.	Sales control.	Gain, loss on asset disposals.	Fixed assets.
	Cash receipts control.		Investments.
	Accounts receivable.	Rental revenue.	Accounts receivable.
Lease revenue.	Capital assets.		Investments.
	Accounts receivable.	Royalty and licence revenue.	Accounts receivable.
Franchise revenue.	Accounts receivable.		Investments.
	Intangibles.	Long-term sales commitments.	Accounts receivable.
Dividends and interest.	Accounts receivable.		Inventory.
	Investments.		

3. Scan the revenue accounts for large and unusual items and for debit entries. Vouch items to supporting documentation.
4. Obtain written client representation about terms of sales, rights of return, consignments and extraordinary, unusual or infrequent transactions.

EXPENSES

5. Obtain schedules of expense accounts comparing the current year with one or more prior years.
   a. Trace amounts to the general ledger.
   b. Compare the current expenses to prior years and seek explanations for significant variations.
   c. Be alert to notice significant variations that could indicate failure to defer or accrue expenses.
6. Compare the current expenses to the company budget, if any. Enquire and investigate explanations for significant variances.
7. Co-ordinate procedures for audit of expenses with evidence obtained in other audit programs:

Purchases, cost of goods sold.	Acquisition control.	Bad debt expense.	Accounts receivable.
	Cash disbursement control.	Depreciation expense.	Fixed assets.
	Inventory.	Property taxes, insurance.	Prepaids and accruals.
Inventory valuation losses.	Inventory.		Fixed assets.
Warranty and guarantee expense.	Inventory.	Lease and rental expense.	Fixed assets.
	Prepaids and accruals.	Repairs and maintenance.	Fixed assets.
	Accounts payable.	Interest expense.	Long-term liabilities.
Royalty and licence expense.	Inventory.	Pension and retirement benefits.	Liabilities.
Marketing and product R&D.	Investments.		Payroll control.
	Intangibles.	Payroll and compensation.	Payroll control.
Investment value losses.	Investments.	Sales commissions.	Payroll control.
Rental property expenses.	Investments.		
Amortization of intangibles.	Intangibles.		

8. Prepare analyses of sensitive expense accounts, such as legal and professional fees, travel and entertainment, repairs and maintenance, taxes, and others unique to the company. Vouch significant items therein to supporting invoices, contracts, reimbursement forms, tax notices and the like for proper support and documentation.
9. Scan the expense accounts for large and unusual items and for credit entries. Vouch items to supporting documentation.
10. Obtain written client representations about long-term purchase commitments, contingencies and extraordinary, unusual or infrequent transactions.

These unusual transactions contain a wide variety of characteristics and are difficult to classify for useful generalization. Controversies have arisen in the past over revenue recognized on the construction percentage-of-completion method, over sales of assets at inflated prices to management-controlled dummy corporations, over sales of real estate to independent parties with whom the seller later associates for development of the property (making guarantees on indemnification for losses) and over disclosure of revenues by source. These revenue issues pose a combination of evidence-gathering problems and reporting-disclosure problems. Three illustrations of such problems are given below.

Expenses

Although many major expense items will have been audited in connection with other account groupings, numerous minor expenses may still remain unaudited. As a brief review, the following major expenses may have been audited in whole or in part as the audit nears its end.

Expenses	Related Account Groups
Purchases, cost of goods sold.	Inventories.
Inventory valuation losses.	Inventories.
Warranty and guarantee expense.	Inventories and liabilities.
Royalty and licence expense.	Inventories.
Marketing and product R&D.	Investments and intangibles.
Investment value losses.	Investments and intangibles.
Rental property expenses.	Investments and intangibles.
Amortization of intangibles.	Investments and intangibles.
Bad debt expense.	Receivables.
Amortization expense.	Capital assets.
Property taxes, insurance.	Capital assets and liabilities.
Lease and rental expense.	Capital assets.
Repairs and maintenance.	Capital assets and liabilities.
Legal and professional fees.	Liabilities and equity.
Interest expense.	Liabilities.
Pension and retirement benefits.	Liabilities, equity and payroll.
Payroll and compensation costs.	Payroll.
Sales commissions.	Payroll.

As with the revenue accounts mentioned in the previous section, if audit work is complete for expense accounts, the working papers should show cross-reference indexing from the working papers to the trial balance. Some of the expenses may not have been audited completely (such as property tax expense), and some finishing-touch vouching of supporting documents may be required.

Audit Procedures

Several minor expenses, such as office supplies, telephone, utilities and similar accounts, are not audited until late in the engagement. Generally, the dollar amounts in these accounts are not material (taken singly), and the relative risk is small that they may be misstated in such a way as to create misleading financial statements. Auditors usually audit these kinds of accounts with substantive **analytical procedures.** These procedures include making a list of the expenses with comparative balances from one or more prior periods. The dollar amounts are then reviewed for unusual changes (or lack of unusual changes if reasons for change are known). This analysis of comparative balances may be enough to decide whether the amounts are fairly presented.

On the other hand, questions may be raised and additional evidence sought. In this case auditors may **vouch** some expenses to supporting documents (invoices and cancelled cheques). Some documentary vouching evidence already may be available about these minor expenses. If the auditors performed detail test of controls procedures on a sample of expenditure transactions in the acquisition and expenditure cycle audit program, a few expense transactions were selected for testing the client's compliance with control objectives (validity, completeness, authorization, accuracy, classification, accounting and proper period). This evidence should be used.

Analytical comparisons to budgets, internal reports and forecasts also may be made. Variations from budget already may have been subject to management explanation, or the auditors may need to investigate variations.

All "miscellaneous" or "other" expense accounts and "clearing" accounts with debit balances should be analysed by listing each important item on a working paper and vouching it to supporting documents. Miscellaneous and other expenses may include abandonments of property, items not deductible for tax purposes and payments that should be

---

Unusual Revenue Transactions

Merger

National Fried Chicken, Inc., a large fast-food franchiser, began negotiations in August to purchase Provincial Hot Dog Company, a smaller convenience food chain. At August 1, 19X6, Provincial's net worth was $7 million, and National proposed to pay $8 million cash for all the outstanding shares. In June 19X7, the merger was consummated and National paid $8 million, even though Provincial's net worth had dropped to $6 million. Consistent with prior years, Provincial lost $1 million in the 10 months ended June 1; as in the past, the company showed a net profit of $1.5 million for June and July. At June 1, 19X7, the fair value of Provincial's net assets was $6 million, and National accounted for the acquisition as a purchase, recording $2 million goodwill. National proposed to show in consolidated financial statements the $1.5 million of post-acquisition income and $50,000 amortization of goodwill.

Audit Resolution. The auditors discovered that the purchase price was basically set at 16 times expected earnings and that management had carefully chosen the consummation date in order to maximize goodwill (and reportable net income after amortization in fiscal 19X7). The auditors required that $1 million of "goodwill" be treated as prepaid expenses which expired in the year ended July 31, 19X7, so that bottom-line income would be $500,000.

Real Estate Deal

In August, a company sold three real estate properties to BMC for $5,399,000 and recognized profit of $550,000. The agreement that covered the sale committed the company to use its best efforts to obtain permanent financing and to pay underwriting costs for BMC. The agreement provided BMC with an absolute guarantee against loss from ownership and a commitment by the company to complete construction of the properties.

According to the provincial securities commission accountant, the terms of this agreement made the recognition of profit improper because the company had not shifted the risk of loss to BMC.

Real Estate Development, Strings Attached

In December 19X6, Black Company sold one half of a tract of undeveloped land to Red Company in an arm's-length transaction. The portion sold had a book value of $1.5 million, and Red Company paid $2.5 million in cash. Red Company planned to build and sell apartment houses on the acquired land. In January 19X7, Black and Red announced a new joint venture to develop the entire tract. The two companies formed a partnership, each contributing its one half of the total tract of land. They agreed to share equally in future capital requirements and profits or losses.

Audit Resolution. The $1 million profit from the sale was not recognized as income in Black's 19X6 financial statements but, instead, was classified as a deferred credit. Black's investment in the joint venture was valued at $1.5 million. Black's continued involvement in development of the property and the uncertainty of future costs and losses were cited as reasons.

---

classified in other expense accounts. Clearing accounts should be analysed and items therein classified according to their nature or source so that all clearing account balances are removed and accounted for properly.

Advertising expense, travel, entertainment expense and contributions are accounts that typically are analysed in detail. These accounts are particularly sensitive to management policy violations and income tax consequences. Travel, entertainment and contributions must be documented carefully if they are to stand the Canada Customs and Revenue Agency auditor's examination. Questionable items may have an impact on the income tax expense and liability. Travel and entertainment sometimes harbour abuses of company policy respecting expense allowances. Minor embezzlements or cheating can be detected by careful auditors. However, a detailed audit of expense-account payments may be of greater interest to the efficiency-minded internal auditor than to the independent auditor. As far as independent auditors are concerned, even if employees did overstate their reimbursable expenses, the actual paid-out amount still is fairly presented as a financial fact. If there is evidence of expense-account cheating, independent auditors may present the data to management. Exhibit 14–1 illustrates some of the common audit procedures for expenses.

R E V I E W
C H E C K P O I N T S

14.1 Certain revenue and expense accounts usually are audited in conjunction with related balance sheet accounts. For the following revenue and expense accounts, list the most likely related balance sheet accounts: lease revenue, franchise revenue, royalty and licence revenue, amortization expense, repairs and maintenance expense, interest expense.

14.2 Why are many of the revenue and expense accounts only audited by analytical procedures and not by other procedures?

14.3 Why can "usual revenue transactions" cause significant audit evidence and reporting problems?

14.4 What procedures can be used to obtain information about the material accuracy of balances in minor expense accounts?

A SEQUENCE OF AUDIT EVENTS

LEARNING OBJECTIVE
3. Explain the use of the client representation letter and the lawyer's letter as an audit is completed.

Based on the material presented on the organization of the audit, you could easily visualize some audit work being done at an interim period sometime before a balance sheet date followed by completion of the work on the magic balance sheet date. True, much audit work is done months before the balance sheet date, with auditors working for a time, leaving the client's offices, and then returning for the year-end work. Actually, auditors may not even do any work on the balance sheet date itself, but they always perform evidence-gathering after that date—sometimes as much as several months afterwards.

Interim and Final Audit Work in Independent Auditing

In the "interim" audit work period, the auditor evaluates internal control with questionnaires, flowcharts and/or written narratives; identifies strengths and deficiencies; and completes the test of controls part of the audit. Some test of controls procedures usually are performed at interim, and tentative judgments about control risk for certain transaction cycles are made early. Also, auditors can apply audit procedures for substantive audit of balances as of an interim date; in this way a significant amount of recalculating, vouching, tracing, observing and confirming can be performed early. (Refer to Chapters 5, 6 and 7 for a more complete discussion.)

When the audit team returns after year-end and receives the final unaudited financial statements (or trial balance) prepared by the client personnel, they can start where they left off at interim and complete the work on control risk assessment and audit of balances.

However, the procedures of obtaining the lawyer's letter and the written client representations are deferred until the end of field work. These written representations are dated at the end of the field work (audit report date) because the auditors are responsible for determining whether important events that occurred after the balance sheet date are properly entered in the accounts or disclosed in the financial statement notes.

Contingencies and Lawyer's Letters

One of the most important confirmations is the response known as the lawyer's representation letter. Some difficulties had arisen over lawyers' willingness to respond to auditors' requests for information about contingencies, litigation, claims and assessments. Lawyers themselves have faced legal liability for failure to respond properly.

Handbook Section 6560, "Communications With Law Firms," requires auditors to make certain enquiries designed to elicit information on claims and possible claims as part of the auditor's examination of financial statements. Exhibit 14–2 is an example of a letter (the enquiry letter) the auditor would request the client to send to all lawyers who had performed work for the client during the period under audit. The client must make this request because it informs the lawyer that his or her client is waiving the privilege of communications between the lawyer and his or her client and giving the lawyer permission to give information to the auditors.

As implied by the client's letter to the lawyers in Exhibit 14–2, questions about contingencies, litigation, claims and assessments should be directed not only to legal counsel but also to management, because an auditor has the right to expect to be informed by management about all material contingent liabilities. Audit procedures useful in this regard include the following:

- Enquire and discuss with management the policies and procedures for identifying, evaluating and accounting for litigation, claims and assessments.

E X H I B I T 14–2   **FROM** *Handbook Section 6560.A, Schedule A*

Schedule A
(Enquiry Letter)[1]

Version 1—when there are claims or possible claims to be listed

(On client letterhead)

(To law firm)   (Date)

Dear Sir(s):

In connection with the preparation and audit of our financial statements for the fiscal period ended (date), (which include the accounts of the following entities)[2], we have made the following evaluations of claims and possible claims with respect to which your firm's advice or representation has been sought:

Description	Evaluation
(name of entity, name of other party, nature, amount claimed and current status)	(indicate likelihood of loss (or gain) and estimated amount of ultimate loss (or gain), if any; or indicate that likelihood is not determinable or amount is not reasonably estimable)

Would you please advise us, as of (effective date of response), on the following points:

   (a) Are the claims and possible claims properly described?

   (b) Do you consider that our evaluations are reasonable?

   (c) Are you aware of any claims not listed above which are outstanding? If so, please include in your response letter the names of the parties and the amount claimed.

This enquiry is made in accordance with the Joint Policy Statement of January 1978 approved by The Canadian Bar Association and the Auditing Standards Committee of the Canadian Institute of Chartered Accountants.

Please address your reply, marked "Privileged and Confidential," to this company and send a signed copy of the reply directly to our auditor, (name and address of auditor).

Yours truly,

c.c. (name of auditor)

[1] The letter should be appropriately modified if the client advises that certain matters have been excluded in accordance with paragraph 12 of the Joint Policy Statement.
[2] Delete if inapplicable. If applicable, refer to paragraph 11 re signing of the enquiry letter.

- Obtain from management a description and evaluation of litigation, claims and assessments.

- Examine documents in the client's possession concerning litigation, claims and assessments, including correspondence and invoices from lawyers.

- Obtain assurance from management that it has disclosed all material unasserted claims that the lawyer has advised them are probable of litigation.

- Read minutes of meetings of shareholders, directors and appropriate committees. Read contracts, loan agreements, leases and correspondence from taxing or other governmental agencies.

- Obtain information concerning guarantees from bank confirmations.

The enquiry letter serves as a major means to learn of material contingencies. Even so, a devious or forgetful management or a careless lawyer may fail to tell the auditor of some important factor or development. Auditors have to be alert and sensitive to all possible contingencies so that they can ask the right questions at the right time.

If management or its lawyers fail to provide adequate information about lawsuit contingencies, the auditor should consider whether this represents a scope limitation on the audit. A serious audit scope limitation requires a qualification in the audit report or a disclaimer of opinion.

Auditors have a natural conservative tendency to look out for adverse contingencies. However, potentially favourable events also should be investigated and disclosed (such as the contingency of litigation for damages wherein the client is the plaintiff). In an effort to assist management in observing the law and to provide adequate disclosure of information in financial statements, the auditor should be alert to all types of contingencies.

Client Representations

LEARNING OBJECTIVE
4. Describe the reasons written client representations are obtained, and list the four items that are included without regard to a materiality criterion.

Management makes numerous responses to auditors' enquiries during the course of an audit. Many of these responses are very important. To the extent that additional evidence is obtainable through other procedures, auditors should corroborate client representations.

In addition, auditors should obtain written client representations on matters of audit importance (ISA 580.3). The written representations take the form of a letter on the client's letterhead, addressed to the auditor, signed by responsible officers (normally the chief executive officer, chief financial officer, and other appropriate managers) and dated as of the date of the auditor's report. Thus, the letter, referred to as the "client's rep letter" in practice, covers events and representations running beyond the balance sheet date up to the end of all important field work. These written representations, however, are not substitutes for corroborating evidence obtainable by applying other auditing procedures.

In most cases the written client representations are merely more assertions, like the ones already in the financial statements (perhaps more detailed, in some cases). In this context they are not "evidence" for auditors. They are not good defences against criticisms for failing to perform audit procedures independently. ("Management told us in writing that the inventory costing method was FIFO and adequate allowance for obsolescence was provided" is not a good excuse for failing to get the evidence from the records and other sources!) However, in some cases the written management representations are the only available evidence about important matters of management intent. For example: (1) "We will discontinue the parachute manufacturing business, wind down the operations and sell the remaining assets" (i.e., accounting for discontinued operations); and (2) "We will exercise our option to refinance the maturing debt on a long-term basis" (i.e., classifying maturing debt as long-term).

One of the major purposes of the management representation letter is to impress upon the management its primary responsibility for the financial statements. These representations also may establish an auditor's defences if a question of management integrity arises later. If the management lies to the auditors, the management representation letter captures the lies in writing. Auditors draft the management representation letter to be prepared on

Interpreting the Lawyers' Letters

Lawyers take great care making responses to clients' requests for information to be transmitted to auditors. This care causes problems of interpretation for auditors. The difficulty arises over lawyers' desire to preserve lawyer-client confidentiality yet co-operate with auditors and the financial reporting process that seeks full disclosure.

The Canadian Bar Association policy statement (HB 6560A.14) observes: It is in the public interest that the confidentiality of lawyer-client communications be maintained. Accordingly, the law firm will not indicate in the response letter any possible claims which are omitted from the enquiry letter.

Consequently, lawyers' responses to auditors may contain vague and ambiguous wording. Auditors need to determine whether a contingency is "likely, unlikely or not determinable" (*Section* 3290.15). Although there are no comparable Canadian guidelines, in the United States the following lawyer responses can be properly interpreted to mean "remote," even though the word is not used:

- We are of the opinion that this action will not result in any liability to the company.
- It is our opinion that the possible liability to the company in this proceeding is nominal in amount.
- We believe the company will be able to defend this action successfully. We believe that the plaintiff's case against this company is without merit.
- Based on the facts known to us, after a full investigation, it is our opinion that no liability will be established against the company in these suits.

However, auditors should view the following response phrases as unclear—providing no information—about the probable, reasonably possible or remote likelihood of an unfavourable outcome for a litigation contingency (adapted from AU 9337):

- We believe the plaintiff will have serious problems establishing the company's liability; nevertheless, if the plaintiff is successful, the damage award may be substantial.
- It is our opinion the company will be able to assert meritorious defences. ["Meritorious," in lawyer language, apparently means "the judge will not summarily throw out the defences."]
- We believe the lawsuit can be settled for less than the damages claimed.
- We are unable to express an opinion on the merits of the litigation, but the company believes there is absolutely no merit.
- In our opinion the company has a substantial chance of prevailing. ["Substantial chance," "reasonable opportunity," and similar phrases indicate uncertainty of success in a defence.]

---

the client's letterhead paper for signature by company representatives. This draft is reviewed with senior client personnel, then finalized.

The management representation letter generally deals only with material matters. Notwithstanding, auditing standards provide that the following four representations must appear in the letter without limitation based on materiality:

1. Management's acknowledgment of primary responsibility for fair presentation of financial statements in conformity with generally accepted accounting principles.

2. Availability of all financial records and related data.

3. Completeness of the minutes of meetings of shareholders, directors and important committees.

4. Irregularities involving management or employees.

ROOM FOR IMPROVEMENT IN LITIGATION CONTINGENCY DISCLOSURES

American research on 126 lawsuits lost by public companies examined the disclosures about the suits in prior years' financial statements. The contingencies involved material, uninsured losses. Subsequent failure in the defence indicates the contingencies to have been "reasonably possible," calling for FASB 5 (comparable to *Section* 3290) disclosure. For the 126 cases, wide disclosure diversity existed. As indicated in the table below, the majority of cases carried satisfactory disclosure while the lawsuits were in progress, but a significant minority did not.

	Number	Percent
Satisfactory disclosure:		
Disclosure conceded the possibility of liability	60	47.6%
Disclosure included an estimate of the related liability	5	4.0
Disclosure along with booked liability	7	5.6
Total	72	57.2%
Unsatisfactory disclosure:		
No mention of the litigation	45	35.7%
Litigation mentioned but with a strong disclaimer of liability	9	7.1
Total	54	42.8%

Among the types of lawsuits covered in the 126 cases, the ones dealing with securities law violations had the highest frequency of satisfactory disclosure (8 out of 11, or 73 percent). The ones dealing with fraud or misrepresentation had the lowest frequency of satisfactory disclosure (2 out of 8, or 25 percent).

Speculations about the reasons company officials and lawyers have difficulty providing auditors with appropriate information include:

- High level of emotion surrounding the lawsuits.
- Fear that financial statement disclosure will be construed as an admission of guilt.
- The legal framework for evaluating litigation outcomes varies significantly from the framework used by auditors.
- More appropriate channels exist for disclosure of litigation information [e.g., business press].
- FASB 5 disclosure requirements are viewed as only a guide and, therefore, need not be taken literally.

Source: "Disclosure of Litigation Contingencies Faulted," *Journal of Accountancy*, July 1990, pp. 15–16.

A U.S. Standard, SAS 19 (AU 333), contains a list of 16 other items and discussions of several other points that may be included. While the *CICA Handbook* does not specifically require a letter of representation (except with regard to law firms), such letters are recommended with prospectuses (*Section* 7100) and review engagements (AUG–20). Exhibit 14–3 shows a typical Canadian representation letter used by the Canadian CA firm of Doane Raymond.

The box on the next page illustrates the serious problems that can arise when the PA firm is no longer able to rely on management's representations.

Audit of Related Party Transactions

One of the questions typically asked in an engagement letter is whether the client has engaged in any related party transactions (see Representation F3 in Exhibit 14–3). Auditors

RITE AID SAYS KPMG QUIT AS AUDITOR DUE TO DOUBTS ABOUT FIRM'S STATEMENTS

Rite Aid Corp. said **KPMG LLP** resigned as the troubled company's outside auditor because the accounting firm decided it was "unable to continue to rely on management's representations."

The nation's third-largest drugstore chain also disclosed late yesterday that the Securities and Exchange Commission has begun a formal investigation of the troubled Camp Hill, Pa. company.

Rite Aid, which has been wracked through much of the year by a series of increasingly grave financial and accounting problems, previously disclosed that it had received informal inquiries from the SEC's enforcement arm.

Earlier this week, Rite Aid gave investors one more piece of unnerving news, when it revealed that KPMG had resigned as its auditor a week before. At the time, the company didn't provide any explanation for the development, but promised it would outline the reasons in an SEC filing.

Rite Aid's fiscal problems, which first became visible in March, are widely considered the consequence of a years-long acquisition spree carried out by former Chief Executive Officer Martin Grass. After succeeding his father, Rite Aid founder Alex Grass, in the top job in 1995, the younger Mr. Grass oversaw a series of rapid-fire transactions which not only expanded and diversified the drug chain, but burdened it with debt.

In March, the fast-growing company's honeymoon with Wall Street ended abruptly, after it stunned investors by announcing that earnings for the fiscal fourth quarter ended Feb. 27 would be well below expectations; the results, when they were reported two weeks later, turned out to be even worse than Rite Aid had warned.

In June—citing questions raised by auditor KPMG—Rite Aid said it would restate its earnings downward for fiscal 1999, reversing some aggressive accounting measures. And as a result of inquiries from the Securities and Exchange Commission, the company said it would restate results for the two prior years as well. The company's chief financial officer soon afterward announced plans to step down.

The company's woes deepened a month ago, when Rite Aid disclosed that it would restate its previous three years' results a second time, this time paring a pretax $500 million from previously reported earnings for the period. Mr. Grass resigned as CEO shortly afterward.

A KPMG official said yesterday evening the company expects to file a formal response to Rite Aid's 8-K with the SEC but declined any comment.

Source: James P. Miller, *The Wall Street Journal*, Friday, November 19, 1999, pg. A3.

have a responsibility to obtain reasonable assurance that related parties have been identified and that there is appropriate disclosure with such parties in the financial statements (*Section* 6010 or ISA 550.2 and ISA 1007.11). Related party transactions are particularly important in Canada because of the high degree of concentration of corporate ownership. The problem with related party transactions is that since they are not arm's length they may not reflect the normal terms of trade that occur with most transactions with external parties. *Handbook Section* 3840 provides the measurement and disclosure standards for related party transactions of profit-oriented enterprises. The major problem for the auditor is identifying related party transactions. The most important procedure is to enquire of management (as in Exhibit 14–3). Other important procedures include reading the minutes of meetings of shareholders', directors', executive and audit committees, as well as acquiring a general knowledge of the client's business (AUG–1, para. 6).

EXHIBIT 14–3

Doane Raymond

Gentlemen:

In connection with your audit of the (consolidated) financial statements of _____ , for the year ending _____ , 20 _____ , we represent, to the best of our knowledge and belief and to the extent that they have or may have a material effect on the financial statements, the following:

A. Financial Statements and Financial Records

1. As members of management of the company, we understand that the purpose of your examination of the (consolidated) financial statements is to express an opinion thereon and that your audit procedures, including your tests of accounting records, were limited to those that you considered necessary in the circumstances. We also understand that such tests would not necessarily detect fraud, irregularities and error even if material in amount.

2. As members of management of the company, we are responsible for the preparation of the (consolidated) financial statements in accordance with generally accepted accounting principles.

3. The significant accounting policies adopted in the preparation of the (consolidated) financial statements are fully and fairly described in the financial statements.

4. We have not knowingly withheld any financial records and related data requested by you.

5. As members of management we believe that the company has an internal control structure adequate to permit the preparation of accurate financial statements in accordance with generally accepted accounting principles.

B. Ownership

1. The company has good title to (or lease interest in), all assets recorded in the accounts and these assets are free from hypothecation, liens and encumbrances (except: [specify]).

C. Valuation

1. Our present plans and intentions are appropriately reflected by the carrying value and classification of the company's assets and liabilities.

2. Adequate provisions have been recorded in the accounts for all anticipated losses (including those related to accounts receivable, inventory and capital assets).

3. The company has considered the effect of environmental matters and the carrying value of the relevant assets is recognized, measured and disclosed as appropriate in the (consolidated) financial statements.

D. Existence and Completeness

1. All assets which are owned by the company are recorded in the accounts.

2. All goods shipped or services rendered prior to the year end have been recorded as sales of that year except that no amount has been included in sales and accounts receivable for goods shipped on consignment, on approval or subject to repurchase agreements.

3. No abnormal returns have been received since the year end or are expected in respect to goods shipped prior to the year end.

4. Inventory does not include:
   a) items not paid for and for which no liability has been recorded in the accounts at year end;
   b) goods on consignment from others; or
   c) goods invoiced to customers.

5. All charges to capital assets (and additions under capital leases) during the year represent actual additions and no expenditures of a capital nature have been charged to expense during the year.

6. All capital assets sold or dismantled (and all capital lease terminations) during the year have been properly accounted for in the accounts.

7. Capital and other assets with a limited life are being depreciated, amortized or otherwise written off as a charge to income in a rational and systematic manner appropriate to the nature of the assets and their use by the company.

8. All liabilities of the company at the year end have been recorded in the accounts (including provisions for such items as salaries, wages and commissions, royalties, employee benefits (including pension costs), warranties, professional service, taxes, etc. and long-term debt and obligations under capital leases).

9. At the year end there were no contingent liabilities (except [specify]) and all claims which are outstanding and possible claims have been disclosed to you, whether or not such claims have been discussed with our lawyers.

10. At the year end, the company had no unusual commitments or contractual obligations of any sort which were not in the ordinary course of business and which might have an adverse effect on the company (except [specify]).

11. There were no material transactions during the year that have not been properly reflected in the accounts.

12. The company has complied with all aspects of contractual agreements that would have a material effect on the financial statements in the event of noncompliance including all covenants, conditions or other requirements of all outstanding debt.

13. With respect to environmental matters
    a) at year end, there were no liabilities or contingencies that have not already been disclosed to you;
    b) liabilities or contingencies have been recognized, measured and disclosed, as appropriate, in the (consolidated) financial statements; and
    c) commitments have been measured and disclosed, as appropriate, in the (consolidated) financial statements.

E X H I B I T   14–3   **(continued)**

E. Consolidated accounts and equity-accounted investments

1. All significant intercompany transactions have been identified and properly eliminated in the consolidated financial statements.
2. The cost of acquisition of investments has been assigned in the financial statements to the purchased assets (including goodwill, after adjustment for minority interest) and liabilities in accordance with their several values at the dates of acquisition.
3. Goodwill is being amortized over its estimated life.
4. Appropriate loss provisions have been provided in the accounts where there has been a permanent impairment in the value of unamortized goodwill.

F. General

1. The minute books presented to you contain complete and authentic minutes of all meetings of shareholders and directors (including committees thereof) held throughout the year to the most recent meetings on the following dates: (specify).
2. None of the directors, officers or shareholders were indebted to the company, other than in the ordinary course of business, at the year end or at any time during the year.
3. With respect to related parties, we have disclosed to you in the financial statements:
   a) all transactions with such parties including sales, purchases, loans, transfers of assets, liabilities and services, leasing arrangements, guarantees, etc. and
   b) all balances due to or from such parties at year end. These are as follows: (specify).
4. No fraud and other irregularities have occurred and nothing has come to light which might reflect upon the honesty or integrity of any employee, agent or officer of the company.
5. There have been no communications from regulatory agencies concerning non-compliance with laws or regulations which could have a material effect on the financial statements except: (specify).
6. We are not aware of any illegal or possibly illegal acts which have not been disclosed to you, the consequences of which should be considered for inclusion in the financial statements as a liability, contingency or commitment.

G. Events subsequent to the year-end

1. No events have occurred or are pending or in prospect and no facts have been discovered as at the present date which are of such significance in relation to the company's affairs as to make the financial statements not present fairly the financial position or results of operations of the company (except: [specify]).

_____   _____

Company/Organization   Date

_____

Per: Officer

Auditors should watch for unusual transactions in the course of the audit. According to *Section* 6010.21:

Example of circumstances that might indicate the existence of undisclosed related parties include

(*a*) abnormal terms of trade, such as unusual prices, interest rates, guarantees and repayment terms;

(*b*) transactions which are unusual as to nature or size, particularly those that:
   (i)   have been recognized at or near the balance sheet date;
   (ii) have been made with unfamiliar enterprises; and

(*c*) transactions whose substance appear to differ from their form;

(*d*) transactions that lack an apparent business reason.

Also, "related parties exist when one party has the ability to exercise directly or indirectly, control, joint control or significant influence over the other. Two or more parties are related when they are subject to common control, joint control or common significant influence. Related parties include management and immediate family members" (*Section* 3840.03).

As noted earlier, auditor's knowledge of the business can help identify transactions between related parties. Procedures that can be used to identify the existence of related party transactions include (ISA 550.7):

(a) review of prior year working papers for related party transactions;

(b) review the entity's procedures for identification of related parties; and

EXHIBIT 14–4   **AUDIT CORRESPONDENCE**

Type	From	To	Time
Engagement letter (acceptance)	Auditor (client)	Client (auditor)	Before engagement
Internal control weaknesses	Auditor	Client	Interim or after audit
Confirmations (replies)	Client (third parties)	Third parties (auditor)	Throughout the audit
Lawyer's letter (reply)	Client Lawyer	Lawyer (auditor)	Near end of audit
Client rep letter	Client	Auditor	End of field work
Management letter	Auditor	Client	After audit
Communication with client audit committee	Auditor	Directors	Before or after audit report

(c) obtaining written representation from management concerning identification and adequacy of related party disclosures (this specific procedure is also required by *Section* 6010.27).

Having identified related party transactions the auditor can perform the following substantive procedures (ISA 550.14 or *Section* 6010.A):

(a) confirm the terms and amounts of the transactions with the related parties;

(b) inspect evidence in possession of the related party; and

(c) confirm or discuss information with persons associated with the transactions, such as banks, lawyers, guarantors and agents.

Section 6010.29 also requires that audit committees be informed of unusual related party transactions or related party transactions that involve significant management judgments.

The box below illustrates how related party transactions can be used to significantly alter the financial statements. The illustration is based on an actual Canadian company trading on NASDAQ and the TSE.

Summary of Audit Correspondence

Many types of formal correspondence have been mentioned in this book. Since you are learning the final procedures to complete the audit, this is a good place to summarize these various correspondence items. Exhibit 14–4 is a summary of audit correspondence. The management letter will be covered later in this chapter.

TURNING EXPENSES INTO REVENUES

CB is a major biotechnology company in Canada that did not like the effect expensing R&D had on its earnings. So, CB proceeded to create a subsidiary, CC, to which it made a capital contribution of $100 million. After a series of share exchanges involving shares of both companies, the net effect on CB's financial statements was to debit retained earnings and credit cash for $100 million. An agreement was then reached in which CC paid CB a fee in exchange for a technology license. CC used the $100 million it had received from CB to repay CB for CB's R&D costs. CB accounted for the amounts received from CC as revenue.

In the words of CB's Chairman of the Board, "This initiative will enable us to leverage our investment in R&D and pursue the ongoing development of exciting new products, without unduly affecting the company's baseline earnings."

R E V I E W
CHECKPOINTS

14.5 What is the purpose of a client representation letter? What representations would you request management to make in a client rep letter with respect to receivables? to inventories? to minutes of meetings? to subsequent events?

14.6 Why are written client representations and lawyers' letters obtained near the end of the audit field work and dated on or near the audit report date?

14.7 In addition to the lawyer's letter, what other procedures can be used to gather evidence regarding contingencies?

14.8 The following was included in a letter auditors received from the client's lawyers, in response to a letter sent to them similar to Exhibit 13–2: "Several agreements and contracts to which the company is a party are not covered by this response since we have not advised or been consulted in their regard." How might the auditor's report be affected by such a statement in a letter from the client's lawyer regarding a pending lawsuit against a client? Explain.

14.9 Why might companies and auditors experience difficulty making appropriate disclosures about litigation contingencies?

EVENTS SUBSEQUENT TO THE BALANCE SHEET DATE

LEARNING OBJECTIVE

5. Given a set of facts and circumstances, classify a subsequent event by type and describe the proper treatment in the financial statements.

Certain material events that occur subsequent to the balance sheet date but before the end of field work (thus, before issuance of the audit report) require disclosure in the financial statements and related notes (ISA 560 and *Handbook Section* 5405). Auditors (and management) are responsible for gathering evidence on these subsequent events and evaluating the proposed disclosure. Material subsequent events have been classified into two types, which are disclosed differently. The first type (Type I) requires adjustment of the dollar amounts in the financial statements and appropriate disclosure (financial statement notes), while the second (Type II) requires note disclosure and sometimes pro forma financial statements.

Type I: Adjustment of Dollar Amounts Required

This type of subsequent event provides new information regarding a financial condition that existed at the date of the balance sheet. The subsequent event information affects the numbers and requires adjustment of amounts in the financial statements for the period under audit.

The following are examples of Type I subsequent events:

- A loss on uncollectible trade accounts receivable as a result of bankruptcy of a major customer. (The customer's deteriorating financial condition existed prior to the balance sheet date.)
- The settlement of litigation for an amount different than estimated (assuming the litigation had taken place prior to the balance sheet date).

Type II: No Adjustment of Financial Statements, but Disclosure Required

The second type of subsequent event involves occurrences that had both their cause and their manifestation arising after the balance sheet date. Recall that the auditor's responsibility for adequate disclosure runs to the date marking the end of the field work. Consequently, even for events that occurred after the balance sheet date and that are not of the first type requiring financial statement adjustment, auditors must consider their importance and may insist that disclosure be made. Type II events that occur after the balance sheet date may be of such magnitude that disclosure is necessary to keep the financial statements from being misleading as of the report date. Disclosure normally is in a narrative note. Occasionally, however, an event may be so significant that the best disclosure is pro forma financial data. **Pro forma** financial data is the presentation of the financial statements "as if" the event had occurred on the date of the balance sheet. Such pro forma data are given in a note disclosure. For example, in addition to historical financial statements, pro forma financial data may be the best way to show the effect of a business purchase or other merger or the sale of a major portion of assets.

Examples of Type II subsequent events are:

- Loss on an uncollectible trade receivable resulting from a customer's fire or flood loss subsequent to the balance sheet date (as contrasted with a customer's slow decline into bankruptcy cited as a Type I event above).
- Sale of a bond or share capital issue.
- Settlement of litigation when the event giving rise to the claim took place subsequent to the balance sheet date.
- Loss of plant or inventories as a result of fire or flood.

The aspect of retroactive recognition of the effect of stock dividends and splits is an exception that may be explained briefly with an example. The problem is one of timing and one of informative communication to financial statement users. When the financial statements reach the users, the stock dividend or split will have been completed, and to report financial data as if it had not occurred might be considered misleading.

Double-Dating in the Audit Report

Double-dating refers to dating the audit report as of the end of field work along with an additional later date attached to disclosure of a significant Type II subsequent event. Sometimes it happens that, after completion of field work but before issuance of the report, a significant event comes to the audit team's attention. For example, imagine that in the illustration given in the following box, field work had been completed on February 1 and the audit report was to be so dated. However, before the report was typed and delivered, the auditors learned of the two-for-one stock split. In this case the report would be dated "February 1 except as to footnote X which is dated February 15" (where footnote X is the disclosure of the stock split). The accounting treatment would be the same as described in the illustration below.

The purpose of double-dating is twofold: (1) to provide a means of inserting important information in the financial statement footnote disclosures learned after field work is complete and (2) to inform users that the auditor takes full responsibility for all subsequent events only up to the end of field work (February 1 in the example) and for the specifically

---

SUBSEQUENT EVENT STOCK SPLIT

The company approved on February 15 a two-for-one stock split to be effective on that date. The fiscal year-end was the previous December 31, and the financial statements as of December 31 showed 50 million shares authorized, 10 million shares issued and outstanding, and earnings per share of $3.

Audit Resolution. Note disclosure was made of the split and of the relevant dates. The equity section of the balance sheet showed 100 million shares authorized, 20 million shares issued and outstanding. The income statement reported earnings per share of $1.50. Earnings per share of prior years were adjusted accordingly. The note disclosed comparative earnings per share on the predividend shares. The audit report was dated February 1, with a double-date of February 15 for the note disclosure.

identified later event (the stock split disclosed in the note in the example, which occurred on February 15). However, responsibility is not taken for other events that may have occurred after the end of field work.

Actually, double-dating in the audit report is not required. In the example the auditors could have used one date (February 15) for the audit report, avoiding the complication of the double-dating. However, the consequence is that the auditors then take responsibility for performing the subsequent event audit procedures through February 15. That is, the auditors extend the field work responsibility two weeks. Double-dating is used to cut off the subsequent event procedural responsibility at the earlier date.

Audit Program for the Subsequent Period

Some audit procedures performed in the period subsequent to the balance sheet date may be part of the audit program for determining cutoff and proper valuation of balances as of the balance sheet date (Part A in Exhibit 14–5). However, the procedures specifically designed for gathering evidence about the two types of subsequent events are different and are apart from the rest of the audit program (Part B in Exhibit 14–5).

EXHIBIT 14–5 **AUDITING PROCEDURES FOR THE PERIOD SUBSEQUENT TO THE BALANCE SHEET DATE**

A. Procedures performed in connection with other audit programs.
  1. Use a cutoff bank statement to:
    a. Examine cheques paid after year-end that are, or should have been, listed on the bank reconciliation.
    b. Examine bank posting of deposits in transit listed on the bank reconciliation.
  2. Vouch collections on accounts receivable in the month following year-end for evidence of existence and collectibility of the year-end balances.
  3. Trace cash disbursements of the month after year-end to accounts payable for evidence of any liabilities unrecorded at year-end.
  4. Vouch write-downs of fixed assets after year-end evidence that such valuation problems existed at the year-end date.
  5. Vouch sales of investment securities, write-downs or write-offs in the months after the audit date for evidence of valuation at the year-end date.
  6. Vouch and trace sales transactions in the month after year-end for evidence of proper sales and cost of sales cutoff.

B. Auditing procedures for subsequent events.
  1. Read the latest available interim financial statements, compare them with the financial statements being reported on and make any other comparisons considered appropriate in the circumstances.
  2. Enquire of officers and other executives having responsibility for financial and accounting matters about whether the interim statements have been prepared on the same basis as that used for the statements under examination.
  3. Enquire of and discuss with officers and other executives having responsibility for financial and accounting matters (limited where appropriate to major locations):
    a. Whether any substantial contingent liabilities or commitments existed at the date of the balance sheet being reported on or at the date of enquiry.
    b. Whether there was any significant change in the share capital, long-term debt or working capital to the date of enquiry.
    c. The current status of items in the financial statements being reported on that were accounted for on the basis of tentative, preliminary or inconclusive data.
    d. Whether any unusual adjustments have been made during the period from the balance sheet date to the date of enquiry.
  4. Read the available minutes of meetings of shareholders, directors and appropriate committees; enquire about matters dealt with at meetings for which minutes are not available.
  5. Request that the client send a letter to legal counsel enquiring about outstanding claims, possible claims and management's evaluation, with the reply to be sent directly to the auditor.
  6. Obtain a letter of representation, dated as of the date of the auditor's report, from appropriate officials, generally the chief executive officer and chief financial officer, about whether any events occurred subsequent to the date of the financial statements that, in the officer's opinion, would require adjustment or disclosure in these statements.
  7. Make such additional enquiries or perform such procedures as considered necessary and appropriate to dispose of questions that arise in carrying out the foregoing procedures, enquiries and discussions.

. . . .

14.10 What are the two types of "subsequent events"? In which way(s) are they treated differently in the financial statements?

14.11 What treatment is given stock dividends and splits that occur after the balance sheet date but before the audit report is issued? Explain.

14.12 What is the purpose of "double-dating" an audit report?

14.13 Generally, what additional actions should auditors take in the period between the audit report date and the effective date of a registration statement?

. . . .

RESPONSIBILITIES AFTER THE AUDIT REPORT HAS BEEN ISSUED

. . . .

LEARNING OBJECTIVE

6. Specify the sequence of decisions and actions auditors must consider upon discovery (after the issuance of the report) of information about facts that may have existed at the date of the auditor's report.

The next two topics do not deal with responsibilities or concerns during the audit, but with responsibilities after the audit is completed and the report has been issued. They are covered here because they are related to subsequent event responsibilities. The topics are (1) subsequent discovery of facts existing at the date of the audit report and (2) consideration of the omission of audit procedures discovered after the report date. The most important thing to remember is that auditors have an active, procedural responsibility for discovering Type I and Type II subsequent events and for their proper disclosure, but they are not required to perform procedures after the audit report date. However, auditors have responsibilities once they become aware of the facts or omitted procedures.

Subsequent Discovery of Facts Existing at the Date of the Auditor's Report

Auditing standards actually deal with two subsequent things: (*a*) events that occur after the balance sheet date and (*b*) knowledge gained after the audit report date of events that occurred or conditions that existed on or before the audit report date. The subsequent event or subsequently acquired knowledge may arise (1) before the end of audit field work, (2) after the end of field work but before issuance of the report, or (3) after the audit report is issued. Exhibit 14–6 shows a time continuum of these combinations with a key to the auditing standards sections that deal with them.

Auditors are under no obligation to continue performing any auditing procedures past the report date (except when engaged on an SEC registration statement). However, when they happen to learn of facts that are important, they have the obligation to (1) determine whether the information is reliable and (2) determine whether the facts existed at the date of the report. When both of these conditions are affirmed and the auditors believe persons are relying on the report, steps should be taken to withdraw the first report, issue a new report and inform persons currently relying on the financial statements. These measures are

E X H I B I T 14–6   SUBSEQUENT EVENTS AND SUBSEQUENT DISCOVERY

NOTIFICATION OF AUDIT REPORT WITHDRAWAL

Endotronics, Inc., reported net income of $1.3 million for its fiscal year ended September 30, 1986. In March 1987 FBI agents who searched the company's warehouses testified that many of the company's cell-replicating machines reported as sold actually remained under Endotronics' control. Soon thereafter (March 1987), Peat, Marwick, Mitchell & Company (KPMG Peat Marwick) withdrew its audit report, saying: "In light of . . . serious questions about the company's revenue figure, we cannot satisfy ourselves about the facts of the situation."

Source: The Wall Street Journal, March 23, 1987.

---

facilitated by co-operation on the part of the client. However, the auditors' duty to notify the public that an earlier report should not be relied on is not relieved by client objections.[1]

A sequence of decisions is explained in Exhibit 14–7. Basically, the decisions relate to the importance and impact of the information, the co-operation of the client in taking necessary action and the actions to be taken.

Consideration of Omitted Procedures After the Report Date

LEARNING OBJECTIVE

7. Specify the considerations and procedures applied by auditors upon concluding (after the audit report date) that one or more auditing procedures were omitted.

Although auditors have no responsibility to continue to review their work after the audit report has been issued, the report and working papers may be subjected to postissuance review by an outside peer review or practice inspection or by the firm's internal inspection program. A peer review is a quality assurance review by another auditing firm of an audit firm's quality control policies and procedures and the compliance thereof. Practice inspection is to ensure that all members in public practice maintain appropriate levels of professional standards. Practice inspection is primarily educational in focus, to help practitioners improve their professional standards where necessary. For example, in Ontario approximately 25 percent of all offices are inspected each year by the Provincial Institutes Office of the Director of Practice Inspection.[2]

Handbook Section 5405, "Date of Auditor's Report," provides guidance for such subsequent discovery of material misstatement situations. A possible sequence of decisions is presented in Exhibit 14–8. Because of legal implications of some of the actions proposed, consultation with the firm's legal counsel is advised. The relevance of the omitted procedure (and the evidence the auditors failed to obtain) should be measured against the auditors' present ability to support the previously expressed opinion. It may be that, after a review of the working papers and discussions with audit staff personnel, other procedures may be shown to have produced the evidence needed. In such circumstances the omitted procedure is not considered to impair the report.

However, if the other procedures did not produce sufficient appropriate evidence, and, therefore the previously expressed opinion cannot be supported, further action is necessary. As with subsequent discovery of facts, the next step is to determine whether the auditors' report is still being relied on. If reliance is still possible, the omitted procedure (or alternative procedures) should be undertaken promptly to provide a basis for the audit opinion.

---

[1] The discussion here is cast in terms of subsequent discovery of facts while the auditor remains engaged by the client. However, the responsibilities to determine whether the subsequent information is reliable and whether the facts existed at the date of the already-issued report remain in force even when the auditor has resigned from the engagement or has been fired by the client.

[2] *Practice Inspection Program,* ICAO, November 1992.

EXHIBIT 14–7   SUBSEQUENT DISCOVERY OF FACTS EXISTING AT THE DATE OF THE AUDITOR'S REPORT

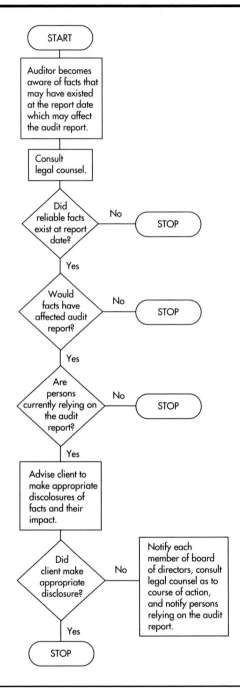

Source: CPA Journal, March 1984, p. 38. Copyright © 1984 by the New York Society of Certified Public Accountants.

If such work reveals facts that existed at the date of the original report, then the actions related to subsequent discovery of facts (Exhibit 14–7) must be taken.

REVIEW
CHECKPOINTS

14.14 What is the difference between a "subsequent event" and a "subsequent discovery of fact existing at the report date"? Describe the auditors' responsibility for each.

E X H I B I T 14–8   CONSIDERATION OF OMITTED PROCEDURES AFTER THE REPORT DATE

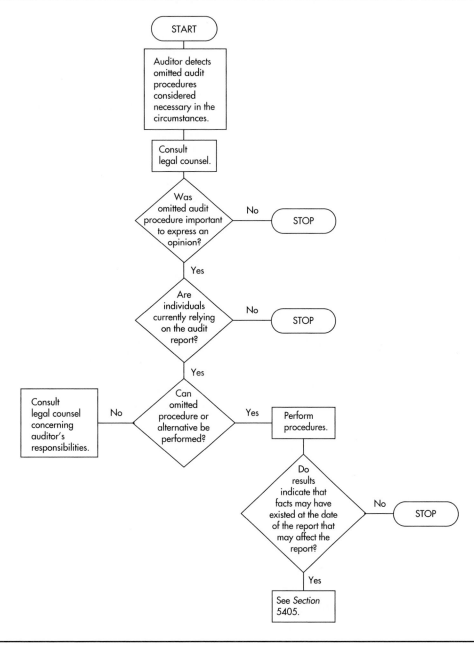

Source: CPA Journal, March 1984, p. 37. Copyright © 1984 by the New York Society of Certified Public Accountants.

14.15 If, subsequent to issuance of a report, the audit partner discovers information that existed at the report date and materially affects the financial statements, what actions should the partner take if the client consents to disclose the information? What action should be taken if the client (including the board of directors) refuses to make disclosure?

14.16 What are the steps an auditor should take if, after the report has been issued, someone discovers that an important audit procedure was omitted?

FINAL WRAP-UP
. . . .

LEARNING OBJECTIVE

8. Explain the final audit steps involving adjusting entries, second-partner review and the management letter.

Several items must be completed before an audit can be considered finished. The client must approve of the proposed adjusting entries and the financial statement notes, and the audit work must be reviewed.

Communications with Audit Committees (or Equivalent)

The auditor should review with management in advance the information to be covered with the audit committee (ISA 1007.18). On certain matters (e.g., company operations), management should report to the audit committee and the auditor then comments; on other matters, such as audit findings, the auditor should report to the audit committee and management then comments. Both should be present in meetings with the audit committee to discuss the reports, which may be written or oral. When the auditor communicates in writing, the report should indicate that it is intended solely for use by the audit committee.

In some instances the auditor may identify matters to discuss with the audit committee without the presence of management.

The auditor should keep notes of audit committee discussions at which the auditor is present. These notes should be compared to the minutes of the audit committee. Any inconsistencies should be resolved with the audit committee or board of directors.

The auditor should communicate all matters affecting approval of the annual financial statements to the board of directors prior to such approval. Normally, the auditor should work within the audit committee's regular cycle of meetings.

The audit committee's expectations need to be clarified and put in writing. The most important matters arising from the audit of financial statements that the auditor should communicate to the audit committee include:

1. Auditor's responsibility under GAAP.
2. The planning of the current audit.
3. Deficiencies in internal controls.
4. Illegal acts.
5. Fraud.
6. Significant accounting principles and policies.
7. Management judgments and accounting estimates.
8. Misstatements.
9. Other information in annual reports (e.g., narrative information).
10. Disagreements with management.
11. Consultation with other accountants by management.
12. Major issues that influence the audit appointment.
13. Difficulties encountered in performing the audit (e.g., unreasonable delays in obtaining information from management).

The auditor's responsibility is to communicate (or determine that management has communicated) matters of concern to the audit committee (*Section* 5220). If the auditor considers the audit committee's action seriously inappropriate, the auditor may need to communicate directly with the board of directors, and in some cases has an obligation to report to outside regulatory authorities. For example, the "well-being reporting requirement" under federal financial institutions legislation described in AUG–17 may require the auditor to report to the Superintendent of Financial Institutions "any significant weaknesses in internal control which have the potential to jeopardize the financial institution's ability to continue as a going concern." Since there is the issue of client confidentiality, the auditor should seek legal advice concerning the best manner of reporting to outside authorities.

Client Approval of Adjusting Entries and Financial Statement Disclosure

The financial statements, including the notes to the financial statements, are the responsibility of management, although auditors frequently draft them. The adjusting entries shown in Exhibit 14–9 are labelled "proposed" to indicate this responsibility of management.

Many of the adjusting entries will be approved by management as they are prepared during the work on an area; others will await the final wrap-up to be approved. A formal list of all approved adjusting entries should be given to the client so that formal entries can be made in the accounting records to bring them into balance with the financial statements.

In a like manner, approval of all disclosure in notes must be obtained from the client. The notes considered necessary usually are drafted as proposed notes by auditors performing the audit procedures. They must be considered carefully by the audit manager and partner before being presented to the client management for acceptance as the company's disclosures.

Exhibit 14–9 is a summary worksheet ("scoresheet") showing the end-of-audit consideration of proposed adjusting journal entries. Auditors can prepare this summary to see how the proposed adjustments affect the financial statements. This review helps auditors decide which adjustments must be made to support an unqualified audit report and which adjustments may be passed. A passed adjustment is a proposed adjustment on which the auditors

EXHIBIT 14–9   PROPOSED ADJUSTING JOURNAL ENTRIES (Illustrative Scoresheet Working Paper)

	Income Statement		Balance Sheet	
	Debit	Credit	Debit	Credit
(1) Unrecorded cash disbursements:				
Accounts payable			$42,000	
Cash				$42,000
(2) Improper sales cutoff:				
Sales	$13,000			
Inventory			7,800	
Cost of goods sold (60%)		$7,800		
Accounts receivable				13,000
(3) Inventory write-off:				
Cost of goods sold	21,000			
Inventory				21,000
(4) Unrecorded liabilities:				
Utilities expense	700			
Commissions expense	3,000			
Wages	2,500			
Accounts payable				700
Accrued expenses payable				5,500
(5) Amortization calculation error:				
Accumulated amortization			17,000	
Amortization expense		17,000		
(6) Reclassify current portion of long-term debt:				
Notes payable			50,000	
Current portion of debt				50,000
(7) Income tax @ 40%:				
Income tax refund receivable			6,160	
Income tax expense		6,160		
	$40,200	$30,960	$122,960	$132,200
Net income change		($9,240)		
Current assets change				($62,040)
Current liabilities change				$14,200
Working capital change				($76,240)

decide not to insist because it does not have a material effect on the financial position and results of operations.

In the exhibit the illustrative proposed adjustments are (1) recording cheques written and mailed but not recorded in the books; (2) reversing recorded sales for goods shipped after the balance sheet date, and reversing the 60 percent cost of goods sold; (3) writing off obsolete and damaged inventory; (4) recording the amounts found in the search for unrecorded liabilities; (5) correcting an amortization calculation error; (6) reclassifying the current portion of long-term debt from the long-term classification; and (6) recording a tax refund asset for overpaid income taxes (could be a debit to tax liability if all the taxes for the year had not already been paid). Some summary effects on income, current assets, current liabilities and working capital are appended to the bottom of the exhibit.

OVERALL EVALUATION OF AUDIT TESTS

The important thing about the audit tests is that they are the basis for deciding if the amount of unadjusted error is material at the end of the audit. The adjusted errors by definition have been corrected, so the real issue at the end of the audit is whether the uncorrected errors are material in amount. A minimal way to estimate this is on the basis of known uncorrected errors as in Exhibit 14–9. We refer to this as minimal because it is based on known errors, not most likely or possible errors (with which the client may disagree). We cover adjustments based on most likely and possible errors in Chapter 20 because they are less common in practice.

The principle of audit decision-making based on known unadjusted errors is to aggregate these in various ways to see if they total to a material amount. If the audit is based on cycles, then special work sheets must be prepared to aggregate errors in specific ways on which the materiality assessment is based. For example, say materiality is based on net income and is assessed to be 10 percent of recorded net income. Then the auditor will need to aggregate all errors affecting net income. This can be done on the basis of either (1) changes in net assets (assets-liabilities), or equivalently, (2) revenues minus expenses. Both approaches should yield the same number. Note that, due to the nature of the double-entry system, in both cases understatements in liabilities/expenses must be *added* to over- or understatements of assets/revenues, while overstatements in liabilities/expenses must be subtracted from over- or understatements of assets/revenues.

Perhaps this is better explained by example than in words. Refer to Exhibit 14–9. The way to compute net effect of unadjusted (uncorrected) known errors on net income in this illustration is as follows:

Errors in net income = Errors in changes in net assets = Errors in changes in assets minus errors in changes in liabilities = $42,000_{(A)} + 13,000_{(A)} + 21,000_{(A)} - 7,800_{(A)} - 17,000_{(A)} - 6,160_{(A)} - (+ 42,000_{(L)} - 700_{(L)} - 5,500_{(L)} + 50,000_{(L)} - 50,000_{(L)}) = 9,240$ = Errors in revenues minus errors in expenses = $13,000_{(R)} - (6,160_{(E)} + 7,800_{(E)} - 21,000_{(E)} - 700_{(E)} - 3,000_{(E)} - 2,500_{(E)} + 17,000_{(E)}) = 9,240$ = Total net errors in net income (overstatement, i.e., to eliminate all error the adjusting entry must reduce client's proposed net income by 9,240). This 9,240 is then compared to predetermined overall materiality. If 9,240 is less than material, then the auditor concludes that he or she does not need to make any more adjustments.

To reiterate, the above analysis is based on known uncorrected errors only and is therefore perfectly appropriate whenever the auditor tests 100 percent of the transactions. This 100 percent testing is likely for cash, capital assets, noncurrent liabilities and the owner's equity section. It is less likely for inventory, receivables and payables, which can represent large populations of individual items, thus the auditor may wish to use sampling theory concepts for adjusting these accounts by most likely and possible error. We cover adjustments and decision making based on these sampling situations in Chapter 20. Another complication in audit evaluation is measurements involving management estimates. Auditors are supposed to keep track of the differences between (1) management estimates and (2) the closest reasonable estimates supported by the audit evidence. And they are supposed to evaluate (1) the differences taken altogether for indications of a systematic bias and (2) the combination of differences with other likely errors in the financial statements found by other audit procedures. An important aspect of SSA audits as discussed in Chapter 13 is that they tend to treat all items as estimates because very little detailed testing is done.

One final point on overall evaluation: how does materiality relate to assertions? Materiality is defined as the amount of errors *from all sources* that would affect a user decision. Thus materiality can be viewed as the minimum error that financial statement users find unacceptable from all assertions that have been violated. In other words, it is presumed users don't care which assertion is violated, only that aggregate violations from all sources are less than material. Again, review Exhibit 14–9 and note the assertions affected by the errors—they include completeness, valuation, existence and presentation assertions.

Working Paper and Report Review

The audit supervisor makes a final review to ensure that all accounts on the trial balance have a working paper reference index (an indication that the audit work has been finished for that account) and that all procedures in the audit program are "signed off" with a date and initials.

The working papers of the audit staff are reviewed soon after being completed by the audit supervisor and sometimes by the audit manager. This review is to ensure that all tick-mark notations are clear, that all procedures performed are adequately documented and that all necessary procedures were performed with due professional care.

The review by the audit manager and engagement partner will focus more on the overall scope of the audit. The audit manager and engagement partner are very involved with the planning of the audit, and they perform some of the field work on difficult areas. However, they are usually not involved in preparing the detail working papers. Even though the working papers are reviewed by the on-site audit supervisor, the review by the partner who is going to sign the audit report is essential. Review "to-do lists" are prepared during these reviews citing omissions or deficiencies that must be cleared before the final work is completed.

Audit firms vary in their treatment of the "to-do lists." Some firms prefer to destroy the lists after the work is performed and documented in the working papers. After all, they want to "clean up" the working papers, and the to-do lists were merely notes directing the staff to tie a neat ribbon around any loose ends or difficult issues. Other firms prefer to keep the lists as signed off and cross-referenced for the work performed. They believe that the lists are "working papers" that show evidence of careful review and completion of the audit. Sometimes, retained to-do lists backfire on auditors by showing questions raised but not resolved.

The working papers and financial statements, including footnotes, are given a final review on large engagements by a partner not responsible for client relations. This **second-partner review** ensures that the quality of audit work and reporting is in keeping with the quality standards of the audit firm.

The final audit time reports must be prepared and the working papers prepared for storage. At the completion of the field work, performance evaluation reports of the staff auditors usually are prepared by the audit supervisor.

Management Letter

During the audit work (especially the evaluation of the control structure and assessment of the control risk), matters are noted that can be made as recommendations to the client. When field work is completed, and in some cases after the audit report is delivered, these items are evaluated and written in a letter (commonly referred to as the **management letter**) to be sent to the client. One firm calls this communication a letter of client advisory comments and characterizes it as a voluntary and constructive dimension of an audit designed to provide clients with an important value-added service. The firm encourages consulting and tax professionals to participate with the auditors in preparing the letter.

The management letter is not required by professional standards and should not be confused with the communication of matters identified during the financial statement audit, which is now required by auditing standards (*Handbook Section* 5750, discussed in Chapter 6) or with significant weaknesses in internal control, which must be reported to the audit committee under *Handbook Section* 5220. Management letters are a service provided as a by-product of the audit (ISA 1007.17 and 1007.20). The management letter is an excellent

---

E X H I B I T 14–10   **MANAGEMENT LETTER**

Anderson, Olds & Watershed
Chartered Accountants
Toronto, Ontario
April 1, 2002

Mr. Larry Lancaster, Chairman
Kingston Company
Kingston, Ontario

Dear Mr. Lancaster:

During our audit of the Kingston Company financial statements for the year ended December 31, 2002, we observed certain matters we believe should be brought to your attention. Our audit work was not designed to be a study of the overall efficiency and economy of the management and operation of Kingston Company, but ordinary audit procedures nevertheless enabled us to notice some actions that could enhance the profitability of the Company.

Summary

When we audited the physical inventory and compared the quantities actually on hand to the quantities shown in the perpetual inventory records, we noted several shortages. Follow-up with your warehouse personnel revealed that the "shortages" were usually in the assembly department, where numerous items of custom lawn maintenance equipment were being assembled for customers prior to delivery. The removal of the inventory from the records was routinely entered when the assembled equipment was delivered. These procedures eventually maintained the records accurately, but the delay in posting the inventory records has resulted in lost sales and some customer dissatisfaction with the custom-assembly service.

The Problem

The warehouse personnel remove parts according to the specification of custom-assembly work orders, moving the parts to the assembly area. If another customer orders these parts soon thereafter, the inventory records show them on hand, and the new customer is told that the order can be filled. Shortly thereafter, warehouse personnel find that the parts are actually not on hand, and the customer is disappointed when informed of a delay. Sales department personnel confirmed that several (20–25 during the last six months) withdrew their orders and bought the parts from a competitor. They estimated that approximately $25,000 was lost in sales during the last six months, amounting to about $9,000 in lost profits.

Custom-Assembly Losses

The inventory "shortages," noticed by warehouse personnel when they try to fill new orders, cause another difficulty. People spend extra time looking around for the parts, and usually their enquiries reach the assembly area, where workers leave their jobs unfinished while trying to help locate the "missing" parts. This helpfulness causes assembly jobs to be delayed, customers get dissatisfied, and, in one case, a customer refused to pay because of late delivery. This one case resulted in lost profits of $10,000 because the equipment had to be disassembled and returned to the inventory.

Recommendation

We discussed the following recommendation with Mr. James Worthy in the warehouse, and he agrees that it can be a practical solution. We recommend that you design a form for "Work in Progress," which will be used to make accounting and inventory entries to remove parts from the main inventory as soon as they are transferred to the assembly area. At that stage, the cost would be classified as "work in progress," which will be entered in cost of goods sold as soon as the assembly is completed and the goods are delivered. Judging from our limited knowledge of the extent of the problem during the year under audit, we estimate that you might produce $20,000–$30,000 additional profit per year, while development and use of the form should cost about $3,000.

Conclusion

AO&W has expertise in system development and operation in our management services department, and we will be happy to assist you in reviewing a new form and a systems plan for your implementation. If you wish to discuss this matter further, please inform Mr. Dalton Wardlaw.

Very truly yours,

Anderson, Olds & Watershed

opportunity to develop rapport with the client and to make the client aware of other business services offered by the accounting firm. Wallace read over 100 management letters and concluded that public accounting firms frequently miss opportunities to impress clients with their wide range of services.[3] Many of the letters failed to "sell." A brief management letter formulated along the lines of her suggestions is shown in Exhibit 14–10.

R E V I E W CHECKPOINTS

14.17 Why are auditors' drafts of adjusting entries and note disclosures always labelled "proposed" near the end of the audit? Why shouldn't auditors just write them in final form and give them to the client?

14.18 What are review "to-do" lists? Cite several items that such lists might contain. Why must such lists be cleared before the field work is considered completed?

14.19 What is a good reason for keeping the "to-do list" in the audit working paper files?

14.20 Describe a "second-partner review." What is its purpose?

14.21 What is a management letter? Is a management letter required by generally accepted auditing standards?

14.22 Which PA firm personnel should participate in preparing a management letter at the end of an audit?

14.23 How can well-prepared management letters lead to additional client services besides audit engagements?

SUMMARY

This chapter covered several aspects of completing an audit. As the work draws to a close, several income and expense accounts may remain to be audited. Analytical comparisons of their balances with prior years and current expectations accomplish this auditing in most cases. Large and significant revenues and expenses usually have already been audited in connection with the audit of other accounts in the cycles. At this late stage in the audit, it is always a good idea to "step back" and review large and unusual revenue and gain transactions recorded near the end of the year. These often have been the vehicles for income statement manipulation. Some examples were given in the chapter.

Two of the most important topics for the audit completion work involve the client's written representation letter and the lawyer's letter. These submissions to the auditors are virtually required for an unqualified audit report. Without them, the audit scope is considered limited. Several requirements for the client representation letter were specified in the chapter. A special insert described particular problems interpreting lawyers' letters. Information from lawyers is especially important for getting evidence about litigation contingencies and their disclosure according to *Handbook Section* 3290. Some descriptive research on *Handbook Section* 3290 disclosure experience in the U.S. was provided to emphasize the difficulties faced by managers and auditors.

"Subsequent events" topics were explained in considerable detail, including (1) procedural responsibility for events following the balance sheet date; (2) the dual-dating alternative for reporting on events that occurred between the end of field work and the delivery of the report; (3) auditors' discovery, after a report was delivered, of facts that existed at the balance sheet date; and (4) auditors' finding, after a report was delivered, that one or more audit procedures they thought were performed were not actually performed.

This chapter closed this text's adventures in auditing with explanation of proposed adjusting journal entries and disclosure notes, working paper review and the management

---

[3] W.A. Wallace, "More Effective Management Letters," *CPA Journal*, December 1983, pp. 18–28.

letter. All that remains is the audit report itself, which was explained in Chapter 3. The next chapter will discuss other types of engagements that are common in public practice.

MULTIPLE-CHOICE QUESTIONS FOR PRACTICE AND REVIEW

Questions 14.24 to 14.26 are located on the CD-ROM that accompanies this textbook.

14.27 When auditing the year-end balance of interest-bearing notes payable, the auditors are most likely to audit at the same time the company's:
   a. Interest income.
   b. Interest expense.
   c. Amortization of goodwill.
   d. Royalty revenue.

14.28 The main purpose of a written client representation letter is to:
   a. Shift responsibility for financial statements from the management to the auditor.
   b. Provide a substitute source of evidence for detail procedures auditors would otherwise perform.
   c. Provide management a place to make assertions about the quantity and valuation of the physical inventory.
   d. Impress upon management its ultimate responsibility for the financial statements and disclosures.

14.29 Which one of these procedures or sources is not used to obtain evidence about contingencies?
   a. Scan expense accounts for credit entries.
   b. Obtain a representation letter from the client's lawyer.
   c. Read the minutes of the board of directors' meetings.
   d. Examine terms of sale in sales contracts.

14.30 A Type I subsequent event involves subsequent information about a condition that existed at the balance sheet date. Subsequent knowledge of which of the following would cause the company to adjust its December 31 financial statements?
   a. Sale of an issue of new shares for $500,000 on January 30.
   b. Settlement of a damage lawsuit for a customer's injury sustained February 15 for $10,000.
   c. Settlement of litigation in February for $100,000 that had been estimated at $12,000 in the December 31 financial statements.
   d. Storm damage of $1 million to the company's buildings on March 1.

14.31 A. Griffin audited the financial statements of Dodger Magnificat Corporation for the year ended December 31, 2002. She completed the audit field work on January 30, and later learned of a stock split voted by the board of directors on February 5. The financial statements were changed to reflect the split, and she now needs to dual-date the audit report before sending it to the company. Which of the following is the proper form?
   a. December 31, 2002, except as to Note X, which is dated January 30, 2003.
   b. January 30, 2002, except as to Note X, which is dated February 5, 2003.
   c. December 31, 2002, except as to Note X, which is dated February 5, 2003.
   d. February 5, 2003, except for completion of field work, for which the date is January 30, 2003.

14.32 In connection with a company's filing a registration statement under most provincial securities acts, auditors have a responsibility to perform procedures to find subsequent events until:
   a. The year-end balance sheet date.
   b. The audit report date.
   c. The date the registration statement and audit report are delivered to the provincial securities commission.
   d. The "effective date" of the registration statement, when the securities can be offered for sale.

14.33 The auditing standards regarding "subsequent discovery of facts that existed at the balance sheet date" refers to knowledge obtained after:
   a. The date the audit report was delivered to the client.
   b. The audit report date.
   c. The company's year-end balance sheet date.
   d. The date interim audit work was complete.

14.34 Which two of the following are not required by U.S. auditing standards?
   a. Client representation letter.
   b. Lawyer's letter.

c. Management letter.
d. Engagement letter.

14.35 Which of these persons generally do not participate in writing the management letter (client advisory comments)?

a. Client's outside lawyers.
b. Client's accounting and production managers.
c. Audit firm's audit team on the engagement.
d. Audit firm's consulting and tax experts.

EXERCISES AND PROBLEMS

14.36 Client Representation Letter. In connection with your audit, you request that management furnish you with a letter containing certain representations. For example:

(1) the client has satisfactory title to all assets;

(2) no contingent or unrecorded liabilities exist except as disclosed in the letter;

(3) no shares of the company's stock are reserved for options, warrants or other rights; and

(4) the company is not obligated to repurchase any of its outstanding shares under any circumstances.

Required:

a. Explain why you believe a letter of representation should be furnished to you.

b. In what way, if any, do these client representations affect your audit procedures and responsibilities?

(AICPA adapted)

14.37 Engagement and Client Representation Letters. The two major written understandings between a PA and client, in connection with an audit of financial statements, are the engagement (arrangements) letter and the client representation letter.

Required:

a. (1) What are the objectives of the engagement (arrangements) letter?

(2) Who should prepare and sign the engagement letter?

(3) When should the engagement letter be sent?

(4) Why should the engagement letter be renewed periodically?

b. (1) What are the objectives of the client representation letter?

(2) Who should sign the client representation letter?

(3) When should the client representation letter be obtained?

(4) Why should the client representation letter be prepared for each examination?

c. A PA's responsibilities for providing accounting services sometimes involve an association with unaudited financial statements. Discuss the need in this circumstance for:

(1) An engagement letter.

(2) Client representation letter.

(AICPA adapted)

14.38 Client Representations Letter Omissions. During the audit of the annual financial statements of Amis Manufacturing, Inc., the company's president, Vance Molar, and Wayne Dweebins, the engagement partner, reviewed matters that were supposed to be included in a written representation letter. Upon receipt of the following representation letter, Dweebins contacted Molar to state that it was incomplete.

To John & Wayne, PAs:

In connection with your examination of the balance sheet of Amis Manufacturing, Inc., as of December 31, 2002, and the related statements of income, retained earnings and cash flows for the year then ended, for the purpose of expressing an opinion on whether the financial statements present fairly the financial position, results of operations and cash flows of Amis Manufacturing, Inc., in conformity with generally accepted accounting principles, we confirm, to the best of our knowledge and belief, the following representations made to you during your audit. There were no:

Plans or intentions that may materially affect the carrying value or classification of assets or liabilities.

Communications from regulatory agencies concerning noncompliance with, or deficiencies in, financial reporting practices.

Agreements to repurchase assets previously sold.

Violations or possible violations of laws or regulations whose effects should be considered for disclosure in the financial statements or as a basis for recording a loss contingency.

Unasserted claims or assessments that our lawyer has advised are probable of assertion that must be disclosed in accordance with Statement of Financial Accounting Standards No. 5.

Capital stock purchase options or agreements or capital stock reserved for options, warrants, conversions or other requirements.

Compensating balance or other arrangements involving restrictions on cash balances.

Vance Molar, President
Amis Manufacturing, Inc.
March 14, 2003

Required:

Identify the other matters that Molar's representation letter should specifically confirm.

(AICPA adapted)

14.39 Subsequent Events. You are nearing the completion of an examination of the financial statements of Jubilee, Inc., for the year ended December 31. You are concerned with ascertaining the occurrence of subsequent events that may require adjustment or disclosure essential to a fair presentation in conformity with generally accepted accounting principles.

Required:

a. Briefly explain what is meant by the phrase "subsequent event."

b. How do those subsequent events which require financial statement adjustment differ from those which require only financial statement disclosure?

c. What are the procedures that should be performed to ascertain the occurrence of subsequent events?

(AICPA adapted)

14.40 Subsequent Events and Contingent Liabilities. Crankwell, Inc., is preparing its annual financial statements and annual report to shareholders. Management wants to be sure that all of the necessary and proper disclosures are incorporated into the financial statements and the annual report. Two classes of items that have an important bearing on the financial statements are subsequent events and contingent liabilities. The financial statements could be materially inaccurate or misleading if proper disclosure of these items is not made.

Required:

a. With respect to subsequent events:
  (1) Define what is meant by a "subsequent event."
  (2) Identify the two types of subsequent events and explain the appropriate financial statement presentation of each type.

b. With respect to contingent liabilities:
  (1) Identify the essential elements of a contingent liability.
  (2) Explain how a contingent liability should be disclosed in the financial statements.

c. Explain how a subsequent event may relate to a contingent liability. Give an example to support your answer.

(CMA adapted)

14.41 Subsequent Events Procedures. You are in the process of "winding up" the field work on Top Stove Corporation, a company engaged in the manufacture and sale of kerosene space heating stoves. To date there has been every indication that the financial statements of the client present fairly the position of the company at December 31 and the results of its operations for the year then ended. Top Stove had total assets at December 31 of $4 million and a net profit for the year (after deducting federal and provincial income taxes) of $285,000. The principal records of the company are a general ledger, cash receipts record, voucher register, sales register, cheque register and general journal. Financial statements are prepared monthly. Your field work will be completed on February 20, and you plan to deliver the report to the client by March 12.

Required:

a. Write a brief statement about the purpose and period to be covered in a review of subsequent events.

b. Outline the program you would follow to determine what transactions involving material amounts, if any, have occurred since the balance sheet date.

(AICPA adapted)

14.42 Subsequent Events—Cases. The following events occurred in independent cases, but in each instance the event happened after the close of the fiscal year under audit but before all members of the audit team had left the office of the client. State in each case what disclosure, if any, you would expect in the financial statements (and notes thereto). The balance sheet date in each instance is December 31.

1. On December 31, commodities handled by the company had been traded in the open market in which the company procures its supplies at $1.40 per pound. This price had prevailed for two weeks, following an official market report that predicted vastly enlarged supplies; however, no purchases were made at $1.40. The price throughout the preceding year had been about $2, which is the level experienced over several years. On January 18 the price returned to $2, following public disclosure of an error in the official calculations of the prior December—correction of which destroyed the expectations of excessive supplies. Inventory at December 31 had been valued on a lower-of-cost-or-market basis.

2. On February 1 the board of directors adopted a resolution accepting the offer of an investment banker to guarantee the marketing of $100 million of preferred shares.

3. On January 22 one of the three major plants of the client burned down, resulting in a loss of $50 million, which was covered to the extent of $40 million by insurance.

4. The client in this case is an investment company of the open-end type. In January a wholly new management came into control. By February 20 the new management had sold 90 percent of the investments carried at December 31 and had purchased others of a substantially more speculative character.

5. This company has a wholly owned but not consolidated subsidiary producing oil in a foreign country. A serious rebellion began in that country on January 18 and continued beyond the completion of your audit work. The press in this country has carried extensive coverage of the progress of the fighting.

(AICPA adapted)

14.43 Subsequent Events—Cases. In connection with your examination of the financial statements of Olars Manufacturing Corporation for the year ended December 31, your post-balance sheet audit procedures disclosed the following items:

1. January 3: The provincial government approved a plan for the construction of an expressway. The plan will result in the appropriation of a portion of the land area owned by Olars Manufacturing Corporation. Construction will be gin late next year. No estimate of the condemnation award is available.

2. January 4: The funds for a $25,000 loan to the corporation made by Mr. Olars on July 15 were obtained by him with a loan on his personal life insurance policy. The loan was recorded in the account loan payable to officers. Mr. Olars's source of the funds was not disclosed in the company records. The corporation pays the premiums on the life insurance policy, and Mrs. Olars, wife of the president, is the owner and beneficiary of the policy.

3. January 7: The mineral content of a shipment of ore en route on December 31 was determined to be 72 percent. The shipment was recorded at year-end at an estimated content of 50 percent by a debit to raw material inventory and a credit to accounts payable in the amount of $20,600. The final liability to the vendor is based on the actual mineral content of the shipment.

4. January 15: A series of personal disagreements have arisen between Mr. Olars, the president, and Mr. Tweedy, his brother-in-law, the treasurer. Mr. Tweedy resigned, effective immediately, under an agreement whereby the corporation would purchase his 10 percent share ownership at book value as of December 31. Payment is to be made in two equal amounts in cash on April 1 and October 1. In December the treasurer had obtained a divorce from Mr. Olars's sister.

5. January 31: As a result of reduced sales, production was curtailed in mid-January and some workers were laid off. On February 5 all the remaining workers went on strike. To date the strike is unsettled.

6. February 10: A contract was signed whereby Mammoth Enterprises purchased from Olars Manufacturing corporation all of the latter's capital assets (including rights to receive the proceeds of any property condemnation), inventories and the right to conduct business under the name "Olars Manufacturing Division." The effective date of the transfer will be March 1. The sale price was $500,000, subject to adjustment following the taking of a physical inventory. Important factors contributing to the decision to enter into the contract were the policy of the board of directors of Mammoth Industries to diversify the firm's activities and the report of a survey con-

ducted by an independent market appraisal firm, which revealed a declining market for Olars's products.

Required:

Assume that the above items came to your attention prior to completion of your audit work on February 15. For each of the above items:

a. Give the audit procedures, if any, that would have brought the item to your attention. Indicate other sources of information that may have revealed the item.

b. Discuss the disclosure that you would recommend for the item, listing all details that should be disclosed. Indicate those items or details, if any, that should not be disclosed. Give your reasons for recommending or not recommending disclosure of the items or details.

(AICPA adapted)

14.44 Subsequent Discovery of Fact. On June 1 Albert Faultless of A.J. Faultless & Co., CAs, noticed some disturbing information about his client, Hopkirk Company. A story in the local paper mentioned the indictment of Tony Baker, whom A.J. knew as the assistant controller at Hopkirk. The charge was mail fraud. A.J. made discreet enquiries with the controller at Hopkirk's headquarters and learned that Baker had been speculating in foreign currency futures. In fact, part of Baker's work at Hopkirk involved managing the company's foreign currency. Unfortunately, Baker had violated company policy, lost a small amount of money, then decided to speculate some more, lost some more, and eventually lost $7 million in company funds.

The mail fraud was involved in his attempt to cover his activity until he recovered the original losses. Most of the events were in process on March 1, when A.J. had signed and dated the unqualified report on Hopkirk's financial statements for the year ended on the previous December 31.

A.J. determined that the information probably would affect the decisions of external users and advised Hopkirk's chief executive to make the disclosure. She flatly refused to make any disclosure, arguing that the information was immate-

rial. On June 17 A.J. provided the subsequent information in question to a news reporter, and it was printed in the *Wall Street Journal* along with a statement that the financial statements and accompanying audit report could not be relied on.

Required:

Evaluate the actions of Faultless & Co., PAs, with respect to the subsequent information discovered. What other action might Faultless & Co. have taken? What are the possible legal effects of the firm's actions, if any?

14.45 Omitted Audit Procedures. The following are independent situations that have occurred in your audit firm, Arthur Hurdman (AH):*

1. During the internal inspection review by the regional office of AH, one of your clients, Wildcat Oil Suppliers, was selected for review. The reviewers questioned the thoroughness of inventory obsolescence procedures, especially in light of the depressed state of the oil exploration industry at the time. They felt that specific procedures, which they considered appropriate, were not performed by your audit team.

2. Top Stove, one of your clients, installed a microcomputer in July 2002 to process part of the accounting transactions. You completed the audit of Top Stove's December 31, 2002 statements on February 15, 2003. During the April 2003 review work on Top Stove's first-quarter financial information, you discovered that during the audit of the 2002 statements only the manual records were investigated in the search for unrecorded liabilities.

3. AH belongs to the private companies practice section (PCPS) of the AICPA division of firms. In keeping with membership requirements of the PCPS, AH contracted with Haskin and Anderson (HA) to conduct a peer review of AH's audit quality control procedures. In HA's report to AH, the audit of Al's Store Organization (ASO) was criticized due to the letterhead on ASO's representation letter. Although the representation letter complied with the requirements of SAS 19, it was prepared on the letterhead of the Palo Alto Garden Club. (Al's wife, Alice, had

---

* Situation derived from examples given in Thomas R. Weirich and Elizabeth J. Ringelberg, "Omitted Audit Procedures," *CPA Journal*, March 1984, p. 36.

been president of the club during the period of the audit.)

Required:

a. Without regard to the specific situation given, answer the following questions:

(1) What are the proper steps auditors should take if it is discovered, after the report date, that an auditing procedure was omitted?

(2) How are auditors' decisions affected if, after review of the workpapers, it is determined that other audit procedures produced the necessary sufficient, appropriate evidence?

(3) If in subsequently applying the omitted procedure, the auditors become aware of material new information that should have been disclosed in the financial statements, how should they proceed?

b. Describe the proper action to take in each situation above, given the additional information provided below:

Case 1: You made a thorough consideration on the scope of the audit of Wildcat Oil Suppliers, and you made a detailed review of the working papers. You have concluded that compensating procedures were conducted sufficient to support the valuation of inventory.

Case 2: Your subsequent investigation of the microcomputer records of Top Stove revealed that material liabilities were not recorded as of December 31.

Case 3: You were requested to investigate the ASO alleged audit procedure deficiency. Your investigations revealed that ASO had a significant loan from the local bank that had received the AH report on ASO's financial statements. The loan is still outstanding, and indeed the representation letter was written on the garden club letterhead.

14.46 Second Partner Review and Dual Dating. You have been assigned to perform a review of a correspondent PA firm's audit of Oxford Millwork Company for the calendar year ending December 31. In the audited financial statements of Oxford Millwork Company, you find the following representations:

> Common shares, $10 par value, 100,000 shares outstanding, 400,000 shares authorized (Note 1) $1,000,000
> Note 1: Subsequent event (dated January 20). The board of directors approved a three-for-one stock dividend effective January 20. At the effective date, the par value of outstanding common shares is $3 million.

You have reviewed the correspondent PA firm's audit report and found the opinion dated "January 15, 2003, except as to Note 1 which is dated January 20, 2003."

Required:

a. What is the purpose of a second partner review?

b. What is the purpose of dual dating?

c. What recommendations would you make to the PA firm concerning presentation of the subsequent event?

DISCUSSION CASES

14.47 Recognizing Income of a Purchased Subsidiary. The following brief dialogue occurred in a controversy wherein a plaintiff claimed that management backdated the effective date of an acquisition in order to pump up earnings improperly. The independent auditors, Eastford and Redwood (E&R), are involved because they signed an unqualified report on the consolidated financial statements in question.

Plaintiff's lawyer: Plaintiff alleges that COSIF Company's purchase of 100 percent of the stock of Prosper, Inc., was effective on April 28, almost four months after the beginning of COSIF's fiscal year on January 1. However, COSIF included in consolidated income the results of Prosper's operations for the full 12 months ended December 31. This was improper accounting which failed to reflect the substance of the transaction.

Eastford and Redwood knew, or should have known, that the effective date was April 28. The evidence shown today proves that the first written agreement concerning the acquisition was a memorandum dated March 5, which set forth the general terms of the transaction. The final written agreement was signed and dated on April 28. Their unqualified opinion was improperly rendered.

Eastford and Redwood's Lawyer: The issue is whether January 1 or some later date should have been used as the acquisition date for accounting purposes. E&R stipulate that the first written memorandum was dated March 5 and the final agreement April 28. However, we have also introduced into evidence written representations from the president of COSIF and COSIF's outside counsel that an oral agreement substantially equivalent to the March 5 memorandum agreement was reached on or about January 1. COSIF's outside counsel is one of the most highly regarded law firms in the Maritimes.

These representations were meaningful to E&R because we were not engaged as COSIF's auditors until November 14 and were not present when the actual negotiations took place.

Plaintiff alleges that applicable accounting principles were misapplied because no written agreement existed on January 1.

We insist that elements of the April 28 agreement, which made the acquisition effective as of January 1, show that the substance of the transaction supports our conclusion that January 1 was the proper accounting date. We cite the following:

1. COSIF and Prosper clearly intended an effective date of January 1.
2. The fixed portion of the purchase price depended on a minimum amount of Prosper's income through December 31 of the year preceding. (At March 5 the audit of Prosper's financial year had not yet been completed.)
3. The contingent portion of the purchase price depended on a minimum amount of Prosper's income for the year beginning January 1 and two years thereafter.
4. Warranties made by Prosper as to assets and liabilities were as of December 31 (just prior to the January 1 effective date).
5. Interest on COSIF's notes issued in the payment package ran from January 1.
6. The full amount of Prosper's earnings from January 1 inured to the benefit of COSIF.

Required:

What is the proper accounting date for COSIF's investment in Prosper?

14.48 Lawyer's Letter Responses. Omega Corporation is involved in a lawsuit brought by a competitor for patent infringement. The competitor is asking $14 million actual damages for lost profits and unspecified punitive damages. The lawsuit has been in progress for 15 months, and Omega has worked closely with its outside counsel preparing its defence. Omega recently requested its outside lawyers with the firm of Wolfe & Goodwin to provide information to the auditors.

The managing partner of Wolfe & Goodwin asked four different lawyers who have worked on the case to prepare a concise response to the auditors. They returned these:

1. The action involves unique characteristics wherein authoritative legal precedents bearing directly on the plaintiff's claims do not seem to exist. We believe the plaintiff will have serious problems establishing Omega's liability; nevertheless, if the plaintiff is successful, the damage award may be substantial.
2. In our opinion, Omega will be able to defend this action successfully, and, if not, the possible liability to Omega in this proceeding is nominal in amount.
3. We believe the plaintiff's case against Omega is without merit.
4. In our opinion Omega will be able to assert meritorious defences and has a reasonable chance of sustaining an adequate defence, with a possible outcome of settling the case for less than the damages claimed.

Required:

a. Interpret each of the four responses separately. Decide whether each is (1) adequate to conclude that the likelihood of an adverse outcome is "remote," requiring no disclosure in financial statements, or (2) too vague to serve as adequate information for a decision, requiring more information from the lawyers or from management.
b. What kind of response do you think the auditors would get if they asked the plaintiff's counsel about the likely outcome of the lawsuit? Discuss.

14.49 Accounting for a Contingency— Lawyer's Letter Information. Central City was involved in litigation brought by MALDEF, a citizens' group, over the creation of single-member voting districts for city council positions. The auditor was working on the financial statements for the year ended December 31, 2002, and had almost completed the field work by February 12, 2003.

The court had heard final arguments on February 1 and rendered its judgment on February 10. The ruling was in favour of MALDEF and required the creation of certain single-member voting districts. While this ruling itself did not impose a monetary loss on Central City, the court also ruled that MALDEF would be awarded a judgment of court costs and legal fees to be paid by Central City.

Local newspaper reports stated that MALDEF would seek a $250,000 recovery from the city. The auditor obtained a lawyer's representation letter dated February 15 that stated the following: "In my opinion the court will award some amount for MALDEF's legal fees. In regard to your enquiry about an amount or range of possible loss, I estimate that such an award could be anywhere from $30,000 to $175,000."

Required:

a. What weight should be given to the newspaper report of the $250,000 amount MALDEF might ask? What weight should be given to the lawyer's estimate?

b. How should this subsequent event be reflected in the 2002 financial statements of Central City? As an accounting adjustment of the amounts presented (Type I)? As a disclosure in the 2002 statements with accounting for the amounts in the 2003 financial statements (Type II)?

14.50 Contingencies. Northern Lights Pulp and Paper Company (NL) has been an audit client of Web & Web, Chartered Accountants, for several years. NL was provincially incorporated in 1975 and has operated two small pulp-and-paper mills in Northern Ontario since that time.

Hard hit by the recession, the company has experienced losses in its last three years, but current-year income projections are optimistic. Like its competitors in the forest industry, NL has managed to cut costs and increase productivity and predicts a significant profit for the year ended December 31, 2004.

It is August 2004. You have just been assigned as the senior-in-charge of NL since the previous senior accepted a position as controller in the private sector. The interim audit was completed by the previous senior. The partner has asked you to become familiar with the client by reviewing the permanent file, the interim file and the many notes prepared by the

previous senior. He would also like you to prepare a memo addressing audit issues you identify based on your review. You noted the following in performing your review of the files:

1. Current year (2004) projected net income is $5,000,000. Prior year (2003) losses were $1,200,000 (2002–$2,000,000, and 2001–$3,500,000). Industry statistics reported total annual losses of $1.4 billion in 2002 to under $200 million in 2003.

2. The controller who had been with the company for 12 years was fired in April 2004. A recently qualified chartered accountant was hired as the new controller.

3. The computerized system was converted during the first six months of the year. No parallel runs were performed since the software package purchased was common to the forest industry. At the interim audit, several accounts were not reconciled. The vice president, finance, believes that the balances were not transferred correctly and has promised to look into this before year-end.

4. A letter was received in May 2004 from the provincial government requiring the company to meet an individual contamination reduction target by 2005. To meet these targets, NL must build a new, secondary biological treatment plant. No action to meet these targets had been taken at the time of the interim audit. The company plans to begin construction of the new treatment plant in September 2004. The letter indicates that heavy fines will be imposed if the company does not comply by the due date.

5. In March 2004, a chemical engineer was hired to help the general manager of each mill establish due diligence standards. This action was taken in response to fears raised by the president, who became aware that Bata Industries and two of its directors were convicted of an environmental offence in 2002. The due diligence standards had not been developed at the time of the interim audit as the chemical engineer had been involved in establishing a way to reduce costs. In 2003, NL was fined $30,000 for failing to meet pollution emission standards.

6. Legal fees increased 150 percent during the first six months of 2004, in comparison to the first six months of 2003.

7. Over the period April to June 2004, NL issued cheques totalling $90,000 to the president and the chemical engineer. According to the new controller, the president and the chemical engineer each earned a $45,000 bonus for the first six months of the year due to the improved financial performance of the company. The president asked the controller to pay the bonus over a three-month period. Therefore, six cheques of $15,000 each were issued.
8. The minute book (shareholders' and directors' meetings) was not updated for the interim audit but is expected to be up to date for the year-end audit.
9. After much hesitation, the president finally agreed to sign the 2003 management representation letter.

Required plan:

Prepare the memo requested by the partner addressing audit issues and their impact on the 2004 audit. The memo should also address risk factors, materiality and the overall audit approach for the 2004 audit.

(ICAO adapted)

14.51 **Contingencies.** You are the senior auditor in charge of the field work for the examination of the financial statements of ABC Chemical Corporation for the year ended December 31, 2005. The company produces chlorine and related products, which are used as bleaching agents, primarily by pulp-and-paper companies.

An analytical review of the company's operation for the current year reveals that recorded sales have increased about 10 percent, and net income about 20 percent relative to the previous year. This is surprising, since demand for the company's products has been weak because of a long and continuing recession in the North American pulp-and-paper industry.

The controller attributes the improvement to an aggressive marketing program directed at foreign companies. In addition, he claims that ABC Chemical has significantly reduced its production costs this year while still remaining, he thinks, within applicable pollution and commercial laws and regulations. He also requests that you not include any of the foreign accounts receivable at year-end in your confirmation sample, since "the practice is not normal in three countries, and is likely to harm our business relationship with these new customers." Fi-

nally, he mentions that because of the unusually good operating results and improving market conditions, the company sold $10,000,000 of common shares in November 2005.

Required:

a. As auditor, do you have any responsibility for determining whether the company actually complies with pollution control laws and regulations in its operations? Briefly explain.
b. Assume the foreign receivables are material in amount at December 31, 2005. Explain how you would deal with the restriction imposed by the controller and how the restriction could affect your auditor's report.
c. Explain how you would design a dollar unit sampling plan to determine the sample size for testing the foreign receivables at year-end. Be specific in identifying relative factors affecting sample size and their likely values (high, medium, or low). (Do not discuss selection or evaluation of the sample.)
d. List four audit procedures you would perform with respect to the sale of common shares during the year.

(CGAAC adapted)

14.52 **Contingencies.** A PA is performing an audit of financial statements of a publicly held company in accordance with generally accepted auditing standards and has completed all the appropriate audit steps up to and through the performance of substantive tests of details of transaction cycles and account balances. She is therefore in the final stages of completing the audit.

Required:

a. With what third parties (if any) is the PA likely to communicate at this stage of the audit process and what would be the purpose of such communication? Explain.
b. Discuss the PA's responsibilities (if any) with respect to subsequent events occurring after the balance sheet date.
c. Discuss the PA's responsibilities (if any) with respect to the MD&A portion of the company's annual report to shareholders.
d. Would it be appropriate to perform analytical procedures at this point in the audit? Explain.

(CGAAC adapted)

14.53 Evaluating Evidence. The purpose of substantive testing is to verify the assertions made by management in the financial statements. An auditor does this by using various evidence gathering methods including inspection, observation, enquiry, confirmation, computation and analysis.

Consider the following six unrelated audit tests that a PA performed in conjunction with the examination of the financial statements of a client whose fiscal year ended December 31, 2004.

1. Sent negative confirmation requests to a sample of the client's customers with unpaid balances at November 30, 2004.
2. Requested statements as of December 31, 2004, from a large sample of vendors with whom the client did business during 2004.
3. Examined invoice copies and shipping documents supporting the first 20 sales transactions recorded in January 2005.
4. Inspected share certificates associated with temporary investments in marketable securities, held in the client's safety deposit box on December 31, 2004.
5. Verified the mechanical accuracy of the "aged" listings, prepared by the chief accountant, of the client's accounts receivable at December 31, 2004.
6. Counted cash on hand at December 31, 2004.

Required:
For each of the six audit tests, list the management assertion(s) which is (are) primarily being verified and comment on the quality (appropriateness) of the evidence obtained. Organize your answer as follows.

Management Assertion(s)	Quality of Evidence

(CGAAC adapted)

14.54 Related Party Transactions. Susan Sharp, PA, audited the financial statements of her continuing client, Octopos Industries, for the year ended December 31, 2003. Octopos is a publicly held company whose shares are traded on the Vancouver Stock Exchange. In discussing the property, plant and equipment accounts with the controller, Sharp learned that a new machine costing $55,000,000 (a material amount) was constructed for the company during the year by an affiliated firm, of which the president of Octopos Industries is the sole shareholder.

In support of this transaction, Sharp examined an invoice from the vendor for $55,000,000 that was stamped "paid." She also examined a memo from the president to the controller of Octopos, authorizing the payment of the invoice. Given the sensitivity of the matter, the president of Octopos instructed the controller not to disclose the transaction in the company's financial statements.

No other problems or unusual situations were encountered during the audit, which was completed on February 25, 2004.

Required:
a. Describe the additional audit procedures (if any) that Sharp should have performed with respect to the machine acquired from the affiliated company.
b. Without prejudice to your answer to part (a), assume that Sharp had obtained sufficient, appropriate evidence with respect to the transaction. Prepare an auditor's report for the case, in good form. Sharp is the managing partner of a firm of PAs whose executive offices are in Vancouver.

(CGAAC adapted)

PART IV

Professional Services and Responsibilities

CHAPTER 15

Learning Objectives

This chapter covers several areas of public accounting practice related to accountants' association with financial information other than complete, audited historical financial statements. PAs often perform work and give reports in these areas of practice:

- Unaudited Financial Statements: Review and Compilation.
- Review of Interim Financial Information.
- Special Reports—Other Comprehensive Bases of Accounting.
- Internal Accounting Control.
- Forecasts and Projections.
- Financial Statements to be Used Outside Canada.

These topics involve assurance standards, auditing standards and accounting and review services standards that were introduced or mentioned briefly in Chapter 2. Your learning objectives related to these topics are to be able to:

1. Write appropriate reports for review and compilation of unaudited financial statements, given specific fact circumstances.

2. List some interim information review procedures and write a report on a review of interim financial information.

3. Define, explain and give examples of "another appropriate disclosed basis of accounting" (AADBA), distinguishing them from GAAP.

4. Explain the content of an auditor's report on supplementary current value financial statements in comparison to a standard report on historical cost financial statements.

5. Describe the various reports on internal control and their connection with public reporting and reporting to a client's audit committee.

6. Define the various financial presentations and levels of service involved in association with financial forecasts and projections, and write compilation and examination reports.

7. Describe the new umbrella standards for assurance engagements.

OTHER PUBLIC ACCOUNTING SERVICES AND REPORTS

INTRODUCTION

Public accountants offer numerous assurance services on information other than the standard historical cost financial statements. These services grow from consumer demand for association by an objective expert. Naturally, business, government and the public want the credibility that goes along with PAs' association. However, PAs need to be careful in their reports on such information that they will not suggest the addition of more credibility than is warranted. As you study the topics in this chapter, you will see the standards for PA association and the care with which reports are worded.

UNAUDITED FINANCIAL STATEMENTS

LEARNING OBJECTIVE

1. Write appropriate reports for review and compilation of unaudited financial statements, given specific fact circumstances.

Many PA firms conduct practice in accounting and review services for small-business clients. These engagements include bookkeeping, financial statement preparation and financial statement review to help small businesses prepare financial communications. Until the late 1970s, auditing standards concentrated on one level of assurance based on a full audit and appeared to deny small clients the full benefit of PAs' services.

The investigations by the Adams Committee in Canada and in the U.S. Congress during 1977–78 highlighted the problem by centring attention on the idea that auditing standards handicapped the business of small public accounting firms and their services to small-business clients. The argument has become known as the "Big GAAS–Little GAAS" question. Big GAAS was portrayed as the villain in the play, with the proposition that existing standards were enacted under the influence of large PA firms whose practice is centred on big business. Even though this proposition is not true, the fact is that small PA firms want to give, and small businesses want to receive, some level of assurance as a result of accountants' work even though an audit in accordance with GAAS is not performed.

A separate part of the *Handbook*, the 8000 sections, and ISA 910 have been set aside to deal with review engagements. *Handbook* section 9100 and ISA 930 deal with compilation engagements.

Review Services

The review services explained in this section apply specifically to accountants' work on the unaudited financial statements. In a review services engagement, an accountant performs some procedures to achieve a moderate level of assurance. This level is not the same that could be attained by performing an audit in accordance with GAAS. According to *Handbook Section* 8100.05:

> Reviews are distinguishable from audits in that the scope of a review is less than that of an audit and therefore the level of assurance provided is lower. A review consists primarily of enquiry, analytical procedures and discussions related to information supplied to the public accountant by the enterprise with the limited objective of assessing whether the information is being reported on appropriate criteria. In this section, the word *plausible* is used in the sense of appearing to be worthy of belief based on the information obtained by the public accountant in connection with the review.

Section 8100.15 identifies standards applicable to a review engagement. They are stated as follows:

Standards Applicable to Review Engagements

General standard

The review should be performed and the review engagement report prepared by a person or persons having adequate technical training and proficiency in conducting reviews, with due care and with an objective state of mind.

Review standards

(*i*) The work should be adequately planned and properly executed. If assistants are employed, they should be properly supervised.

(*ii*) The public accountant should possess or acquire sufficient knowledge of the business carried on by the enterprise so that intelligent enquiry and assessment of information obtained can be made.

(*iii*) The public accountant should perform a review with the limited objective of assessing whether the information being reported on is plausible in the circumstances within the framework of appropriate criteria. Such a review should consist of:

(*a*) enquiry, analytical procedures and discussion; and

(*b*) additional or more extensive procedures when the public accountant's knowledge of the business carried on by the enterprise and the results of the enquiry, and analytical procedures and discussion cause him or her to doubt the plausibility of such information.

Reporting standards

(*i*) The review engagement report should indicate the scope of the review. The nature of the review engagement should be made evident and be clearly distinguished from an audit.

(*ii*) The report should indicate, based on the review:

(*a*) whether anything has come to the public accountant's attention that causes him or her to believe that the information being reported on is not, in all material respects, in accordance with appropriate criteria; or

(*b*) that no assurance can be provided.

The report should provide an explanation of the nature of any reservations contained therein and, if readily determinable, the effect.

A similar set of standards is given in ISA 9109.

These standards suggest that auditors need special training and experience in conducting reviews, especially with respect to working within a plausibility framework. As can be seen by the second review standard, obtaining knowledge of the business is a critical part of the review engagement. Such knowledge is critical to determining whether the information obtained during the course of the engagement is plausible. Sufficient knowledge of the business (and industry) is required to make intelligent enquiries and a reasonable assessment of responses and other information obtained. However, the knowledge of business required for review engagements is normally less detailed than that required in an audit.

The review standards indicate that review work on unaudited financial statements consists primarily of enquiry and analytical procedures. The information gained thereby is similar to audit evidence; but the recommended limitation on procedures (listed below) does not suggest performance of typical auditing procedures of assessing control risk, conducting physical observation of tangible assets, sending confirmations or examining documentary details of transactions.

- Obtain knowledge of the client's business. Know the accounting principles of the client's industry. Understand the client's organization and operations.

- Enquire about the accounting system and bookkeeping procedures.

- Perform analytical procedures to identify relationships and individual items that appear to be unusual.

- Enquire about actions taken at meetings of shareholders, directors and other important executive committees.

- Read (study) the financial statements for indications that they conform with generally accepted accounting principles.

- Obtain reports from other accountants who audit or review significant components, subsidiaries or other investees.

- Enquire of officers and directors about the following: Conformity with generally accepted accounting principles. Consistent application of accounting principles. Changes in the client's business or accounting practices. Matters about which questions have arisen as a result of applying other procedures (listed above). Events subsequent to the date of the financial statements.

- Perform any other procedures considered necessary if the financial statements appear to be incorrect, incomplete or otherwise unsatisfactory.

- Prepare working papers showing the matters covered by the enquiry and analytical review procedures, especially the resolution of unusual problems and questions.

- Obtain a written representation letter from the owner, manager or chief executive officer and from the chief financial officer.

Many firms will perform more detailed procedures such as bank reconciliations and bank confirmations to corroborate information obtained by enquiry. However, there is no requirement to perform such more detailed procedures under current review standards. Reviews have traditionally been supposed to provide negative assurance, or (in the words of the new assurance framework, to be discussed later in this chapter) a moderate level of assurance that indicates the financial information is "plausible" (*Section* 5025.12) or "moderate" (ISA 910.9). The reason the term negative assurance has been traditionally used is because of the "nothing has come to my attention . . ." wording that is used in the review report (see Exhibit 15–1).

A review service does not provide a basis for expressing an opinion on financial statements. Each page of the financial statements should be conspicuously marked as being unaudited. The standards indicate that a report on a review services engagement should include the following:

- Statement on the scope of the review engagement and that a review service was performed in accordance with generally accepted standards for review engagement.

- Statement that a review consists primarily of enquiries of company personnel and analytical procedures applied to financial data.

- Statement that a review service does not constitute an audit, and that an opinion on financial statements is not expressed. (This is a disclaimer of any audit opinion.)

- Statement that the accountant is not aware of any material modifications that should be made; or, if aware, a disclosure of departure(s) from generally accepted accounting principles. (This is a negative assurance.)

When other independent accountants are involved in audit or review of parts of the business, the principal reviewer cannot divide responsibility by referring to the other accountants in the review report, unless the disclosure helps explain the reason for a reservation. You can follow the spirit of the auditing standards to write the form and content of the reference to the work and reports of other auditors (*Section* 6930.22–.23). An example of a review report is given in Exhibit 15–1.

EXHIBIT 15–1   **REVIEW ENGAGEMENT REPORT (from *Handbook Section* 8200.04)**

To (person engaging the public accountant)

I have reviewed the balance sheet of Client Limited as at ...., 20... and the statements of income, retained earnings and changes in financial position for the year then ended. My review was made in accordance with generally accepted standards for review engagements and accordingly consisted primarily of enquiry, analytical procedures and discussion related to information supplied to me by the company.

A review does not constitute an audit and consequently I do not express an audit opinion on these financial statements.

Based on my review, nothing has come to my attention that causes me to believe that these financial statements are not, in all material respects, in accordance with generally accepted accounting principles.

City   (signed) . . . .
Date   CHARTERED ACCOUNTANT

Compilation Services

Compilation is a synonym for an older term—write-up work. Both terms refer to an accountant helping a client "write up" the financial information in the form of financial statements. A compilation service is accounting work in which an accountant performs few, if any, procedures, and it is substantially less than a review service. The description of a compilation of financial statements, according to *Handbook Section* 9200.03 is

> one in which a public accountant receives information from a client and arranges it into the form of a financial statements. The public accountant is concerned that the assembly of information is arithmetically correct, however the public accountant does not attempt to verify the accuracy or completeness of the information provided. Unlike an audit or review engagement in which the public accountant does sufficient work to issue a communication that provides assurance regarding the financial statements, no expression of assurance is contemplated in a compilation engagement.

A similar description is given in ISA 930.3.

Since no assurance credibility is provided by compilation engagements, the public accountant is limited in what action she or he can take. However, the public accountant also has a responsibility to not be associated with misleading information.

> When the public accountant is aware that there are matters which the public accountant believes would cause the financial statements to be false or misleading, she or he should request additional or revised information in order to complete the statements. If the client does not provide the information requested or agree with the statements, the public accountant should not release the statements and should withdraw from the engagement. (*Section* 9200.18, also see ISA 930.14.)

Financial statements may be compiled on a basis other than GAAP if in the auditor's judgment this other basis is appropriate for the circumstances of the engagement. This appropriate non-GAAP basis is referred to as "another appropriate disclosed basis of accounting" or AADBA in the literature. The best way to disclose AADBA statement is through the statement's title (e.g., "Statements Based on Income Tax Accounting") or in a note discussing the statements. The reasons for the compilation are also best achieved through notes to the statements or via the title.

In a compilation service, an accountant should understand the client's business, read (study) the financial statements looking for obvious clerical or accounting principle errors, and follow up on information that is incorrect, incomplete or otherwise unsatisfactory. Each page of the financial statements should be marked **unaudited—see Notice to reader.** The report can be issued by an accountant who is not independent, provided the lack of independence is disclosed, as required by some professional bodies such as the ICAO, which requires disclosure in the Notice to Reader (see Exhibit 15–2). The report should contain the following (see Exhibit 15–2):

- Statement that the public accountant compiled the statement from information provided by management (or proprietor).

- Statement that the public accountant has not audited, reviewed or otherwise attempted to verify the accuracy or completeness of such information.

E X H I B I T   15–2   **NOTICE TO READER (from *Handbook Section* 9200.24)**

I have compiled the balance sheet of Client Limited as at December 31, 20X1, and the statements of income, retained earnings and changes in financial position for the (period) then ended from information provided by management (the proprietor). I have not audited, reviewed or otherwise attempted to verify the accuracy or completeness of such information. Readers are cautioned that these statements may not be appropriate for their purposes.

I am not independent with respect to Client Limited.

City   (printed or signed) . . . .
Date   CHARTERED ACCOUNTANT

- Caution to readers that the statement may not be appropriate for their purposes.
- No expression of any form of opinion or negative assurance.

Exhibit 15–2 illustrates that two kinds of reports on compiled financial statements can be given: (1) a report stating that the accountant is not independent (as in Exhibit 15–2); or (2) a report by an independent public accountant on financial statements prepared using an appropriate basis of accounting such as GAAP. In the second case, the basis of accounting may be an "appropriate disclosed basis of accounting other than GAAP," just like other kinds of accounting services, and reports can cover financial statements presented on such other bases of accounting. (Other appropriate bases of accounting are discussed later in this chapter.)

Although compilation engagements do not provide any attest assurance or credibility, they can be viewed as providing accounting credibility. A public accountant's compilation of the statements as opposed to a nonprofessional's must add some kind of credibility, otherwise there would be no reason to pay the extra cost of a PA to do the compilation.

Note that the Notice to Reader is not a proper place to make non-GAAP AADBA disclosures because the Notice to Reader does not mention GAAP or any other basis of accounting.

Exhibit 15–3 summarizes the major differences between audit, review and compilation engagements.

OTHER REVIEW AND COMPILATION TOPICS

There are several other aspects of review and compilation engagements and reports that differ from audit standards. These topics point out some of the different problems in dealing with unaudited financial statements.

Prescribed Forms

Industry trade associations, banks, government agencies and regulatory agencies often use prescribed forms (standard reprinted documents) to specify the content and measurement of accounting information required for special purposes. Such forms may not request disclosures required by GAAP or may specify measurements that do not conform to GAAP.

When such forms are compiled (not when reviewed) by an accountant, the compilation report does not need to call attention to the GAAP departures or to GAAP disclosure deficiencies.

There's nothing in either *Section* 9200 or in the Guideline, "Compilation Engagements —Financial Statement Disclosures," (AUG-5) requiring public accountants to disclose

EXHIBIT 15–3   **AUDIT VERSUS MAJOR NONAUDIT ENGAGEMENTS SUMMARY**

Compilations	Review	Audit
Prepared for internal use of restricted users	Plausibility, consistency	Conformity with GAAP, GAAS
IC not evaluated	IC not evaluated	Evaluate IC
No independent corroborating evidence	Some evidence	Independent corroborating evidence
Compilation, bookkeeping	Enquiry-based review, discussions, reasonableness	Substantive and compliance testing
Accounting credibility	Negative assurance	Positive assurance, audit credibility
Notice to reader	Accountant's comments or review engagement report	Auditor's report
IC = Internal control		

known departures from GAAP in either the compiled statements or the Notice to Reader. Moreover, in the latter the accountant specifically states that no attempt has been made to determine whether the statements contain GAAP departures. The reason for this is that disclosure of known departures could be confusing or even misleading. If such disclosures were required, readers might assume the accountant is responsible for disclosing *all* GAAP departures in the statements and that the only departures are the disclosed departures. Such a responsibility is beyond the scope of a compilation engagement.

How then does the auditor deal with situations of known departures from GAAP or other AADBA? Well, for one thing the Notice to Reader contains a caution to readers that the financial statements may not be appropriate for their purposes. For another, compiled statements may not be appropriate for general purposes and, hence, are restricted in their use depending on the purpose of the engagement. For example, compiled statements are frequently prepared for management, and they are aware of the limitations. Moreover, "when the accountant is aware that the statements may be misleading for some users or purposes, then the public accountant may need to include appropriate disclosures (in the statements, themselves, not the Notice to Reader) to prevent them from being misleading. Of course, if management will not allow the disclosures considered necessary, he or she has clearly no alternative but to withhold the statements and withdraw from the engagement" (R.J. Johnston, *CA Magazine,* May 1988, p. 53.) Despite this responsibility, keep in mind that with the limited amount of work involved in compilations there is no assurance that the PA can determine whether the financial statements achieve the specified intended purpose.

Communications Between Predecessors and Successors

In the case of audits, successor auditors are required to make certain enquiries of predecessor auditors when a new client is obtained (e.g., Rule 302 of Professional Conduct of ICAO). Rule 302 and similar rules of other accounting bodies in fact apply to all public accounting engagements, including compilation and review work.

Interpretation to Rule 302 gives advice to accountants when communicating with the predecessor. First, the successor accountant should ask the new client to notify the predecessor (incumbent) accountant of the proposed change by the client. The successor should then enquire of the predecessor "whether there are any circumstances that should be taken in account which might influence the potential successors' decision whether or not to accept the appointment" (Interpretation 302). Normally, the successor should await the reply of the predecessor before commencing work for the new client. The Interpretation also requires that the predecessor reply promptly to the successor's queries. When enquiries are made, the successor must obtain the client's permission for the predecessor to disclose confidential information. When confidentiality is in doubt, legal advice should be obtained. An important issue is how much effort the predecessor should make in supplying information to the successor. The interpretation suggests a minimum of discussing with the successor "reasonable information about the work being assumed" and then gives advice on what constitutes "reasonable."

In addition to the rules of professional conduct, PAs should be aware of any federal and provincial legislation, including securities legislation, regulating changes in professional appointments.

Personal Financial Plans

Personal financial planning has become a big source of business for PA firms. Most personal financial plan documentation includes personal financial statements. Ordinarily, an accountant associated with such statements would need to give the standard compilation report (disclaimer), which seems rather awkward in a personal financial planning engagement when the client is the only one using the statements. In Canada a PA who wishes to meet the requirements as a certified financial planner under the Financial Planning Standards

E X H I B I T 15–4   ## QUALIFICATION RESULTING FROM A DEPARTURE FROM GENERALLY ACCEPTED ACCOUNTING PRINCIPLES WHEN THE EFFECTS ARE NOT READILY DETERMINABLE (from *Handbook Section* 8200.B, example A)

REVIEW ENGAGEMENT REPORT

To (person engaging the public accountant)

I have reviewed the balance sheet of Client Limited as at ...., 20... and the statements of income, retained earnings and changes in financial position for the year then ended. My review was made in accordance with generally accepted standards for review engagements and accordingly consisted primarily of enquiry, analytical procedures and discussion related to information supplied to me by the company.

A review does not constitute an audit and consequently I do not express an audit opinion on these financial statements.

Note .... indicates that the investments in companies subject to significant influence have not been accounted for on the equity basis. The effects of this departure from generally accepted accounting principles on the unaudited financial statements have not been determined.

Except for the failure, as described in the preceding paragraph, to account for the investments on an equity basis, based on my review, nothing has come to my attention that causes me to believe that these financial statements are not, in all material respects, in accordance with generally accepted accounting principles

City

Date

(signed . . . .

CHARTERED ACCOUNTANT

Council of Canada must satisfy that body's Rules of Conduct in disclosing any potential conflicts of interest to his or her clients. Although there is no distinction for compilation of personal financial information in Canada, U.S. standards exempt such personal financial statements from the reporting requirement. However, the following report must be given, with each page of the financial report marked "See accountant's report":

> The accompanying Statement of Financial Condition of Edward Beliveau, as of December 31, 2002, was prepared solely to help you develop your personal financial plan. Accordingly, it may be incomplete or contain other departures from generally accepted accounting principles and should not be used to obtain credit or for any purposes other than developing your financial plan. We have not audited, reviewed, or compiled the statements.

E X H I B I T 15–5   ## ADVERSE REPORT RESULTING FROM A DEPARTURE FROM GENERALLY ACCEPTED ACCOUNTING PRINCIPLES (from *Section* 8200.B, example B)

REVIEW ENGAGEMENT REPORT

To (person engaging the public accountant)

I have reviewed the balance sheet of Client Limited as at ...., 20... and the statements of income, retained earnings and changes in financial position for the year then ended. My review was made in accordance with generally accepted standards for review engagements and accordingly consisted primarily of enquiry, analytical procedures and discussion related to information supplied to me by the company.

A review does not constitute an audit and consequently I do not express an audit opinion on these financial statements.

Note .... indicates that commencing this year the company ceased to consolidate the financial statements of its subsidiary companies because management considers consolidation to be inappropriate when there are substantial non-controlling interests. Under generally accepted accounting principles, the existence of such noncontrolling interests is not an acceptable reason for not consolidating the financial statements of subsidiary companies with those of the reporting enterprise. Had consolidated financial statements been prepared, virtually every account in, and the information provided by way of notes to, the accompanying financial statements would have been materially different. The effects of this departure from generally accepted accounting principles on the accompanying financial statements have not been determined.

My review indicates that, because the investment in subsidiary companies is not accounted for on a consolidated basis, as described in the preceding paragraph, these financial statements are not in accordance with generally accepted accounting principles.

City

Date

(signed) . . . .

CHARTERED ACCOUNTANT

E X H I B I T 15–6   **DENIAL OF ASSURANCE (from *Section* 8200.B, example D)**

REVIEW ENGAGEMENT REPORT

To (person engaging the public accountant)

I have reviewed the balance sheet of Client Limited as at ......, 20... and the statements of income, retained earnings and changes in financial position for the year then ended. My review was made in accordance with generally accepted standards for review engagements and accordingly consisted primarily of enquiry, analytical procedures and discussion related to information supplied to me by the company, except as explained below.

A review does not constitute an audit and consequently I do not express an audit opinion on these financial statements.

My review indicated serious deficiencies in the accounting records of the company. As a consequence, I was unable to complete my review. Had I been able to complete my review, I might have determined adjustments to be necessary to these financial statements.

Because of my inability to complete a review, as described in the preceding paragraph, I am unable to express any assurance as to whether these financial statements are, in all material respects, in accordance with generally accepted accounting principles.

City   (signed) ....
Date   CHARTERED ACCOUNTANT

A Note on GAAP Departures and Review Engagement Reports

An accountants' report of known GAAP departures must be treated carefully in review reports.

As in audit reports, the accountant can and should add an explanatory paragraph pointing out known departures from GAAP, including omitted disclosures. The knowledge of GAAP departures means that the accountant must make exception to the departure in the negative assurance sentence, like this: "Except for the failure, as described in the preceding paragraph, to (describe the departure), based on my review nothing has come to my attention . . ."

A separate paragraph describing the departure in more detail would be inserted as the next to last paragraph in the Review Engagement Report. See Exhibit 15–4 for the complete report.

The range of review reports possible is similar to that for audit reports, and they arise for similar reasons. Exhibit 15–5 illustrates an adverse report resulting from a GAAP departure, and Exhibit 15–6 illustrates a denial of assurance report as a result of a newer scope limitation.

· ·

R E V I E W
C H E C K P O I N T S

15.1 Explain what led to the creation of Review and Compilation Standards.

15.2 What considerations should a successor accountant make in accepting a new engagement?

15.3 How should a public accountant disclose misleading statements detected during a compilation engagement?

15.4 What is the difference between a review services engagement and a compilation service engagement regarding historical financial statements? Compare both of these to an audit engagement.

· ·

INTERIM FINANCIAL INFORMATION
· · · · · · · · · · · ·

LEARNING OBJECTIVE

2. List some interim information review procedures and write a report on a review of interim financial information.

Accounting principles do not require interim financial information as a basic and necessary element of financial statements conforming to GAAP. When interim information is presented, however, it should conform to the accounting Recommendation in the *CICA Handbook* (*Section* 1750). Examples of situations where audited interim financial statements might be prepared are buy/sell situations for a business, or to fulfill financial reports required by regulatory authorities, particularly those Canadian companies whose securities are traded in U.S. capital markets and therefore must comply with SEC requirements. On occasion, regulators such as the SEC may insist that the interim financial information be audited, but at the present time interim statements are not normally audited.

A common type of review engagement is the review of interim financial statements or information.

A review of interim financial information differs considerably from an audit. According to *Section* 8200.03, on procedures for review of interim financial statements, a key objective of a review of interim financial statements is to assess whether accounting principles have been applied on a basis consistent with the annual report as well as to the corresponding interim financial statements of the previous year. In particular the auditor is concerned that interim financial statements are not misleading relative to the annualized report. The interim review requires neither a complete assessment of internal control risk each quarter nor the gathering of sufficient, appropriate evidential matter on which to base an opinion on interim financial statements. The nature, timing and extent of review procedures explained below presume that the reviewer has a knowledge base of the company from the audit of the most recent annual financial statements. Note that the presumption of an existing audit knowledge base from the annual audit means there can be significantly more information guiding the review of interim statements than for a review without such a knowledge base. For this reason some observers feel that a review with an audit knowledge base provides more assurance than a review without an audit knowledge base. One significant difference, for example, is that the public accountant has more familiarity with the system of internal controls when there is an existing audit knowledge base.

Nature of Review Procedures

Review procedures consist mainly of enquiry and analytical procedures. *Section* 8200.02 and ISA 910.20 suggest checklists that includes the following:

- Enquire about the accounting system.
- Obtain an understanding of the system. Determine whether there have been any significant changes in the system used to produce interim information.
- Perform analytical procedures to identify relationships and individual items that appear to be unusual.
- Read the minutes of shareholder, board of director and board committee meetings to identify actions or events that may affect interim financial information.
- Read (study) the interim financial information and determine whether it conforms with generally accepted accounting principles.
- Obtain reports from other accountants who perform limited reviews of significant components, subsidiaries or other investees.
- Enquire of officers and executives about the following: Conformity with generally accepted accounting principles. Consistent application of accounting principles. Changes in the client's business or accounting practices. Matters about which questions have arisen as a result of applying other procedures (listed above). Events subsequent to the date of the interim information.
- Obtain written representations from management about interim information matters.

Timing of Review Procedures

Review procedures should be performed at or near the date of the interim information. Starting the engagement prior to the cutoff date will give auditors a chance to deal with problems and questions without undue deadline pressures.

Extent of Review Procedures

The accountant needs to acquire a sufficient knowledge of the client's business, just as if the engagement were a regular audit. Knowledge of strengths and deficiencies in the internal control system and of problem accounting areas obtained during the most recent audit is very useful in judging the extent of review procedures. Basically, the extent of review procedures depends on the accountant's professional judgment about problem areas in the system of internal control, the severity of unique accounting principles problems and the errors that have occurred in the past. With knowledge of these areas, the accountant can direct and fine-tune the review procedures in the interest of improving the quality of the interim information.

Reporting on a Review of Interim Information

An accountant may report on interim information presented separately from audited financial statements, provided that a review has been satisfactorily completed. The basic content of the report is as follows (*Section* 8200.04):

- A statement that a review was made in accordance with standards established for review engagements.
- An identification of the interim information reviewed.
- A description of the review procedures.
- A statement that a review is not an audit.
- A denial of opinion on the interim information.
- Negative assurance about material conformity with the disclosed basis of accounting.
- Each page should be marked "unaudited."

An actual report on reviewed interim information presented in a quarterly report (not within an annual report) is shown in Exhibit 15–7.

When the interim information is presented in a note to audited annual financial statements as supplemental information and when it is presented voluntarily under GAAP and the client has requested a review, the auditors give the standard audit report without mentioning the reviewed interim information, unless there is a reason to take exception. Under this exception basis of reporting, interim information is mentioned in a modified standard audit report only if it departs from *Section* 1750 principles, or if management indicates the auditor performed procedures without also saying the auditor expresses no opinion or if management fails to label interim information in the note to annual audited financial statements as "unaudited."

Additional Interim Information Communication

During the difficult economic times in the 1980s, especially in financial institutions, auditors were criticized in the United States for taking no action when they became aware of material problems with interim financial information. The auditors responded that they

---

E X H I B I T 15–7   **REPORT ON INTERIM INFORMATION IN A COMPANY'S QUARTERLY REPORT**

The Shareholders, XYZ Inc.:

At the request of the Board of Directors and Stockholders, we have made a review of the unaudited condensed balance sheets of Analog Devices, Inc., at April 28, 2000, and April 29, 1999, the related unaudited consolidated statements of income for the three- and six-month periods ended April 28, 2000, and April 29, 1999, and the unaudited consolidated statements of cash flows for the six-month periods ending April 28, 2000, and April 29, 1999, in accordance with standards established by the CICA.

A review of interim financial information consists principally of obtaining an understanding of the system for the preparation of the interim financial information, applying analytical review procedures to financial data and making inquiries to persons responsible for financial and accounting matters. It is substantially less in scope than an examination in accordance with generally accepted auditing standards, the objective of which is the expression of an opinion regarding the financial statements taken as a whole. Accordingly, we do not express such an opinion.

Based on our review, nothing has come to our attention that causes us to believe that the accompanying financial statements are not in all material respects in accordance with generally accepted accounting principles.

Public Accountants
Montreal, Quebec
May 16, 2000

were not required to take any action because they were not engaged to perform an interim review and issue a report.

Several regulatory agencies were distressed that some companies issued misleading interim information—sometimes their auditors knew about it—but nothing was done to inform the public or the regulators. Suggestions were conveyed to the AICPA Auditing Standards Board, and it responded with "Communication of Matters about Interim Financial Information Filed or to Be Filed with Specified Regulatory Agencies—An Amendment to SAS No. 36, Review of Interim Financial Information."

This AICPA standard requires that auditors do something when they learn that interim information filed or to be filed with certain specified agencies is probably materially misstated as a result of a departure from GAAP. The required action is to (*a*) discuss the matter with management as soon as possible, (*b*) inform the company's audit committee if management does not take appropriate and timely action, and (*c*) if the audit committee does not respond appropriately, decide whether to resign from the interim review engagement or resign as the company's auditor. However, auditing standards do not require resignation or direct communication to the "specified agencies." The auditing standard appears to be a compromise between regulators who probably wanted direct reporting and auditors who wanted to handle difficult problems within the affected companies. Again, this requirement only affects Canadian companies falling within the jurisdiction of the SEC.

R E V I E W
C H E C K P O I N T S

15.5   Is interim financial information required to be presented for annual financial statements to be in conformity with GAAP?

15.6   In what respects is a review of the interim financial information similar to a review of the unaudited annual financial statements of a nonpublic company?

15.7   When interim information is presented in a note to annual financial statements, under what circumstances would an audit report on the annual financial statements be modified with respect to the interim financial information?

SPECIAL REPORTS AND AADBA

LEARNING OBJECTIVE

3. Define, explain and give examples of another appropriate disclosed basis of accounting" (AADBA), distinguishing them from GAAP.

For a long time, a small war has been waged over the "Big GAAP–Little GAAP" controversy. Many accountants have been dismayed by the complexity of generally accepted accounting principles and have openly questioned their relevance to small businesses with uncomplicated operations. They believe that business managers and users of the financial statements care little about accounting for such things as pension obligations, capitalized leases, deferred taxes and similar complicated topics. They characterize such topics as "standards overload" that may be necessary for "big business" but are largely superfluous for "small business."

For a while, the "little GAAP" advocates lobbied for formal GAAP exemptions for small businesses. However, resistance was encountered in the counterargument that there was a danger of creating "second-class GAAP" for small business while reserving "real GAAP" for big companies. Bankers and other users of financial statements were not nearly so eager to have "little GAAP" financial statements as some accountants wanted them to be. Anyway, many small businesses aspire to be large businesses, and their managers may not want to be stigmatized by "little GAAP" beginnings. Another reason to distinguish different bases of accounting is that in some industries, notably banks and other financial institutions, there is no GAAP for the industry other than that specified by regulation. For example, in April 1989 in response to the November 1988 CICA Exposure Draft "Banks," the Superintendent of Financial Institutions stated that "until a great deal more work is done my office will not accept the inclusion of banks within the scope of the *Handbook*."[1]

---

[1] *Audit of the Allowance for Credit Losses*, CICA, 1993, p. 3.

In addition, there may be legislative reporting requirements that differ from the *Handbook;* for example, public sector reporting requirements to Parliament may deviate from those reflected in generally accepted public sector accounting principles. Also, some users of financial statements—limited groups of specified users—may have special information needs that necessitate reports deviating from GAAP: for example, financial statements in conformity with contractual requirements or buy/sell agreements. For all of these reasons, reports may be prepared on a basis other than GAAP using another appropriate basis of accounting (AADBA).

The authoritative literature on AADBA is in the form of *Handbook Sections* 5100.05-.06, 5701.14, AUG-12 and AUG-14. In 1996 and 1997 exposure drafts were issued in an attempt to further clarify the criteria for acceptable special reports. However, at the time of this writing (December 1999) it is not clear what the final changes will look like.

Studies in the United States have shown that AADBA financial statements can be less expensive to produce and easier to interpret than full GAAP statements. Surveys report that 50 percent of AADBA financial statements for small businesses are on the "tax basis of accounting," and 49 percent are on the "cash basis." However, these studies also show that AADBA is only appropriate when it meets user needs.

Another Appropriate Disclosed Basis of Accounting

Companies that are not subject to securities regulations and filing requirements can choose to present financial information in accordance with a comprehensive basis of accounting other than GAAP. A comprehensive basis in this context refers to a coherent accounting treatment in which substantially all the important financial measurements are governed by criteria other than GAAP. Examples include (1) treatment applied by financial institutions to statements conforming to the accounting rules of the Office of the Superintendent of Financial Institutions (OFSI) that are not in accordance with GAAP (as discussed in AUG–14, para 8), (2) tax basis accounting, (3) cash basis accounting, and (4) some other fairly well-defined methods, such as constant-dollar, price-level-adjusted financial statements.

AADBA financial statements should not use the titles normally associated with GAAP statements, such as "balance sheet," "statement of financial position," "statement of operations," "income statement," and "statement of cash flows."[2] Even the titles are said to suggest GAAP financial statements. Instead, AADBA statements should use titles like the ones shown in the following box.

SOME NON-GAAP FINANCIAL STATEMENT TITLES USED IN PRACTICE

Statement of Assets and Liabilities—Regulatory Basis.
Statement of Assets and Liabilities—Cash Basis.
Statement of Admitted Assets, Liabilities and Surplus—Statutory Basis Required by the Insurance Superintendent of the Province.

Statement of Assets, Liabilities and Capital—Income Tax Basis.
Statement of Income—Regulatory Basis.
Statement of Revenue and Expenses—Income Tax Basis.
Statement of Revenue Collected and Expenses Paid—Cash Basis.
Statement of Changes in Partners' Capital Accounts—Income Tax Basis.

---

[2] The only exception would be if AADBA were the only available alternatives, such as with the banking industry in Canada. See "GAAP vs. AADBA" by D. Cockburn, *CA Magazine*, January 1992, pp. 35–37.

AADBA statements can be audited, reviewed or compiled like any other financial statements. All the general and field work auditing standards and the standards for review and compilation apply, just as they apply for GAAP financial statements. The reporting standards regarding consistency, adequate disclosure and report responsibility (fourth reporting standard) also apply to AADBA statements. Disclosure requirements are not reduced by AADBA. However, the first reporting standard, which requires the audit report statement on whether the financial statements are presented in conformity with GAAP, is handled differently.

When a non-GAAP accounting method is used, the first reporting standard is satisfied by a sentence in the report that presents the AADBA basis of accounting; and the opinion sentence refers to the AADBA instead of to GAAP. Disclosures in the financial statements should (1) contain an explanation of the AADBA, and (2) describe in general how the AADBA differs from GAAP, but (3) the differences do not have to be quantified—that is, the AADBA does not need to be reconciled to GAAP with dollar amounts. For all practical purposes, the GAAP criteria are replaced by criteria applicable to the AADBA. (See *Handbook Section* 5701.14). An example of a special report on cash basis statements is in Exhibit 15–8.

GAAP, Other Than Historical Cost

You should be aware that GAAP sometimes is not historical cost. The prime examples are market value accounting for the assets in defined benefit pension plans, investment companies (e.g., venture capital companies, small business investment companies, mutual funds), and personal financial statements (e.g., individual or family). In these cases current value accounting is GAAP. The audit report on such financial statements gives an opinion that they are "in conformity with generally accepted accounting principles." No mention is made of an AADBA, because the current value accounting is GAAP and not an AADBA. Indeed, if such financial statements are prepared using the normal historical cost accounting, they contain departures from GAAP, and a qualified audit opinion would be given.

E X H I B I T 15–8   SPECIAL REPORT ON NON-GAAP COMPREHENSIVE BASIS

Independent Auditors' Report

To Trust North Bank Association (Trustee)
and the Unit Holders of the Mega Offshore Trust:

We have audited the accompanying statements of assets, liabilities, and trust corpus—cash basis, of the Mega Offshore Trust as of December 31, 2002 and 2001, and the related statements of changes in trust corpus—cash basis, for each of the three years in the period ended December 31, 2002. These financial statements are the responsibility of the Company's management. Our responsibility is to express an opinion on these financial statements based on our audits.

(Standard scope paragraph here)

As described in Note 2, these financial statements were prepared on the cash receipts and disbursements basis of accounting, which is a comprehensive basis of accounting other than generally accepted accounting principles.

In our opinion, the financial statements referred to above present fairly, in all material respects, the assets, liabilities and trust corpus arising from cash transactions of the Mega Offshore Trust as of December 31, 2002 and 2001, and the related changes in trust corpus arising from cash transactions for each of the three years in the period ended December 31, 2002, on the basis of accounting described in Note 2.

/s/ Auditor signature
March 18, 2003

Note 2 describes a cash basis of accounting and concludes:

This basis for reporting royalty income is considered to be the most meaningful because distributions to the Unit holders for a month are based on net cash receipts for such month. However, it will differ from the basis used for financial statements prepared in accordance with generally accepted accounting principles because, under such accounting principles, royalty income for a month would be based on net proceeds for such month without regard to when calculated or received.

OPINION PARAGRAPH ON LIQUIDATION BASIS STATEMENTS

In our opinion, the financial statements referred to above present fairly, in all material respects, the financial position of Canada Liquidating Corporation at December 31, 2002, and the excess of revenues over costs and expenses and its cash flows for the year then ended, in conformity with generally accepted accounting principles for a company in liquidation.

Another informally recognized basis of accounting that has no formal body of rules is "liquidation basis accounting." Some mention is made of this basis in the literature, but you will not find much official guidance. In fact there is some controversy as to whether the liquidation basis of accounting is GAAP or AADBA when the going concern assumption is no longer appropriate. One of the authors found that there is a split opinion on this within the CICA (as of December 1999). Nevertheless, auditors sometimes give reports on liquidation basis financial statements without referring to them as an AADBA. An excerpt is in the box above. (Be aware, however, that this type of opinion is not illustrated in any standard. It was invented in practice.)

R E V I E W
CHECKPOINTS

15.8   Why does AADBA exist? Can AADBA financial statements be audited?

15.9   Why do you think standard setters have not created "little GAAP" by exempting small businesses from compliance with many complicated accounting standards?

15.10   What should auditors do about the fourth reporting standard when financial statements are presented on a comprehensive basis of accounting other than GAAP?

Current Value Financial Statements

LEARNING OBJECTIVE

4. Explain the content of an auditor's report on supplementary current value financial statements in comparison to a standard report on historical cost financial statements.

Accounting theorists have long favoured various measurements in current value accounting, including discounted present value of cash flows, entry values (replacement cost, current cost), and exit values (disposal value, current cash equivalent) for all types of companies and industries. Measurement by anything other than historical cost received little notice from the practising profession until the mid-1970s, when five things happened: (1) inflation accelerated in Canada and worldwide; (2) critics voiced loud discontent with historical-cost measurement; (3) British, Australian, Dutch and other accountants started promoting accounting measurement alternatives; (4) the SEC issued Accounting Series Release No. 190 requiring disclosure of certain replacement cost information; and (5) the CICA moved into the phase of considering new measurement bases, including some kinds of current value accounting, which culminated in *Handbook Section* 4510 recommending the presentation of supplementary information on both a current cost and price level adjusted basis. (This section was dropped in the early 1990s.)

Interest on the part of accountants in current value and inflation-adjusted financial statements virtually disappeared with the decline in the inflation rate after 1985. However, as the number of failures among banks and trust companies, brokerages and financial services companies surged after 1984, regulators began to beat the drum for "mark to market" (current value) accounting for loans and securities held by financial institutions. In 1992 the FASB made some rules requiring disclosure of market values for financial institution assets. Many regulators also require disclosure of current market values on a supplemental basis.

In the past the real estate and the hotel/motel industries have been particularly interested in reporting the current value of real estate assets. One of the earliest disclosures of cur-

EXHIBIT 15–9   REPORT ON CURRENT VALUE FINANCIAL STATEMENTS

THE ROUSE COMPANY AND SUBSIDIARIES
Consolidated Cost Basis and Current Value Basis Balance Sheets
December 31, 1991 and 1990
(in thousands)

	1991		1990	
	Current Value Basis (note 1)	Cost Basis	Current Value Basis (note 1)	Cost Basis
Assets				
Property (notes 4, 5, 8 and 14):				
Operating properties:				
Current value	$3,638,801		$3,825,882	
Property and deferred costs of projects		$2,482,292		$2,424,003
Less accumulated depreciation and amortization		331,312		287,365
	3,638,801	2,150,980	3,825,882	2,136,638
Development operations:				
Construction and development in progress	59,513	54,290	56,186	49,890
Pre-construction costs, net	14,734	14,734	17,196	17,196
	74,247	69,024	73,382	67,086
Property held for development and sale . . .	192,195	158,472	166,616	125,387
Other property, net (note 14)	18,878	9,004	20,234	9,727
Other assets	87,843	87,843	78,338	78,338
Accounts and notes receivable (note 6) . . .	75,547	75,547	85,153	85,153
Investments in marketable securities	27,505	27,505	41,758	41,578
Cash and cash equivalents	59,077	59,077	70,790	70,790
Total	$4,174,093	$2,637,452	$4,362,153	$2,614,877

Independent Auditors' Report

The Board of Directors and Shareholders,
The Rouse Company:

We have audited the accompanying consolidated cost basis balance sheets of The Rouse Company and subsidiaries as of December 31, 1991 and 1990, and the related consolidated cost basis statements of operations, common stock, and other shareholders' equity and cash flows for each of the years in the three-year period ended December 31, 1991. We have also audited the supplemental consolidated current value basis balance sheets of The Rouse Company and subsidiaries as of December 31, 1991 and 1990, and the related supplemental consolidated current value basis statements of changes in revaluation equity for each of the years in the three-year period ended December 31, 1991. These financial statements are the responsibility of the Company's management. Our responsibility is to express an opinion on these financial statements based on our audits.

We conducted our audits in accordance with generally accepted auditing standards. Those standards require that we plan and perform the audit to obtain reasonable assurance about whether the financial statements are free of material misstatement. An audit includes examining, on a test basis, evidence supporting the amounts and disclosures in the financial statements. An audit also includes assessing the accounting principles used and significant estimates made by management, as well as evaluating the overall financial statement presentation. We believe that our audits provide a reasonable basis for our opinion.

In our opinion, the aforementioned consolidated cost basis financial statements present fairly, in all material respects, the financial position of The Rouse Company and subsidiaries at December 3, 1991 and 1990, and the results of their operations and their cash flows for each of the years in the three-year period ended December 31, 1991, in conformity with generally accepted accounting principles.

As more fully described in note 1 to the consolidated financial statements, the supplemental consolidated current value basis financial statements referred to above have been prepared by management to present relevant financial information about The Rouse Company and its subsidiaries which is not provided by the cost basis financial statements and are not intended to be a presentation in conformity with generally accepted accounting principles. In addition, as more fully described in note 1, the supplemental consolidated current value basis financial statements do not purport to present the net realizable, liquidation or market value of the Company as a whole. Furthermore, amounts ultimately realized by the Company from the disposal of properties may vary from the current values presented.

In our opinion, the aforementioned supplemental consolidated current value basis financial statements present fairly, in all material respects, the information set forth therein on the basis of accounting described in note 1 to the consolidated financial statements.

KPMG Peat Marwick
February 19, 1992

rent asset values was by the Rouse Company, owners of several major mall developments. Excerpts from the balance sheet and the audit report are in Exhibit 15–9. You can see that the audit report contains an unqualified opinion on the historical cost financial statements. It also contains an explanatory paragraph, complete with cautions about the realization of the current values, and a special report opinion on the current value information.

Auditors can accept engagements to audit and report on current value financial statements as long as (1) the company's measurement and disclosure criteria are reasonable and (2) the measurements and disclosures are reasonably reliable. However, auditing standards do not acknowledge general current financial statements to be a stand-alone AADBA. They regard the current value information as supplementary to the GAAP financial statements. (In this regard general current-value financial statements are different from current value as GAAP for defined benefit plans, investment companies and personal financial statements, and also different from a stand-alone AADBA, such as cash basis accounting.)

. . . .

R E V I E W
C H E C K P O I N T S

15.11   What are some examples of AADBA? of entities for which current value is GAAP? of current value financial statements that are supplementary to historical financial statements?

15.12   Insofar as the opinion paragraph in an audit report is concerned, what difference does the client's use of an AADBA make? What difference if the client is one for whom current value is GAAP? What difference if a real estate or manufacturing company presents supplementary current value information?

. . . .

Special Reports—Additional Topics

Auditors may perform a variety of services acting in the capacity of auditor (not as tax adviser or management consultant) that require a report, other than the standard unqualified audit report. Such services involve special reports issued in connection with:

- Engagements to report on specified elements, accounts or items of a financial statement (*Section* 5805 or ISA 800).
- Engagements to report on compliance with contractual agreements or regulatory requirements (*Section* 5815 or ISA 800).
- Limited-scope engagements to perform procedures agreed on by the client (*Section* 9100 or ISA 920).

Specified Elements, Accounts or Items

Auditors may be requested to render special reports on such things as rentals, royalties, profit participations or a provision for income taxes. The fourth CICA reporting standard does not apply because the specified element, account or item does not purport to be a financial statement of financial position or results of operations. The consistency disclosure via footnotes should be made in all cases.

Special engagements with limited objectives enable auditors to provide needed services to clients. *Section* 5805 gives the standards for these engagements. Examples include grant application data, reports relating to amount of sales used in computing rental, reports relating to royalties, reports on a profit participation and a report on the adequacy of a tax provision in financial statements. Exhibit 15–10 contains an illustrative report on a company's accounts receivable.

Compliance with Contractual Agreements or Regulatory Requirements

Clients may have restrictive covenants in loan agreements. Lenders may require a periodic report on whether the client has complied with such contractual agreements. Following a

EXHIBIT 15–10   **EXAMPLE OF A REPORT ON A SCHEDULE OF ACCOUNTS RECEIVABLE**
(from *Handbook Section* 5805.19)

AUDITOR'S REPORT
ON SCHEDULE OF ACCOUNTS RECEIVABLE

To the Directors of Client Limited

I have audited the schedule of accounts receivable of Client Limited as at ...., 20... This financial information is the responsibility of the management of Client Limited. My responsibility is to express an opinion on this financial information based on my audit.

I conducted my audit in accordance with generally accepted auditing standards. Those standards require that I plan and perform an audit to obtain reasonable assurance whether the financial information is free of material misstatement. An audit includes examining, on a test basis, evidence supporting the amounts and disclosures in the financial information. An audit also includes assessing the accounting principles used and significant estimates made by management, as well as evaluating the overall presentation of the financial information.

In my opinion, this schedule presents fairly, in all material respects, the accounts receivable of Client Limited as at ...., 20... in accordance with generally accepted accounting principles.

City   (signed) ....
Date   CHARTERED ACCOUNTANT

---

scope paragraph referring to the report on the audited financial statements, the auditor may give a negative assurance of the following type:

> In connection with our audit, nothing came to our attention that caused us to believe that the company failed to comply with the terms, covenants, provisions, or conditions of sections 32 through 46 of the indenture dated January 1, 1988, with North Country Bank. However, our audit examination was not directed primarily toward obtaining knowledge of such non-compliance.

A similar negative assurance may be given with regard to federal and provincial regulatory requirements. Examples include limitations on investments for mutual funds, and provincial insurance commissioner regulations about the nature of insurance company investments. When the auditor is engaged to provide an audit opinion as to a client's compliance with criteria established by provisions of agreements statutes or regulations, *Section* 5815 provides the appropriate guidance. In this case positive assurance is provided and other than criteria and scope the auditor's report is similar to that for audits of financial statements. An example of an opinion on compliance given in a separate report is provided in Exhibit 15–11.

Regulatory agencies may seek to have auditors sign assertions in prescribed report language that go beyond acceptable professional reporting responsibilities and involve auditors in areas outside their function and responsibility. In such cases auditors should insert additional wording in the prescribed report language or write a completely revised report that reflects adequately their position and responsibility.

Applying Agreed-upon Procedures

In some cases clients may ask auditors to perform a specified set of procedures—the agreed-upon procedures—to examine a particular element, account or item in a financial statement. Such work should not be considered an audit because the specified set of agreed-upon procedures is usually not sufficient to be considered in accordance with generally accepted auditing standards. These special-purpose engagements have a limited scope, so the second and third GAAS examination standards (control risk assessment and sufficient competent evidence for an opinion) and the GAAS reporting standards do not apply.

For example, a client may request procedures on the long-term debt of a company it plans to acquire—not an audit of the company's complete financial statements. *Section* 9100, "Reports on the Results of Applying Specified Auditing Procedures," gives an exam-

EXHIBIT 15–11   **EXAMPLE OF AN OPINION ON COMPLIANCE GIVEN IN A SEPARATE REPORT** (from *Handbook Section 5815.11*)

AUDITOR'S REPORT
ON COMPLIANCE WITH AGREEMENT

To A Trust Company Limited

I have audited Client Limited's compliance as at December 31, 20X1 with the criteria established by (describe nature of provisions to be complied with) described in Sections ...... to ...... inclusive of (name of agreement) dated ...., 20... with (name of party to agreement) and the interpretation of such agreement as set out in note 1 attached. Compliance with the criteria established by the provisions of the agreement is the responsibility of the management of Client Limited. My responsibility is to express an opinion on this compliance based on my audit.

I conducted my audit in accordance with generally accepted auditing standards. Those standards require that I plan and perform an audit to obtain reasonable assurance whether Client Limited complied with the criteria established by the provisions of the agreement referred to above. Such an audit includes examining, on a test basis, evidence supporting compliance, evaluating the overall compliance with the agreement, and where applicable, assessing the accounting principles used and significant estimates made by management.

In my opinion, Client Limited is in compliance, in all material respects, with the criteria established by (the provisions to be complied with) described in Sections ...... to ...... of this agreement.

City   (signed) ....
Date   CHARTERED ACCOUNTANT

EXHIBIT 15–12   **EXAMPLE OF A REPORT ON SPECIFIED AUDITING PROCEDURES CARRIED OUT ON LONG-TERM DEBT** (from *Handbook Section* 9100.13)

To A. Trustee Limited

As specifically agreed, I have performed the following procedures in connection with the above company's certificate dated ...., 20.... as to the amount of the company's Funded Obligations as at ...., 20....:

(list the procedures)

As a result of applying the above procedures, I found no (the following) exceptions (list of exceptions). However these procedures do not constitute an audit of the company's Funded Obligations and therefore I express no opinion on the amount of Funded Obligations as at ...., 20.....

This letter is for use solely in connection with the closing on ...., 20.... of the issue of .... securities of the company.

City   (signed) ....
Date   CHARTERED ACCOUNTANT

---

ple report on such an engagement. The scope paragraph, quoted above in Exhibit 15–12, is clearly not a standard scope explanation describing an audit in accordance with generally accepted auditing standards:

The conclusions paragraph quoted earlier follows the recommendation in *Section* 9100 by (1) denying an audit opinion on the accounts and items, (2) giving a negative assurance as to "no exceptions," (3) listing the procedures, and (4) stating that the report is for restricted use only. You can see how the objectives of this kind of service are very limited and how the report conclusions are also very limited.

REPORTING ON INTERNAL CONTROL
• • • • • • • • • • •

LEARNING OBJECTIVE

5. Describe the various reports on internal control and their connection with public reporting and reporting to a client's audit committee.

Managements and boards of directors have been encouraged to make public reports on internal control, and auditors have been encouraged by the regulators such as Quebec's inspector general of financial institutions to become associated with such reports. Many annual reports of public companies contain a "report from management" that includes brief commentary about internal control responsibilities. Apart from these brief reports, public reports on internal control are not commonplace.

The topic of internal control reports has led a topsy-turvy life. In 1980 the SEC expressed the belief that management's comments in its own report on controls were "other information" and that auditors had a responsibility to disclose any material deficiencies that management did not disclose. This event prompted the Auditing Standards Board to issue an interpretation stating that auditors are responsible for seeing whether a management report contains a material misstatement of fact or fails to be complete insofar as known material weaknesses in internal accounting control are concerned. In 1983 the SEC expressed satisfaction with management's tendency toward volunteering reports on internal accounting control and decided not to require such reports. At the same time, the SEC dropped its consideration of requiring some form of auditor association with management's comments on control. At the time the SEC was in a "deregulation mode" and loath to enact new requirements. In 1988 the SEC once again proposed a rule to require a management report on companies' internal control. Nothing came of this proposal. However, by 1991, with bank failures at an all-time high, Congress passed legislation requiring internal control reports by insured depository institutions. The Auditing Standards Board may delete its current standard on internal control reports and issue a related statement on assurance standards regarding management's report on internal control.

Meanwhile in Canada similar concerns about banks and trust and insurance companies prompted the CICA to issue the Auditing Guideline "Special Reports on Regulated Financial Institutions" in May 1992 (AUG-13).

Regulated financial institutions such as banks, insurance and trust companies, pension funds, mutual funds and investment dealers often include special reporting responsibilities beyond those for financial statements to shareholders. The auditor must sometimes communicate in writing transactions or conditions that come to his or her attention (i.e., negative assurance is provided). This form of communication is referred to as a derivative report. At other times the auditor is required to carry out procedures relating to the matters specified in addition to those required by GAAS. The required communication that reports on such specified procedures is referred to as a nonderivative report.

Especially in the case of derivative reporting, the audit firm should take steps to inform all staff providing services to the financial institution to be sensitized to this reporting responsibility and to be observant concerning potentially relevant transactions or conditions.

When considering an appointment as auditor of a financial institution, the public accountant should obtain an understanding of any special reporting responsibilities and if necessary contact the regulator or obtain interpretation of the regulatory responsibility from legal counsel.

The extent of management involvement will vary with the nature of the special reporting responsibility to the regulator. As a minimum, however, management will need to have an understanding of (*a*) the reporting responsibility, (*b*) the information, including management representation, that the auditor will need, and (*c*) the process the auditor will follow in issuing a report. All understanding should be documented in writing.

Normally, the auditor would send a copy of the report to the board of directors and other members of management before sending the report to the regulator. In some cases the auditor may wish to seek legal advice and report solely to the regulator.

A derivative report is a by-product of the financial statement audit. The only additional audit procedures are (1) understanding and clarifying the derivative reporting responsibility, (2) making all relevant parties aware of it, and (3) reporting separately to the regulator.

The auditor looks for evidence that affects the viability of the financial institution. Unfortunately, the legislation governing auditor's responsibilities often uses such general and subjective terms as "sound financial practices," and "well-being," which are left to the auditor's judgement, and this may differ from the regulator's interpretation (for example, see AUG–17). This may lead to varying interpretations of the matters specified by legislation and to inconsistencies in the types of transactions or conditions identified and reported by auditors.

As a result there are three limitations on the usefulness of derivative reports.

1. The auditor is not required to carry out procedures directed at providing positive assurance on the matters or reportable conditions specified in legislation.

2. There may be no comprehensive and precise interpretation of the matters or reportable conditions.

3. The financial statement audit may not be designed to address such matters.

In deciding on the types of matters or reportable conditions that should go into a derivative report, the auditor should consider not only the significance of individual transactions and conditions encountered, but also whether a combination of insignificant items should be included in the derivative report. The findings should be discussed with appropriate levels of management, including the audit committee.

The derivative report should be titled "Derivative Report by the Auditor." An illustration is given in Exhibit 15–13.

A nonderivative reporting responsibility involves a reporting engagement separate from the audit of the financial statements. Unique features of such engagements are:

1. The auditor may be asked to provide an opinion without a specific assertion from management.

2. The auditor may be required to report directly to the regulator.

3. The matters are often subjective and thus open to different interpretations, and there may be no established criteria for evaluating the matters.

The Special Reports Recommendations can be applied to many of the nonderivative reporting responsibilities specified in legislation. For example, *Sections* 5805, 5815, 8500, 8600, and 9100 can all be relevant for specific nonderivative reporting engagements. AUG–13 focuses on the following nonderivative reporting engagement matters:

1. The methods of management concerning administration and safekeeping of property administered for others.

2. The methods of management adopted by the company to comply with laws relating to self-dealing and conflicts of interest.

3. The procedures adopted by management to safeguard the interests of creditors and members.

E X H I B I T 15–13   **DERIVATIVE REPORT BY THE AUDITOR (from CICA Guideline AUG–13, example A)**

To the Chief Executive Officer of X Financial Institution:

I have audited the financial statements of X Financial Institution as at December 31, 20X1 and for the year then ended, and reported thereon under date of February 19, 20X2.

Pursuant to the requirements of Section XXX of the Y Act (the Act), I am required to report to you any transactions or conditions encountered during the aforementioned audit that (describe matters specified in legislation). For the purposes of understanding the types of transactions or conditions that (describe matters specified in legislation), I have used the following interpretations developed from the following sources:

(Describe the interpretations used and the sources of such interpretations)

During the course of the aforementioned audit, based on the interpretations referred to above, I encountered no relevant transactions or conditions.

No procedures have been carried out in addition to those necessary to form an opinion on the financial statements.

This report has been prepared in accordance with the applicable Auditing and Related Services Guideline issued by the Canadian Institute of Chartered Accountants, and is to be used solely to satisfy the requirements of Section XXX of the Act and should not be referred to or used for any other purpose.

City   (signed) . . . .
Date   CHARTERED ACCOUNTANT

cc: Superintendent of Financial Institutions

Legislation may require an opinion on the adequacy of methods of management, the effectiveness of controls or the adequacy of procedures. However, to do the job the auditor needs to understand a regulator's expectations. The auditor requires reasonable and attainable standards and criteria to serve as benchmarks for evaluating the adequacy of matters to be reported on. Most legislation does not specify the criteria to be used. The auditor may need to consult with the regulator. An agreement reached on appropriate criteria should be put in writing.

It is also desirable to put in writing any other terms of the engagement with the regulator, such as form of opinion and the period to be covered.

If criteria cannot be established in consultation with the regulator, the auditor may agree to (1) industry standards, (2) authoritative literature, (3) other specialists, and (4) management's view on the matters to be reported on. In all cases it is important for the auditor to describe in his or her report the criteria used and the source of the criteria.

The general and applicable examination standards of *Section* 5100 apply to nonderivative reports. The auditor should obtain an understanding of the policies and procedures established by the client to address the matters on which the auditor is to report. The auditor would also obtain sufficient evidence as to whether the policies and procedures existed and operated effectively throughout the period covered by the report; and evaluate the adequacy of policies and procedures against appropriate criteria.

The auditor should obtain a letter of representation from management concerning management's responsibility for the legislated matters and responsibility to inform the auditor of the status of policies and procedures that affect the legislated matters.

The auditor's report is addressed to the party specified in legislation and should be titled "Auditor's Report on [specify matters]." The report consists of an introductory paragraph, a scope paragraph, an opinion paragraph (that there is reasonable assurance that matters being reported on were adequate or effective) and a concluding paragraph stating that the report has been prepared in accordance with this guideline and is to be used solely to satisfy the legislative requirement. (An example of a nonderivative report is given in Exhibit 15-14.)

A reservation in a nonderivative report would be guided by the recommendations in *Section* 5510.

Public and Restricted Reports

Several different kinds of reports on internal control based on a special study of controls have evolved in practice:

- Public reports on control in effect as of a specific date.
- Public reports on control in effect during a specified time period.
- Restricted use reports based on the control risk assessment work during an audit, not sufficient for expressing an opinion on control.
- Restricted use reports based on regulatory agencies' pre-established criteria.
- Restricted use reports based on a review without tests of controls or based on application of agreed-upon procedures.

Some restricted use reports have been illustrated in Exhibits 15–13 and 15–14. Other restricted use internal control reports are covered in *Section* 5900, "Opinions on Control Procedures in Service Organizations," and in *Section* 5750. It is the public reports on internal controls for which we have little authoritative Canadian guidance currently. As an illustration of what we may expect, the Standard (Public) Report on Internal Control in the United States, which is based on a special study of internal controls, is provided in Exhibit 15–15. There, you can see that the last paragraph expresses positive assurance (opinion) on the controls. We will discuss general assurance engagements later in this chapter.

When reporting to a regulatory agency, reports modelled on this standard form may be acceptable. If not, a special report can be issued that, among other things, states the accoun-

E X H I B I T   15–14   **(from CICA Guideline AUG–13, example B)**

Example of a nonderivative report when:

(i) legislation require the auditor to report to the regulator directly on the adequacy of the procedures adopted to safeguard the interests of creditors and members; and

(ii) the auditor has decided on appropriate criteria.

AUDITOR'S REPORT ON PROCEDURES TO SAFEGUARD THE INTERESTS OF CREDITORS AND MEMBERS

To the Superintendent of Financial Institutions:

Pursuant to the requirements of Section XXX of the Act Respecting X Financial Institutions (the Act), I have audited the procedures employed by XYZ Financial Institution (the Company) to safeguard the interests of its creditors and members for the year ended December 31, 20XX. These procedures are the responsibility of the Company's management. My responsibility is to express an opinion on these procedures based on my audit.

I conducted my audit in accordance with generally accepted auditing standards. Those standards require that I plan and perform an audit to obtain reasonable assurance whether the procedures adopted by the Company were adequate to safeguard the interests of its creditors and members based on appropriate criteria. Such an audit includes obtaining an understanding of the procedures employed by management to safeguard the interests of creditors and members, obtaining sufficient appropriate audit evidence to determine whether these procedures operated effectively throughout the year and evaluating the adequacy of the procedures against appropriate criteria. I used the following criteria developed from the sources noted:

(Describe the criteria used and the sources of such criteria)

Because of the inherent limitations of any procedures adopted by a financial institution to safeguard the interests of its creditors and members, only reasonable assurance can be obtained with respect to the adequacy of such procedures.

In my opinion, based on the above criteria, there is reasonable assurance that the procedures adopted by the Company for the year ended December 31, 20XX were adequate to safeguard the interests of its creditors and members.

This report has been prepared in accordance with the applicable Auditing and Related Services Guideline issued by The Canadian Institute of Chartered Accountants, and is intended to be used solely to satisfy the requirements of Section XXX of the Act and should not be referred to or used for any other purpose.

City   (signed) . . . .
Date   CHARTERED ACCOUNTANT

cc: Senior company management

---

tant's conclusions based on the agency's criteria and restricts use of the report to the agency (see Exhibit 15–14). Such reports most often are requested in connection with audits of financial institutions.

Other special-purpose reports on control systems can be issued, but their scope is generally limited. Such reports should (*a*) describe the scope of the engagement, (*b*) disclaim an opinion on the system as a whole, (*c*) state the accountant's findings, and (*d*) restrict the report to management or specified third parties (*Section* 5220).

A problem with the public report noted in Exhibit 15–15 relates to which internal controls should be evaluated. For example, should only accounting controls be evaluated? accounting controls plus operational controls? accounting controls plus operational plus management controls? These questions relate to what should be the internal control objectives for publicly issued internal control reports. Other questions in regard to issuing public general-purpose internal control reports relate to the criteria to be used in evaluating controls. (For example, is effectiveness of management and operating controls too subjective to be measured and evaluated? Current standards focus on accounting controls.) Also, what procedures should the auditors perform in support of such a report, and how should they distinguish between review and examination of internal controls? Some feel these issues can be addressed in a broader attestation/assurance framework rather than in a specific internal control framework.

In May 1990 the CICA sponsored a conference on "criteria of control." The conclusion was that to report on internal control the CICA needed to develop systems criteria for internal control similar to GAAP in accounting. Only with such criteria would auditors be able to address Recommendation 49 of the Macdonald Commission Report (1988) to evaluate

EXHIBIT 15-15   **REPORTING ON INTERNAL ACCOUNTING CONTROL**

To the Company, Directors, Stockholders,
Management, a Regulatory Agency, or Specified Others:

We have made a study and evaluation of the system of internal accounting control of Anycompany and subsidiaries in effect at December 31, 2000. Our study and evaluation was conducted in accordance with standards established by the American Institute of Certified Public Accountants.

The management of Anycompany is responsible for establishing and maintaining a system of internal accounting control. In fulfilling this responsibility, estimates and judgements by management are required to assess the expected benefits and related costs of control procedures. The objectives of a system are to provide management with reasonable, but not absolute, assurance that assets are safeguarded against loss from unauthorized use or disposition, and that transactions are executed in accordance with management's authorization and recorded properly to permit the preparation of financial statements in accordance with generally accepted accounting principles.

Because of inherent limitations in any system of internal accounting control, errors or irregularities may occur and not be detected. Also, projection of any evaluation of the system to future periods is subject to the risk that procedures may become inadequate because of changes in conditions, or that the degree of compliance with the procedures may deteriorate.

In our opinion, the system of internal accounting control of Anycompany and subsidiaries in effect at December 31, 2000, taken as a whole, was sufficient to meet the objectives stated above insofar as those objectives pertain to the prevention or detection of errors or irregularities in amounts that would be material in relation to the consolidated financial statements.

/s/ Auditor signature, PA
February 18, 2001

and report on the design and functioning of internal control systems of financial institutions. With this goal in mind, the CICA's board of governors established the Criteria of Control Committee in 1992. The initial focus of this committee is on financial reporting controls, but an attempt will also be made to develop generic control principles that would also be applicable to operations.

In November 1995 the Criteria of Control Committee of the CICA issued its first publication in the control and governance series, "Guidance on Criteria on Control," or "COCO," for short. The executive summary of the exposure draft provides a useful perspective on the committee's work efforts so far and is therefore reproduced here in full.

The guidance describes and defines control and sets out criteria for its effectiveness. The guidance is applicable to all kinds of organizations, and to part of organizations.

The guidance adopts a broad understanding of control. It involves the coordination of activities toward the achievement of objectives, and includes the identification and mitigation of known risks, the identification and exploitation of opportunities, and the capacity to respond and adapt to the unexpected. Thus, control can provide assurance regarding a broad range of objectives in three general categories: the effectiveness and efficiency of operations, the reliability of financial and management reporting, and compliance with applicable laws and regulations and internal policies.

While people at all levels of an organization participate in control, the decisions and actions of senior management and the board of directors and their level of interest in control set the tone. Management is accountable for control, and therefore needs to assess its overall functioning.

The guidance sets out a control framework, which is a way of looking at an organization so that important aspects of control and relationships between them are apparent. The guidance acknowledges that no one control framework will be perfectly suited to all organizations. It also gives examples of how the criteria can be reorganized into other frameworks, and how other management approaches such as total quality management can be compared to the control framework.

The guidance sets out twenty-three control criteria, stated at a high level in order to be broadly applicable. They address areas such as the culture and values that support good control; objective-setting, risk assessment and planning; control activities that provide assurance that necessary actions are performed; and the monitoring of all aspects of performance to learn what improvements are required. Considerable judgement will be required in applying the criteria, for example, in interpreting them into actionable steps that can be integrated with other management activities; in identifying indicators or early-warning signs so that timely reporting about control can be integrated with reporting about other aspects of performance; and in deciding on the acceptability of risk remaining after control processes have been taken into account.

COCO is written in general, abstract terms in order to provide a flexible framework for future guidelines. The primary intended audience of the guidelines are "auditors who are asked to provide assurance on the reliability of assertions about effectiveness of controls." Control is defined as comprising "those elements of an organization (including its resources, systems, processes, culture, structure and taxes) that, taken together, support people in the achievement of the organization's objectives."

According to the guidance, key concepts in evaluating controls are as follows:

1. Control is effected by people throughout the organization, including the board of directors or its equivalent,[3] management and all other staff.

2. People who are accountable, as individuals or teams, for achieving objectives should also be accountable for the effectiveness of control that supports achievement of those objectives.

3. Organizations are constantly interacting and adapting.

4. Control can be expected to provide only reasonable assurance, not absolute assurance.

5. Effective control demands that a balance be maintained:
   i) Between autonomy and integration—Keeping this balance often involves shifting between centralization and decentralization and between imposing constraints to achieve consistency and granting freedom to act.
   ii) Between the statuus quo and adapting to change—Keeping this balance often involves shifting between demanding greater consistency to gain efficiency and granting greater flexibility to respond to change.

Perhaps the most important features of the guidelines are the 20 control criteria they identify. They are quite detailed but can be summarized by the following categories or components:

1. Purpose groups criteria, which provide a sense of the organization's direction. They address:
   • objectives (including mission, vision and strategy)
   • risks (and opportunities)
   • policies
   • planning
   • performance targets and indicators

2. Commitment groups criteria, which provide a sense of the organization's identity and values. They address:
   • ethical values, including integrity
   • human resource policies
   • authority, responsibility and accountability
   • mutual trust

3. Capability groups criteria, which provide a sense of the organization's competence. They address:
   • knowledge, skills and tools
   • communication processes
   • information
   • co-ordination
   • control activities

---

[3] The governing body of a government or not-for-profit entity may be called by a different name. In a unit within an organization, the equivalent to the board of directors is the senior management or other leadership group.

4. Monitoring and learning groups criteria, which provide a sense of the organization's evolution. They address:
   - monitoring internal and external environments
   - monitoring performance
   - challenging assumptions
   - reassessing information needs and information systems
   - follow-up procedures
   - assessing the effectiveness of control

The basic control framework consists of the definition of control and the criteria as summarized by the broad categories.

Reaction to the criteria appear to be favourable so far. They are consistent with the Canadian philosophy of developing guidelines that are not too detailed so that they resemble a "cookbook" approach to evaluating controls. The committee deliberately crafted the criteria at a high level so that they could be applied to all systems at all organizations. There is considerable scope for experimentation and creativity, and auditors will have to use considerable professional judgement in applying the criteria to specific situations.

There is a comparable effort in the United States titled Internal Control—An Integrated Framework (commonly referred to as COSO). Although both COCO and COSO have the same objective of providing guidance about control and criteria for control, COCO builds on COSO by expanding the notion of what control is and taking a particularly people-oriented approach.

At the present time the guidance will not be included in the *CICA Handbook*. The guidance therefore will not have the authority of *Handbook* accounting or auditing recommendations. A member's decision to use the control guidance to assess internal controls will depend on whether he or she finds the guidance useful and relevant. In this sense the guidance is somewhat experimental.

A second project of the CICA Criteria of Control Committee is the Guidance for Directors—Governance processes for control issued in December 1995. This is the second in a series addressing various aspects of control systems. The purpose of the document is to set out guidance on governance processes to meet the responsibilities of board of directors to control.

It identifies six key areas of board control responsibilities.

1. Establishing and monitoring the organization's ethical values.

2. Approval and monitoring of mission, vision and strategy.

3. Overseeing external communication.

4. Evaluating senior management.

5. Monitoring management control systems.

6. Assessing the board's effectiveness.

The primary focus of the document and of Guidance on Criteria of Control is shown in Exhibit 15–16. This exhibit illustrates the evolving framework for evaluating management and operational controls as part of the internal control framework. To assist auditors in interpreting this guidance relative to other authoritative pronouncements, the Criteria of Control Committee prepared a degree of authoritativeness framework, which is presented in Exhibit 15–17. This exhibit makes clear that the control and governance series are not intended to become *Handbook* recommendations at the current time. Instead, the intent seems to be to get client organizations to experiment with the framework until a more fine-tuned standard can be developed. The resulting framework will probably first be used for internal reporting with an eventual goal of developing sufficiently articulated and supported standards for external reporting purposes. Because of the complexity and pervasiveness of internal controls, the due process for developing reporting and auditing standards on internal control will probably take considerably longer than is usual in developing *Handbook* recommendations.

E X H I B I T 15–16   (from CICA's Criteria of Control Guidance)

E X H I B I T 15–17   DEGREE OF AUTHORITATIVENESS FRAMEWORK
(from CICA's Criteria of Control Guidance)

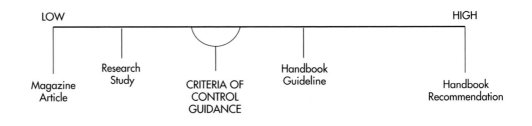

Special Reports: Service Organizations

Occasionally, some clients' transactions are handled by a **service organization**—another business that executes or records transactions, or both, on behalf of the client. Examples of service organizations include computer data-processing service centres, trust departments of banks, insurers that maintain the accounting records for ceded insurance (reinsurance transactions), mortgage bankers and trust companies that service loans for owners, and transfer agents that handle the shareholder accounting for mutual and money market investment funds. An auditor may need information about the service organization's control over their mutual client's transactions. However, the auditor may not have access to do the work when the service organization is not an audit client. This situation is described in Exhibit 15–18.

In such situations all the parties concerned—the user auditor and its client organization, and the service auditor and its client (the service organization)—co-operate to try to enable the user auditor to obtain enough information about controls that affect the audit client's transactions. Certain special-purpose reports on internal accounting control (described more fully in *Section* 5900 and ISA 402.12) can be relied on by the user auditor in connection with the assessment of control risk of the client organization. The reports provide opinions about the service organization's controls as they are applied to the client organization's transactions. Ordinarily, service auditors' reports are not public reports on internal controls. They are used mainly by other auditors.

Section 5900 and ISA 402 describe the form of report under several conditions. In particular, the opinion paragraph should express an opinion on whether the stated internal control objectives were achieved and the control procedures exist either at a point in time or throughout the period covered by the service auditor. Exhibit 15–19 illustrates a report on control procedures at a specified point in time while Exhibit 15–20 illustrates a report on control effectiveness over a specified time period.

E X H I B I T   15–18

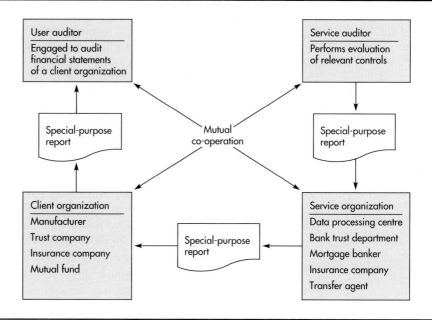

E X H I B I T   15–19   **AUDITOR'S REPORT ON CONTROL PROCEDURES (from *Handbook Section* 5900.12)**

To Y Service Organization

I have examined the accompanying description of the stated internal control objectives of X system of Y Service Organization and the control procedures designed to achieve those objectives and have performed tests of the existence of those control procedures as at June 30, 20X1. My examination was made in accordance with generally accepted auditing standards, and accordingly included such tests and other procedures as I considered necessary in the circumstances.

In my opinion, the control procedures included in the accompanying description were suitably designed to provide reasonable, but not absolute, assurance that the stated internal control objectives of the system described therein were achieved and the control procedures existed as at June 30, 20X1.

As I tested the existence of the control procedures only as at June 30, 20X1, I do not express an opinion on whether the control procedures existed at any other time.

City   (signed) . . . .
July 15, 20X1   CHARTERED ACCOUNTANT

E X H I B I T   15–20   **AUDITOR'S REPORT ON CONTROL PROCEDURES (from *Handbook Section* 5900.12)**

To B Service Organization

I have examined the accompanying description of the stated internal control objectives of A system of B Service Organization and the control procedures designed to achieve those objectives and have performed tests of the effectiveness of those control procedures for the period from January 1, 20X1 to June 30, 20X1. My examination was made in accordance with generally accepted auditing standards, and accordingly included such tests and other procedures as I considered necessary in the circumstances.

In my opinion, the control procedures included in the accompanying description were suitably designed to provide reasonable, but not absolute, assurance that the stated internal control objectives of the system described therein were achieved, and the control procedures operated effectively from January 1, 20X1 to June 30, 20X1.

City   (signed) . . . .
July 15, 20X1   CHARTERED ACCOUNTANT

Other Communication on Control and Other Matters

Regulators, Parliaments, and the public have been concerned about auditors' communication of internal control and other matters to high levels in public corporations, especially in banks and other financial institutions. In response, the CICA issued two Guidelines that address auditors' responsibilities to (1) communicate internal control matters noted in an audit (*Section* 5750), and (2) communicate certain matters to the audit committee of the board of directors (AUG–11, "Communications with Audit Committees (or equivalent)").

When performing an audit, auditors may notice **reportable matters.** These include significant deficiencies in the design or operation of the company's internal control structure, which could adversely affect the organization's ability to record, process, summarize and report financial data in conformity with GAAP (AUG–13, "Special Reports on Regulated Financial Institutions"). Auditing standards do not require auditors to search for reportable matters, but they do require auditors to report the ones that come to their attention (*Section* 5750). The report, preferably in writing, is to be addressed to the management, or the board of directors or its audit committee. An illustration of such a report is in Exhibit 15–21.

Auditors often issue another type of report to management called a management letter. This letter may contain commentary and suggestions on a variety of matters in addition to internal control matters. Examples are operational and administrative efficiency, business strategy and profit-making possibilities. These management letters are not required by auditing standards. They are a type of management advice rendered as a part of an audit. (An illustration of a management letter is shown in Chapter 14, Exhibit 14–10, in connection with completing the audit.)

The concern about reporting control-related matters within a company has spilled over into a set of other important matters that auditors are required to report to companies' audit committees (AUG–11, "Communications with Audit Committees [or equivalent]"). The purpose of these communications is to enhance the audit committees' ability to oversee the audit functions (external and internal) in a company. The auditors are responsible for informing the audit committee about these matters:

- Independent auditors' responsibilities regarding financial statements and other information in documents that include the audited financial statements (e.g., the annual report to shareholders, filings with the regulatory agencies such as the OSC or Superintendent of Financial Institutions).
- Management's significant accounting policies.
- Management judgements about accounting estimates used in the financial statements.
- Significant audit adjustments recommended by the auditors.
- Disagreements with management about accounting principles, accounting estimates, the scope of the audit, disclosures in the notes and the wording of the audit report.

EXHIBIT 15–21   COMMUNICATION OF MATTERS IDENTIFIED DURING THE FINANCIAL STATEMENT AUDIT

During the course of my audit of .... for the year ended .... I identified matters which may be of interest to management. The objective of an audit is to obtain reasonable assurance whether the financial statements are free of material misstatement and it is not designed to identify matters that may be of interest to management in discharging its responsibilities. Accordingly an audit would not usually identify all such matters.

The matters identified were ....

This communication is prepared solely for the information of management and is not intended for any other purpose. I accept no responsibility to a third party who uses this communication.

Source: *Handbook Section* 5750.08

- The auditor's view on accounting matters on which management has consulted with other accountants.
- Major accounting and auditing issues discussed with management in connection with beginning or continuing an auditor-client relationship.
- Illegal acts.
- Difficulties with management encountered while performing the audit—delays in starting the audit or providing information, unreasonable time schedule, unavailability of client personnel and failure of client personnel to complete data schedules.

Internal auditors also have responsibilities for reporting to a company's board of directors. Statement on Internal Auditing Standards No. 7 ("Communicating with the Board of Directors") states that the director of internal auditing should have direct communication with the board. In particular, significant findings about irregularities, illegal acts, errors, inefficiency, waste, ineffectiveness, conflicts of interest and control deficiencies should be reviewed with the management, then communicated to the board of directors and its audit committee. As with the external auditors, these communications are designed to inform the board and the audit committee so that they can fulfil their responsibilities.

R E V I E W
CHECKPOINTS

15.13   Does the standard public report on internal control give the opinion known as "positive assurance?"

15.14   What reports on control and other matters are auditors required to give to a company's management, board of directors or audit committee?

15.15   What two types of engagements can produce an auditor's written report on internal control intended for external use? Describe the reports in general terms.

FORECASTS AND PROJECTIONS

LEARNING OBJECTIVE

6. Define the various financial presentations and levels of service involved in association with financial forecasts and projections, and write compilation and examination reports.

Accountants are associated with prospective financial information when a client requests them to help assemble or submit a report on a forecast or projection. Several provincial securities commissions have encouraged publication of forecasts. For example, the OSC has allowed forecasts since 1984. In September 1989 the CICA issued a new *Handbook* pronouncement (*Section* 4250), dealing with accounting issues involved with forecasts, or more generally, future-oriented financial information (FOFI). At the same time, an auditing and related services guideline was issued covering the examination of a financial forecast or projection included in a prospectus or other public offering document. In February 1993 the CICA issued an auditing guideline for compilation of a financial forecast or projection (AUG–16). Similar guidance is provided in ISA 810.

When accountants have compiled, examined or helped prepare prospective financial statements, they should render a report on them. The characteristics of compilation and examination of prospective financial statements are explored later in this section.

Presentation Guides

Prospective financial statements can be completed in the same format as historical statements or less than complete, but in any event they must contain the following items (if applicable in the circumstances):

a. Sales or gross revenue.

b. Gross profit or cost of sales.

c. Unusual or infrequently occurring items.

> d. Provision for income taxes.
>
> e. Discontinued operations or extraordinary items.
>
> f. Income from continuing operations.
>
> g. Net income.
>
> h. Primary and fully diluted earnings per share.
>
> i. Significant changes in financial position.
>
> j. Statement that assumptions are based on current information, with a warning that the prospective results may not be achieved.
>
> k. Summary of significant assumptions.
>
> l. Summary of significant accounting policies.

These items are what usually appear in historical financial statements for a future period, and so FOFI should be prepared in accordance with the accounting policies expected to be used in the future period (*Section* 4250.18).

Any presentation omitting one or more of the items (*a*) through (*l*) in this list is considered a partial presentation, not a prospective financial statement. Partial and pro forma presentations are not covered by the standards and not recommended for public use.

With the minimum items listed, the nature of prospective financial statements can be one of these:

1. **Financial forecast.** A forecast presents, to the best of the preparer's knowledge and belief, an entity's expected financial position, results of operations and changes in financial position (cash flow). A forecast is based on assumptions about expected conditions and expected courses of action.

2. **Financial projection.** A projection is similar to a forecast, with the important exception that a projection depends on one or more **hypothetical assumption(s).** A hypothetical assumption expresses a condition and course of action the issuer expects could take place. A projection answers the questions: "What might happen if . . . ?" For example, a promoter trying to sell limited partnership interests in a new hotel project might present a cash flow projection based on the hypothetical assumption: "What will be the cash flow if annual hotel room occupancy averages 75 percent?" Financial projections may be multiple projections based on a range of hypothetical assumptions (e.g., hotel room occupancy of 50 percent, 75 percent and 90 percent). A preparer should reasonably expect the future results to fall within the range, however.

Reporting on Prospective Financial Statements

Accountants can report on forecasts and projections three ways. The primary objective of association with forecasts and projections is to lend credibility to them—similar to the assurance objective related to historical financial statements.

1. **Examination of prospective financial statements.** An examination of a forecast or projection is a substantial task. For all practical purposes, it is the equivalent of an audit because the accountant is expected to:

- Evaluate the preparation of the prospective financial statements.

- Evaluate the support underlying the assumptions.

- Evaluate the presentation for conformity with *Section* 4250 presentation recommendations.

- Issue an examination report stating (*a*) whether the prospective financial statements are presented in conformity with CICA standards, (*b*) whether the assumptions provide a reasonable basis for the forecast or projection, and (*c*) a disclaimer as to achievability of the forecast.

Exhibit 15–22 organizes the forecast/projection examination guidelines. You should compare them to the assurance and GAAS standards in Exhibit 2–1.

EXHIBIT 15–22   FORECAST/PROJECTION GUIDELINES

1. The examination should be performed by a person or persons having adequate technical training and proficiency to examine prospective financial statements.
2. In all matters related to the examination of prospective financial statements, the accountant should be independent.
3. Due professional care should be exercised in the performance of the examination and the preparation of the report.
4. The work should be adequately planned and assistants, if any, should be properly supervised.
5. Sufficient appropriate evidence should be obtained to provide a reasonable basis for the examination report.
6. The examination report should be given an opinion that the prospective financial statements are presented in conformity with presentation guidelines and that the underlying assumptions provide a reasonable basis for the forecast.
7. The report should give a caveat that the prospective results may not be achieved.
8. The examination report should identify the prospective financial statements and state that the examination of them was made in accordance with standards established by the CICA.
9. The report should contain a statement that the accountant assumes no responsibility to update the report for events and circumstances occurring after the date of the report.

2. **Compilation of prospective financial statements.** A compilation involves considerably less work than an examination. Compilation procedures mainly facilitate the mechanical preparation of the forecast or projection presentation. The accountants are not expected to gather a significant amount of supporting evidence. However, they are expected to notice assumptions that are obviously inappropriate in the circumstances. These compilation procedures are very similar to the ones specified for a compilation of unaudited historical financial statements.

3. **Application of agreed-upon procedures.** Clients can engage accountants for specified work on forecasts and projections by establishing the nature and scope of the work. In such arrangements (*a*) the users of the statements and accountant's report must take responsibility for the adequacy of the agreed-upon procedures for their purposes, (*b*) the report is to be restricted to these users, and (*c*) the prospective financial statements must contain a summary of significant assumptions. These engagements are the means of obtaining tailored services, so they can take a wide variety of specifications. The accountant's report is similarly tailored to the circumstances.

Reports on Prospective Financial Statements

Standard compilation and examination reports on forecasts are reproduced in Exhibits 15–23 and 15–24. The reports identify the financial statements and describe the accountant's work. The compilation report contains a disclaimer. It offers no conclusions or any other form of assurance. The examination report, in contrast, gives the accountant's conclusions about proper presentation and about the reasonableness of the assumptions.

EXHIBIT 15–23   **NOTICE TO READER ON THE COMPILATION OF A FINANCIAL FORECAST**
                     (from CICA Guideline AUG–16, February 1993, para. 22)

To:.....

I have compiled the financial forecast of .... consisting of a balance sheet as at (date) and statements of income, retained earnings and changes in financial position for the (period) then ending using assumptions with an effective date of ...., and other information provided by management. My engagement was performed in accordance with the applicable guidance on compilation of a financial forecast issued by the Canadian Institute of Chartered Accountants.

A compilation is limited to presenting, in the form of a financial forecast, information provided by management and does not include evaluating the support for the assumptions or other information underlying the forecast. Accordingly, I do not express an opinion or any other form of assurance on the financial forecast or assumptions. Further, since this financial forecast is based on assumptions regarding future events, actual results will vary from the information presented and the variations may be material. I have no responsibility to update this communication for events and circumstances occurring after the date of this communication.

City   (signed) . . . .
Date   CHARTERED ACCOUNTANT

EXHIBIT 15–24 **AUDITOR'S REPORT ON FINANCIAL FORECAST (from CICA Guideline AUG–6, September 1989, para 43)**

To the Directors of ....

The accompanying financial forecast of .... consisting of a balance sheet as at (date) and the statements of income, retained earnings and changes in financial position for the (period(s)) then ending has been prepared by management using assumptions with an effective date of .... I have examined the support provided by management for the assumptions, and the preparation and presentation of this forecast. My examination was made in accordance with the applicable Auditing Guideline issued by the Canadian Institute of Chartered Accountants. I have no responsibility to update this report for events and circumstances occurring after the date of my report.

In my opinion:

- as at the date of this report, the assumptions developed by management are suitably supported and consistent with the plans of the Company, and provide a reasonable basis for the forecast;
- this forecast reflects such assumptions; and
- the financial forecast complies with the presentation and disclosure standards for forecasts established by the Canadian Institute of Chartered Accountants.

Since this forecast is based on assumptions regarding future events, actual results will vary from the information presented and the variations may be material. Accordingly, I express no opinion as to whether this forecast will be achieved.

City (signed) . . . .
Date CHARTERED ACCOUNTANT

In an engagement to examine (audit) and report on a forecast or projection, accountants can give opinions that are unqualified (see Exhibit 15–24), qualified or adverse, or that are disclaimers resulting from scope limitations. The qualified or adverse opinions are given when the forecast or projection omits some information required to be presented by *Section* 4250. The adverse opinion is given when the presentation fails to disclose significant assumptions and when significant assumptions are not reasonable. The disclaimer is given when necessary examination procedures are not performed.

An accountant should not write a report that may lead readers to believe that he or she attests to the achievability of the prospective results. You can see in Exhibit 15–24 that the accountant's report lends credibility and assurance to the forecast, but it does not attest to achievability. Accountants must be independent to give the examination report, and this independence includes independence from all promoters using the forecast to organize or market a venture as well as independence from the entity being promoted.

A recent OSC study found that forecasts issued in 1990 and 1991 were inaccurate by a larger margin than in previous surveys. According to this study, 77 percent of established firms surveyed overestimated their profit, compared with 71 percent in an earlier survey. Moreover, 62 percent overestimated profit by more than 20 percent, up from 51 percent who did so in the previous survey.

In a *Globe and Mail* article, portfolio manager John Saltz of Bolton Tremblay said that management is likely to be biased and optimistic. "I don't pay for stocks based on management's forecast of future earnings."

He also complained about the auditor's role. "The auditor says that the forecast is fine based on underlying assumptions but they don't comment on the underlying assumptions."

The OSC's acting head of corporate finance, Ram Ramachandran, said the audit requirement "may unconsciously add an element of respectability" and lead people to rely too much on the document. Auditors are working in a new area—forecasting—and "the process may not lend itself to crystal ball gazing. As a result, Ontario may ban forecasts altogether."[4]

A recent comprehensive study of financial statement user needs by the AICPA known commonly as the Jenkins Report found that "in general, users do not expect management to provide forecasted financial statements. They are concerned about the reliability of the

---

[4] "Ontario may ban firm's profit forecasts," *The Globe and Mail*, March 1, 1994, p. B3.

information and believe that forecasting financial performance is a function of financial analysis rather than business reporting."[5] Instead, users prefer improved disclosure of risks, uncertainties and opportunities—key aspects on which to base forecasts. The Jenkins Report will probably have a major impact on reporting and ultimately auditing.

The business press and regulators have recently expressed concerns about fraudulent reporting that is designed to meet analysts' quarterly forecasts. (For example, see News Report, *Journal of Accountancy*, December 1999, pg. 17.) The May 2000 Exposure Draft by the Panel on Audit Effectiveness had this to say about fraudulent reporting.

> Frauds often start in one of the first three quarters of a company's fiscal year. Auditors have limited responsibilities for interim financial information (generally quarterly financial reports). Auditors are engaged to review that information, but it is not subjected to the same scrutiny as are the full year's audited financial statements. Furthermore matters potentially material to an interim financial report might not be material to the annual financial statements, and therefore may not receive scrutiny from auditors either in their limited quarterly reviews or the annual audit. Perpetrators may use this fact to their advantage in their efforts at concealment. In addition, manipulations of earnings in interim periods often are rationalized by management as being only temporary "borrowings" since there is plenty of time left in the year to correct the problem. The rationalization also may include a belief that the manipulations are intended to avoid earnings volatility and surprises and therefore are in the shareholders' best interests.[6]

Given this possible latitude with interim information, it is not surprising that if analysts' quarterly expectations are missed by even as little as a penny there can be a loss of millions of dollars in market capitalization. For this reason there has been renewed interest in how materiality is set by the auditor. Both quantitative as well as qualitative factors need to be considered. For example, will a misstatement allow the client to meet analysts' expectations, or will a misstatement convert a loss into a profit? Please review Chapter 5 for more discussion.

R E V I E W
CHECKPOINTS

15.16 How are prospective financial statements defined?

15.17 What are the similarities and differences between examination reports on forecasts and audit reports on historical financial statements? on compilation reports on forecasts? on compilation reports on historical financial statements?

15.18 Why is the OSC considering a ban on financial forecasts?

FINANCIAL STATEMENTS FOR USE IN OTHER COUNTRIES

LEARNING OBJECTIVE

7. Describe the new umbrella standards for assurance engagements.

Auditors practising in Canada are more and more often being asked to report on a Canadian company's financial statements that are intended for use in other countries, especially the United States. Such financial statements may be used by foreign investors or by foreign parent companies for consolidation in foreign financial statements. For many years, American auditors have obtained financial statements of foreign companies and of subsidiaries of U.S.-based multinational companies for consolidation in a U.S. parent company's financial statements. These foreign statements have been prepared on the basis of U.S. GAAP by foreign managements and auditors, even while the foreign company's statements may also be prepared on the basis of foreign GAAP in other countries for use in those countries.

---

[5] AICPA Special Committee on Financial Reporting, "Improving Business Reporting: A Customer Focus—Making the Information Needs of Investors and Creditors" (Jenkins Report), AICPA, 1994, pp. 11–15.

[6] www.pobauditpanel.org on July 7, 2000 para. 3.25

With increasing globalization of corporate ownership, the shoe is on the other foot, and many U.S. companies are owned by foreign parents. Now, the U.S. company's financial statements must be prepared on the basis of accounting principles used in other countries.

In engagements requiring use of foreign standards, Canadian auditors are expected to follow the Canadian general and field work auditing standards, just as they would in any audit. However, some differences in accounting may arise, and these will change some of the audit objectives. For example, some South American countries permit or require general price-level adjusted measurements (because of high rates of inflation), and these management calculations, applied to the Canadian company's account balances, will need to be audited. Likewise, some countries do not permit recognition of deferred taxes, so no deferred tax account balances will exist for audit. Clearly, the auditors must know the accounting principles applied in the country for which the financial statements are intended. The starting place is in the International Accounting Standards established by the International Accounting Standards Committee.

In addition to knowing the foreign accounting principles, the Canadian auditor may be expected to apply foreign auditing standards and procedures. Some countries have codified their auditing standards in professional literature, like Canada, while others put their auditing standards in statutes and legal-like regulations. They may, in some cases, require more auditing of compliance with laws and regulations or other procedures than Canadian standards require. The audit report can take different forms, depending on the circumstances and the distribution of the foreign-GAAP financial statements:

A. Foreign-GAAP financial statements used only outside Canada. The options are:
  1. A Canadian-style report modified to refer to the GAAP of the other country (similar to an AADBA report).
  2. The report form used by auditors in the other country.

B. Foreign-GAAP financial statements that will have more than limited distribution in Canada. The options are:
  1. The CICA standard report, qualified or adverse for departures from Canadian GAAP, with another separate paragraph expressing an opinion on the fair presentation in conformity with the foreign GAAP.
  2. Both (*a*) the report form used by auditors in the other country (A2 above) or a Canadian-style report modified to refer to the GAAP of the other country (A1 above), and (*b*) the qualified or adverse Canadian standard report with an additional paragraph expressing an opinion on the foreign GAAP (B1 above).

C. Two sets of financial statements, foreign GAAP and Canadian GAAP, both of which may be distributed in the foreign country and in Canada. Report on each one:
  1. Report on the foreign-GAAP financial statements as in A1 above, with an additional paragraph notifying users that another report has been issued on Canadian GAAP financial statements.
  2. Report on Canadian-GAAP financial statements as normally done for Canadian financial statements, but add a paragraph notifying users that another report has been issued on foreign-GAAP financial statements.

When a Canadian client must file with the U.S.'s SEC *and* when there is either a disclaimer due to uncertainty or an explanatory paragraph resulting from a change in accounting principle, a CICA Guideline on Canada–U.S. reporting conflicts (AUG-21) should be followed. This Guideline recommends that a Canadian GAAS audit report be issued along with comments that should be added as additional information for American readers.

. . . .

R E V I E W
C H E C K P O I N T S

15.19   Why do you think a Canadian-style report on foreign-GAAP financial statements is similar to a report on AADBA financial statements?

15.20   What precautions should Canadian auditors take when reporting on foreign-GAAP financial statements that will be distributed in the United States?

. . . .

THE ASSURANCE FRAMEWORK

Many of the engagements discussed in the preceding sections fell under the new umbrella framework of the assurance engagements issued by the CICA as *Handbook Section* 5025 in April 1997. This standard was introduced in Chapter 2 and compared to GAAS. You should begin by reviewing the discussion there.

The fundamental concept of *Section* 5025 is that of an accountability relationship: "An accountability relationship exists when one party (the 'accountable party') is answerable to and/or responsible to another party (the 'user') for a subject matter or voluntarily chooses to report to another party on a subject matter" (*Section* 5025.04).

An assurance engagement can take place only when there is an accountability relationship. Therefore *Section* 5025.21 makes clear that the auditor needs to obtain evidence that such a relationship exists before taking on an assurance engagement. The usual form of this evidence is acknowledgment of the existence of the relationship by the accountable party, usually management. Failure to obtain such acknowledgment by the accountable party should be disclosed in the practitioner's report.

The existence of the accountability relationship is what distinguishes assurance engagements from other types of engagements such as tax planning and consulting work (*Section* 5025.15). In our discussions in the appendix to this chapter, and subsequent chapters, we will see that the distinctions between assurance and nonassurance engagements can be very fine indeed. Yet they are very important because assurance engagements with respect to financial statements are what distinguish the PA profession from other professional groups. Thus the assurance standards delineate the unique responsibilities of auditors (or, more generally now, the assurers).

The type of communication provided by the practitioner or assurer depends on the nature of the assurance engagement. The CICA envisions two major categories of assurance engagements. Attestation engagements are those in which the practitioner's (attestation) conclusion will be on a written assertion prepared by the accountable party. The assertion is used to evaluate, using suitable criteria, the subject matter for which the accountable party is responsible. The party making the assertion is sometimes referred to as the asserter.

The other category of assurance engagement is a direct reporting engagement. "In a direct reporting engagement, the practitioners' conclusion will evaluate directly using suitable criteria, the subject matter for which the accountable party is responsible" (*Section* 5025.05). By this definition the essential distinction between an assurance and a direct reporting engagement is that the assertions are written out by the asserter in an assurance engagement but may be only implied by the asserter in a direct reporting engagement. Despite this seemingly straightforward distinction, we will see that what exactly is meant by a written assertion is still considered by some to be a controversial matter in the current standard. We will discuss the ramifications of this in the appendix to this chapter, which covers outstanding issues that some consider remain with the standard.

In order to operationalize the above concepts, it is necessary to clarify additional concepts and relate them to the above assurance framework. This is shown in *Section* 5025.08–.13 as follows:

> The practitioner forms a conclusion concerning a subject matter by referring to suitable criteria. Criteria are benchmarks against which the subject matter and, in an attest engagement, mangement's written assertion on the subject matter, can be evaluated.
>
> In an assurance engagement, the practitioner reduces engagement risk to a level that is appropriate for the assurance provided in his or her report. The term engagement risk is the risk that the practitioner may express an inappropriate conclusion. The three components of engagement risk are inherent risk, control risk and detection risk.
>
> Practitioners should in theory be able to vary infinitely the level of assurance provided in assurance engagements. However, in order to help users understand the level of assurance being provided by the practitioner, the standards in this *Section* limit assurance to two distinct levels—a high level and a moderate level.

In an audit engagement, the practitioner provides a high, though not absolute, level of assurance by designing procedures so that in the practitioner's professional judgment, the risk of an inappropriate conclusion is reduced to a low level through procedures such as inspection, observation, enquiry, confirmation, computation, analysis and discussion. Use of the term "high level of assurance" refers to the highest reasonable level of assurance a practitioner can provide concerning a subject matter. Absolute assurance is not attainable as a result of factors such as the use of judgment, the use of testing, the inherent limitations of control and the fact that much of the evidence available to the practitioner is persuasive rather than conclusive in nature. Assurance will also be influenced by the degree of precision associated with the subject matter itself.

In a review engagement, the practitioner provides a moderate level of assurance by designing procedures so that, in the practitioner's professional judgment, the risk of an inappropriate conclusion is reduced to a moderate level through procedures which are normally limited to enquiry, analysis and discussion. Such risk is reduced to a moderate level when the evidence obtained enables the practitioner to conclude the subject matter is plausible in the circumstances.

Both attest engagements and direct reporting engagements can be completed with either a high or a moderate level of assurance. The level of assurance appropriate for a particular engagement will depend on the needs of users and the nature of the subject matter.

With these concepts and definitions it is now possible to develop meaningful standards for assurance engagements. These have already been listed in Chapter 2 and compared to GAAS. As noted there, the assurance standards are subdivided into (*a*) general standards that relate to attributes of the practitioner and the need for the practitioner to use suitable criteria in evaluating a subject matter (for example, criteria for control discussed in this chapter); (*b*) performance standards relating to obtaining sufficient appropriate evidence to support the practitioner's conclusion and documenting the basis for the conclusion including the concepts of significance (materiality) and engagement risk as used in assurance engagements; and (*c*) reporting standards prescribing the minimum requirements of the practitioner's report, including those for reservations and the conditions for issuing a reservation in an assurance engagement report.

The truly novel aspects of these standards deal with suitability of criteria, significance, engagement risk and the increasing reliance on specialists contemplated by these standards. As we will see in Chapter 18, all of these concepts originated with public sector auditing standards. Given the varied nature of the engagements contemplated by this standard, it is expected that there could be far more reliance on specialists from other fields, and this creates responsibilities on the practitioner to understand the specialists' work to the extent necessary to fulfill the objectives of the engagement. There is an additional responsibility on the part of the specialist to understand the objectives of the engagement at least as to how they relate to the specialists' expertise (*Section* 5025.34). Thus the standards contemplate use of multidisciplinary audit team members to a significantly greater extent than in financial statement audits.

The concept of significance as used in the standard appears to have been influenced by public sector standards (covered in Chapter 18), which use the same concept. Significance can be viewed as an extension of materiality to include broader classes of users whose decisions may be influenced by nonfinancial factors such as, for example, the effectiveness of health care.

Engagement risk is defined in *Section* 5025.54 as:

> the risk that the practitioner will express an inappropriate conclusion in his or her report. This risk consists of (a) risks that are beyond the control of management and the practitioner (inherent risk), (b) the risks that are within control of management (control risk) and (c) risks that are within the control of the practitioner (detection risk). The extent to which the practitioner considers the relevant components of engagment risk will be affected by the nature of the subject matter and the level of assurance to be provided.

An interesting aspect of this definition of engagement risk and its components is that the risk is no longer limited to (*a*) risk of failing to detect significant misrepresentations or omissions, but also explicitly includes (*b*) the possibility that the practitioner may report significant items that in fact are not significant relative to the users. The traditional concept of audit risk is consistent with (*a*), but risk (*b*) has never before been explicitly considered in the audit risk model because it has been assumed this risk is self-correcting. In other words, if the auditor concludes erroneously that there is a material misstatement it's been assumed that additional work will always point out the error to the auditor. The reason risk (*a*) has traditionally been considered the more serious risk is that when this risk occurs the auditor has no evidence to support the proposition of material misstatement when in fact that is the case. Since the auditor's job can be characterized as finding material misstatements, control of risk (*a*) is the reason the auditor was hired in the first place. By extending the risk definition to include risks of the (*b*) type, the standard has potentially changed the risk model for generalized assurance engagements in a significant way that is not completely consistent with the traditional concept of audit risk. The justification for this perhaps is that in the significantly changed environment of assurance engagements auditors need to be explicitly aware of what should be considered significant for various subject matters. A more complete discussion of this risk definition is provided in the appendix.

Perhaps the most important change introduced by *Section* 5025 is the concept of suitable criteria. *Section* 5025.39 identifies five characteristics of suitable criteria: relevance, reliability, neutrality, understandability and completeness. Since these criteria are supposed to apply to all assurance engagements including financial statement audits, these criteria introduce a potentially revolutionary link to accounting theory in that new characteristics of accounting information may now be contemplated. Notably, financial statement concepts listed in *Handbook Section* 1000 do not list completeness as a characteristic of financial statements. Currently, this does not create a problem in the standards because *Section* 5025.02 explicitly exempts existing *Handbook Recommendations* from the assurance engagement standard. But in the longer term it appears that some reconciliation may be necessary. Perhaps the most notable aspect of this development is that assurance and accounting standards are for the first time being linked, albeit in a tentative way. Perhaps this indicates a closer co-ordination between accounting and auditing standard setting in the future—a development some consider a long overdue in an increasingly complicated and interrelated business world. This also relates to the focus on accountability relations in assurance engagements, which also happens to be a primary objective of financial statements. In Chapter 18 we will see that suitable criteria and accountability relations are also central concepts in public sector auditing.

The introduction to the standard makes it clear that existing *Handbook Recommendations* override the current standard, but that nevertheless the long-term objective of the standard is to provide guidelines where standards currently do not exist and to provide future guidance on more specific recommendations in assurance engagements. In the scope of *Section* 5025.01, the long-term overall objective is described as follows:

> These standards establish a framework for all assurance engagements performed by practitioners and for the on-going development of related standards. The standards apply to:
>
> *(a)* engagements in the private and public sectors;
>
> *(b)* attest engagements and direct reporting engagements;
>
> *(c)* engagements designed to provide a high (i.e., audit) level of assurance; and
>
> *(d)* engagements designed to provide a moderate (i.e., review) level of assurance
>
> The assurance standard appendix makes it clear that the standards apply only when the practitioner provides a conclusion on a subject matter. The following services are not considered to provide a conclusion on a subject matter.
>
> *(a)* specified auditing procedure engagements (*Section* 9100)
>
> *(b)* compilation engagements (*Section* 9200)
>
> *(c)* derivative reporting (*Section* 5025.A and AUG-13); and
>
> *(d)* reports on the application of accounting principles, auditing standards, or review standards (*Section* 7600).

A good overview of the various services and the extent of the PA's involvement is provided as *Section* 5020.B, which is reproduced in the box that follows:

The purpose of this . . . is to provide examples of information and the nature and extent of the public accountant's involvement with such information.

NOTE: In addition to the professional responsibilities outlined below, the public accountant would comply with the rules of professional conduct of his or her provincial Institute and would therefore, in all cases, exercise due professional skill and care in the work he or she carries out.

TYPE OF INFORMATION RESPONSIBILITIES	NATURE AND EXTENT OF INVOLVEMENT	NATURE AND EXTENT OF ASSOCIATION	PROFESSIONAL WORK	REPORTING
Information that is the subject matter of an assurance	Assurance engagement	The practitioner has associated himself or herself with the subject matter by virtue of the assurance engagement carried out (see paragraph 5020.04)	The practitioner discharges his or her responsibilities by complying with the Recommendations contained in STANDARDS FOR ASSURANCE ENGAGEMENTS, Section 5025.	Reporting section of STANDARDS FOR ASSURANCE ENGAGEMENTS, Section 5025.
Financial statements REPORT	Audit	The auditor has associated himself or herself with the financial statements by virtue of the audit work carried out (see paragraph 5020.04)	The auditor discharges his or her responsibilities by complying with the Recommendations contained in GENERALLY ACCEPTED AUDITING STANDARDS, Section 5100.	THE AUDITOR'S STANDARD Section 5400.
Financial statements	Review	The public accountant has associated himself of herself with the financial statements by virtue of the review carried out (see paragraph 5020.04).	The public accountant discharges his or her responsibilities by complying with the relevant Recommendations contained in GENERAL REVIEW STANDARDS, Section 8100, or REVIEWS OF FINANCIAL STATEMENTS, Section 8200.	GENERAL REVIEW STANDARDS, Section 8100, or REVIEWS OF FINANCIAL STATEMENTS, Section 8200.
Financial statements	Compilation	The public accountant has associated himself or herself with the financial statements by virtue of compiling the financial statements (see paragraph 5020.04).	The public accountant discharges his or her responsibilities by complying with the relevant Recommendations contained in COMPILATION ENGAGEMENTS, Section 9200.	COMPILATION ENGAGEMENTS, Section 9200
Financing document containing financial information extracted from the audited financial statements.	Consent to use of the auditor's name in the document in connection with the condensed financial information, by consenting to a statement in the document such as, "This condensed financial information has been extracted from the audited financial statements for the year ended December 31, 1986, previously reported on by our auditors ZYX & Co."	The auditor has associated himself or herself with the financial information by consenting to the use of his or her name in connection with that information (see 5020.04).	The auditor discharges his or her responsibilities by complying with paragraph 5020.13.	No reporting standard. See paragraph 5020.10.
Financing document containing financial information prepared by the client and not reported on by the auditor.	Consent to the inclusion of the auditor's name in the document by, for example, consenting to a factual statement in the document naming lawyers, auditors, etc.	The auditor does not associate himself or herself with the information contained in the document by merely consenting to the inclusion of his or her name in the document (see paragraphs 5020.04 and 5020.16).	The auditor discharges his or her responsibilities by complying with paragraph 5020.17.	No reporting standard. See paragraph 5020.10.

Continued

TYPE OF INFORMATION RESPONSIBILITIES	NATURE AND EXTENT OF INVOLVEMENT	NATURE AND EXTENT OF ASSOCIATION	PROFESSIONAL WORK	REPORTING
Financial statements	Typing or reproduction services.	The public accountant has associated himself or herself with the financial statements by virtue of the typing or reproduction services carried out (see paragraph 5020.04)	No professional responsibilities other than those discussed in the Note on the first page of this Appendix.	No reporting standard. See paragraph 5020.10.
Annual report containing audited financial statements.	To determine whether the financial statements and the auditor's report thereon are accurately reproduced in the annual report. To read the other information in the annual report and consider whether any of this information is inconsistent with the financial statements on which the auditor has reported.	The auditor has already associated himself or herself with the financial statements in the annual report by virtue of the audit work carried out. The auditor has also associated himself or herself with the other information in the annual report by virtue of the work carried out under *Section 7500* (see paragraph 5020.04).	The auditor discharges his or her responsibilities by complying with the Recommendations contained in THE AUDITOR'S INVOLVEMENT ANNUAL REPORT, *Section 7500.*	No reporting standard. See paragraph 5020.10.
Tax return and financial statements as attachments to the tax returns.	Preparation of tax return (financial statements were prepared by the client).	The public accountant has associated himself or herself with the tax return by virtue of preparing it and providing related tax advice (see paragraph 5020.04). The public accountant has not associated himself or herself with the financial statements because he or she has not performed services in respect of the financial statements or consented to the use of his or her name in connection with the financial statements (see paragraph 5020.04).	No professional responsibilities other than those discussed in the Note on the first page of this Appendix.	No reporting standard. See paragraph 5020.10.

Keep in mind that *Section* 5025 is intended to be broad enough to include most of the engagements covered in this chapter, and financial statement audits, as well as many other possible engagements, some of which are covered in later chapters. This is a tall order. Much experimentation and experience will be necessary before *Section* 5025 can be refined. The experience in implementing the standards may also suggest future adjustments to the framework itself. The appendix discusses in more detail some of the controversial aspects of the standards and where future adjustments and clarifications are likely. The appendix also reviews trends in the evolution of assurance standards in the United States and internationally.

For more current information on assurance engagements, the following Web sites may prove useful.

www.cica.ca	This is the CICA's general Web site containing all Exposure Drafts and related material outstanding.
www.ifac.org	This is the IFAC's Web site listing their many activities, publications and services.
www.aicpa.org/assurance/ sitemap/index.htm	This the special AICPA Web site on the many facets of their ongoing assurance services project.

568 PART IV   Professional Services and Responsibilities

THE ASSOCIATION FRAMEWORK

The public accounting services covered in this chapter are part of the broadest concept of auditor involvement with information about business enterprises—that of association. Compilation and review engagements are forms of association. *Association* is a term generally used within the profession to indicate a public accountant's involvement with an enterprise or with information issued by that enterprise. General standards for association are covered in *Section* 5020 of the *Handbook.*

Association can arise in three ways:

1. The public accountant associates himself or herself by some action on his or her part with information issued by the enterprise.

2. When the enterprise indicates that the public accountant was involved with information issued by the enterprises without the public accountant's knowledge or consent.

3. A third party assumes the public accountant is involved with information issued by an enterprise.

A public accountant by *Section* 5020.04 associates herself or himself with information when she or he:

(*a*) performs services in respect of that information, or
(*b*) consents to use his or her name in connection with that information.

A public accountant's professional responsibilities when he or she is associated with information are the following:

1. compliance with applicable standards in the *Handbook*;

2. compliance with the rules of professional conduct of his or her provincial institute; and

3. appropriate communication of the extent of his or her involvement with the information.

The public accountant should ensure that the information he or she is associated with is accurate, accurately reproduced and not misleading. If the client attempts to make inappropriate use of the PA's name, the PA should amend the information or get legal advice.

Exhibit 15–25 provides a framework illustrating the relationships of various types of engagements and *Handbook* sections. As a result of the changes to public accounting brought on by *Section* 5025, the concept of association also had to be revised to incorporate the new assurance framework. The new association responsibilities are illustrated in *Section* 5020. A (see the box on page 569).

This revising of the concept of association has also necessitated changes to PA's responses to various client actions with respect to PA communications. The decision tree summarizing a PA's responsibilities with information or subject matters that he or she is inappropriately associated with is reproduced for *Section* 5020.A (see the box on page 570).

Exhibit 15–25 provides a fairly comprehensive association framework for all assurance engagements.

The CICA and provincial institutes are in the process of sorting out what is public accounting: specifically, should public accounting include or exclude compilations? This is an important issue for CGAs and other practitioners because if a provincial public accountancy act excludes CGAs, then what CGAs can practise is determined by the definition of public accountancy. The trend appears to be to exclude compilation from the definition of public accountancy.

A PUBLIC ACCOUNTANT ASSOCIATES HIMSELF OR HERSELF WITH INFORMATION WHEN HE OR SHE

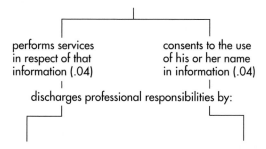

performs services in respect of that information (.04)

consents to the use of his or her name in information (.04)

discharges professional responsibilities by:

a) complying with related rules of professional conduct;
b) complying with applicable Handbook standards;
c) determining whether involvement has been appropriately communicated (.07)

a) determining that the information is an accurate reproduction;
b) determining that any summary or extract of the information is not misleading;
c) determining that his or her communication has been accurately reproduced or reference to his or her name and context in which it is used accurately describes the work carried out (.12 & .13)

are there any reporting standards in the Handbook?

did the public accountant become aware of

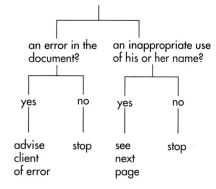

yes

no

communication will describe public accountants involvement (.08 & .10)

is communication necessary to avoid misunderstanding? (.09)

an error in the document?

an inappropriate use of his or her name?

yes

no

yes

no

decide whether it should be oral, written, attached to information, etc. (.10)

stop

advise client of error

stop

see next page

stop

yes

no

Source: Handbook Section 5020.A

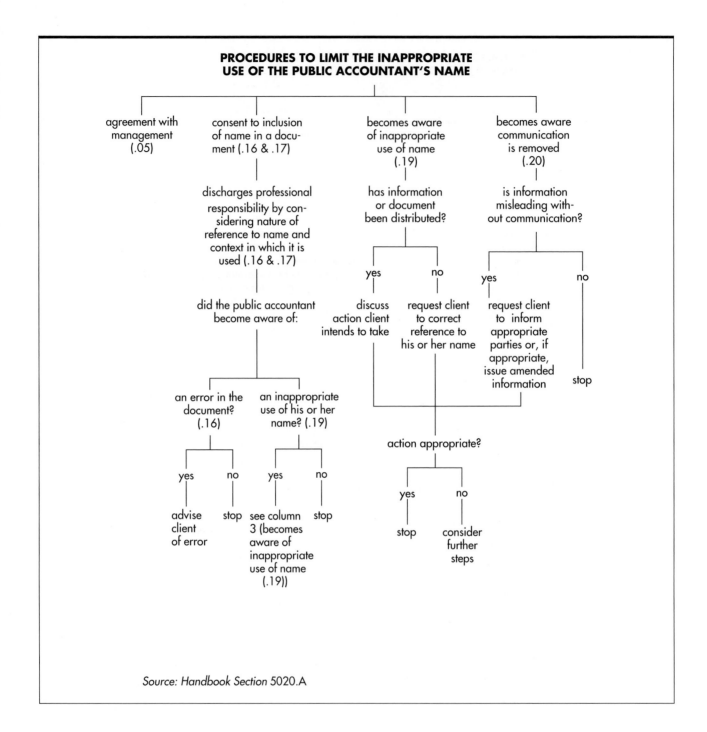

Source: Handbook Section 5020.A

EXHIBIT 15–25   **CURRENT FRAMEWORK FOR ASSOCIATION (as of March 1997)**

Source: *Handbook Section* INTRODUCTION

SUMMARY

· ·

Public accountants are highly regarded for assurance services. Many forms of services, in addition to audits of historical financial statements, have arisen or have been proposed. Managers of companies often develop innovative financial presentations, and they want to give the public some assurance about them, so they engage auditors. Regulators also often become interested in PAs' communication of information and press for assurance involvement.

Guided by auditing, accounting, and review services' standards and the general concepts of assurance, PAs offer services and render reports in several areas. These standards were summarized in Exhibit 15–25.

Unaudited financial statements have been around for a long time. Work on them is known in public practice as review and compilation. The difference lies in the amount of work performed and the level of assurance given in an accountant's report. Review engagements involve less work than an audit, and the report gives a low level of negative assurance instead of an audit opinion. Compilation engagements involve merely writing up the financial statements, which is less work than a review, and the report gives no assurance in the form of an outright denial.

Another type of review is accountants' review of interim financial information (e.g., quarterly financial reports). This review is technically similar to a review of unaudited financial statements, and the report on free-standing interim financial statements gives the negative assurance.

Not everyone wants to produce financial statements fully in conformity with generally accepted accounting principles. Managers have the option to prepare their statements for public use on an "another appropriate disclosed basis of accounting" (AADBA). Auditors can audit and report on such financial statements. This track gives managers an opportunity to avoid the complications of many of the GAAP rules. AADBA audits and reporting are in the auditing standards under the heading of "special reports." Other kinds of special audit reports can be given on parts of financial statements and on current value financial statements.

A special kind of engagement can result in a report on a company's internal control. This report is a positive assurance report on the internal control system. Regulators in some provinces, the SEC, and federal banking agencies have been interested in management reports and audit reports on internal control. This topic of reporting on internal control spills over into auditing standards designed to require auditors to report internally to managers and the board of directors in a company about internal control deficiencies and relations with management in connection with the annual audit.

Innovative managers and promoters frequently use forecasts and projections (known collectively as FOFI) to obtain investors and otherwise inform financial statement users about their estimates of future performance. Auditors can get involved with such presentations by examining or compiling forecasts and projections. In a report on an examination, which is similar to an audit, the accountant gives assurances about the reasonableness of the assumptions underlying the forecast or projection.

The next section in the chapter outlined auditors' responsibilities for reporting on financial statements prepared in accordance with the accounting principles generally accepted in other countries.

Next, the chapter covered the CICA's recent attempt to develop an umbrella framework for many of the PA services via the assurance engagement concept. The chapter concluded with a modified framework for all PA services resulting from introduction of the assurance engagement concept.

MULTIPLE-CHOICE QUESTIONS FOR PRACTICE AND REVIEW

15.21 Which of the following can be considered a prospective financial statement?

a. Balance sheet based on current values of assets and liabilities.

b. Interim-date balance sheet for the first quarter of the fiscal year.

c. Forecasted income statement based on assumptions about expected conditions and expected conditions and expected courses of action.

d. Forecasted valuation of securities held by a venture capital company.

15.22 Which of the following statements is correct?

a. An examination report on prospective financial statements gives the same assurance as an audit report on historical financial statements.

b. An examination report on prospective financial statements does not attest to the achievability of the forecast.

c. In a compilation report on prospective financial statements, an accountant attests to the reasonableness of the underlying forecast assumptions.

d. In reports on prospective financial statements, accountants undertake the obligation to update the reports for important subsequent events.

15.23 Under the Securities and Exchange Commission "safe harbour" rule regarding financial forecasts, persons connected with a company's forecast can be liable for monetary damages if:

a. The plaintiffs are able to prove that the persons connected with the forecast showed lack of good faith and lack of a reasonable basis for belief in the forecast.

b. The plaintiffs are able to prove that the persons connected with the forecast were merely negligent.

c. The persons connected with the forecast had good faith and a reasonable basis for belief in its presentation.

d. The persons connected with a forecast cannot sustain the burden of proof that they acted in good faith and with a reasonable basis for belief in the forecast.

15.24 In a current-value presentation of the balance sheet of a manufacturing company:

a. The basis of valuation must always be explained in notes to the financial statements.

b. The basis of valuation is well known as a "comprehensive basis of accounting other than GAAP."

c. An auditor can attest to the fair presentation of financial position in conformity with GAAP.

d. The company must follow the AICPA guides for presentation of a financial forecast.

15.25 Practice in connection with unaudited historical-cost financial statements is conducted by:

a. International accounting firms only.

b. Regional- and local-size PA firms.

c. Local-size PA firms only.

d. All PA firms.

15.26 The official CICA Recommendations for Compilation and Review services are applicable to practice with:

a. Audited financial statements of public companies.

b. Unaudited financial statements of some companies.

c. Unaudited financial statements of all companies.

d. Audited financial statements of non-public companies.

15.27 A review service engagement for an accountant's association with unaudited financial statements involves:

a. More work than a compilation, and more than an audit.

b. Less work than an audit, but more than a compilation.

c. Less work than a compilation, but more than an audit.

d. More work than an audit, but less than a compilation.

15.28 When an accountant is not independent, the following report can nevertheless be given:

a. Compilation report.

b. Standard unqualified audit report.

c. Examination report on a forecast.

d. Review report on unaudited financial statements.

15.29 An accountant is permitted to express "negative assurance" in which of the following types of reports.

a. Standard unqualified audit report on audited financial statements.

b. Compilation report on unaudited financial statements.

c. Review report on unaudited financial statements.

d. Adverse opinion report on audited financial statements.

15.30 When a company's financial statements in a review or compilation engagement contain a known material departure from GAAP, the accountant's report can:

a. Make no mention of the departure in a compilation report because it contains an explicit disclaimer of opinion.

b. Express the adverse conclusion: "The accompanying financial statements are not presented in conformity with generally accepted accounting principles."

c. Explain the departure as necessary to make the statements not misleading, then give the standard compilation report disclaimer.

d. Explain the departure as necessary to make the statements not misleading, then give the standard review report negative assurance.

15.31 When interim financial information is presented in a note to annual financial statements, the standard audit report on the annual financial statements should:

a. Not mention the interim information unless there is an exception the auditor needs to include in the report.

b. Contain an audit opinion paragraph that specifically mentions the interim financial information if it is not in conformity with GAAP.

c. Contain an extra paragraph that gives negative assurance on the interim information, if it has been reviewed.

d. Contain an extra explanatory paragraph if the interim information note is labelled "unaudited."

15.32 According to auditing standards, financial statements presented on another comprehensive basis of accounting should not:

a. Contain a note describing the other basis of accounting.

b. Describe in general how the other basis of accounting differs from generally accepted accounting principles.

c. Be accompanied by an audit report that gives an unqualified opinion with reference to the other basis of accounting.

d. Contain a note with a quantified dollar reconciliation of the assets based on the other comprehensive basis of accounting with the assets based on generally accepted accounting principles.

15.33 For which of the following reports is an expression of negative assurance not permitted?

a. A review report on unaudited financial statements.

b. An audit report on financial statements prepared on a comprehensive basis of accounting other than GAAP.

c. A report based on applying selected procedures agreed upon by the client and the auditor.

d. A review report on interim financial information.

15.34 Which one of these events is an auditor not required to communicate to a company's audit committee or board of directors?

a. Management's significant accounting policies.

b. Management judgements about accounting estimates used in the financial statements.

c. Immaterial errors in processing transactions discovered by the auditors.

d. Disagreements with management about accounting principles.

EXERCISES AND PROBLEMS

15.35 Review of Forecast Assumptions. You have been engaged by the Dodd Manufacturing Corporation to attest to the reasonableness of the assumptions underlying its forecast of revenues, costs and net income for the next calendar year, 2004. Four of the assumptions are shown below.

a. The company intends to sell certain real estate and other facilities held by Division B at an aftertax profit of $600,000; the proceeds of this sale will be used to retire outstanding debt.

b. The company will call and retire all outstanding 9 percent subordinated debentures (callable at 108). The debentures are expected to require the full call premium given present market interest rates of 8 percent on similar debt. A rise in market interest rates to 9 percent would reduce the loss on bond retirement from the projected $200,000 to $190,000.

c. Current labour contracts expire on September 1, 2004, and the new contract is expected to result in a wage increase of 5.5 percent. Given the forecasted levels of production and sales, aftertax operating earnings would be reduced approximately $50,000 for each percentage-point wage increase in excess of the expected contract settlement.

d. The sales forecast for Division A assumes that the new Portsmouth facility will be complete and operating at 40 percent of capacity on February 1, 2004. It is highly improbable that the facility will be operational before January of 2004. Each month's delay would reduce sales of Division A by approximately $80,000 and operating earnings by $30,000.

Required:

For each assumption, state the evidence sources and procedures you would use to determine the reasonableness.

15.36 Auditing a Current Value Balance Sheet. Your client, the Neighbourhood Paper Company (NPC), has a fiscal year-end of December 31. NPC needs to borrow money from a local bank and believes current value financial statements that report the appreciated value of its assets would be helpful. A loan is needed for working capital purposes.

NPC owns two paper-recycling processors. Old paper is chemically processed, reduced to a wet mass, and then pressed out into thick, semifinished paper mats. The mats are sold to customers who use them for packing material. Recycling processors are fairly complex pieces of integrated machinery and are built on a customized basis by a few specialized engineering companies.

NPC has owned one of the processors for five years. It was appraised last year at $135,000 by a qualified engineering appraiser. The second processor was purchased last month for $125,000—its appraised value—and $10,000 was spent in bringing certain maintenance up to date. Both processors have identical throughput production capabilities.

The other major asset is a nine-acre plot of land NPC bought four years ago when management thought the plant would be moved. The land was purchased for $195,000 and was appraised by a qualified appraiser at $250,000 only 20 months after the purchase date. The nine acres are located near a rapidly expanding industrial area.

Since the recycling processors were appraised/purchased so recently, management does not want to bear the expense of new appraisals this year. No plans have been made to obtain a new appraisal on the land. NPC, however, is a profitable operation. The unaudited income statement for the current year (historical-cost basis) shows net income of $46,000.

Required:

a. What practice standards are applicable to the engagement to review and report on the current value balance sheet?

b. What primary auditing procedures should you apply in addition to those necessary for the audit of the historical-cost financial statements?

c. Will any additional disclosures in footnotes be necessary?

d. Are there any evidential problems in the NPC situation that might prevent your rendering a report on the current value balance sheet?

15.37 Compilation Presentation Alternatives. Jimmy C operates a large service station, garage, and truck stop on Freeway 95 near Plainview. His brother, Bill, has recently joined as a partner, even though he still keeps a small PA practice. One slow afternoon, they were discussing financial statements with Bert, the local PA who operates the largest public practice in Plainview.

Jimmy: The business is growing, and sometimes I need to show financial statements to parts suppliers and to the loan officers at the bank.

Bert: That so.

Jimmy: Yea-boy, and they don't like the way I put 'em together.

Bert: That so.

Bill: Heck, Jimmy, I know all about that. I can compile a jim-dandy set of financial statements for us.

Jimmy: What does Jim Dan over at the café have to do with it?

Bert: Never mind, Jimmy. Bill can't do compiled financial statements for you. He's not independent.

Jimmy: I know, Momma didn't let him outa the house 'til he was 24. The neighbours complained.

Bert: That so.

Bill: Shucks.

Jimmy: But Bert, those fellas are always asking me about accounting policies, contingencies and stuff like that. Said something about "footnotes." I don't want to fool with all that small print.

Required:

Think about the financial disclosure problems of Jimmy and Bill's small business. What three kinds of compiled financial statements can be prepared for them and by whom?

15.38 Negative Assurance in Review Reports. One portion of the report on a review services engagement is the following: Based on my review, I am not aware of any material modifications that should be made to the accompanying financial statements in order for them to be in conformity with generally accepted accounting principles.

Required:

a. Is this paragraph a "negative assurance" given by the PA?

b. Why is "negative assurance" generally prohibited in audit reports?

c. What justification is there for permitting "negative assurance" in a review services report on unaudited financial statements and on interim financial information?

15.39 Reporting on a Forecast. Kingston Company proposed to sell to investors limited partnership interests in 40 new hardware store buildings. Kingston Company would be the general partner. The deal was structured to raise funds for business expansion by offering a real estate investment. As part of the offering material, Kingston management produced a forecast based on the assumption of $1.5 million gross annual revenue for each new location. The lease income to the partnership is to be a base rental fee plus 10 percent of gross revenue in excess of $1 million. Kingston's existing stores have gross revenues ranging from $800,000 to $1.75 million. Kingston also produced related balance sheets and statements of changes in financial position, all in conformity with AICPA forecast presentation guidelines.

Kingston engaged Anderson, Olds & Watershed to examine the forecast and submit a report. One of the assistant accountants on the engagement drafted the opinion paragraph of the report as follows:

In our opinion, the accompanying forecast is presented in conformity with guidelines for presentation of a forecast established by the American Institute of Certified Public Accountants, and the underlying assumption of $1.5 million average revenue per store is sufficient to cover the fixed and variable expenses of store maintenance, taxes and insurance, which are the obligations of the limited partners. However, there will usually be differences between the forecasted and actual results because store revenues frequently do not materialize as expected, and the shortfall may be material. We have no responsibility to update this report for events and circumstances occurring after the date of this report.

Required:

Identify and explain the errors, if any, in this portion of the forecast examination report.

15.40 Current Value Supplement. Ms. Carboy (Kingston's controller) has prepared current cost information following the SFAS 89 guidelines. The information has been placed in a section at the front of the corporate annual report, apart from the audited financial statements. The section declares that Anderson, Olds & Watershed have not performed any review procedures on the information and does not express any opinion on it.

Kingston performs some welding work for customers and uses a ZB40-X-ray machine to inspect the strength of the welds. Kingston bought its ZB40 three years ago for $60,000. Most such X-ray machines last 10 years, so Kingston has recorded $6,000 amortization expense for the current year—the third year the machine has been used. A new ZB40 now costs $75,000. Kingston is planning to purchase a second one because it is the best on the market.

When Ms. Carboy prepared the supplementary current cost information, the BZ40 was reflected as follows:

Current-year amortization expense $75,000

Machinery and equipment $75,000

Accumulated amortization $22,500

Current-year amortization expense $7,500

Required:

a. Should the audit report contain a disclaimer on the current value supplementary information? Explain.

b. Does AOW have any responsibility regarding the current value information?

c. What audit procedures can be performed with regard to supplementary current value information? With reference to the ZB40 machine, explain the procedures.

DISCUSSION CASES

15.41 Prepare a Compilation Report. You have been engaged by the Coffin Brothers to compile their financial schedules from books and records maintained by James Coffin. The brothers own and operate three auto parts stores in Central City. Even though their business is growing, they have not wanted to employ a full-time bookkeeper. James specifies that all he wants is a balance sheet, a statement of operations and a statement of cash flows. He does not have time to write up footnotes to accompany the statement.

James directed the physical count of inventory on June 30 and adjusted and closed the books on that date. You find that he actually is a good accountant, having taken some night courses at the community college. The accounts appear to have been maintained in conformity with generally accepted accounting principles. At least you have noticed no obvious errors.

Required:

You are independent with respect to the Coffin brothers and their Coffin Auto Speed Shop business. Prepare a report on your compilation services engagement.

15.42 Reporting on Comparative Unaudited Financial Statements. Anson Jones, PA, performed a review service for the Independence Company in 2003. He wants to present comparative financial statements. However, the 2002 statements were compiled by Able and Associates, PAs, and Able does not want to co-operate with Jones by reissuing the prior-year compilation report. Jones has no indication that any adjustments should be made to either the 2003 or 2002 statements, which are to be presented with all necessary disclosures. However, he does not have time to perform a review of the 2002 statements. He completed his work on January 15, 2004, for the statement dated December 31, 2003.

Required:

Write Jones' review report and include the paragraph describing the report on the 2002 statements.

15.43 Erroneous Reporting on Interim Financial Information. The report in the box on this page was prepared by Baker & Baker, public accountants, on the interim financial information of Micro Mini Company. The interim financial information was presented in the first quarterly report for the three-month period ended March 31, 2003. No comparative quar-

---

Report of Independent Auditors
The Board of Directors and Stockholders,
Micro Mini Company:

We have made a review of the balance sheet of Micro Mini Company at March 31, 2003, the related statement of income for the three-month period ended March 31, 2003, and the statement of cash flows for the three-month period ended March 31, 2003, in accordance with standards established by the Canadian Institute of Chartered Accountants.

A review of interim financial information consists principally of obtaining an understanding of the system for the preparation of the interim financial information, applying analytical review procedures to financial data and making enquiries to persons responsible for financial and accounting matters.

In our opinion, the accompanying interim financial information presents fairly, in all material respects, the financial position of Micro Mini Company at March 31, 2003, and the results of its operations and its cash flows for the three-month period then ended in conformity with generally accepted accounting principles.

Baker & Baker, PAs
March 31, 2004

terly information of the first quarter of the prior year was presented. Baker & Baker completed a review in accordance with standards established by the CICA and found that, to the best of their knowledge, the information was presented in conformity with CICA requirements. In an audit report dated January 21, 2003, Baker & Baker had given a standard unqualified audit report on Micro Mini's 2002 and 2001 annual financial statements.

Required:
a. Review the report and list, with explanation, the erroneous portions in it.
b. Rewrite the report.

15.44 Report on Comprehensive Basis Other Than GAAP. The Brockville Life Insurance Company prepares its financial statements on a statutory basis in conformity with the accounting practices prescribed and permitted by the Commissioner of Insurance of the Province of Ontario. This statutory basis produces financial statements that differ materially from statements prepared in conformity with generally accepted accounting principles. On the statutory basis, for example, agents' first-year commissions are expensed instead of being partially deferred, and equity securities are reported at market value lower than cost, even if a "permanent impairment" of value is not evident.

The company engaged its auditors, Major and Major Associates, to audit the statutory basis financial statements and report on them. Footnote 10 in the statements contains a narrative description and a numerical table explaining the differences between the statutory basis and GAAP accounting. Footnote 10 also reconciles the statutory basis assets, liabilities, income, expense and net income (statutory basis) to the measurements that would be obtained using GAAP.

Required:
Write the audit report appropriate in the circumstances. The year-end date is December 31, 2002, and the audit field work was completed on February 20, 2003. (The company plans to distribute this report to persons other than the department of insurance regulators.

15.45 Service Bureau Controls. Your firm has been engaged to render an opinion on control procedures at ABC Services Ltd., which is a payroll service bureau.

Required:
a. What type of circumstances might arise that would prevent the auditor of a service organization from issuing an opinion without reservation on control procedures?
b. Identify the two types of engagements for a service bureau and compare and contrast the two types with respect to audit standards and procedures.

(CGAAC adapted)

15.46 Audits vs. Non-audits. Woo, PA, has been engaged to perform an audit of financial statements of FST Inc., which Smith, the owner-manager of FST, intends to submit to the bank in support of a loan application. Woo has applied the audit procedures he considered necessary in the circumstances and is "about halfway" through his collection of audit evidence when Smith informs him that since the bank has just indicated that a review engagement report is sufficient for its purposes, FST does not require a full audit.

Required:
a. Contrast the auditor's overall objective in the performance of an audit with the accountant's overall objective in the performance of a review engagement.
b. Considering that Woo has already applied some audit procedures to and obtained evidence regarding the financial statements of FST, what modifications should Woo make to the standard review engagement report?
c. What are the appropriate criteria against which the financial statements and related disclosures are measured in the case of:
(1) an audit?
(2) a review engagement?
(3) a compilation engagement?

15.47 Special Reports. As well as engagements to examine financial statements in their entirety, a PA may be engaged to prepare other types of special reports for a client.

Required:
a. *Section* 5800 of the *CICA Handbook* provides for two types of special reports.
(1) Identify each type of special report.
(2) Identify the standards governing each type of examination.

(3) Briefly explain how each of the resulting reports differs from an opinion on financial statements.

b. When the auditor is engaged to report on the design, effective operation and continuity of control procedures at a service organization, what are the additional examination responsibilities of the auditor?

(CGAAC adapted)

15.48 Objectives of Different Engagements. Pierre Landret has recently started a landscaping and landscaping supply business. The business is incorporated, with the shareholders being Pierre and his wife. His educational background is a bachelor's degree in agricultural science, and he is unfamiliar with the accounting aspects of his new venture. He has come to you, a CGA, for advice. He says, "I want you to look at the records of my business for the past year. I understand that there are three different types of engagements that you can perform. What are the differences between them as they affect my business, and what purpose might each one serve for my business?

Required:
a. Draft a reply to Mr. Landret.
b. State the two matters that the public accountant must be satisfied about before accepting a review engagement.
c. State the three matters that the public accountant must be satisfied about before accepting a compilation engagement.

(CGAAC adapted)

APPENDIX 15A
A CRITICAL ANALYSIS OF SECTION 5025

Clearly, *Section* 5025 marks only the beginning of a long process of developing audit/assurance standards; it is also a significant attempt to keep auditing relevant in the new century. There are bound to be changes to the section. In indicating possible future trends, we will start by pointing out some contentious areas over the seven years that it took for this section to evolve into its present form.

Section 5025 is the result of a long process that began in 1990, when a group was established to explore the concept of a broad umbrella framework for all assurance engagements. In 1992 the study group came out with a report, "Assurance Based Service Engagements." On the basis of the feedback it received about this report, the CICA in October 1995 issued an Exposure Draft on Standards for Assurance Engagements. This refined the earlier issues paper to create a better integration with public sector auditing standards; perhaps most importantly it also provided, in an extensive appendix, a series of example reports in diverse situations. However, several contentious issues were identified in the resulting feedback from this Exposure Draft so that the final standard was watered down somewhat. Most notably, the *Handbook* section on assurance engagements no longer has illustrations, and the linkage with public-sector auditing standards has been weakened. Nevertheless, this standard is a pioneering one for the profession globally, in that it is the first attempt to establish a coherent framework for all types of audit and audit-related services. The standard can be viewed as a good first step in the development of a reporting framework that will accommodate the needs and concerns of regulators and auditors and meet changing public expectations. Ultimately the framework should (a) clarify the roles and responsibilities of managers, regulators and auditors, (b) outline how auditors discharge their responsibilities, and (c) set out appropriate criteria for use by auditors and regulators in fulfilling their responsibilities. In sum, the result should be a clearer accountability framework for the public and private sectors. It is this focus on an accountability framework that perhaps makes *Handbook Section* 5025 truly unique.

One important difference between the Exposure Draft and the final version of the standard is the lack of illustrative reports in the final version. The Exposure Draft had eight example reports in its Appendix B. Seven of these dealt with attestation engagements on internal control reports, and one was an example of a direct reporting engagement using a public sector illustration.

The box on the next page illustrates a high-level assurance attest engagement report without reservation, with additional information contained in an explanatory paragraph. Note why it was considered an attest engagement: the auditor was reporting on a written management assertion about the state of controls. Note also the use of the words "present fairly" on this new type of assertion and the use of the words "in all significant respects."

EXAMPLE REPORT 1

- High level of assurance.
- Attest engagement.
- Report without reservation.
- Additional information contained in explanatory paragraph.

This and the other examples were dropped, apparently because the CICA did not want to inhibit experimentation, particularly in preparing internal control reports in conformity with COCO.

As we noted in Chapter 15, there are currently no authoritative illustrations of public reports on internal control in Canadian standards. The closest thing we have is example report 1 above.

AUDITORS' REPORT CONCERNING EFFECTIVENESS OF THE SYSTEM OF INTERNAL CONTROL OVER FINANCIAL REPORTING[1]

To the Shareholders of ABC Company

We have audited management's assertion that ABC Company maintained an effective system of internal control over financial reporting as of December 31, 19XX in relation to the criteria [describe criteria or indicate source of criteria].[2] Management's assertion is included in the accompanying report [title of management report]. The maintenance of an effective system of internal control over financial reporting is the responsibility of management. Our responsibility is to express an opinion on management's assertion about the effectiveness of the internal control system based on our audit.

We conducted our audit in accordance with generally accepted auditing standards. Those standards require that we plan and perform an audit to obtain reasonable assurance that management's assertion is free from significant misstatements. An audit includes examining, on a test basis, evidence supporting the content and disclosures in management's assertion. An audit also includes assessing the criteria used and the significant judgements made by management, as well as evaluating the overall presentation of management's assertion.

In our opinion, management's assertion presents fairly, in all significant respects, the effectiveness of the system of internal control over financial reporting of ABC Company as of December 31, 19XX based upon the criteria referred to above.

Because of the inherent limitations in any internal control system, errors or irregularities may occur and not be detected. Also, projections of any evaluation of the internal control system over financial reporting to future periods are subject to the risk that the internal control system may become inadequate because of changes in conditions, or that the degree of compliance with the policies or procedures may deteriorate.[3]

City   . . . .
Date   Chartered Accountants

---

[1] In an attest engagement, the practitioner's report is directly on management's assertion on a subject matter; in a direct reporting engagement the report is directly on the subject matter.

[2] Alternatively, the description of criteria could be attached as an appendix to the report.

[3] Example of additional information and explanations neither required by statute nor intended as a reservation. As such, the opinion paragraph should precede that containing additional information or explanations.

Perhaps the biggest concern with the current authoritative standard as reflected in comments to the Exposure Draft relates to the inconsistencies with existing review standards—specifically the need to make explicit the various risk assessments under 5025. In contrast, existing review standards are more procedurally oriented—for example, they do not require an assessment of internal controls. The chief reason for a risk-oriented framework in *Section* 5025 is that the risk model provides a better theoretical foundation by linking moderate risk to review attest engagements and low risk to audit attest engagements.

Other potential inconsistencies occur between *Section* 5025 and the review standards (5800 series), control procedures in service organizations (*Section* 5900) and public sector exception reporting standards (discussed in Chapter 18).

In addition, there are the inconsistencies explicitly recognized in Appendix A of *Section* 5025, as discussed in the chapter. The rationale for keeping out these engagements is that:

> assurance engagements are intended to provide a conclusion concerning a subject matter of interest to a user. In contrast, in an engagement to provide other services for which guidance is provided in the CICA Handbook, the practitioner communicates the nature of the work carried out with respect to a matter and the factual results of this work. The practitioner provides no conclusion concerning the subject matter. (*Section* 5025.A)

The fact that some users may choose to derive some assurance from the auditor's involvement in these excluded engagements, does not change the fact that the practitioner does not provide assurance consistent with 5025; hence these excluded engagements must have carefully worded reports that clearly communicate the nature of the auditors' involvement (*Section* 5025.A).

As we will see in Chapter 18, many public sector engagements involve a reporting of deficiencies that closely resemble derivative reporting engagements. According to *Section* 5025A, "derivative reporting is not an assurance engagement because the practitioner merely points out matters that have come to his or her attention during the engagement. The practitioner does not provide any assurance that these are the only matters which would be of interest to management, the audit committee or the regulator."

This exclusion has potentially important ramifications for public sector auditors: many of their reports are exception or deficiency reports, and it is unclear whether these should be treated as only moderate assurance engagements or not included as assurance engagements at all. At least theoretically, this would suggest that no assurance is being provided by many public sector engagements. Public sector auditors would be very concerned with such an interpretation, especially considering that the assurance concept was extended primarily to incorporate the direct reporting nature of many public sector engagements. In fact, as noted in Chapter 18, a notable success of public sector auditing is in exception reporting of major waste, inefficiencies or ineffectiveness in government operations. To exclude such obviously important public accountability engagements from the framework of assurance may suggest this framework is incomplete. In fact, *Section* 5025.15 was modified from the Exposure Draft version to specifically exclude mention of public sector mandates requiring legislative auditors. It would appear that some rethinking may be required on whether deficiency reports provide some assurance or not. After all, review engagements provide only negative assurance ("nothing has come to my attention" type of assurance), and yet they are considered assurance engagements by *Section* 5025. This relates, we feel, to the objectives of the engagement in the first place; we will have more to say about this shortly. It is clear that the interface between assurance standards and public sector standards will be an important aspect in the evolution of both sets of standards.

An interesting change in perspective that has taken place within the CICA with the evolution of the assurance engagement standards is that financial statement audits are now increasingly viewed as direct reporting engagements rather than attestation engagements. This is interesting, because the rest of the world views financial statement audits as attestation engagements, so the CICA may be developing a new concept for financial statement auditing. The classification hinges on whether financial statements are treated as written assertions (attest engagements) or as the subject matter of an audit (see D.J. Cockburn, "An Issue of Attestation," *CA Magazine,* November 1992, pp. 35–37). If financial statements are treated as subject matter of the audit, this question arises: What are the written assertions, if any? One may feel that a client representation letter may fulfill this requirement, but the problem here is that when *Section* 5025 refers to written assertions, they appear to mean a public declaration, not something that is just used to document audit working papers. The significance of this distinction is evident from the illustrations the CICA used in its 1995 Exposure Draft. There, all examples of attest engagements referred to a publicly written set of assertions by management (as in, for example, the box above), and only in attest engagements were the words "presents fairly" used in the practitioner's report. In the direct reporting engagement illustration, on the other hand, there was no mention of a client report and there was no use of the words "presents fairly." Perhaps this partly explains why the illustrations were dropped: they suggested a significant change in the nature of the financial statement auditor's report if in fact they were treated as direct reporting engagements. In addition, there would need to be consideration of the fact that suitable criteria may go beyond the current financial accounting framework of *Section* 1000 as noted in the chapter, and the combination of these two interpretations can effectively put the auditor in the position of setting accounting standards on each engagement. This was not likely the result that the CICA standard setters had in mind when they developed *Section* 5025. All of this helps illustrate the fundamental issues being raised by the concept of assurance standards.

The CICA recognizes these and other potential problems with the assurance standard. K. Duggan, in "To Assure or Not to Assure" (*CA Magazine,* January–February 1997, pp. 46–48), identified exception reporting, inconsistency with other *Handbook Sections,* lack of illustrative reports and better clarification of the distinction between moderate and reasonable level of assurance as primary concerns of respondents to the 1995 Exposure Draft. Many of these concerns will be addressed by the CICA in the near future with additional guidelines and *Handbook Recommendations.*

EVOLUTION OF THE ASSURANCE CONCEPT OUTSIDE OF CANADA

In the United States there currently are no assurance standards, although many AICPA groups are working on various aspects of assurance engagements. One of these groups, the Special Committee on Assurance Services (SCAS), has defined assurance services as "independent professional services that improve the quality of information, with context, for decision makers."

We see from this definition that the American concept may be broader than *Section* 5025 because accountability decisions are but one class of decisions. In the SCAS's view, PAs must transform themselves from "certifiers" into "enhancers" of information. The word *quality* in the above definition is presumed to mean reliability and relevance for decision makers' needs. The context refers to how the information is presented in the practitioner's report. According to the SCAS, users can be the client or third parties and the true nature of the engagement is determined by the ultimate goal of the engagement. The SCAS foresees an overlap between assurance and consulting engagements, as indicated in the box below, but it explicitly excludes an overlap between assurance and tax services. In its view, the engagement letter is critical to determining the nature of the engagement.

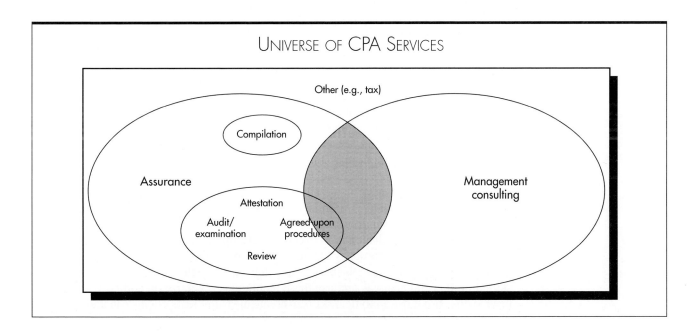

In the view of SCAS, assurance expands the traditional audit function in three major new directions: (1) meeting new needs of the existing client base—for example, risk assessment, performance measurement and information systems reliability; (2) meeting needs of a new client base using existing service expertise—for example, process quality (ISO 9000), product quality and World Wide Web assertions; and (3) providing new services for new clients—for example, elder care, electronic commerce assurance and health care performance measures. The goal of the AICPA is to develop a new conceptual framework for all these areas that is flexible enough for practitioners to use on their own to identify additional assurance service opportunities.

Three boxes follow. The first illustrates a specific user-oriented service. The second provides a discussion of a recent AICPA-proposed assurance standard for Management Discussion & Analysis (MD&A) in annual reports. The third provides a recent overview of assurance services contemplated by the AICPA.

BENCHMARKING AT MOSS ADAMS

Neal West's firm, Moss Adams LLP, began doing benchmarking engagements some 10 years ago, with a pick-up in frequency over the last few. West, the firm's director of business assurance, is a member of the performance measurement task force of the AICPA assurance service committee, and he's ready to help other firms understand what these engagements are about and how to perform them. He told the *Journal* about some of his firm's experiences.

The original and still-popular service starts with a cost of doing business survey for a trade association (for example, an association of marinas or fencing contractors). The association is the client, and its members, the subject of the survey, are the users of the information. The survey allows Moss Adams to create a set of "common size financial statements" based on financial data from all the surveyed members. Association members can compare their performances to the industry-wide performances. The engagement sometimes calls for stratifying the collective data by size of the surveyed entities into three or so sets of financial statements. Association members can compare their performance to the average for the industry or to the group they are closest to within the industry.

Sometimes the survey is used to gather nonfinancial performance data—typically, market, process or workforce data. But the purpose, again, is benchmarking. Another variation is to measure the performance of the top-performing segment of the industry. The data set a standard for association members: they know what is possible and can set targets. Associations can distribute the performance measures to members or provide them for a fee.

The intended use of the data by the associations is always clear when the engagement terms are settled. Many clients know what they want, but Moss Adams always considers what is best for the client's members and will be of most help. In those cases, Moss Adams is designing the engagements with clients by exploring their needs with them.

Moss Adams is doing a growing percentage of its benchmarking for individual firms. Why? Because not all firms fit neatly in an industry category. They may be uncommon in size or have unique geographic characteristics, for example. Moss Adams's Xemplar process, now under development, is designed to set a standard that individual firms of associations can use in such circumstances. Xemplar does not produce an average or an ideal, but an exception example, created in part from experts' views, against which a company can measure its operations.

West believes CPAs have the basic competencies to do this kind of work. They are skilled in financial analysis and use these techniques regularly on audits. What they need to do is use those analytical skills to create measurements clients can understand

and to follow this up with assistance in helping clients improve their operations. Follow-on consulting services of this sort are a very important part of the assurance package, both in terms of benefits to the client and in terms of fees.

West gives this example: Suppose benchmarking shows that personnel turnover is adversely affecting sales and customer retention. Moss Adams would analyze the causes and help the client improve. As West puts it: "We're asking, 'Where are they? Where should they be? And why aren't they there?' Then we help them get there."

CPAs need to have a rich understanding of their clients' businesses and industries in order to do this work, but that is not a new type of demand on them. Basic analytical tools are taught in staff training at Moss Adams, and a synergy exists between analytical reviews that strengthen the audit and the analytical work needed to deliver benchmarking.

"It's a service that meets clients' needs and fits well with our skills base," West concludes.

Source: R.K. Elliott and D.M. Pallais, *Journal of Accountancy,* July 1997, p. 62.

The assurance services that show the most potential are those related to a given firm's existing expertise and client base. Thus, for example, elder care assurance engagements would be most successful as extensions of existing tax or permanent financial planning services. It seems that PAs have a competitive edge when there are tie-ins with existing services. In fact this has been the case traditionally with tax and consulting services, but with the concept now being extended to new assurance engagements. Note, however, that the issue of maintaining auditor independence may grow more complex as the distinctions between their various services become blurred, as is the case under some of the AICPA proposals. It may even become necessary to develop different independence criteria for different assurance engagements.

PROPOSED ATTESTATION STANDARD ON MD&A

Out for exposure is a proposed Statement on Standards for Attestation Engagements (SSAE), *Management's Discussion and Analysis,* that would provide guidance for practitioners examining or reviewing management's discussion and analysis prepared according to Securities and Exchange Commission rules and regulations. "This is a voluntary, value-added service auditors can offer their clients," said Richard Dieter, a task force member and partner of Arthur Andersen LLP.

"The scope of attestation engagements is increasing. People are looking for assurance on matters outside of historical financial statements," said Beth Schneider, a director at Deloitte & Touche LLP, who staffed the auditing standards board task force that drew up the exposure draft. Dieter added, "I think this proposed SSAE is important because it shows we are moving into more subjective and softer information, which includes disclosure of future demands and uncertainties that can face a business. The ASB views the MD&A attest service as a forerunner to some of the services CPAs are—and should be—performing." Emphasizing that such engagements are not required, Dieter said he does not expect the SEC to make it mandatory; he sees the demand for this service coming initially from underwriters in connection with securities offerings.

"The proposed standard also will provide a useful framework for future assurance services in that area."

Source: Journal of Accountancy, April 1997, p. 13.

Where all of this leads is presently hard to tell, but it may be worthwhile to highlight the apparent differences between the CICA and AICPA approaches. The AICPA uses a broader concept of assurance that not only includes items specifically excluded by *Section 5025*, agreed upon procedure, compilation and consulting engagements, but also does not limit itself to accountability frameworks. Whether this is good or bad depends on how well the AICPA will be able to distinguish between assurance and all other PA services. If they aren't able to do a better job, there is a risk that little will be accomplished with a new concept like assurance services, because all it may mean is that assurance services are little different from PA services in general (as discussed in Chapter 1). To further cloud the issue, the current AICPA position seems to treat all unwritten assertion engagements as consulting engagements.

It would appear from our perspective that it would be useful to clearly explain why tax services and some consulting services are not assurance engagements under the AICPA approach. Some indications of the CICA's views on this are given in *Section 5020.B*, repro-

---

A SAMPLE OF ASSURANCE SERVICE POSSIBILITIES

This list of services is taken from the special committee on assurance services survey of 21 large PA firms. (The full survey results, with over 200 entries, are available at www.aicpa.org/asssurance/scas/newsvs/addlposs/index.htm.) The goal of the survey was to establish the breadth of assurance services already offered in practice.

- Assessment of ethics-related risks and vulnerabilities.
- Controls over and risk related to investments.
- Adequacy of controls and policies for derivatives.
- Information systems security reviews.
- Assessment of risk of accumulation, distribution and storage of digital information.
- Fraud and illegal acts risk assessment.
- Management/board salary benchmarking.
- Internal audit quality assurance.
- Adequacy of billing system compared to competitors.
- Advertising rates to be paid vs. those charged.
- Customer satisfaction surveys—reports/validations.
- Review of compliance with investment policy.
- Compliance with trading policies and procedures.
- Compliance with royalty agreements (entertainment).
- Identification of critical items to monitor.
- Examination of software specifications.
- ISO 9000 certification.
- Examination of hardware benchmark test results.
- Newspaper circulation audits.
- Annual environmental report.
- Audit of milestone in long-term incentive plans.
- Compliance with industry standards for additives test labs.
- Verification of contributions under incentive plan.
- Verification of construction costs for incentive grant.

Source: R.K. Elliott and D.M. Pallais, *Journal of Accountancy,* July 1997, p. 63.

duced in the chapter. The advantage of the CICA approach, with its focus on accountability, is the requirement that there be an asserter (the accountable party) whose explicit or implicit assertions are enhanced by the assurer. Thus, for example, one way to distinguish assurance from consulting and tax engagements is that in the latter situations the practitioner acts as an asserter and not as an assurer.

Such an interpretation is supported by the theory of argumentation in philosophy, which would view all PA services as types of dialogue. If the purpose of the argument in a dialogue is to support a conclusion about someone else's assertion, then we have an assurance engagement. If on the other hand we have an argument for the purpose of a different type of conclusion, then we have a non-assurance engagement. Purpose in turn is determined by the context of the dialogue, including the accountability relationship (e.g., see D. Walton, *Argument Structure, A Pragmatic Theory,* Toronto: University of Toronto Press, 1996, for more discussion of arguments and dialogue in philosophy). Thus, if we view PA services as part of a web of dialogue between the practitioner, the accountable party and the users, the CICA approach may be on firmer philosophical ground because of its more precise assurance concept. Theories of philosophy suggest that context should determine the role the auditor plays, and the CICA approach appears to make a finer distinction between different contexts. However, as noted earlier, we need further clarifications on fundamental matters such as whether financial statements are written assertions or the subject matter of audit engagements. As in all dialogue, an agreement on the definition of the terms is a crucial starting point; and what the current controversies suggest is that existing definitions need clarification.

In March 1999 the International Auditing Practices Committee of the International Federation of Accountants (IFAC) issued an Exposure Draft (ED) "Assurance Engagements." The ED has three main parts: (1) Motivation and Background, (2) Framework, and (3) General Principles.

The purpose of this ED is similar to that of the CICA's *Section* 5025—to provide a standards framework for current and future assurance services for practitioners who are carrying out assurance services where no specific standards exist. The ED appears to have been influenced particularly by *Handbook Section* 5025. The biggest differences between the two are as follows:

1. The assurance services can include those provided by internal as well as external auditors.

2. The ED places more stress on getting the acknowledgment of the responsible party for the subject matter.

Generally, the ED is consistent with, and very similar to, *Section* 5025 except for the above. This is evident from the framework as well as from the general principles. For example, the ED framework specifically excludes the following engagements from the framework: agreed upon procedures where no conclusion is expressed; compilation of financial or other information; preparation of tax returns where no conclusion is expressed; and tax consultancy, management consulting and other advisory services.

The ED's framework consists of the following elements of an assurance engagement (RSE):

(*a*) Professional accountant.

(*b*) Subject matter.

(*c*) Responsible party.

(*d*) Intended user.

(*e*) Suitable criteria.

(*f*) Engagement process.

(*g*) Reporting.

The framework provides more details on each of the elements than does *Section* 5025—for example, on qualities of a PA (e.g., integrity, objectivity, condifidentiality). It also provides more illustrations of subject matters (e.g., human resource practices, corporate governance) and of the engagement process (e.g., planning, documentation, subsequent events). Interestingly, the criteria are virtually the same as the CICA's suitability criteria: relevance, reliability, neutrality, understandability and completeness.

An interesting aspect of the IFAC's proposed framework is its definition of an assertion: "The assertion is the responsible party's conclusion about the subject matter based on suitable criteria. In a direct reporting engagement where there is no written assertion by the responsible party, the PA expresses a conclusion on the subject matter using suitable criteria" (ED, para. 39).

The IFAC's ED also provides a set of general principles that further clarify the framework. These principles start with a very important definition of the objective of an assurance engagement: "The objective of an assurance engagement is for a professional accountant to evaluate a subject matter that is the responsibility of another party using identified suitable criteria, and to express a conclusion that provides the intended user with a level of assurance about that subject matter." (ED, para. 2)

The general principle, like the general standard of financial statement auditing, refers to characteristics that the PA should have. The remaining principles deal with the following:

1. Accepting the Engagement.
2. Quality Control.
3. Planning and Conduct.
4. Evidence.
5. Documentation.
6. Subsequent Events.
7. Using the Work of an Expert.
8. Reporting.
9. Format of Report.

Some highlights of the differences between the CICA's *Section* 5025 and these principles include the following:

- The term "materiality" instead of "significance" is used for all assurance engagements.
- The risk model definition of the ED is more consistent with the traditional definition of the audit risk model.
- The ED explicitly states that the documentation "should include the PA's reasoning on all significant matters which require the exercise of professional judgment, together with the professional accountant's conclusion thereon. In areas involving difficult questions of principles or judgment, documentation will record the relevant facts that were known by the professional accountant at the time the conclusion was reached." The key test of this documentation principle appears to be: "What is necessary to provide another PA who has no previous experience with the engagement with an understanding of the work performed and the basis of the principal decisions taken but not the detailed aspects of the engagement?" (ED, para. 65).

The ED thus provides considerably more detailed guidance on what should be documented than the CICA's *Section* 5025.

The ED ends with a discussion of the public sector perspective and some illustrative reports. The ED contends that the basic principles are the same in the public sector and that whatever the public sector mandate, a clear expression is necessary regarding the PA's conclusion about the subject matter. In other words, it is not enough to simply report instances of noncompliance as exceptions to due regard to economy, efficiency and effectiveness. This clarifies that exception reports by themselves are not assurance engagements under the ED's criteria.

Assurance engagements will obviously be an important area of research, standard setting and practitioner innovation in the foreseeable future. We hope this appendix has helped clarify the key issues to watch for in future developments. More detailed discussion of specific types of assurance engagements is provided in Chapters 18 and 19.

We conclude this appendix with two illustrative direct-reporting reports from AICPA-related publications. Exhibits 15A–1 and 15A–2 illustrate assurance reports on risk assessment and performance measurement respectively. Note how difficult it is to distinguish these reports from consulting engagements. The first report, on risk assessments, has more of an assurance orientation as defined by *CICA Handbook, Section* 5025, but it also contains components of what would normally appear in a management letter (see Chapter 14). The second report, on performance measurement, seems much more in line with that of a consulting engagement. Here the auditor appears to be acting more like an asserter than an assurer. However, keep in mind that in the United States there are no standards on assurance engagements yet, and that these reports should be viewed as tentative and experimental. In light of the issues discussed here, you can compare them with the CICA's ED report given earlier in this appendix, and with reports provided in later chapters. It is clear that assurance engagements have the potential to revolutionize the profession, and that this will be a very active area of experimentation and growth over the years.

are the principles that enforce the various series of professional standards. For example, there is usually a specific rule relating to compliance with professional standards.

Compliance with Professional Standards

A member engaged in the practice of public accounting shall perform his or her professional services in accordance with generally accepted standards of practice of the profession (from Rule 206 of ICAO).

Analysis

This rule may be viewed as an extension and refinement of the due care principle. It implies adherence to duly promulgated technical standards in all areas of professional service. These areas include review and compilation (unaudited financial statements), consulting tax and "other" professional services. The practical effect of this rule is to make noncompliance with all technical standards subject to disciplinary proceedings. Thus, failure to follow auditing standards, accounting and review standards, and assurance, compilation and professional conduct standards is a violation of this rule.

Accounting Principles

The compliance rule requires adherence to official pronouncements of accounting principles, with an important exception relating to unusual circumstances where adherence would create misleading statements. The rule itself concedes that unusual circumstances may exist; it permits PAs to decide for themselves the applicability of official pronouncements and places on them the burden of an ethical decision. The rule is not strictly imperative, in that it allows PAs to exercise a utilitarian calculation for special circumstances. The compliance rule requires adherence to official pronouncements unless such adherence would be misleading. The consequences of misleading statements to outside decision makers would be financial harm, so presumably the greater good would be realized by explaining a departure.

As a result of the November 1997 Supreme Court of Canada ruling in *Kripps* v. *Touche Ross,* this compliance rule is likely to become more influential in the future. This is further discussed in Chapter 17.

Confidentiality

The general principle of confidentiality is as follows:

> A member in public practice shall not disclose any confidential information without the specific consent of the client.

This principle shall not be construed (1) to relieve a member of his or her professional obligations[10] to comply with a validly issued and enforceable subpoena or summons, (2) to prohibit a member's compliance with applicable laws and government regulations, (3) to prohibit review of a member's professional practice under *Member's Handbook* bylaws, or (4) to preclude a member from initiating a complaint with or responding to any enquiry made by the ethics division or trial board or a duly constituted investigative or disciplinary body of the members' professional group (CAs, CMAs or CGAs).

Members of any of the bodies identified in (4) above and members involved with professional practice reviews identified in (3) above shall not use to their own advantage or disclose any member's confidential client information that comes to their attention in carrying out those activities. This prohibition shall not restrict members' exchange of information in connection with the investigative or disciplinary proceedings described in (4) above or the professional practice reviews described in (3) above.

---

[10] C. Chazen, R.L. Miller, and K.I. Solomon, "When the Rules Say: See Your Lawyer," *Journal of Accountancy*, January 1981, p. 70.

Confidential information is information that should not be disclosed to outside parties unless demanded by a court or an administrative body having subpoena or summons power. Privileged information, on the other hand, is information that cannot even be demanded by a court. Common-law privilege exists for husband–wife, attorney–client and physician–patient relationships. In all the recognized privilege relationships, the professional person is obligated to observe the privilege, which can be waived only by the client, patient or penitent. (These persons are said to be the holders of the privilege.)

> The duty to keep a client's affairs confidential should not be confused with the legal concept of privilege. The duty of confidentiality precludes the member from disclosing a client's affairs without the knowledge or consent of the client. However, this duty does not excuse a member from obeying an order of a court of competent jurisdiction requiring the member to disclose the information.
>
> A court will determine whether or not a member should maintain the confidentiality of client information depending on the facts of each case. (ICAO Council Interpretation 210.1, paragraph 1)

Accountants and clients have attempted to establish privilege for tax file workpapers so as to shield them from Canada Customs and Revenue Agency summons demands (tax file workpapers contain accountants' analyses of "soft spots" and potential tax liability for arguable tax positions) but have so far been unsuccessful.

The rules of privileged and confidential communication are based on the belief that they facilitate a free flow of information between parties to the relationship. The nature of accounting services makes it necessary for the accountant to have access to information about salaries, products, contracts, merger or divestment plans, tax matters and other data required for the best possible professional work. Managers would be less likely to reveal such information if they could not trust the accountant to keep it confidential. If accountants were to reveal such information, the resultant reduction of the information flow might be undesirable, so no accountants should break the confidentiality rule without a good reason.

Difficult problems arise over auditors' obligations to "blow the whistle" on clients' shady or illegal practices. Generally, the codes indicate that confidentiality in such cases

---

IRS INFORMANT

James C, CPA, was in hot water with the IRS. To get relief, he agreed to tell the IRS about tax cheating by his clients. After all, some of them were practising tax evasion, and James C. knew about it.

Steven N, a client, said: "It's every taxpayer's worst nightmare. I relied on my trusted accountant to keep me out of trouble with the IRS. James C often sat in my living room. We treated him like family. I even gave him power of attorney to represent me before the IRS."

But Steven N had skimmed untaxed income from his restaurant business and was indicted for tax evasion. An AICPA spokesman said: "The accountant's job is to point out errors to the client—not to the IRS."

Postscript: The Missouri State Board of Accountancy revoked James C's CPA certificate, saying: "His action is not only at odds with the role of the CPA, but acts to undermine the very foundation of the professional relationship between an accountant and client. Such duplicity cannot and will not be condoned."

Post Postscript: The U.S. Senate considered a bill making it a crime for federal agents to offer forgiveness of taxes to induce CPAs to inform on their clients. The U.S. Justice Department dropped the tax evasion charges against Steven N.

Source: The Wall Street Journal, February 2, 1990, August 31, 1990, and November 25, 1991.

can be overridden by reason of obtaining or following legal advice. If a client refuses to accept an audit report that has been modified because of inability to obtain sufficient appropriate evidence about a suspected illegal act, failure to account for or disclose properly a material amount connected with an illegal act or inability to estimate amounts involved in an illegal act, the audit firm should withdraw from the engagement and give the reasons in writing to the board of directors. In such an extreme case, the withdrawal amounts to whistle blowing, but the action results from the client's decision not to disclose the information. For all practical purposes, information is not considered confidential if disclosure of it is necessary to make financial statements not misleading.

Auditors are not, in general, legally obligated to blow the whistle on clients. However, circumstances may exist where auditors are legally justified in making disclosures to a regulatory agency or a third party. Such circumstances include (1) when a client has intentionally and without authorization associated or involved a PA in its misleading conduct, (2) when a client has distributed misleading draft financial statements prepared by a PA for internal use only, or (3) when a client prepares and distributes in an annual report or prospectus misleading information for which the PA has not assumed any responsibility.

PAs should not view the rules on confidential information as a licence or excuse for inaction where action may be appropriate to right a wrongful act committed or about to be committed by a client. In some cases auditors' inaction may be viewed as part of a conspiracy or willingness to be an accessory to a wrong. Such situations are dangerous and potentially damaging. A useful initial course of action is to consult with a lawyer about possible legal pitfalls of both whistle blowing and silence. Then, decide for yourself.

Contingency Fees and Service Without Fees

ICAO Rule 215 states, "A member engaged in the practice of public accounting or a related function shall not offer or agree to perform a professional service for a fee payable only where there is a specified determination or result of the service . . . A member engaged in the practice of public accounting or a related function shall not represent that he or she performs any professional service without fee except services of a charitable, benevolent or similar nature . . ."

For a fee to be considered a contingency fee, two characteristics need to be met.

1. Its terms must be contracted for before any services are performed, and

2. The amount paid for the performance must be directly affected by the results obtained.

If one of these characteristics is not present, the fee is not a contingency fee and therefore does not violate the ICAO's Rule 215,[11] or similar rules by other accounting bodies (such as the CGAAC's Rule 802). Fees are not contingent if they are fixed by a court or other public authority or, in tax matters, determined as a result of the finding of judicial proceedings or the findings of government agencies; nor are fees contingent when they are based on the complexity or time required for the work. The current Rule 215 is quite restrictive, conflicting with some statutes such as the Federal Bankruptcy Act and Provincial Trustee Acts, which allow fees based on the results of the PA's work. Because of these conflicts with statutory law, some have called for modifications of the rules to apply to assurance engagements only.[12]

Rule 215 prohibits contingent fees in assurance engagements where users of financial information may be relying on the PAs' work. Acceptance of contingent fee arrangements during the period in which the member or the member's firm is engaged to perform any type of assurance engagement is considered an impairment of independence.

---

[11] C. Schultz, "When Talk Turns to Contingency Fees," *CA Magazine,* May 1988, p. 29.
[12] Ibid. p. 33.

Fee Quotation

ICAO Rule 214 states that "a member shall not quote a fee for any professional services unless requested to do so by a client or prospective client, and no quote shall be made until adequate information has been obtained about the assignment." It is thus against Rule 214 to quote a fee "over the phone" or quote a fixed charge for all audits. There is extensive anecdotal evidence that particularly during economic downturns some firms practice "low balling" or charging a fee that is below cost in order to get an engagement. Low balling would appear to be in violation of at least the spirit of Rule 214 since presumably the need for the information about the assignment is to ensure that an adequate audit is done in which the costs are recovered (no service should be provided for free unless for charitable purposes). The real concern is that auditors may cut back on audit procedures to the point of reducing the quality of audits.[13]

Discreditable Acts

CGAAC's Rule 101 states that "a member shall not permit the member's firm name to be used with, participate in or knowingly provide services to any practice, pronouncement or act which would be of a nature to discredit the profession." We will refer to this and related rules as discreditable act rules.

Analysis

The discreditable acts rules may be called the morals clauses of the Codes, but they are only occasionally the basis for disciplinary action. Penalties usually are invoked automatically under the bylaws, which provide for expulsion of members found by a court to have committed any fraud, filed false tax returns or been convicted of any criminal offence; or found by the Disciplinary Committee to have been guilty of an act discreditable to the profession. Discreditable acts can include (a) withholding a client's books and records when the client has requested their return; (b) practising employment discrimination in hiring, promotion or salary practices on the basis of race, colour, religion, sex or national origin; (c) failing to follow government audit standards and guides in governmental audits when the client or the government agency expects such standards to be followed; and (d) making, or permitting others to make, false and misleading entries in records and financial statements. An extreme example of an actual discreditable act is given in the box below.

Advertising and Other Forms of Solicitation

The rules relating to solicitation state that a member shall not seek to obtain clients by advertising or other forms of solicitation in a manner that is false, misleading or deceptive. Solicitation through coercion, overreaching or harassing conduct is prohibited.

EXTREME EXAMPLE OF A DISCREDITABLE ACT

The Enforcement Committee found that Respondent drew a gun from his desk drawer during a dispute with a client in his office in contravention of Section 501.41 [discreditable acts prohibition] of the [Texas] Rules of Professional Conduct. Respondent agreed to accept a private reprimand to be printed . . . in the Texas State Board Report.

Source: Texas State Board Report, February 1986.

---

[13] M.C. Carscallen, "Fee completion hurts integrity of accounting services," *Bottom Line,* April 1991, p. 20.

Analysis

The Rules permit advertising with only a few limitations. The current rules apply only to PAs practising public accounting and relate to their efforts to obtain clients. Basic guidelines about advertising include the following:

- Advertising may not create false or unjustified expectations of favourable results.
- Advertising may not imply the ability to influence any court, tribunal, regulatory agency or similar body or official.
- Advertising may not contain a fee estimate when the PA knows it is likely to be substantially increased, unless the client is notified.
- Advertising may not contain any representation that is likely to cause a reasonable person to misunderstand or be deceived, or that contravenes professional good taste.

Advertising consists of messages designed to attract business that are broadcast widely (e.g., through print, radio, television, billboards) to an undifferentiated audience. The guidelines basically prohibit false, misleading and deceptive messages.

Solicitation, on the other hand, generally refers to direct contact (e.g., in person, mail, telephone) with a specific potential client. In regard to solicitation, the rules basically prohibit extreme bad behaviour that tends to bring disrepute on the profession.

The advertising rule has undergone many changes over the last two decades. Long ago, all advertising by PAs was prohibited. Then, institutional-type advertising on behalf of PAs in general was permitted. Then, in 1979, in response to the Charter of Rights guarantee to members, the ICAO approved advertising "in good taste," with limitations on style, type size and the like. The other professional bodies followed suit.

Most PAs carry out only modest advertising efforts, and many do no advertising at all. According to a recent article, advertising so far has been very precisely targeted—for example, at CFOs of wholesalers in the food industry. Firms have generally used local rather than national advertising. The biggest problem in advertising so far is that members may make claims they are not able to substantiate.

Firms rarely get new clients through advertising, but it can be effective in generating business in the form of new services for existing clients or from referrals. Overall, other than some isolated examples of creative advertising by some firms, the profession has not pursued advertising aggressively. Nevertheless, it is likely PAs will advertise more in the future.[14] This seems to be especially true as Internet Web sites by PA firms continue to pro-

---

THE ART OF ADVERTISING

In 1987, three charges were brought against "a partner of Ernst & Whinney" in Ontario under subsections (c), (a) and (d). The discipline committee found the member "not guilty" on the first charge, but "guilty" on the second and third. Both guilty charges concerned a 1985 ad he had placed in *The Globe and Mail* which stated, in part, "Canada's Fastest Growing Firm of Business Advisors Announces Its Newest Partners."

The committee found the ad misleading in two ways. First, "accountants do not have a monopoly on the term 'business advisors.'" Second, the claim was made on the basis of statistics that were "accurate as they relate to the participating chartered accountant firms [but] without disclosure of the necessary parameters or basis for the statement, it is misleading."

The member received a written reprimand, was assessed court costs of $6,000, and was fined $5,000.

Source: Tim Falconer, *CA Magazine*, October 1993, p. 46.

---

[14] T. Falconer, "The Art of Advertising," *CA Magazine*, October 1993, pp. 43–46.

liferate (see Chapter 20) and the Internet becomes more popular as an advertising medium. Public practice is generally marked by decorum and a sense of good taste. However, there are exceptions, and they tend to get much attention—most of it disapproving from other PAs and the public in general. The danger in bad advertising is that the advertiser may develop an image as a professional huckster, which may backfire on efforts to build a practice.

Commissions and Referral Fees

A. Prohibited Commissions
A member in public practice shall not for a commission recommend or refer to a client any product or service, or for a commission recommend or refer any product or service to be supplied by a client, or receive a commission, when the member or the member's firm also performs for that client public accounting.

This prohibition applies during the period in which the member is engaged to perform public accounting services and the period covered by any historical financial statements involved in such services.

B. Permitted Commission
A member in public practice is not prohibited by this rule in receiving a commission from the sale or purchase of an accounting practice.

A **commission** is generally defined as a percentage fee charged for professional services in connection with executing a transaction or performing some other business activity. Examples are insurance sales commissions, real estate sales commissions and securities sales commissions. The rules treat such fees as an impairment of independence when received from assurance engagement clients, just like ICAO's Rule 215 treats contingent fees.

However, many PAs perform financial planning for businesses and individuals, and they have seen commissions for insurance, securities, mergers and acquisitions, and other transactions go to other professionals. They want some of this action. The rules permit such commissions, provided the engagement does not involve assurance services.

Most of the commission fee activity takes place in connection with personal financial planning services. PAs often recommend insurance and investments to individuals and families. When the rule change was under consideration, critics pointed out that commission agents (e.g., insurance salespersons, securities brokers) cannot always be trusted to have the best interests of the client in mind when their own compensation depends in large part on clients' buying the product that produces commissions for themselves. These critics bemoaned the demise of the only advisers, PAs, who could not take commissions. They made the point that "fee-only" planning advisers, who do not work on commission, were more likely to have the best interests of the client in mind, directing them to investment professionals who handle a wide range of alternatives. In light of these matters, some PAs make it a point to provide financial planning services on a fee-only basis. This is also the position of the newly organized Financial Planners Standards Council of Canada, which is dedicated to maintaining a licensing system for certified financial planners (CFPs) in Canada. This organization is sponsored by the CICA, CGAAC and SMAC, among other associations.

The rules also include fee arrangements related to commissions. Referral fees are (*a*) fees a PA receives for recommending another PA's services and (*b*) fees a PA pays to obtain a client. Such fees may or may not be based on a percentage of the amount of any transaction. Referral involves the practice of sending business to another PA and paying other PAs or outside agencies for drumming up business. These activities are banned by the Rules of Conduct on the basis that they impair the principle of objectivity.

Form of Organization and Name

General Rule Relating to Form of PA Organization
Each practice office shall be under the personal charge of a member who is a public accountant.

General Rule Relating to Name of PA Organization
A member shall not practice public accounting under a firm name that is misleading. Names of one or more past owners may be included in the firm name of a successor organization.

Analysis

The rules allow members to practise in any form of organization permitted by provincial laws and regulations—proprietorships, partnerships, professional corporations, limited liability partnerships, limited liability corporations, and ordinary corporations. Most provincial accountancy laws prohibit the general corporate form of organization for PAs; however, there has been a recent push for the limited liability partnership form of organization due to increased legal risks. Under the limited liability partnership (LLP) form of organization, most partners do not have their personal assets at risk. The only partners with personal assets at risk are those involved in the litigated engagement; the rest of the partners risk only their investment in the partnership. In the traditional form of partnership, all partners' personal assets are at risk. Thus, the limited liability partnership is a great improvement at a time of increased litigation. Many PA firms are now LLPs.

In 1992 the AICPA approved a move to permit PAs to practise in limited liability corporations and ordinary corporations like other businesses. This has led to non-PA firms such as American Express owning PA firms.

Public accountants have been beset by lawsuits for damages in which they and their insurers are the only persons left with any money (e.g., in cases of business failure), and multimillion-dollar damages have been awarded to plaintiffs against them. In the proprietorship, partnership and professional corporation forms of business, all the business and personal assets of PAs are exposed to loss to such plaintiffs. Many accountants think the tort liability litigation process has gotten out of hand, and so they seek some protection through new forms of organization. See the following box for some consequences that can arise from an attempt at innovative forms of PA firm organization.

The Canadian rules of conduct effectively block persons who are not PAs from being owners. This rule section creates problems for tax and management consulting services personnel who are not PAs. They cannot be admitted to full partnership or become shareholders without causing the other owners who are PAs to be in violation of the rule. Thus, an accounting firm may employ non-PAs who are high on the organization chart, but these persons may not be unrestricted partners or shareholders under current rules.

PAs (Almost) Sell Shares to Public

Nearman & Lents, a Florida PA firm, formed a corporation named Financial Standards Group, Inc., and filed a registration statement with the Securities and Exchange Commission to sell shares to the public. The accounting firm wanted to "go national on a large scale, and . . . raise $3 million or $4 million capital."

The registration became effective, and some shares were actually sold. However, Nearman & Lents withdrew the offering and gave the money back to the purchasers. Florida regulators had raised questions about the company practising public accounting without a license with non-PA ownership, which was prohibited. Financial Standards Group did not become the first publicly held PA firm.

The venture met resistance. Accounting traditionalists and lawyers who specialize in suing accountants for misconduct have generally frowned on letting accountants avail themselves of the limited legal liability provided by a corporation. Regulators have also discouraged accounting firms from issuing shares to outsiders for fear that outside equity partners might taint a firm's ability to judge [audit] a client's books impartially.

Source: New York Times (June 14, 1990) and SEC.

Rules of Conduct and Ethical Principles

Specific rules in the Rules of Conduct may not necessarily be classified under one of the ethics principles. Decisions based on a rule may involve imperative, utilitarian, or generalization considerations, or elements of all three, as well as other considerations discussed in Appendix 16B. The rules have the form of imperatives because that is the nature of a code. However, elements of utilitarianism and generalization seem to be apparent in the underlying rationale for most of the rules. If this perception is accurate, then these two principles may be utilized by auditors in difficult decision problems where adherence to a rule would produce a undesirable result. Appendix 16B discusses other factors to consider.

R E V I E W
CHECKPOINTS

16.5 What ethical responsibilities do members of the provincial institutes have for acts of nonmembers who are under their supervision (e.g., recent university graduates who are not yet PAs)?

16.6 Is an incorporated accounting practice substantially different from an accounting practice organized in the form of a partnership? in the form of a limited liability partnership?

16.7 Define what is meant by a contingency fee and explain how such fees apply to PAs. Do you feel a change is necessary to rules for contingency fees in Canada?

REGULATION AND QUALITY CONTROL

LEARNING OBJECTIVE
3. Name and explain the various professional associations and government agencies that enforce rules of conduct and explain the types of penalties they can impose on accountants.

As a PA, you will be expected to observe rules of conduct published in several codes of ethics. If you are a PA and have a client who issues shares on U.S. stock exchanges, you will be subject to the following:

Source of Rules of Conduct	Applicable to:
Members' Handbook	Persons licensed by province to practise accounting or, if no licence required in province, persons belonging to provincial institutes, societies or organizations
Business Corporations Acts and Securities Acts at federal and provincial levels	Public accountants (usually PAs performing public accounting services) within the various jurisdictions
U.S. Securities and Exchange Commission	Persons who practise before the SEC as accountants and auditors for SEC-registered companies (including auditors of many large Canadian corporations)

If you are an internal auditor, you will be expected to observe the rules of conduct of the Institute of Internal Auditors. As a management accountant, you will be expected to observe the Society of Management Accountants standards of ethical conduct for management accountants. Certified fraud examiners are expected to observe the Association of Certified Fraud Examiners' Code of Ethics.

Regulation and professional ethics go hand in hand. Codes of ethics provide the underlying authority for regulation. Quality control practices and disciplinary proceedings provide the mechanisms of self-regulation. Self-regulation refers to quality control reviews and disciplinary actions conducted by fellow PAs—professional peers. Elements of accountants' self-regulation have been explained in terms of the quality control standards (Chapter 2).

Fraud Examiner Expelled for Fraud

Curtis C was expelled by the board of regents at its regular meeting on August 4, 1991. Mr. C, formerly an internal auditor employed by the City of S, was a member from February 1989 until his expulsion. He was the subject of an investigation by the trial board for falsifying information.

Mr. C wrongfully represented himself as a certified internal auditor, when in fact he did not hold the CIA designation. Such conduct is in violation of Article 1.A.4 of the CFE Code of Professional Ethics.

L. Jackson Shockey, CFE, CPA, CISA, chairman of the board of regents, said: "We are saddened that a member has been expelled for such conduct. However, in order to maintain the integrity of the CFE program, the trial board vigorously investigates violations of the Code of Professional Ethics. When appropriate, the board of regents will not hesitate to take necessary action."

Source: CFE News, September 1991.

Self-Regulatory Discipline

Accounting firms as well as individuals are subject to the Rules of Professional Conduct of the institutes, associations or societies only if they choose to join these organizations. But as a practical matter anyone wishing to practise public accounting finds that the added credibility of belonging to a professional group greatly improves the chances of establishing a successful practice. Thus, enforcement of the Rules of Conduct is an important means of regulating the profession. Regulators can suspend a member's activities on certain exchanges; the professional bodies can initiate other disciplinary proceedings.

An Illustration of Self-Regulation: A Provincial Institute's Disciplinary Process

The provincial institutes' bylaws and rules of professional conduct in the *Member's Handbook* provide the basis for self-regulation. The institutes have a duty to investigate all written complaints received about their members and students, as well as information from the media that may indicate professional misconduct. The Professional Conduct Committee, which represents a broad cross-section of the membership, investigates the complaint and decides whether further action is necessary. The committee considers the respondents' reply and all relevant data in making its decision.

Three conclusions are possible (as per ICAO):

1. The member did not breach the rules and the process is ended.

2. The member did or may have breached the rules, but the infraction is not serious enough to prosecute before the discipline committee; the respondent is informally admonished in writing or at a committee meeting.

3. Charges are laid and the matter is brought up before the discipline committee where a process similar to a civil trial procedure is followed. The discipline committee can reach a decision of not guilty or guilty. There is also an appeal process, which is headed by yet another committee, the Appeal Committee.

In a guilty verdict the penalties can include any one or more of the following (as per ICAO list):

• The member or student be reprimanded.

• The member or student be suspended from the institute.

• The student be struck off the register of students.

• The member be expelled from membership in the institute.

- The member satisfactorily complete a professional development course(s) and/or an examination(s) and/or engage an advisor or tutor.
- The member complete a period of supervised practice.
- The member be reinvestigated by the professional conduct committee.
- The member or student be charged costs and/or fined.
- The member or student be disciplined in such other way as the committee may determine.
- The decision and order(s) be publicized along with the member's or student's name.

The penalties listed above cover a range of severity. In many cases a discipline committee can admonish or suspend a PA and require a number of hours of continuing professional education (CPE) to be undertaken. The goal is to help the PA attain an appropriate level of professional competence and awareness. Although intended as a constructive resolution, the CPE requirement is similar to "serving time." Persons who fail to satisfy CPE conditions will find themselves charged with "actions detrimental to the profession" (violations of rules such as CGAAC's Rule 606 or ICAO's Rule 201) and expelled as "second offenders."

The expulsion penalty, while severe, does not prevent a PA from continuing to practice accounting. Membership in a professional group, while beneficial, is not required. However, a PA must have a valid licence in order to practise public accounting in certain provinces. CGAs are subject to disciplinary action for any offence that constitutes a breach of professional conduct. This disciplinary action is brought on by the member's association or professional corporation, or, if the action is outside these groups, by the board of directors of CGA-Canada (Rule 602.1, CGAAC).

Public Regulation Discipline

Provincial institutes of chartered accountants, provincial associations of CGAs, and provincial societies of CMAs are self-governing agencies. Depending on the province's Public Accounting Act, they issue licences to practise accounting in their jurisdictions or certificates indicating they have met the standards to be a PA. Most provinces require a licence or certification procedure to use the designation *CA* or *Chartered Accountant*, and some limit the assurance (audit) function to licenceholders. Most provinces do not regulate work in areas of management consulting, tax practice or bookkeeping services.

EXAMPLE OF PUBLIC DISCIPLINARY NOTICE

Member Found Guilty of Breaching Rule of Professional Conduct 215
Re: Contingent Fees
A member has been found guilty of a charge of professional misconduct, laid by the professional conduct committee, under Rule of Professional Conduct 215, of agreeing to render professional services for a fee contingent on the results.

It was ordered that the member:
- be reprimanded in writing by the chairman of the hearing,
- be assessed costs of $1,500 to be paid within a specified time; and
- that the decision and order be published in Check Mark.

It was determined that the publication of the member's name was not necessary in the circumstances, as there was no evidence of any intent to breach the rules of professional conduct or moral turpitude on the part of the member, and that this was a matter of first instance.

Provincial institutes, associations and societies have rules of conduct and disciplinary processes as outlined above. Through the disciplinary process, the provincial institutes, associations and societies can admonish a licenceholder; but, more importantly, they can suspend or revoke the licence to practise in some provinces. Suspension and revocation are severe penalties because a person no longer can use the PA title and cannot sign audit reports. When candidates have successfully passed the PA examination or fulfilled other requirements and are ready to become PAs, some provincial institutes administer an ethics examination or an ethics course intended to familiarize new PAs with the rules of professional conduct.

According to a study by Brooks and Fortunato, most disciplinary actions by the ICAO stem from violating the standards affecting the public interest (200 level). Over a roughly three-year period (1988–90), most violations involved just four rules:

Rule 201: Good Reputation of Profession representing 20 percent of all violations   36 violations

Rule 202: Integrity and Due Care representing 16 percent of all violations   29 violations

Rule 205: False and Misleading Representations representing 11 percent of all violations   20 violations

Rule 206: Expressing an Opinion Without Complying with GAAS representing 12 percent of all violations[15]   21 violations

This same study also found that "all but one of the ICAO convictions we examined resulted in disclosure of the convicted member's names, and 95% resulted in levying the costs of hearing on that person. Of those convicted 78% were reprimanded, of which 44% were also suspended; 17% of the total convicted were expelled from the profession." The average fine levied for these cases was $5,695.[16]

The national harmonization of the Rules of Professional Conduct has not only made the self-regulatory processes more comparable across the country for CAs but has also increased the examinability of the Rules of Professional Conduct in the UFE. The appearance of the Rules of Professional Conduct on the UFE in 1994 should serve to reinforce the importance of this topic. CGAAC's rules of conduct have always been national in scope, as noted earlier.

As noted in Chapter 2, the provincial securities commissions sometimes file complaints with the Professional Conduct Committees of the provincial institutes or associations. In addition, some securities commissions, notably the OSC, have been assertive in not accepting financial statements that they consider at odds with GAAP. The OSC now issues staff accounting communiqués (SACs) in which it highlights major problem areas. Any company attempting to use the disfavoured technique may find that its financial statements are unacceptable to the OSC even though there is no reservation in the auditor's report.

The OSC is going even further. "It has a plan to increase its supervision of auditors and other financial advisers and to gain the power to take disciplinary action against them. Although these proposals have yet to be enacted, the OSC already exerts some control over firms via out-of-court settlements, as indicated in the following box.

The SEC also conducts public regulation disciplinary actions. Its authority comes from its rules of practice, one of which, Rule 2(e) provides that the SEC can deny, temporarily or permanently, the privilege of practice before the SEC to any person found (1) not to possess the requisite qualifications to represent others, or (2) to be lacking in character or integrity or to have engaged in unethical or improper professional conduct, or (3) to have willfully violated any provision of the federal securities laws or their rules and regulations. When conducting a "Rule 2(e) proceeding," the SEC acts in a quasijudicial role as an administrative agency.

---

[15] L. Brooks and V. Fortunato, "Disciplines at the ICAO," *CA Magazine*, May 1991, p. 45.
[16] Ibid, pp. 42–43.

PREVENTIVE MEDICINE

"For example, in response to problems arising from the audit of National Business Systems, Inc., the OSC agreed that the partner in charge of that audit would not act as the senior or second partner in charge of the audit of a public company for a year. It was also agreed that procedures and systems would be reviewed by an auditor from another firm and that the results would be resubmitted to the OSC. Moreover, arrangement was made to have the Toronto office inspected by a partner from outside Canada to ensure professional standards were met. The firm agreed to pay $70,000 to cover OSC expenses."

Source: J. Bedard and L. LeBlanc, *CA Magazine,* November 1991, p. 42.

The SEC penalty bars an accountant from signing any documents filed by an SEC-registered company. The penalty effectively stops the accountant's SEC practice. In a few severe cases, Rule 2(e) proceedings have resulted in settlements barring not only the individual accountant but also the accounting firm or certain of its practice offices from accepting new SEC clients for a period of time.

The OSC and other Canadian regulators have been pushing to have similar disciplinary powers within their jurisdictions. Clearly, if the self-regulating process of the institutes is not sufficient to deter bad practices, regulators are willing to step in. In 1991 members of the ICAO approved a proposal giving the institute the power to subject firms to disciplinary action.

In the next chapter we will see how in reaction to a recent Supreme Court of Canada ruling in *Hercules* v. *Ernst & Young,* there are renewed calls in the Canadian press for new securities laws that will hold auditors firmly liable for any negligence in financial statements. Other recent regulatory developments include greater independence and enforcement powers for Ontario and Quebec securities commissions, and increased harmonization procedures between the Alberta and British Columbia commissions. These structural changes in the regulatory climate are likely to increase regulatory disciplinary actions against PAs in the future.

The Canada Customs and Revenue Agency can also discipline accountants as a matter of public regulation. The Canada Customs and Revenue Agency can suspend or disbar from practice before it any PA shown to be incompetent or disreputable or who has refused to comply with tax rules and regulations. The Canada Customs and Revenue Agency can also levy monetary fines for improper practices. The Revenue Ministry has made public its willingness to prosecute those accountants it suspects of "deliberate attempt to defraud the federal treasury."[17]

R E V I E W CHECKPOINTS

16.8   What options does the Canada Customs and Revenue Agency have to discipline PAs?

16.9   What organizations and agencies have Rules of Conduct you must observe when practising public accounting? internal auditing? management accounting? fraud examination?

16.10 What penalties can be imposed by provincial institutes on CAs in their "self-regulation" of ethics code violators?

16.11 What penalties can be imposed by public regulatory agencies on PAs who violate rules of conduct?

---

[17] J. Middleniss, "Too many accountants guilty of fraud, Liberals vow crackdown on shady advisers," *Bottom Line,* March 1994, p. 1.

CONSEQUENCES OF UNETHICAL/ILLEGAL ACTS

Ethics is serious business. Several sectors of professional and public life exist under general clouds of suspicion. Even though many practitioners of accounting, business management, finance, journalism, law, medicine and politics conduct themselves in an exemplary fashion, generally unfavourable perceptions of them are held by some people. Fortunately, accountants generally rate near the top of trustworthy professions (along with the clergy.) Many people, however, think it is a necessity of business life to shade the formal and informal rules of behaviour in order to "get ahead" or "make a buck." Acting on this belief can have catastrophic consequences for the profession. Without the public's confidence, the accounting profession cannot meet the public interest.

However, conforming to rules of behaviour is not always easy because of potential conflicts in the rules. The most troublesome area lies in the potential conflict between rules related to confidentiality on the one hand, and the prohibition against association with misleading information on the other. Whenever there is a conflict of interest situation for the auditor there is a potential to create a threat to the auditor's independent state of mind. Brooks (1995, p. 126) identified the following deficiencies in professional Codes of Conduct.

- No or insufficient prioritization is put forward to resolve conflicting interests.
- Consultation on ethical matters is encouraged for some members, but is inhibited for others.
- A fair reporting/hearing process is not indicated, so members are uncertain whether to come forward.
- Protection is not offered to a whistle blower.
- Sanctions are often unclear, and their applicability is not defined.
- Resolution mechanisms for conflicts between professionals and firms, or employers, or employing corporations are not put forward.

According to an article in the November 13, 1997, issue of the *Finincial Post* by Sandra Rubin, the latest round of mergers among the accounting firms is making these deficiencies even more critical to the integrity of the financial reporting system. The problem is the perception of increased conflict of interest and the fact that the merged firms will be so big that no single nation (or national body) will be able to regulate them. The role of the International Organization of Securities Commissions (IOSCO) will likely increase the future regulation of the huge international PA firms.

SUMMARY

This chapter began with considerations of moral philosophy, explained the provincial institutes' Rules of Professional Conduct and ended with the agencies and organizations that enforce the rules governing PAs' behaviour.

Professional ethics for accountants is not simply a matter covered by a few rules in a formal Rule of Professional Conduct. Concepts of proper professional conduct permeate all areas of practice. Ethics and its accompanying disciplinary potential are the foundation for public accountants' self-regulatory efforts.

Your knowledge of philosophical principles in ethics—the imperative, the utilitarian and generalization—will help you make decisions about the provincial Rules of Professional Conduct. This structured approach to thoughtful decisions is important not only when you are employed in public accounting but also when you work in government, industry and education. The ethics rules may appear to be restrictive, but they are intended for the benefit of the public as well as for the discipline of PAs.

Public accountants must be careful in all areas of practice. Regulators' views on ethics rules may differ in several aspects from the provincial institute views. As an accountant, you must not lose sight of the nonaccountants' perspective. No matter how complex or technical a decision may be, a simplified view of it always tends to cut away the details of special technical issues to get directly to the heart of the matter. A sense of professionalism coupled with a sensitivity to the impact of decisions on other people is invaluable in the practice of accounting and auditing.

Finally, it should be noted that there is a strong link between codes of conduct and GAAS. In fact, codes of conduct can be viewed as a means of fufilling auditor responsibilities for GAAS and assurance standards. For example, the first GAAS standard, which relates to the personal attributes of the auditor (see Chapter 2), closely corresponds to the ethical principles of integrity, objectivity, independence, professional competence and due care discussed above. The dominance of ethical issues over accounting or auditing techniques is increasingly being recognized throughout the profession. Most audit failures appear to be attributable to poor professional judgment, at least in hindsight, that arise from improper consideration of conflicts of interest on various disclosure and measurement issues. In this regard, see L.J. Brooks, *Professional Ethics for Accountants,* West Publishing, 1995, p. 69; and S. Gunz and J. McCutcheon, "Some Unresolved Ethical Issues in Auditing," *Journal of Business Ethics,* 1991.

MULTIPLE-CHOICE QUESTIONS FOR PRACTICE AND REVIEW

16.12 Auditors are interested in having independence in appearance because:
  a. They want to impress the public with their independence in fact.
  b. They want the public at large to have confidence in the profession.
  c. They need to comply with the standards of field work of GAAS.
  d. Audits should be planned and assistants, if any, need to be properly supervised.

16.13 If a PA says she always follows the rule that requires adherence to CICA pronouncements in order to give a standard unqualified audit report, she is following a philosophy characterized by:
  a. The imperative principle in ethics.
  b. The utilitarian principle in ethics.
  c. The generalization principle in ethics.
  d. Reliance on one's inner conscience.

16.14 Which of the following "committees" have been authorized to discipline members in violation of the rules of professional conduct?
  a. CICA Committee on Professional Ethics.
  b. Appeals Committee.
  c. Discipline Committee.
  d. Professional Conduct Committee.

16.15 Which of the following bodies does not have any power to punish individual members for violations of the Rules of Professional Conduct?

  a. CICA.
  b. Canada Customs and Revenue Agency.
  c. OSC.
  d. ICAO.

16.16 Phil Greb has a thriving practice in which he assists lawyers in preparing litigation dealing with accounting and auditing matters. Phil is "practising public accounting" if he:
  a. Uses his CA designation on his letterhead and business card.
  b. Is in partnership with another PA.
  c. Practises in a limited partnership with other PAs.
  d. Never lets his clients know that he is a PA.

16.17 The ICAO should remove its general prohibition against PAs' taking commissions and contingent fees because:
  a. CAs prefer more price competition to less.
  b. Commissions and contingent fees enhance audit independence.
  c. The Charter of Rights will force the change anyway.
  d. Objectivity is not always necessary in accounting and auditing services.

16.18 PA Smith is the auditor of Ajax Corporation. Her audit independence will not be considered impaired if she:
  a. Owns a $1,000 worth of Ajax shares.
  b. Has a husband who owns $2,000 worth of Ajax shares.

c. Has a sister who is the financial vice president of Ajax.

d. Owns $1,000 worth of the shares of Pericles Corporation, which is controlled by Ajax as a result of Ajax's ownership of 40 percent of Pericles's shares, and Pericles contributes 3 percent of the total assets and income in Ajax's financial statements.

16.19 When a client's financial statements contain a material departure from a *CICA Handbook* Accounting Recommendation and the PA believes that disclosure is necessary to make the statements not misleading:

a. The PA must qualify the audit report for a departure from GAAP.

b. The PA can explain why the departure is necessary, and then give an unqualified opinion paragraph in the audit report.

c. The PA must give an adverse audit report.

d. The PA can give the standard unqualified audit report with an unqualified opinion paragraph.

16.20 Which of the following would not be considered confidential information obtained in the course of an engagement for which the client's consent would be needed for disclosure?

a. Information about whether a consulting client has paid the PA's fees on time.

b. The actuarial assumptions used by a tax client in calculating pension expense.

c. Management's strategic plan for next year's labour negotiations.

d. Information about material contingent liabilities relevant for audited financial statements.

16.21 Which of the following would probably not be considered an "act discreditable to the profession":

a. Numerous moving traffic violations.

b. Failing to file the PA's own tax return.

c. Filing a fraudulent tax return for a client in a severe financial difficulty.

d. Refusing to hire Asian Canadians in an accounting practice.

16.22 The U.S. Securities and Exchange Commission would consider an audit firm's independence not impaired when:

a. A partner completed the client's audit in January, retired from the firm in March, and became a member of the former client's board of directors in August.

b. A partner who had been in charge of the firm's national audit co-ordination office retired in May 2000, and became a member of the board of directors of one of the firm's clients in August 2002.

c. A partner in the firm has a father-in-law who is the warehouse supervisor for an audit client.

d. The audit firm helped the client perform data processing for three months during the current year in connection with preparing financial statements to be filed with the SEC.

16.23 A PA's legal licence to practise public accounting can be revoked by:

a. The CICA.

b. Provincial Institute of PAs.

c. Auditing Standards Board.

d. Provincial securities commissions.

16.24 An auditor's independence would not be considered impaired if he had:

a. Owned common shares of the audit client but sold them before the company became a client.

b. Sold short the common shares of an audit client while working on the audit engagement.

c. Served as the company's treasurer for six months during the year covered by the audit but resigned before the company became a client.

d. Performed the bookkeeping and financial statement preparation for the company, which had no accounting personnel, and the president had no understanding of accounting principles.

16.25 When a PA knows that a tax client has skimmed cash receipts and not reported the income in the federal income tax return but signs the return as a PA who prepared the return, the PA has violated which Rule of Professional Conduct?

a. Confidential Client Information.

b. Integrity and Objectivity.

c. Independence.

d. Accounting Principles.

EXERCISES AND PROBLEMS

. . . .

16.26 Independence, Integrity and Objectivity Cases. Knowledge of the rules of conduct and related interpretations on independence, integrity and objectivity will help you respond to the following cases. For each case, state whether the action or situation shows violation of the Rules of Professional Conduct, explain why, and cite the relevant rule or interpretation.

a. PA R. Stout performs the audit of the local symphony society. Because of her good work, she was elected an honorary member of the board of directors.

b. N. Wolfe, a retired partner of your PA firm, has just been appointed to the board of directors of Palmer Corporation, your firm's client. Wolfe is also an ex officio member of your firm's income tax advisory committee, which meets monthly to discuss income tax problems of the partnership's clients, some of which are competitors of Palmer Corporation. The partnership pays Wolfe $100 for each committee meeting attended and a monthly retirement benefit, fixed by a retirement plan policy, of $1,000.

(AICPA adapted)

c. PA Archie Goodwin performs significant day-to-day bookkeeping services for Harper Corporation and supervises the work of the one part-time bookkeeper employed by Marvin Harper. This year, Marvin wants to engage PA Goodwin to perform an audit.

d. PA Fritz's wife owns 20 percent of the common shares of Botacel Company, which wants Fritz to perform the audit for the calendar year ended December 31, 2007.

e. Fritz's wife gave her shares to their 10-year-old daughter on July 1, 2007.

f. Fritz's daughter, acting through an appropriate custodian, sold the shares to her grandfather on August 1, 2007. His purchase, as an accommodation, took one-half of his retirement savings.

g. Fritz's father managed to sell the shares on August 15 to his brother, who lives in Brazil. The brother fled there 20 years ago and has not returned.

h. Clyde Brenner is a manager in the Regina office of a large national PA firm. His wife, Bonnie, is assistant controller in ATC Corporation, a client of the firm whose audit is performed by the New York office. Bonnie and Clyde live in Rhode Island and commute to their respective workplaces.

i. Clyde Brenner just received word that he has been admitted to the partnership.

j. The Rockhard Trust Company, a client of your firm, privately told your local managing partner that a block of funds would be set aside for home loans for qualified new employees. Rockhard's president is well aware that your firm experiences some difficulty hiring good people in the midsize but growing community and is willing to do what he can to help while mortgage money is so tight. Several new assistant accountants obtained home loans under this arrangement.

16.27 Independence, Integrity and Objectivity Cases. Knowledge of the rules of conduct, interpretations thereof, and related rulings on independence, integrity and objectivity will help you respond to the following cases. For each case, state whether the action or situation shows violation of the Rules of Professional Conduct, explain why, and cite the relevant rule or interpretation.

a. Your client, Contrary Corporation, is very upset over the fact that your audit last year failed to detect an $800,000 inventory overstatement caused by employee theft and falsification of the records. The board discussed the matter and authorized its lawyers to explore the possibility of a lawsuit for damages.

b. Contrary Corporation filed a lawsuit alleging negligent audit work, seeking $1 million in damages.

c. In response to the lawsuit by Contrary, you decided to start litigation against certain officers of the company, alleging management fraud and deceit. You are asking for a damages judgment of $500,000.

d. The Allright Insurance company paid Contrary Corporation $700,000 under fidelity bonds covering the employees involved in the inventory theft. Both you and Contrary Corporation have dropped your lawsuits. However, under subrogation rights, Allright has sued your audit firm for damages on the grounds of negligent performance of the audit.

e. Your audit client, Science Tech, Inc., installed a cost accounting system devised by the consulting services department of your firm. The system failed to account properly for certain product costs (according to management), and the system had to be discontinued. Science Tech management was very dissatisfied and filed a lawsuit demanding return of the $10,000 consulting fee. The audit fee is normally about $50,000, and $10,000 is not an especially large amount for your firm. However, you believe that Science Tech management operated the system improperly. While you are willing to do further consulting work at a reduced rate to make the system operate, you are unwilling to return the entire $10,000 fee.

f. A group of dissident shareholders filed a class-action lawsuit against both you and your client, Amalgamated, Inc., for $30 million. They allege there was a conspiracy to present misleading financial statements in connection with a recent merger.

g. PA Anderson, a partner in the firm of Anderson, Olds & Watershed, (a professional accounting corporation), owns 25 percent of the common shares of Dove Corporation (not a client of AO&W). This year Dove purchased a 32 percent interest in Tale Company and is accounting for the investment using the equity method of accounting. The investment amounts to 11 percent of Dove's consolidated net assets. Tale Company has been an audit client of AO&W for 12 years.

h. Durkin & Panzer, PAs, regularly perform the audit of the North Country Bank, and the firm is preparing for the audit of the financial statements for the year ended December 31, 2007.

i. Two directors of the North Country Bank became partners in D&P, PAs, on July 1, 2007, resigning their directorship on that date. They will not participate in the audit.

j. During 2007, the former controller of the North Country Bank, now a partner of D&P, was frequently called on for assistance regarding loan approvals and the bank's minimum chequing account policy. In addition, he conducted a computer feasibility study for North Country.

(AICPA adapted)

k. The Cather Corporation is indebted to a PA for unpaid fees and has offered to give the PA unsecured interest-bearing notes. Alternatively, Cather Corporation offered to give two shares of its common stock, after which 10,002 shares would be outstanding.

(AICPA adapted)

l. Johnny Keems is not yet a PA but is doing quite well in this first employment with a large PA firm. He's been on the job two years and has become a "heavy junior." If he passes the PA exam in September, he will be promoted to senior accountant. This month, during the audit or Row Lumber Company, Johnny told the controller about how he is remodelling an old house. The controller likes Johnny and had a load of needed materials delivered to the house, billing Johnny at a 70 percent discount—a savings over the normal cash discount of about $300. Johnny paid the bill and was happy to have the materials, which he otherwise would not have been able to afford on his meager salary.

m. PA Lily Rowan inherited $1 million from her grandfather, $100,000 of which was the value of shares in the North Country Bank. Lily practises accounting in Hamilton, and several of her audit clients have loans from the bank.

n. Groaner Corporation is in financial difficulty. You are about to sign the report on the current audit when your firm's office manager informs you that the audit fee for last year has not yet been paid.

o. Your audit client, Glow Company, is opening a plant in a distant city. Glow's president asks that your firm's office in that city recruit and hire a new plant controller and a cost accountant.

p. Colt & Associates, PAs, audit Gore Company. Ms. Colt and Bill Gore (president) found a limited real estate partnership deal that looked too good to pass up. Colt purchased limited partnership interests amounting to 23 percent of all such interests, and Gore personally purchased 31 percent. Unrelated investors held the remaining 46 percent. Colt and Gore congratulate themselves on the opportunity and agree to be passive investors with respect to the partnership.

16.28 General and Technical Rule Cases. Knowledge of the rules of conduct, interpretations thereof and resolutions of Council related to general and technical standards will help you respond to the following cases. For each case, state whether the action or situation shows violation of the ICAO Rules of Professional Conduct, explain why, and cite the relevant rule or interpretation.

a. PA P. Stebbins helped Price Corporation prepare a cash flow forecast of hospital operations. The forecast was presented by Stebbins at a city council hearing for approval under the city's health services ordinance. Stebbins's report, which accompanied the forecast, consisted entirely of a full description of the sources of information used and the major assumptions made but did not include a disclaimer on the achievability of the forecast.

b. Kim Philby of Philby & Burgess, PAs, received a telephone call from his friend John, who is financial vice-president of U.K. Auto Parts. U.K. distributes parts over a wide area and does about $40 million in business a year. U.K. is not a client but is audited by Anderson, Olds & Watershed CAs, a venerable firm in the city. Kim has been hoping that John would switch auditors. Today John wants to get Kim's opinion about accounting for lease capitalizations related to a particularly complicated agreement with franchise dealers. Kim makes notes and promises to call John tomorrow.

c. PA Maclean gave a standard unqualified audit report on the financial statements of Anglo Korp. The annual report document did not contain supplementary oil and gas reserve information required by the *Handbook.*

d. Saul Panzer is a former university football player. Saul is a PA who works for Aggregate Corporation, which owns controlling interests in 42 other corporations. Theodolinda Bonner, president of Aggregate, has assigned Saul the task of performing audits of these corporations and submitting audit opinions directly to her for later presentation to the board of directors.

e. PA Blunt audits the Huber Hope Company. Huber's controller, also a PA, has conducted his own audit of Little Hope, Inc., Huber's single subsidiary, which amounts to 10 percent of the total assets, revenue and income

of the consolidated entity. Blunt has written an audit report that carefully explains reliance on "part of examination made by other independent auditors," with added language to explain the controller's role.

16.29 Responsibilities to Clients Cases. Knowledge of the rules of conduct and interpretations thereof on confidential client information and contingent fees will help you respond to the following cases. For each case, state whether the action or situation shows violation of the ICAO Rules of Professional Conduct, explain why and cite the relevant rule or interpretation.

a. PA Sally Colt has discovered a way to eliminate most of the boring work of processing routine accounts receivable confirmations by contracting with the Cohen Mail Service. After the auditor has prepared the confirmations, Cohen will stuff them in envelopes, mail them, receive the return replies, open the replies and return them to Sally.

b. Cadentoe Corporation, without consulting its PA, has changed its accounting so that it is not in conformity with generally accepted accounting principles. During the regular audit engagement, the PA discovers that the statements based on the accounts are so grossly misleading that they might be considered fraudulent. PA Cramer resigns from the engagement after a heated argument. Cramer knows that the statements will be given to John Cairncross, his friend at the Last National Bank, and knows that John is not a very astute reader of complicated financial statements. Two days later, Cairncross calls Cramer and asks some general questions about Cadentoe's statements and remarks favourably on the very thing that is misrepresented. Cramer corrects the erroneous analysis, and Cairncross is very much surprised.

c. A PA who had reached retirement age arranged for the sale of his practice to another public accountant. Their agreement called for the transfer of all working papers and business correspondence to the accountant purchasing the practice.

d. Martha Jacoby, PA, withdrew from the audit of Harvard Company after discovering irregularities in Harvard's income tax returns. One week later, Ms. Jacoby was telephoned by Jake Henry, PA, who explained that he had just been retained by Harvard Company to replace Ms. Jacoby. Mr. Henry asked Ms. Jacoby why she withdrew from the Harvard engagement. She told him.

e. David Moore, PA, offers a consulting service to clients in which he reviews their needs for computer-related supplies (magnetic tapes, disks, cards, paper and so on) and places their orders with Computographics, Inc. This supplier offers a special discount price because of the volume of business generated by Moore. David is considering two alternative billing arrangements:

1. Charge the clients no fee and instead accept a 3 percent commission from Computographics, Inc.
2. Charge his regular consulting rate of $160 per hour.

f. Amos Fiddle, PA, prepared an uncontested claim for a tax refund on Faddle Corporation's amended tax return. The fee for the service was 30 percent of the amount that the Canada Customs and Revenue Agency rules to be a proper refund. The claim was for $300,000.

g. After Faddle had won a $200,000 refund and Fiddle collected the $60,000 fee, Jeremy Faddle, the president, invited Amos Fiddle to be the auditor for Faddle Corporation.

16.30 Other Responsibilities and Practices Cases. Knowledge of the rules of conduct and interpretations thereof regarding various other responsibilities and practices will help you respond to the following cases. For each case, state whether the action or situation shows violation or potential for violation of the ICAO Rules of Professional Conduct, explain why, and cite the relevant rule or interpretation.

a. PA R. Stout completed a review of the unaudited financial statements of Wolfe Gifts. Ms. Wolfe was very displeased with the report. An argument ensued, and she told Stout never to darken her door again. Two days later, she telephoned Stout and demanded he return (1) Wolfe's cash disbursement journal, (2) Stout's working paper schedule of adjusting journal entries, (3) Stout's inventory analysis working papers, and (4) all other working papers prepared by Stout. Since Wolfe had not yet paid her bill, Stout replied that provincial law gave him a lien on

all the records and that he would return them as soon as she had paid his fee.

b. The PA firm of Durkin & Panzer had received promissory notes in payment of the Henshaw Hacksaw company tax return preparation fee. Six months after the notes were due, PA Durkin notified Dave Henshaw that the notes had been turned over to the North Country Bank for collection.

c. PA Panzer has been invited to conduct a course in effective tax planning for the City Chamber of Commerce. The C. of C. president said a brochure would be mailed to members giving the name of Panzer's firm, his educational background and degrees held, professional society affiliations, and testimonials from participants in the course held last year comparing his excellent performance with that of other PAs who have offered competing courses in the city.

d. PA Philby is a member of the provincial bar. Her practice is a combination of law and accounting, and she is heavily involved in estate planning engagements. Her letterhead gives the affiliations: Member, Provincial Bar of —, and Member, CICA.

e. The PA firm of Burgess & Maclean has made a deal with Cairncross & Company, a firm of management consulting specialists, for mutual business advantage. B&M agreed to recommend Cairncross to clients who need management consulting services. Cairncross agreed to recommend B&M to clients who need improvements in their accounting systems. During the year both firms would keep records of fees obtained by these mutual referrals. At the end of the year, Cairncross and B&M would settle the net differences based on a referral rate of 5 percent of fees.

f. Sturm & Drang, PAs, conduct an aggressive, growing practice in Middle City. The firm pays 20 percent of first-year fees to any staff member (below partner) who brings in a new client.

g. Jack Robinson and Archie Robertson (both PAs) are not partners, but they have the same office, the same employees, and a joint bank account, and they work together on audits. A letterhead they use shows both their names and the description "Members, ICAO."

h. PA Dewey retired from the two-person firm of Dewey & Cheatham. One year later, D&C merged practices with Howe & Company, to form a regional firm under the name of Dewey, Cheatham & Howe Company.

i. Fritz Brenner, PA, died and widow Brenner inherited the interest he had in the PA firm of Brenner & Horstmann, P.C. Can widow Brenner share in the partnership as a passive investment? She is not a PA.

16.31 Rules of Professional Conduct

Required:

For each of the following completely independent situations, describe the rules of professional conduct that are relevant. Have they been violated? Support your conclusion.

Situation A

Randi Woode, PA, was working on the year-end audit of her client, Pads N' Pens (PNP). PNP is an office stationery retailer with a July 31 year-end. She was having difficulty completing the audit because some accounting records for the months of April and May had been destroyed in a fire.

She told the owner-manager of PNP, Joe Smith, that she might have to qualify her audit report because of her inability to substantiate some of the balances on the financial statements. Joe pointed out that he had been her client for eight years and that she knew him to be honest and trustworthy. He also said a qualified report would harm his negotiations with the bank for additional loans. After considering PNP's need for additional financing, as well as their long-standing relationship, Randi agreed to issue an unqualified report.

Situation B

Lori Wilkes is an audit senior with a large PA firm in Toronto. She has learned that one of her largest clients, Superior Motors Ltd. (SML), is planning to acquire Steelco Inc. SML is Canada's largest automobile manufacturer, and Steelco is one of SML's biggest steel suppliers. Lori is confident that SML's acquisition of Steelco will reduce SML's costs dramatically, and that as a result, SML's share price will rise. She

has, therefore, encouraged her boyfriend, Tom, to buy some shares while being careful not to divulge the real reasons behind her recommendation.

Situation C

After obtaining his PA designation, Larry Wilde decided to set up his own public accounting practice. He reasoned that naming his practice "Quality Chartered Accountancy Services" would best attract new clients.

(ICAO adapted)

16.32 Rules of Professional Conduct.

In mid-May, Aileen Macdonald, PA, received a phone call from one of her largest clients, a manufacturer. The client wanted to know more details about the impact that the GST would have on his 2001 operations and financial statements. When Aileen and the client had discussed the results of the 1999 audit last February, part of their conversation had dealt with the tax. Aileen had indicated that she would be sending a newsletter about the tax by July 1.

Since February there had been more changes to the legislation, which Aileen and her partners hadn't had time to absorb. However, Aileen had registered for the annual June provincial conference, where she would attend the four technical sessions on the GST. She planned to ask questions about her client's situation during the question-and-answer periods that followed each session.

Aileen explained to the client that she would have more information within a month and would contact him then. At that time, she will ask the client for names of firms that might be interested in receiving her newsletter.

Required:

Which rules of professional conduct are relevant to the above situation? Discuss the rules with which Aileen Macdonald is in compliance as well as those she may have violated.

(ICAO adapted)

DISCUSSION CASES

· ·

16.33 **General Ethics.** Is there any moral difference between a disapproved action in which you are caught and the same action that never becomes known to anyone else? Do many persons in business and

professional society make a distinction between these two circumstances? If you respond that you do (or do not) perceive a difference while persons in business and professional society do not (or do), then how do you explain the differences in attitudes?

16.34 Ethics Decision Problem. You are treasurer of a church. A member approaches you with the following proposition: "I will donate shares to the church on December 31, if, on January 1, you will sell them back to me. All you will need to do is convey the certificate with your signature to me in return for my cheque, which will be for the asking price of the shares quoted that day without reduction for commissions."

The member's objective, of course, is to obtain the income tax deduction as of December 31, but he wants to maintain his ownership interest. The policy of the church board is not to hold any shares but to sell shares within a reasonably short time.

Consider:

a. Should the treasurer accommodate the member? Would you if you were treasurer?

b. Would your considerations and conclusions be any different if:
   1. The church were financially secure and the gift were small in amount?
   2. The church were financially secure and the gift were large?
   3. The church would be in deficit position for the year were it not for the gift?

16.35 Competition and Audit Proposals. Accounting firms are often asked to present "proposals" to companies' boards of directors. These "proposals" are comprehensive booklets, accompanied by oral presentations, telling about the firm's personnel, technology, special qualifications and expertise in hope of convincing the board to award the work to the firm.

Dena has a new job as staff assistant to Michael, chairman of the board of Granof Grain company. The company has a policy of engaging new auditors every seven years. The board will hear oral proposals from 12 accounting firms. This is the second day of the three-day meeting. Dena's job is to help evaluate the proposals. Yesterday, the proposal by Anderson, Olds & Watershed was clearly the best.

Then Dena sees Michael's staff chief, a brash go-getter, slip a copy of the AOW written proposal into an envelope. He tells Dena to take it to a friend who works for Hunt and Hunt, a PA firm scheduled to make its presentation tomorrow. He says: "I told him we'd let him glance at the best proposal." Michael is absent from the meeting and will not return for two hours.

What should Dena do? What should PA Hunt do if he receives the AOW proposal, assuming he has time to modify the Hunt and Hunt proposal before tomorrow's presentation?

16.36 Engagement Timekeeping Records. A time budget is always prepared for audit engagements. Numbers of hours are estimated for various segments of the work—for example, internal control evaluation, cash, inventory, report review and the like. Audit supervisors expect the work segments to be completed "within budget," and staff accountants' performance is evaluated in part on ability to perform audit work efficiently within budget.

Sarah is an audit manager who has worked hard to get promoted. She hopes to become a partner in two or three years. Finishing audits on time weighs heavily on her performance evaluation. She assigned the cash audit work to Craig, who has worked for the firm for 10 months. Craig hopes to get a promotion and salary raise this year. Twenty hours were budgeted for the cash work. Craig is efficient, but it took 30 hours to finish because the company had added seven new bank accounts. Craig was worried about his performance evaluation, so he recorded 20 hours for the cash work and put the other 10 hours under the internal control evaluation budget.

What do you think about Craig's resolution of his problem? Was his action a form of lying? What would you think of his action if the internal control evaluation work was presented "under budget" because it was not yet complete, and another assistant was assigned to finish that work segment later?

16.37 Audit Overtime. All accountants' performance evaluations are based in part on their ability to do audit work efficiently and within the time budget planned for the engagement. New staff accountants, in particular, usually have some early difficulty learning speedy work habits, which demand that no time be wasted.

Elizabeth started work for Anderson, Olds & Watershed in September. After attending the staff training school, she was assigned to the Rising Sun Company audit. Her first work assignment was to complete the extensive recalculation of the inventory compilation, using the audit test counts and audited unit prices for several hundred inventory items. Her time budget for the work was six hours. She started at 4 p.m. and was not finished when everyone left the office at 6 p.m. Not wanting to stay downtown alone, she took all the necessary working papers home. She resumed work at 8 p.m. and finished at 3 a.m. The next day, she returned to the Rising Sun offices, put the completed working papers in the file, and recorded six hours in the time budget/ actual schedule. Her supervisor was pleased, especially about her diligence in taking the work home.

What do you think about Elizabeth's diligence and her understatement of the time she took to finish the work? What would you think of the case if she had received help at home from her husband? What would you think of the case if she had been unable to finish and had left the work at home for her husband to finish while he took off a day from his job interviews?

16.38 Form of Practice, Technical Standards and Confidentiality. Knowledge of the rules of conduct and interpretations thereof will help you respond to this case problem.

Gilbert and Bradley formed a corporation called Financial Services, Inc. Each took 50 percent of the authorized common shares. Gilbert is a PA and a member of the provincial institute. Bradley is a CPCU (Chartered Property Casualty Underwriter). The corporation performs auditing and tax services under Gilbert's direction and insurance services under Bradley's supervision. The opening of the corporation's office was announced in a full-page advertisement in the local newspaper.

One of the corporation's first audit clients was the Grandtime Company. Grandtime had total assets of $600,000 and total liabilities of $270,000. In the course of the audit, Gilbert found that Grandtime's building with a book value of $240,000 was pledged as a security for a 10-year term note in the amount of $200,000. The client's statement did not mention that the building was pledged as security for the 10-year term note. However, as the failure to disclose the lien did not affect either the value of the assets or the amount of the liabilities, and the audit was satisfactory in all other respects, Gilbert rendered an unqualified opinion on Grandtime's financial statements. About two months after the date of his opinion, Gilbert learned that an insurance company was planning to loan Grandtime $150,000 in the form of a first-mortgage note on the building. Realizing the insurance company was unaware of the existing lien on the building, Gilbert had Bradley notify the insurance company of the fact that Grandtime's building was pledged as security for the term note.

Shortly after the events described above, Gilbert was charged with several violations of professional ethics.

Required:

Identify and discuss the Rules of Professional Conduct violated by Gilbert and the nature of the violations.

(AICPA adapted)

16.39 Rules of Professional Conduct. You and Laura Cooper are the two partners of a PA firm in Ottawa. After your two-week Caribbean vacation, you return to the office to discover that your secretary is busily preparing to mail some brochures. You have never seen the brochures before and your secretary explains that Laura had them printed during your absence. The brochures are colourful and glossy and the name of your firm is boldly displayed on the front cover. You pick up a brochure and notice that it describes your firm as "the PA firm where clients always come first." On the last page of the brochure, readers are advised that new audit clients will not be charged a fee for any management consulting services provided in the first full year.

You ask Laura about the brochures, and she tells you that she had them specially designed and printed to increase the firm's profile and competitiveness. She believes that mailing these brochures to all the top companies in Ottawa will not only increase the firm's client base but will also help it develop a high-quality image by getting a reputation for obtaining the "best clients." Furthermore, she plans to contact all recipients of the brochure in a few weeks to arrange a "follow-up" meeting to discuss their accounting and auditing needs.

Required:

Describe which rules of professional conduct may have been violated and indicate your professional responsibilities and course of action.

(ICAO adapted)

16.40 Conflict of Clients' Interests. Jon Williams, PA, has found himself in the middle of the real-life soap opera "Taxing Days of Our Lives."

The cast of characters:

Oneway Corporation is Jon's audit and tax client. The three directors are the officers and also the only three shareholders, each owning exactly one-third of the shares.

President Jack founded the company and is now nearing retirement. As an individual, he is also Jon's tax client.

Vice president Jill manages the day-to-day operations. She has been instrumental in enlarging the business and its profits. Jill's individual tax work is done by PA Phil.

Treasurer Bill has been a long-term, loyal employee and has been responsible for many innovative financial transactions and reports of great benefit to the business. He is Jon's close personal friend and also an individual tax client.

The conflict:

President Jack discussed with PA Jon the tax consequences to him as an individual of selling his one-third interest in Oneway Corporation to vice president Jill. Later, meeting with Bill to discuss his individual tax problems, Jon learns that Bill fears that Jack and Jill will make a deal, put him in a minority position, and force him out of the company. Bill says: "Jon, we have been friends a long time. Please keep me informed about Jack's plans, even rumours. My interest in Oneway Corporation represents my life savings and my resources for the kids' university. Remember, you're little Otto's godfather."

Thinking back, Jon realized that vice president Jill has always been rather hostile. Chances are that Phil would get the Oneway engagement if Jill acquires Jack's shares and controls the corporation. Nevertheless, Bill will probably suffer a great deal if he cannot learn about Jack's plans, and Jon's unwillingness to keep him informed will probably ruin their close friendship.

Later, on a dark and stormy night:

Jon ponders the problem. "Oneway Corporation is my client, but a corporation is a fiction. Only a form. The shareholders personify the real entity, so they are collectively my clients, and I can transmit information among them as though they were one person. Right? On the other hand, Jack and Bill engage me for individual tax work, and information about one's personal affairs is really no business of the other. What to do? What to do?

Required:

Give Jon advice about alternative actions, considering the constraints of the ICAO's Rules of Conduct.

16.41 Failure to Follow GAAS. It's going to be a long night! First thing this morning, the senior partner of your three-partner firm, Peters, Peters and Paul ("PPP"), called you into her office to tell you that she had a confidential but exciting assignment for you. The firm has been retained to review the audit working papers of another firm in connection with its audit of TVB Software (TVB), a public company. That firm, Yeller, Louder and Soft (YLS), had performed the audit of TVB for the last two years, since the date it went public. It appears that the bank did not renew TVB's loan when it matured some six months ago and TVB was unable to obtain other financing. As a result, your firm's client lost a good portion of the $2 million he had invested in the shares of TVB. Your client is suing the auditors of TVB, alleging that they failed to perform the audit in accordance with generally accepted auditing standards (GAAS), and that as a result, your client relied on financial statements that were not correct when he made his decision to hold on to his TVB shares. The last audited statements are included in Exhibit 16.41–1.

Victoria Smyth, the partner, has reviewed the contents of YLS's working papers. Her notes are in Exhibit 16.41–2. You have been asked to review these notes and prepare a report identifying any departures from GAAS to support your client's view that the audit was not conducted in accordance with GAAS. In this regard, you should note whether each instance is a clear departure from GAAS or whether the matter is grey and, therefore, subject to potential challenge in court. Victoria is also concerned that your firm may have some professional responsibilities under the Rules of Professional Conduct in connection with this agreement. She would like you to identify these for her.

Required

Prepare the report requested by Victoria Smyth.

(ICAO adapted)

EXHIBIT 16.41–1   **EXTRACTS FROM AUDITED FINANCIAL STATEMENTS**

TVB Software
Balance Sheet
As at December 31
(in thousands of dollars)

	20–3	20–2
Assets		
Current Assets		
Prepaids	$ 237	$ 410
Accounts receivable	6,146	5,410
Inventory	13,904	9,382
	20,287	15,202
Other Assets		
Fixed assets	13,640	14,975
Goodwill	4,084	4,310
Other assets	6,950	7,010
	24,674	26,295
	$44,961	$41,497
Liabilities and Shareholder Equity		
Current Liabilities		
Bank indebtedness	$ 4,940	$ 1,749
Accounts payable	10,641	5,940
Deferred revenue	140	3,643
Current portion of long-term debt	1,400	1,400
	17,121	12,732
Long-term Debt	18,210	19,990
Share capital	8,500	8,500
Retained Earnings	1,130	275
Total Liabilities and Capital	$44,961	$41,497

TVB Software
Income Statement
For the years ended December 31
(in thousands of dollars)

	20–3	20–2
Sales	$21,724	$31,490
Cost of Sales	15,908	20,130
Gross Margin	5,816	11,360
Sales and Administrative Expenses		
Salaries	1,760	3,170
Research costs	304	3,775
Marketing and sales	501	2,607
Interest	1,739	1,889
Other	657	16
	4,961	11,457
Net Income Before Taxes	855	(97)
Income Taxes	—	203
Net Income	$ 855	($ 300)

E X H I B I T 16.41–1 **(continued)**

TVB Software
For the year ended December 31, 2003

From Note 1—Accounting Policies
  Goodwill
    Goodwill is amortized to income over its 40-year life.
From Note 7—Fixed Assets
  Fixed assets comprises.

	Cost	December 31, 2003 Accumulated Debt	Book Value
Computer Equipment	$29,790	$26,100	$ 3,690
Furniture and Fixtures	10,650	7,700	2,950
Building	11,000	4,000	7,000
Total	$51,440	$37,800	$13,640

E X H I B I T 16.41–2 **TVB SOFTWARE**

"PRIVILEGED"

Victoria Smyth's notes on review of audit working papers of TVB Software prepared by Yeller, Louder & Soft

1. I reviewed YLS's working papers at their office. The audit report for the year ended December 31, 2003 was signed by YLS on February 20, 2004.

   The working papers were neat and appeared to be well organized. All of the files have been prepared by audit staff and have been reviewed by a YLS junior audit partner, though not the one who signed the financial statements. This is the only public company audited by YLS.

   I asked to review the files of the previous year but was told that YLS only retains one year of files. The 2002 files had been destroyed. I reminded YLS that the 2002 files had now been subpoenaed by the Court.

2. The audit was staffed by two YLS CAs. Neither had performed audits of a software company before, but one of them had several years of auditing experience. The other CA had recently qualified and had spent the previous two years working for a government internal auditor's department. The audit partner told me that he wasn't concerned about this other CA because he was related to TVB's CFO and, hence, had a good knowledge of some of the workings of the company.

3. The audit was fully substantive in nature. All three of YLS's files contain working papers documenting the results of its substantive testing. Each section of the work contains a checklist of substantive tests. The tests appear to have been developed specifically for this assignment. The steps on the checklists appear to be signed off and cross-referenced to the appropriate working papers.

4. The first file is called the "TOP FILE" and contains several memos to file. The most significant of these are as follows:
   a) Materiality. A short memo sets materiality at $400,000. The memo notes that the company is not currently profitable although it is expected to be in the near future. As a result, it is more appropriate to use balance sheet numbers to determine materiality. Once the company becomes profitable, YLS would expect to use normalized income as a basis for materiality. Thus, one per cent of total assets is approximately $400,000.
   b) Plan. A short memo sets out that the audit will be fully substantive against a materiality of $400,000 and follow the approach used in the previous year, including the tailored audit programs developed that year.
   c) Engagement letter, signed by the client.
   d) Legal letters to each of TVB's lawyers, each with a standard reply.
   e) A standard management representation letter, containing no unusual or tailored paragraphs.

5. Prepaids. As these amounts were not material, YLS only compared this year's schedule to that of the previous year. There were no unusual items on either of the schedules.

6. Accounts receivable. The audit work in this section included a confirmation of the 15 largest accounts and 10 other accounts selected at random, covering 79% of the population. All but two of the confirmations (totalling $326,000) were received back with no problems noted. In view of the satisfactory result on the other confirmations, no additional procedures were carried out in relation to these two items.

   A review was done to identify subsequent payments, and as at the date of the audit opinion, 85% of the receivables had been collected. Of the remaining accounts, none were above $100,000, so no further work was carried out.

   Procedures were carried out to ensure that balances outstanding at year end related to shipments before year-end. These procedures included agreeing amounts to invoices and shipping documents.

E X H I B I T 16.41–2   **TVB SOFTWARE (continued)**

7. Inventory. The inventory consisted of software packages, most of which were manufactured by TVB, and some purchased for modification and resale.

   YLS attended the inventory count at year-end and reviewed the procedures necessary to achieve a proper cut-off. As a result of these procedures, YLS found cut-off errors that resulted in an overstatement of sales of $182,500. They concluded that, as this amount was not material, no adjustment was necessary. They also reviewed the inventory valuation by reviewing the process for allocating costs to specific products. This is a very complex process and the audit work seems to be detailed and thorough with much recomputation and testing in the files. They concluded that the allocation methodology was appropriate in the circumstances. They did not identify any errors.

8. Fixed assets. YLS's work was limited to reviewing the schedule of purchases (there were none above $100,000) and recomputing the depreciation for the year.

9. Goodwill. YLS recomputed the amortization for the year.

10. Bank indebtedness. YLS confirmed the amount of the bank indebtedness and the long-term debt, which is also owing to the bank. The confirmation noted that the debt was up for renewal in June of the following year. There is a note in the file that company management was confident that the debt would be renewed for a five-year term. As well, the file contained copies of some internal TVB memoranda, written over a four-month period in 2003, summarizing management's meetings with the bank and supporting the view that the debt would likely be renewed. On this basis, YLS concurred with management's view that the debt should continue to be classified as long-term debt.

11. Accounts payable. The files contained a confirmation of 100% of the accounts payable. All of the replies were in the file and all discrepancies had been followed up. As a result of these procedures, YLS concluded that accounts payable were understated by $232,000 but that, as this amount was immaterial, no adjustment was required.

12. Income taxes. Very detailed work was carried out in this section by a tax manager from YLS. The review appears very thorough and amounts are reconciled down to the penny.

13. Profit and loss. YLS carried out analytical procedures, comparing the current year's results to those of the previous year on an account-by-account basis. Explanations were obtained from management for all variances over $50,000 or 5 per cent of the previous year's balance.

   The file includes a detailed review of all invoices paid to outside consultants, including several other accounting firms, and copies of their reports. One of the assignments relates to a "business review" of TVB carried out at the request of the bank. The report for that assignment is not in the file.

16.42 CGA Code of Ethics. The issue of ethical conduct is becoming more and more important in the professional practice of PAs.

Required:
a. Identify the sequence of steps that have been proposed for an auditor to follow in attempting to resolve an ethical dilemma.
b. What are the two broad aims of the CGA Code of Ethics?
c. Briefly describe the three mechanisms by which the CGA Code of Ethics and Rules of Professional Conduct work.

(CGAAC adapted)

16.43 Independence. You are an audit manager with the firm of Wu, Potter and McKinley, PAs. You and Ray St. Claire, a manager with another PA firm, are having a discussion about auditor independence. Ray says, "On the one hand, the public seems to be demanding more and more assurance from us about more and more aspects of a client's operations, but to maintain our practice in today's environment we have to be competitive to be able to attract new clients."

Required:
a. Identify and briefly explain the competitive practice on the part of auditors to which Ray is referring.
b. Why is this perceived as a threat to auditor independence and the quality of audits?
c. With reference to parts *a.* and *b.*, what could a client do, at least in theory, to take advantage of this situation? What is the reason this strategy might not work?
d. What does the CGA-Canada Code of Ethics say about this issue?

(CGAAC adapted)

16.44 Audit Proposals. Smith and Mulberry (S&M) were asked by Behometh Ltd. to submit a proposal for its audit. This involved a 30-minute presentation to the board of directors and a written submission. The submission included a fixed fee quote for the first two years, a detailed outline of the proposed audit strategy, and a list of the qualifications of the audit team to be assigned. Five other PA firms were invited to bid on the engagement. S&M put in a "lowball" bid because the partners saw this as a golden opportunity to get exposure in this industry.

Several weeks later, Edgar Brown, chairman of the board, telephoned Mike Mulberry, congratulating him on being awarded the audit. The conversation went as follows:

Edgar: I'm pleased to offer you the engagement, Mike, and I want you to know you weren't the lowest bid. What really impressed us was your attitude and promise to give us personal attention. It's so refreshing to find an auditor who openly states there needs to be a completely harmonious relationship between auditor and client.

Mike: We're really pleased to be your auditors, Edgar. We were a little apprehensive about not having any experience in your industry.

Edgar: Well Mike, since you did indicate you would hire someone experienced to oversee the engagement, I really see no problem. I certainly support your idea of Stan Biggs, since he knows the industry inside out. We're a little sorry to lose him. He had only been with us two years since obtaining his PA and was a fine controller.

Mike: Yes, his knowledge of your operations should allow us to complete the audit in the minimal time.

Edgar: There is one favour you can do us right away, Mike. We would like to start a national ad campaign that depicts our auditor slashing prices to the bone on our products. We would like you to be the auditor in that ad.

Mike: Acting's not really my strong suit, Edgar, but I'm sure we can accommodate you on that.

Edgar: By the way Mike, to show how much we value our auditors, I want to give you a key to the executive washroom, a special pass that allows you to park in restricted zones and a letter that will give you folks an additional 25 percent off our employee store prices.

Mike: Thanks very much, Edgar.

(ICAO adapted)

The following week Mike went out to review the working papers of the predecessor auditors. He was shocked at the poor quality of work evident in these files. However, given the rule against criticism of fellow members, he believed it would be inappropriate to mention this to Behometh.

The audit went very smoothly. In fact, with Biggs in charge, S&M even managed to turn a profit on the job.

Several months later some information came to light, which Mike was not sure if he should worry about. Although Biggs had severed all employment ties with Behometh prior to joining S&M, apparently he still retained 1,000 shares of voting stock in the company.

Required:

Discuss the ethical issues in this case.

(ICAO adapted)

APPENDIX 16A

THE SEC ON INDEPENDENCE

. . . .

LEARNING OBJECTIVE

3. Identify and explain the major differences between AICPA and SEC views on auditors' independence.

The Securities and Exchange Commission was established in 1934 to administer the Securities Act of 1933, the Securities Exchange Act of 1934, and several other regulatory acts. In addition to administrative powers, the SEC has rule-making and judicial powers. The SEC relies heavily on the accounting profession and has a great interest in auditing standards and standards of professional conduct.

The SEC rule on independence is in Rule 2-01(b) of Regulation S-X. Except for differences in the choice of words, the content of the SEC rule appears to be very similar to Rules of Conduct. The SEC and provincial institutes define *member* essentially the same with reference to independence matters. However, these surface similarities mask some substantive differences in the ways the two agencies interpret their rules. The main differences are in the areas of bookkeeping, family relations, financial interests and former partners.

BOOKKEEPING
. . . .

The SEC prohibits the combination of bookkeeping (accounting) and auditing services. The provincial institutes do not consider independence impaired if an accountant first prepares the client's books and then audits the financial statements prepared from them. However, the client must be able to accept responsibility for accounting decisions and for the financial statements. The SEC views the two services as incompatible, believing that an auditor cannot appear to be independent when auditing the bookkeeping work he or she has done. In the SEC's eyes, independence is impaired even if the PA keeps clients' books by offering computerized accounting services. However, exceptions can be made in the case of emergency, in other unusual situations and when computer services for first-time registrants were merely routine and mechanical, and did not involve the most recent fiscal year in the financial statements.

FAMILY RELATIONS
. . . .

The SEC tends to go further than provincial institutes in attributing family relations to a "member." The SEC considers independence impaired in most cases when a spouse, dependent person or someone else in the member's household has a direct or material indirect financial interest, or when nondependent close relatives (children, brothers, sisters, grandparents, parents, parents-in-law and the spouses of each of the foregoing) have material direct financial interests or managerial relationships in an audit client. The provincial institutes make allowances for the "audit sensitivity" of a relative's employment, letting independence be considered intact if the position is not sensitive. However, the provincial institute interpretations warn members to be aware of the appearances no matter what the specific facts may be. Overall, the provincial institutes' position appears to be flexible and permits assessment of the circumstances in each case. In contrast, the SEC position tends to prohibit most relationships involving close relatives, especially when the relative holds an executive position or is in a position to influence the content of the financial statements.

FINANCIAL INTERESTS
. . . .

The SEC tends to be stricter than the provincial institutes on matters of prohibited indirect financial interests. The tendency is to be conservative and to consider most financial relationships, investments in concert with client's officers and directors and other joint business ventures as impairments of independence.

FORMER PARTNERS

The SEC is stricter than the provincial institutes about the effect of a retired or resigned partner's association with his or her former firm's appearance of independence. Broadly, the SEC considers the firm's independence impaired if (*a*) a former partner who was closely associated with an audit becomes a member of the board of directors of the auditee within two years after resignation or retirement, (*b*) a former partner who was "prominent in his or her firm" becomes a director of a client of the accounting firm within five years, and (*c*) a former partner becomes an executive of a client of the accounting firm without a total separation, including settlement of retirement benefits, from the firm. However, former partners can become directors of auditees and still receive retirement benefits from the accounting firm so long as the benefits were fixed at the time of retirement. The provincial institutes' rules are similar but do not contain the specific time limits.

SEC VIEWS

The SEC has emphasized an important facet of factual independence, saying: "Perhaps the most critical test of the actuality of an accountant's independence is the strength of his insistence upon full disclosure of transactions between the company and members of its management as individuals; accession to the wishes of management in such cases must inevitably raise a serious question [of] whether the accountant is, in fact, independent," The provincial institutes' rules do not emphasize this point. This SEC view casts a cloud of suspicion over the practice of negotiating with the client the nature and amount of financial statement adjustments proposed by auditors.

SEC interpretations on independence are made by staff members in the Office of the Chief Accountant. In the past, accountants presented fact situations and requested decisions about their independence in a particular situation. The staff prepared letters expressing case-specific conclusions. Periodically, some of these conclusions were compiled and published. At present, they can be found in Financial Reporting Release No. 1, Section 602, published by the SEC. These case decisions are used by accountants as analogies to new fact situations and as guides to figuring out the SEC position.

Accountants are always welcome to submit their independence questions to the chief accountant for a decision. It is much better to settle a question before an audit is conducted than to have an issue of independence raised later. Accountants' letters describing fact situations and letters containing SEC conclusions are routinely released to the public.

R E V I E W
CHECKPOINTS

16.45 Compare the ICAO and SEC views on independence. How are they similar? How do they differ?

APPENDIX 16B

SOME ADDITIONAL BACKGROUND IN PHILOSOPHY, ETHICS AND LOGIC IN THE CONTEXT OF AUDITING

This appendix is intended to provide a better understanding of the rules of professional conduct, their justification and the logic of audit decision making. The appendix has three sections. We begin by providing an overview of the nature of philosophy. Next, we review some key philosophical concepts as they relate to the study of ethics. Finally, we provide a brief overview of logic, how logic is used in ethics and how logical argumentation pervades the entire audit process.

SECTION 1: INTRODUCTION TO PHILOSOPHY

Philosophy's importance arises from the fact that philosophy includes the formal study of reasoning in all its forms, including audit reasoning. Philosophy can be defined as the study of processes governing thought and conduct. Philosophy is the study of wisdom in all its many forms. This is reflected by the many fields which have their own distinctive philosophies, for example, philosophy of law, of history, of art, of human relationships. There is even a classic book on the philosophy of auditing by Mautz and Sharaf (1961). In short there is a philosophy underlying every discipline. And since philosophy deals with the underlying rationality of all disciplines, it is worthwhile to be aware of some of its basic features.

Philosophy can be thought of as a second order discipline that has as its object of study first order disciplines such as those of the sciences, arts, theology, psychology and management. Basic philosophy, however, is distinguished by its method rather than by its subject matter. The core of philosophy is generally considered to consist of metaphysics (the nature of being or reality), epistemology (the study of knowledge and how it can be obtained), and logic (the study of reasoning). Since logic is a major source of knowledge, it and epistemology are closely linked. From this core, philosophy branches out into less general areas such as philosophy of science, moral philosophy and aesthetics and these then become the basis of philosophies of more specific areas such as auditing. These various areas of philosophy are only vaguely defined as there is much overlap not only among the core areas but in some cases the more specialized areas, for example, moral philosophy affects auditing via the professional code of conduct. However, as we branch out into more specialized areas such as the philosophy of auditing we find that auditing depends on the core areas such as epistemology without the need for epistemology to rely on auditing. In this sense the core areas are foundational.

SECTION 2: A PHILOSOPHICAL FRAMEWORK FOR ETHICS

Ethics is the philosophical study of morality. Although there are many dimensions to morality, the main ones are what objectives in life should human beings have and what principles should determine our choices and goals. Kant's imperative principle and utilitarianism discussed in the chapter are examples of principles that govern right actions. Ethics involves belief systems about how we should conduct our lives. Such philosophical systems involve aspects of metaphysics, epistemology and logic. To know whether or not an action is ethical involves whether it can be justified. This follows from the generally accepted idea in epistemology that knowledge implies a justified true belief. Something cannot be considered knowledge unless it is believed, the belief must be justified (that is, it cannot be an arbitrary belief to be considered knowledge), and the belief must be considered to be true. Ethics tends to focus on choices and actions. In ethics, knowledge simplifies to justification of actions since in taking an action it is generally assumed that the action occurs and is believed to have occurred (unless our senses are completely misleading us!). Thus if we had to identify the central issue in ethics as applied to auditing, justification would be a good choice.

Justification relies on logic. There are two major categories of logic, formal logic and informal logic. Formal logic abstracts principles as much as possible from the specific context in which the reasoning takes place. The goal is to develop more universal principles regardless of the context or field in which the reasoning takes place (that is, the field-independent aspects of reasoning are emphasized). Informal logic, on the other hand, deals with the application of logic to specific contexts and thus also incorporates the additional complexities of practical decision making such as the natural language (for example, French or Mandarin) in which the reasoning takes place, as well as the background knowledge about the field that helps give the reasoning its strength.

Informal logic is especially common in moral reasoning. Moral reasoning deals with judgements about right or wrong, fair or unfair, about how people ought to be treated. Some skeptics equate moral reasoning with tastes, or likes and dislikes because they feel moral judgements cannot be justified. One difference between moral judgements and tastes is that the former are generalizable whereas the latter are not.

Radical skeptics claim there are no premises or principles of morality on which to justify moral judgements. A foundational problem in moral reasoning is that moral skeptics can't prove that moral criteria do not exist whereas their opponents can't prove that they do exist. But this problem exists for many fundamental principles of mathematics and science, and so the radical skeptical approach is not very pragmatic. This of course doesn't mean we have to argue on foundational principles, we can disagree and be skeptical and withhold judgement, it is part of rational inquiry.[18]

The two most common types of principles in the philosophy of moral reasoning are teleological (utilitarianism) and deontological (based on imperatives such as the biblical commandments). Both utilitarianism and Kantian theories attempt to develop a theory based on a single dominant principle (such theories are called monistic). But the problem with practical ethics is that monistic theories are not sufficient to handle the complexities of most real-life ethical problems. Frequently, there are multi-dimensional aspects to an issue and these different aspects or viewpoints are reflected by different approaches that have evolved over the centuries. For example, an influential approach is character ethics which focuses on the virtues a person needs to take the most ethical action. Generous, caring, compassionate and sympathetic individuals are more likely to understand what should be done. This is because "when the feelings, concerns and attitudes of others are the morally relevant matters, rules and principles are not as likely as human warmth and sensitivity to lead us to notice what should be done. Even a seldom noticed virtue, such as cheerfulness or tactfulness, can be far more significant than standard rules in some contexts. Furthermore, forms of loyalty, reliability and commitment to other persons can, across time, be more integral to an adequate or full moral life than following principles or rules."[19]

Another important approach to ethics are rights based theories. Rights are justified claims that individuals and groups can make upon others or upon society (for example, childrens' rights or the right to health care). The claims can be viewed as rules based: the rules determine the claim or entitlement in question. The rules can be legal, institutional or based on social norms. For some justifications rights are the dominant principle. For example, rights theory underlies much of international law, treaties and constitutional law related to human rights such as freedom of the press and freedom of religious expression.

Another important approach to ethics is community-based theory or communitarianism. Communitarian theories view everything fundamental in ethics as deriving from communal values, the common good, social goals, traditional practices and the cooperative virtues. In other words, the primacy is put on social practices.

[18] W. Hughes, *Critical Thinking* (Peterborough. Ont.: Broadview Press, 1997), pp. 207–209.
[19] T.L. Beauchamp and J.F. Childress, *Principles of Biomedical Ethics*, 4th ed. (Oxford: Oxford University Press, 1994), p. 69.

Yet another approach to ethics is the ethics of care. Ethics of care emphasizes emotional commitment to, and willingness to act on behalf of persons with whom one has a significant relationship. Emphasis is put on human bonding and friendship and responsibilities derived from attachment to others. Taking care of others is the core notion, and it is modelled on relationships such as those between parent and child. Some noted psychologists and philosophers maintain that women's moral development is different from men's and it is largely the ethic's of care that reflects this difference.[20] By incorporating a care ethic into a moral framework a more balanced approach may result that combines abstract principles and emotions.

The need to balance different approaches to ethics and the possibility of conflicts in the approaches to specific situations has led to calls for a case-based reasoning approach in a variety of fields, including biomedical ethics. Biomedical ethics may be a useful test case of applied ethics in all fields because technological advances in medicine and technology have created novel ethical problems on matters involving life and death. For example, at what point is failure to give an experimental treatment or costly treatment that prevents death tantamount to negligence or even murder? Biomedical ethics thus forces one to take moral reasoning more seriously and not to dismiss ethics as the exclusive domain of religion or mysticism. For example, the decision whether or not to end painful treatment for a terminal illness can't be left to mysticism or religion. While these may help, it is also important to justify one's actions as much as possible. Since ethical problems in other fields are not nearly as dramatic, biomedical ethics may provide the broadest practical ethical framework.

An influential approach to reasoning in biomedical ethics is case-based reasoning "Casuistery, as it is called, focuses on practical decision making in particular cases. Casuists are skeptical of rules, rights and theories divorced from history, precedent and circumstances. Appropriate moral judgements occur, casuists say, through an intimate understanding of particular situations, and the historical record of similar cases."[21]

Casuists follow the distinction first made by Aristotle between reasoning in the sciences, which ideally follows an axiomatic (deductive) approach, and in ethics, which is based on social norms and therefore does not have first foundational principles that have first priority. This ancient ideal for the sciences has never been achieved, only approximated. Thus practical disciplines like auditing have to recognize the sometimes extensive limitations of the idealized approaches. As in bioethics, audit reasoning may need to incorporate the broader principles of classical logic and rhetoric that are over 2000 years old because this is still the only way of capturing the full meaning of much practical reasoning. "We can only echo what rhetoricians since Aristotle have said: Every argument depends on three appeals—its *logos* (logic), its *pathos* (emotional quality), and its *ethos* (the writer's perceived character) and our reader's conviction (i.e. the user of the auditor's report) is woven of all three."[22]

All reasoning in natural language has rhetorical aspects. Explicit acknowledgement of qualifications or weaknesses in the reasoning strengthens these rhetorical aspects, and therefore the strength of the reasoning (because it helps demonstrate that all the evidence has been considered). For example, in auditing the *ethos* aspect of reasoning is what explains the importance of maintaining the appearance of independence to the public.

The modern versions of casuistery appear to capture the logical as well as the rhetorical features of practical ethical reasoning. "Casuists maintain that some forms of moral reasoning and judgement make no appeal to principles, rules, rights or virtues. These forms include appeals to narratives, paradigm, cases, analogies, models, classification schemes, and even immediate intuition and discerning insight."[23]Casuists maintain that moral judgements are possible even when reliance on principles is not possible, such as when principles conflict. It is claimed that actual professional ethical reasoning is more consistent

[20] Ibid., p. 69.
[21] Ibid., p. 94.
[22] W.C. Booth, G.G. Colomb and J.M. Williams, *The Craft of Research* (Chicago: University of Chicago Press, 1995), p. 145.
[23] Beauchamp and Childress, *Principles of Biomedical Ethics*, p. 94.

with casuistery than with any other approach. For example, a recent study of Ethics Commissioners (our equivalent of standard setters) in biomedical and behavioural research showed that they rely on reasoning by casuistery. Although the commissioners nominally use moral principles to justify their conclusions, they usually appeal to paradigms, particular cases and families of cases. Reasoning by analogy is often used to closely relate precedents about which social consensus has formed. "The commission's deliberations and conclusions are best understood, then, as examples of dialectical reasoning in which principles become interpreted, modified and specified in context by the force of examples and counterexamples drawn from real life cases."[24]

Casuistery is thus very much dependent on the specific context of the case. Context helps determine which principle should dominate the case and to what extent. If several principles are involved the relative weighing and balancing of the principles or social norms is also determined by the context. For example, biomedical ethicists have identified the following principles of common morality: respect for autonomy, nonmalificence, beneficence and fairness or justice. These lead to rules and corresponding virtues and ideals of action: truthfulness, confidentiality, respect for privacy, faithfulness, exceptional forgiveness, exceptional generosity, exceptional compassion and exceptional kindness to name a few.[25]

Justice in this system is based on a right of some type and injustice is viewed as taking away this right. For example, the right to being treated equally before the law or in the democratic voting process (each person having a single, equal vote). Frequently justice is based on a process rather than an outcome. For example, the justice of a democracy is frequently easier to verify than the fairness of the outcome of a democratic process. This explains why the process of justification in practical ethics so important. Justification in practical ethics is provided by good reasons in the sense of coherence with principles, social norms and other aspects of social life such as character ethics, moral emotions, virtues and rights.[26] The implementation of such an approach requires considerable balancing, judgement, expertise, and sensitivity to social norms and virtues.

Despite obvious risks of incoherence in the eclectic approach represented by casuistry, in practice considerable consensus and convergence is usually achievable. This practical success helps explain why casuistry is so influential in the health care field and why it may also be useful for making ethical decisions in an assurance engagement context. This success in building consensus also explains why practical ethics is equated with casuistery even though there is no single overarching principle that is used in all circumstances. Practical ethics is thus a pluralistic approach as opposed to a monastic approach stressing one principle (such as obligations) as in utilitarianism or Kantianism.

Practical ethics via casuistery thus attempts to provide a balance by not getting so abstract that it becomes difficult to apply a principle in many situations, yet not to overspecify a principle or rule because it then becomes too rigid and insensitive to the circumstances. The solution then is to use a pluralistic approach but to attempt to identify which principles are most appropriate for the circumstances of a given engagement. Advocates therefore characterize practical ethics in medicine and psychology as principle based but not limited to a single type of principle. This seems very similar to the way PA's rules of professional conducts are derived and applied as discussed in this chapter.

The need for a practical approach to ethics arises from the fact that often there is no straightforward way to move from theory to practice and it is necessary to consider a number of issues and factors simultaneously to develop a coherent support for a conclusion of a practical moral argument. Additional uncertainty is introduced by the need to interpret the facts in deciding what principles are most relevant. A particular specification of a code of ethics is justified only if it is more coherent with the whole set of relevant norms than any other available specification. We can expect only as much simplification in a code of ethics as the subject matter permits, and in practice no single non-pluralistic approach is sufficient.

"In moral reasoning we often blend appeals to principles, rules, rights, virtues, passions, analogies, paradigms, parables and interpretations. To assign priority to one of these factors as the key ingredient is a dubious project, as is the attempt to dispense with ethical theory altogether. The more general (principles, rules, theories, etc.) and the more particular (feelings, perceptions, case judgements, practices, parables, etc.) should be linked together in our moral thinking."[27]

SECTION 3: ROLE OF LOGIC IN AUDITING

Logic is the study of reasoning. Reasoning is not the same as thinking, however. Thinking includes things like daydreaming and playing tennis whereas reasoning is the active organization of thoughts to either support a conclusion or to provide an explanation. When reasoning is expressed in statements it is called an argument. In particular an argument consists of a set of statements one or more of which support (or provide reasons for) another statement called the conclusion. The truthfulness of a conclusion (for example an audit opinion) is dependent on the truthfulness of the other statements (reasons, or in philosophy frequently referred to as premises). If the premises are rationally acceptable and the argument has logical strength, then we have a sound argument. The strength of the link between the premises and the conclusion is the central issue in the study of logic. This strength can be measured by the inductive probability of an argument, which is the probability the conclusion is true if the premises are true. Inductive probabilities apply to the entire argument.

The auditor however is usually interested in the truthfulness of the conclusion itself. This probability is referred to as the epistemic probability.[28] Epistemic probability is based on our stock of knowledge, which in turn influences the strength of our argument. In particular, the epistemic probability is a function of the truthfulness of the premises used in the argument, and the inductive probability of the argument itself. If the premises can be assumed to be 100% true, then epistemic probability = inductive probability. In this sense the stronger the argument the stronger the conclusion.

Since the central problem in auditing is the strength of the auditor's conclusion as reflected in his or her opinion, it should immediately be apparent why argumentation is so critical to auditing. The audit opinion, if it is to be justified, should be the conclusion of an audit argument incorporating moral reasoning as well as reasoning with the evidence gathered in the audit.

As in biomedical ethics, informal logic appears to be the general reasoning model for supporting audit conclusions. Informal logic also dominates in law, other professions, and, in fact, in everyday reasoning. Perhaps it is for this reason that philosophy has recently shown increased interest in informal logic and it is rapidly evolving as a specialized branch of logic. Public sector auditors have already adopted a variant of informal logic, and so we will use a simplified version of their model here. We simplify their model of audit argumentation by using only the following concepts: warrants, data, conclusion and qualifiers, defined as follows.

Conclusion

The statement representing the claim of a logical argument. The conclusion can be supported either 100 percent (deductive argument) by the other statements in the argument, or something less than 100 percent (inductive argument). In auditing (and all assurance engagements) the opinion statement represents a conclusion that is warranted (supported

---

[27] Ibid., p. 111.
[28] B. Skyrms, *Choice and Chance*, 3rd ed. (Irvine, Calif.: University of California at Irvine, 1986), ch. 1.

by the evidence). In order to be socially justified an opinion needs to be warranted. Mere feelings cannot be the basis for socially justifiable professional opinions. Logical arguments justify professional opinions (and such arguments are also, or should be, an integral part of professional judgment).

Warrants

The statements in an argument that explain the connection between the data and the conclusion. Warrants are the major premises of an argument because they determine what data are relevant to the argument. Warrants include not only explanations of the relevance of the data, but also concepts, principles, rules, social norms, definitions and conventions. Examples of warrants used in auditing are the not only the utilitarian and imperative principles of this chapter, but also risk and materiality, assertions and the audit risk model of earlier chapters. Warrants determine whether qualitative features such as reliability and relevance (e.g., assertions) are met, as well as quantitative features such as sufficiency (e.g., risk and materiality). The warrants used in an audit thus pervade the entire audit process.

Data

The evidence from audit procedures including observation, analysis and knowledge of the client's business and industry. Data is considered the minor premise of an argument because it is dependent on the warrant (major premise) to determine its relevance for the conclusion. Thus in the simplest complete argument using data premises we have: 1). Major Premise (warrant) 2). Minor Premise (data) and 3). Conclusion.

Qualifiers

The constraints, limitations or exception with using the warrants. Explicitly acknowledging the qualifications of one's argument helps strengthen the argument. "Your credibility requires that you limit the scope of your arguments by hedging the uncertainty of your claims and evidence with modifying words and phrases"[29]

It is widely recognized in informal logic that the form or soundness of an argument depends on the context. In particular "given the same set of grounds (e.g., data), one can generate different claims (i.e., conclusions) depending upon the warrant (e.g., explanatory link) chosen. This is important both to the critic and to the creator of arguments. There is no single "correct" warrant to be attached to any set of grounds. Choice of warrant is a matter of the process of argumentation and is governed by the types and strength of claim sought as well as the audience—readers or listeners—to whom the argument is addressed." Thus in many respects arguments are "field dependent," that is, they are governed by specific rules of procedures or "due process" that greatly shape the argument and its accepted soundness. However, there are more universal "field invariant" rules of procedure that apply to rational criticism in all fields and forums. These "field invariant" features are based on the more traditional formal logic.

Specifically, S. Toulmin and others identify the following field invariant features:

1. The claims put forward and criticized in any particular context.
2. The grounds by which these claims are supported and the warrants by which grounds and claims are connected.
3. The backing available to establish the soundness and acceptability of these warrants.
4. The modal qualifiers that indicate the strength and/or conditions of rebuttal of the initial claim.[30]

It is noteworthy that public sector auditors used these field invariant features as a basis for developing an evidence framework for auditing.[31] This represents the first attempt to tai-

---

[29] Booth, et al. *The Craft of Research*, p. 140.
[30] S. Toulmin, R. Rielke, and A. Jainke, *An Introduction to Reasoning*, 2nd ed. (New York: Macmillan, 1984), p. 271.
[31] D.M. Barnes, *Value-for-Money Audit Evidence*, (Toronto: Canadian Institute of Chartered Accountants, 1991).

lor the argumentation framework to auditing. While the above features may be common to arguments in all fields, the strength or soundness of a particular argument within a field is determined by the "field dependent" characteristics such as what warrants are applicable and reliable. The warrants in turn determine the relevance of the evidence used and what kind of expertise is needed to work with the warrants. Informal logic thus incorporates the field dependent as well as the field independent aspects of argumentation. It should also be noted that the rhetorical features of argumentation noted above would be part of the field dependent features. For example, the appearance of independence is very important to maintaining the credibility of auditor argumentation.

In evaluating an informal argument a simplified scheme consists of only three steps: (1) acceptability of premises, (2) relevance of premises, and (3) the argument. Considered together, they provide good grounds for the conclusion.[32] It is clear from even this simplified scheme that practical argument evaluation requires much more than a decontextualized artificial language such as formalized symbolic logic. For example, how does one establish acceptability of premises without the use of natural language and common-sense background knowledge about the world? Thus informal logic is indispensable to the evaluation of all professional arguments.

To better understand the nature of formal versus informal, and deduction versus induction, it would perhaps be useful to clarify their relationships. They are not synonymous, but there is considerable overlap. The basic nature of deductive reasoning (a prime example is mathematical proofs) is that it is a type of argument that derives all its strength from form (syntax). Deduction is truth preserving in the sense that it guarantees the truth of its conclusion assuming the truth of its premises. In addition, because deduction focuses on the structure (syntax) of the argument it is independent of context and can therefore be more formally abstract. For these reasons deductive inferences have been considered the ideal form of knowledge in classical philosophy.

Inductive arguments lack this ability to guarantee conclusions because they involve a claim by the conclusion that goes beyond the claim made by the premises. This risk of error is the price we pay for gaining new knowledge. Genuinely new knowledge must rely on inductive reasoning because deductive reasoning is limited to exploring the implications of what we already know or assume to be true. Thus the truth-preserving qualities of deduction come with a price: we cannot go beyond the knowledge already contained in the premises. Induction is generally not independent of context and so it is closely related to informal logic. The only time informal logic is not inductive is when a natural language argument is purely deductive, for example, "all persons are mortal, Socrates is a person, therefore Socrates is mortal." If a natural language argument includes both inductive and deductive subarguments in its exposition, the argument as a whole is always inductive by definition. Informal logic using induction is thus the primary means of justifying audit conclusions. This is true regardless of whether the conclusion relates to ethical issues (this chapter), evidential issues (most of the other chapters), or to the audit opinion (Chapter 3).

Of course, the overall audit conclusion should be consistent with the audit opinion and supported by the auditor's entire argument. The auditor's argument is reflected in the audit working papers. The overall audit argument is a complex argument with some premises supporting an intermediate conclusion (e.g., that inventory is fairly presented), and the intermediate conclusions then become premises in the next step of argumentation. Thus each of the intermediate steps of reasoning which are linked together to form a complex argument can be an argument in its own right. Ethical arguments are thus intermediate arguments that help support the audit opinion. Generally, audit evidence is used to form auditor beliefs about fairness of presentation and decisions as to auditor actions, such as the wording of the opinion, are ethical decisions. Ethical reasoning is thus part of the complex audit argumentation that is needed to justify the audit opinion. The complexity of ethical argumentation in auditing should be evident, for example, from the boxes and discussion in the chapter related to independence and objectivity.

---

[32] T. Govier, *A Practical Study of Argument*, 3rd ed. (Belmont Calif.: Wadsworth, 1992), p. 84.

Justification is generally viewed in philosophy as an evaluation of how a conclusion was reached. This is usually done by looking at the reasons offered. There are two basic philosophies to justification, coherentism and foundationalism. Foundationalism focuses on individual beliefs as the ultimate source of justification, whereas coherentism looks at whole systems of belief for justification. Casuistery, which uses a pluralistic approach, relies on a coherence theory to justification. As a starting point casuistery uses social norms that are accepted without recourse to other judgments. These initial norms must, however, cohere with one another. This approach is dialectical in the sense that justification is viewed as a discourse among the affected parties. In a dialectic the starting points of justification are the premises conceded by the participants followed by a search for conclusions that can be derived from the agreed-to premises (keep in mind that these agreed-to premises can include observation statements and the data premises). Experience, background knowledge, character, as well as general principles are brought to bear in deciding how to resolve ethical issues within the dialectical framework.

A coherent approach is a combination of inductive approaches (reasoning from the particular to the general) as well as deductive approaches (deriving particulars from the most general assertions or principles). As in argumentation, a deductive approach has traditionally been promoted as the best model for justification. For example, particular judgements may be derivable from rules, which in turn are derivable from principles. In practice, however, combining deductive and inductive approaches using different principles, rules, theories and judgements depending on the circumstances results in a system more amenable to the dialectical framework, where not all premises may be acceptable to all parties. Thus the concept of coherentism better captures the justification needed to help resolve the conflicts of interest that can arise in ethical dialectics. As a famous ethics philosopher, J. Rawls, has noted, justification is a "matter of mutual support of many considerations, everything fitting together into one coherent whole."[33] Principles in this context are more general guides that leave considerable room for judgement in specific cases that provide substantive guidance for the development of more detailed rules and policies.

In summary, philosophical justification for audit conclusions, whether ethical or otherwise, are based on informal, inductive arguments using a coherentist approach.

[33] Beauchamp and Childress, *Principles of Biomedical Ethics*, p. 23.

CHAPTER 17

Learning Objectives

As noted in Chapter 16, auditors have three sources of responsibility: moral, professional and legal.

The previous chapter on professional ethics dealt mainly with accountants' self-regulation. This chapter focuses on public regulation through the courts. The discussion will help you to understand accountants' legal liability for professional work. Your learning objectives are to be able to:

1. List some ways that auditors can get into civil and criminal legal trouble.

2. Specify the characteristics of accountants' liability under common law, and cite some specific case precedents.

3. Specify the characteristics of accountants' liability under statutory law.

Legal Liability

The Legal Environment

LEARNING OBJECTIVE
1. List some ways that auditors can get into civil and criminal legal trouble.

"Tort reform" has been a hot topic in the business and popular press. Record-setting damages have been awarded and professional liability insurance premiums have increased dramatically, and in some cases insurance is difficult to obtain. The problems affect everyone, from manufacturers to rock concert promoters. Accountants are likewise affected. In the 1990s payments for litigation were over four times greater than in the 1980s. Payments in the U.S. now run into the billions. Twenty-seven medium-sized accounting firms formed their own offshore captive insurance company in Bermuda to get adequate liability insurance.

Accountants are potentially liable for monetary damages and even subject to criminal penalties (e.g., under SEC rules), including fines and jail terms, for failure to perform professional services properly. They can be sued by clients, clients' creditors, investors and the government. Exposure to large lawsuit claims is possible through class actions permitted under federal rules of court procedure in Canada and the United States. In a class action suit, a relatively small number of aggrieved plaintiffs with small individual claims can bring suit for large damages in the name of an extended class. After a bankruptcy, for example, 40 bondholders who lost $40,000 might decide to sue, and they can sue on behalf of the entire class of bondholders for all their alleged losses (say $40 million). In some jurisdictions, lawyers will take such suits on a contingency fee basis (a percentage of the judgement, if any). The size of the claim and the zeal of the lawyers make the class action suit a serious matter. In the United States this has become such a problem that it threatens the existence of many firms, and one regional firm has already been forced into bankruptcy as a result of litigation.

Lawsuit Causes and Frequency

One study of law cases showed that accountants' and auditors' legal troubles arose from five major types of errors. In 129 cases 334 errors were found, classified as follows: (1) 33 percent involved misinterpretation of accounting principles, (2) 15 percent involved misinterpretation of auditing standards, (3) 29 percent involved faulty implementation of auditing procedures, (4) 13 percent involved client fraud, and (5) 7 percent involved fraud by the auditor.[1] These data suggest that accountants' and auditors' exposure to liability for failure to report known departures from accounting principles, for failure to conduct audits properly, for failure to detect management fraud and for actually being parties to frauds. Threat of lawsuits has also affected how public accountants conduct their work in consulting services and tax practice. Lest you believe audit practice bears all the liability, be aware that about 35 percent of civil damage suits arise from tax practice disputes.

Another study of accountants' litigation showed how lawsuits against auditors have increased. During the 1960–72 period, 181 cases were found, compared to 291 cases during the 1973–85 period.

All litigation is serious and results in expenses for defence, but not all cases result in payments for damage. In fact, about 40 percent of the lawsuits in the 1960–85 period were dismissed or settled with no payment by the accounting firm. Another 30 percent were settled by payment of approximately $1 million or less. This leaves about 30 percent of the

---

[1] K. St. Pierre and J. Anderson, "An Analysis of Audit Failures Based on Documented Legal Cases," *Journal of Accounting, Auditing, and Finance,* Spring 1982, pp. 236–37.

cases where the auditors paid significant damage awards. All these data relate to lawsuits over audit services, to the exclusion of lawsuits about nonaudit services and other matters.[2]

Audit Responsibilities

Many users of audit reports expect auditors to detect fraud, theft and illegal acts, and to report them publicly. Auditors take responsibility for detecting material misstatements in financial statements; but they are very cautious about taking responsibility for detecting all manner of fraud, and are especially cautious about accepting a public reporting responsibility. Fraud and misleading financial statements loom large among the concerns of financial statement users. They are afraid of information risk, and they want it to be reduced, even eliminated. Some of their expectations are very high, and for this reason an expectation gap often exists between the diligence users expect and the diligence auditors are able to accept.

The audit responsibility for detection of fraud in financial statements is a complex topic, and Chapter 19 (Fraud Awareness Auditing) is devoted entirely to it. Auditors take some responsibility but not as much as many users expect (e.g., see *Handbook Sections* 5135 and 5136). This disparity leads to lawsuits, even when auditors have performed well.

<table>
<tr><td>R E V I E W
CHECKPOINTS</td><td>17.1 What are class action lawsuits, and why should auditors be concerned about them?

17.2 What are some causes of auditors' involvement in lawsuits as defendants?

17.3 What proportion of lawsuits against accountants relate to tax practice?</td></tr>
</table>

The next parts of this chapter cover accountants' legal liabilities under common law and statutory law. The principle of *stare decisis* or "to stand by a previous decision" is an important principle of common law. The practical problem in many cases, however, is whether the facts in a given case are similar enough to a precedent-setting one. It's rare that the facts are exactly the same. Common law is all the cases and precedents that govern judges' decisions in previous lawsuits. Common law is "common knowledge," in the sense that judges tend to follow the collective wisdom of past cases decided by themselves and other judges. Common law is not enacted in statutes by a legislature. In contrast, statutory law is all the prohibitions enacted by a legislature—for example, the Canadian Business Corporation Acts and related provincial Corporation Acts.

LIABILITY UNDER COMMON LAW

LEARNING OBJECTIVE
2. Specify the characteristics of accountants' liability under common law, and cite some specific case precedents.

Legal liabilities of professional accountants may arise from lawsuits brought on the basis of the law of contracts or as tort actions for negligence. Breach of contract is a claim that accounting or auditing services were not performed in the manner agreed. This basis is most characteristic of lawsuits involving public accountants and their clients. Tort actions cover the civil complaints (e.g., fraud, deceit and injury), and such actions are normally initiated by users of financial statements.

Tort refers to a private or civil wrong or injury. The rule of the law of torts is to compensate victims for harm suffered from the activities of others. The problem for tort law is to identify those actions which create a right to compensation. In doing so the law takes into account the fault or blame of the defendant (breach of duty) and whether the defendant's conduct could be considered the cause of the harm (causation). Both breach of a duty

---

[2] Zoe-Vonna Palmrose, "An Analysis of Auditor Litigation and Audit Service Quality," *Accounting Review,* January 1988, pp. 55–73.

to the plaintiff and causation must be established in order for the defendant to be found liable for damages. However, the burden of proof for tort actions varies depending on social policy. For example, under "no fault" schemes the burden of compensation is spread widely to all automobile owners (Smith, Soberman, and Easson, *The Law and Business Administration in Canada,* 7th Edition, 1995, pp. 76–79).

Suits for civil damages under common law usually result when someone suffers a financial loss after relying on financial statements later found to be materially misleading. In the popular press, such unfortunate events are called audit failures. However, a distinction should be made between a business failure and an audit failure. A business failure is a bankruptcy or other serious financial difficulty experienced by an auditor's client. Business failures arise from many kinds of adverse economic events. An audit failure is an auditor's faulty performance, a failure to conduct an audit in accordance with generally accepted auditing standards (GAAS) with the result that misleading financial statements get published.

Characteristics of Common Law Actions

When an injured party considers himself or herself damaged by an accountant and brings a lawsuit, he or she generally asserts all possible causes of action, including breach of contract, tort, deceit, fraud or whatever else may be relevant to the claim.

Burden of Proof on the Plaintiff

Actions brought under common law place most of the burdens of affirmative proof on the plaintiff, who must prove (1) that he or she was damaged or suffered a loss, (2) the necessary privity or beneficiary relationship, (3) that the financial statements were materially misleading or that the accountant's advice was faulty, (4) that he or she relied on the statements or advice, (5) that they were the direct cause of the loss, and (6) that the accountant was negligent, grossly negligent, deceitful or otherwise responsible for damages. Appendix 17A reviews the U.S. securities acts, a type of U.S. statutory law that regulates the PA profession. There you will that some of the U.S. statutes shift some of these burdens of affirmative proof to the PA.

Clients may bring a lawsuit for breach of contract. The relationship of direct involvement between parties to a contract is known as *privity*. When privity exists, a plaintiff usually need only show that the defendant accountant was negligent. (Ordinary negligence—a lack of reasonable care in the performance of professional accounting tasks—is usually meant when the word *negligence* stands alone.) If negligence is proved, the accountant may be liable, provided the client has not been involved in some sort of contributory negligence in the dispute—that is, that it can be shown that the client contributed to his own harm.

Smith v. London Assurance Corp. (1905)

> This was the first American case involving an auditor. The auditor sued for an unpaid fee, and the company counterclaimed for a large sum that had been embezzled by one of its employees, which they claimed would not have occurred except for the auditor's breach of contract. The evidence indicated that the auditors indeed failed to audit cash accounts at one branch office as stipulated in an engagement contract. The court recognized the auditors as skilled professionals and held them liable for embezzlement losses that could have been prevented by nonnegligent performance under the contract.

Fifty years ago, it was very difficult for parties, other than contracting clients, to succeed in lawsuits against auditors. Other parties not in privity had no cause of action for breach of contract. However, the court opinion in the case known as *Ultramares* expressed the view that, if negligence were so great as to constitute gross negligence—lack of minimum care in performing professional duties, indicating reckless disregard for duty and responsibility—grounds might exist for concluding that the accountant had engaged in constructive fraud. Actual fraud is characterized as an intentional act designed to deceive, mislead or injure the rights of another person.

Ultramares Corporation v. Touche (1931)

The *Ultramares* decision stated criteria for an auditor's liability to third parties for deceit (a tort action). In order to prove deceit, (1) a false representation must be shown, (2) the tort-feasor must possess scienter—either knowledge of falsity or insufficient basis of information, (3) intent to induce action in reliance must be shown, (4) the damaged party must show justifiable reliance on the false representation, and (5) there must have been a resulting damage. The court held that an accountant could be liable when he did not have sufficient information (audit evidence) to lead to a sincere or genuine belief. In other words, an audit report is deceitful when the auditor purports to speak from knowledge when he has none. The court also wrote that the degree of negligence might be so gross, however, as to amount to a constructive fraud. Then the auditor could be liable in tort to a third-party beneficiary.

Another important result of the *Ultramares* case was that the accountants were not liable to third parties for ordinary negligence. This had two ramifications for public accountants: (1) auditors were not liable to third parties under common law for the next 35 years and (2) this decision had a major impact on the U.S. Congress and influenced its passage of the SEC Acts of 1933 and 1934, creating a statutory responsibility to third parties where none existed under common law (see Appendix 17A).

Most auditor legal responsibilities arise from the law of negligence, which is the part of the common law known as the law of torts. Negligence is the failure to perform a duty with the requisite standard care (due care). The standard relates to one's public calling or profession.

Under the common law of torts for negligence (which is based on fault theory and causation as discussed above), all of the following four elements of negligence must be established by the plaintiff if she or he is to successfully sue the auditor.

I. Four Elements of Negligence

1. There must exist a legal duty of care to the plaintiff.
2. There must be a breach in that duty (e.g., failure to follow GAAS and GAAP).
3. There must be proof that damage resulted (otherwise the plaintiff is limited to the amount of audit fee).
4. There must be a reasonably proximate connection between the breach of duty and the resulting damage (e.g., losses must occur subsequent to firm's audit).

The auditor's defence is to demonstrate that at least one of the above elements is missing. The auditor may also use a contributory negligence argument that the plaintiff contributed to his own loss by, for example, not correcting internal control weaknesses. However, the contributory negligence defence applies only to parties having a contractual relationship with the auditor. Just to keep things straight the auditor is the first party, the contractual client (who hires the auditor for the audit engagement and thus has privity of contract with the auditor) is the second party, and other audited financial statement users are third parties.

II. Due Care to Whom?

A key issue in establishing liability against auditors is to whom do they owe a duty of care? The contractual client (the second party to the contract) is owed a duty of care due to privity of contract. The client is the organization that appoints the auditor, a corporation, a proprietorship or a partnership. The engagement letter is critical in specifying the contractual obligation, particularly for nonaudit engagements. This explains the importance of having the engagement letter in the first place—it is the basis for establishing the liability of the auditor to second parties.

Under the *Foss* v. *Harbottle* (1842) principle, financial stakeholders cannot sue for losses suffered simply because the corporation in which they hold the stake has suffered losses. This is the flipside of the protection that the stakeholder gets from suits by the corporation's creditors. Just as a creditor can't sue the corporation's owners, the owners can't sue on behalf of the corporation. The corporation itself has to claim any damages. In the case of auditors, the owners are not viewed as having privity of contract with the auditors; only the corporation has privity of contract. Thus, shareholders can only take action as third parties, and then they must establish damages separate from that to the corporation. It turns out that the difficulty of establishing this latter point has greatly limited legal liability to Canadian accountants from shareholders (even though the auditors' report is addressed to the shareholders).

The most important source of liability to auditors, however, is from third parties. This relates to a principle of common law that got transplanted from third-party liability for acts causing injury or physical damage (*Heaven* v. *Pender*, 1883). Until recently, courts were unwilling to compensate for pure economic losses—that is, where there was no physical injury or damage to a plaintiff's person or property. However, that situation has changed dramatically. The *Ultramares* v. *Touche* case (1931) confirmed that there is no third-party liability for financial losses caused by ordinary auditor negligence. Only in the case of fraud or constructive fraud (gross negligence) could the auditor be held liable to third parties.

The leading case for extending tort law to cover pure economic loss is *Hedley Byrne* v. *Heller and Partners*, which is described in the following box:

Hedley Byrne & Co. Ltd. v. *Heller & Partners Ltd.*
[1964] A.C. 562 (H.L.)

In *Hedley Byrne,* the National Provincial Bank telephoned and wrote to Heller & Partners on behalf of Hedley Byrne to find out whether Easipower Ltd., a customer of Heller & Partners, was of sound financial position and thus a company with which Hedley Byrne would want to do business. Heller & Partners, disclaiming all responsibility to both enquiries by National Provincial Bank, said Easipower Ltd. was of sound financial shape. Hedley Byrne, in reliance on those statements, entered into a contract with Easipower Ltd., which subsequently thereafter sought liquidation.

The House of Lords, in deciding that Heller & Partners Ltd. would have been liable except for the disclaimer, established the modern role governing liability for professional advisers whose negligence gives rise to economic loss. A professional adviser has an implied duty of care in making an oral or written statement to another person whom he or she knows or should know will rely on it in making a decision with economic consequences.

Source: L.J. Brooks. *Professional Ethics for Accountants,* West Publishing, 1995, p. 113. Reprinted with permission.

Another reason that *Hedley Byrne* v. *Heller* is so important to the public accounting profession is that it established the precedent of third-party liability for (ordinary) negligence to "reasonably foreseeable third-parties." These third parties would include eventually, as a result of subsequent cases, present shareholders and lenders as well as limited classes of prospective shareholders and prospective lenders.

This precedent-setting decision was upheld by the Supreme Court of Canada in *Haig* v. *Bamford* (1976). The Supreme Court concluded that auditors owe a duty to third parties of which they have "actual knowledge of the limited class that will use and rely on the statements." The details of this are given in the following box:

HAIG V. BAMFORD ET. AL. (1976) 72 D.L.R. (3D) 68

In *Haig,* the Saskatchewan Development Corporation agreed to advance a $20,000 loan to a financially troubled company in part based on the conditional production of satisfactory audited financial statements. The company engaged Bamford's accountants to prepare the statements. The accountant knew that the statements would be used by Saskatchewan Development Corporation. Relying on the accountant's information, Saskatchewan Development Corporation advanced $20,000 to the company. Later investigation disclosed that a $28,000 prepayment on two uncompleted contracts had been treated as if the contracts had been completed, thereby showing a profit instead of a loss, and the accountants failed to spot the error. The court held that where an accountant has negligently prepared financial statements and a third party relies on them to his or her detriment, a duty of care in an action for negligent misstatement will arise in the following circumstances: the accountant knows that it will be shown to a member of a limited class of which the plaintiff is a member and which the accountant actually knows will use and rely on the statement; the statements have been prepared primarily for guidance of that limited class and in respect of a specific class of transactions for the very purpose for which the plaintiff did in fact rely on them; the fact that the accountant did not know the identity of the plaintiff is not material as long as the accountant was aware that the person for whose immediate benefit they were prepared intended to supply the statements to members of the very limited class of which the plaintiff is a member.

Source: L.J. Brooks, *Professional Ethics for Accountants,* West Publishing, 1995; p. 113. Reprinted with permission.

The contemporary *Toromont* v. *Thorne* case (1975) also upheld the *Hedley Byrne* precedent, as it applied to Canada, of liability to known third parties (in this case a prospective investor, Toromont). Auditor's liability in Canada was further extended to prospective investors (reasonably foreseeable third parties) in *Dupuis* v. *Pan American Mines* (1979), the details of which are given in the following box:

DUPUIS V. PAN AMERICAN MINES

On June 15, 1971, a draft prospectus pertaining to Pan American Mines Ltd. and its wholly owned subsidiary, Central Mining Corporation, was filed with the Quebec Securities Commission. Included in the prospectus was a consolidated balance sheet of Pan Am and its subsidiary, which had been audited by the accounting firm of Thorne, Gunn, Helliwell & Christenson, and on which Thorne, Gunn had expressed an unqualified opinion. On June 16, 1971, the securities commission authorized trading in Pan Am shares and distribution of the prospectus. Pan Am was then listed on the Canadian Stock Exchange, but in November 1971 trading in the shares was suspended, and in February 1972 Pan Am was delisted.

The plaintiff, Albert Dupuis, brought an action claiming that he had suffered a loss on shares of Pan Am purchased between the time the shares were listed and the time trading was suspended. His action was based on the alleged falsity of some of the information contained in the prospectus, including the auditors' report and the notes to the considated financial statement.

The judges' decision was worded in part as follows: "When an auditor prepares a balance sheet which he knows is going to be inserted in a company prospectus offering stock for sale, *I believe he has a duty to make sure that the contents of that balance sheet are accurate* so that prospective investors will not be led into error by it" (emphasis added).

In conclusion, the judge gave the plaintiff judgment against Thorne, Gunn for $89,266.91, with interest from October 15, 1971, and costs.

Source: H. Rowan, "Legal Cases," *CA Magazine,* August 1979, pp. 36–39.

In summary, through 1979 Canadian courts had gradually widened auditor's liability under common law to include limited classes of third parties.

The recent *Caparo Industries Plc.* v. *Dickman* case (1989) in the United Kingdom, however, has the potential to reverse this increasing liability to third parties, since it limits liability to those third parties of which auditors have knowledge.[3]

CAPARO INDUSTRIES PLC. V. PICKMAN ET AL. [1991] 2. W.L.R. 358 (H.L.)

Caparo, in its takeover of Fidelity plc, had Touche Ross & Co. audit the financial statements of Fidelity. Caparo later alleged that its purchase of shares and subsequent takeover were made in reliance on the accounts, which they claimed were misleading and inaccurate in that they showed a pre-tax profit of £1.3 million instead of a loss of £400,000. Caparo sued Touche Ross for negligence, maintaining that Touche Ross owed them a duty of care as shareholders and potential investors with respect to the audit and certification of the accounts.

The House of Lords decided that Touche Ross owed no duty of care to Caparo either as a potential investor before it was registered or as a shareholder thereafter, for the following reasons:

While there is no general principle that will determine the existence and scope of a duty of care in all cases, in order for a duty of care to arise, there must be: the harm said to result from the breach of duty must have been reasonably foreseeable; there must be a relationship of sufficient "proximity" between the party said to owe the duty and the party to whom it is said to be owed; and the situation must be one in which, on policy grounds, the court considers it fair, just and reasonable that the law should impose a duty of a given scope on the part of one party for the benefit of the other.

Source: L.J. Brooks, *Professional Ethics for Accountants,* West Publishing, 1995, pp. 113–114. Reprinted with permission.

A related Canadian case is given in the following box:

FLANDERS V. MITHA

In August 1992 Justice Holmes of the B.C. Supreme Court ruled in *Flanders* v. *Mitha* (1992) that "disgruntled investors suing a BC accounting firm Buckett & Sharpley for negligently preparing a housing co-op's financial statements must show that they actually relied on those statements when making their investment decision." During

---

[3] M. Paskelle-Mede, "Duty of Care Revisited," *CA Magazine,* December 1993, pp. 34–35.

> the court proceedings none of the plaintiffs was found to have actually relied on the financial statements in purchasing an apartment. They either relied on the realtor or had made the purchase decision prior to requesting and receiving the financial statements from the realtor. *Flanders* v. *Mitha* (1992) thus limits the auditor's liability when his or her work is used by a client to solicit investments from the public.

The interesting questions are whether the Canadian Courts will continue to take this narrow approach (some other recent British Columbia decisions suggest so), and whether regulatory agencies such as the Ontario Securities Commission (OSC) will succeed in convincing legislatures to make companies, their directors and auditors legally responsible to shareholders under revised securities acts for all misleading documents (as in the United States). Currently, Canadian auditors' legal liability to third parties follows largely from common law. (The four elements of negligence above were identified in *Toromont* v. *Thorne et al.* [1975], in which the auditors were found negligent but the plaintiffs could not prove that they suffered losses as a result.) Nevertheless, some recent articles in the financial press make it clear that litigation against auditors in Canada is reaching alarming proportions.

In summary, the current status of auditor third-party legal liability under common law appears to be as follows: The courts have attempted to strike a fair balance between reliable information for users of financial statements and unreasonable risk to the auditor. This balance has resulted in Canadian auditors currently being liable for negligent error to limited classes of third parties. Third parties are often classified in the following categories:

(a) Known third parties.

(b) Reasonably foreseeable third parties.

(c) All third parties relying on financial statements.

The trend in litigation suggests the courts will most likely draw the line between categories (*b*) and (*c*) for purposes of deciding to whom auditors owe a duty of care under common law.

Fraudulent misrepresentation is a basis for liability in tort (established in *Haig* v. *Bamford*), so parties not in privity with the accountant may have causes of action when negligence is gross enough to amount to constructive fraud. These other parties include primary beneficiaries, actual foreseen and limited classes of persons, and all other injured parties.

State Street Trust Co. v. Ernst (1938)

> Accountants, however, may be liable to third parties, even without deliberate or active fraud. A representation certified as true to the knowledge of the accountants when knowledge there is none, a reckless misstatement or an opinion based on grounds so flimsy as to lead to the conclusion that there was no genuine belief in its truth, are all sufficient upon which to base liability. A refusal to see the obvious, a failure to investigate the doubtful, if sufficiently gross, may furnish evidence leading to an inference of fraud so as to impose liability for losses suffered by those who rely on the balance sheet. In other words, heedlessness and reckless disregard of consequences may take the place of deliberate intention. In this connection we are to bear in mind the principle already stated, that negligence or blindness, even when not equivalent to fraud, it nonetheless evidence to sustain an inference of fraud. At least, this is so if the negligence is gross.

Primary beneficiaries are third parties for whose primary benefit the audit or other accounting service is performed. Such a beneficiary will be identified to, or reasonably foreseeable by, the accountant prior to or during the engagement, and the accountant will know that his or her work will influence the primary beneficiary's decisions. For example, an audit firm may be informed that the report is needed for a bank loan application at the North Land Bank in the Kingston Company case (located on the accompanying CD-ROM).

Many cases indicate that proof of ordinary negligence may be sufficient to make accountants liable for damages to primary beneficiaries.

CIT Financial Corp. v. Glover (1955)

> Auditors are liable to third parties for ordinary negligence if their reports are for the primary benefit of the third party. Thus, the privity criterion may not serve as a defense when third-party beneficiaries are known.

Accountants may also be liable to foreseeable beneficiaries—creditors, investors or potential investors who rely on accountants' work. If the accountant is reasonably able to foresee a limited class of potential users of his or her work (e.g., local banks, regular suppliers), liability may be imposed for ordinary negligence. This, however, is an uncertain area, and liability in a particular case depends entirely on the unique facts and circumstances. Beneficiaries of these types and all other injured parties may recover damages if they are able to show that an accountant was grossly negligent and perpetrated a constructive fraud.

Rusch Factors, Inc. v. Levin (1968)

> With respect to the plaintiff's negligence theory, this case held that an accountant should be liable in negligence for careless financial misrepresentations relied upon by actually foreseen and limited classes of persons. According to the plaintiff's complaint in the case, the defendant knew that his certification was to be used for, and had as its very aim and purpose, the reliance of potential financiers of the Rhode Island corporation.

Rosenblum, Inc. v. Adler (1983)

> Giant Stores Corporation acquired the retail catalog showroom business owned by Rosenblum, giving stock in exchange for the business. Fifteen months after the acquisition, Giant Stores declared bankruptcy. Its financial statements had been audited and had received unqualified opinions on several prior years. These financial statements turned out to be misstated because Giant Stores had manipulated its books.
>
> In finding for the plaintiffs on certain motions, the New Jersey Supreme Court held that Independent auditors have a duty of care to all persons whom the auditor should reasonably foresee as recipients of the statements from the company for proper business purposes, provided that the recipients rely on those financial statements . . . It is well recognized that audited financial statements are made for the use of third parties who have no direct relationship with the auditor . . . Auditors have responsibility not only to the client who pays the fee but also to investors, creditors and others who rely on the audited financial statements.
>
> [The case went back to the trial court for further proceedings.]

Defences of the Accountant

The defendant accountant in a common law action presents evidence to mitigate or refute the plaintiff's claims and evidence. For example, the accountant might offer evidence that the plaintiff was not in privity or not foreseen, that the financial statements were not misleading or that the plaintiff contributed to the negligence. The primary defence against a negligence claim is to offer evidence that the audit had been conducted in accordance with GAAS with due professional care.

Some courts hold plaintiffs to a strict privity criterion to have a standing in court. In New York courts the general rule is that these conditions must be met: (1) the accountants must have been aware that the financial reports were to be used for a particular purpose, (2) the accountants must have known that a particular third party was going to rely on the reports, and (3) some action by the accountants must link them with the third party and must demonstrate that the accountants knew of the reliance on the reports. In response to these conditions, some users of financial statements have invented a request for a "reliance letter." Users have requested accountants to sign letters saying that they have been notified that a particular recipient of the financial statements and audit report intends to rely upon them for particular purposes.

The AICPA has warned accountants to be careful when signing such letters so that they do not become an automatic proof of users' actual reliance.

In several Canadian cases the auditors successfully argued that clients should not have relied on the financial statements to make their investment decision.[4] A good example is when banks claim that they have been mislead by the financial statements. A key issue in this instance is the fourth element of negligence: Did the banks' losses follow from the auditor's breach of duty with regard to auditing the financial statements? Peskelle-Mede notes that "the courts carefully review the degree of reliance plaintiff bankers have on misleading financial statements. Banks usually have available to them not only their customers' financial statements but a great deal of other information as well. Their decision to continue a loan is very often based on considerations quite apart from any reliance they may place on the opinion of the customer's auditors. In these circumstances the auditors ought not to be found liable—or at least not entirely—for the bank's losses." In general, "it's refreshing to see a court carefully reviewing the degree of reliance plaintiff bankers place on misleading financial statements."[5]

Liability in Compilation and Review Services

You may find it easy to think about common law liability in connection with audited financial statements. Do not forget, however, that accountants also render compilation and review services and are associated with unaudited financial information (see Chapter 15). People expect public accountants to perform these services in accordance with professional standards, and courts can impose liability for accounting work judged to be substandard. Accountants have been assessed damages for work on such statements, as shown in *1136 Tenants' Corporation* v. *Max Rothenberg & Co.* Approximately 11 percent of losses in the AICPA professional liability insurance plan involve compilation and review engagements relating to unaudited financial statements.

1136 Tenants' Corporation v. Max Rothenberg & Co. (1967)

> Despite defendant's claims to the contrary, the court found that he was engaged to audit and not merely write up plaintiff's books and records. The accountant had, in fact, performed some limited auditing procedures including preparation of a worksheet entitled "Missing Invoices 1/1/63–12/31/63." These were items claimed to have been paid but were not. The court held that, even if accountants were hired only for write-up work, they had a duty to inform plaintiffs of any circumstances that gave reason to believe that a fraud had occurred (e.g., the record of "missing invoices"). The plaintiffs recovered damages of about $237,000.

One significant risk is that the client may fail to understand the nature of the service being given. Accountants should use a conference and an engagement letter to explain clearly that a compilation service ("write-up") involves little or no investigative work, and that it is lesser in scope than a review service. Similarly, a review service should be explained in terms of being less extensive than a full audit service. Clear understandings at the outset can enable accountants and clients to avoid later disagreements.

Yet even with these understandings, public accountants cannot merely accept client-supplied information that appears to be unusual or misleading. A court has held that a public accountant's preparation of some erroneous and misleading journal entries without sufficient support was enough to trigger common law liability for negligence, even though the accountant was not associated with any final financial statements. CICA and ISA standards for compilations require accountants to obtain additional information if client-supplied accounting data are incorrect, incomplete or otherwise unsatisfactory. Courts may hold accountants liable for failure to obtain additional information in such circumstances.

[4] "Auditing in Crisis," *Bottom Line*, March 1990.
[5] H. Rowan, "Are Banks Looking to Pin the Blame?" *CA Magazine*, June 1988.

When financial statements are reviewed, public accountants' reports state: "Based on my review, nothing has come to my attention that causes me to believe that these financial statements are not, in all material respects in accordance with generally accepted accounting principles" (*Handbook Section* 8200.04 and ISA 910 Appendix 3). Courts can look to the facts of a case and rule on whether the review was performed properly. Generally, the same four elements of negligence must be met for review engagements as for audit engagements. The only difference is that "due care" in review engagements should follow the standards for review engagements rather than the standards for audits. Generally, it would appear that third-party liability continues to flow to the same classes of persons who would be relying on the financial statements.[6] Some courts might decide an accountant's review was substandard if necessary adjustments or "material modifications" should have been discovered. These risks tend to induce more work by accountants beyond superficial looking-it-over and enquiry procedures.

A 1987 New York case, however, may create an attitude more favourable for PAs' review work on unaudited financial statements. In 1985 William Iselin & Company sued the Mann Judd Landau (MJL) accounting firm, claiming damages for having relied on financial statements reviewed by MJL. Iselin had used the financial statements of customers for its factoring–financing business. A customer had gone bankrupt and Iselin's loans became worthless. A New York appeals court dismissed the case, saying that third parties (Iselin) cannot rely on reviewed financial statements as they can on audited financial statements to assure themselves that a company is financially healthy. The court observed that MJL expressed no opinion on the reviewed financial statements. Iselin's lawyer was reported to have observed: "Accountants and their clients will find that reviews are useless, since no one can rely on them."

R E V I E W
CHECKPOINTS

17.4 What must be proved by the plaintiff in a common law action seeking recovery of damages from an independent auditor of financial statements? What must the defendant accountant do in such a court action?

17.5 What legal theory is derived from the *Ultramares* decision? Can auditors rely on the *Ultramares* decision today?

17.6 Define and explain *privity*, *primary beneficiary* and *foreseeable beneficiary* in terms of the degree of negligence on the part of an accountant that would trigger the accountant's liability.

17.7 What proportion of lawsuits against accountants relate to compilation and review (unaudited financial statements) practice?

III. DUE CARE: ITS MEANING

A key aspect to the second element of negligence is the meaning of due care. What is it that the auditor must be breaching? Due professional care implies the careful application of all the standards of the profession (GAAS, GAAP) and observance of all the rules of professional conduct. The courts have interpreted due care to be that of a reasonably prudent practitioner, neither the extremes of the highest possible standards nor the lowest acceptable or minimum standards would be considered due care. This suggests that looking at *Rules of Professional Conduct* or the *Handbook* may not always be sufficient in the view of the courts since these would be viewed as minimal standards. In fact, over the years the courts have helped shape audit practice by their interpretation of what is due care. For example, the concept of testing (less than 100 percent examination of the accounts) was first accepted as reasonable by the progressive decision in *London and General Bank* (1895). This case was also the first to acknowledge that there is some limit on the auditor's responsibility for the detection of fraud and the *duty* to take increased care in the presence of

[6] "The Jury's Still Out on Review Engagement Liability," *CA Magazine*, June 1988.

suspicious circumstances. This case influenced the development of later professional announcements and hundreds of subsequent cases (e.g., *1136 Tennants* [1967]).

Another example of the influence of the courts in setting auditing standards (and therefore influencing due care provisions) is the requirement that the auditor corroborate management assertions with his or her own evidence. The auditor can't just rely on words of management; he or she must justify reliance through checking, testing and other audit procedures. This practice following from the third examination standard has been shaped by decisions in many court cases, such as *Continental Vending* (1969) and the Canadian *Toromont* v. *Thorne* (1975).

An obvious example of court influence in determining what constitutes auditor due care is *McKesson Robbins* (1939) (discussed in Appendix 17A). This can be viewed as ultimately influencing the creation of *Handbook Section* 6030 and ISA 501 (and similar sections in U.S. standards). In that case, the auditor failed to observe inventory or confirm receivables. It should thus be evident that the due care provision of negligence has significantly shaped and probably will continue to influence the development of audit standards. One impact of the *Continental Vending* case, discussed in Appendix 17A, is that the courts did not accept the auditor's defence that they were following GAAP (i.e., the auditors were able to establish that the footnote in the financial statement was in accordance with GAAP); instead, the courts expected the auditor to use some higher standard of fairness in deciding on proper disclosure. This has led to much greater diligence on the part of standard setters when it comes to matters of disclosing various types of information.

A sense of urgency on this issue of fairness has recently been introduced to Canadian courts, as indicated in the following box:

ACCOUNTING PROFESSION HAS A DUTY TO SHAREHOLDERS

Before buying shares in a company, investors usually rely on an important safeguard—the auditor's opinion of its financial statements. And that opinion usually declares that the statements are both "presented fairly" and are "in accordance with generally accepted accounting principles (GAAP)." For decades, though, auditors have tried to duck legal liability to the investors they serve. Auditors appear to want what doesn't exist: authority without responsibility.

This spring two Canadian lawsuits promise to clarify the trust that investors can place in auditors. One case, *Stephen Kripps et al.* v. *Touche Ross* (now Deloitte Touche) *et al.*, emerged from the B.C. Court of Appeal last month. In 1985, Kripps et al. relied on the audited financial statements of a mortgage company to buy $1.9 million of its debentures. The company went into receivership and the investors lost $2.7 million including interest. The investors sued the auditor, lost in a lower court, and won at appeal.

A 2-to-1 appeal court majority ruled that "Touche had actual knowledge that a simple application of GAAP would . . . lead to financial statements that could not be said to have fairly represented the financial position" of the company. "Auditors cannot hide behind [the formula] 'according to GAAP' " the court declared, "if the auditors know . . . that the financial statements are misleading." It ruled against Touche. The court's point is correct—GAAP is too loose a standard to be a sufficient safeguard by itself. That's why the financial statements must also be "presented fairly," to use the actual language of the auditor's opinion. Despite the ruling's validity, some accountants want the Canadian Institute of Chartered Accountants (CICA) to support an appeal by Touche to the Supreme Court.

Postscript: On November 6, 1997, the Supreme Court of Canada denied Deloitte & Touche's right to appeal the negligence ruling against it by the B.C. Court of Appeal. The *Kripps* v. *Touche Ross* decision thus may make it easier for investors to sue Canadian auditors in the future. The other case referred to in the above editorial is discussed at the end of this chapter.

Source: Editorial, *The Financial Post,* May 20, 1997.

IV. OTHER ELEMENTS OF NEGLIGENCE

. . . .

The two other elements of negligence have also proven to be material issues in various court cases. The third element requires that some damage must occur to the third party—otherwise, they are limited to recovering the audit fee only. This was the situation in *Toromont* v. *Thorne*. The last element of negligence requires that there be a causal link between the breach of duty and the resulting damage. Thus, for example, if losses occur before the time of the audit, or if it can be proven in some other way that the plaintiff did not rely on the audited information to any significant degree, the lawsuit will fail.

Perhaps at this point it is useful to note the relationship between joint and several liability and the fourth element of evidence. In Canada and the United States we have what's called joint and several liability, meaning any of several defendants that have caused part of the damages are liable to the plaintiffs for the entire amount of damages. This system was set up to protect plaintiffs from having to sue several different parties to recover the full amount of damages. Under joint and several liability, the courts can force the defendant with the "deepest pockets" to pay all the damages even though they may have contributed, say, only 1 percent to the losses. It is, of course, then up to the defendant auditor to recover from the other defendants its share of the losses. If the other defendants are in bankruptcy, however, this can leave the auditor stuck with all the losses. The box below, from a *Bottom Line* article, indicates the problems that joint and several liability can cause in Canada.

LOW COVERAGE LIMITS LEAVE MAJOR FIRMS EXPOSED

Major accountancies are in "near crisis" because of high deductibles and low coverage limits in their malpractice insurance.

"From the point of view of current planning, the (large) firms are looking at this as if there is really no insurance going to be available," said William Broadhurst, head of a national task force on accountants' professional liability.

No Canadian insurer is writing policies large enough. So the six largest Canadian accounting firms insure through international markets, usually as part of international groups.

They do not negotiate separately as Canadian firms.

Ten years ago, a typical deductible was about $2 million. Now it is around $50 million, according to Broadhurst.

Too Small

Consequently, all recent payouts in Canada on settlements and judgements have been too small to be covered by insurance.

"There may have been [some for] a couple of million [dollars] here and there," he said.

So far, there has been nothing even close to the settlements in 1988 and 1989 on the Alberta bank failures claims, "generally said to be in the order of $100 million."

Even if there is no payout on a claim, there are litigation costs.

"With this large deductible, you're into your own resources from dollar one, right up," Broadhurst said.

Until the mid-80s, coverage of $200 million was available, and the risks could be adequately provided for. Premiums, deductibles and coverage have all steadily worsened (senior CA partners are reportedly paying as much as $30,000 a year for limited professional insurance).

Now, there is no true, commercial insurance for more than $100 million. But even for the band of liability between $50 million and $100 million, coverage is now "spotty," said Broadhurst.

Different syndicates cover different "layers"—one for $50–60 million, say, and another for $60–75 million. The upshot is that a large firm is likely to be insured for about 50 percent of this whole range: only about $25–30 million.

As for the $100–$150 million range, there are two kinds of "self-insurance." First, international firms have formed "pools" for their various national components. Second, large Canadian firms have joined in a mutual fund.

But they can only draw out what they put in (plus interest). If the payouts exceed the pooled assets, they have to be pro-rated among the firms.

Beyond $150 million, there is no protection at all.

In Canada there are now two much larger sets of claims, "the only two of threatening size," as Broadhurst put it: one for about $900 million from the failure of Castor Holdings Ltd., the other concerning Standard Trust, for about $1.5 billion."

Warm Feeling

Broadhurst professed ignorance on the merits of these cases. But he said, "If they were substantially successful, the [defendant accounting] firms would not be able to deal with these numbers. Now, I make the assumption they won't be. But they don't give you a good warm feeling."

Hard numbers on Canadian settlements don't exist, said Broadhurst, and if they did, they might not be "hugely impressive."

The insurance market reflects international experience, and Canadian potential, not yet the actuality.

But according to Broadhurst, insurers rate Canada towards the high end of risk, close to the U.S., the U.K. and Australia. "Presumably in the underwriters' mind, there's no significant difference between us and the others . . . The risks in Canada mirror [those] other jurisdictions."

The litigation environments of the U.S. and Canada do differ.

But Canada has fewer, larger financial institutions. The risk to the auditors increases with the size of the institution. Broadhurst concluded that the factors are all in place for exposure to claims as big as in the U.S., U.K. and Australia.

"We view the insurance situation as basically a disaster," he said. On the other hand, he said, "We would have a hard time saying there's a disaster situation in Canada."

"We have a near-crisis situation . . . It could turn into a crisis any day."

Crisis Any Day

"Do we have to have a bankruptcy of a major firm, before someone looks at the problem and decides whether or not there is some action required?"

"We're hoping we don't have to go that route."

Broadhurst saw no prospect for a turnaround in insurance, unless legislation limits auditors' liability to their proportion of fault.

Source: Gerald Owen, *The Bottom Line*, March 1995.

A recent development in the profession in light of these potential legal liabilities has been the creation of limited liability partnerships (LLPs). In 1998 Ontario was the first province to enact legislation allowing the use of the LLP form of organization, followed by Alberta in 1999. LLPs limit the legal liability of most partners only to the assets of the LLP. With the traditional partnership form of organization, the partners themselves are liable for all debts and liabilities incurred by their firm. In an LLP the negligent partner is still liable to the extent of his or her own personal assets. The personal assets of nonnegligent partners, however, are not threatened in the LLP form of organization. Thus the LLP form of organization can generally reduce the risk to partners of legal liability.

AUDITOR'S LIABILITY WHEN AUDITOR IS ASSOCIATED WITH MISLEADING FINANCIAL INFORMATION

If the courts conclude that the auditor is associated with misleading financial statements, even if such statements are in conformity with GAAP, they may conclude that the auditors are fraudulently negligent. If auditors are found guilty of a fraudulent misrepresentation, then there are no limits on third-party liability. In U.S. courts the concepts of gross negligence–constructive fraud has been used to expand auditor liability to larger classes of third parties. This is done not only through U.S. common law but also in statutory law via the U.S. Securities Acts. As a result there have been several cases in the United States in which auditors have been found guilty of fraud when they otherwise would have been found to be only negligent (see, e.g., *Continental Vending* in Appendix 17A).

Interestingly, the Ontario Securities Commission appears to be interested in increasing auditors' legal responsibility to shareholders by revising the securities acts in Ontario. This may be a way of expanding auditor liability to wider classes of third parties in Ontario (e.g., see subsequent discussion of "Auditing in Crisis"). This combined with the increasing influence of Charter of Rights and Freedoms legislation on the courts may make the Canadian legal environment more comparable to that of the United States in the near future. In addition, class action legislation has recently been approved in Quebec (1979), Ontario (1993) and British Columbia (1995). Contingency fees are another issue being considered by the Ontario Law Society; implementing them would also make the Ontario environment more comparable to that of the United States. Thus many of the problems of high litigation rates and insurance premiums and costly court decisions may soon be imported to at least parts of the Canadian legal environment. Recent requirements to expand auditor responsibilities for detecting money-laundering schemes will further add to the liabilities burden.

AUDITOR'S LIABILITY UNDER STATUTORY LAW

LEARNING OBJECTIVE

3. Specify the characteristics of accountants' liability under statutory law.

A great deal of liability for American auditors arises from statutory law under the SEC. These SEC laws give the SEC the legal right to decide what is GAAP. There is nothing comparable in Canadian legislation, yet increasingly the OSC and Quebec regulators are seeking more enforcement power over professionals such as accountants operating in the capital markets. We will discuss the latest developments at the time of this writing at the end of the chapter.

What is unique about Canadian statutory law is the Canadian Business Corporation Act (CBCA) and related provincial corporation acts.

The highlights of the CBCA are as follows (to be covered in more detail in your business law course).

1. The CBCA identifies conditions under which the auditor is not considered independent (Section 161).

2. It identifies conditions of appointing and retiring the auditor (Sections 162 and 163).

3. It identifies the auditor's rights and responsibilities (Section 168):
   (*a*) to attend shareholder meetings
   (*b*) to provide a written statement of reasons for a resignation
   (*c*) to make an audit examination unimpeded and gain access to data the auditor considers necessary

4. Sections 44–47 of the CBCA identify the financial statements subject to audit, and specify that the financial statements must be in conformity with the *CICA Handbook*. (Note that this represents a stark contrast with U.S. securities law, which allows the SEC to decide what is GAAP. The important point is that the ultimate authority in the United States is the SEC, whereas here in Canada the ultimate authority on accounting issues is the CICA via the *Handbook*. This gives *Handbook* standards much higher legal status than comparable standards in the United States.)

5. Until 1994 the CBCA applied to all companies incorporated under the act, having revenues in excess of $10 million or assets greater than $5 million. Under amendments to the CBCA made in 1994, privately held companies are no longer required to have their financial statements audited or disclosed. The Ontario Business Corporations Act requires audits only for companies having $100 million of either assets or revenues; other provincial corporations acts vary in their reporting requirements.

   Another important Canadian statutory law is Bill C-61, which met with controversy when it was first proposed, as described in the next box.

"PROPOSED FEDERAL CRIME LEGISLATION PUTS ACCOUNTANTS AT RISK OF BEING PROSECUTED"

VANCOUVER: Amendments to Canada's Criminal Code could jeopardize unwary financial professionals, legal experts warn.

Bill C-61, known informally as the "proceeds of crime" legislation, is so sweeping that unsuspecting accountants could be guilty of a criminal offence for simply giving advice, the lawyers say.

The proceeds of crime legislation, which is now contained in Part XII.2 of the Criminal Code, is based on American antiracketeering statutes and is designed to deprive criminals of their ill-gotten gains.

But, although the new law may seem well intentioned, Bill C-61 is so broadly worded that, if accountants know or even suspect that a client has illegal profits, they could be guilty of a crime if they act for that client.

The amendments contained in the Bill create two new offences—money laundering and possessions of property derived through drug trafficking.

Money laundering is defined as dealing with any property with intent to conceal or convert it while knowing that it was derived as a result of a "designated drug offence" or an "enterprise crime."

The Criminal Code describes "designated drug offences" as virtually any drug infraction other than simple possession. "Enterprise crime" are generally profit-motivated offences and include things such as bribery, fraud, gambling and stock manipulation.

Under the criminal law doctrine of "wilful blindness," people are deemed to know they are dealing with the proceeds of crime if they are suspicious about the source of any property but choose to remain ignorant rather than make further inquiries.

The effect of the legislation is that accountants who accept any property, including fees, from a client, knowing or being wilfully blind to the fact the property was obtained illegally, could be charged with possession or laundering.

Problems could also arise if accountants become suspicious about a client's finances during an ongoing engagement. If they continue to act and their advice relates to property obtained through a crime, they could be committing an offence.

Accountants will be particularly vulnerable because they are often aware of the intimate details of a client's financial dealings.

Source: Brad Dusley, *The Bottom Line*, November 1990, p. 6. Reprinted with permission.

Interestingly, the CICA has proposed an Exposure Draft on auditor responsibilities concerning money-laundering activities. This reflects increasing recognition that auditors should take responsibility for money laundering.

OTHER ISSUES

1. Fiduciary Duty of Accountants

According to an article by G. McLennan, a unique feature of Canadian common law that may precipitate a litigation crisis here is the expanding concept of fiduciary duty as it applies to accountants. An accountant may be a fiduciary in many different situations, including when he or she acts as a trustee, receiver, auditor or simply an adviser to a peculiarly vulnerable client. Accountants may also be liable for simply assisting someone who is a fiduciary to another, although this would only be the case where a PA knows the fiduciary relationship and knows it is being dishonestly breached.

Allegations of a breach of fiduciary duty have become increasingly common in lawsuits against accountants in Canada. If a court concludes that an accountant is a fiduciary, he or she may be held responsible for damages, even though (1) the PA's conduct did not cause the damage, (2) the plaintiff failed to take reasonable steps to mitigate those damages, or (3) the plaintiff was partially at fault or other third parties contributed to the damages suffered. Thus, common defences to a negligence action, such as contributory negligence, remoteness of damages, failure to mitigate and no duty of care, do not apply to an action in breach of fiduciary duty.

Literally, fiduciary means "trust-like" but the term has been used in so many contexts in the courts that it is applied as if it related to, among other things, all breaches of duty by accountants.

The closest thing to legal definition is that set forth in the Supreme Court of Canada decision concerning *LAC Minerals* v. *Corona Resources*. In *LAC Minerals* the court stated there were three factors to consider when determining if a fiduciary duty exists:

1. The fiduciary has scope for the exercise of some discretion or power.
2. The fiduciary can unilaterally exercise that power or discretion so as to affect the beneficiary's legal or practical interests.
3. The beneficiary is peculiarly vulnerable to or at the mercy of the fiduciary who is holding the discretion or power.

Case law provides illustrations when such a duty exists; the article by M. Paskell-Mede reviews several of these cases. Generally, when an accountant acts as a receiver/manager or trustee in insolvency situations, he or she owes a fiduciary duty to creditors of an insolvent corporation. Where an accountant has an established relationship with one lender, it may be that it is a breach of fiduciary duty to also act as a trustee or receiver of the insolvent borrower. Accountants that act as financial advisers or tax advisers also have a fiduciary duty. Accountants that have successfully defended themselves in lawsuits involving breach of fiduciary duty have done so by showing that either factors 1 or 3 in the definition were not present.[7]

2. Confidentiality Versus Misleading Financial Statements

In Chapter 15 we noted that there may be a potential conflict between rules dealing with confidentiality and rules dealing with association with misleading financial statements. There is a conflict between similar rules in the U.S. code that has been the focus of two

---

[7] G. McLennan, "Trust Not," *CA Magazine*, June-July, 1993, pp. 40–43 and M. Paskell-Mede, "Adviser Relationships," *CA Magazine*, May 1995, pp. 27–32.

court cases there: *Consolidata Services* v. *Alexander Grant* (1981) and *Fund of Funds* v. *Arthur Andersen* (1982). In *Consolidata* the courts ruled that auditors should have preserved confidentiality, and in *Fund of Funds* the courts ruled that the confidential information should have been used to prevent misleading reports. The inconsistent legal results from these two cases illustrate that the rules can be just as difficult to resolve for the courts as they are for practising auditors. In both cases, however, it was the auditors who lost—and paid. (The court awarded damages to Fund of Fund's shareholders in the amount of $80 million, the largest judgment ever made against a public accounting firm until that time.)

3. Legal Liability Implications for Auditor Practice

As a result of the increasingly litigious climate, auditors ought to

(*a*) Be wary of what kind of clients are accepted.

(*b*) Know (thoroughly) the client's business (KNOB).

(*c*) Perform quality audits.
(*i*)   Use qualified personnel, properly trained and supervised, and motivated.
(*ii*) Obtain sufficient evidence (including proper elicitation of oral evidence and documentation of client's oral evidence).
(*iii*) Prepare good working papers.
(*iv*) Obtain engagement and representation letters.

The increased litigation has also caused improvements in audit working paper files through:

(*a*) Use of forceful management letters that are "unambiguous and couched in terms of alarm with respect to problematic internal controls or sloppy bookkeeping.

(*b*) Use of detailed memos in the working papers describing the conversation with the client and accompanied by a follow-up letter to the client.

(*c*) Use of a letter to the client or note to the file documenting discussions to reduce audit fees or changing to a review engagement." (M. Pashell-Mede, "So Sue Me," *CA Magazine*, February 1991, pp. 36–38).

Legal Liability for Failure to Disclose Illegal Acts

Handbook Section 5136, "Misstatements—illegal acts," provides expanded guidance on detecting and disclosing illegal acts or possibly illegal acts. One of the objectives of this *Handbook Section* is to reduce the auditor's exposure to legal liability. It does this (1) by reducing the risk that GAAS will be misinterpreted by auditors and the courts; (2) by establishing recommendations for the auditors to follow, such as that of obtaining written representation from management about illegal acts, that reduce the likelihood of an audit failing to detect a material misstatement arising from the consequences of an illegal act; and (3) by providing a defence for the auditor if he or she fails to detect a material misstatement despite conducting the audit in accordance with the standards.[8]

Illegal acts is another area where potential ethical and legal conflicts may now be expected to grow. According to an article by M. Paskell-Mede, the whistle-blowing responsibility of the auditor to third parties may be expected to grow even in the absence of a regulator since plaintiffs are raising the issues of association more frequently in lawsuits. It is Paskell-Mede's impression that plaintiffs whose lawyers recognize that their case is weak—as a result of inability to demonstrate either actual reliance on the financial statements or that a direct duty of care was owed with respect to those statements—are now compensating for this weakness by presenting the claim as one based on association. In such instances, the plaintiff's lawyer will argue that their client relied on the auditor's reputation. However, the courts so far have upheld the obligation for auditors to maintain client confidentiality. For example, in *Transamerica Financial Corporation, Canada* v. *Dunwoody*

---

[8] V. Murusalu, "Drawing the Line," *CA Magazine*, Jan/Feb. 1995, pp. 68–69.

& Company, the judge decided that client confidentiality overrode whistle-blowing to a third-party plaintiff especially since the plaintiff was already aware of irregularities at the client. For Paskell-Mede this is evidence that the courts are becoming more careful about assigning blame to auditors—that they are becoming more sophisticated in analysing the causal connection between the illegal misrepresentation and damages.[9]

Is There an Auditor Liability Crisis in Canada?

Some people argue that there is no auditor's legal liability crisis in Canada. M. Paskell-Mede takes this position and gives a review of the differences between the American and Canadian legal systems concerning auditors' legal liability. In the United States pending suits against auditors total about US$20 billion. There is a definite crisis there. Do we have a problem of the same magnitude in Canada?

The author doesn't think so and identifies important differences.

1. Jury trials are common in the United States for civil cases but "virtually extinct" for auditor liability suits in Canada. American juries tend to be more sympathetic to plaintiffs and swayed by factors other than the evidence. Judges are less influenced by the drama of the courtroom setting, and tend to be better experienced and better trained in dealing with commercial disputes.

2. Punitive damages are not available in Canada for mere negligence. Moreover, any damages awarded are only a fraction of the compensatory damages assessed (instead of the multiples used in the United States).

3. In Canada the unsuccessful party must pay up to 50 to 60 percent of the legal fees of the opposing side and possible other costs (e.g., 1 percent of the amount claimed). This tends to discourage frivolous suits.

4. Class actions (a few suing on behalf of many) are much rarer in Canada because of the belief here that each plaintiff may rely on the accountant's work differently. But this may change, with more provinces allowing class actions, as noted earlier.

5. The U.S. national regulator, the SEC (nothing comparable in Canada), uses the "fraud on the market" theory, which assumes that the entire market for shares is affected by misrepresentations. This greatly increases the liability exposure of auditors of publicly traded companies.

"Faced with these differences it seems safe to assume that Canadian accountants will not face lawsuits of the same magnitude and frequency as those experienced by U.S. accountants, assuming no fundamental changes to our legal systems. On the other hand, lawsuits in Canada are getting larger and some CA firms may soon exceed their insurance limits and be forced into bankruptcy. Thus it may simply be a matter of time before we, too, face a liability crisis."[10]

Others argue that we already are facing a liability crisis. In a series of articles entitled "Auditing in Crisis" in the March 1990 issue of the *Financial Post*, the following points were made.

A vicious cycle had started by 1990 in that due to severe competition (partly caused by the many mergers in the 1980s) audit fees had been lowered, resulting in lower-quality audits. This combined with more aggressive reporting resulted in more problem audits, which in turn increased lawsuits. Plaintiffs also were increasingly of the type that can litigate indefinitely (financial institutions, government agencies). This came at a time of increased policing of accounting firms by regulators such as the OSC. As a result, the total number of lawsuits increased dramatically starting in the 1980s. For example, there were 18 major lawsuits initiated between 1985 and 1990. Compare this to a total of 9 between 1917 and 1984. In addition to the increased lawsuits, the damage awards per lawsuit have increased dramatically. This, combined with an exponential growth in lawsuits in the

---

[9] M. Paskell-Mede, "Tales of Sherwood Forest," *CA Magazine*, August 1994, pp. 47–48.
[10] M. Paskell-Mede, "What Liability Crisis," *CA Magazine*, May 1994, pp. 42–43.

United States, has greatly increased North American professional liability insurance premiums (premiums have risen by 10 percent per year).

The series of articles also provides much anecdotal evidence that there are serious problems in many auditor–client relationships. For example, according to a vice president of finance of a major Canadian company, "it's very easy for management to browbeat an auditor at any time in the audit," and "anything goes unless there is a rule to the contrary (in the *Handbook*)."

To combat these problems, key recommendations developed in an article by M.F. Murray were that the auditors report to a company's audit committee, that standard setters should reduce the number of accounting alternatives in GAAP, that auditors need more guidance on how to report on a company's ability to continue and that auditors need to better document high-risk clients and be ready to take immediate defensive measures. Some firms now even talk about "firing" their troublesome clients. Some warning signs of potentially troublesome clients include financial or organizational difficulty, involvement in suspicious transactions, unco-operativeness, fee pressures, refusal to sign engagement and representation letters, and frequent involvement in litigation.

Before accepting clients, PAs should ask why clients are changing accountants, visit the client's business, meet their accounting and tax personnel and check their references. A useful client acceptance checklist could be used that documents whether a client should be accepted for an engagement. This form should be prepared before the engagement letter is submitted. If this screening does not result in rejection of an existing or prospective client, it may also be used to identify engagements that require extra precautions, such as very precise engagement letters and advance collection of fees.[11]

SOME DEVELOPMENTS CONCERNING THE LIABILITY CRISIS

In December 1995 the American accounting profession was successful in getting the U.S. Congress to pass (over President Clinton's veto) the Private Securities Litigation Reform Act, which changes auditor liability under SEC section 10b (discussed in the appendix). There are three objectives to the act. First, it is intended to "discourage abusive claims of investors' losses due to fraudulent misstatements or omissions by issuers of securities" (and professionals associated with the misstatements or omissions, such as auditors). Second, the act provides more protection against securities fraud. Third, the act increases the flow of forward-looking financial information." The act meets these objectives by imposing specific pleading requirements; by reducing the effectiveness of discovery in coercing settlements; by mandating sanctions for frivolous claims; by giving the plaintiff class far more control of class actions; by providing for proportionate liability except in cases of knowing fraud; by creating a safe harbour for forward-looking information; and by codifying auditor's responsibilities to search for and disclose fraud.[12]

For the purposes of this chapter, the most important feature of the act concerns the reform of "joint and several liability," which under SEC law now only applies to auditors who knowingly commit a violation of the security law. "A defendant (auditor) whose conduct is less culpable is liable only for a percentage of the total damages corresponding to the percentage of responsibility allocated to the defendant (auditor) by the jury . . . Thus, for example, if a PA firm is found 10 percent responsible for an injury and insolvent corporate management is allocated 90 percent the PA firm no longer will have to make up all of the management's share (as long as the PA firm did not engage in knowing fraud)."[13]

A recent Supreme Court of Canada decision may cause a dramatic shift in Canadian auditors' liability in the near future, as indicated in the following box.

---

[11] M.F. Murray, "When a Client Is a Liability," *Journal of Accountancy*, September 1992, pp. 54–58.

[12] A.R. Andrews and G. Simonette Jr., "Tort Reform Revolution," *Journal of Accountancy*, September 1996, p. 54.

[13] Ibid., p. 50.

Auditors Not Legally Liable to Investors, Top Court Rules

An auditor who signs a company's financial statements has no legal liability to shareholders or investors.

That's the thrust of a ruling by the Supreme Court of Canada brought down Thursday in the case of *Hercules Managements Ltd. et al.* v. *Ernst & Young et al.*

The court's concern, observers say, is to protect auditors from unlimited liability to thousands of investors who may use the audit opinion for many different purposes.

The annual financial statement is now a joke, says Al Rosen, a professor of accounting at York University in Toronto and a partner in Rosen & Vettese Ltd., forensic accountants.

"Public accountants may think this is a wonderful win for them," Rosen added. "But in the long run I see this as a disaster. Who really needs an audit of financial statements that is not useful for investor decision-making?"

The court's ruling was applauded by Michael Rayner, president of the Canadian Institute of Chartered Accountants. "The decision leaves the profession in a legal environment in which it can maximize its contribution to the capital markets," Rayner said yesterday.

The court has "tried to provide a reasonable amount of liability for auditors," he added.

"We believe the responsibility of auditors is important . . . and there are still significant redresses available through the courts for auditors who are engaged in a situation where there is clear negligence on their part."

The effect of the court's ruling could be short-lived. Brenda Eprile, executive director of the Ontario Securities Commission—Canada's leading securities regulator—says provincial regulators are working on a legal framework that will re-establish the legal liability of auditors to investors.

Hercules Managements was the 80 percent shareholder of Manitoba-based Northguard Acceptance Ltd., which lent money on mortgages in the 1970s and early 1980s. Ernest & Young was the auditor.

In 1984, Northguard went into receivership. Hercules sued Ernst & Young, alleging negligence.

The action was dismissed by the Manitoba Court of Queen's Bench, and by the Manitoba Appeal Court. It was heard by the Supreme Court on December 6. The Canadian Institute of Chartered Accountants gained status with the court to argue in favor of protecting auditors from liability.

The court's ruling does not declare whether Ernst & Young was negligent.

On the issue of liability, the court said audited financial reports only call for "a duty of care" by the auditors when they are used "as a guide for the shareholders, as a group, in supervising or overseeing management."

For this reason, there appears to be no direct liability to the shareholders for any reduction in value of their equity, jointly or individually.

"The law in Canada in respect of the responsibility of auditors is basically consistent with the United Kingdom, the United States and many other countries," Rayner said.

"I feel that I have been run over by a truck," said Mark Schulman, of the Winnipeg law firm of Schulman and Schulman, who acted for Hercules.

He points out that one motions judge, three judges of the court of appeal and seven judges in the Supreme Court all ruled against Hercules, and thoroughly entrenched the principle of no general auditor liability.

Eprile pointed out that auditors are already liable, under securities acts to investors, in the narrow case when the audited financial statements appear in a prospectus.

> "We are recommending that we amend our securities legislation . . . to call for liability in the [entire] secondary market," she said.
>
> That would mean that the public company, the auditor, the directors and possibly the underwriters would be liable for any negligent disclosure when investors buy a company's shares through a stock exchange.
>
> The legislation has been drafted, Eprile said. It would be uniform across Canada and may take a year or two to get through provincial legislatures, she said.
>
> *Source:* Philip Mathias, *The Financial Post,* May 24, 1997, p. 3.

The legislation referred to in the box is still pending at the time of this writing (February 2000). The legislation would create statutory law civil liability for PAs and others accused of misleading the public. The proposed legislation would allow class action lawsuits against PAs and put the burden of proof on the defendant PA that a drop in the client's share price was due to a financial statement misrepresentation (the "fraud on the market" theory used by the SEC in the U.S.). In other words, once a misrepresentation has been identified it is up to the auditor to show that any losses suffered by investors was not due to the misrepresentation. The plaintiff would not have the burden of proving negligence by the PA. However, the proposed legislation would put caps on the PA's liability, as well as use the proportionate rather than the joint and several liability rule. However, these limitations on liability would not apply if the PA knowingly deceived the market. (See M. Paskell-Mede, *CA Magazine*, November 1998, pp. 35–36 for more details.)

This proposed legislation seems to be inspired by U.S. statutory law covered in Appendix 17A. It should be noted that PAs in Canada already have similar liabilities for initial public offerings of securities. The proposed legislation extends the liability to subsequent financial statements of companies already listed on the TSE. But such an extension would expose the Canadian PA to far more potential legal liability than is currently the case.

SUMMARY

Litigation against accountants has virtually exploded in the United States and to a lesser extent in Canada. Damage claims of hundreds of millions of dollars have been paid by PA firms and their insurers. Insurance is expensive and hard to obtain. A mid-sized national PA firm in the United States, Laventhol & Horwath, declared bankruptcy in 1990 as a result of losses from litigation. Accountants are not alone in this rash of litigation, which affects manufacturers, architects, doctors and people in many other walks of life. The professional accounting organizations have joined with other interest groups pushing for "tort reform" of various types (e.g., limitation of damages, identification of liability) in an effort to stem the tide. Other effects of this climate take the form of changing the nature of organizations in which public accountants practice (such as to LLPs).

Accountants' liability to clients and third parties under common law has expanded. Fifty years ago, a strict privity doctrine required other parties to be in a contract with and known to the accountant before they could sue for damages based on negligence.

Of course, if an accountant was grossly negligent in such a way that his or her actions amounted to constructive fraud, liability exists as it would for anyone who committed a fraud. Over the years the privity doctrine was modified in many jurisdictions, leading to liability for ordinary negligence to primary beneficiaries (known users) of the accountants' work product, then to liability based on ordinary negligence to foreseen and foreseeable beneficiaries (users not so easily known). While the general movement has been to expand accountants' liability for ordinary negligence, some jurisdictions have held closer to the privity doctrine of the past. The treatment can vary from province to province. The *Kripps* v. *Touche Ross* case discussed in this chapter has also called into question the sufficiency of conformity with GAAP defense in Canada, but it is unclear what alternative standards auditors will be held to. Future court cases will likely clarify this issue.

Accountants' liability under statutory law is also onerous, especially the potentially wide application of Bill C-61, which can label accountants as "racketeers." Regulatory laws in the United States greatly changed the obligations of public accountants. Canadian PAs whose clients obtain financing from the United States may be affected by these laws, and these laws also have had an influence on Canadian laws such as Bill C-61.

Under common law a plaintiff suing an accountant had to bring all the proof of the accountant's negligence to the court and convince the judge or jury. In the case of a public offering of securities registered in a registration statement filed under a U.S. Securities Act (and as proposed in some Canadian securities legislation), the plaintiff only needs to show evidence of a loss and that the financial statements were materially misleading. Case rested. Then, the accountant shoulders the burden of proof of showing that the audit was performed properly or that the loss resulted from some other cause. The burden of proof has thus shifted from the plaintiff to the defendant. The securities acts also impose criminal penalties in some cases. As indicated throughout the chapter, many commentators feel that the profession is in the midst of a liability crisis that has many causes and may take a long time to resolve.

Appendix 17A reviews U.S. statutory law in some detail because many court cases setting legal precedents for accountants were launched as a result of these statutory laws.

MULTIPLE-CHOICE QUESTIONS FOR PRACTICE AND REVIEW

. . . .

17.8 Under the Foreign Corrupt Practices Act of 1977:
   a. Companies must refrain from bribing foreign politicians for commercial advantage.
   b. Independent auditors must audit all elements of a company's internal control system.
   c. Companies must establish control systems to keep books, records and accounts properly.
   d. Independent auditors must establish control systems to keep books, records and accounts properly.

17.9 The management accountants employed by Robbins, Inc., wrongfully charged executives' personal expences to the overhead on a government contract. Their activities can be characterized as:
   a. Errors in the application of accounting principles.
   b. Irregularities of the type of independent auditors should plan an audit to detect.
   c. Irregularities of the type independent auditors have no responsibility to plan an audit to detect.
   d. Illegal acts of a type independent auditors should be aware might occur in government contract business.

17.10 Which of these laws does the U.S. Securities and Exchange Commission not administer?
   a. Securities Act of 1933.
   b. Securities and Exchange Act of 1934.
   c. Racketeer Influenced and Corrupt Organization Act.
   d. Foreign Corrupt Practices Act of 1977.

17.11 Good Gold Company sold $20 million of preferred shares. The company should have registered the offering under the Securities Act of 1933 if it were sold to:
   a. 150 accredited investors.
   b. One insurance company.
   c. 30 investors all resident in one state.
   d. Diverse customers of a brokerage firm.

17.12 When a company registers a security offering under the Securities Act of 1933, the law provides an investor with:
   a. An SEC guarantee that the information in the registration statement is true.
   b. Insurance against loss from the investment.
   c. Financial information about the company audited by independent PAs.
   d. Inside information about the company's trade secrets.

17.13 A group of investors sued Anderson, Olds & Watershed, PAs, for alleged damages

suffered when the company in which they held common shares went bankrupt. In order to avoid liability under the common law, AOW must prove which of the following?
a. The investors actually suffered a loss.
b. The investors relied on the financial statements audited by AOW.
c. The investors' loss was a direct result of their reliance on the audited financial statements.
d. The audit was conducted in accordance with generally accepted auditing standards and with due professional care.

17.14 The Securities and Exchange Commission document that governs accounting in financial statements filed with the SEC is:
a. Regulation D.
b. Form 8-K.
c. Form S-18.
d. Regulation S-X.

17.15 Able Corporation plans to sell $10 million common shares to investors. The company can do so without filing an S-1 registration statement under the Securities Act (1933) if Able sells the shares:

a. To an investment banker who then sells them to investors in its national retail network.
b. To no more than 75 investors solicited at random.
c. Only to accredited investors.
d. Only to 35 accredited investors and an unlimited number of unaccredited investors.

17.16 A "public company" subject to the periodic reporting requirements of the Exchange Act (1934) must file an annual report with the SEC known as the:
a. Form 10-K.
b. Form 10-Q.
c. Form 8-K.
d. Form S-3.

17.17 When investors sue auditors for damages under Section 11 of the Securities Act (1933), they must allege and prove:
a. Scienter on the part of the auditor.
b. That the audited financial statements were materially misleading.
c. That they relied on the misleading audited financial statements.
d. That their reliance on the misleading financial statements was the direct cause of their loss.

Discussion Cases

17.18 **Responsibility for Errors and Irregularities.** Huffman & Whitman, a large regional PA firm, was engaged by the Ritter Tire Wholesale Company to audit its financial statements for the year ended January 31. Huffman & Whitman had a busy audit engagement schedule from December 31 through April 1, and they decided to audit Ritter's purchase vouchers and related cash disbursements on a sample basis. They instructed staff accountants to select a random sample of 130 purchase transactions and gave directions about the important deviations, including missing receiving reports. Boyd, the assistant in charge, completed the working papers, properly documenting the fact that 13 of the purchases in the sample had been recorded and paid without the receiving report (required by stated internal control procedures) being included in the file of supporting documents. Whitman, the partner in direct charge of the audit, showed the findings to Lock, Ritter's chief accountant. Lock appeared surprised but promised that the missing re-

ceiving reports would be inserted into the files before the audit was over. Whitman was satisfied, noted in the workpapers that the problem was solved, and did not say anything to Huffman about it.

Unfortunately, H&W did not discover the fact that Lock was involved in a fraudulent scheme in which he diverted shipments to a warehouse leased in his name and sent the invoices to Ritter for payment. He then sold the tires for his own profit. Internal auditors discovered the scheme during a study of slow-moving inventory items. Ritter's inventory was overstated by about $500,000 (20 percent)—the amount Lock had diverted.

Required:
a. With regard to the 13 missing receiving reports, does a material weakness in internal control exist? If so, does Huffman & Whitman have any further audit responsibility? Explain.
b. Was the audit conducted in a negligent manner?

17.19 Responsibility for Errors and Irregularities. Herbert McCoy is the president of McCoy Forging Corporation. For the past several years, Donovan & Company, PAs, has done the company's compilation and some other accounting and tax work. McCoy decided to have an audit. Moreover, McCoy had recently received a disturbing anonymous letter that stated: "Beware, you have a viper in your nest. The money is literally disappearing before your very eyes! Signed: A friend." He told no one about the letter.

McCoy Forging engaged Donovan & Company, PAs, to render an opinion on the financial statements for the year ended June 30, 2003. McCoy told Donovan he wanted to verify that the financial statements were "accurate and proper." He did not mention the anonymous letter. The usual engagement letter providing for an audit in accordance with generally accepted auditing standards (GAAS) was drafted by Donovan & Company and signed by both parties.

The audit was performed in accordance with GAAS. The audit did not reveal a clever defalcation plan. Harper, the assistant treasurer, was siphoning off substantial amounts of McCoy Forging's money. The defalcations occurred both before and after the audit. Harper's embezzlement was discovered by McCoy's new internal auditor in October 2003, after Donovan had delivered the audit report. Although the scheme was fairly sophisticated, it could have been detected if Donovan & Company had performed additional procedures. McCoy Forging demands reimbursement from Donovan for the entire amount of the embezzlement, some $40,000 of which occurred before the audit and $65,000 after. Donovan has denied any liability and refuses to pay.

Required:
Discuss Donovan's responsibility in this situation. Do you think McCoy Forging would prevail in whole or in part in a lawsuit against Donovan under common law? Explain your conclusions.

(AICPA adapted)

17.20 Common Law Liability Exposure. A PA firm was engaged to examine the financial statements of Martin Manufacturing Corporation for the year ending December 31. Martin needed cash to continue its operations and agreed to sell its common share investment in a subsidiary through a private placement. The buyers insisted that the proceeds be placed in escrow because of the possibility of a major contingent tax liability that might result from a pending government claim against Martin's subsidiary. The payment in escrow was completed in late November. The president of Martin told the audit partner that the proceeds from the sale of the subsidiary's common shares, held in escrow, should be shown on the balance sheet as an unrestricted current account receivable. The president was of the opinion that the government's claim was groundless and that Martin needed an "uncluttered" balance sheet and a "clean" auditor's opinion to obtain additional working capital from lenders. The audit partner agreed with the president and issued an unqualified opinion on the Martin financial statements, which did not refer to the contingent liability and did not properly describe the escrow arrangement.

The government's claim proved to be valid, and, pursuant to the agreement with the buyers, the purchase price of the subsidiary was reduced by $450,000. This adverse development forced Martin into bankruptcy. The PA firm is being sued for deceit (fraud) by several of Martin's unpaid creditors who extended credit in reliance on the PA firm's unqualified opinion on Martin's financial statements.

Required:
a. What deceit (fraud) do you believe the creditors are claiming?
b. Is the lack of privity between the PA firm and the creditors important in this case?
c. Do you believe the PA firm is liable to the creditors? Explain.

(AICPA adapted)

17.21 Common Law Liability Exposure. Risk Capital Limited, an Alberta corporation, was considering the purchase of a substantial amount of treasury shares held by Sunshine Corporation, a closely held corporation. Initial discussions with the Sunshine Corporation began late in 2002.

Wilson and Wyatt, Sunshine's accountants, regularly prepared quarterly and annual unaudited financial statements. The most recently prepared financial statements were for the year ended September 30, 2002.

On November 15, 2002, after extensive negotiations, Risk Capital agreed to purchase 100,000 shares of no par, class A capital shares of Sunshine at $12.50 per share. However, Risk Capital insisted on audited statements for calendar year 2002. The contract that was made available to Wilson and Wyatt specifically provided:

Risk Capital shall have the right to rescind the purchase of said shares if the audited financial statements of Sunshine for the calendar year 2002 show a material adverse change in the financial condition of the corporation.

The audited financial statements furnished to Sunshine by Wilson and Wyatt showed no such material adverse change. Risk Capital relied on the audited statements and purchased the treasury shares of Sunshine. It was subsequently discovered that, as of the balance sheet date, the audited statements were incorrect and that in fact there had been a material adverse change in the financial condition of the corporation. Sunshine is insolvent, and Risk Capital will lose virtually its entire investment.

Risk Capital seeks recovery against Wilson and Wyatt.

Required:

Assuming that only ordinary negligence is proved, will Risk Capital prevail:

a. Under the *Ultramares* decision?

b. Under the *Rusch Factors* decision?

17.22 Common Law Liability Exposure. Smith, PA, is the auditor for Juniper Manufacturing Corporation, a privately owned company that has a June 30 fiscal year. Juniper arranged for a substantial bank loan, which was dependent on the bank receiving, by September 30, audited financial statements showing a current ratio of at least 2 to 1. On September 25, just before the audit report was to be issued, Smith received an anonymous letter on Juniper's stationery indicating that a five-year lease by Juniper, as lessee, of a factory building that was accounted for in the financial statements as an operating lease was in fact a capital lease. The letter stated that there was a secret written agreement with the lessor modifying the lease and creating a capital lease.

Smith confronted the president of Juniper, who admitted that a secret agreement existed but said it was necessary to treat the lease as an operating lease to meet the current ratio requirement of the pending loan and that nobody would ever discover the secret agreement with the lessor. The president said that, if Smith did not issue his report by September 30, Juniper would sue Smith for substantial damages that would result from not get-

ting the loan. Under this pressure and because the working papers contained a copy of the five-year lease agreement supporting the operating lease treatment, Smith issued his report with an unqualified opinion on September 29. In spite of the fact that the loan was received, Juniper went bankrupt. The bank is suing Smith to recover its losses on the loan and the lessor is suing Smith to recover uncollected rents.

Required:

Answer the following, setting forth reasons for any conclusions stated:

a. Is Smith liable to the bank?

b. Is Smith liable to the lessor?

c. Was Smith independent?

(AICPA adapted)

17.23 Common Law Liability Exposure. Farr and Madison, PAs, audited Glamour, Inc. Their audit was deficient in several respects:

1. Farr and Madison failed to audit properly certain receivables, which later proved to be fictitious.

2. With respect to other receivables, although they made a cursory check, they did not detect many accounts that were long overdue and obviously uncollectible.

3. No physical inventory was taken of the securities claimed to be in Glamour's possession, which in fact had been sold. Both the securities and cash received from the sales were listed on the balance sheet as assets.

There is no indication that Farr and Madison actually believed the financial statements were false. Subsequent creditors, not known to Farr and Madison, are now suing based on the deficiencies in the audit described above. Farr and Madison moved to dismiss the lawsuit against it on the basis that the firm did not have actual knowledge of falsity and therefore did not commit fraud.

Required:

May the creditors recover without demonstrating that Farr and Madison had actual knowledge of falsity? Explain.

17.24 Liability in a Review Engagement. Mason and Dilworth, PAs, were the accountants for Hotshot Company, a closely held corporation owned by 30 residents of the area. M&D had been previously engaged by Hotshot to perform some compilation and tax work. Bubba Crass, Hotshot's president and holder of 15 percent of the shares, said he needed something more than these services. He told Mason, the partner in charge, that he wanted financial statements for internal use, primarily for management purposes, but also to obtain short-term loans from financial institutions. Mason recommended a "review" of the financial statements. Mason did not prepare an engagement letter.

During the review work, Mason had some reservations about the financial statements. Mason told Dilworth at various times he was "uneasy about certain figures and conclusions," but that he would "take Crass's word about the validity of certain entries since the review was primarily for internal use in any event and was not an audit." M&D did not discover a material act of fraud committed by Crass. The fraud would have been detected had Mason not relied so much on the unsupported statements made by Crass concerning the validity of the entries about which he had felt so uneasy.

Required:

a. What potential liability might M&D have to Hotshot Company and other shareholders?

b. What potential liability might M&D have to financial institutions that used the financial statements in connection with making loans to Hotshot Company?

(AICPA adapted)

17.25 Regulation D Exemption. One of your firm's clients, Fancy Fashions, Inc., is a highly successful, rapidly expanding company. It is owned predominantly by the Munster family and key corporate officials. Although additional funds would be available on a short-term basis from its bankers, this would only represent a temporary solution of the company's need for capital to finance its expansion plans. In addition, the interest rates being charged are not appealing. Therefore, John Munster, Fancy's chairman of the board, in consultation with the other shareholders, has decided to explore the possibility of raising additional equity capital of approximately $15 million to $16 million. This will be Fancy's first public offering to investors, other than the Munster family and the key management personnel.

At a meeting of Fancy's major shareholders, its lawyers and a PA from your firm spoke about the advantages and dis-

advantages of "going public" and registering a share offering in the United States. One of the shareholders suggested that Regulation D under the Securities Act of 1933 might be a preferable alternative.

Required:

a. Assume Fancy makes a public offering for $16 million and, as a result, more than 1,000 persons own shares of the company. What are the implications with respect to the Securities Exchange Act of 1934?

b. What federal civil and criminal liabilities may apply in the event that Fancy sells the securities without registration and a registration exemption is not available?

c. Discuss the exemption applicable to offerings under Regulation D, in terms of two kinds of investors, and how many of each can participate.

(AICPA adapted)

17.26 Applicability of Securities Act and Exchange Act.

1. The partnership of Zelsch & Company, PAs, has been engaged to audit the financial statements of Snake Oil, Inc., in connection with filing an S-1 registration statement under the Securities Act (1933). Discuss the following two statements made by the senior partner of Zelsch & Company.

   a. "The partnership is assuming a much greater liability exposure in this engagement than exists under common law."

   b. "If our examination is not fraudulent, we can avoid any liability claims that might arise."

2. Xavier, Francis & Paul is a growing, medium-sized partnership of PAs located in the Midwest. One of the firm's major clients is considering offering its shares to the public. This will be the firm's first client to go public. State whether the following are true or false. Explain each.

   a. The firm should thoroughly familiarize itself with the securities acts, Regulation S-X, and Regulation S-K.

   b. If the client is unincorporated, the Securities Act (1933) will not apply.

   c. If the client is going to be listed on an organized exchange, the Exchange Act (1934) will not apply.

   d. The Securities Act (1933) imposes an additional potential liability on firms such as Xavier, Francis & Paul.

e. So long as the company engages in exclusively intrastate business, the federal securities laws will not apply.

17.27 Section 11 of Securities Act (1933) Liability Exposure. The Chriswell Corporation decided to raise additional long-term capital by issuing $20 million of 12 percent subordinated debentures to the public. May, Clark & Company, PAs, the company's auditors, were engaged to examine the June 30, 1993, financial statements, which were included in the bond registration statement.

May, Clark & Company completed its examination and submitted an unqualified auditor's report dated July 15, 1993. The registration statement was filed and became effective on September 1, 1993. On August 15 one of the partners of May, Clark & Company called on Chriswell Corporation and had lunch with the financial vice president and the controller. He questioned both officials on the company's operations since June 30 and enquired whether there had been any material changes in the company's financial position since that date. Both officers assured him that everything had proceeded normally and that the financial condition of the company had not changed materially.

Unfortunately, the officers' representation was not true. On July 30 a substantial debtor of the company failed to pay the $400,000 due on its account receivable and indicated to Chriswell that it would probably be forced into bankruptcy. This receivable was shown as a collateralized loan on the June 30 financial statements. It was secured by shares of the debtor corporation, which had a value in excess of the loan at the time the financial statements were prepared but was virtually worthless at the effective date of the registration statement. This $400,000 account receivable was material to the financial condition of Chriswell Corporation, and the market price of the subordinated debentures decreased by nearly 50 percent after the foregoing facts were disclosed.

The debenture holders of Chriswell are seeking recovery of their loss against all parties connected with the debenture registration.

Required:
Is May, Clark & Company liable to the Chriswell debenture holders under Section 11 of the Securities Act (1933)? Explain. (Hint: Review the *BarChris* case in Chapter 5.)

(AICPA adapted)

17.28 Rule 10b-5 Liability Exposure under the Exchange Act (1934). Gordon & Groton, PAs, were the auditors of Bank & Company, a brokerage firm and member of a national stock exchange. G&G examined and reported on the financial statements of Bank, which were filed with the Securities and Exchange Commission.

Several of Bank's customers were swindled by a fraudulent scheme perpetrated by Bank's president, who owned 90 percent of the voting shares of the company. The facts establish that Gordon & Groton were negligent in the conduct of the audit but neither participated in the fraudulent scheme nor knew of its existence.

The customers are suing G&G under the antifraud provisions of Section 10(b) and Rule 10b-5 of the Exchange Act (1934) for aiding and abetting the fraudulent scheme of the president. The customers' suit for fraud is predicated exclusively on the negligence of G&G in failing to conduct a proper audit, thereby failing to discover the fraudulent scheme.

Required:
Answer the following, setting forth reasons for any conclusions stated:
a. What is the probable outcome of the lawsuit?
b. What might be the result if plaintiffs had sued under a common law theory of negligence? Explain.

(AICPA adapted)

17.29 Foreign Corrupt Practices Act. Major Manufacturing Company is a large diversified international corporation whose shares trade on the New York Stock Exchange. The U.S. Department of Justice and the SEC have investigated the Global Oil Well Equipment Company, a subsidiary of Major. The agencies allege that Global has engaged in activities clearly in violation of the Foreign Corrupt Practices Act.

Tobias (Global president), Wilton (vice president), and Clark (regional manager of operations in Nogoland) have conspired to make payments to influential members of Nogoland's Parliament in order to influence legislation in Global's favour. The agencies allege that Tobias, Wilton and Clark met secretly in Geneva and decided to give inducements to Mr. Rock, the Speaker of Nogoland's Parliament. They made a $750,000 loan to Mr. Rock's manufacturing business at a 2 percent interest rate. They gave a $10,000 diamond to Mrs. Rock as a memento of the Rock's wedding anniversary. They paid Jeremy Rock's tuition to medical school. These expenditures were classified as investments, commissions and promotion expenses in the Global financial statements. Their nature and purpose were not otherwise disclosed.

Required:

a. What provisions of the FCPA have apparently been violated by these actions by Global and its officers?

b. What penalties might be assessed on the corporation, if convicted? on Tobias, Wilton and Clark?

(AICPA adapted)

17.30 Management Fraud Probability Assessment. This is an exercise designed to reveal some facts of reasoning and decision making. The "fraud involvement test" is fictional.

A team of accountants and psychologists has developed a procedure to test for the existence of management involvement in fraudulent activities. The procedure consists of developing a personality profile of key managers and relating this profile to a master profile compiled from interviews conducted by clinical psychologists with a substantial number of individuals who have admitted to perpetrating material frauds. If the manager's profile is sufficiently similar to the master profile, the test signals "fraud." If there is not sufficient similarity, the test signals "no fraud." In the last 18 months, the procedure has been tested extensively in the field by a national public accounting firm and it has found the following:

- If a key manager has been involved in a material fraud, the test procedure indicates "fraud" 8 times out of 10.
- If a key manager has not been involved in a material fraud, the test will nonetheless indicate "fraud" 20 times out of 100.
- The evidence indicates that about 10 key managers in 100 have been involved in material fraud.

Based on these results, what is your assessment of the probability that a key manager who receives a "fraud" test signal is actually involved in fraudulent activities?

17.31 Audit Report and Legal Liabilities. The auditor's report below was drafted by

Smith, a staff accountant at the firm of Wong & Wilson, PAs, at the completion of the audit of the financial statements of PPC Ltd., a publicly held company, for the year ended March 31, 2003. The report was submitted to the engagement partner, who reviewed the audit working papers and properly concluded that an unqualified opinion should be issued. In drafting the report, Smith considered the following:

- During the fiscal year, PPC changed its amortization method for capital assets. The engagement partner concurred with this change in accounting principles and its justification, and Smith included an explanatory paragraph in the auditor's report.
- The 2003 statements are affected by an uncertainty concerning a lawsuit, the outcome of which cannot presently be estimated. Smith has included an explanatory paragraph in the auditor's report.
- The financial statements for the year ended March 31, 2002 are to be presented for comparative purposes. Wong & Wilson had previously audited these statements and expressed an unqualified opinion.

The report which Smith drafted appears below:

Independent Auditor's Report
To the Board of Directors of PPC Ltd.:
We have audited the accompanying balance sheet of PPC Ltd., as of March 31, 2003 and 2002, and statements of income and retained earnings for the year then ended. These financial statements are the responsibility of the company's management.

We conducted our audits in accordance with generally accepted auditing standards. Those standards require that we plan and perform the audit to obtain reasonable assurance about whether the financial statements are fairly presented. An audit includes examining, on a test basis, evidence supporting the amounts and disclosures in the financial statements. An audit also includes assessing significant estimates made by management, as well as evaluating the overall financial statement presentation. We believe that our audits provide a basis for determining whether any material modifications should be made to the accompanying financial statements.

As discussed in Note X to the financial statements, the company changed its method of computing amortization in fiscal 2003.

In our opinion, except for the accounting change, with which we concur, the financial statements referred to above present fairly, in all material respects, the financial position of PPC Ltd. as of March 31, 2003, and the results of its operations for the year then ended in conformity with generally accepted accounting principles.

As discussed in Note Y to the financial statements, the company is a defendant in a lawsuit alleging infringement of certain copyrights. The company has filed a counteraction, and preliminary hearings on both actions are in progress. Accordingly, any provision for liability is subject to adjudication of this matter.

Wong & Wilson, PAs
May 5, 2003

Required:

Identify the deficiencies in the order in which they appear in the auditor's report as drafted by Smith. Do not redraft the report.

(CGAAC adapted)

17.32 Liability for Auditor Negligence. You have been called to testify as an expert witness in a negligence action brought against another public accounting firm, Muss, Tache & Co. (Muss). Briefly, the facts of the case are:

- Muss's client is insolvent.
- A major cause of the insolvency was overvaluation of the net assets of a wholly owned subsidiary, which led to its failure.
- The subsidiary was audited by another PA firm, Able & Co. (Able).
- The primary auditor (Muss) accepted the work of Able without examination of either the subsidiary's accounting records or Able's working papers.
- The action was initiated by the bank that was the primary creditor.
- Muss's defence hinged on these factors:
  (a) There was no need to examine the other auditor's working papers, since the other firm was in good standing with the Institute.
  (b) Since the subsidiary constituted only 12 percent of consolidated net income, it was not material anyway.

Required:

a. Discuss whether or not the bank will be successful in its suit for damages, with reference to the factors the court would consider in arriving at its decision.

b. If Muss, Tache & Co. had made an internal quality control review several weeks after the issue of the audit report and the review indicated that Muss should have performed some work on the subsidiary, what action should Muss, Tache & Co. have taken at the time? Assume that the review had occurred before Muss's client's insolvency became known and before that bank's negligence action was initiated.

c. Discuss the factors that Muss, Tache & Co. should have considered when determining the materiality for this engagement.

(ICAO adapted)

17.33 Liability in a Prospectus Engagement. Alex P. Keaton Jr. has just returned to the office after an exhausting "busy season." His partner, Malory Dowell, called Alex into her office.

"Alex, I have good news and bad news. First the good news! I've just returned from Expansion Exploration Ltd. and they are going public to help finance their Arctic activities. Therefore, you finally get a chance to work on a prospectus engagement! The bad news is that they want to have the prospectus and the underwriting agreement signed by next Friday, the 31st of March.

"Fortunately, we have been their auditors for the past five years, so we won't have any problems there. Also, I'm quite certain that all five years have had "clean" opinions.

"They have provided me with a copy of their interim financial statements for the five months ended February 28, 1999. As you may recall, their last year-end was September 30, 1998.

"What I would like you to do now, is to provide me with a memo for our planning file briefly outlining what our involvement is to be on this prospectus and describing what communications we are going to have to provide to the securities commission as a result of this involvement."

Required:

a. Assume the role of Alex P. Keaton Jr. and prepare the memo requested by Malory Dowell.

b. Indicate the parties to whom it could be shown that the auditors owe a legal duty of care in this particular situation, and discuss the implications.

(ICAO adapted)

17.34 Litigation Resulting from Bankruptcy of Client. A bank that lent considerable funds to a "high-flying" and, until its recent bankruptcy, highly successful real estate development company has hired your firm to investigate the company's long-time auditors, a medium-sized PA firm. The bank has claimed that the financial statements did not fairly represent the company's financial position. The senior partner in your firm in charge of the investigation has been provided with full access to the complete working papers of the initial auditor in order to complete the investigation. If the matter ultimately goes to court, the case will likely be very high in profile and will likely receive significant media coverage.

The senior partner in your firm has assigned you, a manager with considerable auditing experience, to assist him in evaluating the auditors' quality of work and actions.

Required:

a. Outline what you would do to help your senior partner prepare for the investigation. You should give details of those items he should consider in his preparation as well as the guidelines that would be used to develop an opinion as to the appropriateness of the auditors' actions.

b. On what basis (bases) will the court decide the auditors' liability in this situation?

(ICAO adapted)

APPENDIX 17A
U.S. STATUTORY LAW

. . . .

Appendix Objective
Acquaint students (whose future clients may come under the jurisidiction of U.S. law) of U.S. statutory and common law. Some influential U.S. cases are reviewed as well as the statutory law.

TWO IMPORTANT LAWS

. . . .

Numerous laws affect accountants and business people in the United States, but two of them deserve special mention. The Foreign Corrupt Practices Act of 1977 (FCPA) and the Racketeer Influenced and Corrupt Organization Act (RICO) have changed the landscape of much audit practice and have influenced the nature of lawsuits. These are the focus of this appendix. However, some recent developments perhaps should also be mentioned at this point. One is a change in SEC rules that requires the auditor to inform the SEC of material illegal acts if a client fails to inform the SEC within one business day of the auditor's discovery of the illegal acts. Another development (to be discussed in Chapter 19) is the increased global concern about corruption and auditors' responsibility to report on it. The United States was the first nation to make it illegal to bribe foreign officials. This was implemented through the landmark Foreign Corrupt Practices Act of 1977, discussed below.

Foreign Corrupt Practices Act of 1977

In 1976, under a program of voluntary disclosure, some 250 American companies notified the Securities and Exchange Commission (SEC) that they had made illegal or questionable payments in the United States and abroad. Millions of dollars were involved in some cases, as were high officials in the United States, Europe and Japan. The pattern of payments involved contributions to American and foreign politicians, bribes to win overseas contracts and under-the-table payments to expedite performance of services. Some payments were made with the apparent consent of chief executive officers, while others were authorized at lower management levels without the knowledge of top executives. Some disbursements came from general corporate funds and others from secret "slush funds" maintained off the books.

A rising tide of public indignation and impatience with wrongdoing prompted enactment of the Foreign Corrupt Practices Act of 1977 (FCPA). This law—an amendment of the Securities Exchange Act of 1934—makes it a criminal offence for American companies to bribe a foreign official, a foreign political party or a candidate for foreign political office for the purpose of influencing decisions in favour of the business interests of the company. Companies may be fined up to $2 million; individuals may be fined up to $100,000 and imprisoned up to five years for violations.

The law also amended the Securities Exchange Act of 1934 to include some accounting and internal control standards. These provisions require companies registered with the SEC to keep books, records and accounts which, in reasonable detail, accurately and fairly reflect the transactions and dispositions of the company's assets. Companies must also devise and maintain a system of internal accounting control. The effect of the Foreign Corrupt Practices Act of 1977 was to make a company's failure to establish and maintain a control system a violation of federal law in addition to being a mere matter of poor business practice. However, the monetary fines and prison terms that apply to bribes do not apply to violations of the accounting and internal control requirements.

The law gives the Securities and Exchange Commission another way to bring action against companies and accountants. Only three months after the law was passed, the SEC charged a company's officers with making false entries in the books and records and failing to maintain an adequate accounting control system. The case was settled with an injunction—the SEC's most frequent settlement method—in which the company, without admitting or denying a violation of law, agreed not to violate the law in the future. Accountant's disciplinary proceedings are also settled frequently with an injunction. You might think this kind of agreement is not a harsh penalty. However, the public notoriety of the proceedings singles out the defendants, and an injunction has some teeth. If a company or an accountant later breaks the law, the persons can be charged with criminal contempt of court. Penalties for such contempt can be severe.

When companies or accountants are taken to court with FCPA or other charges of securities acts violations, the case is litigated (decided by a judge). The SEC got its first litigated decision under FCPA in 1983 and won. However, the SEC is not interested in harassment or in unnecessarily expensive responses to internal control needs. In the first five years, the SEC brought only 26 FCPA cases against American companies, and the U.S. Justice Department brought only 8 cases. The principal purpose of FCPA is to reach knowing and reckless managerial misconduct and managers' efforts to "cook the books." As one judge put it, FCPA was enacted on the principle that reasonably accurate recordkeeping is essential to promote management responsiblity and thwart management misfeasance, misuse of corporate assets and other conduct reflecting adversely on management's integrity.

The FCPA is a law directed at company managements. Independent auditors have no direct responsibility under the law. They may advise clients about faulty control systems, but they are under no express obligation to report on deficient systems. The law cast a spotlight on companies and their internal auditors. It had the effect of making internal audit departments more important and more professional. The internal auditors often got the assignment to see that their companies complied with FCPA.

Racketeer Influenced and Corrupt Organization Act

RICO is not a law administered by the Securities and Exchange Commission. It is a general federal law, and it has both civil and criminal features. Lawsuits are often characterized as "civil RICO" or "criminal RICO." The original intent of the law was to provide an avenue for criminal prosecution of organized crime activities. However, clever lawyers have found ways to apply it in other cases, including malpractice lawsuits against accountants. As noted in the chapter, this legislation appears to have influenced comaprable legislation initiatives in Canada (e.g., Bill C-61).

The civil RICO provisions permit plaintiffs to allege and attempt to prove (a) fraud in the sale of securities and (b) mail or wire (e.g., telephone) fraud related to audit or tax practice; but RICO provides a perverse twist. If the plaintiffs in a lawsuit can prove a "pattern of racketeering activity," they can, if successful, win triple damages, court costs and legal fees' reimbursement. These potential losses raise considerably the risk of the lawsuit.

You might think that accountants may not be in great danger of being found to have participated in a "pattern of racketeering activity." Think again! Such a "pattern" can be established if a defendant accountant has engaged, whether convicted or not, in two racketeering acts—fraud in the sales of securities, mail fraud, wire fraud—within the past 10 years. An accounting firm can meet this test by losing a malpractice lawsuit that involved clients' mailing misleading financial statements and using the telephone during the audit. Since all the major PA firms have lost malpractice lawsuits, they are exposed to civil RICO lawsuits. In fact, RICO has been included among the charges in numerous lawsuits against accountants, and one accounting firm lost such a lawsuit resulting in a judgment of about $10 million.

RICO is hated and feared not only because of the monetary effect on a lawsuit. PAs do not wish to be characterized as "racketeers." It's not good for business. When the RICO threat is included in a lawsuit, PAs are more eager to settle with the plaintiffs before trial, paying damages that might not be won in a courtroom.

LIABILITY UNDER STATUTORY LAW

. . . .

Several federal statutes provide sources of potential liability for accountants, including the Federal False Statements Statute, Federal Mail Fraud Statute, Federal Conspiracy Statute, Securites Act of 1933 ("Securities Act") and Securities and Exchange Act of 1934 ("Exchange Act").

The securities acts contain provisions defining certain civil and criminal liabilities of accountants. Because a significant segment of accounting practice is under the jurisdiction of the securities acts, the following discussion will concentrate on duties and liabilities under these laws. First, however, you should become familiar with the scope and function of the securities act and the Securities and Exchange Commission (SEC).

Federal securities regulation in the United States was enacted in 1933 not only as a reaction to the events of the early years of the Great Depression but in the spirit of the New Deal era and as a culmination of attempts at "blue-sky" regulation by the states. The Securities Act of 1933 and the Securities and Exchange Act of 1934 require disclosure of information needed for informed investment decisions. The securities acts and the SEC operate for the protection of investors and for the facilitation of orderly capital markets. Even so, no government agency, including the SEC, rules on the quality of investments. The securities acts have been characterized as "truth-in-securities" law. Their spirit favours the otherwise uninformed investing public, while caveat vendor is applied to the issuer—let the seller beware of violations.

SEC Regulation of Accountants and Accounting

The SEC has made rules governing the conduct of persons practising before it. Rule 2(e) of its Rules of Practice provides a means of public regulation discipline. Through these rules, the SEC can apply direct regulatory authority to individual accountants and accounting firms.

Both the Securities Act (1933) and the Exchange Act (1934) give the SEC power to establish accounting rules and regulations. Regulation S-X contains accounting requirements for audited annual and unaudited interim financial statements filed under both the Securities Act and the Exchange Act. Equally important, Regulation S-K contains requirements relating to all other business, analytical and supplementary financial disclosures. In general, Regulation S-X governs the content of the financial statements themselves, and Regulation S-K governs all other disclosures in financial statement footnotes and other places in reports required to be filed.

For more than 50 years, the SEC has followed a general policy of relying on the organized accounting profession to establish generally accepted accounting principles (GAAP). However, the SEC makes its influence and power known in the standard-setting process. Its chief accountant monitors the development of FASB standards, meets with FASB staff, and decides whether a proposed pronouncement is reasonable. The SEC view is communicated to the FASB, and the two organizations try to work out major differences before a new Statement on Financial Accounting Standards (SFAS) is made final. Usually the two bodies reach agreement.

In the past, however, the SEC itself has made a few accounting rules because (1) the SEC could act faster when an emerging problem needed quick attention and (2) the SEC thought GAAP was deficient and wanted to prod the FASB to act. Consequently, GAAP and Regulation S-X differ in a few respects, but not many. Examples where Regulation S-X requires more than GAAP include nonequity classification of redeemable preferred shares, separate presentation of some income tax details and additional disclosures about compensating balances, inventories and long-term debt maturities. Otherwise, "SEC accounting" is not fundamentally different from GAAP accounting. The spirit of the force and effect of accounting principles and the respective roles of FASB and SEC are explained by an early SEC policy statement as follows:[14]

1. When financial statements filed with the commission are prepared according to principles that have no authoritative support, they will be presumed to be misleading. Other disclosures or footnotes will not cure this presumption.

2. When financial statements involve a principle on which the commission disagrees but has promulgated no explicit rules or regulations, and the principle has substantial authoritative support, then supplementary disclosures will be accepted in lieu of correction of the statements.

3. When financial statements involve a principle that (*a*) has authoritative support in general, but (*b*) the commission has ruled against its use, then the statements will be presumed misleading. Supplementary disclosures will not cure this presumption.

The biggest difference between SEC practice and other accounting practice involves the disclosures required by Regulation S-K. These requirements are detailed, and accountants must be well aware of them. In many respects, Regulation S-K goes beyond GAAP because FASB pronouncements usually do not specify as much detail about footnote disclosures. Also, accountants must keep up to date on the SEC's Financial Reporting Releases (FRR—a new name for the Accounting Series Releases issued through 1982), which express new rules and policies about accounting and disclosure. Finally, accountants must keep up to date on the SEC's Staff Accounting Bulletins (SAB), which are unofficial but important interpretations of Regulation S-X and Regulation S-K.

Integrated Disclosure System

Under the integrated disclosure system, companies must give annual reports to shareholders, file annual reports on Form 10-K (discussed later in this appendix) and file registration statements (also discussed later in this appendix) when securities are offered to the public. However, companies can prepare the annual report to shareholders in conformity with Regulation S-X and Regulation S-K, and use it to provide most of the other information required for the Form 10-K annual report. Some companies can also use these reports as the basic reports required in a Securities Act registration statement because the integrated disclosure system basically has made the 10-K requirements the same as the registration statement disclosure requirements.

The integrated disclosure system is intended to simplify and co-ordinate various reporting requirements. It also has had the not-too-subtle effect of making most of Regulation S-X and Regulation S-K required in annual reports to shareholders, making them GAAP for companies that want to obtain the benefits of integration.

Regulation of Auditing Standards

In contrast to its concern for the quality of accounting principles, the SEC's involvement in auditing standards and procedural matters has been minimal since the developments of the McKesson and Robbins affair. Following an investigation of *McKesson*, the SEC ruled that auditors' reports must state that an audit was performed in accordance with "generally accepted auditing standards." At that time (1938) the 10 standards had not yet been issued by the AICPA. They were written and adopted soon afterward.

McKesson & Robbins, Inc.
An SEC investigation resulted in these conclusions expressed in Accounting Series Release No. 19 (1940): First, the auditors failed to employ that degree of vigilence, inquisitiveness, and

---

[14] Accounting Series Release No. 4 (1938). Also, Accounting Series Release No. 150 (1973) affirmed that pronouncements of the FASB will be considered to constitute substantial authoritative support of accounting principles, standards and practices (FRR No. 1, Section 101). Other sources of authoritative support are enumerated in SAS 5 (see Chapter 2, Exhibit 2–3).

Enthusiasm for Private Stock Offerings

Ariad Pharmaceuticals, Inc., raised $46 million in a private share sale. Specialists in small-company finance say the sale is a sign of growing interest in private financings that could benefit many companies.

Ariad's shares were offered only to a small number of wealthy investors. They had to attest that they had a net worth of at least $1 million (excluding homes) or otherwise met government tests (SEC Regulation D) aimed at protecting small investors. Ariad obtained about 21 percent from institutional investors and the rest from individuals.

Many companies prefer to sell shares privately to avoid the need for public disclosure about proprietary technology or trade practices.

Source: The Wall Street Journal, March 27, 1992.

---

analysis of the evidence available that is necessary in a professional undertaking and is recommended in all well-known and authoritative works on auditing. Meticulous verification was not needed to discover the inventory fraud. Second, although the auditors are not guarantors and should not be responsible for detecting all fraud, the discovery of gross overstatements in the accounts is a major purpose in an audit, despite the fact that every minor defalcation might not be disclosed.

The SEC's chief accountant also monitors the development of auditing standards by the AICPA Auditing Standards Board (ASB). A member of the chief accountant's staff attends ASB meetings, analyses new proposals and decides whether an issue of relevance to SEC-registered public companies is involved. The chief accountant discusses differences of opinion with the ASB, and the two try to work them out. Ordinarily, the SEC does not get as involved with technical auditing standards and ASB proceedings as it does with accounting standards and FASB proceedings. The SEC has rules about audit reports that corresond with generally accepted auditing standards (GAAS), but the SEC has no body of technical rules similar to the Statements on Auditing Standards.

Regulation of Securities Sales

For the most part, the Securities Act (1933) regulates the issue of securities, and the Exchange Act (1934) regulates trading in securities. Neither these securities laws nor the SEC approves or guarantees investments. The laws and the SEC's regulation concentrate on disclosure of information to investors, who have the responsibility for judging investment risk and reward potential. The Securities Act provides that no person may lawfully buy, sell, offer to buy or offer to sell any security by the means of interstate commerce

---

General SEC Definitions

Nonpublic Offering ("Private Placement"). Sale of securities to a small number of persons or institutional investors (usually not more than 35), who can demand and obtain sufficient information without the formality of SEC registration.

Nonpublic Company. Company with less than $5 million in assets and fewer than 500 shareholders. Not required to register and file reports under the Exchange Act.

Accredited Investors. Financial institutions, investment companies, large tax-exempt organizations, directors and executives of the issuer and individuals with net worth of $1 million or more or income of $200,000 or more.

unless a registration statement is "effective" (a legal term meaning, essentially, "filed and accepted"). This prohibition should be interpreted literally: No person can buy or sell any security by means of interstate commerce (e.g., telephone, mail, highway, national bank) unless a registration statement is effective.

A registration statement must be filed and must be effective before a sale is lawful. The SEC has adopted a series of forms for use in registrations. The forms most commonly used for general public offerings are Forms S-1, S-2 and S-3. These forms are related to the integrated disclosure system discussed earlier. They are not sets of "forms" as in an income tax return, however. A "registration form" is a list of financial statement and disclosure requirements cross-referenced to Regulation S-X and Regulation S-K.

Form S-1 is the general registration form. It is available to all issuers but must be used by issuers who do not qualify to use Forms S-2 or S-3. A certain set of financial statements and disclosures (Part I) in an S-1 is known as the prospectus, which must be distributed to all purchasers. Investors can obtain the complete S-1, containing all the required information, from the SEC.

Form S-3 represents the SEC's acknowledgment of "efficient markets" for widely distributed information about well-known companies. Part I (the prospectus) can be concise—containing information about the terms of the securities being offered, the purpose and use of proceeds, the risk factors and some other information about the offering. The remainder of the financial information is "incorporated by reference." Financial statements are not enclosed with the prospectus, but reference is merely made to reports filed earlier (10-K, 10-Q, and 8-K reports, which will be discussed later). The information in these reports is presumed to have been obtained and used by securities analysts and already impounded in current securities prices. Form S-3 can be used by companies that have made timely reports under the Exchange Act for 36 months, that have not recently defaulted on obligations, and that have $150 million of shares trading or $100 million of shares trading with annual trading volume of 3 million shares. These requirements describe reasonably large, "seasoned" companies.

There are other forms as well: S-2 is for smaller seasoned companies and S-18 is for smaller companies making an initial public offering (IPO). These forms are simpler and processed much faster in order to facilitate access to public securities markets by smaller companies.

Regulation of Periodic Reporting

The Exchange Act primarily regulates daily trading in securities and requires registration of most companies whose securities are traded in interstate commerce. Companies having total assets of $5 million or more and 50 or more shareholders are required to register under the Exchange Act. The purpose of these size and share criteria is to define securities in which there is a significant public interest. (From time to time, these criteria may be changed.)

For auditors and accountants, the most significant aspect of the Exchange Act is the requirement for annual reports, quarterly reports and periodic special reports. These reports are referred to by the form numbers 10-K, 10-Q, and 8-K, respectively. Under the integrated disclosure system, a company's regular annual report to shareholders may be filed

---

SECURITIES ACT (1933) REGISTRATION FORMS	
Form S-1	General registration form available to all companies.
Form S-2	Registration form for small "seasoned" companies.
Form S-3	Registration form for large "seasoned" companies.
Form S-18	Registration form for relatively small initial public offerings (IPOs).

EXCHANGE ACT (1934) PERIODIC REPORTS

Form 10-K Annual report.
Form 10-Q Quarterly report.
Form 8-K Periodic report of selected special events.

---

as a part of the 10-K to provide part or all of the information required by law. The 10-Q quarterly report is filed after each of the first three fiscal quarters, and its contents are largely financial statement information. Form 8-K, the "special events report," is required whenever certain significant events occur, such as changes in control, legal proceedings and changes in accounting principles. These 8-K reports are "filed" with the SEC but are not usually sent to all shareholders and creditors. They can be obtained from the SEC and, therefore, are considered publicly available information. Frequently, 8-Ks consist of news releases distributed by the company. Commercial information services also obtain the filings and disseminate the information to clients and newsletter subscribers. Anyone can obtain the filings by requesting them and paying a fee.

One of the events considered significant for an 8-K report is a change of auditors. Companies that change auditors must report the reasons for the change. Most often they cite personality conflicts, high fees, growth of the business and need for a larger audit firm, geographical expansion and need to have a firm with several offices, new international operations and need for a firm with foreign offices or affiliates and other similar reasons. When companies grow and "go public" for the first time, investment bankers involved in the public offering often suggest changing to a Big Six firm for added credibility. This bias to large PA firms has long been a sore point with the other PA firms. They and the AICPA have declared that audits by firms other than the Big Six are professionally competent and that the investment bankers should recognize the fact. Nevertheless, large and growing companies often switch to the larger PA firms.

In the past some auditor changes have occurred for the purpose of getting an auditor who will agree with management's treatment of a troublesome revenue recognition or expense deferral treatment. Such changes are suspect, and a few of them have turned out to be cases of audit failure on the part of the new auditor. Thus, auditor changes in the context of a disagreement with management are thought to be of interest to investors. Whenever a company changes auditors, the company must report the fact and state whether in the past 24 months there has been any disagreement with the auditors concerning matters of accounting principles, financial statement disclosure or auditing procedure. At the same time, the former auditor must submit a letter stating whether the auditor agrees with the explanation and, if the auditor disagrees, giving particulars. These documents are available to the public on request, and their purpose is to make information available about client–auditor conflicts that may have a bearing on financial presentations and consequent investment decisions. Reported disagreements have included disputes over recoverability of asset cost, revenue recognition timing, expense recognition timing, amounts to be reported as liabilities and necessity for certain auditing procedures. These disclosures must also provide information about "opinion shopping" consultations with a new auditor.

LIABILITY PROVISIONS: SECURITIES ACT OF 1933

. . . .

Section 11 of the Securities Act is of great interest to auditors because it alters significantly the duties and responsibilities otherwise required by common law. This section contains the principal criteria defining civil liabilities under the statute. Portions of Section 11 pertinent to auditors' liability are discussed next.

Section 11—General Liability

The Securities Act (1933) is applicable only when a company files a registration statement (e.g., S-1, S-2, S-3, S-18) to issue securities. The sections that follow explain the practical meaning of the act.

In Section 11 the accountant is considered the "expert" on the financial statements that are covered by the audit report and, therefore, must perform a reasonable investigation—an audit in accordance with GAAS using due professional care. All other people who might be included in a registration legal action do not need to prove that they made a "reasonable investigation" of the financial statements, since they relied on the authority of the expert (the accountant who provided the audit report). Thus, the other parties would like the accountant to expand the audit report to cover as much as possible, while the accountant must be careful to specify exactly which statements, including footnotes, are covered by the audit report.

The effect of Section 11 is to shift the major burdens of affirmative proof from the injured plaintiff to the expert accountant. Recall that under the common law, the plaintiff had to allege and prove damages, misleading statements, reliance, direct cause and negligence. Under Section 11, the plaintiff still has to show that he or she was damaged and has to allege and show proof that financial statements in the registration statement were materially misleading, but here the plaintiff's duties essentially are ended. Exhibit 17A–1 summarizes these common-law and statutory duties.

Privity Not Required

The plaintiff does not have to be in privity with the auditor. Section 11 provides that any purchaser may sue the accountant. The purchaser–plaintiff does not need to prove that he or she relied on the financial statements in the registration statement. In fact, the purchaser may not have even read them.[15] The purchaser is not required to show that the misleading statements caused him or her to make an unwise decision and, thus, suffer a loss.

EXHIBIT 17A–1   COMPARISON OF COMMON-LAW AND STATUTORY LITIGATION

Under Common Law	Under Securities Act, Section 11	Under Exchange Act, Section 10(b)
Plaintiff		
Proves damages or loss.	Same as common law.	Same as common law.
Proves necessary privity or beneficiary relationship.	Any purchaser may sue the accountant.	Any purchaser or seller may sue the accountant.
Alleges, shows evidence and the court decides whether financial statements were misleading.	Same as common law.	Same as common law.
Proves reliance on misleading statements.	Not required.*	Same as common law.
Proves misleading statements the direct cause of his loss.	Not required.	Same as common law.
Proves the requisite degree of negligence by the accountant.	Not required.	Must allege and prove that the accountant knew about the scheme or device to defraud.
Defendant Accountant		
Offers evidence to counter above, such as: no privity, statements not misleading and that the audit was conducted in accordance with GAAS with due care.†	Must prove a reasonable investigation was performed (due diligence)†	Must prove acted in good faith and had no knowledge of the misleading statements.†

*Proof of purchaser's reliance may be required if a 12-month earnings statement had been issued.
†Upon failing to prove a proper audit, due diligence or good faith, the accountant may try to prove that the plaintiff's loss was caused by something other than the misleading financial statements, for example, actions by the plaintiff such as contributory negligence or loss from some other cause.

[15] This matter of reliance is modified by Section 11(a) to the extent that when enough time has elapsed and the registrant has filed an income statement covering a 12-month period beginning after the effective date, when the plaintiff must prove that he or she purchased after that time in reliance on the registration statement. However, the plaintiff may prove reliance without proof of actually having read the registration statement.

Section 11 was written with the protection of the investing public in mind, not the protection of the expert auditor. The first significant court case under Section 11 was *Escott et al. v. BarChris Construction Corporation et al.* The ruling in this case was that the auditors did not conduct a reasonable investigation and, thus, did not satisfy Section 11(b)(B).

Escott v. BarChris Construction Corp. (1968)
The court ruled that the auditors were the only experts under Section 11 and specifically ruled that the attorneys were not considered experts. In individual findings against all defendants (except the auditors), the court generally ruled that they had not conducted reasonable investigations to form a basis for belief and that they had not satisfied the diligence upon the portions of the prospectus expertised by the auditors [a lesser diligence requirement under Section 11(b)(C)]. The court ruled that the auditors had also failed to perform a diligent and reasonable investigation [Section11(b)(B)]. The court found that the auditor had spent "only" 20.5 hours on the subsequent events review, had read no important documents, and "He asked questions, he got answers that he considered satisfactory and he did nothing to verify them . . . He was too easily satisfied with glib answers to his inquiries." The court also said: "Accountants should not be held to a standard higher than that recognized in their profession. I do not do so here. The senior accountant's review did not come up to that standard. He did not take some of the steps [the] written program prescribed. He did not spend an adequate amount of time on a task of this magnitude."

Section 11 Exemption

Financial reporting has changed since 1933. The SEC now requires some larger companies to present interim financial statements and encourages the presentation of forecasts. To remove the legal liability barrier to auditor association with such information, the SEC has exempted auditors from Section 11 liability related to interim information and has enacted a "safe harbour" with respect to forecasts. (A *safe harbour* means that plaintiffs in a lawsuit must show that the auditor did not act in good faith when reporting on a forecast, effectively placing the burden of proof on the plaintiff.) The FASB requires some kinds of supplementary information outside the basic financial statements (oil and gas reserve information), and auditing standards require implicit reporting. (*Implicit reporting* means that auditors modify the standard audit report only when some exception is taken to the presentation of the supplementary information; otherwise, the report is silent.) The SEC has not exempted auditors' implicit reports on supplementary information from Section 11 liability exposure.

Statute of Limitations

Section 13 of the Securities Act defines the statute of limitations in such a way that suit is barred if not brought within one year after discovery of the misleading statement or omission, or in any event if not brought within three years after the public offering. These limitations and the reliance limitation related to a 12-month earnings statement restrict auditors' liability exposure to a determinable time span. Oftentimes, the statute of limitations is the best defence available to auditors. (In 1991 proposals were made to extend the time span to two years after discovery and five years after the fraudulent act occurred.)

Due Diligence Defence

Section 11 also states the means by which auditors can avoid liability. Section 11(b) describes the "due diligence" defence. If the auditor can prove that a reasonable examination was performed, then the auditor is not liable for damages. Section 11(c) states the standard of reasonableness to be that degree of care required of a prudent person in the management of his or her own property. In a context more specific to auditors, a reasonable investigation would be shown by the conduct of an audit in accordance with generally accepted auditing standards in both form and substance.

Section 11 also gives a diligence defence standard for portions of a registration statement made on the authority of an expert. Any person who relies on an "expert" is not required to conduct a reasonable investigation of his or her own, but only to have no reasonable grounds for disbelief. Thus, the auditor who relies on the opinion of an actuary or engineer need not make a personal independent investigation of that expert's area. Similarly, any officer, director, attorney or underwriter connected with a registration has a far lesser diligence duty for any information covered by an auditor's expert opinion. In the *BarChris* judgment, officers, directors, attorneys and underwriters were found lacking in diligence except with respect to audited financial statements.

Causation Defence

Section 11(e) defines the last line of defence available to an auditor when lack of diligence has been proved. This defence is known as the causation defence. Essentially, if auditors can prove that the plaintiff's damages (all or part) were caused by something other than the misleading and negligently prepared registration statement, then all or part of the damages will not have to be paid. This defence may create some imaginative "other reasons." In the *BarChris* case, at least one plaintiff had purchased securities after the company had gone bankrupt. The presumption that the loss in this instance resulted from events other than the misleading registration statement is fair, but this claim was settled out of court, so there is no judicial determination for reference.

Section 17—Antifraud

Section 17 of the Securities Act is the antifraud section. The wording and intent of this section is practically indentical to Section 10(b) and Rule 10b-5 under the Exchange Act. The difference between the two acts is the Securities Act references to "offer or sale" and the Exchange Act reference to "use the securities exchanges."

SECTION 24—CRIMINAL LIABILITY
• • • • • • • • • • • •

Section 24 sets forth the criminal penalties imposed by the Securities Act. Criminal penalties are characterized by monetary fines or prison terms, or both. The key words in Section 24 are wilful violation and wilfully causing misleading statements to be filed.

> *United States v. Benjamin (1964)*
> The judgement in this case resulted in conviction of an accountant for willingly conspiring by use of interstate commerce to sell unregistered securities and to defraud in the sale of securities, in violation of Section 24 of the 1933 Securities Act. The accountant had prepared "pro forma" balance sheets and claimed that use of the words *pro forma* absolved him of responsibility. He also claimed that he did not know his reports would be used in connection with securities sales. The court found otherwise, showing that he did in fact know about the use of his reports and that certain statements about asset values and acquisitions were patently false and that the accountant knew they were false. The court made two significant findings: (1) that the wilfulness requirements of Section 24 may be proved by showing that due diligence would have revealed the false statements and (2) that use of limiting words such as *pro forma* does not justify showing false ownership of assets in any kind of financial statements.

LIABILITY PROVISIONS: SECURITIES AND EXCHANGE ACT OF 1934
• • • • • • • • • • • •

Section 10 of the Exchange Act is used against accountants quite frequently. Like Section 17 of the Securities Act, Section 10 is a general antifraud section.

The *Fischer* v. *Kletz* ruling and the *Hochfelder* decisions have more to say about Section 10. An important point about Section 10 liability is that plaintiffs must prove scienter—that an accountant acted with intent to deceive—in order to impose liability under the rule. Mere negligence is not enough cause for liability. The basic comparison of Section 10 with common law and with Section 11 of the Securities Act is shown in Exhibit 17A–1.

> *Fischer* v. *Kletz* (popularly known as the "Yale Express" case, 1967)
> The judge ruled that "aiding and abetting" allegations were sufficient grounds for proceeding to trial on the merits of the lawsuit. This decision is the court's ruling to deny the defendant's motion to dismiss the suit. No other public record exists because the suit was later settled without trial. Plaintiff's allegations were based on common-law deceit, Section 18 of the Exchange Act, and Section 10(b), and Rule 10B-5 under the Exchange Act. The case was complicated by the accounting firm's involvement in a consulting services engagement after the financial statement audit.
>
> The court's findings dealt with the following subjects: (1) The accounting firm's role of consultant may have interfered with duties as statutory independent auditor; (2) silence and inaction rather than affirmative misrepresentations may be criteria for deceit; (3) "aiding and abetting" may trigger Section 10(b) and Rule 10b-5 liability; and (4) auditors may have public responsibilities in connection with unaudited interim financial statements.
>
> *Ernst & Ernst* v. *Hochfelder* (U.S. Supreme Court, 1976)
> The decision in this case established precedent for plaintiff's needs to allege and prove scienter—intent to deceive—to impose Section 10(b) liability under the Exchange Act. The point of law at issue in the case was whether scienter is a necessary element for a cause of action under 10(b) or whether negligent conduct alone is sufficient. "Scienter" refers to a mental state embracing intent to deceive, manipulate or defraud. Section 10(b) makes unlawful the use or employment of any manipulative or deceptive device or contrivance in contravention of Securities and Exchange Commission rules. The respondents (*Hochfelder*) specifically disclaimed any allegations or fraud or intentional misconduct on the part of Ernst & Ernst, but they wanted to see liability under 10(b) imposed for negligence.
>
> The Court reasoned that Section 10(b) in its reference to "employment of any manipulative and deceptive device" meant that intention to deceive, manipulate or defraud is necessary to support a private cause of action under Section 10(b), and negligent conduct is not sufficient. This decision is considered a landmark for accountants because it relieved them of liability for negligence under Section 10(b) of the Exchange Act and its companion SEC Rule 10b-5. Mere negligence is not enough. However, reckless professional work might yet be a sufficient basis for 10(b) liability even though scienter is not clearly established.

Section 18—Civil Liability

Section 18 sets forth pertinent civil liability definition under the Exchange Act.

> Section 18, Securities and Exchange Act of 1934
> Section 18(a): Any person who shall make or cause to be made any statement . . . which . . . was at the time and in the light of the circumstances under which it was made false or misleading with respect to any material fact shall be liable to any person (not knowing that such statement was false or misleading) who, in reliance upon such statement, shall have purchased or sold a security at a price which was affected by such statement, for damages caused by such reliance, unless the person sued shall prove that he acted in good faith and had no knowledge that such statement was false or misleading.

Good Faith Defence

Under Rule 10b-5 and Section 18, a plaintiff has to prove reliance on misleading statements and damages caused thereby—the same requirement as under common law. As a defence, the auditor must then prove action in good faith and no knowledge of the misleading statement. This requirement appears to be the *Ultramares* rule written into statute, to the extent that proving good faith is equivalent to showing that any negligence was no greater than ordinary negligence. (A note on the *Ultramares* decision was presented earlier in this chapter.)

Section 32—Criminal Liability

Section 32 states the criminal penalties for violation of the Exchange Act. Like Section 24 of the Securities Act, the critical test is whether the violator acted "wilfully and knowingly."

The defendant accountants in the *Continental Vending* case (*United States* v. *Simon*) and in *United States* v. *Natelli* were charged with violation of Section 32.

United States v. *Simon* (popularly known as the "*Continental Vending* case, 1969)
The circumstances were judged to be evidence of wilful violation of the Exchange Act. Generally accepted accounting principles were viewed by the judge as a persuasive but not necessarily conclusive criteria for financial reporting.

In affirming the conviction, the appeals court stated that it should be the auditor's responsibility to report factually whenever corporate activities are carried out for the benefit of the president of the company and when "looting" has occurred.

United States v. *Natelli* (popularly known as the "*National Student Marketing*" case, 1975)
Circumstances and actions on the part of accountants were construed to amount to wilful violation of the Exchange Act.

The court stated: "It is hard to probe the intent of a defendent . . . When we deal with a defendant who is a professional accountant, it is even harder at times to distinguish between simple errors of judgment and errors made with sufficient criminal intent to support a conviction, especially when there is no financial gain to the accountant other than his legitimate fee."

Nevertheless, the court affirmed one accountant's conviction by the lower trial court because of his apparent motive and action to conceal the effect of some accounting adjustments. A footnote in particular, as it was written, failed to reveal what it should have revealed—the write-off of $1 million of "sales" (about 20 percent of the amount previously reported) and the large operating income adjustment ($210,000 compared to $388,031 originally reported). The court concluded that the concealment of the retroactive adjustments to the company's 1968 revenues and earnings were properly found to have been intentional for the very purpose of hiding earlier errors.

EXTENT OF LIABILITY

You may be interested in knowing about who suffers exposure and penalties in lawsuits—the accounting firm, partners, managers, senior accountants, staff assistants or all of these. Most lawsuits centre attention on the accounting firm and on the partners and managers involved in the audit or other accounting work. However, court opinions have cited the work of senior accountants, and there is no reason that the work of new staff assistant accountants should not come under review. All persons involved in professional accounting are exposed to potential liability.

U.S. Auditing Standards titled "Planning and Supervision" offer some important thoughts for accountants who question the validity of some of the work. Accountants can express their own positions and let the working paper records show the nature of the disagreement and the resolution of the question. SAS 22 expressed the appropriate action as follows:

The auditor with final responsibility for the examination [partner in charge of the audit] and assistants should be aware of the procedures to be followed when differences of opinion concerning accounting and auditing issues exist among firm personnel involved in the examination. Such procedures should enable an assistant to document his disagreement with the conclusions reached if, after appropriate consultation, he believes it necessary to disassociate himself from the resolution of the matter. In this situation, the basis for the final resolution should also be documented.

CHAPTER 18

Learning Objectives

This chapter introduces governmental and internal auditing in the context of comprehensive auditing. These fields differ in important respects from financial statements auditing practiced by independent CAs in public accounting. However, you will find that all the fields of auditing share many similarities. The explanations and examples in this chapter will help you understand the working environment, objectives and procedures that characterize governmental and internal auditing. Your learning objectives are to be able to:

1. Describe the public sector and internal audit institutions (II), and tell how public sector and internal audit work interacts with independent audits.

2. Define public sector auditing and internal auditing.

3. Compare aspects of public sector, internal and external auditors' independence problems.

4. Specify the elements of expanded scope auditing in both public sector and internal audit practice.

5. Describe the coverage of public sector and internal audit standards.

6. Describe a sequence of work in governmental and internal audits in terms of preliminary survey, evaluation of administrative control, evidence-gathering field work and report preparation.

7. Explain the function of standards and measurements in economy and efficiency and program results audits.

8. List and explain several requirements for public sector and internal audit reports.

Comprehensive Auditing: Public Sector

and Internal Audits

"External," Public Sector and Internal Audits

LEARNING OBJECTIVE

1. Describe the public sector and internal audit institutions (II), and tell how public sector and internal audit work interacts with independent audits.

Public sector and internal auditing is an extensive subject. This chapter explains some of the main features. Even though points of similarity and difference in comparison to "external" auditing would be useful, space does not permit presentation of a detailed comparison. Many such similarities and differences will be apparent, however, when you study this chapter after having studied Chapters 1 and 2.

Perhaps you have already noticed the reference to "external" auditing. Ordinarily, you can refer to public sector, internal and independent auditors—the latter referring to CAs in public practice, or PAs. Yet labels are potentially confusing. Many public sector and internal auditors are PAs, and take pride in their independence in mental attitude. For purposes of this chapter, therefore, "external" auditing will be used to refer to auditing performed by PAs in public accounting firms and thereby to distinguish public practice from public sector and internal practice.

Internal Auditing

Internal auditing is practised by auditors employed by an organization, such as a bank, hospital, city government or industrial company. The Institute of Internal Auditors (IIA) is the international organization that governs the standards, continuing education and general rules of conduct for internal auditors as a profession. (The IIA Standards for the practice of internal auditing are summarized in Appendix 18A.) The IIA also sponsors research and development of practices and procedures designed to enhance the work of internal auditors wherever they are employed. For example, the IIA actively provides courses in numerous internal audit and investigation subjects and promotes its massive, multivolume Systems Auditability and Control guide for dealing with computerized information systems.

The IIA also controls the Certified Internal Auditor (CIA) program. This certification is a mark of professional achievement that has gained widespread acceptance throughout the world. To become a CIA, a candidate must hold a university degree and pass a two-day examination covering these areas: theory and practice of internal auditing; management, quantitative methods and information systems; and accounting, finance and economics. Candidates must also have two years of audit experience (internal audit or public accounting audit) obtained before or after passing the examination. Holders of masters' degrees need only one year of experience.

Public Sector Auditing

The public sector auditors discussed in this chapter are auditors employed by federal, provincial and municipal levels of government.

The Office of the Auditor General (OAG) is headed by the Auditor General of Canada. In one sense OAG auditors are the highest level of internal auditors for the federal government as a whole. Provincial (and other federal agencies and other local governmental units) use the CICA Public Sector Standards to guide their audits. These standards are published in separate *Handbook* sections. We will use the acronym *PS* for public sector

NOVATEL, OR THE CHAMBER OF HORRORS

Provincial auditors' reports have always cited cases of waste, flagrant mismanagement and not-so-flagrant cover-ups as springboards for recommendations on better accounting and accountability systems. Typically, such disclosures give rise to a flurry of damning articles in the provincial press—not to speak of indignant reactions from the opposition. As horror tales go, however, few have been more politically charged, brought more coverage in the national media, or served as a greater catalyst for improvements to a government's accounting systems than that of Novatel Communications Ltd., as documented in a special 1992 report by Alberta auditor general Donald Salmon.

Novatel was a joint venture created in 1983 between government-owned Alberta Government Telephones (AGT) and energy giant Nova Corp. The company's cellular systems and subscriber equipment business were to serve as a mainstay for the province's high-technology industry—a safeguard for the day when the oil revenues ran dry. By the end of 1988, however, it had accumulated losses of $148.7 million. In 1990, it issued a forecast in which it predicted a second-half profit of $16.9 million—which it had to revise eight days later into a $4.1-million shortfall. Shortly thereafter plans to find a strategic partner were scuttled when the German company Robert Bosch GmbH backed off from an agreement to buy 50% of Novatel. The government ended up with the company on its own hands, and the drain continued. In May 1992, it finally sold off part of the business to Northern Telecom Ltd. and another part to Telexel Holding Ltd., admitting to a $566-million loss on the deal.

By this time, the need to determine exactly what went wrong over Novatel's nine-year history was painfully apparent to all. Conscious of the expense that a full public inquiry would entail, Alberta's Executive Council chose instead to ask Don Salmon to conduct a review. Although this decision was criticized by the opposition as a deliberate attempt on the government's part to avoid a full probe, Salmon promised that the report would speak for itself. And that it did. Issued in September 1992, two weeks after Premier Donald Getty announced his resignation, the 201-page document described in exacting detail the events that ultimately led to what Salmon calculated as a $614-million tab for Alberta's taxpayers. It showed how mismanagement, cronyism and lack of strategic direction ultimately turned the Conservative government's much-touted ticket to the future into an albatross of loss, and how this could have been prevented. More important, it offered broad recommendations designed to strengthen accountability systems in the province.

The recommendations were as follows:

1. The province should consider using the expertise of the public service commissioner to short-list suitable candidates for appointments to the boards of all provincial agencies and Crown corporations. The primary criterion should be "proven relevant expertise."

2. All provincial agencies and Crown-controlled organizations, including subsidiaries, should be required to prepare annual budgets as a basis for comparison with actual results.

3. The public accounts should include the financial statements of all provincial agencies and Crown-controlled organizations and their subsidiaries.

4. The public accounts committee should consider the reasons why actual results are significantly worse than budgeted results.

5. The definition of a Crown-controlled organization should be widened to include a 50% interest in, or equal control of, an organization.

Although Getty officially stepped down shortly after the report's release, Salmon says he nevertheless indicated that he "was pleased and accepted the recommendations." But the story did not quite end there: In January 1993, after Ralph Klein had taken over as premier, the AG had a further opportunity to admonish the government when he released his 1991–92 report. That report was rife with additional horror stories, including the fact that the government had lost $80.8 million on Gainers Inc. since it took the meatpacking plant over from Peter Pocklington in 1989. The stories were so numerous, in fact, that they prompted *Calgary Herald* columnist Don Braid to quip: "Salmon could truly destroy the government if he ever decided to get annoyed about the dismal facts in his reports . . . [He] probably figures that the information in his reports is damning enough. If so, he's right."

Indeed, further developments tended to confirm Braid's assessment. In that same annual report, Salmon made eight main recommendations—five of which were the same as those put forward in the Novatel report. Klein, who was planning an election later in the year, hastened to accept virtually all of them. Salmon recalls: "So here for the first time we have a government that accepts all of our recommendations."

In Salmon's view, this link between the Novatel report and the ensuing acceptance of his recommendations is not a chance occurrence. He concludes in these terms: "In Alberta we were fortunate—we were given that special assignment on Novatel, which was much broader than our normal work. And because of the large loss in one organization we were able to then give some strong and broad recommendations. I think this has helped the government focus on financial accountability—and that, of course, is what we're interested in."

Source: M. Criag Bourdin, "On Guard for Thee," *CA Magazine,* January/February 1994, pp. 30–31.

auditing standards developed by the CICA. Because of the wide adoption of the PSs, you will be introduced to them in this chapter.

Many provinces also have provincial auditors similar to the OAG. They answer to provincial legislatures and perform the same types of work described herein as OAG auditing. In another sense OAG and similar provincial agencies are really external auditors with respect to government agencies they audit because they are organizationally independent.

Many government agencies have their own internal auditors and auditor general. Well-managed local governments also have internal audit departments. For example, many federal agencies (Health Canada, the Canada Customs and Revenue Agency, Natural Resources Canada), provincial agencies (education, welfare, health), and local governments (cities, regions, townships) have internal audit staffs. In the private sector some huge industrial companies have revenues and assets as large as some governments, and the corporate internal auditors are in the same position relative to such a company as a whole as the auditor general is to the federal government. Both in matters of scale and the positions they occupy, governmental and internal auditors have much in common. The discussion in this chapter combines and compares their activities. The box above illustrates the unique influence that public sector auditors have in Canada.

Interaction with External Auditors

External auditors often find themselves working with internal auditors on an independent audit of a company's financial statements. They also often take engagements to perform audits in accordance with the CICA standards (PS 5200 to PS 6430 in the *CICA Handbook*).

Considering the Internal Audit Function in an Independent Audit of Financial Statements
External auditors consider the internal audit function in two contexts: (1) internal audit is part of a company's control environment and external auditors must understand how it operates in order to gain an understanding of the company's control structure (second GAAS examination standard) and (2) internal auditors may help the external auditors

gather evidence about internal control and about balances in accounts (third GAAS examination standard). External auditors can make their audits more efficient by utilizing the work of a company's internal auditors and, thereby, avoiding duplication of effort.

External auditors must obtain an understanding of a company's internal audit department and its program of work. This task is part of the understanding of the entire control structure. If a preliminary review of the internal audit function shows that the internal auditors have developed, monitored and made recommendations about internal controls, the external auditors will probably decide that it will be efficient to use internal audit information to reduce their own work on the audit. When this decision is made, the external auditors are obligated to investigate the competence and objectivity of the internal auditors. These investigations become a part of the external auditors' work program.

Internal auditors' competence is investigated by obtaining evidence about their educational and experience qualifications, their certification (CIA) and continuing education status, the department's policies and procedures for work quality and for making personnel assignments, the supervision and review activities and the quality of reports and working paper documentation. This evidence enables the external auditors to make an evaluation of internal auditors' performance.

Internal auditors' objectivity is investigated by learning about their organizational status and lines of communication in the company. The theory is that objectivity is enhanced when the internal auditors are responsible to high levels of management and can report directly to the audit committee of the board of directors. Objectivity is questioned when the internal auditors report to divisional management, line managers or other persons with a stake in the outcome of their findings. Objectivity is especially questioned when managers have some power over the pay or job tenure of the internal auditors. Likewise, objectivity is questioned when individual internal auditors have relatives in audit-sensitive areas or are scheduled to be promoted to positions in the activities under internal audit review.

Favourable conclusions about competence and objectivity enable external auditors to accept the internal auditors' documentation and work on review, assessment and monitoring of a company's internal control procedures. This information, combined with other evidence obtained through the external auditors' own work, leads to an assessment of control risk that is used in the remainder of the external audit planning.

Competent, objective internal auditors may also have performed some external audit–like procedures to obtain evidence about the dollar balances in accounts (substantive procedures). For example, they often confirm accounts receivable and make observations during interim counts of physical inventory. By relying in part on this work, external auditors may be able to relax the nature, timing or extent of their own procedures in the same areas. Be careful to note, however, that this utilization of internal auditors' work may not be a complete substitute for the external auditors' own procedures and evidence related to accounting judgments and material financial statement balances.

The external auditors cannot share responsibility for audit decisions with the internal auditors and must supervise, review, evaluate and test the work performed by the internal auditors. This requirement applies both to the work of obtaining an understanding of the internal control structure and to the work of using internal auditors' evidence about financial statement balances.

Compliance Auditing Applicable to Governmental Entities and Other Recipients of Governmental Financial Assistance

When independent accountants in public practice take engagements governed by the OAG audit standards, they are supposed to conduct the work in accordance with PSs. In fact, failure to follow PSs in such engagements is an "act discreditable to the profession." Some parliamentary regulatory laws require auditors to test and report on an entity's compliance with laws and regulations. This work is known as compliance auditing, and it has a special relevance in government-standard audit engagements.

External auditors have responsibilities under the CICA's generally accepted auditing standards for detecting material errors, irregularities and certain illegal acts in connection

---

UNIVERSITY OF XYZ, PROVINCE OF XYZ

University Student Loan Program:

Finding: Of the 50 student records tested for a total dollar amount of $94,181, fifteen loan application forms were completed incorrectly . . . These applications must be completed correctly to ensure that the students will not be overawarded. These errors resulted in 1 student being overawarded by a total amount of $1,387; 2 students being underawarded by a total of $631; and with no effect on the awarded amount for the remaining 12 students.

Recommendations: Management should ensure that the costs and estimates are calculated correctly. The loan applications should be reviewed.

University's response: The overaward resulted because one student's Student Aid Report was received late. The award was based on preliminary information from the Comprehensive Financial Aid Report. Underawards were the result of clerical errors. Management will monitor the completion of the loan applications more closely.

---

with the independent audits of commercial and not-for-profit financial statements. These are detailed in the appendixes to Chapter 19 in this textbook. However, governmental entities and government fund recipients contend with many more laws and regulations, especially ones concerned with eligibility, procedure and payment of amounts under various entitlements and programs. Auditors must study the laws and regulations and get the management to give a list of all the ones applicable in the circumstances. Auditors can then determine whether to perform specific procedures to obtain evidence about compliance with the laws and regulations.

The public sector sometimes requires reports on compliance. The auditors can give positive assurance on areas tested with compliance procedures and negative assurance on areas not tested. An example of part of a report on compliance test results is shown in the box above.

Some public sector agencies also require reports on internal control. (Some aspects of such reports for nongovernmental entities were discussed in Chapter 15.) The reports on internal control must describe the entity's control structure, report the scope of the auditors' work, and describe any reportable conditions and material control weaknesses. The requirements for such reports can be very detailed and go beyond the scope of this textbook.

REVIEW CHECKPOINTS

18.1 What special professional certification is available for internal auditors? for OAG auditors?

18.2 What must external auditors do to use the work of internal auditors in the audit of a company's financial statements?

18.3 Why do you think special attention is paid to compliance auditing for governmental-type audits when independent PAs may perform compliance procedures in all types of audits anyway?

DEFINITIONS AND OBJECTIVES

LEARNING OBJECTIVE
2. Define public sector auditing and internal auditing.

The Institute of Internal Auditors (IIA) defined internal auditing and stated its objective as follows:

Internal auditing is an independent appraisal function established within an organization to examine and evaluate its activities as a service to the organization. The objective of internal auditing is to assist members of the organization in the effective discharge of their obligations. To this end, internal auditing furnishes them with analyses, appraisals, recommendations, counsel and information concerning the activities reviewed.

Operational Auditing

Internal auditors perform audits of financial reports for internal use, much as external auditors audit financial statements distributed to outside users. Thus, much internal auditing work is similar to the auditing described elsewhere in this textbook. However, some internal auditing activity is known as **operational auditing**. Operational auditing (also known as **performance auditing** and **management auditing**) refers to auditors' study of business operations for the purpose of making recommendations about economic and efficient use of resources, effective achievement of business objectives and compliance with company policies. The goal of operational auditing is to help managers discharge their management responsibilities and improve profitability. Operational auditing, thus, is included in the definition of internal auditing given above. In a similar context, an operational or effectiveness audit performed by independent PA firms is a distinct type of consulting service having the goal of helping a client improve the use of its capabilities and resources to achieve its objectives. So, internal auditors consider operational auditing an integral part of internal auditing, and external auditors define it as a type of consulting service offered by public accounting firms.

Independence

LEARNING OBJECTIVE

3. Compare aspects of public sector, internal and external auditors' independence problems.

Internal auditors hold independence, and the objectivity thus obtained, as a goal. Although internal auditors cannot be disassociated from their employers in the eyes of the public, they seek operational and reporting independence. Operationally, internal auditors should be independent when obtaining evidence in the sense of being free from direction or constraint by the managers of the business unit under audit (e.g., program, division, subsidiary). Independence and objectivity are enhanced when internal auditors have the authority and responsibility to report to a high executive level and to the audit committee of the board of directors. The goal here is a measure of practical independence from the control or direct influence of operating managers whose functions, operations and results they may be assigned to audit. Practical independence enables internal auditors to be objective in reporting findings without having to fear for their jobs. (See the IIA Code of Ethics in Appendix 18B.)

Public sector auditors, like external and internal auditors, hold independence as a goal. PS 5000.04 and IFAC Public Sector Guidelines recommend that public sector auditors should adhere to established rules of professional conduct such as those embodied in the Rules of Conduct of each provincial institute. This relates to maintaining integrity and objectivity as well as to the independence-damaging appearance of financial and managerial involvement. As a public sector auditor, one must be aware that such personal factors as preconceived ideas about programs, political or social convictions and loyalty to a level of government may impair the integrity and objectivity that is the foundation of real independence. Like internal auditors, public sector auditors must be alert to external sources of independence impairment, such as interference by higher-level officials and threats to job security.

Organizational separation from such influences is essential for independence so that auditors can report directly to top management without fear of job or compensation retribution. Auditors of governmental units are presumed independent when they are (1) free from sources of personal impairment, (2) free from sources of external impairment, (3) organizationally independent, (4) independent under Provincial Rules of Professional Conduct, (5) elected or appointed and reporting to a legislative body of government, or (6) auditing in a level or branch of government other than the one to which they are normally assigned.

On any particular assignment, public sector auditors may perform services for the benefit of several interested parties—the management of the auditee, officials of the agency requiring the audit, officials of one or more agencies that fund the auditee's programs, members and committees of local governments, a provincial legislature, and/or the national Parliament and the public. All such parties should receive the audit report unless laws or regulations restrict public distribution (e.g., for reasons of national security). In fact, the annual reports of the OAG and provincial auditors to their respective parliaments are widely reported media events—which suggests that public sector auditors do not face the expectations gap of external auditors. In contrast, standard audit reports on financial statements given by independent external auditors are addressed to the client and distributed only by the client to whomever the client wishes (except in the case of securities commission–registered companies, where the law usually requires the reports to be filed for public inspection).

Scope of Service

LEARNING OBJECTIVE

4. Specify the elements of expanded scope auditing in both public sector and internal audit practice.

The stated objective of internal auditing is phrased in terms of service to "the organization," not just to management or some narrow internal interest group. Internal auditors, exercising their objectivity, function for the benefit of the whole organization—whether it is represented by the board of directors, the chief executive officer, the chief financial officer or other executives. The services provided by internal auditors include (1) audits of financial reports and accounting control systems; (2) reviews of control systems that ensure compliance with company policies, plans and procedures and with laws and regulations; (3) appraisals of the economy and efficiency of operations; and (4) reviews of effectiveness in achieving program results in comparison to established objectives and goals. Internal auditors often make recommendations that result in additional profits or cost savings for their companies. In this capacity they function like management consultants.

The Office of the Auditor General of Canada shares with internal auditors these same elements of expanded-scope services. The OAG, however, emphasizes the accountability of public officials for the efficient, economical and effective use of public funds and other resources. The OAG defines and describes expanded scope governmental auditing in terms of the types of government audits that can be performed, which are as follows:

1. Financial Statement Audits (PS 5200)
   a. Financial statement audits determine (1) whether the financial statements of an audited entity present fairly the financial position, results of operations and cash flows or changes in financial position in conformity with generally accepted accounting principles and (2) whether the entity has complied with laws and regulations for transactions and events that may have a material effect on the financial statements.

INTERNAL AUDITORS PRODUCE INTEREST INCOME

During an audit of the cash management operations at branch offices, internal auditors found that bank deposits were not made until several days after cash and cheques were received. Company policy was to complete the bookkeeping before making the deposit.

The auditors showed branch managers a cost-efficient way to capture the needed bookkeeping information that would permit release of the cash and cheques. Management agreed to implement the timely deposit of cheques and transfer to headquarters through an electronic funds transfer system from local banks to the headquarters bank, performing the bookkeeping afterward.

The change resulted in additional interest income in the first year in the amount of $150,000.

2. **Compliance Audits (PS 5300).**
Compliance audits are those in which audit mandates are required to do one or more of the following:
   a. Express an opinion on whether an entity complied with specified authorities or whether its transactions were carried out in compliance with specified authorities.
   b. Express an opinion on whether the transactions that have come to their notice in the cause of discharging their other audit responsibilities were carried out in compliance with specified authorities.
   c. Report instances of noncompliance with authorities observed in the course of discharging their audit responsibilities.

3. **Value for Money (Performance) Audits (PS 5400)**
   a. Economy and efficiency audits include determining (1) whether the entity is acquiring, protecting and using its resources (such as personnel, property and space) economically and efficiently; (2) the causes of inefficiencies or uneconomical practices; and (3) whether the entity has complied with laws and regulations concerning matters of economy and efficiency.
   b. Effectiveness or program audits include determining (1) the extent to which the desired results or benefits established by the legislature or other authorizing body are being achieved; (2) the effectiveness of organizations, programs, activities or functions; and (3) whether the agency has complied with laws and regulations applicable to the program.

The audit of a governmental organization, program, activity or function may involve one or more of these types of audits. The term "comprehensive audit" is used to describe engagements that include all three types of the audits described above. The OAG, however, and other public sector auditors do not require comprehensive audits. Most public sector engagements involve just one or two of the above three types of audits. The scope of the work is supposed to be determined according to the needs of the users of the audit results. However, the OAG recommends observance of PSAS standards in audits of governmental units by external auditors as well as by governmental auditors at federal, state and local levels.

REVIEW CHECKPOINTS

18.4 What is operational auditing, and why can it be called a type of consulting service?

18.5 How can internal auditors achieve practical independence?

18.6 What general auditing services do internal auditors provide?

18.7 What general auditing services do governmental auditors provide?

18.8 What factors should governmental auditors consider in determining whether they are independent?

INTERNAL AUDITING STANDARDS

LEARNING OBJECTIVE
5. Describe the coverage of public sector and internal audit standards.

The Standards for the Professional Practice of Internal Auditing were issued by the Institute of Internal Auditors (IIA) in 1978 (see Appendix 18A). The IIA now issues Statements on Internal Auditing Standards (SIAS) intended to provide authoritative interpretations of the 1978 standards.

The 1978 standards are classified into five major categories. Altogether, 25 different guiding standards are included, under the following headings:

1. Independence.
2. Professional Proficiency.

  a. The Internal Auditing Department.

  b. The Internal Auditor.

3. Scope of Work.

4. Performance of Audit Work.

5. Management of the Internal Auditing Department.

Students usually learn CICA generally accepted auditing standards (GAAS) first, then study other auditing standards. The IIA standards include the spirit of all the general and field work standards of the CICA generally accepted auditing standards. On the assumption that GAAS, including the CICA Statements on Auditing Standards, are familiar, we will look only at the IIA standards that are significantly different.

Internal auditors are expected to comply with the Institute of Internal Auditors' standards of professional conduct (see Appendix 18B). IIA audit standards are recommended and encouraged, but compliance with them depends on their acceptance, adoption and implementation by practising internal auditors. The IIA standards require internal auditors to be skilled in dealing with people and in communicating effectively. Such a requirement may be considered implicit in GAAS related to training and proficiency, but little is said in GAAS about effective communication, perhaps because the audit report language is so standardized. External auditors tend to believe that the public has the responsibility to learn how to understand their audit reports, while internal auditors believe that it is their own responsibility to see that their reports are understood properly.

Three of the IIA standards call for (1) review of compliance with policies, plans, procedures, laws and regulations; (2) review of economy and efficiency in the use of resources; and (3) review of the results of programs for effectiveness. These standards all go considerably beyond the requirements of generally accepted auditing standards and closely resemble those of two of the three types of public sector audits.

The IIA standards include a requirement for following up to ascertain that appropriate action is taken on reported audit findings or ascertaining that management or the board of directors has taken the risk of not taking action on reported findings. CICA standards have no comparable follow-up requirement because external audit reports do not make recommendations related to financial statements.

Ten of the IIA standards deal with the organization and management of the internal audit department. Accountants in public practice have similar standards, but their standards are in the quality control standards, rather than in GAAS. However, observance of quality control standards is considered essential for proper auditing practice in accordance with GAAS. The quality control standards are "incorporated by reference" in GAAS and enforced through practice inspections of provincial institutes and quality control reviews of accounting firms.

The four reporting standards are comprehensive insofar as audit reports on financial statements are concerned, but the related IIA standard merely says, "Internal auditors should report the results of their audit work." Since the details under this standard are similar to the public sector standards, further explanation will be given later in the discussion of the public sector standards.

PUBLIC SECTOR STANDARDS

The Public Sector Assurance Sections (PSs) incorporate the CICA generally accepted auditing standards but also include terminology and concepts unique to the public sector. Many PAs accept engagements to audit government grants and programs that must follow the public sector sections. Therefore, these sections are important to PAs. Indeed, these public sector sections control all the government audit work performed by PA firms. The seven current Public Sector Assurance Sections (PSs) are as follows:

Public Sector Assurance Section PS 5000: Assurance in the Public Sector (Similar to IFAC Public Sector Guideline 1)

This first recommendation provides background information useful in interpreting the subsequent statements.

In the public sector, legislatures and other elected or appointed bodies provide authority for the management of financial resources. Management is responsible for the administration of a government entity and is accountable to the governing body and ultimately to the public the governing body represents. In the federal and provincial governments, management consists of the executive (i.e., Cabinet) and appointed officials (e.g., deputy ministers). Similarly, in local governments management consists of various combinations of elected and appointed officials.

Responsibilities of management include measuring the effectiveness of programs, directing operations and activities with due regard for economy and efficiency, maintaining adequate systems of control, ensuring compliance with applicable authorities, selecting and applying appropriate accounting policies and safeguarding assets.

To the extent required by their mandates, auditors help legislatures and other governing bodies to fulfill their responsibility by providing assurances as to the credibility of management reports, assessments of various administrative practices and other information. To fulfill these responsibilities, auditors must be independent of those they audit. They must be qualified and have access to all information pertinent to their mandate. Auditors must respect the confidentiality and sensitivity of the information that comes to their attention.

Government and other entities in the public sector employ resources to achieve a variety of social and economic goals, and while their audited financial statements provide an accounting of their financial operations, these statements by themselves may not adequately report management performance. The governing bodies of such entities may therefore be interested in information relating to:

1. Compliance with legislative and related authorities.
2. Accounting for and safeguarding of assets.
3. Adequacy of management control systems.
4. Economy and efficiency in the administration of resources.
5. Effectiveness of programs.

Auditors of governments and other entities in the public sector may be directed to report to the government bodies on these matters. Management, however, may not be required to make public representations on them. In such circumstances auditors provide their own assessments to governing bodies rather than attesting to the credibility of representation by management. This kind of reporting is a unique feature of public sector auditing.

Auditors in the public sector report in accordance with their mandates. Audit mandates specify what is required of auditors and give them the authority to carry out their work. These mandates are either established by contract or included in legislation.

The audit and reporting requirements specified in audit mandates establish the audit objectives. These objectives vary in accordance with the concerns of legislatures or other governing bodies. Most require auditors to examine and express opinions on the financial statements. Some may also require auditors to examine and report on the information listed above. Audits that fulfill these broad-scope mandates are often referred to as comprehensive audits. Some jurisdictions authorize auditors to bring any other matters to their attention that in the auditor's judgment should be reported: for example, questionable or nonproductive payments, or the adverse effects of specific legal requirements on the financial statements. Some auditors in the public sector are required to report deficiencies on an exception basis. In such circumstances the auditor's report should describe the nature of the mandate and any mitigating factors or other relevant context of the exception.

Auditors in the public sector should adhere to established rules of professional conduct such as those embodied in the codes of each provincial institute. The *CICA Handbook* sets out GAAS when expressing opinions on financial statements. Public Sector Assurance Sections supplement GAAS to recognize special circumstances in the public sector.

Summary of PS 5200:
Audit of Financial Statements in the Public Sector (Similar to IFAC's Public Sector Guideline 2)

This section deals with the application of generally accepted auditing standards to audits of financial statements of governments and other entities in the public sector. The public sector auditor should use GAAS as set out in *Section* 5100 of the *CICA Handbook*.

In some circumstances the public sector financial statements may have information different from that set out in *Section* 5100 (e.g., comparison of expenditures in the period with limits established by legislation). In these situations appropriate modifications may be required in the wording of the auditor's report.

Many public sector entities such as governments do not use GAAP but rather another appropriate disclosed basis of accounting (AADBA) considered appropriate by management or specifically prescribed by legislation. In the absence of GAAP appropriate for the reporting entity, auditors should express a reservation of opinion on any accounting policies that they believe result in misleading financial statements together with the reasons and, when practicable, quantification of the effect on the financial statements. In applying this statement the auditor needs to be satisfied that the AADBA does not result in misleading statements. It is not sufficient for auditors to conclude only that alternatives to the AADBA result in more appropriate presentations.

The statement ends with a discussion of the use of the words *present fairly* in conjunction with AADBA. This statement discourages use of the words *present fairly* with accounting policies that arise from legislated requirements, unless the auditor can explain in the report the context in which the term *present fairly* is used. Effectively, this statement says that there are two opinions when using AADBA in the public sector: (1) an opinion on conformity with AADBA, and (2) an opinion on the fairness of AADBA. Theoretically, therefore, it is possible to have a reservation on only one of these two opinions. (This is sometimes referred to as a two-part opinion.)

Summary of PS 5300:
Auditing for Compliance with Legislative and Related Authorities (Similar to IFAC Public Sector Study 3)

This section provides guidance for audit mandates that are required to:

1. Express an opinion on whether an entity complied with specified authorities or whether its transactions were carried out in compliance with specified authorities.
2. Express an opinion on whether the transactions that came to the auditors' notice in the course of discharging their other audit responsibilities were carried out in compliance with specified authorities.
3. Report instances of noncompliance with authorities observed in the course of discharging audit responsibilities.

In this section the word *authorities* refers to legislation, regulations, orders-in-council, directives, municipal bylaws, corporate bylaws and other instruments through which powers are established and delegated. Governments and other entities in the public sector may be subject to numerous authorities. Auditors of such entities require knowledge and familiarity of the authorities that apply to the entity being audited and to the transactions for which the entity is responsible.

E X H I B I T   18–1   **OPINIONS ON COMPLIANCE WITH SPECIFIED AUTHORITIES AUDITOR'S REPORT**

To the honourable Minister responsible for Entity Inc.

I have made an examination to determine whether Entity Inc. complied with the provisions of Part IV of the Government Agencies Act during the year ended March 31, 2001. My examination was made in accordance with generally accepted auditing standards, and accordingly included such tests and other procedures as I considered necessary in the circumstances.

In my opinion, Entity Inc. has complied, in all significant respects, with the provisions of Part IV of the Government Agencies Act during the year ended March 31, 2001.

City

Date   _____

                                                                        PA

The same general and examination standards apply to opinions on compliance as to opinions on financial statements (see *Section* 5100). However, since an opinion on compliance does not relate specifically to financial statements, different reporting standards are required.

In an opinion on compliance, the words *in all significant respects* are used because there may be minor instances of noncompliance that either may not be detected by the audit or may not be worthy of inclusion in the report. Significance is closely related to the materiality concept, and both terms encompass a broader concept than solely quantitative considerations. Auditors must exercise professional judgment when assessing the significance of noncompliance.

Depending on their mandates, auditors may examine and report on only a portion of the entity such as a program, a class of transactions or even a simple transaction. Accordingly, the auditor's report should clearly identify the entity or portion of its examination.

PS 5300 recommends that when expressing an opinion on compliance with specified authorities, the auditor's report should:

1. describe the scope of the audit by:
   (*a*) identifying the entity or portion thereof being reported on;
   (*b*) specifying the authorities against which compliance is being reported; and

E X H I B I T   18–2   **OPINIONS ON TRANSACTIONS COMING TO THE AUDITOR'S NOTICE IN THE COURSE OF DISCHARGING OTHER AUDIT RESPONSIBILITIES**

Auditor's Report

To the honourable Minister responsible for ABC Crown corporation

I have examined the balance sheet of ABC Crown Corporation as at March 31, 2001 and the statements of income, retained earnings and changes in financial position for the year then ended. My examination was made in accordance with generally accepted auditing standards, and accordingly included such tests and other procedures as I considered necessary in the circumstances.

In my opinion, these financial statements present fairly the financial position of the Corporation as at March 31, 2001 and the results of its operations and the changes in its financial position for the year then ended in accordance with generally accepted accounting principles applied on a basis consistent with that of the preceding year.

Further, I have examined the transactions that came to my notice in the course of the above mentioned examination of the financial statements of ABC Crown Corporation for the year ended March 31, 2001, to determine whether they were in accordance with Part XII of the Financial Administration Act, the regulations, the charter and bylaws of the corporation (and any directives given to the corporation pursuant to the Act). My examination of these transactions was made in accordance with generally accepted auditing standards, and accordingly included such tests and other procedures as I considered necessary in the circumstances. In my opinion, these transactions were, in all significant respects, in compliance with the authorities specified.

City

Date   _____

                                                                        PA

VFM audit mandates also have different reporting requirements. Many mandates require direct reporting about the entity. For example, auditors may report deficiencies, or provide an opinion on whether there is reasonable assurance, based on specified criteria, that there are no significant deficiencies in the system and practices examined. Auditors may be asked to attest to management assertions. When the mandate does not specify the reporting requirements, auditors would choose, often in consultation with their clients, how the results of the audit will be reported. The reporting requirements affect the nature and extent of work that must be performed in the audit.

PS 6420: Knowledge of the Entity in VFM Audits

Knowledge of the entity is important for audit planning. This knowledge is initially obtained on a first-time audit during the preliminary review of survey. On subsequent audits the preliminary review is a way of updating knowledge of the entity. The knowledge required in the preliminary review permits the auditor to identify the areas to be addressed in more depth later in the audit. The process of obtaining knowledge about the entity continues throughout the audit and subsequent information may have an effect on the initial planning decisions.

In conducting the preliminary review the auditor would examine the important features of the entity including (1) the nature of the entity, (2) accountability relationships, (3) program, operations and activities, (4) performance (5) resources, (6) systems controls and practices, (7) work environment, (8) government priorities, (9) external environment, (10) risks, (11) constraints, and (12) constituents.

In order to avoid possible misunderstanding, it is desirable for auditors to communicate their understanding of the entity to management and, when possible, to their clients. This may be a verbal or written communication, such as a report of the preliminary review.

Audit objectives and scope must be established for all VFM audits to provide a framework for the audit. They are closely linked. Audit objectives relate to why the audit is being conducted and are based on the audit mandate. Audit scope is defined in terms of the entity or portion thereof, the matters and the time period subject to audit.

Auditors generally consider factors such as significance, risk, auditability, resource requirements and timing when establishing or assessing the objectives and scope of a VFM audit. These factors are interrelated, and the sequence in which they are assessed depends on the circumstances of the audit.

Significance and Risk

In VFM auditing, significance (materiality) consists of qualitative and quantitative considerations, including (1) financial magnitude, (2) importance, (3) economic, social and environmental impact, (4) management action with respect to important issues previously raised, (5) interest expressed in the matters, and (6) impact of centralized function. These are discussed in paragraph 19 of the interpretation.

In setting the objectives and scope of a VFM audit, the auditor needs to consider components of audit risk, including the likelihood of an occurrence of a lack of due regard for money (inherent risk) and the likelihood of an inadequacy in a system, control or practice designed to ensure VFM (i.e., control risk).

Audit risk is affected by many factors, including (1) the diversity, consistency and clarity of the entity's objectives and goals, (2) the complexity of operations, (3) the complexity and quality of management information and control systems and external reporting, (4) the nature and degree of change in the environment or within the entity, (5) the program delivery method, (6) and the nature of transactions. These are discussed in paragraph 21 of the interpretation.

The auditor should identify all areas of the entity that are significant and/or high risk when establishing or assessing the audit objectives and scope. In doing so significance and risk would be assessed together. The auditor should plan to examine significant areas where the risk is high and other areas that are significant in terms of achieving VFM, even where the risk is judged low. Insignificant areas, whether the risk is high or low, may be reviewed to confirm the auditor's judgment, but would not generally be examined in detail.

Auditability relates to whether an audit can be done. The auditor needs to assess whether an audit with the proposed objectives and scope can be conducted. To accomplish this the auditor would consider whether:

- There are relevant approaches, methodologies and criteria available.
- The information or evidence required is likely to be available and can be obtained efficiently.

Criteria

Auditors need criteria against which to evaluate matters subject to audit. Criteria are reasonable and attainable standards of performance and control against which the adequacy of systems and practices and the extent of VFM can be assessed. Reasonable and attainable criteria are those that management can be realistically expected to meet.

Criteria must be suitable, or else inappropriate conclusions may be drawn. Suitability of criteria depends on factors such as (1) the audit objectives, (2) the activity, and (3) the approach to audit.

Characteristics of suitable criteria are the same as that for assurance engagements (*Sections 5025.36–.45*):

1. reliability
2. neutrality (freedom from bias)
3. relevance
4. understandability
5. completeness

These characteristics are considered together in identifying criteria and assessing their suitability. The relative importance of the characteristics in different circumstances is a matter of professional judgment. The level of detail of the audit conclusions is affected by the level of detail at which audit criteria are specified. At the planning stage criteria may be identified at a relatively general level. However, more specific criteria would generally be identified for audit examination. Criteria can be developed from many sources but may require interpretation and modification to ensure their suitability.

Audit Evidence

When planning a VFM audit, it is important that the auditor identify the probable nature, sources and availability of audit evidence required. Factors to consider include:

1. The effect of the audit approach.
2. The ability to integrate audit work with other audits or studies (e.g., work of internal auditors).
3. The effect of the reporting requirements. The amount of evidence required to form an overall opinion on an entity may be relatively greater than that needed to identify and report audit deficiencies.
4. The cost of obtaining evidence.

Audit Plan

The results of audit planning would be reflected in an audit plan. The audit plan documents key planning information and decisions such as:

- The auditor's understanding of the entity.
- The audit objectives.

- The scope of the audit (i.e., the entity or portion thereof, the matters and time period subject to audit).
- The planned criteria.
- The probable nature, sources and availability of evidence.
- The resources required.
- The work schedule.
- The reporting requirements and timing of the report.

As additional information becomes available during the audit, the audit plan may need to be modified. Inclusion of the above information in the audit plan provides evidence of compliance with VFM auditing standards on planning.

The VFM engagement concept relies extensively on the assurance engagement concept (*Section* 5025). An interesting feature of the Exposure Draft of *Section* 5025 was an illustration of a direct reporting engagement report using a VFM audit as an example. Although this illustration was dropped from the final version of 5025, we include it here as Exhibit 18–4 to show what a VFM audit report might look like when characterized as an assurance engagement. Note that this is not just a report of deficiencies, since an overall conclusion on the "subject-matter" is also provided.

PS 6430: Engaging and Using Specialists in VFM Audits

Because of the many potential subject matters involved, public sector auditors are very likely to require the assistance of experts in other fields in order to perform a competent audit. The auditor may therefore need to engage a specialist. In engaging a specialist the auditor needs to obtain reasonable assurance that the specialist is qualified for the engagement. This is done, for example, by considering the specialist's reputation, experience and any professional certification. The auditor also needs to consider the specialist's knowledge and proficiency in auditing. Generally, the more involved in the audit, the greater the degree of audit knowledge required of the specialist.

The auditor also needs to assess the objectivity of the specialist. In particular to determine that the specialist is free of conflicts of interest that could impair, or appear to impair, the specialist's professional judgment. The auditor should not engage a specialist whose objectivity may be impaired.

The auditor should also obtain a written confirmation of the specialist's understanding and agreement to the terms of the engagement.

The auditor needs to obtain reasonable assurance of the quality and reliability of the specialist's work and conclusions. This assurance is obtained for example by: understanding how the specialist's work relates to the audit objectives, considering other corroborating evidence, observing the specialist at work and discussing the findings with the specialist. The auditor needs to document how the specialist's work supports the audit opinion. The auditor's report may or may not refer to the reliance on the specialist. However, the auditor must always accept overall responsibility for all conclusions.

Summary of the Differences Between Traditional Auditing and VFM Auditing

1. In traditional audits, the objective is to render an opinion on the financial statements, and scope restrictions can result in qualification. In VFM audits, the auditor's mandate may provide the auditor with the discretion to establish the audit objectives and scope.

   In most cases VFM audits have mandates established through legislation or contracts. These mandates specify what is required for the auditor.

2. In VFM audits the objectives and scope vary from one audit to another, depending on the function and characteristics of the organization being audited.

E X H I B I T 18–4   **CICA EXPOSURE DRAFT STANDARDS FOR ASSURANCE ENGAGEMENTS—OCTOBER 1995 EXAMPLE REPORT 8**

- long-form report
- high level of assurance
- direct report engagement
- significant weakness
- qualification
- additional information contained in explanatory paragraphs

(This report would be one of several value-for-money audits reported together in an Auditor General's report. A cover page to the report would show the addressee as the Members of the Legislative Assembly and would be signed by the Auditor General. The report might also include detailed explanations of recommended remedial action and the Ministry's responses to each of the recommendations.)

CHAPTER Y
Value-For-Money Audit
Ministry of XY-COMMERCIALIZATION OF INTELLECTUAL PROPERTY

Audit objectives

We had two objectives for this audit. First, we assessed whether the Ministry of XY adequately identified, protected and developed the commercial potential of intellectual property arising from its research and development activities. Second, we assessed whether the Ministry collected royalties owed to the Crown.

During the period of January 1 to November 1, 19XX, we examined all significant activities of the Ministry in this regard, in particular the work of its Commercialization Unit.

Audit Criteria

We assessed the Ministry's performance against the following criteria.

1. The Ministry should recognize the commercial potential of intellectual property as early as possible in the life cycle of a research project.
2. The Ministry's rights over intellectual property should be safeguarded.
3. The commercial application of intellectual property should be fully developed at least cost.
4. All royalties due the Crown should be collected.

These criteria are discussed more fully in the detailed findings following the conclusion paragraph.

Management's responsibilities

In 1993–94, the Ministry spent $250 million on research and development. Since 1985, it has been the policy of the Ministry to protect and exploit the commercial potential of the intellectual property arising from its research work. The Ministry's Commercialization Unit is responsible for:

(a) assisting in the identification of intellectual property with promising commercial potential;
(b) safeguarding the ownership of intellectual property resulting from research funded by the Ministry;
(c) developing commercial application of the Ministry's intellectual property; and
(d) collecting royalties.

Once intellectual property has been identified, the Unit works in partnership with private sector contractors to develop its commercial potential. The Ministry collects $15 million in royalties annually.

Auditor's responsibility

Our responsibility is to express an opinion on the Ministry's performance in carrying out these responsibilities. To do so, we examined a representative sample of research projects underway during our audit that were at various stages in their life cycle. We also examined relevant management processes and practices.

We conducted our audit in accordance with generally accepted auditing standards for value-for-money audit engagements promulgated by the Canadian Institute of Chartered Accountants. Those standards require that we plan and perform an audit to obtain reasonable assurance in support of our conclusion. An audit includes examining evidence, on a test basis, in order to conclude on the audit objective based on the criteria. Our audit work was completed on December 31, 19XX.

Significant weakness

Our audit revealed that the Ministry was taking little action to systematically identify the commercial potential of its intellectual property. As a result, there was a considerable risk that the commercial potential of intellectual property was not recognized at all, or was recognized much later than it could have been.

Conclusion

In our opinion, except for the effect of the significant weakness described above, once the commercial potential of intellectual property had been recognized, the Ministry adequately protected and developed it, and adequately collected royalties due based on the criteria described above.

Detailed Findings

For the projects we examined, we found many instances where the Ministry had only recognized the commercial potential of its intellectual property several years after the discoveries had been made. There were also several instances where research papers had already been published although no assessment of the commercial potential had been done, thereby jeopardizing the possibility of protecting the Ministry's rights over any potential applications that might have resulted. There are two reasons for this. First, the Ministry does not consider whether a research project might result in intellectual property with commercial potential when these projects are initiated. Second, the Ministry does not attempt to monitor projects as they progress; for example, by assessing their commercial potential at pre-determined intervals. Instead, when commercial potential was identified, it was because a research team had recognized, or is recognized much later than it could be.

For those research projects that we examined where the potential for commercialization had been identified, we found that appropriate legal steps had been taken to protect the Ministry's legal rights. For the most part, this was accomplished through patent applications as well as license agreements and copyrights. We also found that appropriate security arrangements were in place. However, as discussed above, there may be other projects when protection might have been appropriate but had not been sought.

The Ministry contracts with private sector firms to develop the commercial application of intellectual property. If a commercial product results, the development firm receives an exclusive license to exploit it. The Ministry receives royalties in return (usually 30%). In this way, the Ministry passes on the cost, and the risk, of development to its partner. Although a high failure rate would normally be expected, we found that fully three-quarters of the intellectual property that contractors had attempted to develop had resulted in a marketable product.

We found that the Ministry collects the royalties owed to the Crown. The Ministry is exercising satisfactory control over this income. It receives an annual return from contractors on royalties due and takes appropriate action to verify these amounts are correct and are collected on a timely basis. [further background and elaboration of the findings]

According to PS 6410.07, an auditor always has to use his or her professional judgment when faced with a broad mandate and define it in specific terms with specific objectives. In the case where the mandate is specific, an auditor must still assess the objectives' appropriateness.

3. In VFM audits much of the audit focuses on matters that are not necessarily financial, such as human resource management.

4. There is no body of standards analogous to GAAP. Standards may be management-defined, legislative or defined by professions and associations.

5. The nature and sources of evidence may differ from those in financial statement auditing. PS 6410.25 states that sufficient appropriate evidence should be obtained to afford a reasonable basis to support the content of the auditor's report.

   Since a VFM audit can be required to report deficiencies rather than to form an overall opinion, the amount of evidence needed may be lower.

   The fact that a VFM audit can focus more on processes than results also influences the nature of the evidence.

6. A VFM audit will tend to use a multidisciplinary audit team with expertise in different areas (like economics, statistics, engineering). The make-up of the group will depend on the type of organization being audited and the needs of the mandate.

7. VFM audits may not relate to a standard time period, such as a year-end.

8. There is no standard audit report for VFM audits. The form of the report will depend on the mandate, and can take the form of a report on deficiencies, or an overall opinion or an attestation of management assertions. By contrast, an audit of the financial statements of an entity has a standard report prescribed by the *CICA Handbook*.

9. VFM audits use the concept of "significance" rather than materiality. Significance, broadly defined, will include the following considerations:
   a. *Financial magnitude.* Areas with larger dollar amounts will receive greater attention.
   b. *Importance.* Some programs, operations and activities are more important than others in the entity's strategy to achieve its objectives.
   c. *Economic, social and environmental impact.* A project or program with a small budget may have a significant impact on the population, or the environment.
   d. *Previous VFM recommendations.* The auditor may choose to emphasize deficient areas previously pointed out that appear not to have improved.

10. The concept of "audit risk" takes on unique meanings in a VFM audit. "Inherent risk" is the probability of lack of due regard to value-for-money. "Control risk" is the probability that a system, control or practice designed to ensure that VFM will fail. "Detection risk" is the risk that the auditor will fail to detect significant errors.

In summary, there are many differences between traditional financial statement and VFM audits. However, as noted in Chapter 15, the assurance engagement concept introduced in *Handbook Section* 5025 incorporates, with modifications, many of the concepts of VFM audits. This is understandable, since an objective of *Section* 5025 is to provide an umbrella framework for *all* audits, including VFM audits.

ECONOMY, EFFICIENCY AND EFFECTIVENESS AUDITS

Economy and efficiency measures are fairly straightforward. Auditors can use these tools and techniques to evaluate them: financial and organizational analysis; computer-assisted data analysis and EDP testing; value analysis; productivity measurement and quantitative analysis; methods analysis using work study techniques; work measurement; and productivity–opportunity matrices. Economy is related to the price variance, while efficiency is related to the efficiency variance of standard variance analysis in managerial accounting for control. The products here, however, are usually services or activities instead of tangible goods, and thus it may not be possible to measure them as discrete units.

Effectiveness is more difficult to define and evaluate, but it may be helpful to view it as a type of "volume" or "capacity" variance where "volume(s)" are measured relative to some objective or objectives of the organization. The Canadian Comprehensive Auditing Foundation (CCAF) prepared a report called *Effectiveness Reporting and Auditing in the Public Sector* to deal with the question of effectiveness. The report enumerated 12 different "attributes" of effectiveness that the auditor must examine in performing a value-for-money audit. The attributes are:

1. *Management direction.* How well integrated are the organization's objectives and component programs with management decision making?

2. *Relevance.* Does the program still serve the originally intended purpose?

3. *Appropriateness.* Is the program's structure appropriate considering its purpose?

4. *Achievement of results.* Has the program realized its goals and objectives?

5. *Acceptance.* How well have constituents or customers received the service or output of the organization?

6. *Secondary impacts.* Has the organization caused any other intended or not-intended results?

7. *Costs and productivity.* How efficient has the organization been?

8. *Responsiveness.* Has the organization adapted well to changes in its environment?

9. *Financial results.* Has the organization accounted properly for revenues and expenses, and valued assets and liabilities properly?

10. *Working environment.* Is the work environment appropriate, given the organization's purpose, and does it promote initiative and achievement?

11. *Protection of assets.* Does the organization safeguard valuable assets?

12. *Monitoring and reporting.* Does the organization know where it stands with regard to key performance indicators?

Effectiveness can mean much more than the extent to which program objectives are being met and encompasses all the above characteristics.

When defining effectiveness, the client (Parliament or other legislative bodies) may have completely different perceptions than the stakeholder (the program recipient).

Audit mandates specify what is required of auditors and provide auditors with the authority to carry out their work and report. The amount of discretion an auditor has in establishing the objectives and scope of the VFM audit varies. Some VFM audit mandates embodied in legislation provide only general direction about objectives and scope. In such cases the auditor decides on audit objectives and scope for a particular VFM audit. Other legislated mandates, such as that for special examinations of federal Crown corporations, may be more specific in defining objectives and scope. In contractual mandates, audit objectives and scope are usually specified by the client. In such cases the auditor would assess the appropriateness of the audit objectives and scope before accepting the engagement.

VFM audit mandates also have different reporting requirements. Many mandates require direct reporting about the entity. For example, auditors may report deficiencies, or provide an opinion on whether there is reasonable assurance, based on specified criteria, that there are no significant deficiencies in the systems and practices examined. Auditors may be asked to attest to management assertions. When the mandate does not specify the reporting requirements, auditors would choose, often in consultation with their clients, how the results of the audit will be reported. The reporting requirements affect the nature and extent of work that must be performed in the audit.

Government audits require more work on compliance and reporting on internal control than external auditors normally do in an audit of financial statements of a private business.

The reason is the public's concern for laws, regulations and control of expenditures. One-third of the Canadian economy and over $100 billion of federal funds used is represented by the public sector, so the stakes are high.

R E V I E W
CHECKPOINTS

18.9   Identify the twelve attributes of effectiveness.

18.10   What is a comprehensive audit?

18.11   Explain the difference between compliance and VFM audits.

18.12   Compare and contrast economy, efficiency and effectiveness measures of performance. Which of these is the hardest to audit? Explain.

AUDIT ASSIGNMENTS

One question you might ask is this: "How are public sector and internal auditors assigned to an audit job in the first place?" Herbert pointed out that government auditors are assigned as a result of:

- Specific statutory or policy requirements for audits.

- Legislative, audit committee or executive department requests.

- Auditors' own initiative resulting from recognition of the importance of a program, activity or organization because of the size of its revenues, expenditures or investment in assets.

- Auditors' own initiative resulting from recognition of the potential importance of a new program or activity.

- Auditors' response to a request for proposal to audit a specific organization, program, activity or function.[1]

Internal auditors undertake specific assignments for similar reasons. Corporate policy or the audit committee of the board of directors may require certain audits, or executives may request them. Also, a well-managed internal audit department will often take the initiative to recommend an agenda or schedule of audit assignments.

Accountants in public practice most often get involved in public sector audits as a result of responding to an agency's request for proposal (RFP). Well-prepared RFPs specify the audit work requested, making clear what extent of expanded scope auditing is needed. When responding to an RFP, a public accountant is effectively bidding for the job in competition with other respondents. The response to an RFP will specify the engagement objectives and nature of services, the engagement scope and limitations, the roles and responsibilities of the auditee's personnel and other consultants, the engagement approach and methods, the manner and timing of reporting, the work schedule and the fee.

The process of getting the assignment is important because it includes an understanding and definition of the objectives of the audit. Auditors must know these objectives—whether they relate to financial reports, compliance audit, internal control review or economy, efficiency and effectiveness studies—in order to plan and manage the evidence-gathering activities. Governmental and internal auditors do not need to reply to an RFP but must take similar care in planning the assignment.

---

[1] Adapted from Leo Herbert, *Auditing the Performance of Management* (Belmont, Calif.: Lifetime Learning Publications, 1979), p. 24.

Evidence Gathering
· · · · · · · · · · · ·

LEARNING OBJECTIVE

6. Describe a sequence of work in governmental and internal audits in terms of preliminary survey, evaluation of administrative control, evidence-gathering field work and report preparation.

The evidence-gathering field work can best be described in general terms as an application of a practical audit method for solving audit problems.

- *Problem recognition.* Ascertain the pertinent facts and circumstances. In addition to overall engagement objectives, identify specific objectives in detail. Define problem areas or opportunities for improvement. Define program goals.
- *Evidence collection.* Select and perform procedures designed to produce information related to problem areas, opportunities for improvement or achievement of program goals.
- *Evidence evaluation.* Evaluate activities in terms of economy, efficiency and goal achievement. Report findings and recommendations.[2]

Preliminary Survey

Most government and many internal audit engagements begin with a **preliminary survey**. A preliminary survey is an auditor's familiarization with the organization, program or activity being audited, gained by gathering information, but without detailed investigation or verification procedures. It is designed to identify problem areas needing additional review in order to plan and accomplish the audit.[3] Sawyer has pointed out that the preliminary survey is a logical means of salvaging order out of a complex chaos of information by answering these questions: What is the job? Who does it? Why is it done? How is it done?[4] These questions require auditors to have a business sense about the audit objectives so that they can get the big picture.

Using interview techniques, auditors can learn about the nature of the entity under audit and its program goals, the organizational structure of the entity, its policies and procedures, its administrative and internal control systems, its financial data and its nonfinancial measurement system. In many respects VFM audits depend on the administrative controls of the entity and the nonfinancial measures of its program results. For example, efficiency, economy and effectiveness may be measured not only in terms of monetary expenditure but, more importantly, in terms of employee productivity, student educational achievement, medical service delivered, research and development achievement, environmental effectiveness or other outputs.

As a part of the preliminary survey, auditors must determine the specific standards for economy, efficiency and effectiveness results relevant in the circumstances. Some of these standards for government agencies can be found in laws, legislative committee reports, legislative or administrative orders and resolutions, local ordinances and resolutions, grant proposals and contracts made by a grantee or agency. Similarly, business units may be under orders from the board of directors or may be undertaking a project resulting from an internal proposal that sets forth budgets and objectives.

Standards for economy and efficiency are sometimes hard to determine. Auditors' challenges are to determine the appropriate standards as objectively as possible. An increasing number of sources are available. For example, the publications of the Urban Institute, the International City Management Association, and the National Planning Association are sources of standards. These organizations have produced data about various city services and social services, transportation, energy and environmental protection programs. Also, it would appear that the various publications of the Criteria for Control Committee of the CICA should provide useful guidance on control issues (see below). Auditors should not

---

[2] Adapted from *Guidelines for CPA Participation in Government Audits to Evaluate Economy, Efficiency, and Program Results*, MAS Guideline Series No. 6 (New York: AICPA, 1977), p. 19.

[3] Adapted from *Public Sector Audit Guidelines #1: "Planning VFM Audits"* (March 1990).

[4] Lawrence B. Sawyer, *Sawyer's Internal Auditing* (Altamonte Springs, Fla.: The Institute of Internal Auditors, 1988), p. 129.

overlook available reference books and should also be able to apply good management principles to recognize underutilized facilities, nonproductive work, costly procedures and overstaffing or understaffing in particular circumstances.

The preliminary survey should be an organized activity, with a written plan or program. It should not be a haphazard "get acquainted" activity conducted loosely. It should lead to a program for study and evaluation of the administrative controls of the business unit, program, activity or function being audited.

Emphasis on Administrative Controls

Auditors have classified controls into two broad categories: administrative controls and internal accounting controls. **Administrative control** has been defined as the plan of organization and all methods and procedures that are concerned mainly with operational efficiency and adherence to managerial policies and that usually relate only indirectly to financial records. This management function is directly associated with the responsibility for achieving the organization's objectives. It is the starting point for establishing accounting control of transactions. Administrative control sets the stage for detailed accounting control.

Another aspect of control is **internal accounting control**. It consists of the plan of organization and procedures designed to prevent, detect and correct accounting errors that may occur and get recorded in ledger accounts and financial statements. The external auditors' assessment of control risk is a fairly complicated subject covered in Chapter 6 and other chapters in this textbook.

In connection with governmental and internal audits, however, auditors are very concerned with the administrative controls because they directly affect economy, efficiency and effectiveness of activities. Administrative control is a broad concept involving all management activities, such as responsibilities for production, quality control, transportation, research and development, personnel relations and many other areas. The focus is not limited to accounting-related activities. This breadth makes it difficult to express specific standards and objectives for administrative control.

The new guidance provided by the Criteria of Control Committee (discussed in Chapter 14) will be equally useful in evaluating administrative controls. The Control Criteria Study views internal controls much more broadly than previous recommendations and in particular includes behavioural factors, objective setting, values, visions and ethics as part of the control system.[5]

Chapter 6 explained specific standards and objectives of internal control used by auditors of financial statements. As a reminder, you should think of accounting controls as being very specific and accounting-related and of administrative controls as being more general and management-related. Some examples illustrating the contrast are given in Exhibit 18–5.

One key question is this: Given the lack of specific standards, how can you cope with the need to study and evaluate administrative control? Answer: It is not easy! You need to rely on knowledge of marketing, management, production, finance, statistics, business law, economics, taxation, operations research, political science, physical sciences and other subjects. These are some of the nonaccounting courses you can take in your university curriculum. Such studies are important because they serve as a foundation for organizing your early practical experiences and your development of a common sense in business management. Last, but far from least, you will also need to be able to exercise imagination to adapt your classroom and on-the-job experience to specific audit engagement circumstances. You can expect very little to be routine in a study and evaluation of administrative control, and that is what makes governmental and internal audit assignments such exciting challenges.

---

[5] B.J. Zimmerman, "Message in a Hologram," *CA Magazine*, June/July 1995, p. 52.

EXHIBIT 18–5   **ACCOUNTING AND ADMINISTRATIVE CONTROLS**

Accounting Control Techniques	Administrative Control Techniques
Cash	
Establish a control total of cash receipts as soon as they are received, so that subsequent deposits, journal entries, and ledger entries can be compared to the total.	Prepare timely forecasts of cash flow and provide for temporary borrowing to cover needs, or for temporary investment to generate interest income.
Accounts Receivable	
Reconcile customers' subsidiary ledger accounts with the control account total to control bookkeeping accuracy.	Prepare an aged trial balance of customer receivables for the credit manager's collection efforts.
Inventory	
Assign physical control responsibility to a storekeeper to safeguard inventory from theft or other unauthorized removal.	Co-ordinate inventory purchases with sales and production forecasts so that stockout losses and inventory carrying costs can be optimized.

Audit Procedures

LEARNING OBJECTIVE

7. Explain the function of standards and measurements in economy and efficiency and program results audits.

The general evidence-gathering procedures in governmental and internal audits are about the same as the ones used by external auditors in the audit of financial statements. These procedures are explained in general in Chapter 4 and in more specific terms in other chapters in this textbook. However, the audit problems are usually different in audits of economy, efficiency and program results.

Governmental and internal auditors must be as objective as possible when developing conclusions about efficiency, economy and effectiveness results. This objectivity is achieved by (1) finding standards for evaluation and (2) using measurements of actual results so that the actual results can be compared to the standards. Finding standards and deciding on relevant measurements takes imagination. Sawyer has presented two examples, one rather routine and the other very unusual, to illustrate the role of standards and measurements.[6]

Routine Problem.   Evaluate the promptness with which materials pass through a receiving inspection before being accepted and placed in inventory.

- *Source of a standard.* Management policy about acceptable delay between date of receipt and date of inspection approval.
- *Measurement unit.* Number of days between date of receipt and date of inspection approval.
- *Audit procedures.* Select a sample of inspection reports and record the two relevant dates and the number of elapsed days. Develop descriptive statistics of the sample data. Compare these measurements to the management policy standard. Report the findings and conclusions.

Unusual Problem.   Determine whether the company's test pilots are reporting aircraft defects properly.

- *Background information.* Test pilots fill out check sheets as they fly, recording such things as pressure instrument readings under various flight conditions. If a reading is outside acceptable limits, the pilot is supposed to prepare a report, which will trigger an investigation of the reason for the unacceptable instrument reading.
- *Source of a standard.* Engineering specifications of acceptable limits for pressure readings under specific flight conditions. For example, the fuel pressure at 20,000 feet and a power setting of 85 percent should be between 90 and 100 pounds.

---

[6] Lawrence B. Sawyer, *Sawyer's Internal Auditing* (Altamonte Springs, Fla.: The Institute of Internal Auditors, 1988), pp. 229–30.

AUDITOR'S REPORT A LIFE-AND-DEATH STORY

Provincial Auditor Douglas Archer has made a damning indictment of Ontario's social services system.

The auditor usually reports on areas where the government of the day has wasted money. That always provides interesting reading.

But money is just money, not usually a matter of life and death.

Yesterday, Archer's annual report was chillingly different.

The auditor's staff inspected six institutions which are supposed to care for developmental handicapped adults—those who used to be called retarded people. Three are operated by the government and three by nonprofit agencies.

Here is what the auditors found.

- In one nonprofit agency, 15 residents had died over two years as a result of problems associated with "feeding and nutrition."

  That is three times the usual mortality rate for such institutions. When auditors attempted to check with the Ministry of Community and Social Services about the deaths, they found it blithely unworried.

  Indeed, the ministry—which is responsible for inspection—could initially find written reports on only five of the 15 deaths. (It later found six more reports in another filing cabinet.)

  Later, in the Legislature, Premier Bob Rae identified the institution as the Brantwood Residential Development Centre in Brantford.
- In another instance, auditors found residents in one non-profit agency had gone 10 years without vision or hearing checkups.

  In two of the three nonprofit agencies audited, residents had gone for more than a year without medical or dental examinations.

  All this occurred in spite of the fact that the agencies had been inspected by the ministry—and in spite of the fact that inspectors are required to ensure all residents receive annual checkups.
- Ministry inspection reports were misleading. Inspectors reported that all "serious occurrences" involving the care of residents at the nonprofit agencies were reported.

  But the auditors stated flatly that serious occurrences were "seldom reported."
- Abuse. The auditors said they had evidence to suggest that abuse of residents of provincially run institutions is more widespread than reported.

  The auditors say that statistics on abuse are "questionable" and found that in one year, 17 cases of abuse had not been reported.

  They add that staff members said they feared reprisals from their co-workers if they reported cases of abuse.

  Indeed, unlike nonprofit institutions, provincially run centres for adult developmentally handicapped people are not inspected at all.

  That's bad since, as the auditors note, residents of these institutions are "particularly susceptible and vulnerable to abuse."
- Inadequate inspection of old-age homes. These institutions for the care of the elderly are run by municipalities and charitable organizations but supervised by government.

However, the auditors found that inspections were carried out by bureaucrats rarely qualified to judge matters such as diet and nursing care.

Government inspectors made no effort to ensure that required fire safety and sanitary inspections were carried out.

Usually, homes were given too much advance notice of inspections, they were able to clean up their act beforehand, the report says.

All of this is disturbing information. What disturbs particularly is the way in which attempts to oversee these institutions seem to have failed.

> In the case of provincially run institutions for retarded adults, there simply is no outside inspection, beyond the usual ones required by, for instance, the fire code.
>
> Here the ministry seems to think government operation provides its own safeguards.
>
> In the case of government-regulated, nonprofit institutions, inspection seems to be haphazard at best.
>
> The question of inspection is particularly crucial now. For the government has been engaged in an effort to shift people from large institutions—such as residences for the developmentally handicapped—into smaller, community-based group homes.
>
> Done right, this could be of great advantage to the individual.
>
> But to be done right, this so-called deinstitutionalization requires vigilant inspection. Society must be sure these people are not merely dumped and forgotten.
>
> Given the inadequate way in which Queen's Park is able to monitor even its existing institutions, the future for this particular path does not look bright.
>
> *Source:* Thomas Walkom, *The Toronto Star*, November 28, 1990, A23. Reprinted with permission—The Toronto Star Syndicate.

- *Measurement unit.* Number of times an instrument reading is reported improperly by a test pilot.
- *Audit procedures.* Select a sample of check sheets and related test pilot reports. Compare each instrument reading on the check sheet to the engineering specifications. Read the test pilot's reports and look for no unfavourable mention of acceptable readings and for appropriate mention of unacceptable readings. Tally and describe all report deficiencies. Summarize the findings and report the conclusions. (Notice that the procedure involves reading the test pilot's reports for two possible deficiencies— inappropriate reporting of acceptable readings as well as failure to report unacceptable readings.)

When dealing with standards, measurements and comparisons, auditors must keep inputs and outputs in perspective. Evidence about inputs—personnel hours and cost, materials quantities and cost, asset investment—are most important in connection with reaching financial audit conclusions. For economy, efficiency and effectiveness conclusions, however, output measurements are equally important. Management has the responsibility for devising information systems to measure output. Such measurements should correspond to program objectives set forth in laws, regulations, administrative policies, legislative reports and other such sources. Auditors must realize that output measurements are usually not expressed in financial terms—for example, water quality improvement, educational progress, weapons effectiveness, materials-inspection time delays and test pilot reporting accuracy.

Many economy and efficiency audits and most effectiveness audits are output-oriented. Auditors need to be careful not to equate program activity with program success without measuring program results. (In contrast, with respect to financial statement audits, the auditor's primary concern is with reporting on the accounting for inputs.) An outstanding example of the difference is illustrated in the box above. It deals with a newspaper article by Thomas Walkom of the *Toronto Star* about a provincial auditor's report that shocked Ontario taxpayers several years ago. Part of what caused the media sensation was that it was not medical officers or health officials who made this discovery but auditors merely trying to assess effectiveness of nursing home care.

. . . .

R E V I E W
CHECKPOINTS

18.13   What is a request for proposal (RFP)? And what significance does it have in a governmental audit engagement performed by an independent PA in public practice?

18.14   Specify and describe a general analytical approach that can be used in audits of economy, efficiency and program results.

18.15   Which four major blocks of work characterize governmental and internal audit engagements?

18.16   What information can an auditor expect to obtain in a preliminary survey?

18.17   Where can an auditor expect to find information about economy, efficiency and program results standards for governmental agencies? for business units? for municipal services and social programs?

18.18   What is administrative control? What does it accomplish?

18.19   How can governmental and internal auditors try to achieve objectivity when developing conclusions about economy, efficiency or program results?

. . . .

REPORTING
. . . .

LEARNING OBJECTIVE

8. List and explain several requirements for public sector and internal audit reports.

Public sector and internal audit reports are not standardized like external auditors' reports on financial statements. Each report is different because governmental and internal auditors need to communicate findings on a variety of assignments and audit objectives. The key criterion for such a report is its ability to communicate clearly and concisely.

Public Sector Audit Report

Exhibit 18–6 contains an example of findings from a report by government auditors. This example is condensed from a more lengthy report in the *1994 Annual Report by the Office of the Provincial Auditor of Ontario*. It shows the nature and emphasis of a governmental audit report.

The emphasis is on the effectiveness of a drinking water surveillance program for Ontario. The general audit assignment was to assess how well the program was working. One feature of effectiveness is highlighted in the excerpts in Exhibit 18–6: priority should be given to those plants identified as having significant compliance problems. The report consists of a general description of the objectives of the surveillance program, the objective of the audit, the resulting recommendations (which are numbered—here recommendation 3.06), and the ministry responses.

As noted in Chapter 15, such reports may not be considered assurance engagements under *Section* 5025 if all they do is report on deficiencies found. With exception reporting there is always the risk that readers may draw unwarranted conclusions (such as, for example in this case, concluding that the drinking water is unsafe). Therefore, it is important that a clear description of the specific objectives and scope of the particular audit be included in the report and that the report emphasize that deficiencies are reported in relation to them. "The more readers are told about what was done, for what purpose, and the results, the less likely they will be to reach unwarranted conclusions."[7] This seems to be the case with Exhibit 18–6, and therefore it likely meets the conditions of an assurance engagement as defined in *Section* 5025. Also see K. Duggan, "To Assure or Not to Assure," *CA Magazine,* January–February 1997, pp. 46–48.

Unfortunately, in this particular instance the provincial auditor recommendations were not followed up. Instead after a change in provincial government in 1995, the Ontario Environment Ministry budget was cut 43 per cent. This is now widely suspected to have contributed to the Walkerton Ontario water contamination tragedy in mid-May 2000 in

---

[7] D. Hillier, "VFM Audit Standards," *CA Magazine,* October 1987, p. 48.

EXHIBIT 18–6   **QUALITY OF DRINKING WATER**
Drinking Water Surveillance Program

The Drinking Water Surveillance Program for Ontario was established to monitor and provide reliable current information on drinking water quality. The program was started in 1986 and is intended to eventually include all water treatment plants in Ontario.

The program tests water samples for the presence and levels of 180 substances including bacteria, inorganic chemicals, organic chemicals such as PCB and dioxin, and radioactive substance. Sampling frequency ranges from monthly for new plants to semi-annually for established plants with underground water sources. The Ministry publishes the results of this program annually.

As of December 31, 1993, 120 of the 490 (23 percent) water treatment plants were covered by the program. However, it should be noted that these two plants serve about seven million people or 70 percent of Ontario's population. The Ministry plans to extend this program to about 15 new plants every year. In general, the results have indicated that water treatment plants monitored to date by the program are producing water of acceptable quality.

Inspection Program

Water treatment plants collect samples of their intake and outflow for laboratory tests to assess the quality of their treatment processes. The Ministry inspects all treatment plants every two years to verify compliance with Ministry guidelines.

A 1992 summary report by the Ministry on the inspection of 490 water treatment plants indicated that over 120 of them had significant compliance problems, including:

- not performing sufficient sample testing for bacteria and toxic chemicals;
- not conforming with minimum guidelines for treating bacteria; and
- not meeting Ministry guidelines on treated water quality.

We observed that the plants with significant compliance problems were mainly smaller plants serving about 10 percent of Ontario's population. Furthermore, over 90 percent of these plants were not yet covered by the Drinking Water Surveillance Program.

Our review of 23 current water treatment inspection files indicated similar problems. We noted that problems which were not followed up at the time of our audit had been outstanding for approximately 17 months on average.

We are concerned about the lack of timely followup action on problems identified by inspection staff and the inadequate monitoring of plants not covered by the Drinking Water Surveillance Program.

Recommendations:

Instead of relying on a two-year inspection cycle of all water treatment plants, the Ministry should give priority to follow-up on those plants identified as having significant compliance problems.

Plants having significant compliance problems should be brought into the Drinking Water Surveillance Program as quickly as is practical.

Ministry Response

The Ministry has created a new, proactive inspections unit in each district that will be responsible for plant inspections along with other facilities. Inspection frequency will be based on risk assessment factors rather than routine cycles so that plants with historic problems will be inspected more frequently. Improved reporting and abatement followup is an important element of this new approach to inspections.

The correction of problems at water treatment plants often requires capital work, etc., which may take two or more years to complete. During this time, however, abatement work is ongoing and staff do not wait for the next scheduled inspection to follow-up.

Priority of additions to the Drinking Water Surveillance Program is now being given to plants presently not meeting the sampling guidelines.

Abatement staff will continue to work with plants to obtain conformance with provincial guidelines and policy.

Source: 1994 Annual Report by the Office of the Provincial Auditor of Ontario, pp. 80–81. © Queen's Printer for Ontario, 1994. Reproduced with permission of The Office of the Provincial Auditor of Ontario.

which six people died and 2000 others had fallen ill. In addition, by mid-July 2000 a watch-list had been prepared pinpointing 120 cities, towns, seniors' residences, schools and camp-sites across Ontario that had problems with their water supply. Also following Walkerton, an inspection blitz on Ontario's water treatment plants found almost two-thirds of them to be deficient, ranging from inadequate monitoring to insufficient chlorination. This suggests that the budget cuts may have led to a major reduction in water quality relative to 1993 as described in Exhibit 18-6. This rather dramatically illustrates the relevance of Provincial Auditors in government accountability. However, if a government fails to act on the audi-tor recommendations then that is the fault of the government not the auditor.

Internal Audit Report

The reporting stage is the internal auditor's opportunity to capture management's undivided attention. To be effective, a report cannot be unduly long, tedious, technical or laden with minutiae. It must be accurate, concise, clear and timely. There is no standard form for inter-nal audit reports, and there will likely never be one, given the diversity of assignments and the diversity of managers' abilities and interests. Unlike external audit reports, internal audit reports are usually considered "open" until a formal written reply to the recommen-dations is received from the management of the audited unit or department. This reply, which would also go to the same people as the audit report, such as the audit committee, would indicate which recommendations were implemented or which were considered not cost-efficient. Only after the written response is received is the audit considered closed. Another procedure unique to internal (and public sector) audit reporting is that the criti-cisms and recommendations are usually reviewed with the audit management before they are included in the final report.

Exhibit 18–7 contains an example of an internal audit report on the study of a trans-portation operation. The report begins with a summary or overall conclusion that conveys the essential findings and captures the reader's attention.

Consulting Engagement Reports by PAs

In contrast to the well-defined areas of audit and tax practice, public accountants' practice in consulting services can be described only by cataloguing a variety of such services. On a specific engagement basis, independent accountants, acting as management consultants, perform services in areas as diverse as those performed by governmental and internal audi-tors. Consultants may accent engagements to evaluate compliance, economy and efficiency, and program results. Consequently, consulting engagement reports exhibit the same char-acteristics as internal audit reports and public sector reports: The problem is identified, some explanation of the investigation is given, and the findings and recommendations are expressed clearly and concisely.

The consulting report in Exhibit 18–8 is the full text of an actual report. The assignment was a relatively uncomplicated one—evaluation of the system for controlling inventory—and the resultant report is a good example of clarity and direct communication.

The consulting report, like the governmental and internal audit reports, gets to the main problem quickly, identifying the source of trouble as the warehouse operation. The con-sultants found and reported that the trouble was not the result of a basic system weakness. The report makes specific points and recommendations on inventory-handling procedures as well as on record-keeping procedures. This particular engagement required not only ordinary expertise as an accountant but also an ability to perceive some elementary mate-rials-handling problems and offer good managerial solutions.

E X H I B I T 18–7   **INTERNAL AUDIT REPORT (excerpts)**

XYZ /Corporation
Audit Project Rbx-18 August 16, 20XX

	Audit Highlights
Highway Transportation Department (A regularly scheduled review)	
Prior Audit	No deficiency findings
Audit Coverage	1. Equipment maintenance and vehicle dispatching.
	2. Fuel, parts and repair services.
Overall Opinion	In general, the operation was functioning in a reasonably satisfactory manner.
	We found some control weaknesses. The most serious involved the lack of separation of duties in the procurement of parts and services. Steps are being taken to correct these weaknesses.
Executive Action Required	None

Summary Report

Foreward:

   This report covers the result of our regularly scheduled review of the activities of the Highway Transportation Department. Our last review of the department's activities disclosed no deficiencies.

   The department's primary responsibilities are (1) to transport personnel and materials and (2) to maintain and repair automotive equipment.

   At the time of our review, about 50 employees were assigned to the department. Operating costs (not including labor) for equipment rental, repair parts and services, and fuel and oil are projected to reach about $900,000 for 20XX. Mileage for the year will total about 5 million miles.

   During this review, we issued one progress report to bring to management attention certain matters requiring prompt corrective action.

Purpose:

We have made an examination of the Highway Transportation Department's principal activities to determine whether they were being controlled adequately and effectively. In performing our review, we examined the system of controls concerning the following activities.

   1. Equipment maintenance and vehicle dispatching, including (a) scheduling preventive maintenance inspections, (b) performing regular maintenance and repairs, and (c) dispatching cars and trucks.
   2. Ordering, receiving, and disbursing fuel and parts and obtaining automotive repair services.

Opinions and Findings:

   We formed the opinion that adequate controls had been provided over the activities we reviewed, except for lack of separation of duties in the procurement of parts and services. (Some) other matters of lesser significance likewise involved control weaknesses.

   We also formed the opinion that despite the control weaknesses we had discovered, the functions we reviewed were being performed in a generally satisfactory manner.

   Our conclusions and findings on each of the groups of activities covered in our examination are summarized in the following paragraphs.

Equipment Maintenance and Vehicle Dispatching:

   Adequate controls have been provided to make sure that (1) automotive equipment would receive inspection and preventive maintenance in accordance with manufacturers' recommendations and (2) truck and car dispatching would be accomplished in accordance with established procedures.

   We examined preventive maintenance reports and related control records and satisfied ourselves that maintenance was being properly scheduled, monitored, and performed. We also examined documentation supporting vehicle dispatching and observed the dispatching operations; we concluded that dispatching was being adequately controlled and performed.

E X H I B I T 18–7   (concluded)

Ordering, Receiving, and Disbursing Fuel and Parts, and Obtaining Vehicle Repair Services:

Controls had been provided to make sure that fuel, parts, and outside repair services were (1) ordered when needed, (2) recorded upon receipt, and (3) properly approved for payment, and that the disbursement of fuel and parts was adequately documented.

We found, however, (1) a lack of appropriate separation of duties in the procurement of parts and services, and (2) what we considered to be inadequate surveillance over the withdrawal of gas and oil by vehicle operators. These matters are discussed more fully in the Supplement to this Summary Report.

We examined representative samples of (1) reports, records, and blanket purchase orders covering the procurement and receipt of supplies and services, and (2) the logs and records covering fuel withdrawals. Despite the control weaknesses, we concluded on the basis of our tests that the functions were being performed in a reasonably satisfactory manner. We made an analysis of the fuel pump meter records and compared them with the amounts of fuel recorded by vehicle operators. The results showed little variance between the two, indicating that fuel withdrawals were being properly recorded.

The deficiency findings previously mentioned are discussed in the Supplement which follows and are summarized at the end of the Supplement, along with the referrals for completion of corrective action.

/s/Auditor-in-Charge
/s/Supervising Auditor
/s/Manager of Internal Auditing

Details of Deficiency Findings:

1. *There was no separation of functional authority in the procurement of parts and services, and effective administration of labor-hour agreements was beyond the Highway Transportation Department's resources.*

Blanket Purchase Orders (BPOs) have been issued for the procurement of parts and services. The . . . purchasing department has assigned to the Highway Transportation Department all authority and responsibility for controlling (a) release of orders under the BPOs to suppliers; (b) receipt, inspection, and acceptance upon delivery; and (c) approvals of invoices for payment.

In practice, all of these functions are performed by the department manager or by one or two people under his direct control and supervision. Thus, there is none of the protection normally afforded by the separation of such functions among personnel of independent departments, such as establishing requirements, ordering, receiving, inspection, and approving for payment.

Because of the lack of separation of duties, we made an extensive examination of the system and of transactions, but we found no basis for questioning any of the charges. Nevertheless, we recommend that branch management review this condition with a view toward implementing some reasonable control through assignment of some of the key functions to other departments.

We discussed this matter with management personnel, and they informed us they intend to review the methods used at other major divisions of the company to determine whether any of their practices may warrant adoption.

2. *Gasoline and oil were being withdrawn by company employees without adequate surveillance.*

Since our last examination, the department reassigned the service station attendant who had recorded gasoline and oil disbursements on the form provided for that purpose. Under present practice, the vehicle operator serves himself and records his own withdrawals of gasoline and oil, without surveillance. There is no assurance, therefore, that the records are maintained accurately or that the information is always entered. Hence, the dangers of misappropriations are increased. We estimate that the total yearly gasoline withdrawal will approximate 300,000 gallons at a cost of about $66,000.

We recognize that the benefits of control must be weighed against the costs of control. Nevertheless, we recommend that management consider some of means of surveillance—even on a spot-check basis—to provide minimum elements of control.

We discussed this matter with management personnel and they indicated that appropriate surveillance would be conducted over fuel pump operations.

Summary of Findings Requiring Corrective Action

The matters requiring corrective action are summarized as follows:

1. There was no separation of functional authority in the procurement of parts and services.
2. Gasoline and oil were being withdrawn by company employees without adequate surveillance.

Finding 1 is referred jointly to the management of the Procurement Department and the manager of the Highway Transportation Department for completion of corrective action. Finding 2 is referred to the manager of the Highway Transportation Department for completion of corrective action.

Source: Lawrence B. Sawyer, *Sawyer's Internal Auditing*, rev. ed. (pp. 667–71). Copyright 1988 by The Institute of Internal Auditors, Inc., 249 Maitland Avenue, Altamonte Springs, Florida 32701 U.S.A. Reprinted with permission.

EXHIBIT 18–8   **CONSULTING REPORT BY A PUBLIC ACCOUNTING FIRM**

Mr. C. D. Derfin
Control Instruments, Inc.

Dear Mr. Derfin:

We have completed our review of the cost accounting system of Control Instruments, Inc., as outlined in our engagement letter to you. The primary objective of our review was to determine if your new system should be modified. Our conclusion is that the present system for controlling inventory is sound. It is simple, but it should provide for good control of inventory. The problem is one of improper utilization of the existing system.

We believe that control of inventory is vital to company operations. We understand there are numerous shortages of parts which delay the assembly process. However, we do not believe this problem is primarily due to a system weakness. We observed that additions to inventory are properly entered on the perpetual records when receiving reports are received by the inventory control clerk. Items are deducted from the records when they are pulled from the warehouse, and an adequate system exists for keeping track of material shortages. We believe that the warehouse operation is the primary source of inventory control problems. Our observations and recommendations in this area are summarized below.

Warehouse Operations

Warehouse personnel are currently taking cycle counts of raw materials to locate differences between perpetual records and actual quantities on hand. We noted there were many such discrepancies. In an attempt to find a reason for these discrepancies, we unpacked three pulled orders in the warehouse and compared actual items packed with the amounts indicated as being packed on the bills of material. In each case, we found discrepancies.

In order to identify the source of these errors, we recommended the warehouse be required to initial the bills of material for the orders they pull. They have already been instructed to do this. The production supervisor currently unpacks all pulled orders and counts the contents before the orders go to the production line. We believe he should take the additional step of reporting the exact discrepancies daily to John Roberts. Additional recommendations to improve the warehouse operation are summarized below. Some of these recommendations are already being implemented.

1. Continue the cycle count procedure, but take time to resolve differences daily. Report reasons for differences to John Roberts.
2. Temporarily assign a person full time to maintain inventory records.
3. Stock inventory in the correct locations or attach a note to the bin stating where additional items are located.
4. Adopt a "last bag" system for control of "C" items.
5. When an order for several units on the small line requires more than one box, pack all of one type of part in the same box.
6. When pulling an order for several units on the large line, pack as many complete units as possible and limit the shortages to the remaining units.
7. Require warehouse personnel to pack orders neatly, particularly general kits.
8. Adopt a daily routine in the warehouse as follows:
    a. Stock the items received.
    b. Fill short orders.
    c. Fill remaining orders.
    d. Work on special projects.

We noted that physical control of inventory has been substantially improved by constructing a chain-link fence around the warehouse area. Since access to the warehouse is now very limited, it will be difficult for unauthorized personnel to remove parts.

General Observation

While most of our time was spent in the warehouse, we also noted some opportunities to improve the general operation of the Control Instruments facility. Our recommendations are summarized below:

1. Revise the cost book to contain an accurate description and the current cost of each item.
2. Revise the Bills of Material to make them accurate and adopt a formal procedure for keeping them current.
3. Redesign the forms used for Bills of Material. They can be changed to indicate more clearly the number of items packed versus the number of item specified. They could also indicate which items are used in the electrical subassembly process, so these items could be packed together. These forms should be ordered as snap-out multiple part forms.
4. Redesign the "owe sheets" to make them consistent and easy to understand.
5. Assign part numbers to all purchased parts except common nuts and bolts.
6. Assign part numbers to sheet metal parts and include these parts in the cost book and Bills of Material.
7. Adopt a tag method for keeping track of labor-hours spent on individual units and revise labor time standards as appropriate.

EXHIBIT 18-8   (concluded)

Accounting Procedures

There is some confusion over exactly what accounting procedures have been employed in the past. We recommend the following procedures be used in the future to account for cost of materials and labor. We believe most of these procedures are already understood by accounting personnel and are being used.

1. Record raw materials purchased at standard cost and maintain a purchase price variance account. For internal financial statements, the variance can be treated as part of cost of goods sold.

2. Charge labor to cost of goods sold at standard time. Charge the difference between standard and actual to labor efficiency variance, which is part of cost of goods sold.

3. At the end of each month, count the finished goods inventory and estimate work-in-process inventory.

We would be pleased to discuss this letter further at your convenience.

We appreciate this opportunity to be of service to you.

Very truly yours,

Burr & Hamilton,

PAs

R E V I E W
C H E C K P O I N T S

18.20   What are the major differences between independent auditors' reports on financial statements and internal, public sector and consulting reports on efficiency, economy and effectiveness audits?

18.21   Why do you think the public sector reporting standards permit the report to include "pertinent views of responsible officials" of the auditee concerning the auditor's findings, conclusions and recommendations?

SUMMARY

Governmental and internal auditing standards include the essence of the CICA generally accepted auditing standards (GAAS) and go much further by expressing standards for audits of economy, efficiency and effectiveness of program results. In addition, the internal auditing standards contain many guides for the management of an internal audit department within a company.

All auditors hold independence as a primary goal, but internal auditors must look to an internal organization independence from the managers and executives whose areas they audit. Public sector auditors must be concerned about factual independence with regard to social, political and level-of-government influence.

Public sector auditing is complicated by the special context of audit assignments intended to accomplish accountability by agencies that handle federal funds—grants, subsidies, welfare programs and the like. The requirements of the public sector auditing standards impose on the audit function the responsibility for compliance audit work designed to determine agencies' observance of laws and regulations, of which there are many. Auditors must report not only on financial statements but also on internal control, violations of laws and regulations, fraud, abuse and illegal acts. These elements are all part of Ottawa's oversight of federal spending, facilitated by auditors.

Audit engagements are an application of the practical audit method—essentially a fact-finding approach. Auditors start the work with an understanding of the audit objectives involved in the assignment and carry them out through the major blocks of work—preliminary survey, study and evaluation of administrative control, application of audit procedures and reporting of the audit conclusions and recommendations. Auditors try to achieve objectivity by determining appropriate standards for economy, efficiency and effectiveness of program results, by measuring their evidence, and by comparing their measurements to the standards in order to reach objective conclusions.

Public sector and internal audit reports and similar reports on public accountants' consulting services are not standardized like the GAAS reports on audited financial statements. Auditors must be very careful that their reports communicate their conclusions and recommendations in a clear and concise manner. The variety of assignments and the challenge of reporting in such a free-form setting contribute to making governmental auditing, internal auditing and consulting services exciting fields for career opportunities.

A useful website for this chapter is http://www.rutgers.edu/accounting/raw/IIA. This Institute of Internal Auditors site includes association news releases on ethics, professional standards and membership options.

MULTIPLE-CHOICE QUESTIONS FOR PRACTICE AND REVIEW

18.22 Which of the following is considered different and more limited in objectives than the others?
  a. Operational auditing.
  b. Performance auditing.
  c. Management auditing.
  d. Financial statement auditing.

18.23 A typical objective of an operational audit is for the auditor to:
  a. Determine whether the financial statements fairly present the company's operations.
  b. Evaluate the feasibility of attaining the company's operational objectives.
  c. Make recommendations for achieving company objectives.
  d. Report on the company's relative success in attaining profit maximization.

18.24 A government auditor assigned to audit the financial statements of the provincial highway department would not be considered independent if the auditor:
  a. also held a position as a project manager in the highway department.
  b. Was the provincial audit official elected in a general provincewide election with responsibility to report to the legislature.
  c. Normally works as a provincial auditor employed in the department of human services.
  d. Was appointed by the provincial minister with responsibility to report to the legislature.

18.25 Government auditing can extend beyond audits of financial statements to include audits of an agency's efficient and economical use of resources and:
  a. Constitutionality of laws and regulations governing the agency.
  b. Evaluation of the personal managerial skills shown by the agency's leaders.
  c. Correspondence of the agency's performance with public opinion regarding the social worth of its mission.
  d. Evaluations concerning the agency's achievements of the goals set by the legislature for the agency's activities.

18.26 Which of the following best describes how the detailed audit program of the external auditor who is engaged to audit the financial statements of a large publicly held company compares with the audit client's comprehensive internal audit program?
  a. The comprehensive internal audit program covers areas that would normally not be reviewed by the external auditor.
  b. The comprehensive internal audit program is more detailed although it covers fewer areas than would normally be covered by the external auditor.
  c. The comprehensive internal audit program is substantially identical to the audit program used by the external auditor because both review substantially identical areas.
  d. The comprehensive internal audit program is less detailed and covers fewer areas than would normally be reviewed by the external auditor.

18.27 Which of the following would you not expect to see in an auditor's report(s) on the financial statements of an independent government agency?
  a. A statement that the audit was conducted in accordance with generally accepted government audit standards.
  b. A report on the agency's compliance with applicable laws and regulations.
  c. Commentary by the agency's managers on the audit findings and recommendations.
  d. A report on the agency's internal control structure.

18.28 Public Sector Auditing Standards require auditors to determine and report several things about provincial and local governments that receive federal funds. Which of the following is not normally required to be reported?

a. An opinion on the fair presentation of the financial statements in accordance with generally accepted accounting principles.

b. A report on the government's internal control structure related to the federal funds.

c. The government's performance in meeting goals set in enabling legislation.

d. A report on the government's compliance with applicable laws and regulations.

18.29 In government and internal performance auditing, which of the following is the least important consideration when performing the field work?

a. Determining the applicable generally accepted government accounting principles pronounced by the GASB.

b. Defining problem areas or opportunities for improvement and defining program goals.

c. Selection and performance of procedures designed to obtain evidence about operational problems and production output.

d. Evaluation of evidence in terms of economy, efficiency and achievement of program goals.

18.30 Which of the following is the least important consideration for a government auditor who needs to be objective when auditing and reporting on an agency's achievement of program goals?

a. Measure the actual output results of agency activities.

b. Compare the agency's actual output results to quantitative goal standards.

c. Perform a comprehensive review of administrative controls.

d. Determine quantitative standards that describe goals the agency was supposed to achieve.

18.31 When an external auditor obtains an understanding of a client's internal control structure in connection with the annual audit of financial statements, the external auditor must obtain information and evaluate:

a. The competence and objectivity of the internal auditors.

b. The education, experience and certification of the internal auditors.

c. The employment of internal auditors' relatives in management positions.

d. The internal audit department and its program of work.

18.32 Compliance auditing in audits performed in accordance with public sector auditing standards is necessary for an auditor's:

a. Report on the auditee's internal control, including reportable conditions and material weaknesses.

b. Opinion on the auditee's observance, or lack thereof, of applicable laws and regulations.

c. Opinion on the auditee's financial statements.

d. Report of a supplementary schedule of federal assistance programs and amounts.

EXERCISES AND PROBLEMS

18.33 **Identification of Audits and Auditors**. Audits may be characterized as (a) financial statement audits, (b) compliance audits, (c) economy and efficiency audits, and (d) program results audits. The work can be done by independent (external) auditors, internal auditors or governmental auditors (including Canada Customs and Revenue Agency auditors and federal bank examiners). Below is a list of the purpose or products of various audit engagements.

1. Determining the equity of interest rates charged on federally guaranteed loans to students.

2. Determining the fair presentation in conformity with GAAP of an advertising agency's financial statements.

3. Study of Ministry of Natural Resources (MNR) policies and practices on grant-related income.

4. Determination of costs of municipal garbage pickup services compared to comparable service subcontracted to a private business.

5. Audit of tax shelter partnership financing terms.

6. Study of a private aircraft manufacturer's test pilot performance in reporting on the results of test flights.

7. Periodic Superintendent of Financial Institution examination of a bank for solvency.

8. Evaluation of the promptness of materials inspection in a manufacturer's receiving department.

9. Report of how better care and disposal of vehicles confiscated by drug enforcement agents could save money and benefit law enforcement.

10. Rendering a public report on the assumptions and compilation of a revenue forecast by a sports stadium/ racetrack complex.

Required:

Prepare a three-column schedule showing (1) each of the engagements listed above; (2) the type of audit (financial statement, compliance, economy and efficiency, or program results); and (3) the kinds of auditors you would expect to be involved.

18.34 Organizing a Preliminary Survey. You are the director of internal auditing of a large municipal hospital. You receive monthly financial reports prepared by the accounting department, and your review of them has shown that total accounts receivable from patients has steadily and rapidly increased over the past eight months.

Other information in the reports shows the following conditions:

a. The number of available hospital beds has not changed.

b. The bed occupancy rate has not changed.

c. Hospital billing rates have not changed significantly.

d. The hospitalization insurance contracts have not changed since the last modification 12 months ago.

Your internal audit department audited the accounts receivable 10 months ago. The working paper file for that assignment contains financial information, a record of the preliminary survey, documentation of the study and evaluation of administrative and internal accounting controls, documentation of the evidence-gathering procedures used to produce evidence about the validity and collectibility of the accounts and a copy of your report which commented favourably on the controls and collectibility of the receivables.

However, the current increase in receivables has alerted you to a need for another audit so that things will not get out of hand. You remember news stories last year about the manager of the city water system who got into big trouble because his accounting department double-billed all the residential customers for three months.

Required:

You plan to perform a preliminary survey in order to get a handle on the problem, if indeed a problem exists. Write a memo to your senior auditor listing at least eight questions he should use to guide and direct the preliminary survey. (Hint: The questions used in the last preliminary survey were organized under these headings: (1) Who does the accounts receivable accounting? (2) What data processing procedures and policies are in effect? and (3) How is the accounts receivable accounting done? This time, you will add a fourth category: What financial or economic events have occurred in the last 10 months?)

(CIA adapted)

18.35 Study and Evaluation of Administrative Control. The study and evaluation of administrative controls in a governmental or internal audit is not easy. First, auditors must determine the controls subject to audit. Then, they must find a standard by which performance of the control can be evaluated. Next, they must specify procedures to obtain the evidence on which an evaluation can be based. Insofar as possible, the standards and related evidence must be quantified.

Students working on this case usually do not have the experience or theoretical background to figure out control standards and audit procedures, so the description below gives certain information that internal auditors would know about or be able to figure out on their own. Fulfilling the requirement thus amounts to taking some information from the scenario below and figuring out other things by using accountants' and auditors' common sense.

The Scenario: Ace Corporation ships building materials to more than a thousand wholesale and retail customers in a five-province region. The company's normal credit terms are net/30 days, and no cash discounts are offered. Fred Clark is the chief financial officer, and he is concerned about maintaining control over customer credit. In particular, he has stated two administrative control principles for this purpose.

1. Sales are to be billed to customers accurately and promptly. Fred knows that errors will occur but thinks company personnel ought to be able to hold quantity, unit price and arithmetic errors down to 3 percent of the sales invoices. He considers an invoice error of $1 or less not to matter. He believes that prompt billing is important since customers are expected to pay within 30 days. Fred is very strict in thinking

that a bill should be sent to the customer one day after shipment. He believes that he has staffed the billing department well enough to be able to handle this workload. The relevant company records consist of an accounts receivable control account; a subsidiary ledger of customers' accounts in which charges are entered by billing (invoice) date and credits are entered by date of payment receipts; a sales journal that lists invoices in chronological order; and a file of shipping documents cross-referenced by the number on the related sales invoice copy kept on file in numerical order.

2. Accounts receivable are to be aged and followed up to ensure prompt collection. Fred has told the accounts receivable department to classify all the customer accounts in categories of (*a*) current, (*b*) 31–59 days overdue, (*c*) 60–90 days overdue, and (*d*) more than 90 days overdue. He wants this trial balance to be complete and to be transmitted to the credit department within five days of each month-end. In the credit department, prompt follow-up means sending a different (stronger) collection letter to each category, cutting off credit to customers over 60 days past due (putting them on cash basis), and giving the over-90-days accounts to an outside collection agency. These actions are supposed to be taken within five days after receipt of the aged trial balance. The relevant company records, in addition to the ones listed above, consist of the aged trial balance, copies of the letters sent to customers, copies of notices of credit cutoff, copies of correspondence with the outside collection agent and reports of results—statistics of subsequent collections.

Required:
Take the role of a senior internal auditor. You are to write a memo to the internal audit staff to inform them about comparison standards for the study and evaluation of these two administrative control policies. You also need to specify two or three procedures for gathering evidence about performance of the controls. The body of your memo should be structured as follows:

1. Control: Sales are billed to customers accurately and promptly.
   a. Accuracy.
      (1) Policy standard . . .
      (2) Audit procedures . . .
   b. Promptness.
      (1) Policy standard . . .
      (2) Audit procedures . . .
2. Control: Accounts receivable are aged and followed up to ensure prompt collection.
   a. Accounts receivable aging.
      (1) Policy standard . . .
      (2) Audit procedures . . .
   b. Follow-up prompt collection.
      (1) Policy standard . . .
      (2) Audit procedures . . .

18.36 Analytical Review of Inventory. External auditors usually calculate inventory turnover (cost of goods sold for the year divided by average inventory) and use the ratio as a broad indication of inventory age, obsolescence or overstocking. External auditors are interested in evidence relating to the material accuracy of the financial statements taken as a whole. Internal auditors, on the other hand, calculate turnover by categories and classes of inventory in order to detect problem areas that might otherwise get overlooked. This kind of detailed analytical review might point to conditions of buying errors, obsolescence, overstocking and other matters that could be changed to save money.

The data shown in Exhibit 18.36–1 are turnover, cost of sales and inventory investment data for a series of four historical years and the current year. In each of the historical years, the external auditors did not recommend any adjustments to the inventory valuations.

Required:
Calculate the current year inventory turnover ratios. Interpret the ratio trends and point out what conditions might exist, and write a memo to the vice president for production explaining your findings and the further investigation that can be conducted.

18.37 PA Involvement in an Expanded-Scope Audit. A public accounting firm received an invitation to bid for the audit of a local food commodity distribution program funded by the Ministry of Agriculture. The audit is to be conducted in accordance with the public sector audit standards published by the CICA. The accountants have become familiar with the public sector standards and recognize that the public sector standards incorporate the CICA generally accepted auditing standards (GAAS).

The public accounting firm has been engaged to perform the audit of the pro-

E X H I B I T 18.36–1 **INVENTORY DATA**

	Inventory Turnover				Current-year Inventory (000)	
	20X1	20X2	20X3	20X4	Beginning	Ending
Total inventory	2.1	2.0	2.1	2.1	$3,000	$2,917
Materials and parts	4.0	4.1	4.3	4.5	1,365	620
Work in process	12.0	12.5	11.5	11.7	623	697
Finished products:						
Computer games	6.0	7.0	10.0	24.0	380	500
Floppy disk drives	8.0	7.2	7.7	8.5	64	300
Semiconductor parts	4.0	3.5	4.5	7.0	80	400
Electric typewriters	3.0	2.5	2.0	1.9	488	400

Additional Information

	Current Year (000)				
	Transfers	Sales	Cost of Goods Sold	Gross Profit	Compared to 20X4
Materials and parts	$3,970*	NA	NA	NA	
Work in process	7,988†	NA	NA	NA	
Computer games	2,320‡	$2,000	$2,200	$<200>	Sales volume declined 60%§
Floppy disk drives	2,236‡	3,000	2,000	1,000	Sales volume increased 35%
Semiconductor parts	2,720‡	4,000	2,400	1,600	Sales volume increased 40%
Electric typewriters	712‡	1,000	800	200	Sales volume declined 3%

NA means not available.
* Cost of materials transferred to Work in Process.
† Cost of materials, labour and overhead transferred to Finished Goods.
‡ Cost of goods transferred from Work in Process to Finished Product Inventories.
§ Selling prices also were reduced and the gross margin declined.

gram, and the audit is to encompass both financial and performance audits that constitute the expanded scope of a public sector audit.

Required (See Appendix 18C):
a. The accountants should perform sufficient audit work to satisfy the financial and compliance element of the GAO standards. What is the objective of such audit work?
b. The accountants should be aware of general and specific kinds of uneconomical or inefficient practices in such a program. What are some examples?
c. What might be some standards and sources of standards for judging program results?

DISCUSSION CASES

· ·

18.38 Operational Audit: Customer Complaints. Danny Deck, the director of internal auditing for the Rice Department Stores, was working in his office one Thursday when Larry McMurray, president of the company, burst in to tell about a problem. According to Larry: "Customer complaints about delays in getting credit for merchandise returns are driving Sally Godwin up the wall! She doesn't know what to do because she has no control over the processing of credit memos."

Sally is the manager in charge of customer relations, and she tries to keep everybody happy. Upon her recommendation, the company adopted an advertising motto: "Satisfaction Guaranteed and Prompt Credit When You Change Your Mind." The motto is featured in newspaper ads and on large banners in each store.

Danny performed a preliminary review and found the following:
1. Sally believes that customers will be satisfied if they receive a refund cheque

or notice of credit on account within five working days.

2. The chief accountant described the credit memo processing procedure as follows: When a customer returns merchandise, the sales clerks give a smile, a "returned merchandise receipt," and a promise to send a cheque or a notice within five days.

The store copy of the receipt and the merchandise is sent to the purchasing department, where buyers examine the merchandise for quality or damage to decide whether to put it back on the shelves, return it to the vendor or hold it for the annual rummage sale. The buyers then prepare a brief report and send it with the returned merchandise receipt to the customer relations department for approval. The buyer's report is filed for reference and the receipt, marked for approval in Sally's department, is sent to the accounting department. The accounting department sorts the receipts in numerical order, checking the numerical sequence, and files them in readiness for the weekly batch processing of other transactions than sales and cash receipts, both of which are processed daily. When the customer has requested a cash refund, the cheques and cancelled returned merchandise receipt are approved by the treasurer, who signs and mails the cheque. When the credit is on a customer's charge account, it is shown on the next monthly statement sent to the customer.

3. The processing in each department takes two or three days.

Required:

a. Analyse the problem. How much time does it take the company to process the merchandise returns?

b. Formulate a recommendation to solve the problem. Write a brief report explaining your recommendation.

18.39 Public Sector Auditor Independence (Study of Chapter 16 on Professional Ethics is recommended for this problem). The public sector reporting standards for VFM audits state that each report should include "recommendations for action to correct the problem areas and to improve operations." For example, an audit of the Metropolitan Area Transit Authority found management decision deficiencies affecting some $230 million in provincial funds. The public sector auditors recommended that the transit authority improve its management control over subway car procurement through better enforcement of contract requirements and development of a master plan to test cars.

Suppose the transit authority accepted and implemented specific recommendations made by the OAG auditors. Do you believe these events would be enough to impair the independence of the OAG auditors in a subsequent audit of the transit authority? Explain, and tell if it makes any difference to you whether the same or a different person performs both the first and subsequent audits.

18.40 Marketing Audit I. During your eight years with a PA firm based in Winnipeg with offices in four other provinces, you had developed an increasing interest and reputation in the field of marketing. On one of your monthly trips to the Calgary office, you were invited to have lunch with James, the president and CEO of Vulcan Pharmaceuticals Inc. (VPI), which you knew as a strong competitor in a very competitive field. Your host came to the point over coffee:

"Your firm and your name were suggested to me by an executive at Chugalug Beverages, who credits your marketing recommendations with the turnaround in Chugalug's sales and profitability. It is no secret that the "drug game" is a competitive jungle. Products, distribution, prices, promotion, all have to be watched very carefully; otherwise you can wake up to discover you have been left behind by the competition. The picture at Vulcan is troubling. In 2003, we led the competition with net income of $102 million on sales of $850 million; prospects seemed very rosy. But in 2004, sales dropped to $760 million and our net income to $48 million. I have just seen the forecast for 2005, and it is not good; specifically, the vice president finance is forecasting a further decline in sales to $680 million and net income just in the black at $10 million; I think he is being optimistic. The chairman is not happy at all, and neither am I.

"We have studied the problem at length, and remain convinced that we have the best research and franchise arrangements in Canada and that, building on these strengths, our products still lead the field. We are also convinced that our distribution arrangements are superior to those of all our major competitors. Where we seem vulnerable is in two areas: promotion, which is all advertising in this "game"; and pricing.

"I would like to make a presentation to our board, next week if possible, on how you would go about a management audit of marketing at VPI, including a brief outline of the sort of criteria you would use for advertising and pricing."

Required:

Prepare the marketing audit proposal to the board.

(CGAAC adapted)

18.41 Marketing Audit II. As director of management audit in the Ministry of Labour, Skills and Employment Training, you had always been uneasy about the large contractual grants awarded for job training to the 67 provincial colleges and the large number of small training organizations—some commercial, some not-for-profit—that had recently been established. There was a rudimentary process of assessing applications, but essentially the ministry just paid the bill submitted by the training organizations. As a professional auditor, and, you hoped, a good public servant, you were very concerned about control and accountability.

There were two points of focus in your concern. First, you believed that current arrangements provided no incentives to efficiency in resource utilization or effectiveness in training program delivery. Second, while you considered that the required external financial audit by the provincial legislative auditor provided reasonable assurance of fiscal propriety, you also knew that the external auditors did not actually look for fraud, but only reported it if they came across it in the course of their audit of the financial statements. So you continued to have some concern about some scandal that would reflect on the ministry and your own department. To your surprise and relief, you found that the senior assistant deputy minister, who was also a PA, shared your concerns. Her note to you suggested a course of action:

"I share your concerns about the hand-out program for job training. The colleges have a reasonable tradition of accountability, and I can live with that; it is the large number of small training organizations that concerns me. They are not accountable in any serious way to us, and, consequently, we cannot be accountable in any serious way to Treasury Board for the resources we transfer to them—although we are sure to be blamed for something even though we cannot control it! The issue of the actual effectiveness of these programs is a matter I intend to avoid for the moment, but I would like to begin to deal with two accountability issues.

"The first issue relates to efficiency in resource utilization, and I would like you to work with two consultants who will arrive next week to write a planning memorandum for an efficiency audit of training programs in the large group of commercial and not-for-profit training organizations with which we had contractual arrangements. The part of the memorandum on which I want you to concentrate is the question of evidence. What constitutes evidence of efficiency in these organizations? How would you get that evidence?

"The second issue on which I would like to have your thoughts about the nature of evidence and how to get it, is with respect to fraud. I have received two unsigned notes over the last two months, and I got another one today, alleging that there is serious fraud in many of these training organizations, and that much of the information we get as justification for payment may be false. I want you to approach this matter as a confidential by-product of the efficiency audit and summarize your thoughts in a confidential memo. You should indicate what evidence would be needed and how it should be collected."

Required:

Prepare the two planning documents, one public, one confidential, as requested.

(CGAAC adapted)

18.42 DracuLab Inc. Six years as an audit manager in a PA firm, then five more as assistant director, management audit, in the provincial Ministry of Health had given you an appetite for new challeges in the health field. So you were pleased to be offered the position of executive director, management audit, reporting to the vice-president, finance and administration, in DracuLab Inc., a rapidly growing drug and medical equipment corporation with net income of $115 million on sales of $805 million in 2004. Your enthusiasm increased further during your first detailed briefing session with the vice-president:

"Welcome to DracuLab Inc. I have been arguing for a larger role for management audit for five years—your predecessor left in frustration when my attempt to increase her budget last year fell on stoney ground and the CEO and board have finally come around to my point of view (helped, I should add, by a note in the last management letter from our external auditor). You have a current staff of nine, consisting of seven accountants and two administrative people. I have secured a commitment for you to hire three more professional staff as soon as possible and to provide considerable flexibility to extend your staff on a contractual basis as needed over the next year.

"As you know, this is a very technical multiproduct corporation with a wide range of technical professional staff. My sense is that these people see management audit as simply a minor extension of the accounting department, and they doubt that you have the skills to say anything intelligent and helpful about their specialized tasks. And it is precisely in these technical areas that the external auditor and I have strong reservations about our management controls.

"While you are working on your staffing, I would also like you to take a first step towards building confidence in your area by coming to the executive meeting and making a presentation that focuses directly on the professional skills of your department, including the hiring of supplementary personnel and the use of specialists on a contractual basis."

Required:
Prepare the presentation for the Executive meeting.

(CGAAC adapted)

18.43 Natran Inc., a Crown Corporation. In your role as director of internal audit for Natran, Inc., a federal Crown corporation with revenues of $3 billion in 2003–04 and 37,000 employees across the country, you employed your 15 professional and six support staff in a variety of functions. In the last three years, the proportions of your work related to compliance with legislation and regulations, and to value-for-money questions, had risen to 30 percent and 40 percent, respectively. When the vice president summoned you to a meeting just after the presentation of your proposed audit plan and budget for the forthcoming year, you anticipated having to defend what you considered a barely sufficient audit plan in the light of the risks facing Natran. The vice president was concerned about audit budgets, but concern was focused on the soaring cost of the independent external audit that Natran was obliged by statute to undergo each year.

"I have always been unhappy with what I consider the ridiculously high fees we have to pay for the traditional external attest audit of our financial statements.

But things are getting much worse. Now we are faced with much higher costs as the external auditor feels obliged not only to address the compliance issues that get a lot of public attention, but also, as a consequence of the revisions to the Financial Administration Act, to get into a host of value-for-money issues and to more or less insist that management prepare a set of auditable assertions on value for money, broadly defined. The proposed bill for all this work is staggering, and I need your advice on how we can minimize the costs of our external audit.

"Specifically, I want your advice on how we can co-ordinate the roles of internal audit and external audit to accomplish the total audit effort in the most effective and efficient way. The Financial Administration Act obliges the external auditor to use your work and to indicate the extent of reliance. What I want to see is a very large degree of reliance. I would like you to make a presentation to the audit committee of the board in a couple of weeks on the issue. You should introduce the topic by pointing to the benefits to Natran of coordinated audit work, and tell the committee what your Internal Audit Standards say on the topic. That should take about one-third of your presentation.

"For the balance of your presentation I would like you to present a proposal to maximize the potential usefulness of your department to the external auditor in his areas of responsibility. Indicate what you do now that would be helpful, and also indicate how you could adapt your work program using existing resources to be even more helpful since there is no way I can get you additional staff this year. I know the external auditor has the highest regard for you and your staff, and would almost certainly welcome more audit co-ordination. But the ball is, I believe, in our court. It is our responsibility to act. I look forward to your help in reducing this burden."

Required:
Prepare the requested presentation.

(CGAAC adapted)

18.44 TechNet, a Software Company. Your role as vice president, management audit, in TechNet, Inc., was always challenging and occasionally trying. TechNet had become the biggest software corporation in Canada three years ago when it took over two strong competitors. Profit in 2003–04 was $103 million on total revenue of just over $3 billion. The CEO's philosophy was that competitive pressure was essential both externally and internally. While the three major divisions representing the original TechNet and its two corporate acquisitions were carefully co-ordinated, they were also required to compete against one another. There were no entitlements at TechNet. Even within each division, the CEO had established a belief in competitive survival, and managers of staff areas were required to demonstrate that their services were the most cost-effective available. Your role was to monitor this highly competitive corporate environment with 14 professionals—accountants and engineers—and six administrative staff. The management audit department was used to introduce bright new managers to the whole corporate environment at TechNet and to offer occasional revitalization to executives after a period on the "front line."

In one of your recent performance audits, you had been quite severe on the vice president (marketing) in one of the divisions, and she had responded angrily, accusing you of bias. She re-enforced this claim by arguing that the management audit staff member who had led the audit had joined the audit staff only eight months previously from one of the other divisions. She and her colleagues had also been heard to remark that it was time your department was "outsourced"—the current term for "contracted out"! Your meeting with the CEO to discuss the matter ended with his making the following proposal:

> "I think that our senior staff need to trust your department and we need to reassure them in this respect. I would therefore like you to come to the senior staff meeting and make a presentation about the independence of your operations. The statement could actually take the form of a departmental policy statement on independence. By all means include the usual information on organizational status, but spend at least half your time on that difficult but critical concept of objectivity. I would be pleased to comment on your draft."

Required:
Draft the proposed presentation.

(CGAAC adapted)

18.45 Health Care Audit. You are director of management audit in United Metro Hospitals (UMH), which is a group of four hospitals with a total of 800 acute care and long-term care beds. Your role has been really that of a troubleshooter. When a problem arose (usually a systems problem of some sort), you were dispatched to

fix it. The new CEO had been appointed with a mandate to change things, and he came to the point with you quite quickly.

"I have just come from a group of hospitals in southern Ontario, where the head of management audit served as my eyes and ears on areas of corporate risk, kept a strong internal evaluative tone, and was my major source of suggestions for change. I want you to play the same sort of reflective role here. I would like you to start with a part of traditional management audit. We are all going to have to build a value-for-money culture in our primary services, but that is going to take some time. Where I want to start is with our support services, and, within that group, specifically the purchasing department. Excluding capital purchases, we spent nearly $15 million last year on the host of items we need to keep the hospital running—drugs, minor equipment, food and so on—and that figure has been growing by ten percent each year for the last four years. We have a Purchasing Department with an impressive director—Mary Thompson—four professionals and two administrative support staff, who are responsible for making sure that all necessary items of the appropriate quality are obtained at the best prices in town. With our market clout, we should have no problems. But I have heard more complaints from administrative and clinical staff about the Purchasing Department than any other support area.

"Obviously, I discount the usual nonsense from those who claim that their brother-in-law working out of his basement can offer a better deal, but there is certainly a broad perception that something is wrong. So I want you to begin with Purchasing. Please come to the hospital executive committee next week with a presentation, which should include the following: first, a brief comment on the current role and main activities of purchasing in UMH; second, and as the core of your presentation, a discussion of the purchasing activities you propose to audit and the approach you would follow in conducting the audit (including some illustrative criteria); and, finally, some preliminary reflections (which might actually help you in suggesting audit criteria) on how purchasing might grow into sophisticated supply management at UMH. Frankly, I think we need to bring the department into the 2000s, and your audit should be designed with such changes in mind."

Required:
Prepare the requested presentation.

(CGAAC adapted)

APPENDIX 18A

SUMMARY OF GENERAL AND SPECIFIC STANDARDS FOR THE PROFESSIONAL PRACTICE OF INTERNAL AUDITING*

. . . .

100 **Independence. Internal auditors should be independent of the activities they audit.**

    110 Organizational Status. The organizational status of the internal auditing department should be sufficient to permit the accomplishment of its audit responsibilities.

    120 Objectivity. Internal auditors should be objective in performing audits.

200 **Professional Proficiency. Internal audits should be performed with proficiency and due professional care.**

THE INTERNAL AUDITING DEPARTMENT

. . . .

    210 Staffing. The internal auditing department should provide assurance that the technical proficiency and educational background of internal auditors are appropriate for the audits to be performed.

    220 Knowledge, Skills, and Disciplines. The internal auditing department should possess or should obtain the knowledge, skills, and disciplines needed to carry out its audit responsibilities.

    230 Supervision. The internal auditing department should provide assurance that internal audits are properly supervised.

THE INTERNAL AUDITOR

. . . .

    240 Compliance with Standards of Conduct. Internal auditors should comply with professional standards of conduct.

    250 Knowledge, Skills, and Disciplines. Internal auditors should possess the knowledge, skills, and disciplines essential to the performance of internal audits.

    260 Human Relations and Communications. Internal auditors should be skilled in dealing with people and in communicating effectively.

    270 Continuing Education. Internal auditors should maintain their technical competence through continuing education.

    280 Due Professional Care. Internal auditors should exercise due professional care in performing internal audits.

300 Scope of Work. **The scope of the internal audit should encompass the examination and evaluation of the adequacy and effectiveness of the organization's system of internal control and the quality of performance in carrying out assigned responsibilities.**

    310 Reliability and Integrity of Information. Internal auditors should review the reliability and integrity of financial and operating information and the means used to identify, measure, classify, and report such information.

    320 Compliance with Policies, Plans, Procedures, Laws, and Regulations. Internal auditors should review the systems established to ensure compliance with

* From *Summary of Standards for the Professional Practice of Internal Auditing*, by the Institute of Internal Auditors, Inc. Copyright 1978 by The Institute of Internal Auditors, Inc., 249 Maitland Avenue, Altamonte Springs, Florida, 32701 U.S.A. Reprinted with permission.

those policies, plans, procedures, laws, and regulations which could have a significant impact on operations and reports and should determine whether the organization is in compliance.

330 Safeguarding of Assets. Internal auditors should review the means of safeguarding assets, and, as appropriate, verify the existence of such assets.

340 Economical and Efficient Use of Resources. Internal auditors should appraise the economy and efficiency with which resources are employed.

350 Accomplishment of Established Objectives and Goals for Operations or Programs. Internal auditors should review operations or programs to ascertain whether results are consistent with established objectives and goals and whether the operations or programs are being carried out as planned.

400 **Performance of Audit Work. Audit work should include planning the audit, examining and evaluating information, communicating results, and following up**.

410 Planning the Audit. Internal auditors should plan each audit.

420 Examining and Evaluating Information. Internal auditors should collect, analyze, interpret, and document information to support audit results.

430 Communicating Results. Internal auditors should report the results of their audit work.

440 Following Up. Internal auditors should follow up to ascertain that appropriate action is taken on reported audit findings.

500 **Management of the Internal Auditing Department. The director of internal auditing should properly manage the internal auditing department**.

510 Purpose, Authority, and Responsibility. The director of internal auditing should have a statement of purpose, authority, and responsibility for the internal auditing department.

520 Planning. The director of internal auditing should establish plans to carry out the responsibilities of the internal auditing department.

530 Policies and Procedures. The director of internal auditing should provide written policies and procedures to guide the audit staff.

540 Personnel Management and Development. The director of internal auditing should establish a program for selecting and developing the human resources of the internal auditing department.

550 External Auditors. The director of internal auditing should coordinate internal and external audit efforts.

560 Quality Assurance. The director of internal auditing should establish and maintain a quality assurance program to evaluate the operations of the internal auditing department.

APPENDIX 18B
THE INSTITUTE OF INTERNAL AUDITORS CODE OF ETHICS*

PURPOSE

A distinguishing mark of a profession is acceptance by its members of responsibility to the interests of those it serves. Members of The Institute of Internal Auditors (Members) and Certified Internal Auditors (CIAs) must maintain high standards of conduct in order to effectively discharge this responsibility. The Institute of Internal Auditors (Institute) adopts this Code of Ethics for Members and CIAs.

APPLICABILITY

This Code of Ethics is applicable to all Members and CIAs. Membership in The Institute and acceptance of the "Certified Internal Auditor" designation are voluntary actions. By acceptance, Members and CIAs assume an obligation of self-discipline above and beyond the requirements of laws and regulations.

The standards of conduct set forth in this Code of Ethics provide basic principles in the practice of internal auditing. Members and CIAs should realize that their individual judgement is required in the application of these principles.

CIAs shall use the "Certified Internal Auditor" designation with discretion and in a dignified manner, fully aware of what the designation denotes. The designation shall also be used in a manner consistent with all statutory requirements.

Members who are judged by the Board of Directors of The Institute to be in violation of the standards of conduct of the Code of Ethics shall be subject to forfeiture of their membership in The Institute. CIAs who are similarly judged also shall be subject of forfeiture of the "Certified Internal Auditor" designation.

STANDARDS OF CONDUCT

I. Members and CIAs shall exercise honesty, objectivity, and diligence in the performance of their duties and responsibilities.

II. Members and CIAs shall exhibit loyalty in all matters pertaining to the affairs of their organizations or to whomever they may be rendering a service. However, Members and CIAs shall not knowingly be a party to any illegal or improper activity.

III. Members and CIAs shall not knowingly engage in acts or activities which are discreditable to the profession of internal auditing or to their organization.

IV. Members and CIAs shall refrain from entering into any activity which may be in conflict with the interest of their organization or which would prejudice their ability to carry out objectively their duties and responsibilities.

* Adopted by Board of Directors, July 1988. From *The Institute of Internal Auditors, Inc., Code of Ethics.* Copyright 1988 by the Institute of Internal Auditors, Inc., 249 Maitland Avenue, Altamonte Springs, Florida, 32701 U.S.A. Reprinted with permission.

V. Members and CIAs shall not accept anything of value from an employee, client, customer, supplier, or business associate of their organization which would impair or be presumed to impair their professional judgment.

VI. Members and CIAs shall undertake only those services which they can reasonably expect to complete with professional competence.

VII. Members and CIAs shall adopt suitable means to comply with the Standards for the Professional Practice of Internal Auditing.

VIII. Members and CIAs shall be prudent in the use of information acquired in the course of their duties. They shall not use confidential information for any personal gain not in any manner which would be contrary to law or detrimental to the welfare of their organization.

IX. Members and CIAs, when reporting on the results of their work, shall reveal all material facts known to them which, if not revealed, could either distort reports or operations under review or conceal unlawful practices.

X. Members and CIAs shall continually strive for improvement in their proficiency, and in the effectiveness and quality of their service.

XI. Members and CIAs, in the practice of their profession, shall be ever mindful of their obligation to maintain the high standards of competence, morality, and dignity promulgated by The Institute. Members shall abide by the bylaws and uphold the objectives of The Institute.

APPENDIX 18C

ABRIDGED SUMMARY OF U.S. STANDARDS FOR AUDIT OF GOVERNMENTAL ORGANIZATIONS, PROGRAMS, ACTIVITIES AND FUNCTIONS

SCOPE OF AUDIT WORK

Audits may have a combination of financial and performance audit objectives, or may have objectives limited to only some aspects of one audit type. Auditors should follow the appropriate generally accepted government audit standards (GAGAS) that are applicable to the individual objectives of the audit.

1. Financial Statement Audits.
    a. Financial statement audits determine (1) whether the financial statements of an audited entity present fairly the financial position, results of operation, and cash flows or changes in financial position in accordance with generally accepted accounting principles, and (2) whether the entity has complied with laws and regulations for those transactions and events that may have a material effect on the financial statements.

2. Performance Audits.
    a. Economy and efficiency audits include determining (1) whether the entity is acquiring, protecting, and using its resources (such as personnel, property, and space) economically and efficiently, (2) the causes of inefficiencies or uneconomical practices, and (3) whether the entity has complied with laws and regulations concerning matters of economy and efficiency.
    b. Program audits include determining (1) the extent to which the desired results or benefits established by the legislature or other authorizing body are being achieved, (2) the effectiveness of organizations, programs, activities, or functions, and (3) whether the agency has complied with laws and regulations applicable to the program.

GENERAL STANDARDS

1. *Qualifications.* The staff assigned to conduct the audit should collectively possess adequate professional proficiency for the tasks required.
2. *Independence.* In all matters relating to the audit work, the audit organization and the individual auditors, whether government or public, must be free from personal and external impairments to independence, should be organizationally independent, and should maintain an independent attitude and appearance.
3. *Due professional care.* Due professional care should be used in conducting the audit and in preparing related reports.
4. *Quality Control.* Audit organizations conducting government audits should have an appropriate internal quality control system in place and participate in an external quality control review program.

FINANCIAL AUDITS

· · · · · · · · · · · ·

Field Work Standards for Financial Audits

1. The GAGAS standards of field work incorporate the AICPA standards of field work for financial audits (GAAS) and prescribe supplemental standards to satisfy the unique needs of government financial audits.

2. Planning shall include consideration of the requirements of all levels of government.

3. A test should be made of compliance with applicable laws and regulations, including: (*a*) the auditor should design audit steps and procedures to provide reasonable assurance of detecting errors, irregularities, and illegal acts that could have a direct and material effect on the financial statement amounts or the results of financial related audits, and (*b*) the auditor should also be aware of the possibility of illegal acts that could have an indirect and material effect on the financial statements or the results of financial related audits.

4. A record of the auditors' work should be retained in the form of working papers, which should:
   a. Contain a written audit program cross-referenced to the working papers.
   b. Contain the objective, scope, methodology, and results of the audit.
   c. Contain sufficient information so that supplementary oral explanations are not required.
   d. Be legible with adequate indexing and cross-referencing, and include summaries and lead schedules, as appropriate.
   e. Restrict information included to matters that are materially important and relevant to the objectives of the audit.
   f. Contain evidence of supervisory reviews of the work conducted.

Reporting Standards for Financial Audits

1. The GAGAS standards of reporting incorporate the AICPA standards of reporting for financial audits (GAAS) and prescribe supplemental standards to satisfy the unique needs of government financial audits.

2. A statement should be included in the auditors' report that the audit was made in accordance with generally accepted government auditing standards (GAGAS).

3. The auditors should prepare a written report on their tests of compliance with applicable laws and regulations. This report should contain a statement of positive assurance on those items which were tested for compliance and negative assurance on those items not tested. It should include all material instances of noncompliance, and all instances or indications of illegal acts that could result in criminal prosecution.

4. The auditors should prepare a written report on their understanding of the entity's internal control structure and the assessment of control risk made as part of the financial statement audit, or a financial related audit. This report should include as a minimum: (*a*) the scope of the auditor's work, (*b*) the entity's significant internal controls or control structure including the controls established to ensure compliance with laws and regulations that have a material impact on the financial statements, and (*c*) the reportable conditions, including the identification of material weaknesses identified as a result of the auditors' work in understanding and assessing the control risk.

5. Written reports are to be prepared giving the results of each financial-related audit regarding financial presentations other than complete financial statements.

6. If certain information is prohibited from general disclosure, the report should state the nature of the information omitted and the requirement that makes the omission necessary.

7. Written audit reports are to be submitted by the audit organization to the appropriate officials of the organization audited and to the appropriate officials of the organizations requiring or arranging for the audits, including external funding organizations, unless legal restrictions, ethical considerations, or other arrangements prevent it. Copies of the reports should also be sent to other officials who have legal oversight authority or who may be responsible for taking action and to others authorized to receive such reports. Unless restricted by law or regulation, copies should be made available for public inspection.

Performance Audits

Field Work Standards for Performance Audits

1. Work is to be adequately planned.
2. Staff are to be properly supervised.
3. An assessment is to be made of compliance with applicable requirements of laws and regulations when necessary to satisfy the audit objectives: (*a*) Auditors should design the audit to provide reasonable assurance of detecting abuse or illegal acts that could significantly affect the audit objectives, and (*b*) auditors should be alert to situations or transactions that could be indicative of abuse or illegal acts.
4. An assessment should be made of applicable internal controls when necessary to satisfy the audit objectives.
5. Sufficient, competent, and relevant evidence is to be obtained to afford a reasonable basis for the auditors' judgments and conclusions regarding the organization, program, activity, or function under audit. A record of the auditors' work is to be retained in the form of working papers, which may include tapes, films, and disks.

Reporting Standards for Performance Audits

1. Written audit reports are to be prepared communicating the results of each government audit.
2. Reports are to be issued promptly so that the information is available for timely use by management, legislative officials, and other interested parties.
3. The report should include:
   a. A statement that the audit was made in accordance with GAGAS and disclose when applicable standards were not followed.
   b. A statement of the audit objectives and a description of the audit scope and methodology.
   c. A full discussion of the audit findings and, where applicable, the auditor's conclusions.
   d. A description of the cause of problem areas noted in the audit, and recommendations for actions to correct the problem areas and to improve operations when called for by the audit objectives.
   e. An identification of the significant internal controls that were assessed, the scope of the auditors' assessment work, and any significant weaknesses found during the audit.
   f. All significant instances of noncompliance and abuse and all indications or instances of illegal acts that could result in criminal prosecution that were found during or in connection with the audit.
   g. Pertinent views of responsible officials of the organization, program, activity, or function audited concerning the auditors' findings, conclusions, and recommendations, and what corrective action is planned.

h. A description of any significant noteworthy accomplishments, particularly when management improvements in one area may be applicable elsewhere.

i. A listing of any significant issues needing further study and consideration.

j. A statement about any pertinent information that was omitted because it is deemed privileged or confidential. The nature of such information should be described, and the basis under which it is withheld should be stated.

4. The report should be complete, accurate, objective, and convincing, and be as clear and concise as the subject matter permits.

5. Written audit reports are to be submitted by the audit organization to the appropriate officials of the organization audited, and to the appropriate officials of the organizations requiring or arranging for the audits, including external funding organizations, unless legal restrictions, ethical consideration, or other arrangements prevent it. Copies of the reports should also be sent to other officials who may be responsible for taking action on audit findings and recommendations and to others authorized to receive such reports. Unless restricted by law or regulation, copies should be made available for public inspection.

CHAPTER 19

Learning Objectives

Fraud auditing can be very exciting. It has the aura of detective work—finding things people want to keep hidden. However, fraud auditing and examination are not easy and are not activities to be pursued without training, experience and care. Fraud awareness, thus, is the focus of this chapter. Having worked through this chapter, you will have accomplished these learning objectives:

1. Define and explain the differences among several kinds of fraud, errors, irregularities and illegal acts that might occur in an organization.

2. Explain the various auditing standards regarding external, internal and governmental auditors' responsibilities with respect to detecting and reporting errors, irregularities and illegal acts.

3. List and explain some conditions that can lead to frauds.

4. Describe ways and means for preventing frauds.

5. Describe some common employee fraud schemes and explain some audit and investigation procedures for detecting them.

6. Describe some common financial reporting fraud features and explain some audit and investigation procedures for detecting them.

7. Explain the use of some extended audit procedures for finding fraud.

8. Describe how PAs can assist in prosecuting fraud perpetrators.

FRAUD AWARENESS AUDITING

INTRODUCTION

This chapter is not intended to make you a fraud examiner or fraud auditor. Its purpose is to heighten your familiarity with the nature, signs, prevention, detection and reaction to fraud that can enable you to perform financial statement audits with awareness of fraud possibilities.

Users of audited financial statements generally believe that one of the main objectives of audits is fraud detection. External auditors know the issue is very complex, and they fear the general view that their work should ferret out all manner of major and minor fraud and misstatement in financial statements. This difference in viewpoints is one of the chronic "expectation gaps" between external auditors and users of published financial statements.

Part of the gap arises from the ability and expertise needed to be a fraud examiner or fraud auditor. Most of the trained and experienced fraud examiners come from government agencies, such as Revenue Canada, the Royal Canadian Mounted Police (RCMP), the Office of the Auditor General of Canada (OAG), provincial securities commissions (especially the OSC), the Minister of Justice and various police departments. Alumni of these agencies often practise as consultants and fraud examiners, but few of them enter public accounting to become financial statement auditors. So, what are most financial statement auditors to do? One option is to become more aware of fraud possibilities so that they can perform a limited set of procedures and determine when it is necessary to call upon people with greater fraud examination expertise. Financial statement auditors need to understand fraud and potential fraud situations, and they need to know how to ask the right kinds of questions during an audit. We know this is not impossible because there has always been the odd investigative job to be done by accountants. For example, one of the best known of fraud auditors in Canada got started doing an investigative audit of a former owner of the Toronto Maple Leafs hockey team.

DEFINITIONS RELATED TO FRAUD

LEARNING OBJECTIVE

1. Define and explain the differences among several kinds of fraud, errors, irregularities and illegal acts that might occur in an organization.

There are several kinds of "fraud." Some are defined in laws, while others are matters of general understanding. Exhibit 19–1 shows some acts and devices often involved in financial frauds. Collectively, these are known as white-collar crime—the misdeeds done by people who wear ties to work and steal with a pencil or a computer terminal. In white-collar crime there are ink stains instead of bloodstains.

Fraud consists of knowingly making material misrepresentations of fact, with the intent of inducing someone to believe the falsehood and act upon it and, thus, suffer a loss or damage. This definition encompasses all the varieties by which people can lie, cheat, steal and dupe other people.

Employee fraud is the use of fraudulent means to take money or other property from an employer. It usually involves falsifications of some kind—false documents, lying, exceeding authority or violating an employer's policies. It consists of three phases: (1) the fraudulent act, (2) the conversion of the money or property to the fraudster's use, and (3) the cover-up.

Embezzlement is a type of fraud involving employees' or nonemployees' wrongfully taking money or property entrusted to their care, custody and control, often accompanied by false accounting entries and other forms of lying and cover-up.

EXHIBIT 19-1   AN ABUNDANCE OF FRAUDS

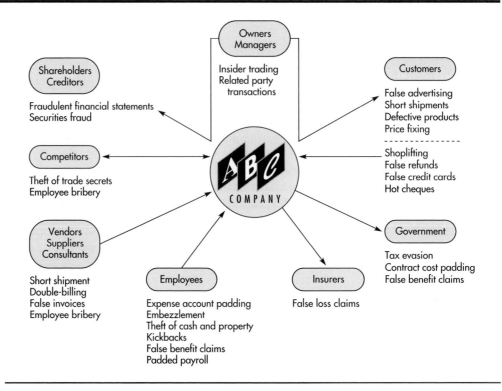

Defalcation is another name for employee fraud and embezzlement. Technically, defalcation is the term used when somebody in charge of safekeeping the assets is doing the stealing.

Management fraud is deliberate fraud committed by management that injures investors and creditors through materially misleading financial statements. The class of perpetrators is management; the class of victims is investors and creditors; and the instrument of perpetration is financial statements.[1] Sometimes management fraud is called "fraudulent financial reporting." **Fraudulent financial reporting** was defined by the National Commission on Fraudulent Financial Reporting (1987) as intentional or reckless conduct, whether by act or omission, that results in materially misleading financial statements.

The *CICA Handbook Section* 5135.02–.03 defines fraud as follows:

Fraud and other irregularities refer to an intentional misstatement in financial statements, including an omission of amount or disclosure, or to a misstatement arising from theft of the entity's assets. Fraud also involves:

(*i*) the use of deception such as manipulation, falsification, or alteration of accounting records or documentation;

(*ii*) misrepresentation or intentional omission of events, transactions, or other significant information; or

(*iii*) intentional misapplication of accounting principles relating to amount, classification, or manner of presentation of disclosure.

The word *fraud* is used in this section, although in practice the auditor will normally be concerned with a suspected rather than a proven fraud. Final determination of whether fraud has occurred will probably be made by a court of law.

---

[1] R. K. Elliott and J. J. Willingham, *Management Fraud: Detection and Deterrence* (New York: Petrocelli Books, Inc., 1980), p. 4.

Errors are unintentional misstatements or omissions of amounts or disclosures in financial statements. Irregularities are intentional misstatements or omissions in financial statements, including fraudulent financial reporting (management fraud) and misappropriations of assets (defalcations). Direct-effect illegal acts are violations of laws or government regulations by the company or its management or employees that produce direct and material effects on dollar amounts in financial statements.

Fraud auditing has been defined in courses conducted by the Association of Certified Fraud Examiners as a proactive approach to detect financial frauds using accounting records and information, analytical relationships and an awareness of fraud perpetration and concealment schemes. A good overview of the nature and scale of the fraud problem in Canada is provided by KPMG's Annual Fraud Report. For example, the 1999 report included the findings listed in the box below.

KPMG 1999 CANADIAN FRAUD SURVEY REPORT

Executive Summary

- Fifty-seven percent of survey participants drawn from Canada's 1,000 largest companies reported that fraud had taken place in their organization in 1998.

- Twenty-six percent of all respondents believe that fraud is a major problem for their business.

- The average amount of money reported lost to fraud by each of Canada's largest companies in 1998 was $958,927. One company reported that it had been defrauded out of $25 million.

- The sectors that are most affected by fraud, and where the level of concern among respondents is the highest, are financial services and retail and consumer products.

- Respondents stated that their own employees are the greatest source of fraud.

- The average amount of money lost to companies from cheque fraud was $234,936. Most companies reported that they absorbed the losses from cheque frauds.

- Most fraud was discovered by the company through existing internal controls, internal audits, whistle-blowers or by accident. Only 5 percent of all frauds were discovered through external audits.

- Sixty-one percent of respondents conduct business internationally. Of these, 21 percent stated that they had been a victim of international fraud.

- Nigeria, China and Russia are the countries where the highest number of respondents were either affected by international fraud or refuse to conduct business due to concerns about fraud.

- Thirty-six percent of respondents stated that organized crime represented a threat to their industry while 32 percent stated that it posed a threat to their company. The most frequently mentioned threats to respondents' companies by organized crime were fraud, theft, money laundering and the corruption of employees.

- Thirteen percent of respondents stated their company's computer network had been penetrated by external hackers.

Source: www.kpmg.ca as of Feb. 21, 2000.

Characteristics of Fraudsters

White-collar criminals are not like typical bank robbers, who are often described as "young and dumb." Bank robbers and other strong-arm artists often make comic mistakes like writing the holdup note on the back of a probation identification card, leaving the get-away car keys on the convenience store counter, using a zucchini as a holdup weapon and timing the holdup to get stuck in rush-hour traffic. Then there's the classic about the robber who ran into his own mother at the bank (she turned him in!).

Burglars and robbers average about $400–$500 for each hit. Employee frauds average $20,000, on up to $500,000 if a computer is used. Yet, employee frauds are not usually the intricate, well-disguised ploys you find in espionage novels. Who are these thieves wearing ties? What do they look like? Unfortunately, they "look like" most everybody else, including you and me. They have these characteristics:

- Likely to be married.
- Not likely to be divorced.
- Probably not tattooed.
- Member of a church.
- Educated beyond high school.
- No arrest record.
- Range in age from teens to over 60.
- Socially conforming.
- Employment tenure from 1 to 20 or more years.
- Usually act alone (70 percent of incidents).

White-collar criminals do not make themselves obvious, although there may be telltale signs, which will be described later as "red flags." Unfortunately, the largest frauds are committed by people who hold high executive positions, have long tenure with an organization and are respected and trusted employees. After all, these are the people who have access to the largest amounts of money and have the power to give orders and override controls.

The Art of Fraud Awareness Auditing

Fraud examination work combines the expertise of auditors and criminal investigators. Fraud examiners are fond of saying that their successes are the result of accident, hunches or luck. Nothing can be further from the reality. Successes come from experience, application of logic and the ability to see things that are not obvious (as Sherlock Holmes noticed the dog that did not bark). Fraud awareness auditing, broadly speaking, involves familiarity with many elements: the human element, organizational behaviour, knowledge

---

WHO DOES IT?

Alex W. was a 47-year-old treasurer of a credit union. Over a seven-year period, he stole $160,000. He was a good husband and the father of six children, and he was a highly reputed official of the credit union. His misappropriations came as a stunning surprise to his associates. He owed significant amounts on his home, cars, university for two children, two side investments and five different credit cards. His monthly payments significantly exceeded his take-home pay.

Source: National Association of Certified Fraud Examiners (NACFE), "Auditing for Fraud."

THE CASE OF THE EXTRA CHECKOUT

The district grocery store manager could not understand why receipts and profitability had fallen and inventory was hard to manage at one of the largest stores in her area. She hired an investigator who covertly observed the checkout clerks and reported that no one had shown suspicious behaviour at any of the nine checkout counters. Nine? That store only has eight, she exclaimed! (The store manager had installed another checkout aisle, not connected to the cash receipts and inventory maintenance central computer, and was pocketing all the receipts from that register.)

---

of common fraud schemes, evidence and its sources, standards of proof and sensitivity to red flags.[2]

Independent auditors of financial statements and fraud examiners approach their work differently. While there are many differences, these are some of the most important and obvious ones:

- Financial auditors follow a program/procedural approach designed to accomplish a fairly standard job, while fraud examiners float in a mind-set of sensitivity to the unusual where nothing is standard.

- Financial auditors make note of errors and omissions, while fraud examiners focus as well on exceptions, oddities and patterns of conduct.

- Financial auditors assess control risk in general and specific terms to design other audit procedures, while fraud examiners habitually "think like a crook" to imagine ways that controls could be subverted for fraudulent purposes.

- Financial auditors work to a level of materiality (dollar size big enough to matter) that is usually much higher than the amounts that fraud examiners consider worth pursuing. Financial auditors use materiality as a measure of importance one year at a time, whereas fraud examiners think in terms of cumulative materiality. (Theft of $20,000 per year may not loom large each year, but after a 15-year fraud career, $300,000 is a considerable loss.)

- Financial audits are based on theories of financial accounting and auditing logic, while fraud examination has a theory of behavioural motive, opportunity and integrity.

External and internal auditors get credit for finding about 20 percent of discovered frauds. Larger percentages are discovered by voluntary confessions, anonymous tips and other haphazard means. Fraud examiners have a higher success rate because they are called in for a specific purpose when fraud is known or highly suspected.

Some aspects of audit methodology make a big difference in the fraud discovery success experience. Financial auditors often utilize inductive reasoning—that is, they sample accounting data, derive audit findings and project ("induct") the finding to a conclusion about the population of data sampled. Fraud examiners often enjoy the expensive luxury of utilizing deductive reasoning—that is, after being tipped off that a certain type of loss occurred or probably occurred, they can identify the suspects, make clinical observations (stakeouts), conduct interviews and interrogations, eliminate dead-end results and concentrate on running the fraudster to ground. They can conduct covert activities that usually

---

[2] These and other aspects of the art of fraud auditing are more fully developed in G.J. Bologna and R.J. Lindquist, *Fraud Auditing and Forensic Accounting* (New York: John Wiley & Sons, 1987), pp. 27–42; W.S. Albrecht, M.B. Romney, D.J. Cherrington, I.R. Payne, and A.J. Roe, *How to Detect and Prevent Business Fraud* (New York: Prentice-Hall, 1982); R. White and W.G. Bishop, III, *The Role of the Internal Auditor in the Deterrence, Detection, and Reporting of Fraudulent Financial Reporting* (The Institute of Internal Auditors); and M.J. Barrett and R.N. Carolus, *Control and Internal Auditing* (The Institute of Internal Auditors).

are not in the financial auditors' tool kit. The "expensive luxury" of the deductive approach involves surveying a wide array of information and information sources, eliminating the extraneous and retaining the selection that proves the fraud.

R E V I E W
CHECKPOINTS

19.1 What are the defining characteristics of white-collar crime? employee fraud? embezzlement? defalcation? management fraud? errors? irregularities? illegal acts?

19.2 What does a fraud perpetrator look like? And how does one act?

19.3 Compare and contrast the type of work performed by external auditors (auditing financial statements to render an audit report) and fraud examiners.

AUDITORS' AND INVESTIGATORS' RESPONSIBILITIES

LEARNING OBJECTIVE

2. Explain the various auditing standards regarding external, internal and governmental auditors' responsibilities with respect to detecting and reporting errors, irregularities and illegal acts.

Audit standards from several sources explain the responsibilities for errors, irregularities and illegal acts. The term "external auditors" refers to independent PAs who audit financial statements for the purpose of rendering an opinion; internal auditors and certified internal auditors are references to persons, who can be both independent and PAs, employed within organizations; "government auditors" refers to auditors whose work is governed by the public sector sections of the audit standards, whether they be audit employees of governments or public accounting firms engaged to perform government audits; and "fraud examiners" refers to people engaged specifically for fraud investigation work. Forensic or investigative accounting deals with the relationship and application of financial facts to legal problems, particularly in use of the findings at a trial. "The involvement of the forensic accountant is almost always on a reactive basis which distinguishes the forensic accountant from the fraud auditor, who more usually tends to be involved on an active basis with the aspects of prevention and detection in a corporate or regulatory environment.[3]

External Auditors' Responsibilities

The CICA auditing standards are rigorous. Relevant standards concern misstatements (*Section* 5135), misstatements due to illegal acts by clients (*Section* 5136), auditing accounting estimates (*Section* 5305), communication with audit committees or equivalent (AUG–11), and communication of matters identified during the financial statement audit (*Section* 5750).

Auditor's Responsibility to Detect and Report Errors and Irregularities
Section 5135 presents an extensive array of audit responsibilities. The details are in Appendix 19A. Basically, *Section* 5135 requires auditors to understand errors and irregularities, assess the risk of their occurrence, design audits to provide reasonable assurance of detecting material ones and report on findings to management, directors, users of financial statements (sometimes) and outside agencies (certain conditions).

Illegal Acts by Clients
Section 5136 does not distinguish between the two kinds of illegal acts identified in U.S. standard SAS 53:

(1) Direct-effect illegal acts produce direct and material effects on financial statement amounts (e.g., violations of tax laws and government contracting regulations for cost and revenue recognition), and they come under the same responsibilities as errors and irregularities; and
(2) Indirect-effect illegal acts is the term used to refer to violations of laws and regulations that are far removed from financial statement effects (e.g., violations relating to insider securities

---

[3] G.J. Bologna and R.J. Lindquist, *Fraud Auditing and Forensic Accounting* (Wiley, 1987), p. 85.

trading, occupational health and safety, food and drug administration, environmental protection and equal employment opportunity).

In the United States the far-removed illegal acts come under a responsibility for general awareness, particularly in matters of contingent liability disclosure, but not routine responsibility for detection and reporting. Details of U.S. standards are in Appendix 19A.

Section 5136, on the other hand, requires auditors to consider the consequences of the illegal acts and the best way of disclosing such consequences. If failures to disclose would result in a material misstatement, then the auditor should attempt to reduce this risk to an appropriately low level. *Section* 5136 acknowledges that illegal acts may be difficult to detect because of (1) efforts made to conceal them, and (2) questions about whether an act is illegal, which are complex and may only be resolved by a court of law. For these reasons *Section* 5136.10 recommends that the engagement letter inform management of limitations in detecting illegal acts through the audit.

The auditor should use knowledge of the business and make enquiries of management to identify laws and regulations that could result in material misstatements if violated and not reported (*Section* 5136.11). In addition, auditors should enquire and obtain representations about awareness and disclosure of possibly illegal acts (*Section* 5136.21). Discovery of material possibly illegal acts should be communicated to the audit committee and other appropriate levels of management. *Section* 5136.23 gives a list of circumstances that may indicate illegal acts.

Auditing Accounting Estimates

Section 5305 is related to fraudulent financial reporting because numerous fraud cases have involved manipulation of estimates. This area is difficult because an accounting estimate is an approximation of a financial statement element, item or account made by an organization's management. (Examples include allowance for loan losses, net realizable value of inventory, percentage-of-completion revenue and fair value in nonmonetary exchanges.)

Management is responsible for making the accounting estimates, and auditors are responsible for evaluating their reasonableness in the context of the financial statements taken as a whole. Auditors are supposed to keep track of the differences between (1) management's estimates and (2) the closest reasonable estimates supported by the audit evidence. And they are supposed to evaluate (1) the differences taken altogether for indications of a systematic bias and (2) the combination of differences with other likely errors in the financial statements found by other audit procedures.

Communication with Audit Committees

The *Guideline of Communication with Audit Committees* (or equivalent) (AUG–11) sets forth requirements intended to ensure that audit committees are informed about the scope and results of the independent audit. The auditing standards place great faith in audit committees and boards of directors, although their effectiveness has been questioned elsewhere.[4] *Section* 5750 requires external auditors to make oral or written communication on the following matters: (a) misstatements other than trivial errors; (b) fraud; (c) misstatements that may cause future financial statements to be materially misstated; (d) illegal or possibly illegal acts, other than ones considered inconsequential; and (e) significant weaknesses in internal control.

Appendix 19A provides additional details on these and related U.S. standards.

P.J. Cockburn, in an article titled "Closing the Gap" in the November 1993 issue of *CA Magazine* (pp. 31–32), noted that there is some inconsistency in the *Handbook* regarding responsibility to detect material misstatements due to error and those due to fraud. Specifically, *Section* 5000.04 states: "The auditor seeks reasonable assurance whether the

---

[4] Wechsler reported the findings of the National Commission on Fraudulent Financial Reporting: that of the 120 fraudulent financial reporting cases brought by the SEC between 1981 and 1986, two-thirds involved companies that had audit committees. This caused Professor Briloff to remark: "Now I see that they are not functioning as they should." (D. Wechsler, "Giving the Watchdog Fangs," *Forbes*, November 13, 1989, p. 130.) However, these observations beg the question of the thousands of companies with and without audit committees that did not get involved in fraudulent financial reporting.

financial statements are free of material misstatement" without qualifying the sources of misstatement, whereas *Section* 5135.16 explains that an auditor is "less likely" (because of concealment) to detect misstatement arising from fraud than he or she would be to detect misstatement from error. In addition, *Section* 5136 suggests that some illegal acts such as building code violations may have an even lower chance of being detected by an external auditor. These would appear to correspond to indirect-effect illegal acts.

In contrast to these CICA Standards, AICPA Standard SAS No. 82, "Consideration of Fraud in a Financial Statement Audit" (effective for periods ending after December 15, 1997), requires U.S. auditors to take the same responsibility for detecting material misstatement due to fraud (intentional misstatement) as for material misstatement due to error (unintentional misstatement). SAS 82 requires auditors to specifically assess the risk of material misstatement due to fraud in every audit. The SAS identifies two types of fraud: fraudulent financial reporting and misappropriation of assets. When the auditor finds fraud, he or she needs to consider the implications for other aspects of the audit, arrange discussions with the appropriate level of management and the audit committee and suggest that the client consult legal counsel for any regulatory requirements.

A recent study by American researchers provides more specific guidance on fraud warning signs. "The lack of awareness of the warning signs of fraud is a frequently cited cause of audit failure. If auditors better understood the signs and applied professional scepticism, they would decrease their risk of not detecting fraud. Knowing the most important warning signs should help auditors do a better job of assessing fraud risk." A survey of 130 auditors asked them to rank 30 commonly cited warning signals of fraud according to their relative importance. The auditors ranked client dishonesty as the most important factor. The survey revealed an interesting pattern. Auditors generally perceived "attitude" factors to be more important warning signs of fraud than "situational" factors.

The top 15 warning signs are listed in the box on the next page.

Internal Auditors' Responsibilities

Internal auditors' attitudes about fraud responsibilities cannot be usefully generalized. Some hesitate to get involved because they believe that a watchdog role will damage their image and effectiveness as internal consultants. Others have flocked to the fraud investigation education programs run by the National Association of Certified Fraud Examiners because they want to add the fraud expertise dimension to their skills.

The scope-of-work sections of the internal audit standards (Appendix 18A in this book) give the basic charge to internal auditors for fraud awareness auditing: Internal auditors review the reliability and integrity of financial and operating information (section 310); review the systems established to ensure compliance with policies, plans, procedures, laws and regulations (section 320); and review the means of safeguarding assets and verify the existence of assets (section 330). This charge was expanded in Statement on Internal Auditing Standards No. 3, "Deterrence, Detection, Investigation and Reporting of Fraud." An abbreviated list of some specifications from SIAS 3 is in Appendix 19A.

The internal auditing standards appear to be carefully written to impose no positive obligation for fraud detection and investigation work in the ordinary course of assignments. However, internal auditors are encouraged to be aware of the various types of frauds, their signs (red flags) and the need to follow up the notice of signs and control weaknesses to determine whether a suspicion is justified; then, alert management to call in the experts. SIAS 3 cautions that internal auditors are not expected to guarantee that fraud will be detected in the normal course of most internal audit assignments.

Public Sector Auditing Standards

As discussed in Chapter 18, public sector standards are applicable for audits conducted by government employees and by public accounting firms engaged to perform audits on

AUDITORS' RANKING OF THE RELATIVE IMPORTANCE OF FRAUD WARNING SIGNS

Auditors' rankings	Fraud warning signs
1.	Managers have lied to the auditors or have been overly evasive in response to audit enquiries.
2.	The auditor's experience with management indicates a degree of dishonesty.
3.	Management places undue emphasis on meeting earnings projections or the quantitative targets.
4.	Management has engaged in frequent disputes with auditors, particularly about aggressive application of accounting principles that increases earnings.
5.	The client has engaged in opinion shopping.
6.	Management's attitude toward financial reporting is unduly aggressive.
7.	The client has a weak control environment.
8.	A substantial portion of management compensation depends on meeting quantified targets.
9.	Management displays significant disrespect for regulatory bodies.
10.	Management operating and financial decisions are dominated by a single person or a few persons acting in concert.
11.	Client managers display a hostile attitude toward the auditors.
12.	Management displays a propensity to take undue risks.
13.	There are frequent and significant difficult-to-audit transactions.
14.	Key managers are considered highly unreasonable.
15.	The client's organization is decentralized without adequate monitoring.

Source: V.B. Heiman-Hoffman, K.P. Morgan, and J.M. Patton, "The Warning Signs of Fraudulent Financial Reporting," *Journal of Accountancy*, October 1996, pp. 76–77.

governmental organizations, programs, activities and functions. Consequently, the public sector standards control a significant portion of audits by public accountants. The basic governmental audit requirements are to know the applicable laws and regulations, design the audit to detect abuse or illegal acts and report to the proper level of authority. Some more detailed guidance from a variety of sources is provided in Appendix 19A.

Auditors are supposed to prepare a written report on their tests of compliance with applicable laws and regulations, including all material instances of noncompliance and all instances or indications of illegal acts that could result in criminal prosecution. (More discussion of compliance auditing and reports relating to laws and regulations is in Chapter 18.) Reports should be directed to the top official of an organization and, in some cases to an appropriate oversight body, including other government agencies and audit committees. Persons receiving the audit reports are responsible for reporting to law enforcement agencies.

The following box illustrates the dramatic impact that fraud can have in the public sector.

FORMER CHIEF MOUNTIE HIRED AFTER SUN EXPOSE BLITZ ON HEALTH-CARE FRAUD

Ontario Health Minister Jim Wilson contracted Inkster, now president of KPMG Investigation and Security, after widespread cheating was exposed by Sun columnist Christie Blatchford yesterday.

"The number of reported fraud cases quoted in (The) Toronto Sun are of great concern to me," Wilson said in a statement hand-delivered by aide Cynthia Janzen yesterday.

Blatchford revealed every single day, between 30 and 50 people show up at Ontario's hospitals and clinics seeking treatment with bogus health cards, and the government ignores it. In February, stolen health cards were presented for treatment 1,057 times, she wrote.

Despite promises to crack down on fraud in the 1995 throne speech and fall economic statement, Ontario's health ministry employs just one fraud investigator for every 1.6 million provincial residents. Wilson employs more political staff than enforcement officers in his $18-billion ministry, which has prosecuted only one case of fraud this year.

Janzen said Wilson was motivated after reading Blatchford's column. A 1993 internal governmental report found that fraud costs the health ministry $284 million a year. And, unfortunately, the Conservative government has failed in its promise to weed out health-care fraud, Tory and Liberal MPPs said.

"Basically, there is no enforcement," Tory MPP and Crown attorney Toni Skarica said in an interview.

"There are virtually no resources put into fraud investigations or prosecutions. As a result, we could get major frauds that undermine the economy," Skarica said.

Liberal critic Dominic Agostino said the province is losing "hundreds of millions a year" to illegitimate hucksters.

Source: Jeff Harder, *The Toronto Sun,* May 31, 1997, p. 5. Copyright 1997, *The Toronto Sun,* a division of Sun Media Corporation.

Fraud Examiner Responsibilities

If you try to make an informal ranking of the strength of commitment to fraud matters, it appears that the external auditors (GAAS) come first, followed by the public sector auditors, then the internal auditors (SIAS 3). Of course, fraud examiners have the strongest spirit of fraud detection and investigation. They differ significantly from other kinds of auditors. When they take an assignment, fraud is already known or strongly suspected. They do not fish around for fraud while performing "normal" work. In fact, the Association of Certified Fraud Examiners teaches that assignments are not begun without predication, which means a reason to believe fraud may have occurred. (The Professional Standards and Practices for Certified Fraud Examiners are reproduced in Appendix 19B.)

Fraud examiners' attitudes and responsibilities differ from those of other auditors in two additional respects—internal control, and materiality. Their interest in internal control policies and procedures lies not so much in evaluating their strengths but in evaluating their weaknesses. Fraud examiners "think like crooks" to imagine fraud schemes for getting around an organization's internal controls. They imagine scenarios of white-collar crime in situations where controls are not in place.

Fraud examiners have a different attitude about "materiality." While other auditors may have a large dollar amount as a criterion for an error that is big enough to matter, fraud examiners have a much lower threshold. An oddity is an oddity no matter the amount of money involved, and small oddities ought not be passed by just because "$5,000 isn't mate-

---

No Separation of Duties

An electronic data processing employee instructed the company's computer to pay his wife rent for land she had allegedly leased to the company by assigning her an alphanumeric code as a lessor and then ordering the payments. The control lesson: Never let a data entry clerk who processes payment claims also have access to the approved vendor master file for additions or deletions.

Source: G.J. Bologna and R.J. Lindquist, *Fraud Auditing and Forensic Accounting* (New York: John Wiley & Sons, 1987), p. 70–71.

Money, Money, Money Case

Brian Money, a 29-year-old assistant branch manager and lending officer of a large downtown Toronto bank, defrauded the bank of some $10.2 million over a 20-month period. He fabricated loans to real and fictitious customers and gambled away the proceeds at an Atlantic City casino. Money was such a valued customer that the casino flew its corporate jet to Toronto to pick him up for weekend jaunts.

The defalcation came to light when Canadian law enforcement authorities arrested Money for a traffic violation on his return from a trip to Atlantic City. A search of his person disclosed that he was carrying about $29,000 in currency. That information was passed on to the bank, which then conducted an audit and found the fictional loans and transfers of funds to the casino. The bank is suing the casino to recover at least part of its loss.

Money used a *lapping scheme* to keep auditors off his trail—that is, he paid off earlier loans with subsequent loans so that no delinquencies would show. However, the fictional loan balances grew and grew. Money's superior at the branch had approved the larger loans because "he had no reason to mistrust him." The branch manager was subsequently suspended along with the assistant branch manager for administration, a credit officer and an auditor.

Source: G.J. Bologna and R.J. Lindquist, *Fraud Auditing and Forensic Accounting* (2nd ed.), New York: John Wiley & Sons, 1995, pp. 230–231. Reprinted by permission of John Wiley & Sons, Inc.

---

rial to the financial statements taken as a whole." External auditors comprehend materiality in relation to each year's financial statements, so that, for example, a $50,000 misstatement of income might not be big enough to matter. Fraud examiners think of materiality as a cumulative amount. A fraud loss of $20,000 this year may not be material to an external auditor, but $20,000 each year for a 15-year fraud career amounts to $300,000 in the fraud examiner's eyes—and it is big enough to matter!

REVIEW CHECKPOINTS

19.4 What are the CICA auditing standards requirements regarding (*a*) awareness of fraud, (*b*) procedural audit work, (*c*) professional skepticism, and (*d*) reporting? Do these standards differ for (1) errors, irregularities, and direct-effect illegal acts; and (2) far-removed-effect illegal acts?

19.5 To what extent would you say internal auditors include fraud detection responsibility in their normal audit assignments?

19.6 How does the requirement for design of audit procedures differ in public sector audit work from external auditors' work on financial statement audits (not involving governmental auditing)? Consider both errors/irregularities and illegal acts aspects.

19.7 Why might it be said that the order of strength of commitment to fraud matters is (1) government auditors, (2) external auditors, (3) internal auditors?

19.8 Why might fraud examiners have attitudes about control systems and materiality different from those of other auditors?

· ·

CONDITIONS THAT MAKE FRAUD POSSIBLE, EVEN EASY

· · · · · · · · · · · ·

LEARNING OBJECTIVE

3. List and explain some conditions that can lead to frauds.

When can fraud occur? Imagine the probability of fraud being a function of three factors—motive, opportunity and lack of integrity. When one or two of these factors weigh heavily in the direction of fraud, the probability increases. When three of them lean in the direction of fraud, it almost certainly will occur.[5] As Bologna and Lindquist put it: Some people are honest all the time, some people (fewer than the honest ones) are dishonest all the time, most people are honest some of the time, and some people are honest most of the time.[6]

Motive

A **motive** is some kind of pressure experienced by a person and believed unshareable with friends and confidants. Psychotic motivation is relatively rare; but is characterized by the "habitual criminal," who steals simply for the sake of stealing. Egocentric motivations drive people to steal to achieve more personal prestige. Ideological motivations are held by people who think that their cause is morally superior, and that they are justified in making someone else a victim. However, economic motives are far more common in business frauds than the other three.

The economic motive is simply a need for money, and at times it can be intertwined with egocentric and ideological motivations. Ordinarily honest people can fall into circumstances where there is a new or unexpected need for money, and the normal options for talking about it or going through legitimate channels seem to be closed. Consider these needs:

- Pay college tuition.
- Pay hospital bills for a parent with cancer.
- Pay gambling debts.
- Pay for drugs.
- Pay alimony and child support.
- Pay for high lifestyle (homes, cars, boats).
- Finance business or stock speculation losses.
- Report good financial results.

Opportunity

An **opportunity** is an open door for solving the unshareable problem in secret by violating a trust. The violation may be a circumvention of internal control policies and procedures, or it may be simply taking advantage of an absence or lapse of control in an organization. We have no police state where every person is shadowed by an armed guard. Everyone has some degree of trust conferred for a job, even if it is merely the trust not to shirk and procrastinate. The higher the position in an organization, the greater the degree of trust; and, hence, the greater the opportunity for larger frauds. Here are some examples:

- Nobody counts the inventory, so losses are not known.
- The petty cash box is often left unattended.

---

[5] For further reference, see D.R. Cressey, "Management Fraud, Accounting Controls, and Criminological Theory," pp. 117–47, and Albrecht et al., "Auditor Involvement in the Detection of Fraud," pp. 207–61, both in R.K. Elliott and J.J. Willingham, *Management Fraud: Detection and Deterrence* (New York: Petrocelli Books, Inc., 1980).; J.K. Loebbecke, M.M. Eining, and J.J. Willingham, "Auditors' Experience with Material Irregularities: Frequency, Nature, and Detectability," *Auditing: A Journal of Practice and Theory*, Fall 1989, pp. 1–28.

[6] Bologna and Lindquist, *Fraud Auditing*, p. 8.

I COULDN'T TELL ANYONE

An unmarried young woman stole $300 from her employer to pay for an abortion. Coming from a family that strongly disdained premarital sex, she felt that her only alternative was to have the secret abortion. Once she realized how easy it was to steal, however, she took another $86,000 before being caught.

Source: W.S. Albrecht, "How CPAs Can Help Clients Prevent Employee Fraud," *Journal of Accountancy*, December 1988, p. 113.

- Supervisors set a bad example by taking supplies home.
- Upper management considered a written statement of ethics but decided not to publish one.
- Another employee was caught and fired, but not prosecuted.
- The finance vice president has investment authority without any review.
- Frequent emergency jobs leave a lot of excess material just lying around.

Lack of Integrity

Practically everyone, even the most violent criminals, knows the difference between right and wrong. Unimpeachable integrity is the ability to act in accordance with the highest moral and ethical values all the time. Thus, it is the lapses and occasional lack of integrity that permit motive and opportunity to take form as fraud. But people normally do not make deliberate decisions to "lack integrity today while I steal some money." They find a way to describe (rationalize) the act in words that make it acceptable for their self-image. Here are some of these rationalizations:

- I need it more than the other person (Robin Hood theory).
- I'm borrowing the money and will pay it back.
- Nobody will get hurt.
- The company is big enough to afford it.
- A successful image is the name of the game.
- Everybody is doing it.

It is noteworthy that lack of integrity appears to be the most important factor affecting the risk of management fraud. This is evident from the list in the box on page 757, which primarily reflect on management integrity. This perhaps should not be too surprising since given their authority, responsibilities and incentives, the other factors of motive and opportunity are already largely present for management, and so management integrity is the only

---

SHE CAN DO EVERYTHING

Mrs. Lemon was the only bookkeeper for an electrical supply company. She wrote the cheques and reconciled the bank account. In the cash disbursements journal, she coded some cheques as inventory, but she wrote the cheques to herself, using her own true name. When the cheques were returned with the bank statement, she simply destroyed them. She stole $416,000 over five years. After being caught and sentenced to prison, she testified to having continuous guilt over doing something she knew was wrong.

Source: NACFE, "Auditing for Fraud."

The Most Common Computer-Related Crimes

Whereas computer hacking (pranksters breaking into computers) has received most of the recent media attention, the most prevalent computer crime is the fraudulent disbursement of funds, which is generally preceded by the submission of a spurious claim in the following forms:

- False vendor, supplier or contractor invoice.
- False governmental benefit claim.
- False fringe benefit claim.
- False refund or credit claim.
- False payroll claim.
- False expense claim.

Fraudulent disbursement of funds usually requires a data entry clerk in accounts payable, payroll or the benefits section, acting either alone or in collusion with an insider or outsider (depending on how tight the internal controls are). From an accountant's perspective, the claim is a false debit to an expense so that a corresponding credit can be posted to the cash account for the issuance of a cheque. Auditors assert that such disbursement frauds represent more than half of all frauds by lower-level employees.

At higher management levels, the typical fraud involves overstating profits by the fabrication of such data as sales, which are increased arbitrarily (sales booked before the sales transaction is completed), and the understatement of expenses, which are arbitrarily reduced or disguised as deferrals to the next accounting period. There are numerous variations on these two main themes: overstatement of sales, and understatement of expenses. One of the more common ploys to overstate profits is to arbitrarily increase the ending inventory of manufactured goods or merchandise held for sale. That ploy results in understating the cost of goods sold and thereby increasing the net profit.

The executive compensation system often provides the incentive to overstate profits. If bonus awards depend on profits, executives have an economic incentive to fudge the numbers. They may also be tempted to do so if they own a great many company shares, whose value depends on investors' perceptions of profitability. If profits are down, investors are unhappy and may rush to sell, thus causing a lowered share price and depressing the value of the executive's own shares.

Manipulations of this type often require line executives and personnel in accounting and data processing capacities to conspire together. Such conspiracies have become a recurring theme in business. The pressure on executives for high performance grows each year. We are therefore likely to see more such frauds in the future.

Source: G.J. Bologna and A.J. Lindquist, *Fraud Auditing and Forensic Accounting* (2nd Edition), Wiley, 1995, pp. 176–179. Reprinted by permission of John Wiley & Sons, Inc.

---

factor remaining that can prevent fraud at the top levels of the organization. This may be one of the reasons why the "tone at the top" is one of the most important aspects of good internal controls.

R E V I E W CHECKPOINTS

19.9 What are some of the pressures that can cause honest people to contemplate theft? List some egocentric and ideological ones as well as economic ones.

19.10 What kinds of conditions provide opportunities for employee fraud? for financial statement fraud?

19.11 Give some examples of "rationalizations" that people have used to excuse fraud. Can you use them?

· ·

FRAUD PREVENTION
· · · · · · · · · · · ·

LEARNING OBJECTIVE

4. Describe ways and means for preventing frauds.

Accountants and auditors have often been exhorted to be the leaders in fraud prevention by employing their skills in designing "tight" control systems. This strategy is, at best, a short-run solution to a large and pervasive problem. Business activity is built on the trust that people at all levels will do their jobs properly. Control systems limit trust and, in the extreme, can strangle business in bureaucracy. Imagine street crime being "prevented" by enrolling half the population in the police force to control the other half! Managers and employees must have freedom to do business, which means giving them freedom to commit frauds as well.[7] Effective long-run prevention measures are complex and difficult, and involve the elimination of the causes of fraud by mitigating the effects of motive, opportunity and lack of integrity.

Managing People Pressures in the Workplace

From time to time, people will experience financial and other pressures. The pressures cannot be eliminated, but the facilities for sharing them can be created. Some companies have "ethics officers" to serve this purpose. Their job is to be available to talk over the ethical dilemmas faced in the workplace and help people adopt legitimate responses. However, the ethics officers are normally not psychological counsellors.

Many companies have "hot lines" for anonymous reporting of ethical problems. Reportedly, the best kind of hot-line arrangement is to have the responding party be an agency outside the organization. In the United States some organizations are in the business of being the recipients of hot-line calls, co-ordinating their activities with the management of the organization.

The most effective long-run prevention, however, lies in the practice of management by caring for people. Managers and supervisors at all levels can exhibit a genuine concern for the personal and professional needs of their subordinates and fellow managers, and subordinates can show the same concern for one another and for their managers. The approach is idealistic and calls for the elimination of interpersonal competition, of climbing up over the bodies of colleagues and of office "politics." Nevertheless, it is practised in many organizations in the form of staff meetings, personal counselling and "quality circles" (groups of employees from all levels who plan production, selling and administrative activities together). Some organizations have daycare centres, alcohol and drug counselling, financial counselling and other programs to help people share their problems with experts.

When external auditors are engaged in the audit of financial statements, they must obtain an understanding of the company's "control structure." The control structure includes the "control environment," which relates to the overall scheme of management activity in the company. Management that considers carefully the people pressures in the workplace, using some of the devices mentioned above, has a good control environment and the beginnings of a good control structure.

Control Procedures and Employee Monitoring

Auditors would be aghast at an organization that had no control policies and procedures, and rightly so. Controls in the form of job descriptions and performance specifications are indeed needed to help people know the jobs they are supposed to accomplish. Almost all people need some structure for their working hours. An organization whose only control is

---

[7] Cressey, "Management Fraud," p. 124.

DISHONESTY IS BAD POLICY

Now be honest. When fixing your car following an accident, your body shop includes extra repairs and puts them on the insurance company's tab. Do you say thanks and let the insurer pay?

According to an ethics poll conducted recently for the **Canadian Coalition Against Insurance Fraud,** 25 percent of those surveyed said they'd go along with the mechanic's bill padding.

For the property and casualty insurers who make up the membership of the coalition, this ethical laxity adds up to an estimated $1.3-billion-a-year problem, including the cost of police and fire officials' investigations.

That's how much is lost on fraudulent claims relating to homes. Insurance fraud is second only to illegal drug sales as a source of criminal profit.

Put another way, fraud accounts for 10 percent to 15 percent of all claims paid out—money that ends up being covered by honest policyholders in the form of increased premiums.

The coalition is conducting a study to analyse the kinds of insurance fraud that are most frequently perpetrated, says executive director Mary Lou O'Reilly.

She says a link has been found between the ethical decisions people make in their everyday lives and opportunistic fraud.

"Fraud for the average Canadian is an opportunity to 'get back' some of what they feel is rightfully theirs when they have a legitimate claim."

Sometimes, for example, they inflate a claim to cover the deductible. "But these are not seasoned criminals," she says. "These are honest people who just don't recognize that fraud is a crime."

Or people who get clumsy when they veer from the straight and narrow. Insurers have dozens of anecdotes about people whose 12-inch televisions suddenly develop 29-inch screens once they're lost. Then there was the one about the policyholder with the damaged 20-foot boat that turned out to have been stored in an 18-foot garage.

The coalition has helped cut down on fraud through an alliance with Crime Stoppers, which are volunteer-run, privately funded, anonymous telephone-tip services operated in co-operation with local police forces.

Under the arrangement, a tip called in to Crime Stoppers about a possible fraud is relayed to the Insurance Crime Prevention Bureau and investigated. Police may also be called in.

If a claim is denied, Crime Stoppers receives 5 percent of the damage claim up to $1,500, which is then passed on to the tipster at the discretion of Crime Stoppers.

Source: Susan Yellin, *The Financial Post,* May 23, 1997, p. 10.

"trustworthy employees" has no control.[8] Unfortunately, "getting caught" is an important consideration for many people when coping with their problems. Controls provide the opportunity to get caught.

Without going into much detail about controls at this point, let it be noted that procedures for recognizing and explaining red flags are important for nipping frauds in the bud before they get bigger. Controls that reveal the following kinds of symptoms are necessary:[9]

- Missing documents.
- Second endorsements on cheques.

---

[8] W.S. Albrecht, "How CPAs Can Help Clients Prevent Employee Fraud," *Journal of Accountancy,* December 1988, pp. 110–14.
[9] Ibid., pp. 113–14.

HOW TO ENCOURAGE FRAUD

Practice autocratic management.
Orient management to low trust and power.
Manage by crisis.
Centralize authority in top management.
Measure performance on a short-term basis.
Make profits the only criterion for success.
Make rewards punitive, stingy and political.
Give feedback that is always critical and negative.
Create a highly hostile, competitive workplace.
Insist that everything be documented with a rule for everything.

Source: Adapted from G.J. Bologna and R.J. Lindquist, *Fraud Auditing and Forensic Accounting* (New York: John Wiley & Sons, 1987), pp. 47–49.

- Unusual endorsements.
- Unexplained adjustments to inventory balances.
- Unexplained adjustments to accounts receivable.
- Old items in bank reconciliations.
- Old outstanding cheques.
- Customer complaints.
- Unusual patterns in deposits in transit.

The problem with control systems is that they are essentially negative restrictions on people. The challenge is to have a bare minimum of useful controls and to avoid picky rules that are "fun to beat." The challenge of "beating the system," which can lead to bigger and better things, is an invitation to fraudulent types of behaviour. (How many university students find ways to get into course registration before their scheduled times?)

Integrity by Example and Enforcement

The key to integrity in business is "accountability"—that is, each person must be willing to put his or her decisions and actions in the sunshine. There must be norms for these decisions and actions. Many organizations begin by publishing codes of conduct. Some of these codes are simple, and some are very elaborate. Government agencies and defence contractors typically have the most elaborate rules for employee conduct. Sometimes they work, sometimes they don't. A code can be effective if the "tone at the top" supports it. When the chairman of the board and the president make themselves visible examples of the code, then other people will believe it is real. Subordinates will tend to follow the boss's lead.

Hiring and firing are important. Background checks on prospective employees are advisable. A new employee who has been a fox in some other organization's hen house will probably be a fox in a new place. Organizations have been known to hire private investigators to make these background checks. Fraudsters should be fired and, in most cases, prosecuted. They have a low rate of recidivism (repeat offences) if they are prosecuted, but they have a high rate if not.[10] Prosecution delivers the message that management does not believe that "occasional dishonesty" is acceptable.

---

[10] Ibid., p. 114.

REGULATORS UNITE TO FIGHT TELEMARKETING SCAMS

Two Canadian securities commissions have joined regulators from 21 U.S. states and the U.S. Federal Trade Commission in an offensive on telemarketing scams that cost investors about $40 billion a year.

Securities regulators in Quebec and British Columbia are taking part in the campaign, "Project Field of Schemes," by publicizing some of the most significant cases of the past three months.

Frauds over the Internet are a new source of concern, an extension of the telemarketing campaigns that target old people.

"The Internet is like a huge classified ad section, with a money wanted column showing you where to invest, and it becomes a perfect medium for conveying investment offers," said Mark Griffin, president of the North American Securities Administrators Association.

The British Columbia Securities Commission supported the campaign because it knows all regulators deal with the same types of scams, often orchestrated by the same people.

"Frauds are similar wherever you go—and often the perpetrators have crossed jurisdictional boundaries so they can start fresh in a new place where they are not known," said Barbara Barry, communications manager at the BCSC.

"Basically, people and their greed are universal."

She noted a recent case involving a company called Goldman-Stanley consultants, which controlled four other firms. Its name was purposely similar to that of the well-known New York investment house and its stationery had a similar look.

"People who bought believed that Goldman-Stanley consultants were agents that were placing foreign exchange contract purchases for legitimate companies in other jurisdictions," Berry said.

Goldman-Stanley also used a storefront location to mimic a well-known Hong Kong investment firm in a successful attempt to solicit Asian clients.

Source: Ian Karleff, *The Financial Post,* July 3, 1997, p. 8.

WHERE DID HE COME FROM?

The controller defrauded the company for several million dollars. As it turned out, he was no controller at all. He didn't know a debit from a credit. The fraudster had been fired from five previous jobs where money had turned up missing. He was discovered one evening when the president showed up unexpectedly at the company and found a stranger in the office with the controller. The stranger was doing all of the accounting for the bogus controller.

Source: NACFE, "Auditing for Fraud."

R E V I E W
CHECKPOINTS

19.12   Make a two-column list with fraud-prevention management-style characteristics in one column and, opposite each of these, management-style characteristics that might lead to fraud.

FRAUD DETECTION
. . . .

Since an organization cannot prevent all fraud, its auditors, accountants and security personnel must be acquainted with some detection techniques. Frauds consist of the fraud act itself, the conversion of assets to the fraudster's use and the cover-up. Catching people in the fraud act is difficult and unusual. The act of conversion is equally difficult to observe, since it typically takes place in secret away from the organization's offices (e.g., fencing stolen inventory). Many frauds are investigated by noticing signs and signals of fraud, then following the trail of missing, mutilated or false documents that are part of the accounting records cover-up.

This chapter has already mentioned signs and signals in terms of red flags, oddities and unusual events. Being able to notice these takes some experience, but this book can give some starting places.[11]

Red Flags

LEARNING OBJECTIVE
5. Describe some common employee fraud schemes and explain some audit and investigation procedures for detecting them.

Employee Fraud.   Employee fraud usually, but not always, involves people below the top executive levels. Observation of persons' habits and lifestyle and changes in habits and lifestyle may reveal some red flags. Fraudsters in the past have exhibited these characteristics:

- Lose sleep.
- Take drugs.
- Can't relax.
- Can't look people in the eye.
- Go to confession (e.g., priest, psychiatrist).
- Work standing up.
- Drink too much.
- Become irritable easily.
- Get defensive, argumentative.
- Sweat excessively.
- Find excuses and scapegoats for mistakes.
- Work alone, work late.

HIGH STYLE IN THE MAILROOM

A female mailroom employee started wearing designer clothes (and making a big deal about it). She drove a new BMW to work. An observant manager, who had known her as an employee for seven years and knew she had no outside income, became suspicious. He asked the internal auditors to examine her responsibilities extra carefully. They discovered she had taken $97,000 over a two-year period.

Source: NACFE, "Auditing for Fraud."

---

[11] Long lists of red flags can be found in Bologna and Lindquist, *Fraud Auditing*, pp. 49–56; Albrecht et. al., in *Management Fraud*, pp. 223–26; Statement on Auditing Standard 82; "Auditing for Fraud" courses of the Association of Certified Fraud Examiners; and courses offered by other organizations, such as the CICA and the Institute of Internal Auditors.

Personality red flags are problematic because (1) honest people sometimes show them and (2) they often are hidden from view. It is easier to notice changes, especially when a person changes his or her lifestyle or spends more money than the salary justifies—for example, on homes, furniture, jewellery, clothes, boats, autos, vacations and the like.

Often, telltale hints of the cover-up are visible. These generally appear in the accounting records. The key is to notice exceptions and oddities, such as transactions that are at odd times of the day, month or season; too many or too few; in the wrong branch location; and in amounts too high, too low, too consistent or too different. Exceptions and oddities can appear in these forms:

- Missing documents.
- Cash shortages and overages.
- Excessive voids and credit memos.
- Customer complaints.
- Common names or addresses for refunds.
- Adjustments to receivables and payables.
- General ledger that does not balance.
- Increased past due receivables.
- Inventory shortages.
- Increased scrap.
- Alterations on documents.
- Duplicate payments.
- Employees who cannot be found.
- Second endorsements on cheques.
- Documents being photocopied.
- Dormant accounts becoming active.

Broker Vows to Repay Huge Client Losses

A former investment-market whiz kid facing multi-million-dollar lawsuits and fraud charges has vowed to reimburse client's losses, his lawyer says.

Mr. X faces 15 fraud charges totalling $22 million and lawsuits from more than 20 ex-clients claiming $10 million . . .

Investors accused Mr. X, 33, of misrepresenting the value of their funds, negotiating without their knowledge and not repaying loans. His ex-employers and wife are also being sued.

After retirees, a taxi owner, a dentist, accountants, a builder and an actress told First Marathon Securities Ltd. and Midland Walwyn Capital Inc of unusual losses, Mr. X was fired and his licence suspended. Charged Monday in one of Canada's largest brokerage frauds, he was freed on bail.

Gone are the couple's Porsche, Jaguar and lavish parties, the couple's lawyer said. Their $1.3 million Forest Hill home and their Cobourg house are so heavily mortgaged "there might be no equity."

Two Toronto retirees claimed US$582,121 was lost with Mr. X, court documents say.

Eight clients in million dollar claims cite Mr. X for "deceit, fraud . . . negligence and breach of contract," said their lawyer, Neil Gross. "All of them have suffered devastating losses."

Source: Ian Robertson, *The Toronto Sun,* June 12, 1997, p. 2. Copyright 1997, *The Toronto Sun,* a division of Sun Media Corporation.

Management Fraud (Fraudulent Financial Reporting)

LEARNING OBJECTIVE

6. Describe some common financial reporting fraud features and explain some audit and investigation procedures for detecting them.

Fraud that affects financial statements and causes them to be materially misleading often arises from the perceived need to "get through a difficult period." The difficult period may be characterized by a cash shortage, increased competition, cost overruns and similar events. Managers usually view these conditions as "temporary," believing they can be overcome by getting a new loan, selling shares or otherwise buying time to recover. In the meantime, falsified financial statements are used to "benefit the company." These conditions and circumstances have existed along with frauds in the past:

- Unfavourable industry conditions.
- Excess capacity.
- High debt.
- Profit squeeze.
- Strong foreign competition.
- Lack of working capital.
- Rapid expansion.
- Product obsolescence.
- Slow customer collections.
- Related party transactions.

By both fraud and "creative accounting," companies have caused financial statements to be materially misleading by (1) overstating revenues and assets, (2) understating expenses and liabilities, and (3) giving disclosures that are misleading or that omit important information. Generally, fraudulent financial statements show financial performance and ratios that are better than current industry experience or better than the company's own history. Sometimes the performance meets exactly the targets announced by management months earlier.

Because of the double-entry bookkeeping system, fraudulent accounting entries always affect two accounts and two places in financial statements. Since many frauds involve improper recognition of assets, there is a theory of the "dangling debit," which is an asset amount that can be investigated and found to be false or questionable. Frauds may involve the omission of liabilities, but the matter of finding and investigating the "dangling credit" is normally very difficult. It "dangles" off the books. Misleading disclosures also present difficulty, mainly because they involve words and messages instead of numbers. Omissions may be hard to notice, and misleading inferences may be very subtle.

OVERSTATED REVENUE, RECEIVABLES AND DEFERRED COSTS

Cali Computer Systems, Inc., sold franchises enabling local entrepreneurs to open stores and sell Cali products. The company granted territorial franchises, in one instance recording revenue of $800,000 and in another $580,000. Unfortunately, the first of these "contracts" for a territorial franchise simply did not exist, and the second was not executed and Cali had not performed its obligations by the time it was recorded. In both cases the imaginary revenue was about 40 percent of reported revenues. These franchises were more in the nature of business hopes than completed transactions.

Cali was supposed to deliver computer software in connection with the contracts and had deferred $277,000 of software development cost in connection with the programs. However, this software did not work, and the contracts were fulfilled with software purchased from other suppliers.

Source: SEC Accounting and Auditing Enforcement Release 190, 1988.

A client's far-removed illegal acts may cause financial statements to be misleading, and external auditors are advised to be aware of circumstances that might indicate them. Below is a list of some signs and signals of the potential for illegal acts:

- Unauthorized transactions.
- Government investigations.
- Regulatory reports of violations.
- Payments to consultants, affiliates, employees for unspecified services.
- Excessive sales commissions and agent's fees.
- Unusually large cash payments.
- Unexplained payments to government officials.
- Failure to file tax returns, to pay duties and fees.

BRIBERY AND CORRUPTION: A NEW GLOBAL SOCIAL CONCERN

An article in the *White Paper* (May/June 1997), a publication of the Association of Certified Fraud Examiners, titled "The Global Explosion of Corruption—the Misuse of Public Power for Private Profit or Political Gain," identifies corruption as a major challenge in the new global, high-tech economy. A long section of the article talks about Transparency International, a unique organization dedicated to fighting global corruption. This section is reproduced in full below.

Transparency International Encourages Governments to Fight Corruption

In 1993, Dr. Peter Eigen, former World Bank director, founded Transparency International (TI) in Berlin as a not-for-profit, non-governmental organization, "to counter corruption . . . in international business transactions," according to its mission statement.

The small group, which has organized over 60 chapters throughout the world, says that it encourages governments to establish laws, policies and anti-corruption programs. TI is funded by multilateral groups (including the World Bank), national programs and private companies.

TI says that corruption is causing vast sums of money to be misallocated by public officials in dozens of countries. The group says that funds which were originally earmarked for new schools, hospitals and institutions to serve the most needy, are often channelled into projects of negligible social value by officials receiving kickbacks from commercial contractors.

Corruption is also the enemy of progress, TI says. Corrupt leaders cling to power, opposing efforts to open government, curbing personal freedoms and abusing human rights, the group says. Also, the honest business person goes broke, the rules of a healthy economic system become twisted, and companies addicted to paying bribes become rotten, TI says.

The group says there are too many countries where corporations can pay bribes abroad and claim these as tax deductible expenses in their home countries. "We will do our best to get our house in order," said Ethiopian Prime Minister Meles Zenawi at an international conference a year ago, "but our Northern friends: please do not support the bribery by your exporters by giving them tax deductions for their bribes."

One of the most effective ways that TI has publicized the corruption problem is through its annual Corruption Perception Index based on the experience of multinational corporations. See the box below. This index is increasingly used to develop international efforts to fight worldwide corruption and bribery.

THE TRANSPARENCY INTERNATIONAL CORRUPTION PERCEPTION INDEX (CPI), 1998 (85 COUNTRIES)

Country rank	Selected countries	CPI score (out of 10)
1	Denmark	10.0
6	Canada	9.2
11	UK	8.7
17	USA	7.5
21	France	6.7

Higher-risk countries (5.0 or less) in which
Canadian companies are most likely to do business

39	Italy	4.6
43	South Korea	4.2
46	Brazil	4.0
52	China	3.5
55	Mexico	3.3
55	Philippines	3.3
61	Argentina	3.0
66	India	2.9
71	Pakistan	2.7
76	Russia	2.4
80	Indonesia (pre-Suharto overthrow)	2.0

Source: S. Chester and D. Selley, "Giving Kickbacks the boot," *CAmagazine*, August 1999, Exhibit 1, p. 22.

"The mounting support for anti-corruption action in the international organizations is a vital requirement in raising this issue to highest political levels in governments around the globe," said Eigen. "But these initiatives only have an impact if they are followed up at the national level and if organizations like TI constantly monitor the official agencies to see their bold rhetoric is matched by meaningful action."

Electronic trading and funds transfer systems [see Chapter 21] combined with offshore banking havens and new financial instruments have facilitated the laundering of criminal and illegal funds. It has been estimated that up to 25 percent of financial instruments and foreign currency trading involves some kind of illegal money laundering scheme. Cross border capital flows now amount to $1.25 trillion per day. The illegitimate amounts are so huge that they threaten world financial markets. The only way to deal with money laundering of this scale is through international efforts.

As part of an international fight against bribery sponsored by TI and the Organization for Economic Cooperation and Development (OECD), early in 1999 Canada made it illegal to pay foreign bribes. Modelled on the US's Foreign Corrupt Practices Act, Canada's Corruption of Foreign Public Officials Act makes foreign bribes illegal and a nondeductible business expense. Thus foreign bribes now fall under *Section* 5136 "Misstatements—Illegal Acts." This makes auditors responsible for the detection of foreign bribes that can have a material effect on the financial statements. Auditors now need to assess the risk of such material misstatements by, for example, checking to see how much and the nature of business done in "high risk" countries in the corruption index. Other risk factors to consider include a past record of having to pay bribes and unnecessarily complex or unusual payment methods.[12]

---

[12] S. Chester and D. Selley, "Giving Kickbacks the boot," *CAmagazine*, August 1999, pp. 20–24.

WORTH A CLOSER LOOK

Consider the following audit procedures when the combined
inherent and control risk is assessed as "not low"

- Examine all relevant contracts and source documents thoroughly. Discuss them with management to assess whether they reflect the transaction's substance.

- When applicable, check documentation concerning the bidding process for major contracts in foreign countries, including the inclusion of unusually large agency fees or other amounts that do not appear to relate directly to the contract's substance.

- Review banking records for large and unusual transactions or cash transactions. Consider using analytical procedures such as data-mining techniques.

- If local auditors are involved (whether affiliates of the Canadian auditor or not), discuss the risk assessment with them and obtain their views of the likelihood of a bribe having been paid; also discuss the procedures they have carried out or might perform. Be aware, too, that the position of such auditors may be very sensitive in their local environment and that telephone and other communications may not be secure. It may be appropriate to visit the locations concerned.

- If payments are made through offshore companies or bank accounts, obtain information about the companies and financial institutions to assess their legitimacy.

- If inexplicably large payments are made to an agent, attempt to contact the agent to determine how the fees were disbursed. This will often be a fruitless exercise, but a refusal to answer on the agent's part significantly increases the likelihood that the Corruption of Foreign Public Officials Act has been breached. An agent should not be contacted without the client's permission.

Source: S. Chester and D. Selley, "Giving Kickbacks the Boot," *CAmagazine*, August 1999, Exhibit 2, p. 23.

Controls to compensate for these high inherent risks include a corporate code of conduct with specific policies and procedures designed to avoid violating the Act, and effective monitoring and communication of these procedures. If combined inherent and control risks are assessed as too high, then the auditor would consider additional procedures as listed in the box above.

REVIEW
CHECKPOINTS

19.13 Is there anything odd about these situations? (1) Auditors performed a surprise payroll distribution, and J. Jones, S. Smith, and D. Douglas were absent from work. (2) A cheque to Larson Lectric Supply was endorsed with "Larson Lectric" above the signature of "Eloise Garfunkle." (3) Numerous cheques were issued dated January 1, May 22, July 1, September 4, October 9, and December 25, 2000.

19.14 What account could you audit to determine whether a company had recorded fictitious sales?

Internal Control

A study by KPMG showed that 50 percent of all frauds are detected by the internal control system. An important feature of internal control is the separation of these duties and responsibilities: (1) transaction authorization, (2) recordkeeping, (3) custody of, or access to, assets, and (4) reconciliation of actual assets to the accounting records. Generally, a per-

THE TRUSTED EMPLOYEE

A small business owner hired his best friend to work as his accountant. The friend was given full unlimited access to all aspects of the business and was completely responsible for the accounting. Five years later, the owner finally terminated the friend because the business was not profitable. Upon taking over the accounting, the owner's wife found that cash receipts from customers were twice the amounts formerly recorded by the accountant "friend." An investigation revealed that the friend had stolen $450,000 in cash sales receipts from the business, while the owner had never made more than $16,000 a year. (The friend had even used the stolen money to make loans to the owner and to keep the business going!)

NO LOCKS ON THE DOOR

Perini Corporation kept blank cheques in an unlocked storeroom, where every clerk and secretary had access. Also in the storeroom was the automatic cheque-signing machine. The prenumbered cheques were not logged and restricted to one person. The bookkeeper was very surprised to open the bank statement one month and find that $1.5 million in stolen cheques had been paid on the account.

Source: NACFE, "Auditing for Fraud."

son who, acting alone or in a conspiracy, can perform two or more of these functions also can commit a fraud by taking assets, converting them and covering up. (Other control features were explained in Chapter 6.)

Fraud awareness auditing involves perceptions of the controls installed (or not installed) by a company, plus "thinking like a crook" to imagine ways and means of stealing. When controls are absent, the ways and means may be obvious. Otherwise, it may take some scheming to figure out how to steal from an organization.

WHEN YOUR IDENTITY IS STOLEN

Even your utility bills can be turned to fraudulent use.

A 22-year-old secretary realizes she's got an evil twin travelling around the country when Revenue Canada begins demanding she cough up unpaid taxes. Her imposter—who'd apparently applied for and received a social insurance number under her name years earlier—has been moving from job to job without paying taxes.

The names of children who died years ago are used to set up phony businesses that collect GST refunds. An Etobicoke man, who is eventually jailed for tax fraud, collected the names from tombstones.

Another con man opens a number of accounts at Vancouver-area banks using someone else's SIN and birth certificate. He defrauds the banks of more than $170,000 by depositing phony cheques and withdrawing the money from ATMs.

Identity thieves take over someone else's identity to commit fraud—either by applying for a credit card or loan, opening a bank account or using social insurance numbers to hide from the taxman.

These are some of the stories on the growing list of Canadian cases involving identity theft as identified by privacy commissioner Ann Cavoukian.

The victim often doesn't find out what's happened until months later and by that time his or her credit report is such a mess it can take years to sort out.

Cavoukian has just released a report on some of the steps she believes need to be taken to stop the crime. Some of the less obvious ones include the following:

Tips to prevent identity theft

- Shred or tear up sensitive documents before throwing them away. These include phone and utility bills, pre-approved credit applications and anything that provides credit card number, bank account number, tax information, your driver's license number or your birth date.
- Install a locked mailbox.
- Obtain a copy of your credit report regularly to check for fraudulent accounts and false address changes. Contact Equifax Canada Inc at 1-800-465-7166.
- Don't leave a paper record behind after using bank machines.
- Avoid writing your credit card number or SIN on a cheque.
- Don't give your credit card number out over the phone unless you know the company you're dealing with well. It's especially important not to provide personal information over cordless or cellular phones.

Source: Valeries Lawton, *Toronto Star,* July 6, 1997, B5. Reprinted with permission—The Toronto Star Syndicate.

REVIEW CHECKPOINTS

19.15 What could happen if a person could authorize medical insurance claims and enter them into the system for payment without supervisory review?

19.16 What could happen if the inventory warehouse manager also had responsibility for making the physical inventory observation and reconciling discrepancies to the perpetual inventory records?

SCHEMES AND DETECTION PROCEDURES

An article by J. Hall, titled "How to Spot Fraud," first printed in the October 1996 issue of *Journal of Accountancy,* is quoted in full in the following box:

1. Focus on Fraud Possibilities

Hard as it is to accept, most preventive controls can be beaten by a motivated thief. And when thieves are inside the organization, they may be part of the control effort itself.

Ask yourself how management steps such as reengineering, downsizing, outsourcing, computerization and globalization affect the reliability of controls—as well as the attitudes of those who have access to the assets.

Other places to look are industry resources. Many industry organizations maintain data on fraud cases. Since banks, insurers and others all support fraud prevention, contact your industry association's security professionals for guidance.

Keep files of news reports of fraud. These articles often contain enough detail to allow you to understand how the deed was done. But be careful not to get caught up in the drama of the fraud: Put less emphasis on the thieves and their reasons for stealing, focusing instead on the modus operandi.

Typical questions you should ask:

- What jobs are likely to provide opportunities for fraud?
- What opportunities exist for employees, executives, vendors, contractors' agents, customers and others?
- How could they get around approval or transaction confirmation controls?
- What general ledger account and cost center could the fraud be charged to?
- How could the thief deceive the manager in charge of those cost centers when the month-end reports are reviewed?

2. Know the Symptoms

Here's a short list of some fraud symptoms:

- Multiple endorsements on commercial cheques.
- The use of common or repetitive names for refunds—such as Smith or Jones or a commercial name that is very similar to one in your industry but is spelled slightly differently.
- Line items in standard reconciliations that don't go away.
- Customer complaints about having paid invoices for which they are being dunned.
- Adjustments to either inventory records or customer accounts.
- The addresses of vendors that are the same as employee addresses.
- No proceeds from the disposition of used assets.

When one of these symptoms appears, use caution. Often there are reasonable explanations and they usually don't lead to a thief—just an error or an ill-designed process. So don't jump to conclusions. Instead, track down the cause for the symptom.

Be especially cautious when reacting to a person's suspicious lifestyle. While such signs should sound an alarm, by themselves they prove nothing, but certainly more investigation is warranted.

3. Design Controls and Audit Procedures

In developing procedures, be sure to include specific steps calculated to look for fraud symptoms. And while measuring fraud exposure, assess the reliability of such controls.

4. Follow Through on All Symptoms Observed

Whoever finds a symptom of fraud—the external or internal auditor or a company manager—should resolve the situation before going on. Operate with an attitude of healthy professional skepticism. Beware of pressures to complete work within unreasonable deadlines. Be aware that the single symptom you are looking at may not be an isolated occurrence, it may be one of many.

If you believe the follow-up is beyond your capabilities, consider giving the problem to a professional investigator. There are legal liability dangers inherent in mishandling possible fraud cases."

The same article provides a case study reproduced in the following box:

THE REBATE SCAM

A construction company's project manager engineered a simple scam that earned him about $250,000 before he was unmasked. Here's how he did it—and how he was tripped up:

The project manager opened a bank account using a name very similar to the name of the construction project he was managing. He then approached three major suppliers and requested cash rebates in excess of normal industry practice. In exchange, he guaranteed each would be the sole source for their respective products. In addition, he promised they would be paid promptly for all materials delivered. He told them the rebates were due on the first of each month for all transactions of the proceeding month. The cheques were to be made payable to the name on the bogus bank account.

The suppliers agreed to the unusual terms in order to secure the business. None questioned the name on the cheques because it was close enough to the actual project name.

The arrangement worked smoothly for several months. Rebate cheques were delivered to the project manager each month and he deposited them into his account. After the cheques cleared, he withdrew most of the funds using cashier's cheques.

The scheme came to light when a supervisor in the construction company's accounts payable department questioned why prompt-payment discounts weren't being made to the three suppliers. She had just attended a fraud-awareness seminar and remembered that such an unusual arrangement might be a symptom of fraud. Rather than question either the project manager or the suppliers, she correctly referred the matter to the corporate audit department for investigation.

The auditors made simultaneous unannounced visits to all three suppliers. Two wouldn't talk, but the third explained the relationship and provided copies of the cancelled rebate cheques.

Lessons learned from the case:

- It's relatively easy to open unauthorized bank accounts because most banks have limited ability to verify the identity of the person opening an account.
- Scam artists know how to cash cheques—to any payee, in any amount.
- Schemes that involve relationships with suppliers are particularly hard to prevent and detect.
- When contracting with suppliers, try to secure the right to review any appropriate records. While this is fairly common in the contracting environment, it's also something to consider for other relationships in which purchase orders are used.

The importance of internal control in preventing and detecting fraud cannot be underestimated. In designing a system of controls it's important to identify weaknesses or improper utilization of materials, people or equipment. A good first step is to investigate the company's historical experience with losses and how to prevent the losses. A system of checks and balances should be designed to address these risks. To the extent possible every transaction should be authorized, initiated, approved, executed and recorded. No transaction should be handled by one person. Preprinted serial numbered documents such as purchase orders, sales and purchases invoices, receiving reports, cheques and debit or credit memos should be used. All policies and procedures should be documented, including procedures in the event of an internal control breakdown. Once implemented, the internal con-

---

A Simple Internal Controls Checklist for Companies

- Allow for a system of checks and balances. Every transaction should be authorized, initiated, approved, executed and recorded.
- Divide or segregate duties. Do not allow one person to handle all aspects of a transaction from beginning to end.
- Do not allow the same person to have custody of an asset (i.e. cash and inventory) and the responsibility to record transactions.
- Use serial numbers on debit or credit memos, sales and purchases invoices, cheques, tickets, purchase orders and receiving reports.
- Use a safe, and maintain adequate safekeeping of all assets. Make deposits on a daily basis, and if necessary, several times per day.
- Use a budget or forecast to detect whether goals are achieved. Investigate the differences—what happened and why.
- Incorporate hiring policies and practices, which include drug testing and background checks. Subscribe to an ethics hot line, such as the Association's *EthicsLine*, to provide a way for employees to report anonymously suspected infractions or violations within a company to an independent party.

Safeguarding Small Businesses

The minimum controls for a small organization are as follows:

- deposit all cash receipts intact daily;
- make all payments by serial-numbered cheques with the exception of small transactions by petty cash;
- reconcile bank accounts monthly;
- record all cash receipts immediately;
- balance ledgers at regular intervals; and
- prepare comparative financial statements in sufficient detail every month to disclose significant variations in revenue and expense categories.

Source: D. A. Sebert, "Repeat After Me: Internal Controls, Internal Controls, Internal Controls . . ." *The White Paper*, September/October 1998, p. 33.

---

trol system should be communicated orally and in writing to all employees. The policies should communicate firmly and clearly that fraud will not be tolerated and the consequences of fraud involvement. The internal control system should be evaluated periodically for cost effectiveness, and employee feedback should be encouraged and rewarded. The box above gives a basic system of controls to deter common types of fraud.

SOME NEWER APPROACHES TO FRAUD DETECTION

The SSA audits discussed in Chapter 13 have been promoted as a means to increase the auditor's effectiveness in detecting fraud. "The use of complex analytical procedures comprising an SSA knowledge acquisition framework, coupled with an assessment of other fraud risk factors, should improve the auditor's ability to detect and diagnose anomalies associated with management fraud. And, a comprehensive knowledge decision frame will serve to heighten the auditor's level of professional skepticism when appropriate, e.g., by enabling the auditor to develop his own hypotheses about unusual financial-statement trends and fluctuations without relying exclusively on management's explanations."[13]

Another recent development in the auditor's fraud detection arsenal is the use of Benford's Law to detect anomalies in the accounting records as indicated in the box below.

In this section of the chapter we will consider some "casettes" (little cases). They will follow a standard format in two major parts: (1) Case Situation, and (2) Audit Approach. Some problems at the end of the chapter will give the case situation, and you will be assigned to write the audit approach section. The first three casettes deal with employee fraud, and the last two deal with management fraud. With the first three casettes, you can practise on learning objective 5: Describe some common employee fraud schemes and explain some audit and investigation procedures for detecting them. With the last two casettes, you can practise on learning objective 6: Describe some common financial reporting fraud features and explain some audit and investigation procedures for detecting them.

BENFORD'S LAW AND AUDITING

Do financial statements universally "favor" some numbers over others? The idea seems to defy logic. In a random string of numbers pulled from a company's books, each digit, 1–9, would seem to have one chance in nine of starting a given number. But according to a 60-year-old formula making its way into the accounting field, some numbers really *are* more "popular" than others. A disruption in the pattern may reveal an inefficient process, an honest mistake or outright fraud. Benford's Law is the newest tool in the auditor's arsenal.

According to Mark J. Nigrini, PhD, "Benford's Law gives us the expected patterns of the digits in a list of numbers . . . These patterns would appear in accounts payable invoices and accounts receivable numbers, for example." When patterns vary from those set down by Benford, there may be a problem. "Variations may reveal employees are listing expenses as $24 to avoid a $25 voucher limit. Or consider a manager who has a $3,000 signing authority. Benford's Law tells me that say, only 0.6 percent of all numbers should start with 29. If I get more than that, maybe a manager is approving too many $2,900 invoices right under his limit." . . . "Maybe managers are breaking down one project into several pieces to circumvent a higher level of oversight for some reason. Clients want to know when employees are going around their control systems." . . . Sometimes, said Nigrini, patterns change because of an error. "Invoices entered more than once will change the frequencies."

"At other times we see spikes—digit frequencies that violate Benford's Law—at $15 or $25," said Ernst & Young partner James Searing. "Even though these are low-dollar items, that might mean a client is writing a separate check for each express-mail delivery. That is a very expensive way to process invoices and write checks." By advising the client to arrange for monthly billing for express mail, E&Y can make the audit a value-added service.

Benford's Law may also catch fraud, thanks to psychology, said Nigrini. "People just don't think 'Benford-like.' If someone is cutting a $400 check every week for nonexistent janitorial services, those checks will skew the digit distribution. A thorough application of the law will find the fraud."

E&Y has developed proprietary software that applies Benford's Law to a client's data. "The more we use such analytical tools, the more we find," said Searing. "In the long term, advanced analytical tools, such as application of Benford's Law, will be part of the audit. They may very well help us reduce the overall risk of auditing, increase the reliability of the audit opinion and increase value to the client."

Source: "Numerology for Accountants," *Journal of Accountancy*, November 1998, p. 15.

---

[13] T. Bell, F. Marrs, I. Solomon and H. Thomas, *Auditing Organizations Through a Strategic-Systems Lens*, KPMG, 1997, p. 69.

CASETTE 19.1
CASE OF THE MISSING PETTY CASH

Problem

Petty cash embezzlement.

Method

The petty cash custodian (1) brought postage receipts from home and paid them from the fund, (2) persuaded the supervisor to sign blank authorization slips the custodian could use when the supervisor was away, and using these to pay for fictitious meals and minor supplies, (3) took cash to get through the weekend, replacing it the next week.

Paper Trail

Postage receipts were from a distant post office station the company did not use. The blank slips were dated on days the supervisor was absent. The fund was cash short during the weekend and for a few days the following week.

Amount

The fund was small ($100), but the custodian replenished it about every two working days, stealing about $20 each time. With about 260 working days per year and 130 reimbursements, the custodian was stealing about $2,600 per year. The custodian was looking forward to getting promoted to general cashier and bigger and better things!

AUDIT APPROACH

Objective

Obtain evidence of the existence and validity of petty cash transactions.

Control

A supervisor is assigned to approve petty cash disbursements by examining them for validity and signing an authorization slip.

Test of Controls

Audit for transaction authorization and validity. Select a sample of petty cash reimbursement cheque copies with receipts and authorization slips attached; study them for evidence of authorization and validity (vouching procedure). Notice the nature and content of the receipts. Obtain supervisor's vacation schedule and compare dates to authorization slip dates.

Audit of Balance

On Friday count the petty cash and receipts to see that they add up to $100. Then, count the fund again later in the afternoon. (Be sure the second count is a surprise and that the custodian and supervisor sign off on the count working paper so the auditor will not be accused of theft.)

Discovery Summary

Knowing the location of the nearby post office branch used by the company, the auditor noticed the pattern of many receipts from a distant branch, which was near the custodian's apartment. Several authorizations were dated during the supervisor's vacation, and he readily admitted signing the forms in blank so his own supervisor "wouldn't be bothered." The second count on the same day was a real surprise, and the fund was found $35 short.

CASETTE 19.2
THE LAUNDRY MONEY SKIM

Problem

Stolen cash receipts skimmed from collection.

Albert owned and operated 40 coin laundries around town. As the business grew, he could no longer visit each one, empty the cash boxes, and deposit the receipts. Each location grossed about $140 to $160 per day, operating 365 days per year. (Gross income about $2 million per year.)

Method

Four part-time employees each visited 10 locations, collecting the cash boxes and delivering them to Albert's office, where he would count the coins and currency (from the change machine) and prepare a bank deposit. One of the employees skimmed $5 to $10 from each location visited each day.

Paper Trail

None, unfortunately. The first paper that gets produced is Albert's bank deposit, and the money is gone by then.

Amount

The daily theft does not seem like much, but at an average of $7.50 per day from each of 10 locations, it was about $27,000 per year. If all four of the employees had stolen the same amount, the loss could have been about $100,000 per year.

AUDIT APPROACH

Objective

Obtain evidence of the completeness of cash receipts—that is, that all the cash received is delivered to Albert for deposit.

Control

Controls over the part-time employees were nonexistent. There was no overt or covert surprise observation and no times when two people went to collect cash (thereby needing to agree, in collusion, to steal). There was no rotation of locations or other indications to the employees that Albert was concerned about control.

Test of Controls

With no controls there are no test of control procedures. Obviously, however, "thinking like a crook"

leads to the conclusion that the employees could simply pocket money.

Audit of Balance

The "balance" in this case is the total revenue that should have been deposited, and auditing for completeness is always difficult. Albert marked a quantity of coins with an etching tool and marked some $1 and $5 bills with ink. Unknown to the employees, he put these in all the locations, carefully noting the coins and bills in each.

Discovery Summary

Sure enough, a pattern of missing money emerged. When confronted, the employee confessed.

CASETTE 19.3
THE WELL-PADDED PAYROLL

Problem

Embezzlement with fictitious people on the payroll.

Method

Maybelle had responsibility for preparing personnel files for new hires, approval of wages, verification of time cards and distribution of payroll cheques. She "hired" fictitious employees, faked their records and ordered cheques through the payroll system. She deposited some cheques in several personal bank accounts and cashed others, endorsing all of them with the names of the fictitious employees and her own.

Paper Trail

Payroll creates a large paper trail with individual earnings records, T-4 tax forms, payroll deductions for taxes and insurance and payroll tax reports. Maybelle mailed all the T-4 forms to the same post office box.

Amount

Maybelle stole $160,000 by creating some "ghosts," usually three to five out of 112 people on the payroll, and paying them an average of $256 per week for three years. Sometimes the ghosts quit and were later replaced by others. But she stole "only" about 2 percent of the payroll funds during the period.

AUDIT APPROACH

Objective

Obtain evidence of the existence and validity of payroll transactions.

Control

Different people should be responsible for hiring (preparing personnel files), approving wages and distributing payroll cheques. "Thinking like a crook"

leads an auditor to see that Maybelle could put people on the payroll and obtain their cheques.

Test of Controls

Audit for transaction authorization and validity. Random sampling might not work because of the small number of ghosts. Look for the obvious. Select several weeks' cheque blocks, account for numerical sequence (to see whether any cheques have been removed), and examine cancelled cheques for two endorsements.

Audit of Balance

There may be no "balance" to audit, other than the accumulated total of payroll transactions, and the total may not appear out of line with history because the fraud is small in relation to total payroll and has been going on for years. Conduct a surprise payroll distribution, follow up by examining prior cancelled cheques for the missing employees. Scan personnel files for common addresses.

Discovery Summary

Both the surprise distribution and the scan for common addresses provided the names of two or three exceptions. Both led to prior cancelled cheques (which Maybelle had not removed and the bank reconciler had not noticed), which carried Maybelle's own name as endorser. Confronted, she confessed.

CASETTE 19.4
FALSE SALES, ACCOUNTS RECEIVABLE AND INVENTORY

Problem

Overstated sales and accounts receivable caused overstated net income, retained earnings, current assets, working capital and total assets.

Method

Q.T. Wilson was a turnaround specialist who took the challenge at Mini Marc Corporation, a manufacturer of computer peripheral equipment. He set high goals for sales and profits. To meet these goals, managers shipped bricks to distributors and recorded some as sales of equipment to retail distributors and some as inventory out on consignment. No real products left the plant. The theory was that actual sales would grow, and the bricks would be replaced later with real products. In the meantime, the distributors may have thought they were holding consignment inventory in the unopened cartons.

Paper Trail

All the paperwork was in order because the managers had falsified the sales and consignment invoices, but they did not have customer purchase orders for all the false sales. Shipping papers were in order, and several shipping employees knew the boxes did not contain disk drives.

Amount

Prior to the manipulation, annual sales were $135 million. During the two falsification years, sales were $185 million and $362 million. Net income went up from a loss of $20 million to $23 million (income), then to $31 million (income); and the gross margin percent went from 6 percent to 28 percent. The revenue and profit figures outpaced the industry performance. The accounts receivable collection period grew to 94 days, while it was 70 days elsewhere in the industry.

AUDIT APPROACH

Objective

Obtain evidence about the existence and valuation of sales, accounts receivable and inventory.

Control

Company accounting and control procedures required customer purchase orders or contracts evidencing real orders. A sales invoice was supposed to indicate the products and their prices, and shipping documents were supposed to indicate actual shipment. Sales were always charged to the customer's account receivable.

Test of Controls

There were no glaring control omissions such that "thinking like a crook" would have pointed to fraud possibilities. Sensitive auditors might have noticed the high tension created among employees by concentration on meeting profit goals. Normal selection of sales transactions with vouching to customer orders and shipping documents might turn up a missing customer order. Otherwise, the paperwork would seem to be in order. The problem lay in the managers' power to override controls and instruct shipping people to send bricks. Most auditors do not ask the question: "Have you shipped anything, other than company products, this year?"

Audit of Balance

Confirmations of distributors' accounts receivable might have elicited exception responses. The problem was to have a large enough confirmation sample to pick up some of these distributors or to be skeptical enough to send a special sample of confirmations to distributors who took the "sales" near the end of the accounting period. Observation of inventory should include some inspection of goods not on the company's premises.

Discovery Summary

The overstatements were not detected. The confirmation sample was small and did not contain any of the false shipments. Tests of detail transactions did not turn up any missing customer orders. The inventory out on consignment was audited by obtaining a written confirmation from the holders, who apparently had not opened the boxes. The remarkable financial performance was attributed to good management.

CASETTE 19.5
OVERSTATE THE INVENTORY, UNDERSTATE THE COST OF GOODS SOLD

Problem

Overstated inventory caused understated cost of goods sold, overstated net income and retained earnings, and overstated current assets, working capital and total assets.

Method

A division manager at Doughboy Foods wanted to meet his profit goals and simply submitted overstated quantities in inventory reports. The manager (a) inserted fictitious count sheets in the independent auditors' working papers, (b) handed additional count sheets to the independent auditors after the count was completed saying "these got left out of your set," and (c) inserted false data into the computer system that produced a final inventory compilation (even though this ploy caused the computer-generated inventory not to match with the count sheets).

Paper Trail

In general, management reports should correspond to accounting records. The manager's inventory reports showed amounts larger than shown in the accounts. He fixed the problem by showing false inventory that was "not recorded on the books."

Amount

The food products inventory was overstated by $650,000. Through a two-year period, the false reports caused an income overstatement of 15 percent in the first year and would have caused a 39 percent overstatement the second year.

AUDIT APPROACH

Objective

Obtain evidence of the existence, completeness and valuation of inventory.

Control

Inventory counts should be taken under controlled conditions, but not under the control of managers who might benefit from manipulation. (However, if these managers are present, auditors should nevertheless be prepared to perform the audit work.) Inventory-takers should be trained and follow instructions for recording quantities and condition.

Test of Controls

Auditors should attend the inventory-taker training sessions and study the instructions for adequacy. Observation of the inventory-taking should be conducted by managers and by auditors to ensure compliance with the instructions.

Audit of Balance

For evidence of existence, select a sample of inventory items from the perpetual records and test-count them in the warehouse. For evidence of completeness, select a sample of inventory items in the warehouse, test-count them, and trace them to the final inventory compilation. For evidence of valuation, find the proper prices of inventory for one or both of the samples, calculate the total cost for the items, and compare to their amounts recorded in the books. Compare book inventory amounts to management reports. Control the working papers so that only members of the audit team have access. Analytical procedures gave some signals. The particular manager's division had the lowest inventory turnover rate (6.3) among all the company divisions (comparable turnover, about 11.1) and its inventory had consistently increased from year to year (227 percent over the two-year period).

Discovery Summary

In the second year, when the manager handed over the count sheets "that got left out of your set," the auditor thanked him, then went to the warehouse to check them out. Finding them inaccurate, she compared book inventories to his management reports and found an overstatement in the reports. This prompted further comparison of the computer-generated inventory with the count sheets and more evidence of overstated quantities on 22 of the 99 count sheets.

R E V I E W
C H E C K P O I N T S

19.17 If the petty cash custodian were replaced and the frequency of fund reimbursement decreased from every two days to every four days, what might you suspect?

19.18 Give some examples of control omissions that would make it easy to "think like a crook" and see opportunities for fraud.

19.19 If sales and income were overstated by recording a false cash sale at the end of the year, what "dangling debit" might give the scheme away?

19.20   What three general descriptions can be given to manipulations that produce materially misleading financial statements?

. . . .

DOCUMENTS, SOURCES AND "EXTENDED PROCEDURES"

References are often made in the auditing literature to "extended procedures," but these are
rarely defined and listed. Authorities are afraid that a list will limit the range of such procedures, so "extended procedures" is generally left undefined as an open-ended set to refer
vaguely to "whatever is necessary in the circumstances." This section describes some of the
"extended procedures" with the proviso that (1) some auditors may consider them ordinary
and (2) other auditors may consider them unnecessary in any circumstances. Even so, they
are useful detective procedures in either event.

Content of Common Documents

Auditing textbooks often advise beginner auditors to "examine cheques," and to "check the
employees on a payroll." It helps to know something about these common documents and
the information that can be seen on them.

Information on a Cheque
Exhibit 19–2 describes the information found on a typical cheque. Knowledge of the codes
for federal reserve districts, offices, states and bank identification numbers could enable an
auditor to spot a crude cheque forgery. Similarly, a forger's mistakes with the optical identification printing or the magnetic cheque number might supply a tipoff. If the amount of a
cheque is altered after it has cleared the bank, the change would be noted by comparing the
magnetic imprint of the amount paid to the amount written on the cheque face. The back of
a cheque carries the endorsement(s) of the payees and holders in the due course; the date and
the name and routing number of the bank where the cheque was deposited; and the date,
identification of the federal reserve office, and its routing number for the federal reserve
cheque clearing. (Sometimes there is no federal reserve clearing identification when local
cheques are cleared locally without going through a federal reserve office.) Auditors can
follow the path of a cancelled cheque by following the banks where it was deposited and
cleared. This route may or may not correspond with the characteristics of the payee. (For
example, ask why a cheque to a local business in Mississauga, Ontario, should be deposited
in a small Missouri bank and cleared through the St. Louis federal reserve office.)

Information on a Bank Statement
Most of the information shown on the bank statement in Exhibit 19–3 is self-explanatory.
However, auditors should not overlook the usefulness of some of the information: the
bank's count and dollar amount of deposits and cheques can be compared to the detail data
on the statement; the account holder's business identification number is on the statement,
and this can be used in other databases (for individuals, this is a place to get a person's
Social Insurance number); and the statement itself can be studied for alterations.

Valid Social Insurance Numbers
In Canada, social insurance numbers (SINs) have become a universal identification number. They can be useful to auditors when checking the personnel files and the validity of
people on the payroll. Here are some characteristics of SINs:[14]

---

[14] Caution: Human Resources Development Canada periodically adds numbers that have been issued and may use num-
bers assigned to one geographic area for another. If the validity of an SIN becomes important in an audit, check with Human
Resources Development Canada to ascertain the current status of numbers issued. For further reference, see M. L. Levy,
"Financial Fraud: Schemes and Indicia," *Journal of Accountancy*, August 1985, p. 85; E. J. Pankau, *Check it Out* (Houston:
Cloak & Data Press, 1990), pp. 20–27.

EXHIBIT 19–2   HOW TO READ A CANCELLED CHEQUE AND ENDORSEMENT

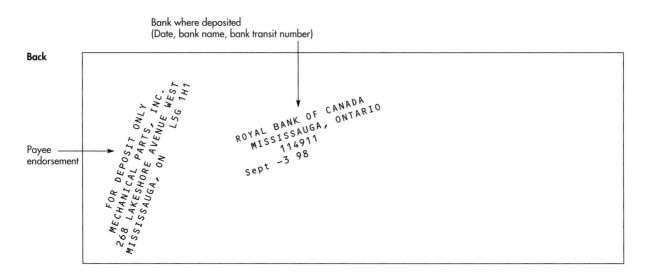

- The SIN number is a nine-digit number, the ninth digit is a check digit that is calculated using the first eight digits.
- There are two types of SIN numbers, regular numbers and distinctive numbers. Regular numbers are issued to Canadian citizens, Registered Indians and permanent residents. Distinctive numbers start with digit 9. They are issued to people who do not have status as above, e.g., foreign workers, visitors.
- If the first digit is not a nine, then it is used to indicate the province or territory where the number was issued.
- The middle seven digits are issued in generally ascending numerical order. This makes it feasible to apply Benford's Law to analyzing these digits.

EXHIBIT 19-3   **SMALL BUSINESS BANK STATEMENT**

```
                                                                        27
            ⊠ North Country Bank

            MISSISSAUGA, ON                                      ACCOUNT
            P.O. BOX 908                       ---              604017-526-5
            KINGSTON, ON   K5G 2H3             ---    ---

                                              ---                  PAGE
                                              ---                    1


            CAULCO INC                                        SIN/TAX ID
            BLDG 1 OFFICE F                                   74-2076251
            5450 BEE CAVE RD
            MISSISSAUGA, ON                               CYC MC FREQ
            L5G 1H2                                       01 01 M0000

            **  YOUR CHECKING ACCOUNT      01-29-88 THRU 02-29-88 **

      TO YOUR PREVIOUS BALANCE OF - - - - - - - -       7,559.06
      YOU ADDED       1 DEPOSITS FOR  - - - - -          5,654.16
      YOU SUBTRACTED   26 WITHDRAWALS FOR - - - - -     10,838.29
      GIVING YOU A CURRENT BALANCE OF - - - - - - -      7,374.93

      NUMBER OF DAYS USED FOR AVERAGES  - - - - - -            31
      YOUR AVERAGE LEDGER BALANCE - - - - - - - - -      4,014.67
      YOUR LOW BALANCE OCCURRED ON 02-22 AND WAS  -      2,374.93

                      THANK YOU


      -----------------------------------------------------------------
      -----------------------------------------------------------------
                    DEPOSITS AND OTHER ADDITIONS

          DATE    AMOUNT
          0204    5654.16 ✓
      -----------------------------------------------------------------
                    CHECKS AND OTHER WITHDRAWALS

      CHECK DATE      AMOUNT CHECK DATE      AMOUNT CHECK DATE      AMOUNT
      2201 0211        57.83✓ 2214 0203      403.92✓ 2225 0217     ✓182.77
        **                    2215 0203      135.59✓   **
      2205 0222        16.72✓ 2216 0216        6.16✓ 2231 0205     ✓254.37
      2206 0203       533.28✓ 2217 0217      138.43✓ 2232 0210     ✓ 60.61
      2207 0203      1312.15✓ 2218 0217      131.92✓
        **                    2219 0217       82.97✓ 2234 0217     ✓ 64.69
      2209 0203       247.10✓ 2220 0217       87.49✓ 2235 0218     ✓279.97
      2210 0203       249.98✓ 2221 0217       85.68✓   **
      2211 0203       255.26✓ 2222 0217       84.69✓ 2238 0219     ✓ 90.00
      2212 0203       242.09✓   **
      2213 0203       384.91✓ 2224 0217      449.71✓
```

- Working with Human Resources Development Canada, an auditor may be able to detect fictitious SIN numbers.

R E V I E W
CHECKPOINTS

19.21 How could you tell whether the amount on a cheque had been raised after it was paid by a bank?

19.22 If a false social insurance number of a new employee is entered in the payroll system, and the employee receives a paycheque, what control in the system is not being used?

Sources of Information

A wide variety of records and information is available for various kinds of investigations ranging from personal background checks to business enquiries. Our concern here is with public records and ways to get them. Only a few of the hundreds of sources are described briefly below.

General Business Sources

City and county tax assessor–collectors keep files on real property by address and legal description, owner, taxable value, improvements and amount of taxes and delinquencies. Province (and some city) regulatory agencies have directories of liquor licences, and various professionals (e.g., PAs, dentists, doctors, plumbers, electricians). Provincial building ministries and ministers of public housing may have a central index file of appraisers, real estate brokers and most components of the building industry. The industry and trade ministries have data on companies that apply for import and export licences. The federal Ministry of Transportation maintains files on the chain of ownership of all civil aircraft in Canada. Provincial securities commissions have extensive financial information on registered companies and their properties, principal officers, directors and owners. Local Better Business Bureaus keep information about criminal rackets, cons and their operators, and can provide information about the business reputation of local businesses. Standard & Poor's Register of Corporations, Directors and Executives lists about 37,000 public and private companies and the names and titles of over 400,000 officials. The Internet and various on-line information sources are becoming increasingly important not only in investigative accounting but as part of gaining familiarity with a new client in a normal audit.[15]

Business and Asset Identification Sources

According to Pankau, each region and province has a system for registering businesses—corporations, joint ventures, sole proprietorships and partnerships. They keep files on registered "assumed names" (DBA, or "doing business as" names). Some businesses may be registered with a province and not a region, or with a region and not a province. All real corporations are chartered by a province or federal government, and each province's ministry of consumer and corporate affairs keeps corporate record information, such as the date of registration and the initial officers and owners. (Using these sources, you can find the assets or business "hidden" in the spouse's name.) Crooks often work through a labyrinth of business entities, and you can find all the registered ones in these sources. You can find phony vendor companies created by real employees to bilk employers with false billings. Banks, finance companies and other creditors often file Uniform Commercial Code (UCC) records to record the interest of the creditor in assets used as collateral for a loan so that other parties cannot claim interest in the assets (e.g., boats, business equipment, appliances). UCCs are found in regional clerks' offices and in the province's office of the ministry of consumer and/or commercial affairs. (They are also on-line in some commercial data bases.)[16]

Federal and Provincial Revenue Agencies

Ever wonder how revenue agents find tax evaders? One accountant described the following sources of tips for possible big audit findings. (1) Police arrest records point to people who may have illicit unreported income. (2) Real estate sales records may identify people who "forget" to put their sales in a tax return. (3) Auto registrations of expensive cars point to people who have a lot of money to spend—maybe some unreported income. (4) Com-

---

[15] Hundreds of sources and directories under the categories of business, finance, people, property and electronic databases are listed and described in the U.S. General Accounting Office publication *Investigators' Guide to Sources of Information* (GAO/OSI-88-1, March 1988, updated periodically).

Also, insider information is increasingly difficult to "keep under the lid" as investors form on-line investor forums to assist each other in passing on "hot tips." See J.A. Abbey, "Fools and Their Money," *Time*, June 17, 1996, pp. 51–54). Auditors may find these on-line services useful sources of information on risks and uncertainties facing their clients.

[16] These and other sources of business and personal information are described in Pankau, *Check It Out*.

Quota Reports Fishy?

HALIFAX—New recruits to the ranks of the federal fisheries enforcement program are to be given courses in accounting so they can net fishermen who have been cooking their books. And inspectors currently on the payroll of the Fisheries and Oceans Department will be given crash courses in audit procedures over the next several months that will teach them to focus on crooked practices in the fishing industry. A 1994 audit suggested that much of the fish caught on the country's coasts slips through the federal quota system as a result of misreporting of black market trading. The report by federal auditors was obtained by The Canadian Press news service under the *Access to Information Act.*

It is said the inspectors, who tend to concentrate on the mesh sizes of nets and the species and volumes of fish in a trawler's hold, should focus more on the records and catch reports maintained by fishermen. Authors of the report suggested the inspectors attend commercial-crime courses conducted by the RCMP. The audit pointed to some fishermen, provided with individual quotas, as possible villains who have taken advantage of procedural gaps in enforcement to cheat the quota system.

Over the last few years, individual quotas have replaced the shared quota system which set overall limits on catches within designated fisheries. The new system reduced competition for the total allowable catches and extended the season for fishermen who survived devastation of the east coast cod fishery. It was eventually extended to the west coast and Lake Erie fisheries.

Despite its shortcomings, however, the bureaucrats who reviewed the process hailed the individual quota system as a stabilizing factor in the fragile fishing industry.

Source: The Bottom Line, September 1996, p. 6.

---

parison of provincial sales tax returns with income tax revenue amounts may reveal discrepancies (depending on which tax collector is feared the most). (5) Agents have used university-town newspaper rental ads to identify people who rent rooms, garage apartments, duplex halves and the like, but forget to report the income. The boxes above and below provide illustrations of procedures used in public sector auditing and by insurance fraud auditors, respectively.

Forensics on Front Lines in War on Insurance Frauds

TORONTO—Forensic accountants play an increasingly important role in documenting, proving and reducing insurance fraud.

Insurance adjusters and lawyers have long used accountants to document clearly fraudulent claims. However, many insurance companies, concerned about huge losses to fraud—about $1.3 billion a year in property and casualty (P&C) claims alone—have recently set up their own fraud-busting Special Investigation Units (SIUs).

The SIUs, staffed mostly by ex commercial crime unit police officers, work proactively to reduce fraud by investigating all claims above a certain amount, as well as suspicious claims.

Once they have established the possibility of fraud, the SIUs (or insurance counsel, if the claim has already progressed to the litigation stage) turn to forensic accountants for the hard proof. "It's just starting to happen," said Ted Baskerville of

Lindquist Avey MacDonald Baskerville. "Our role up to now has always been to deal with claims that are overstated—or appear to be—or with arson, or staged theft."

In suspected arson or staged theft cases, Lindquist Avey's forensic specialists determine the insured's possible financial motive by looking at details of ownership or management, historical financial results, past and future obligations, profitability and cash flow.

They prepare a general profile of the company, including its relationship with creditors, and try to answer the following: Do owners have financial needs they can't satisfy legitimately through the business? What do the owners withdraw from the company, or how do they benefit from it in other ways?

In cases of possible theft, it's important to look at other businesses owned by the insureds; maybe they're trying to run down one business for the benefit of another.

The growing use of electronic document storage systems can have unexpected benefits for the forensic sleuth.

According to Ken Gibson of Mintz & Partners in Toronto, "people sometimes don't realize what they have stored." Many systems automatically back up computer communications like e-mail.

Aspiring fraud perpetrators may destroy the e-mail record in their own computers, but forget, or don't know, that investigators can read the backup disk.

Gibson typically deals with commercial damage claims—theft for example, where inventory appears to be gone, but there's little evidence of a break-in.

In those sorts of cases, he said, investigators try to establish whether anything is in fact missing and, if so, whether it had any real value.

Often, a line of goods, such as video or electronic products, isn't selling, and then it allegedly disappears.

The forensic investigator looks at sales figures, dealings with suppliers and interviews employees or others involved.

Fraud by employees, leading to fidelity bond claims, is a growth industry, according to Ivor Gottschalk of Ernst & Young's Toronto-based forensic and litigation accounting group.

Often, an employee in a company's purchasing department orders an unnecessary or nonexistent material or service, and gets a kickback for the order.

Other types of fraud include setting up fake suppliers, fictitious employees on a payroll or phony accounts payable.

"People are getting more and more creative," said Gottschalk.

"We're seeing fraud on the other side, where there's actually fraud in collusion with customers. Companies will normally control their purchasing departments quite closely because they're aware that purchasing is very vulnerable to outside forces.

"But generally, you wouldn't think of your accounts receivable clerk as being in a position to benefit somebody outside the company, writing off invoices to customers, for example."

Many forensic accountants are members of the Association of Certified Fraud Examiners, based in the U.S., but with more than 900 Canadian members in nine chapters.

Source: Copyright 1996 by Derek Lundy. Reprinted with permission.

REVIEW CHECKPOINTS

19.23 Where could you find information about real estate valuation? aircraft ownership? names of licensed doctors? assumed (fictitious) business names? liens on personal property?

Extended Procedures

LEARNING OBJECTIVE

7. Explain the use of some extended audit procedures for finding fraud.

The nature of extended procedures is limited only by an auditor's imagination and, sometimes, the willingness of management to co-operate in extraordinary audit activities. Next is a short series of extended procedures, with some brief explanations.[17]

Count the Petty Cash Twice in a Day

The second count is unexpected, and you might catch an embezzling custodian short.

Investigate Suppliers (vendors)

Check the Better Business Bureau for reputation, the telephone book for a listing and address and the provincial corporation records for owners and assumed names. You may find fictitious vendors being used to make false billings or companies related to purchasing department employees.

Investigate Customers

As with vendors, investigation may reveal companies set up by insiders, with billings at below-list prices so that the insiders can "buy" goods and resell them at a profit.

Examine Endorsements on Cancelled Cheques

Look for second endorsements, especially the names of employees. Most business payments are deposited with one endorsement. Be sure to include cheques payable to "cash" or to a bank for purchase of cashiers' cheques. The second endorsee indicates that the payee may not have received the benefit of the payment.

Add Up the Accounts Receivable Subsidiary

Cash payments on customer accounts have been stolen, with receipts given credit entry to the customer account, but no cash deposit and no entry to the control account.

Audit General Journal Entries

Experience has shown that the largest number of accounting errors requiring adjustment are found in nonroutine, nonsystematic journal entries. (Systematic accounting is the processing of large volumes of day-to-day ordinary transactions.)

Match Payroll to Life and Medical Insurance Deductions

Ghosts on the payroll seldom elect these insurance coverages. Doing so reduces the embezzler's take and complicates the cover-up.

Match Payroll to Social Insurance Numbers

Fictitious SINs may be chosen at random; if so, the fraudster will have made the mistake of using an unissued number or one that does not match with the birthdate. Sort the payroll SINs in numerical order and look for false, duplicate or unlikely (e.g., consecutive) numbers.

Match Payroll with Addresses

Look for multiple persons at the same address.

Retrieve Customers' Cheques

If an employee has diverted customer payments, the cancelled cheques showing endorsements and deposits to a bank where the company has no account are not available because

---

[17] Further explanation of these and other procedures can be found in the books and articles cited in preceding footnotes and in these sources: *AICPA Technical Practice Aids* (TPA 8200.02); D. Churbuck, "Desktop Forgery," *Forbes*, November 27, 1989, pp. 246–254; O. Hilton, *Scientific Examination of Questioned Documents*, rev. ed. (New York: Elsevier North Holland, 1982); A.C. Levinston, "40 Years of Embezzlement Tracking," *Internal Auditor*, April 1991, pp. 51–55.

WANT TO FUDGE YOUR TAX DEDUCTIONS?

Don't try to turn that $300 receipt into $800 with the stroke of a ballpoint pen. The IRS has ultraviolet scanners, ink chromatographers, densitometers and argon-ion lasers that can identify the brand of pen, the age of the paper and the source of the paper. Something printed on a laser printer is harder, but they're working on it.

Source: D. Churbuck, "Desktop Forgery," *Forbes*, November 27, 1989, p. 252.

---

they are returned to the issuing organization (customer). Ask the customer to give originals or copies, or to provide access for examination.

Use Marked Coins and Currency
Plant marked money in locations where cash collections should be gathered for turning over for deposit.

Measure Deposit Lag Time
Compare the dates of cash debit recording and deposit slip dates to dates credited by the bank. Someone who takes cash, then holds the deposit for the next cash receipts to make up the difference, causes a delay between the date of recording and the bank's date of deposit.

Document Examination
Look for erasures, alterations, copies where originals should be filed, telltale lines from a copier when a document has been pieced together, handwriting and other oddities. Professional document examination is a technical activity that requires special training (e.g., RCMP), but crude alterations may be observed, at least enough to bring them to specialists' attention.

Enquire, Ask Questions
Be careful not to discuss fraud possibilities with the managers who might be involved. It gives them a chance to cover up or run. Wells described fraud audit questioning (FAQ) as a nonaccusatory method of asking key questions of personnel during a regular audit to give them an opportunity to furnish information about possible misdeeds. Fraud possibilities are addressed in a direct manner, so the FAQ approach must have the support of management. Example questions are "Do you think fraud is a problem for business in general?" "Do you think this company has any particular problem with fraud?" "In your department, who is beyond suspicion?" "Is there any information you would like to furnish regarding possible fraud within this organization?"[18]

Covert Surveillance
Observe activities while not being seen. External auditors might watch employees clocking onto a work shift, observing whether they use only one time card. Travelling hotel auditors may check in unannounced, use the restaurant and entertainment facilities and watch the employees skimming receipts and tickets. (Trailing people on streets and maintaining a "stakeout" should be left to trained investigators.)

Horizontal and Vertical Analyses
This is analytical review ratio analysis and is very similar to the preliminary analytical procedures explained in Chapter 5. Horizontal analysis refers to changes of financial statement numbers and ratios across several years. Vertical analysis refers to financial statement

---

[18] Joseph T. Wells, "From the Chairman: Fraud Audit Questioning," *The White Paper*, National Association of Certified Fraud Examiners, May-June 1991), p. 2. This technique must be used with extreme care and practice.

amounts expressed each year as proportions of a base, such as sales for the income statement accounts and total assets for the balance sheet accounts. Auditors look for relationships that do not make sense as indicators of potential large misstatement and fraud.

Net Worth Analysis

This is used when fraud has been discovered or strongly suspected, and the information to calculate a suspect's net worth can be obtained (e.g., asset and liability records, bank accounts). The method is to calculate the suspect's net worth (known assets minus known liabilities) at the beginning and end of a period (months or years), then try to account for the difference as (1) known income less living expenses and (2) unidentified difference. The unidentified difference may be the best available approximation of the amount of a theft.

Expenditure Analysis

This is similar to net worth analysis, except the data are the suspect's spending for all purposes compared to known income. If spending exceeds legitimate and explainable income, the difference may be the amount of a theft.

It should be noted that an analysis like this normally represents only indirect (circumstantial) evidence in a court of law and normally by itself it cannot prove the "guilt beyond a reasonable doubt" that is required in criminal cases.

Valuation Services

Forensic accounting and fraud auditing frequently involve quantification of economic losses resulting from illegal activities. This may require the specialized services of chartered business valuators. For example, see the CICA practice aid, *Investigative and Forensic Accounting Practice Issues* (1995).

R E V I E W
C H E C K P O I N T S

19.24   What is the difference between a "normal procedure" and an "extended procedure"?

19.25   What might be indicated by two endorsements on a cancelled cheque?

19.26   What three oddities might be found connected with ghosts on a padded payroll?

19.27   What can an auditor find using horizontal analysis? vertical analysis? net worth analysis? expenditure analysis?

AFTER DISCOVERING A FRAUD

Building a case against a fraudster is a task for trained investigators. Most internal and external auditors take roles as assistants to fraud examiners, who know how to conduct interviews and interrogations, perform surveillance, use informants and obtain usable confessions. In almost all cases, the postdiscovery activity proceeds with a special prosecutorial assignment with the co-operation or under the leadership of management. A Crown attorney and police officials may be involved. Prosecution of fraudsters is advisable because, if left unpunished, they often go on to steal again. This is no place for "normal" auditing, but auditors have been given some guidelines related to relevant communications.

CICA and Internal Audit Standards

Standards for external auditors contain materiality thresholds related to reporting auditors' knowledge of errors, irregularities and illegal acts. Immaterial errors are supposed to be reported to management at least one level above the people involved (*Section* 5135.19). The idea is that small matters can be kept in the management family. However, errors material to the financial statements must be adjusted and handled by management persons respon-

sible for the financial statements to the satisfaction of auditors, or else the audit report will
be qualified.

Irregularities get slightly different treatment, but there is still a materiality standard in
effect. The auditors should inform the audit committee of the board of directors of all irregularities, except ones that are "clearly inconsequential." Irregularities involving senior
management are never "inconsequential." In the CICA audit standards, room is always left
for auditors' discretion in determining whether something is minor enough not to matter
and not to report. However, management and directors must deal with irregularities to the
satisfaction of the auditors. If uncertainties persist about the irregularities and management's actions, the audit report should be qualified, explaining all the unsavoury reasons,
or the auditors may withdraw from the engagement.

Clients' illegal acts also come under the "clearly inconsequential" materiality standard.
Ones that amount to more than this should be reported to the organization's audit committee, and the financial statements should contain adequate disclosures about the organization's illegal acts (*Section* 5136.04). External auditors always have the option to withdraw
from the engagement if management and directors do not take action satisfactory in the
circumstances.

Under the CICA audit standards, disclosures of irregularities and clients' illegal acts to
outside agencies are limited. If the auditors get fired, the firm can cite these matters in the
letter attached to the provincial securities commission, which may require explanation of

FRAUDULENT FINANCIAL REPORTING: 1987–1997 AN ANALYSIS OF U.S. PUBLIC COMPANIES

Summary of Research Commissioned by the Committee of Sponsoring Organizations (COSO) of the Treadway Commission

- The companies committing fraud generally were small, and most were not listed on the New York or American Stock Exchanges.

- The frauds went to the very top of the organizations. In 72 percent of the cases, the CEO appeared to be associated with the fraud.

- The audit committees and boards of the fraud companies appeared to be weak. Most audit committees rarely met, and the companies' boards of directors were dominated by insiders and others with significant ties to the company.

- A significant portion of the companies was owned by the founders and board members.

- Severe consequences resulted when companies committed fraud, including bank-ruptcy, significant changes in ownership, and delisting by national exchanges.

- Cumulative amounts of fraud were relatively large for the many small compa-nies involved, for example, resulting in an average financial misstatement of 25 percent of total assets.

The study results highlight the need for an effective control environment, or "tone at the top." The risk of fraud is much higher in small companies. A strong CEO, with significant share ownership in a small organization, needs an experienced, independ-ent board to insure objectivity.

COSO's mission is to improve the quality of financial reporting through internal controls, governance, and ethics. This study validates the need for continued focus on all three areas. We believe the study will provide a platform for those responsible for financial reporting to improve their effectiveness.

Source: www.aicpa.org as of April 15, 1999.

an organization's change of auditors. A fired auditor can tell the successor auditor about them when the successor makes the enquiries required by professional ethics.

Auditors must respond when answering a subpoena issued by a court or other agency with authority, which will happen in a lawsuit or prosecution. When performing work under public sector audit standards, auditors are required to report irregularities and illegal acts to the client agency under the audit contract, which may be an agency or office different from the organization audited.

SIAS No. 3 requires internal auditors to inform management of suspected wrongdoing. They are expected to report fraud findings to management, the board of directors, or the audit committee of the board, being careful not to report to persons who might be involved in a fraud scheme. But as the preceding box indicates, much can still be done to improve the financial fraud record of companies even in the highly regulated securities markets of North America.

Recently SEC Chairman Arthur Levitt has been criticizing the profession for allowing "hocus-pocus accounting" that facilitates financial statement fraud. The box below summarizes the most common forms of "hocus-pocus" accounting.

Consulting and Assisting

LEARNING OBJECTIVE
8. Describe how PAs can assist in prosecuting fraud perpetrators.

While engaged in the audit work, auditors should know how to preserve the chain of custody of evidence. The chain of custody is the crucial link of the evidence to the suspect, called the "relevance" of evidence by lawyers and judges. If documents are lost, mutilated, coffee-soaked or compromised (so that a defence lawyer can argue that they were altered

---

HOCUS-POCUS ACCOUNTING

Executive Summary

- Public companies that fail to report quarterly earnings which meet or exceed analysts' expectations often experience a drop in their stock prices. This can lead to practices that sometimes include fraudulent overstatement of quarterly revenue.

- One of the most common schemes is the bill-and-hold sales transaction. While it's not necessarily a GAAP violation, it's often associated with financial frauds and calls for deeper investigation. The SEC says that all of the following conditions must be met for revenue recognition to be appropriate:
  - The risks of ownership must have passed to the buyer.
  - The customer must have a commitment to purchase, preferably in writing.
  - The buyer must request the bill-and-sale transaction and substantiate a business purpose for it.
  - A fixed delivery date must exist.
  - The seller must not retain any significant specific performance obligations.
  - The goods must be complete and ready for shipment and not subject to being used to fill other orders.

- Deals called sham transactions refer specifically to sales schemes that appear genuine but actually are rigged for the purpose of letting the seller recognize revenue. Other indicators that fraudulent financial reporting might exist include bogus shipping dates, revenue figures that always meet analysts' expectations and transactions with unusual payment terms.

- Auditors with a good understanding of the client, the business and its products are well prepared to see the warning signs of revenue-recognition fraud.

D.R. Carmichael, "Hocus-Pocus Accounting," *Journal of Accountancy*, October 1999, p. 60.

FIRMS SHOULD TAKE FRAUD SERIOUSLY

Company managers are increasingly aware of fraud and have taken initiatives to address its costly consequences, but there is no reason for complacency.

KPMG Investigation and Security Inc. says 62 percent of respondents to its survey of 1,000 of the country's largest companies as ranked by FP reported that fraud had taken place in their organization in the past year, up from 52 percent in the 1996 survey. Better detection is responsible for some of the rise, KPMG says, but a large part is attributable to an actual increase in the incidence of fraud.

Those surveyed see a host of factors as key in allowing fraud to take place, such as poor hiring practices, management override of internal controls and collusion between employees and third parties. However, poor internal controls are viewed as the leading factor.

Internal fraud remains a huge problem. The survey indicates that based on dollar losses 55 percent of all scams are from inside companies. Management accounts for 17 percent of all fraud—usually phoney expense accounts. Employee fraud—38 percent—is predominantly cheque forgery or counterfeiting. What is equally disturbing is that almost half the respondents conduct business in such a way as to be vulnerable to money laundering.

The sad fact is many companies—25 percent of those surveyed—haven't taken even basic measures to shrink the possibility of fraud. These include devising a corporate code of conduct and checking new employees. With the incidence of fraud rising, this is hardly a responsible way to manage a company.

Source: Editorial, *The Financial Post,* May 16, 1997, p. 14.

---

to frame the suspect), they can lose their effectiveness for the prosecution. Auditors should learn to mark the evidence, writing an identification of the location, condition, date, time and circumstances as soon as it appears to be a signal of fraud. This marking should be on a separate tag or page, the original document should be put in a protective envelope (plastic) for preservation, and audit work should proceed with copies of the documents instead of originals. A record should be made of the safekeeping and of all persons who use the original. Any eyewitness observations should be timely recorded in a memorandum or on tape (audio or video), with corroboration of colleagues, if possible. There are other features to the chain of custody relating to interviews, interrogations, confessions, documents obtained by subpoena and other matters, but these activities usually are not conducted by auditors.

Independent PAs often accept engagements for litigation support and expert witnessing. This work can be termed forensic accounting, which means the application of accounting and auditing skills to legal problems, both civil and criminal. Litigation support can take several forms, but it usually amounts to consulting in the capacity of helping lawyers document cases and determine damages. Expert witness work involves testifying to findings determined during litigation support and testifying about accounting principles and auditing standards applications. The CICA and the Institute of Internal Auditors conduct continuing education courses for auditors who want to become experts in these fields.

The CICA plans to offer as its first specialization a certificate in investigative and forensic accounting (IFA). This will probably be available beginning in 2001 or 2002.

FRAUD AUDITS AS ASSURANCE ENGAGEMENTS

An obvious question is whether investigations and audits of the types discussed in this chapter are assurance or consulting engagements. Much depends on the nature of the engagement and whether there exists an accountability relationship. But if we view every employee including management as being accountable for resources entrusted to them by the company, many fraud audits would appear to be of the direct reporting types, with an implied assertion that defalcations are not occurring.

Currently, the only authoritative guidance on fraud audit reports is that developed by the Association of Certified Fraud Examiners in their Fraud Examiners Manual. Exhibit 19–4 illustrates a "clean" opinion on a fraud audit. Note, however, that although the term *opinion* is used, suggesting high assurance for the assertion "there is no fraud," the wording of the opinion paragraph is more in the nature of the moderate-assurance, "nothing came to our attention" type that is used in review engagements. This is probably because there is no agreed-upon set of standardized procedures such as GAAS that can provide high assurance for this particular type of assertion.

The equivalent of an adverse opinion, on the other hand, which is given in Exhibit 19–5, provides much higher assurance for the assertion that a fraud did occur (especially if there is a signed confession satisfying all legal requirements). But note that the high assurance is provided in part because of the way the opinion is worded. The opinion does not state that the fraud can be proven legally—that is, "beyond a reasonable doubt," as would be required in a criminal court. Instead the conclusion is a much milder one—"if proven in a court of law," the actions would be considered fraudulent. In other words, the fraud auditor is not claiming that there is fraud beyond a reasonable doubt, which is something only the courts can decide. Rather, the auditor is saying that he or she is providing high assurance that a fraud may have taken place. Thus, by properly wording the conclusion the auditor can provide high assurance for the conclusion, and the use of the word "opinion" would appear to be warranted in this case under *Section* 5025.

There are two important lessons to be learned from these illustrative reports: one is that the level of assurance depends very much on the ability to identify suitable criteria—for example, a signed confession; the other is that the level of assurance depends very much

---

EXHIBIT 19–4

Investigation Appendix	Engagement Contracts/Opinion Letters

FRAUD EXAMINATION OPINION
(evidence does not support allegation)

[Date]

[   ], Esq.
[Law Department]
[Company Name]
[Address]
[City, State, Zip Code]

RE: [Fraud Examination]

Dear Mr./Mrs. [   ]:

We have conducted a fraud examination concerning a possible misappropriation of assets of the [Company Name]. This examination was predicated upon information resulting from a routine audit of the company's books by the company's internal auditors.

Our examination was conducted in accordance with lawful fraud examination techniques, which include, but are not limited to: examination of books and records; voluntary interviews of appropriate personnel; and other such evidence-gathering procedures as necessary under the circumstances.

Because concealment and trickery are elements of fraud, no assurance can be given that fraud does not exist. However, based on the results of our examination, we have found no evidence to indicate a violation of criminal and/or civil fraud-related statutes in connection with this matter.

Very truly yours,

Source: Fraud Examiner's Manual © 1993 Association of Certified Fraud Examiners, Austin, TX—Revised 10/1/93.

EXHIBIT 19–5

Investigation Appendix	Engagement Contracts/Opinion Letters

FRAUD EXAMINATION OPINION
(evidence supports allegation)

[Date]

[   ], Esq.
[Law Department]
[Company Name]
[Address]
[City, State, Zip Code]

RE: [Fraud Examination]

Dear Mr./Mrs. [   ]:

We have conducted a fraud examination concerning a possible misappropriation of assets of the [Company Name]. This examination was predicted upon information resulting from a routine audit of the company's books by the company's internal auditors.

Our examination was conducted in accordance with lawful fraud examination techniques, which include, but are not limited to: examination of books and records; voluntary interviews of appropriate witnesses/personnel; and other such evidence-gathering procedures as necessary under the circumstances.

During the pendency of this fraud examination, Mr. [   ] voluntarily furnished a signed statement indicating that he misappropriated $..................... to his personal benefit.

Based on the results of our examination and the confession of Mr. [ ], it is our opinion that his actions, if proven in a court of law, could constitute a violation of relevant criminal and/or civil fraud-related statutes.

Very truly yours,

Source: Fraud Examiner's Manual © 1993 Association of Certified Fraud Examiners, Austin, TX—Revised 10/1/93.

---

on the specific phrasing of the conclusion. For example, if in Exhibit 19–5 the auditor had concluded that fraud had taken place, such an opinion would provide only low assurance because fraud is a legal matter that must be proven in the courts. In addition, because the fraud assertion has not yet been proven in the courts—and because fraud is a matter to be proven under criminal law—the auditor might even be found guilty of libel! There is the related issue that even if the auditor *does* have high assurance that a fraud has been perpetrated, high audit assurance does not necessarily equate to the "beyond a reasonable doubt" burden of proof that is required by the Criminal Code. On the other hand, under civil law, if, for example, the client's company is only expecting to recover damages or trying to obtain sufficient cause to fire the employee, then the burden of proof is considerably lower. In civil law the burden of proof is "on balance of probabilities" and an opinion such as in Exhibit 19–5 may very well satisfy this requirement. So the amount of assurance depends on the circumstances, and the wording should properly reflect the circumstances.

For example, since fraud is a legal term and legal conditions must be met before the term is assigned to anyone, a perhaps better term for use in an assurance report is "irregularities," which is a term defined by the PA profession. An auditor can then reach a conclusion about the likelihood of irregularities occurring (including but not limited to fraud) without being encumbered with legal definitions and the responsibilities inherent in using specific legal terms such as fraud. As long as there is ambiguity between the level of assurance provided by the assurance engagement, and legal assurance required by terms such as "on balance of probabilities" and "proof beyond a reasonable doubt," it is probably in the auditor's best interest to use terminology that does not have a precise legal meaning but instead reflects the standards of the PA profession. Otherwise the auditors will need to be very careful when the legal terms are used in the report, or risk being caught in libel suits.

Hopefully this section has illustrated some of the complexities of expanding assurance engagements into new areas not familiar to most PAs.

19.28 Why is prosecution of fraud perpetrators generally a good idea?

19.29 What are the CICA materiality guidelines for reporting errors, irregularities and illegal acts?

19.30 Why must care be taken with evidence of fraudulent activity?

SUMMARY

Fraud awareness auditing starts with knowledge of the types of errors, irregularities, illegal acts and frauds that can be perpetrated. External, internal and governmental auditors all have standards for care, attention, planning, detection and reporting of some kinds of errors, irregularities and illegal acts. Fraud examiners, on the other hand, have little in the way of standard programs or materiality guidelines to limit their attention to fraud possibilities. They float on a sea of observations of exceptions and oddities that may be the tip of a fraud iceberg.

Fraud may be contemplated when people have motives, usually financial needs, for stealing money or property. Motive, when combined with opportunity and a lapse of integrity, generally makes the probability of fraud or theft very high. Opportunities arise when an organization's management has a lax attitude about setting an example for good behaviour and about maintenance of a supportive control environment. The fear of getting caught by control procedures deters some fraudsters. Otherwise, attentive management of personnel can ease the pressures people feel and, thus, reduce the incidence of fraud.

Auditors need to know about the red flags, those telltale signs and indications that have accompanied many frauds. When studying a business operation, auditors' ability to "think like a crook" to devise ways to steal can help in the planning of procedures designed to determine whether fraud occurred. Often, imaginative "extended procedures" can be employed to unearth evidence of fraudulent activity. However, technical and personal care must always be exercised because accusations of fraud are always taken very seriously. For this reason, after preliminary findings indicate fraud possibilities, auditors should enlist the co-operation of management and assist fraud examination professionals in bringing an investigation to a conclusion.

For information on the Association of Certified Fraud Examiners (CFEs), visit their website at www.cfenet.com.

MULTIPLE-CHOICE QUESTIONS FOR PRACTICE AND REVIEW

19.31 One of the typical characteristics of management fraud is:
  a. Falsification of documents in order to steal money from an employer.
  b. Victimization of investors through the use of materially misleading financial statements.
  c. Illegal acts committed by management to evade laws and regulations.
  d. Conversion of stolen inventory to cash deposited in a falsified bank account.

19.32 CICA auditing standards do not require auditors of financial statements to:
  a. Understand the nature of errors and irregularities.
  b. Assess the risk of occurrence of errors and irregularities.
  c. Design audits to provide reasonable assurance of detecting errors and irregularities.
  d. Report all finding of errors and irregularities to police authorities.

19.33 Which of the following types of auditors have the highest expectations in their audit standards regarding the detection of fraud?
  a. External auditors of financial statements.
  b. Government auditors of financial statements, programs, activities and functions.

c. Internal auditors employed by companies.

d. Management advisory consultants engaged to design a company's information system.

19.34 Which two of the following characterize the work of fraud examiners and are different from the typical attitude of external auditors?

a. Analysis of control weaknesses for opportunities to commit fraud.

b. Analysis of control strengths as a basis for planning other audit procedures.

c. Determination of a materiality amount that represents a significant misstatement of the current-year financial statements.

d. Thinking of a materiality amount in cumulative terms—that is, as becoming large over a number of years.

19.35 When auditing with "fraud awareness," auditors should especially notice and follow up employee activities under which of these conditions?

a. The company always estimates the inventory but never takes a complete physical count.

b. The petty cash box is always locked in the desk of the custodian.

c. Management has published a company code of ethics and sends frequent communication newsletters about it.

d. The board of directors reviews and approves all investment transactions.

19.36 The best way to enact a broad fraud-prevention program is to:

a. Install airtight control systems of checks and supervision.

b. Name an "ethics officer" who is responsible for receiving and acting upon fraud tips.

c. Place dedicated "hot line" telephones on walls around the workplace with direct communication to the company ethics officer.

d. Practise management "of the people and for the people" to help them share personal and professional problems.

19.37 Which of the following gives the least indication of fraudulent activity?

a. Numerous cash refunds have been made to different people at the same post office box address.

b. Internal auditor cannot locate several credit memos to support reductions of customers' balances.

c. Bank reconciliation has no outstanding cheques or deposits older than 15 days.

d. Three people were absent the day the auditors handed out the paycheques and have not picked them up four weeks later.

19.38 Which of the following combinations is a good means of hiding employee fraud but a poor means of carrying out management (financial reporting) fraud?

a. Overstating sales revenue and overstating customer accounts receivable balances.

b. Overstating sales revenue and overstating bad debt expense.

c. Understating interest expense and understating accrued interest payable.

d. Omit the disclosure information about related party sales to the president's relatives at below-market prices.

19.39 Which of these arrangements of duties could most likely lead to an embezzlement or theft?

a. Inventory warehouse manager has responsibility for making the physical inventory observation and reconciling discrepancies to the perpetual inventory records.

b. Cashier prepared the bank deposit, endorsed the cheques with a company stamp, and took the cash and cheques to the bank for deposit (no other bookkeeping duties).

c. Accounts receivable clerk received a list of payments received by the cashier so that he could make entries in the customers' accounts receivable subsidiary accounts.

d. Financial vice president received cheques made out to suppliers and the supporting invoices, signed the cheques, and put them in the mail to the payees.

19.40 If sales and income were overstated by recording a false credit sale at the end of the year, where could you find the false "dangling debit?" In the:

a. Inventory?

b. Cost of goods sold?

c. Bad debt expense?

d. Accounts receivable?

19.41 Which of these is an invalid social insurance number?

a. 462 003 335.

b. 473 09 7787.

c. 506 98 5529.

d. 700 051 135.

19.42 Public records from which of these sources could be used to find the owner of an office building?

a. Ministry of Industry and Trade export/import licence files.
b. Transport Canada records.
c. City and county tax assessor-collector files.
d. Securities commission filings.

19.43 Experience has shown that the largest number of accounting errors requiring adjustment are found in:
a. Systematic processing of large volumes of day-to-day ordinary transactions.

b. Payroll fraudsters' mistakes in using unissued social insurance numbers.
c. Petty cash embezzlements.
d. Nonroutine, nonsystematic journal entries.

19.44 The type of financial analysis that expresses balance sheet accounts as percentages of total assets is known as:
a. Horizontal analysis.
b. Vertical analysis.
c. Net worth analysis.
d. Expenditure analysis.

EXERCISES AND PROBLEMS

19.45 **Give Examples of Errors, Irregularities and Frauds.** This is an exercise concerning financial reporting misstatements, not employee theft. Give an example of an error, irregularity or fraud that would misstate financial statements to affect the accounts as follows, taken one case at a time. (Note: "overstate" means the account has a higher value than would be appropriate under GAAP, and "understate" means it has a lower value.)
a. Overstate an asset, state another asset.
b. Overstate an asset, overstate shareholder equity.
c. Overstate an asset, overstate revenue.
d. Overstate an asset, understate an expense.
e. Overstate a liability, overstate an expense.
f. Understate an asset, overstate an expense.
g. Understate a liability, understate an expense.

19.46 **Overall Analysis of Accounting Estimates.** Oak Industries, a manufacturer of radio and cable TV equipment and an operator of subscription TV systems, had a multitude of problems. Subscription services in a market area, for which $12 million cost had been deferred, were being terminated, and the customers were not paying on time ($4 million receivables in doubt). The chances are 50–50 that the business will survive another two years.

An electronic part turned out to have defects that needed correction. Warranty expenses are estimated to range from $2 million to $6 million. The inventory of this part ($10 million) is obsolete, but $1 million can be recovered in salvage; or, the parts in inventory can be rebuilt at a cost of $2 million (selling price of the inventory on hand would then be $8 million, with 20 percent of selling price required to market and ship the products, and the normal profit expected is 5 percent of the selling price). If the inventory were scrapped, the company would manufacture a replacement inventory at a cost of $6 million, excluding marketing and shipping costs and normal profit.

The company has defaulted on completion of a military contract, and the government is claiming a $2 million refund. Company lawyers think the dispute might be settled for as little as $1 million.

The auditors had previously determined that an overstatement of income before taxes of $7 million would be material to the financial statements. These items were the only ones left for audit decisions about possible adjustment. Management has presented the analysis below for the determination of loss recognition:

Write-off deferred subscription costs	$ 3,000,000
Provide allowance for bad debts	4,000,000
Provide for expected warranty expense	2,000,000
Lower of cost or market inventory write-down	2,000,000
Loss on government contract refund	—
Total write-offs and losses	$11,000,000

Required:
Prepare your own analysis of the amount of adjustment to the financial statements. Assume that none of these estimates have been recorded yet, and give the adjusting entry you would recommend. Give any supplementary explanations you believe necessary to support your recommendation.

19.47 **Select Effective Extended Procedures.** Given below are some "suspicions," and you have been requested to select some effective extended procedures designed to confirm or deny the suspicion.

Required:
Write the suggested procedures for each case in definite terms so that another person can know what to do.

a. The custodian of the petty cash fund may be removing cash on Friday afternoon to pay for his weekend activities.

b. A manager has noticed that eight new vendors have been added to the purchasing department approved list since the assistant purchasing agent was promoted to chief agent three weeks ago. She suspects that all or some of them may be phony companies set up by the new chief purchasing agent.

c. The payroll supervisor may be stealing unclaimed paycheques of people who quit work and don't pick up the last cheque.

d. Although no customers have complained, cash collections on accounts receivable are down, and the counter clerks may have stolen customers' payments.

e. The cashier may have "borrowed" money, covering it by holding each day's deposit until cash from the next day(s) collection is enough to make up the shortage from an earlier day, then sending the deposit to the bank.

19.48 Horizontal and Vertical Analysis. Horizontal analysis refers to changes of financial statement numbers and ratios across two or more years. Vertical analysis refers to financial statement amounts expressed each year as proportions of a base, such as sales for the income statement accounts,

EXHIBIT 19.48–1 **RETAIL COMPANY**

	Prior Year Audited		Current Year		Change	
	Balance	Common Size	Balance	Common Size	Amount	Percent
Assets:						
Cash	$ 600,000	14.78%	$ 484,000	9.69%	(116,000)	−19.33%
Accounts receivable	500,000	12.32	400,000	8.01	(100,000)	−20.00
Allowance doubt accts.	(40,000)	−0.99	(30,000)	−0.60	10,000	−25.00
Inventory	1,500,000	36.95	1,940,000	38.85	440,000	29.33
Total current assets	$2,560,000	63.05	2,794,000	55.95	234,000	9.14
Capital assets	3,000,000	73.89	4,000,000	80.10	1,000,000	33.33
Accum. depreciation	(1,500,000)	−36.95	(1,800,000)	−36.04	(300,000)	20.00
Total assets	$4,060,000	100.00%	$4,994,000	100.00%	934,000	23.00%
Liabilities and equity:						
Accounts payable	$ 450,000	11.08%	$ 600,000	12.01%	150,000	33.33%
Bank loans, 11%	0	0.00	750,000	15.02	750,000	NA
Accrued interest	50,000	1.23	40,000	0.80	(10,000)	−20.00
Accruals and other	60,000	1.48	10,000	0.20	(50,000)	−83.33
Total current liab.	560,000	13.79	1,400,000	28.03	840,000	150.00
Long–term debt, 10%	500,000	12.32	400,000	8.01	(100,000)	−20.00
Total liabilities	1,060,000	26.11	1,800,000	36.04	740,000	69.81
Share capital	2,000,000	49.26	2,000,000	40.05	0	0
Retained earnings	1,000,000	24.63	1,194,000	23.91	194,000	19.40
Total liabilities and equity	$4,060,000	100.00%	$4,994,000	100.00%	934,000	23.00%
Statement of operations:						
Sales (net)	$9,000,000	100.00%	$8,100,000	100.00%	(900,000)	−10.00%
Cost of goods sold	6,296,000	69.96	5,265,000	65.00	(1,031,000)	−16.38
Gross margin	2,704,000	30.04	2,835,000	35.00	131,000	4.84
General expense	2,044,000	22.71	2,005,000	24.75	(39,000)	−1.91
Amortization	300,000	3.33	300,000	3.70	0	0
Operating income	360,000	4.00	530,000	6.54	170,000	47.22
Interest expense	50,000	0.56	40,000	0.49	(10,000)	−20.00
Income taxes (40%)	124,000	1.38	196,000	2.42	72,000	58.06
Net income	$ 186,000	2.07%	$ 294,000	3.63%	108,000	58.06%

NA means not applicable.

EXHIBIT 19.48-2   **RETAIL COMPANY**

	Prior Year	Current Year	Percent Change
Balance sheet ratios:			
Current ratio	4.57	2.0	−56.34%
Days' sales in receivables	18.40	16.44	−10.63
Doubtful accounts ratio	0.0800	0.0750	−6.25
Days' sales in inventory	85.77	132.65	54.66
Debt/equity ratio	0.35	0.56	40.89
Operations ratios:			
Receivables turnover	19.57	21.89	11.89
Inventory turnover	4.20	2.71	−35.34
Cost of goods sold/sales	69.96%	65.00%	−7.08
Gross margin %	30.04%	35.00%	16.49
Return on equity	6.61%	9.80%	48.26

and total assets for the balance sheet accounts. Exhibit 19.48–1 contains the Retail Company's prior year (audited) and current year (unaudited) financial statements, along with amounts and percentages of change from year to year (horizontal analysis) and common-size percentages (vertical analysis). Exhibit 19.48–2 contains selected financial ratios based on these financial statements. Analysis of these data may enable auditors to discern relationships that raise questions about misleading financial statements.

Required:
Study the data in Exhibits 19.48–1 and 19.48–2. Write a memo identifying and explaining potential problem areas where misstatements in the current year financial statements might exist. Additional information about Retail Company is as follows:
- The new bank loan, obtained on July 1 of the current year, requires maintenance of a 2:1 current ratio.
- Principal of $100,000 plus interest on the 10 percent long-term note obtained several years ago in the original amount of $800,000 is due each January 1.
- The company has never paid dividends on its common shares and has no plans for a dividend.

19.49 Expenditure Analysis. Expenditure analysis is used when fraud has been discovered or strongly suspected, and the information to calculate a suspect's income and expenditures can be obtained (e.g., asset and liability records, bank accounts). Expenditure analysis consists of establish-

ing the suspect's known expenditures for all purposes for the relevant period, subtracting all known sources of funds (e.g., wages, gifts, inheritances, bank balances and the like), and calling the difference the expenditures financed by unknown sources of income.

***FORENSIC ACCOUNTING
CONSULTING ENGAGEMENT 1***
You have been hired by the law firm of Gleckel and Morris. The lawyers have been retained by Blade Manufacturing Company in a case involving a suspected kickback by a purchasing employee, E. J. Cunningham.

Cunningham is suspected of taking kickbacks from Mason Varner, a salesman for Tanco Metals. He has denied the charges, but Lanier Gleckel, the lawyer in charge of the case, is convinced the kickbacks have occurred.

Gleckel filed a civil action and subpoenaed Cunningham's books and records, including his last year's bank statements. The beginning bank balance January 1 was $3,463, and the ending bank balance December 31 was $2,050. Over the intervening 12 months, Cunningham's gross salary was $3,600 per month, with a net of $2,950. His wife doesn't work at a paying job. His house payments were $1,377 per month. In addition, he paid $2,361 per month on a new Mercedes 500 SEL and paid a total of $9,444 last year toward a new Nissan Maxima (including $5,000 down payment). He also purchased new state-of-the-art audio and video equipment for $18,763, with no down payment, and total payments on the equipment last year of $5,532. A reasonable estimate of his household expenses during the period is $900 per month ($400 for food, $200 for utilities and $300 for other items).

Required:
Using expenditure analysis, calculate the amount of income, if any, from "unknown sources."

19.50 Net Worth Analysis. Net worth analysis is used when fraud has been discovered or strongly suspected, and the information to calculate a suspect's net worth can be obtained (e.g., asset and liability records, bank accounts). The procedure is to calculate the person's change in net worth (excluding changes in market values of assets), and to identify the known sources of funds to finance the changes. Any difference between the change in net worth and the known sources of funds is called "funds from unknown sources," which may be ill-gotten gains.

FORENSIC ACCOUNTING
CONSULTING ENGAGEMENT 2
C. Nero has worked for Bonne Consulting Group (BCG) as the executive secretary for administration for nearly 10 years. His dedication has earned him a reputation as

an outstanding employee and has resulted in increasing responsibilities. C. Nero is a suspect in fraud.

This is the hindsight story. During Nero's first five years of employment, BCG subcontracted all of its feasibility and marketing studies through Jackson & Company. This relationship was terminated because Jackson & Company merged with a larger, more expensive consulting group. At the time of termination, Nero and his supervisor were forced to select a new firm to conduct BCG's market research. However, Nero never informed the accounting department that the Jackson & Company account had been closed.

Since his supervisor allowed Nero to sign the payment voucher for services rendered, Nero was able to continue to process cheques made payable to Jackson's account. Nero was trusted to be the only signature authorizing payments less than $10,000. The accounting department continued to write the cheques and Nero would take responsibility for delivering them. Nero opened a bank account in a nearby city under the name of Jackson & Company, where he would make the deposit.

NERO'S RECORDS

	Year One	Year Two	Year Three
Assets:			
Residence	$100,000	$100,000	$100,000
Shares and bonds	30,000	30,000	42,000
Automobiles	20,000	20,000	40,000
Certificate of deposit	50,000	50,000	50,000
Cash	6,000	12,000	14,000
Liabilities:			
Mortgage balance	90,000	50,000	—
Auto loan	10,000	—	—
Income:			
Salary		34,000	36,000
Other		6,000	6,000
Expenses:			
Scheduled mortgage payments		6,000	6,000
Auto loan payments		4,800	—
Other living expenses		20,000	22,000
Hint:			
Set up a working paper like this:			
	End Year 1	End Year 2	End Year 3

Assets (list)
Liabilities (list)
Net worth (difference)
Change in net worth
Add total expenses
= Change plus expenses
Subtract known income
= Funds from unknown sources

Required:
C. Nero's financial records have been obtained by subpoena. You have been hired to estimate the amount of loss by estimating Nero's "funds from unknown sources" that financed his comfortable lifestyle. Below is a summary of the data obtained from Nero's records.

DISCUSSION CASES

GENERAL INSTRUCTIONS FOR CASES 19.51–19.56:
These cases are designed like the ones in the chapter. They give the problem, the method, the paper trail, and the amount. Your assignment is to write the Audit Approach portion of the case organized around these sections:

Objective: Express the objective in terms of the facts supposedly asserted in financial records, accounts and statements.

Control: Write a brief explanation of desirable controls, missing controls and especially the kinds of "deviations" that might arise from the situation described in the case.

Test of controls: Write some procedures for getting evidence about existing controls, especially procedures that could discover deviations from controls. If there are no controls to test, then there are no procedures to perform; go then to the next section. A "procedure" should instruct someone about the source(s) of evidence to tap and the work to do.

Audit of balance: Write some procedures for getting evidence about the existence, completeness, valuation, ownership or disclosure assertions identified in your objective section above.

Discovery summary: Write a short statement about the discovery you expect to accomplish with your procedures.

19.51 Employee Embezzlement via Cash Disbursements and Inventory. Follow the instructions at the beginning of this Discussion Cases section.

STEALING WAS EASY
Problem: Cash embezzlement, inventory and expense overstatement.

Method: Lew Marcus was the only bookkeeper at the Ace Plumbing Supply Company. He ordered the supplies and inventory, paid the bills, collected the cash receipts and cheques sent by customers and reconciled the bank statements. The company had about $11 million in sales, inventory of $3 million, and expenses that generally ran about $6–7 million each year. Nobody checked Lew's work, so sometimes when he received a bill for goods from a supplier (say, for $8,000) he would make an accounting entry for $12,000 debit to inventory, write an $8,000 cheque to pay the bill, then write a $4,000 cheque to himself. The cheque to Lew was not recorded, and he removed it from the bank statement when he prepared the bank reconciliation. The owner of the business considered the monthly bank reconciliation a proper control activity.

Paper trail: No perpetual inventory records were kept, and no periodic inventory count was taken. The general ledger contained an inventory control account balance that was reduced by 60 percent of the amount of each sale of plumbing fixtures (estimated cost of sales). The bank statements and reconciliations were in a file. The statements showed the cheque number and amount of Lew's cheques to himself, but the cheques themselves were missing. The cheques to vendors were in the amounts of their bills, but the entries in the cash disbursements journal showed higher amounts.

Amount: Over an eight-year period, Lew embezzled $420,000.

19.52 Employee Embezzlement via Cash Receipts and Payment of Personal Expenses. Follow the instructions at the beginning of this Discussion Cases section. In this case you can assume that you have received the informant's message.

THE EXTRA BANK ACCOUNT
Problem: Cash receipts pocketed and personal expenses paid from business account.

Method: The Ourtown Independent School District, like all others, had red tape about school board approval of cash disbursements. To get around the rules, and to make timely payment of some bills possible, the superintendent of schools had a school bank account that was used in the manner of a petty cash fund. The board knew about it and had given blanket approval in advance for its use to make timely payment of minor school expenses. The board, however, never reviewed the activity in this account. The business manager had sole responsibility for the account, subject to the annual audit. The account got money from transfers from other school accounts and from deposit of cafeteria cash receipts. The superintendent did not like to be bothered with details, and he often signed blank cheques so that the business manager would not need to run in for a signature all the time. The business manager sometimes paid her personal American Express credit card bills, charged personal items to the school's VISA account, and pocketed some cafeteria cash receipts before deposit.

Paper trail: An informant called the state education audit agency and told the story that this business manager had used school funds to buy hosiery. When told of this story, the superintendent told the auditor to place no credibility in the informant, who is "out to get us." The business manager had in fact used the account to write unauthorized cheques to "cash," put her own American Express bills in the school files (the school district had a VISA card, not American Express) and signed on the school card for gasoline and auto repairs during periods of vacation and summer when school was not in session. (As for the hosiery, she purchased $700 worth with school funds one year.) The superintendent was genuinely unaware of the misuse of funds.

Amount: The business manager had been employed for six years, was trusted, and stole an estimated $25,000.

19.53 Employee Embezzlement via Padded Payroll. Follow the instructions at the beginning of this Discussion Cases section. In this case your assignment is to analyse the payroll register and see if you can identify any of the ghosts.

GHOST RIDERS ON THE PAYROLL
Problem: Embezzlement with fictitious people on the payroll.

Method: Billy Joe had responsibility for preparing personnel files for new hires, approval of wages, verification of time cards and distribution of payroll cheques. He "hired" fictitious employees, faked their records and ordered cheques through the payroll system.

Paper trail: The payroll department produces a payroll register listing various items of information about employees. A selection from the register is in Exhibit 19.53–1. Reading the columns from left to right, it shows the employee identification number, employee name, employees'

section number (retail store location), social insurance number and bank addresses (account numbers for electronic funds transfer).

Amount: Billy Joe stole $160,000 over a three-year period.

Required:
Analyse the payroll register in Exhibit 19.53–1 and identify the questionable employees who might be ghosts on the payroll.

19.54 Employee Embezzlement: Medical Claims Fraud. Follow the instructions at the beginning of this Discussion Cases section.

DOCTOR! DOCTOR!
Problem: Fictitious medical benefit claims were paid by the company, which self-insured up to $50,000 per employee. The expense account that included legitimate and false charges was "employee medical benefits."

Method: As manager of the claims payment department, Martha Lee was considered one of Beta Magnetic's best employees. She never missed a day of work in 10 years, and her department had one of the company's best efficiency ratings. Controls were considered good, including the verification by a claims processor that (1) the patient was a Beta employee, (2) medical treatments were covered in the plan, (3) the charges were within approved guidelines, (4) the cumulative claims for the employee did not exceed $50,000 (if over $50,000 a claim was submitted to an insurance company), and (5) the calculation for payment was correct. After verification processing, claims were sent to the claims payment department to pay the doctor directly. No payments ever went directly to employees. Martha Lee prepared false claims on real employees, forging the signature of various claims processors, adding her own review approval, naming bogus doctors who would be paid by the payment department. The payments were mailed to various post office box addresses and to her husband's business address.

Nobody ever verified claims information with the employee. The employees received no reports of medical benefits paid on their behalf. While the department had performance reports by claims processors, these reports did not show claim-by-claim details. No one verified the credentials of the doctors.

E X H I B I T 19.53–1   **PAYROLL REGISTER**

I.D. No.	Name	Sect.	Social Ins. Number	Address
5592	Annalee, Michele	1990	455411471	6205193611
8961	Avondale, Richard	1990	435315873	4723265701
186	Bryce, Sharon	1990	449435042	2763431893
3553	Gorman, Thalia	1990	459497264	1565644635
6521	Gordon, Marshall	1990	463355479	8999781365
6999	Harvey, Kevin	1990	396546363	7409894998
8920	Mazzini, Virgil	1990	461785493	2012719362
4534	Paperton, Karen	1990	453491250	6371802086
6204	Peterman, Jennifer	1990	473600914	7818539686
5481	Brione, Kimberly	2000	461635205	5622472908
5363	Brione, Douglas	2000	137567089	4286008036
7891	Jones, Jonothan	2000	464373412	3890567269
9491	Jones, Michael	2000	464373413	3890567269
527	Jones, Thomas	2000	464373413	4609659041
4042	Bull, Lisa	2000	466471495	2797567256
6041	Bushman, Jolle	2000	451355503	9103080617
590	Camp, Liana	2000	455690418	4237338557
3054	Cantraz, Luan	2000	460594645	7894813997
8063	Churchman, Matt	2000	466232740	6977367072
2964	Allford, Eric	2010	444782904	2935968014
9293	Altzheimer, Jeff	2010	453493495	6349921488
6729	Ameston, Jackie	2010	483889548	2722529584
3154	Arrgon, Mary	2010	452535653	8213209536
852	Bulling, John	2010	325462648	5587231055
7219	Chidid, Adam	2010	124491704	7443759037
9346	Chu, Song	2010	465350881	2171962355
5261	Cooker, Scott	2010	459983822	4634865235
4987	Coolman, Maury	2010	458531820	1291047566
1667	Daughterford, Debby	2010	461478070	8223680929
6145	Butterby, Laura	2020	462237424	3463748143
9265	Butterby, Leigh	2020	462236725	3463748143
1231	Butterby, L.A.	2020	462236726	3463748143
6919	Cevil, John	2020	453454988	9781429093
6840	Chung, Hihnno	2020	483113789	4888874664
7489	Cordon, Andy	2020	497605588	5129368143
9111	Coward, Clay	2020	452639707	49242627
4873	Cranehook, Mary	2020	275643410	1622537823
9362	Diercheski, Ward	2020	460496149	7641205905
378	Fineman, Bryan	2020	459679356	8703966421
4613	Deitrick, James	2025	135635583	6947113473
5361	Larson, Kermit	2025	221156649	6947113473
3276	Newman, Paul	2025	601669984	6947113473
3493	Robertson, Jack	2025	680623358	6947113473
8857	Rosingale, Patricia	2025	460654900	6609741958
7103	Ruhle, Mabry	2025	397804404	6940593886
7559	Ruffinio, Jill	2025	461394849	2874916590
8494	Rummsfell, Judith	2025	466539183	4621454720
43	Smith, Michael	2025	442641436	6504510060
1948	Shultze, Robert	2025	457020330	9202701679

Paper trail: The falsified claim forms were in Beta's files, containing all the fictitious data on employee names, processor signatures, doctors' bills and phony doctors and addresses. The cancelled cheques were returned by the bank and were kept in Beta's files, containing "endorsements" by the doctors. Martha Lee and her husband were somewhat clever: They deposited the cheques in various banks in accounts opened in the names and identification of the "doctors."

Martha Lee did not stumble on the paper trail. She drew the attention of an auditor who saw her take her 24 claims processing employees out to an annual staff appreciation luncheon in a fleet of stretch limousines.

Amount: Over seven years, Martha Lee and her husband stole $3.5 million, and, until the last, no one noticed anything unusual about the total amount of claims paid.

19.55 Financial Reporting: Overstated Sales and Profits. Follow the instructions at the beginning of this Discussion Cases section. For this case, give the recommended adjusting journal entry as well as the audit approach.

THANK GOODNESS IT'S FRIDAY

Problem: Overstated sales caused overstated net income, retained earnings, current assets, working capital and total assets. Overstated cash collections did not change the total current assets or total assets, but they increased the amount of cash and decreased the amount of accounts receivable.

Method: Alpha Brewery Corporation has generally good control policies and procedures related to authorization of transactions for accounting entry, and the accounting manual has instructions for recording sales transactions in the proper accounting period. The company regularly closes the accounting process each Friday at 5 p.m. to prepare weekly management reports. The year-end date (cutoff date) is December 31, and in 2001 December 31 was a Monday. However, the accounting was performed through Friday as usual, and the accounts were closed for the year on January 4.

Paper trail: All the entries were properly dated after December 31, including the sales invoices, cash receipts, and shipping documents. However, the trial balance from which the financial statements were prepared was dated December 31, 2001. Nobody noticed the slip of a few days because the Friday closing was normal.

Amount: Alpha recorded sales of $672,000 and gross profit of $268,800 over the January 1–4 period. Cash collections on customers' accounts came in the amount of $800,000.

19.56 Financial Reporting: Overstated Inventory and Profits (duplicated in Chapter 10: Case 10.68). Follow the instructions at the beginning of this Discussion Cases section. For this case recalculate the income (loss) before taxes using the correct inventory figures. (Assume the correct beginning inventory two years ago was $5.5 million.)

THE PHANTOM OF THE INVENTORY

Problem: Overstated physical inventory caused understated cost of goods sold and overstated net income, current assets, total assets and retained earnings.

Method: All Bright Company manufactured lamps. Paul M, manager of the State Street plant, was under pressure to produce profits so that the company could maintain its loans at the bank. The loans were secured by the inventory of 1,500 types of finished goods, work in process and parts used for making lamps (bases, shades, wire, nuts, bolts and so on). Paul arranged the physical inventory counting procedures and accompanied the external audit team while the external auditors observed the count and made test counts after the company personnel had recorded their

SCHEDULE FOR 19.56

	Two Years Ago	One Year Ago	Current Year
Sales	$25,000	$29,000	$40,500
Cost of goods sold	(20,000)	(22,000)	(29,000)
Expenses	(5,000)	(8,000)	(9,000)
Income (loss) before taxes	—	$(1,000)	$2,500
Ending inventory	$6,000	$8,000	$10,200
Other current assets	9,000	8,500	17,500
Total assets	21,000	21,600	34,300
Current liabilities	5,000	5,500	13,000
Long-term debt*	5,500	6,600	9,300
Shareholder equity	10,500	9,500	12,000

*Secured by inventory pledged to the bank.

counts on tags attached to the inventory locations. At the auditors' request, Paul directed them to the "most valuable" inventory for their test counts, although he did not show them all of the most valuable types. When the auditors were looking the other way, Paul raised the physical count on inventory tags the auditors would not include in their test counts. When everyone had finished each floor of the multistory warehouse, all the tags were gathered and sent to data processing for computer compilation and pricing at FIFO cost.

Paper trail: All Bright had no perpetual inventory records. All the records of the inventory quantity and pricing were in the count tags and the priced compilation, which was produced by the data processing department six weeks later. The auditors traced their test counts to the compilation and did not notice the raised physical quantities on the inventory types they did not test-count. They also did not notice some extra (fictitious) tags Paul had handed over to data processing.

Amount: Paul falsified the inventory for three years before the company declared bankruptcy. Over that period the inventory was overstated by $1 million (17 percent, two years ago), $2.5 million (31 percent, one year ago), and $3 million (29 percent, current year). The financial statements showed the information in the schedule provided on the previous page (dollars in 000).

19.57 Role of Control, Analytical Procedures and Extended Procedures in Fraud Detection

CORRUPT CAPERS IN THE CHICKEN BUSINESS

After fathering six children and completing 14 years of employment with a variety of federal law enforcement and regulatory agencies with whom I had served in audit, compliance, investigative and supervisory capacities, I fell prey to the need to earn more money. So I accepted an executive position with a new fast-food chain in Nashville, Tennessee, then called Minnie Pearl Chicken Systems, Inc. The company bore the name of that great lady of Grand Old Opry fame, but she herself was only a small shareholder and inactive in day-to-day management. The year was 1969, and any celebrity with national name recognition was in the fast-food business. But that's another story.

I was given the job of managing a company division called Nashco Equipment and Supply. Nashco was organized as a profit centre. It supplied both company-owned and franchised restaurants with restaurant decor, furniture, cooking equipment and utensils, uniforms, signage and ad specialties. Nashco's operations were located about a mile from corporate headquarters in a leased warehouse and office facility of some 60,000 square feet. Nashco's major functional components at that site included purchasing, inventory control, sales and physical distribution.

Nashco's physical distribution function included warehousing, receiving and shipping activities. The latter included a fleet of leased trucks used to deliver restaurant equipment, supplies and certain construction materials to new restaurant sites throughout the United States and Canada.

On the day I arrived to take over the division, the president of the company briefed me on his expectations. In simple terms his demand was, "Make money." He didn't say "or else." But I instinctively knew the implications. I inferred that because he made it clear that the division had lost money the year before—about $500,000.

The profit-centre manager who had incurred the loss was still employed by the company. In fact he had been demoted and made an assistant—to me! However, the president suggested I could terminate him at any time if I so desired.

It seemed to me that terminating the poor man should have been handled by someone either above me or by the corporate personnel director. At any rate I was stuck with him for the time being, mainly because I didn't know what else to do.

When I did meet my assistant, he seemed like a pleasant-enough chap. His previous experience and his education were in aeronautical engineering—a little odd perhaps, since we were in the fast-food business. I didn't give it much further thought. Why should I? What did I know about the restaurant business? I was as green as he was—greener! He had been with the company for nine months.

My first day on the job, after my "executive briefing" with the president, was spent meeting all the members of my staff. Most of these folks were also relatively new at their jobs and showed evidence of insecurity in their roles. The only people who seemed secure in job roles were the warehousing people—stevedores, truck drivers and the traffic manager. They at least knew their jobs and their place. They even showed great deference to me when I met them. But I didn't know why. (Was it typical of Southern culture to show deference for the boss? Perhaps. But here it seemed more than just deference. They almost feigned servility when I met them.)

As it turned out these were no gentlemen of the South. They were crooks. The evidence of their scams began to surface after I had had enough time to become better educated in my job. I spent my first two months learning as much as I could about the fast-food industry, franchising restaurant layouts and designs, and restaurant equipment purchasing and sales. I finally moved through the area I knew least and began to concentrate on what I knew best—accounting, finance, audits, controls, investigations, management and security.

My first effort to reverse the previous year's loss was to review the previous year's operating statements and search for causes. Two items glared at me. Cost of sales was out of line the year before because of a large inventory shrink. Inventory per books was $200,000 higher than the physical count had indicated. The variance was about 10 percent—far more than anyone had expected. But nothing had been done to investigate the loss. The outside auditors made the appropriate adjustments, and the matter was left at that.

Another item was the high cost of transportation expense. I divided the total cost of transportation by the number of miles Ryder Truck Systems had billed us during the previous year. The resultant cost per mile was about double the national average for that time period.

So I had two things to work on now that I was freed from learning how to run a fried-chicken restaurant.

The inventory control group that reported to me consisted of three young ladies, two recent high school graduates and a supervisor, a woman of about 25 who appeared bright and hard-working.

One day when things seemed quiet (which wasn't very often in the halcyon days of fast food in Nashville in 1969), I visited with the inventory control supervisor and asked that she give me a briefing on what she and her crew did. She explained she manually kept perpetual inventory control system to me as best she could, after apologizing that she really was neither an accountant nor an auditor. She said she took a year of high school bookkeeping and had worked in the office

of a moving company for several years before we hired her. At Minnie Pearl her training consisted of a four-hour briefing given by a member of the controller's staff. She apologized for the condition of the inventory records, saying there was more work than she and her staff could handle on a timely basis. So she often had to work overtime to catch up (for which she said she was not paid).

A cursory review of her in-process work and a few inventory ledger cards made my knees feel weak. She had not yet entered shipments of goods made three weeks earlier. And her recording of inbound merchandise was about equally tardy. For all intents and purposes we had no real inventory control system. Some goods were received and shipped out two weeks before any entry was made on the appropriate inventory ledger card.

What was worse, I discovered that a number of ledger cards contained red-ink entries. She explained that the procedure was recommended by a member of the controller's staff who informed her that she should make such an entry whenever she went to the warehouse to make a spot check of certain inventory items. She hadn't fully understood the rationale for cycle counting of selected items, so whenever she noted a discrepancy—the balance shown on the card disagreed with her count—she merely made a red-ink entry on whichever side of the card the discrepancy favoured. But she never advised anyone of the discrepancy or investigated any further, and she never reconciled her pluses and her minuses to determine whether she had a net of more or less. At the year-end, however, she did total the minuses and pluses out, she said. But not during the working year.

On one such ledger card there was a succession of red-ink entries. The ledger card related to large electric chicken fryers that cost the company over $1,000 each. Each of our restaurants needed four fryers. I quickly tallied her pluses and minuses and found the minuses were ahead by some 40 units, or by over $40,000!

A little investigating showed that an equipment serviceman for the company occasionally called from the field and ordered a replacement fryer for one that was in such a state of disrepair it needed to be sent back to the manufacturer on a warranty-claim basis. The warehousemen, lacking any prohibiting instructions, accommodated him.

What the serviceman did in fact was repair the chicken fryer on site, and when the new one arrived he would tell the restaurant manager the warehouse erred, and he himself would return the fryer—no problem. However the fryer never got back to the warehouse. It ended up in his garage, which was filled with other company property as well—refrigerator cabinets, heated cabinets and even a knocked-down walk-in cooler.

As soon as it became apparent that something was wrong by way of the ledger card for chicken fryers, I began calling franchises and asking them whether anyone had offered to sell them chicken fryers at reduced prices. On the fifth call a franchisee mentioned that the serviceman had offered to sell him several fryers for a new restaurant at very "reasonable" prices. The serviceman told him the fryers were brand new and still in the manufacturer's carton.

"Sure enough and so they were," said the franchisee.

"Where did he say he got them?" I asked.

"He didn't say and I didn't ask him," said the franchisee.

"But I know where he kept them."

"Where's that?" I asked.

"In his garage," he said.

Armed with the franchisee's statement and our garbled inventory card, we got a search warrant for the serviceman's garage. There we found a treasure trove of restaurant equipment and supplies that belonged to the company.

So first things first, we developed a real inventory control system and hired an experienced person to supervise the function.

Transportation costs were next on the agenda. Our transport costs were horrendous. I tried the "rant and rave" approach to reduce costs early on but saw no real reduction. After the theft matter had settled down, I tried to find why transportation costs were so high.

I found that our truck fleet, after making deliveries of restaurant equipment, deadheaded back to Nashville, bypassing equipment manufacturers along the route. I thought that was strange, so I talked to the traffic manager. He said it was illegal for us to pick up our own inbound freight, that we were not common carriers and restaurant equipment was not an exempt commodity like farm produce. Our ICC permits allowed us to handle our own goods only after title had passed to us,

which he said occurred after we received them at our warehouse.

So I called several manufacturers who sold us equipment and asked whether we could pick up our equipment purchases at their plant sites with our own fleet. They each said they would accommodate us, but we should change our purchase orders to show FOB their plant sites so as to not run afoul of ICC regulations. Changing the shipment for FOB destination point to FOB origination point caused title to pass to us at their plant so we could haul our own merchandise back and thus save the freight-in charges.

Feeling buoyed by this cost-cutting discovery, I called in the traffic manager and told him to co-ordinate his driver's return trips with the purchasing director and to pick up our equipment along the routes back to Nashville.

A month went by. No real reduction in transportation costs. The traffic manager skirmished with the purchasing director whenever he was told to have a returning truck make a pickup.

Then information came our way that indicated our truck drivers were unhappy about the notation of return loads. It kept them on the road a day or two longer, and away from their wives and children—or so they claimed. At least four of our drivers sought union representation from the Teamsters, as did a half-dozen warehouse employees.

What I didn't fully grasp was that I was ruining something a lot of people had a financial stake in. The drivers didn't want to pick up chicken fryers in Dallas or stainless steel sinks in St. Louis on their way back from Los Angeles because they already had a load to carry. What they were carrying back to Nashville was head lettuce and other fresh fruits and vegetables from California.

Several things tripped up the scheme. The first was collect phone calls made by our drivers to the traffic manager from strange places in California, places where we had neither existing restaurants nor new ones under construction; for example, Salinas has been known for its head lettuce ever since William Saroyan and John Steinbeck made it famous for that.

The Salinas calls caught my attention first. But then when Bakersfield showed up (potatoes) and Ventura/Oxnard (oranges, lemons), I knew something strange was happening. We had no restaurants within miles of these places and they weren't exactly along the route back to Nashville from San Francisco and Los Angeles, where we did have a large number of restaurants.

The strange calls piqued my curiosity, but they weren't evidence of anything yet. My next move was to review the expense claims submitted by the drivers after their returns. That had been the responsibility of my assistant. When I asked that he send the vouchers directly to me from then on, he seemed miffed, as though I had insulted his integrity. He said it was a Mickey Mouse chore, better left to him or the traffic manager, who really knew how to check the excesses of truck drivers who crib on their expense vouchers. When I insisted, he pouted but agreed to send me the vouchers.

I then visited the controller's office at corporate headquarters and asked to see all documentation that supported truck driver expense reports for the preceding six months.

In reviewing the documents submitted by drivers, I noted a recurring oddity. Weight statements at entry points on the Arizona border coming in from California seemed to be smudged, erased, written over, or just plain undecipherable. I selected about a half-dozen examples, made copies of the statements, and returned to my office. I then sent copies to a friend who was an Arizona state trooper, and asked him to secure for me copies of the state's own originals of the weight slips. Sure enough, when I got them back, the weights written on our copies were 20,000 or more pounds lower, indicating that the truck was loaded with something on its way back home.

Next we made phone calls to the numbers in Salinas, Oxnard, and Bakersfield. They were offices of produce growers, merchants and shippers. One claimed he sold lettuce to Minnie Pearl restaurants in St. Louis. When told we had opened no restaurants in Saint Louis yet, he stammered and hung up.

We thought we could piece together what had happened at that point, but we needed confirmation. Our theory of the case was that the traffic manager through contacts with produce merchants in Nashville and St. Louis and growers and shippers in California was doing a little moonlighting with our fleet.

Shipping fresh produce by rail or by truck from California is not cheap. But because the federal government has attempted to support agricultural econom-ics by making special rules for farm products, such products are generally exempt commodities from the standpoint of certain ICC regulations. Truckers who haul farm products are subject to far fewer requirements and regulations.

But because California ships out so much more produce than it takes in, its growers are chronically short of transportation mediums. So growers and shippers are eager to find any poor and lonesome trucker heading east with excess capacity. A thriving bootleg trucking business therefore existed that utilized the trucks of companies that could not find legitimate return loads.

The Minnie Pearl trucks were "sleepers" and carried two drivers so as to expedite deliveries and returns. The typical bootleg arrangement consisted of a $400 fee paid in cash to the two drivers by the grower or shipper. The drivers in turn took $100 each and gave $200 to our traffic manager, who had brokered the deal to begin with.

We cracked the case by asking one pair of driver-partners to explain the discrepancy between the weight slips they had submitted with their expense vouchers and the originals of those slips that we had secured from the state of Arizona. They laid out the scheme and implicated other drivers, and the traffic manager as the master-mind. Both confessed mainly because they were on parole—a report of the incident to parole authorities might have caused them to complete their prison sentences.

The traffic manager then implicated several other managers in the company as deriving benefits from his scheme.

(Source: G.J. Bologna and R.J. Lindquist, Fraud Auditing and Forensic Accounting (New York: John Wiley & Sons, 1987), pp. 227–33. Reprinted with permission of the publisher.)

Required:

a. Identify any potential management or personnel problems that might contribute to or facilitate fraud.

b. Identify the analytical procedures and findings that raised signals for further investigation and management work.

c. Identify some detail (extended) procedures performed to give signals and definite information about operational and fraudulent problems in connection with the inventory write-downs (shrink).

d. Identify some detail (extended) procedures performed to give signals and definite information about operational and fraudulent problems in connection with the high transportation costs.

19.58 Bank Reconciliation. Chapter 19 covers a wide range of fraud topics. The audit of bank reconciliations is in Chapter 9. Discussion Case 9.63 deals with a manipulated bank reconciliation and refers to Exhibit 19–3 in Chapter 19. You may wish to use Case 9.63 as an assignment for Chapter 19.

19.59 Payroll Fraud. You had established a national reputation as head of management audit at Henry Vanier Inc., a food manufacturing and processing corporation based in Calgary, with 40,000 employees in eight plants across the country and profits in 2003–04 of $92 million on revenue of $900 million. Your reputation had been based on innovations inspired by your financial control system audits and your performance audits in such areas as investment in new technology, costing and quality assurance. Vanier had also avoided the embarrassing public revelations of fraud suffered over the last two years by your major competitor—Top Brands, which is based in Montreal. You were due to present your updated three-year audit plan to the board meeting next month, and the CEO dropped into your office as you were pondering your draft presentation.

"I have been watching the debacle at Top Brands with dismay," he said. "I realize that they are our competitors, but this fraud business affects the whole industry. Your approach to fraud is, I understand from our previous chats, really to keep an eye open for any signs while you conduct your financial control, compliance and performance audits, and, as far as we all know, that has kept us from serious problems. But I wonder if we should build on that good public record by actually taking a careful pre-emptive look at fraud, and possibly even adding to our mission statement what I would like to call our corporate 'fraud policy.' To this end, I would like you to take an additional hour at the forthcoming board meeting to do three things: first, I would like a short statement on the definition of fraud and the responsibilities of management and auditors; then you should give the board a brief overview, but with all the stages defined, on how you would conduct a fraud investigation at Vanier. Finally, for, say, the last third of your presentation, I would like you to present a draft of the components that could go into a fraud policy statement for consideration by the board. I would envisage that this statement would be given to all employees and board members, and indeed widely publicized."

While you were working on this presentation, you received a call from Susan, one of your staff. Apparently, in a routine review of the payroll system, she had encountered a possible case of fraud, and she wanted you to review her findings. As part of the routine review, Susan extracted payroll records for the last quarter from the mainframe computer into a dBASE file. She then used ACL to analyse the payroll records. The dBASE file contains the following fields that are of relevance for the audit:

Field	Description
EMPNUM	Employee number
NAME	Name of employee
ADDRESS	Address of employee
DEPT	Department
SUPRVSOR	Supervisor name
PERIOD	Payroll period (1 for January, 2 for February, and so on)
BANK	Bank for payroll deposit
BANKACCT	Account number of payroll deposit
PAY	Amount of payment

The following is a partial printout from the dBASE file that Susan found disturbing:

EMPNUM	BANK	BANKACCT
691023	BNS	71029-2
701932	HKB	8923-12
702595	BNS	78910-3
710941	RBC	81-234
711120	HKB	9012-15
720187	BNS	73015-2
720198	TDB	1-29305
729510	BOM	128-412
729102	BNS	71029-2
730194	RBC	81-234
732103	BNS	72076-3
732461	RBC	81-234
732518	BOM	128-412
732892	TDB	1-29305
733019	HKB	8923-12
740125	BNS	72076-3
742957	TDB	1-29305
744910	BOM	128-412
751025	BNS	78910-3
760120	HKB	9012-15

Required:
a. Prepare the presentation on fraud for the forthcoming meeting.
b. Explain what conclusions can be drawn from the partial ACL printout.
c. What additional computer-assisted audit techniques would you use to make the printout more useful? You do not need to provide the ACL commands.
d. What audit procedures are required to follow up these payroll records?

(CGAAC adapted)

APPENDIX 19A

DETAILS OF VARIOUS AUDIT STANDARDS CONCERNING ERRORS, IRREGULARITIES, ILLEGAL ACTS, FRAUD, ABUSE AND INEFFICIENCY

Auditor's Responsibility to Detect and Communicate Misstatements (from *Section* 5135.09)

Because the auditor maintains an attitude of professional scepticism when performing the audit, he or she will consider whether circumstances encountered indicate the possibility of a material misstatement existing in the financial statements. Examples of circumstances which, either individually or in combination, may make the auditor suspect misstatements exist are:

a. Unrealistic time deadlines for audit completion imposed by management.

b. Reluctance by management to engage in frank communication with appropriate third parties, such as regulators and bankers.

c. Limitation in audit scope imposed by management.

d. Identification of important matters not previously disclosed by management.

e. Conflicting or unsatisfactory evidence provided by management or employees.

f. Unusual documentary evidence such as handwritten alterations to documentation or handwritten documentation that would usually be electronically printed.

g. Information provided unwillingly or after unreasonable delay.

h. Seriously incomplete or inadequate accounting records.

i. Unsupported transactions.

j. Unusual transactions, by virtue of their nature, volume or complexity, particularly if they occurred close to the year-end.

k. Significant unreconciled differences between control accounts and subsidiary records, or between physical count and the related account balance, that were not appropriately investigated and corrected on a timely basis.

l. Inadequate control over computer processing. For instance, too many processing errors, or delays in processing results and reports.

m. Significant differences from expectations disclosed by analytical procedures.

n. Fewer confirmation responses than expected, or significant differences revealed by confirmation responses.

If the auditor confirms or is unable to dispel the suspicion that the financial statements are materially misstated, he or she needs to consider the implications for the audit. The auditor would refer to Materiality and Audit Risk in Conducting an Audit, *Section* 5130; Reservations in the Auditors' Report, *Section* 5510; and Communication of Matters Identified During the Financial Statement Audit, *Section* 5750, for guidance on the evaluation and disposition of misstatements and the effect on the auditor's report.

From AICPA, SAS 82, "Consideration of Fraud in a Financial Statement Audit."

Numerous aspects of responsibility for detecting and reporting errors and irregularities include the following:

1. Understand the characteristic causes and signs of errors and fraud. Risk factors that relate to misstatements arising from fraudulent financial reporting may be grouped in the following three categories:

a. *Management's characteristics and influence over the control environment.* These pertain to management's abilities, style and attitude relating to internal control and the financial reporting process.

b. *Industry conditions.* These involve the economic and regulatory environment in which the entity operates.

c. *Operating characteristics and financial stability.* These pertain to the nature and complexity of the entity and its transactions, the entity's financial condition and its profitability.

2. Assess the risk that errors or fraud may cause a company's financial statements to contain a material misstatement.

3. Design the audit to provide reasonable assurance of detecting material errors and fraud.

4. Exercise due care in planning, performing and evaluating the results of audit procedures.

5. Have the proper degree of professional scepticism, assuming neither dishonesty nor unquestioned honesty of management.

6. Assign significant engagement responsibilities to audit personnel with the experience and training indicated as needed by the risk assessment. (Higher risk requires more experienced auditors and more extensive supervision.)

7. Determine whether accounting policies (revenue recognition, asset valuation, capitalization versus expensing) are acceptable in the circumstances.

8. Audit large and unusual transactions, particularly those that occur at or near year-end.

9. Evaluate the quantitative and qualitative significance of differences between the accounting records and the underlying facts and circumstances.

10. Accumulate potential audit adjustments and summarize and evaluate the combined effect.

11. Report immaterial fraud to a level of management at least one level above the people involved.

12. Insist that financial statements affected by a material fraud be revised, or else give a qualified report explaining all the substantive reasons.

13. Withdraw from the engagement if uncertainties about fraud cannot be resolved and management co-operation is unsatisfactory, and communicate the reasons for withdrawal to the audit committee of the board of directors.

14. Inform the company's audit committee of frauds, except those that are clearly inconsequential. (Frauds involving senior management are never "inconsequential.")

15. Disclose fraud to outside agencies in limited circumstances by:

- Reporting a change of auditors on SEC Form K-8.
- Responding to a subpoena.
- Responding to a successor auditor's enquiries.
- Communicating with a funding or other agency when required in audits of entities that receive governmental financial assistance.
- Communicate to the SEC any detection of a fraudulent act if the client fails to do so.

External auditors are not responsible for:

- Authenticating documents (lack of training).
- Finding intentional misstatements concealed by collusion* when using procedures designed to find unintentional misstatements.

---

* Collusion is the circumstance in which two or more people conspire to conduct fraudulent activity in violation of an organization's internal control policies and procedures.

- Ensuring or guaranteeing that all material misstatements will be discovered.
- General reporting of fraud to outside agencies or parties.
- Detecting and reporting errors and fraud in areas outside the scope of an engagement limited to parts or elements of financial statements.

Section 5136, Illegal Acts by Clients

Auditors have these responsibilities regarding illegal acts:

1. *a.* The auditor should apply his or her knowledge of the entity's business and make enquiries of management to identify laws and regulations which, if violated, could reasonably be expected to result in a material mistatement in the financial statements.
   b. The auditor is more likely to identify such laws and regulations if they:
      (i) Enter into the determination of financial statement amounts or disclosures, for example, the Income Tax Act for taxable entities or the Bank Act for chartered banks.
      (ii) Have a fundamental effect on the entity's industry and its operations, for example, an environmental law or regulation for a company which produces toxic chemicals.
   c. The auditor should enquire whether management is aware of any such laws and regulations.

2. When performing procedures in the normal course of the audit, the auditor will be alert to the possible existence of laws and regulations which, if violated, could reasonably be expected to result in a material misstatement in the financial statements.

3. The auditors should assess inherent risk. Example procedures should include:
   a. Obtaining evidence by reading the minutes of meetings of the board of directors or from reading the response to an enquiry letter to a law firm.
   b. Enquiring of and obtaining a written representation from management.
   c. Identifying factors that could indicate the likelihood of violation is other than low. These include:
      (i) Violations of such laws or regulations by the entity in the current or a prior period.
      (ii) Recent, well-publicized violations of such laws or regulations by other entities within the industry.
      (iii) Active monitoring of such laws or regulations by a regulatory agency or other groups.
      (iv) The complexity of such laws or regulations.
      (v) Management's lack of experience in interpreting or applying such laws or regulations, for example, because the law or regulation is unusual or recently enacted.
   d. If the auditor assessed inherent risk as above low, the procedures might include:
      (i) Obtaining a more detailed understanding of laws or regulations identified, for example, by enquiry of management, other knowledgeable employee or the entity's legal counsel or by reviewing the laws or regulations.
      (ii) Enquiring of management about policies and procedures implemented by management to help discharge its responsibility to prevent and detect illegal acts.
      (iii) Testing of controls of the policies and procedures implemented by management (if the auditor plans to assess control risk below maximum).
      (iv) Consulting with the entity's legal counsel or other specialists about the application of laws or regulations and the possible effect on the financial statements.
      (v) Reading correspondence and reports from a regulatory agency or other similar authority.
      (vi) Reading minutes of meetings of the board of directors or committees established to monitor compliance with those laws or regulations identified.

4. The auditor should enquire and obtain written representation from management to confirm that either:
    a. management is not aware of any illegal or possibly illegal acts; or
    b. management has disclosed to the auditor all facts related to illegal or possibly illegal acts. [Jan. 1995]

5. When the auditor has obtained evidence that indicates an illegal or possibly illegal act, other than one considered inconsequential, may have occurred, the auditor should ensure that the audit committee and other appropriate levels of management are informed.

6. Auditors should also watch for the following:
    a. Comments made in the response letter obtained in accordance with "Communications with Law Firms," *Section* 6560.
    b. Investigation by a government agency, an enforcement proceeding or payment of unusual fines or penalties.
    c. Violations of laws or regulations cited in correspondence and reports issued by regulatory agencies made available to the auditor.
    d. Unusually large cash receipts or payments, transfers to numbered bank accounts or accounts in financial institutions with which the entity does not normally do business.
    e. Unsupported payments.
    f. Increased or unusual legal or consulting fees.
    g. Allegations about illegal acts made by suppliers, creditors or employees.
    h. Media comment.

External auditors are not responsible for:

- Final determination that a particular act is illegal (lack of legal, judicial expertise).
- Ensuring that illegal acts will be detected or that related contingent liabilities will be disclosed.
- Designing audit procedures to detect illegal acts in the absence of specific information brought to the auditors' attention.
- General reporting of illegal acts to outside agencies or parties.

Auditor Communications to the Audit Committee (AUG–11)

1. The audit committee may expect the auditor to communication such matters as:
    a. illegal acts;
    b. significant transactions that appear to be inconsistent with the ordinary course of business;
    c. unusual actions which significantly increase the risk of loss to the entity; and
    d. actions which, if they became public knowledge, might cause serious embarrassment to the entity, such as breaches of the corporate code of conduct.

2. The auditor's responsibility under generally accepted auditing standards and planning the audit include discussion of the following:
    a. the general approach to the audit, such as the cyclical coverage of branches and stock-taking in various locations;
    b. areas of the financial statements identified as having a high risk of material mistatement and the auditor's response thereto;
    c. the materiality and audit risk levels on which the audit is based (as noted in "Materiality and Audit Risk in Conducting an Audit," paragraph 5130.31, the question of whether to communicate these levels is a matter for the professional judgment of the auditor);
    d. weaknesses in internal control;
    e. fraud;

  f. significant accounting principles and policies;

  g. management judgments and accounting estimates;

  h. misstatements;

  i. disagreements with management;

  j. consultation with other accountants;

  k. major issues discussed that influence audit appointment; and

  l. difficulties encountered in performing the audit.

Section 5750, Communication of Matters Identified During the Financial Statement Audit

The auditor has the responsibility to report during the course of the financial statement audit the following matters to the appropriate level of management.

  a. misstatements, other than trivial errors;

  b. fraud;

  c. misstatements that may cause future financial statements to be materially misstated;

  d. illegal or possibly illegal acts, other than ones considered inconsequential; and

  e. significant weaknesses in internal control.

The type and significance of the matter to be communicated will determine the level of management to which the communication is directed.

The auditor would review matters communicated as a result of the previous financial statement audit. If, in the auditor's professional judgment, the matters have not been satisfactorily addressed, the auditor would consider recommunicating these matters and, when appropriate, communicating them to a higher level of management. Periodically, the auditor would consider whether because of changes in circumstances, such as a change in management, or simply because of the passage of time, it is appropriate to recommunicate matters communicated as a result of a previous financial statement audit.

The communication should preferably be in writing (para. 09) on a timely basis (para. 14). When no such matters have been identified there is no requirement to communicate the fact.

APPENDIX 19B

PROFESSIONAL STANDARDS AND PRACTICES FOR CERTIFIED FRAUD EXAMINERS (DECEMBER 31, 1994)

I. GENERAL STANDARDS

A. **Independence and Objectivity**

CFEs are responsible for maintaining independence in attitude and appearance, approaching and conducting fraud examinations in an objective and unbiased manner, and assuring that examining organizations they direct are free from impairments to independence.

B. **Qualifications**

CFEs must possess skills, knowledge, abilities and appearance needed to perform examinations proficiently and effectively. CFEs responsible for directing fraud examinations must assure they are performed by personnel who collectively possess the skills and knowledge necessary to complete examinations in accordance with these Standards. CFEs must maintain their qualifications by fulfilling continuing education requirements and adhering to the Code of Ethics of the Association of Certified Fraud Examiners.

C. **Fraud Examinations**

CFEs must conduct fraud examinations using due professional care, with adequate planning and supervision to provide assurance that objectives are achieved within the framework of these Standards. Evidence is to be obtained in an efficient, thorough and legal manner; and reports of the results of fraud examinations must be accurate, objective and thorough.

D. **Confidentiality**

CFEs are responsible for assuring they and the examining organizations they direct exercise due care to prevent improper disclosure of confidential or privileged information.

II. SPECIFIC STANDARDS

A. **Independence and Objectivity**

1. Attitude and Appearance

   Independence of attitude requires impartiality and fairness in conducting examinations and in reaching resulting conclusions and judgments. CFEs must also be sensitive to the appearance of independence so that conclusions and judgments will be accepted as impartial by knowledgeable third parties. CFEs who become aware of a situation or relationship that could be perceived to impair independence, whether or not actual impairment exists, should inform management immediately and take steps to eliminate the perceived impairment, including withdrawing from the examination, if necessary.

2. Objectivity

   To assure objectivity in performing examinations, CFEs must maintain an independent mental attitude, reach judgments on examination matters without undue influence from others and avoid being placed in positions where they would be unable to work in an objective professional manner.

3. Organizational Relationship

   The CFE's reporting relationship should be such that the attitude and appearance of independence and objectivity are not jeopardized. Organizational independence is achieved when the CFE's function has a mandate to conduct independent examinations throughout the organization, or by a reporting relationship high enough in the organization to assure independence of action.

B. **Qualifications**

1. Skills, Knowledge, Abilities and Experience

   CFEs cannot be expected to have an expert level of skill and knowledge for every circumstance that might be encountered in a fraud examination.

Nevertheless, CFEs must have sufficient skill and knowledge to recognize when additional training or expert guidance is required. It is the responsibility of a CFE to assure that necessary skills, knowledge, ability and experience are acquired or available before going forward with a fraud examination.

CFEs must be skilled in obtaining information from records, documents and people; in analyzing and evaluating information and drawing sound conclusions; in communicating the results of fraud examinations, both orally and in writing; and in serving as an expert witness when appropriate.

CFEs must be knowledgeable in investigative techniques, applicable laws and rules of evidence, fraud auditing, criminology and ethics.

2. Continuing Education

CFEs are required to fulfill continuing education requirements established by the Association of Certified Fraud Examiners. Additionally, CFEs are responsible for securing other education necessary for specific fraud examinations and related fields in which they are individually involved.

3. Code of Ethics

CFEs are to adhere to the Code of Professional Ethics of the Association of Certified Fraud Examiners.

C. **Fraud Examinations**

1. Due Professional Care

Due professional care is defined as exercising the care and skill expected of a prudent professional in similar circumstances. CFEs are responsible for assuring that there is sufficient predication for beginning a fraud examination; that said examinations are conducted with diligence and thoroughness; that all applicable laws and regulations are observed; that appropriate methods and techniques are used; and that said examinations are conducted in accordance with these Standards.

2. Planning and Supervision

CFEs must plan and supervise fraud examinations to assure that objectives are achieved within the framework of these Standards.

3. Evidence

CFEs must collect evidence, whether exculpatory or incriminating, that supports fraud examination results and will be admissible in subsequent proceedings, by obtaining and documenting evidence in a manner to ensure that all necessary evidence is obtained and the chain of custody is preserved.

4. Reporting

CFE reports of the results of fraud examinations, whether written or verbal, must address all relevant aspects of the examination, and be accurate, objective and understandable.

In rendering reports to management, clients or others, CFEs shall not express judgments on the guilt or innocence of any person or party, regardless of the CFE's opinion of the preponderance of evidence. CFEs must exercise due professional care when expressing other opinions related to an examination, such as the likelihood that a fraud has or has not occurred, and whether or not internal controls are adequate.

D. **Confidentiality**

CFEs, during fraud examinations, are often privy to highly sensitive and confidential information about organizations and individuals. CFEs must exercise due care so as not to purposefully or inadvertently disclose such information except as necessary to conduct the examination or as required by law.

Source: Association of Certified Fraud Examiners, 716 West Avenue, Austin, Texas, 78701.

PART V

SPECIALIZED TOPICS

CHAPTER 20

Learning Objectives

Chapter 20 contains more mathematical–statistical details related to the test of controls sampling introduced in Chapter 7. In fact, Chapter 20 is like a technical appendix on test of controls sampling and substantive testing. In Chapter 20 you will find more specific explanation of how to do statistical sampling in the test of controls phase of the control risk assessment work and for substantive tests of details. After studying this chapter in conjunction with Chapter 7, you should be able to:

PART I

1. Explain the role of professional judgement in assigning numbers to risk of assessing control risk too low, risk of assessing control risk too high and tolerable deviation rate.

2. Use statistical tables or calculations to determine test of controls sample sizes.

3. Calculate the effect on test of controls sample sizes of subdividing a population into two relevant populations.

4. Use your imagination to overcome difficult sampling unit selection problems.

5. Use tables and calculations to compute statistical results (UEL, the computed upper error limit) for evidence obtained with detail test of controls procedures.

6. Use the discovery sampling evaluation table for assessment of audit evidence.

7. Choose a test of controls sample size from among several equally acceptable alternatives.

PART II

8. Calculate a risk of incorrect acceptance, given judgements about inherent risk, control risk and analytical procedures risk, using the audit risk model in the Handbook Guideline on Materiality and Audit Risk (paragraph 23).

9. Explain the considerations in controlling the risk of incorrect rejection.

10. Explain the characteristics of dollar-unit sampling and its relationship to attribute sampling.

11. Calculate a dollar-unit sample size for the audit of the details of an account balance.

12. Describe a method for selecting a dollar-unit sample, define a "logical unit," and explain the stratification effect of dollar-unit selection.

13. Calculate an upper error limit for the evaluation of dollar-value evidence, and discuss the relative merits of alternatives for determining an amount by which a monetary balance should be adjusted.

STATISTICAL SAMPLING CONCEPTS FOR TESTS OF

CONTROLS AND TESTS OF BALANCES

PRELIMINARY CONCEPTS

Brief Overview of Basic Formulas Used in This Chapter

We start with some basic formulas used throughout this chapter to provide an overview of the most fundamental mechanics. There are two key points at which the formulas and tables are used in statistical sampling: (1) sample size planning and (2) sample evaluation. They are briefly summarized as follows.

I. Sample Size Planning

The most important concept of this chapter is the formula: $n = R/P$ because it clearly illustrates the relationship between the confidence level (as reflected by the R value) and materiality (as reflected by P), and the extent of audit testing (as reflected in sample size n). That is, the amount of audit work is directly proportional to the confidence level and inversely proportional to the materiality level used. The equation $n = R/P$ thus summarizes the key factors that affect the sufficiency of audit evidence.

For both tests of controls and substantive tests, solve for n in the formula: $R = nP$. So that $n = R/P$, where $R = {}_{CL}R_k$ is a confidence level factor which is unique for each combination of confidence level (CL) and acceptable number of errors (k) from the table of values for R given in Appendix 20A, and P is materiality, or something based on materiality, that is represented as a rate or proportion. P is also referred to as UEL, which stands for upper error limit. The auditor must use professional judgment in specifying k, CL and P.

Note: as will be discussed later in this chapter $1 - CL$ = beta risk, and k implicitly controls the alpha risk. The higher the k value used in sample size planning, the greater the alpha risk control and the larger the sample size.

P is the amount, in terms of a rate, that the auditor considers material for the population being tested. It has to be set considering additive effect of errors in other accounting populations representing other balances or transaction streams. Planned P as used in this stage of sampling might be an amount lower than materiality so that the auditor can reduce alpha risk. Firm practice varies: firms can (indirectly) control alpha risk through using the *planned* k value, through the *planned* P value, or through a combination of the two. The most common strategy appears to be to use $k = 0$ and to use a *planned* P in the range of half to full materiality.

II. Sample Evaluation

Sample evaluation essentially involves solving for P in the formula $R = nP$ so that $P = R/n$. When P is solved this way, it is referred to as the achieved P or as the achieved upper error limit (UEL). This achieved UEL or achieved P is calculated after the sample has been taken and the results of the sample are known. This means that the number of errors (k) detected by the sample is already known, the confidence level (CL = 1 – beta risk) is known, and the sample size taken is already known as well. Thus we can solve for achieved UEL = achieved $P = R/n$, where $R = {}_{CL}R_k$ and CL is the specified confidence level, and k is the number of errors *found* in the sample (not the number expected as in Part I below).

Achieved P can be interpreted as the maximum error rate for the specified confidence level. There are additional complications for substantive testing but the formulas already given are all one really needs to know to get a conceptual understanding. And it took less than two pages! We hope this convinces you that statistical auditing is not that hard.

The reason for this simplicity is that we use the easiest approach to statistical sampling in auditing. It is called dollar-unit sampling or DUS for short. These formulas are so simple and so effective that they are now the most widely used in audit practice. This is why we focus on DUS in this chapter. The next section covers some basic concepts underlying the formulas above and, in fact, all statistical applications. Later sections cover the above formulas in more detail, including various refinements.

How Risk and Materiality Are Used in Statistical Auditing

Materiality and risk are key concepts in statistical sampling and in auditing. This is illustrated by the *Handbook Section* 5130.25 quote that "Decisions concerning materiality and audit risk are the most significant made in the course of an audit because they form the basis for determining the extent of the auditing procedures to be undertaken." Hence, professional judgement concerning these concepts is critical to audit practice.

In order to better understand why this is so, it's useful to imagine what the audit would be like if it were a purely scientific endeavour in which the management assertions were treated as hypotheses which had to be either supported (verified) or contradicted by the evidence. Perhaps a good analogy, but one not to be taken too literally, is to think of auditor opinions as being similar to the opinion polls one frequently encounters in the media.

A recent opinion poll in *The Toronto Star* reported that a mayoral candidate M.L. led candidate B.H. with 51 percent and 46 percent support, respectively, of decided voters. This poll was the result of surveying 400 Toronto residents. A sample of this size is considered accurate to within 5 percentage points, 19 times out of 20. In other words, due to the uncertainties associated with the representatives of the sample of 400, the best the statistician can conclude about M.L.'s prospects is that there is a 95 percent confidence level that his actual support is in the range 51% + or − 5% = 46% to 56%. The width of this band around the best point estimate (the 51%) is frequently referred to as sampling precision, which is related to materiality, and the confidence level is related to the amount of audit assurance.

Conceptually, an auditor can make a similar statement about financial statements. For example, after audit testing the auditor may conclude that a client's net income number is 200,000 + or − 10,000, 19 times out of 20. It would be possible for the auditor to make this kind of statement if the appropriate statistical samples were drawn from all the various accounting components making up net income. In this statistical sampling framework, materiality is compared to the degree of accuracy or precision of the sample (i.e., the + or − 10,000 for the client or + or − 5 percent of the *Star* poll); and audit assurance is related to the statistical confidence (the 19 times out of 20 statement, which means the same as 95 percent = 19/20). Thus, if a purely statistical interpretation were to be put on the auditor's report, "presents fairly in all material respects" means that the difference between the audit estimate (the audit value or AV) based on audit testing and the reported amount (the book value or BV) is less than material. The level of audit assurance is assumed to be captured by the words *in our opinion* in the auditor's report. The standard audit report supplies the highest, but unspecified, level of assurance with the adverse opinion the lowest level of assurance that the financial statements are fairly presented in accordance with GAAP.

The standard audit report can therefore be interpreted to mean there is a high level of assurance that there are no material misstatements in the financial statements. Conversely, we can look at the complement of assurance, which is audit risk (*Section* 5130.02), and interpret the standard audit report to mean there is a low level of risk that there are material misstatements in the financial statements after the audit.

In terms of a statistical sampling framework, the auditor's decision on the form of this report will be based on doing a sufficient amount of testing so that the auditor will be able to construct a confidence interval around his or her best estimate AV such that if BV is included in this interval *and* this interval is smaller than materiality, the auditor will have achieved the planned level of assurance from his or her testing. An equivalent but perhaps more intuitive approach can be developed which constructs an interval of possible errors around BV and if this precision is smaller than materiality, then the auditor has achieved the stated confidence that there is no material error. For example, assume the auditor has done enough testing at a client with a reported net income of $198,000 to conclude that the auditor has 95 percent confidence (assurance) that GAAP income is in the interval 198,000 + or – 10,000. Assume materiality is set at 8 percent of reported income so that materiality equals .08 * 198,000 = 15,840. Since the achieved precision of 10,000 is less than materiality of 15,840, the auditor can conclude with at least 95 percent assurance that there is no material error in the reported net income of $198,000.

In order that the auditor can reach such a conclusion, he or she will have to plan the testing so that achieved precision is no larger than materiality. Note that if BV – AV is greater than materiality, then the auditor has not obtained the 95 percent assurance from testing and will either have to do more audit work or insist on an adjustment. The details of this are discussed in the rest of the chapter. We begin by discussing the concepts of sampling risks and hypothesis tests.

How Sampling Risks Are Controlled in Statistical Auditing

When using statistical sampling concepts in auditing, we need to develop a decision rule, which must be used consistently if we are to control risks objectively. It is the assumption of the consistent use of a strict decision rule that allows the risks to be predicted and thus controlled via the sample size. The decision rule is frequently referred to as a hypothesis test, and the auditor is typically interested in distinguishing between two hypotheses:

Hypothesis 1: There exists a material misstatement in the total amount recorded for the accounting population (e.g., accounts receivable file).

Hypothesis 2: There exists no misstatement in the amount recorded for the accounting population.

The decision rule the auditor uses in statistical auditing is to select one of these two simplified hypotheses based on the results of the statistical sample. The mechanics of this will be discussed later in this chapter. For now we are interested in depicting what happens to sampling risk (risk that arises when testing only a portion of the population statistically) when a consistent decision rule is used. This is when the concept of a probability of acceptance curve becomes useful.

Probability of Acceptance Curve (or acceptance curve, for short)

Consider Figure 20–1, which plots the probability of acceptance of the recorded amount against total misstatement within the recorded amount of some accounting population, such as aggregate accounts receivable. The horizontal axis reflects total misstatement while the vertical axis reflects probability.

In a perfect world of no uncertainty, auditors would want to have a zero probability of accepting a recorded amount having material misstatement (MM). However, the concept of testing or sampling only a part of a population requires the auditor to be willing to accept some uncertainty concerning the total population value. This is reflected in the fact that the probability of acceptance cannot be zero at MM with sampling. However, the auditor can, or course, design his or her audit so that this probability is appropriately low (see "X" in Figure 20–1).

An auditor using a consistent decision rule selecting one of the hypotheses discussed above with a given sample size over a range of possible errors will experience varying probabilities of acceptance, as indicated in Figure 20–2. This is what we mean by a probability of acceptance curve.

F I G U R E 20–1

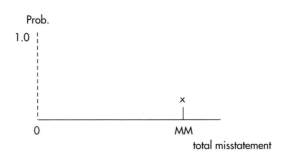

Note an important feature of this curve: as the error amount increases (in the direction of the arrow), the probability of acceptance goes down (as one would expect). How fast it drops depends on a variety of factors including the statistical model, the sample size and the error pattern.

Concepts of Sampling Risk

The probability of acceptance curve is useful for depicting the full range of sampling risks that the auditor may experience with a given test. This is summarized in Figure 20–3.

To understand these risks, let's consider some scenarios. First, assume there is an immaterial amount of misstatement (i.e., to the left of MM in Figure 20–3), say ½ MM. The probability of acceptance curve in Figure 20–3 tells us what the probability is of accepting any given amount of misstatement (including .5MM).

Is acceptance the correct decision with this amount of misstatement? The answer is yes because the amount of misstatement is less than material. Thus, the probability of acceptance gives us the probability of making the correct decision at .5MM. Since the only other alternative in this simple framework is to reject the reported amount, an incorrect decision, this probability of making the incorrect decision must then be one minus the probability of acceptance. This risk of incorrect decision when there is less than material misstatement is referred to as the alpha risk in auditing.

A completely different error is possible when there happens to be a material misstatement, that is, at or to the right of MM in Figure 20–3. Now, accepting the reported amount is the incorrect decision and the probability of accepting the recorded amount is thus the risk of accepting a material misstatement. This risk of accepting a material misstatement is referred to in auditing as the beta risk. The correct decision is to reject the reported amount

F I G U R E 20–2

F I G U R E 20–3

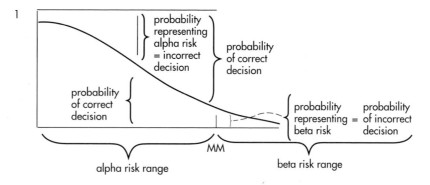

when there is a material misstatement and this equals one minus the probability of accepting the reported amount when there is a material misstatement, or one minus beta risk.

To recap: alpha risk can only occur when there is less than material misstatement and alpha risk = one minus the probability of acceptance when there is less than material misstatement. On the other hand, beta risk can only take place when there is a material misstatement and beta risk = the probability of acceptance of the recorded amount when there is material misstatement.

Another important thing to note is that as error increases, the probability of acceptance decreases and therefore, beta risk decreases. The maximum beta risk is thus at the smallest amount of material misstatement, which is at the point MM itself. That is, maximum beta risk is at MM. Hence if the auditor controls beta risk at a specified level at MM, he or she automatically controls it at a lower level for errors greater than MM.

This is not true for alpha risk, however. An analysis of Figure 20–3 should make clear that as probability of acceptance decreases with increasing errors in the immaterial error range, alpha risk is increasing. Maximum alpha risk therefore occurs at just below MM and equals (at the limit) one minus beta risk at MM. For a numerical example assume beta risk is controlled at .05 at MM. Then we know that maximum alpha risk = 1 − .05 = .95. In practice, alpha risk is frequently controlled only at zero errors by controlling alpha risk at its minimum level. Note that this concept of risk control is completely different from that of beta risk control, which is always controlled via the beta risk's maximum value.

Positive and Negative Approaches and Confidence Level
In the statistical literature there is frequent reference to the concept of confidence level of a statistical test. How does this relate to alpha and beta risks as used in auditing?

The answer is, it all depends.

It depends on the way the hypothesis tests are constructed. Confidence level is related to the primary or null hypothesis of the test. Specifically, confidence level equals one minus risk of rejecting the null hypothesis when it is true. Thus, confidence level is dependent on the null hypothesis used. In auditing a distinctive statistical terminology has evolved over the years. If hypothesis 1 above is the null hypothesis, then we are using the negative approach to hypothesis testing, and if hypothesis 2 is the null hypothesis, then we are using the positive approach to hypothesis testing.

Under the negative approach, confidence level equals one minus beta risk while under the positive approach, confidence level equals one minus alpha risk.

The negative approach is the more important and common approach in auditing. In particular, it underlies all attribute sampling tables and formulas. Dollar unit sampling always uses the negative approach. The positive approach frequently underlies formulas using the normal distribution assumption; this is briefly discussed at the end of the chapter. Because of its simplicity and straightforward relationship to audit objectives, the negative approach is used throughout the remainder of the chapter. However, it should be noted that the positive approach is much more important in the sciences, and, in particular, the alpha risk when associated with the null hypothesis of "no difference" is the more important risk of the sciences. In contrast, the beta risk is more important in auditing because it is related to the more important hypothesis of "material misstatement" or "significant difference," which it is the auditor's job to detect. In fact, some have characterized the purpose of the auditing profession as that of "controlling beta risk" associated with financial statements. For this reason beta risk is associated with audit effectiveness.

Effect of Changing the Sample Size under the Negative Approach

Under the negative approach, the confidence level = 1 − beta risk. Under some interpretations auditors can equate the confidence level with audit assurance, and so these auditors work with assurance or confidence factors rather than risk factors. The underlying principles remain essentially the same, however, whether the auditor works with risk or confidence levels.

What if the auditor varies the sample size while keeping the confidence level constant?

Figure 20–4 illustrates what happens: Curve A is the probability of acceptance with the smallest sample size possible for given beta risk, Curve B results from using twice the Curve A sample size, and Curve C results from four times the Curve A sample size, whereas Curve D represents a "perfect acceptance curve" with no sampling risk. Curve D occurs when a population is examined 100 percent. From Figure 20–4 it is evident that if confidence level (and thus beta risk under the negative approach) and MM are held constant while changing the sample size, it is the alpha risk that changes with the sample size—specifically, alpha risk is reduced throughout its range when the sample size is increased, and the converse. This illustrates that if the auditor wishes to reduce alpha risk while keeping beta risk and MM unchanged, then a larger sample size needs to be used. In fact, if any one of alpha risk, beta risk or MM were to be reduced, sample size would need to be increased, and the converse.

F I G U R E 20–4   **ACCEPTANCE CURVES FOR DUS**

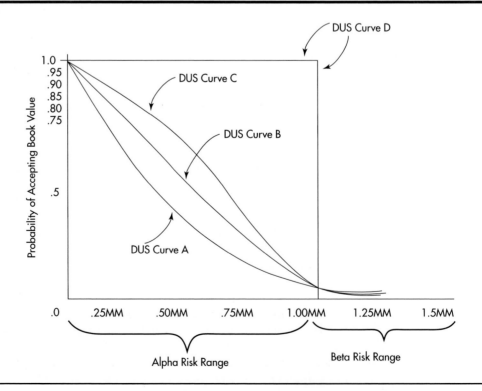

Curve A reflects the acceptance curve with the smallest sample size possible with dollar unit sampling for a given beta risk. This smallest sample size is called a discovery sample. If the auditor wishes to control alpha risk to a lower level than indicated by Curve A, the sample size should be increased. Sample size increases in practice are normally implemented through formulas by one of two major approaches: (1) increase the number of errors to be accepted by the sample, or (2) increase the planned expected error rate in computing the sample size. Sometimes a combination of the two approaches is used in computing the sample size. More rigorous methods are available for controlling alpha risk for an explicit amount of expected errors, but we will not cover these methods here because the additional complexity does not change the nature of the basic judgments that must be made and the necessary cost-benefit tradeoffs that are required. The concepts of beta risk, alpha risk, and their relationship to confidence level described here applies with some modification to all statistical procedures. In this sense they are very general, and Figures 20–1 to 20–4 are suggestive of sampling risk associated with all statistical hypothesis testing. Auditors have developed their own terminology for the risks associated with different audit procedures. As we review various statistical procedures, we will identify new risk terms associated with these procedures, but we will see that for the most part these risks relate to the more important sampling risk in auditing, that of beta risk.

Finally, it should be noted that these acceptance curves are not the same thing as probability distributions that you may be familiar with from your statistics courses. Probability distributions measure the probability of various risks by calculating *areas* under the curve (for example, the normal probability distribution). The acceptance curves that we have discussed here represent the probabilities as the *vertical distance* from the curve to the horizontal axis (representing the probability of one or zero, respectively). Acceptance curves make it easier to visualize the sampling risks for different amounts of errors. Acceptance curves are a type of what statisticians call power curve, where the shape of the power curve varies, like the confidence level, with the null hypothesis.

PART I: TEST OF CONTROLS WITH ATTRIBUTE SAMPLING RISK AND RATE QUANTIFICATIONS

LEARNING OBJECTIVE
1. Explain the role of professional judgement in assigning numbers to risk of assessing control risk too low, risk of assessing control risk too high and tolerable deviation rate.

The quantification of sampling risk is an exercise of professional judgement. When using statistical sampling methods, auditors must quantify the two risks of decision error. The risk of assessing control risk too low is generally considered more important than the risk of assessing control risk too high. Auditors must also exercise professional judgement to determine the extent of deviation allowable (tolerable rate) in assessing control risk.

Tolerable Deviation Rate: A Professional Judgement

Auditors should have an idea about the correspondence of rates of deviation in the population with control risk assessments. Perfect control compliance is not necessary, so the question is: What rate of deviation in the population signals control risk of 10 percent? 20 percent? 30 percent? and so forth, up to 100 percent? To answer this question, you need to relate material misstatement of an account to a tolerable deviation rate for the control procedures affecting that account.

Assume that material dollar misstatement of $30,000 is used in planning the audit of accounts receivable for possible overstatement. This amount is relevant to the audit of control over sales transactions because uncorrected errors in sales transactions misstate the financial statements by remaining uncorrected in the accounts receivable balance. In other words, we test the controls over sales transaction processing in order to determine the control risk relevant to our audit of the accounts receivable balance. Therefore, if sales transactions are in error by $30,000 or more, the accounts receivable balance may be materially misstated.

However, a deviation in a sales transaction (e.g., one unsupported by shipping documents) does not necessarily mean the transaction amount is totally in error. After all, missing paperwork may be the only problem. Perhaps a better example is a mathematical accuracy deviation: If a sales invoice is computed incorrectly to charge the customer $2,000 instead of $1,800, there is a 100 percent control deviation (the inaccuracy), but it does not describe a 100 percent dollar error. Therefore, more than $30,000 in sales transactions can be "exposed" to control deviation without generating $30,000 dollar error in the sales and the accounts receivable balances. This "exposure" is sometimes called the **smoke/fire concept**, meaning that there can be more exposure to error (smoke) than actual error (fire), just as in a conflagration.

Smoke/fire thinking produces a multiplier to apply to the tolerable dollar misstatement assigned to the account balance, $30,000 in our example. We know that a multiplier of 1 is not reasonable (i.e., $30,000 on invoices with deviations produces $30,000 of misstatement in the accounts receivable), and a multiplier of 100 or 200 is probably also not reasonable (too large). Some auditors say a multiplier of 3 is reasonable, having no other basis than a mild conservatism. Some PA firms have sampling policies with implicit multipliers that range from 3 to 14. A multiplier of 3 has the practical effect of producing the conclusion that $90,000 on sales invoices could be exposed to control deviations. If the total gross sales on all invoices is $8.5 million, the implied **tolerable deviation** rate is $90,000/$8.5 million = 0.0106, or approximately 1 percent.

This 1 percent tolerable deviation rate now represents a theoretical anchor. It is the deviation rate that marks low control risk (say, 0.05 control risk). When this tolerable deviation rate seems too low for practical audit work, auditors can "accept" a higher tolerable rate. The only thing that happens is that auditors are implicitly saying that a higher control risk is ultimately satisfactory for the audit of the account balance. Higher tolerable rates signal greater control risk in this scheme of thinking, like the example in Exhibit 20–1.

The point in this demonstration of smoke/fire and tolerable rate thinking is to show that tolerable rate is a decision criterion that helps auditors assess a control risk. The association of tolerable rates with different control risks is the important point. To achieve a low control-risk assessment (e.g., 10 percent), the sample size of transactions will be very large, but the sample size required to obtain a moderate control risk assessment (e.g., 50 percent) can be much smaller. Therefore, sample size varies inversely with the tolerable rate—the lower the rate (and the lower the "desired control risk assessment"), the larger the sample size. Some auditors express the tolerable rate as a number (necessary for statistical calculations of sample size), while others do not put a number on it.

The audit strategy is to think about the audit plan, including a consideration of the sample size of balances the team wants to audit. For example, Exhibit 20–2, column 3, shows

E X H I B I T 20–1   ILLUSTRATIVE CONTROL RISK AND TOLERABLE RATE RELATIONSHIPS

Tolerable Rate	Control Risk	Control Risk
1–% (anchor)	0.05	
2	0.10	
4	0.20	Low control risk.
6	0.30	
8	0.40	
10	0.50	Moderate control risk.
12	0.60	
14	0.70	
16	0.80	Control risk slightly below maximum.
18	0.90	
20	1.00→	Maximum control risk.

Note: The tolerable rate increases 1 percentage point for each additional 0.05 control risk in this example.

EXHIBIT 20–2   CONTROL RISK INFLUENCE ON SUBSTANTIVE BALANCE-AUDIT SAMPLE SIZE

Control Risk Categories	(1) Possible Control Risk Assessments (CR)	(2) Related Risk of Incorrect Acceptance (RIA)*	(3) Number of Balance Items to Select for Substantive Audit
Low control risk	0.10	0.50	51
	0.20	0.25	81
	0.30	0.167	96
Moderate control risk	0.40	0.125	107
	0.50	0.10	117
	0.60	0.083	125
Control risk slightly below the maximum	0.70	0.071	130
	0.80	0.0625	136
	0.90	0.0556	140
Maximum control risk	1.00	0.05	143

*Assuming AR = 0.05, IR = 1.0, AP = 1.0. Therefore, RIA = $0.05/(1.0 \times CR \times 1.0)$.

various numbers of customer accounts. Suppose the audit manager plans to select 107 for confirmation and other procedures. This decision suggests that control risk needs to be as good as 40 percent (Exhibit 20–2, column 1), and the tolerable rate for this assessment is 8 percent (Exhibit 20–1). Thus, the auditors need to select a sample of sales transactions for test of controls audit sufficient to justify a decision about an 8 percent tolerable rate.

Risk of Erroneous Control Risk Assessments: Another Professional Judgement

Assessing control risk too low causes auditors to rely on control too much (overreliance) and audit the related account balances less than is necessary. The risk in "risk of assessing control risk too low" relates to the effect of the erroneous control evaluation. This effect is produced in the substantive audit by influencing the sample size for auditing the account balances related to the controls being evaluated.

Internal control is evaluated, and control risk is assessed, on the environment, the accounting system and the client control procedures related to particular account balances. For example, auditors will evaluate control over the processing of sales and cash receipts transactions because these are the transactions that produce the debits and credits to the customer accounts receivable. Some other examples are shown in Exhibit 20–3. The ultimate purpose of the control risk assessment is to decide how much work to do when auditing the general ledger accounts—for example, cash accounts receivable, inventory, sales revenue and expenses. The question of "how much work" relates directly to the sample size of the general ledger account details to audit—for example, how many bank accounts to reconcile, how many customer accounts receivable to confirm, how many inventory items to count and recalculate for correct costing. The control risk assessment provides supporting information for the balance-audit work. We will proceed, using the audit of accounts receivable as an occasional example.

When planning the audit of the accounts receivable balance, auditors make judgements and estimates of the overall risk of failing to detect material misstatements in the balance (AR, audit risk related to the receivables audit), the probability that errors entered the accounts (IR, inherent risk), and the effectiveness of their analytical procedures for detecting material errors in the receivables (APR, analytical procedures risk). At this stage the remaining elements of the risk model are the control risk (CR) and the substantive sample risk of incorrect acceptance (RIA). The internal control evaluation task is directed to assessing the control risk, and the risk of incorrect acceptance is then derived using the expanded risk model: RIA = $AR/(IR \times CR \times APR)$. As the acronym indicates, RIA is the same as beta risk discussed earlier in this chapter.

EXHIBIT 20–3   EXAMPLES OF CLASSES OF TRANSACTIONS FLOWING INTO GENERAL LEDGER BALANCES

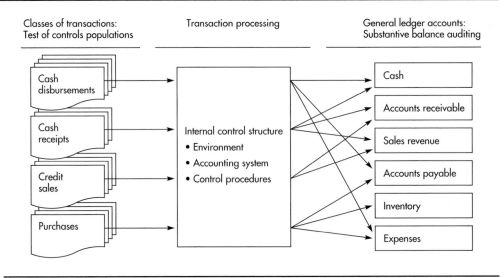

Since control risk is the probability that the client's controls will fail to detect material misstatements, provided any enter the accounting system in the first place, control risk itself can take on values ranging from very low probability (say, 0.10) to maximum probability (1.0). Using the audit risk model (AUG-7: Applying Materiality and Audit Risk Concepts in Conducting An Audit), there exists a risk of incorrect acceptance (RIA, also known in the literature as "test of details risk") for every possible control risk assessment (CR). These RIAs affect the sample sizes for the substantive audit work on the account balances.

Exhibit 20–2 shows a range of possible control risk assessments in column (1). To their left are some labels commonly used in public accounting practice. (PA firms deal with a few control risk categories instead of a full range of control risk probabilities.)[1] Column (2) contains the risks of incorrect acceptance (RIA) derived from the audit risk model for the balance-audit substantive sample, and column (3) shows the substantive sample sizes based on these RIAs. The sample sizes in column (3) are the substantive balance-audit sample sizes (e.g., number of customer accounts, number of inventory items), not the test of controls samples. (The actual calculation of these substantive sample sizes is explained later in this chapter.)

These relationships are evident in Exhibit 20–2: (1) for higher control risk, the related RIA is lower; (2) for lower RIAs, the substantive samples are larger; and (3) therefore, the higher the control risk, the larger the substantive sample size required for the audit of the related balance sheet account. These are the relationships suggested by the second examination standard—that is, the understanding of the control structure and the assessment of control risk is for the purpose of planning the nature, timing and extent of substantive tests to be performed.

Erroneous decisions leading to assessing control risk too high also should be avoided in the interest of audit efficiency.

For the following explanation, you need to be introduced to the concept of the upper error limit (UEL). The UEL is a statistical estimate of the population deviation rate computed from the test of controls sample evidence. It consists of the actual sample deviation rate (number of deviations found in the sample divided by the test of controls sample size) plus a statistical allowance for sampling error. The UEL is similar to the upper confidence limit of a statistical confidence interval. (You probably studied confidence intervals in your

---

[1] PA firms that use quantitative test of controls sampling policies have quantified probabilities underlying their categories, and they fall in the ranges indicated in Exhibit 20–1.

statistics course.) It is used in statistical evaluation of test of controls sample results as the estimate of the population deviation rate. It is compared to the tolerable deviation rate when auditors assess the control risk.

If the number of deviations in a test of controls sample causes the UEL to be higher than the tolerable deviation rate, when the population deviation rate is actually equal to or lower than the tolerable deviation rate, the auditors may assess control risk too high. This causes them to perform more substantive audit work on the related account balance than they would have performed had they obtained better information about the control risk.

Conversely, if achieved sample UEL is too low (specifically below tolerable error), the auditor may assess control risk too low. This causes the auditor to do less substantive audit work on the related account balance than she or he would have performed had he or she obtained better information on the control risk. This is a much more serious risk for the auditor because it ultimately relates to audit effectiveness. Note also that since this risk affects adversely the auditor's ability to detect material misstatement, assessing control risk too low is the beta risk associated with tests of control.

PA firms frequently use a risk of assessing control risk too low of 10 percent. This is a rather arbitrary policy that eases the burden of the number of judgements auditors need to make. The implication is that auditors are willing to take a 1 in 10 chance of assessing control risk too low and suffer the consequences of auditing a substantive sample smaller than they would have audited had the decision error not been made. However, less arbitrary methods can be devised that link CR missassessments to the extent of substantive testing of details. These refined methods are not discussed here.

. . . .

R E V I E W
C H E C K P O I N T S

20.1 If inherent risk (IR) is assessed as 0.90 and the detection risk (DR) implicit in an audit plan is 0.10, what audit risk (AR) is implied when the assessed level of control risk is 0.10? 0.50? 0.70? 0.90? and 1.0?

20.2 What general considerations are important when an auditor decides on an acceptable risk of assessing control too high?

20.3 What general considerations are important when an auditor decides on an acceptable risk of assessing control risk too low?

20.4 What considerations are important when an auditor decides on an acceptable risk of assessing control risk too high? What is the probability of finding one or more deviations in a sample of 100 if the population deviation rate is actually 2 percent?

20.5 What is the probability of finding one or more deviations in a sample of 100 units if the deviation rate in the population is only 0.5 percent?

20.6 What is the connection between possible assessments of control risk and a judgement about tolerable rate, both considered prior to performing test of controls audit procedures?

20.7 What is the connection between material dollar misstatement assigned for the substantive audit of a balance and tolerable deviation rate used in a test of controls sample?

20.8 What professional judgement and estimation decisions must be made by auditors when applying statistical sampling in test of controls audit work?

. . . .

SAMPLE SIZE DETERMINATION
. . . .

As noted in the introduction to this chapter, we will use the simplest formulas and tables to plan and evaluate statistical sampling in auditing. These formulas are based on dollar unit sampling (DUS) theory. One of the advantages of DUS is that the same formula and tables can be used for planning sample sizes for tests of controls (attribute sampling) as well as substantive tests of details. The key formula is $R = nP$. Solving for n in this formula: $n = R/P$ yields the sample size that would be used with DUS. In this formula R is the (beta) risk factor or, equivalently, the confidence level factor, P is the precision, and n is the sample size. This same formula is used for sample planning and evaluation: if the formula is used to solve n, then it is being used for sample planning; if the formula is used to solve for P, then it is being used for sample evaluation.

The risk level factor, R, is unique for each combination of risk level (or, equivalently, confidence level) and number of errors. Since we are using the negative approach, confidence level = 1 – beta risk. The less serious alpha risks are frequently controlled indirectly in practice through the number of errors that are considered acceptable. For a given RIA and MM, the greater the number of errors to be considered acceptable by a sample, the greater the sample size required (and, as discussed earlier, the lower the alpha risk). In case you are interested, R is the mean of a Poisson distribution with a Poisson process that captures the essence of the attributes sampling distribution underlying DUS theory. Here we are using the Poisson distribution to approximate the binomial or hypergeometric distributions that underlie the attribute sampling theory that forms the basis for statistical tests of controls. This approximation is quite good for most audit applications, and so we can exploit the simplifications possible with the Poisson distribution.

P stands for precision and is referred to as planned precision at the sample determination stage. In tests of controls, P is tolerable error or some fraction of it at the sample determination stage. P is also referred to as the planned upper error limit (or planned UEL) at the sample determination stage. The auditor must use professional judgement in specifying the number of errors, RIA and P in planning sample sizes for tests of controls using the formula and Appendix 20A.

To illustrate the calculation of sample size for tests of controls, assume the following:

1. Your risk of assessing control risk too low is 1 percent. That is, beta risk for tests of controls is 1 percent.

2. Your tolerable rate is 6 percent. That is, the P value in the formula is 6 percent = .06.

3. Your expected population deviation rate is zero, so we expect zero errors in the sample.

4. Your sample size is 77 calculated using the formula $R = nP$ and Appendix 20A as follows:

   Sample size = $n = R/P$ = using Poisson risk factor for zero errors and beta risk of .01, divided by tolerable deviation rate = 4.61/.06 = 77 (to be conservative always round up to the nearest integer).

The sample sizes using the formula are reliable in that they closely approximate but do not understate the sample sizes necessary to achieve audit objectives. (This is because the Poisson is a conservative approximation of the binomial and hypergeometric distributions on which attribute sampling is based.) However, since it is much easier to work with the Poisson table of R values, we will base all our calculations on Appendix 20A.

We can now also illustrate control of alpha risk. If we wish to reduce alpha risk, one method is to use a higher number of errors—that is, let errors = 1 in Appendix 20A and all else in the illustration remains unchanged. Then sample size (n) = 6.64/.06 = 111. Be sure you can confirm this using the formula and Appendix 20A. Since beta risk is still the same (1 percent) and so is tolerable deviation rate (6 percent), what we get for the increased sample size is a reduction in alpha risk (as illustrated in Figure 20–4). The auditor can make this alpha risk control explicit by using more complex formulas, but most firms follow a policy of controlling alpha risk indirectly based on subjectively estimating the number of errors or using a planned precision P that is less than the tolerable deviation rate.

The effect of using a lower planned precision in sample determination can also be illustrated. Let's assume the auditor uses a planned precision of 3 percent rather than the tolerable error rate of 6 percent. Now we get a sample size n = 4.61/.03 = 154. Again, beta risk is 1 percent, tolerable error rate is still 6 percent (it will be used in the sample evaluation decision rule for deciding if the sample error rate is acceptable) so that what the auditor obtains with the increased sample size is, again, a reduction in alpha risk. Since sample size can be increased to virtually any amount, most audit firms put a restriction on planned precision by not letting it get below one half the tolerable deviation rate.

20.9   What facts, estimates and judgments do you need to figure a test of controls sample size using the Appendix 20A tables? What other relevant judgment is not used?

20.10   Test yourself to see whether you can get the sample size of 87 from Appendix 20A with these specifications: beta risk = 5 percent, tolerable deviation rate = 9 percent, expected errors = 3.

20.11   What facts, estimates and judgments do you need to figure a test of controls sample size using the Appendix 20A Poisson risk factors? What other relevant judgment is not used?

20.12   Test yourself to see whether you can get the sample size of 70 using the Poisson risk factor equation with these specifications: beta risk = 5 percent, tolerable deviation rate = 9 percent, expected errors = 2.

MORE ABOUT DEFINING POPULATIONS: STRATIFICATION

LEARNING OBJECTIVE
3. Calculate the effect on test of controls sample sizes of subdividing a population into two relevant populations.

Auditors can exercise flexibility when defining populations. Accounting populations are often **skewed**, meaning that much of the dollar value in a population is in a small number of population units. For example, the **80/20 "rule"** is that 80 percent of the value tends to be in 20 percent of the units. Many inventory and accounts receivable populations have this skewness. Sales invoice, cash receipt and cash disbursement populations may be skewed, but usually not as much as inventory and receivables balances.

Theoretically, a company's control procedures should apply to small-dollar as well as to large-dollar transactions. Nevertheless, many auditors believe that evidential matter is better when more dollars are covered in the test of controls part of the audit. This inclination can be accommodated in a sampling plan by subdividing (stratifying) a population according to a relevant characteristic of interest. For example, sales transactions might be subdivided into foreign and domestic; accounts receivable might be subdivided into sets of customers with balances of $5,000 or more and those with smaller balances; payroll transactions might be subdivided into supervisory payroll (salaried) and hourly payroll.

Nothing is wrong with this kind of stratification. However, you must remember that (1) an audit conclusion based on a sample applies only to the population from which the sample was drawn and (2) the sample should be representative—random for statistical sampling. If 10,000 invoices represent 2,000 foreign sales and 8,000 domestic sales, and you want to subdivide the population this way, you will have two populations. You can establish decision criteria of acceptable risk of assessing control risk too low and tolerable deviation rate for each population. You also can estimate an expected population deviation rate for each one. Suppose your specifications are these:

	Foreign	Domestic
Risk of assessing control risk too low	5%	10%
Tolerable deviation rate	5	5
Expected population deviation rate	2	1
Then, sample size (Appendix 20A and assume *P* is adjusted for expected error rate, e.g., foreign *P* = .05 − .02 = .03).	100	58

You can evaluate each sample separately using the appropriate risk of assessing control risk too low, or you can combine the sample. To combine the sample sizes effectively, one would have to make the most conservative assumptions among the strata objectives. In the illustration this means using an overall combined risk of assessing control risk too low of 10 percent and an expected combined population (strata) deviation rate of 1 percent so that both alpha and beta risks are at the lower of the two sample sizes.

Interestingly, if the population had not been stratified but treated as one population of 10,000 invoices, and the criteria had been beta risk = 10 percent, tolerable deviation rate = 5 percent, expected error rate = 1 percent, the sample size would be 58. Subdividing in two a population subject to test of controls sampling has the practical effect of doubling the extent of sampling. This is the price we pay for being able to make separate statistical statements about each strata—so the audit issue is how important is it to evaluate the strata separately.

A LITTLE MORE ABOUT SAMPLING UNIT SELECTION METHODS

LEARNING OBJECTIVE

4. Use your imagination to overcome difficult sampling unit selection problems.

Audit sampling can be wrecked on the shoals of auditors' impatience. Planning an imaginative selection method takes a little time, and auditors are sometimes in a big hurry to grab some units and audit them. A little imagination goes a long way. For example, suppose an auditor of a newspaper publishing client needs to audit the controls over the completeness of billings—specifically, the control procedure designed to ensure that customers were billed for classified ads printed in the paper. You have seen classified ad sections, so you know they consist of different-size ads, and you know that ad volume is greater on weekends than on weekdays. How can you get a random sample that can be considered representative of the printed ads?

The physical frame of printed ads defines the population. You probably cannot obtain a population count (size) of the number of ads. However, you know that the paper was printed on 365 days of the year, and the ad manager can probably show you a record of the number of pages of classified ads printed each day. Using this information, you can determine the number of ad pages for the year, say 5,000. For a sample of 100 ads, you can choose 100 random numbers between 1 and 5,000 to obtain a random page. Then you can choose a random number between 1 and 10 to identify one of the 10 columns on the page, and another random number between 1 and 500 (the number of lines on a page). The column-line coordinate identifies any ad on the random day. (This method approximates randomness because larger ads are more likely to be chosen than smaller ads. In fact, the selection method probably approximates a sample selection stratified by the size of the ads.)

You can judge the representativeness by noticing the size of the ads selected. Also, since you will know the number of Friday-Saturday-Sunday pages (say, 70 percent of the total, or 3,500 pages), you can expect about 70 of the ads to come from weekend days.

Random Number Table

The most accurate although most time-consuming sampling unit selection device is a table of random digits. (See Appendix 20B.) This table contains rows and columns of digits from 0 to 9 in random order. When items in the population are associated with numbers in the table, the choice of a random number amounts to choice of a sampling unit, and the resulting sample is random. Such a sample is called an **unrestricted random sample**. For example, in a population of 10,000 sales invoices, assume the first invoice in the year was 32071 and the last one was 42070. By obtaining a random start in the table and proceeding systematically through it, 100 invoices may be selected for audit.[2] Assume that a random start is obtained at the five-digit number in the second row, 50 column—number 29094—and

---

[2] A random start in a table may be obtained by poking a pencil at the table, or by checking the last four digits on your $10 bill to give row and column co-ordinates for a random start.

E X H I B I T 20–4   RANDOM NUMBER TABLE USED AS AUDIT WORKING PAPER

Index _____

Prepared by _____
Reviewed by _____

Kingston Company
Random Selection of Sales Invoices
12/31/92

Population: 10,000 invoices numbered 32701-42070.
Method: unrestricted selection of 5-digit random invoice numbers.
Random Start: _____

(32942)	95416	42339	59045	26693	49057	87496	20624	14819
07410	99859	83828	21409	29094	65114	36701	25762	12827
59981	68155	45673	76210	58219	45738	29550	24736	09574
46251	25437	69654	99716	11563	08803	86027	51867	12116
65558	51904	93123	27887	53138	21488	09095	78777	71240
99187	19258	86421	16401	19397	83297	(40111)	49326	81686
(35641)	00301	16096	(34775)	21562	97983	45040	19200	16383
14031	00936	81518	48440	02218	04756	19506	60695	88494
60677	15076	92554	26042	23472	69869	62877	19584	(39576)
66314	05212	67859	89356	20056	30648	87349	20389	53805
20416	87410	75646	64176	82752	63606	(37011)	57346	69512
28701	56992	70423	62415	(40807)	98086	58850	28968	45297
74579	(33844)	(33426)	07570	00728	07079	19322	56325	84819
62615	52342	82968	75540	80045	53069	20665	21282	07768
93945	06293	22879	08161	01442	75071	21427	94842	26210
75689	76131	96837	67450	44511	50424	82848	(41975)	71663
02921	16919	(35424)	93209	52133	87327	95897	65171	20376
14295	(34969)	14216	03191	61647	30296	66667	10101	63203
05303	91109	82403	(40312)	62191	67023	90073	83205	71344
57071	90357	12901	08899	91039	67251	28701	03846	94589
78471	57741	13599	84390	(32146)	00871	09354	22745	65806
89242	79337	59293	47481	07740	43345	25716	70020	54005
14955	59592	97035	80430	87220	06392	79028	57123	52872
42446	(41880)	(37415)	47472	04513	49494	08860	08038	43624
18534	22346	54556	17558	73689	14894	05030	19561	56517

Selection path: down each column to bottom, top next right column, then to top of column at left
◯ Sampling unit selection.

that the reading path in the table is down to the bottom of the column, then to the top of the next column, and so on. The first usable number and first invoice is 40807, the second is 32146, and so forth. Note that several of the random numbers were skipped because they did not correspond with the invoice number sequence.[3] A page of random digits like the one in Appendix 20A can be annotated and made into your sample selection working paper to document the selection, as shown in Exhibit 20–4.

Systematic Random Selection

Another selection method used commonly in auditing because of its simplicity and relative ease of application is **systematic selection**. This method is employed when direct association of the population with random numbers is cumbersome. Systematic selection

---

[3] Most auditors will not allow the same sample item to appear twice in a selection—duplicate selections are counted only once. Strictly speaking, this amounts to sampling without replacement and the hypergeometric probability distribution is appropriate instead of the binomial distribution. The binomial probabilities are exact only when each sample item is replaced after selection, thus giving it an equally likely chance of appearing in the sample more than once. For audit purposes the practice of ignoring the distribution is acceptable because the difference is mathematically insignificant.

DANGER IN SYSTEMATIC SELECTION

Western Products Company has a stable payroll of 50 hourly employees, paid weekly, for a total of 2,600 pay transactions in the year under audit. The auditors decided to select a systematic sample of 104 paycheques for detail test of controls audit procedures. The skip interval was $k = 2600/104 = 25$. The auditors carefully chose a random start in the first week at ?3 on the payroll register (Wyatt Earp) and selected every 25th payroll entry thereafter. They got 52 entries for Wyatt Earp and 52 entries for Bat Masterson. The audit manager was disgusted over the failure to get a representative sample!

---

consists of (*a*) dividing the population size by the sample size, obtaining a quotient k (a "skip interval"); (*b*) obtaining a random start in the population file; and (*c*) selecting every kth unit for the sample. A file of credit records provides a good example. These may be filed alphabetically with no numbering system. Therefore, to select 50 from a population of 5,000, first find $k = 5,000/50 = 100$, then obtain a random start in the first 100 of the set of physical files and pull out every 100th one thereafter, progressing systematically to the end of the file and returning to the beginning of the file to complete the selection. This method only approximates randomness, but the approximation can be improved by taking more than one random start in the process of selection. When more than one start is used, the interval k is changed. For example, if five starts are used, then every 500th item would be selected. Five random starts give you five systematic passes through the population, and each pass produces 10 sampling items, for a total of 50.

Auditors usually require five or more random starts. You can see that when the number of random starts equals the predetermined sample size, the "systematic" method becomes the same as the unrestricted random selection method. Multiple random starts are a good idea because a population may have a nonrandom order that could be embedded in a single-start systematic method.

Computerized Selection

Most audit organizations have computerized random number generators available to cut short the drudgery of poring over printed random number tables. Such routines can print a tailored series of numbers with relatively brief turnaround time. Even so, some advance planning is required, and knowledge of how a random number table works is useful.

You can also use random number generators in popular electronic spreadsheet programs, like Excel. The RAND function in Excel generates a list of random numbers in a desired range. A custom list using an electronic spreadsheet or another random number generator can eliminate the problem of numerous discards (unusable numbers) that is encountered when a printed random number table is used. (Notice the numerous discards skipped in the procedure shown in Exhibit 20–4.)

. . . .

R E V I E W
C H E C K P O I N T S

20.13   When you subdivide a population into two populations for attribute sampling, how do the two samples compare to the one sample that would have been drawn if the population had not been subdivided?

20.14   Are you required to use all five digits of a random number when you have a random number table like the one in Appendix 20B?

20.15   What steps are involved in selecting a sample using the systematic random selection method?

. . . .

STATISTICAL EVALUATION

LEARNING OBJECTIVE

5. Use tables and calculations to compute statistical results (UEL, the computed upper error limit) for evidence obtained with detail test of controls procedures.

To accomplish a statistical evaluation of test of controls audit evidence, you must know the tolerable rate and the acceptable beta risk. These are your **decision criteria**—the standards for evaluation in the circumstances. You also need to know the size of the sample that was audited and the number of deviations. Now you can use Appendix 20A in making the evaluation. Again you use the Poisson risk factors in Appendix 20A except now you use the $R = nP$ formula to solve for P to get achieved precision = computed upper error limit = UEL: $P = R/n$. You already know n since now you already have selected the sample; R is obtained from Appendix 20A with your knowledge of the number of errors found and planned beta risk.

For example, suppose you audited a sample of 90 sales transactions and found 2 of them without proper shipping documents. Previously, you had decided a beta risk of 5 percent was appropriate.

Using the formula above, UEL = Poisson risk factor for number of errors, beta risk divided by sample size.

For example: The Poisson risk factor for beta risk = 5 percent and 2 errors (deviations) found in a sample is 6.30; thus, with a sample of 90: UEL = 6.30/90 = 0.07, or 7 percent.

Applying a Decision Rule

After you calculate the UEL, you can compare it to your previously determined tolerable deviation rate and apply an appropriate decision rule. Note you don't compare the computed UEL to the planned precision that you used in determining the sample size if the planned precision was less than the tolerable rate. As discussed earlier, the sole reason for using a planned precision less than tolerable was to control for alpha risk through a larger sample size. In sample evaluation the planned precision has no role to play because we use the achieved precision resulting from the actual sample results obtained.

A higher control risk assessment decision is not the same as a "rejection" decision. You can take the UEL derived from your sample and use it to assess the control risk. For example, assume you audited 30 sales transactions (tolerable deviation rate criterion of 8 percent, a beta risk criterion of 10 percent, and an expectation of zero deviations) to try to evaluate control risk at 0.40 (see Exhibit 20–5) and justify the audit of 107 customer accounts in the accounts receivable total (see Exhibit 20–6). You can achieve this control risk assessment if you find no deviations in the sample of 30 transactions (see Appendix 20A). If you find one actual deviation in the sample of 30, your computed upper error limit is 14 percent (see Appendix 20A and use the formula), and according to the decision rule, you should not assess control risk at 0.40. However, you can take UEL = 14 percent, assess a higher control risk (0.70 according to Exhibit 20–1), and audit a sample of 130 customer

---

TEST OF CONTROLS DECISION RULE

If UEL (computed upper error limit) is less than your tolerable deviation rate, you can conclude that the population deviation rate is low enough to meet your tolerable rate decision criterion, and you can assess the control risk at the level associated with the tolerable deviation rate. (Alternatively, you can assess the control risk at the level associated with the UEL, or you can calculate a probability associated with the tolerable deviation rate based on the sample data.)

If UEL exceeds your tolerable deviation rate, you can conclude that the population deviation rate may be higher than your decision criterion, and you should assess a higher control risk—for example, the control risk associated with the UEL.

accounts, which is appropriate for control risk of 0.70, instead of the sample of 107 appropriate if control risk had been assessed at 0.40.

The **computed upper error limit** is a statistical calculation that takes sampling error into account. You know that a sample deviation rate (number of actual deviations in the sample divided by sample size) cannot be expressed as the exact population deviation rate. According to common sense and statistical theory, the actual but unknown population rate might be lower or higher. Since auditors are mainly concerned with the risk of assessing control risk too low (because it relates to the more serious beta risk), the higher limit is calculated to show how high the estimated population deviation rate may be.

Auditing standards tell you to "consider the risk that your sample deviation rate can be lower than your tolerable deviation rate for the population, even though the actual population rate exceeds the tolerable rate." In statistical evaluation you accomplish this consideration by holding the risk of assessing the control risk too low constant at the acceptable level while computing UEL, then comparing UEL to your tolerable deviation rate. In short, if achieved UEL > tolerable error for tests of controls, then reject reliance at planned level; otherwise you can rely. How much reliance depends on the auditor's judgement and the decision rule he or she uses. (Exhibit 20–1 is an example of such a decision rule.)

Example of Satisfactory Results

Suppose you selected 200 recorded sales invoices and vouched them to supporting shipping orders. You found no shipping orders for one invoice. When you followed up, no one could explain the missing documents, but nothing about the sampling unit appeared to indicate an intentional irregularity. You have already decided that a 10 percent risk of assessing control risk was too low—that is, beta risk for test of controls = 10 percent, and a 3 percent tolerable deviation rate, adequately define your decision criteria for the test of controls audit. Calculate UEL using the $R = nP$ formula and Appendix 20A. From $R = nP$ solve for P: $P = R/n$. From Appendix 20A find the appropriate value for R using beta risk = 10 percent and 1 error: $R = 3.89$. so the calculated upper error limit = UEL = 3.89/200 = 1.945 percent.

> **Audit conclusion:** The probability is 10 percent that the population deviation rate is greater than 2 percent. This finding (UEL of 2 percent, less than tolerable rate of 3 percent) satisfies your decision criteria, and you can assess control risk as you had originally planned.

Example of Unsatisfactory Results

The situation is the same as above, except you found four invoices with missing shipping orders. Now, $P = R/n = 8/200 = 4$ percent = computed upper error limit = UEL.

> **Audit conclusion:** The probability is 10 percent that the population deviation rate is greater than 4 percent. This UEL finding exceeds your tolerable rate criterion of 3 percent, and you ought to assess a higher control risk than you had originally planned.

Discovery Sampling—Fishing for Fraud

LEARNING OBJECTIVE

6. Use the discovery sampling evaluation table for assessment of audit evidence.

Discovery sampling is essentially another kind of sampling design directed toward a specific objective. However, discovery sampling statistics also offer an additional means of evaluating the sufficiency of audit evidence in the event that no deviations are found in a sample.

A discovery sampling table is obtainable from Appendix 20A by simply reading the entries for the zero errors line. That is, no errors are considered acceptable in the sample—as indicated in Figure 20–4, this results in the highest alpha risk over the range of immaterial errors. A discovery sampling plan deals with the following kind of question: If I believe some important kind of error or irregularity might exist in the records, what sample size will I have to audit to have assurance of finding at least one example? Ordinarily, discovery sampling is used for designing procedures to search for such things as examples of forged cheques or intercompany sales improperly classified as sales to outside parties. However, discovery sampling may be used effectively whenever a low deviation rate is expected. Auditors must quantify a desired **probability of at least one occurrence** when the specified tolerable deviation rate occurs. In discovery sampling the tolerable deviation rate is frequently referred to as the **critical rate of occurrence**. Generally, the critical rate is very low because the deviation is something very sensitive and important, such as a sign of fraud.

The probability in this case represents the desired probability of finding at least one occurrence (example of the deviation) in a sample. In Appendix 20A you can read across the zero errors column for the desired beta risk (the beta risk in the zero errors row represents the probability of at least one occurrence), and critical rate is simply the P value in our formula: $R = nP$.

To illustrate, suppose that in the test of controls audit of recorded sales, you are especially concerned about finding an example of a deviation of as few as 50 outright fictitious sales (intentional irregularities) existed in the population of 10,000 recorded invoices (a critical rate of 0.5 percent). Furthermore, suppose you want to achieve at least 0.99 probability (or in percentage terms, 99 percent probability) of finding at least one. Appendix 20A and our formula indicate a required sample size of 922 recorded sales invoices, as follows: $n = R/P = 4.61/0.005 = 922$. If a sample of this size were audited and no fictitious sales were found, you could conclude that the actual rate of fictitious sales in the population was less than 0.5 percent with 0.99 probability of being right.

This feature of discovery sampling evaluation provides the additional means of evaluating the sufficiency of audit evidence whenever an attribute sample turns up zero deviations. You can scan across the different beta risk tables in Appendix 20A until you find an R value in the zero errors row that comes just below the one associated with the lowest beta risk. As an illustration, suppose 200 sales invoices were audited and no deviations of missing shipping orders were found. Appendix 20A shows that, if the population deviation rate were 2 percent, the probability of including at least 1 deviation in a sample of 200 is 0.98 (i.e., $R = nP = 200 * 0.02 = 4$—the highest R value in the zero errors rows of Appendix 20A not exceeding 4 occurs with beta risk = 0.02—the complement of this risk is the probability of finding more than zero errors). None was found, so, with 0.98 probability, you can believe that the occurrence rate of missing shipping orders is 2 percent or less.

R E V I E W
C H E C K P O I N T S

20.16   What is the auditing interpretation of the sampling error-adjusted deviation rate (UEL)?

20.17   What is the UEL for these data: sample size audited = 46, actual deviations found = 3, beta risk = 35 percent?

20.18   What is the proper interpretation of the probability in discovery sampling?

Putting It All Together

LEARNING OBJECTIVE
7. Choose a test of controls sample size from among several equally acceptable alternatives.

To this point, you have learned some of the theoretical details about defining populations, perceiving control risk (CR) as a probability ranging from low (e.g., 0.10) to high (e.g., 1.0), using smoke/fire multiple thinking to determine an anchor tolerable deviation rate and using tables and Poisson risk factor calculations to determine the test of controls sample size (n). You also learned about an assignment of successively higher tolerable deviation rates to successively higher CRs as a means of identifying each control risk level with a tolerable deviation rate.

You also have learned about the links that connect tests of controls sampling for control risk assessment to substantive sampling for the audit of an account balance. These links are

(1) the smoke/fire multiplier judgement that relates tolerable dollar misstatement in the substantive balance-audit sample to the anchor tolerable deviation rate in the test of controls sample and (2) methods that relate an audit judgment of risk of incorrect acceptance for the substantive balance-audit sample to the risk of incorrect acceptance consequences of assessing control risk too low. There is one more link: (3) considering the cost of the substantive balance-audit sample to decide the test of controls sample size and the planned control risk assessment. The **planned control risk assessment**, with the emphasis on *planned*, is the auditors' selection of a control risk level for which they want to justify a control risk assessment after completing the test of controls audit work. Conceptually, the auditor should pick that strategy of control testing combined with substantive tests of detail that minimizes total audit cost. This can be done formally through use of explicit cost assumptions or informally, for example, as in Exhibit 20–6. Most firms use the informal approach, probably to help facilitate implementation and a certain consistency and audit quality across all clients, and because cost estimates may not be that accurate.

R E V I E W
CHECKPOINTS

20.19   What are the links that connect test of controls sample planning with substantive balance-audit sample planning?

20.20   When you have several alternative test of controls sample sizes to choose from, how do you choose the one to audit?

Summary of Sampling for Tests of Controls

Statistical sampling for attributes in test of controls auditing provides quantitative measures of deviation rates and risks of assessing control risk too low. The statistics support the auditors' professional judgements involved in control risk assessment. The most important judgements are the numbers assigned to the tolerable rate of deviation, the risk of assessing control risk too low and the risk of assessing control risk too high. With these specifications and an estimate of the deviation rate in the population, a preliminary sample size can be predetermined. However, nothing is magic about a predetermined sample size. It will turn out to be too few, just right or too many, depending on the evidence produced by it and the control risk assessment supported by it.

The easy part of attribute sampling is the statistical evaluation. The hard parts are (1) specifying the controls for audit and defining deviations, (2) quantifying the decision criteria, (3) using imagination to find a way to select a random sample, and (4) associating the quantitative evaluation with the assessment of control risk. The structure and formality of the steps involved in statistical sampling force auditors to plan the procedures exhaustively. This same structure and formality also contribute to good working paper documentation because they clearly identify the things that should be recorded in the working papers. Altogether, statistical sampling facilitates auditors' plans, procedures and evaluations of defensible evidence.

Part II: Audit of an Account Balance

Most of the account balances that appear in financial statements consist of numerous subsidiary accounts, some more numerous than others. Many of these accounts may be audited with sampling methods—auditing less than 100 percent of the subsidiary accounts within a control account balance or financial statement total for the purpose of determining the fair presentation of one or more of the financial statement assertions. Some examples of such accounts include:

- Cash: Usually not audited by sampling because there are few accounts. Might be sampled if a company has a large number of bank accounts.

- Accounts receivable: Usually audited by sampling when there are a modest to large number of customers.
- Inventory: Usually audited by sampling when there are a modest to large number of different inventory items.
- Fixed assets: Sampling may be used to audit numerous additions or an "inventory-taking" of fixed assets.
- Accounts payable: Some sampling used, but normally a judgement sample for missing payables.
- Notes payable: Usually not audited by sampling because of small number.

This short list and description of accounts, however, is not a description of relevant data populations for all assertions. For example, you would select a sample from the recorded accounts receivable to audit for the existence, rights, valuation and presentation and disclosure assertions, but not for the completeness assertion. To audit for missing accounts receivable, the recorded ones are the wrong population! (A selection of shipping documents to determine whether receivables from customers had been recorded, or an audit of cash receipts in the period after year-end to detect receipts applicable to the prior year, could be proper samples for auditing for accounts receivable completeness.) Likewise, a selection of recorded accounts payable does not produce evidence of completeness of liabilities recordings. After all, the unrecorded liabilities are not in that population. (A selection of cash disbursements made after the year-end to identify ones applicable to year-end liabilities could be one proper sample for auditing for liability completeness.)

The audit of an account balance with dollar-value sampling has a different objective than test of controls auditing with attribute sampling. Test of controls sampling has the main objective of producing evidence about the rate of deviation from company control procedures for the purpose of assessing the control risk. Measuring the dollar effect of control deviations is a secondary consideration. On the other hand, a test of an account balance has the objective of producing direct evidence of dollar amounts of error in the account. This is called dollar-value sampling to indicate that the important unit of measure is dollar amounts. Sometimes, dollar-value sampling is called variables sampling just to distinguish it from attributes sampling and the control risk assessment objective.

There are two main types of dollar-value sampling. The one most frequently used in financial auditing is called dollar-unit sampling. This method is the subject covered here. The other method is known as classical sampling—a name attached merely to distinguish it from dollar-unit sampling. Classical sampling is discussed briefly at the end of this chapter. The method is called "classical" because it was used before dollar-unit sampling was developed, and because it depends on the well-known statistical mathematics of the normal distribution. Dollar-unit sampling, by contrast, does not depend upon the normal distribution statistics.

Before we get to the techniques of dollar-unit sampling, however, two topics of common application need to be expanded—the risk of incorrect acceptance and the risk of incorrect rejection.

RISK OF INCORRECT ACCEPTANCE
· · · · · · · · · · · ·

LEARNING OBJECTIVE

8. Calculate a risk of incorrect acceptance, given judgements about inherent risk, control risk and analytical procedures risk, using the audit risk model in the Handbook Guideline on Materiality and Audit Risk (paragraph 23).

In Chapter 7 you saw the audit risk model expanded to include these terms:

$$AR = IR \times CR \times APR \times RIA$$

Dollar-value sampling for account balance auditing is primarily concerned with the risk of incorrect acceptance (RIA) in the risk model. The RIA is also called the test of details risk because it is the sampling risk of failing to detect a materiality magnitude of monetary error with audit procedures applied to the details (subsidiary units) in a control account. The other elements of the model are products of auditors' professional judgement.

The audit risk (AR) is the overall risk the auditor is willing to take of failing to discover material misstatement in the account. PA firms that quantify this risk usually set it at 0.05 or 0.10. Their policies are somewhat arbitrary because there is no overall theory acceptable in the practice world to justify any particular quantification of the audit risk. Five percent and 10 percent just seem to work adequately.

The inherent risk (IR) is the auditors' assessment of general factors relating to the probability of erroneous transactions entering the accounting system in the first place. It is hard to assess, often consisting of auditors' memory of no problems in previous audits or other aspects of the knowledge of the business. Some PA firms have questionnaires to document the findings of the know-the-business procedures and to translate them into an inherent risk assessment. PA firms that quantify this risk assign values from 0.30 to 1.00.

Analytical procedures were introduced in Chapter 4. They basically consist of all evidence-gathering procedures other than direct audit of account details. They are substantive procedures, as are the substantive tests of details, but they are not applied on a sample basis. Thus, there is frequently no mathematical way to measure their risk of failure. The analytical procedures risk in the model (APR) is the auditors' judgement of the probability that these nondetail procedures will fail to detect misstatement in the amount of tolerable misstatement in the account. PA firms that quantify this risk assign values from 0.30 to 1.0.

The control risk (CR) is the auditors' assessment of the quality of the client's control structure. Control risk assessment was explained in detail in Chapters 6 and 7. Some PA firms combine the inherent risk judgement and the control risk assessment into one factor.

These risk elements are considered independent, meaning that their combined risk can be a product (multiplication). While theoretical arguments of the validity of the model rage, several PA firms have built it into their sampling plans. They determine the risk of incorrect acceptance for a sampling application by first making AR, IR, CR, and APR judgements and assessments, then calculate the RIA:

$$\text{Maximum RIA} = 0.50, \text{ if the equation produces RIA} > 0.50.$$

However, be forewarned: Not all PA firms or other audit organizations use the model in this fashion. Some quantify RIA for statistical sampling in the context of the client situation without reference to the model. Some say they do sampling without quantifying RIA. Some say they do audit sampling, but not statistical sampling. Practice varies.

The risk of incorrect acceptance influences statistical sample size calculations, and thus it is a prime determinant of the extent of substantive audit work. Exhibit 20–2 was presented to emphasize the effect of the audit risk model and its production of RIA on the substantive balance-audit sample sizes, as affected by the range of possible control risk assessments.

Notice the nonlinear change in sample size in relation to the evenly spaced (linear) control risk levels. From CR = 0.10 to CR = 0.20, the sample size increases by 30 sampling units (81 – 51), but from CR = 0.90 to CR = 1.00, the sample size increases by only 3 sampling units (143 – 140). The sample sizes are based on dollar-unit calculations for an account balance of $300,000 with a tolerable misstatement of $10,000.

. . . .

R E V I E W
C H E C K P O I N T S

20.21 What is the objective of test of controls auditing with attribute sampling? test of a balance with dollar-value sampling?

20.22 Does use of the audit risk model to calculate RIA remove audit judgement from the risk determination process?

20.23 Is there any benefit to be gained from using the audit risk model to calculate RIA?

20.24 If audit risk (AR) is 0.015, inherent risk (IR) is 0.50, control risk (CR) is 0.30, and analytical procedures risk (APR) is 0.50, what risk of incorrect acceptance (RIA) is suggested by the expanded risk model?

. . . .

RISK OF INCORRECT REJECTION

. . . .

LEARNING OBJECTIVE
9. Explain the considerations in controlling the risk of incorrect rejection.

The other risk auditors accept in audit sampling is to decide that an account balance is misstated by more than the material misstatement when, in fact, but unknown to the auditors, it is not misstated by that much. Note this is the alpha risk. This can happen when the sample is not actually representative of the population from which it was drawn. An initial incorrect rejection decision will create an audit inefficiency because additional work will be done to determine the amount of an adjustment, and the auditors ordinarily will discover that the recorded amount was not materially misstated all along. The planning goal is to keep the risk of incorrect rejection low and also to keep the cost of the audit work within reasonable bounds. When planning the size of an audit sample, the judgement about the acceptable risk of incorrect rejection amounts to an incremental cost analysis.

You can minimize the risk of incorrect rejection by auditing a large sample—spending time and effort at the beginning with the initial sample size. Alternatively, you can take a smaller sample size and save time and cost; but this strategy will increase the risk of incorrect rejection. Taking more risk of incorrect rejection increases the likelihood of "rejection," in which case you may need to expand the sample or otherwise perform work later that you could have performed at the beginning with the initial sample. Thus, your cost trade-off relationship involves (*a*) the cost saved by taking a smaller initial sample, reduced by (*b*) the probability-weighted expected cost of needing to expand the sample or perform other types of audit procedures. These two elements taken together are the expected cost saving from taking more risk of incorrect rejection. Taking a chance on needing to expand the sample is important only if the cost (per item) is lower in the initial sample and higher (per item) when sample units are added later. (If these costs were equal, you could simply audit sample items one at a time until you reached a justifiable conclusion.)

The cost trade-off is based on probabilities, and these sometimes are hard to estimate. An audit manager may prefer to incur the additional cost in the first phase of work to avoid any possibility of additional cost of subsequent work. Cost aside, the auditors may not have time to select and audit additional items before the report deadline. For example, auditors may not have time to mail additional accounts receivable confirmations and wait two weeks for replies. Assessment of the risk of incorrect rejection also depends on the audit manager's preferences for cost and certainty, and on the time deadlines for completing the audit.

The risk of incorrect rejection pertains to audit efficiency. However, GAAS does not present a model or method for determining or thinking about this risk. GAAS also does not have anything to say about a "base RIR" or an "alternative RIR" used in planning a dollar-value audit sample.

. . . .

R E V I E W
C H E C K P O I N T S

20.25   Why is the risk of incorrect acceptance considered more critical than the risk of incorrect rejection in connection with audit decisions about an account balance?

20.26   What considerations are important for determining the risk of incorrect rejection?

20.27   What position is taken in generally accepted auditing standards with respect to the risk of incorrect rejection?

. . . .

DOLLAR-UNIT SAMPLING FOR ACCOUNT BALANCE AUDITING

. . . .

LEARNING OBJECTIVE
10. Explain the characteristics of dollar-unit sampling and its relationship to attribute sampling.

Dollar-unit sampling (DUS) is a modified form of attributes sampling that permits auditors to reach conclusions about dollar amounts as well as compliance deviations. Variations are called combined attributes-variables sampling (CAV), cumulative monetary amount sampling (CMA), monetary unit sampling (MUS) and sampling with probability proportional to size (PPS).

Recall the discussion of the point that the test of controls audit of control procedures based on attribute statistics did not directly incorporate dollar measurements. Hence, conclusions were limited to decisions about the rate of control deviations, which helped auditors assess the control risk. DUS is a sampling plan that attaches dollar amounts to attribute statistics. DUS is used widely by many accounting firms and other audit organizations for account balance auditing (variables sampling).

The unique feature of DUS is its definition of the population as the number of dollars in an account balance or class of transactions. Thus, in our example of auditing accounts receivable with a recorded amount (book value) of $300,000, the population is defined as 300,000 dollar units instead of as 1,500 customer accounts for classical sampling applications.

With this definition of the population, the audit is theoretically conducted on a sample of dollar units, and each of these sampling units is either right or wrong. This is the type of treatment given to control procedures in attribute sampling: a control procedure is either performed or not performed and there is either a deviation or no deviation, thus a rate of deviation is the statistical measure. However, DUS sampling adopts a convention for assigning dollar values to the deviations, and we will cover these calculations a little later in this chapter.

DUS was significantly enhanced for audit practice by Canadian practitioners, who wrote the first widely published manual on the techniques.[4] It is now the first choice of auditors throughout their domestic and international practices.

Use of Dollar-Unit Sampling (DUS)

All dollar-value sampling methods, including DUS, require basic audit judgments for audit risk (AR), inherent risk (IR), control risk (CR) and analytical procedures risk (APR) for the purpose of deriving the risk of incorrect acceptance (RIA). All these sampling methods, including DUS, require an audit judgment of material dollar misstatement (MM) for the account and an estimate of the misstatement (EM) the auditors think might exist in the account.

DUS has advantages in the form of overcoming some of the difficulties inherent in classical sampling plans, such as:

- An accurate estimate of a normal distribution standard deviation is required for classical sampling. DUS does not require this estimate because the statistical basis is the binomial distribution.

- Classical statistics estimators suffer problems of bias because a sufficient number of errors may not be found in a sample to permit proper use. DUS imposes no requirements for a minimum number of errors.

- Large sample sizes: DUS sample sizes are generally smaller than classical sampling sample sizes. (Smaller sample sizes are considered more efficient in most situations.)

- Complicated stratification plans: DUS sample selection methods accomplish stratification by automatically selecting a large proportion of high-value items.

There are still some critics of DUS, and here is their purported list of disadvantages (along with rebuttals to their arguments):

- Criticism: The DUS assignment of dollar amounts to errors is conservative (high) because rigorous mathematical proof of DUS upper error limit calculations has not yet been accomplished. Rebuttal: On the other hand, this provides the auditor with assurance that achieved RIA < planned RIA, and this helps ensure that actual or achieved audit risk is within the planned level. In fact, some practitioners treat this feature of DUS as an advantage because they know their primary objective of risk control is virtually guaranteed of being met.

---

[4] D.A. Leslie, A.D. Teitlebaum, and R.J. Anderson, *Dollar-Unit Sampling: A Practical Guide for Auditors* (Toronto: Copp Clark Pitman, 1979).

• Criticism: DUS is not designed to evaluate financial account understatement very well. Rebuttal: On the other hand, no sampling estimator is considered very effective for understatement error. Auditors control this problem the same way that they control for the completeness assertion—through audits of related populations such as subsequent payments or subsequent collections.

The use of DUS in account balance auditing can be inferred from the advantages and disadvantages indicated above. DUS is clearly the best method to use when auditors expect to find few or no errors, and where the greatest risk of error is the risk that the book value is overstated. DUS has also been found to be a reliable estimator in more varied situations where there are more errors, and modifications are available for dealing with both understatement and overstatement of book values. As in any formal techniques, care is needed in using the procedure to make sure the formal requirements of the model are satisfied.

R E V I E W
C H E C K P O I N T S

20.28 What are some of the other names for types of dollar-unit sampling (DUS)?

20.29 What is the unique feature of dollar-unit sampling?

20.30 What are the advantages and disadvantages of DUS?

20.31 In what way does dollar-unit sampling resemble attribute sampling for control deviations?

DUS Sample Size Calculation

LEARNING OBJECTIVE

11. Calculate a dollar-unit sample size for the audit of the details of an account balance.

The same formula is used for substantive testing of details as for testing of controls: $n = R/P$. The only adjustment is that planned precision must be converted from a dollar amount to a rate or percentage as is used in control testing. This is achieved by simply dividing the planned precision in dollars by the recorded amount of the account balance.

The basic equation for calculating a DUS sample size for substantive testing of details is:

$$n = (BV * R)/MM$$

where:

BV = Total book value (recorded amount) of the account balance.
 R = Poisson risk factor appropriate for the risk of incorrect acceptance (RIA or beta risk).
MM = Material misstatement for the account balance.

Note that the above formula follows from $n = R/P$ if we let $P = MM/BV$. That is, planned precision P is represented as a rate in testing of details by dividing material misstatement by the reported amount of the account balance.

The recorded amount (BV) is the book balance of the account under audit—for example, a \$300,000 accounts receivable total for 1,500 customers, subject to auditing by sampling.

The concept of material misstatement was covered in Chapter 5.

As in attributes sampling, alpha risk (RIR) is usually controlled indirectly following either or both of the following approaches: (*a*) select a number of errors greater than zero, and/or (*b*) use a planned precision that has been reduced by the amount of expected misstatement. For example, in using approach (*b*) assume that expected misstatement is EM, then planned precision to be used in the denominator in sample determination would be (MM/BV – EM/BV) = (MM – EM)/BV. Auditors that use this technique don't allow planned precision to get below one half of MM/BV. Note that firms using this rule and setting the number of errors = zero in Appendix 20A never plan higher than twice the discovery sample for the given RIA (RIA = 1 – confidence level). To illustrate, assume as before in Chapter 7 that MM = \$10,000. Then a discovery sample size (the smallest possible for RIA = 1 percent) is $n = 4.61/(10000/300000) = 4.61/0.0334 = 139$ (round up to be conservative). If the auditor wishes to accept a sample with one error and all else remains unchanged, the sample size will be $n = 6.64/0.0334 = 199$. Note that since RIA and materiality are the same, what the auditor gets for this increased work is a reduction in RIR. (Remember Figure 20–4.)

The other way to reduce RIR is by adjusting planned precision P for expected misstatements (*EM*). As an illustration, assume $EM = 4000$, then sample size can be increased to $n = 4.61/((10000 - 4000)/300000) = 4.61/(0.0334 - 0.0134) = 4.61/0.02 = 231$.

Note that in the numerator we use the R value with zero errors since we are already controlling RIA through the tighter precision (0.02 vs. 0.0334) in the denominator. There is thus little need to combine the adjustment of planned precision approach with the zero errors approach in controlling RIR with DUS.

More formal, explicit approaches are available for controlling RIR and RIA simultaneously, but since the basic principles are the same, we do not cover these refinements here.

R E V I E W
C H E C K P O I N T S

20.32 All other factors remaining the same, will DUS sample size be larger, smaller or the same for a larger book balance?

20.33 All other factors remaining the same, will DUS sample size be larger, smaller or the same for a larger risk of incorrect acceptance?

20.34 All other factors remaining the same, will DUS sample size be larger, smaller or the same for a larger expected misstatement?

20.35 All other factors remaining the same, will DUS sample size be larger, smaller or the same for a larger tolerable misstatement?

Selecting the Sample

LEARNING OBJECTIVE

12. Describe a method for selecting a dollar-unit sample, define a "logical unit" and explain the stratification effect of dollar-unit selection.

DUS sampling unit selection is a type of systematic selection, very similar to the systematic selection method introduced for attribute sampling.

However, before sampling is started, auditors usually take some defensive auditing measures. They identify the individually significant units in the whole population and remove them for a 100 percent audit. In our example of auditing the $400,000 accounts receivable in the balance sheet of Kingston Company, the auditors could identify the six customer accounts over $10,000 (total amount of $100,000) and set them aside for audit. The cutoff size of $10,000 in this case corresponds to the material misstatement assigned to the accounts receivable audit. By being sure to audit each customer account whose balance exceeds the material misstatement, the auditors guard against the possibility of missing a material misstatement that might exist in a single subsidiary account. This leaves the remaining $300,000 of accounts receivable as the dollar value population (BV) subject to auditing by sampling.

To carry out a systematic DUS selection, you must calculate the sample size (n), then divide the population size (BV) by 1 minus the sample size to get a "skip interval" (k):

$$k = BV/(n - 1).$$

For example, in the audit of the Kingston Company accounts receivable, if the sample is 96 the skip interval is:

$$k = \$300,000/95 = \$3,157.90 \text{ (rounded to 3158)}$$

You use $n - 1$ as the denominator because the method of choosing the first and last random selections adds 1 to the sample size.

With one random start, you select every 3,158th dollar unit. Each time a $1 unit is selected, it hooks the logical unit that contains it. A **logical unit** is the ordinary accounting subsidiary unit that contains the dollar unit selected in the sample. In this example the logical unit is a customer's account. Obviously, all customer accounts with balances of $3,158 or more will be selected, and the larger units have a proportionally larger likeli-

---

MINI-EXAMPLE OF DUS SYSTEMATIC SAMPLE SELECTION

This example is a takeoff on the Kingston Company example. Everything is reduced so that you can see the entire sample selection. See the accompanying box on the next page.

Assume Kingston II has $30,000 accounts receivable in 15 customer accounts, and you want to select a sample of 10 dollar units, which gives you a skip interval, $k = 30,000/9 = 3,333$.

We still start with a random number between 1 and 3,333, say 722, and this random number identifies the first sampled dollar. (The first one will not necessarily fall in the first account.)

You identify subsequent logical units by starting an "accumulator." The accumulator first takes a value of zero minus the starting number. In our example the accumulator is zero $- 722 = - 722$.

You then add the next logical unit account balances to the accumulator until it turns into a positive number. On the first round, when the balance in the second account is added, the accumulator turns positive: $- 722 + 3,500 = 2,778$. When the accumulator turns positive, the logical unit contains a dollar for the sample.

On the next round, you go to the "modified accumulator" by subtracting the skip interval; then add the subsequent logical unit balances until the accumulator turns positive again. The modified accumulator is $2,778 - 3,333 = - 555$, then the accumulator next becomes $- 555 + 1,965 = 1,410$, and this positive number identifies another sample dollar. (See the table in the next box.)

The process is repeated.

If the modified accumulator remains positive after subtracting the sampling interval, as it does at account #12, you have selected two dollar units in the same logical unit. Subtract the skip interval again before adding the next account balance.

---

hood of selection than the smaller units. These phenomena of the selection method give DUS its high degree of stratification, with automatic selection of the high-value logical units. DUS samplers say the DUS selection hooks the largest logical units and places them in the sample.

In contrast, the classical sampling methods define the population as 1,500 logical units and gives each of them an equal likelihood of being selected for the sample. Thus, very large and very small customer balances will be in a classical sample of customer accounts receivable. On average, the number of dollars of the account balance in a classical sample will be smaller than the number hooked in a DUS sample. Indeed, the DUS systematic selection guarantees that all customer accounts larger than the skip interval (k) will be in the sample, but classical sampling selection of logical units carries no such guarantee. In our Kingston example all customers with balances over $3,158 will be in the sample. Furthermore, each logical unit has a probability of being in the sample in proportion to its size. That is, a $500 customer balance has twice the probability of selection as a $250 customer balance.

A mini-example of DUS selection is shown in the box above.

· ·

R E V I E W
C H E C K P O I N T S

20.36 What effect does the identification of individually significant logical units have on the size of the recorded amount population for dollar-unit sampling (DUS)?

20.37 How does DUS sample selection produce an automatic stratification of choosing the high-value logical units in a control account balance?

20.38 What happens when two dollar units for the sample fall in the same logical unit?

· ·

E X H I B I T 20.68–1   GOODWIN MANUFACTURING COMPANY

Control Risk Categories		CR	TDR	RIA	RACRTL	Test of Control		Balance-Audit		
						n[c]	Cost	n[s]	Cost	Total
Low control risk	{	0.10						25		
		0.20						46		
		0.30						60		
Moderate control risk	{	0.40						71		
		0.50						71		
		0.60						87		
Control risk below maximum	{	0.70						91		
		0.80						96		
		0.90						101		
Maximum risk		1.00						101		

RIA = Risk of incorrect acceptance for the substantive balance-audit sample.

Wolfe believes the inventory balance can be misstated by as much as $2 million without causing the financial statements as a whole to be materially misstated. The overall materiality judgment is $8 million misstatement of operating income before taxes, and $2 million is the amount assigned to the audit of the inventory balance.

The audit staff recently attended a training session where Wolfe learned about the concepts of a smoke/fire multiplier and an incremental risk of incorrect acceptance used to judge the risk of assessing control risk too low. Inventory purchase pricing errors can be numerous, yet not affect the dollar amounts very much, so Wolfe decided that a smoke/fire multiplier of 7 was appropriate. (The firm's policy is to use the multiplier to figure an anchor tolerable deviation rate for control risk = 0.05, and round the anchor up to 1 percent if the multiplier produces an anchor less than 1 percent. After that, each tolerable deviation rate is 1 percentage point higher for each 0.05 control risk level increment.)

The firm's policy about an incremental risk of incorrect acceptance resulting from assessing control risk too low has not yet been published, but Wolfe thinks that a 0.02 change should not make much difference.

The problem is deciding the size of the test of controls sample for the audit of the purchase-pricing transactions. Wolfe partially completed the worksheet shown in Exhibit 20.68–1. She handed it over to you.

Required:
Copy the worksheet. Complete it and decide the size of the sample for the detail test of accuracy control over the pricing of purchases (additions to the inventory). [Round the risk of incorrect acceptance and risk of assessing control risk too low probabilities to two decimal places.]

MULTIPLE-CHOICE QUESTIONS FOR PRACTICE AND REVIEW: PART II

Exercises 20.69 and 20.70 are located on the accompanying CD-ROM.

20.71 When audit risk (AR) is 0.015, inherent risk (IR) is 0.50, control risk (CR) is 0.30, and analytical procedures risk (AP) is 0.50, the risk of incorrect acceptance (RIA) is:
a. 0.20.
b. 0.02.
c. 2.00.
d. Not determinable.

20.72 Which of the following elements in the audit risk model is/are a product of the auditors' professional judgement?
a. Control risk.
b. Analytical procedures risk.
c. Test of details risk of incorrect acceptance.
d. All the above.

20.73 When making a sample-based decision about the dollar amount in an account balance, the incorrect acceptance decision error is considered more serious than the incorrect rejection decision error because:
a. The incorrect rejection decision impairs the efficiency of the audit.
b. Auditors will do additional work and discover the error of the incorrect decision.
c. The incorrect acceptance decision impairs the effectiveness of the audit.
d. Sufficient, competent evidence will not have been obtained.

20.74 "Overauditing" can be defined as:
a. Auditing too small a sample size.
b. Auditing a larger sample size than necessary.
c. Taking more risk than is professionally acceptable.
d. Giving an inappropriate unqualified report on financial statements.

20.75 The characteristic(s) that distinguishes dollar-unit sampling (DUS) from classical variables sampling is (are):
a. Classical sampling requires an estimate of the standard deviation and DUS does not.
b. Classical sampling depends upon the statistics of the normal distribution and DUS does not.
c. DUS is not concerned with the audit of logical units in the population as is classical sampling.
d. Classical sampling requires calculation of an upper limit of dollar error.

Dollar-Unit Sampling Questions

20.76 The unique feature of dollar-unit sampling (DUS) insofar as sample design is concerned is:
a. Sampling units are not chosen at random.
b. A dollar unit selected in a sample is not replaced before the sample selection is completed.
c. Auditors need not worry about the risk of incorrect acceptance decision error.

d. The population is defined as the number of $1 units in an account balance or class of transactions.

20.77 When calculating a dollar-unit (DUS) sample size, an auditor does not need to make a judgement or estimate of:
a. Audit risk.
b. Tolerable misstatement.
c. Estimate misstatement.
d. Standard deviation of misstatement.

20.78 Which of these combinations will produce the largest DUS sample size:

	RIA	Errors	Recorded Amount	Tolerable Misstatement
a.	0.03	2	$1,000,000	$50,000
b.	0.03	1	1,000,000	35,000
c.	0.06	0	1,500,000	65,000
d.	0.10	4	1,500,000	65,000

20.79 Which of the following statements is correct about dollar-unit sampling (DUS)?
a. The risk of incorrect acceptance must be specified.
b. Smaller logical units have a greater probability of selection in the sample than larger units.
c. The systematic sampling "skip interval" is the same as the "average sampling interval" used for quantitative evaluation.
d. Projected likely misstatement cannot be calculated in the quantitative evaluation when one or more errors are discovered.

20.80 One of the primary advantages of dollar-unit sampling (DUS) is the fact that:
a. It is a good method of sampling for evidence of understatement in asset accounts.
b. The sample selection automatically achieves high-dollar selection and stratification.
c. The sample selection provides for including a representative number of small-value population units.
d. Expanding the sample for additional evidence is very easy.

Exercises and Problems

20.81 Selecting a Dollar-Unit Sample. You have been assigned the task of selecting a dollar-unit sample from the Whitney Company's detail inventory records as of September 30, 1992. Whitney's controller has given you a list of the 23 different inventory items and their recorded book amounts. The senior accountant has told you to select a sample of 10 dollar units and the logical units that contain them.

Required:

Prepare a working paper showing a systematic selection of 10 dollar units and the related logical units. (Arrange the items in their numerical identification number order, and take a random starting place at the 1,210th dollar.)

ID	Amount	ID	Amount	ID	Amount	ID	Amount
1	$1,750	7	$1,255	13	$ 937	19	$2,577
2	1,492	8	3,761	14	5,938	20	1,126
3	994	9	1,956	15	2,001	21	565
4	629	10	1,393	16	222	22	2,319
5	2,272	11	884	17	1,738	23	1,681
6	1,163	12	729	18	1,228		

20.82 When Acceptable Risk Exceeds 50 Percent. Write an explanation of the auditing theory and generally accepted auditing standards regarding sampling plans when the risk model causes the calculation of RIA (acceptable risk of incorrect acceptance) to exceed 50 percent.

DISCUSSION CASES

20.83 Relation of Dollar-Unit Sample Sizes to Audit Risk Model. Prepare tables like the one in Exhibit 20–2 under different assumptions for the three combinations given below. Calculate dollar-unit sample sizes using the Poisson risk factors for a dollar value of the balance of $300,000 and a tolerable misstatement of $10,000. Assume zero expected misstatement. (These are the recorded amount and tolerable misstatement underlying Exhibit 20–2.) Round your RIAs to two decimal places to use the Poisson risk factor tables.

1. AR = 0.10, IR = 1.00, AP = 1.00
2. AR = 0.05, IR = 0.50, AP = 1.00
3. AR = 0.05, IR = 1.00, AP = 0.50

Required:

Explain the differences or similarities among the different or same sample sizes produced by your calculations.

20.84 Determining an Efficient Risk of Incorrect Rejection (DUS). Your audit firm is planning the audit of a company's accounts receivable, which consists of 1,032 customer accounts with a total recorded amount (book value) of $300,000. You have already decided that the accounts receivable can be overstated by as much as $10,000, and the financial statements would not be considered materially misstated. Judging by the experience of past audits on this client, only a negligible amount of misstatement is expected to exist in the account.

Preliminary calculations of sample sizes have been made for several possible

control risk levels. These calculations were based on a "base" risk of incorrect rejection of 0.01. Minimum sample sizes based on the alternative risks of incorrect rejection shown below also were calculated.

Audit work on the accounts will cost $8 per sampling unit when the accounts are selected for the initial sample. However, if the sample indicates a rejection (material overstatement) decision, the audit of additional sampling units will cost $19 each.

Control Risk	"Base" Sample	Alternative RIR	Alternative (minimum) Sample
0.20	80	0.02	41
0.30	96	0.02	53
0.40	107	0.03	62
0.50	116	0.03	68
0.60	122	0.03	74
0.70	128	0.03	78
0.80	133	0.03	82
0.90	137	0.03	86
1.00	141	0.03	89

Required:

For each of the control risk levels shown above, calculate the expected cost savings from auditing the initial alternative (minimum) sample. Assume that the action in the event of a rejection decision is to expand the work by selecting additional units up to the number in the base sample. Discuss the potential audit efficiencies and possible inefficiencies from beginning the audit work with the alternative (minimum) sample size.

20.85 Different Sampling Methods Compared. The trial balance of 50 of Kingston Company's accounts receivable ("balance" column) in Exhibit 20.85–1 was extracted from the population of 1,506 customer accounts you have seen in previous assignments. (However, the customer account numbers have been changed to run consecutively from 1 to 50.) This small population represents the accounts kept by a division of the company, although they are included in the population of 1,506 for financial statement presentation. The small population normally would not be audited separately and normally would not be treated by statistical sampling methods. However, it is presented here to enable you to try out some of the sample selection methods and calculations. You also are given hypothetical audit findings for all the accounts, as if all of the errors in them were known. The requirements below are a kind of "final exam" on account balance audit sampling.

Required:

a. Select an unrestricted random sample (without replacement) of the customer accounts by associating account numbers with random numbers. Start in the first row, first column, of the Table of Random Digits in Appendix 20A. Use two-digit random numbers, reading down the first column until you have identified 10 customer accounts.

b. Select a systematic random sample of 10 customer accounts using two random starts. Select a random number between 1 and 10 and select every 10th account, then select another random number between 1 and 10 and select every 10th account again. (Your instructor's solution is based on random starts of 3 and 5.)

c. Select a systematic random dollar-unit sample of 10 dollars, identifying the associated logical units. For the given sample size of 10, the average sampling interval is $1,947 ($17,523/9). Select a random number between 1 and 1,947. (Your instructor's solution is based on a random starting number of 0741. At the end of the population you will need to cycle back to the beginning to get the 10th selection.)

d. Which customer account(s) in the trial balance will always be included in a systematic dollar-unit sample of 10?

e. Prepare a table comparing the results of each of the samples in *a*, *b*, and *c* above. The columns should be titled (*a*) Random Unit Sample, (*b*) Systematic Unit Sample, and (*c*) Dollar-Unit Sample. Label the rows for the following data and calculations: Population size, population dollar total, sample size, recorded amount in sample, number of error accounts in sample, projected likely misstatement (difference method, ratio method, dollar-unit method). Produce all the values for the rows for each kind of sample.

f. Calculate the upper error limit (finitely corrected) for the 2.0 percent risk of incorrect acceptance for each sample. Add a line for UEL to the table you started in (*e*) above. Assume the relevant standard deviations are standard deviation of random unit sample and systematic unit sample difference amounts = $181.

EXHIBIT 20.85–1 **POPULATION OF 50 ACCOUNTS RECEIVABLE**

Account No.	Balance	Wrong Quantity	Wrong Math	Wrong Date	Monetary Error	Audit Amount
1	$ 141				$ 0	$ 141
2	346				0	346
3	1,301				0	1,301
4	683				0	683
5	1,555			$ 600	600	955
6	105				0	105
7	1,906	$ 200			200	1,706
8	102				0	102
9	634				0	634
10	116				0	116
11	77				0	77
12	51				0	51
13	320				0	320
14	178				0	178
15	188				0	188
16	482			137	137	345
17	183	59			59	124
18	130		$ 8		8	122
19	683				0	683
20	141				0	141
21	57				0	57
22	161				0	161
23	145				0	145
24	210				0	210
25	461	111			111	350
26	508			136	136	372
27	656				0	656
28	193		11		11	182
29	98				0	98
30	177				0	177
31	103				0	103
32	503			115	115	388
33	500			107	107	393
34	104				0	104
35	157				0	157
36	388				0	388
37	98				0	98
38	621	106			106	515
39	394				0	394
40	134				0	134
41	80				0	80
42	91				0	91
43	65				0	65
44	10				0	10
45	470			117	117	353
46	156				0	156
47	703				0	703
48	378			72	72	306
49	312				0	312
50	268				0	268
Number	50	$ 4	2	7	13	50
Total	$17,523	$ 476	$ 19	$ 1,284	$1,779	$15,744
Average	$350.46	$119.00	$9.50	$183.43	$35.58	$314.88
Standard deviation	$374.28				$94.31	$320.88

APPENDIX 20A
R VALUE TABLES

Gives a unique R value for every combination of confidence level (CL) or beta risk (= 1 – CL) and number of errors (K value)

BETA RISKS (= 1– Confidence levels)

K Errors	50% (CL = 50%) R	50% (CL = 50%) PGW	45% (CL = 55%) R	45% (CL = 55%) PGW	40% (CL = 60%) R	40% (CL = 60%) PGW	35% (CL = 65%) R	35% (CL = 65%) PGW
0	0.70	—	0.80	—	0.92	—	1.05	—
1	1.70	0.00	1.84	0.04	2.02	0.10	2.22	0.17
2	2.70	0.00	2.88	0.04	3.11	0.09	3.35	0.13
3	3.70	0.00	3.92	0.04	4.18	0.07	4.45	0.10
4	4.70	0.00	4.95	0.03	5.24	0.06	5.55	0.10
5	5.70	0.00	5.97	0.02	6.29	0.05	6.63	0.08
6	6.70	0.00	7.00	0.03	7.34	0.05	7.71	0.08
7	7.70	0.00	8.02	0.02	8.39	0.05	8.78	0.07
8	8.70	0.00	9.04	0.02	9.43	0.04	9.85	0.07
9	9.70	0.00	10.06	0.02	10.47	0.04	10.91	0.06
10	10.70	0.00	11.08	0.02	11.51	0.04	11.97	0.06
11	11.70	0.00	12.10	0.02	12.55	0.04	13.03	0.06
12	12.70	0.00	13.12	0.02	13.59	0.04	14.09	0.06
13	13.70	0.00	14.14	0.02	14.62	0.03	15.14	0.05
14	14.70	0.00	15.15	0.01	15.66	0.04	16.19	0.05
15	15.70	0.00	16.16	0.01	16.69	0.03	17.24	0.05
16	16.70	0.00	17.18	0.02	17.72	0.03	18.29	0.05
17	17.70	0.00	18.19	0.01	18.75	0.03	19.33	0.04
18	18.70	0.00	19.21	0.02	19.78	0.03	20.38	0.05
19	19.70	0.00	20.22	0.01	20.81	0.03	21.42	0.04
20	20.70	0.00	21.24	0.02	21.84	0.03	22.47	0.05

K Errors	30% (CL = 70%) R	30% (CL = 70%) PGW	25% (CL = 75%) R	25% (CL = 75%) PGW	20% (CL = 80%) R	20% (CL = 80%) PGW	19% (CL = 81%) R	19% (CL = 81%) PGW
0	1.21	—	1.39	—	1.61	—	1.66	—
1	2.44	0.23	2.70	0.31	3.00	0.39	3.06	0.40
2	3.62	0.18	3.93	0.23	4.28	0.28	4.36	0.30
3	4.77	0.15	5.11	0.18	5.52	0.24	5.61	0.25
4	5.90	0.13	6.28	0.17	6.73	0.21	6.82	0.21
5	7.01	0.11	7.43	0.15	7.91	0.18	8.01	0.19
6	8.12	0.11	8.56	0.13	9.08	0.17	9.19	0.18
7	9.21	0.09	9.69	0.13	10.24	0.16	10.35	0.16
8	10.31	0.10	10.81	0.12	11.38	0.14	11.51	0.16
9	11.39	0.08	11.92	0.11	12.52	0.14	12.65	0.14
10	12.47	0.08	13.03	0.11	13.66	0.14	13.79	0.14
11	13.55	0.08	14.13	0.10	14.78	0.12	14.92	0.13
12	14.63	0.08	15.22	0.09	15.90	0.12	16.04	0.12
13	15.70	0.07	16.31	0.09	17.02	0.12	17.17	0.13
14	16.77	0.07	17.40	0.09	18.13	0.11	18.28	0.11
15	17.84	0.07	18.49	0.09	19.24	0.11	19.39	0.11
16	18.90	0.06	19.57	0.08	20.34	0.10	20.50	0.11
17	19.97	0.07	20.65	0.08	21.44	0.10	21.61	0.11
18	21.03	0.06	21.73	0.08	22.54	0.10	22.71	0.10
19	22.09	0.06	22.81	0.08	23.64	0.10	23.81	0.10
20	23.15	0.06	23.89	0.08	24.73	0.09	24.91	0.10

BETA RISKS (= 1– Confidence levels)

K Errors	18% (CL = 82%) R	18% (CL = 82%) PGW	17% (CL = 83%) R	17% (CL = 83%) PGW	16% (CL = 84%) R	16% (CL = 84%) PGW	15% (CL = 85%) R	15% (CL = 85%) PGW
0	1.71	—	1.77	—	1.83	—	1.90	—
1	3.13	0.42	3.21	0.44	3.29	0.46	3.38	0.48
2	4.44	0.31	4.53	0.32	4.63	0.34	4.73	0.35
3	5.70	0.26	5.80	0.27	5.90	0.27	6.02	0.29
4	6.92	0.22	7.03	0.23	7.15	0.25	7.27	0.25
5	8.12	0.20	8.24	0.21	8.36	0.21	8.50	0.23
6	9.31	0.19	9.43	0.19	9.57	0.21	9.71	0.21
7	10.48	0.17	10.61	0.18	10.75	0.18	10.90	0.19
8	11.64	0.16	11.78	0.17	11.92	0.17	12.08	0.18
9	12.79	0.15	12.93	0.15	13.09	0.17	13.25	0.17
10	13.93	0.14	14.08	0.15	14.24	0.15	14.42	0.17
11	15.07	0.14	15.23	0.15	15.39	0.15	15.57	0.15
12	16.20	0.13	16.36	0.13	16.54	0.15	16.72	0.15
13	17.33	0.13	17.49	0.13	17.67	0.13	17.86	0.14
14	18.45	0.12	18.62	0.13	18.80	0.13	19.00	0.14
15	19.57	0.12	19.74	0.12	19.93	0.13	20.13	0.13
16	20.68	0.11	20.87	0.13	21.06	0.13	21.26	0.13
17	21.79	0.11	21.98	0.11	22.17	0.11	22.39	0.13
18	22.90	0.11	23.09	0.11	23.29	0.12	23.51	0.12
19	24.00	0.10	24.20	0.11	24.40	0.11	24.63	0.12
20	25.10	0.10	25.30	0.10	25.52	0.12	25.74	0.11

K Errors	14% (CL = 86%) R	14% (CL = 86%) PGW	13% (CL = 87%) R	13% (CL = 87%) PGW	12% (CL = 88%) R	12% (CL = 88%) PGW	11% (CL = 89%) R	11% (CL = 89%) PGW
0	1.97	—	2.04	—	2.12	—	2.21	—
1	3.46	0.49	3.56	0.52	3.66	0.54	3.77	0.56
2	4.83	0.37	4.94	0.38	5.06	0.40	5.18	0.41
3	6.13	0.30	6.25	0.31	6.39	0.33	6.53	0.35
4	7.39	0.26	7.53	0.28	7.67	0.28	7.83	0.30
5	8.63	0.24	8.77	0.24	8.93	0.26	9.09	0.26
6	9.85	0.22	10.00	0.23	10.17	0.24	10.34	0.25
7	11.05	0.20	11.21	0.21	11.38	0.21	11.57	0.23
8	12.24	0.19	12.41	0.20	12.59	0.21	12.78	0.21
9	13.41	0.17	13.59	0.18	13.78	0.19	13.99	0.21
10	14.58	0.17	14.77	0.18	14.97	0.19	15.18	0.19
11	15.75	0.17	15.94	0.17	16.14	0.17	16.36	0.18
12	16.90	0.15	17.10	0.16	17.31	0.17	17.54	0.18
13	18.05	0.15	18.26	0.16	18.47	0.16	18.70	0.16
14	19.19	0.14	19.41	0.15	19.63	0.16	19.87	0.17
15	20.33	0.14	20.55	0.14	20.78	0.15	21.02	0.15
16	21.46	0.13	21.69	0.14	21.92	0.14	22.18	0.16
17	22.59	0.13	22.83	0.14	23.07	0.15	23.33	0.15
18	23.72	0.13	23.96	0.13	24.21	0.14	24.47	0.14
19	24.84	0.12	25.09	0.13	25.34	0.13	25.61	0.14
20	25.97	0.13	26.21	0.12	26.47	0.13	26.75	0.14

BETA RISKS (= 1– Confidence levels)

K Errors	10% (CL = 90%)		5% (CL = 95%)		4% (CL = 96%)		3% (CL = 97%)	
	R	PGW	R	PGW	R	PGW	R	PGW
0	2.31	—	3.00	—	3.22	—	3.51	—
1	3.89	0.58	4.75	0.75	5.01	0.79	5.36	0.85
2	5.33	0.44	6.30	0.55	6.60	0.59	6.98	0.62
3	6.69	0.36	7.76	0.46	8.09	0.49	8.51	0.53
4	8.00	0.31	9.16	0.40	9.51	0.42	9.96	0.45
5	9.28	0.28	10.52	0.36	10.89	0.38	11.37	0.41
6	10.54	0.26	11.85	0.33	12.24	0.35	12.75	0.38
7	11.78	0.24	13.15	0.30	13.57	0.33	14.10	0.35
8	13.00	0.22	14.44	0.29	14.87	0.30	15.42	0.32
9	14.21	0.21	15.71	0.27	16.16	0.29	16.73	0.31
10	15.41	0.20	16.97	0.26	17.43	0.27	18.02	0.29
11	16.60	0.19	18.21	0.24	18.69	0.26	19.30	0.28
12	17.79	0.19	19.45	0.24	19.94	0.25	20.57	0.27
13	18.96	0.17	20.67	0.22	21.18	0.24	21.83	0.26
14	20.13	0.17	21.89	0.22	22.42	0.24	23.08	0.25
15	21.30	0.17	23.10	0.21	23.64	0.22	24.32	0.24
16	22.46	0.16	24.31	0.21	24.86	0.22	25.56	0.24
17	23.61	0.15	25.50	0.19	26.07	0.21	26.78	0.22
18	24.76	0.15	26.70	0.20	27.27	0.20	28.00	0.22
19	25.91	0.15	27.88	0.18	28.47	0.20	29.22	0.22
20	27.05	0.14	29.07	0.19	29.67	0.20	30.42	0.20

K Errors	2% (CL = 98%)		1% (CL = 99%)	
	R	PGW	R	PGW
0	3.91	—	4.61	—
1	5.83	0.92	6.64	1.03
2	7.52	0.69	8.41	0.77
3	9.08	0.56	10.05	0.64
4	10.58	0.50	11.61	0.56
5	12.03	0.45	13.11	0.50
6	13.44	0.41	14.58	0.47
7	14.82	0.38	16.00	0.42
8	16.17	0.35	17.41	0.41
9	17.51	0.34	18.79	0.38
10	18.83	0.32	20.15	0.36
11	20.13	0.30	21.49	0.34
12	21.42	0.29	22.83	0.34
13	22.71	0.29	24.14	0.31
14	23.98	0.27	25.45	0.31
15	25.24	0.26	26.75	0.30
16	26.50	0.26	28.04	0.29
17	27.74	0.24	29.31	0.27
18	28.98	0.24	30.59	0.28
19	30.22	0.24	31.85	0.26
20	31.42	0.20	33.11	0.26

APPENDIX 20B

TABLE OF RANDOM DIGITS

32942	95416	42339	59045	26693	49057	87496	20624	14819
07410	99859	83828	21409	29094	65114	36701	25762	12827
59981	68155	45673	76210	58219	45738	29550	24736	09574
46251	25437	69654	99716	11563	08803	86027	51867	12116
65558	51904	93123	27887	53138	21488	09095	78777	71240
99187	19258	86421	16401	19397	83297	40111	49326	81686
35641	00301	16096	34775	21562	97983	45040	19200	16383
14031	00936	81518	48440	02218	04756	19506	60695	88494
60677	15076	92554	26042	23472	69869	62877	19584	39576
66314	05212	67859	89356	20056	30648	87349	20389	53805
20416	87410	75646	64176	82752	63606	37011	57346	69512
28701	56992	70423	62415	40807	98086	58850	28968	45297
74579	33844	33426	07570	00728	07079	19322	56325	84819
62615	52342	82968	75540	80045	53069	20665	21282	07768
93945	06293	22879	08161	01442	75071	21427	94842	26210
75689	76131	96837	67450	44511	50424	82848	41975	71663
02921	16919	35424	93209	52133	87327	95897	65171	20376
14295	34969	14216	03191	61647	30296	66667	10101	63203
05303	91109	82403	40312	62191	67023	90073	83205	71344
57071	90357	12901	08899	91039	67251	28701	03846	94589
78471	57741	13599	84390	32146	00871	09354	22745	65806
89242	79337	59293	47481	07740	43345	25716	70020	54005
14955	59592	97035	80430	87220	06392	79028	57123	52872
42446	41880	37415	47472	04513	49494	08860	08038	43624
18534	22346	54556	17558	73689	14894	05030	19561	56517
39284	33737	42512	86411	23753	29690	26096	81361	93099
33922	37329	89911	55876	28379	81031	22058	21487	54613
78355	54013	50774	30666	61205	42574	47773	36027	27174
08845	99145	94316	88974	29828	97069	90327	61842	29604
01769	71825	55957	98271	02784	66731	40311	88495	18821
17639	38284	59478	90409	21997	56199	30068	82800	69692
05851	58653	99949	63505	40409	85551	90729	64938	52403
42396	40112	11469	03476	03328	84238	26570	51790	42122
13318	14192	98167	75631	74141	22369	36757	89117	54998
60571	54786	26281	01855	30706	66578	32019	65884	58485
09531	81853	59334	70929	03544	18510	89541	13555	21168
72865	16829	86542	00396	20363	13010	69645	49608	54738
56324	31093	77924	28622	83543	28912	15059	80192	83964
78192	21626	91399	07235	07104	73652	64425	85149	75409
64666	34767	97298	92708	01994	53188	78476	07804	62404
82201	75694	02808	65983	74373	66693	13094	74183	73020
15360	73776	40914	85190	54278	99054	62944	47351	89098
68142	67957	70896	37983	20487	95350	16371	03426	13895
19138	31200	30616	14639	44406	44236	57360	81644	94761
28155	03521	36415	78452	92359	81091	56513	88321	97910
87971	29031	51780	27376	81056	86155	55488	50590	74514
58147	68841	53625	02059	75223	16783	19272	61994	71090
18875	52809	70594	41649	32935	26430	82096	01605	65846
75109	56474	74111	31966	29969	70093	98901	84550	25769
35983	03742	76822	12073	59463	84420	15868	99505	11426

Source: The Rand Corporation, *A Million Random Digits with 100,000 Normal Deviates* (Glencoe: Free Press, 1955), p. 102.

APPENDIX 20C

OTHER TOPICS IN STATISTICAL AUDITING: REGRESSION FOR ANALYTICAL REVIEW

Auditors sometimes use statistical models with analytical review procedures. The most common such statistical model is regression. In a regression model a linear mathematical relationship is assumed between one dependent variable and one or more independent variables based on a set of values for these variables. An illustration of a relationship that may be used in auditing is to set the dependent variable equal to sales, the independent variable to cost of sales. The data set may consist of monthly recorded amounts for each of the 36 months preceding the current year. A scatter graph of these variables may suggest a linear relationship, which the auditor might exploit in order to get audit assurance from such a relationship.

The simple regression model assumes a linear relationship and "fits" a line that reflects this relationship and estimates two parameter values necessary to model the line. The regression model is represented as follows:

$$y = a + bx + E$$

where y = the dependent variable values, e.g., sales values, which vary depending on the independent variable.

where x = the independent variable, e.g., cost of sales, which is the variable assumed "to explain" the dependent variable. From an audit point of view it can be any variable that plausibly provides an explanation for the dependent variable based on past historical relationships.

where a = a constant and represents one of the parameters, the intercept (value of y when $x = 0$), estimated by the regression of the linear equation; where b = another constant estimated by the regression model called the coefficient of the independent variable and represents the slope of the regression line. Both constants a and b are needed to define the regression line mathematically.

where E = the residual unexplained difference and reflects the fact that the regression line is not a perfect predictor of y given the x variable. If this residual gets too large for any given month observation it is termed an *outlier.*

After constructing a regression line statistically with one or more independent variables, the auditor can use this model to predict the adequacy of the reported amount for the dependent variable for the months covering the current audit period.

For an illustration we use an example from an influential book on statistical regression by K.W. Stringer and J.R. Steward of the former Deloitte Haskins Sells.[7] Their Gamma Company example used data from the 36 months preceding the current fiscal year to estimate a linear equation using regression of the following form:

$$y = -366.46 + .8906\, x_1 + 1.3578\, x_2$$

where y here represents revenues for a software firm
  x_1 = programming hours at standard and
  x_2 = expenses

Assume also that the model has successfully passed the usual tests for regression, e.g., t test and F test, and the usual diagnostics that are normally built into the software used by auditing firms. With such a model the auditor can develop expectations for the current audit period on revenues by month; for example, say the client reports revenues of 2,698 for June and the auditor wishes to get some assurance on the accuracy of this amount. The above regression model can be used to make a prediction about what revenues should be, given

---

[7] K.W. Stringer and J.R. Stewart, *Statistical Techniques for Analytical Review (STAR)*, Deloitte, Haskins & Sells, New York, 1985.

historical relationships. So, plugging standard hours of 2013 for June and expenses of 1157 for June into the equation, we get predicted revenues of:

$$y = -336.96 + .8906 \,(2013) + 1.3578 \,(1157) = 3027$$

The difference between the expected amount provided by the model and the actual amount proposed by the client (3027 – 2698 = 329) is the amount of variation unexplained by expected relationships. If the auditor feels this difference is significant he or she would investigate revenue for the month of June in more detail. Note how regression can be used to identify problem areas and to help plan the audit of the revenue amount in this case.

GRAPH OF TYPICAL REGRESSION APPLICATION

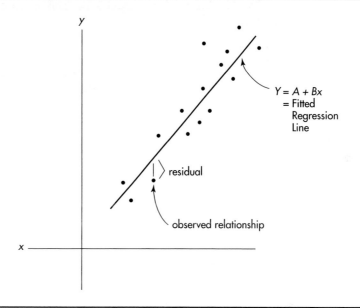

Several technical implementation issues have to be addressed in developing models like the one above. First, and most importantly, the auditor has to determine plausible business relationships for use in the regression to determine expectations for the amounts being audited. This includes identifying the appropriate dependent and independent variables to use in the model. The auditor would start by using his/her professional judgement in selecting the variables to use in the model. This can be supplemented by various statistical tests to further refine the model. For example, the initial set of independent variables considered for this regression included hours worked by programmer, senior programmer and analysts as well as the hourly rates for each of these groups, and expenses charged to clients and cost of services.

It takes a high level of audit judgement and good knowledge of the client's business to develop cost-effective regression models for analytical procedures. Such statistical models are used primarily at the planning stage, when they are of most use to the auditor. As noted in Chapter 10, analytical procedures have proven to be very effective procedures for detecting material errors in audits. And they can be used for a variety of accounts, particularly when sufficiently desegregated monthly data are conveniently available from the client.

However, caution is advisable since research has also shown that while statistical analytical review can be used to provide some audit assurance for client accounts, it should not be used to provide a high level or the sole amount of assurance for anything other than immaterial amounts.

Another caution is that because of the sensitivity of the regression results to materiality, the planned level of assurance (the confidence level), and the need to use the negative approach, auditors need to develop a special interface in applying regression models to audit practice. In other words, you can't just take a regression package available from, say, Excel and apply it to your audit data. Keep in mind that audit assurance is related to 1-RIA, not 1-RIR. Specifically, in most scientific applications the null hypothesis relates to there being no difference because the scientist is usually interested in the effects of some experimental treatment. In auditing because the crucial null hypothesis assumes there is a material difference, the confidence level is the complement of the opposite risk that is normally used in the sciences. Specifically, in the sciences (and therefore in most statistical tables) it is the positive approach that is used rather than the negative approach that is relevant to the auditor.

As a result special adjustments normally need to be made for classical statistical estimators, and that includes the regression model. That is why audit firms have developed a special audit interface to be used with the regression models. And you should be aware of the need for such an interface before applying off-the-shelf regression packages to audit applications. In fact it's far better to obtain a package specially tailored for auditor use. Most of the large firms already have such packages, thus making use of statistical analytical procedures very feasible.

Research has shown that the negative approach for analytical review in auditing is preferred to the positive approach in controlling both alpha and beta risks. (See Y. Chen and R.A. Leitch, "An Analysis of the Relative Power Characteristics of Analytical Procedures," *Auditing, A Journal of Practice and Theory*, Fall 1999, pp. 35–69.)

DUS for Tests of Controls

Although we have noted that DUS formulas can be used for tests of controls applications, we implicitly assumed in all our illustrations that the test of controls sampling was based on physical unit selection. Some auditors argue that a more appropriate way of evaluating controls is to use dollar unit sampling rather than physical unit selection. The reason for this is that automatic stratification of the population results from DUS and the evaluation of controls can then be based on the maximum proportion of dollars (rather than maximum proportion of physical units) in the population that is likely to contain errors. Research has shown that compliance deviation rates per recorded dollar can be substantially different from compliance deviation rates for physical units such as sales invoices or shipping documents.

For example, in the stratification example in Chapter 7 compliance deviations for strata 3, 4, 5 may be much higher than for the high valued items, in strata 1 and 2. The auditor can incorporate such differences judgementally or let the sampling technique DUS automatically account for this effect in evaluating controls. Note such differences in controls for different strata could affect auditor strategies as noted in Exhibit 14–2. In fact, we can take the position that unstratified physical units sampling for attributes ignores possible differing strengths of controls based on the value of items recorded—unstratified physical unit sampling for tests of controls implicitly assumes controls are equally strong for high-value items and low-value items. Limited empirical evidence on this issue suggests this is not the case in practice. Nevertheless, unstratified physical units is the most commonly used method in practice currently. A Canadian research study has called for a change in this practice and increased reliance on DUS for control testing.[8] As the importance of auditor reports on internal controls increases, perhaps this issue will gain increasing prominence.

For example, the increasingly important concept of continuous auditing (discussed in Chapter 21) allows a way to calculate sample size and sampling interval without knowing the recorded amount for the entire period. That is, without knowing the recorded amount (BV) of an entire population, such as sales or purchases for the period. Tests of controls and substantive tests with DUS addresses this problem of continuous audits by allowing the calculation of sampling interval and sample size without knowing the BV for the population in advance. All that's required is the auditor to specify materiality in dollar terms.

[8] D.A. Leslie, *Materiality, The Concept and Its Application to Auditing*, CICA, 1985, Ch. 8.

But this is simply P*BV, that is, MM = P*BV. Note that if the auditor can directly specify MM (= P*BV), then the auditor can also determine the average sampling interval: BV/n. This is possible because n = R/P, and the sampling interval is algebraically equivalent to BV/(R/P) = (BV*P)/R = MM/R.

Thus the auditor can determine the sampling interval without specifying BV itself or knowing BV in advance. This can be an important advantage in practice if the client has not yet compiled a total BV for his or her population, as would be the case in continuous audits involving continuous on-line real-time reporting of sales and purchases as may be demanded in e-commerce audits. The auditor can take a systematic sample as he or she simply adds through the population of transactions as the transactions occur. This, however, would require embedded software as discussed in Chapter 21.

We can now try to summarize all the various sampling risks with the audit risk model.

SAMPLING RISKS AND THE AUDIT RISK MODEL

The basic goal of the audit can be characterized as providing a high degree of assurance that there are no material errors, where:

Level of assurance = Probability that there is no material error after the audit = 1 − Probability of material error existing after the audit = 1 − Audit risk, and where audit risk according to the *Handbook* can be represented as audit risk = IR * CR * DR where IR = inherent risk, CR = control risk and DR = detective risk. DR in turn is sometimes split up into a substantive testing of details risk (RIA) and risk of other audit procedures including analytical review (APR). Some auditors prefer to stress the audit assurance aspect provided by these various sources so that they refer to assurance from substantive testing of details risk (= 1 − RIA) or assurance from analytical procedures (= 1 − APR). This is just a different way of looking at these factors, and the amount of work would not be affected since the assessments are still the same.

Now, how do all these risks relate to sampling risk?

IR = inherent risk has nothing to do with sampling risk, but note it relates to risk of having material errors, i.e., the negative approach null hypothesis underlying beta risk.

RIA = beta risk for substantive tests of details.

CR = beta risk for tests of control under some approaches; however, since there are usually several tests of control, CR does not automatically equal a beta for a given test. Professional judgement is also required in combining the results of several procedures on internal control (some statistical, some not) to assess CR for a given application.

APR = beta risk for regression equations for analytical review, but if combined with other nonstatistical analytical procedures (which is normally the case), additional professional judgement is required to assess APR.

Now we can better appreciate why same practitioners say "minimization of the overall beta risk is the reason for the existence of the public accounting profession." Statistical auditing provides a more objective means of controlling these beta risks for different procedures. Note moreover that alpha risk is not directly considered anywhere in the risk model. Perhaps this explains why auditors are less likely to directly quantify alpha risk in practice.

KEY TERMS

account analysis   identification of each important item and amount in an account followed by document vouching and enquiry to determine whether amounts should be classified elsewhere. *(Chapter 14)*

account balance audit program   a specification (list) of procedures designed to produce evidence about the assertions in financial statements. *(Chapter 6)*

accounting (as a control objective)   a general category concerned with ensuring that the accounting process for a transaction is completely performed and in conformity with GAAP. *(Chapter 6)*

accounting estimate   an *approximation* of a financial statement element, item, or account made by an organization's management. *(Chapters 14 and 20)*

accounting system (as element of a control structure)   an organization of policies and procedures for recording transactions properly *(Chapter 6)*

accuracy (as a control objective)   refers to ensuring that dollar amounts are figured correctly. *(Chapter 6)*

act-utilitarianism (in moral philosophy)   emphasis on the individual act is it is affected by the specific circumstances of a situation. *(Chapter 16)*

administrative control   the plan of organization and all methods and procedures that are concerned mainly with operational efficiency and adherence to managerial policies and usually relate only indirectly to financial records. *(Chapter 18)*

adverse opinion   the opposite of an unqualified opinion, stating that financial statements are *not* in conformity with GAAP. *(Chapter 2)*

analytical procedures   audit evaluation of financial statement accounts by studying and comparing relationships among financial and nonfinancial data. *(Chapters 4 and 14)*

analytical procedures risk (AP)   the probability that analytical procedures will *fail* to detect material errors. *(Chapter 7)*

application description   (in computer system documentation) system flowcharts, description of all inputs and outputs, record formats, lists of computer codes and control features. *(Chapter 8)*

associated with financial statements   circumstance in which a PA's name is used in connection with financial statements, or a PA has prepared the statements, even if the PA's name is not used in any written report. *(Chapter 3)*

assurance engagement   an engagement by a practitioner designed to report on the credibility of information, which is the responsibility of another party and which is referred to as the subject-matter, by evaluating that information against identified suitable criteria and expressing a conclusion. *(Chapters 2 and 15)*

assurance standards   a general set of standards intended to guide assurance engagements. *(Chapter 2)*

attestation   the lending of some credibility to financial or other information involving written assertions by professional auditors who serve as objective intermediaries. *(Chapter 1)*

attributes sampling   another name for test of controls audit sampling. *(Chapter 7)*

audit objective   expression of a financial statement *assertion* for which evidence needs to be obtained. *(Chapter 9)*

audit of balances   ordinary and extended *substantive procedures designed to find signs* of errors, irregularities and frauds in account balances and classes of transactions. *(Chapter 7)*

audit procedure (nature)   actions described as the general audit procedures of recalculation, physical observation, confirmation, verbal enquiry, document examination, scanning and analytical review. *(Chapter 7)*

audit procedures   particular and specialized actions auditors take to obtain evidence in a specific audit engagement. *(Chapter 2)*

audit program   a list of the audit procedures believed necessary to obtain sufficient, competent evidence that will serve as the basis for the audit report. *(Chapters 2, 4 and 5)*

audit risk (global)   the probability that an auditor will give an inappropriate opinion on financial statements. *(Chapter 5)*

audit risk (account level)   probability that an auditor will fail to find misstatement equal to, or greater than, the tolerable misstatement assigned to an account. *(Chapter 5)*

audit standards   audit quality guides that remain the same through time and for all audits, including audits of computerized accounting systems. *(Chapter 2)*

auditee   the company or other entity whose financial statements are being audited. *(Chapter 1)*

auditing around the computer   auditors' attempt to isolate the computer and to find audit assurance by vouching data from output to source documents and by tracing from source documents to output. *(Chapter 8)*

auditing through the computer   auditors' actual evaluation of the hardware and software to determine the reliability of operations that cannot be viewed by the human eye. *(Chapter 8)*

auditing with the computer   audit techniques such as the use of the client's computer hardware and software to process real or simulated transactions or the use of specialized audit software to perform other audit tasks. *(Chapter 8)*

auditing without the computer   using visible evidence such as the input source data, the machine-produced error listings, the visible control points and the detailed printed output. *(Chapter 8)*

authorization (as a control objective)   ensuring that transactions are approved before they are recorded. *(Chapter 6)*

average sampling interval (ASI)   the recorded dollar amount of a population being sampled divided by the sample size. *(Chapter 20)*

backup   a retention system for files, programs and documentation so that master files can be reconstructed in case of accidental loss and processing can continue at another site if the computer centre is lost to fire or flood. *(Chapter 8)*

batch control totals   totals of dollar numbers, nonsense numbers or count of documents. *(Chapter 6)*

batch processing (also **serial** or **sequential processing**) all records to be processed are collected in groups (batches) of like transactions before computer processing. *(Chapter 8)*

bill of materials   a specification of the materials authorized for production; the source of authorization for the preparation of materials requisitions. *(Chapter 11)*

block sampling   choosing segments of contiguous transactions for a sampling application. *(Chapter 7)*

breach of contract   a claim that accounting or auditing services were not performed in the manner agreed. *(Chapter 17)*

capital budget   management document that contains the plans for asset purchases and business acquisitions. *(Chapter 12)*

cash flow forecast   forecast that informs the board of directors and management of the business plans, the prospects for cash inflows and the needs for cash outflows. *(Chapter 12)*

categorical imperative (in moral philosophy)   Kant's specification of an unconditional obligation. *(Chapter 16)*

Certified General Accountants   persons who have met the Certified General Accountants Association of Canada criteria for CGA credentials. *(Chapter 1)*

Certified Internal Auditors   persons who have met the Institute of Internal Auditors' criteria for professional CIA credentials. *(Chapter 18)*

Certified Management Accountants   persons who have met the Society of Management Accountants of Canada criteria for CMA credentials. *(Chapter 1)*

chain of custody   the crucial link of the evidence to the suspect, called the "relevance" of evidence by lawyers and judges. *(Chapter 19)*

check digit   an extra number, precisely calculated, that is tagged onto the end of a basic identification number, such as an employee number. *(Chapter 6)*

cheque kiting   the illegal practice of building up apparent balances in one or more bank accounts based on uncollected (float) cheques drawn against similar accounts in other banks. *(Chapter 9)*

class of transactions   a group of transactions having common characteristics, such as cash receipts or cash disbursements, but which are not simply added together and presented as an account balance in financial statements. *(Chapter 7)*

classification (as a control objective)   ensuring that transactions are recorded in the right accounts, charged or credited to the right customer (including classification of sales to subsidiaries and affiliates) entered in the correct segment product line or inventory description and so forth. *(Chapter 6)*

client   person (company, board of directors, agency or some other person or group) who retains the auditor and pays the fee. *(Chapter 1)*

collusion   circumstance in which two or more people conspire to conduct fraudulent activity in violation of an organization's internal control policies and procedures. *(Chapter 19)*

commission   a percentage fee charged for professional services in connection with executing a transaction or performing some other business activity. *(Chapter 16)*

common law   all the cases and precedents that govern judges' decisions in lawsuits for monetary damages. Common law is "common knowledge" in the sense that judges tend to follow the collective wisdom of past cases decided by themselves and other judges. *(Chapter 17)*

compensating control   a control feature used when a standard control procedure (such as strict segregation of functional responsibilities) is not specified by the company. *(Chapter 12)*

competent (characteristic of evidence) evidence that is valid, relevant and unbiased. *(Chapter 4)*

completeness (as a control objective) ensuring that valid transactions are *not omitted entirely* from the accounting records. *(Chapter 6)*

computed upper limit (CUL) a statistical estimate of the population deviation rate computed from the test of controls sample evidence. *(Chapter 20)*

conflict of interest any relationship whereby an individual or his or her relative may benefit from a transaction within the individual's business relations where he or she has influenced the transaction or relationship. *(Chapter 1)*

contingent fee a fee established for the performance of any service in an arrangement in which no fee will be charged unless a specific finding or result is attained, or the fee otherwise depends on the result of the service. *(Chapter 16)*

control environment a set of characteristics that defines good management control features other than accounting policies and control procedures. *(Chapter 6)*

control procedures specific error-checking routines performed by company personnel. *(Chapter 6)*

control risk the probability that a material misstatement (error or irregularity) could occur and not be prevented or detected on a timely basis by the company's internal control structure policies and procedures *(Chapters 2, 5 and 6)*

internal control structure consists of a company's control environment, accounting system and control procedures. The existence of a satisfactory internal control structure reduces the probability of errors and irregularities in the accounts. *(Chapter 2)*

controlled reprocessing (also **parallel simulation**) auditors' determination of whether output from the computer program the client actually used in processing data produces satisfactory accounting output when compared to the output from the auditors' controlled copy of the program. *(Chapter 21)*

cross-reference computer program provide printed listings of every occurrence of each name used in an application program or a list of every file used in an application system. *(Chapter 21)*

cutoff bank statement auditors' information source for vouching the bank reconciliation items; a complete bank statement including all paid cheques and deposit slips received directly by the auditors. *(Chapter 9)*

cycle set of accounts and business activities that go together in an accounting system. *(Chapter 4)*

database administrator (DBA) person responsible for determining who should have access to data elements. *(Chapter 21)*

data elements individual pieces of information such as employee number, address, pay rate, balance in a computer system. *(Chapter 21)*

data redundancy indicates the same data stored in several separate files. *(Chapter 21)*

decision criteria standards for decision and evaluation in specific circumstances. *(Chapter 20)*

defalcation another name for employee fraud and embezzlement. *(Chapter 19)*

detail test of control procedure consists of (1) identification of the data population from which a sample of items will be selected for audit and (2) an expression of the action that will be taken to produce relevant evidence. In general, the *actions* in detail test of control audit procedures involve vouching, tracing, observing, scanning and recalculating. *(Chapters 9, 10 and 11)*

detection rate ratio of the number of exceptions reported to auditors to the number of account errors. *(Chapter 9)*

detection risk the probability that audit procedures will fail to produce evidence of material misstatement, provided any have entered the accounting system in the first place and have not been detected and corrected by the client's control policies and procedures. *(Chapter 5)*

deviation (as in **control failure,** also error, occurrence and exception) refers to a departure from a prescribed internal control procedure in a particular case. *(Chapter 7)*

direct-effect illegal acts violations of laws or government regulations by the company or its management or employees that produce direct and material effects on dollar amounts in financial statements. *(Chapter 19)*

direct personal knowledge audit evidence obtained by eyewitness and physical inspection. *(Chapter 4)*

disclaimer of opinion lowest level of assurance; "no assurance." Auditors explicitly state that they give no opinion and no assurance, thus taking no responsibility for a report on the fair presentation of financial statements in conformity with GAAP. *(Chapters 2 and 3)*

dollar-value estimation objective in statistical sampling the job of helping a client obtain an estimate of an amount. *(Chapter 20)*

dual-purpose procedure an audit procedure that simultaneously serves the *substantive* purpose (obtain direct evidence about the dollar amounts in account balances) and the *test of controls* purpose (obtain evidence about the company's performance of its own control procedures). *(Chapter 9)*

echo check   a magnetic read after each magnetic write, "echoing" back to the sending location and comparing results. *(Chapter 8)*

80/20 "rule"   the rule of thumb about population skewness that 80 percent of the value tends to be in 20 percent of the units. *(Chapter 20)*

embezzlement   a type of fraud involving employees' or nonemployees' wrongfully taking money or property entrusted to their care, custody and control, often accompanied by false accounting entries and other forms of lying and coverup. *(Chapter 19)*

employee fraud   the use of fraudulent means to take money or other property from an employer. *(Chapter 19)*

engagement letter   letter from the auditor to the management of an audit client setting forth the terms of the engagement. *(Chapter 4)*

errors (as in **errors and irregularities**)   unintentional misstatements or omissions of amounts or disclosures in financial statements. *(Chapter 19)*

error (as in **control failure,** also **deviation, occurrence** and **exception**)   refers to a departure from a prescribed internal control procedure in a particular case. *(Chapter 7)*

error analysis   investigation of each deviation from a prescribed control procedure to determine its nature, cause and probable effect on financial statements. *(Chapter 7)*

event driven (also **transaction driven**)   computer data processing system that is started with each transaction event; individual transactions trigger the processing activity and all relevant files are updated. *(Chapter 8)*

evidence   all the influences upon the minds of auditors which ultimately guide their decisions. *(Chapter 2)*

exception (as in **control failure,** also **deviation, error** and **occurrence**)   a departure from a prescribed internal control procedure in a particular case. *(Chapter 7)*

expectation about the population deviation rate   an estimate of the ratio of the number of expected deviations to population size. *(Chapter 7)*

extending the audit conclusion   performing substantive-purpose audit procedures on the transactions in the remaining period and on the year-end balance to produce sufficient competent evidence for a decision about the year-end balance. *(Chapter 7)*

extent (of audit procedures)   refers to the *amount* of work done when the procedures are performed. *(Chapters 6 and 7)*

existence (as a **financial statement assertion**)   management representation that assets, liabilities, equities, revenue and expenses exist in reality. *(Chapter 4)*

expanded scope governmental auditing   auditing that goes beyond an audit of financial reports and compliance with laws and regulations to include economy and efficiency and program results audits. *(Chapters 1 and 18)*

expert witness   testifying to findings determined during litigation support and testifying as to accounting principles and auditing standards applications. *(Chapter 19)*

external auditors   independent PAs who audit financial statements for the purpose of rendering an opinion. *(Chapter 1)*

external evidence   documentary evidence obtained directly from independent external sources. *(Chapter 4)*

external-internal evidence   documentary evidence that has originated outside the client's data processing system but which has been received and processed by the client. *(Chapter 4)*

fidelity bond   an insurance policy that covers most kinds of cash embezzlement losses. *(Chapter 9)*

financial forecast   presents, to the best of the preparer's knowledge and belief, an entity's expected financial position, results of operations, and changes in financial position; based on assumptions about expected conditions and expected courses of action. *(Chapter 15)*

financial projection   similar to a forecast, with the important exception that a projection depends on one or more hypothetical assumptions. *(Chapter 15)*

financial reporting   broad-based process of providing statements of financial position (balance sheets), statements of results of operations (income statements), statements of changes in financial position (cash flow statements), and accompanying disclosure notes (footnotes) to outside decision makers who have no internal source of information like the management of the company has. *(Chapter 1)*

Financial Reporting Releases (FRR)   SEC publications of rules and policies about accounting and disclosures. *(Chapter 17)*

finitely corrected   sample size calculation that incorporates the population size in such a way that sample sizes larger than the population size cannot be produced. *(Chapter 20)*

forensic accounting   application of accounting and auditing skills to legal problems, both civil and criminal. *(Chapter 19)*

foreseeable beneficiaries   creditors, investors or potential investors who rely on accountant's work. *(Chapter 17)*

fraud action of knowingly making material misrepresentations of fact with the intent of inducing someone to believe the falsehood and act upon it and thus suffer a loss or damage. *(Chapter 19)*

fraud auditing a proactive approach to detect financial frauds using accounting records and information, analytical relationships and an awareness of fraud perpetration and concealment efforts (ACFE). *(Chapter 19)*

fraud examiners people engaged specifically for fraud investigation work. *(Chapter 19)*

fraudulent financial reporting (see also **management fraud**) intentional or reckless conduct, whether by act or omission, that results in materially misleading financial statements (National Commission on Fraudulent Financial Reporting, 1987). *(Chapter 19)*

generalization argument (in moral philosophy) a judicious combination of the imperative and utilitarian principles. *(Chapter 16)*

generalized audit software (GAS) set of software functions that may be utilized to read, compute and operate on machine-readable records. *(Chapter 8)*

government auditors auditors whose work is governed by the GAO audit standards, whether they be audit employees of governments or public accounting firms engaged to perform government audits. *(Chapter 18)*

gross negligence lack of even minimum care in performing professional duties, indicating reckless disregard for duty and responsibility. *(Chapter 17)*

haphazard selection any unsystematic way of selecting sample units. *(Chapter 7)*

harmonization accountants' and regulators' interest in making accounting and auditing standards coordinated, if not uniform, throughout the world. *(Chapter 2)*

horizontal analysis study of changes of financial statement numbers and ratios across two or more years. *(Chapters 5 and 19)*

hypothesis testing auditors hypothesize that an account balance is materially accurate as to existence, ownership and valuation and test the hypothesis with sample-based evidence. *(Chapter 7)*

hypothetical assumption expression of a condition and course of action the issuer of a financial projection expects could take place. *(Chapter 15)*

illegal acts violations of laws and regulations that are far removed from financial statement effects. *(Chapter 19)*

information risk risk (probability) that the financial statements distributed by a company will be materially false and misleading. *(Chapter 1)*

inherent risk probability that material misstatements have occurred in transactions entering the accounting system used to develop financial statements. *(Chapter 5)*

injunction legal settlement in which a person or company, without admitting or denying a violation of law, agrees not to violate the law in the future. *(Chapter 17)*

inspection (as in **test of controls procedures**) auditors look to see whether the documents were marked with an initial, signature or stamp to indicate they had been checked. *(Chapter 6)*

integrity ability to act in accordance with the highest moral and ethical values all the time. *(Chapter 19)*

interim audit work procedures performed several weeks or months before the balance sheet date. *(Chapter 4)*

interim date a date some weeks or months before the auditee's fiscal year-end. *(Chapters 2 and 7)*

internal accounting control the plan of organization and procedures designed to prevent, detect and correct accounting errors that may occur and get recorded in ledger accounts and financial statements. *(Chapter 18)*

internal auditors persons employed within organizations for audit assignments. *(Chapters 1, 18 and 19)*

internal auditing (see also **management auditing, operational auditing, performance auditing**) study of business operations for the purpose of making recommendations about the economic and efficient use of resources, effective achievement of business objectives and compliance with company policies. *(Chapters 1 and 18)*

internal control questionnaire a checklist used in a formal interview with knowledgeable managers. *(Chapter 6)*

internal evidence documents that are produced, circulated and finally stored with the client's information system. *(Chapter 4)*

International Federation of Accountants (IFAC) an organization dedicated to developing international auditing standards. IFAC publishes its own handbook on auditing standards referred to as international standards on auditing (ISAs). ISAs cover such issues as basic principles of auditing, auditor's reports, professional independence, reliance on other auditors abroad and professional qualifications. *(Chapter 1)*

international standard on auditing (ISA) an auditing standard promulgated by IFAC and included in the IFAC Handbook. *(Chapter 1)*

irregularities intentional misstatements or omissions in financial statements, including fraudulent financial reporting (management fraud) and misappropriations of assets (defalcations). *(Chapter 19)*

known misstatement the actual monetary error found in a sample. *(Chapter 7)*

levels of assurance standard unqualified report with opinion on financial statements, review report with negative assurance and compilation report with no expression of opinion or assurance. *(Chapter 3)*

likely misstatement the projected amount of misstatement in a population based on sample evidence. *(Chapter 7)*

litigated settlement of a controversy by a judge in the civil justice system. *(Chapter 17)*

litigation support consulting in the capacity of helping lawyers document cases and determine damages. *(Chapter 19)*

logical unit ordinary accounting subsidiary unit that contains the dollar unit selected in a dollar-unit sample. *(Chapter 20)*

management auditing (see also **internal auditing, operational auditing, performance auditing**) study of business operations for the purpose of making recommendations about the economic and efficient use of resources, effective achievement of business objectives and compliance with company policies. *(Chapters 1 and 18)*

management fraud (see also **fraudulent financial reporting**) deliberate fraud committed by management that injures investors and creditors through materially misleading financial statements. *(Chapter 19)*

material weakness in internal control condition in which the design or operation of the specific internal control structure elements (environment, accounting system, control procedures) does not reduce to a relatively low level the risk that errors or irregularities in amounts that would be material to the financial statements being audited may occur and may not be detected within a timely period by employees in the normal course of performing their assigned functions. *(Chapter 6)*

materials requisitions requests that create authorizations for the inventory custodian to release raw materials and supplies to the production personnel; documents that are the inventory recordkeepers' authorizations to update the raw materials inventory files to record reductions of the raw materials inventory. *(Chapter 11)*

mathematical computations (as **audit evidence**) auditors' own calculations. *(Chapter 4)*

mitigating factors elements of financial flexibility (salability of assets, lines of credit, debt extension, dividend elimination) available as survival strategies in circumstances of going concern uncertainty which may reduce the financial difficulty problems. *(Chapter 3)*

motive (with reference to fraud) pressure experienced by a person and believed to be unsharable with friends and confidants. *(Chapter 19)*

nature (of audit procedures) refers to the seven general procedures: recalculation, physical observation, confirmation, verbal enquiry, document examination, scanning and analytical procedures. *(Chapter 6)*

negative assurance "Based on our review, we are not aware of any material modifications that should be made to the accompanying financial statements in order for them to be in conformity with generally accepted accounting principles;" permitted in reviews of unaudited financial statements, letters to underwriters and reviews of interim financial information. *(Chapter 3)*

negative confirmations confirmation letter that requests a reply only if the account balance is considered incorrect. *(Chapter 4)*

nonpublic company company with less than $5 million in assets and fewer than 500 shareholders. Not required to register and file reports under the Exchange Act. *(Chapter 17)*

nonpublic offering (see also **private placement**) sale of securities to a small number of persons or institutional investors (usually not more than 35), who can demand and obtain sufficient information without the formality of registration. *(Chapter 17)*

nonsampling risk all risk other than sampling risk. *(Chapter 7)*

nonstatistical sampling audit sampling in which auditors do not utilize statistical calculations to express the results. *(Chapter 7)*

occurrence (as in **control failure,** also **deviation, error,** and **exception**) refers to a departure from a prescribed internal control procedure in a particular case. *(Chapter 7)*

operational auditing (see also **internal auditing, management auditing, performance auditing**) study of business operations for the purpose of making recommendations about the economic and efficient use of resources, effective achievement of business objectives and compliance with company policies. *(Chapter 1)*

opportunity (with reference to fraud) an open door for solving the unshareable problem in secret by violating a trust. *(Chapter 19)*

ordinary negligence lack of reasonable care in the performance of professional accounting tasks. *(Chapter 17)*

overreliance (obsolete term)   the result of assessing control risk too low and restricting other audit procedures when they actually should perform more work. *(Chapter 7)*

ownership (as a financial statement assertion) another name for the *rights* assertion, suggesting auditee's possession of legal title to assets. *(Chapter 4)*

paper trail   set of telltale signs of erroneous accounting, missing or altered documents or a "dangling debit" (the false or erroneous debit that results from an overstatement of assets). *(Chapters 9, 10, 11 and 12)*

parallel simulation   reprocessing live data to test program controls. *(Chapter 21)*

parity check   electronic function that ensures the coding of data internal to the computer does not change when it is moved from one internal storage location to another. *(Chapter 8)*

payroll accounting   preparation of individual paycheques, pay envelopes or electronic transfers using rate and deduction information supplied by the personnel function and base data supplied by the timekeeping-supervision functions. *(Chapter 11)*

payroll distribution   (as an employer's procedure) control of the delivery of pay to employees so that unclaimed cheques, cash or incomplete electronic transfers are not returned to persons involved in any of the other payroll functions. *(Chapter 11)*

peer review   study of a firm's quality control policies and procedures, followed by a report on a firm's quality of audit practice. *(Chapters 1 and 13)*

performance auditing (see also **internal auditing, management auditing, operational auditing**)   study of business operations for the purpose of making recommendations about the economic and efficient use of resources, effective achievement of business objectives and compliance with company policies. *(Chapter 1)*

personnel or **labour relations department**   function having transaction initiation authority to add new employees to the payroll, delete terminated employees, obtain authorizations for deductions (such as insurance, saving bonds and withholding tax exemptions on federal forms) and transmit authority for pay rate changes to the payroll department. *(Chapter 11)*

physical observation (as an audit procedure)   auditors' actual eyewitness inspection of tangible assets and formal documents. *(Chapter 4)*

physical representation of the population   auditor's frame of reference for selecting a sample. *(Chapter 7)*

planned control risk assessment   emphasis on *planned*; the auditors' selection of a control risk level for which they want to justify a control risk assessment after completing the test of controls audit work. *(Chapter 20)*

planning materiality   the largest amount of uncorrected dollar misstatement the auditors believe could exist in published financial statement without causing them to be considered materially misleading. *(Chapter 5)*

population   set of all the elements that constitute an account balance or class of transaction. *(Chapter 7)*

population unit   one element in a population. *(Chapter 7)*

positive confirmation   confirmation letter requesting a reply in all cases, whether the account balance is considered correct or incorrect. *(Chapter 4)*

possible misstatement   the further misstatement remaining undetected in units not selected in a sample. *(Chapter 7)*

predication (with reference to fraud examination)   a reason to believe fraud may have occurred. *(Chapter 19)*

preliminary survey   an internal auditor's familiarization with the organization, program or activity being audited, gained by gathering information, but without detailed investigation or verification procedures. *(Chapter 18)*

primary beneficiaries   third parties for whose primary benefit an audit or other accounting service is performed. *(Chapter 17)*

private placement (see also **nonpublic offering**)   sale of securities to a small number of persons or institutional investors (usually not more than 35), who can demand and obtain sufficient information without the formality of registration. *(Chapter 17)*

privity   the relationship of direct involvement between parties to a contract. *(Chapter 17)*

problem-recognition (as an audit method phase)   phase of formulating an audit objective related to a financial assertion. *(Chapter 7)*

pro forma financial date   presentation of financial statements "as if" an event had occurred on the date of the balance sheet. *(Chapter 14)*

production orders   internal documents that specify the materials and labour required and the timing for the start and end of production. *(Chapter 11)*

program description (computer program documentation) contains a program flowchart, a listing of the program source code (such as COBOL) and a record of all program changes. *(Chapter 21)*

program driven   computer data processing system that is started when a specific program is loaded into the computer to process all transactions that fit that program and its related files; characterized by batch processing. *(Chapter 8)*

projected likely misstatement (PLM)   auditors' best estimate of misstatement based on the errors found in a sample. *(Chapter 20)*

prospectus   set of financial statements and disclosures distributed to all purchasers in an offering registered under Securities Law. *(Chapter 17)*

qualified audit report   audit report other than the standard unqualified audit report; contains an opinion paragraph that does not give the positive assurance that everything in the financial statements is in conformity with GAAP. *(Chapter 3)*

quality review   study of a firm's quality control policies and procedures; an "audit" of a firm's quality of audit practice. *(Chapter 1)*

racketeering acts   engagement in illegal activities such as fraud in the sales of securities, mail fraud, wire fraud. *(Chapter 17)*

random sample   set of sampling units chosen so that each population item has an *equal likelihood* of being selected in a sample. *(Chapter 7)*

reasonable assurance   concept that recognizes that the cost of any entity's internal control structure should not exceed the benefits that are expected to be derived. *(Chapter 6)*

referral fees   (a) fees a CPA receives for recommending another CPA's services and (b) fees a CPA pays to obtain a client. Such fees may or may not be based on a percentage of the amount of any transaction. *(Chapter 16)*

registrar   fiduciary who keeps the shareholder list and from time to time determines the shareholders eligible to receive dividends (shareholders of record on a dividend record date) and those entitled to vote at the annual meeting. *(Chapter 12)*

relative risk   conditions of more or less inherent risk. *(Chapter 5)*

reperformance   (in test of controls procedure) auditors perform again the arithmetic calculations and the comparisons the company people were supposed to have performed. *(Chapter 6)*

replication   process of reperforming a selection procedure and getting the same sample units. *(Chapter 7)*

reportable condition   significant deficiency in the design or operation of a company's internal control structure which could adversely affect the organization's ability to record, process, summarize and report financial data in conformity with GAAP. *(Chapter 15)*

representative sample   sample that mirrors the characteristics of the population. *(Chapter 7)*

response rate   for positive confirmations is the proportion of the number of confirmations returned to the number sent, generally after the audit team prompts recipients with second and third requests. Research studies have shown response rates ranging from 66 to 96 percent. *(Chapter 9)*

review services   accountant performs some procedures lesser in scope than an audit for the purpose of giving a negative assurance report on financial statements. *(Chapter 14)*

risk model $AR = IR \times CR \times DR$ *(Chapter 12);* $AR = IR \times CR \times AP \times RIA.$ *(Chapter 20)*

risk of assessing the control risk too high   probability that the test of controls (compliance) evidence in the sample indicates high control risk when the actual (but unknown) degree of compliance would justify a lower control risk assessment. *(Chapter 7)*

risk of assessing the control risk too low   probability that the test of controls (compliance) evidence in the sample indicates low control risk when the actual (but unknown) degree of compliance does not justify such a low control risk assessment. *(Chapter 7)*

risk of incorrect acceptance (RIA)   probability that test of detail procedures will fail to detect material errors. *(Chapter 7)*

risk of incorrect rejection   probability that test of detail procedures will indicate that a balance *is* materially misstated when, in fact, it is not. *(Chapter 7)*

rule-utilitarianism (in **moral philosophy**)   emphasis on the centrality of rules for ethical behaviour while still maintaining the criterion of the greatest universal good. *(Chapter 16)*

run-to-run   sequential computer processing operations (runs) using the same data. *(Chapter 6)*

safe harbour   plaintiffs in a lawsuit must show that the auditor did not act in good faith when reporting on a forecast, effectively placing the burden of proof on the plaintiff. *(Chapter 16)*

sales forecast   estimated future sales. *(Chapter 11)*

sample   set of sampling units. *(Chapter 7)*

sample audit review file (SARF)   technique similar to systems control audit review file, except instead of programming auditors' test criteria, a random sampling selection scheme in programmed. *(Chapter 21)*

sampling error   amount by which a projected likely misstatement amount could differ from an actual (unknown) total as a result of the sample not being exactly representative. *(Chapter 7)*

sampling error-adjusted upper limit   sample deviation rate adjusted upward to allow for the idea that the actual population rate could be higher. *(Chapter 7)*

sampling risk   probability that an auditor's conclusion based on a sample might be different from the conclusions based on an audit of the entire population. *(Chapter 7)*

sampling unit   one logical unit from a population, such as a customer's account, an inventory item, a debt issue, a cash receipt, a cancelled cheque and so forth. *(Chapter 7)*

schema   entire set of data elements in a computerized data base. *(Chapter 21)*

scienter   person's action with knowing intent to deceive. *(Chapter 17)*

scope limitation   condition in which the auditors are unable to obtain sufficient competent evidence. *(Chapter 3)*

search for unrecorded liabilities   set of procedures designed to yield audit evidence of liabilities that were not recorded in the reporting period. *(Chapter 10)*

second audit partner   one who reviews the work of the audit team. *(Chapter 4)*

second partner review   working papers and financial statements, including footnotes, are given a final review on large engagements by a partner not responsible for client relations. *(Chapter 14)*

self-checking number   a basic code number with its check digit. *(Chapter 6)*

service organization   another business that executes and/or records transactions on behalf of the client. *(Chapter 15)*

simple extension   calculation of projected likely misstatement based on sample evidence using the difference and ratio methods. *(Chapter 20)*

skewness   concentration of a large proportion of the dollar amount in an account in a small number of the population items. *(Chapter 7)*

smoke/fire concept   means there can be more exposure to error (smoke) that actual error (fire), in analogy to test of controls sampling determination of a tolerable deviation rate. *(Chapter 20)*

specialists   persons skilled in fields other than accounting and auditing who are not members of the audit team. *(Chapter 4)*

standard deviation   a measure of population variability. *(Chapter 7)*

statistical sampling   audit sampling that uses the laws of probability for selecting and evaluating a sample from a population for the purpose of reaching a conclusion about the population. *(Chapter 7)*

statutory law   all the prohibitions enacted by a legislature. *(Chapter 17)*

strategic systems approach to auditing (SSA audits)   an auditing approach that has a top-down focus, starting with an in-depth understanding of the auditee's business. This focus enables the auditor to understand the strategic objectives of the auditee, the risks the auditee faces in relation to these objectives and the controls necessary for the business to respond to these risks. After obtaining an understanding of the business as a whole, the SSA auditor then proceeds to look at the details of the risky transactions in the context of the knowledge gained at the broader level. *(Chapter 13)*

stratification   in relating to account balances and audit sampling, refers to subdividing a population. *(Chapter 7)*

subschema   certain portions of a computerized database. *(Chapter 21)*

substantive audit procedures   transaction detail audit and analytical procedures designed to detect material misstatements in account balances and footnote disclosures. *(Chapters 5 and 6)*

substantive-purpose audit program   list of account balance- related procedures designed to produce evidence about assertions in financial statements. *(Chapter 7)*

substantive tests of details auditing   performance of procedures to obtain direct evidence about the dollar amounts and disclosures in financial statements. *(Chapter 7)*

supervision   (in payroll processing) authorization of all pay base data (hours, job number, absences, time off allowed for emergencies, etc.) by an employee's immediate supervisor. *(Chapter 11)*

systematic random sample   random sample chosen by calculating a skip interval and selecting every kth population unit in a frame. *(Chapter 7)*

systems control audit review file (SCARF)   method in which auditors build into the data processing programs special limit, reasonableness or other audit tests for selection of transactions for audit. *(Chapter 21)*

systems development and documentation standards manual   computer documentation containing standards that ensure (1) proper user involvement in the systems design and modification process, (2) review of the specifications of the system, (3) approval by user management and data processing management, and (4) controls and auditability. *(Chapter 8)*

tainting percentage   ratio of misstatement in a sampling unit to the recorded amount of the sampling unit. *(Chapter 20)*

test data   auditor-produced transactions used to audit programmed control procedures with simulated data. *(Chapter 21)*

test deck   sample of one of each possible combination of data fields that may be processed through the client's actual computer system. *(Chapter 21)*

test of controls   ordinary and extended procedures designed to produce evidence about the effectiveness of client controls that should be in operation. *(Chapters 6, 7, 9, 10, 11 and 12)*

timing (of audit procedures)   refers to when procedures are performed: at "interim" before the balance sheet date, or at "year-end" shortly before and after the balance sheet date. *(Chapters 6 and 7)*

timekeeping   payroll function of producing time cards or time sheets that provide the basis for payment to hourly workers. *(Chapter 11)*

tolerable deviation rate   decision criterion of the frequency of control failure for assessing control risk. *(Chapter 7)*

tolerable misstatement   decision criterion of the amount of dollar misstatement that can exist undetected in an account and not cause financial statements to be considered materially misleading. *(Chapter 5)*

tort   legal action covering civil complaints other than breach of contract; normally initiated by users of financial statements. *(Chapter 17)*

tracing   auditor selects sample items from basic source documents and proceeds forward through the accounting and control system to find the final recording of the accounting transactions. *(Chapter 4)*

transaction driven (also **event driven**)   computer data processing system that is started with each transaction event; individual transactions trigger the processing activity and all relevant files are updated. *(Chapter 21)*

transfer agent   fiduciary who handles the exchange of shares, cancelling the shares surrendered by sellers and issuing new certificates to buyers. *(Chapter 12)*

trap doors   unauthorized computer program modules used solely for fraudulent purposes. *(Chapter 21)*

underreliance (obsolete term)   the result of assessing control risk too high and expanding other audit procedures, performing more audit work when less work would suffice. *(Chapter 7)*

unrestricted random sample   items in a population are associated with numbers in a random number table or computer program for selection of a sample; no population stratification. *(Chapter 20)*

upper error limit (UEL)   largest amount of monetary misstatement that can be calculated, using the coefficient for the decision criterion risk of incorrect acceptance. *(Chapter 20)*

validity (as a control objective)   ensuring that recorded transactions are ones that should have been recorded. *(Chapter 6)*

verbal and written representations (audit evidence)   responses to audit enquiries given by the client's officers, directors, owners and employees. *(Chapter 4)*

vertical analysis   study of financial statement amounts expressed each year as proportions of a base such as sales for the income statement accounts and total assets for the balance sheet accounts. *(Chapters 5 and 19)*

vouching   auditor selects sample items from an account and goes backward through the accounting and control system to find the source documentation that supports the item selected. *(Chapter 4)*

walk-through   act of following one or a few transactions through the accounting system and control system in order to obtain a general understanding of the client's systems. *(Chapter 7)*

white collar crime   misdeeds done by people who wear ties to work and steal with a pencil or a computer terminal. *(Chapter 19)*

year-end audit work   audit procedures performed shortly before and after the balance sheet date. *(Chapter 4)*

INDEX